CW00821864

A TREATISE

OF

CELESTIAL MECHANICS,

BY P. S. LAPLACE,

MEMBER OF THE NATIONAL INSTITUTE, AND OF THE COMMITTEE OF LONGITUDE, OF FRANCE; THE ROYAL SOCIETIES OF LONDON AND GOTTINGEN; OF THE ACADEMIES OF SCIENCES OF RUSSIA, DENMARK, AND PRUSSIA, &c.

PART THE FIRST—BOOK THE FIRST.

TRANSLATED FROM THE FRENCH, AND ELUCIDATED WITH *EXPLANATORY NOTES.*

BY THE REV. HENRY H. HARTE, F.T.C.D. M.R.I.A.

DUBLIN:

PRINTED FOR RICHARD MILLIKEN, BOOKSELLER TO THE UNIVERSITY; AND FOR LONGMAN, HURST, REES, ORME AND BROWNE, LONDON.

1822.

TO

THE REV. CHARLES WILLIAM WALL,

THIS TREATISE

IS DEDICATED,

BY

HIS FRIEND, AND FORMER PUPIL,

HENRY H. HARTE.

PREFACE.

IT has been made a matter of surprise, that considering the great capabilities of many individuals in these countries, so few are conversant with the contents of a work of such acknowledged eminence, as the Celestial Mechanics. Without adverting to other causes, it may be safely asserted, that the chief obstacle to a more general knowledge of the work, arises from the summary manner in which the Author passes over the intermediate steps in several of his most interesting investigations. To remove this obstacle, is the design of the present treatise, in which the translator endeavours to elucidate every difficulty in the text, and to expand the different operations which are taken for granted. He has not attempted to follow the principles into all their details; but he has occasionally adverted to some useful applications of them, which occur in different Authors. He is aware that those conversant with such subjects will find much observation that may be dispensed with; but when it is considered that his object was to render this work accessible to the general class of readers, he trusts that he will not be deemed unnecessarily diffuse, if he has insisted longer on some points than the experienced reader may think necessary. As many of the propositions which Newton announced *separately* are so many different results, which are all comprised under the same general law *analytically* investigated, he has also taken occasion to notice, in the notes, those propositions of Newton, which are embraced in the general analysis of the text, which he was induced to do, in order to show the great superiority of the analytic mode of investigating problems. The Work will be divided into five parts, which will be published in separate volumes. The first volume contains the first book, which treats of the general principles of the equilibrium and motion of bodies. The number of notes which was necessary for the elucidation of these principles is much greater than will be required in any of the subsequent volumes. The second volume will contain the second and third books of the original; the third volume, the fourth and fifth books; the fourth volume will contain the sixth, seventh, and eighth books; and the last volume will contain the ninth and tenth books, together with the supplement to the tenth book.

Trin. Coll.
April, 1822.

TABLE OF CONTENTS.

BOOK I.

A TREATISE

OF

CELESTIAL MECHANICS,

&c. &c,

NEWTON published, towards the close of the seventeenth century, the discovery of universal gravitation. Since that period, Philosophers have reduced all the known phenomena of the system of the world to this great law of nature, and have thus succeeded in giving to the theories and astronomical tables a precision which could never have been anticipated. I propose in this present treatise to exhibit in one point of view, these theories which are scattered through a great number of works, of which the whole comprising the results of universal gravitation, on the equilibrium and motion of the bodies both solid and fluid, composing the solar and similar systems, constitutes *The Celestial Mechanics.* Astronomy, considered in the most general manner, is a great problem of Mechanics, of which the arbitrary quantities are the elements of the motions of the heavenly bodies; its solution depends, at the same time, on the precision of the observations, and on the perfection of analysis; and it is of the last importance to banish all empiricism, and to reduce it, so that it may borrow nothing from observation, but the indispensable data. The object of this work, is, as far as it is in my power, to accomplish this interesting end. I trust that, in consideration of the difficulties and importance of the subject, Philosophers and Mathematicians will receive it with indulgence, and that they will find the results sufficiently simple to be employed in their investigations. It will be divided into two parts. In the first, I will give the methods, and formulæ, for determining the motions of the centres of gravity of the heavenly bodies, their figures, the oscillations of the fluids which are spread over them, and their motions about their proper centres of gravity. In the second part, I will apply the formulæ which have been found in the first, to the planets, the satellites and the comets; and I will conclude with a discussion of several questions relative to the system of the world, and by a historical notice of the labours of Mathematicians on this subject. I will adopt the decimal division of the quadrant, and of the day, and I will refer the linear measures, to the length of the metre, determined by the arc of the terrestrial meridian comprised between Dunkirk and Barcelona.

ERRATA.

Page Line

3, 23, *for* the new forces, *read* these forces.

6, 12, *for* reluctant, *read* resultant.

12, 15, *for* (*c*) *read* (*b*).

17, 1, *for* equation, *read* equations.

23, 14, *for* $\varphi(f')$, *read* $\varphi'(f)$.

21, 14, *for* *a* and *b*, *read* *c* and *b*, and line 17, *for* angle, *read* angled.

32, 10, *for* $dy^2 dz^2$, *read* $dy^2 + dz^2$.

33, 2, from bottom, *after* A^2, *add* $=$; and last line, *after* the differential of the, add square of the, and *for* $s^n ds$, *read* $\frac{s^n ds}{n+1}$.

35, 2, from bottom, *for* first the order, *read* the first order.

40, 18, *after* centrifugal, *add* force.

47, last line, *for* *dt* constant, *read* *dx* constant.

49, 11, *for* $2h.\cos.\theta.$ *read* $2h.\cos.^2\theta.$; and in lines 21, 22, *dele* the 2 which occur in the Den[r].

50, 14, *dele* the 2 by which the values of *dt*, *dz*, *dx*, are multiplied.

51, 11, *for* $g2t$, *read* gt^2.

65, 1, *for* ds_2, *read* ds^2, ; line 16, *for* $\log.n.(s+q)\frac{1}{n})$, *read* $\log.n.(s+q))\frac{1}{n}$; line 17, *for* $(s'+q^n)$ *read* $s'+q$.

72, 14, *for* $\frac{ds}{S\,ds}$ *read* $\frac{ds}{S.dt}$.

82, 4, *for* *P*, *read* $-P$.

83, 2, *for* they, *read* it.

84, 23, *for* *k*, *k*, *k*, *read* *R*, *R*, *R*.

86, 3 from bottom, *for* $\frac{\partial y}{\partial x}$ *read* $\frac{\partial s}{\partial x}$.

94, 2, *after* centre, *read* of gravity.

99, 12, *for* figure, *read* figures.

105, *for* $\partial\varrho$, *read* ∂p; 20, *after* each, *read* other.

ERRATA.

Page	Line
138,	16, *for* sin. θ. sin. ψ.+cos. ψ. sin. ϕ. *read* sin. θ. sin. ψ. cos. ψ. sin. ϕ; line 19, *for* makes *read* make.
142,	16, *for* Σmx, Σmy, Σmz, *read* $\Sigma mx_,$, $\Sigma my_,$, $\Sigma mz_,$.
148,	18, *for* $\Sigma m.(2\Sigma m.fm.\ Pdx+Qdy+Rdz)$, *read* $\Sigma m.\ 2\Sigma.fm,(Pdx+Qdy+Rdz$ and in line 19, *for* $fmm'_, fdf$, *read* $fmm'.Fdf$.
149,	2, *after* velocities, *read* of the bodies.
168,	15, to the second x''^2 prefix + and line 19, *for* $+x''$ *read* $+x''^2$.
197,	20, *for* $+r'$, *read* $+r'^2$.
204,	21, *for* parallel, *read* perpendicular.
214,	2, *for* to coincide very nearly with the plane of x' and $y'_,$, *read* to be very nearly perpendicular to the plane of x' and y'.
217,	26, *for* dy, *read* dy'.
218,	19, *for* z''^2 sin. θ. *read* z''^2. sin. $^2\theta$.
229,	2, *for* $\frac{dx}{db}$, *read* $\frac{dz}{dc}$.
230,	3, *for* dx, *read* dx, line 11, *for* the first $\frac{dy}{db}.\frac{dz}{da}$, *read* $\frac{dy}{da}.\frac{dz}{db}$.
231,	20, *for* $\frac{du}{dz}.\mathrm{V}+$ *read* $\left(\frac{du}{dx}\right)u$.
233,	4, *for* $\frac{dy.+dw.dt}{dz}$ *read* $\frac{dy+dv.dt}{dx}$
234,	2, multiply the first member by dt, line 11, prefix — to dt, and *for* — V *read* — $V.dt$.
235,	17, *for* k *read* $\frac{1}{k}$.
236,	17, *for* δr, *read* $\delta \varrho$, and for homogenous, *read* homogeneous.
240,	16, *for* dz, *read* dz^2.
241,	12, *for* the second $\frac{d^2\phi}{dx^2}$, *read* $\frac{d^2\phi}{dz^2}$.
251,	16, *for* ra^2, *read* r^2a.
252,	8, *for* numbers, *read* members.
256,	17, *for* $r^2.(\sin.\theta+au.\cos.\theta)$; *read* $r'^2(\sin.\theta+au\cos\theta)$; line 19, *for* $2as$, *read* $2ars$.
265,	17, *for* $\frac{n}{2}$, *read* $\frac{n^2}{2}$.

A

TREATISE

ON

CELESTIAL MECHANICS,

&c. &c.

PART I.—BOOK I.

IN this book, the general principles of the equilibrium and motion of bodies are established, and those problems in Mechanics are solved, the solution of which is indispensable in the theory of the system of the world.

CHAPTER I.

Of the equilibrium and of the composition of forces which act on a material point.

1. A body appears to us to move, when it changes its situation with respect to a system of bodies which we suppose to be at rest; but as all bodies, even those which seem to us to be in a state of the

most absolute rest, may be in motion; we, in imagination, refer the position of bodies to a space which is supposed to be boundless, immoveable, and penetrable to matter; and when they answer successively to different parts of this real or ideal space, we conceive them to be in motion.

The nature of that singular modification, in consequence of which a body is transferred from one place to another is, and always will be, unknown: we have designated it by the name force; but we can only determine its effects and the laws of its action. The effect of a force acting on a material point, is, if no obstacle opposes, to put it in motion; the direction of the force is the right line which it tends to make the point describe. It is evident that when two forces act in the same direction, their effect to move the point is the sum of the two forces, and that when they act in opposite directions, the point is moved by a force represented by their difference. If their directions form an angle with each other, a force results, the direction of which is intermediate between the directions of the composing forces. Let us investigate this resultant and its direction.

For this purpose, let us consider two forces x and y acting at the same time on the material point M, and forming a right angle with each other. Let z represent their resultant, and θ the angle which it makes with the direction of the force x; the two forces x and y being given, the angle θ will be determined, and also the resultant z, so that there exists between these three quantities x, y, z, a relation which it is required to ascertain.

Let us suppose at first the forces x and y infinitely small, and equal to the differentials dx and dy; let us suppose afterwards that x becoming successively dx, $2dx$, $3dx$, &c. y becomes dy, $2dy$, $3dy$, &c. it is evident that the angle θ will always remain the same, and that the resultant z will become successively dz, $2dz$, $3dz$, &c.; thus in the successive increments of the three forces x, y, and z, the ratio of x to z will be constant, and can be expressed by a function of θ which we will designate by $\varphi(\theta)$; therefore we shall have $x = z\,\varphi(\theta)$, in which equation x may be changed into y, provided that in like manner the angle θ is changed into $\frac{\pi}{2}-\theta$, π being the semi-circumference of a circle whose radius is equal to unity.

Now, we can consider the force x as the resultant of two forces x' and x'', of which the first x' is in the direction of the resultant z, the second x' being perpendicular to this resultant. The force x which results from these two new forces, forming the angle θ with the force x', and the angle $\frac{\pi}{2}-\theta$, with the force x'' we shall have

$$x' = x\varphi(\theta) = \frac{x^2}{y};\; x'' = x\varphi\left(\frac{\pi}{2}-\theta\right) = \frac{xy}{z}$$

therefore we can substitute these two forces, for the force x. In like manner we can substitute for the force y, two new forces y' and y'', of which the first is equal to $\frac{y^2}{z}$ and in the direction of z, and of which the second is equal to $\frac{xy}{z}$ and perpendicular to z, thus we shall have in place of the two forces x and y the four following,

$$\frac{x^2}{z}, \frac{y^2}{z}, \frac{xy}{z}, \frac{xy}{z};$$

the two last acting in opposite directions, destroy each other; the two first acting in the same direction, when added together constitute the resultant z; we shall have therefore

$$x^2+y^2=z^2;$$

from which it follows that the resultant of the two forces x and y is represented in quantity by the diagonal of a rectangle, of which the sides represent the new forces.

Let us now proceed to determine the angle θ. If the force x is increased by its differential, without altering the force y,* this angle will be diminished by the indefinitely small quantity $d\theta$, but it is possible to suppose the force dx resolved into two, one dx' in the direction of z, the other dx'' perpendicular to z; the point M will then be acted on by the forces $z+dx'$ and dx'' perpendicular to each other, and the resultant of those two forces, which we represent by z', will make with dx'' the angle $\frac{\pi}{2}-d\theta$; therefore by what precedes we shall have $dx''=z'.\,\varphi\left(\frac{\pi}{2}-d\theta\right)$, consequently the function $\varphi\left(\frac{\pi}{2}-d\theta\right)$ is indefinitely small, and of the form $-Kd\theta$; K being a constant quantity independent of the angle θ; therefore we have $\frac{dx''}{z'}=-Kd\theta$; z' differing by an indefinitely small quantity from z; moreover as dx'' forms an angle with dx equal to $\frac{\pi}{2}-\theta$ we have

$$dx''=dx\,\varphi\left(\frac{\pi}{2}-\theta\right)=y.\,dx;$$

therefore

$$d\theta=\frac{-ydx}{Kz^2},$$

* Since the direction of the resultant depends on the relation which exists between composing forces, if one force be increased, while the other remains unaltered, the angle contained between the direction of the increased force and resultant, will be diminished by a quantity of the same order with that by which the force was increased. And when the force y receives the increase, the angle contained between the resultant and this increased force, will be diminished, therefore its complement, the angle θ, will be increased by the same quantity; and this is the reason why the expressions for the variations of θ corresponding to the respective variations of x and y are affected with contrary signs. If x and y are increased or diminished simultaneously, $d\theta$ will always vanish when dx, dy are respectively proportional to the quantities varied; this follows immediately from the expression for $d\theta$.

If the force y is varied by its differential dy, x being supposed to be constant, we shall have the corresponding variation of the angle θ, by changing x into y, y into x, and θ into $\frac{\pi}{2}-\theta$, in the preceding equation; which then gives

$$d\theta = \frac{xdy}{Kz^2}$$

therefore by making x and y to vary at the same time, the total variation of the angle θ will be $\frac{xdy-ydx}{Kz^2}$ and we shall have

$$\frac{xdy-ydx}{z^2} = Kd\theta$$

If we substitute for z^2 its value x^2+y^2, and then * integrate we shall have

$$\frac{y}{x} = \tan.\ (K\theta+\rho)$$

ρ being a constant arbitrary quantity. This equation being combined with the equation $x^2+y^2=z^2$ gives

$$x = z.\cos.\ (K\theta+\rho)$$

$$\frac{xdy-y\,dx}{x^2+y^2} = \frac{\frac{xdy-y\,dx}{x^2}}{1+\frac{y^2}{x^2}} = \frac{d.\left(\frac{y}{x}\right)}{1+\frac{y^2}{x^2}} = \frac{du}{1+u^2} \quad \text{(by putting}$$

$$\left.\frac{y}{x}=u\right) \quad \text{therefore} \int\frac{du}{1+u^2} \quad (=\text{arc tang.} = u) = \int K\,d\theta =$$

$$K\theta+\varrho \quad \because u = \left(\frac{y}{x}\right) = \tan.\ (K\theta+\varrho) = \frac{\sin.\ K\theta+\varrho}{\cos.\ K\theta+\varrho} \quad \therefore y^2 \ (=z^2-x^2) =$$

$$x^2\frac{\sin.^2(K\theta+\varrho)}{\cos.^2(K\theta+\varrho)} \quad \therefore z^2\cos.^2(K\theta+\varrho) = x^2\left((\sin.^2(K\theta+\varrho)+\cos.^2(K\theta+\varrho)\right) = x^2$$

It is only now required to know the two constant quantities K and ρ; but if we suppose y to vanish we have evidently $z = x$, and $\theta = o$, therefore cos. $\rho = 1$ and $x = z$. cos. $K\theta$. If we suppose x to vanish, then $z = y$, and $\theta = \frac{1}{2}\varpi$; cos. $K\theta$ being then equal to nothing, K *must be equal to $2n+1$, n being an integral number; and in this case x will vanish as often as θ will be equal to $\frac{\frac{1}{2}\varpi}{2n+1}$; but x being nothing we have evidently $\theta = \frac{1}{2}\varpi$; therefore $2n+1 = 1$, or $n = o$, consequently

$$x = z.\ \cos.\ \theta.$$

From which it follows that the diagonal of a rectangle described on the right lines which represent the forces x and y, represents not only the quantity but also the direction of their reluctant. Thus we can substitute for any force whatever two other forces which form the sides of a rectangle, of which that force is the diagonal; and it is easy to infer from thence that it is possible to resolve a force into three others, which form the sides of a rectangular parallelipiped of which it is the diagonal.†

Let therefore a b and c represent the three rectangular coordinates of the extremity of a right line, which represents any force whatever, and of which the origin is that of the coordinates; this force will be represented by the function $\sqrt{a^2+b^2+c^2}$, and by resolving it

* In this case $K\theta$ is some odd multiple of $\frac{\pi}{2}$ and therefore K must be of the form $2n+1$.

† The given force being resolved into two, of which one is perpendicular to a plane given in position, the other being parallel to this plane, if this second partial force be decomposed into two others, parallel to two axes situated in this plane, and perpendicular to each other; it is evident that the three partial forces will be at right angles to each other, and that the sum of the squares of the lines representing these forces, will be equal to the square of the line representing the given force, therefore this last force is the diagonal of a rectangular parallelbpiped, of which the partial forces constitute the sides.

parallel to the axes of a of b and of c, the partial forces will be expressed respectively by these coordinates.

Let a', b', c', be the coordinates of a second force; $a+a'$, $b+b'$, $c+c'$, will be the coordinates of the resultant of the two forces, and will represent the partial forces into which it can be resolved parallel to the three axes, from whence it is easy to conclude that this resultant is the diagonal of a parallelogram, of which the two forces are the sides.*

In general a, b, c; a', b', c'; a'', b'', c''; &c. being the coordinates of any number of forces; $a+a'+a''+$, &c. $b+b'+b''+$, &c. $c+c'+c''+$ &c. will be the coordinates of the resultant; the square of which will be equal to the sum of the squares of these last coordinates; thus we shall have both the quantity and the position of the resultant.†

* The coordinates of the extremity of this diagonal are evidently equal to $a+a'$, $b+b'$, $c+c'$, therefore this diagonal must be equal to the resultant of the two forces. We are enabled to derive an expression for the cosine of the angle, contained between the given forces, in terms of the cosines of the angles which these forces make with the coordinates, for calling the forces S and S', and the angles which S makes with the three axes, A, A', A'', and B, B', B'', the angles which S' makes with the same axes we have $a=S\cos. A$, $b=S\cos. A'$, $c=S\cos. A''$, $a'=S'\cos. B$, $c'=S'\cos. B'$, $c'=S'\cos. B''$, the square of the line connecting the extremities of S and $S'=S^2-2SS'.\cos.\Delta+S'^2$; Δ being the angle contained between S and S', the square of this line is also equal to

$$(S\cos. A-S'\cos. B)^2+(S\cos. A'-S'\cos. B')^2+(S\cos. A''-S'\cos. B'')^2;$$

$$=S^2+S'^2-2SS'(\cos. A.\cos. B+\cos. A'.\cos. B'+\cos. A''.\cos. B'',)$$

consequently we have

$$\cos.\Delta=\cos. A.\cos. B+\cos. A.\cos. B'+\cos. A''.\cos. B'',$$

therefore when the two forces are perpendicular to each other, the second member of this equation is equal to nothing.

† Let S S' S'', &c. represent the forces of which the coordinates are respectively a, b, c; a', b', c'; a'', b'', c'', &c. then by what precedes $a+a'$, $b+b'$, $c+c'$, are the coordinates of the resultant of S and S', $a+a'+a''$, $b+b'+b''$, $c+c'+c''$, are the coordinates of the resultant of this last force, and the force S'' &c.: therefore the resultant V of any number of forces is the diagonal of a rectangular parallelipiped of which

2. From any point whatever of the direction of a force S, which point we will take for the origin of this force, let us draw a right line, which we will call s, to the material point M; let x, y, z, be the three rectangular coordinates which determine the position of the point M, and a, b, c, the coordinates of the origin of the force; we shall have

$$S = \sqrt{(x-a)^2+(y-b)^2+(z-c)^2}.$$

If we resolve the force S parallel to the axes of x, of y, and of z, the corresponding partial forces will be by the preceding number

$$S.\frac{(x-a)}{s};\ S.\frac{(y-b)}{s};\ S.\frac{(z-c)}{s};\quad \text{or } S.\left(\frac{\delta s}{\delta x}\right);\ S.\left(\frac{\delta s}{\delta y}\right);\ S.\left(\frac{\delta s}{\delta z}\right);^{*}$$

the coordinates are equal respectively to the sum of the coordinates of the composing forces,

$$\therefore V^2 = (a+a'+a''+\&c.)^2 + (b+b'+b''\ \&c.)^2 + (c+c'+c''+\ \&c.)^2.$$

Let m, n, p = the angles which V makes with the rectangular axes

$$\cos. m = \frac{a+a'+a''+\ \&c.}{V}\quad \cos. n = \frac{b+b'+b''+\ \&c.}{V}\quad \cos. p = \frac{c+c'+c''+\&c.}{V}$$

$\therefore$ we have both the quantity and direction of the resultant.

From the preceding composition of forces it follows, that if a polygon is constructed, of which the sides, (which may be in different planes) are respectively proportional to these forces, and parallel to their directions, the last side of this polygon represents the resultant of all the forces in quantity and in direction.

* S being considered as a function of x, y, and z, $\delta s = \left(\frac{\delta s}{\delta x}\right)\delta x + \left(\frac{\delta s}{\delta y}\right)\delta y + \left(\frac{\delta s}{\delta z}\right)\delta z$

and when $s = \sqrt{(x-a)^2+(y-b)^2+(z-c)^2}$ $\left(\frac{\delta s}{\delta x}\right) = \frac{x-a}{s}$, $\frac{\delta s}{\delta y} = \frac{y-b}{s}$, $\frac{\delta s}{\delta z} = \frac{z-c}{s}$

$\frac{x-a}{s}$ $\frac{y-b}{s}$, &c. are evidently the expressions for the cosines of the angles which s makes with the coordinates x, y, and z, since

$$V.\left(\frac{\delta u}{\delta x}\right) = S\left(\frac{\delta s}{\delta x}\right) + S'\left(\frac{\delta s'}{\delta x}\right) + S''\left(\frac{\delta s''}{\delta x}\right) + \&c.;$$

$\left\{\frac{\partial s}{\partial x}\right\}$; $\left\{\frac{\partial s}{\partial y}\right\}$; $\left\{\frac{\partial s}{\partial z}\right\}$, expressing according to the received notation the coefficients of the variations of ∂x, ∂y, ∂z, in the variation of the preceding expression of s.

If, in like manner, we name s' the distance of M from any point in the direction of another force S', that point being taken for the origin of this force; $S'.\left\{\frac{\partial s'}{\partial x}\right\}$ will be this force resolved parallel to the axes of x, and just so the rest; therefore the sum of the forces S, S', S'', &c.

$$V.\left(\frac{\partial u}{\partial y}\right) = S.\left(\frac{\partial s}{\partial y}\right) + S'.\left(\frac{\partial s'}{\partial y}\right) + S''.\left(\frac{\partial s''}{\partial y}\right) + \&c.$$

$$V.\left(\frac{\partial u}{\partial z}\right) = S.\left(\frac{\partial s}{\partial z}\right) + S'.\left(\frac{\partial s'}{\partial z}\right) + S''.\left(\frac{\partial s''}{\partial z}\right) + \&c.$$

by multiplying these equations by ∂x, ∂y, ∂z, respectively, and adding them together, we get

$$V.\left(\left(\frac{\partial u}{\partial x}\right).\,\partial x + \left(\frac{\partial u}{\partial y}\right).\,\partial y + \left(\frac{\partial u}{dz}\right).\,\partial z\right) =$$

$$V.\,\partial u = S.\left(\left(\frac{\partial s}{\partial r}\right).\,\partial x + \left(\frac{\partial x}{\partial y}\right).\,\partial y + \left(\frac{\partial s}{\partial z}\right).\,\partial z\right)$$

$$+ S'.\left(\left(\frac{\partial s'}{\partial x}\right).\,\partial x + \left(\frac{\partial s'}{\partial y}\right).\,\partial y + \left(\frac{\partial s'}{\partial z}\right)\partial z.\right)$$

$$+ S''.\left(\left(\frac{\partial s''}{\partial x}\right)\partial x + \left(\frac{\partial s''}{\partial y}\right)\partial y + \left(\frac{\partial s''}{\partial z}\right)\right),\ \partial z + \&c. = S.\partial s + S'\partial s' + S''\partial s'' + \&c. = \Sigma.S.\partial s.$$

Now since these equation have place whatever be the variations ∂x, ∂y, ∂z, one of them may exist while the other two vanish, therefore the equation (a) is equivalent to the three equations which precede it. We shall see hereafter that the introduction of the coefficient $\left(\frac{\partial s}{\partial x}\right)$ is of the greatest consequence, for from the equation (b) which follows immediately from the equation (a), we deduce the equation (l) of No. 14, which involves the principle of vertual velocities, and this principle combined with that of D'Alembert, has given to Mechanics all the perfection of which it was susceptible, for by means of it the investigation of the motions of any system of bodies is reduced to the integration of differential equations. See No. 18.

resolved parallel to this axis will be $\Sigma.\ S.(\frac{\delta s}{\delta x})$, the characteristic Σ of finite integrals expressing the sum of the terms $S.(\frac{\delta s}{\delta x})$, $S'.\left\{\frac{\delta s'}{\delta x}\right\}$; &c.

Let V be the resultant of all the forces S, S', &c. and u the distance of the point M from any point in the direction of this resultant, which is taken for its origin; $V.\left\{\frac{\delta u}{\delta x}\right\}$ will be the expression of this resultant resolved parallel to the axis of x; therefore by the preceding number we shall have $V.\left\{\frac{\delta u}{\delta x}\right\} = \Sigma.\ S.\left\{\frac{\delta s}{\delta x}\right\}$,

we shall have in like manner

$$V.\left\{\frac{\delta u}{\delta y}\right\} = \Sigma.\ S.\left\{\frac{\delta s}{\delta y}\right\};\quad V.\left\{\frac{\delta u}{\delta z}\right\} = \Sigma.\ S.\left\{\frac{\delta s}{\delta z}\right\}$$

from which we may obtain, by multiplying these equations respectively by δx, δy, δz, and adding them together

$$V.\delta u = \Sigma.\ S.\ \delta s;$$

As this last equation has place whatever be the variations δx, δy, δz it is equivalent to the three preceding. If its second member is an exact variation of a fuction φ, we shall have $V.\ \delta u = \delta\varphi$, and consequently

$$V.\left\{\frac{\delta u}{\delta x}\right\} = \frac{\delta\varphi}{\delta x}$$

which indicates that the sum of all the forces resolved parallel to the axis of x is equal to the partial difference $\left\{\frac{\delta\varphi}{\delta x}\right\}$. * This case ob-

* If we multiply δs the variation of any quantity by any function of that quantity, such as $\frac{g}{s.^m}$, $g.s^m$, &c. the product is evidently an exact variation, however this is not true of every species of function, for there are some transcendental and exponential functions, such as $\frac{\delta s}{\log.\ s.}$ which are not exact variations.

tains generally, when the forces are respectively functions of the distance of their origin from the point M. In order to have the resultant of all these forces resolved parallel to any right line whatever, we shall take the integral $\Sigma. \int. S. \delta s$, and naming φ this integral, we shall consider it as a function of x, and of two right lines perpendicular to each other and to x; the partial difference $\left\{\frac{\delta \varphi}{\delta x}\right\}$ will be the resultant of the forces $S\, S'\, S''$, &c. resolved parallel to the right line x.

3. When the point M is in equilibrio, in consequence of the action of the forces which solicit it; their resultant vanishes, and the equation (a) becomes

$$O = \Sigma. S. \delta s \quad (b)$$

which indicates, that in the case of the equilibrium of a point acted on by any number of forces, the sum of the products of each force by the element of its direction is nothing.*

* Since the forces parallel to the coordinates x, y, z, are independant of each other, it follows from the notes to the preceding number, that when the point M is in equilibrio

$\Sigma. S \left\{\frac{\delta s}{\delta x}\right\}$ $\Sigma. S. \left\{\frac{\delta s}{\delta y}\right\}$ $\Sigma. S. \left\{\frac{\delta s}{\delta z}\right\}$ are = respectively to nothing.

$$i.\,e.\ S. \cos. A + S'. \cos. B + S'' \cos. C + \&c. = 0$$

$$S. \cos A' + S' \cos. B' + S'' \cos. C' + \&c. = 0.$$

$$S. \cos. A'' + S'. \cos. B'' + S'' \cos. C'' = 0.$$

(A, A', A''; B, B', B'', &c. are the angles which the directions of S, S', &c. make with x, y, z,); these are the equations of equilibrium of a system of forces applied to a material point which is entirely free The independence which exists between these equations is extremely advantageous, it only obtains when the forces are resolved parallel to three rectangular coordinates. $\Sigma. S. \left\{\frac{\delta s}{\delta x}\right\} = 0$ indicates that M is at an invariable distance from the plane of y, z; in this case the forces are reducible to two rectangular ones, in the plane y, z.

When the point M is in equilibrio any one of the forces acting on it is equal and contrary to the resultant of all the remaining forces, for naming V the resultant of the forces S', S''+&c. and a, b, c, the angles which it makes with the coordinates x, y, z, by

If the point M is forced to be on a curved surface, it will experience a reaction, which we will designate by R. This reaction is equal and directly contrary to the pressure with which the point presses on the surface; for by conceiving it acted on by two forces R and $-R$, it is possible to suppose that the force R is destroyed by the reaction of the surface, and that thus the point presses the surface with the force R; but the force of pressure of a point on a surface is perpendicular to it, otherwise it might be resolved into two, one perpendicular to the surface, which would be destroyed by it, the other parallel to the surface, in consequence of which the point would have no action on this surface, which is contrary to the hypothesis; consequently if r be the perpendicular drawn from the point M to the surface, and terminated in any point whatever of its direction, the force R will be directed along this perpendicular; therefore it will be necessary to add $R.\delta r$ to the second member of the equation (c) which thus becomes

$$0 = \Sigma.\, S.\, \delta s + R.\delta r \quad (c)$$

$-R$ being then the resultant of all the forces S, S', &c. it is perpendicular to the surface.

If we suppose that the arbitrary variations δx, δy, δz belong to the curved surface on which the point is subjected to remain, we shall have $\delta r = 0$, since r is perpendicular to the surface, therefore $R.\delta r$ vanishes from the preceding equation, in consequence of which the equation (b) obtains in this case, provided that one of the three variations δx, δy, δz, be eliminated by means of the equation to the surface; but then, the

what precedes we shall have $V'.\cos a = S'\cos. B + S''\cos C +$&c. $V'\cos. c = S'\cos B' + S'.\cos. C' +$&c. and since $S.\cos. A + S'.\cos. B + S''.\cos. C +$&c. $= 0$. We have $V'.\cos. a = -S.\cos. A$; in like manner it may be shewn that $V'\cos. b = -S.\cos. B$, and $V'.\cos. c = -S.\cos. C$: if we add together the squares of these equations we shall obtain $V'^2 = S^2$, because $\cos.^2 a + \cos.^2 b + {}^2 c = 1 = \cos.^2 A + \cos.^2 B + \cos.^2 C$ ∴ we have $\cos. a = -\cos. A$ &c. ∵ $a = 200' - A$, in like manner it follows, that $b = 200 - B$, $c = 200 - C$, ∵ the forces S and V' are equal, and act in opposite directions.

equation (b) which in the general case is equivalent to three, is only equivalent to two distinct equations, which may be obtained by putting the coefficients of the two remaining differentials separately equal to nothing. Let $u = 0$ be the equation of the surface, the two equations $\delta r = 0$, and $\delta u = 0$ will have place at the same time; this requires that δr should be equal to $N\delta u$, N being a function of x, y, and z. Naming a, b, c, the coordinates of the origin of r we shall have to determine it

$$r = \sqrt{(x-a)^2+(y-b)^2+(z-c)^2}$$

from which we may obtain $\left\{\frac{\delta r}{\delta x}\right\}^2 + \left\{\frac{\delta r}{\delta y}\right\}^2 + \left\{\frac{\delta r}{\delta z}\right\}^2 = 1$, and consequently

$$N^2.\left\{\left\{\frac{\delta u}{\delta x}\right\}^2 + \left\{\frac{\delta u}{\delta y}\right\}^2 + \left\{\frac{\delta u}{\delta z}\right\}^2\right\} = 1,$$

therefore by making

$$\lambda = \frac{R}{\sqrt{\left\{\frac{\delta u}{\delta x}\right\}^2 + \left\{\frac{\delta u}{\delta y}\right\}^2 + \left\{\frac{\delta u}{\delta z}\right\}^2}}$$

the term $R.\delta r$ of the equation (c) will be changed into $\lambda\delta u$, and this equation will become

$$0 = \Sigma.\ S.\ \delta s + \lambda\delta u$$

in which equation we ought to put the coefficients of the variations δx, δy, δz, separately equal to nothing, which gives three equations; but on account of the indeterminate quantity λ, which they contain, they are equivalent to only two between x, y, and z. Therefore instead of extracting from the equation (b) one of the variations δx, δy, δz, by means of the differential equation of the surface, we may add to it this equation multiplied by the indeterminate quantity λ, and then consider the variations δx, δy, and δz, as independant. This method, which also results from the theory of elimination combines the advantage of simplifying the calculation with that of indicating the force $-R$ with which the point M presses the surface.*

* When the point M is on a curved surface, then all that is required for its equilibrium is, that the direction of the resultant of all the forces which act on it should be perpendicular to this surface, but the intensity of this resultant is altogether undetermined, since the reaction is equal and contrary to the pressure of the point on the surface, by adding to $\Sigma.\ S.\ \delta s$ the quantity $R.\ \delta r$ we may consider the material point as entirely free.

δr vanishes because the perpendicular is the shortest line which can be drawn from a given point to the surface.

Since the same values of x, y, and z, satisfy the equations $\delta r = 0$ $\delta u = 0$, it follows from the theory of equations that $N = \frac{\delta r}{\delta u}$ is a function of x, y, and z,

$$\text{this function} = \frac{1}{\sqrt{\left\{\frac{\delta u}{\delta x}\right\}^2 + \left\{\frac{\delta u}{\delta y}\right\}^2 + \left\{\frac{\delta u}{\delta z}\right\}^2}}$$

it follows from the expression that is given for δr, that the cosines of the angles which the normal makes with the coordinates are equal respectively to $N\left\{\frac{\delta u}{\delta x}\right\} N.\left\{\frac{\delta u}{\delta y}\right\} N.\left\{\frac{\delta z}{\delta u}\right\}$.

See notes to No 9.

$$\text{Let } X = S.\left\{\frac{\delta s}{\delta x}\right\} + S'.\left\{\frac{\delta s'}{\delta y}\right\} + S''\left\{\frac{\delta s''}{\delta z}\right\} + \&c.$$

$$Y = S.\left\{\frac{\delta s}{\delta y}\right\} + S'\left\{\frac{\delta s'}{\delta y}\right\} + S''\left\{\frac{\delta s''}{\delta y}\right\} + \&c.$$

$$Z = S.\left\{\frac{\delta s}{\delta z}\right\} + S.\left\{\frac{\delta s'}{\delta z}\right\} + S''\left\{\frac{\delta s''}{\delta z}\right\} + \&c.$$

then $\Sigma.\ S.\ \delta s + \lambda \delta u = 0$ will be equal to $X.\ \delta x + Y.\ \delta y + Z.\ \delta z +$

$$\lambda\left\{\frac{\delta u}{\delta x}\right\}\delta x + \lambda\left\{\frac{\delta u}{\delta y}\right\}\delta y + \lambda\left\{\frac{\delta u}{\delta z}\right\}\delta z = 0.$$

and on account of the independance of the variables x, y, z, we shall have

$$X + \lambda\left\{\frac{\delta u}{\delta x}\right\} = 0, \quad Y + \lambda\left\{\frac{\delta u}{\delta y}\right\} = 0, \quad Z + \lambda\left\{\frac{\delta u}{\delta z}\right\} = 0,$$

eliminating λ we have the following equations:

$$Y.\frac{\delta u}{\delta x} - X.\frac{\delta u}{\delta y} = 0, \quad Z.\frac{\delta u}{\delta z} - X.\frac{\delta u}{\delta z} = 0.$$

Let us conceive this point to be contained in a canal of simple or double curvature; the reaction of the canal which we will denote by k, will be equal and directly contrary to the pressure with which the point acts against the canal, the direction of which is perpendicular to its side; but the curve formed by this canal, is the intersection of two surfaces of which the equations express its nature, therefore we may consider the force k as the resultant of two forces R, R', which express the reactions of the two surfaces on the point M; since the directions of the three forces R, R', k, being respectively perpendicular to the side of the curve they are in the same plane, therefore by naming δr, $\delta r'$ the elements of the directions of the forces R, R', which directions are respectively perpendicular to each surface; we must add to the equation (b) the two terms $R\delta r$, $R'\delta r'$, which will change it into the following:

$$0 = \Sigma . S\delta s + R.\delta r + R'.\delta r'. \quad (d)$$

These are the equations of equilibrium of a material point solicited by any number of forces S, S', S', and constrained to move on a curved surface: if the position of M on the surface is not given, then the two equations, resulting from the elimination of λ, combined with the equation of the surface, $u = 0$, are sufficient to determine the three coordinates of the point. When the forces and position of the point are given we obtain λ by means of one of the three preceding equations, from which we can collect immediately the value of R, and consequently the pressure; the investigation of R would be considerably abridged by making the axis of x to coincide with the normal, for then $\lambda . \left\{ \frac{\delta u}{\delta y} \right\}$, $\lambda . \left\{ \frac{\delta u}{\delta z} \right\}$, are equal respectively to nothing, and $\lambda \left\{ \frac{\delta u}{\delta x} \right\} = RN. \left\{ \frac{\delta u}{\delta x} \right\} = R$, for in this case $N. \left\{ \frac{\delta u}{\delta x} \right\} = \left\{ \frac{\delta r}{\delta x} \right\} = 1$; since $\lambda \left\{ \frac{\delta u}{\delta y} \right\}$, $\lambda \left\{ \frac{\delta u}{\delta z} \right\}$, are $=$ to nothing, we shall have $Y = 0$, $Z = 0$, which indicate that the forces resolved respectively parallel to two lines in the plane which touches the surface in the given point, are equal to nothing; this also follows from considering that the resultant of the forces is necessarily perpendicular to the surface. If the variations δx, δy, δz, are supposed to belong to the surface then we shall have $X\delta x + Y\delta y + Z\delta z = 0$, and substituting for δz its value in terms of δx and δy, which we get by means of the equation $\left\{ \frac{\delta u}{\delta x} \right\} . \delta x + \left\{ \frac{\delta u}{\delta y} \right\} . \delta y + \left\{ \frac{\delta u}{\delta z} \right\} . \delta z = 0$, we can obtain *immediately* the equations of condition

$$Y . \frac{\delta u}{\delta x} - X . \frac{\delta u}{\delta y} = 0. \quad Z . \frac{\delta u}{\delta x} - X . \frac{\delta u}{\delta z} = 0.$$

If we determine the variations δx, δy, δz, so that they may appertain at the same time to the two surfaces, and consequently to the curve formed by the canal; δr and $\delta r'$ will vanish, and the preceding equation will be reduced to the equation (b) which therefore obtains in the case where the point is constrained to move in a canal; provided that we make two of the variations δx, δy, δz, to disappear by means of the two equations which express the nature of this canal.

Let us suppose that $u=0$, $u'=0$ are the equations of the two surfaces whose intersection forms the canal. If we make

$$\lambda = \frac{R}{\sqrt{\left(\frac{\delta u}{\delta z}\right)^2 + \left(\frac{\delta u}{\delta y}\right)^2 + \left(\frac{\delta u}{\delta z}\right)^2}}$$

$$\lambda' = \frac{R'}{\sqrt{\left(\frac{\delta u'}{\delta x}\right)^2 + \left(\frac{\delta u'}{\delta y}\right)^2 + \left(\frac{\delta u'}{\delta z}\right)^2}}$$

the equation (d) will become

$$0 = \Sigma.\, S.\, \delta s. + \lambda.\, \delta u + \lambda'.\delta u',$$

in which the coefficients of each of the variations δx, δy, δz, will be separately equal to nothing; thus three equations will be obtained, by means of which the values of λ and λ' may be determined, which will give R and R' the reaction of the two surfaces, and by composing them we shall have the reaction k of the canal on the point M, and consequently the pressure of this point against the canal. The reaction resolved parallel to the axis of x is equal to

$$R.\left(\frac{\delta r}{\delta x}\right) + R'.\left(\frac{\delta r'}{\delta x}\right), \text{ or to } \lambda.\left(\frac{\delta u}{\delta x}\right) + \lambda'.\left(\frac{\delta u'}{\delta x}\right):^*$$

* When the point is forced to be on a canal of simple or double curvature there is only one equation of condition, which is obtained by eliminating λ and λ'; this equation combined with the equations $u = 0$, $u' = 0$ are sufficient to detrmine the coordinates of the

therefore the equation of condition $u=0$, $u'=0$, to which the motion of the point M is subjected, express by means of the partial differentials of functions, which are equal to nothing in consequence of these equations, the resistances with which the point is affected in consequence of the conditions of its motion.

It appears from what precedes that the equation (b) of equilibrium obtains universally, provided, that the variations δx, δy, δz, are subjected to the conditions of equilibrium. This equation may be made the foundation of the following principle.

" If an indefinitely small variation be made in the position of the " point M, so that it still remains on the curve or surface along which " it ought to move, if it is not entirely free; the sum of the forces " which solicit it, each multiplied by the space through which the " point moves in its direction, is equal to nothing, in the case of an " equilibrium."*

The variations δx, δy, δz, being supposed arbitrary and independant, it is possible to substitute for the coordinates x, y, z, in the equation (a), three other quantities which are functions of them, and to equal the coefficients of the variations of these quantities to nothing. Thus naming ρ the radius drawn from the origin of the coordinates, to the

point of the canal where the given forces constitute an equilibrium, in this case it is only required for the equilibrium of the point that the resultant of the forces should exist in a plane perpendicular to the element of the curve on which the point is situated, from whence it appears that the position of the resultant is more undetermined than when the point exists on a curved surface. See Notes to No. 9.

We might simplify the investigation of the pressures and obtain immediately the equation of equilibrium between the forces by taking two of the axes in the plane of the normals of the surfaces whose intersection constitutes the curve, for then we shall have at once $Z=0$, the third axis is in the direction of the tangent to the curve formed by the intersection of the two given surfaces.

* The equation (b) obtains universally, but under different circumstances, according as the point is free, or constrained to move on a surface; in the former case V the resultant of all the forces vanishes, and $\therefore \Sigma. S.\delta s. = V.\delta u$ must vanish; in the latter case V has a

projection of the point M, on the plane of x and y, and π the angle formed by ρ and the axis of x, we shall have

$$x = \rho.\cos.\pi;\quad y = \rho.\sin.\pi.$$

If, therefore in the equation (a), we consider u, s, s' as functions of ρ, π, and z; and then compare the coefficients of $\delta\pi$, we shall have

$$V.\left\{\frac{\delta u}{\delta\varpi}\right\} = \Sigma.S.\left\{\frac{\delta s}{\delta\varpi}\right\};\quad (e)$$

$\frac{V}{\rho}.\left\{\frac{\delta u}{\delta\varpi}\right\}$ is the expression for the force V resolved in the direction of the element $\rho.\delta\varpi$. Let V' be this force resolved parallel to the plane of x and y, and P the perpendicular demitted from the axis of z on direction of V', parallel to the same plane; $\frac{PV'}{\rho}$ will be a second expression for the force V' resolved in the direction of the element $\rho\delta\varpi$; therefore we shall have

$$PV'. = V.\left\{\frac{\delta u}{\delta\varpi}\right\}.$$

If we conceive the force V' to be applied to the extremity of the perpendicular P, it will tend to make it turn about the axis of Z; the product of this force, by the perpendicular, is denominated the moment of the force V with respect to the axis of z; therefore this moment is equal to $V.\left\{\frac{\delta u}{\delta\varpi}\right\}$; and it appears from the equation (e), that the moment of the resultant of any number of forces is equal to the sum of the moments of these forces.*

finite value, but its direction being perpendicular to the surface δr the variation of this perpendicular must be equal to nothing, and consequently in this case also $\Sigma.S\delta s = V\delta u$ must vanish.

* The force V resolved parallel to the axis of $x = \frac{V.(x-a)}{u} =$, by substituting for

x its value $V.\frac{(\varrho.\cos.\varpi-a)}{u}$, this last force resolved in the direction of the element $\varrho.\partial\varpi$, i. e. perpendicular to $\varrho = V.\frac{(\varrho.\cos.\varpi-a)}{u}.\frac{y}{\varrho}$ = (by substituting for y its value) $V.\frac{(\varrho.\cos.\varpi-a)}{u}.\sin.\varpi$ in like manner if we resolve the force V parallel to the axis of y, and then this last force in the direction of $\varrho\,\partial\varpi$, it will be equal to $V.\frac{(\varrho.\sin.\varpi-b)}{u}.\cos.\varpi$ These forces in the direction of $\varrho.\,\partial\varpi$ act in opposite directions, therefore their difference $=\frac{V.}{u}\Big((\varrho.\sin.\varpi-b).\cos.\varpi-(\varrho.\cos.\varpi-a).\sin.\varpi)\Big)$ is the expression for that part of the force V in the direction of the element $\varrho.\partial\varpi$, which is really efficient, this expression $=\frac{V.}{\varrho}\left\{\frac{\partial u}{\partial\varpi}\right\}$; for $u^2=(\varrho.\cos.\varpi-a)^2+(\varrho.\sin.\varpi-b^2+(z-c)^2$ (by substituting for x and y their values); therefore taking the derivitive function, ϖ being considered as the variable, we shall have, $u.\left\{\frac{\partial u}{\partial\varpi}\right\}=-\varrho.\sin.\varpi.(\varrho.\cos.\varpi-a)+\varrho.\cos.\varpi.(\varrho.\sin.\varpi-b)$. $\therefore\frac{V.}{\varrho}\left\{\frac{\partial u}{\partial\varpi}\right\}=\frac{V.}{u}\Big((\cos.\varpi.(\varrho.\sin.\varpi-b)-\sin.\varpi.(\varrho.\cos.\varpi-a)\Big),=\frac{PV''}{\varrho}$, for conceiving the force V' to be resolved into two, of which one is perpendicular to ϱ, the other being in the direction of ϱ, the triangle constituted by these forces will be similar to a triangle, two of whose sides are ϱ and P, and the third side $= V''$ produced to meet P. $\therefore$ that part of the force V' which is perpendicular to ϱ is to V'' as P to ϱ $\therefore$ it is equal to $\frac{PV''}{\varrho}$.

From the definition that has been given in this No. of the moment of a force with respect to an axis, it appears that it can be geometrically exhibited by means of a triangle, whose vertex is in this axis, and whose base represents the intensity of the force, it vanishes when the resultant V vanishes, and also when P vanishes, i. e. when the resultant passes through the origin of the coordinates. See Notes to No. 6.

Let X and Y indicate, as in the preceding notes, the force V, resolved respectively parallel to the axes of x and y, $X=V.\frac{(x-a.)}{u}$, $Y=V.\frac{(y-b)}{u}$, the expression for these forces resolved perpendicular to $\varrho=V.\frac{(x-a)}{u}.\frac{y}{\varrho}$, $V.\frac{(y-b)}{u}.\frac{x}{\varrho}$, their difference $=\frac{PV'}{\varrho}=\frac{Yx-Xy}{\varrho}$; we are enabled by means of this expression to deduce the equation of the right line, along which the resultant is directed, for the equations of its projection V' on the plane of $x\,y$ is $y-b=\frac{Y'}{X}.(x-a)$. $Xy-Xb=Yx-Y.a$. Let L be equal to $Yx-Xy$, and the preceding equation will become $b=\frac{Y}{X}.a-\frac{L}{X}$. we might derive similar expressions for the projection of V on the planes of x and z, and y and z, from whence it is easy to collect the equation of the right line along which V is directed, $-\frac{L}{X}$ indicates the distance of the origin of the coordinates from the intersection of V' with the axis of y, and $\frac{L}{Y}$ indicates the distance of the origin of the coordinates from the intersection of the resultant V' with the axis of x. $Yx-Xy=Ya-Xb$ shews that it is indifferent what point of the direction of V' is considered. $Yx-Xy=0$ when $V'=0$, and also when its direction passes through the axis o z.

CHAPTER II.

Of the motion of a material point.

4. A point in repose cannot excite any motion in itself, because there is nothing in its nature to determine it to move in one direction in preference to another. When solicited by any force, and then left to itself, it will move constantly, and uniformly in the direction of that force, if it meets with no resistance. This tendency of matter to persevere in its state of motion or rest, is what is termed its *inertia*; it is the first law of the motion of bodies.

The direction of the motion in a right line follows necessarily from this, that there is no reason why the point should deviate to the right, rather than to the left of its primitive direction; but the uniformity of its motion is not equally evident. The nature of the moving force being unknown, it is impossible to know *a priori*, whether this force should continue without intermission or not. Indeed, as a body is incapable of exciting any motion in itself, it seems equally incapable of producing any change in that which it has received, so that the law of inertia is at least the most natural and the most simple which can be imagined; it is also confirmed by experience. In fact, we observe on the earth that the motions are perpetuated for a longer time, in proportion as the obstacles which oppose them are diminished; which induces us to think that if these obstacles were entirely removed, the motions would never cease. But the inertia of matter is most remarkable in the motions of the heavenly bodies, which for a great number of ages have not experienced any perceptible alteration. For these reasons we shall consider the inertia of bodies as a law of nature; and when we observe any change in the motion of a body we shall conclude that it arises from the action of some foreign cause.

In uniform motions the spaces described are proportional to the times. But the times employed in describing a given space are longer or shorter according to the magnitude of the moving force. From these differences has arisen the idea of *velocity*, which, in uniform motions is the ratio of the space to the time employed in describing it. Thus s representing the space, t the time, and v the velocity, we have $v = \frac{s}{t}$. Time and space being heterogeneal and consequently not comparable quantities, a determinate interval of time, such as a second, is taken for a unit of time, and in like manner a portion of space, such as a metre for an unit of space, and then time and space become abstract numbers, which express how often they contain units of their species, and thus they may be compared one with another. By this means the velocity becomes the ratio of two abstract numbers, and its unity is the velocity of a body which describes a metre in one second.

5. Force being only known to us by the space which it causes to be described in a given time, it is natural to take this space for its measure, but this supposes, that several forces acting in the same direction, would cause to be described in a second of time, a space equal to the sum of the spaces which each would have caused to be described separately in the same time, or in other words, that the force is proportional to the velocity; but of this we cannot be assured *a priori*, in consequence of our ignorance of the nature of the moving force. Therefore it is necessary on this subject also to have recourse to experience, for whatever is not a necessary consequence of the few data which we have on the nature of things, must be to us the result of observation.

Let us name v the velocity of the earth, which is common to all the bodies on its surface, let f be the force with which one of these bodies M is actuated in consequence of this velocity, and let us suppose that $v = f.\varphi(f)$ is the relation which exists between the velocity and the force, $\varphi(f)$ being a function of f which must be determined by experience. Let a, b, c. be the three partial forces into which the force f may be resolved parallel to three axes which are perpendicular to each other. Let us then suppose the moving body M to be solicited by a new force, f', which may be resolved into three others a', b', c', parallel to the same axis. The forces by which this body will be solicited parallel to these axis will be $a+a'$, $b+b'$, $c+c'$, naming F the sole resulting force, by what precedes we shall have

$$F = \sqrt{\overline{a+a'}|^2 + (b+b')^2 + (c+c')^2}$$

If the velocity corresponding to F be named U; * $\frac{(a+a').\ U}{F}$ will be this velocity resolved parallel to the axes of a, thus the relative velocity of the body on the earth parallel to this axis will be $\frac{(a+a')U}{F} - \frac{a}{f}$ or $(a+a').\ \varphi.(F) - a.\ \varphi.f.$ The most considerable forces which can be impressed on bodies at the surface of the earth being much smaller than those by which they are actuated in consequence of the motion of the earth, we may consider a', b', c', as indefinitely small quantities relative to f; therefore we shall have $F = f + \frac{aa' + bb' + cc'}{f}$ † and φ $(F) = \varphi.\ (f) + \frac{(aa' + bb' + cc').}{f}\ \varphi'(f)$; $\varphi.(f')$; being the differential

* The velocity of a body moving in a given direction is to *its* velocity, *estimated* in any other direction, as radius to the cosine of the angle which the two directions make with one another, that is, in this case as F to $a+a'$, therefore the velocity U resolved parallel to the axis of a will be equal to $U\ \frac{(a+a')}{F}$.

† $F. = \sqrt{(a+a')^2+(b+b')^2+(c+c')^2} = \sqrt{a^2+b^2+c^2+2aa'+2bb'+2cc'}$, the squares of a', b', and c' being rejected as indefinitely small, if this radical is expanded by the binomial theorem (all the terms except the two first being neglected as involving the squares, products, and higher powers of a', b', c',) it will become

$$\sqrt{a^2+b^2+c^2} + \frac{2\,(aa'+bb'+cc')}{2\sqrt{a^2+b^2+c^2},} = f + \frac{aa'bb'+cc'}{f},$$

$$\text{and } \varphi\ (F) = \varphi.\left(f + \frac{aa'+bb'+cc'}{f}\right) \text{ equal by Taylor's theorem to}$$

$$\varphi(f) + \frac{aa'+bb'+cc'}{f}.\ \varphi'\ (f).$$

of $\varphi.(f)$ divided by $d.f.$ The relative velocity of M in the direction of the axis of a will thus become

$$a'.\varphi.(f) + \frac{a}{f}\left\{ aa' + bb' + cc' \right\}.\varphi'.(f)$$

its relative velocities in the directions of b and c will be

$$b'.\varphi.(f) + \frac{b}{f}\left\{aa' + bb' + cc'\right\}.\varphi'.(f);$$

$$c'\varphi.(f) + \frac{c}{f}\left\{aa' + bb' + cc'\right\}\varphi'(f);$$

The position of the axes of a of b and of c being arbitrary, we may take the direction of the impressed force for the axis of a, and then b and c will vanish; the preceding relative velocities will be changed into the following

$$a\left\{\varphi.(f) + \frac{a^2}{f}.\varphi'(f)\right\}; \frac{ab}{f}. a'.\varphi'(f); \frac{ac}{f}. a'\varphi'(f).$$

If $\varphi'(f)$ does not vanish, the moving body in consequence of the impressed force a' will have a relative velocity perpendicular to the direction of this force, provided that a and b do not vanish,—that is to say, provided that the direction of this force does not coincide with that of the motion of the earth. Thus, conceiving that a globe at rest upon a very smooth horizontal plane is struck by the base of a right angle cylinder, moving in the direction of its axis, which is supposed to be horizontal, the apparent relative motion of the globe will not be parallel to this axis in all positions of this axis relative to the horizon. We have thus an easy means of determining by experiment whether $\varphi'(f)$ has a perceptible value on the earth; but the most accurate experiments have not indicated in the apparent motion of the globe any deviation from the direction of the force impressed; from which it follows that on the earth $\varphi'(f)$ is very nearly nothing. If its value was at all perceptible, it would particularly be shewn in the duration of the oscillations of a pendulum, which duration would alter according as the position of the plane of its motion differed from the direction of the motion of the earth. As the most exact observations have not evinced any such difference, we ought to conclude that $\varphi'(f)$ is insensible, and at the surface of the earth ought to be supposed equal to nothing.*

If the equation $\varphi'(f) = 0$ has place whatever be the magnitude of the force f, $\varphi.(f)$ will be constant, and the velocity will be proportional to the force; it will be also proportional to it if the function $\varphi.(f)$ is composed of only one term, as otherwise $\varphi'.(f)$ would not vanish unless f did; therefore if the velocity is not proportional to the force, it is necessary to suppose that, in nature, the function of the velocity which expresses the force consists of several terms, which is very improbable; we must moreover suppose that the velocity of the earth is exactly such as corresponds to the equation $\varphi'(f) = 0$,† which is contrary to all probability. Besides, the velocity of the earth varies during the different seasons of the year; it is a thirtieth part greater in winter than in summer. This variation is even more considerable if, as every thing appears to indicate, the solar system be in motion in space; for according as this progressive motion conspires with that of the earth, or is contrary to it, there must result in the course of the year, very sensible variations in the absolute motion of the earth, which would alter the equation which we are considering, and the ratio of the force impressed to the absolute velocity which results from it, if this equation and this ratio were not independant of the motion of the earth. Nevertheless, the smallest difference has not been discovered by observation.

E

* These experiments evince that the appearances of bodies in motion are independant of the direction of the motion of the earth; and from the preceding investigation it follows, that in order this should be the case, the small increase of the force by which the earth is actuated should be to the corresponding increase of the velocity, in the ratio of the quantities themselves; thus our experiments only prove the reality of this proportion, which if it had place, whatever the velocity of the earth might be, would give the law of the velocity proportional to the force.

† $\varphi'(f) = 0$, not only when $\varphi(f)$ is constant, but also in other cases, such as when $\varphi(f)$ is a maximum or minimum, in the former case the force f may be of any magnitude whatever; in the latter case the value of f is *unique*; but since the velocity

Thus we have two laws of motion; the law of inertia, and that of the force proportional to the velocity, which are both given by observation. They are the most natural and the most simple which can be imagined, and are, without doubt, derived from the nature itself of matter, but this nature being unknown, they are, with respect to us, solely the result of observation, and the only observed facts which the science of Mechanics borrows from experience.*

6. The velocity being proportional to the force, those two quantities may be represented one by the other, and we may apply to the composition of velocities all that has been previously established respecting the composition of forces.† Thus it follows, that the relative motions of a system of bodies actuated by any force whatever, are the same whatever be their common motion, for this last motion decomposed into three others, parallel to three fixed axes, only increases by the same quantity the partial velocities of each body parallel to these axes, and as their relative velocities only depend on the difference of these partial velocities, it will be the same whatever be the motion common to all bodies; it is therefore impossible to judge of the absolute motion of the system, of which we make a part by the appearances which can be observed, which circumstance characterises the law of the force proportional to the velocity.

of the earth is different in different points of its orbit, the value of f corresponding to this velocity must also vary.

If $\varphi(f)$ is an algebraic function of f, and consists of only one term, then $\varphi'(f)$ will not vanish unless f vanishes; but if φ was a transcendental function, then f might have a finite value, $\varphi'(f)$ vanishing, or *vice versa*.

* In this respect, therefore, the theory of motion is less extensive than the theory of equilibrium, which does not involve any hypothesis whatever.

† Let v, v', v'', represent the uniform velocities parallel to the coordinates x, y, z, after any time t, $x = vt$, $y = v't$, $z = v''t$, the resulting motion will be uniform, and its direction rectilinear, the equation of s, the line described, will be $s = t\sqrt{v^2+v'^2+v''^2}$, the velocity in the direction of $s = \sqrt{v^2+v'^2+v''^2}$, the cosines of the angles which this direction makes with x, y, and z, are equal respectively to

$$\frac{v}{\sqrt{v^2+v'^2+v''^2}}, \quad \frac{v'}{\sqrt{v^2+v'^2+v''^2}}, \quad \frac{v''}{\sqrt{v^2+v'^2+v''^2}};$$

thus the composition and resolution of velocities are effected in the same manner as the

It follows also from No. 3, that, if we project each force and their resultant on a fixed plane, the sum of the moments of the composing forces thus projected with respect to a fixed point taken on the plane, is equal to the moment of the projection of the resultant; but if we draw from this point to the moving body a radius, which we shall call the *radius vector*, this radius projected on a fixed plane will trace, in consequence of each force acting separately, an area equal to the product of the projection of the line which the moving body is made to describe, into half the perpendicular let fall from the fixed point on this projection; therefore this area is proportional to the time; it is also in a given time* proportional to the moment of the projection of the force; thus the sum of the areas which the projection of the radius vector would describe, if each composing force acted separately, is equal to the area which the resultant makes this radius to describe. It follows from this, that if a body is first projected in a right line, and then solicited by any forces whatever, directed towards a fixed point, its radius vector will always describe about this point areas proportional to the times, because the areas which the new composing forces† make this radius to describe will vanish. It appears conversely, that if the moving body describes areas proportional to the times about the fixed point, the resultant of the new forces which solicit it is constantly directed towards this point.‡

* The area varies as the base multiplied into the altitude; the base varies as the time multiplied into the projection of the force; therefore the area varies as the continued product of the altitude, projection of force, and time, or (by substituting the moment for the altitude multiplied into the projection of the force) as the moment multiplied into the time.

† If the forces directed to the fixed point did not act, the moving point would evidently describe areas proportional to the times; but these forces being supposed to act. the areas which are described about the fixed point, in consequence of the action of these forces, are nothing; for the perpendicular from the fixed point on the direction of the force in this case vanishes, consequently the proportionality of the areas to the times is not disturbed by the action of those forces.

‡ By means of the equations, $\frac{d^2x}{dt^2}=P$; $\frac{d^2y}{dt^2}=Q$. which are established in the subsequent number, we can exhibit immediately the relation which exists between the areas

7. Let us now consider the motion of a material point solicited by forces which seem to act continually, such as gravity. The causes of this and similar forces which have place in nature being unknown, it is impossible to know whether they act without interruption, or whether their successive actions are separated by imperceptible intervals of time;

and moments; for if we multiply the first of these equations by y, and the second by x, and then subtract, we shall have, by concinnating $\frac{d^2y.x-d^2x.y}{dt^2} + yP-xQ) = 0$; if this equation be integrated, we shall obtain $\frac{xdy-ydx}{dt} + \int . dt\,(yP-xQ) = c$; $yP-xQ$. is the moment of the projection of the force on the plane x and y (see last note to No. 3); it vanishes when the force is directed to the origin of the coordinates, and also when P and Q vanish, that is when the point is not solicited by any accelerating foree,-consequently in both these cases, $xdy-ydx = cdt$ and is ∵ proportional to the time. in the second case the origin of the coordinates may be any point whatever; but in the first case, the origin must be in the *fixed* point, to which the forces soliciting the point are directed; ($xdy-ydx$ = the elementary area which the projection of the radius vector on the plane $x\ y$ describes in dt; for $x = \varrho .\cos .\varpi$, $y = \varrho .\sin .\varpi$; therefore $dx = d\varrho .\cos \varpi - d\varpi .\sin .\varpi .\varrho$. $dy = d\varrho .\sin .\varpi + d\varpi .\cos .\varpi .\varrho$. consequently $xdy - y.dx = d\varrho .\sin .\varpi .\cos .\varpi .\varrho + d\varpi .\cos .^2\varpi .\varrho^2 - d\varrho .\sin .\varpi .\cos .\varpi .\varrho + d\varpi .\sin .^2\varpi .\varrho^2 = d\varpi .\varrho^2$; but since $\varrho d\varpi$ is the elementary arc described by the projection of the radius vector on the plane x, y, $\varrho .^2 d\varpi$ will be the expression for the elementary area.) Since, when the areas are proportional to the times $yP-xQ = 0$, it follows that the magnitude of the area described in a given time is not affected by the intensity of the accelerating force.

By a similar process of reasoning it may be shewn, that the projections of the elementary area on the plane x, z, y, z, which are equal to $xdz - zdx$, $ydz - zdy$ generally, are equal respectively to $c'.dt$, $c''.dt$. when the forces soliciting the point are directed towards the origin of the coordinates. When the areas are proportional to the times, the curve described is of single curvature, for then we have $xdy-ydx=cdt$, $xdz-zdx=c'dt$, $ydz-zdy=c''dt$; if the first of these equations be multiplied by z, the second by y, and the third by x, we shall obtain, by adding them together, the equation $cz+c'y+c''x = 0$, which belongs to a plane.

The velocities are inversly as the perpendiculars when the areas are proportional to the times; for if we call the perpendicular p, and the elementary arc of the curve described ds, we will have $p.ds = x.dy - y.dx = c.dt$ ∵ $p = \frac{cdt}{ds} = \frac{c}{v}$.

The constant quantities c, c', c'', depend on the species of the curve described; in conic sections when the force is directed to the focus, they are to the square roots of the parameters as the cosines of inclinations of the planes x,y, x,z, yz, to the plane of the section to radius. See No. 3. book 2.

but it is easy to be assured that the phenomena ought to be very nearly the same on the two hypotheses; for if we represent the velocity of a body solicited by a force whose action is continued by the ordinate of a curve of which the abscissa represents the time, this curve, on the second hypothesis will be changed into a polygon, having a great number of sides, which for this reason may be confounded with the curve. We shall, with geometers, adopt the first hypothesis, and suppose that the interval between two consecutive actions is equal to the element dt of the time, which we will denote by t. It is evident that the action of a force ought to be more considerable according as the interval is greater which separates its successive actions, in order that after the same time t the velocity may be always the same. Therefore the instantaneous action of a force ought to be supposed to be in the ratio of its intensity, and of the element of time during which it is supposed to act. Thus P, representing this intensity at the commencement of each instant, dt, the point, will be solicited by the force Pdt, and its motion will be uniform during this instant. This being agreed upon,

All the forces which solicit a point M may be reduced to three, P, Q, R, acting parallel to three rectangular coordinates x, y, z, which determine the position of this point;* we shall suppose these forces to act in a contrary direction from the origin of the coordinates, or to tend to increase them. At the commencement of a new instant dt, the moving point receives in the direction of each of its coordinates increments of force or velocity, Pdt, $Q.dt$, Rdt. The velocities of the point M, parallel to these coordinates, are $\frac{dx}{dt}$, $\frac{dy}{dt}$, $\frac{dz}{dt}$,† for during an inde-

* By thus referring the position of a point in space to rectangular coordinates, all curvilinear motion may be reduced to two or three rectilinear motions, according as the curve described is of simple or double curvature. For the position of the moving point is completely determined when we are able to assign the position of its projections on three rectangular axes, each coordinate represents the rectilinear space described by the point parallel to the axes to which it is referred, it will consequently be a given function of the time; and if we could determine these functions with respect to the three coordinates, the species of the curve described might be assigned by eliminating the time by means of the three equations between the coordinates and the time.

finitely small portion of time, they may be considered as uniform, and therefore equal to the elementary spaces divided by the element of the time. Consequently the velocity with which the moving body is solicited at the commencement of a new instant, is

$$\frac{dx}{dt}+P.dt\,;\quad \frac{dy}{dt}+Q.dt\,;\,\frac{dz}{dt}+R dt\,;$$

or

$$\frac{dx}{dt}+d.\frac{dx}{dt}-d.\frac{dx}{dt}+P.dt\,;$$

$$\frac{dy}{dt}+d.\frac{dy}{dt}-d.\frac{dy}{dt}+Q.dt;$$

$$\frac{dz}{dt}+d.\frac{dz}{dt}-d.\frac{dz}{dt}+R.dt\,;$$

but in this new instant, the velocities with which the moving body is actuated parallel to the coordinates x, y, z, are evidently

$$\frac{dx}{dt}+d.\frac{dx}{dt}\,;\quad \frac{dy}{dt}+d.\frac{dy}{dt};\quad \frac{dz}{dt}+d.\frac{dz}{dt}\,;$$

ment of the space, when dt becomes indefinitely small; we can assign the actual value by means of Taylor's theorem; for if t receive the increment dt, then ($x=f(t)$ becomes $x'=f(t+dt)$ $\because\ x'-x=f(t+dt)-f(t)=\frac{dx}{dt}.dt+\frac{d^2x}{dt^2}.\frac{dt^2}{1.2}+\frac{d^3x}{dt^3}.\frac{dt^3}{1.2.3}+$ &c. by making dt indefinitely small all the terms but the two first may be rejected; and since $\frac{dx}{dt}$ is the coefficient of dt it represents the velocity, and since $\frac{d^2x}{dt^2}$ is the coefficient of dt^2, it is proportional to the force; consequently. if the action of the forces soliciting the point should cease suddenly $\frac{d^2x}{dt^2}$ would vanish, and the point would move with an uniform velocity, if instead of vanishing $\frac{d^2x}{dt^2}$ became constant, then $\frac{d^3x}{dt^3}$, and all subsequent coefficients would vanish, and the motion of the point would be composed of an uniform motion, and of one uniformly accelerated, both commencing at the same instant.

therefore the forces

$$-d.\frac{dx}{dt}+P.dt,\ -d.\ \frac{dy}{dt}+Q.dt,\ -d.\ \frac{dz}{dt}+R.dt,$$

must be destroyed, so that, if the point was actuated by these sole forces it would be in equilibrium. Thus if we denote by δx, δy, δz, any variations whatever of the three coordinates x, y, z, which variations are not necessarily the same with the differentials dx, dy, dz, that express the spaces described by the moving body parallel to the three coordinates during the instant dt, the equation (b) of No. 3, will become

$$0=\delta x.\left\{d.\ \frac{dx}{dt}-P.dt.\right\}+\delta y.\left\{d.\ \frac{dy}{dt}-Q.dt.\right\}+\delta z.\left\{d.\ \frac{dz}{dt}-R.dt\cdot\right\}.\ (f)^{*}$$

We may put the coefficients of δx, δy, δz, separately equal to nothing; if the point M be free, and the element dt of the time being supposed constant, the differential equations will become

$$\frac{d^2x}{dt^2}=P\ ;\quad \frac{d^2y}{dt^2}=Q;\quad \frac{d^2z}{dt^2}=R.\dagger$$

* From the equation (f) it appears that the laws of the motion of a material point may be reduced to those of their equilibrium, we shall see in No. 18, that the laws of the motion of any system of bodies are reducible to the laws of their equilibrium.

† If P, Q, R, are given in functions of the coordinates, then by integrating twice we shall obtain the values of x, y, and z, in functions of the time; two constant quantities are introduced by these integrations, the first depends on the velocity of the point at a given instant, the second depends on the position of the point at the same instant.

If the values of the coordinates x, y, z, which are determined by these integrations, give equations of this form, $x=a.f(t)$, $y=b.f(t)$, $z=c.\ f(t)$, the point will move in a right line, the cosines of the angles which the direction of this line makes with x, y, and z, are respectively equal to $\frac{a}{\sqrt{a^2+b^2+c^2}}$, $\frac{b}{\sqrt{a^2+b^2+c^2}}$, $\frac{c}{\sqrt{a^2+b^2+c^2}}$, the constant quantities a, b, c, depend on the nature of the function $f(t)$, if $f(t)=t$; a, b, c, represent the uniform velocities parallel to x, y, and z, the uniform velocity of the point $=\sqrt{a^2+b^2+c^2}$, if $f(t)=t^2$, then a, b, c, are proportional to the accelerating forces parallel to x, y, z, and the point will be moved with a motion uniformly accelerated, repre-

If the point M be not free, but subjected to move on a curve or on a surface, then by means of the equations to the curve or surface, there must be eliminated from the equation (f) as many of the variations δx, δy, δz, as there are equations, and the coefficients of the remaining variations must be put separately equal to nothing.*

8. We may suppose the variations δx, δy, δz, in the equation (f) equal to the differentials dz, dy, dz, since these differentials are necessarily subjected to the conditions of the motion of the point M. By making this supposition, and then integrating the equation (f), we shall have†

$$\frac{dx^2+dy^2 dz^2}{dt^2}=c+2.\int(P.dx+Q.dy+Rdz,$$

sented by $\sqrt{a^2+b^2+c^2}$. If $x=a.f(t)+b f'(t)$, $y=c\ f(t)+d.(f't)$, $z=\epsilon.\ f(t)+g.\ f'(t)$, the point will move in a curved line, however, this curve is of single curvature; for by eliminating t we obtain an equation of the form $a'x+b'y+c'z=0$, which is the equation of a plane. The simplest case of this form is $x=a\ (t)+b\ (t^2)$, $y=b\ (t)+d\ (t^2)$, $z=\epsilon.\ (t)+g\ (t^2)$, eliminating t between the two first equations we shall obtain an equation of the second order between x and y, and from the relation which exists between the coefficients of the three first terms of this equation, it is evident that the curve is a parabola. If $x=f(t)$, $y=F(t)$, $z=ff(t)$, all the points of the curve will not exist in the same plane.

* The law of the force being given, the investigation of the curve which this force makes the body describe, is much more difficult than the reverse problem of determining the velocity, and force the nature of the curve described being given; as the integrations which are required in the first case, are much more difficult than the differentials which determine the velocity and force in the second case.

† We have seen in No. 7, that when a point moves in a right line, its velocity is equa to the element of the space divided by the element of the time; this is also true when the motion is curvilinear; for if $P.Q.R$, the forces soliciting the point parallel to the three coordinates, should suddenly cease, then the velocity in the direction of each of the coordinates will be uniform, and equal to $\frac{dx}{dt}$, $\frac{dy}{dt}$, $\frac{dz}{dt}$, respectively, (see second note to the preceding number) consequently the motion of the point will become uniform, and its direction rectilinear, ∵ if v express this velocity we will have, by first note to No. 6.

$$v.=\frac{\sqrt{dx^2+dy^2+dz^2}}{dt}=\frac{ds}{dt}\text{ for }ds=\sqrt{dx^2+dy^2+dz^2}.$$

c being a constant quantity. $\frac{dx^2+dy^2+dz^2}{dt^2}$ is the square of the velocity of M, which velocity we will denote by v; therefore if $Pdx, + Q.dy, + Rdz,$ is an exact differential of a function φ, we shall have

$$v^2=c+2\varphi. \quad (g)$$

This case obtains when the forces which solicit the point M are functions of the distances of their origins from this point. In fact, if S, S', &c.* represent these forces, s, s', being the distances of the point M

F

(See Lacroix Traite Elementaire, No 139.) The rectilinear direction is that of the tangent, for if A, B, C, denote the angles which this direction makes respectively with x, y, z, we shall have $v.\cos. A=\frac{dx}{dt}$, $v.\cos. B=\frac{dy}{dt}$, $v.\cos. C=\frac{dz}{dt}$, by substituting for v. its value, which has been given above, and then dividing we obtain $\cos. A=\frac{dx}{ds}$, $\cos. B=\frac{dy}{ds}$, $\cos. C=\frac{dz}{ds}$; but these are the cosines of the angles which the tangent makes with the coordinates $\because$ the tangent coincides with the line along which the point moves when the forces cease.

* If $P.dx+Q.dy+Rdz=f(x, y, z,)$ then $v^2=c+2.f(x, y, z,)$ let A be the velocity corresponding to the coordinates a, b, c; then $A^2=c+2.f(a, b, c,)$ $\because v^2-A^2=2.f(x, y, z)-2.f(a, b, c,)$ $\because$ the difference of the squares of the velocities depends only on the coordinates of the extreme points of the line described; consequently when the point describes a curve, the pressure of the moving point on the curve does not affect the velocity.

The constant quantity c depends on the values of v, and of x, y, z, at any given instant.

When the moving point describes a curve returning into itself, the velocity is always the same at the same point.

If the velocities of two points, of which one describes a curve, while the other describes a right line, are equal at equal distances from the centre of force in any one case, they will be equal at all other equal distances.

If the force varies as the nth power of the distance from the centre, then s and s' being any two distances, φ or $f(x, y, z,)=s^{n+1}$, $\because v^2-A^2$, $s^{n+1}-s'^{n+1}$.

In this case also the differential of the velocity $=s.^n ds$, therefore by erecting ordinates

from their origins; the resultant of all these forces multiplied by the variation of its direction will, by No. 2, be equal to $\Sigma.S.\delta s$; it is also equal to $P.\delta x+Q.\delta y+R.\delta z$; therefore we have

$$P.\delta x+Q.\delta y+R.\delta z=\Sigma.S.\delta s.$$

and as the second member of this equation is an exact variation, the first will be so likewise.

From the equation (g)* it follows, 1st, that if the point M is not

proportional to s^n, we can exhibit the figure which represents the square of the velocity, when n is positive the figure is of the parabolic species, when negative it is hyperbolic.

If the distances increase in arithmetical progression, while the force decreases in geometric progression, the figure representing the square of the velocity will be the logarithmic curve. See Principia Matthematica, lib. 1, prop. 40, 39.

If $Pdx+Q\,dy+Rdz$ be an exact differential, then $\frac{dP}{dy}=\frac{dQ}{dx}$; $\frac{dP}{dz}=\frac{dR}{dx}$ + &c. P,Q,R, must be functions of x, y, and z, independant of the time ∵ if the centres to which the forces were directed had a motion in space, the time would be involved, and consequently $P.dx+Q.dy+R.dz$, would *not* be an exact differential, for then the equations $\frac{dP}{dz}=\frac{dR}{dx}$ + &c. would not obtain.

When the forces P,Q,R, arise from friction or the resistance of a fluid, the equation $P.dx+Q\,dy+R.dz$, does not satisfy the preceding conditions of integrability, for since $P.Q,R$, depend on the velocities $\frac{dx}{dt}$, $\frac{dy}{dt}$, $\frac{dz}{dt}$ in this case; it is evident that $P.dx+Q.dy+Rdz$ cannot be an exact differential of a function of x, y, and z, considered as independant variables ∵ to integrate $P\,dx+Q.dy+R.dz$, we should substitute the values of these variables and their differentials in a function of the time, which supposes that we have solved the problem; consequently when the centre to which the force is directed is in motion, and when the force arises from friction or resistance, the velocity is not independant of the curve described.

* The velocity is constant when $f(x,y,z)$ is constant; and also when $f(x,y,z,)$ vanishes, when the point is put in motion by an initial impulse, the motion is uniform, and its direction rectilinear, and $v^2=A^2$, $\frac{dx}{dt}=c$, $\frac{dy}{dt}=c'$ $\frac{dz}{dt}=c''$, for then $\left\{\frac{d^2x}{dt^2}\right\}=P$, $\left\{\frac{d^2y}{dt^2}\right\}=Q$, $\left\{\frac{d^2z}{dt^2}\right\}=R$, are equal respectively to nothing.

The velocity lost by a body, in its passage from one plane to another, is proportional to

solicited by any forces, its velocity is constant, because then $\varphi=0$. It is easy to be assured of this otherwise, by observing, that a body moving on a surface or on a curved line, looses, at each rencounter with the indefinitely small plane of the surface, or indefinitely small side of the curve, but an indefinitely small part of its velocity of the second order. 2dly. That the point M, in passing from a given point with a given velocity, will have, when it attains another point, the same velocity, whatever may be the curve which it shall have described.

But if the point is not constrained to move on a determined curve, then the curve described possesses a singular property, to which we have been led by metaphysical considerations, and which is, in fact, but a remarkable consequence of the preceding differential equations. It consists in this, that the integral $\int v.ds$ comprised between the two extreme points of the curve described, is less than on any other curve if the point is free, or than on any other curve subjected to the same surface if the point is not entirely free.

To make this appear we shall observe, that $P.dx+Q.dy+Rdz$ being supposed an exact differential, the equation (g) gives

$$v.\delta v = P.\delta x+Q.\delta y+R\delta z.$$

in like manner the equation (f) of the preceding number becomes,

$$0=\delta x.\, d.\frac{dx}{dt}+\delta y.d.\frac{dy}{dt}+\delta z.d.\frac{dz}{dt}-v.dt.\,\delta v.$$

naming ds the element of the curve described by the moving point, we shall have

$$v.dt=ds;\ ds=\sqrt{dx^2+dy^2+dz^2},$$

the difference between radius and cosine of the inclination of the planes, i. e. to the versed sine, or to the square of the sine; and when the curvature is continuous the sine is an indefinitely small quantity of first the order, ∵ the velocity lost, is an indefinitely small quantity of the second order.

consequently

$$0 = \delta x.d.\frac{dx}{dt} + \delta y.d.\frac{dy}{dt} + \delta z.d.\frac{dz}{dt} - ds.\delta v, \quad (h)$$

by differentiating with respect to δ, the expression for ds, we have

$$\frac{ds}{dt}.\delta.ds. = \frac{dx}{dt}.\delta.dx + \frac{dy}{dt}.\delta.dy + \frac{dz}{dt}.\delta.dz.$$

The characteristics d and δ being independant, it is indifferent which precedes the other; therefore the preceding equation may be made to assume the following form:

$$v.\delta.ds = d.\frac{(dx\,\delta x + dy.\delta y + dz.\delta z)}{dt} - \delta x.d.\frac{dx}{dt} - \delta y.d.\frac{dy}{dt} - \delta z.d.\frac{dz}{dt},$$

by substracting from the first member of this equation the second member of the equation (h) we shall have

$$\delta\,(vds) = \frac{d.(dx.\delta x + dy.\delta y + dz.\delta z)}{dt}*$$

This last equation integrated with respect to the characteristic d, gives

$$\delta.\int v.ds = \text{const.} + \frac{dx.\delta x + dy.\delta y + dz.\delta z}{dt},$$

* For $d.\frac{(dx.\delta x+dy.\delta y+dz.\delta z)}{dt} = d.\frac{dx}{dt}\delta x. + d.\frac{dy}{dt}\delta y + d.\frac{dz}{dt}\delta z; + \frac{dx}{dt}d.\delta x + \frac{dy}{dt}d.\delta y + \frac{dz}{dt}d.\delta x \left\{ = \frac{dx}{dt}\delta.dx + \frac{dy}{dt}\delta.dy + \frac{dz}{dt}\delta.dz.\right\}$, ∵ by performing the operations prescribed in the text, we obtain $v.\delta.ds + ds.\delta v = \delta.(v.ds) = d.\left\{\frac{dx.\delta x + dy.\delta y + dz.\delta z}{dt}\right\}$. This equation being integrated with respect to the characteristic d gives $\int.\delta.(v.ds.)$ const. $+ \frac{dx.\delta x + dy.\delta y + dz.\delta z}{dt}$; when the two extreme points of the curve are fixed, the variations δx, δy, δz, of the coordinates must be equal to nothing at these points; consequently the variation of $\int.(v.ds)$ is equal to nothing, and ∵ $\int(v.ds)$ is either a maximum or minimum; but it is evident from the nature of function $\int.(v.ds.)$ that it does not

If we extend this integral to the entire curve described by the moving point, and if we suppose the extreme points of this curve invariable, we will have $\delta.\int v.ds = 0$, that is to say, of all the curves, which a point solicited by the forces P, Q, R, can describe in its passage from one given point to another, it describes that in which the variation of the integral $\int v.ds$, is equal to nothing, and in which, consequently, this integral is a *minimum*.

If the point moves on a given surface without being solicited by any force, its velocity is constant, and the integral $\int v.ds$ becomes $v.\int ds$. Therefore in this case the curve described by the moving point is the shortest which it is possible to trace on the surface from the point of departure to that of arrival.*

9. Let us determine the pressure of a point moving on a curved surface. Instead of eliminating from the equation (f) of No. 7, one of the variations δx, δy, δz, by means of the equation to the surface, we can by No. 3 add to this equation, the differential equation of the sur-

* When the velocity is constant the integral $\int v.ds$, becomes $v.\int.ds = v.s$, and since s is a minimum, the time of describing s, which is proportional to s in consequence of the uniformity of the motion, will be a minimum in like manner. Since the equation $\delta.\int.(v.ds) = 0$, has place when $Pdx + Qdy + R.dz$ is an exact differential, it belongs to all curves that are described by the actions of forces directed to *fixed* centres, the forces being functions of the distance from those centres; and if the form of these functions was given we could determine the species of the curve described, by substituting for v its value in terms of the force, (which we have by a preceding note), and then investigating by the calculus of variations, the relation existing between the coordinates of the curve which answers to the minimum of the expression $\int(v.ds)$. If S the force varied as $\frac{1}{s^2}$ by making use of Polar coordinates we would arrive at the polar equation of a conic section, in which the origin of the coordinates would be at the focus of the section; if S was proportional to s the resulting equation would be also that of a conic section, the origin of the coordinates being at the centre of the section. From the preceding property the known laws of refraction and reflection have been deduced. Mr. Laplace has also successfully applied it to the investigation of the law of double refraction of Iceland chrystal, which was first announced by Huyghens, and afterwards confirmed by the celebrated experiments of Malus on the polarization of light. See a paper of Laplace's in the volume of the Institute for the year 1809.

face multiplied by the indeterminate—λdt, and then consider the three variations δx, δy, δz, as independant quantities. Therefore let $u=0$ be the equation of the surface, by adding to the equation (f) the term $-\lambda\delta u.\,dt.$ the pressure will, by No. 3, be equal to

$$\lambda.\sqrt{\left\{\frac{du}{dx}\right\}^2+\left\{\frac{du}{dy}\right\}^2+\left\{\frac{du}{dz}\right\}^2}$$

At first let us suppose that the point is not solicited by any force; its velocity v will be constant, and since $v.dt=ds$; the element of the time being supposed constant, the element ds of the curve will be so likewise, and by adding to the equation (f) the term $-\lambda.\delta u.dt$, we will obtain the three following:

$$0=v.^2\frac{d^2x}{ds^2}-\lambda.\left\{\frac{du}{dx}\right\};\quad 0=v^2\frac{d^2y}{ds^2}-\lambda.\left\{\frac{du}{dy}\right\};$$

$$0=v.^2\frac{d^2z}{ds^2}-\lambda.\left\{\frac{du}{dz}\right\},^*$$

from which we may collect

$$\lambda.\sqrt{\left\{\frac{du}{dx}\right\}^2+\left\{\frac{du}{dy}\right\}^2+\left\{\frac{du}{dz}\right\}^2}=v.^2\frac{\sqrt{(d^2x)^2(+d^2y^2)+(d^2z^2)}}{ds^2},$$

but ds being constant, the radius of curvature of the curve described by the moving point is equal to

$$\frac{ds^2}{\sqrt{(d^2x)^2+(d^2y)^2+(d^2z)^2}}\;\dagger$$

* By substituting for dt^2 its value $\frac{ds^2}{dv^2}$, we eliminate the time t, if the resulting equations be squared, we obtain, by adding their corresponding members,

$$\frac{v.}{ds^4}(d^2x^2+d^2y^2+d^2z^2)=\lambda^2\left\{\frac{du}{dx}\right\}^2+\left\{\frac{du}{dy}\right\}^2+\left\{\frac{du}{dz}\right\}^2.$$

† This expression for the radius of the osculating curve may be thus investigated: let

∴ by naming this radius r we shall have

$$\lambda.\sqrt{\left\{\frac{du}{dx}\right\}^2+\left\{\frac{du}{dy}\right\}^2+\left\{\frac{du}{dz}\right\}^2}=\frac{v^2}{r},$$

then $r^2=(x-a)^2+(y-b)^2+(z-c)^2$; $dx.(x-a)+dy.(y-b)+dz.(z-c)$, the differential of this equation is equal to nothing, as any one of these coordinates may be considered as a function of the two remaining, we can obtain the following equations of partial differences $dx.(x-a)+dz.(z-c)=0$, $dy.(y-b)+dz.(z-c)=0$, (the values of dz in these equations are evidently different,) consequently we have $d^2x.(x-a)+d^2z.(z-c)+dx^2+dz^2=0$; $d^2y\,(y-b)+d^2z.(z-c)+dy^2+dz^2=0$, ∵ $(x-a)=-\frac{dz}{dx}(z-c)$, $(y-b)=-\frac{dz}{dy}$, $(z-c)$, and since ds is supposed to be constant, we have $d^2x.dx+d^2y.dy+d^2z.dz=0$, ($d^2z$ in this equation refers to the entire variation of dz,) consequently z being considered as a function of x and y, we obtain

$$d^2x.\,dx+d^2z.dz=0;\; d^2y.\,dy+d^2z.dz=0;\; ∵ \frac{dz}{dx}=-\frac{d^2x}{d^2z};\; \frac{dz}{dy}=-\frac{d^2y}{d^2z};$$

these values being substituted in place of $\frac{dz}{dx}\,\frac{dz}{dy}$; in the preceding equations we shall have

$$x-a=\frac{d^2x}{d^2z}\,(z-c),\;(y-b)=\frac{d^2y}{d^2z}.\,(z-c),$$

∵ by adding together the two preceding differential equations of the second order, substituting for $(x-a)\,(y-b)$ their values, and observing that the whole variation of z is equal to the sum of the partial ones in these equations, we obtain,

$$\frac{d^2x^2+d^2y^2+d^2z^2}{d^2z}.\,(z-c)+dx^2+dy^2+dz^2=0, \text{ consequently}$$

$$(z-c)^2=\frac{(dx^2+dy^2+dz^2)^2}{d^2x^2+d^2y^2+d^2z^2)}.\,d^2z^2;\text{ and as } r^2=(x-a)^2+(y-b)^2+(z-c)^2.$$

by substituting for $(x-a)^2\,(y-b^2$ their values $\frac{d^2x^2}{d^2z^2}.)z-c)^2$; $\frac{d^2y^2}{d^2z^2}.(z-c^2)$, which have been given, we obtain

$$(x-a)^2+(y-b)^2+(z-c)^2=\frac{(dx^2+dy^2+dz^2)^2}{d^2x^2+d^2y^2+d^2)^2}.\,(d^2x^2+d^2y^2+d^2z^2)$$

$$∵ r=\sqrt{(x-a)^2+(y-b)^2+(z-c)^2}=\frac{ds^2}{\sqrt{d^2x^2+d^2y^2+d^2z^2}}.$$

consequently the pressure which the point exercises against the surface is equal to the square of the velocity divided by the radius of curvature of the curve described.

If the point moves on a spheric surface,* it will describe the circumference of a great circle of the sphere, which passes through the primitive direction of its motion; since there is no reason why it should deviate to the right rather than to the left of the plane of this circle; therefore its pressure against the surface, or what amounts to the same, against the circumference which it describes, is equal to the square of the velocity divided by the radius of this circle.

If we conceive the point attached to the extremity of a thread destitute of mass, having the other extremity fastened to the centre of the surface, it is evident that the force with which the point presses the circumference is equal to the force with which the string would be tended if the point was retained by it alone. The effort which this point would make to tend the string, and to increase its distance from the centre of the circle, is denominated the centrifugal force; therefore the centrifugal is equal to the square of the velocity divided by the radius.

The centrifugal force† of a point moving on any curve whatever is

* If the point move on a spherical surface, the motion will be necessarily performed on a great circle, for the deflection can only take place in the direction of radius, and in the plane in which the body moves.

† If the body moves on any curve whatever, the centrifugal force $=\frac{v^2}{r}$, this force acts in the direction of a normal to the curve, and if all the accelerating forces which act on the point be resolved into two, of which one is in the direction of the normal, and the other in the direction of the tangent, the resultant of the centrifugal force, and of the former of these decomposed forces, is the entire pressure with which the point acts against the curve, and the resistance of the curve is an accelerating force equal and contrary to this resultant. If we denote this normal force by L, and if A, B, C, be the angles which it makes with the coordinates x, y, z, respectively, then by the equation (f) and No. 3, we have

$$\frac{d^2x}{dt^2}=P+L.\cos.A;\ \frac{d^2y}{dt^2}=Q+L.\cos.B;\ \frac{d^2z}{dt^2}=R+L.\cos.C;$$

equal to the square of the velocity divided by the radius of curvature of the curve; because the indefinitely small arc of this curve is confounded with the circumference of the osculating circle. Therefore we shall

and since $\frac{dx}{ds}$, $\frac{dy}{ds}$, $\frac{dz}{ds}$, express the cosines of the angles which the tangent makes with x, y, and z, $\frac{dx}{ds}.\cos A+\frac{dy}{ds}.\cos. B+\frac{dz}{ds}.\cos. C.=0$; because the tangent is perpendicular to the normal. (See last note to No. 1). We have also $\cos{}^2 A+\cos.{}^2 B+\cos.{}^2 C=1$, and the four undetermined quantities L, A, B, C, being eliminated between the five preceding equations, the resulting equation will be one of the second order between x, y, z, and t; this equation combined with the two equations of the trajectory which are given in each particular case, are sufficient to determine the coordinates in a function of the time. See notes to No. 3, and No. 7.

The elimination of L, A, B, C, might be effected by one operation; for multiplying the three preceding equations by dx, dy, dz, respectively, and adding them together, we obtain the following equation:

$$\frac{dx.d^2x+dy.d^2y+dz.d^2z}{dt^2}=P.dx+Q.dy.+R.dz+L.(\cos. A.dx+\cos. B.dy+\cos. C.dz.)$$

(the latter part of this second member is equal to nothing, as has been already remarked;) and since $ds^2=dx^2+dy^2+dz^2$, $d^2s.ds=d^2x.dx+d^2y.dy+d^2z.dz$, ∴ we shall have

$$\frac{d^2s}{dt^2}=P.\frac{dx}{ds}+Q.\frac{dy}{ds}+R.\frac{dz}{ds};$$

from this last equation it appears that the accelerating force resolved in the direction of the tangent, is equal to the second differential coefficient of the arc considered as a function of the time, ∵ this expression for the force has place whatever be the nature of the line along which the point moves. See Notes to No. 7. In like manner it appears that the expression for the force in the direction of the tangent is altogether independant of L. It is also evident, that when there is no accelerating force $\frac{d^2s}{dt^2}=0$, this also follows from the circumstance of the velocity being uniform when P, Q, R, are equal to nothing.

Let V denote the resultant of all the accelerating forces which act on the point, and θ the angle which this resultant makes with the normal, then $V.\cos.\theta$ will be the expression of the resultant resolved in the direction of the normal; and when all the points of the curve exist in the same plane, the entire pressure will be equal to the sum or difference of $\frac{v^2}{r}$, and $V.\cos.\theta$, according as these two forces act in the same or in con-

have the pressure of the point on the curve which it describes by adding to the square of the velocity, divided by the radius of curvature, the pressure produced by the forces which solicit this point.*†

trary directions, $\therefore +L = \pm \frac{v^2}{r} + V.\cos.\theta$. We can express this pressure otherwise by means of the rectangular coordinates; for since P, Q, are the expressions for the force V resolved parallel to x and y, these forces resolved in the direction of the normal are equal respectively to $P.\frac{dy}{ds}$; $Q.\frac{dx}{ds}$, (the signs of $\frac{dx}{ds}$, and $\frac{dy}{ds}$, are evidently different) consequently we have

$$V.\cos.\theta = +P.\frac{dy}{ds} + Q.\frac{dx}{ds}, \text{ and } \because L = \frac{v^2}{r} + P.\frac{dy}{ds} + Q.\frac{dx}{ds},$$

therefore if we know the equation of the trajectory, and if we have also the values of P and Q in terms of the coordinates, we can determine the velocity, and consequently L, and substituting this value of L in the expressions for $\frac{d^2x}{dt^2}$, $\frac{d^2y}{dt^2}$, $\frac{d^2z}{dt^2}$, which have been given in the foregoing part of this note, we might by integrating determine the velocity in the direction of each of the coordinates, and also the position of the point at a given moment.

If the point be attached to one extremity of a thread supposed without mass, of which the other extremity is fixed in the evolute of the curve described, then the point receiving such an impulse, that the string remaining always tended, may unroll itself in the plane of the evolute, it will describe the given curve; the direction of the string is always perpendicular to the curve, and its tension is equal to the normal pressure on the trajectory, and consequently equal to $\frac{v^2}{r} + \frac{P.dy + Q\,dx}{ds}$. By equating this expression of L to nothing, we can derive the equation of those trajectories in which the motion is free, or in which the trajectory may be described freely, i. e. it is not necessary to retain the point on the curve by means of a thread, or a canal, or any perpendicular force.

* If the motion is performed in a resisting medium, this resistance may be considered as a force acting in a direction contrary to that of the motion of the body, consequently it must tend to some point in the tangent. If we denote this resistance by I its moment is equal $-I.\delta i$ ($i = \sqrt{(x-l)^2+(y-m)^2+(z-n)^2}$, l, m, n, are the coordinates of the centre of the force I, therefore $\delta i = \frac{(x-l)}{i}.\delta x + \frac{(y-m)}{i}.\delta y + \frac{(z-n)}{i}.\delta z$; if we suppose the centre of force in the tangent, then $i = \sqrt{dx^2+dy^2+dz^2} = ds \because \frac{x-l}{i} = \frac{dx}{ds}$;

$\frac{y-m}{i} = \frac{dy}{ds}$; $\frac{z-n}{i} = \frac{dz}{ds}$; and $\delta i = \frac{dx}{ds}.\delta x + \frac{dy}{ds}.\delta y + \frac{dz}{ds}.\delta z$, if the resisting medium was in motion, its motion must be compounded with the motion of the body, in order to have the direction of the resisting force. If da, db, dc, be the spaces described by the medium, while the body describes ds, these quantities must be added or subducted from dx, dy, dz, in order to have the relative motions, and as $ds = \sqrt{dx^2+dy^2+dz^2}$, if we make $d\sigma = \sqrt{(dx-da)^2+(dy-db)^2+(dx-dc)^2}$, we shall have $\delta i = \frac{dx-da}{d\sigma}.\delta x + \frac{dy-db}{d\sigma}.\delta y + \frac{dz-dz}{d\sigma}.\delta z$. The resistance I in general $= \psi(v)$, a function of the velocity, in this case it is a function of the relative velcoity.

By the preceding investigation we are enabled to apply our general formula to motions made in resisting mediums without entering into a *particular* consideration of this species of motion. However the analysis becomes very complicated when the forces which compose P, Q. R, exist in different planes, and as in this case, the causes on which the variation of the velocity depends, arise in some measure from the velocities themselves, we are not permitted to regard $P.dx + Q.dy + R.dz$, as an exact differential of three independant variables, which facilitates our investigations when the motion is performed in a vacuo. See Notes to Nos. 8.

We might also reduce to our general formula, the differential equations of motion, when the retardation arises from the friction against the sides of the canal.

† If the body moved on a surface we might, as before, abstract from the consideration of the surface, and consider the material point entirely free by adding to the given forces another accelerating force, of which the intensity is unknown, and of which the direction is normal to the surface, ∵ if this force be denoted by L we shall have, by the equation (f) of No. 7, and by No. 3, the following equations:

$$\frac{d^2x}{dt^2} = P + L.N.\left\{\frac{\delta u}{\delta x}\right\};\quad \frac{d^2y}{dt^2} = Q. + L.N.\left\{\frac{\delta u}{\delta y}\right\};\quad \frac{d^2z}{dt^2} = R. + L.N.\left\{\frac{\delta u}{\delta z}\right\};$$

($u=0$ is the equation of the suface. See Notes to No. 3).

If we eliminate L between these three equations, N will also disappear; and if the two differential equations of the second order, which result from this elimination, be combined with the equation $u=0$ of the surface, we can determine the three coordinates of the point in a function of the time. If we multiply the preceding equations by dx, dy, dz. respectively, and then add together the corresponding members, we will obtain

$$\frac{d^2x.dx + d^2y.dy + d^2z.dz}{dt^2} = P.dx + Q.dy + Rdz + N.L.\left\{\frac{\delta u}{\delta x}\right\}dx + \left\{\frac{\delta u}{\delta y}\right\}dy +$$

$\left\{\frac{\delta u}{\delta z}\right\}dz$; but the last part of the second member is = to nothing,

When the point moves on a *surface*,* the pressure due to the centrifugal force, is equal to the square of the velocity, divided by the radius of the osculating circle, and multiplied by the sine of the inclination of the plane of this circle, to the plane which touches the surface; therefore, if we add to this pressure, that which arises from the action of the forces which solicit the point, we shall have the entire force with which the point presses the surface.

$\Big\{$since $du = 0$, and $\left\{\frac{du}{dx}\right\} = \left\{\frac{\delta u}{\delta x}\right\}$ ∵ if $P.dx + Q.dy + R.dz$ is an exact differential, we shall have $\frac{d^2s}{dt^2} = P.\frac{dx}{ds} + Q.\frac{dy}{dt} + R.\frac{dz}{ds}$, as before, and $\frac{ds^2}{dt^2} = v^2 = C + \int(P.dx + Q.dy + R.dz)$, and if P, Q, R, and consequently v were given in terms of the coordinates, we might obtain immediately the differential equations of the trajectory by multiplying the equation $\frac{d^2x}{dt^2} = P + L.N.\left\{\frac{\delta u}{\delta x}\right\}$, by dy and dz successively, and then subducting it from the two remaining equations multiplied by dx; by concinnating the resulting equations, substituting for dt its value $\frac{ds}{v}$, and for v its value in a function of the coordinates, we obtain two differential equations of the second order, from which eliminating the quantities LN there results a differential equation of the second order between the three coordinates x, y, z, solely; this equation, and the equation $u=0$ of the surface will be the two equations of the *trajectory*.

* If a point moves on any curve the centrifugal force is always directed along the radius of the osculating circle; and since the pressure on the surface is always estimated in the direction of a normal to the surface, (see No. 3) if the plane of the trajectory is not at right angles to the surface, the radius of the osculating circle will not coincide with the normal to the surface, and consequently the part of the centrifugal which produces a pressure on the surface is equal to $\frac{v^2}{r}$, multiplied into the cosine of the angle which the radius makes with the normal, but this angle is evidently the complement of the angle which the plane of the osculating circle makes with the plane which touches the surface. If the forces soliciting the point are resolved into two, of which one is perpendicular to the trajectory, then the resultant of this last force, and of the centrifugal force, will express the whole force of pressure on the curve; if this curve was fixed, it would be sufficient for the pressure to be counteracted, that its direction was in a plane perpendicular to this curve, but if the curve be one traced on a given surface, then, in order that the pressure should be counteracted, it is necessary that the resultant of the forces should be in the direction of a *normal* to the surface. See note to page 16.

We have seen that when the point is not solicited by any forces, its pressure against the surface, is equal to the square of the velocity, divided by the radius of the osculating circle; therefore the plane of this circle, that is to say, the plane which passes through two consecutive sides of the curve described by the point is then perpendicular to the surface. This curve on the surface of the earth is called the perpendicular to the meridian; and it has been proved (in No. 8) that it is the shortest which can be drawn from one point to another on the surface.*

* If we make the axis of one of the coordinates to coincide with the normal to the surface, we can *immediately* determine the inclination of the plane of the osculating circle to the plane touching the surface; for if we denote by A, B, the angles which the radius of the osculating circle makes with the normal and with the coordinate which is in the plane of the tangent, and by m, n, l, the angles which the resultant V of all the forces makes with the three coordinates, the force $\frac{v^2}{r}$ resolved parallel to these coordinates is equal to $\frac{v^2}{r}.\cos. A$, $\frac{v^2}{r}.\cos. B$, $+\frac{v^2}{r}.\cos. 100°$, (because the angle between the radius and tangent to the curve is equal to $100°$) in like manner the force V. resolved parallel to these coordinates equals $V.\cos. m$, $V.\cos. n$, $V.\cos. l$, since A and m denote the inclinations of the radius of curvature, and of the resultant to the normal, $\frac{v^2}{r}.\cos. A+V.\cos. m$, express the pressure of the point on the surface, $V.\cos. n+\frac{v^2}{r}.\cos. 100°$, or $V.\cos. n$ is the force by which the body is moved; and since this motion is performed in the direction of the tangent, $V.\cos. l+\frac{v^2}{r}.\cos. B$, which expresses the motion perpendicular to the tangent must vanish; consequently we have $V.\cos. l+\frac{v^2}{r}.\cos. B=0$, ∵ if V. l, v, and r were given we might determine B, which is = to the inclination of the plane of the osculating circle to the plane touching the surface, it also follows, that when the point is not solicited by any accelerating force, $\frac{v^2}{r}.\cos. B=0$, ∴ $B=100°$, or the plane of the osculating circle is perpendicular to the surface, which we have previously established from other considerations.

If the plane whose intersection with the surface produces the given curve is not *perpendicular* to the surface, then the radius of curvature is equal to the sine of the inclination of the cutting plane to the plane touching the surface, multiplied into the radius of curvature of the section made by a plane passing through the normal to the surface, and through the intersection of the plane touching the surface and the cutting plane. See Lacroix, No. 324. ∴ the pressure is the same whether the point move in a greater or

10. Of all the forces that we observe on the earth, the most remarkable is gravity; it penetrates the most inward parts of bodies, and would make them all fall with equal velocities, if the resistance of the air was removed. Gravity is very nearly the same at the greatest heights to which we are able to ascend, and at the lowest depths to which we can descend; its direction is perpendicular to the horizon, but on account of the small extent of the curves which projectiles describe relatively to the circumference of the earth, we may, without sensible error, suppose that it is constant, and that it acts in parallel lines. These bodies being moved in a resisting fluid, we shall call b the resistance which they experience; it is directed along the side ds of the curve which they describe; moreover we will denote the gravity by g. This being premised, let us resume the equation (f) of No. 7, and suppose that the plane of x and y is horizontal, and that the origin of z is at the most elevated point; the force b will produce in the direction of the coordinates x, y, z, the three forces $-b.\frac{dx}{ds}$, $-b.\frac{dy}{ds}$, $-b.\frac{dz}{ds}$ ∵ by No. 7 we shall have $P=-b.\frac{dx}{ds}$; $Q=-b.\frac{dy}{ds}$; $R=-b.\frac{dz}{ds}+g.$* and the equation (f) becomes

$$0=\delta x.\left\{d.\frac{dx}{dt}+b.\frac{dx}{ds}dt.\right\}+\delta y.\left\{d.\frac{dy}{dt}+b.\frac{dy}{ds}dt.\right\}$$
$$+\delta z.\left\{d.\frac{dz}{dt}+b.\frac{dz}{ds}dt.-g.dt.\right\}*$$

less circle, for the sine of inclination occurs both in the numerator and denominator of the expression, this also follows from considering the proportion of the sagitta of curvature in a perpendicular and oblique plane.

The investigation of the shortest line which can be drawn between two given points on a curved surface, whose equation is $u=0$, by the method of variations, leads us to the same conclusions. See Lacroix. The consideration of the shortest line which can be traced on a spheroidical surface is of great importance in the theory of the figure of the earth. (See Book 3, No. 38.)

* Since the force b acts in the direction of the tangent or of the element ds of the curve (see note to No. 9,) this force resolved parallel to the three coordinates x, y, z, $= b.\frac{dx}{ds}$, $b.\frac{dy}{ds}$, $b.\frac{dz}{ds}$, for $\frac{dx}{ds}$, $\frac{dy}{ds}$, $\frac{dz}{ds}$ are $=$ to the cosines of the angles

If the body be entirely free we shall have the three equations

$$0=d.\frac{dx}{dt}+b.\frac{dx}{ds}.dt;\ 0=d.\frac{dy}{dt}+b.\frac{dy}{ds}.dt;$$
$$0=d.\frac{dz}{dt}+b.\frac{dz}{ds}.dt-g.dt,$$

The two first give

$$\frac{dy}{dt}.\ d.\frac{dx}{dt}-\frac{dx}{dt}.\ d.\frac{dy}{dt}=0.$$

from which we obtain by integrating, $dx=fdy$, f being a constant arbitrary quantity. This equation belongs* to an horizontal right line, therefore the body moves in a vertical plane.

By taking this plane for that of x, z, we shall have $y=0$, the two equations,

$$0=d.\frac{dx}{dt}+b.\frac{dx}{ds}.dt;\ 0=d.\frac{dz}{dt}.+b.\frac{dz}{ds}.dt-g.dt,$$

will give, by making dx constant,

$$b=\frac{ds.d^2t}{dt^3},\ 0=\frac{d^2z}{dt}-\frac{dz.d^2t}{dt^2}+b.\frac{dz}{ds}.dt-g.dt.$$

From* which we obtain $g.dt^2=d^2z$, and by taking the differential

which the tangent makes with the three coordinates; they are affected with negative signs because they tend to diminish the coordinates.

* Dividing $\frac{dy}{dt}.d.\frac{dx}{dt}-\frac{dx}{dt}.d.\frac{dy}{dt}=0$, by $\frac{dy^2}{dt^2}$ it becomes $d.\left\{\frac{\frac{dx}{dt}}{\frac{dy}{dt}}\right\}=0$, ∴ by integrating $\frac{\frac{dx}{dt}}{\frac{dy}{dt}}=f$ and $dx=fdy$, since the equation of the projection of the line which the projectile describes on a horizontal plane, is that of a right line, the body must have moved in a vertical plane, otherwise its projection on an horizontal plane would not be a right line; this circumstance we might have anticipated from the manner in which the forces act on the body.

* If we make dt constant in the equation $d.\frac{dx}{dt}+b.\frac{dx}{ds}.dt=0$, we get $-\frac{dx.d^2t}{dt^2}$

$2g.dt.d^2t = d^3z$, if we substitute for d^2t its value $\frac{b.dt^3}{ds}$, and for dt^2 its value $\frac{d^2z}{g}$, we shall have

$$\frac{b}{g} = \frac{ds.d^3z}{2(d^2z)^2}.$$

This equation gives the law of the resistance b, which is necessary to make the projectile describe a given curve.

If the resistance be * proportional to the square of the velocity, b is equal to $h.\frac{ds^2}{dt^2}$, h being constant, when the density of the medium is uniform. We shall have then

$$\frac{b}{g} = \frac{h.ds^2}{g.dt^2} = \frac{h.ds^2}{d^2z},$$

therefore $h.ds = \frac{d^3z}{2.d^2z}$, which gives by integrating $\frac{d^2z}{dx^2} = 2a.c^{2hs}$.†

$+b.\frac{dx}{ds}.dt = 0$, $\therefore b = \frac{ds.d^2t}{dt^3}$, by substituting this quantity in place of b, and differentiating, we get the expression

$$\frac{d^2z}{dt} - \frac{dz.d^2t}{dt^2} + \frac{ds.d^2t}{dt^3}.\frac{dz}{ds}dt - g.dt = \frac{d^2z}{dt} - \frac{dz.d^2t}{dt^2} + \frac{dz.d^2t}{dt^2} - g.dt. =$$

$\frac{d^2z}{dt} - g.dt = 0$, $\therefore$ by differentiating we obtain $d^3z = 2g.dt.d^2t$, and substituting for d^2t its value $b.\frac{dt^3}{ds}$, and for dt^2 its value $\frac{d^2z}{g}$, we arrive at the following equation,

$d^3z = \frac{2g.b.}{ds}\left\{\frac{d^2z}{g}\right\}^2 \therefore \frac{b}{g} = \frac{d^3z}{2(d^2z)^2}.ds.$

* The value of the constant coefficient h is obtained by experiment; it is different in different fluids, and when bodies of different figures move in the same fluid.

† Since the square of the velocity is equal to $\frac{ds^2}{dt^2}$, the resistance is expressed by $h.\frac{ds^2}{dt^2}$, $\therefore$ by substituting for dt^2 its value $\frac{d^2z}{g}$, $\frac{hds^2}{d^2z} = \frac{ds.d^3z}{2(d^2z)^2}$, $\therefore 2h.ds. = \frac{d^3z}{d^2z}$,

a being a constant arbitrary quantity, and c being the number whose hyperbolic logarithm is unity. If we suppose the resistance of the me-

H

$\because 2h.s = \log. d^2z + \log. F \because c^{2hs} = F.d^2z, \because \frac{c^{2hs}}{F.dx^2} = \frac{d^2z}{dx^2}$. (Let $2a = \frac{1}{F.dx^2}$) and we shall have $2ac^{2hs} = \frac{d^2z}{dx^2}$; dx being constant it is permitted to introduce dx^2 as a divisor. The constant quantity a depends on the velocity of projection, and on the angle which its direction makes with the horizon; for by substituting $-g.dt^2$ in place of d^2z we shall have $-\frac{dx^2}{dt^2} = \frac{g}{2a}.c^{-2hs}, \frac{dx^2}{dt^2}$ is the velocity of the body in the direction of the axis of x at the end of the time t; let u be the velocity of projection, and θ the angle which its direction makes with the horizon, we shall have at the same time $t = 0$, $x=0$, $z=0$, and $\frac{dx}{dt} = u. \cos. \theta, \because u^2. \cos.^2\theta = -\frac{g}{2a}$. Let h be the height due to the velocity u, $u^2 = 2gh$, $\because$ by substituting for u^2 its value, we deduce $a = \frac{-1}{4h} \frac{}{\cos.^2\theta}$

By making $dz = pdx$, ds becomes equal to $dx.\sqrt{1+p^2}$, $\because -c^{2hs}. ds = 2h. \cos.^2 \theta. dp. \sqrt{1+p^2}, \left\{\text{for } dp = \frac{d^2z}{dx}\right\} \because$ by integrating $\frac{-c^{2hs}.}{2h} + C = 2h. \cos.^2 \theta. \int dp.\sqrt{1+p^2}$,

$$\left\{= 2h. \cos.^2 \theta. \int \frac{dp}{\sqrt{1+p^2}} + 2h. \cos. \theta. \int \frac{dp.p^2}{\sqrt{1+p^2}}\right\} = h. \cos.^2 \theta. \log. (p+\sqrt{1+p^2}),$$

$+h. \cos.^2 \theta. p. \sqrt{1+p^2}$, the constant quantity C is easily found; for since p is the derivitive function of z considered as a function of x, at the commencement of the motion, when $s=0$, $p=$ the tangent of the angle of projection which is given, $\because C$ is equal to

$$h. \cos.^2 \theta. \left\{(\log. (\tan. \theta + \sec. \theta) + \tan. \theta. \sec. \theta.)\right\} + \frac{1}{2h}.$$

By substituting for $-\frac{c^{2hs}}{2h}$ its value, which we obtain from the equation $-\frac{c^{2hs}}{2h} = 2.. \cos.^2 \theta. \frac{dp}{dx}$, we deduce

$$dx = \frac{dp}{2h.\{(\log.(p+\sqrt{1+p^2})+p\sqrt{1+p^2})-C\}}, \text{ and } dz =$$

$$p.dx = \frac{p.dp}{2h\{(\log. (p+\sqrt{1+p^2})+p.\sqrt{1+p^2})-C\}}$$

and since $g.dt^2 = d^2z = dp.dx$ we have $dt^2 = \frac{dp.dx}{g}$,

dium to vanish, h is equal to 0; then by integrating* we will obtain the equation to the parabola $z=ax^2+bx+c$, b and c being constant arbitrary quantities.

The differential equation $d^2z=g.dt^2$, will give $dt^2=\frac{2a}{g}.dx^2$, from

$$\therefore dt=\frac{dp}{\{2gh\,(\log.\,(p+\sqrt{1+p^2})+p.\sqrt{1+p^2})-C\}^{\frac{1}{2}}}.$$

If the integrals for these values of dx, dy, dt, could be exhibited in a finite form, the problem would be completely solved, for the integrations of the two first equations would give the values of x and z in functions of p; and if p be eliminated between the resulting equations, the relation between x and y would be had; those integrations have hitherto baffled the skill of the most celebrated analysts. However by means of the expressions for dx and dz, we can describe the curve by a series of points, and the approximation will be always more accurate, according as we divide the interval between the extreme values of p into a greater number of parts. We might collect some of the remarkable properties of the curve described from the preceding values of dx, dz; for if p be very great, log. $(p+\sqrt{1+p^2})$ vanishes with respect to p, and $\therefore$ the limit of dx, dz, and dt are $\frac{dp}{2h.p^2}$, $\frac{dp}{2h.p}$, and $\frac{dp}{\sqrt{2gh.p}}$, $\therefore$ by integrating we get $x=a-\frac{1}{p}$, $z=a'+\log.\,p$, $t=a''+\frac{1}{2gh}$. log. p, the first equation indicates that x has a limit, the vertical ordinate increases indefinitely, but in a less ratio than p, therefore the descending branch has a vertical asymptote. By eliminating log. p in the expression for t we get an expression for z from which we may collect, that according as the direction of the motion approaches towards the vertical, the motion of the body tends to become uniform.

When the angle of projection is very small, we can find by approximation the relation which exists between x, and z, for that portion of the trajectory which is situated above the horizontal axis; in this case the tangent is very nearly horizontal, $\therefore$ p is very small, and $\sqrt{1+p^2}=1$, q.p. $\therefore ds=dx.\sqrt{1+p^2}=dx$, q.p. and $s=x$, for they commence together, and substituting x in place of s, we have $\frac{dp}{dx}=-\frac{c^{2hx}}{2h\cos.^2\theta}$, but θ being by hypothesis very small, $\cos.^2\theta=1$, $\therefore dp=-\frac{c^{2hx}}{2h}.\,dx$, by integrating this equation, when we know the value of the constant arbitrary quantity which is introduced by the integration we obtain the value of p and $\therefore$ of $z=\int p.dx$. See a memoir of Legendre's in the Transactions of the Academy of Berlin for the year 1782.

* In this case $\frac{d^2z}{dx^2}=2a$, $\therefore \frac{dz}{dx}=2ax+b$, $\therefore z=ax^2+bx+c$.

which we may obtain $t=x.\sqrt{\frac{2a}{g}}+f'$. If x, z, and t, commence together, we shall have $c=0$, $f'=0$, and consequently

$$t=x\sqrt{\frac{2a}{g}};\quad z=ax^2+bx,$$

which gives

$$z=\frac{gt^2}{2}+b.t.\sqrt{\frac{g}{2a}}$$

These three equations contain the whole theory of projectiles in a vacuum; it follows, from what precedes, that the velocity is uniform in an horizontal direction,* and that in the vertical direction the velocity is the same as if the body fell down the vertical. If the body moves from a state of repose b will vanish, and we shall have

$$\frac{dz}{dt}=gt;\quad z=\frac{1}{2}.g^2t;$$

therefore the velocity acquired increases as the time, and the space increases as the square of the time.

It is easy by means of these formulæ to compare the centrifugal force with that of gravity. For v being the velocity of a body moving in the circumference of a circle, of which the radius is r, it appears from No. 9, that its centrifugal force is equal to $\frac{v^2}{r}$. Let h be the height from which the body must fall to acquire the velocity v; by what precedes we shall have $v^2=2g.h$; from which we obtain $\frac{v^2}{r}=g.\frac{2h}{r}$. The centrifugal

* For $\frac{dx}{dt}$ = the velocity in an horizontal direction $=\sqrt{\frac{g}{2a}}$, and $\frac{dz}{dt}$ = the velocity in a vertical direction $=gt\,,\,b.\sqrt{\frac{g}{2a}}$.

force will be equal to the gravity g, if $h=\frac{r}{2}$. Therefore* a heavy body attached to the extremity of a thread, which is fixed at its other extremity, on an horizontal plane, will tend the string with the same force as if it was suspended vertically; provided that it moves on this plane, with a velocity equal to that which the body would acquire in falling down a height equal to half the length of the thread.

11. Let us consider the motion of a heavy body on a spherical surface, denoting its radius by r, and fixing the origin of the coordinates at its centre, we shall have $r^2-x^2-y^2-z^2=0$; this equation being compared with that of $u=0$, gives $u=r^2-x^2-y^2-z^2$; therefore if we add to the equation (f) of No. 7, the function δu multiplied by the indeterminate quantity $-\lambda.dt$, we shall have

$$0=\delta x.\left\{d.\frac{dx}{dt}+2\lambda.x.dt.\right\}+\delta y.\left\{d.\frac{dy}{dt}+2\lambda.y.dt.\right\}$$

$$+\delta z.\left\{d.\frac{dz}{dt}+2.\lambda.z.dt-g.dt.\right\}^{\dagger}$$

In this equation we can put the coefficients of each of the variations δx, δy, δz, equal to nothing, which gives the three following equations:

$$0=d.\frac{dx}{dt}+2\lambda.xdt,$$

$$0=d.\frac{dy}{dt}+2\lambda.y.dt.$$

$$0=d.\frac{dz}{dt}+2\lambda.z.dt-g.dt.$$

* The plane of the motion being horizontal, the force with which the string is tended arises entirely from the centrifugal force.

† For $\left\{\frac{\delta u}{\delta x}\right\}=-2x$, $\left\{\frac{\delta u}{\delta y}\right\}=-2y$, $\left\{\frac{\delta u}{\delta z}\right\}=-2z$.

The indeterminate λ makes known the force with which the point presses on the surface. This pressure by No. 9 is equal to

$$\lambda.\sqrt{\left\{\frac{du}{dx}\right\}^2+\left\{\frac{du}{dy}\right\}^2+\left\{\frac{du}{dz}\right\}^2};$$

consequently it is equal to $2\lambda r$; but by No. 8 we have

$$c+2gz=\frac{dx^2+dy^2+dz^2}{dt^2},$$

c being a constant arbitrary quantity; by adding this equation to the equations (A) divided by dt, and multiplied respectively by x, y, z, and then observing that $x.dx+y.dy+z.dz=0$, $x.d^2x+y.d^2y+z.d^2z+dx^2+dy^2+dz^2=0$, are the first and second differential equations of the surface, we shall obtain*

$$2\lambda.r=\frac{c+3gz}{r}.$$

* For performing these operations we get $c+2gz=$

$\frac{dx^2+dy^2+dz^2}{dt^2}+\frac{x.d^2x}{dt^2}+\frac{y.d^2y}{dt^2}+\frac{z.d^2z}{dt^2}+2\lambda.(x^2+y^2+z^2)-gz$, therefore we have

$2\lambda r^2=c+3gz$, and $2\lambda r=\frac{c+3gz}{r}$, $\because$ the pressure is equal to $\frac{c+3gz}{r}$, when the initial velocity c vanishes, the tension of the pendulum vibrating in a quadrantal arc is, at the lowest point, $=$ to three times the force of gravity; $\frac{z}{r}=$ the cosine of the angle which the radius r makes with the vertical, therefore it follows that when a body falls from a state of rest, the pressure on any point is proportional to the cosine, of the distance from the lowest point, it is easy to collect, in like manner, that the accelerating force varies as the right sine of the angular distance from the lowest point, we might from the preceding expression for the pressure determine the point where this pressure is in a given ratio to the force of gravity.

If we multiply the first of the equations (A) by $-y$, and add it to the second, multiplied by x, and then integrate their sum, we shall have

$$\frac{x.dy-y.dx}{dt}=c';\ *$$

c' being a new arbitrary quantity.

Thus the motion of the point is reduced to three differential equations of the first order,

$$x.dx+y.dy=-z.dz,$$

$$x.dy-y.dx=c'.dt,$$

$$\frac{dx^2+dy^2+dz^2}{dt^2}=c+2gz.$$

By squaring each member of the two first equations,† and then adding them together, we shall have

$$(x^2+y^2)\,(dx_2+dy^2)=c'^2dt^2+z^2dz^2.$$

* $x.dy-y.dx=c'.dt$ shews that the area described by a body moving on a spherical surface, and projected on the plane x, y, is proportional to the time; the same area projected on the plane x, z, or y, z, is not constant in a given time; for if we add to the first of the equations (A) multiplied by $-z$, the third multiplied by x, and then integrate their sum, it becomes equal to $\frac{x.dz-z.dx}{dt}=c''+\int.(gx.dt)$, this might have been anticipated, as the force g does not pass perpetually through the origin of the coordinates, $\because$ $x.dz-z.dx$, $y.dz-z.dy$ are not proportional to the time, but as there is no force acting parallel to the horizontal plane, $x.dy-y.dx$ must be proportional to the time.

† For we have in this case

$$x^2.dx^2+y^2.dy^2+2x.y.dx.dy=z^2.dz^2.$$
$$x^2dy^2+y^2.dx^2-2x.y.dx.dy=c'^2dt^2.$$
$$\because(x^2+y^2)(dx^2+dy^2)=c'^2dt^2+z^2.dz^2.$$

$\because$ by substituting for x^2+y^2, and $\frac{dx^2+dy^2}{dt^2}$, their values we obtain (r^2-z^2).

If we substitute in place of x^2+y^2, and $\frac{dx^2+dy^2}{dt^2}$, their respective values r^2-z^2, and $c+2gz-\frac{dz^2}{dt^2}$; we shall have on the supposition that the body departs from the vertical

$$dt=\frac{-r.dz}{\sqrt{(r^2-z^2).(c+2gz)-c'^2}}.$$

The function* under the radical may be made to assume the form $(a-z).(b-z).(2gz+f)$; $a, b, f,$ being determined by the equations

$(cdt^2+2gz.dt^2-dz^2) = c'^2\,dt^2+z^2.dz^2$, therefore $(r^2-z^2).(c+2gz)-c'^2).dt^2 = r^2.dz^2+z^2dz^2-z^2.dz^2$, consequently

$$dt=\frac{-r.dz}{\sqrt{(r^2-z^2).(c+2gz)-c'^2}},$$

dz is affected with a negative sign, because the motion commencing when the body is at the lowest point, z decreases according as t increases.

* If we multiply the factors of the expression, and range them according to the dimensions of z, we get $-2gz^3-cz^2+2r^2.gz+r^2c-c'^2$, if the same operation be performed on the expression $(a-z).(z-b).(2gz+f)$ we will obtain $-2gz^3+(2g(a+b)-f).z^2+(f.(a+b)-2g.ab)\,z-fab$, these two expressions being *always* equal, their corresponding terms must be *identical*, consequently, by comparing the coefficients of z, we have $f=2g.\frac{(r^2+ab)}{a+b}$, by comparing the coefficients of z^2, and substituting for f its value we get

$$2.g\left\{(a+b)-\frac{r^2+ab}{a+b}\right\}=-c \because \text{ by concinnating}$$

$$2g.\frac{a^2+2ab+b^2-r^2+ab}{a+b}=-c=2g.\left\{\frac{r^2-a^2-ab-b^2}{a+b}\right\},$$

the comparison of the absolute quantities, gives, by substituting for f and c their values, which have been already found,

$$2g.r^2\left\{\frac{r^2-a^2-ab-b^2}{a+b}\right\}-c'^2=-2g.ab.\left\{\frac{r^2+ab}{a+b}\right\}, \because c'^2=$$

$$2g.\left\{\frac{r^4-r^2.a^2-r^2ab-r^2.b^2+r^2.ab+a^2b^2}{a+b}\right\}=2g.\frac{(r^2-a^2).(r^2-b^2)}{a+b},$$

$$f = 2g.\frac{(r^2+ab)}{(a+b)}$$

$$c = 2g.\frac{(r^2-a^2-ab-b^2)}{a+b}$$

$$c'^2 = 2g.\frac{(r^2-a^2).(r^2-b^2)}{a+b}$$

We can thus substitute for the arbitrary quantities c and c', a and b, which are also arbitrary, of which the first is the greatest value of z, and the second the least. Then, by making

$$\sin.\theta = \sqrt{\frac{a-z}{a-b}},$$

the preceding differential equation will become

$$dt = \frac{r.\sqrt{2(a+b)}}{\sqrt{g\{(a+b)^2+r^2-b^2\}}} \cdot \frac{d\theta}{\sqrt{1-\gamma^2.\sin.^2\theta}}, \quad *$$

these values of f, c, c' being possible, we are permitted to substitute the expression $(a-z).(z-b).(2gz+f)$ in place of $(r^2-z^2).(c+2gz)-c'^2$, therefore $\frac{r.dz}{dt} = -\sqrt{(a-z).(z-b).(2gz+f)}$, z being a function of t, this differential coefficient vanishes when $a=z$, and also when $z=b$; $\frac{r\,z}{dt} = -\sqrt{(a-z).(z-b).(2gz+f)} = 0$, has at least *two* real roots; for as the point is constrained to move on the surface of the sphere, the trajectory has necessarily a maximum and a minimum; and as impossible roots enter equations by pairs, it follows that all the roots are real, moreover it is manifest from the variations of the signs, that one root is negative: $\frac{dz}{dt}$ expresses the velocity of the point in the direction of the vertical.

* The transformation $\sin.\theta = \sqrt{\frac{a-z}{a-b}}$ is made in order to facilitate the integration. $\sin.^2\theta = \frac{a-z}{a-b}$, and $\cos.^2\theta = \frac{z-b}{a-b}$ $\because z = a.\cos.^2\theta + b.(1-\cos.^2\theta) = a\cos.^2\theta + b\sin.^2\theta$,

γ^2 being equal to

$$\frac{a^2-b^2}{(a+b)^2+r^2-b^2},$$

The angle θ gives the coordinate z by means of the equation;

$$z=a.\cos.^2\theta+b.\sin.^2\theta,$$

I

$$d\theta.\cos.\theta=\frac{-dz}{2.\sqrt{(a-z).(a-b)}}\therefore -dz=2d\theta.\sqrt{(a-z).(z-b)}$$

and $\frac{-r.dz}{\sqrt{(a-z).(z-b).(2gz+f)}}=$ (substituting for f its value)

$$\frac{2r.d\theta\sqrt{(a-z).(z-b)}}{\sqrt{2g.(a-z).(z-b)\left(z+\frac{r^2+ab}{a+b}\right\}}}=\frac{2r.d\theta}{\sqrt{2g.\left\{z+\frac{r^2+ab}{a+b}\right\}}};$$

(substituting for z its value $a.\cos.^2\theta+b.\sin.^2\theta$) we obtain

$$\frac{2r.d\theta\sqrt{a+b}}{\sqrt{2g.(a^2.\cos.^2\theta+ab.\cos.^2\theta+ab.\sin.^2\theta+b^2.\sin.^2\theta+r^2+ab}}$$

$$=\frac{2r.d\theta.\sqrt{a+b}}{\sqrt{2g.((a^2+2ab+b^2)+(r^2-b^2)+(b^2-a^2).)\sin.^2\theta}}$$

$$=\frac{2r.d\theta.\sqrt{a+b}}{\sqrt{2g.(a+b)^2+(r^2-b^2)+(b^2-a^2).\sin.^2\theta)}},$$

and if $\gamma^2=\frac{a^2-b^2}{(a+b)^2+r^2-b^2)}$, $b^2-a^2=-((a+b)^2+(r^2-b^2)).\gamma^2$, $\therefore$ substituting for b^2-a^2 in the preceding expression we shall have $dt=$

$$\frac{2r.d\theta.\sqrt{a+b}}{\sqrt{2g.((a+b^2)+(r^2-b^2)-((a+b)^2+(r^2-b^2)).\gamma^2.\sin.^2\theta.}}$$

$$=\frac{r.\sqrt{2.(a+b)}}{\sqrt{g.((a+b)^2+(r^2-b^2)}.}\times\frac{d\theta}{\sqrt{1-\gamma^2.\sin.^2\theta.}}$$

and the coordinate z divided by r, expresses the cosine of the angle which the radius r makes with the vertical.

Let ϖ be the angle which the vertical plane passing through the radius r, makes with the vertical plane which passes through the axis of x; we shall have

$$x = \sqrt{r^2 - z^2}. \cos. \varpi; {}^{*} \quad y = \sqrt{r^2 - z^2}. \sin. \varpi;$$

which give

$$xdy - ydx = (r^2 - z^2). d\varpi,$$

$\therefore$ the equation $xdy - ydx = c'dt$ will give

$$d\varpi = \frac{c'.dt}{r^2 - z^2},$$

we will obtain the angle ϖ in a function of θ, by substituting for z and dt their preceding values in terms of θ; thus we may know at any time whatever, the two angles θ and ϖ, which is sufficient to determine the position of the moving point.

Let us name, $\frac{T}{2}$, the time employed † in passing from the greatest

* $x =$ the product of the projection of r, on the plane x, y, into the cosine of the angle which x makes with the projected line, $\therefore$ as, $\sqrt{r^2 - z^2} = r$ so projected, and $\varpi =$ the angle which x makes with $\sqrt{r^2 - z^2}$, $x = \cos. \varpi. \sqrt{r^2 - z^2}$, $dx = -\sqrt{r^2 - z^2}. \sin. \varpi.$ $d\varpi. - \frac{zdz. \cos. \varpi}{2\sqrt{r^2 - z^2}}$, $y = \sqrt{r^2 - z^2}. \sin. \varpi$, $\therefore dy = \sqrt{r^2 - z^2}. d\varpi. \cos. \varpi - \frac{zdz. \sin. \varpi}{2. \sqrt{r^2 - z^2}}$,

$$xdy - ydx = (r^2 - z^2)\, d\varpi \cos.^2 \varpi. - \frac{zdz. \sin. \varpi. \cos. \varpi}{2} + (r^2 - z^2) d\varpi. \sin.^2 \varpi$$

$$+ \frac{z.dz. \sin. \varpi \cos. \varpi.}{2} = (r^2 - z^2). \; d\varpi.$$

† For evolving the expression for dt into a series, it becomes,

$$\frac{r. \sqrt{2(a+b)}}{\sqrt{g. ((a+b)^2 + r^2 - b^2}}. d\theta + \frac{1}{2}\gamma^2. \sin.^2 \theta. d\theta + \frac{1.3}{2.4}\gamma^4. \sin.^4. \theta. d\theta + \frac{1.3.5}{2.4.6}\gamma^6. \sin.^6 \theta d\theta + \&c.$$

$$\text{but } \sin.^2 \theta = -\frac{\cos. 2\theta}{2} + \frac{1}{2}, \sin.^4 \theta = \frac{\cos. 4\theta}{8} - \frac{4. \cos. 2\theta}{8} + \frac{3}{2.4}$$

to the least value of z, a semi-oscillation. In order to determine it, we should integrate the preceding value of dt from $\theta=0$ to $\theta=\frac{1}{2}.\pi$, π

I 2

$$\sin.^6\theta = -\frac{\cos 6\theta}{32}+\frac{6.\cos.4\theta}{32}-\frac{15.\cos.2\theta}{32}+\frac{10}{32}, \text{ \&c.}$$

$$\therefore \int\sin.^2\theta.\,d\theta=-\frac{\sin.2\theta}{4}+\frac{\theta}{2};\int\sin.^4\theta.\,d\theta=\frac{\sin.4\theta}{32}-\frac{4\sin.2\theta}{16}+\frac{3\theta}{2.4},$$

$$\int\sin.^6\theta.\,d\theta=-\frac{\sin 6\theta}{192}+\frac{6.\sin.4\theta}{128}-\frac{15.\sin.2\theta}{64}+\frac{10\,\theta}{32}, \text{ \&c.}$$

(See Lacroix, Traite Elementaire, No. 200.)

These quantities being integrated between the limits $\theta=0$, and $\theta=\frac{1}{2}.\pi$, or between sin. $\theta=0$, and sin. $\theta=1$, i. e. between the greatest and least values of z, become respectively $\frac{\pi}{2}.\frac{1}{2}, \frac{3\pi 1}{2.4.2}, \frac{10\pi}{32}.\frac{1}{2}=\left\{\frac{3.5.\pi}{2.4.6}.\frac{1}{2}\right\}$ &c. for the parts in which the sines of the multiple arcs occur, vanish, being respectively $=$ to sin. (2π), sin. (4π), sin. (6π), the numeral co-efficients of $\frac{\pi}{2}$ are equal to the corresponding coefficients in the expanded radical; $\therefore$ these integrals being substituted in the preceding series we obtain

$$\frac{T}{2}=\sqrt{\frac{r}{g}}.\sqrt{\frac{2r(a+b)}{(a+b)^2+(r^2-b^2)}}.\left\{\frac{\pi}{2}+\frac{1}{2}.\gamma^2\frac{1}{2}.\frac{\pi}{2}+\frac{1.3}{2.4}.\gamma^2.\left\{\frac{1.3}{2.4}\frac{\pi}{2}\right\}\right.$$
$$\left.+\frac{1.3\,5}{2.4.6}\gamma^4.\left(\frac{1.3.5}{2.4.6}\,\frac{\pi}{2}\right)+\text{\&c.}\right.$$

$$\therefore T=\pi.\sqrt{\frac{r}{g}}\sqrt{\frac{2r.(a+b)}{(a+b)^2+(r^2-b^2)}}\left\{1+\left\{\frac{1}{2}\right\}^2.\gamma^2+\left\{\frac{1.3}{2.4}\right\}^2.\gamma^4+\right.$$
$$\left.\left\{\frac{1.3.5}{2.4.6}\right\}^2.\gamma^6+\text{\&c.}\right.$$

If in the series, $d\theta+\frac{1}{2}.\gamma^2.\sin.^2\theta.d\theta+\frac{1.3}{2.4}.\gamma^4.\sin.^4\theta.\,d\theta+\frac{1.3.5}{2.4.6}.\gamma^6\sin.^6\theta.\,d\theta+$&c. the integrals being taken as above, between the limits sin. $\theta=0$, sin. $\theta=\pm 1$; $\theta=k\pi$, $\theta=\frac{1}{2}(2n+1).\pi$, (where k and n are any numbers whatever) will satisfy these conditions; from which indetermination of k and n, it follows, that the vertical coordinate passes through its maximum and minimum an indefinite number of times, and consequently, when all obstacles are removed, the number of oscillations is infinite; we would obtain an expression for the time intervening between the commencement of the motion, and the successive transits through the greatest and least values of z, by taking θ successively $=\frac{1}{2}\pi, \frac{3}{2}\pi, \frac{5}{2}\pi$, these quantities differing by π, and as in the preceding integral, the first power of θ only occurs, it is evident that the times of all oscillations are equal.

being the semi-circumference of a circle, of which the radius is unity; we shall thus find

$$T=\pi.\sqrt{\frac{r}{g}}.\sqrt{\frac{2r.(a+b)}{(a+b)^2+r^2-b^2}}.\left\{1+\left(\frac{1}{2}\right)^2.\gamma^2+\left\{\frac{1.3}{2.4}\right\}^2.\gamma^4+\left\{\frac{1.3.5}{2.4.6}\right\}^2.\gamma^6+\&c\right.$$

Supposing the point suspended at the extremity of a thread without mass, of which the other extremity is firmly fixed; if the length of the thread is r, the motion of the point will be the same as in the interior of a spherical surface; it will constitute with the thread a pendulum, of which the cosine of the greatest deviation from the vertical will be $\frac{b}{r}$. If we suppose that in this state, the velocity of the point is nothing;* it will vibrate in a vertical plane, and in this case we shall

* $\frac{z}{r}$ expressing the cosine of the angle which the radius makes with the vertical, when the deviation from the vertical is the greatest, z is then least, and consequently it is equal to b, $\therefore \frac{b}{r}$ is the cosine of the greatest deviation, and as generally $\frac{\sin.^2 A}{2}=\frac{1-\cos. A}{2}$, in this case it is $=$ to $\frac{r-b}{2r}$, γ^2 $=$ this quantity, for making $a=r$ in the expression for γ^2, it becomes

$$\frac{r^2-b^2}{2r^2+2rb}=\frac{(r-b)(r+b)}{2r.(r+b)}=\frac{r-b}{2r}.$$

The pendulum described in the text is merely ideal, as every body has weight. However, philosophers have given a rule, by means of which we are able to determine the length of the imaginary pendulum, such as has been described, from the compound pendulum which is isochronous with it. (See No. 31 of this book.)

From the equation $d\varpi.(r^2-z^2)=c'.dt$ it follows that the angular velocity is inversly as the square of the distance; this is universally true, whenever the areas are proportional to the times, for we have then $\varrho^2.d\varpi.=c'dt \therefore d\varpi=\frac{c.dt}{\varrho^2}$. See note to No. 6.

From the equation $c+2gz=\frac{dx^2+dy^2+dz^2}{dt}=\frac{ds^2}{dt^2}$, we derive $dt=\frac{ds}{\sqrt{c+2gz}}$, when the velocity $\frac{ds}{dt}$ vanishes before the tangent becomes a second time horizontal,

have, $a=r$; $\gamma^2=\frac{r-b}{2r}$. The fraction $\frac{r-b}{2r}$ is the square of the sine of half the greatest angle which the thread makes with the vertical; the entire duration T of an oscillation of the pendulum will therefore be

$$T=\pi.\sqrt{\frac{r}{g}}.\left\{1+\left\{\frac{1}{2}\right\}^2.\left\{\frac{r-b}{2r}\right\}+\left\{\frac{1.3}{2.4}\right\}^2.\left\{\frac{r-b}{2r}\right\}^2+\left\{\frac{1.3.5}{2.4.6}\right\}.\left\{\frac{r-b}{2r}\right\}^3+\&c.\right\}$$

If the oscillation is very small, $\frac{r-b}{2r}$ is a very small fraction, which may be neglected, and then we shall have

$$T=\pi.\sqrt{\frac{r}{g}};$$

therefore the very small oscillations are isochronous, or of the same duration, whatever may be their extent; and by means of this duration, and of the corresponding length of the pendulum, we can easily determine the variations of the intensity of gravity, in different parts of the earth's surface.

Let z be the height through which a body would fall by the action of gravity in the time T; by No. 10 we shall have $2z=gT^2$, and consequently $z=\frac{1}{2}\pi.^2r$; thus we can obtain with the greatest precision, by means of the length of a pendulum which vibrates seconds, the space through which bodies descend by the action of gravity in the first second of their fall. It appears from experiments, very accurately made,

the point describes only a part of a circle of the sphere, but if $\frac{ds}{dt}$ be finite, when the tangent becomes a second time horizontal, then the point describes the entire circumference. These circumstances may be determined by means of the equation

$$c+2gz=\frac{dx^2+dy^2+dz^2}{dt^2}$$

that the length of the pendulum which vibrates seconds is the same, whatever may be the substances which are made to oscillate. From which it follows that gravity acts equally on all bodies, and that it tends, in the same place, to impress on them the same velocity, in the same time.

* When the oscillations are very small $T = \pi.\sqrt{\frac{r}{g}}$, and if a body vibrated in a cycloid whose length was equal to $2r$, the time of an entire vibration would be equal to $\pi.\sqrt{\frac{r}{g}}$, *whatever be the amplitude* of the arc, for the equation of this curve is $s^2 = az$. (See Lacroix Traite Elementaire, No. 102) $\therefore ds = \sqrt{a}\frac{-dz}{\sqrt{z}}$, and $\sqrt{2g(h-z)} = -\frac{ds}{dt}$, ($h$ equal to the value of z when $t=0$) $\therefore dt = \frac{1}{\sqrt{2g}}.\frac{-ds}{\sqrt{h-z}} = \frac{1}{2}.\sqrt{\left(\frac{2a}{g}\right)} \times -\frac{dz}{\sqrt{hz-z^2}}$, $\therefore t = \frac{1}{2}.\sqrt{\left(\frac{2a}{g}\right)}$. arc cos.$\left(\frac{2z-h}{h}\right) + C$, if we take this integral between the limits $z=h$, $z=0$, $\frac{T}{2} = \frac{\pi}{2}.\sqrt{\frac{2a}{g}}$, $\therefore$ if $2a=r$, *i*, *e*, if the radius of the osculating circle be equal to $2a$, the small oscillations in this circle are equal to the oscillations in the cycloid, and since h does not occur in this integral, the time of describing all arcs of the cycloid are equal, provided one extremity of these arcs be at the *lowest* point.

It appears from the foregoing investigation, that the time of vibration in a cycloidal arc, is the limit to which the time in a circular arc approaches, when the latter becomes indefinitely small. When great accuracy is required, all the terms after the two first in the series expressing the time in a circular arch are rejected, and then the expression for $T = \pi.\sqrt{\frac{r}{g}}\left\{1 + \left(\frac{1}{2}\right)^2.\left(\frac{r-b}{2r}\right);\right\}$ from which it appears that the aberration from isochronism varies, as the square of the sine of half the amplitude.

We might determine the time of describing any given arc of a circle, if we knew the coordinates a and b, and also z the coordinate of the extremity of the arc required, for then the angle θ would be determined. We might also, derive a general expression for the time of describing any given arc of a *cycloid*. For if in the initial velocity be such, as would be acquired in falling down a height equal to A, we shall have at any point in the cycloid $v^2 = 2g.(H+h-z)$ consequently $\frac{ds}{dt} = \sqrt{2g(H+h-z)}$ $\therefore dt = \frac{-ds}{\sqrt{2g.(H+h-z)}} =$ (by substituting for ds its value $\sqrt{a.}\left(\frac{dz}{\sqrt{z}}\right)$

12. The isochronism of the oscillations of the pendulum, being only an approximation; it is interesting to know the curve on which a heavy body ought to move, in order to arrive at the point where the motion ceases, in the same time, whatever may be the arc which it shall have described from the lowest point. But to solve this problem in the most general manner, we will suppose, conformably to what has place in nature, that the point moves in a resisting medium. Let s represent the arc described from the lowest point of the curve; z the vertical abscissa reckoned from this point; dt the element of the time, and g the gravity. The retarding force along the arc of the curve will be,

$$\sqrt{\frac{a}{2g}} \times \frac{dz}{\sqrt{z.(H+h-z)}} = \sqrt{\frac{a}{2g}} \frac{\left\{ \frac{dz}{\frac{1}{2}(H+h)} \right\}}{\sqrt{1-\left(\frac{z-\frac{1}{2}H+h}{\frac{1}{2}(H+h)}\right)^2}} =$$

$$\sqrt{\frac{a}{2g}}.d. \text{ arc.} \left\{ \cos. = \frac{z-\frac{1}{2}(H+h)}{\frac{1}{2}(H+h)} \right\} \therefore t =$$

$\sqrt{\frac{a}{2g}}.\text{arc. cos.} = \frac{z-\frac{1}{2}(H+h)}{\frac{1}{2}(H+h)} + C$; we determine C by making $t = 0$, and $z = H$, we might deduce from this general expression, the time of describing the whole cycloidal arch; C is equal to $= \sqrt{\frac{a}{2g}} \left\{ \text{arc} \left\{ \cos. = \frac{h-H}{h+H}, \right.\right.$ $\therefore$ when the initial velocity vanishes $C = 0$, for then H vanishes.

In the preceding investigations the motions are supposed to be performed in a *nonresisting* medium, but this is not essentially necessary, in order that the oscillations should be isochronous in the cycloid, or *nearly* so in the circle. For it is proved in No. 12, that the oscillations of a body moving in a medium, of which the resistance is as the velocity, are isochronous when the curve described is a cycloid, and it has been demonstrated by M. Poisson, that when a body describes a small *circular* arch, in a medium of which the resistance varies as the square of the velocity, or as the two first powers of the velocity, the oscillations are isochronous, the analytical expression indicates that the time of describing the first arc is as much lengthened by the resistance, as the time of describing the ascending arc is diminished, so that the time of the entire vibration remains the same as if the body moved in a vacuo, the amplitude of the arc perpetually lessens; and it may be proved, that if the intervals of time are taken in arithmetic progression, the amplitudes of the arcs described decrease in geometric proportion.

1st, the gravity resolved along the arc ds, which thus becomes equal to $g.\frac{dz}{ds}$; 2dly, the resistance of the medium, which we will express by $\varphi.\left\{\frac{ds}{dt}\right\}$, $\frac{ds}{dt}$ being the velocity of the point, and $\varphi.\left\{\frac{ds}{dt}\right\}$ being any function of this velocity. By No. 7 the differential of this velocity will be equal to $-g.\frac{dz}{ds}-\varphi.\left\{\frac{ds}{dt}\right\}$; therefore, by making dt constant we shall have

$$0=\frac{d^2s}{dt^2}+g.\frac{dz}{ds}+\varphi.\left\{\frac{ds}{dt}\right\}. \qquad (i)$$

Let us suppose that $\varphi.\left\{\frac{ds}{dt}\right\}=m.\frac{ds}{dt}+n.\frac{ds^2}{dt^2}$, and $s=\psi(s')$; denoting by $\psi'(s')$ the differential of $\psi(s')$ divided by ds'; and by $\psi''(s')$ the differential of $\psi'(s')$ divided by ds', we shall have

$$\frac{ds}{dt}=\frac{ds'}{dt}.\ \psi'(s')$$

$$\frac{d^2s}{dt^2}=\frac{d^2s'}{dt^2}.\ \psi'(s')+\frac{ds'^2}{dt^2}.\psi''(s');$$

the equation (i) will become

$$0=\frac{d^2s'}{dt^2}+m\frac{ds'}{dt}+\frac{ds'^2}{dt^2}.\left\{\frac{\psi''(s')+n\{\psi'(s')\}^2}{\psi'(s')}\right\}+\frac{g.dz}{ds'\{\psi'(s')\}^2};^*(l)$$

* Substituting for $\varphi.(ds)$ its value in the equation (i), it becomes

$$0=\frac{d^2s}{dt^2}+g.\frac{dz}{ds}+m.\frac{ds}{dt}+n.\frac{ds^2}{dt^2};\ \frac{d^2s}{dt^2}=\frac{d^2s'}{dt^2}.\ \psi'(s')+\frac{ds'^2}{dt^2}.\ \psi'(s'),\ \text{and as}$$

$$ds=ds'.\psi'(s');\ \frac{ds^2}{dt^2}=\frac{ds'^2}{dt^2}.\ \psi'(s')^2$$

substituting these values for $\frac{ds^2}{dt^2}$, and $\frac{d^2s}{dt^2}$, we shall have

$$0=\frac{d^2s'}{dt^2}.\psi'.(s')+\frac{ds'^2}{dt^2}.\psi''.(s')+n.\frac{ds'^2}{dt^2}.\ \psi'(s')^2+m.\frac{ds'}{dt}.\ \psi'.(s')+\frac{g.dz}{ds'.\psi'.(s')}$$

We make the term multiplied by $\frac{ds^2}{dt^2}$, to disappear by means of the equation

$$0 = \psi''.(s') + [\psi'(s')]^2;$$

which gives by integrating

$$\psi\,[s') = \log.\ \{(h(s'+q)^{\frac{1}{n}}\} = s;$$

h and q being arbitrary quantities. By making s' commence with s we shall have $hq^{\frac{1}{n}} = 1$, and if, for greater simplicity we make, $h = 1$, we shall have $s' = c^{ns} - 1$.*

K

$\because$ dividing all the terms by $\psi'.(s')$ and concinnating we obtain

$$0 = \frac{d^2s'}{dt^2} + m.\frac{ds'}{dt} + \frac{ds'^2}{dt^2}.\left\{\frac{\psi''.(s') + n.(\psi'.(s'))^2}{\psi'.(s')}\right\} + \frac{g.dz}{ds'(.\psi(s'))^2}.$$

* From the value of d^2s which has been already given, we get

$$\psi''.(s') = \frac{d^2s}{ds'^2} - \frac{d^2s'.ds}{ds'^3}$$

$$\because 0 = \psi''.(s') + n\psi'.(s')^2 = \frac{d^2s}{ds'^2} - \frac{d^2s'}{ds'^3}.\ ds + n.\frac{ds^2}{ds'^2} = \frac{d^2s}{ds} - \frac{d^2s'}{ds'} + n.ds,$$

and by integrating we obtain, $\log.\ ds - \log.\ ds' + ns = e$ or $\log.\ \frac{ds}{ds'} = e - ns$;

$\because \frac{ds}{ds'} = \frac{c^e}{c^{ns}}$, and $ds' = \frac{ds.c^{ns}}{c^e}$, integrating again we shall have $s' + q = \frac{c^{ns-e}}{n}$,

$\because \log.(n.(s'+q)) = ns - e$ or dividing both sides by n; $\frac{\log\,(n(s'+q)}{n}) = ((\log.(n.(s+q)^{\frac{1}{n}}))$ $= s - \frac{e}{n}$, and if $\frac{e}{n}$, be made equal to $\frac{h}{n^{\frac{1}{n}}}$ we obtain $\log.((h.(s'+q^n))^{\frac{1}{n}} = s$. If we suppose s' to commence with s, they are $=$ to 0 at the same instant, $\because \log.\ h.q^{\frac{1}{n}} = 0$, at this instant, and consequently $h.q^{\frac{1}{n}} = 1$, q must be equal to unity since n is a constant indetermined coefficient, $\because \log.\ (s'+1)^{\frac{1}{n}} = s = \psi(s')$, and $s' = c^{ns} - 1$.

c being the number whose hyperbolic logarithm is unity; the differential equation (l) becomes then

$$0 = \frac{d^2s'}{dt^2} + m.\frac{ds'}{dt} + n^2g.\frac{dz}{ds'}.(1+s')^2.$$

By supposing s' very small, we may develope the last term of this equation into a series ascending according to the powers of s' which will be of this form, $ks'+ls'^i+$, &c.; i being greater than unity; the last equation then becomes

$$0 = \frac{d^2s'}{dt^2} + m.\frac{ds'}{dt} + ks' + ls'^i + \text{ \&c.*}$$

This equation multiplied by $c^{\frac{mt}{2}}.(\cos.\gamma t + \sqrt{-1}.\sin.\gamma t)$, and then integrated, becomes (γ being supposed equal to $\sqrt{k-\frac{m^2}{4}}$)

$$c^{\frac{mt}{2}}.\left\{\cos.\gamma t+\sqrt{-1}.\sin.\gamma t\right\}.\left\{\frac{ds'}{dt}+\left(\tfrac{m}{2}-\gamma\sqrt{-1}.s'\right\}\right. =$$

$$-l.\int s'^i dt.c^{\frac{mt}{2}}\left\{\cos.\gamma t+\sqrt{-1}.\sin.\gamma t.\right\} - \text{\&c.}\dagger$$

* For since $s' = c^{ns}-1$, $\frac{ds}{ds'} = \psi'(s') = \frac{1}{n.c^{ns}} = \frac{1}{n.(1+s')} \because \psi'(s')^2 = \frac{1}{n^2.(1+s')^2}$, $\because$ the equation (l) becomes $\frac{d^2s'}{dt^2} + m.\frac{ds'}{dt} + n^2g.\frac{dz}{ds'}.(1+s')^2$, when s' is very small the variable part of the last term of this equation may be expanded into a series proceeding according to the ascending powers of s', for substituting in place of s' it becomes $= \frac{dz}{ds}.c^{ns}$, when s is very small s' is also very small, as is evident from the equation $s' = c^{ns}-1 \because \frac{dz}{ds}$ = the sine of the inclination of the tangent to the horizon is very small, and as all the terms which occur in the expression $\frac{dz}{ds}.(1+s')^2$ are very small it can be developed in a series of the form given in the text.

† $\text{Cos.}\gamma t+\sqrt{-1}.\sin.\gamma t = c^{\gamma t\sqrt{-1}}$. See Lacroix Traite Elementaire, No. 164.) $\because$ by substituting $c^{\gamma t\sqrt{-1}}$ in place of the circular function, we obtain

By comparing separately the real and imaginary parts, we will have two equations by means of which we can eliminate $\frac{ds'}{dt}$; but it will be

K 2

$$c^{(\frac{m}{2}+\gamma\sqrt{-1})t}.\frac{d^2s}{dt^2}+m\,c^{(\frac{m}{2}+\gamma\sqrt{-1})t}.\frac{ds'}{dt}+ks'c^{(\frac{m}{2}\gamma+\sqrt{-1})t}=-l.s''.\,c^{(\frac{m}{2}+\gamma\sqrt{-1})t}$$

&c. If we multiply both sides of this equation by dt, and then partially integrate, we shall have

$$c^{(\frac{m}{2}+\gamma\sqrt{-1})t}.\frac{ds'}{dt}-\left(\frac{m}{2}+\gamma.\sqrt{-1}\right)\int ds'.c^{(\frac{m}{2}+\gamma.\sqrt{-1})t}+ms'.\,c^{(\frac{m}{2}+\gamma.\sqrt{-1})t}$$

$$-m\left(\frac{m}{2}+\gamma.\sqrt{-1}\right).\int s'\,c^{(\frac{m}{2}+\gamma.\sqrt{-1})t}.\,dt.$$

$$+k.\int s'dt.\,c^{(\frac{m}{2}+\gamma.\sqrt{-1})t}=-l.\int s''dt.c^{(\frac{m}{2}+\gamma.\sqrt{-1})t}\ \&c.$$

(the integral of $ds'c^{(\frac{m}{2}+\gamma.\sqrt{-1})t}=s'c^{(\frac{m}{2}+\gamma.\sqrt{-1})t}$

$$-\left(\frac{m}{2}+\gamma.\sqrt{-1}\right).\int s'c^{(\frac{m}{2}+\gamma\sqrt{-1})}dt,)$$

substituting this value of $\int ds'.c^{(\frac{m}{2}+\gamma.\sqrt{-1})t}$ in the second term of the preceding integral, and for k its value $\gamma^2+\frac{m^2}{4}$, we obtain

$$c^{(\frac{m}{2}+\gamma.\sqrt{-1}).t}.\frac{ds'}{dt}+\left(\frac{m}{2}-\gamma\sqrt{-1}\right)s'.c^{(\frac{m}{2}+\gamma.\sqrt{-1})t}+\left(\frac{m^2}{4}+m.\gamma.\sqrt{-1}-\gamma^2\right)\times$$

$$\int(s'dt.c^{(\frac{m}{2}+\gamma\sqrt{-1})t}.\ \left(-\frac{m^2}{2}-m\gamma.\sqrt{-1}+\frac{m^2}{4}+\gamma^2\right).\int s'dt.c^{(\frac{m}{2}+\gamma.\sqrt{-1})t}$$

$$-\left(-\frac{m}{4}-m\gamma.\sqrt{-1}+\gamma^2.\int s'.dt.c^{(\frac{m}{2}+\gamma.\sqrt{-1})t}\right)=-l\int s''c^{(\frac{m}{2}+\gamma.\sqrt{-1})t}\ \&c.$$

If we substitute for $c^{\gamma\sqrt{-1}\,t}$ its value $\cos.\gamma t+\sqrt{-1}\sin.\gamma t$, and concinnate, we will obtain

$$c^{\frac{mt}{2}}\left(\cos.\gamma t+\sqrt{-1}.\sin.\gamma t\right)\left(\frac{ds'}{dt}+\left(\frac{m}{2}-\gamma.\sqrt{-1}\right).s'\right)=-l\int s''.dt.c^{\frac{mt}{2}}$$

$$(\cos.\gamma t.+\sqrt{-1}.\sin.\gamma t.)\ \&c.$$

sufficient to consider here the following*

$$c^{\frac{mt}{2}}.\frac{ds'}{dt}.\ \sin.\gamma t+c^{\frac{mt}{2}}.s'.\left\{\frac{m}{2}.\ \sin.\ \gamma t-\gamma.\cos.\gamma t.\right\}$$

$$=-l.\int s'^{i}dt.c^{\frac{mt}{2}}.\sin.\gamma t\text{—\&c.}$$

the integrals of the second member being supposed to commence with t. Naming T the value of t at the end of the motion, when $\frac{ds}{dt}$ vanishes, at that instant we shall have

$$c^{\frac{mT}{2}}.s'.\left\{\frac{m}{2}.\sin.\gamma T-\gamma.\cos.\gamma T.\right\}=-l.\int s'^{i}.\ dt.\ c^{\frac{mt}{2}}.\sin.\gamma t\text{—\&c.}$$

When s' is indefinitely small, the second member of this equation vanishes, when compared with the first, and we shall have;

$$0=\frac{m}{2}.\sin.\gamma T-\gamma.\cos.\gamma T,\text{*}$$

* As the imaginary parts of this equation cannot be equated with the real parts, the real and imaginary parts must be compared separately, which gives two distinct equations, the part of this equation which is considered, is the part which was multiplied by $\sqrt{-1}$

† Partially integrating the expression $-l.\int s'^{i}.c^{\frac{mt}{2}}.\sin.\gamma t.dt+$ &c. we obtain

$$\frac{l.}{\gamma}.\ c^{\frac{mt}{2}}.\cos.\gamma t.s'^{i}-\frac{lm}{2\gamma}\int.c^{\frac{mt}{2}}.dt.\cos.\gamma t.s'^{i}-\frac{li}{\gamma}\int.c^{\frac{mt}{2}}.\cos.\gamma t.s'^{i-1}ds',$$

if we integrate the second term of this expression, as before, we shall have

$$-\frac{lm}{2\gamma^2}.\ c^{\frac{tm}{2}}.\ \sin.\ \gamma t.\ s'^{i}+\frac{lm^2}{4\gamma^2}\int.c^{\frac{mt}{2}}dt.\sin.\gamma t.s'^{i}+\frac{lmi}{2\gamma^2}\int c^{\frac{mt}{2}}.\sin.\gamma t.s'^{i-1}ds',$$

in like manner the integration of the term in this last expression, which contains dt, would give terms of the same form as in the preceding integral; consequently the value of $-l\int.s'^{i}dt.c^{\frac{mt}{2}}.\sin.\gamma t+$&c. cannot be exhibited in a finite number of terms, but if the preceding intervals are taken from $t=0$ to $t=T$, then the value of $-l\int s'.c^{\frac{mt}{2}}.\ dt.\ \sin.$

consequently

$$\text{tang.}\ \gamma T = \frac{2\gamma}{m},$$

and as the time T is, by hypothesis independant of the arc described,

$\gamma t=0$, for by substituting in place of $\cos.\ \gamma T$ its value $\frac{m}{2\gamma}\ \sin.\ \gamma T$, in the terms where ds occurs, these terms in two succeeding expressions will be equal, and affected with contrary signs, consequently they destroy each other; with respect to those terms which are free from the sign of integration $\int$, we may remark that they resolve themselves into two decreasing geometric series, which are respectively of the following forms

$$\frac{l}{\gamma}.\cos.\gamma t.c^{\frac{mt}{2}}.s'^{\iota}-\frac{lm^2}{4\gamma^3}.\cos.\gamma t.c^{\frac{mt}{2}}.s'^{\iota}+\frac{lm^4}{16.\gamma^5}.\cos.\gamma t.c^{\frac{mt}{2}}.s'^{\iota}, \text{ \&c. ad infinitum,}$$

$$-\frac{lm}{2\gamma^2}.\sin.\gamma t.c^{\frac{mt}{2}}.s'^{\iota}+\frac{lm^3}{8\gamma^4}.\sin.\gamma t.c^{\frac{mt}{2}}.s'^{\iota}-\frac{lm^5}{32\gamma^6}.\sin.\gamma t.c^{\frac{mt}{2}}.s'^{\iota}+\text{\&c. ad infinitum,}$$

by summing these series they come out equal respectively to

$$\frac{\frac{l}{\gamma}}{1+\frac{m^2}{4\gamma^2}}.\cos.\gamma t.c^{\frac{mt}{2}}.s'^{\iota}-\frac{\frac{lm}{2\gamma^2}}{1+\frac{m^2}{4\gamma^2}}.\sin.\gamma t.c^{\frac{mt}{2}}.s'^{\iota},$$ by substituting

for $\cos.\ \gamma T$ its value $\frac{m}{2\gamma}.\sin.\gamma T$, the first expression becomes

$$\frac{\frac{lm}{2\gamma^2}}{1+\frac{m^2}{4\gamma^2}}.\sin.\gamma T.c^{\frac{mT}{2}}.s'^{\iota},$$ which is equal to the second with a contrary sign, consequently it follows that whatever be the magnitude s'^{ι}—$l.\int s'^{\iota}.\ dt.c^{\frac{mt}{2}}.\ \sin.\ \gamma t=0$, when the integral is taken from $t=0$ to $t=T$. The same reasoning applies to the other terms of the series, which contain powers of s' superior to ι.

l being independant of s', if it is equal to nothing when s' is very small it will be always equal to nothing; and since neither $\sin.\gamma t$, nor $c^{\frac{mt}{2}}$ change their signs from $t=0$, to $t=T$, it is evident that the evanescence of $\int s'^{\iota}.c^{\frac{mt}{2}}.\ \sin.\ \gamma t$ can only arise from l being equal to nothing, in this case also the coefficients of the powers of s' greater than s'^{ι}. i. e. the subsequent terms of the series vanish.

this value of tang. γT has place for any arc whatever, therefore whatever be the value of s', we have

$$0 = l.\int s'^{i}.\ dt.c^{\frac{mt}{2}}.\ \sin.\ \gamma t + \&c.$$

the integral being taken from $t=0$ to $t=T$. If we suppose s' very small the second member of this equation will be reduced to its first term, and it can only be satisfied by making $l=0$; for the factor $c^{\frac{mt}{2}}$. sin. γt, being constantly positive from $t=0$ to $t=T$, the preceding integral is necessarily positive in this interval. Therefore the tautochronism is only possible on the supposition of

$$n^{2}.g.\frac{dz}{ds'}.(1+s')^{2}=ks',^{*}$$

which gives for the equation of the tautochronous curve

$$g.dz = \frac{k.ds}{n}.\ (1-c^{-ns})$$

In a vacuum, and when the resistance is proportional to the velocity, n

* Substituting for $1+s'$ its value c^{ns}, and ds' its value $n.ds.c^{ns}$, we obtain

$$\frac{n^{2}g.dz.}{n.ds.c^{ns}}\ c^{2ns} = k(c^{ns}-1)\ \because g.dz = \frac{k.ds}{n}\left\{1-c^{-ns}\right\},\ \because$$

when the body moves in a vacuo, or in a medium of which the resistance is proportional to the velocity, $n=o \because gdz = \frac{k.ds}{0}\ (1-c^{-0s}) = ks.\frac{0}{0}$, but if we express c^{-ns} in a series it becomes $=1-\frac{ns}{1}+\frac{n^{2}s^{2}}{1.2}$, &c. $\because$ the general expression for

$$g.dz = \frac{k.ds}{n}\left(1-1+\frac{ns}{1}-\frac{n^{2}s^{2}}{1.2}+\frac{n^{3}s^{3}}{1.2.3}-\&c.\right)=,$$

when $n=0$, $k.ds.s$. From this equation it follows that $k=\frac{g.dz}{ds.s}$, this is also q.p true, when n has a finite value, if s be taken very small, as is evident from the preceding series.

is nothing; and this equation becomes $g.dz = ks.ds$; which is the equation of the cycloid.

It is remarkable * that the coefficient n of the part of the resistance, which is proportional to the square of the velocity, does not enter into the expression of the time T; and it is evident from the preceding analysis that this expression will be the same, even though we should add to the expression for the law of the resistance, which has been given above, the terms,

$$p.\frac{ds^3}{dt^3} + q.\frac{ds^4}{dt^4} + \&c.$$

If in general, R represents the retarding force along the curve, we shall have

$$0 = \frac{d^2s}{dt^2} + R.$$

s being a function of t, and of the entire arc described, which consequently, is a function of t and of s. By differentiating this last function, we obtain a differential equation of this form,

$$\frac{ds}{dt} = V.$$

V being a function of t and of s, which, by the conditions of the problem must vanish, when t has a determinate value, which is independant of the whole arc described. Suppose, for example, $V = S.T$, S

* Since the value of T is the same when the terms $P.\frac{ds^3}{dt^3} + q.\frac{ds^4}{dt^4} +$ &c. are added to $m.\frac{ds}{dt} + n.\frac{ds^2}{dt^2}$, it follows that the generality of the conclusion is not affected by substituting $m.\frac{ds}{dt} + n.\frac{ds^2}{dt^2}$ in place of $\varphi\left\{\frac{ds}{dt}\right\}$.

being a function of s only, and T being a function of t only; we shall have

$$\frac{d^2s}{dt^2} = T.\frac{dS}{ds}.\frac{ds}{dt} + S.\frac{dT}{dt} = \frac{dS}{S.ds}.\frac{ds^2}{dt^2} + S.\frac{dT}{dt};*$$

but the equation $\frac{ds}{dt} = ST$, gives t, and consequently $\frac{dT}{dt}$ equal to a function of $\frac{ds}{S.dt}$, which function we will denote by $\frac{ds^2}{S^2dt^2}.\psi\left\{\frac{ds}{S.dt}\right\}$ therefore we shall have

$$\frac{d^2s}{dt^2} = \frac{ds^2}{S.dt^2}\left\{\frac{dS}{ds} + \psi\left(\frac{ds}{S.dt}\right)\right\} = -R.$$

Such is the expression for the resistance which corresponds to the differential equation $\frac{ds}{dt} = ST$; and it is easy to perceive that it involves the case of the resistance proportional to the two first powers of the velocity, multiplied respectively by constant coefficients. Other differential equations would give different laws of resistance.†

* S being a function of s, which is a function of t, the differential coefficient of S, with respect to $t = \frac{dS}{ds}.\frac{ds}{dt}$, and substituting for T its value $\frac{ds}{S.ds}$ we obtain

$$\frac{d^2s}{dt^2} = \frac{dS}{S.ds}.\frac{ds^2}{dt^2} + S.\frac{dT}{dt}.$$

† In the preceding investigation the body is supposed to ascend from the lowest point, and the curve which then satisfies the condition of tautochronism is *unique* in a given medium; but if the body descended from the highest point, then it would oscillate at the other side of the point where the tangent was horizontal, and the problem becomes somewhat more indeterminate, in this case it may be announced more generally thus; to find the lines, the time of describing which will be given, whatever be the amplitude of the arch described; the discussion of this problem is too long to be inserted here, the reader will find a complete investigation of it by Euler in the Transactions of the Academy of Petersburgh for the years 1764 and 1734, he demonstrates that the arcs at each side of the lowest point are not necessarily equal and similar, however, the sum of these arcs

is proportional to the square root of the vertical coordinate, ∴ the curve whose length is equal to the sum of these arcs will be the common cycloid, in like manner, if we have the differential equation of one of these arcs, we can determine the differential equation of the other; if the first arc be a cycloid, the second will also be the arc of a cycloid; in this case the time of describing *each* of the cycloidal arcs will be constant, however the generating circle of the second cycloid is not necessarily equal to that of the first. If we combine the condition of tautochronism, with the condition of the two branches at each side of the lowest point, being equal and similar, the curve will be then the vulgar cycloid, therefore this is the only *plane* curve in which the sum of the times of the ascent and descent is always the same in a vacuo; but this property belongs to an indefinite number of curves of double curvature which are formed by applying the cycloid to a vertical cylinder of any base, the altitude of the curve above the horizon remaining the same as before, for $v^2 = \frac{ds^2}{dt^2} = c - 2gz$, ∴ $dt = -\frac{\pm ds}{\sqrt{c-2gz}}$, consequently the value of t depends on the initial velocity, and on the relation between the vertical ordinates and arc of the curve ∴ whatever changes are made in the curve compatible with the continuity, the value of dt will not be changed, provided the preceding relation remains; and it follows conversely, that the projection of any tautochronous curve of double curvature, on a vertical plane, will be a cycloid with a horizontal base.

In the cycloid, if a body falls freely, the accelerating force along the tangent varies as the distance from the lowest point, for $s^2 = 4az$, ∴ $g.\frac{dz}{ds}$ ($=$ accelerating force $= \frac{gs}{2a}$,) the pressure arising from gravity $= g.\frac{\sqrt{4a^2 - z^2}}{2a}$, and the pressure which is produced by the centrifugal force $= \frac{2.g.(a-z)}{2.\sqrt{a(a-z)}}$, for radius of curvature $= 2\sqrt{a(a-z)}$, and the square of the velocity $= 2.g.(a-z)$, see No. 9, (the coordinates of z are reckoned from the lowest point;) it follows from the preceding expression that the *whole* pressure at the lowest point, and consequently the tension at this point of a body vibrating in a cycloid is $=$ to twice the gravity.

When a body describes a cycloid, the accelerating force varies as the distance from the lowest point, as has been stated above; and if a body was solicited by a force varying according to this law, the time of falling to the centre will be given, for we have

$$\frac{dv}{dt} = -As ∴ \frac{dvv}{dt} = -As.\frac{ds}{dt}, ∴ v^2 = -As^2 + C, \; v=0, \; s = S, ∴ C = AS^2, ∴$$

$$v = A^{\frac{1}{2}}\sqrt{S^2 - s^2} \;\&\; A^{\frac{1}{2}}.dt = \frac{ds}{\sqrt{S^2 - s^2}}, ∴ A^{\frac{1}{2}}t = \text{arc. cos.}\frac{s}{S}, \text{ and when } s=0, \; t=T$$

$= \frac{\pi}{2A^{\frac{1}{2}}}$, consequently the time of descent to the centre, is the same from whatever point, the body begins to fall. From the preceding expression, it follows, that the time of describing any space s, varies as the arc, and the velocity acquired varies as the right sine. See Princip. Mat. Prop. 38, Book 1st.

CHAPTER III.

Of the equilibrium of a system of bodies.

13. The simplest case of the equilibrium of several bodies, is that of two material points meeting each other with equal and directly contrary velocities; their mutual impenetrability evidently annihilates their motion, and reduces them to a state of rest.

Let us now suppose a number m of contiguous material points, arranged in a right line, and moving in its direction with the velocity u, and also another number m' of contiguous points, disposed in the same line, and moving with the velocity u', directly contrary to u, so that the two systems may strike each other; there must exist a certain relation between u and u', when both the systems remain at rest after the shock.

In order to determine this condition, it may be observed that the system m, moving with the velocity u, will constitute an equilibrium with a single material point, moving in a contrary direction with the velocity mu; for every point of the system would destroy in this last point, a velocity equal to u, and consequently the m points would destroy the whole velocity mu; we may therefore substitute for this system a single point, moving with the velocity mu. In like manner we may substitute for the system m', a single point moving with the velocity $m'u'$; now* the two systems being supposed to constitute an equilibrium, the two points which are substituted in their place, ought to be also in equilibrio, therefore their velocities must be equal; consequently we

* These two systems of contiguous material points, may be supposed to represent two bodies M, M', of different masses, equal respectively to the sum of all the ms, and m',s.

have for the condition of the equilibrium of the two systems, $mu = m'u'$.

The mass of a body is the number of its material points, and the product of the mass by the velocity, is what is termed its *quantity of motion*; this is also what we understand by the force of a body in motion. In order that the two bodies, or two systems of points which strike each in contrary directions, may be in equilibrio, the quantities of motion or the opposite forces must be equal, and consequently the velocities must be inversely as the masses.

The density of bodies depends on the number of material points which they contain in a given volume. In order to determine their absolute density, we should compare their masses with that of a body† which has no pores; but as we know no such body, we can only determine the relative density of bodies, that is to say, the ratio of their density, to that of a given substance. It is evident that the mass is in the ratio of the volume and density; therefore, if we denote the mass of the body by M, its volume by U, and its density by D, we shall have generally $M = U.D$; in this equation the quantities M, D, U, relate to the units of their respective species.

In what precedes, we suppose that bodies are composed of similar material points, and that they only differ in the relative situation of these points. But the intimate nature of matter being unknown, this supposition is at least very precarious, and it is possible that there may be essential differences‡ in their integrant molecules. Fortunately, the truth of this hypothesis is of no consequence to the science of mechanics, and we may adopt it without any apprehension of

† Distilled water, at its greatest density, is the substance which has been selected for the term of comparison, as being one of the most homogeneous substances, and that which may be readily reduced to a pure state.

‡ By the integrant molecules of bodies, as contradistinguished from their constituent parts, we understand those which arise from the subdivision of the body, into minuter portions; by the constituent parts are understood the elementary substances of which a body is composed.

error, provided that *by similar material points*, we understand points which, when they meet with equal and opposite velocities, mutually constitute equilibrium, whatever their nature may be.*

14. Two material points, of which the masses are m and m', can only act on each other in the direction of the line joining them. Indeed, if the two points are connected by a thread passing over a fixed pully, their reciprocal action cannot be directed along this line ; but the fixed pully may be considered as having at its centre a mass of infinite density, which reacts on the two bodies, so that their mutual action may be considered as indirect.

Let p denote the action which is exerted by m on m' by means of the right line which joins them, which line we suppose to be inflexible and without mass. Conceive this line to be actuated by two equal and opposite forces p and $-p$; the force $-p$ will destroy in the body m a force equal to p, and the force p of the right line will be communicated entirely to the body m'. This loss of force in m, occasioned by its action on m', is termed the *reaction* of m' ; therefore in the communication of motions, *the reaction is always equal and contrary to the action.* It appears from observation that this principle obtains for all the forces of nature.†

* If there be actually *essential* differences in the integrant molecules, then it is not inconsistent to suppose, with some philosophers, that the planetary regions are filled with a very subtle fluid destitute of pores, and of such a nature as not to oppose any resistance to the motions of the planets. We can thus reconcile the permanency of these motions, which is evinced by observation, with the opinion of those philosophers who regard a vacuum as an impossibility ; however the plenum, for which De-Cartes contended, is not confirmed by the preceding hypothesis, as he held that all matter was homogeneous, and that the ether, which, according to him filled the planetary regions, differed from other substances only in *the form of the matter.* See Princip. Math. Book 2, Prop. 40 ; Exper. 14, and Book 3, Prop. 6, Cor. 2 and 3 ; Newton's Optics, Query 18 ; and Systeme de Monde, page 166. However, as extension and motion are the only properties which are taken into account in Mechanics, it is indifferent whether matter be considered as homogeneous or not.

† This equality does not suppose any particular force inherent in matter, it follows necessarily from this, that a body cannot be moved by another body, without depriving this body of the quantity of motion which is acquired by the first body, in the same manner as when two vessels communicate with each other, one cannot be filled but at the expense of the other.

Let us suppose two heavy bodies m and m' attached to the extremities of an horizontal right line, supposed to be inflexible and without mass, which can turn freely about a point assumed in this right line. In order to conceive the action of those bodies on each other, when they are in equilibrio, we must suppose the right line to be bent by an indefinitely small quantity at the assumed point, so as to be formed of two right lines, constituting at this point an angle, which differs from two right angles by an indefinitely small quantity ω. Let f and f' represent the distances of m and m' from the fixed point; if we resolve the weight of m into two forces, one acting on the fixed point, and the other directed towards m', this last force will be represented by $\frac{mg.(f+f')}{\omega f'}$*, g being the force of gravity. In like manner the action of m' on m will be represented by $\frac{m'g.(f+f')}{\omega f}$, the two bodies constituting an equilibrium, these two expressions will be equal, consequently we will have $mf=m'f'$; this gives the known law of the equilibrium of the lever, and at the same time, enables us to conceive the reciprocal action of parallel forces.

Let us now consider the equilibrium of a system of points actuated by any forces whatever, and reacting on each other. Let f represent the distance of m from m'; f' the distance of m from m'', f'' the distance of m' from m'', &c.

* Gravity must be distinguished from weight; the weight of a bedy is the product of the gravity of a single particle, by the number of particles.

If we conceive a line drawn from the fixed point, parallel to the direction of gravity, meeting a line connecting m and m', this last line will be $q.p.$ horizontal, and therefore perpendicular to the vertical line, which will ∵ be equal to f multiplied into the sine of the angle which f makes with the horizontal line, but as the sides are as the sines of the opposite angles, we have the sine of the angle which f makes with the horizontal line, to the sine of ω, or its supplement, as $f':f+f'$ ∴ it is equal to $\frac{f'.\sin.\omega}{f+f'}=q.p.\frac{f\omega}{f+f'}$, now if the weight be represented by the vertical line, then mg divided by sine of the angle which f makes with the horizontal line, *i. e.* $\frac{m.g.(f+f')}{\omega f'}$ will be the force in the direction of f.

also let p be the reciprocal action of m on m'; p' that of m on m''; p'' that of m' on m'', &c. and lastly, let mS, $m'S'$, $m''S''$, be the forces which act on m, m', m''; &c. s, s', s'', lines drawn from any fixed points in the direction of these forces, to the bodies m, m', m'', &c.; this being premised, we may consider the point m as perfectly free, and in equilibrio in consequence of the action of the force mS, and of the forces, which the bodies m, m', m'', communicate to it; but if it was subjected to move on a curve or on a surface, it would be necessary to add to these forces, the reaction of the curve or of the surface. Therefore, let δs be the variation of s, and let $\delta_{,} f$, denote the variation of f, taken on the supposition that m' is fixed. In like manner let $\delta_{,} f'$, be the variation of f', on the supposition that m'' is fixed, &c. Let R, R', represent the reactions of the two surfaces, which form by their intersection the curve on which the point is constrained to move, and let δr, $\delta r'$ be the variations of the directions of these last forces. The equation (d) of No. 3, will give:

$$0 = mS.\delta s + p.\delta_{,} f + p'.\delta_{,} f' + \&c. + R\delta r + R'\delta r' + \&c.$$

In the same manner m' may be considered as a point perfectly free, retained in equilibrio by means of the force $m'S'$, of the actions of the bodies m, m', m'', and of the reactions of the surfaces on which m' is constrained to move, which reactions we will denote by R'', and R'''. Let, therefore, the variation of s' be called $\delta s'$, and the variations of f, and f'', taken on the supposition that m and m'' are fixed, be respectively $\delta_{,,} f$, $\delta_{,} f''$; in like manner, let $\delta r''$, $\delta r'''$, be the respective variations of the directions of R'', R''', and we shall have for the equilibrium of m'

$$0 = m'S.\delta s' + p.\delta_{,,} f + p''.\delta_{,} f'' + \&c. + R''.\delta r'' + R'''.\delta r'''.$$

If we form similar equations relative to the equilibrium of m'', and m''', &c. by adding them together, and observing that $\delta f = \delta_{,} f + \delta_{,,} f$; $\delta f' = \delta_{,} f' + \delta_{,,} f'$; * &c. δf, and $\delta f'$, being the total

* $\delta f = \delta_{,} f + \delta_{,,} f$; $\delta f' = \delta_{,} f' + \delta_{,,} f'$ + &c.; for f and f' are respectively functions of the coordinates of their extreme points, and when these are moved by an indefinitely small quantity, all the powers of the increments of the coordinates, after the first may be rejected, and then the entire increment of f is equal to the sum of the partial increments

variations of f and f' + &c. we shall have

$$0 = \Sigma.m.S.\delta s + \Sigma p.\delta f + \Sigma R.\delta r; \qquad (k)$$

in this equation, the variations of the coordinates of the different points of the system are entirely arbitrary. It should be observed here, that in consequence of the equation (a) of No. 2, we may substitute in place of $mS.\delta s$, the sum of the products of all the partial forces by which m is actuated, multiplied by the respective variations of their directions. The same may be observed of the products $m'S\delta s'$; $m''.S''.\delta s''$; + &c.*

If the distances of the bodies from each other be invariable, *i. e.* if f, f', f'', + &c. are constant, this condition may be expressed by making $\delta f = 0$, $\delta f' = 0$, &c. The variations of the coordinates in the equation (k) being arbitrary, they may be subjected to satisfy these last equations, and then the forces p, p', p'', &c. which depend on the reciprocal action of the bodies composing the system, will disappear from this equation; we can also make the terms $R.\delta r$, $R'.\delta r'$. + &c.† to disappear, by subjecting the variations of the coordinates to satisfy the equations of the surfaces, on which the body is constrained to move. The equation (k) will then become

$$0 = \Sigma.mS.\delta s; \qquad (l)$$

from which it follows that in case of equilibrium, the sum of the varia-

which are due to the separate variation of each coordinate, ∵ the entire variation of f is equal to the sum of the partial variations, which correspond to the characteristics $\delta_{,}$ and $\delta_{,,}$.

* From this it appears, that the conditions of the equilibrium of a system of bodies, may be always determined by the law of the composition of forces; for we can conceive the force by which each point is actuated to be applied to the point in its direction, where all the forces concurring, constitute an equilibrium when the point is entirely free, or which constitute a resultant, which is destroyed by the fixed points of the system, when the point is not altogether free.

† See Notes to No. 3.

The equation (l) obtains, whether the points are all free, or are subjected to move on

tions of the products of the forces, into the elementary variations of their directions will be equal to nothing, whatever changes be made in the position of the system compatible with the conditions of the connection of the parts of the system.

We have arrived at this theorem, on the particular supposition of the parts of the system being at invariable distances from each other; however it is true whatever may be the conditions of the connection of the parts of the system. In order to prove this, it will be sufficient to shew that when the variations, of the coordinates, are subjected to those conditions, we have in the equation (k)

$$0 = \Sigma.p.\delta f + \Sigma.R.\delta r;$$

but it is evident that δr, $\delta r'$, &c. are equal to nothing, when these conditions are satisfied; therefore it is only necessary to prove that in the same circumstances we have

$$0 = \Sigma.p.\delta f.$$

Let us therefore suppose the system actuated by the sole forces p, p', $p_{\prime}$ &c. and that the bodies are subjected to move on the curves, which they can describe in consequence of the same conditions; these forces may be resolved into others, some of which q, q', q'', &c. acting in the direction of f, f', f'', &c. will mutually destroy each other, without producing any action on the curves described; others will be perpendicular to those curves; and others again will act in the direction of tangents to those curves, by the action of which the bodies may be moved; but it is easy to perceive that the sum of these last forces ought to be equal to nothing; since the system being by hypothesis at liberty to move in their directions, they are not able to produce either pressure on the curves described, or reaction between the bodies;

curved surfaces; in the former case, the forces S, S', S'', constitute an equilibrium; in the latter case, these forces have a resultant, of which the direction is perpendicular to the surface. (See Note to page 17.)

consequently they cannot constitute an equilibrium with the forces $-p, -p', -p''$, &c. q, q', q'', &c. T, T', T''; therefore they must vanish, and the system must be in equilibrio in consequence of the sole forces $p, -p', -p''$, &c.; q, q', q'', &c.; T, T', &c. Now, if $\delta i, \delta i'$, &c. represent the variations of the directions of the forces T, T', &c. we shall have in consequence of the equation (k)

$$0 = \Sigma.(q-p).\delta f + \Sigma.T.\delta i;$$

but the system being supposed to be at rest, in consequence of the sole action of the forces q, q', &c. without any action being produced on the curves described, the equation (k) gives us also $0 = \Sigma.q.\delta f$;* consequently we have

$$0 = \Sigma.p.\delta f - \Sigma.T.\delta i;$$

but as the variations of the coordinates are subjected to satisfy the conditions of the curves described, we have $\delta i, = 0$, $\delta i', = 0$, &c.; therefore the preceding equation becomes

$$0 = \Sigma.p.\delta f;\dagger$$

as the curves described are themselves arbitrary, and are only subjected to the conditions of the connection of the system, the preceding equation obtains, provided that we satisfy these conditions, and then the equation (k) will be changed into the equation (l). The following principle, known by the name of the principle of virtual velocities, when analytically expressed, is represented by this equation. It is thus an-

* $0 = \Sigma\, q.\delta f$, for q, q', q'', are directed along the lines f, f', f''; and are supposed to *destroy* each other without producing *any* action on the curves described.

† The object of the second part of this demonstration is to shew, that if the system is at rest, and acted on by the sole forces p, p', p'', these forces may be so decomposed as to afford forces equivalent to the reciprocal actions of the respective bodies, and that the remaining portions of the forces, as well as these reciprocal actions, will balance each other, in case of equilibrium, according to the terms of the proposition.

Since the equation (k) is reduced to the equation (l), when we subject the variations of the coordinates to satisfy the equations of the surfaces, on which the bodies are constrained to move, it follows that it is not necessary to compute the forces p, p', &c. in order to derive the equations of equilibrium in each particular case.

nounced: "If we make an indefinitely small variation in the position* of a system of bodies, which are subjected to the conditions they ought to fulfil, the sum of the forces which solicit it, multiplied respectively by the space that the body to which it is applied, moves along its direction, should be equal to nothing in the case of the equilibrium of the system."

This principle not only obtains in the case of equilibrium, but it also insures its existence. Let us suppose, in fact, that whilst the equation (l) obtains, the points m, m', &c. acquire the velocities v, v', in consequence of the action of the forces mS, $m'S'$, which are applied to them. The system will be in equilibrio in consequence of the action of these forces, and of $-mv$, $-m'v'$, &c.; denoting by δv, $\delta v'$, &c. the variations of the directions of these new forces, we shall have in consequence of the principle of virtual velocities

$$0 = \Sigma.mS.\delta s - \Sigma.mv.\delta v,$$

but by hypothesis $\Sigma.mS.\delta s. = 0$, therefore we have $0 = \Sigma.mv.\delta v$. We may suppose the variations δv, $\delta v'$, &c. equal to $v.dt$, $v'dt$, &c. since they are necessarily subjected to the conditions of the system, and then we have $0 = \Sigma.mv^2$, and consequently $v = 0$, $v' = 0$, &c. that is to say, the system is in equilibrio in consequence of the sole forces mS, m',S', &c.

The conditions of the connection of the parts of the system may be always reduced to equations between the coordinates of the several bodies. Let $u = 0$, $u' = 0$, &c. be these different equations, by No. 3, we can add to the equation (l), the function $\lambda\delta u$, $\lambda'\delta u'$, &c. or $\Sigma\lambda\delta u$; λ, λ', being indeterminate functions of the coordinates of the bodies, the

* When an indefinitely small change is made in the position of the system, so that the conditions of the connections of the points of the system may be preserved, each point advances in the direction of the force which solicits it by a quantity equal to a part of this direction, contained between the first position of this point, and a perpendicular demitted from the second position on this direction; these indefinitely small lines are termed the virtual velocities; they have been denominated vertual, because the system being in equilibrio, these changes may obtain without the equilibrium being disturbed.

equation will then become

$$0 = \Sigma.mS.\delta s + \Sigma.\lambda\delta u\;;*$$

in this case the variations of all the coordinates are arbitrary, and we may equal their coefficients to nothing; which will give as many equations, by means of which we can determine the functions λ, λ'. If we compare this equation with the equation (k) we shall have

$$\Sigma.\lambda.\delta u = \Sigma.p.\delta f + \Sigma.R.\delta r\;;$$

by means of which we can easily determine the reciprocal actions of the bodies m, m', &c. on each other, and also the forces $-R$, $-R'$, with which they press against the surfaces on which they are constrained to move.

15. If all the bodies of the system are firmly united to each other, its position will be determined by that of three of its points which are not in the same right line; the position of each of these points depends on three coordinates; this produces nine indeterminate quantities; but we can reduce them to six others, because the mutual distances of the three points are given and invariable; these being substituted in the equation (l), will introduce six arbitrary variations; by supposing their coefficients to vanish, we shall obtain six equations, which will contain all the conditions of the equilibrium of the system: let us proceed to develope these equations.†

* By means of the formulæ which are given in the notes to No. 3, page 14 and 15, we can determine λ, λ', &c. when S, S', S'', are given for each individual point; and therefore p, p', p'', k, k', k'', by means of the equation $\Sigma.\lambda.\delta u = \Sigma.p.\delta f + \Sigma.R.\delta r$; in the equation $\Sigma\, m.S\delta s + \Sigma.\lambda.\delta u$, m, m', m'', &c. may be considered as entirely free; and if we put the coefficients of the variation of each variable equal to nothing, and then eliminate the indeterminate quantities, λ, λ', λ'', &c. between these equations, the expressions which result, will give the relations which must exist between S, S', S'', &c. and the coordinates, when the system is in equilibrio.

† It follows immediately, from the demonstration of the principle of virtual velocities, that it has place for all the indefinitely small motions which can be given to a solid body, which is either free or constrained to certain conditions, for in all these motions the respective distances of the points of the body remain the same.

For this purpose, let x, y, z, be the coordinates of m; x', y', z', those of m'; x'', y'', z'', those of m''; &c.; we shall have then

$$f = \sqrt{(x'-x)^2+(y'-y)^2+(z'-z)^2}$$

$$f' = \sqrt{(x''-x)^2+(y''-y)^2+(z''-z)^2}$$

$$f'' = \sqrt{(x''-x')^2+(y''-y')^2+(z''-z')^2} \quad \&c.$$

and if we suppose

$$\delta x = \delta x' = \delta x'' = \&c.$$

$$\delta y = \delta y' = \delta y'' = \&c.;$$

$$\delta z = \delta z' = \delta z'' = \&c.;$$

we shall have $\delta f = 0$, $\delta f' = 0$, $\delta f'' = 0$, &c.;* the required conditions will therefore be satisfied, and from the equation (l) we may infer

$$0 = \Sigma.m.S.\left\{\frac{\delta s}{\delta x}\right\};\quad 0 = \Sigma.mS.\left\{\frac{\delta s}{\delta y}\right\};\quad 0 = \Sigma.m.S.\left\{\frac{\delta s}{\delta z}\right\};\quad (m)$$

we have thus obtained three of the six equations, which contain the conditions of the equilibrium of the system. The second members of these equations are the sum of the forces of the system, resolved parallel to the three axes of x, y, and z, therefore each of these sums must vanish in the case of equilibrium.

And as the number of the equations of equilibrium, which are derived from the principle of virtual velocities, is always equal to the number of possible motions, this number being equal to six, in the case of a solid body, or of a body whose parts are invariably connected, the number of equations of equilibrium will be six in like manner.

* $$\delta f = \frac{(x'-x).(\delta' x-\delta x)+(y'-y)(\delta y'-\delta y)+(z'-z)(\delta z'-\delta z)}{f} + \&c.$$

consequently when $\delta x'=\delta x$, $\delta y'=\delta y$, $\delta z'=\delta z$, &c. $\delta f=0$, therefore $\Sigma m.S.\left\{\frac{\delta s}{\delta x}\right\}=0$, $\Sigma m.S.\left\{\frac{\delta s}{\delta y}\right\}=0$. &c.; for when $\delta x=\delta x'=\delta x''$; $\delta y=\delta y'=\delta y''$; $\delta z=\delta z'=\delta z''=$ &c.;

The equations $\delta f_{,} = 0$, $\delta f' = 0$, $\delta f'' = 0$, &c. will be also satisfied, if we suppose, z, z', z'', invariable, and then make

$$\delta x = y\delta\omega; \qquad \delta y = -x.\delta\omega;$$

$$\delta x' = y'.\delta\omega, \text{ \&c.} \qquad \delta y' = -x'.\delta\omega, \text{ \&c.}$$

$\delta\omega$ being any variation whatever. By substituting these values in the equation (l), we shall have

$$*0 = \Sigma.mS.\left\{y.\left(\frac{\delta s}{\delta x}\right) - x.\left(\frac{\delta s}{\delta y}\right)\right\}.$$

It is evident that we may, in this equation, change either the coordinates x, x', x'', &c. or the coordinates y, y', y'', &c, into z, z', z'', which will give two other equations, and these reunited with the preceding equation, will constitute the following system of equations:

$$0 = \Sigma mS.\left\{y.\left(\frac{\delta s}{\delta x}\right) - x\left(\frac{\delta s}{\delta y}\right)\right\};$$

$$0 = \Sigma mS.\left\{z.\left(\frac{\delta s}{\delta x}\right) - x\left(\frac{\delta s}{\delta z}\right)\right\}; \quad (n)$$

$$0 = \Sigma mS.\left\{y.\left(\frac{\delta s}{\delta z}\right) - z.\left(\frac{\delta s}{\delta y}\right)\right\};$$

$\Sigma m.S.\delta s = 0$, is equivalent to $\Sigma mS.\left\{\frac{\delta s}{\delta x}\right\}.\delta x = 0$, $\Sigma mS.\left\{\frac{\delta s}{\delta y}\right\}.\delta y = 0$, $\Sigma.m.S.\left\{\frac{\delta s}{\delta z}\right\}.\delta z = 0$. See Note to No. 2, page 9.

* In like manner, if we suppose, $\delta x = y.\delta\omega$, $\delta x' = y'.\delta\omega$, $\delta y = -x\delta\omega$, $\delta y' = -x'\delta\omega$, δf, $\delta f'$, &c. $= 0$, for substituting in the preceding expression for δf, which has been given, for δx, $\delta x'$, δy, $\delta y'$, and it becomes

$$= \frac{(x'-x).(y'-y) + (y'-y).(x-x')}{f} + \text{\&c.} = 0, \quad \delta z = 0.$$

By substituting in the equation, $\Sigma m.S\delta s = 0$, for δx, δy, &c. their values it becomes $\Sigma m.S.\left\{y.\frac{\delta y}{\delta x}\right\} - x\left\{\frac{\delta s}{\delta y}\right\}\delta\omega = 0.$

When all the forces are applied to the same point, the three first equations suffice for the equilibrium; but when these forces act in different points of space, or when they are

by No. 3, the function $\Sigma m S y . \left\{ \frac{\partial s}{\partial x} \right\}$ is the sum of the moments of all the forces, parallel to the axes of x, which would cause the system to revolve about the axis of z. In like manner, the function $\Sigma m . S x . \left\{ \frac{\partial s}{\partial y} \right\}$ is the sum of the moments of all the forces parallel to the axes of y, which would cause the system to revolve round the axis of z, but in a direction contrary to that of the former forces; therefore the first of the equations (n) indicates that the sum of the moments of the forces is nothing with respect to the axis of z. The second and third equations indicate, in a similar manner, that the sum of the moments of the forces is nothing with respect to the axes of y and x, respectively. If we combine these three conditions with those, in which the sum of the forces parallel to those axes, was nothing with respect to each of them; we shall have the six conditions of the equilibrium of a system of bodies invariably connected together.*

If the origin of the coordinates is fixed, and firmly attached to the system, it will destroy the forces parallel to the three axes, and the conditions of the equilibrium of the system about this origin, will be reduced to the following, that the sum of the moments of the forces which would make it turn about the three axes, be equal to nothing, with respect to each of them.†

applied to different parts of the same solid body, it is also requisite that the moments of the forces with respect to axis of x, y, and z, should be respectively equal to nothing.

* If all the points exist in the plane of x, y, then ∂z, $\partial z'$, $\partial z''$, are equal respectively to nothing, consequently the equations of equilibrium are reduced to the three following:

$$\Sigma . m\, S . \left\{ \frac{\partial s}{\partial x} \right\} = 0, \quad \Sigma . m . S . \left\{ \frac{\partial s}{\partial y} \right\} = 0, \quad \Sigma . m . S . \left\{ y . \left(\frac{\partial s}{\partial x} \right) \right\} - x . \left(\frac{\partial s}{\partial y} \right) \Big\}$$

† When the origin of the coordinates is fixed and invariably attached to the system, the number of possible motions is reduced to three, therefore the number of equations of equilibrium will be three; this also appears from considering that the number of indeterminate quantities may be reduced to three, because the distances of any three assumed points in the system, not existing in the same right line, from the fixed origin of the coordinates, are given.

† In *this* case, the resultant of all the forces which act on the body passes through the fixed point, which resultant is therefore destroyed by the resistance of the fixed point, and it expresses the force with which this point is pressed. (See last note to No. 3.) When there are two points of the system fixed and invariable, then the only possible motion, which can be impressed on the body, is that of rotation, about the line joining the given points, consequently if this line be taken for the axis of z, there will be but one equation of equilibrium, *i. e.* $\Sigma.mS.\left\{y.\left(\frac{\delta s}{\delta x}\right)-x.\left(\frac{\delta s}{\delta y}\right)\right\}=0$, this is also manifest from the circumstances of the indeterminate quantities, which were six in number when there was no fixed point, being reducible to one, when the origin of the coordinates, and also another point of the system, were fixed and invariable. The forces parallel to the axes of z cannot produce any motion in the system, ∵ it is only necessary to consider those which exist in the plane of x, y, and as to those, it is evident, from the equation $\Sigma m.S.\left\{y.\left(\frac{\delta s}{\delta x}\right)-x.\left(\frac{\delta s}{\delta y}\right)\right\}=0$; that their resultant passes through the origin of the coordinates, its direction will be perpendicular to the axis of z, and its intensity will express the force with which it presses on this axis. When the number of fixed points is three, there is evidently no equation of equilibrium.

If the forces S, S', S'', &c. do not constitute an equilibrium, in order to reduce them to the least possible number, we should resolve them into three systems of forces, parallel respectively to the axes of x, of y, and of z, then reducing the forces parallel to the axes of x, and y, to forces = to them respectively, but acting in the same plane, which is always possible, if this last system of forces, and also the forces parallel to the axis of z, have separately unique resultants; and if these resultants exist in the same plane, we can compose them into one sole force, which will be the resultant of the given forces, but if the forces directed in the plane x, y, can only be reduced to two parallel forces, not reducible into one, then if we combine them with the force parallel to the axis of z, the entire system of forces, will be reduced to two parallel ones acting in different planes, consequently irreducible into a unique force. Denoting

$\Sigma.m.S.\left\{\frac{\delta s}{\delta x}\right\}$; $\Sigma.m.S.\left\{\frac{\delta s}{\delta y}\right\}$; $\Sigma.m.S.\left\{\frac{\delta s}{\delta z}\right\}$, by P, Q, R; respectively, and

$\Sigma.m.S.\left\{y.\left\{\frac{\delta s}{\delta x}\right\}-x.\left\{\frac{\delta s}{\delta y}\right\}\right\}$; $\Sigma.m.S.\left\{z.\left\{\frac{\delta s}{\delta x}\right\}-x.\left\{\frac{\delta s}{\delta z}\right\}\right\}$; $\Sigma.m.S.\left\{y.\left\{\frac{\delta s}{\delta z}\right\}-z.\left\{\frac{\delta s}{\delta y}\right\}\right\}$, by L, M, N; if $x_{,}$, $y_{,}$ be the coordinates of that point in which the resultant of all the forces meets the plane of the axes of x, y, we shall have by the last note to No. 3, $P.y_{,} - Q x_{,} = L$, $R.x_{,} = M$, $-Q.y_{,} = N$; therefore $x_{,} = \frac{M}{R}$; $y_{,} = -\frac{N}{R}$, substituting these expressions for $x_{,}$ and $y_{,}$ in the equation $P.y_{,} - Q.x_{,} = L$, we will obtain the equation $L.R+M.Q+N.P=0$, which may be considered as an equation of condition which must be satisfied, when the forces which act on the different points of the system, have an unique resultant. We must however except the case where P, Q, R, are respectively equal to nothing; for then the forces are reducible to two parallel forces $=$, but not *directly* opposed to each other. If only P, and Q vanish, then in order that the preceding equation may be satisfied, it is necessary that L should vanish, consequently since P, Q, and L vanish, the forces which are directed in the plane, x, y, constitute an equilibrium, ∵ the unique resultant of the forces S, S', S'', &c. must be the same with the resultant R, of the forces parallel to the axes of z, ∵ we conclude that if L does not vanish when P and Q vanish, the forces have not an unique resultant, since the forces in the plane of x, y, are in this case evidently irreducible to one sole force, if however only one of the three sums P, Q, R, vanish, then the forces in the plane x, y, and those parallel to the axes of z, would have respectively unique resultants, consequently the preceding equation of condition would apply to this case.

When the forces have an unique resultant, it is very easy to determine its position with respect to the coordinates, for if we denote this resultant by V, we shall have $V^2=P^2+Q^2+R^2$, and $\frac{P}{V}, \frac{Q}{V}, \frac{R}{V}$, $=$ the cosines of the angles which V makes with the axes of x, y, and z, respectively, and $\frac{M}{R}, -\frac{N}{R}$, are the distances of the intersection of V with the plane of x, y, from the axes of x and y, respectively.

Supposing the system to revolve round the axis of z, the elementary variations of x and y, &c. are $=$ respectively to $y\delta\omega$, $-x\delta\omega$; if y be made the axis of rotation, and $\delta\phi$ the variation of the angle, then we shall have $\delta x=-z\,\delta\phi$; $\delta z=+x.\delta\phi$; in like manner, x being the axis of rotation, and $\delta\psi$ the corresponding variation of the angle, $\delta y=+z.\delta\psi$; $\delta z=-y.\delta\psi$; &c.; now if the three rotations be supposed to take place together, we shall have the entire variation of $x=y.\delta\omega-z.\delta\phi$, of $y=z.\delta\psi-x.\delta\omega$ of $z=x.\delta\phi-y.\delta\psi$, and similar expressions may be derived for the variations of x', y', z', x'', &c.; now if we substitute these values for δx, δy,+ &c. in the equation (l), we shall have the equation $L.\delta\phi+M.\delta\psi, N.\delta\omega=0$, L, M, N, indicating the same quantities as before; this equation is evidently equivalent to the equation (n); when the coordinates x, y, z, of any point of the system are proportional to the elementary variations $\delta\psi$, $\delta\phi$, $\delta\omega$, $z\,\delta\phi=y.\delta\omega$, $z.\delta\psi=x\delta\omega$, $x\delta\phi=y\delta\psi$.

And consequently $\delta x=0$, $\delta y=0$, $\delta z=0$; ∵ this point and all others which have the same property are immoveable, during the instant the point describes the angles $\delta\phi$, $\delta\psi$, $\delta\omega$, by turning round the axes of x, y, and z; all points possessing this property exist in a right line passing through the origin of the coordinates, see No. 28, as the cosines of the angles m, n, l, which this line make with the axes of x, y, and z, are

$$\frac{x}{\sqrt{x^2+y^2+z^2}}=\text{ in this case }\frac{\frac{z.\delta\psi}{\delta\omega}}{\sqrt{\frac{z^2.\delta\psi^2}{\delta\omega^2}+\frac{z^2.\delta\phi^2}{\delta\omega^2}+z^2}}.$$

Let us suppose that the bodies m, m', m'', are subject to the sole force

$$\frac{z}{\sqrt{x^2+y^2+z^2}}=\left\{\frac{\delta\psi}{\sqrt{(\delta\psi^2+\delta\omega^2+\delta\varphi^2)}}\right\};$$

∵ the right line which makes with the axes, angles whose cosines are equal to those expressions, is the locus of all the points, which are quiescent during the instantaneous rotation of the system. Making $\delta\theta=\sqrt{\delta\psi^2+\delta\varphi^2+\delta\omega^2}$, we obtain $\delta\psi=\delta\theta.\cos. m$; $\delta\varphi=\delta\theta. \cos. n$; $\delta\omega=\delta\theta.\cos. l$; consequently $\delta x=(y.\cos. l-z.\cos. n).\delta\theta$; $\delta y=(z.\cos. m-x.\cos. l.)\delta\theta$; $\delta z.=(x.\cos. n-y.\cos. m.)\delta\theta$, substituting for δx, δy, δz, these values in the expression $\delta x^2+\delta y^2+\delta z^2$, which is equal to the indefinitely small space described by the point whose coordinates are x, y, z, and observing that $\cos.^2 l+\cos.^2 m+\cos.^2 n=1$, it becomes equal to $(x^2+y^2+z^2-(x.\cos. m+y\cos. n+z\cos. l.)^2).\delta\theta^2$; $x.\cos. l+y.\cos. m+z.\cos. n.$ is proportional to the cosine of the angle which the line whose coordinates are x, y, z, makes with the right line which makes the angles l, m, n, with the axes of x, y, z, ∵ when the line drawn from the origin of the coordinates to the point whose coordinates are x, y, z, is perpendicular, to the instantaneous axis of rotation, the elementary space described by a point so circumstanced $=\sqrt{x^2+y^2+z^2}.\delta\theta$, this agrees with what is demonstrated in No. 28. If we suppose $\delta\psi$, $\delta\varphi$, $\delta\omega$, proportional to L, M, N, and make $H=\sqrt{L^2+M^2+N^2}$, then

$$\frac{L}{H}=\frac{\delta\psi}{\delta\theta}=\cos. m;\quad \frac{M}{H}=\frac{\delta\varphi}{\delta\theta}=\cos. n.\quad \frac{N}{H}=\frac{\delta\omega}{\delta\theta}=\cos l.$$

∵ $L=H.\cos m$; $M=H.\cos. n$; $N=H.\cos. l$; ∵ if $H=L$, $m=0$, $n=100°$, $l=100°$; ∵ L, the moment of the force is a maximum when $=H$, and the moments whose axes are perpendicular to the axis of H, will be equal to nothing. This will be more fully explained in Nos. 21, and 28, it is mentioned here in order to shew how the conditions of the equilibrium of a solid body may be expressed by means of the greatest moment, and unique resultant; if this resultant, and this moment respectively vanish, then $R=0$, $H=0$, i. e. P, Q, R; L, M, N, which are equivalent to the equations $(m)(n)$, are equal respectively to nothing; consequently the evanescence of H and R contains the six equations of the equilibrium of a system, whose parts are invariably connected; and as by No. 3, the sum of the moments of the composing forces with respect to an axis, is equal to the moment of the projection of the resultant of these forces; this resultant must necessarily exist in that plane, in which the moment is the greatest possible, ∵ the perpendicular to this plane must be at right angles to the resultant, consequently, as $\frac{L}{H}, \frac{M}{H}, \frac{N}{H}$, are equal to the cosines of the angles which the axis of the greatest moment make with the axis of x, y, and z, and as $\frac{P}{V}, \frac{Q}{V}, \frac{R}{V}$, are equal to the cosines of the angles which V, the unique resultant makes with the same axes; by note to No. 2, page 7, we have $LR+MQ+NP=0$, which is the equation indicating that the forces have an unique resultant

of gravity, as its acts equally on all bodies; and as we may conceive, that its direction is the same, for all the bodies of the system, we shall have

$$S, = S', = S'', = \&c.;$$

$$\left\{\frac{\delta s}{\delta x}\right\} = \left\{\frac{\delta s}{\delta x'}\right\} = \left\{\frac{\delta s}{\delta x'}\right\} = \&c.;$$

$$\left\{\frac{\delta s}{\delta y}\right\} = \left\{\frac{\delta s}{\delta y'}\right\} = \left\{\frac{\delta s}{\delta y''}\right\} = \&c.;$$

$$\left\{\frac{\delta s}{\delta z}\right\} = \left\{\frac{\delta s}{\delta z'}\right\} = \left\{\frac{\delta s}{\delta z'}\right\} = \&c.;$$

whatever may be supposed the direction of s, or of the gravity, we shall satisfy the three equations *(n)*, by means of the three following :*

$$0 = \Sigma.m.x;\ 0 = \Sigma.m.y;\ 0 = \Sigma.m.z;\ (o)$$

* The force of gravity being uniform, and the direction of its action being always the same, $S=S'=S''=\&c.$, $\left\{\frac{\delta s}{\delta x}\right\} = \left\{\frac{\delta s'}{\delta x'}\right\} = \&c. \left\{\frac{\delta s}{\delta y}\right\} = \left\{\frac{\delta s'}{\delta y'}\right\}$, (for these quanties $\left\{\frac{\delta s}{\delta x}\right\}$ &c. indicate the cosines of the angles which the directions of gravity makes with the three coordinates,) the three equations (*n*) may be made to assume the following form :

$$0 = S.\left\{\left\{\frac{\delta s}{\delta x}\right\}.\ \Sigma.my - \left\{\frac{\delta s}{\delta x}\right\}\Sigma.mx.\right\};\ 0 = S.\left\{\left\{\frac{\delta s}{\delta s}\right\}.\ \Sigma.mz - \left\{\frac{\delta s}{\delta z}\right\}.\ \Sigma.mx.\right\};$$

$$0 = S.\left\{\left\{\frac{\delta s}{\delta z}\right\}.\ \Sigma.my - \left\{\frac{\delta s}{\delta y}\right\}.\ \Sigma.mz.\right\};$$

they are satisfied by means of the three following: $0=\Sigma.mx$, $0=\Sigma.my$; $0=\Sigma.mz$. The equations (*m*) will be reduced to the following

$$0 = S.\left\{\frac{\delta s}{\delta x}\right\}.\ \Sigma m;\ 0 = S.\left\{\frac{\delta s}{\delta y}\right\}.\ \Sigma m;\ 0 = S.\left\{\frac{\delta s}{\delta z}\right\}.\ \Sigma m;$$

The origin of the coordinates, being supposed fixed, it will destroy parallel to each of the three axes, the forces

$$S.\left\{\frac{\delta s}{\delta x}\right\}\Sigma m\,;\quad S.\left\{\frac{\delta s}{\delta y}\right\}\Sigma.m\,;\quad S.\left\{\frac{\delta s}{\delta z}\right\}.\ \Sigma m\,;$$

by composing these three forces, we shall obtain an unique force, equal to $S.\Sigma.m.$ i. e. to the weight of the system.

This origin of the coordinates about which we suppose the system in equilibrio, is a very remarkable point in it, on this account, that being supported, the system actuated by the sole force of gravity remains in equilibrio, whatever position it may be made to assume about this point, which is from thence denominated the *centre of gravity* of the system. Its position may be determined by this property, that if we make any plane whatever pass through this point, the sum of the products of each body,* by its distance from this plane, is equal to nothing; for this

these forces admit a resultant, see note to page 89, and as $\frac{\delta s}{\delta x}, \frac{\delta s}{\delta y}, \frac{\delta s}{\delta z}$, are equal to the cosines of the angles which its direction makes with the axes of x, of y, and of z, combining those three expressions, the resultant is evidently $=$ to $S\Sigma m$; consequently the force with which the fixed origin is pressed, in this case equals the weight of the bodies composing the systems. $S.\Sigma m.$ answers to the expression $m\,g.$ in the first note to page 78.

It follows from note to page 88, that the resultant of all the forces must pass through the origin for $\Sigma.mx$; $\Sigma.my$; $\Sigma.mz$; are equal respectively to nothing. If another point in the system besides the centre of gravity was fixed, then $0 = S.\left\{\frac{\delta s}{\delta z}\right\}\Sigma.my - \frac{\delta s}{\delta y}.\Sigma.mz.\}$ is the sole equation of equilibrium; in this case the fixed axis of rotation must be vertical.

* If $Ax' + By' + Cz' = 0$, be the equation of a plane passing through the centre of gravity, the cosines of the angles which this plane makes with the plane of the axes $x\,y$, of $x\,z$, and of $y\,z$, respectively, i. e. the cosines of the angles which a perpendicular to this plane makes with the axis of x, and of y, of $z =$

$$\frac{A}{\sqrt{A^2+B^2+C^2}},\ \frac{B}{\sqrt{A^2+B^2+C^2}},\ \frac{C}{\sqrt{A^2+B^2+C^2}};$$

see Lacroix, tom. 1. No. 269,

in like manner the cosines of the angles, which lines drawn, from the point, whose coordinates are x, y, z, make with the axes of x, of y, and of z,

distance is a linear function of the coordinates $x, y, z,$ of the body; consequently by multiplying it by the mass of the body, the sum of these products will be equal to nothing in consequence of the equations. (o)

In order to determine the position of the centre of gravity, let $X, Y, Z,$ represent its three coordinates with respect to a given origin; let $x, y, z,$ be the coordinates of m with respect to the same point; $x', y', z',$ those of m', &c. the equations (o) will then give

$$0 = \Sigma.m.(x - X.)$$

but we have $\Sigma.m.X = X.\Sigma.m$, $\Sigma.m$ being being the entire mass of the system, therefore we have

$$X = \frac{\Sigma.m.x}{\Sigma.m},$$

we shall have in like manner

$$Y = \frac{\Sigma.m.y}{\Sigma.m}; \quad Z = \frac{\Sigma.m.z}{\Sigma.m};$$

$$= \frac{x}{\sqrt{x^2+y^2+z^2}}, \frac{y}{\sqrt{x^2+y^2+z^2}}, \frac{z}{\sqrt{x^2+y^2+z^2}},$$

∵ by note to No. 2, page 7, the cosine of the angle which the perpendicular to the given plane, makes with the line whose coordinates are $x, y, z,$

$$= \frac{xA+yB+zC}{\sqrt{A^2+B^2+C^2} \times \sqrt{x^2+y^2+z^2}},$$

let this angle $= a$ and $\sqrt{x^2+y^2+z^2} \times \cos. a = \frac{xA+yB+zC}{\sqrt{A^2+B^2+C^2}} =$ the distance of the point from the given plane, consequently, the sum of all the distances multiplied respectively into their masses

$$= \frac{A.\Sigma.mx + B.\Sigma.my + C.\Sigma.mz}{\sqrt{A^2+B^2+C^2}} = 0,$$

in consequence of the equation (o).

thus, as the coordinates X, Y, Z, determine only one point, it follows that the centre of a system of bodies is an unique point.

The three preceding equations give

$$X^2+Y^2+Z^2 = \frac{(\Sigma\, m.x)^2+(\Sigma.m.y)^2+(\Sigma\, m.z)^2}{(\Sigma.m)^2}$$

this equation may oe made to assume the following form :*

$$X^2+Y^2+Z^2 = \frac{\Sigma.m\,(x^2+y^2+z^2)}{\Sigma.m} - \frac{\Sigma mm'\{(x'-x)^2+(y'-y)^2+(z'-z)^2\}}{(\Sigma.m)^2};$$

the finite integral $\Sigma mm'\{(x'-x)^2+(y'-y)^2+(z'-z)^2\}$ expresses the sum of all the products similar to that, which is contained under the characteristic Σ, and which is formed by considering all the combinations of

* The square of the sum of any number of quantities, being equal to the sum of the squares of those quantities, and twice the sum of the products of all the binary combinations of the different quantities, we have

$$(\Sigma(mx))^2 = \Sigma(m^2x^2)+2\,\Sigma(mm'.xx'),\ \Sigma mm'.(x-x')^2)$$

denotes the products which are obtained, by taking on one part all the binary combinations of the bodies mm', &c. in which the quantities mm' are affected with different accents, and then multiplying these by the square of $(x-x')$, in which the terms have respectively the same accents as the bodies which they are multiplied by, thus $\Sigma.(x-x')^2 = x^2+x'^2+x''^2+$ &c. $-2xx'-2xx''-2x'x''-$ &c and $\Sigma(mm'(x-x')^2) = mm'x^2+mm'x'^2+mm''.x^2+mm''.x''^2+m'm''x'^2+m'm''.x''^2+$ &c. $-2mm'xx'-2mm''xx''-2m'm''x'x''$; &c. $=\Sigma(mm'.x^2)$ $-2\Sigma(mm'.(xx'))$ and as $\Sigma(mx^2) =, mx^2+m'x'^2+m''x''^2+$ &c. $\Sigma(m.x^2).\Sigma m.$ $=(mx^2+m'x'^2+m''x''^2+$ &c.$).(m+m'+m''+m'''+$ &c.$) = m^2x^2+m'^2x'^2+m''^2x''^2+$ &c. $+mm'x^2+mm'x^2+mm'x'^2+m''m'.x'^2+mm''.x''^2+m'm''.x''^2+$ &c. $=\Sigma(m^2x^2)+\Sigma(mm'x^2)$ ∵ $(\Sigma mx)^2 = \Sigma(m^2x^2)+2\Sigma(mm'xx') = \Sigma(mx^2).\ \Sigma m - \Sigma(mm'x^2) - \Sigma.mm'.(x-x')^2 + \Sigma mm')x^2) = \Sigma(mx^2).\Sigma m - \Sigma mm'(x-x)^2$, (by substituting for $\Sigma(m^2x^2)$ its value $\Sigma(mx^2)\,\Sigma m - \Sigma mm'.(x^2)$, and for $2\Sigma(mm'\,xx')$. its value $\Sigma(mm'.(x^2),) - \Sigma(mm'.(x-x')^2)$ ∵ the value of X^2

$$\frac{(\Sigma mx)^2}{(\Sigma m)^2} = \frac{(\Sigma mx^2)}{\Sigma m} - \frac{\Sigma mm'(x-x)^2}{(\Sigma m)^2},$$

we might derive corresponding expressions for Y^2, and Z^2.

This method gives the position of the centre of gravity of any body of a given form, without being obliged, to refer the position of its molecules to coordinate planes.

the different bodies of the system. We shall thus obtain the distance of the centre of gravity from any fixed point, by means of the distances of the bodies of the system, from the same fixed axis, and of their mutual distances. By determining in this manner the distance of the centre of gravity from any three fixed points, we shall have its position in space; which suggests a new way of determining this point.

The denomination of centre of gravity has been extended to that point, of any system of bodies, either with or without weight, which is determined by the three coordinates X, Y, Z.

16. Is is easy to apply the preceding results to the equilibrium of a solid body of any figure, by conceiving it made up of an indefinite number of points, firmly united together. Therefore let dm be one of these points, or an indefinitely small molecule of the body, and let x, y, z, be the rectangular coordinates of this molecule; also let P, Q, R, represent the forces by which it is actuated parallel to the axis of x, of y, and of z, the equations (m) and (n) of the preceding number will be changed into the following:

$$0 = \int P.dm\,;\quad 0 = \int Q.dm\,;\quad 0 = \int R.dm\,;^*$$

$$0 = \int (Py - Qx).\,dm\,;\quad 0 = \int (Pz - Rx).\,dm\,;\quad 0 = \int (Ry - Qz).\,dm\,;$$

The sign of integration $\int$ is relative to the molecule dm, and ought to be extended to the entire mass of the solid.

* $\left\{\frac{\delta s}{\delta x}\right\}$ being the cosine of the angle which the direction of the force S makes with the axis of x, $S.\left\{\frac{\delta s}{\delta x}\right\}$ = the force resolved parallel to the axis of x, ∵ it is equal to P; and as $\Sigma.m = \int dm$, $\Sigma m.\ S.\left\{\frac{\delta s}{\delta x}\right\} = \int P.dm$, and since $\Sigma.S.\left\{\frac{\delta s}{\delta x}\right\} ym = \int Py.dm$;

$\Sigma.m.S.\left\{ y.\left\{\frac{\delta s}{\delta x}\right\} - x.\left\{\frac{\delta s}{\delta y}\right\}\right\} = \int (Py - Qx)\,dm$, &c.

From the values which have been given in the text for the coordinates of the centre of gravity, it is manifest that the position of this centre remains unaltered, whatever change may take place in the absolute force of gravity, ∵ when bodies are transferred from one latitude to another on the surface of the earth, though the absolute weight varies, still the position of the centre of gravity is fixed.

If the body could only turn about the origin of the coordinates, the three last equations will be sufficient for its equilibrium.*

* When any system of homogeneous bodies is in equilibrio, the centre of gravity is then the highest or lowest possible; this is immediately evident from the principle of virtual velocities, for let the weights of any number of bodies m, m', m'', be denoted by S, S', S'', &c. and let s, s', s'', &c. represent lines demitted from the centres of the several bodies m, m', m'', &c. on the horizontal plane; now if the position of the system be disturbed in an indefinitely small degree, we shall have, when the bodies of the system are in equilibrio, the equation of virtual velocities

$$S\delta s + S'.\delta s' + S.\delta s'' + \&c. = 0,$$

consequently the quantity of which this expression is the variation, i. e. $Ss + S's' + S''s'' +$ &c. (= the entire weight of all the bodies composing the system, multiplied by the distance of the centre of gravity of the system from the horizontal plane, $= s_{,}.S.\Sigma m.$) is a maximum or minimum, and as the weight of all the bodies of the system is always given, the distance of the centre of gravity of the system from the horizontal plane must be either a maximum or a minimum when the system is in equilibrio; this being established, it is interesting to know the equation of the curve, in which the centre of gravity is lower than in any other curve whose points of suspension and length are given; the investigation of this curve, which is termed the catenary, is very easy, it occurs in all the elementary treatises, the differential equation is of the following form $(y+g).dx = g \cos. c.\sqrt{dx^2 + y^2}$.

It might be proved conversely, that when the distance of the centre of gravity from an horizontal plane is the greatest or least possible, the system is in equilibrio, for we shall have $S.\delta s + S'.\delta s' + S''\delta s'' + \&c. = G.\delta s_{,} = 0$, however there is an essential difference between their states of equilibrium; in the first case, the equilibrio is denominated instable, in the second, it is termed stable, in order to determine these two different states, we should attend to the species of the motion when the centre deviates by an indefinitely small quantity from the vertical, see No. 30.

* In Physical and Astronomical problems, the method that is generally employed, to determine the mean value between several observed ones, of which some are greater, and some less than the true one, is to divide the sum of all the observed values by their number. This comes, in fact, to determine the distance of the centre of gravity from a given plane. For if z, z', z'', &c. represent the observed quantities, then $\frac{z + z' + z'' +}{n}$, &c. is the expression for the mean value, but if z, z', z'', denote the distances of the centres of gravity of n masses, equal each to m from the plane, then $\frac{zm + z'm' + z''m'' +}{nm}$, &c. =

the distance of the centre of gravity of the system of m masses from this plane $= \frac{z+z'+z''+}{m}$, &c. = the required mean value.

If several forces concurring in a point constitute an equilibrium, then supposing that, at the extremities of lines, in the directions of these forces, and respectively proportional to them, we place the centres of gravity of bodies equal to each other, the common centre of gravity of these masses will be the point where all the forces concur. For since the forces are by hypothesis represented by lines taken their direction, and concurring in one point, it is evident that by making this point the origin of the coordinates, we shall have the sum of the forces parallel to the three rectangular axes proportional to $\Sigma(x)$, $\Sigma(y)$, $\Sigma(z)$, these sums are ∴ by the conditions of the problem = to nothing, see note to page 11; and since the masses are all equal we shall have $\Sigma(x).m = \Sigma(mx) = 0$, this also obtains for the other axes, consequently we shall have $\Sigma(m.x) = 0$, $\Sigma(my) = 0$, $\Sigma(mz) = 0$, ∴ the origin of the coordinates coincides with the centre of gravity of the system of masses respectively equal to m.

The centre of gravity of a body, or system of bodies, is that point in space from which if lines be drawn to the molecules of the body, the sum of their squares is the least possible. For if X, Y, Z, represent the coordinates of such a point, then the sum of the squares of the distances of all the molecules of the system from this point is equal to $\Sigma((x-X)^2+(y-Y)^2(z-Z)^2)$, if we take the differential of this expression with respect to each of the coordinates, and multiply each of the terms of the sums which are respectively equal to nothing, by the element of the mass, we shall have $\Sigma.m.(x-X) = 0$, $\Sigma.m.(y-Y)=0$, $\Sigma.m.(z-Z,) = 0$,

$$\therefore X = \frac{\Sigma(mx)}{\Sigma m}, \quad Y=\frac{\Sigma my}{\Sigma m}; \quad Z=\frac{\Sigma mz}{\Sigma m}:$$

and from what has been demonstrated in the preceding note it follows, that if we apply to all the points of the system, forces directed towards the centre of gravity, and proportional to the distances between those points and the centre of gravity, these forces will constitute an equilibrium; consequently when several forces constitute an equilibrium, the sum of the squares of the distances of the point of concourse of these forces, from the extremities of lines representing these forces, *i. e.* the sum of the squares of these lines, is a minimum.

From the preceding property it appears, that if several observations give different values for the position of a point in space, the mean position, *i. e*, the position which deviates the least from the observed positions, is that in which the sum of the squares of its distances from the observed positions is the least possible. The problem is altogether similar when we wish to combine several observations of *any* kind whatever; for the distances of the points correspond to the differences between the particular results and their mean value; and since it is impossible entirely to exterminate these differences, we are obliged to select a mean result, such that the sums of the squares of these differences may be a minimum; this is the principal of the method of the least squares, which was devised by Le Gendre to combine the equations of conditions between the errors deduced from a comparison of the astronomical tables with observation; it comes in fact to find the centre of gravity of the observations which we compare together.

The general form of the equations of condition is as follows:

$0 = a + bx + cy + dz + \&c.$ when we pass into one member all the terms which compose them, a, b, c, are given numerical coefficients, if all these equations could be satisfied exactly, by the values of x, y, z, their first members would be necessarily reduced to nothing by substituting for x, y, z, their values, but as this substitution does not render them accurately equal to nothing, let E, E', E'', represent the errors which remain, then we shall have $E = a + bx + cy + dz + \&c.$, $E' = a' + b'x + c'y + d'z + \&c.$, $E'' = a'' + b''x + c''y + \&c.$ the quantities x, y, z', &c. are to be determined by the condition that the values E, E', are either nothing, or very small; the sum of the squares of the errors =

$$E^2 + E^2 + E^2 + \&c. = (a^2 + a'^2 + a''^2 + \&c.) + (b^2 + b'^2 + b''^2).x^2 + (c^2 + c'^2 + c''^2 + \&c.)y^2 + (d^2 + d'^2 + d''^2 + \&c.)z^2 + .$$

$$2(ab + a'b' + a''b'' + \&c.)x + 2(ac + a'c' + a''c'')y + 2(ad + a'd' + a''d'' + \&c.)z:$$

$$+ 2(bc + b'c' + b''c'' + \&c.)xy + 2(bd + b'd' + b''d'') + 4z + \&c.$$

the minimum of this expression, with respect to x, will be 0

$$= \Sigma.ab + x\,\Sigma.b^2 + y\,\Sigma.bc + z.\,\Sigma.bd + \&c.$$

the minimum with respect to $y = \Sigma.ac + x\Sigma.bc + y\Sigma c^2 + x.\Sigma.dc = 0$, we derive a corresponding value for the minimum of z, hence in order to form the equation of the minimum with respect to one of the unknown quantities, we must multiply all the terms of each proposed equation by the coefficient of the unknown term in that equation, and then put the sum of the products equal to nothing. Though this method requires more numerical calculations, in order to form the particular equation relative to each unknown quantity, than the method suggested by Mayer; it is more direct in its application, and requires no tentation on the resulting equations. Laplace has shewn in his Theory of Probabilities, that when we would take the mean between a great number of observations of the same quantity, obtained by *different* means, this is the only method which the theory permits us to employ, see Le Gendres Memoir on the determination of the orbits of the comets, and Biot's Astronomie Physique, tome 2, page 200.

CHAPTER IV.

Of the equilibrium of fluids.

17. In order to determine the laws of the equilibrium, and of the motion of *each* of the molecules of a fluid, it would be necessary to ascertain their figure, which is impossible; but we have no occasion to determine these laws, except for fluids* considered in a mass, and for this purpose the knowledge of the figures of their molecules is useless. Whatever may be the nature of these figures, and the properties which depend on them in the integrant molecules, all fluids, considered in the aggregate, ought to exhibit the same phenomena in their equilibrium, and also in their motions, so that from the observation of these phenomena, we are not able to discover any thing respecting the configuration of the fluid molecules. These general phenomena depend on

* Although the figure of the molecules of fluids are unknown to us, still there can be no question but that they are material, and consequently that the general laws of the equilibrium and motion of solid bodies are applicable to them. If we were able analytically to express their characteristic property, to wit, extreme smallness, and perfect mobility, no particular theory would be required in order to determine the laws of their equilibrium and motion; they would be then only a particular case of the general laws of Statics and Dynamics. But as we are not able to effect this, it is proposed to derive the theory of their equilibrium and motion from the property which is peculiar to them, of transmitting equally, and in every direction, the pressure to which their surface is subjected; this property is a necessary consequence of the perfect mobility of the molecules of the fluids. In the definition which has been given in the text there is no account made of the tenacity or adhesion of the molecules, which is an obstacle to this free separation; this adhesion exists however between the molecules of most of the fluids with which we are acquainted.

the perpect mobility of these molecules, which are thus able to yield to the slightest force. This mobility is the characteristic property of fluids; it distinguishes them from solid bodies, and serves to define them. It follows from this, that when a fluid mass is in equilibrio each molecule must be in equilibrio in consequence of the forces which * solicit it, and of the pressures to which it is subjected by the action of the surrounding particles. Let us proceed to develope the equations which may be deduced from this property.

For this purpose, let us consider a system of fluid molecules, constituting an indefinitely small rectangular parallelepiped. Let x, y, z, denote the three rectangular coordinates of that angle of the parallelopiped, which is nearest to the origin of the coordinates. Let dx, dy, dz, represent the three dimensions of this parallelepiped; let p repre-

* When a fluid is contained in a vessel, the pressure to which it is subjected at its surface is transmitted in every direction, as has been just stated, but since the molecules are material, they must have weight, therefore it also presses the sides of the vessel with a force arising from the weight of the molecules, and different in every point of the sides; and if the fluid is contained in a vessel closed in every side, when the molecules are solicited by any given accelerating forces, then the pressure is different for every particular point, its direction is always perpendicular to the surface, since by No. 3, when the resistance of a surface destroys the pressure on it, the direction of this pressure must be normal to the surface. The intensity of this pressure depends on the given forces, and on the position of the point.

Therefore it appears, that in the equilibrium of a fluid contained in a vessel, the entire pressure in each point of the sides is the sum of two pressures altogether distinct; one of which arises from the pressure, exerted on the surface, and is the same on all the points; the other is owing to the motive forces of the particles of the fluids, and varies from one point to another.

Fluids are generally distinguished into two classes, incompressible, and elastic; with respect to the last class, they may press against the sides of the vessel in which they are enclosed, although no motive forces act on the particles, or without any pressure urging the surface of the fluid. For from their elasticity they tend perpetually to dilate themselves, which gives rise to a pressure on the sides of the vessel; however this is a constant pressure in the same fluid; it depends on the matter of the fluid, its density and tem-

sent the mean of all the pressures, to which the different points of the side $dy.\,dz$ of the parallelepiped, which is nearest to the origin of the coordinates, is subjected; and let p' be the corresponding quantity on the opposite side. The parallelepiped, in consequence of the pressure to which it is subjected, will be urged in the direction of x, by a force equal to $(p-p').\,dy.dz$; $p'-p$ is the difference of p, taken on the hypothesis that x alone is variable; for although the pressure p' acts in a direction contrary to p, nevertheless the pressure to which a point is subject being the same in every direction, $p'-p$ may be considered as the difference of two forces infinitely near, and acting in the same direction; consequently we have*

$$p'-p=\left\{\frac{dp}{dx}\right\}.dx, \text{ and } (p-p').\,dy.\,dz=-\left\{\frac{dp}{dx}\right\}.\,dx.\,dy.\,dz.$$

Let P, Q, R, be the three accelerating forces which solicit the molecules of the fluid, independently of their connexion, parallel to the axes of x, of y, and of z; if the density of the parallelepiped be denoted by ρ, its mass will be equal to $\rho.\,dx.\,dy.\,dz.$ and the product of the force P by this mass, will represent the whole motive force, which is derived from

* Since $p, \rho.\ P, Q, R$, generally vary from one point to another of the fluid mass, they must be considered as functions of x, y, z. We distribute the fluid into parallelepipeds, in order more easily to express in analytical language the fact of the equality of pressure, which, as has been stated, is the fundamental principle from which we deduce the whole theory of their equilibrium, and by supposing these parallelepipeds indefinitely small, we are permitted to consider all the points of the same side as equally pressed, and also ρ, P, Q, R, as constant for each side respectively, by means of which we are able to determine the pressure p. x, y, z, being the coordinates of the angular point next the origin, and p being a function of these coordinates, we shall have

$$\partial p=\left\{\frac{dp}{dx}\right\}.\,\partial x+\left\{\frac{dp}{dy}\right\}.\,\partial y+\left\{\frac{dp}{dz}\right\}.\,\partial z.$$

the coefficient $\left\{\frac{dp}{dx}\right\}=\left\{\frac{\partial p}{\partial x}\right\}$ &c. they are taken negatively because they tend to diminish the coordinates.

it; consequently this mass will be solicited parallel to the axes of x, by the force $\left\{\rho P - \left\{\frac{dp}{dx}\right\}\right\}.\,dx.dy.dz.$ For similar reasons it will be solicited parallel to the axes of y, and of z, by the forces

$$\left\{\rho.Q - \left\{\frac{dp}{dy}\right\}\right\}.\ dx.dy.dz. \text{ and } \left\{\rho.R - \left\{\frac{dp}{dz}\right\}\right\}.\ dx.\ dy.\ dz. \ \&c.$$

therefore, by the equation (b) of No. 3, we shall have

$$0 = \left\{\rho P - \left\{\frac{dp}{dx}\right\}\right\}.\,\delta x + \left\{\rho Q - \left\{\frac{dp}{dy}\right\}\right\}.\,\delta y + \left\{\rho R - \left\{\frac{dp}{dz}\right\}\right\}.\,\delta z;$$

$$\text{or } \delta p = \rho(P.\delta x + Q.\delta y + R.\delta z).$$

The first member of this equation being an exact variation, the second must be so likewise; from which we may deduce the following equation of partial differentials,*

$$\left\{\frac{d.\rho P}{dy}\right\} = \left\{\frac{d.\rho Q}{dx}\right\};\ \left\{\frac{d.\rho P}{dz}\right\} = \left\{\frac{d.\rho R}{dx}\right\};\ \left\{\frac{d.\rho Q}{dz}\right\} = \left\{\frac{d.\rho R}{dy}\right\};$$

* When $\varrho\ (P.\delta x + Q\,\delta y + R.\delta z.)$ is an exact differential, $\left\{\frac{d.\varrho P}{dy}\right\} = \left\{\frac{d.\varrho Q}{dx}\right\}$ &c. (see Lacroix Traite Elementaire, Calcul. Differential and Integral, No. 261.)

$$\therefore \frac{\varrho.dP}{dy} + \frac{P.d\varrho}{dy} = \frac{\varrho.dQ}{dx} + \frac{Q.d\varrho}{dx};\ \frac{\varrho.dP}{dz} + \frac{P.d\varrho}{dz} = \frac{\varrho.dR}{dx} + \frac{R.d\varrho}{dx};$$

$\frac{\varrho.dQ}{dz} + \frac{Q.d\varrho}{dz} = \frac{\varrho.dR}{dy} + \frac{R.d\varrho}{dy}$, if we multiply the first equation by R, the second by $-Q$, and the third by P, we shall obtain,

$$\frac{\varrho.R.dP}{dy} + \frac{R.P.d\varrho}{dy} = \frac{R.\varrho.dQ}{dx} + \frac{R.Q.d\varrho}{dx};\ -\frac{\varrho.Q.dP}{dz} - \frac{Q.P.d\varrho}{dz} = -\frac{\varrho.Q.dR}{dx}$$

$$-\frac{R.Q.d\varrho}{dx};\ \frac{\varrho.P.dQ}{dz} + \frac{P.Q.d\varrho}{dz} = \frac{\varrho.P.dR}{dy} + \frac{R.P.d\varrho}{dy}.$$

from which we may obtain

$$0 = P.\left\{\frac{dQ}{dz}\right\} - Q.\left\{\frac{dP}{dz}\right\} + R.\left\{\frac{dP}{dy}\right\} -$$
$$P.\left\{\frac{dR}{dy}\right\} + Q.\left\{\frac{dR}{dx}\right\} - R.\left\{\frac{dQ}{dx}\right\}.$$

This equation expresses the relation which must exist between the forces P, Q, and R, in order that the equilibrium may be possible.

If the fluid be free at its surface, or in certain parts of this surface, the value of p will be equal to nothing in those parts; therefore we shall have $\delta p = 0$, provided that the variations δx, δy, δz, appertain to this surface; consequently when these conditions are satisfied, we shall have

$$0 = P.\delta x + Q.\delta y + R.\delta z.$$

If $\delta u = 0$, be the differential equation of the surface, we shall have

$$P.\delta x + Q.\delta y + R.\delta z = \lambda.\delta u,$$

λ being a function of x, y, z; from which it follows, by No. 3, that

by reducing all the terms in which $\delta\rho$ is involved to one side, and then adding them together, we get

$$\rho.\left\{\frac{R.dP}{dy} - \frac{R.dQ}{dx} - \frac{Q.dP}{dz} + \frac{Q.dR}{dx} + \frac{P.dQ}{dz} - \frac{P.dR}{dy}\right\} =$$

$$-\frac{RP.\delta\rho}{dy} + \frac{RQ.d\rho}{dx} + \frac{QP.d\rho}{dz} - \frac{RQ.d\rho}{dx} - \frac{PQ.\delta\rho}{dz} + \frac{RP.d\rho}{dy} = 0.$$

by concinnating

$$P.\left\{\frac{dQ}{dz}\right\} - Q.\left\{\frac{dP}{dz}\right\} + R.\left\{\frac{dP}{dy}\right\} - P.\left\{\frac{dR}{dy}\right\} + Q.\left\{\frac{dR}{dx}\right\} - R.\left\{\frac{dQ}{dx}\right\} = 0.$$

This equation shews whether the equilibrium is possible, though we are unable to ascertain the density ρ.

the resultant of the forces $P,Q,R,$* must be a perpendicular to those parts of the surface, in which the fluid is free.

Let us suppose that the variation $P\delta x + Q.\delta y + R.\delta z$ is exact, this is the case when $P,Q,R,$ are the result of attractive forces. Denoting this variation by $\delta\varphi$, we shall have $\delta p = \rho\delta\varphi$; therefore ρ must be a function of p and of φ, and as the integration of this differential equation gives φ

If the relation indicated by this equation does not obtain between the forces $P, Q, R,$ the fluid will be in a perpetual state of agitation, whatever figure it may be made to assume; but when this relation is satisfied, the equilibrium will be *possible*, and *vice versa;* and as $P,Q,R,$ are functions of the coordinates, we can integrate the expression $\rho.(P.\delta x + Q.\delta y + R.\delta z.)$ by the method of quadratures, by means of which we can find the value of the pressure for any given place of the fluid; consequently we can obtain the force with which any side of the vessel in which the fluid is enclosed is pressed. But though the relation which exists between the forces must be such as to satisfy the preceding equation, when there is an equilibrium, still this is not sufficient, in most cases, to insure the equilibrium, for the fluid must also assume a determined figure, depending on the nature of the forces $P, Q, R,$ which solicit the molecules.

* When an incompressible fluid is free at its surface, and in a state of equilibrium, p must vanish, $\because \delta p = 0$, if the fluid is elastic this condition can never be satisfied, because ρ being proportional to p, whilst the density has a finite value, p can never vanish. When p vanishes, $0 = \delta p = P.\delta x + Q.\delta y + R.\delta z$, $\because$ when $\delta x, \delta y, \delta z,$ appertain to the surface, by substituting for $P, Q, R,$ their values, the resulting expression will be the equation of the surface. It follows from No. 3, that the resultant of the forces $P, Q, R,$ must be perpendicular to the surface; it may be proved directly thus:

$$\frac{P}{\sqrt{P^2+Q^2+R^2}},\ \frac{Q}{\sqrt{P^2+Q^2+R^2}},\ \frac{R}{\sqrt{P^2+Q^2+R^2}},$$

are equal to the cosines of the angles, which the resultant makes with the axes of x, of y, and of z, but since $P.\delta x + Q.\delta y + R.\delta z$, is the equation of the surface, they also express the cosines of the angles which the normal make with the same axes respectively; see Notes to page 14; consequently the normal coincides with the resultant. This coincidence of the resultant with the normal is the second condition, which must be satisfied, in order, as has been stated above, to insure the equilibrium; and it is this condition which enables us in each particular case to determine the figure corresponding to the equilibrium of the fluid, and if there be one only attractive force directed towards a fixed point, then the surface will be of a spherical form, the fixed point being the centre of the sphere; if this point

in a function of p, we shall have p in a function of ρ. Therefore the pressure is the same, for all molecules whose density is the same; thus $\delta\rho$ must vanish with respect to those strata of the fluid, in which the density is constant, and with regard to these surfaces, we have,

$$0 = P.\delta x + Q.\delta y + R.\delta z.^{*}$$

consequently, the resultant of the forces, which solicit each molecule

P

be at an infinite distance the surface will degenerate into a plane, ∵ if the planets were originally fluid, and if their molecules attracted each other with forces, varying as $\frac{1}{d^2}$ they would assume a spherical form. See No. 12, Book 2[d].

* If $P.\delta x + Q.\delta y + R.\delta z$ is an exact variation, $\delta\varphi$, $\delta p = \rho\delta\varphi$, ∵ ρ must be some function of φ, otherwise it would not be an exact variation; however, the form of this function is undetermined, see note to page 10, consequently p will be a function of φ, and p and ρ will be the same for all those molecules in which the value of φ is given, i. e. for the molecules in the same strata of level, therefore when the density varies, an equilibrium cannot subsist unless each stratum is homogeneous during its entire extent; for when this is the case, ρ, and consequently p is the same; ∵ $\delta p = 0$, for the surfaces in which ρ is constant, ∵ for such surfaces $0 = P.\delta x + Q.\delta y + R.\delta z$, and the resultant coincides with the normal. If we integrate the preceding equation, by putting φ equal to a constant arbitrary quantity, we derive an equation which appertains to an indefinite number of surfaces, differing from each only by the value of this constant arbitrary quantity. If we make this quantity increase by insensible gradations, we will have an infinite series of surfaces, distributing the entire mass into an indefinite number of strata, and constituting between any two successive surfaces, what have been denominated *strata of Level.* The law of the variation of the density ρ, in the transit from one strata to another, is altogether arbitrary, as it depends on what function of φ, ρ is, but this is undetermined. It appears from what precedes, that there are two cases, in which $\delta p = 0$, when it is at the free surface, in which case p must vanish of itself, and also when p is constant, i. e. for all surfaces of the same level, consequently when the fluid is homogeneous, the strata to which the resultant of the forces is perpendicular, are then necessarily of the same density.

When the fluid is contained in a vessel, closed in on every side, it is only necessary that all strata of the same level must have the same density; in elastic fluids, the first condition to wit, that p should vanish, or that $P.\delta x + Q.\delta y + R.\delta z = 0$, can never obtain, ∵ unless this fluid extends indefinitely into space, so that ρ may be altogether insensible it cannot be in equilibrium, except in a vessel closed in on every side.

of the fluid, is in the state of equilibrium, perpendicular to the surfaces of these strata, and on this account they have been termed strata of level. This condition is *always* satisfied, if the fluid is homogeneous, and incompressible, because then the strata, to which this resultant is perpendicular, are all of the same density.

For the equilibrium of an homogeneous fluid mass, of which the extreme surface is free, and covers a fixed solid nucleus of any figure whatever, it is necessary and sufficient, first, that the variation $P\delta x + Q.\delta y + R + .\delta z$ be exact; secondly, that the resultant of the forces at the exterior surface be directed perpendicularly *towards* this surface.*

* If two different fluids are in equilibrio, then the surface which separates them must be horizontal; if the denser fluid is superior, the centre of gravity of *all* the molecules will be highest; if it be inferior, then the centre will be lower than in any other position, ∵ that the equilibrium may be stable, the denser strata should be inferior. See Notes to No. 15.

When p is constant, the equation $\varphi = C$, gives the relation which must exist for each stratum of level between the coordinates of the different molecules of the surface which answers to the preceding equation; in this case $\delta\varphi = 0$, which shews that φ is either a maximum or minimum, and generally when $P.\delta x + Q.\delta y + R.\delta z$ is an exact variation, ρ is a function of φ, ∵ the equation of equilibrium $\delta p - \rho.\delta\varphi = 0$, shews that in the state of equilibrium there is a function of p and of x, y, z, which is either a maximum or a minimum. Though in the state of equilibrium all the molecules in the same strata of level have necessarily the *same* density, and experience the same pressure, still the converse is not true, for in homogeneous incompressible fluids, ρ is constant in those sections of the fluid in which neither $\delta\varphi$, nor $\delta p = 0$.

In elastic fluids, the density ρ is observed to be proportional to the compressing force, ∵ $p = k.\rho$; k depends on the temperature and matter of the fluid, by substituting for ρ, in the equation $\delta p = \rho\delta\varphi$, we obtain $\delta p = \frac{p}{k}.\ \delta\varphi$, ∵ by integrating we get $\log. p + C = \frac{\varphi}{k}$, because when the matter and temperature are given, k will be constant, ∴ by making $C = -\log. E$, we obtain $p = Ec^{\frac{\varphi}{k}}$, ∵ since p and ρ, $= \left\{\frac{\varphi}{k}\right\}$, are respectively functions of φ, the pressure and density will be constant for each stratum of level, but the law of the variation of the density is not arbitrary, as in the case of incompressible fluids, for the equation $\rho = \frac{p}{k} = \frac{E}{k}.\ c^{\frac{\varphi}{k}}$, *determines* the law. If the matter of the fluid remaining homogeneous, the temperature undergoes any alteration, k will be a function of the variable temperature, but in order that the equation $\frac{\delta p}{p} = \frac{\delta \varphi}{k}$ may be an exact variation, it is necessary that k, and $\because$ the temperature should be functions of φ, these functions are altogether arbitrary; consequently we conclude, that when the fluid is in a state of equilibrium, the temperature of each stratum is uniform, and that the law of the variation of temperature is arbitrary; but this law being given, we are able to integrate the expression $\frac{\delta \varphi}{k}$, from which integral we can conclude the law of the densities and pressures by means of the equations $p = E.\,c^{\int \frac{\delta \varphi}{k}}$; $\varrho = \frac{E}{k}.\,c^{\int \left\{ \frac{\delta \varphi}{k} \right\}}$.

In incompressible fluids, if the force varies as the nth power of the distance from the centre, by fixing the origin of the coordinates at this point, we have $P = A\varrho r^{n-1}.\,x$, $Q = A\varrho r^{n-1}\ y$, $R = A\varrho r^{n-1}.\,z$, $\because P.\delta x + Q.\delta y + R.\delta z = A\varrho r^{n-1}.\,(x.\delta x + y.\delta y + z.\delta z) = A\varrho r^{n}.\,\delta r, = \delta p$, $\because \frac{A\varrho r^{n+1}}{n+1}$ when ϱ is given, $\pm \varphi = p + C$, when $n = -2$, $\frac{A\varrho r^{n+1}}{n+1} = p = -\frac{A\varrho}{r}$, if gravity is the sole force acting on the molecules, by making the axis of z vertical, P and Q, will vanish, and $R = g$, $\because P.\delta x + Q.\delta y + R.\delta z$ is reduced to the equation $g.\delta z = 0$, $\because gz = C$, consequently the surface is horizontal, since $R = (A\varrho r^{n-1}.\,z) = g$, $\int (g.\delta z) = p$ $\because$ the pressure varies as the height. Since when the force varies as the nth power of the distance from the centre $\delta \varphi = Ar^{n}.\delta r$, by substituting in the equation of elastic fluids $\frac{\delta p}{p} = \frac{\delta \varphi}{k}$ for $\delta \varphi$, and integrating, we get log. $p = \frac{Ar^{n+1}}{k.(n+1)}$, consequently, if the $(n+1)^{th}$ powers of the distance be taken in arithmetic progression, the pressures and the densities proportional to them, will be in geometric progression, $\because$ if n is negative, and if in the radius, ordinates be erected proportional to the pressures or densities, the locus of their extremities will be a curve of the hyperbolic species, and the radius produced, will be an asymptote to the curve, if n is positive, the locus of the extremities of the coordinates, will be a curve of the parabolic species, if $n = 0$, i. e. if the force is constant, the locus will be the logarithmic curve. See Princip. Matth. Liber 2. Prop. 22, et Scholium.

CHAPTER V.

The general principles of the motions of a system of bodies.

18. We have, in No. 7,* reduced the laws of the motion of a point, to those of its equilibrium, by resolving the instantaneous motion into two others, of which one remains, while the other is destroyed by the action of the forces which solicit the point; we have derived the differential equations of its motion, from the equilibrium which subsists between these forces, and the motion lost by the body. We now proceed to employ the same method, in order to determine the motion of a system of bodies m, m', m'', &c. Thus, let mP, mQ, Rm, be the forces which solicit m parallel to the axes of the rectangular coordinates x, y, z; let $m'P'$, $m'Q'$, $m'R'$, be the forces which solicit m', parallel to the same axes, and so on of the rest; and let us denote the time by t. The partial forces $m.\frac{dx}{dt}$, $m.\frac{dy}{dt}$, $m.\frac{dz}{dt}$ of the body m at any instant whatever will become in the following:†

* The principle established in this number, has been termed *the principle of D'Alembert*, by it the laws of the motion of a system are reducible to one sole principle, in the same manner as the laws of the equilibrium of bodies have been reduced to the equation (l) of No. 14.

† In consequence of the mutual connection which subsists between the different bodies of the system, the effect, which the forces immediately applied to the respective bodies would produce, is somewhat modified, so that their velocities, and the directions of their motions, are different from what would take place, if the bodies composing the system were altogether free; consequently, if at any point of time we compute the motions which

$$m.\frac{dx}{dt}+m.d.\frac{dx}{dt}-m.d.\frac{dx}{dt}+mP.dt;$$

$$m.\frac{dy}{dt}+m.d.\frac{dy}{dt}-m.d.\frac{dy}{dt}+mQ.dt;$$

$$m.\frac{dz}{dt}+m.d.\frac{dz}{dt}-m.d.\frac{dz}{dt}+mR.dt;$$

the bodies would have at the subsequent instant, if they were not subjected to their mutual action; and if we also compute the motions, which they have in the subsequent instant, in consequence of their mutual action, the motions which must be compounded with the first of these, in order to produce the second, are such as if they acted on the system alone, would constitute an equilibrium between the bodies of the system; for if not, the second of the abovementioned motions would not be those which actually obtain, contrary to the hypothesis. But as these motions, which must be compounded with the motions which actually have place, in order to produce the first, are altogether unknown; in the analytical expressions, we substitute expressions equivalent to them, i. e. the quantities of motion which have actually place, taken in a direction contrary to their true one, and the motions which would take place, taken in the true direction, by means of this we are able to establish immediately equations of equilibrium between the first and second of the abovementioned species of motion, and also to determine the velocities which would take place, if the bodies composing the system were altogether free. Now if we suppose the preceding motions, resolved respectively into three others parallel to three rectangular coordinates, mP, mQ, mR, $m'P'$, &c. will represent the motions parallel to the three axes which the bodies would assume, if they were altogether free.

$$m.\frac{d^2x}{dt^2},\ m.\frac{d^2y}{dt^2},\ m.\frac{d^2z}{dt^2},\ m'.\frac{d^2x'}{dt^2},\ \&c.$$

represent the motions parallel to the same axes, which the bodies actually have, at the commencement of the secondinstant. Since the motions which actually take place, are to be taken in a direction contrary to their true one, they are affected with negative signs.

We might by means of this principle, without introducing the consideration of virtual velocities, derive several important consequences; but it is the combination of this principle with that of virtual velocities, which has contributed so much to the perfection of Mechanics; this combination was first suggested by L'Agrange, who by this means has reduced the investigation of the motion of any system of bodies, to the integration of differential equations; thus we can reduce into an equation every problem relating to Dynamics, and it belongs to pure analysis to complete the solution; so that it appears that the only bar to the complete solution of every problem of Mechanics, arises from the imperfection of the analysis.

and as the forces

$$m.\frac{dx}{dt} + m.d.\frac{dx}{dt};\ m.\frac{dy}{dt} + m.d.\frac{dy}{dt};\ m.\frac{dz}{dt} + m.d.\frac{dz}{dt};$$

of the velocity, that the changes in the motions of the body are made by insensible degrees.

The inspection of the equation (P) shews that it consists of two parts entirely distinct, of which one is the quantity which we ought to put equal to nothing, when the forces P, Q, R, P', &c. which are applied to the different points of the system, constitute an equilibrium, the other part arises from the motion which is produced by the forces P, Q, R, P', &c. when they do not constitute an equilibrium; therefore we may express the equation (P) in this manner:

$$0 = \Sigma.(m.(P.\delta x + Q.\delta y + R.\delta z) - \Sigma m.\left\{\frac{d^2x}{dt^2}.\delta x + \frac{d^2y}{dt^2}.\delta y + \frac{d^2z}{dt^2}.\delta z.\right\}$$

and the equation (l) of No. 14, is only a particular case of the equation (P); thus the principle of virtual velocities may be considered as an universal instrument which is necessary for the solution of all problems relating to Mechanics. The expression

$$m.\frac{d^2x}{dt^2}.\ \delta x + m.\frac{d^2y}{dt^2}.\ \delta y + m.\frac{d^2z}{dt^2}.\ \delta z.$$

by which the equation (P) differs from the equation (l) is entirely independant of the *position* of the axes of the coordinates; for by substituting the coordinates x', y', z', in place of the preceding coordinates x, y, z, by the known formulæ we have

$$x = ax' + by' + cz',$$

$$y = a'x' + b'y' + c'z',$$

$$z = a''x' + b''y' + c''z',$$

the origin being the same, by differentiating the preceding expression twice, the coefficients a, b, c, a', &c. being constant, we obtain

$$d^2x = a.d^2x' + b.d^2y' + c.d^2z',$$

$$d^2y = a'.d^2x' + b'.d^2y' + c'.d^2z',$$

$$d^2z = a''.d^2x' + b''.d^2y' + c''.d^2z'.$$

only remain; the forces

$$-m.d.\frac{dx}{dt}+P.dt;-m.d.\frac{dy}{dt}+Q.dt;\ -m.d.\frac{dz}{dt}+R.dt,$$

will be destroyed.

By distinguishing, in this expression, the characters m, x, y, z, P, Q, R, by one, two, marks, &c. successively, we shall have an expression for the forces destroyed in the bodies m', m'', &c. This being premised, if we multiply these forces by the respective variations of their directions δx, δy, δz, &c. we shall obtain, by means of the principle of virtual velocities, laid down in No. 14, the following equation, in which dt is supposed to be constant.

$$\left.\begin{array}{l}0=m.\delta x.\left\{\frac{d^2x}{dt^2}-P.\right\}+m.\delta y.\left\{\frac{d^2y}{dt^2}-Q.\right\}+m.\delta z.\left\{\frac{d^2z}{dt^2}-R.\right\}\\ +m'.\delta x'\left\{\frac{d^2x'}{dt^2}-P'.\right\}+m'.\delta y'.\left\{\frac{d^2y'}{dt^2}-Q'.\right\}+m'\delta z'.\left\{\frac{d^2z'}{dt^2}-R'.\right\}\end{array}\right\};(P)$$

From this equation we may eliminate, by means of the particular conditions of the system, as many variations as we have conditions; and then by making the coefficients of the remaining variations separately

and also,

$$\delta x=a.\delta x'+b.\delta y'+c.\delta z',$$

$$\delta y=a'.\delta x'+b'.\delta y+c'.\delta z',$$

$$\delta z=a''.\delta x'+b''.\delta y''+c''.\delta z';$$

∵ by substituting for these expressions in the expression

$$m.\frac{d^2x}{dt^2}.\delta x+m.\frac{d^2y}{dt^2}.+m.\frac{d^2z}{dt^2}.\text{ we get }m.\frac{d^2x'}{dt^2}.\delta x'+m.\frac{d^2y'}{dt^2}.\delta y'+m.\frac{d^2z'}{dt^2}.\delta z'.$$

for $a^2+a'^2+a''^2=1$, $ab+ac+bc=0$, &c. see Notes to page 7; the same substitutions being made in the expressions of the mutual distances between the bodies, the coefficients a, b, c, a', &c. will disappear for the same reasons.

equal to nothing, we shall obtain all the equations necessary for determining the motions of the several bodies of the system.

19. The equation (p) involves several general principles of motion, which we shall examine in detail. The variations δx, δy, δz, will be subjected to all the conditions of the connection of the * parts of the forces, by supposing them equal to the differentials dx, dy, dz, dx', &c.

* If the equation of condition involves the time explicitly, then we are not permitted to suppose the variations δx, δy, δz, equal to the differentials dx, dy, dz, as for instance, if one of the bodies composing the system, always existed on a given surface, which surface moved according to a given law; or if the body moved in a resisting medium, which medium was in motion, then there will exist an equation between the coordinates of the body and the time which will also be at any instant, the differential equation of the surface, the most general equation expressing the preceding condition, is of the following form:

$$\varphi.(x, y, z;\ x', y', z', \text{ \&c. } t) = 0,$$

at the following instant the coordinates will be varied by the quantities δx, δy, δz, $\delta x'$, $\delta y'$, &c and the equation of condition will become

$$\varphi.(x+\delta x,\ y+\delta y,\ z\,\delta z;\ x'+\delta x',\ y'+\delta y',\ z'+\delta z', \text{ \&c. } t) = F = 0,$$

∵ the difference of these two expressions, i. e.

$$\left\{\frac{dF}{dx}\right\}.\delta x+\left\{\frac{dF}{dy}\right\}.\delta y+\left\{\frac{dF}{dz}\right\}.\delta z+\left\{\frac{dF}{\delta x}\right\}.\delta x+ \text{ \&c.} = 0.$$

but the complete differential of the preceding function =

$$\left\{\frac{dF}{dx}\right\}.dx+\left\{\frac{dF}{dy}\right\}.dy+\left\{\frac{dF}{dz}\right\}.dz+\left\{\frac{dF}{dx'}\right\}.dx', \text{ \&c.} + T.dt;$$

T is the differential coefficient of F, taken on the hypothesis that the time varies. consequently, if F involves the time explicitly, when we subject the variations δx, δy, &c. to satisfy the conditions of the connection of the parts of the system, we are not permitted to regard the expression

$$\left\{\frac{dF}{dx}\right\}.dx+\left\{\frac{dF}{dy}\right\}.dy+\left\{\frac{dF}{dz}\right\}.dz+\left\{\frac{dF}{dx'}\right\}.dx'+\text{\&c.}$$

as equal to nothing.

This supposition is consequently permitted, and then the integration of the equation (P) gives

$$\Sigma.m.\frac{(dx^2+dy^2+dz^2)}{dt^2}=c+2.\Sigma.\textstyle\int m.(P.dx+Q.dy+R.dz);\quad (Q)$$

c being a constant arbitrary quantity introduced by the integration.

If the forces P, Q, R, are the results of attractive forces, directed towards fixed centres, and of a mutual attraction between the bodies; the function $\Sigma.\int m.(P.dx+Q.dy+Rdz)$* is an exact integral. For the

Q

* In fact, the accelerating force of m, produced by the action of m' in the direction of the line f, $=m'\,F$, (F is always a given function of f,) ∵ the components of this force parallel to the axes of x, y, z, are $m'F.\frac{(x'-x)}{f}$, $m'F.\frac{(y'-y)}{f}$, $m'F.\frac{(z'-z)}{f}$, ∵ the parts of $P.dx+Q.dy+R.dz$, which answers to this force alone are
$m'F.((x'-x).dx+(y'-y).dy+(z'-z).dz)$, and as the accelerating force of m', arising from the action of m, resolved parallel to the coordinates x, y, z, respectively $=$
$m.F.\frac{(x-x')}{f}+m.F.\frac{(y-y')}{f}+m.F.\frac{(z-z')}{f}$, the corresponding part of $P'.dx'+Q'.dy'+R'.dz'$, is, $F.m.\left\{\frac{(x-x')}{f}.dx'+\frac{(y-y')}{f}.dy'+\frac{(z-z')}{f}.dz'\right\}$, therefore in order to have the motive force arising from the mutual action of the bodies m and m' we must multiply the first expression by m, and the second by m', and adding them together, they will become

$$mm'.F.\,(x'-x).\,dx+(y'-y).\,dy+(z-z).dz+(x-x').dx'+(y-y').\,dy'+(z-z'),\,dz')=$$
$$mm'.F.fdf,\ \text{for as } f^2=(x-x')^2+(y-y')^2+(z-z')^2,\ fdf=$$
$$(x-x').(dx-dx')+(y-y).(dy-dy')+(z-z').(dz-dz'),$$

consequently as F is given to be a function of f, $Ff.df$. is an exact differential. If the centres to which the forces are directed have a motion in space, then $P.dx+Q.dy+Rdz$, is not an exact differential, though the law according to which the forces vary should be a function of the distance, see Note to page 34.

The sum of the living forces at any instant will be given by the equation (Q), when we know the value of this sum at a determined instant, and the coordinates of the bodies composing the system in the two positions of the system. And when the system returns to the same position, the living forces will be the same as before.

part which depends on the attractions directed towards fixed points, are exact integrals by No. 8. This is equally the case, with respect to those parts, which depend on the mutual attractions of the bodies composing the system; for if we name f, the distance of m from m', $m'F$, the attraction of m' on m; the part of $m(P.dx+Q.dy+R.dz)$ which arises from the attraction of m' on m, will be, by the above cited No. equal to $-mm'Fdf$, the differential df being taken on the supposition, that the coordinates x, y, z, only vary. But reaction being equal and contrary to action, the part of $m'(P'.dx'+Q'.dy'+R'dz')$ which is due to the attraction of m on m', is equal to $-mm'.Fdf$, the coordinates x', y', z', being the only quantities which are supposed to vary, consequently df being the differential of f on the supposition that both the coordinates x, y, z, and x', y', z', vary simultaneously, the part of the function $\Sigma.m(P.dx+Q.dy+R.dz)$ which depends on the reciprocal action of m on m' is equal to $-mm'.F.df$. Therefore this quantity is an exact differential when F is a function of f, or when the attraction varies as some function of the distance, which we shall always suppose; consequently the function $\Sigma.m.(P.dx+Q.dy+R.dz)$ is an exact differential, as often as the forces which act on the different bodies of the system, are the result of their mutual attraction, or of attractive forces directed towards fixed points. Let then $d\varphi$ represent this differential, and naming v the velocity of m, v' the velocity of m', &c. we shall have

$$\Sigma.mv^2 = c+2\varphi. \quad (R)$$

This equation corresponds to the equation (g) of No. 8, it is the analytical expression of the principle of the conservation of living forces. The product of the mass of a body by the square of its velocity, is termed the living force, or the vis viva of a body. The principle just announced consists in this, that the sum of the living forces, or the entire living force of the system is constant, if the system is not solicited by any forces; and if the bodies are actuated by any forces whatever, the sum of the increments of the entire living force is the same whatever may be the nature of the curves described, provided that their points of departure and arrival be the same.*

However this principle is only applicable, when the motions of the bodies change by imperceptible gradations.† If these motions undergo abrupt changes, the living force is diminished by a quantity which may be thus determined. The analysis which has conducted us to the equation (P) of the preceding number, gives us in this case, instead of that equation, the following:

$$0 = \Sigma.m. \left\{ \frac{\delta x}{dt}.\Delta.\frac{dx}{dt} + \frac{\delta y}{dt}.\Delta.\frac{dy}{dt} + \frac{\delta z}{dt}.\Delta.\frac{dz}{dt} \right\};*$$

* What has been demonstrated respecting the mutual attraction of the bodies of the system, is equally true respecting repulsive forces which vary as some function of the distance; it is true also when the repulsions are produced by the action of springs interposed between the bodies, for the force of the spring must vary as some function of the distance between the points, ∵ in the impact of perfectly elastic bodies though the quantity of motion communicated may be increased indefinitely, still the living force after the impact is the same as before; indeed *during* the impact, the vis viva varies as the coordinates of the respective points vary, but after its completion, from the nature of perfectly elastic bodies they resume their original position, and consequently the value of the vis viva will be the same as before, but if the elasticity is not perfect, in order to have the value of the vis viva at any instant, we should know the law of the elasticity, or the relation which exists between the compressive and restitutive force.

‡ When the motions of the bodies of the system, are modified by friction, or the resistance of the medium in which the motion is performed, the expression $P.dx + Q.dy + R.dz$ is not an exact differential, see note to page 34, and the living forces must be diminished. This is indeed evident of itself, for when the bodies of the system are actuated by no other forces but those of resistance, the sum of the living forces must be *gradually* diminished, in order to determine the actual loss experienced after any time, we should know the law according to which the resistance varies, which is very difficult to be determined; but there is another cause of diminution of the living force, in which we are able to determine accurately the loss sustained, to wit, the case adverted to in the text, when the bodies undergo an *abrupt* change in their motions.

‡ The characteristic Δ designates according to the received notation, the *difference* which exists between two consecutive states of the same quantity.

$$-\Sigma.m.(P.\delta x + Q.\delta y + R.\delta z)\,;$$

$\Delta.\frac{dx}{dt}$, $\Delta.\frac{dy}{dt}$, $\Delta.\frac{dz}{dz}$, being the differences of $\frac{dx}{dt}$, $\frac{dy}{dt}$, $\frac{dz}{dt}$, from one instant to another; differences which become finite, when the motions of the bodies undergo finite alterations in an instant. In this

The equation (P) may be made to assume the following form:

$$\Sigma.m.\left\{\frac{d^2x}{dt^2}.\delta x + \frac{d^2y}{dt^2}.\delta y + \frac{d^2z}{dt^2}.\delta z.\right\} - \Sigma m.(P.\delta x + Q.\delta y + Q.\delta z).$$

in which the changes that are produced in the motions of the bodies composing the system, are made by insensible degrees, as is evident from the circumstance, that the differential of the velocities is expressed by $\frac{d^2x}{dt^2}$, see note to page 30; now, if instead of this gradual diminution, bodies experience abrupt changes in their motions $\Delta.\frac{dx}{dt}.\Delta.\frac{dy}{dt}$, &c. expressing those changes, the preceding expression will be changed into the following:

$$\Sigma.m.\left\{\left\{\Delta.\frac{dx}{dt}.\frac{\delta x}{dt}\right\} + \left\{\Delta.\frac{dy}{dt}.\frac{\delta y}{dt}\right\} + \left\{\Delta.\frac{dz}{dt}.\frac{\delta z}{dt}\right\}\right\}$$
$$-\Sigma.m.(P.\delta x + Q.\delta y + R.\delta y\,;$$

and as in this case $m\Delta.\frac{dx}{dt}$ is the variation of the force of the body, on the supposition that it is entirely free, and $m.P.dt$ is the variation which actually takes place in consequence of the action of the bodies of the system, the reasoning in No. 18 is applicable to this case, consequently the preceding expression may be put equal to nothing; and since the values of dx, dy, dz, are changed in the following instant into $dx+\Delta.dx$, $dy+\Delta.dy$. $dz+\Delta dz$, we shall satisfy the conditions of the connection of the parts of the system, by making the variations δx, δy, δz, equal to these expressions respectively; and then the preceding equation will assume this form

$$\Sigma.m.\left\{\Delta.\frac{dx}{at} + \frac{dx}{dt}\right\}\Delta.\frac{dx}{dt} + \left\{\Delta.\frac{dy}{dt} + \frac{dy}{dt}\right\}\Delta.\frac{dy}{dt} +$$
$$\left\{\Delta.\frac{dz}{dt} + \frac{dz}{dt}\right\}\Delta.\frac{dz}{dt} -$$
$$\Sigma.m.(P.(dx + \Delta.dx) + Q.(dy + \Delta.dy) + R.(dz + \Delta.dz), = 0,$$

equation we may suppose

$$\delta x = dx + \Delta.dx\,;\ \delta y = dy + \Delta.dy\,;\ \delta z = dz + \Delta.\,dz\,;$$

because the values of dx, dy, dz, being changed in the following instant into $dx + \Delta.dx$, $dy + \Delta.dy$, $dz + \Delta.dz$, these values of δx, δy, δz, satisfy the conditions the connection of the parts of the system; therefore we shall have

$$0 = \Sigma.m.\left\{\left\{\frac{dx}{dt} + \Delta.\frac{dx}{dt}\right\}\Delta.\frac{dx}{dt} + \left\{\frac{dy}{dt} + \Delta.\frac{dy}{dt}\right\}\Delta.\frac{dy}{dt} + \left\{\frac{dz}{dt} + \Delta.\frac{dz}{dt}\right\}.\Delta\frac{dz}{dt}\right\}$$

$$- \Sigma.m.(P.(dx + \Delta.dx) + Q.(dy + \Delta.dy + R.(dz + \Delta.dz))$$

This equation should be integrated as an equation of finite differences relative to the time t, of which the variations are infinitely small, as well as the variations of x, y, z, x', &c. Let $\Sigma_{,}$ denote the finite integrals resulting from this integration, in order to distinguish them from the preceding finite integrals, which refer to the aggregate of all the bodies of the system. The integral of $mP.(dx + \Delta.dx)$ is evidently equal to $\int mP.dx$; therefore we shall have const. =

$$\Sigma.m.\frac{dx^2 + dy^2 + dz^2}{dt^2} + \Sigma_{,}.\Sigma m.\left\{\left(\Delta.\frac{dx^2}{dt^2}\right) + \left(\dot{\Delta}\frac{dy^2}{dt^2}\right) + \left(\Delta.\frac{dz^2}{dt^2}\right)\right\}^{*}$$

$$-2\Sigma.\int m.(P.dx + Q.dp + R.dz);$$

* In this equation, though the value of $\Delta.\frac{dx}{dt}$ may be finite, still $dx + \Delta.dx$, and the variation of the time may be indefinitely small, and ∵ integrating with respect to *this* quantity, $\Sigma_{,}\Sigma.m.\left\{\frac{dx}{dt}.\Delta.\frac{dx}{dt}\right\} = \Sigma.m.\frac{dx^2}{dt^2}$, or it may be otherwise expressed thus, $\Delta.(x^2) =$ (see Lacroix No. 344) $2xh + h^2$, and if h be made equal to Δx, it becomes $2x.\Delta x + (\Delta x)^2$, ∵ $2.\ \Sigma_{,}(x\Delta.x + (\Delta x)^2) = \Sigma_{,}(2x.\Delta.x + (\Delta x)^2) + \Sigma_{,}(\Delta x)^2 = x^2 + \Sigma_{,}(\Delta x^2)$, consequently, if we multiply the preceding equation by two, and substitute dx in place of x, and then integrate, we obtain the expression which has been given in the text.

therefore v, v, v'' denoting the velocities of m, m', m'', &c. we shall have

$$\Sigma.mv^2 = \text{Const.} - \Sigma_{,}\Sigma.m.\left\{\left\{\Delta.\frac{dx}{dt}\right\}^2 + \left\{\Delta.\frac{dy}{dt}\right\}^2 + \left\{\Delta.\frac{dz}{dt}\right\}^2\right\}$$

$$+ 2\Sigma.\textstyle\int m.(P.dx+Q.dy+R.dz).$$

The quantity contained under the sign $\Sigma_{,}$ being necessarily positive, we may perceive that the living force of the system is diminished by the mutual action of the bodies, as often as during the motion, any of the variations $\Delta.\frac{dx}{dt}$, $\Delta.\frac{dy}{dt}$, &c. are finite. Moreover, the preceding equation affords a simple means of determining the quantity of this diminution.

At each abrupt variation of the motion of the system,* the velocity

* At every abrupt change in the motion of the system, the velocity is not always diminished for *every* body, but the expression which is here given may be considered as general, by supposing that when the velocity is increased, a negative portion of it has been destroyed, and the square of the velocity after the shock is equal to

$$\Sigma.m.\frac{(dx^2+2dx\Delta.dx+(\Delta.dx)^2+dy^2+2dy.\Delta.dy+(\Delta.dy)^2+dz^2+2dz\Delta.dz+(\Delta dz.)^2}{dt^2}$$

and as

$$\Sigma m.\frac{2.dx\Delta.dx+2(\Delta.dx)^2+2.dy\Delta.dy+2(\Delta.dy)^2+2dz\Delta.dz+2(\Delta.dz)^2,}{dt^2}$$

$=0$, by subtracting this equation from the preceding, we obtain the square of the velocity after the shock, equal to

$$\Sigma.m.\frac{(dx^2+dy^2+dz^2)}{dt^2} - \Sigma.m.\frac{(\Delta.dx)^2+(\Delta.dy)^2+(\Delta.dz)^2}{dt^2}$$

and as the square of the velocity before the shock is equal to $\Sigma.mv^2 = \Sigma.m.\frac{dx^2+dy^2+dz^2}{dt^2}$, the square of the velocity lost by the shock $=\Sigma.m.V^2$

$$=\Sigma m.\frac{(\Delta.dx)^2+(\Delta.dy)^2+(\Delta.dz)^2}{dt^2};$$

consequently the loss which the living forces experience, is equal to the sum of the living forces, which would belong to the system, if each body was actuated by that velocity which it loses by the shock.

of m, may be conceived to be resolved into two others, of which one v subsists in the following instant, the other V being destroyed by the action of the other bodies, but the velocity of m before the decomposition being $\frac{\sqrt{dx^2+dy^2+dz^2}}{dt}$, and changing afterwards into

$$\frac{\sqrt{(dx+\Delta.dx)^2+(dy^2+\Delta.dy)^2+(dz+\Delta.dz)^2}}{dt}$$

it is easy to perceive that

$$V^2=\left\{\Delta.\frac{dx}{dt}\right\}^2+\left\{\Delta.\frac{dy}{dt}\right\}^2+\left\{\Delta.\frac{dz}{dt}\right\}^2;$$

consequently the preceding equation may be made to assume the following form,

$$\Sigma.mv^2=\text{const.}-\Sigma_{,}.\Sigma.m.V^2-2.\Sigma.\textstyle\int m.(P.dx+Q.dy+.dz),^*$$

* The variation of the vis viva of the system, is equal to $2\Sigma m.(P.dx+Q.dy+R.dz)$ consequently when this expression vanishes, i. e. when $d.\Sigma.(mv^2)$ vanishes, the vis viva of the system, equal to $\Sigma.(mv^2)$, is a maximum, or a minimum; but it appears from the principle of virtual velocities, that $\Sigma m.(P.\delta x+Q.\delta y+R.\delta z)$ is equal to nothing, when the forces P, Q, R, P', constitute an equilibrium; and since the differentials dx, dy, dz, may be substituted for the variations δx, δy, δz, when they are subjected to satisfy the conditions of the connection of the parts of the system, $\Sigma m.(P.dx+Q.dy+R.dz)$ is equal to nothing, in the same circumstances; ∵ when the forces P, Q, R, P', constitute an equilibrium, the vis viva of the system is a maximum or a minimum.

And as it appears from note to page 96, that the positions of equilibrium of a system of heavy bodies, correspond to the instants, when the centre of gravity is the highest or lowest possible, the sum of the living forces is always a maximum or a minimum when the centre ceases to ascend, and commences to descend, and when it ceases to descend and commences to ascend. The value of the vis viva is a minimum in the first case, and a maximum in the second, for $\Sigma m.(P.dx+Q.dy+R.dz)$ corresponds to the expression $S.\delta s+S'.\delta s'+S''\delta s''+\&c.$ in page 96, and ∵ by substitution we have $\Sigma mv^2=c+s_{,}.S\Sigma m.$ consequently $\Sigma.mv^2$ is a maximum or minimum, when $s_{,}$ is a maximum or minimum. When $\Sigma.mv^2$. is a maximum, the equilibrium is stable; when a minimum, the equilibrium is instable. For from the definition of stability, (see No. 28) it appears that if the system is only agitated by one sole species of simple oscillation, the bodies composing it will perpe-

20. If in the equation (P) of No. 18, we suppose,

$$\delta x' = \delta x + \delta x_{/}' ; \quad \delta y' = \delta y + \delta y_{/}' ; \quad \delta z' = \delta z + \delta z_{/}' ;$$

tually tend to revert to the position of equilibrium, consequently their velocities will diminish according as their distance from the position of equilibrium is increased, and ∵ the sign of the second differential of φ will be negative, consequently Σmv^2. will be a maximum in this case; and it may be shewn by a like process of reasoning, that the vis viva of the system is a minimum, when the equilibrium is instable.

From a comparison of this observation with the note to page 96, it appears that in a system of heavy bodies, when the vis viva is a maximum, the centre of gravity is the lowest possible, and highest when the vis viva is a minimum.

This may be more strictly demonstrated thus: if the system be disturbed by an indefinitely small quantity from the position of equilibrium, by substituting for P, Q, R, P', &c. their values in terms of the coordinates, and then expanding the resulting expressioninto a series ascending according to the variations of these coordinates, the first term of the series will be the value of φ, when the system is in equilibrio; and since it is given, it may be made to coalesce with the constant quantity c, which was introduced by the integration; the second term vanishes by the conditions of the problem; and when $\Sigma.mv^2$. is a maximum, the theory of maxima and minima shews that the third term of the expansion may be made to assume the form of a sum of squares, affected with a negative sign, see Locroix, No. 134; the number of terms in this sum, being equal to the number of variations, or independant variables; the terms whose squares we have assumed, are linear functions of the variations of the coordinates, and vanish at the same time with them; they are therefore greater than the sum of all the remaining terms of the expansion. The constant quantity being equal to the sum of c, and of the value of $\Sigma.mv^2$. when the forces P, Q, R, P', &c. constitute an equilibrium, it is necessarily positive, and may be rendered as small as small as we please, by diminishing the velocities; but it is always greater than the greatest of the quantities whose squares have been substituted in place of the variations of the coordinates; for if it were less, this quantity being negative, would exceed the constant quantity, and therefore render the value of Σmv^2. negative, consequently these squares, and the variations of the coordinates, of which they are linear functions, must always remain very small, ∵ the system will always *oscillate* about the position of equilibrium, and this equilibrium will be stable. But in the case of a minimum it is not requisite that the variations should be always constrained to be very small, in order to satisfy the equation of living forces when φ is a minimum; this, indeed, does not prove that there is no limit then to these variations which is necessary, in order that the equilibrium may be instable; in order to shew this we should substitute for these variations, their values in functions of the time, and then shew from the form of these functions, that they increase indefinitely with the time, however small the primi-

$$\delta x'' = \delta x + \delta x''_{,}\,; \quad \delta y'' = \delta y + \delta y''_{,}\,; \quad \delta z'' = \delta z + \delta z''_{,}\,;^{*}$$

&c. by substituting these variations, in the expressions of the variations δf, $\delta f'$, $\delta f''$, &c. of the mutual distances of the bodies composing the system, the values of which have been given in No. 15; we shall find that the variations δx, δy, δz, will disappear from those expressions. If the system be free, that is, if it have none of its parts connected with foreign bodies, the conditions relative to the mutual connection of the bodies, will only depend on their mutual distances, and therefore the variations δx, δy, δz, will be independent of these conditions; consequently when we substitute in place of $\delta x'$, $\delta y'$, $\delta z'$, $\delta x''_{,}$, &c. their preceding values in the equation (P), we should put the coefficients of the

R

tive velocities may be. For a complete solution of the problem of the small oscillations of a system, the reader is referred to the Mechanique Analytique of Lagrange, 5th and 6th section, seconde partie, where the important problem of coexisting oscillations is discussed in all its generality, and all difficulties are cleared up; see also Notes to No. 23 and 30, of this book.

* It is always possible to make these substitutions, for it in fact comes to transferring the origin of the coordinates to a point of which the coordinates are equal to x, y, z, respectively; as the expression for δf,

$$= \frac{(x'-x)\,(\delta x'-\delta x)+(y'-y).(\delta y'-\delta y)+(z'-z).(\delta z'-\delta z)}{f}$$

equal by substituting for x', y', z', $\delta x'$, $\delta y'$, $\delta z'$, their values,

$$\frac{(x+x'_{,}-x).(\delta x+\delta x'_{,}-\delta x)+(y+y'_{,}-y).(\delta y+\delta y'_{,}-\delta y)+(z+z'_{,}-z).(\delta z+\delta z'_{,}-\delta z)}{f}+$$

$$= \frac{x'_{,}\delta x'_{,}+y'_{,}.\delta y'_{,}+z'_{,}.\delta z'_{,}}{f}$$

consequently as δx, δy, δz, disappear from the expressions of the variations δf, $\delta f'$, and as when the system is at liberty, the conditions relating to the mutual connexion of its parts, depend only on their distance from each other, the variations δx, δy, δz, will be independent of these conditions, ∴ substituting for $\delta x'$, $\delta y'$, $\delta z'$ in the equation (P), the values which have been just given for them, the coefficients δx, δy, δz, must be put equal to nothing.

variations δx, δy, δz, separately equal to nothing; which gives the three following equations:

$$0 = \Sigma m.\left\{\frac{d^2x}{dt^2} - P\right\};\quad 0 = \Sigma m.\left\{\frac{d^2y}{dt^2} - Q\right\};\quad 0 = \Sigma m.\left\{\frac{d^2z}{dt^2} - R\right\}^*$$

Let us suppose that X, Y, Z, are the three coordinates of the centre of gravity of the system; by No. 15 we shall have,

$$X = \frac{\Sigma.mx}{\Sigma.m};\quad Y = \frac{\Sigma.my}{\Sigma.m};\quad Z = \frac{\Sigma.mz}{\Sigma.m};$$

consequently

$$0 = \frac{d^2X}{dt^2} - \frac{\Sigma.mP}{\Sigma.m};\quad 0 = \frac{d^2Y}{dt^2} - \frac{\Sigma.mQ}{\Sigma.m};\quad 0 = \frac{d^2Z}{dt^2} - \frac{\Sigma.mR}{\Sigma.m},\ \dagger$$

therefore the motion of the centre of gravity of the system is the same

* By actually substituting for $\delta x'$, $\delta y'$, $\delta z'$, $\delta z''$, &c. in the equation (P) we obtain 0=.

$$m.\delta x.\left\{\frac{d^2x}{dt^2} - P\right\} + m.\delta y.\left\{\frac{d^2y}{dt^2} - Q\right\} + m.\delta z.\left\{\frac{d^2z}{dt^2} - R\right\}$$

$$+ m'.\delta x.\left\{\frac{d^2x'}{dt^2} - P'\right\} + m'.\delta x'_{,}.\left\{\frac{d^2x'}{dt^2} - P'\right\}$$

$$+ m'\delta y.\left\{\frac{d^2y'}{dt^2} - Q'\right\} + m'\delta y'_{,}.\left\{\frac{d^2y'}{dt^2} - Q'\right\};$$

the terms in this expression which are multiplied by δx, δy, δz, respectively, are by adding them together

$$\Sigma.m.\left\{\frac{d^2x}{dt^2} - P\right\};\ \Sigma\,m.\left\{\frac{d^2y}{dt^2} - Q\right\};\ \Sigma.m.\left\{\frac{d^2z}{dt^2} - R\right\}$$

and being independent of the conditions of the connection of the system, they must be put severally equal to nothing.

† Since $X = \dfrac{\Sigma.m.x}{\Sigma.m}$, $Y = \dfrac{\Sigma.my}{\Sigma.m}$, &c. $\dfrac{d^2X}{dt^2} = \dfrac{\Sigma.m.\frac{d^2x}{dt^2}}{\Sigma m} = \dfrac{\Sigma.mP}{\Sigma.m}$,

because

$$\Sigma.m.\frac{d^2x}{dt^2} - \Sigma m.P = 0.$$

as if all the bodies m, m', &c. were concentrated in this point, the forces which solicit the system being applied to it.

If the system is only subjected to the mutual action of the bodies which compose it, and to their reciprocal attractions, we shall have

$$0=\Sigma.mP\,;\;0=\Sigma.mQ\,;\;0=\Sigma.mR\,;$$

for p designating the reciprocal action of m on m', whatever its nature may be, and f denoting the mutual distance of these two bodies; we shall have, in consequence of this sole action,

$$mP=p.\frac{(x-x')}{f}\,;\;mQ=p.\frac{(y-y')}{f};mR=p.\frac{(z-z')}{f}\,;$$

$$m'P'=p.\frac{(x'-x)}{f};\;m'Q'=p.\frac{(y'-y)}{f};\;m'R'=p.\frac{(z'-z)}{f};$$

from which we collect

$$0=mP+m'P'\,;\;0=mQ+m'Q'\,;\;0=mR+m'R'\,;\;*$$

and it is evident that these equations obtain, even in the case in

* $x'-x$, $y'-y$, $z'-z$, being the coordinates of m relative to the new origin of the forces, and the action of p being directed along the line

$$f(=\sqrt{(x'-x)^2+(y'-y)^2+(z'-z)^2},$$

the part of mP, which corresponds to the force p resolved parallel to the axis of $x=p\,\frac{(x-x')}{f}$, the analogous parts of mQ, and mR, are $p.\frac{(y-y')}{f}$, $p.\frac{(z-z')}{f}$ respectively, in like manner the forces soliciting m' parallel to the coordinates, arising from the action of p,

$$=p.\frac{(x'-x)}{f},\,p.\frac{(y'-y)}{f},\,p.\frac{(z'-z)}{f};$$

∴ when the sole force soliciting m and m' arises from p, which expresses the reciprocal action of m on m', we have $mP+m'P',=p\,\frac{(x-x'+x'-x)}{f}=0$.

Action being equal to reaction, and its direction being contrary thereto, when two bo-

which the bodies exercise on each other, a finite action in an instant. Their reciprocal action disappears from the integrals $\Sigma.mP$, $\Sigma.mQ$, $\Sigma.mR$, and consequently, these expressions vanish, when the system is not solicited by any extraneous forces. In this case we have

$$0=\frac{d^2X}{dt^2};\ 0=\frac{d^2Y}{dt^2};\ 0=\frac{d^2Z}{dt^2};$$

and by integrating

$$X=a+bt:\ Y=a'+b't;\ Z=a''+b''t;^*$$

a, b, a', b', a'', b'', being constant arbitrary quantities. By eliminating the time t, we shall have an equation of the first order, between either X and Y, or X and Z; consequently the motion of the centre of gravity is rectilinear. Moreover, its velocity being equal to

$$\sqrt{\left\{\frac{dX}{dt}\right\}^2+\left\{\frac{dY}{dt}\right\}^2+\left\{\frac{dZ}{dt}\right\}^2};$$

or to $\sqrt{b^2+b'^2+b''^2}$, it is constant, and the motion is uniform.

It is manifest, from the preceding analysis, that this invariability of the motion of the centre of gravity of a system of bodies, whatever their mutual action may be,† subsists even in the case in which any one

dies concurring, exercise on each other a finite action in an instant, their reciprocal action will disappear in the expressions $\Sigma.mP$, $\Sigma.mQ$, &c. in fact, as we can always suppose the action of the bodies to be effected by means of a spring, interposed between them, which endeavours to restore itself after the shock, the effect of the shock will be produced by forces of the same nature with p, which, as we have seen, disappear in the expressions $\Sigma.mP$, $\Sigma.mQ$, $\Sigma.mR$.

* By integrating once we get $\frac{dX}{dt}=b$, $\therefore dX=bdt$, and $X=bt+a$; the constant quantities a, a', a'', are equal to the coordinates of the centre of gravity when $t=0$, and b, b', b'', are equal to the velocity of the centre of gravity resolved parallel to the coordinates See notes to page 31.

† In fact, from what has been observed, in the note to page 116, it is evident that the principle of D'Alembert is true, whether the velocities acquired by the bodies be finite, after a given time, or indefinitely small, or whether the velocities be partly finite, and partly infinitely small, such as arise from the action of accelerating forces, and both

of the bodies loses in an instant, by this action, a finite quantity of motion.*

21. If we make

$$\delta x' = \frac{y'.\delta x}{y} + \delta x_{,}'; \; \delta x'' = \frac{y.''\delta x}{y} + \delta x_{,}''; \text{ \&c.}$$

$$\delta y = -\frac{x.\delta x}{y} + \delta y_{,}; \; \delta y' = -\frac{x'.\delta x}{y} + \delta y_{,}'; \; \delta y'' = -\frac{x''.\delta x}{y} + \delta y_{,}''; \text{ \&c.} \dagger$$

the variation δx will again disappear from the expressions δf, $\delta f'$, $\delta f''$, &c.; therefore, by supposing the system free, the conditions relative

before and after the impact, we have $0 = \frac{d^2 X}{dt^2}$, $0 = \frac{d^2 Y}{dt^2}$, &c. and also $\frac{dX}{dt} . \Sigma.m = \Sigma.m. \frac{dx}{dt}$, &c. = the quantity of motion, and since by hypothesis the quantity of motion lost, equal to the difference between $\Sigma m. \frac{dx}{dt}$ before and after impact, should be = to nothing, such as would cause an equilibrium in the system, it follows that $\frac{dX}{dt}.\Sigma.m.$ before and after impact must be the same, but $\Sigma.m$ being given, $\frac{dX}{dt}$ equal to the velocity of the centre of gravity, will be the same before and after impact.

* As the centre of gravity of a system, moves in the same manner as a body equal to the sum of the bodies would move, if placed in the centre of gravity, provided that the same momenta were communicated to it, which are impressed on the respective bodies of the system, the motion and direction of the centre of gravity, may be always determined by the law of composition of forces.

If the several bodies of a system were only subjected to their mutual action, then they would meet in the centre of gravity, for the bodies must meet, and the centre of gravity remains at rest.

† The fractional part of these expressions for $\delta x'$, $\delta x''$, δy, $\delta y'$, $\delta y''$, &c. arises from the rotatory motion of the system about an axis parallel to z, for it appears from Nos. 22 and 25. that when the direction of the impulse does not pass through the centre of gravity, the body acquires both a rotatory and rectilinear motion, now if the only motion impressed on the system was that of rotation, then the element of the angle described by the body m, is equal to the variation of the sine divided by the cosine $= \frac{\sqrt{x^2+y^2}}{y} . \delta x$, the elementary angle described by

to the connection of the parts of the system will only influence the variations $\delta f'$, $\delta f''$ &c.; the variation δx is independent of them, and entirely arbitrary; thus by substituting in the equation (P) of No. 18, in the place of $\delta x'$, $\delta x''$, $\delta x'''$, &c. $\delta y'$, $\delta y''$, $\delta y'''$, &c. their preceding values,

$$m' = \frac{\sqrt{x^2+y^2}}{y}. \frac{\sqrt{x'^2+y'^2}}{\sqrt{x^2+y^2}}.\delta x = \frac{\sqrt{x'^2+y'^2}}{y}.\delta x,$$

$\therefore$ the variation of x' will be equal to

$\frac{\sqrt{x'^2+y'^2}}{y}.\frac{y'}{\sqrt{x'^2+y'^2}}.\delta x = \frac{y'}{y}.\delta x$ the same may be proved of the other variations $\delta x'$, $\delta x''$,

$\sqrt{x^2+y^2}$ = the distance of m from the axis of z, $\therefore \frac{x}{\sqrt{x^2+y^2}}$ is equal to the sine of the angle which $\sqrt{x^2+y^2}$ makes with y. If the expression $\frac{\delta x \sqrt{x^2+y^2}}{y}$ be considered with respect to the cosine y, the variation $\delta y = -\delta x. \frac{\sqrt{x^2+y^2}}{y}.\frac{x}{\sqrt{x^2+y^2}}$ $= -\frac{\delta x.x}{y}$, for the variation of the cosine is equal to the variation of the arc affected with a negative sign, and divided by the sine, and as the variation of the angle described by $m' = \frac{\sqrt{x'^2+y'^2}}{y}.\delta x$, this expression being referred to the cosine is equal to $-\frac{\sqrt{x'^2+y'^2}}{y}.$ $\frac{x'}{\sqrt{x'^2+y'^2}}.\delta x = -\frac{x'}{y}.\delta x.$

If in the expression

$$\delta f = \frac{(x'-x).(\delta x'-\delta x)+(y'-y).(\delta y'-\delta y)+(z'-z).(\delta z'-\delta z)}{f}$$

we substitute for $\delta x'$, $\delta x''$, δy, $\delta y'$, $\delta y''$, &c. their values, it becomes

$$\frac{(x'-x).\left(\frac{y'.\delta x}{y}+\delta x_{,}'-\delta x\right)+(y'-y).\left(-\frac{x'.\delta x}{y}+\delta y_{,}'+\frac{x.\delta x}{y}-\delta y_{,}\right)}{f}=$$

$$\frac{x'y'\delta x}{y}-\frac{xy'\delta x}{y}-x'.\delta x+x.\delta x+x'.\delta x_{,}'-x.\delta x_{,}'-\frac{y'x'.\delta x}{y}+\frac{y.x'\delta x}{y}+\frac{y'x.\delta x}{y}$$

$$-\frac{yx\,\delta x}{y}+y'\delta y_{,}'-y.\delta y_{,}'-y'\delta y_{,}+y\delta y_{,}\div f=\frac{(x'-x).\delta x_{,}'+(y'-y).(\delta y_{,}'-\delta y_{,})}{f}$$

therefore the variation δx disappears from the expressions δf, $\delta f'$, &c.

Making the same substitutions in the equation (P) it becomes

we should put the coefficient of δx separately equal to nothing, which gives

$$0=\Sigma.m.\frac{(xd^2y-yd^2x)}{dt^2}+\Sigma.m.\ (Py-Qx);$$

from which we deduce by integrating with respect to the time t,

$$c=\Sigma.m.\frac{(xdy-ydx)}{dt}+\Sigma.\int.m.(Py-Qx).\ dt;$$

c being a constant arbitrary quantity.

In this integral, we may change the coordinates y, y', &c. into z, z', provided that we substitute in place of the forces Q, Q', &c. parallel to the axis of y, the forces R, R', parallel to the axis of z, which gives,

$$c'=\Sigma.m.\frac{(ydz-zdy)}{dt}+\Sigma.\int.m.(Pz-Rx).\ dt;$$

c' being a new arbitrary quantity. In like manner we shall have

$$c''=\Sigma.m.\frac{(ydz-zdy)}{dt}+\Sigma.\int.m.(Qz-Ry).\ dt;$$

c'' being a third arbitrary quantity.

$$0=\delta x.\left\{m.\left\{\frac{d^2x}{dt^2}-P\right\}-\frac{x}{y}.m.\left\{\frac{d^2y}{dt^2}-Q\right\}+\frac{y'}{y}m'.\left\{\frac{d^2x'}{dt^2}-P'\right\}\right.$$
$$\left.-\frac{x'}{y}.m'.\left\{\frac{d^2y'}{dt^2}-Q'\right\}\right\}$$

$$+m.dy_{,}\left\{\frac{d^2y}{dt^2}-Q\right\}+m'.\delta x'_{,}\left\{\frac{d^2x'}{dt^2}-P'\right\}+m'.\delta y'_{,}.\left\{\frac{d^2y'}{dt^2}-Q'\right\}\&c.=$$

$$\frac{\delta x}{y}.\left\{m.\left\{\frac{y.d^2x-x.d^2y}{dt^2}\right\}+m'.\left\{\frac{y'\ d^2x'-x'd^2y'}{dt}\right\}-mPy+mQx-m'P'y'+m'Q'x',\ \&c.\right.$$

therefore if this expression is extended to all the coordinates, it will become

$$=\frac{\delta x}{y}.\left\{\Sigma.m.\frac{y\ d^2x-xd^2y}{dt^2}+\Sigma.m.(Q.x-P.y)\right\}+m.\delta y_{,}\left\{\frac{d^2y}{dt^2}-Q\right\}$$
$$\left.+m'.\delta x'_{,}\left(\frac{d^2x'}{dt^2}-P'\right)+(m'.\delta y'_{,}(.\frac{d^2y'}{dt^2}-Q')\right\}$$

Let us suppose, that the bodies of the system are only subjected to their mutual action, and to a force directed towards the origin of the coordinates. Let p denote, as before, the reciprocal action of m on m', we shall have in consequence of this sole action,

$$0 = m.(Py - Qx) + m'.(P'y' - Q'x');$$

thus the mutual action of the bodies disappears from the finite integral $\Sigma.m.(Py - Qx)$. Let S be the force which solicits m towards the origin of the coordinates; in consequence of this sole force, we shall have

$$P = \frac{-S.x}{\sqrt{x^2 + y^2 + z^2}}; \quad Q = \frac{-S\,y}{\sqrt{x^2 + y^2 + z^2}};$$

consequently the force S disappears from the expression $Py - Qx$, thus, in the case in which the different bodies composing the system are only solicited by their action and mutual attraction, and by forces directed towards the origin of the coordinates, we have

$$c = \Sigma.m.\frac{(xdy - ydx)}{dt}; \quad c' = \Sigma.m.\frac{(xdz - zdx)}{dt}; \quad c'' = \Sigma.m.\frac{(ydz - zdy)}{dt}$$

If we project the body m, on the plane of x and of y, the differential $\frac{xdy - ydx}{2}$, will represent the area which the radius vector, drawn from the origin of the coordinates to the projection of m, describes in the time dt; consequently the sum of the areas, multiplied respectively by the masses of the bodies, is proportional to the element of the time, from which it follows, that in a finite time, it is proportional to the time. It is this which constitutes the principle of the conservation of areas.*

* When the bodies are only subjected to their reciprocal action,

$$\Sigma.m.(Py - Qx) = m.(Py - Qx) + m'\,(P'y' - Q'x') + \&c. =$$

by substituting for $m\,P$, $m\,Q$, their values, given in page 122,

$$p.\left\{\frac{(xy - x'y - yx + xy')}{f} + \frac{x'y' - xy' - y'x' + x'y)}{f}\right\} = 0.$$

The fixed plane of x and of y being arbitrary, this principle obtains for any plane whatever, and if the force S vanishes, i. e. if the bodies are only subjected to their reciprocal action and mutual attraction, the origin of the coordinates is arbitrary, and may be in any point whatever. Finally, it is evident from what precedes, that this principle subsists, even when by the mutual action of the bodies composing the system, they undergo sudden changes in their motions.

There exists a plane, with respect to which c' and c'' vanish, and which, for this reason, it is interesting to know, for it is manifest that

S

see preceding number. If the bodies are solicited by forces directed towards a fixed point, then making this point the origin of the coordinates,

$$P = \frac{-Sx}{\sqrt{x^2+y^2+z^2}},\; Q = \frac{-Sy}{\sqrt{x^2+y^2+z^2}},\; \therefore\; Py-Qx = S.\,\frac{(xy-xy)}{\sqrt{x^2+y^2+z^2}} = 0,$$

consequently this force will also disappear from the expression $Py-Qx$, $\therefore$ in these two cases we have $c = \Sigma\, m.\, \frac{xdy-ydx}{dt}$, &c ; $\frac{xdy-ydx}{2}$ = the area which the projection of the radius vector on the plane of x, y, describes in the time dt, see notes to No. 6, page 27. $\Sigma.m.(Py-Qx) = 0$, also when P and Q, &c. vanish, i. e. when the system is not actuated by any accelerating force, but only moved by an initial impulse ; $\therefore$ the principle of the conservation of the areas obtains in these three cases ; 1st. when the forces are only the result of the mutual action of the bodies composing the system; 2ndly, when the forces pass through the origin of the coordinates ; and 3dly, when the system is moved by a primitive impulse. In the first and last case, the origin of the coordinates may be any point whatever. If there is a *fixed* point in the system, the equations (Z) are only true when this point is made the origin of the coordinates, any other point being made the origin, the moment $Py-Qx$ will not disappear, see notes to No. 3, page 12 ; if $\therefore$ in these circumstances the bodies are solicited by forces directed towards a given centre, this centre coincides with the fixed point of the system, when the equations (Z) obtain ; if there are *two fixed* points in the system, only one of the equations (Z) will subsist, to wit, that which contains those coordinates, the plane of which is perpendicular to line joining the given points, the origin of the coordinates may be any point whatever in this line, see notes to No. 15, page 88.

The constant quantities c, c', c'', may be determined at any instant, when the velocities and the coordinates of the bodies of the system, are given at that instant.

*

the equality of c' and c'' to nothing, ought to simplify considerably the investigation of the motion of a system of bodies. In order to determine this plane, we must refer the coordinates $x,y,z,$ to three other axes having the same origin as the preceding. Let therefore θ represent the inclination of the required plane, formed by two of the new axes, with the plane of x and of y, and ψ the angle which the axis of x constitutes with the intersection of these two planes, so that $\frac{\pi}{2}-\theta$ may be the inclination of the third new axis with the plane of x and of y, and $\frac{\pi}{2}-\psi$ may represent the angle which its projection on the same plane, makes with the axis of x, π being the semi periphery.

In order to assist the imagination, let us suppose the origin of the coordinates to be at the centre of the earth; and that the plane of x and of y coincides with the plane of the ecliptic, and that the axis of z is the line drawn from the centre of the earth to the north pole of the ecliptic: moreover, let us suppose that the required plane is that of the equator, and that the third new axis, is the axis of rotation of the earth, directed towards the north pole; θ will represent the obliquity of the ecliptic, and ψ will be the longitude of the fixed axis of x, relative to the moveable equinox of spring. The two first new axes will be in the plane of the equator, and by calling φ, the angular distance of the first of those axes from this equinox, φ will represent the rotation of the earth reckoned from the same equinox, and $\frac{\pi}{2}+\varphi$ will be the angular distance of the second of these axes from the same equinox. We will name these three new axes, *principal axes.*

Let $x_{,}, y_{,}, z_{,}$ represent the coordinates of m referred, first to the line drawn from the origin of the coordinates, to the equinox of spring; $x_{,}$ being reckoned positive on this side of the equinox; 2dly, to the projection of the third principal axis on the plane of x and of y; 3dly to the axis of z, we shall have

$$x = x_{,}.\ \cos.\ \psi + y_{,}.\ \sin.\ \psi\,;$$

$$y = y_{,}.\ \cos.\ \psi - x_{,}.\ \sin.\ \psi\,;^{*}$$

$$z = z_{,}.$$

Let $x_{,,}$, $y_{,,}$, $z_{,,}$, be the coordinates referred, 1st to the line of the equinox of spring; 2dly, to the perpendicular to this line in the plane of the equator; 3dly, to the third principal axis; we shall have

$$x_{,} = x_{,,}\,;$$

$$y_{,} = y_{,,}.\ \cos.\ \theta + z_{,,}.\ \sin.\ \theta\,;$$

$$z_{,} = z_{,,}.\ \cos.\ \theta - y_{,,}.\ \sin.\ \theta.$$

Finally, let $x_{,,,}$, $y_{,,,}$, $z_{,,,}$, be the cooordinates of m, referred to the first,

* As the axes of the coordinates $x_{,}$, $y_{,}$ exist in the plane of x, y, and as the angle which the axis of x makes with the axis of $x_{,}$ is equal to ψ, we have by the known formulæ for the transformation of one system of rectangular coordinates, into another system existing in the same plane,

$x = x_{,}.\cos.\psi + y_{,}.\sin.\psi$; $y = y_{,}.\cos.\psi - x_{,}.\sin.\psi$; and because the axis of z coincides with the axis of $z_{,}$, we have $z = z_{,}$. Comparing the coordinates, $x_{,}, y_{,}, z_{,}$, with the coordinates $x_{,,}, y_{,,}, z_{,,}$, it appears that the axis of $x_{,}$ coincides with the axis of $x_{,,}$, and consequently $x_{,} = x_{,,}$; and as the axis of $y_{,}$ is in the plane of the ecliptic, perpendicular to the line of equinox of spring, and as the axis of $y_{,,}$ exists in the plane of the equator perpendicular to the same line, it is manifest that the angle formed by these axes is equal to the angle θ, the inclination of the two planes, and that these two lines and the axes of $z_{,}$ and $z_{,,}$, which are respectively perpendicular to those planes, exist in the same plane, consequently we have, as before, $y_{,} = y_{,,}.\ \cos.\ \theta. + z_{,,}.\ \sin.\ \theta$, $z_{,} = z_{,,}.\ \cos.\ \theta.\ - y_{,,}\ \sin.\ \theta$. Lastly, it appears that the axis of $z_{,,}$ coincides with the axis of $z_{,,,}$, and consequently that $z_{,,} = z_{,,,}$; and as the axis of $x_{,,}$ and $y_{,,}$ and of $x_{,,,}$ and $y_{,,,}$ are in the plane of equator; and as by hypothesis, φ is equal to the angle which the axis of $x_{,,,}$ makes with the line of equinox of spring, which line is supposed to coincide with the axis of $x_{,,}$, we have $x_{,,} = x_{,,,}.\cos.\ \varphi - y_{,,,}.\ \sin.\ \varphi$; $y_{,,} = y_{,,,}.\ \cos.\ \varphi + x_{,,,}.\ \sin\ \varphi$. By substituting for $x_{,}$, $y_{,}$, $x_{,,}$, $y_{,,}$, their values, we obtain $x = x_{,}.\ \cos\ \psi + y_{,}\ \sin.\ \psi = (x_{,,}.\ \cos.\ \psi + y_{,,}\ \cos.\ \theta.\ \sin.\ \psi + z_{,,}.\ \sin.\ \theta.\ \sin.\ \psi) = (x_{,,,}.\ \cos.\ \varphi.\ \cos.\ \psi - y_{,,,}.\ \cos.\ \psi.\ \sin\ \varphi + y_{,,,}.\ \cos.\ \theta.\ \sin.\ \psi.\ \cos.\ \varphi.\ + x_{,,,}.\ \cos.\ \theta.\ \sin.\psi.\ \sin.\ \varphi + z_{,,,}.\ \sin\ \theta.\ \sin.\ \psi)$, ∵ by concinnating we obtain $x = x_{,,,}.(\cos.\ \theta.\ \sin.\ \psi.\ \sin.\ \varphi + \cos.\ \varphi.\ \cos.\ \psi) + y_{,,,}\ (\cos.\ \theta.\ \sin.\ \psi.\ \cos.\ \varphi. - \cos.\ \psi.\ \sin.\ \varphi) + z_{,,,}.\ \sin.\ \theta.\ \sin.\ \psi$, which is the expression given in the text; by a similar process we could derive values for y and z.

second, and third principal axes; we shall have

$$x_{,,} = x_{,,,}.\cos.\varphi - y_{,,,}.\sin.\varphi;$$

$$y_{,,} = y_{,,,}.\cos.\varphi + x_{,,,}.\sin.\varphi;$$

$$z_{,,} = z_{,,,}.$$

From which it is easy to deduce

$$x = x_{,,,}.(\cos.\theta.\sin.\psi.\sin.\varphi + \cos.\psi.\cos.\varphi) +$$
$$y_{,,,}.(\cos.\theta.\sin.\psi.\cos.\varphi - \cos.\psi.\sin.\varphi)$$
$$z_{,,,}.(\sin.\theta.\sin.\psi);$$

$$y = x_{,,,}.(\cos.\theta.\cos.\psi.\sin.\varphi - \sin.\psi.\cos.\varphi) +$$
$$y_{,,,}.(\cos.\theta.\cos.\psi.\cos.\varphi + \sin.\psi.\sin.\varphi)$$
$$+ z_{,,,}(\sin.\theta.\cos.\psi);$$

$$z = z_{,,,}.\cos.\theta - y_{,,,}.\sin.\theta.\cos.\varphi - x_{,,,}\sin.\theta.\sin.\varphi.*$$

If we multiply these values of x, y, z, by the respective coefficients of

* If any line x is drawn from the origin of the coordinates $x_{,,,}$, $y_{,,,}$, $z_{,,,}$, and if A, B, C, represent the cosines of the angles which x makes with $z_{,,,}$, $y_{,,,}$, $z_{,,,}$, respectively, then $x = Ax_{,,,} + By_{,,,} + Cz_{,,,}$, for if a perpendicular erected from the extremity of x meets a line r, whose coordinates are $x_{,,,}$, $y_{,,,}$, $z_{,,,}$, then $\frac{x}{r}$ is equal to the cosine of the angle which x makes with r, and $\frac{x_{,,,}}{r}$, $\frac{y_{,,,}}{r}$, $\frac{z_{,,,}}{r}$, are equal to the cosines of the angles which r makes with $x_{,,,}$, $y_{,,,}$, $z_{,,,}$, ∵ we have by note to page 7, $\frac{x}{r} = A.\frac{x_{,,,}}{r} + B.\frac{y_{,,,}}{r} + C.\frac{z_{,,,}}{r}$, ∵ $x = Ax_{,,,} + By_{,,,} + Cz_{,,,}$. Consequently we infer that the coefficients of $x_{,,,}$, $y_{,,,}$, $z_{,,,}$, in the expression given in the text for x, y, z, are equal to the cosines of the angles which the axis of x, y, z, make with the principal axes respectively; therefore $\sin.\theta.\sin.\psi$, is equal to the cosine of the angle which the axis of $z_{,,,}$, makes with the axis of

$x_{,,,}$, in the preceding expressions; we shall have, by adding them together,

$$x_{,,,} = x.(\cos.\theta.\sin.\psi.\sin.\varphi+\cos.\psi.\cos.\varphi)+$$

$$y.(\cos.\theta.\cos.\psi.\sin.\varphi-\sin.\psi.\cos.\varphi)-z.\sin.\theta.\sin.\varphi.$$

By multiplying in like manner the values of x, y, z, by the respective coefficients of $y_{,,,}$ in the same expression, and afterwards by the coefficients of $z_{,,,}$, we shall have

$$y_{,,,} = x.(\cos.\theta.\sin.\psi.\cos.\varphi-\cos.\psi.\sin.\varphi.)+$$

x, ∵ equal to the cosine of the angle which the plane of $y_{,,,}$, $x_{,,,}$, makes with the plane y, z; in like manner $\sin.\theta.\cos.\psi$, is equal to the cosine of the angle contained between the axis of $z_{,,,}$ and of y, = the cosine of the inclination of the plane $x_{,,,}$, $y_{,,,}$ to the plane x, z, also $\sin.\theta.\sin.\varphi$, $\sin.\theta.\cos.\varphi$, $\cos.\theta$. are equal to the cosines of the angles which the axis of z makes with the axes of $x_{,,,}$, $y_{,,,}$, and $z_{,,,}$, respectively, see No. 27.

We may observe that in the general expressions for the transformations of one system to another of rectangular coordinates, which are of the following form:

$$x = Ax_{,,,}+By_{,,,}+Cz_{,,,},$$
$$y = A_{,}.x_{,,,}+B_{,}.y_{,,,}+C_{,}.z_{,,,},$$
$$z = A_{,,}x_{,,,}+B_{,,}.y_{,,,}+C_{,,}.z_{,,,},$$

there are six equations of condition, i. e.

$$A^2+A_{,}^2+A_{,,}^2,=1 \qquad AB+A_{,}B_{,}+A_{,,}B_{,,}=0,$$
$$B^2+B_{,}^2+B_{,,}^2,=1 \qquad AC+A_{,}C_{,}+A_{,,}C_{,,}=0,$$
$$C^2+C_{,}^2+C_{,,,}^2,=1 \qquad BC+B_{,}C_{,}+B_{,,}C_{,,}=0,$$

which are derived from the identity between the expressions $x^2+y^2+z^2$, and $x_{,,,}^2+y_{,,,}^2+z_{,,,}^2$, for they are respectively equal to the square of the distance of the same point, from the common origin of the coordinates, ∵ three of the nine coefficients which are introduced by the transformation, may be regarded as undetermined; these three undetermined quantities are, in fact, the angles θ, ψ, and φ; for, by substituting in the six preceding equations of condition for A, B, C, $A_{,}$, &c. their values in functions of the angles θ, ψ, and φ, the resulting equations will become identical, and there arises no relation between θ, ψ, and φ.

$$y.(\cos.\theta.\cos.\psi.\cos.\varphi+\sin.\psi.\sin.\varphi)-z.\sin.\theta.\cos.\varphi;$$

$$z_{,,,}=x.\sin.\theta.\sin.\psi+y.\sin.\theta.\cos.\psi.+z.\cos.\theta.$$

These different transformations will be very useful hereafter, we will obtain the coordinates corresponding to the bodies m', m'', &c.: by placing one, two, &c. marks above the coordinates $x_{,}$, $y_{,}$, $z_{,,,}$, $y_{,,,}$, $z_{,,}$.*

* If we actually perform this operation we shall obtain

$$x.(\cos.\theta.\sin.\psi.\sin.\varphi+\cos.\psi\cos.\varphi)=x_{,,,}.(\cos.^2\theta.\sin.^2\psi.\sin.^2\varphi+\cos.^2\psi.\cos.^2\varphi+ 2\cos.\theta.\sin.\psi.\cos.\psi.\sin.\varphi.\cos.\varphi.)$$

$$+y_{,,,}.(\cos.^2\theta.\sin.^2\psi.\sin.\varphi.\cos.\varphi+\cos.\theta.\sin.\psi.\cos\psi.\cos.^2\varphi-\cos.\theta.\sin.\psi.\cos.\psi\sin.^2\varphi -\cos.^2\psi.\sin.\varphi.\cos.\varphi.)$$

$$+z_{,,,}.(\sin.\theta.\cos.\theta.\sin.^2\psi.\sin.\varphi+\sin.\theta.\sin.\psi.\cos.\psi.\cos.\varphi);$$

$$y.(\cos.\theta.\cos.\psi.\sin.\varphi-\sin.\psi.\cos.\varphi.)$$

$$=x_{,,,}.(\cos.^2\theta.\cos.^2\psi.\sin.^2\varphi+\sin.^2\psi.\cos.^2\varphi-2(\cos.\theta.\sin.\psi.\cos.\psi.\sin.\varphi.\cos.\varphi)$$

$$+y_{,,,}.(\cos.^2\theta.\cos.^2\psi.\sin.\varphi.\cos.\varphi+\cos.\theta.\sin.\psi.\cos.\psi.\sin^2\varphi-\cos.\theta.\sin.\psi.\cos.\psi \cos.^2\varphi-\sin.^2\psi.\sin.\varphi.\cos.\varphi.)$$

$$+z_{,,,}.(\sin.\theta.\cos.\theta.\cos.^2\psi.\sin.\varphi-\sin.\theta.\sin\psi.\cos.\psi.\cos.\varphi)$$

$$-z.\sin.\theta.\sin.\varphi=-z_{,,,}.\sin.\theta.\cos.\theta.\sin.\varphi+y_{,,,}.\sin.^2\theta.\sin.\varphi.\cos.\varphi+x_{,,,}.\sin^2\theta.\sin.^2\varphi;$$

adding these three equations together, and making the terms which are at the right hand side to coalesce, we shall get the coefficients of $x_{,,,}$= to $\cos.^2\theta.\sin.^2\varphi+\cos^2\varphi.+\sin.^2\theta\sin.^2\varphi$, $(=\sin.^2\varphi-\sin.^2\theta.\sin.^2\varphi+\cos^2\varphi+\sin.^2\theta.\sin.^2\varphi)=1$, the coefficients of $y_{,,,}$ will be equal to $\cos.^2\theta.\sin.\varphi.\cos.\varphi-\sin.\varphi.\cos.\varphi+\sin.^2\theta.\sin.\varphi.\cos.\varphi=0$, in like manner the coefficient of $z_{,,}=\sin.\theta.\cos.\theta.\sin.\varphi-\sin.\theta.\cos.\theta.\sin.\varphi=0$; the terms at the other side are those which have been given in the text. In like manner to obtain the value of $y_{,,,}$, a corresponding multiplication gives

$$x.(\cos.\theta.\sin.\psi.\cos.\varphi-\cos.\psi.\sin.\varphi)=$$

$$x_{,,,}.(\cos.^2\theta.\sin.^2\psi.\sin.\varphi.\cos.\varphi+\cos.\theta.\sin.\psi.\cos.\psi.\cos.^2\varphi-\cos.\theta.\sin.\psi.\cos.\psi.\sin.^2\varphi- \cos.^2\psi.\sin.\varphi.\cos.\varphi)$$

$$+y_{,,,}(\cos.^2\theta.\sin.^2\psi.\cos^2\varphi+\cos.^2\psi.\sin.^2\varphi-2.\cos\theta.\sin.\psi.\cos.\psi.\sin.\varphi.\cos.\varphi)$$

$$+z_{,,,}(\sin.\theta.\cos.\theta.\sin.^2\psi.\cos.\varphi-\sin\theta.\sin.\psi.\cos.\psi.\sin.\varphi)$$

From what precedes, it is easy to conclude, by substituting c, c', c'', in place of

$$\Sigma.m.\frac{(xdy-ydx)}{dt}, \Sigma.m.\frac{(xdz-zdx)}{dt}, \Sigma m.\frac{(ydz-zdy)}{dt},$$

$$y.(\cos.\theta.\cos.\psi.\cos.\varphi+\sin.\psi.\sin.\varphi)$$

$$=x_{,,,}(.\cos.^2\theta.\cos.^2\psi.\sin.\varphi.\cos.\varphi-\cos.\theta.\sin.\psi.\cos.\psi.\cos.^2\varphi+\cos.\theta.\sin.\psi.\cos.\psi.\sin.^2\varphi-\sin.^2\psi.\sin.\varphi.\cos.\varphi)$$

$$+y_{,,,}(\cos.^2\theta.\cos.^2\psi.\cos.^2\varphi+\sin.^2\psi.\sin.^2\varphi+2.\cos.\theta.\sin.\varphi.\cos.\varphi.\sin.\psi.\cos.\psi)$$

$$+z_{,,,}.\sin.\theta.\cos.\theta.\cos.^2\psi.\cos.\varphi+\sin.\theta.\sin.\psi.\cos.\psi.\sin.\varphi.)$$

$$-z.\sin.\theta.\cos.\varphi=$$

$$-z_{,,,}\sin.\theta.\cos.\theta.\cos.\varphi+y_{,,,}.\sin.^2\theta.\cos.^2\varphi+x_{,,,}.\sin.^2\theta.\sin.\varphi.\cos.\varphi,$$

adding those quantities together, and concinnating as before, we obtain

$$x.(\cos.\theta.\sin.\psi.\cos.\varphi-\cos.\psi.\sin.\varphi)+y.(\cos.\theta.\cos.\psi.\cos.\varphi+\sin.\psi.\sin.\varphi)$$

$$-z.\sin.\theta.\cos.\varphi=$$

$$x_{,,,}.(\cos.^2\theta.\sin.\varphi.\cos.\varphi-\sin.\varphi.\cos.\varphi+\sin.^2\theta.\sin.\varphi.\cos.\varphi)=0,$$

$$+y_{,,,}(\cos.^2\theta.\cos.^2\varphi+\sin.^2\varphi+\sin.^2\theta.\cos.^2\varphi)=y_{,,,}$$

$$+z_{,,,}(\sin.\theta.\cos.\theta.\cos.\varphi-\sin.\theta.\cos.\theta.\cos.\varphi)=0.$$

For the value of $z_{,,,}$ by performing similar operations, we obtain $x.\sin.\theta.\sin.\psi=$

$$x_{,,,}(\sin.\theta.\cos.\theta.\sin.^2\psi.\sin.\varphi+\sin.\theta.\sin.\psi.\cos.\psi.\cos.\varphi)$$

$$+y_{,,,}.(\sin.\theta.\cos.\theta.\sin.^2\psi.\cos.\varphi-\sin.\theta.\sin.\psi.\cos.\psi.\sin.\varphi)$$

$$+z_{,,,}.(\sin.^2\theta.\sin.^2\psi.$$

$$y.\sin.\theta.\cos.\psi=$$

$$x_{,,,}.(\sin.\theta.\cos.\theta.\cos.^2\psi.\sin.\varphi-\sin.\theta.\sin.\psi.\cos.\psi.\cos.\varphi)$$

$$+y_{,,,}.(\sin.\theta.\cos.\theta.\cos.^2\psi.\cos.\varphi+\sin.\theta.\sin.\psi.\cos.\psi.\sin.\varphi)+z_{,,,}(\sin.^2\theta.\cos.^2\psi.)$$

$$z.\cos.\theta=-x_{,,,}\sin.\theta.\cos.\theta.\sin.\varphi-y_{,,,}(\sin.\theta.\cos.\theta.\cos.\varphi+z_{,,,}.(\cos.^2\theta),$$

∴ adding the corresponding quantities together, we obtain

that $\Sigma m. \frac{(x_{,,,}dy_{,,,}-y_{,,,}dx_{,,,})}{dt} = c. \cos. \theta - c'. \sin. \theta. \cos \psi + c''. \sin. \theta. \sin \psi$;

$$\Sigma m. \frac{x_{,,,}.dz_{,,,}-z_{,,,}.dx_{,,,}}{dt} = c. \sin. \theta. \cos. \varphi \; *$$

$$x. (\sin. \theta. \sin. \psi) + y. \sin. \theta. \cos. \psi + z. \cos. \theta =$$

$$x_{,,,}.(\sin. \theta. \cos. \theta. \sin. \varphi - \sin. \theta. \cos. \theta. \sin. \varphi.) = 0,$$

$$+ y_{,,,}.(\sin. \theta. \cos. \theta. \cos. \varphi - \sin. \theta. \cos. \theta. \cos. \varphi) = 0, \; + z_{,,,}.(\sin.^2 \theta. + \cos.^2 \theta) = z_{,,,}.$$

* When we substitute for the expression $x_{,,,}dy_{,,,}-y_{,,,}dx_{,,,}$, the respective values of $x_{,,,}$, $dx_{,,,}$, $y_{,,,}$, $dy_{,,,}$, in functions of x, dx, y, dy, and of the angles θ, ψ, and φ, it is not necessary to take into account any expression, in which the variable part is the product of a coordinate into its own differential, because this expression occurs again, affected with a sign, the opposite to that, with which it was affected before. By performing the prescribed multiplication of the value of $x_{,,,}$ into the value of $dy_{,,,}$ of $y_{,,,}$ into $dx_{,,,}$ we obtain

$$x_{,,,}.dy_{,,,} = x.dy.(\cos.^2 \theta. \sin. \psi. \cos \psi. \sin. \varphi. \cos. \varphi + \cos. \theta. \sin.^2 \psi. \sin.^2 \varphi + \cos. \theta. \cos.^2 \psi. \cos.^2 \varphi + \sin. \psi. \cos. \psi. \sin. \varphi \cos \varphi),$$

$$+ y.dx.(\cos.^2 \theta. \sin. \psi. \cos. \psi. \sin. \varphi. \cos. \varphi - \cos. \theta. \cos.^2 \psi. \sin.^2 \varphi - \cos. \theta. \sin.^2 \psi. \cos.^2 \varphi + \sin. \psi. \cos. \psi. \sin. \varphi. \cos. \varphi),$$

$$- z.dx.(\sin. \theta. \cos. \theta. \sin. \psi. \sin. \varphi. \cos. \varphi - \sin. \theta. \cos. \psi. \sin.^2 \varphi),$$

$$- z.dy.(\sin. \theta. \cos. \theta. \cos. \psi. \sin. \varphi. \cos. \varphi + \sin. \theta. \sin. \psi. \sin.^2 \varphi),$$

$$- x.dz.(\sin. \theta. \cos. \theta. \sin. \psi. \sin. \varphi. \cos. \varphi + \sin. \theta. \cos. \psi. \cos.^2 \varphi),$$

$$- y.dz.(\sin. \theta. \cos. \theta. \cos. \psi. \sin. \varphi. \cos. \varphi - \sin. \theta. \sin. \psi. \cos.^2 \varphi),$$

$$y_{,,,}.dx_{,,,} = x.dy.(\cos.^2 \theta. \sin. \psi. \cos. \psi. \sin. \varphi. \cos. \varphi - \cos. \theta. \sin.^2 \psi. \cos.^2 \varphi - \cos. \theta. \cos.^2 \psi. \sin.^2 \varphi + \sin. \psi. \cos. \psi. \sin. \varphi. \cos. \varphi),$$

$$+ y.dx.(\cos.^2 \theta. \sin. \psi. \cos. \psi. \sin. \varphi. \cos. \varphi + \cos. \theta. \cos.^2 \psi. \cos.^2 \varphi + \cos. \theta. \sin.^2 \psi. \sin.^2 \varphi + \sin. \psi. \cos. \psi. \sin. \varphi. \cos. \varphi),$$

$$- z.dx.(\sin. \theta. \cos. \theta. \sin. \psi. \sin. \varphi. \cos. \varphi + \sin. \theta. \cos. \psi. \cos.^2 \varphi),$$

$$- z.dy.(\sin. \theta. \cos. \theta. \cos. \psi. \sin. \varphi \cos. \varphi - \sin. \theta. \sin. \psi. \cos.^2 \varphi),$$

$$- x.dz.(\sin. \theta. \cos. \theta. \sin. \psi. \sin. \varphi. \cos. \varphi - \sin. \theta. \cos. \psi. \sin.^2 \varphi),$$

$$- y.dz.(\sin. \theta. \cos. \theta. \cos. \psi. \sin. \varphi. \cos. \varphi + \sin. \theta. \sin. \psi. \sin.^2 \varphi);$$

$c'.$ (sin. ψ. sin. φ+cos. θ. cos. ψ. cos. φ)+c''. (cos. ψ. sin. φ—cos. θ. sin. ψ. cos. φ); $\frac{\Sigma m. y_{,,,}.dz_{,,,}.-z_{,,,}.dy_{,,,}}{dt} = -c.$ sin. θ. sin. φ.

$+c'$.(sin. ψ. cos. φ—cos. θ. cos. ψ. sin. φ)
$+c''$. cos. ψ. cos. φ+cos. θ. sin. ψ. sin. φ).

If we determine ψ and θ, so that we may have sin. θ. sin. ψ

$$= \frac{c''}{\sqrt{c^2+c'^2+c''^2}}; \text{ sin. } \theta. \text{ cos. } \psi = \frac{-c'}{\sqrt{c^2+c'^2+c''^2}},$$ which gives

$$\cos. \theta = \frac{c}{\sqrt{c^2+c'^2+c''^2}}$$ we shall have *

$$\Sigma m. \frac{x_{,,,}.dy_{,,,}.-y_{,,,}.dx_{,,,}}{dt} = \sqrt{c^2+c'^2+c''^2} \dagger$$

T

∵ subducting $x_{,,,}.dy_{,,,}$ from $y_{,,,}.dx_{,,,}$, and making the terms whose variable parts are the same coalese, we obtain $x_{,,,}.dy_{,,,}-y_{,,,}.dx_{,,,} = (x.dy-y.dx)$. cos. θ+ $(x.dz-z.dx)$. sin. θ. cos. ψ+$(y.dz-z.dy)$. sin. θ. sin. ψ; and substituting for $x.dy-y.dx$, $x.dz-z.dx$, &c. their values $c', c''_{,}$, we obtain c. cos. θ.—c'. sin. θ. cos. ψ,+c''. sin. θ. sin. ψ; $=x_{,,,}.dy_{,,,}-y_{,,,}.dx_{,,,}$, by a similar analysis we arrive at the expressions for $x_{,,,}.dz_{,,,}-z_{,,,}.dx_{,,,}$, $y_{,,,}.dz_{,,,}-z_{,,,}.dy_{,,,}$, which are given in the text.

* For sin.^{2} θ. sin.^{2} ψ +sin.^{2} θ. cos.^{2} ψ= sin.^{2} $\theta = \frac{c''^2+c'^2}{c^2+c'^2+c''^2}$ ∴ cos.^{2} θ.=1—sin.^{2} θ $= \frac{c^2}{c^2+c'^2+c''^2}$.

† For substituting in place of cos. θ, sin. θ. cos. ψ, sin. θ. sin. ψ, these values, we shall have

$$\Sigma.m. \frac{x_{,,,}dy_{,,,}-y_{,,,}dx_{,,,}}{dt} = \frac{c^2}{\sqrt{c^2+c'^2+c''^2}} + \frac{c'^2}{\sqrt{c^2+c'^2+c''^2}} + \frac{c''^2}{\sqrt{c^2+c'^2+c''^2}}$$

$=\sqrt{c^2+c'^2+c''^2}$, and if we substitute for c, c', c'', their values, $\sqrt{c^2+c'^2+c''^2}$, cos. θ, $-\sqrt{c^2+c'^2+c''^2}$, sin. θ. cos. ψ. $+\sqrt{c^2+c'^2+c''^2}$, sin. θ. sin. ψ, the expression $\Sigma.m. \frac{x_{,,,}.dz_{,,,}-z_{,,,}.dx_{,,,}}{dt}$ will become $\sqrt{c^2+c'^2+c''^2}$, (sin. θ. cos. θ. cos. φ,—sin. θ. sin. ψ,

$$\Sigma m. \frac{x_{,,,}.dz_{,,,}-z_{,,,}.dx_{,,,}}{dt}=0;\ \Sigma m. \frac{y_{,,,}.dz_{,,,}-z_{,,,}.dy_{,,,}}{dt}=0;$$

$\therefore$ the values of c' and c'' vanish with respect to the plane of $x_{,,,}$ and $y_{,,,}$, determined in this manner. There exists only one plane, which possesses this property, for supposing that it is the plane of x and y, we shall have

$$\Sigma m. \frac{x_{,,,}.dz_{,,,}-z_{,,,}.dx_{,,,}}{dt}=c.\sin.\theta.\cos.\varphi;\ \Sigma m. \frac{y_{,,,}.dz_{,,,}-z_{,,,}.dy_{,,,}}{dt}= -c.\sin.\theta.\sin.\varphi;$$

If these two functions are put equal to nothing, we shall have $\sin.\theta=0$, which shews that the plane of $x_{,,,}$ and $y_{,,,}$ then coincides with the plane of x and y. Since the value of $\Sigma m. \frac{x_{,,,}.dy_{,,,}-y_{,,,}.dx_{,,,}}{dt}$ is equal to $\sqrt{c^2+c'^2+c''^2}$, whatever may be the plane of x and y, it follows that the quantity $c^2+c'^2+c''^2$ is the same, whatever this plane may be, and that the plane of $x_{,,,}$ and $y_{,,,}$, determined by the preceding analysis is that, with respect to which the function $\Sigma m. \frac{x_{,,,}.dy_{,,,}-y_{,,,}.dx_{,,,}}{dt}$ is a maximum; therefore, this plane * possesses these remarkable pro-

$\cos.\psi.\sin.\varphi-\sin.\theta.\cos.\theta.\cos.^2\psi.\cos.\varphi+\sin.\theta.\sin.\psi+\cos.\psi.\sin.\varphi-\sin.\theta.\cos.\theta.\sin.^2\psi.\cos.\varphi)=\sqrt{c^2+c'^2+c''^2}$, $(\sin.\theta.\cos.\theta.\cos.\varphi-\sin.\theta.\cos.\theta.\cos.\varphi)=0$ the same is true respecting the expression $\Sigma.m. \frac{y_{,,,}dz_{,,,}-z_{,,,}dy_{,,,}}{dt}$.

* As the cosines of the angles which the axes of $z_{,,,}$ makes with the axes z, y, x, i. e. the cosines of the angles which the plane $x_{,,,}, y_{,,,}$ makes with the planes x, y; x, z; y, z, (see note to page 133,) are equal to $\cos.\theta$, $\sin.\theta.\cos.\psi$, $\sin.\theta.\sin.\psi$, it follows that when we have the projections c, c', c'', of any area on three coordinate planes, we have its projection $\Sigma m.(x_{,,,}.dy_{,,,}-y_{,,,}.dx_{,,,})$ on the plane $x_{,,,}y_{,,,}$ whose position, with respect to the three planes x,y; x,z; y,z, is given. In like manner it follows from the exression, $\Sigma.m.\left\{\frac{x_{,,,}dy_{,,,}-y_{,,,}dx_{,,,}}{dt}\right\}$, which has been given in the text, that for all planes equally inclined to the plane on which the projection is the greatest, the values of the projection of the area are equal, for supposing the plane of x, y to be the invariable plane, then $\Sigma.m.\left\{\frac{x.dy-y.dx}{dt}\right\}$, will be the greatest possible, $\Sigma.m.\left\{\frac{x.dz-z.dx}{dt}\right\}$,

perties—first, that the sum of the areas traced by the projection of the radii vectores of the respective bodies, and multiplied by their masses, is the greatest possible; secondly, that the same sum, vanishes relative to any plane, which is perpendicular to it, because the angle φ is undetermined. By means of these properties, we shall be able to find this plane at any instant, whatever variations may be induced in the respective positions of the bodies by their mutual action; we can, in like manner very easily

T 2

$\Sigma.m. \left\{ \frac{y.dz-z.dy}{dt} \right\}$, are respectively equal to nothing, $\because\ \Sigma.m. \left\{ \frac{x_{,,,}.dy_{,,,}-y_{,,,}dx_{,,,}}{dt} \right\}$ $= \Sigma.m. \left\{ \frac{x.dy-y\,dx}{dt} \right\}. \cos.\theta.$

Since c, c', c'', are constant quantities, and proportional to the cosines of the angles which the plane on which the projection of the area is a maximum, makes with the coordinate planes, it follows, that the position of *this* plane is always fixed and *invariable*; and as the quantities c, c', c'', depend on the coordinates of the bodies at any instant, and on the velocities $\frac{dx}{dt}$, &c. parallel to the coordinates, when these quantities are given, we can determine the position of this invariable plane; we have termed this plane invariable, because it depends on the quantities c, c', c'', which are constant during the motion of the system, provided that the bodies composing it are only subjected to this mutual action, and to the action of forces directed towards a fixed point. (See page, 128.)

Since the plane x, y is indetermined in the text, we conclude, that the sum of the squares of the projections of any area, existing in the invariable plane, on any three coordinate planes passing through the same point in space is constant; consequently, if we take on the axes to any coordinate planes y, z; x, z; x, y, lines proportional to c, c', c'', then the diagonal of a parallepiped, whose sides are proportional to those lines, will represent the quantity and direction of the greatest moment, and this direction is the same whatever three coordinate planes be assumed, but the *position* in absolute space is undetermined, for the projections on all *parallel* planes are evidently the same. The conclusions to which we have arrived, respecting the projections of areas on coordinate planes, are in like manner applicable to the projections of moments, since as has been observed in Note, page 28, these moments are geometrically exhibited by triangles of which the bases represent the projected force, the altitudes being equal to perpendiculars let fall from the point to which the moments are referred, on the direction of the bases.

When the forces applied to the different points of the system have an unique resultant, V; then since the sum of the moments of any forces projected on a plane is equal to the moment of the projection of their resultant, it follows necessarily, that

find at all times the position of the centre of gravity of the system, and for this reason it is as natural to refer the position of the coordinates x and y to this plane, as to refer their origin to the centre of gravity.*

22. The principles of the preservation of living forces, and of areas, obtain when the origin of the coordinates has a uniform rectilinear motion in space. To demonstrate this, let X, Y, Z, represent the coordinates of this origin, supposed to be in motion, with reference to a fixed point, and let us suppose

$$x = X + x_{,}; \; y = Y + y_{,}; \; z = Z + z_{,};$$

$$x' = X + x'_{,}; \; y' = Y + y'_{,}; \; z = Z + z'_{,}; \; \&c.$$

$x_{,}$, $y_{,}$, $z_{,}$; $x'_{,}$, &c. will be the coordinates of m, m', &c. relative to the

the unique resultant V and the point to which the moments are referred, must exist in the invariable plane; ∴ the axis of this plane must be perpendicular to this resultant, and as $\frac{P}{V}$, $\frac{Q}{V}$, $\frac{R}{V}$, are equal to the cosines of the angles which V makes with the coordinates, and as

$$\frac{c}{\sqrt{c^2+c'^2+c''^2}}, \; \frac{c'}{\sqrt{c^2+c'^2+c''^2}}, \; \frac{c''}{\sqrt{c^2+c'^2+c''^2}},$$

are equal to the cosines of the angles which the axes to the invariable plane makes with the same coordinates, we have

$$\frac{cP+c'Q+c''R}{\sqrt{c^2+c'^2+c''^2}} = 0, \; \because \; cP+c'Q+c''R = 0. \text{ (See note to No. 1, page 7.)}$$

* Besides the advantages adverted to in the text, it may be observed, that our investigations are considerably simplified by the circumstance of two of the constant arbitrary quantities c, c', c'', vanishing when we make the plane of projection the invariable plane. It may also be remarked that this plane always subsists when the bodies composing the system are not solicited by any forces beside those of mutual attraction, and of forces directed towards fixed points; nor is the position of this plane affected in any respect when two or any number of bodies impinge on each other; for as we have before observed, these impacts dont cause any change in the expressions $Py - Qx$, &c.—on the equality of which to nothing depends, the principle of the conservation of areas, and the

moveable origin. We shall have by hypothesis,

$$d^2X = 0;\ d^2Y = 0;\ d^2Z = 0;$$

but we have by the nature of the centre of gravity, when the system is free

$$0 = \Sigma m.(d^2X + d^2x_{,}) - \Sigma m.P.dt^2;^*$$

$$0 = \Sigma m.(d^2Y + d^2y_{,}) - \Sigma m.Q.dt^2;$$

$$0 = \Sigma m.(d^2Z + d^2z_{,}) - \Sigma m.R.dt^2;$$

position of this invariable plane. The practical rule for the determination of this plane is given in the exposition, Du Systeme du Monde, page 207, the investigation of this rule will be given in No. 62, of the second book.

We shall see in No. 26, chapter 7, that the consideration of this plane is of great service in the determinations of the motions of a body of any figure whatever.

* $0 = \Sigma.m.d^2x - \Sigma.m.P.dt^2$; $0 = \Sigma.m.d^2y - \Sigma.m.Q.dt^2$; $0 = \Sigma.m.dz^2 - \Sigma.m.R.dt^2$; substituting in place of d^2x, d^2y, d^2z, we obtain the expression in the text; and since d^2X is by hypothesis equal to 0, the expression, $0 = \Sigma.m.(d^2x_{,} + d^2X - \Sigma.P.dt^2) = \Sigma.m. d^2x_{,} + d^2X.\ \Sigma.m. - \Sigma.m.P.dt^2 = \Sigma.m.dx_{,}^2 - \Sigma.m.Pdt_{,}^2$, &c.; in like manner, substituting for δx, δy, &c. in the equation (P), we obtain

$$0 = \Sigma.m. \left\{ \delta X + \delta x_{,} \right\} \frac{d^2x}{dt^2} - P. \Big\} + \Sigma.m.(\delta Y + \delta y_{,} \left\{ \frac{d^2y}{dt^2} - Q. \right\} + \&c. =$$

$$\Sigma.m\delta x_{,}. \left\{ \frac{d^2x}{dt^2} - P. \right\} + \Sigma.m. \left\{ \frac{d^2x}{dt^2} - P. \right\}.\ \delta X + \Sigma.m\,\delta y_{,}. \left\{ \frac{dy^2}{dt^2} - Q \right\}$$

$$\left\{ + \Sigma.m. \left\{ \frac{d^2y}{dt^2} - Q. \right\} \delta Y + \&c. \right.$$

but as by the nature of the centre of gravity

$\Sigma.m. \left\{ \frac{d^2x}{dt^2} - P. \right\}$, $\Sigma.m. \left\{ \frac{d^2y}{dt^2} - Q. \right\}$, &c. are respectively equal to nothing, and also $d^2x = d^2x_{,}$, $d^2y = d^2y_{,}$, &c. the preceding expression becomes

$$0 = \Sigma.m.\delta x_{,}. \left\{ \frac{d^2x_{,}}{dt^2} - P. \right\} + \Sigma.m.\delta y_{,}. \left\{ \frac{d^2y_{,}}{dt^2} - Q. \right\} \&c.$$

and by substituting $\delta X+\delta x_{,}$ $\delta Y+\delta y_{,}$ $\delta Z+\delta z_{,}$ &c. in place of δx, δy, δz, &c. the equation (P) of No. 18, will also become

$$0=\Sigma m.\delta x_{,}.\left\{\frac{d^2x_{,}}{dt^2}-P.\right\}+\Sigma m.\delta y_{,}\left\{\frac{d^2y_{,}}{dt^2}-Q.\right\}$$

$$+\Sigma m.\delta z_{,}.\left\{\frac{d^2z_{,}}{dt^2}-R\right\};$$

which is precisely of the same same form as the equation (P), if the forces P, Q, R, P', depend only on the coordinates $x_{,}$, $y_{,}$, $z_{,}$, $x'_{,}$, &c. Therefore by applying to it the preceding analysis, we can obtain the principle of the preservation of living forces and of areas, relative to the moveable origin of the coordinates.

If the system is not acted on by any extraneous forces, its centre of gravity will move uniformly in a rectilinear direction in space as we have seen in No. 20; therefore, by fixing the origin of the coordinates x, y and z at this centre these principles will always have place, X, Y, and Z, being in this case the coordinates of the centre of gravity, by the nature of this point, we shall have

$$0=\Sigma.mx\,;\ 0=\Sigma m.y\,;\ 0=\Sigma m.z\,;$$

consequently we have

$$\Sigma.m.\left\{\frac{x.dy-y.dx}{dt}\right\}=\frac{X.dY-Y.dX}{dt}.\,\Sigma.m+\Sigma m.\,\frac{x_{,}.dy_{,}-y_{,}.dx_{,}}{dt};^*$$

$$^*\ \Sigma.m.\left\{\frac{X+x_{,}).dY+dy_{,})-(Y+y_{,})(dX+dx_{,})}{dt}\right\}=\frac{\Sigma.m.X.dY+\Sigma mx_{,}dY+\Sigma.m.Xd.y_{,}+\Sigma.m.x_{,}dy_{,}}{dt}$$

$$-\frac{\Sigma.m.Y.dX-\Sigma.m.y_{,}dX-\Sigma m.Y.dx_{,}-\Sigma.my_{,}dx_{,}}{dt},$$ and as $\Sigma.mx_{,}$, $\Sigma.my_{,}$, $\Sigma m.dx_{,}$, $\Sigma.m.dy_{,}$ are respectively equal to nothing by the nature of the centre of gravity, the preceding

$$\Sigma.m. \frac{dx^2+dy^2+dz^2}{dt^2} = \frac{dX^2+dY^2+dZ^2}{dt^2}\Sigma.m.$$

$$+\Sigma.m. \left\{\frac{dx_{,}^2+dy_{,}^2+dz_{,}^2}{dt}\right\};*$$

thus the quantities which result from the preceding principles are com-

expression becomes equal to

$$\frac{X.dY-Y.dX.}{dt}\Sigma m. + \Sigma.m. \frac{x_{,}dy_{,}-y_{,}.dx_{,}}{dt} = c, \text{ \&c.}$$

* $\Sigma.m.dx^2 = \Sigma.m.dX^2 + 2\Sigma.m.dx_{,}.dX + \Sigma.m.dx_{,}^2$, and as $2dX.\ \Sigma.m.dx_{,} = 0$, we have $\Sigma.m.dx^2 = dX^2.\ \Sigma.m + \Sigma.m.dx_{,}^2$, ∵

$$\Sigma.m. \frac{dx^2+dy^2+dz^2}{dt^2} = \frac{dX^2+dY^2+dZ^2}{dt^2},\ \Sigma.m + \Sigma.m. \frac{dx_{,}^2+dy_{,}^2+dz_{,}^2}{dt^2} \text{ \&c.} = c+2\varphi.$$

If all the bodies were concentrated in their common centre of gravity, $x_{,}, y_{,}$; $dx_{,}, dy_{,}$; would vanish, therefore the second part of the first members of the preceding equation would vanish, and we would have $\frac{X.dY-Y.dX}{dt}\Sigma.m. = c$, $\frac{dX^2+dY^2+dZ^2}{dt^2}.\Sigma m = c+2\varphi$. Consequently, it appears from what has been established in this number, that when the bodies composing the system are not acted on by foreign forces, the quantities which are concerned in the principles of living forces, and of areas are composed of quantities which would have existed, if all the bodies of the system were concentrated in their centre of gravity; and 2dly, of quantities which would obtain if the centre of gravity quiesced, the former description of quantities are represented respectively by $\frac{dX^2+dY^2+dZ^2}{dt^2}\Sigma.m$, $\Sigma m.\frac{XdY-YdX}{dt}$, and the latter by $\Sigma.m. \frac{dx_{,}^2+dy_{,}^2+dz_{,}^2}{dt^2}$, $\Sigma m. \frac{x_{,}dy_{,}-y_{,}.dx_{,}}{dt}$, the first indicates what obtains in consequence of the progressive motion of the system, the second what arises from a rotatory motion, about an axis passing through the centre of gravity. (See No. 25.)

If the origin of the coordinates $x_{,}, y_{,}, z_{,}$ be transferred to a point of which the coordinates are A, B, C, the expression for the projection of area on the plane x, y, becomes $\Sigma m. \frac{(x-A)\ dy-(y-B).\ dx}{dt} = \Sigma.m\left\{\frac{xdy-y.dx}{dt}\right\} - \frac{A.\Sigma m.\ dy+B.\Sigma m\ dx}{dt}$, but as $\Sigma m.\ dy$, $\Sigma m.\ dx = dY\Sigma m,\ dX.\Sigma m$; $-\frac{A\Sigma m\ dy+B\Sigma m.dx}{dt}$ becomes$-\frac{A.dY+B.\ dX}{dt}.\Sigma.m.$

posed, 1st of quantities which would obtain, if all the bodies of the system were concentrated in the centre of gravity; 2dly, of quantities relative to the centre of gravity supposed immoveable; and since the first described quantities are constant, we may perceive the reason why the principles in question have place with respect to the centre of gravity. Therefore if we place the origin of the coordinates at this point, the equation Z, of the preceding number will always subsist; from which it follows that the plane which constantly passes through this centre, and with respect to which the function $\Sigma.m.\left\{\frac{x.dy-y.dx}{dt}\right\}$

∴ the projection of the area on the plane x, y, with respect to the new origin becomes equal to $c+\frac{B.\,dX-A.\,dY,}{dt}.\Sigma m$, and similar expressions may be derived for the projections on the planes x,z,y,z, From this it appears, that for all points in which $\frac{B.dX-A.dY}{dt}.\Sigma m=0$ the value of c will remain constantly the same, but it is evident that this equation will be satisfied, if the locus of the origin of the coordinates be either the right line described by the centre of gravity, or any line parallel to this line, consequently for all such lines the position of the invariable plane will remain constantly parallel to itself; however, though for all points of the *same* parallel the position of the invariable plane is constant, yet in the transit from one parallel to another the *direction* of this plane changes.

If the forces which act on the several points of the system are reducible to an unique resultant, by making the origin of the coordinates any point in this resultant, the quantities c, c', c'', and therefore the plane with respect to which the projection of the areas is a maximum, will vanish, if the locus of the origin of the coordinates be a line parallel to this resultant, the value of the projection of the area with respect to this line on the plane x, y, will be constant and equal to $\frac{B.dX-A.dY}{dt}.\Sigma m$ for c in this case vanishes, if the locus of the origin of the coordinates be a right line *diverging* from this resultant, the expression $\frac{Bd\,X-A\,dY}{dt}.\Sigma m$ is susceptible of perpetual increase. From these observations it appears that when the forces admit an unique resultant, that point with respect to which the value of $\sqrt{c^2+c'^2\,c''^2}$ is least of all is a point so circumstanced, that the axis or perpendicular to the plane of greatest projection passing through this point, is parallel to the direction of the unique resultant;

is a maximum, remains always parallel to itself, during the motion of the system, and that the same function relative to every other plane which is perpendicular to it, is equal to nothing.

The principles of the conservation of areas, and of living forces, may be reduced to certain relations between the coordinates of the mutual distances of the bodies composing the system. In fact, the origin of the coordinates x, y, z, being supposed always to be at the centre of gravity; the equations (Z) of the preceding number, may be made to assume the following form

$$c.\Sigma.m = \Sigma mm'.\left\{\frac{(x'-x).)dy'-dy)-(y'-y).(dx'-dx)}{dt}\right\};$$

$$c'.\Sigma m = \Sigma.mm'.\left\{\frac{(x'-x).(dz'-dz)-(z'-z).)dx'-dx)}{dt}\right\};$$

$$c''.\Sigma.m = \Sigma.mm'.\left\{\frac{(y'-y).dz'-dz)-(z'-z).(dy'-dy)}{dt}\right\}.^{*}$$

It may be remarked, that the second members of these equations

U

* This expression is proved to be true with respect to three bodies in the following manner and as the same reasoning is applicable to any number of bodies whatever, it may be considered as a general proof

$$\Sigma mm'\left\{\frac{(x'-x).(dy'-dy)-(y'-y).(dx'-dx)}{dt}\right\} = mm'x'\frac{dy'}{dt} - mm'x\frac{dy'}{dt} - mm'x'.\frac{dy}{dt}$$

$$+ mm'.x\frac{dy}{dt} - mm'y'.\frac{dx'}{dt} + mm'y'.\frac{dx}{dt} + mm'.y\frac{dx'}{dt} - mm'y.\frac{dx}{dt} + mm''.x''\frac{dy''}{dt}$$

$$- mm''.x.\frac{dy''}{dt} - mm''.x''.\frac{dy}{dt} + mm''.x\frac{dy}{dt} - mm''.y''.\frac{dx''}{dt} + mm''.y''.\frac{dx}{dt} + mm''.y.\frac{dx''}{dt}.$$

$$- mm''.y\frac{dx}{dt} + m''.m'.x''.\frac{dy''}{dt} - m''.m'.x'\frac{dy''}{dt} - m''m'x''\frac{dy'}{dt} + m'm''.x'.\frac{dy'}{dt}$$

$$- m''m'.y''.\frac{dx''}{dt} + m''m'.y''.\frac{dx'}{dt} + m''m'y'.\frac{dx''}{dt} - m'm''.y'.\frac{dx'}{dt}$$

multiplied by dt, express the sum of the projections of the elementary areas, traced by each line which joins the two bodies of the system, of which one is supposed to move round the other, considered as immoveable, each area being multiplied by the product of the two masses, which are connected by the right line.

and by concinnating it comes out equal to

$$mm'.\left\{\frac{x'dy'-y'dx'}{dt}\right\}+mm'\left\{\frac{xdy-y.dx}{dt}\right\}-mm'.\left\{\frac{x'dy-y'dx}{dt}\right\}$$

$$-mm'.\left\{\frac{xdy'-y.dx'}{dt}\right\}+mm''.\left\{\frac{x''dy''-y''.dx''}{dt}\right\}+mm''.\left\{\frac{xdy-y.dx}{dt}\right\}$$

$$-mm''.\left\{\frac{xdy''-y.dx''}{dt}\right\}-mm''.\left\{\frac{x''.dy-y''dx}{dt}\right\}+m''m'.\left\{\frac{x''dy''-y''.dx''}{dt}\right\}$$

$$+m'm''.\left\{\frac{x'dy'-y'.dx'}{dt}\right\}-m''m'.\left\{\frac{x'.dy''-y'dx''}{dt}\right\}-m''.m'.\left\{\frac{x''dy'-y''dx'}{dt}\right\}$$

and as in the case of three bodies

$$c=\Sigma m.\left\{\frac{xdy-y.dx}{dt}\right\}=m.\left\{\frac{xdy-y.dx}{dt}\right\}+m'.\left\{\frac{x'dy'-y'dx'}{dt}\right\}$$

$$+m''.\left\{\frac{x''.dy''-y''.dx''}{dt}\right\}\therefore c.\Sigma m=c(m+m'+m'')=m^2\left\{\frac{xdy-y.dx}{dt}\right\}$$

$$+m'.^2\left\{\frac{x'.dy'-y'.dx'}{dt}\right\}+m''.^2\left\{\frac{x''.dy''-y''.dx''}{dt}\right\}+mm'\left\{\frac{xdy-y.dx}{dt}\right\}$$

$$+mm''\left\{\frac{xdy-y.dx}{dt}\right\}+mm'\left\{\frac{x'dy'-y'.dx'}{dt}\right\}+m'm''.\left\{\frac{x'dy'-y'.dx'}{dt}\right\}$$

$$+mm''\left\{\frac{x''dy''-y''.dx''}{dt}\right\}+m'm''\left\{\frac{x''.dy''-y''.dx''}{dt}\right\}.$$

By the nature of the centre of gravity we have $mx+m'x'+m''x''=0$ and also $mdy+m'dy'+m''.dy''=0$ $\therefore$ their product vanishes *i, e,* $m^2xdy+m'^2x'dy'+m''^2x''.dy''+mm'x'.dy+mm''.x''.dy+mm'.xdy'+m'm''.x'dy'+m.m''.xdy''+m''m'.x'.dy''=0$ $\therefore$ we have $m^2xdy+m'^2x'.dy'+m''.^2x''.dy''=-mm'.x'dy-mm''.x''.dy-mm'.xdy'-m'm''.x''dy-mm''.xdy''.-m''.m'.x'dy'$, and by multiplying $my+m'y'+m''y'$, into $mdx+m'dx'+m''dx''$;$-m^2ydx$

By applying to the preceding equations, the analysis of No. 21, it will appear, that the plane passing constantly through any of the bodies of the system, and with respect to which the function

$$\Sigma.mm'.\left\{\frac{(x'-x).(dy'-dy)-(y'-y).(dx'-dx)}{dt}\right\}$$

is a *maximum*, remains always parallel to itself, during the motion of the system, and that this plane is parallel to the plane passing through

$-m'^2\ y'.dx'-m''^2\ y''.\ dx''=+\ mm'.y'.\ dx+mm''\ y''.\ dx+mm'y.dx'+m'm''y''dx'+mm''.y.dx''+m''.m'.y'.dx''$, $\therefore$ adding these quantities together we obtain

$$m^2\left\{\frac{xdy-ydx}{dt}\right\}+m'^2\left\{\frac{x'.dy'-y'.dx'}{dt}\right\}+m''^2\left\{\frac{x''dy''-y''.dx''}{dt}\right\}$$

$$=-mm'.\left\{\frac{x'.dy-y'.dx}{dt}\right\}-mm''\left\{\frac{x''.dy-y''.dx}{dt}\right\}-mm'.\left\{\frac{x.dy'-y.dx'}{dt}\right\}$$

$$-mm''\left\{\frac{xdy''-ydx''}{dt}\right\}-m''m'.\left\{\frac{x'dy''-y'.dx''}{dt}\right\}-m''m'.\left\{\frac{x''.dy'-y''.dx'}{dt}\right\}$$

$\therefore$ if in the expression for $c(m+m'+m'')$ we substitute in place of the sum of the functions which are multiplied by the squares of the masses, the quantities which are equivalent to them we shall obtain $c\ (m+m'+m'')=$

$$mm'\left\{\frac{xdy-y.dx.}{dt}\right\}+mm''.\left\{\frac{xdy-y.dx}{dt}\right\}+mm'.\left\{\frac{x'dy'-y'.dx'}{dt}\right\}$$

$$+m'm''.\left\{\frac{x'dy'-y'.dx'}{dt}\right\}+mm''\left\{\frac{x''dy''-y''\ dx''}{dt}\right\}+m'.m''.\left\{\frac{x''.dy''-y''\ dx''}{dt}\right\}$$

$$-mm'\left\{\frac{x'dy-y'.dx}{dt}\right\}-mm''\left\{\frac{x''.dy-y''dx}{dt}\right\}-mm'.\left\{\frac{xdy'-y\ dx'}{dt}\right\}$$

$$-m''m'.\left\{\frac{x''\ dy'-y''dx'}{dt}\right\}-m''m.\left\{\frac{xdy''-ydx''}{dt}\right\}-m''.m'\left\{\frac{x'.dy''-y'.dx''}{dt}\right\}$$

which is equal to to the expression which has been given above for the value of $\Sigma m.m'.$ $\left\{\frac{(x'-x)\ dy'-dy)-y'-y\ (dx'-dx}{dt}\right\}$

the centre of gravity, and relatively to which, the function $\Sigma.m.\ \frac{(x.dy-y.dx)}{dt}$ is a *maximum*. It will also appear that the second members of the preceding equations vanish with respect to all planes passing through the same body, and perpendicular to the plane in question.†

The equation (Q) of No. 19, can be made to assume the form*

$$\Sigma.mm'.\left\{\frac{(dx'-dx)^2+(dy'-dy)^2+(dz'-dz)^2}{dt}\right. = \text{const.} - 2\Sigma.m.$$

$\Sigma.fmm'.\ Fdf$; this equation respects solely the coordinates of the mu-

* When there are but three bodies $\Sigma.m.dx^2 = mdx^2 + m'dx'^2 + m''.dx''^2$, but by the nature of the centre of gravity we have $mdx + m'dx' + m''.dx'' = 0$ and $\therefore m^2dx^2 + m'^2.dx'^2 + m''^2.dx''^2 + 2m.m'.dx.dx' + 2mm''.dx.dx'' + 2m'm''.dx'.dx'' = 0$, and multiplying $\Sigma.m.dx^2$ by Σm, we obtain, $m^2dx^2 + m'^2.dx'^2 + m''^2.dx''^2 + mm'dx'^2 + m'm''.dx'^2 + m'm.dx^2 + m''.m\,dx^2 + mm''.dx''^2 + m'm''.dx''^2$, if we substract the previous equation from this we get, $mm'.dx'^2 + m'm''.dx'^2 + m'm.dx^2 + m''.m.dx^2 + mm''.dx''^2 + m'm''.dx''^2 - 2mm'.dx\,dx' - 2mm''.dx.dx'' - 2m'.m''.dx'.dx'' = mm'.(dx'-dx)^2 + m'm''(dx''-dx')^2 + mm''(dx''-dx)^2 = \Sigma.mm'.(dx'-dx)^2 = \Sigma.m.(\Sigma m.(dx^2)$, and in like manner we derive $\Sigma.mm'(dy'-dy)^2 = \Sigma m.(\Sigma m.dy^2)$, $\Sigma.mm'.(dz'-dz)^2 = \Sigma m.(\Sigma m.dz^2)$, $\therefore$ we have $\Sigma mm'\left\{\frac{dx'-dx)^2+(dy'-dy)^2+(dz'-dz^2}{dt^2}\right\} = c.\Sigma m + \Sigma.m.(2.\Sigma m.fm.(P.dx+Qdx+Qdy) = \text{const.} - 2\,\Sigma m.\,\Sigma.fmm'fdf$, (substituting $-\Sigma f\,mm'.fdf$ in place of $\Sigma.fm.(Pdx+Q.dy+Rdz)$. (See No. 19, page 113.)

† When the origin of the coordinates is in the centre of gravity of the system, the quantities $c\ c'\ c''$, are constant and $\therefore$ the position of the plane, with respect to which the function $\Sigma m.\left\{\frac{xdy-y\,dx}{dt}\right\}$ is a maximum, remains the same during the motion of the system, $\therefore$ as the quantity Σm, would occur both in the numerator and denominator of the expression for the cosines of the angles which the plane with respect to which the function $\Sigma.m.m'\left\{\frac{(x'-x(\ (dy'-dy-(y'-y)\ (dx'-dx)}{dt}\right\}$ is a maximum, makes with the three coordinate planes, it is evident that the values of the angles which the invariable plane makes with three coordinate planes, is the same in both cases, from these considerations it appears that the invariable plane may be determined at each instant by means of the *relative* velocities of the system, without a knowledge of their *absolute* velocities in space. (See Notes to page 139.)

tual distances of the bodies, in which the first member expresses the sum of the squares of the relative velocities of the system about each other, considering them two by two, and supposing at the same time that one of them is immoveable, each square being multiplied by the product of the two masses which are considered.

23. If we resume the equation (R) of No. 19, and differentiate it with respect to the characteristic δ, we shall have

$$\Sigma.m\, v.\, \delta v = \Sigma m.\, (P.\delta x + Q.\delta y + R\delta z)\,;$$

and the equation (P) of No. 18, will then become

$$0 = \Sigma.m. \left\{ \delta x.\, d.\frac{dx}{dt} + \delta y.\, d.\,\frac{dy}{dt} + \delta z.\, d.\,\frac{dz}{dt} \right\} - \Sigma.m.dt.v\delta v.$$

Denoting by ds, ds' &c. the elements of the curves described by m, m' &c.; we shall have

$$vdt = ds\,;\;\; v'dt = ds'\,;\;\text{\&c.}$$

$$ds = \sqrt{dx^2 + dy^2 + dz^2}\,;\;\text{\&c.}$$

from which we can obtain, by following the same process as in the analysis of No. 8,

$$\Sigma.m.\delta.\,(vds) = \Sigma.m.\, d.\left(\frac{dx.\,\delta x + dy.\,\delta y + dz.\,\delta z}{dt}\right).$$

By integrating with respect to the differential characteristic d, and making the integrals extend to the entire curves described by the bodies m,m', &c. we shall have

$$\Sigma.\delta.\textstyle\int mvds = \text{const.} + \Sigma.m. \left(\frac{dx.\delta x + dy.\delta y + dz.\,\delta z.}{dt}\right);$$

in this equation the variations δx,δy,δz, &c and also that part of its second member, which is constant, 'refer to the extreme points of the curves described by m,m', &c.

From which it appears that when these points are invariable, we shall have

$$0 = \Sigma.\delta.\int mvds\,;^*$$

which indicates that the function $\Sigma.\int mvds$ is a minimum. It is in this, that the principle of the least action, in the motion of a system of bodies, consists; a principle, which, as we have seen, is only a mathematical result of the primitive laws of the equilibrium and motion of bodies. It is also apparent, that this principle combined with the principle of living forces, gives the equation (P) of No. 18, which contains all that is necessary for the the determination of the motions of the system. Finally, it appears from No. 22, that this principle obtains, even when the origin of the coordinates is in motion; provided that the motion is uniform, its direction rectilinear and the system entirely free.†

* By substituting for ds, ds' their values $v.dt$, $v'dt$, the expression $\Sigma.\int v.ds$ will become $\Sigma.\int mv.^2 dt$, and as $\int mv.^2 dt$ is the sum of the living forces of the body m during the motion; $\Sigma.\int mv.^2 dt$ will express the sum of the living forces of *all* the bodies of the system during the same time; therefore the principle of the least action, in fact indicates, that the sum of the living forces of the system, during its transit from one given position to another, is a minimum, and when the bodies are not actuated by any accelerating forces, the velocities v, v', and the sum of the living forces at each instant, are constant, (see No. 18, page 114.) $\therefore$ $\Sigma.\int mv.^2 dt = \Sigma mv.^2 \int dt$, and the sum of the living forces for any interval of time is proportional to this time, consequently in this case the system passes from one position to another in the shortest time. Since therefore the expression $\Sigma\int v.ds$ is the same as $\Sigma.\int mv^2 dt$ La Grange proposed to alter the denomination of the principle of least action, and to term it the principle of the greatest or least living force, for by contemplating in this manner, it is equally applicable to the states of equilibrium and motion, since it has been demonstrated in the notes page 119, that in case of equilibrium the vis viva is either a maximum or a minimum; from what precedes it appears that, as La Place observes in his Systeme du Monde, the true economy of nature is that of the living force, and it is this economy which we should always have in view in the construction of machines, which are always more perfect according as less living force is consumed in producing a given effect.

† With respect to the extent of the different principles which are treated of in this fifth chapter, it is important to remark, that the principles of the conservation of the motion of the centre of gravity, and of the conservation of areas subsist, even when by the mutual action of the bodies, they undergo sudden changes in their motions, which renders these principles extremely useful in several circumstances, but the principles of the conservation

of the vis viva, and of the least action, require that the variations of the motion of the system, be made by imperceptible gradations.

The principle of the least action differs from the other principles in this, that the other principles are the *real integrals* of the differential equations of the motion of bodies, whereas this of the least action is only a singular combination of these equations, in fact it being established that $\Sigma.\int mv.ds$ is a minimum by seeking by the known rules, the conditions which render it such, and making use of the general equation of the conservation of living forces, we should find all the equations which are necessary to determine the motion of each body.

The principle established in this number was first *assumed* as a metaphysical truth, and was applied by Maupertius to the discovery of the laws of reflection and refraction, however it ought not to be deemed a *final* cause, for we can infer analogous results from all relations mathematically possible between the force and the velocity, provided that we substitute in this principle, in place of the velocity, that *function* of the velocity by which the force is expressed, (see next chapter, page 154,) and so far from having been the origin of the laws of motion, it has not even contributed to their discovery, without which we should be still debating what was to be understood by the least action of nature.

CHAPTER VI.

Of the laws of motion of a system of bodies, in all the relations mathematically possible between the force and the velocity.

24. It has been already remarked in No. 5, that there are an infinite number of ways of expressing the relation between force and velocity, which do not imply a contradiction. The simplest of all these relations is that of the force proportional to the velocity, which as we have observed, is the law of nature. It is from this law that we have derived, in the preceding chapter, the differential equations of the motion of a system of bodies; but it is easy to apply the same analysis, to all relations mathematically possible, which may exist, between the force and the velocity, and thus to exhibit under a new point of view the general principles of motion. For this purpose, let F represent the force and v the velocity, we have $F=\varphi(v)$; $\varphi(v)$ being any function whatever of v; let $\varphi'(v)$ denote the difference of $\varphi(v)$ divided by dv. The denominations of the preceding numbers always remaining, the body m will be solicited parallel to the axis of x by the force $\varphi(v).\frac{dx}{ds}$. *

In the following instant, this force will become $\varphi(v).\frac{dx}{ds}+d.\left\{\varphi(v).\frac{dx}{ds}\right\}$

* ds being the differential of the line described by the body, the cosine of the angle which the direction of the motion makes with the axis of x is equal to $\frac{dx}{ds}$, $\therefore$ the force F or $\varphi(v)$ resolved in the direction of the axis of $x=\varphi(v).\frac{dx}{ds}$.

or $\varphi(v).\ \frac{dx}{ds} + d.\left(\frac{\varphi(v).}{v}\ .\ \frac{dx}{dt}\right)$, because $\frac{ds}{dt} = v$. Moreover, P, Q, R, being the forces which solicit the body m parallel to the axes of the co-ordinates; the system will, by No. 18, be in equilibrio in consequence of these forces, and of the differentials,

$$d.\left\{\frac{dx}{dt}.\frac{\varphi(v)}{v}\right\},\ d.\left\{\frac{dy}{dt}.\ \frac{\varphi\ (v)}{v}\right\},\ d.\left\{\frac{dz}{dt}.\frac{\varphi(v)}{v}\right\},$$

taken with a contrary sign; therefore in place of the equation (P) of the same number we shall have the following:

$$0=\Sigma.m.\left\{\delta x.\ d.\left\{\frac{dx}{dt}.\frac{\varphi(v)}{v} - Pdt\right\} + \delta y.\ d.\left\{\frac{dy}{dt}.\frac{\varphi.(v)}{v}\right.\right.$$

$$\left.\left. - Q.dt\right\} + \delta z.\ d.\left\{\frac{dz}{dt}.\frac{\varphi(v)}{v} - Rdt\right\}\right\};\ (S)$$

which only differs from it in this respect, that $\frac{dx}{dt}, \frac{dy}{dt}, \frac{dz}{dt}$, are multiplied by the function $\frac{\varphi(v)}{v}$, which in the case of the force proportional to the velocity, may be assumed equal to unity. However this difference renders the solution of the problems of mechanics very difficult. Notwithstanding, we can obtain from the equation (S), principles analogous to those of the conservation of living forces, of areas, and of the centre of gravity.

By changing δx into dx, δy into dy, δz into dz, &c., we shall have

$$\Sigma.m.\left\{\delta x.d.\left\{\frac{dx}{dt}.\frac{\varphi(v)}{v}\right\} + \delta y.\ d.\left\{\frac{dy}{dt}.\frac{\varphi(v)}{v}\right\} + \delta z.\ d.\left\{\frac{dz}{dt}.\frac{\varphi(v)}{v}\right\}\right\} =$$

$$\Sigma.m.\ v.\ dv.\ dt.\ \varphi'\ (v);\ ^*$$

X

* Substituting ds in place of $v.dt$, the expression

$$\Sigma.m.\left\{dx.d.\left\{\frac{dx}{dt}.\frac{\varphi\ (v)}{v}\right\} + dy.\ d.\left\{\frac{dy}{dt}.\frac{\varphi\ (v)}{v}\right\} + dz.d.\left\{\frac{dz}{dt}.\frac{\varphi\ (v)}{v}\right\}\right.$$

and consequently

$$\Sigma.\int mv.dv.\varphi'(v)=\text{const.}+\Sigma.\int m.\ (P.dx+Q.dy+R.dz),$$

If we suppose that $\Sigma m.(P.dx+Q.dy+R.dz)$ is an exact differential equal to $d\lambda$, we shall have

$$\Sigma.\int mv.dv.\varphi'(v) = \text{const.} + \lambda\,;\ (T)$$

which equation is analogous to the equation (R) of No. 19, into which it is changed in the case of the law of nature, or of $\varphi'(v)=1$. Therefore, the principle of the conservation of living forces obtains in all laws mathematically possible between force and velocity, provided that we understand by the living force of a body, the product of its mass by double the integral of its velocity, multiplied by the differential of the function of the velocity which expresses the force.

If in the equation (S), we make $\delta x'=\delta x+\delta x'_{,}$, $\delta y'=\delta y+\delta y'_{,}$, $\delta z'=\delta z+\delta z'_{,}$, $\delta x''=\delta x+\delta x''_{,}$; &c. we shall have by putting the coefficients of δx, δy, δz, respectively equal to nothing

$$0=\Sigma.m.\left\{d.\left(\frac{dx}{dt}.\frac{\varphi(v)}{v}\right)-Pdt\right\},\ 0=\Sigma.m.\left\{d.\left(\frac{dy}{dt}.\frac{\varphi(v)}{v}\right)-Qdt\right\},$$

$$0=\Sigma m.\left\{d.\left(\frac{dz}{dt}.\frac{\varphi(v)}{v}\right)-Rdt\right\},$$

becomes

$$\Sigma.m.\left\{dx.d.\left\{\frac{dx}{ds}.\varphi(v)\right\}+dy.d.\left\{\frac{dy}{ds}.\varphi(v)\right\}+dz.d.\left\{\frac{dz}{ds}.\varphi(v)\right\}\right\}$$

and by taking the differential it becomes.

$$\Sigma.m.\left\{\frac{dx.d^2x+dy.d^2y+dz.d^2z}{ds}\right\}.\varphi(v)-\Sigma.m.\left\{\frac{dx^2+dy^2+dz^2}{ds^2}\right\}.d^2s.\varphi(v)+$$

$$\Sigma.m.\left\{\frac{dx^2+dy^2+dz^2}{ds}\right\}.d.\varphi(v)=\Sigma.m.d^2s.\varphi(v)-\Sigma.m.d^2s.\varphi(v)+\Sigma.m.ds.d.\varphi(v)$$

and this last quantity is equal by substitution to $\Sigma.m.\ v.dt.dv.\varphi'(v)$.

These three equations are analogous to those of No. 20, from which we have inferred, the conservation of the motion of the centre of gravity, in the case of nature, when the system is not subjected to any forces but those of the mutual action and attraction of the bodies of the system. In this case $\Sigma.m.P$, $\Sigma.m.Q$, $\Sigma.m.R$, vanish, and we have

$$\text{const.} = \Sigma.m.\frac{dx}{dt}.\frac{\varphi(v)}{v};\ \text{const.} = \Sigma m.\frac{dy}{dt}.\frac{\varphi(v)}{v};$$

$$\text{const.} = \Sigma m.\frac{dz}{dt}.\frac{\varphi(v)}{v};\ m.\frac{dx}{dt}.\frac{\varphi(v)}{v}\ \text{is} = m.\varphi(v).\frac{dx}{ds}.$$

and this last quantity is the finite force of the body, resolved parallel to to the axis of x; the force of a body being the product of its mass by the function of the velocity which expresses the force. Therefore in this case the sum of the finite forces of the system, resolved parallel to any axis, is constant whatever may be the relation between the force and the velocity, and what distinguishes the state of motion from that of repose, is, that in this last state, the same sum vanishes. These results are common to all laws mathematically possible between the force and the velocity; but it is only in the law of nature, that the centre of gravity moves with an uniform motion in a rectilinear direction. *

Again let us make in the equation (S)

$$\delta x' = \frac{y'.\delta x}{y} + \delta x'_{,};\ \delta x'' = \frac{y''.\delta x}{y} + \delta x''_{,}\ \ \&c.$$

$$\delta y = -\frac{xdx}{y} + \delta y_{,}\ \delta y' = -\frac{x'.\delta x}{y} + \delta y'_{,};\ \&c.$$

the variation δx will disappear from the variations of the mutual distances

X 2

* It is evident that the centre of gravity does not move uniformly in a right line when P, Q, R, vanish, except when $\frac{\varphi(v)}{v}$ is equal to unity, for it is only in this case that we could prove from the expression, const. $= \Sigma.m.\frac{dx}{dt}.\frac{\varphi v}{v}$, that dX the differential of the co-ordinate of the centre of gravity is constant.

f, f', &c. of the bodies composing the system, and of the forces which depend on these quantities. If the system is not affected by extraneous obstacles, we shall have, by putting the coefficient of δx equal to nothing

$$0 = \Sigma.m. \left\{ x.d.\left(\frac{dy}{dt}.\frac{\phi(v)}{v}\right) - y.\,d.\left(\frac{dx}{dt}.\frac{\phi(v)}{v}\right) \right\} +$$

$\Sigma m.(Py - Q.x)dt$, from which we deduce by integrating,

$$c = \Sigma.m.\left(\frac{xdy - ydx}{dt}\right).\frac{\phi(v)}{v} + \Sigma.\int m\,(Py - Qx).dt, *$$

we shall have in like manner

$$c' = \Sigma.m.\left(\frac{xdz - zdx}{dt}\right).\frac{\phi(v)}{v} + \Sigma.\int m\,(Pz - Rx).dt;$$

$$c'' = \Sigma.m.\left(\frac{ydz - zdy}{dt}\right).\frac{\phi(v)}{v} + \Sigma\int m\,(Qz - Ry).dt;$$

c, c', c'', being constant arbitrary quantities.

If the system is only subjected to the mutual action of its component parts, we have, by No. 21, $\Sigma m.\ (Py - Qx) = 0$; $\Sigma m.\ (Pz - Rx) = 0$ $\Sigma m.\ (Qz - Ry) = 0$; also $m\left\{x\,\frac{dy}{dt} - y.\frac{dx}{dt}\right\}.\frac{\phi(v)}{v}$ is the moment of the finite force by which the body is actuated, resolved parallel to the plane of x and y, which tends to make the system turn about the axis of z; therefore the finite integral $\Sigma.m.\left\{\frac{xdy - ydx}{dt}\right\}.\frac{\phi(v)}{v}$ is equal to the sum of the moments of all the finite forces of the bodies of the system

* The integral of this expression is equal to $\Sigma.m \left\{ x.\frac{dy}{dt}.\frac{\phi(v)}{v} - \int dx.\left(\frac{dy}{dt}.\frac{\phi(v)}{v}\right)\right.$

$$\left. - y.\frac{dx}{dt}.\frac{\phi(v)}{v} + \int\left(\frac{dy.dx}{dt}.\frac{\phi(v)}{v}\right)\right\} = \Sigma.m.\frac{xdy - y.dx}{dt}.\frac{\phi(v)}{v}.$$

to make it revolve round the same axis; consequently this sum is constant. It vanishes in the case of equilibrium; therefore, there is the same difference between these two states as there is relatively to the sum of the forces parallel to any axis. In the law of nature, this property indicates that the sum of the areas described about a fixed point, by the projections of the radii vectores of the bodies is constant in a given time, but this constancy of the areas described does not obtain in any other law.*

By differentiating with respect to the characteristic δ, the function $\Sigma.\int m.\varphi(v).ds$;

we shall obtain

$$\delta.\Sigma.\int m.\varphi(v)\,ds = \Sigma.\int m.\varphi(v).\delta.ds + \Sigma.\int m.\delta v.\varphi'(v).ds;$$

but we have

$$\delta ds = \frac{dx.\delta dx + dy.\delta dy + dz.\delta dz}{ds} = \frac{1}{v}\left\{\frac{dx}{dt}.\,d.\delta x + \frac{dy}{dt}.d.\,\delta y + \frac{dz}{dt}.\,d.\,\delta z\right\};$$

therefore by partial integration we shall obtain

$$\delta.\Sigma.\int m.\varphi(v).ds = \Sigma.\,\frac{m\varphi(v)}{v}\left\{\frac{dx}{dt}.\delta x + \frac{dy}{dt}.\delta y + \frac{dz}{dt}.\delta z\right\}$$

$$-\Sigma.\int m\left\{\delta x.d.\left(\frac{dx}{dt}.\frac{\varphi(v)}{v}\right) + \delta y.d.\left(\frac{dy}{dt}.\frac{\varphi(v)}{v}\right) + \delta z.d.\left(\frac{dz}{dt}.\frac{\varphi(v)}{v}\right)\right\}$$

$$+\Sigma.\int m.\delta v.\varphi'(v).ds.$$

The extreme points of the curves described by the bodies of the system

* As the factor $\frac{\varphi(v)}{v}$ is variable in every other case beside that of nature, it follows that though the quantity $\Sigma.m.\left\{\frac{x\,dy - y\,dx}{dt}\right\}.\frac{\varphi(v)}{v}$ is constant and equal to c, still that part of it $\Sigma.m.\left\{\frac{xdy - y.dx}{dt}\right\}$ is not constant.

being supposed fixed, the term which is not affected by the sign $\int$ must disappear in this equation; therefore we shall have in consequence of the equation (S),

$$\delta.\,\Sigma.\int m.\varphi(v).ds=\Sigma.\int m.\delta v.\varphi'(v).ds-\Sigma.\int mdt(P\delta x+Q.\delta y+R.\delta z)$$

but the equation (T) differentiated with respect to δ gives

$$\Sigma.\int m.\delta v.\varphi'(v).ds=\Sigma.\int mdt\,(P\delta x+Q.\delta y+R.\delta z)\;;$$

therefore we have

$$0=\delta.\,\Sigma.\int m.\varphi(v).ds.$$

This equation corresponds to the principle of the least action in the law of nature. $m.\varphi(v)$ is the entire force of the body m, thus the principle comes to this, that the sum of the integrals of the finite forces of the bodies of the system, respectively multiplied by the elements of their directions, is a minimum, presented in this manner, it answers to all laws mathematically possible between the force and velocity. In the state of equilibrium the sum of the forces multiplied by the elements of their directions vanishes, in consequence of the principle of virtual velocities, what therefore in this respect distinguishes the state of equilibrium, from that of motion is that the same differential function, which in the state of equilibrium vanishes, gives in a state of motion by its integration a minimum.

CHAPTER VII.

Of the motions of a solid body of any figure whatever.

25. The differential equations of the motions of translation and rotation of a solid body, may be easily deduced from those which have been given in the fifth chapter; but from their importance in the theory of the system of the world we are induced to develope them in detail.

Let us suppose a solid body of which all the parts are solicited by any forces whatever. Let x, y, z, represent the orthogonal coordinates of its centre of gravity, and let $x+x', y+y', z+z'$, be the coordinates of any molecule dm of the body, then x', y', z', will be the coordinates of this molecule with respect to the centre of gravity of the body. Moreover, let P, Q, R, be the forces which solicit the molecule parallel to the axes of x, of y, and of z,. The forces destroyed at each instant in the molecule, parallel to these axes, will be by No. 18,

$$-\left\{\frac{d^2x+d^2x'}{dt}\right\}.\,dm+P.dt.\,dm;$$

$$-\left\{\frac{d^2y+d^2y'}{dt}\right\}.\,dm+Q.dt.\,dm;$$

$$-\left\{\frac{d^2z+d^2z'}{dt}\right\}.\,dm+R.dt.dm;$$

(the element dt of the time being considered as constant.)

Therefore it follows that all the molecules actuated by similar forces should mutually constitute an equilibrium. We have seen in No. 15, that for this purpose, it is necessary that the sum of the forces parallel to the same axes, should vanish which gives the three following equations

$$S.\left\{\frac{d^2x+d^2x'}{dt^2}\right\}.dm = S.Pdm;$$

$$S.\left\{\frac{d^2y+d^2y'}{dt^2}\right\}.dm = S.Qdm;$$

$$S.\left\{\frac{d^2z+d^2z'}{dt^2}\right\}.dm = S.Rdm;$$

the letter S being here a sign of integration relative to the moelcule dm, which we should extend to the entire mass of the body. The variables x, y, z, are the same for all the molecules, therefore we can bring them from under the sign S; thus, denoting the mass of the body by m, we shall have

$$S.\frac{d^2x}{dt^2}.dm = m.\frac{d^2x}{dt^2}; \; S.\frac{d^2y}{dt^2}.dm = m.\frac{d^2y}{dt^2}; \; S.\frac{d^2z}{dt^2}.dm = m.\frac{d^2z}{dt^2}.$$

Moreover by the nature of the centre of gravity, we have,

$$S.x'.dm = 0; \; S.y'.dm = 0; \; Sz'.dm = 0\,*$$

therefore

$$S.\frac{d^2x'}{dt^2}.dm = 0; \; S.\frac{d^2y'}{dt^2}.dm = 0; \; S.\frac{d^2z'}{dt^2}.dm = 0;$$

* $S.\frac{d^2x}{dt^2}.dm = \frac{d^2x}{dt^2}.Sdm = \frac{d^2x}{dt^2}.m$ &c.

$S.x'.dm = 0$ $S.y'.dm = 0$ because x', y', &c. are the coordinates of the body referred to the centre of gravity, see No. 15, page 91.

consequently we shall have

$$\left.\begin{aligned} m.\frac{d^2x}{dt^2}&=S.Pdm\,; \\ m.\frac{d^2y}{dt^2}&=S.Qdm\,; \\ m.\frac{d^2z}{dt^2}&=S.Rdm\,; \end{aligned}\right\}; \qquad (A)$$

these three equations determine the motion of the centre of gravity of the body ; they correspond to the equations of No. 20, which relate to the motion of the centre of gravity of a system of bodies.

We have seen in No. 15, that for the equilibrium of a solid body the sum of the forces parallel to the axis of x, multiplied by their distances from the axis of z, minus the sum of the forces parallel to the axis of y, multiplied by their distances from the axis of z, should be equal to nothing ; thus we shall have

$$S.\left\{(x+x').\left(\frac{d^2y+d^2y'}{dt^2}\right)-(y+y').\left(\frac{d^2x+d^2x'}{dt^2}\right)\right\}.dm$$

$$=S.\{(x+x')\,Q-(y+y').\,P.\}.dm\,; \qquad (1\cdot)$$

but we have

$$S.\,(x.d^2y-y.d^2x).\,dm=m.(x.d^2y-y.d^2x)\,;$$

in like manner we have

$$S.\,(Qx-Py).\,dm=x.\int Qdm-y.\int Pdm$$

finally we have

$$S.\,(x'.d^2y+x.d^2y'-y'.d^2x-y.d^2x').\,dm=d^2y.\,S.x'dm-d^2x.\,Sy'dm$$

$$+x.S.d^2y'.dm-y.\ S.d^2x'.dm\ ;\ ^*$$

by the nature of the centre of gravity, each of the terms of the second member of this equation vanishes; therefore the equation (1) will become in consequence of the equations A,

$$S.\left\{\frac{x'.d^2y'-y'.d^2x'}{dt^2}\right\}.dm=S.\ (Qx'-Py').dm\ ;$$

* By performing the multiplication,

$$S.\left\{(x+x').\frac{(d^2y+d^2y')}{dt^2}-(y+y').\frac{(d^2x+d^2x')}{dt^2}\right\}.dm$$

$$=S.\left\{(x+x').\ Q-(y+y').\ P\right\}.dm\ ;=S.\left\{\frac{x d^2y-y.d^2x}{dt^2}\right\}.dm+$$

$$S.\left\{\frac{x'.d^2y+xd^2y'-y'.d^2x-y.d^2x'}{dt^2}\right\}.dm+S.\left\{\frac{x'.d^2y'-y'.d^2x'}{dt^2}\right\}.dm=$$

$.(Qx-Py).dm+S.(Q.x'-Py').dm$, $\therefore$ by substituting for

$$S.\frac{d^2y}{dt^2}.dm=\frac{d^2y}{dt^2}.m,\quad S.\frac{d^2x}{dt^2}.dm=\frac{d^2x}{dt^2}.m$$

the expressions $S.P.dm$, $S.Q.dm$, to which they are respectively equal as appears from the equations (A), and freeing the quantities d^2y, d^2x, x, y, from the sign S, the preceding equation will be changed into the following

$$x.\ S.Q.\ dm-y.\ SP.\ dm+\frac{d^2y}{dt^2}.\ Sx'.dm+x.\ S.\frac{d^2y'}{dt^2}.dm-\frac{d^2x}{dt^2}.\ Sy'.dm$$

$$-y.S.\frac{d^2x'}{dt^2}.dm+S\left\{\frac{x'd^2y'-y'.d^2x'}{dt^2}\right\}.\ dm=x.\ S.\ Q.\ dm-y.\ S.P.dm+$$

$S\ (Q.x'-Py').\ dm$, and omitting quantities which destroy each other, and also those which by the nature of the centre of gravity, vanish, we will obtain the equation

$$S.\left\{\frac{x'd^2y'-y'.d^2x'}{dt^2}\right\}.dm=S.\ (Qx'-Py').dm\ ;$$

this equation involves the principle of the conservation of areas, for if the forces which solicit the molecules arise from their mutual action, and from the action of forces directed towards fixed points, $S(Qx'-Py')\ dm=0$.

this equation integrated with respect to the time, gives

$$S.\left\{\frac{x'dy'-y'.dx'}{dt}\right\}.\,dm = S.\textstyle\int(Qx'-Py').\,dt.\,dm\,;$$

the sign of integration $\int$ being relative to the time t.

From what precedes it is easy to infer that if we make

$$S.\textstyle\int(Q.x'-Py').\,dt.\,dm=N\,;$$

$$S.\textstyle\int(Rx'-Pz').\,dt.\,dm=N'\,;$$

$$S.\textstyle\int(Ry'-Q.z').\,dt.\,dm=N''\,;$$

we shall obtain the three following equations

$$\left.\begin{array}{l} S.\left\{\dfrac{x'.dy'-y'.dx'}{dt}\right\}.dm=N\,; \\ S.\left\{\dfrac{x'dz'-z'.dx'}{dt}\right\}.dm=N'\,; \\ S.\left\{\dfrac{y'dz'-z'dy'}{dt}\right\}.dm=N''\,; \end{array}\right\}; \quad (B)$$

these three equations contain the principle of the conservation of areas; they are sufficient to determine * the motion of rotation of a body about its centre of gravity; combined with the equations (A), they completely determine the motions of translation and rotation of a body.

* In our investigations relative to the invariable plane in the 5th chapter, we have seen that when a body or system of bodies are not solicited by any extraneous forces, the motion may be distinguished into two others, of which one is progressive and the same for all points, the other is rotatory about a point in the body or system, the first determined by the equation (A), and the second by the equation(B); by thus distinguishing the motion into two others, we can represent with more clearness the motion of a solid body in space,for these two motions are entirely independent of each other, as is evident from the inspection of the equations which indicate them, so that the equations (A) may vanish, while the equations (B) have a finite

If the body is constrained to turn about a fixed point; it follows from No. 15, that the equations (B) are sufficient for this purpose; but then it is necessary to fix the origin of the coordinates x', y', z', at this point.*

value or vice versa. The centre of the rotatory motion may be any point whatever, however when we would wish to determine these two kind of motions it is advantageous to assume for this point, the centre of gravity of the body, because in most cases its motion may be determined directly, and independently of that of the other points of the body.

Dividing the equations (A) by m, we may perceive by a comparison of the resulting expressions, with the equations of the motion of a material point, which have been given in No. 7, page 31, that the motion of the centre of gravity is the same, as if the entire mass of the body was concentrated in it, and the forces of all the points and in their respective directions were applied to it; this rectilineal motion is common to all the points of the body, and the same as the motion of *translation.*

* If a solid body is acted on by forces which act *instantaneously,* in general it acquires the two kinds of motions, of translation and of rotation; which are respectively determined by the equations (A) and (B); when the equations (A) vanish, the forces are reducible to two parallel forces, equal, and acting in opposite directions, when the rotatory motion vanishes the instantaneous forces have an unique resultant passing through the centre of gravity, see notes to page 143, when the molecules of the body are solicited by accelerating forces, their action in general will alter the two motions which have been produced by initial impulse, however if the resultant of the accelerating forces passes through the centre of gravity of the body, the rotatory motion will not be affected by the action of these forces, this is the case of a sphere acted on by forces which vary as the distance, or in the inverse square of the distance from the molecules, see Newton prin. Vol. 1. Section 12, or Book 2, No. 12, of this work, consequently if the planets were spherical bodies, the motive force arising from the mutual action of the sun and planets would pass through the centre of gravity, and the rotatory motion would not be affected, but the direction of this force does not always pass accurately through this centre, in consequence of the oblateness of the planets, therefore the axis of rotation does not remain accurately parallel to itself, however the *velocity* of rotation is not sensibly affected, see Systeme du Monde, Chapter 14, Book 4, and Book 5, No. 7 and 8. It is in this slight oscillation of the axis of the earth arising principally from the attractions of the sun and moon, that the phenomena of the precession of the equinoxes and of the nutation of the earths axis consist. (See Nos. 28, 29.

If the body be moved in consequence of initial impulses, the directions of the forces, their intensities and points of application been given, we might by the formula of No. 21, determine the principal moment of the forces with respect to the centre of gravity, and the direction of the plane to which this moment is referred, which would completely determine the moment of rotation about the centre of gravity, and it is evident that the same data would be sufficient to determine the rectilinear motion of the centre of gravity, and consequently

26. Let us attentively consider these equations, the origin of the coordinates being supposed fixed at any point, the same or different from the centre of gravity. Let us refer the position of each molecule to three axes perpendicular to each other, fixed in the body, but moveable in space. Let θ be the inclination of the plane formed by the two first axes to the plane of x, y, ; let φ be the angle formed by the line of intersection of these two planes and by the first axis ; finally, let ψ be the complement of the angle which the projection of the third axis on the plane of x, y, makes with the axis of x. We will term these three axes principal axes, and we will denote the three coordinates of the molecule dm, referred to those axes by x'', y'', z'', ; then by No. 21, the following equations will obtain

$$x'=x''.(\cos.\theta.\sin.\psi.\sin.\varphi+\cos.\psi.\cos.\varphi)+$$

$$y''.(\cos.\theta.\sin.\psi.\cos.\varphi-\cos.\psi.\sin.\varphi)+z''.\sin.\theta.\sin.\psi;$$

$$y'=x''.(\cos.\theta.\cos.\psi.\sin.\varphi-\sin.\psi.\cos.\varphi)+$$

$$y''.(\cos.\theta.\cos.\psi.\cos.\varphi+\sin.\psi.\sin.\varphi)+z''.\sin.\theta.\cos.\psi;$$

$$z'=z''.\cos.\theta-y''.\sin.\theta.\cos.\varphi-x''.\sin.\theta.\sin.\varphi.$$

By means of these equations, we are enabled to develop the the first members of the equations (B) in functions of θ, ψ, φ and their differentials. But this investigation will be considerably simplified, by observing that the position of the three principal axes depends on three arbitrary quantities, which we can always determine so as to satisfy these three equations.

$$S.x''y''.dm=0\,;\ S.x''z''.dm=0\,;\ S.y''z''.dm=0.\ *$$

* In deducing the values of $-$N, $-$N', in functions of θ,ψ,φ, and the coordinates x'', y'', z'', it is assumed that there are three axes possessing this property of having $S y''z''.dm$, $S\,x''y''.dm=0$, $S\,x''z''.dm=0$. However it is afterwards *demonstrated* that there exists three such axes in every body.

Since by hypothesis the principal axes preserve their initial positions, being moveable in space though fixed in the body, while the axes of x', y', and z', are fixed *in space*, it follows

then let us make

$$S.\,(y''^2+z''^2).\,dm=A;\ S.\,(x''^2+z''^2).\,dm=B;\ S.\,(x''^2+y''^2)\,dm\ C;$$

and in order to abridge let us make

$$d\varphi-d\psi.\cos.\theta=p.dt;$$

$$d\psi.\sin.\theta.\sin.\varphi-d\theta.\cos.\varphi=q.dt;$$

$$d\psi.\sin.\theta.\cos.\varphi+d\theta.\sin.\varphi=r.dt.$$

The equations (B) will, after all reductions, be changed into the three following;

$$\left.\begin{array}{l} A.q.\sin.\theta.\sin.\varphi+Br.\sin.\theta.\cos.\varphi-Cp.\cos.\theta=-N; \\ \mathrm{Cos}.\psi.\,\{Aq.\cos.\theta.\sin.\varphi+Br.\cos.\theta.\cos.\varphi+Cp.\sin.\theta\} \\ +\sin.\psi.\,\{Br.\sin.\varphi-Aq.\cos.\varphi\}=-N'; \\ \mathrm{Cos}.\psi.\,\{Br.\sin.\varphi-Aq.\cos.\varphi\} \\ -\sin.\psi.\{Aq.\cos.\theta.\sin.\varphi+Br.\cos.\theta.\cos.\varphi+Cp.\sin.\theta\}=-N'' \end{array}\right\};\ (C)\ *$$

that the coordinates x'', y'', z'', are constantly the same for the same molecule, and vary only in passing from one molecule to another, but the coordinates $x'\ y'\ z'$ vary with the time ∴ they are functions of the time, as are also the angles θ, ψ, φ, since they depend on the position of the principal axes with respect to the fixed axes ∴ when we take the differential of x', y', and z', with respect to the time in terms of $x''\ y''\ z''$ and the angles θ, ψ, φ, we should not take the differentials of x'', y'', z'', it may likewise be observed that we can omit the consideration of those quantities of which one of the factors is the product of two different coordinates, for such quantities disappear from the expression $x'dy-y'dx'$, as they occur in the two parts of it affected with contrary signs, these considerations enable us to abridge considerably the investigation of the value of $\frac{x'dy'-y'dx'}{dt}$ in terms of $x''y''z''$ and functions of the angles θ, ψ, φ, for we shall not take into account, those terms which would eventually disappear in the expression $\frac{x'dy'-y'.dx'}{dt}$.

* $dx'==x''.(-d\theta.\sin.\theta.\sin.\psi\sin.\varphi+d\psi.\cos.\psi.\cos.\theta.\sin.\varphi$

$+d\varphi.\cos.\varphi.\sin.\psi.\cos.\theta-d\psi.\sin.\psi.\cos.\varphi-d\varphi.\sin.\varphi.\cos.\psi)$

these three equations give by differentiating them and then supposing $\psi = 0$, after the differentiations, which is equivalent to assuming the

$$+y''(-d\theta.\sin.\theta.\sin.\psi.\cos.\varphi + d\psi.\cos.\psi.\cos.\varphi.\cos.\theta$$

$$-d\varphi.\sin.\varphi.\sin.\psi.\cos.\theta + d\psi.\sin.\psi.\sin.\varphi - d\varphi.\cos.\varphi.\cos.\psi)$$

$$+z''.(d\theta.\cos.\theta.\sin.\psi + d\psi.\cos.\psi\sin.\theta);$$

$$dy' = x''.(-d\theta.\sin.\theta.\cos.\psi.\sin.\varphi - d\psi.\sin.\psi.\sin.\varphi.\cos.\theta$$

$$+d\varphi.\cos.\varphi.\cos.\psi.\cos.\theta - d\psi.\cos.\psi.\cos.\varphi + d\varphi.\sin.\varphi.\sin.\psi)$$

$$+y''(-d\theta.\sin.\theta.\cos.\psi.\cos.\varphi - d\psi.\sin.\psi.\cos.\varphi.\cos.\theta$$

$$-d\varphi.\sin.\varphi.\cos.\psi.\cos.\theta + d\psi.\cos.\psi.\sin.\varphi + d\varphi.\cos.\varphi.\sin.\psi)$$

$$+z''.(d\theta.\cos.\theta.\cos.\psi - d\psi.\sin.\psi.\sin.\theta)$$

$$dz' = -z''.d\theta.\sin.\theta - y''.d\theta.\cos.\theta.\cos.\varphi + y''.d\varphi.\sin.\varphi.\sin.\theta$$

$$-x''.d\theta.\cos.\theta.\sin.\varphi - x''.d\varphi.\cos.\varphi.\sin.\theta$$

$$\therefore x'dy' =$$

$$(x''.\cos.\theta.\sin.\psi.\sin.\varphi + x''\cos.\psi.\cos.\varphi + y''.\cos.\theta.\sin.\psi.\cos.\varphi$$

$$-y''.\cos.\psi.\sin.\varphi + z''.\sin.\theta.\sin.\psi)\times$$

$$(-x''.d\theta.\sin.\theta.\cos.\psi.\sin.\varphi - x''.d\psi.\sin.\psi.\sin.\varphi.\cos.\theta + x''d\varphi.\cos.\varphi.\cos.\psi.\cos.\theta$$

$$-x''d\psi.\cos.\psi.\cos.\varphi + x''d\varphi.\sin.\varphi.\sin.\psi$$

$$-y''.d\theta.\sin.\theta.\cos.\psi.\cos.\varphi - y''.d\psi.\sin.\psi.\cos.\varphi.\cos.\theta$$

$$-y''.d\varphi.\sin.\varphi.\cos.\psi.\cos.\theta + y''.d\psi.\cos.\psi.\sin.\varphi + y''.d\varphi.\cos.\varphi,\sin.\psi$$

$$+z''.d\theta.\cos.\theta.\cos.\psi - z''.d\psi.\sin.\psi.\sin.\theta) =$$

$$-x''.^2d\theta.\sin.\theta.\cos.\theta.\sin.\psi.\cos.\psi.\sin.^2\varphi - x''.^2d\theta.\sin.\theta.\cos.^2\psi.\sin.\varphi.\cos.\varphi$$

$$-x''.^2d\psi.\sin.^2\psi.\sin.^2\varphi.\cos.^2\theta. - x''.^2d\psi.\sin.\psi\cos.\psi.\sin.\varphi.\cos.\varphi.\cos.\theta$$

$$+x''.^2d\varphi.\sin.\varphi.\cos.\varphi.\sin.\psi.\cos.\psi.\cos.^2\theta + x''.^2d\varphi.\cos.^2\varphi.\cos.^2\psi.\cos.\theta$$

$$-x''.^2d\psi.\sin.\psi.\cos.\psi.\sin.\varphi.\cos.\varphi.\cos.\theta - x''.^2d\psi.\cos.^2\psi.\cos.^2\varphi$$

$$+x''.^2d\varphi.\sin.^2\varphi.\sin.^2\psi.\cos.\theta + x''.^2d\varphi.\sin.\varphi.\cos.\varphi.\sin.\psi.\cos.\psi.$$

$$-y''^2.d\theta.\sin.\theta.\cos.\theta.\sin.\psi.\cos.\psi.\cos.^2\varphi + y''.^2d\theta.\sin.\theta.\cos.^2\psi.\sin.\varphi.\cos.\varphi$$

$$-y''.^2d\psi.\sin.^2\psi.\cos.^2\varphi\cos.^2\theta. + y''.^2d\psi.\sin.\psi.\cos.\psi.\sin.\varphi.\cos.\varphi.\cos.\theta$$

axis of x' indefinitely near the line of intersection of the plane of x' and y', with that of x'' and y'',

$$-y''^{.2}\,d\phi.\sin.\phi.\cos.\phi.\sin.\psi.\cos.\psi.\cos.^2\theta.+y''^{.2}d\phi.\sin.^2\phi\cos.^2\psi.\cos.\theta$$

$$+y''^{.2}d\psi.\sin.\psi.\cos.\psi.\sin.\phi.\cos.\phi.\cos.\theta-y''^{.2}d\psi.\cos.^2\psi.\sin.^2\phi$$

$$+y''^{.2}d\phi.\cos.^2\phi.\sin.^2\psi.\cos.\theta-y''^{.2}d\phi.\sin.\phi.\cos.\phi.\sin.\psi.\cos.\psi$$

$$+z''^{.2}.d\theta.\sin.\theta.\cos.\theta.\sin.\psi.\cos.\psi-z''^{.2}d\psi.\sin.^2\psi.\sin.^2\theta$$

$$y'.dx'.=$$

$$(x''.\cos.\theta.\cos.\psi.\sin.\phi-x''\sin.\psi.\cos.\phi+y''.\cos.\theta.\cos.\psi.\cos.\phi$$

$$+y''.\sin\,\psi.\sin.\phi+z''.\sin.\theta.\cos.\psi)\times$$

$$(-x''.d\theta.\sin.\theta.\sin.\psi.\sin.\phi+x''.d\psi.\cos.\psi.\sin.\phi.\cos.\theta+x''.d\phi.\cos.\phi.\sin.\psi.\cos.\theta$$

$$-x''.d\psi.\sin.\psi.\cos.\phi-x''.d\phi.\sin.\phi.\cos.\psi$$

$$-y''.d\theta.\sin.\theta.\sin.\psi.\cos.\phi+y''.d\psi\,\cos.\psi.\cos\,\phi.\cos.\theta-y''.d\phi.\sin.\phi.\sin.\psi.\cos.\theta$$

$$y''.d\psi.\sin.\psi.\sin.\phi-y''.d\phi.\cos.\phi.\cos.\psi.$$

$$+z''.d\theta.\cos.\theta.\sin.\psi.+z''d\psi.\cos.\psi.\sin.\theta)=$$

$$-x''^{.2}d\theta.\sin.\theta.\cos.\theta.\sin.\psi.\cos.\psi.\sin.^2\phi-x''^{.2}d\theta.\sin.\theta.\sin.^2\psi.\sin.\phi.\cos.\phi$$

$$+x''^{.2}d\psi.\cos.^2\psi.\sin.^2\phi.\cos.^2\theta-x''^{.2}d\psi.\sin.\psi.\cos.\psi.\sin.\phi.\cos.\phi.\cos.\theta$$

$$+x''^{.2}d\phi.\sin.\phi.\cos.\phi.\sin.\psi.\cos.\psi.\cos.^2\theta.-x''^{.2}d\phi\,\cos.^2\phi.\sin.^2\psi.\cos.\theta$$

$$-x''^{.2}d\psi.\sin.\psi.\cos.\psi.\sin.\phi.\cos.\phi.\cos.\theta+x''^{.2}d\psi.\sin.^2\psi.\cos.^2\phi$$

$$-x''^{.2}d\phi.\sin.^2\phi.\cos.^2\psi.\cos.\theta+x''.d\phi.\sin.\phi.\cos\,\phi.\sin.\psi.\cos.\psi.$$

$$-y''^{.2}d\theta.\sin.\theta.\cos.\theta.\sin.\psi.\cos.\psi.\cos.^2\phi-y''^{.2}d\theta.\sin.\theta.\sin.^2\psi.\sin.\phi.\cos.\phi$$

$$+y''^{.2}d\psi.\cos.^2\psi.\cos.^2\theta.\cos\,^2\phi.+y''^{.2}d\psi.\sin\,\psi.\cos.\psi.\sin.\phi.\cos.\phi.\cos.\theta.$$

$$-y''^{.2}d\phi\,\sin.\phi.\cos.\phi.\sin.\psi.\cos.\psi.\cos.^2\theta.-y''^{.2}d\phi.\sin.^2\phi\,\sin.^2\psi.\cos.\theta$$

$$+y''^{.2}d\psi.\sin.\psi.\cos\,\psi.\sin.\phi.\cos.\phi.\cos.\theta+y''^{.2}d\psi.\sin.^2\psi.\sin.^2\phi$$

$$-y''^{.2}d\phi.\cos.^2\phi.\cos.^2\psi.\cos.\theta-y''^{.2}d\phi.\sin.\phi.\cos\,\phi.\sin.\psi.\cos.\psi,$$

$$+z''^{.2}d\theta.\sin.\theta.\cos.\theta.\sin.\psi.\cos.\psi.+z''^{2}d\psi.\cos.^2\psi.\sin.^2\theta.$$

$$d\theta.\cos.\theta.(Br.\cos.\varphi+Aq.\sin.\varphi)+\sin.\theta.d.(Br.\cos.\varphi+Aq.\sin.\varphi)$$
$$-d.(Cp.\cos.\theta)=-dN;$$

$$d\psi.(Br.\sin.\varphi-Aq.\cos.\varphi)-d\theta.\sin.\theta.(Br.\cos.\varphi+Aq.\sin.\varphi)+\cos\theta.$$
$$d.(Br\cos.\varphi+Aq.\sin.\varphi)+d.(Cp.\sin.\theta)=-dN';$$

$$d.(Br\sin.\varphi-Aq.\cos.\varphi)-d\psi.\cos.\theta.(Br\cos.\varphi+Aq.\sin.\varphi)$$
$$-Cp.d\psi.\sin.\theta=-dN''$$

making

$$Cp=p';\ Aq=q';\ Br=r';$$

Z

∴ observing the terms which coalesce and those which destroy each other in the expression for $x'dy'-y'dx'$, this function becomes equal to

$$-x''.^2\,d\theta.\sin.\theta.\sin.\varphi.\cos.\varphi-x''.^2d\psi.\sin.^2\varphi.\cos.^2\theta-x''.^2d\psi.\cos.^2\varphi$$
$$+(x''.^2\,d\varphi.\cos.^2\varphi.\cos.\theta+x''.^2\,d\varphi.\sin.^2\varphi.\cos.\theta)=(x''.^2d\varphi.\cos.\theta.)$$
$$+y''.^2d\theta.\sin.\theta.\sin.\varphi.\cos.\varphi-y''.^2d\psi.\cos.^2\varphi.\cos.^2\theta-y''.^2d\psi.\sin.^2\varphi$$
$$+(y''.^2d\varphi.\sin.^2\varphi.\cos\theta+y''.^2d\varphi.\cos.^2\varphi.\cos.\theta)=(y''.^2d\varphi.\cos.\theta).$$
$$-z''.^2d\psi.\sin.^2\theta.$$

This equation when extended to all the molecules of the body is identical with the equation,

$$A.q.\sin.\theta.\sin.\varphi+Br.\sin.\theta.\cos.\varphi-C.p.\cos.\theta.=-N;$$

taken with a contrary sign, for substituting in place of A, B, C, p, r, q, their values, in this equation, it becomes for one molecule

$$(y''+z'')^2\left\{\frac{d\psi.\sin.^2\theta.\sin.^2\varphi)-d\theta.\sin.\theta.\sin.\varphi.\cos\varphi}{dt}\right\}+(x''^2+z''^2).$$

$$\frac{(d\psi.\sin.^2\theta.\cos.^2\varphi+d\theta.\sin.\theta.\sin.\varphi.\cos.\varphi)-(x''^2+y''^2)(d\varphi.\cos.\theta-d\psi.\cos.^2\theta),}{dt}$$

equal by making all the quantities by which y''^2, z''^2, x''^2 are respectively multiplied coalesce so that they may be respectively factors of these coordinates these three differential equations give the following ones *

$$\left.\begin{array}{l} dp' + \left\{\frac{B-A}{AB}\right\} q'r'.dt = dN.\cos.\theta - dN'.\sin.\theta; \\ dq' + \left\{\frac{C-B}{CB}\right\} .r'p'.dt = -(dN.\sin.\theta + dN'.\cos.\theta).\sin.\varphi \\ \qquad\qquad + dN''.\cos.\varphi; \\ dr' + \left\{\frac{A-C}{CA}\right\} .p'q'.dt = -(dN.\sin.\theta + dN'.\cos.\theta).\cos.\varphi. \\ \qquad\qquad - dN''.\sin.\varphi. \end{array}\right\} ; (D)$$

$$y''^{2}.d\psi\,(\sin.^2\theta.\sin.^2\varphi + \cos.^2\theta) - y''^{2}.d\theta.\sin.\theta.\sin.\varphi.\cos.\varphi - y''^{2}.d\varphi.\cos.\theta$$

$$= y''^2.d\psi.\cos.^2\varphi.\cos.^2\theta + y''^{2}.d\psi.\sin.^2\varphi - y''^2.d\theta.\sin.\theta.\sin.\varphi.\cos.\varphi - y''^2.d\varphi.\cos.\theta$$

$$z''^2.d\psi\,\sin.^2\theta.\sin.^2\varphi - z''^2.d\theta.\sin.\theta.\sin.\varphi.\cos.\varphi + z''^2.d\psi.\sin.^2\theta.\cos.^2\varphi$$

$$+ z''^{2}.d\theta.\sin.\theta.\sin.\varphi\,\cos.\varphi = z''^{2}.d\psi.\sin.^2\theta$$

$$+ x''^2.d\psi.\sin.^2\theta.\cos.^2\varphi + x''^2.d\theta.\sin.\theta.\sin.\varphi.\cos.\varphi - x''^2.d\varphi.\cos.\theta + x''^2.d\psi.\cos.^2\theta$$

$$= x''^2.d\psi.(\sin.^2\varphi.\cos.^2\theta) + x''^2.d\psi.\cos.^2\varphi - x''^2.d\varphi.\cos.\theta + x''^2.d\theta.\sin.\theta.\sin.\varphi.\cos.\varphi.$$

Since the angle ψ vanishes after the differentiations, wherever $\sin.\psi$ occcurs as a factor this quantity must be rejected, and wherever $\cos.\psi$ occurs it becomes equal to unity, keeping these circumstances in view it will immediately appear that the expressions for $-dN - dN'' - dN'''$ should be such as are given in the text.

* The first differential equation being multiplied by $-\cos.\theta$ becomes equal to

$$-d\theta.\cos.^2\theta\,(Br.\cos.\varphi + Aq.\sin.\varphi) - \sin.\theta.\cos.\theta.\,d.(Br.\cos.\varphi + Aq.\sin.\varphi)$$

$$+ \cos.\theta.\,d.(Cp.\cos.\theta) = dN.\cos.\theta$$

and multiplying the second equation by $\sin.\theta$, we have

$$d\psi.\sin.\theta.(Br.\sin.\varphi - Aq.\cos.\varphi) - d\theta.\sin.^2\theta.(Br.\cos.\varphi + Aq.\sin.\varphi) + \sin.\theta.\cos.\theta.$$

$$d.(Br.\cos.\varphi + Aq.\sin.\varphi) + \sin.\theta\,d.(Cp.\sin.\theta) = -dN'.\sin.\theta$$

$$\therefore dN.\cos.\theta - d.N'.\sin.\theta = -d\theta.(Br.\cos.\varphi + Aq.\sin.\varphi) + d\psi.\sin.\theta.(Br.\sin.\varphi - Aq.\cos.\varphi)$$

$$+ \cos.^2\theta.\,d.(C.p) - d\theta.\sin.\theta.\cos.\theta.(Cp) + \sin.^2\theta.\,d(Cp) + d\theta\,\sin.\theta.\cos.\theta.(Cp); =$$

these three equations are very convenient for determining the motion of rotation of a body, when it turns very nearly about one of the principal axes, which is the case of the celestial bodies.

27. The three principal axes to which we have referred the angles

by substituting for r and q their values

$$=\frac{-B.(d\theta.d\psi.\sin.\theta.\cos.^2\varphi+d\theta.^2\sin.\varphi.\cos.\varphi)-A(d\theta.d\psi.\sin.\theta.\sin.^2\varphi-d\theta.^2\sin.\varphi.\cos.\varphi)}{dt}$$

$$\frac{+B.(d\psi.^2\sin.^2\theta.\sin.\varphi.\cos.\varphi+d\psi.d\theta.\sin.\theta.\sin.^2\varphi)-A.(d\psi.^2\sin.^2\theta.\sin.\varphi.\cos.\varphi}{dt}$$

$$\frac{-d\psi.d\theta.\sin.\theta.\cos.^2\varphi)}{dt}+d.(C.p.)=$$

$$\frac{(B-A.).(d\psi.^2\sin.^2\theta.\sin.\varphi.\cos.\varphi)-d\theta.^2\sin.\varphi.\cos.\varphi+d\psi.d\theta.(\sin.\theta.\sin.^2\varphi-\sin.\theta.\cos.^2\varphi))}{dt}$$

$$+d.(C.p.)=(B-A).\ q.r.dt+dp'=\frac{B-A}{AB}.q'.r'.dt+dp'$$

in like manner, multiplying the first of the differential equations by sin. θ. sin. φ, the second cos. θ. sin. φ. and the third by—cos. φ, and then adding them together we obtain

$$-dN.\sin.\theta.\sin.\varphi-dN'.\cos.\theta.\sin.\varphi-dN''.\cos.\varphi=\text{ to}$$

$$d\theta.\sin.\theta.\cos.\theta.\sin.\varphi.(Br.\cos.\varphi+Aq.\sin.\varphi)+\sin.^2\theta.\sin.\varphi.d.(Br.\cos.\varphi+Aq.\sin.\varphi)$$

$$-\sin.\theta.\sin.\varphi.d.(C.p.\cos.\theta)$$

$$+d\psi.\cos.\theta.\sin.\varphi(Br.\sin.\varphi-Aq.\cos.\varphi)-d\theta.\sin.\theta.\cos.\theta.\sin.\varphi(Br.\cos.\varphi+Aq.\sin.\varphi)$$

$$+\cos.^2\theta.\sin.\varphi.d.(Br.\cos.\varphi+Aq\ \sin.\varphi)+\cos.\theta.\sin.\varphi.d.(Cp.\sin.\theta)$$

$$-\cos.\varphi.d.(Br.\sin.\varphi-Aq.\cos.\varphi)+d\psi.\cos.\theta.\cos.\varphi.(Br.\cos.\varphi+Aq.\sin.\varphi)$$

$$+Cp.d\psi.\sin.\theta.\cos.\varphi=\text{ by concinnating}$$

$$\sin.\varphi.d.(Br.\cos.\varphi+Aq.\sin.\varphi)+d\psi.\cos.\theta.Br-\cos.\varphi.d.(Br.\sin.\varphi-Aq.\cos.\varphi)$$

$$-\sin.\theta.\cos.\theta.\sin.\varphi.d.(Cp)+d\theta.\sin.^2\theta.\sin.\varphi.(Cp)+\sin.\theta.\cos.\theta.\sin.\varphi.d.(Cp)$$

$$+d\theta.\cos.^2\theta.\sin.\varphi.(Cp.)+(Cp.)d\psi.\sin.\theta.\cos.\varphi;$$

$$=\sin.\varphi.\cos.\varphi.d.(Br)+\sin.^2\varphi.d.(Aq)-Br.d\varphi.\sin.^2\varphi.+Aq.d\varphi.\sin.\varphi.\cos.\varphi.$$

$$+d\psi.\cos.\theta.Br-\sin.\varphi.\cos.\varphi.d.(Br)+\cos.^2\varphi.d.(Aq)-Br.d\varphi.\cos.^2\varphi-Aq.d\varphi.\sin.\varphi.\cos.\varphi.$$

$$+d\theta.\sin.\varphi.(C.p.)+(Cp).d\psi.\sin.\theta.\cos.\varphi=d.(Aq)-Br.d\varphi+d\psi.\cos.\theta.Br$$

θ, φ, ψ, deserve particular consideration; we now proceed to determine their position in any solid whatever. From the values of x' y' z', which have been given in the preceding number we may obtain the following expressions by No. 21.

$$x'' = x'(\cos.\theta.\sin.\psi.\sin.\varphi + \cos.\psi.\cos.\varphi) + y'.(\cos.\theta.\cos.\psi.\sin.\varphi - \sin.\psi.\cos.\varphi) - z'.\sin.\theta.\sin.\varphi;$$

$$y'' = x'(\cos.\theta.\sin.\psi.\cos.\varphi - \cos.\psi.\sin.\varphi) + y'.(\cos.\theta.\cos.\psi.\cos.\varphi + \sin.\psi.\sin.\varphi) - z'.\sin.\theta.\cos.\varphi;$$

$$z'' = x'.\sin.\theta.\sin.\psi + y'.\sin.\theta.\cos.\psi + z'.\cos.\theta;$$

From which may be obtained,

$$x''.\cos.\varphi - y''.\sin.\varphi = x'.\cos.\psi - y'\sin.\psi;$$

$$x''.\sin.\varphi + y''.\cos.\varphi = x'.\cos.\theta.\sin.\psi + y'.\cos.\theta.\cos.\psi - z'.\sin.\theta;$$

and making

$$S.x'.^2dm = a^2;\quad S.y'.^2dm = b^2;\quad S.z'.^2dm = c^2;$$

$$S.x'y'.dm = f;\quad S.x'z'.dm = g;\quad S.y'z'.dm = h;$$

we shall have

$$\cos.\varphi.S.x''z''.dm - \sin.\varphi.S.y''z''.dm = (a^2 - b^2)\sin.\theta.\sin.\psi.\cos.\psi$$

but by substitution $d.(Aq) + Br.(-d\varphi + d\psi.\cos.\theta) + d\theta.\sin.\varphi.Cp. + d\psi.(Cp.)\sin.\theta.\cos.\varphi. =$

$$d.(Aq)\frac{-Bd\psi.d\varphi.\sin.\theta.\cos.\varphi - d\varphi.d\theta.\sin.\varphi + d\psi.^2\sin.\theta.\cos.\theta\cos.\varphi + d\psi.d\theta.\cos.\theta.\sin.\varphi.}{dt}$$

$$\frac{+C.(d\theta\, d\varphi.\sin.\varphi - d\theta.d\psi.\cos.\theta.\sin.\varphi) + C.d\psi.d\varphi.\sin.\theta.\cos.\varphi - C.d\psi.^2\sin.\theta.\cos.\theta.\cos.\varphi.}{dt}$$

$$\frac{= (C-B).d\varphi.d\psi.(\sin.\theta.\cos.\varphi.) + (d\varphi.d\theta.\sin.\varphi) - d\psi.^2\sin.\theta.\cos.\theta.\cos.\varphi - d\theta.d\psi.\cos.\theta\sin.\varphi)}{dt}$$

$$+ d(Aq.) = (C-B).p.r.dt + d.(Aq.) = \frac{C-B}{CB}p'.r'dt + dq'$$

$$+f. \sin. \theta. (\cos.^2 \psi - \sin.^2\psi)$$

$$+\cos. \theta. (g. \cos.\psi - h. \sin. \psi);$$

$$\sin. \varphi. S. x''z''dm + \cos. \varphi. S. y''z''.dm =$$

$$\sin. \theta. \cos. \theta. (a.^2 \sin.^2\psi + b.^2 \cos.^2\psi - c^2 + 2f. \sin. \psi. \cos. \psi)^*$$

$$+(\cos.^2\theta - \sin.^2\theta). (g. \sin. \psi + h. \cos. \psi).$$

$* x''. \cos. \varphi = x'. (\cos. \theta. \sin. \psi. \sin. \varphi. \cos. \varphi + \cos. \psi. \cos.^2\varphi)$

$+y'. (\cos. \theta. \cos. \psi. \sin. \varphi. \cos. \varphi - \sin. \psi. \cos.^2\varphi) - z'. \sin. \theta. \sin. \varphi. \cos. \varphi.$

$y''. \sin. \varphi = x'. (\cos. \theta. \sin. \psi. \sin. \varphi. \cos. \varphi - \cos. \psi. \sin.^2\varphi)$

$+y'. (\cos. \theta. \cos. \psi. \sin. \varphi. \cos. \varphi + \sin. \psi. \sin.^2\varphi) - z'. \sin. \theta. \sin. \varphi. \cos. \varphi,$

$\therefore x''. \cos. \varphi - y''. \sin. \varphi = x'. \cos. \psi - y'. \sin. \psi$

$x''. \sin. \varphi = x' (\cos. \theta. \sin. \psi. \sin.^2\varphi + \cos. \psi. \sin. \varphi. \cos. \varphi)$

$+y' (\cos. \theta. \cos. \psi. \sin.^2\varphi - \sin \psi. \sin. \varphi. \cos. \varphi) - z'. \sin. \theta. \sin.^2\varphi.$

$y''. \cos. \varphi = x' (\cos. \theta. \sin. \psi. \cos.^2\varphi - \cos. \psi. \sin. \varphi. \cos. \varphi)$

$+y'. (\cos. \theta. \cos. \psi. \cos.^2\varphi + \sin. \psi. \sin. \varphi. \cos. \varphi) - z'. \sin. \theta. \cos.^2\varphi$

$\therefore x''. \sin. \varphi + y''. \cos. \varphi = x'. \cos. \theta. \sin. \psi + y'. \cos. \theta. \cos. \psi - z'. \sin. \theta;$

multiplying the first member of the equation $x''. \cos. \varphi - y''. \sin. \varphi = x'. \cos. \psi - y'. \sin. \psi.$ by z'' and the second member by the value of z'' we obtain

$\cos. \varphi. x''z'' - \sin. \varphi. y''.z'' = x'.^2 \sin. \theta. \sin. \psi. \cos. \psi - x'y'. \sin. \theta. \sin.^2\psi$

$+x'y'. \sin. \theta. \cos.^2\psi - y'.^2 \sin. \theta. \sin. \psi. \cos. \psi.$

$+z'. x'. \cos. \theta. \cos. \psi - z'y'. \cos. \theta. \sin. \psi,$

substituting for x'^2, y'^2, $x'y'$, $z'y'$, $z'x'$, their values and concinnating we obtain

$\cos. \varphi. x''z'' - \sin. \varphi. y'' z'' = (x'^2 - y'^2) \sin. \theta. \sin. \psi. \cos. \psi + x'y'. \sin. \theta. (\cos.^2\psi - \sin.^2\psi.)$

$+z'x'. \cos. \theta. \cos. \psi - z'y'. \cos. \theta. \sin. \psi,$

this expression being extended to all the molecules of the body, will give by substituting for Sx'^2dm $Sy'.^2dm$, &c. their respective values a^2, b^2, f, g, h, &c. the expression in the text, in like manner $\sin. \varphi. x'' z''$

by equalling the second members of these two equations to nothing, we shall obtain

$$\tan.\theta = \frac{h.\sin.\psi - g.\cos.\psi}{(a^2-b^2).\sin.\psi.\cos.\psi + f.(\cos.^2\psi - \sin.^2\psi)};$$

$$\tfrac{1}{2}\tan.2\theta = \frac{g.\sin.\psi + h.\cos.\psi}{c^2 - a^2.\sin.^2\psi - b^2.\cos.^2\psi - 2f.\sin.\psi.\cos.\psi};$$

but we have always

$$\tfrac{1}{2}\tan.2\theta = \frac{\tan.\theta}{1-\tan.^2\theta};$$

by equalling these two values of tan. 2θ, and substituting in the last expression, in place of tan. θ. its value, which has been given in a function of ψ; and then in order to abridge, making tan. $\psi = u$; we shall obtain after all reductions, the following equation of the third order.*

$$0 = (gu+h).(hu-g)^2$$

$$+\{(a^2-b^2).u + f.(1-u^2)\}.\{hc^2 - ha^2 + fg).u + gb^2 - gc^2 - hf\}.$$

$$+\cos.\varphi.y''.z'' = x'^2\sin.\theta.\cos.\theta.\sin.^2\psi + x'y'.\sin.\theta.\cos.\theta.\sin.\psi.\cos.\psi - z'x'.\sin.^2\theta.\sin.\psi$$

$$+x'y'.\sin.\theta.\cos.\theta.\sin.\psi.\cos.\psi + y'.^2\sin.\theta.\cos.\theta.\cos.^2\psi - z'y'\sin.^2\theta.\cos.\psi$$

$$+z'x'.\cos.^2\theta.\sin.\psi + z'y'.\cos.^2\theta.\cos.\psi - z'.^2\sin.\theta.\cos.\theta =$$

$$\sin.\theta.\cos.\theta.(x'.^2\sin.^2\psi + y'.^2\cos.^2\psi - z'^2) + 2x'y'.\sin.\theta.\cos.\theta.\sin.\psi.\cos.\psi)$$

$$+(\cos.^2\theta - \sin.^2\theta.)(z'x'.\sin.\psi. + z'y'.\cos.\psi.)$$

by extending this expression to all the molecules and substituting $a^2, b^2, c^2, h, f\,g$, &cæt. for Sx'^2dm and Sy'^2dm &c. we shall obtain the expression which has been given in the text.

* The second members are put equal to nothing because by the conditions of the problem, the first members respectively vanish, consequently we have 0 =

$$((a^2-b^2).\sin.\psi.\cos.\psi + f.(\cos^2\psi - \sin.^2\psi)).\sin.\theta + (g.\cos.\psi - h.\sin.\psi).\cos.\theta;$$

$$0 = \sin.\theta.\cos.\theta.(a^2\sin.^2\psi + b.^2\cos.^2\psi - c^2 + 2f.\sin.\psi.\cos.\psi)$$

As this equation has at least one real root we may perceive that it is always possible to make these two subsequent expressions, and consequently the sum of their squares, to vanish at the same time

$$\therefore \frac{\sin.\theta}{\cos.\theta} = \tan.\theta = \frac{h\sin.\psi - g.\cos.\psi}{(a^2-b^2).\sin.\psi.\cos.\psi + f.(\cos.^2\psi - \sin.^2\psi)},$$

$$\frac{\sin.\theta.\cos.\theta}{\cos.^2\theta - \sin.^2\theta} = \frac{\frac{\sin.\theta}{\cos.\theta}}{1 - \frac{\sin.^2\theta}{\cos.^2\theta}} = \frac{\tan.\theta}{1-\tan.^2\theta} = \tfrac{1}{2}\tan.2\theta =$$

$$\frac{g.\sin.\psi. + h.\cos.\psi}{c^2 - a.^2\sin.^2\psi - b.^2\cos.^2\psi - 2f.\sin.\psi.\cos.\psi}$$

these fractions being divided cos. ψ, become by substituting u in place of

$$\frac{\sin.\psi}{\cos.\psi},\quad \frac{hu-g}{((a^2-b^2).u + f.(1-u^2)).\cos.\psi},\quad \frac{gu+h}{((c.^2(1+u^2) - a^2u^2 - b^2 - 2fu).\cos.\psi}$$

if we call the factors of cos. ψ in the denominators of these respective fractions m and n we shall have

$$\tan.\theta. = \frac{hu-g}{m.\cos.\psi} \therefore \tfrac{1}{2}.\tan.2\theta =$$

$$\frac{\frac{hu-g}{m.\cos.\psi}}{1-\left\{\frac{hu-g}{m.\cos.\psi}\right\}^2} = \frac{(hu-g).m.\cos.\psi}{\overline{m.\cos.\psi}^2 - \overline{hu-g}^2} = \frac{gu+h}{n.\cos.\psi} \therefore$$

by reducing we obtain

$$(hu-g).mn.\cos.^2\psi = (gu+h).(.(m\cos\psi)^2 - (hu-g)^2)$$

and consequently $0 =$

$$\cos.^2\psi.(m.(hu-g).n - (gu+h).m) + (hu-g).^2(gu+h,)\ \text{now}\ (hu-g)n. =$$

by substituting for n, $(c.^2(1+u^2) - a^2u^2 - b^2 - 2fu)$ and then multiplying

$$hc^2u + hc^2u^3 - ha^2u^3 - hb^2u - 2fhu^2 - gc^2 - gc^2u^2 + ga^2u^2 + gb^2 + 2fgu,$$

in like manner

$$\cos.\ \varphi.\ S.\ x''z''.dm - \sin.\ \varphi.\ S.\ y'.z''.dm\,;$$

$$\sin.\ \varphi.\ S.\ x''z''.dm + \cos.\ \varphi.\ S.\ y''z''.dm\,;$$

and this requires that we should have $S.\ x''z''.dm$; $S\,y''z''.dm$ separately equal to nothing.

The value of u gives that of the angle ψ, and consequently the value of tang. θ, and of the angle θ. It is only now required to determine the angle φ and this will be effected by means of the condition $S.\ x''y''.dm=0$, which we have yet to satisfy. For this purpose it may be observed, that if we substitute in $S.x''y'.dm$ * in place of x'', y'',

$$-(gu+h).\,m = (-(gu+h).(a^2-b^2).\,u+f(1-u^2)) =$$

$$-a^2gu^2+gb^2u^2-gfu+gfu^3-ha^2u+hb^2u-hf+hfu^2\ \therefore$$

the preceding equation becomes, to by making the similar factors of u and its powers to coalesce, equal to,

$$(hc^2 u.(1+u^2)-ha^2 u.(1+u^2)-fh.(1+u^2)-gc.^2(1+u^2)+fgu.(1+u^2)$$

$$+gb.^2(1+u^2)).\left\{\frac{(a^2-b^2)u+f.(1-u^2)}{1+u^2}\right\}$$

$$\text{for } \cos.\ ^2\psi.\ m.(hu-g) = \frac{(a^2-b^2).u+f.(1-u^2)}{1+u_2}$$

$$+(hu-g)^2.\ (gu+h) =$$

$$((a^2-b.)^2\,u+f.(1-u^2)).\,((hc^2-ha^2+fg).u-fh-gc^2+gb^2))+(hu-g).^2(gu+h)=0,$$

which is the expression given in the text.

$$*\ x''.\cos.\ \varphi-y''.\sin.\ \varphi=x'.\cos.\ \psi-y'.\sin.\ \psi. = P$$

$$x''.\sin.\ \varphi+y''.\cos.\ \varphi=x'.\cos.\ \theta.\sin.\ \psi+y'.\cos.\ \theta.\cos.\ \psi-z.\sin.\ \theta = Q$$

$$\therefore x''.\cos.\ ^2\varphi-y''.\sin.\ \varphi.\cos.\ \varphi=x'.\cos.\ \psi.\cos.\ \varphi-y'.\sin.\ \psi.\cos.\ \varphi = P.\cos.\ \varphi$$

$$x''.\sin.\ ^2\varphi+y''.\sin.\ \varphi.\cos.\ \varphi = x'.\cos.\ \theta.\sin.\ \psi.\sin.\ \varphi+y'.\cos.\ \theta.\cos.\ \psi.\sin.\ \varphi$$

$$-z'\sin.\ \theta.\sin.\ \varphi = Q.\sin.\ \varphi$$

$$\therefore x''. = x'.(\cos.\ \theta.\sin.\ \psi.\sin.\ \varphi+\cos.\ \psi.\cos.\ \varphi)+y'(\cos.\ \theta.\cos.\ \psi.\sin.\ \varphi-\sin.\ \psi.\cos.\ \varphi)$$

$$-z'.\sin.\ \theta.\sin.\ \varphi = P.\cos.\ \varphi+Q.\sin.\ \varphi$$

their preceding values, this function will assume this form, $H.\sin 2\phi + L.\cos.\ 2\phi$; H and L being functions of the angles θ and ψ, and of the constant quantities a^2, b^2, c^2, f, g, h, by putting this expression equal to nothing, we shall obtain $\tan.\ 2\phi = \frac{-L}{H}$.

The three axes determined by means of the preceding values of θ, ψ, and ϕ, satisfy the three equations,

A A

also

$$x''.\sin.\phi.\cos.\phi - y''.\sin.^2\phi = x'.\cos.\psi.\sin.\phi - y'.\sin.\psi\sin.\phi = P.\sin.\phi$$

$$x''.\sin.\phi.\cos.\phi + y''\cos.^2\phi = x'.\cos.\theta.\sin.\psi.\cos.\phi + y'.\cos.\theta.\cos.\psi.\cos.\phi -$$

$$z'\sin.\theta.\cos.\phi = Q.\cos.\phi$$

$$\therefore y'' = x'.(\cos.\theta.\sin.\psi.\cos.\phi - \cos.\psi.\sin.\phi) + y'(\cos.\theta.\cos.\psi.\cos.\phi + \sin.\psi.\sin.\phi)$$

$$+ z'.\sin.\theta.\cos.\phi = Q.\cos.\phi - P.\sin.\phi\ \therefore$$

$x''y'' = PQ.\cos.^2\phi - PQ.\sin.^2\phi + Q.^2\sin.\phi.\cos.\phi - P.^2\sin.\phi.\cos.\phi$ $\therefore$ if $S\,x''y''.dm = 0$, we shall have

$$SPQ.dm(\cos.^2\phi - \sin.^2\phi) + S(Q^2 - P^2).dm\sin.\phi.\cos.\phi = 0. \text{ and } \frac{S.PQdm}{S(Q^2 - P^2)dm}$$

$$= \frac{\sin.\phi.\cos.\phi}{\cos.^2\phi - \sin.^2\phi},$$

$$\text{making } H = S(Q^2 - P^2)dm \text{ and } \frac{L}{2H} = S.PQ\,dm \text{ we shall have } -\frac{L}{2L} =$$

$$\frac{\sin.2\phi.}{2.\cos.2\phi}\ \therefore \frac{-L}{H} = \tan.2\phi;$$

this equation determines a real value for, $\tan.\ 2\phi$ and $\therefore$ for ϕ, and as the equation which determines the value of u has at least one real root, $\tan.\ \psi$ and $\therefore$ $\tan.\ \theta$. are real, consequently we are justified in assuming as we have done

$$Sx''y''.dm,\ Sy''z''.dm,\ Sx''z''.dm,$$

respectively equal to nothing, and therefore we shall have at least one system of principal axes existing in every body.

$$S.x''y''.dm=0\,;\ S.x''z''.dm=0\,;\ S.y''z''.dm=0.^*$$

The equation of the third order in u, seems to indicate three systems of principal axes, similar to the preceding; but it ought to be observed

* All the roots in the equation which determines the value of u are real, and this equation must be of the third dimension, for in the investigation of the angles θ, ψ, ϕ, there is no difference between the principal axes, nor is there any condition to determine which of the three principal planes we assume, ∴ the solution must be applicable equally to the angle contained between the axes of x', and either of the three intersections formed by the plane of x', y', with the three principal planes of the body respectively, consequently the roots of the equation must be all real, it also follows that there is only one system of principal axes in every body, for as each system would give three values of u, the dimension of the resulting equation which determines the value of u, should be equal to three multiplied into the number of systems, but the equation does not transcend the third order, ∴the number of systems is only one, indeed if the equations which give the values of θ ψ and ϕ are identical, the number of principal axes is infinite, this will evidently be the case where the terms which compose the equation in u vanish without supposing any relations existing between the terms i, e, when $a^2=b^2=c^2$, and f, g, h, respectively vanish we shall have for the coordinates x', y', z', $S.x'y'.dm=0$, $S\,x'z'dm=0$, $S.y'z'.dm=0$ ∴ they are principal axes, and as in this case tan. $\theta=\frac{0}{0}$, the position of these axes is entirely undetermined ∴ all systems of rectangular axes are principal axes and their number is infinite; from the expression for tan. θ it appears in like manner, that this angle is $100°$, when $a^2=b^2$ and $f=0$, and consequently that the plane of the axes of y' and x' must pass through the axis of z''.

For all bodies symmetrically constituted, one of the principal axes, is the axis of the figure i, e, a line perpendicular to the plane dividing the bodies into two parts perfectly equal and similar, for supposing this plane to be that of x, y, then if we take two equal molecules, similarly situated with respect to this plane, it is evident that if the coordinates of one molecule be x, y, z, the coordinates of the other will be x, y, $-z$, and the indefinitely small elements of the integrals $S.xz.dm$, $S.yz.dm$, which correspond to these molecules will be $xz.dm$, $-xz\,dm$, $yz.dm$ $-yz.dm$, ∴ the sum of all the indefinitely small quantities $xz.dm$, $-xz.dm$, $yz.dm-yz,dm$, at one side of the plane will be equal to the sum of the indefinitely small quantities at the other side affected with a contrary sign, ∴ their respective aggregates $S.xzdm$, $S.yz.dm$ are equal to nothing, ∴ the axis of z is a principal axis, and if the molecules of the body be symmetrically arranged with respect to a plane passing through the axis of z' perpendicular to the first mentioned plane, we shall have $S.xy.dm=0$ ∴ the axes of x, y, z, will be principal axes.

What has been established in the preceding note is of great importance, as the investi-

that u is the tangent of the angle formed by the axis of x', and by the intersection of the plane of x' and y' with the plane of x'' and y'', and it is evident that one of the three axes of x'', of y'', and of z'' may be changed in another, since the three preceding equations will be always satisfied; therefore the equation in u ought to determine indifferently, the tangent of the angle formed by the axis of x', with the intersection of the plane x', y', either with the plane x'' y'', or the plane x'', z'', or finally with the plane y'', z'',. Thus the three roots of the equation in u are real, and they belong to the same system of axes.

It follows from what precedes, that generally a solid has only one system of axes, which possess the property in question. These axes

A A 2

gation of the position of the principal axes is considerably facilitated by making one of them to coincide with one of three coordinates x' y' z', whose position is entirely arbitrary, for supposing the axis of x'' to coincide with the axis of x', then since φ=the angle which the intersection of the plane of x'' and y'', with the plane x', y', makes with the axis of x', and since ψ = the complement of the angle, which the projection of the third axis on the plane of x' and y' makes with the axes of x', these angles are severally equal to nothing

$$\therefore \tan.\theta = \frac{h.\sin.\psi - g.\cos.\psi}{(a^2-b^2)\sin.\psi.\cos.\psi + f.(\cos.^2\psi - \sin.^2\psi)}$$

becomes equal to

$$-\frac{g'}{f'} \text{ and } \tfrac{1}{2}.\tan.2\theta = \frac{g.\sin.\psi + h.\cos.\psi}{c^2 - a^2.\cos.^2\psi - b^2.\sin.^2\psi - 2f.\sin.\psi.\cos.\psi} = \frac{h'^2}{c'^2 - b'^2},$$

n which c', b', f', g', h' indicate what c, b, f, g, h, become when x' coincides with x'', and as $\tan.2(\theta+100) = \tan.(2\theta+200) = \tan.2\theta$, it follows that the other two axes must be taken in the plane y', z', one making the angle θ and the other the angle $\theta + 100$ with the axis of y', now if we made the axes of y'', and z'', to coincide with the axes of y' and z' respectively, θ, and $\therefore h'$ would vanish, and consequently $S(y'z'.)dm$ would be equal to nothing. But if h' remaining equal to nothing, b' and c' would be equal to each other then $\tan.2\theta = \frac{h'}{c'^2-b'^2}$ would be equal to $\frac{0}{0}$ $\therefore$ θ would be indeterminate and every line in the plane y' z', and passing through the origin of the coordinates would be a principal axis, see notes to page 184.

have been named principal axes of rotation, on account of a property which is peculiar to them and which will be noticed in the sequel.

The sum of the products of each molecule of the body, into the square of its distance, from an axis, is called the *moment of inertia* of a body with respect to this axis. Thus the quantities A, B, C, are the moments of inertia of the solid, which we have considered, with respect to axis of x'', of y'', and of z''. Naming C' the moment of inertia of the same solid with respect to the axis of z', by means of the values of x', y', and z', which are given in the preceding number, we shall find

$$C' = A.\sin.^2\theta.\sin.^2\varphi + B.\sin.^2\theta.\cos.^2\varphi + C.\cos.^2\theta. \ *$$

The quantities $\sin.^2\theta.\ \sin.^2\varphi$, $\sin.^2\theta$, $\cos.^2\varphi$, $\cos.^2\theta$, are the squares of the cosines of the angles, which the axes of x'', of y'', and of z'', make with the axis of z'; hence it follows in general that, if we multiply the moment of inertia relative to each principal axis of rotation,

* Since $S.(x''^2+y''^2+z''^2)\,dm = S.(x'^2+y'^2+z'^2).\,dm$ by substituting the value of $z',^2$ in terms of $x'',^2\,y'',^2\,z''.^2$ and observing that $S.x''y''.dm$, $Sx''z''.dm$, $Sy''z''.dm$, are equal to nothing, we have

$$Sx''.^2dm + Sy''.^2dm + Sz''.^2dm = S.x'.^2dm + S.y'.^2dm + S.x''.^2\sin.^2\theta.\sin.^2\varphi\,dm$$

$$+ S\,y''.^2\sin.^2\theta.\cos.^2\varphi\,dm + Sz''.^2\cos.^2\theta.dm \therefore Sx''^2(1-\sin.^2\theta.\sin.^2\varphi)dm$$

$$+ Sy^{2''}.(1-\sin.^2\theta.\cos.^2\varphi).dm +$$

$$Sz''.^2(1-\cos.^2\theta).dm = S(x'^2+y'^2).dm \therefore = S.x''.^2(\cos.^2\theta+\sin.^2\theta.\cos.^2\varphi).dm$$

$$+ S'y'.^2(\cos.^2\theta+\sin.^2\theta.\sin.^2\varphi)dm$$

$$+ S.z''.^2\sin.^2\theta.\sin.^2\varphi\,dm + S.z''.^2\sin.^2\theta.\cos.^2\theta.dm$$

and making the like factors coalesce we obtain C'

$$S.(y''.^2+z''^2).\sin.^2\theta.\sin.^2\varphi.dm + S.(x''^2+z''^2).\sin.^2\theta.\cos.^2\varphi.dm + S\,(x''^2+y''^2).\cos.^2\theta.\,dm \quad \text{i, e,}$$

$$C' = A.\sin.^2\theta.\sin.^2\varphi + B.\sin.^2\theta.\cos.^2\varphi + C.\cos.^2\theta.;$$

$\sin.\theta.\sin.\varphi$, $\sin.\theta.\cos.\varphi$, $\cos.\theta$, are equal to the cosines of the angles which the axes of x'', of y'' and of z'' make with the axes of z', see Note, page 132.

by the square of the cosine of the angle which it makes with any axis, the sum of the three products, will be the moment of inertia of the solid, relative to this last axis.

The quantity C' is less than the greatest, and greater than the least of the three quantities * A, B, C,; therefore the greatest and least moments of inertia appertain to the principal axes. †

* Let A be the greatest and C the least moment of inertia, the value of C' may be made to assume the following form

$$C' = A + (B-A).\sin.^2\theta.\cos.^2\phi + (C-A).\cos.^2\theta,$$

∴ since the moments of inertia are always affirmative, the two last terms of the second member of this equation will be negative, consequently C' is less than A, let C be the greatest moment of inertia and the expression for C' will become

$$C + (A-C)\ \sin.^2\theta.\sin.^2\phi + (B-C).\sin.^2\theta.\cos.^2\phi,$$

in this case also the two last terms of the second member are negative, ∴ C' is less than C; the moment of inertia C' is greater than the least of the three principal moments, for if A be the least of the three moments which refer to the principal axes, we have as before

$$C' = A + (B-A).\sin.^2\theta.\cos.^2\phi + (C-A).\cos.^2\theta,$$

and as the differences are on the present hypothesis affirmative, C' is greater than A, let C be the least of the three moments, and we have

$$C' = C + (A-C).\sin.^2\theta\,\sin.^2\phi + (B-A).\sin.^2\theta.\cos.^2\phi,$$

the terms which compose the second members are always affirmative, ∴ we conclude that C' is greater than the least of the three moments, A, B, C,

From what has been established in the preceding note, it appears that when the three principal moments of inertia are unequal there is only one system of principal axes, for let there be another system and make A', B', C', the moments of inertia relative to these axes, then we shall have at the same time $A > A'$ and $A' > A$ which is impossible, see note to page 178.

† For $S(x'-X)^2.dm = Sx'.^2dm - 2X.Sx'.dm + X^2m = Sx'.^2dm - 2X^2m + X^2m$, for $Sx'.dm = X.m$. and as the quantity $-m.(X^2+Y^2)$ is essentially negative, the moment of inertia with respect to the centre of gravity must be less than the corresponding moment for any axis not passing through the centre of gravity. If the moments are referred to an axis passing through a point different from the centre of gravity and of which the coordinates are a, b, c,

Let X, Y, Z, be the coordinates of the centre of gravity of the solid, relatively to the origin of the coordinates which we fix at the point about which the body is subjected to revolve, if it is not free; $x'-X$, $y'-Y$, $z'-Z$, will be coordinates of the molecule of the body, with respect to the centre of gravity; therefore the moment of inertia, relative to an axis passing through the centre of gravity, and parallel to the axis of z' will be

$$S.\left\{(x'-X)^2+(y'-Y)^2\right\}.dm;$$

but from the nature of the centre of gravity, we have $S.\,x'.dm=m\,X$, $S.\,y'.dm=mY$; $\therefore$ the preceding expression will be reduced to

$$-m.\,(X \quad Y^2)+S.(x'^2+y'^2).\,dm.$$

Consequently we shall have the moments of inertia of the solid, with respect to an axis passing through any point whatever; when these moments are known for axes passing through the centre of gravity. At the same time it appears that the minimum minimorum of the moments of inertia appertains to one of the three principal axes, passing through this centre.

Let us suppose the nature of the body to be such, that the two moments of inertia A and B are equal, then we shall have

$$C'=A.\,\sin.^2\theta+C.\,\cos.^2\theta;\ *$$

the value of the moment of inertia with respect to this point is equal to

$$A-2.(aX+bY).\,m+(a^2+b^2).m$$

It is evident from an inspection of their values, that the greatest moment of inertia with respect to any point, is less than the sum of the other two moments.

* When $A=B$ the moment of inertia with respect to any other axis $=A.\,\sin,^2\theta+C.\,\cos.^2\theta$, and as neither ψ or φ occur in this expression, the moment of inertia for all axes making the same angle, with the axis of z' are equal, and if θ be a right angle $C'=A$, therefore in this case there is an indefinite number of principal axes, but they have all a common axis z'', when $\theta=100°$ we have $a^2=b^2$ and $f=0$ i, e, $Sx'^2dm=Sy'^2dm$ and $Sx'y'.dm=0$ this also

and by making θ equal to a right angle, which will render the axis of z' perpendicular to the axis of z'', we shall have $C'=A$; therefore the moments of inertia relative to all axes situated in the plane perpendicular to the axis of z'' are then equal to each other. But it is easy to be assured that we have in this case for the system of the axis of z'', and of any two axes perpendicular to each other, and to this axis,

$$S.\,x'y'.dm=0\,;\quad S.\,x'z''.dm=0\,;\quad S.\,y'z''.dm=0\,;$$

for if we denote by x'' and y'' the coordinates of a molecule dm referred to the principal axes, taken in the plane perpendicular to the axis of z'', and with respect to which the moments of inertia are supposed equal, we shall have

$$S.(x''^2+y''^2).dm=S.\,(y''^2+z''^2).dm\,;$$

or simply $S.x''^2.dm=S.\,y''^2.dm$; but by naming ϵ the angle which the axis of x' makes with the axis of x'', we have

$$x'=x''.\cos.\,\epsilon+y''.\sin.\,\epsilon\,;$$

$$y'=y''.\cos.\,\epsilon-x''.\sin.\,\epsilon\,;$$

consequently we have

$$S.\,x'y'.dm=S.\,x''y''.dm\,(\cos.^2\epsilon-\sin.^2\epsilon)$$

$$+\,S.\,(y''^2-x''^2).\,dm.\,\sin.\,\epsilon.\,\cos.\,\epsilon=0$$

we shall find in like manner $S.\,x'z''.dm=0$; $S.\,y'z''.dm=0$; therefore all axes perpendicular to the axis of z'', are in this case principal axes; and in this case the solid has an infinite number of similar axes.

follows from the equations $x'=x''.\cos.\,\epsilon+y''\sin.\,\epsilon$, $y'=y''.\cos.\,\epsilon-x''\sin.\,\epsilon$ for $S.\,x'^2dm=S.(x''^2\cos.^2\epsilon+Sy''^2\sin.^2\epsilon).=S.x''^2dm=Sy''^2dm$, since $Sx''y''.dm=0$, in the case of an ellipsoid generated by the revolution of an ellipse above its minor axis, we have always two of the principal moments of inertia equal, the moment which is the greatest is referred to the minor axis.

If we have at the same time $A=B=C$; we shall have generally $C'=A$; * that is to say, all the moments of inertia of the solid are equal, but then we have generally,

$$S.x'y'.dm=0;\ S.x'z'.dm=0;\ S.y'z'.dm=0;$$

whatever may be the position of the plane of x' and of y'; so that all the axes are principal axes. This is the case of the sphere, and we shall see in the sequel that this property belongs to an infinite number of other solids of which the equation will be given.†

* Since by hypothesis $A=B=C$, $Sx''.^2dm=Sy''.^2dm=Sz''.^2dm$, $\therefore$ if in the expression for z'^2 in terms of x''^2, y''^2, z''^2 and of the angle θ, ψ, φ, we take this into account and also observe that $S.x''y''.dm$, $Sx''z''.dm$. $S.y''z''.dm$, are equal to nothing, we shall find $S.z'^2\,dm=Sz''^2\,dm$ for $z'=z''.\cos.\theta-y''.\sin.\theta.\cos.\varphi-x''.\sin.\theta.\sin\varphi$ $\therefore$ $z'^2=z''^2\cos.^2\theta+y''^2\sin.^2\theta.\cos.^2\varphi+x''^2\sin.^2\theta.\sin^2\varphi=$ (when $x''^2=y''^2=z''^2$) z''^2, the same is true respecting y'^2 and x'^2, on the other hand if we equate z''^2 and its value in a function of x' y', z' and the angles θ, ψ, φ, and also satisfy the equations $Sx'^2\,dm=Sy'^2\,dm=Sz'^2\,dm$, we must equate $Sx'y'.dm$, $Sx'z'dm$, $Sy'z'dm$ to nothing. (See Book V. Chap. I. No. 2.)

† x'' y'' z'' being the coordinates with respect to the principal axes of any point of the solid, if we transfer the origin to a point of which the coordinates are a, b, c, then the coordinates relative to the new origin will be $x''-a, y''-b, z''-c$, now if we suppose that the three principal moments of inertia with respect to this new origin are equal, then all rectangular axes, and $\therefore$ the axes of $x''-a, y''-b, z''-c$, will be principal axes, consequently we shall have

$$\Sigma.(x''-a)(y''-b).dm=\Sigma.x''y''.dm-a\,\Sigma.y''.dm-b\,\Sigma.x''dm+a\,b\,\Sigma dm=0$$

$$\Sigma.(x''-a).(z''-c).dm=\Sigma x''z''.dm-a\,\Sigma.z''.dm-c\,\Sigma x''.dm+a\,c.\,\Sigma dm=0$$

$$\Sigma.(y''-b).(z''-c).dm=\Sigma.y''.z''.dm-b\,\Sigma.z''.dm-c\,\Sigma.y''.dm+bc\,\Sigma dm=0$$

now if we suppose the origin of the coordinates x'', y'', z'', to be at the centre of gravity the preceding equations will be reduced to $ab.\,\Sigma dm=0$, $a\,c.\,\Sigma dm=0$, $bc.\,\Sigma dm=0$ $\therefore$ two of the preceding quantities must vanish, let b, c, be equal to nothing and a will be undetermined, $\therefore$ the point required will be at a distance equal to a from the origin by a foregoing note the moments of inertia with respect to this point will be $A, B+ma^2, C+ma^2$ and by the conditions of the problem they are supposed to be equal $\therefore$ we have $a=\pm\sqrt{\dfrac{A-C}{m}}$, $\therefore$ A being greater than C we have two values of a equally distant on

28. The quantities p, q, r, which we have introduced in the equations (C) of No. 26. have this remarkable property, that they determine the position of the real and instantaneous axis of rotation with respect to the principal axes. In fact, we have relatively to all points situated in the axis of rotation, $dx'=0$; $dy'=0$; $dz'=0$; if we difference the values of x', y', z', of No. 26, and then make sin. $\psi=0$ after the dif-

opposite sides from the centre of gravity, but a is also equal to $\frac{\sqrt{A-B}}{\sqrt{m}}$ ∴ in order that these two values of a should be possible, it is requisite that B should be equal to C, ∴ when A B C are unequal there is no point which satisfies the required conditions and when two of the moments are equal, the third must be greater than either of them, and in this case the point required is situated on the axis relative to which the principal moment of inertia is the greatest, when the three moments of inertia are equal the two points are concentrated in the common centre of gravity. When $B=C$ we have $S.y''.^2dm=Sz''.^2dm$.

In an ellipsoid generated by the revolution of an ellipse of an ellipse round its minor axis two of the three principal moments relative to the principal diameters are equal, and the greatest moment is relative to the minor axis, see note page 181, ∴ we shall have two points existing on this axis relatively to which all the moments of inertia are equal, it is easy to shew that the distance of those points from the centre of the ellipsoid is = to the square root of the fifth part of the difference between the squares of the semi-axes, and ∴ they may be within the ellipsoid, at its surface, or finally without this surface.

We might have inferred a priori that there is an axis with respect to which the moment of inertia is a maximum and a minimum, for from their nature all moments of inertia are positive and have a finite magnitude, and most authors deduce the properties of principal axes from the moments of inertia which are the greatest and least, the general expression for $S.(x''^2+y''^2).dm$ in terms of x' y' and z' is equal to

$$S.x'^2.dm.\cos.^2\theta\sin.^2\psi+S.x'^2dm.\cos.^2\psi+S.y'.^2dm\cos.^2\theta.\cos.^2\psi+Sy'.^2dm\sin.^2\psi$$

$$+S.z'^2.dm\sin.^2\theta+2\,Sx'y'dm.\cos.^2\theta.\sin.\psi.\cos.\psi$$

$$-2S.x'y'.dm.\sin.\psi.\cos.\psi-2S.z'x'.dm\sin.\theta.\cos.\theta.\sin.\psi-2\,S.z'y'dm.\sin.\theta.\cos.\theta.\cos.\psi.$$

When the law of the variation of the density and the equation of the generating curve of a solid of revolution are given, the value of $S.(x'^2+y'^2).\ dm$ may be computed by a method similar to that by which the centre of gravity of a body is determined; the value of $S(x^2+y'^2).dm$ is computed for the earth in Book V. Chapter I. No. 2.

ferentiations which we are permitted to do, since the position of the axis of x' on the plane of x', y', is indeterminate, we shall have

$$dx' = x''.\{d\psi.\cos.\theta.\sin.\varphi - d\varphi.\sin.\varphi) + y''.\{d\psi.\cos.\theta.\cos.\varphi$$

$$-d\varphi.\cos.\varphi\} + z''.d\psi.\sin.\theta = 0;$$

$$dy' = x''.\{d\varphi.\cos.\theta.\cos.\varphi - d\theta.\sin.\theta.\sin.\varphi - d\psi.\cos.\varphi\}$$

$$+ y''.\{d\psi.\sin.\varphi - d\varphi.\cos.\theta.\sin.\varphi - d\theta.\sin.\theta.\cos.\varphi\}$$

$$+ z''.d\theta.\cos.\theta = 0;$$

$$dz' = -x''.(d\theta.\cos.\theta.\sin.\varphi + d\varphi.\sin.\theta.\cos.\varphi)$$

$$-y''.(d\theta.\cos.\theta.\cos.\varphi - d\varphi.\sin.\theta.\sin.\varphi) - z''.d\theta.\sin.\theta = 0.$$

If we multiply the first of these equations by $-\sin.\varphi$; the second by $\cos.\theta.\cos.\varphi$, and the third by $-\sin.\theta.\cos.\varphi$; we shall have by adding them together,

$$0 = px'' - qz''.$$

Multiplying the first of the same equations by $\cos.\varphi$; the second by $\cos.\theta.\sin.\varphi$, and the third by $-\sin.\theta.\sin.\varphi$, and then adding them together we shall obtain

$$0 = py'' - rz''.$$

Finally, if we multiply the second of those equations by $\sin.\theta$, and the third by $\cos.\theta$, and then add them together, their addition will give *

$$0 = qy'' - rx.''$$

* In taking the differentials of dx', dy', dz', we may omit those quantities in which $\sin.\psi$ occurs after the differentiations, and where $\cos.\psi$ occurs, we may substitute unity; multiplying the value of dx' which results by $-\sin.\varphi$, it becomes

$$-dx'.\sin.\varphi = -x''.(d\psi.\cos.\theta.\sin.^2\varphi - d\varphi.\sin.^2\varphi) - y''.(d\psi.\cos.\theta.\sin.\varphi\cos.\varphi$$

$$-d\varphi.\sin.\varphi.\cos.\varphi) - z''.d\psi.\sin.\theta.\sin.\varphi;$$

This last equation evidently results from the two preceding; thus the three equations $dx'=0$, $dy'=0$, $dz'=0$ reduce themselves to these two equations which belong to a right line, forming with the axes of x'',

B B 2

and in like manner multiplying dy' and its value by cos. θ. cos φ, we have

$$dy'.\cos.\theta.\cos.\varphi = x''(d\varphi.\cos.^2\theta.\cos.^2\varphi - d\theta.\sin.\theta.\cos.\theta\sin.\varphi.\cos.\varphi - d\psi.\cos.\theta.\cos.^2\varphi)$$

$$+y''.(d\psi.\sin.\varphi\cos.\varphi.\cos.\theta - d\varphi.\cos.^2\theta.\sin.\varphi.\cos.\varphi - d\theta.\sin.\theta.\cos.\theta.\cos.^2\varphi)$$

$$+z''.d\theta.\cos.^2\theta.\cos.\varphi$$

and the multiplication of dz', and its value by—sin. θ. cos. φ, gives

$$-dz'.\sin.\theta.\cos.\varphi = x''(d\theta.\sin.\theta.\cos.\theta.\sin.\varphi.\cos.\varphi + d\varphi.\sin.^2\theta.\cos.^2\varphi)$$

$$+y''(d\theta.\sin.\theta.\cos.\theta.\cos.^2\varphi - d\varphi.\sin.^2\theta.\sin.\varphi.\cos.\varphi) + z''.d\theta.\sin.^2\theta.\cos.\varphi$$

adding these quantities together and making the factors of the differentials of θ, ψ, φ, which belong to the same coordinates coalesce we obtain

$$-x''.(d\psi.\cos.\theta + d\varphi) + z''.(d\theta.\cos.\varphi - d\psi.\sin.\theta.\sin.\varphi) = 0 =$$

(by substituting p and q instead of their values) $x''.p - z''.q$; multiplying the first equation by cos. Φ. the second by cos. θ. sin. φ, and the third by—sin. θ. sin. φ, we obtain

$$dx'.\cos.\varphi = x''.(d\psi.\cos.\theta.\sin.\varphi.\cos.\varphi - d\varphi.\sin.\varphi.\cos.\varphi)$$

$$+y''(d\psi.\cos.\theta.\cos.^2\varphi - d\varphi.\cos.^2\varphi) + z''.d\psi.\sin.\theta.\cos.\varphi$$

$$dy'.\cos.\theta.\sin.\varphi, = x''(d\varphi.\cos.^2\theta.\sin.\varphi.\cos.\varphi - d\theta.\sin.\theta.\cos.\theta.\sin.^2\varphi$$

$$-d\psi.\sin.\varphi.\cos.\varphi.\cos.\theta)$$

$$+y'(d\psi.\sin.^2\varphi.\cos.\theta - d\varphi.\cos.^2\theta.\sin.^2\varphi - d\theta.\sin.\theta.\cos.\theta.\sin.\varphi.\cos.\varphi)$$

$$+z''.d\theta.\cos.^2\theta.\sin.\varphi$$

$$-dz'.\sin.\theta.\sin.\varphi = x''.(d\theta.\sin.\theta.\cos.\theta.\sin.^2\varphi + d\varphi.\sin.^2\theta.\sin.\varphi.\cos.\varphi)$$

$$+y''.(d\theta.\sin.\theta.\cos.\theta.\sin.\varphi.\cos.\varphi - d\varphi.\sin.^2\theta.\sin.^2\varphi) + z''.d\theta.\sin.^2\theta.\sin.\varphi$$

adding and concinnating as before we obtain

$$y''.(d\psi.\cos.\theta. - d\varphi) + z''.(d\psi.\sin.\theta.\cos.\varphi + d\theta.\sin.\varphi) = 0 = -y''p + z''.r$$

of y'' and of z'', angles of which the cosines are

$$\frac{q}{\sqrt{p^2+q^2+r^2}},\quad \frac{r}{\sqrt{p^2+q^2+r^2}},\quad \frac{p}{\sqrt{p^2+q^2+r^2}}\ *$$

multiplying the second equation by sin. θ, and the third by cos. θ, we obtain

$$dy'.\sin.\theta = x''.(d\varphi.\cos.\varphi.\sin.\theta.\cos.\theta - d\theta.\sin.^2\theta.\sin.\varphi - d\psi.\sin.\theta.\cos.\varphi)$$

$$+y''.(d\psi.\sin.\theta.\sin.\varphi - d\varphi.\sin.\theta.\cos.\theta.\sin.\varphi - d\theta.\sin.^2\theta.\cos.\varphi) + z''.d\theta.\sin.\theta.\cos.\theta.$$

$$dz'.\cos.\theta = -x''.(d\theta.\cos.^2\theta.\sin.\varphi + d\varphi.\sin.\theta.\cos.\theta.\cos.\varphi)$$

$$-y''.(d\theta.\cos.^2\theta.\cos.\varphi - d\varphi.\sin.\theta.\cos.\theta.\sin.\varphi) - z''.d\theta.\sin.\theta.\cos.\theta$$

∴ adding and concinnating we have

$$-x''.(d\theta.\sin.\varphi + d\psi.\sin.\theta.\cos.\varphi) - y''.(d\theta.\cos.\varphi - d\psi.\sin.\theta.\sin.\varphi) = -x''r + y''.q.$$

* The equations $px'' - qz'' = 0$ — &c. are the equations of the projections of the line, relatively to which dx' dy' are equal to nothing at any instant, on the planes x'' z'', y'' z'', &c. ∴ the cosines of the angles which this line makes with the axes are respectively

$$\frac{q}{\sqrt{p^2+q^2-r^2}},\quad \frac{r}{\sqrt{p^2+q^2+r^2}}\quad \frac{p}{\sqrt{p^2+q^2+r^2}}.$$

For these cosines are equal to

$$\frac{x''}{\sqrt{x''^2+y''^2+z''}} = \frac{\dfrac{qz''}{p}}{\sqrt{\dfrac{q^2z''^2}{p^2}+\dfrac{r^2z''^2}{p^2}+z''^2}} = \frac{q}{\sqrt{p^2+r^2+q^2}}$$

and the same is true of the other cosines.

From the preceding analysis it follows, that the locus of all the points whose velocity is nothing at any given moment is a right line, whose position with respect to the principal axes is determined by p, q, r, ∴ the preceding equations both evince the existence of such a line and indicate its position, and a body revolving about a fixed point may be considered as revolving about an axis determined in this manner, but as in general p, q, r, vary from one instant to another, being functions of the time, the *position* of this axis will also vary, and hence it is that this axis has been termed by some authors the axis of instantaneous rotation; when p, q, r, are constant, the axis of rotation will remain immoveable during the motion of the system.

Therefore this right line quiesces, and constitutes the real axis of rotation of the body. *

* The values which have been given for $px''-qz''$, $py''-rz''$, $qy''-rx''$, enables us to determine the linear velocity of each point resolved parallel to the axes of x' y' and z' for if we multiply the first of the preceding equations by cos. θ. cos. φ. the second by cos. θ. sin. φ. and the third by sin. θ. we shall obtain by adding them together

$$-dx'.\cos.\theta.\sin.\varphi.\cos.\varphi+dy'.\cos.^2\theta.\cos.^2\varphi-dz.\sin.\theta.\cos.\theta.\cos.^2\varphi$$

$$+dx'.\cos.\theta.\sin.\varphi.\cos.\varphi+dy'.\cos.^2\theta.\sin.^2\varphi-dz'.\sin.\theta.\cos.\theta.\sin.^2\varphi+dy'.\sin.^2\theta$$

$$+dz'.\sin.\theta.\cos.\theta=dy'=(px''-qz'').\cos.\theta.\cos.\varphi+(py''-rz'').\cos.\theta.\sin.\varphi$$

$$+(qy''-rx'').\sin.\theta\text{; if we multiply } px''-qz'' \text{ by}-\sin.\varphi \text{ and } py''-rz''$$

by cos. φ we shall obtain

$$dx'.\sin.^2\varphi-dy'.\cos.\theta.\sin.\varphi.\cos.\varphi+dz'.\sin.\theta.\sin.\varphi.\cos.\varphi+dx'.\cos.^2\varphi$$

$$+dy'.\cos.\theta.\sin.\varphi.\cos.\varphi-dz.\sin.\theta.\sin.\varphi.\cos.\varphi=dx'$$

$$=-(px''-qz'').\sin.\varphi+(py''-rz'').\cos.\varphi\text{, multiplying } px''-qz'' \text{ by}-\sin.\theta.\cos.\varphi,$$

$$py''-rz'' \text{ by}-\sin.\theta.\sin.\varphi. \text{ and } qy''-rx'' \text{ by } \cos.\theta,$$

we shall obtain

$$dx'.\sin.\theta.\sin.\varphi.\cos.\varphi-dy'\sin.\theta.\cos.\theta.\cos.^2\varphi+dz'.\sin.^2\theta.\cos.^2\varphi$$

$$-dx'.\sin.\theta.\sin.\varphi.\cos.\varphi-dy.\sin.\theta.\cos.\theta.\sin.^2\varphi+dz'.\sin.^2\theta.\sin.^2\varphi+dy'.\sin.\theta.\cos.\theta.$$

$$+dz'\cos.^2\theta=dz'=-(px''-qz'')\sin.\theta.\cos.\varphi-(py''-rz'').\sin.\theta.\sin.\varphi+(qy''-rx'').\cos.\theta\text{;}$$

we might in like manner obtain the value of the accelerating forces resolved parallel to the axes of x' y' and z', by taking the differentials of dz', dy', dz', and of their respective values.

Since as has been observed, in note, page 166, the coordinates of x'', y'', z'', do not vary with the time, and as the angles θ, ψ, φ, are functions of the time, it follows that when we take the differential of x'' y'' and z'' respectively in terms of the coordinates x', y', z', and of the angles θ, ψ, φ, the sines and cosines of these angles must be considered as constant, ∴ keeping this in view and also that sin. $\psi=0$ after the differentiations we shall obtain

$$dx''=dx'.\cos.\varphi+dy'.\cos.\theta.\sin.\varphi-dz'.\sin.\theta.\sin.\varphi\text{; } dy''=-dx'.\sin.\varphi+dy'.\cos.\theta.\cos.\varphi$$

$$-dz'.\sin.\theta.\cos.\varphi\text{; } dz''=dy'.\sin.\theta+dz'.\cos.\theta\text{;}$$

In order to determine the velocity of rotation of the body, let us consider that point of the axis of z'', of which the distance from the origin of the coordinates is represented by a quantity equal to unity. We shall have the velocities parallel to the axes of x' of y' and of z', by making $x''=0$, $y''=0$, $z''=1$, in the preceding expressions of dx', dy', dz', and then dividing them by dt, which gives for these partial velocities

$$\frac{d\psi}{dt}.\sin.\theta;\ \frac{d\theta}{dt}.\cos.\theta;\ \frac{-d\theta}{dt}.\sin.\theta;$$

therefore the entire velocity of the point in question, is $\frac{\sqrt{d\theta^2+d\psi^2.\sin.^2\theta}}{dt}$

or $\sqrt{q^2+r^2}$, and dividing this expression by the distance of the point from the instantaneous axis of rotation, we shall have the angular velocity of rotation of the body; but this distance is evidently equal to the sine of the angle, which the real axis of rotation makes with the axis of z'', and the cosine of this angle is equal to $\frac{p}{\sqrt{p^2+q^2+r^2}}$;

but it is evident from what precedes that the second members of these equations are equal respectively to

$$(py''-rz'',).\,dt,\ (px''-qz''.).\,dt,\ (qy''-rx'').\,dt$$

∴ we have

$$\frac{dx''}{dt}=py''-rz'',\ \frac{dy''}{dt}=px''-qz'',\ \frac{dz''}{dt}=qy''-rx'',$$

consequently the quantities p, q, r, which determine the position of the axes of rotation, give also for any other point the linear and angular velocities of the different points of the body resolved parallel to the coordinates x'', y'', and z''.

therefore $\sqrt{p^2+q^2+r^2}$ will be equal to the angular velocity of rotation.*

It appears from what precedes that whatever may be the rotatory motion of a body, about a fixed point, or a point considered as fixed; this motion must be considered as a motion of rotation about a fixed axis *during* an instant, but which may vary from one moment to another. The position of this axis with respect to the principal axes, and the angular velocity of rotation depend on the variables p, q, r, the determination of which is most important in these investigations, and as they express quantities independent of the situation of the plane of x' and y', are themselves independent of this situation.

29. Let us proceed to determine these variables in functions of the time, in that case in which the body is not solicited by any accelerating forces. For this purpose, let us resume the equations (D) of No. 26, existing between the variables p', q', r', which are in a given ratio to

* $$\frac{p}{\sqrt{p^2+q^2+r^2}}$$

= the cosine of the angle which the axis of z' makes with the instantaneous axis of rotation ∴

$$1-\frac{p^2}{p^2+q^2+r^2}=\frac{q^2+r^2}{p^2+q^2+r^2}$$

is equal to the square of the sine of the same angle, and since z'' is by hypothesis equal to unity we have the perpendicular distance of the point in question from the axis of rotation equal to this sine, ∴ dividing $\sqrt{q^2+r^2}$ by this distance the quote will be equal to $\sqrt{p^2+q^2+r^2}$, and as the axis during an instant may be considered as fixed the angular velocity of all points during this instant will be the same, the selection of the point so circumstanced that $x''=0$, $y''=0$, $z''=1$ is made in order to simplify the calculus, ∴ it appears from an inspection of the value of the angular velocity, that it is constant when p q and r are constant, *i, e,* when the axis of rotation is immoveable, but the converse of this proposition is not true for it is possible that the function $\sqrt{p^2+q^2+r^2}$ should be constant, while at the same time its component parts may vary, see page 197.

the variables $p, q, r,$.* In this case, the differentials dN, dN', dN'' vanish, and these equations being multiplied by p', q', and r' respectively and then added together give

$$0 = p'.dp' + q'.dq' + r'.dr';$$

and integrating them we shall obtain

$$p'^2 + q'^2 + r'^2 = k^2;$$

k being a constant arbitrary quantity.

If we multiply the equations (D) by $AB.p'$, $BC.q'$, and $AC.r'$, and then add them together, we shall obtain by integrating their sum,

$$AB.p'^2 + BC.q'^2 + AC.r'^2 = H^2;$$

H being a constant arbitrary quantity; this equation involves the principle of the conservation of living forces. † By means of the two pre-

* $p : p' :: 1 : C :: 1 : S(x''^2 + y''^2).dm$, but this is a constant ratio, because the position of the principal axes being given, the quantity $S(x''^2 + y''^2).\ dm$ is constant, and when no exterior forces act on the body, the quantities N, N', N'', are constant and $\therefore$ $dN\ dN'\ dN''$ vanish.

† For substituting for p', q', r', their values, we obtain

$$A.B.C(Cp^2 + Aq^2 + Br^2) = H^2, \therefore S(x''^2 + y''^2)dm.\ p^2 + S\,(y''^2 + z''^2)dm''.q^2$$
$$+ S(x'' + z''^2)\,dm.\ r^2 =$$

a constant quantity, now we have seen in a preceding note, that the velocity of any point resolved parallel to the axes of x'' of y'' and of z'' is equal to $rx'' - qz''$, $py'' - rz''$, $qy'' - rx''$

and the sum of the squares of these quantities

$$= p^2x''^2 + q^2z''^2 + p''^2y''^2 + r^2z''^2 + q^2y''^2 + r^2x''^2 - 2pq.\ x''z'' - 2pr.y''z'' - 2qry''x'', =$$

the square of the velocity of the point whose coordinates are x'', y'', z'', $\therefore$ this expression multiplied by dm equals the living force of this molecule, now as the quantities p, q, r, are the same for all molecules at the same instant, the sum of the living forces of all the

ceding integrals we shall obtain

$$q'^2 = \frac{AC.k^2 - H^2 + A.(B-C).\,p'^2}{C.\,(A-B)} \,*$$

$$r'^2 = \frac{H^2 - BC.k^2 - B.(A-C).p'^2}{C(A-B)}$$

thus, we shall have q' and r' in functions of the time, when p' will be determined, but from the first of the equations (D) we have

$$dt = \frac{AB.dp'}{(A-B).q'r'.} \;;$$

consequently

molecules will be equal to

$$p^2.\smallint(x''^2+y''^2).dm + q^2\smallint(y''^2+z'')^2.dm + r.^2\smallint x''^2+z''^2).dm$$

$$-2pq\smallint x''z''.dm - 2pr\smallint y''z''.dm - 2qr\smallint y''x''.dm,$$

but these latter quantities vanish, x'', y'', z'', belonging to the principal axes consequently

$$p^2\smallint(x''^2+y''^2).dm + q^2\smallint y''^2+z''^2)dm + r^2\smallint(x''^2+z''^2).dm$$

is equal to the sum of the living forces, and being constant as has been just shewn, it follows that the expression

$$AB.p'^2 + BC.\,q'^2 + AC.\,r'^2 = H^2,$$

involves the principal of the conservation of living forces.

$$*\; r'^2 = k^2 - p'^2 - q'^2 = \frac{H^2 - AB.\,p'^2 - BC.\,q'^2}{AC}$$

$\therefore\; AC.k^2 - ACp'^2 - AC.q'^2 = H^2 - AB.p'^2 - BC.\,q'^2$ therefore $q'^2 =$

$$\frac{AC.k^2 - H^2 + A.(B-C)p'^2}{C.(A-B)},$$

the value of r'^2 is derived in a similar manner.

$$dt = \frac{ABC.dp'}{\sqrt{\{AC.k^2 - H^2 + A.(B-C).p'^2\}.\{H^2 - BC.k^2 - B.(A-C).p'^2\}}}*$$

* When $A = B$, $dt = \dfrac{ABC.dp'}{\sqrt{(AC.k^2 - H^2 + A.(A-C)p'^2).(H^2 - ACk^2 - A(A-C).p'^2)}}$

$$= \frac{ABC.dp'}{\sqrt{-(AC.k^2 - H^2 + A(A-C)p'^2)^2}} =$$

$$\frac{ABC.dp'}{ACk^2 - H^2 + A(A-C)p'^2}$$

and it may be made to assume the form

$$C_{,}.\frac{a^2.dp'}{a^2+p'^2}\left(C_{,} \text{ being equal to } \frac{ABC}{AC.k^2 - H^2}\right)$$

and a^2 being equal to $\dfrac{ACk^2 - H^2}{A.(A-C)}$

and the integral of this expression $= t = C_{,}$. (arc tangent$=p'$ to radius$= a$. the constant quantity is equal to nothing because $t=0$ at the same time with p'. When $A = C$ the expression for dt becomes

$$\frac{AB.C.dp'}{\sqrt{(A^2k^2 - H^2 + A.(B-A)p'^2).(H^2 - BAk^2)}}$$

this expression may be reduced to the form

$$C_{,}.\frac{dp'}{\sqrt{a^2+p'^2}}\left(\text{in which } C_{,} \text{ is equal to } \frac{A^2B}{A(B-A).(H^2 - BAk)}\right)$$

and $a^2 = \dfrac{Ak^2 - H^2}{A.(B-A)}$

the integral $= C_{,}.\log(p' + \sqrt{a^2+p'^2}$

If $B = C$ then $dt \dfrac{AB^2dp'}{\sqrt{(AC.k^2 - H^2)(H^2 - B^2k^2 - B)(A-B)).p^2}} = \quad -C_{,} - \dfrac{a.dp'}{\sqrt{a^2 - p'^2}}$

and the integral will be arc sine $= p'$ rad $= a$

$C_{,}$ being equal to $\dfrac{AB^2}{\sqrt{ACk^2 - H^2.(H^2 - B^2k^2)}}$.

and $a^2 = \dfrac{(ACk^2 - H^2).(H^2 - Bk^2)}{-B.(A-B)}$

if $ACk^2 = H^2$ then

this equation is only integrable in one of the three following cases, $B=A$, $B=C$, $A=C$.

The determination of the three quantities p', q', r', involves three arbitrary quantities, H^2, k^2 and that which the integration of the preceding differential equation introduces. But these quantities only give the position of the instantaneous axis of rotation of the body, on the surface, *i, e,* with respect to the three principal axes, and its angular velocity of rotation. In order to have the real motion of the body, about the fixed point, we must also know the position of the principal axes in space; * this should introduce three new arbitrary quantities

C C 2

$$q'^2_{\;} = \frac{A.(B-C).p'^2}{C(A-B)} \text{ and } dt = \frac{ABC\, dp'}{\sqrt{A(B-C)p'^2(H^2-BCk^2-B.(A-C)p'^2}}$$

$$= C_, \frac{2adp}{p'\sqrt{a^2-p'^2}}$$

in which $2C_, = \dfrac{ABC}{\sqrt{(A(B-C)\,H^2-BC.\,k^2)}}$

and $a^2 = \dfrac{A(B-C).(H^2-BCk^2)}{-B.(A-C)}$

its integral will be equal to $C_, .\log. \dfrac{a-\sqrt{a^2-p^2}}{a+\sqrt{a^2-p^2}}$

See Lacroix, page 256, No. 174. and if $H^2=BC.k^2$ then

$$dt = \frac{ABC.dp'}{\sqrt{ACk^2-H^2+A(B-C)p'^2)(-B(A-C)p'^2)}}$$

$$= C_, \frac{2adp'}{p'.\sqrt{a+p'^2}} \text{ and } t = C_, .\log. \frac{\sqrt{a^2+p'}-a}{\sqrt{a^2+p'^2}+a},$$

the constant quantities vanish for these integrals, beeause as has been already mentioned $p'=0$ when t vanishes. The value of dt eannot be exhibited in a finite form except in the cases already specified, and when all the moments of inertia are equal, in every other case, the value of the integral of dt must be obtained by the method of quadratunes.

* From the quantities p', q', r', we can collect the values of p, q, r, which are in a given ratio to them, and from these last quantities we obtain the cosines of the angles which the axis of instantaneous rotation makes with the principal axes, but as these axes though fixed in the body are moveable in space, we must know the position of these axes at the com-

which depend on the initial position of these axes, and which require three new integrals, which being joined to the preceding quantities will

mencement of the motion, in order to have the real motion of the body, which gives three constant quantities.

Substituting in the values of $-N, -N', -N''$, p' for Cp, q' for Aq, r' for Br we shall have

$$q'.\sin.\theta.\sin.\phi+r'.\sin.\theta.\cos.\phi-p'.\cos.\theta.=-N$$

$$q'.\cos.\theta.\sin.\phi.\cos.\psi+r'.\cos.\theta.\cos.\phi.\cos.\psi+p'.\sin.\theta.\cos.\psi$$

$$+r'.\sin\phi\sin.\psi-q'.\cos.\phi.\sin.\psi=-N'$$

$$-q'.\cos.\theta.\sin.\phi.\sin.\psi-r'.\cos.\theta.\sin.\psi.\cos.\phi-p'.\sin.\theta.\sin.\psi$$

$$+r'.\sin.\phi.\cos.\psi-q'.\cos.\phi.\cos.\psi=-N''$$

squaring these quantities we obtain

$$q'.^2\sin.^2\theta.\sin.^2\phi+r'.^2\sin.^2\theta.\cos.^2\phi+p'.^2\cos.^2\theta+2q'r'.\sin.^2\theta.\sin.\phi.\cos\phi$$

$$-2p'q'.\sin.\theta.\cos.\theta.\sin.\phi-2p'r'.\sin.\theta.\cos.\theta.\cos.\phi=N^2$$

$$q'.^2\cos.^2\theta.\sin.^2\phi\cos.^2\psi+r'.^2\cos.^2\theta.\cos.^2\phi.\cos.^2\psi+p'.^2\sin.^2\theta.\cos.^2\psi$$

$$+2q'r'.\cos.^2\theta.\sin.\phi.\cos.\phi.\cos.^2\psi+2p'r'.\sin.\theta.\cos.\theta.\cos.\phi.\cos.^2\psi$$

$$+2p'q'.\sin.\theta.\cos.\theta.\sin.\phi.\cos.^2\psi)$$

$$+r'.^2\sin.^2\phi.\sin.^2\psi+q'.^2\cos.^2\phi.\sin.^2\psi-2q'.r'.\sin.\phi.\cos.\phi.\sin.^2\psi=N'^2$$

$$q'.^2\cos.^2\theta.\sin.^2\phi.\sin.^2\psi+r'.^2\cos.^2\theta.\sin.^2\psi.\cos.^2\phi+p'.^2\sin.^2\theta.\sin.^2\psi$$

$$+2q'r'.\cos.^2\theta.\sin.^2\psi.\sin.\phi.\cos.\phi+2p'r'\sin.\theta.\cos.\theta.\sin.^2\psi.\cos.\phi$$

$$+2p'q'\sin.\theta.\cos.\theta.\sin.^2\psi.\sin.\phi)$$

$$+r'.^2\sin.^2\phi.\cos.^2\psi+q'.^2\cos.^2\phi.\cos.^2\psi-2q'r'.\sin.\phi.\cos.\phi\cos.^2\psi=N''^2$$

$\therefore$ adding the first members of these equations together we obtain

$$q'.^2\sin.^2\theta.\sin.^2\phi+q'.^2\cos.^2\theta.\sin.^2\phi+q'.^2\cos.^2\phi=(q'^2)+r'.^2\sin.^2\theta.\cos.^2\phi$$

$$+r'.^2\cos.^2\theta.\cos.^2\phi+r'.^2\sin.^2\phi=(r'^2)+p'.^2\cos.^2\theta+p'.^2\sin.^2\theta.\cos.^2\psi$$

$$+p'.^2\sin.^2\theta.\sin.^2\psi=p'^2;$$

the parts of these squares which are the products of two different quantities vanish when added together and in the expressions for N'^2, N''^2 we omit the product $(q'.\cos.\theta.\sin.\phi\cos.\psi+r'\cos.\theta.\cos.\phi.\cos.\psi+p'.\sin.\theta.\cos.\psi).(r'.\sin.\phi.\sin.\psi-q.\cos.\phi.\sin.\psi)$ for this product occurs in N'^2 and N''^2 affected with contrary signs, $\therefore$ it must vanish from $N'^2+N''^2$ $\therefore$ we shall have

$$p'^2+q'^2+r'^2=+N^2+N'^2+N''^2.$$

completely solve the problem. The equations (C) of No. 26, involve three arbitrary quantities N, N', N'', ; but they are not entirely distinct from the arbitrary quantities H and k. In fact, if we add together the squares of the first members of the equations (C), we shall have

$$p'^2+q'^2+r'^2=N^2+N'^2+N''^2;$$

and consequently

$$k^2=N^2+N'^2+N''^2.$$

The constant quantities N, N', N'', correspond to the constant quantities c, c', c'', of No. 21, and the function $\frac{1}{2}.\ t.\ \sqrt{p'^2+q'^2+r'^2}$ expresses the sum of the areas described in the time t, by the projection of each molecule of the body on the plane relatively to which this sum is a *maximum*. N', N'', vanish with respect to this plane, ∴ if we put their values, which have been found in No. 26, equal to nothing we shall have

$$0=Br.\ \sin.\ \varphi-Aq.\ \cos.\ \varphi\ ;$$

$$0=Aq.\ \cos.\ \theta.\ \sin.\ \varphi+Br.\ \cos.\ \theta.\ \cos.\ \varphi+Cp.\ \sin.\ \theta\ ;\text{*}$$

* From the equation $Br.\sin.\ \varphi-Aq.\ \cos.\ \varphi=0$ we obtain by substitution

$$\tan.\ \varphi=\frac{q'}{r'}\ \therefore\ \cos.\ \varphi.=\frac{r'}{\sqrt{q'^2+r'^2}}\text{ and }\sin.\ \varphi=\frac{q'}{\sqrt{q'^2+r'^2}}$$

consequently we have $\frac{q'^2+r'^2}{\sqrt{q'^2+r^2}}.\ \cos.\ \theta.$

$$=\sqrt{(q'^2+r'^2)}.\ \cos.\ \theta=p'.\ \sin.\ \theta.\ \therefore\ (q'^2+r'^2).\ \cos.^2\theta=p'^2-p'^2\cos.^2\theta\ \therefore$$

$$\cos.\ \theta=\frac{p'}{\sqrt{p'^2+q'^2+r'}},$$

if we multiply the first of the preceding equations by $\cos.\ \theta.\ \sin.\ \varphi.$ and the second by $\cos.\ \varphi.$ we shall obtain by adding them together $r'.\ \cos.\ \theta+p'.\ \sin.\ \theta.\ \cos.\ \varphi=0$ ∴ substituting for $\cos.\ \theta$ its value we obtain

from which we deduce

$$\cos.\ \theta = \frac{p'}{\sqrt{p'^2+q'^2+r'^2}};$$

$$\sin.\ \theta.\ \sin.\ \varphi = \frac{-q'}{\sqrt{p'^2+q'^2+r'^2}};$$

$$\sin.\ \theta.\ \cos.\ \varphi = \frac{-r'}{\sqrt{p'^2+q'^2+r'^2}}.$$

By means of these equations, we can determine the values of θ and φ in functions of the time with respect to the fixed plane which we have considered. We have only now to determine the angle ψ, which the intersection of this plane, and that of the two first principal axes, constitutes with the axis of x'; but this requires a new integration.

From the values of q and of r which have been given in No. 26 we derive

$$d\psi.\ \sin.\ ^2\theta = q.dt.\ \sin.\ \theta.\ \sin.\ \varphi + r.dt.\ \sin.\ \theta.\ \cos.\ \varphi;$$

from which we deduce

$$\sin.\ \theta.\ \cos.\ \varphi = \frac{-r'}{\sqrt{p'^2+q'^2+r'^2}},$$

and if we multiply the first of the preceding equations by cos. θ. cos. φ, and the second by sin. φ, and then substract the first from the second we shall obtain

$$q'.\ \cos.\ \theta + p'.\ \sin.\ \theta.\ \sin.\ \varphi = 0$$

∴ substituting for cos. θ its value, we obtain

$$\sin.\ \theta.\ \sin.\ \varphi = \frac{-q'}{\sqrt{p'^2+q'^2+r'^2}}.$$

$$d\psi = \frac{-k.dt.(Bq'^2 + Ar'^2)}{AB.(q'^2+r'^2)} *$$

but from what precedes, we have

$$q'^2+r'^2=k^2-p'^2 \ ; \ Bq'^2+Ar'^2=\frac{H^2-AB.p'^2}{C};$$

therefore we shall have

$$d\psi = \frac{-k.dt(H^2-AB.p'^2)}{ABC(k^2-p'^2)}$$

By substituting in place of dt, its value which has been given above; we shall have the value of ψ in a function of p'; thus the three angles θ, ϕ, and ψ will be determined in functions of the variables p', q', r', which will be themselves determined in functions of the time t.†

Consequently we can have at any instant the values of these angles with respect to the plane of x', and y', which we have considered, and it will be easy by means of the formulæ of spherical trigonometry, to

* If we multiply the values of qdt, rdt, given in page 166, respectively by sin. θ. sin. ϕ, sin. θ. cos. ϕ, and then add them together we shall have

$$d\psi.\sin.^2\theta = q.dt.\sin.\theta.\sin.\phi + rdt.\sin.\theta.\cos.\phi =$$

$$\left(-\frac{q'^2dt}{A.k}-\frac{r'^2dt}{B.k}=-\frac{(Bq'^2+A.r'^2)}{AB.k}.dt \text{ and as } \sin.^2\theta.=\frac{q'^2+r'^2}{k^2},\right.$$

the value of $d\psi$ will be

$$-\frac{k.dt.(Bq'^2+Ar'^2)}{A.B(q'^2+r'^2)}.$$

† Cos. θ—sin. θ. sin. ϕ,—sin. θ. cos. ϕ, are the cosines of the angles which a perpendicular to the fixed plane or the axis of z' makes the principal axes, see page 180, and

$$\frac{p'}{\sqrt{p'^2+q'^2+r'^2}} \quad \frac{q'}{\sqrt{p'^2+q'^2+r'^2}} \quad \frac{r'}{\sqrt{p'^2+q'^2+r'^2}}$$

are the cosines of the angles which the principal axes, z'', y'', x'', make with the axis of the plane, on which the projection of the area is a maximum, consequently the cosine of the angle which the axis of the plane on which the projection of the area is a maximum makes

determine the values of the same angles with respect to any other plane; * this will introduce two new arbitrary quantities, which combined with the four preceding quantities will constitute the six arbitrary quantities, which ought to give the complete solution of the problem which we have discussed. But it is evident that the consideration of the above mentioned plane simplifies considerably this problem.

The position of the three principal axes on the surface, being supposed to be known; if at any instant, the position of the real axis of rotation on this surface, is given and also the angular velocity of rotation, we

with the axis of the fixed plane, (see note to page 7).

$$=\frac{p'.\cos.\theta-q'.\sin.\theta.\sin.\varphi-r'.\sin.\theta.\cos.\varphi}{\sqrt{p'^2+q'^2+r'^2}}=\frac{N,}{k}$$

we might by a similar process shew that the cosine of the angle which the axis of the plane of greatest projection makes with y', and x', are respectively proportional to N' and N'', consequently the position of this plane with respect to the fixed axes of x' y', and z' is given, therefore this plane remains fixed during the motion, and the values of N, N', N'', are the three quantities which determine the position of the fixed axes, with respect to the plane of greatest projection.

* The determination of p', q', r', which give the position of the instantaneous axis of rotation requires three arbitrary quantities and the determination of θ, ψ, φ, which give the position of the principal axes with respect to the fixed axes requires three more arbitrary quantities, these are, H, h, and the constant quantities which are introduced by the integration of dt and $d\psi$, the two remaining quantities are determined by the values of $\cos.\theta$, $\sin\theta.\sin.\varphi$, $\sin.\theta.\cos\varphi$, for any other fixed plane beside the invariable plane, ∴ by making the plane of greatest projection, to coincide with the fixed plane; these new arbitrary quantities vanish, and the number of constant arbitrary quantities will be reduced to four.

The values of θ, φ, ψ, with respect to the plane on which the projection of the area is a maximum being given, and also the value of the angle which this plane makes with any other plane, it will be easy to deduce the cosine of the angle which each of the principal axes makes with the assumed plane, in fact by means of the values of N N' N'' we can determine the angles θ, ψ, φ, where we have the values of the same angles for the plane on which the projection of the area is a maximum, *i, e,* where we have p', q', r', and substituting p, q, r, in place of p', q', r', in these expressions we obtain the cosine of the angle which the axis of instantaneous rotation makes with the axis of the fixed plane, the three quantities N, N', N'', are not undetermined, for if N' and N'' have definite values the value of N is determined by means of the equation $N^2+N'^2+N''^2=k^2$.

shall have the values of p, q, r, at this instant because these values divided by the angular velocity of rotation express the cosines of the angles, which the real axis of rotation constitutes with the three principal axes; $\therefore$ we shall have the values of p', q', r', but these last values are proportional to the sines of the angles which the three principal axes constitute with the plane x' and y', relatively to which the sum of the areas of the projections of the molecules of the body, multiplied respectively by these molecules, is a *maximum*; therefore we can determine at all instants, the intersection of the surface of the body with the invariable plane; and consequently find the position of this plane, by the actual conditions of the motion of the body.

Let us suppose, that the motion of rotation of the body arises from a primitive impulse, of which the direction does not pass through its centre of gravity. It follows from what has been demonstrated in Nos. 20 and 22, that the centre of gravity will acquire the same motion, as if this impulse was immediately applied to it, and that the body will move round this centre with the same rotatory motion as if this centre quiesced. The sum of the areas described about this point, by the radius vector of each molecule projected on a fixed plane, and multiplied respectively by these molecules will be proportional to the moment of the principal force projected on the same plane; but this moment is evidently the greatest possible for the plane which passes through its direction and through the centre of gravity; consequently this plane is the invariable plane. If the distance of the primitive impulse from the centre of gravity be f and if v be the velocity which is impressed on this point, m representing the mass of the body, mfv * will be the moment of this im-

* v being the velocity of the centse of gravity, and m being the mass of the body, the measure of the force will be equal to mv, and its moment with respect to the centre of gravity will be equal to $mf.v$, see No. 3, and the motion of all the molecules of the body arising solely from this impulse it is evident from the principle of D'Alembert, which has been established in No. 18, that the quantities of motion which these molecules have at the

pulse and being multiplied by $\frac{1}{2}.t$, the product will be equal to the sum of the areas described in the time t, but by what precedes this sum is equal to $\frac{t}{2} \cdot \sqrt{p'^2+q'^2+r'^2}$; consequently we have

$$\sqrt{p'^2+q'^2+r'^2} = m,fv.$$

If at the commencement of the motion we know the position of the principal axes with respect to the invariable plane, i, e, * the angles θ and φ; we shall have at this commencement the values of p' q' and r' and consequently those of p, q, r, therefore at *any* instant we shall have the values of the same quantities. †

constitute an equilibrium with the force mv consequently the principal plane i, e, the plane with respect to which the moment is a maximum is the plane passing through the centre of gravity, and the direction of the primitive impulsion $\therefore$ the sum of the areas described in the time $t = \frac{1}{2}\, t.\, m,fv$.

* The constant quantity $k = m,fv$; in order to determine H, it may be remarked that the position of the principal axes at the commencement of the motion, with respect to the plane passing through the fixed point and the direction of the impulse being given, we have the the values of p' q', r', being proportional to the cosines of the angles which the principal axes make with the axis to the invariable plane. Consequently we have the *constant* quantity

$$H = \sqrt{AB.\,p'^2+BC.q'^2+ACr'^2};$$

the third constant quantity will be determined by integrating the value of dt, which will be equal to a function of p'+ a constant arbitrary quantity; p' which is proportional to the cosine of the angle which the axis of x' makes with the axis to the plane of greatest moment has a determined value when $t=0$ $\therefore$ by means of this value we are enabled to find the value of the third constant quantity; with respect to the fourth constant quantity which arises from the integration of the value of $d\psi$, this gives $\psi =$ to a function of p' plus a constant quantity, p' being proportional to cos. θ, we shall obtain the fourth constant quantity which is necessary to complete the solution of the problem, if we know what value of ψ corresponds to a given value of θ.

† When a solid body is not solicited by any accelerating forces and can revolve freely about a point we shall have

$$dx = y d\varpi - z d\phi,\ dy = z d\psi - x d\varpi,\ dz = x d\phi - y d\psi, \text{ \&c.}$$

By means of this theory, we are enabled to explain the double motion of rotation and of revolution, of the planets, by one initial impulse. In fact, let us suppose that a planet is an homogenous sphere whose radius is

See page 89, if we multiply the equations (*Z*) of No. 21, by

$$\frac{d\varpi}{dt},\ \frac{d\phi}{dt},\ \frac{d\psi}{dt},$$

respectively we shall obtain

$$c.\frac{d\varpi}{dt}+c'.\frac{d\phi}{dt}+c''.\frac{d\psi}{dt}=\Sigma m.\left\{\frac{xd\varpi.dy-y.d\varpi.dx}{dt^2}\right\}+\Sigma.\left\{\frac{zd\phi.dx-xd\phi.dz}{dt^2}\right\}$$

$$+\Sigma m.\left\{\frac{y.d\psi.dz-z.d\psi dy}{dt^2}\right\}=\Sigma m.\left\{\frac{xd\varpi-z.d\psi}{dt^2}\right\}.dy+\Sigma m.\left\{\frac{z.d\phi-y.d\varpi}{dt^2}\right\}.dx$$

$$+\Sigma m.\frac{(y.d\psi-xd\phi)}{dt^2}.dz=\Sigma m.\frac{(dx^2+dy^2+dz^2)}{dt^2}=$$

const. (see No. 19) now if we substitute for c, c', c'',

$$\sqrt{c^2+c'^2+c''^2}\ \cos.\ \theta,\ \sqrt{c^2+c'^2+c''^2}\ \sin.\ \theta.\ \sin.\ \psi,\ -\sqrt{c^2+c'^2+c''^2}\ \sin.\ \theta.\ \cos.\ \psi,$$

to which they are respectively equal, and also for

$d\varpi$, $d\phi$, $d\psi$, $d\theta.\cos.l$, $d\theta.\cos.n$, $d\theta.\cos.m$, see page 90, we shall obtain

$$\Sigma m.\ \left\{\frac{dx^2+dy^2+dz^2}{dt^2}\right\}=\sqrt{c^2+c'^2+c''^2}.\frac{d\theta}{dt}.$$

$$(\cos.\theta.\cos.l+\sin.\theta.\sin.\psi.\cos.n-\sin.\theta.\cos.\psi.\cos.m)$$

$$=\text{const. as }\cos.\theta,\ \sin.\theta.\sin.\psi,\ \sin.\theta.\cos.\psi,$$

are equal to the cosines of the angles which the axis of the plane of greatest projection, makes with three fixed axes, and as $\cos.l$, $\cos.n$, $\cos.m$, are the cosines of the angles which the axis of instantaneous rotation makes with the same axes, the last factor of the second member of the equation is equal to the cosine of the angle, which the axis of rotation makes with the axis of the plane on which projection of the areas is the greatest possible, ∴ as $\frac{d\theta}{dt}$ is the exponent of the velocity of rotation for any instant, this expression multiplied

equal to R, and that it revolves about the sun with an angular velocity equal to U; r being supposed to express its distance from the sun, we shall have $v=r\ U$; moreover if we conceive that the planet is put in motion by a primitive impulse, of which the direction is distant from its centre by a quantity equal to f, it is evident that it will revolve about an axis perpendicular to the invariable plane; therefore if we suppose that this axis coincides with the third principal axis * we shall have $\theta=0$, and consequently $q'=0$, $r'=0$; therefore $p'=mfv$ *i, e,* $Cp=mfrU$. But in the sphere, we have $C=\frac{2}{5}mR^2$; consequently,

$$f=\frac{2}{5}.\frac{R^2}{r}.\frac{p}{U};$$

which gives the distance of the direction of the primitive impulsion from the centre of the planet, and satisfies the ratio which is observed to obtain between p the angular velocity of rotation, and U the angular velocity of the revolution of the planet round the sun. With respect to the earth, we have $\frac{p}{U}=366{,}25638$; the parallax of the sun gives $\frac{R}{r}=0.000042665$, and consequently $f=\frac{1}{160}.R$ very nearly.

into the cosine of the angle, which the axis of instantaneous rotation makes with the axis of the plane, on which the projection is a maximum, is a constant quantity. When the plane of $x\,y$ coincides with the plane passing through the direction of the impulse, and the point about which the rotation is performed $\cos.\theta=1$ and $\sin.\theta=0$ ∴ we shall have $c'\frac{d\varphi}{dt}, c''\frac{d\psi}{dt}=0$; constant quantity$=c.\frac{d\theta}{dt}.\cos.l$ consequently the velocity of rotation, *i. e,* parallel to the axis of z, $=\frac{d\theta}{dt}.\cos.l$ is constant.

* All the diameters of a sphere being principal axes, if we suppose that the axis of revolution which is evidently the axis of the invariable plane coincides with the axis of z'', $\theta=0$ ∴ $\cos.\theta=1$ ∴ q' and $r'=$ respectively to $\sin.\theta.\sin.\varphi$, $\sin.\theta.\cos.\varphi$ vanish and this considerably simplifies the calculus.

The planets are not homogenous; but we may suppose them to be composed of concentrical spherical strata of unequal density. Let ρ denote the density of one of those stratas of which the radius is equal to R, we shall have

$$C = \frac{2m}{3} \cdot \frac{\int \rho . R.^4 dR}{\int \rho . R.^2 dR} . *$$

* The moment of inertia for a sphere is calculated in Book V. No. II. in a general manner, but as it involves some steps which are demonstrated in the second and third books, it will be necessary to give here a special demonstration, let there be two concentrical circles, whose radii are q, $q+dq$, the circumference of the interior is equal to $2\pi.q$, and the area of the annulus contained between the peripheries of those circles is equal $2\pi.q.dq$ ∴ $2\pi.q.^3dq$ is equal to the moment of inertia of this annulus and $\frac{1}{2}\pi.q,^4$ is the moment of inertia of a concentrical annulus of a finite breadth, ∴ when the preceding integral is taken between the limits $q=0$, $q=R$ the expression becomes $\frac{1}{2}\pi R^4$, which is the moment of inertia for the entire circle, now in order to obtain the moment of inertia for the entire sphere, let us conceive a plane parallel to the axis of rotation cutting the sphere at a distance from the axis equal to x, its intersection with the surface of the sphere will a lesser circle of the sphere, let $y=$the radius of this circle, the moment of inertia of this circle with respect to its centre is equal by what precedes to $\frac{1}{2}\pi y,^4$ ∴ the moment of inertia of an indefinitely small slice is equal to $\frac{1}{2}\pi.y^4.dx = \frac{1}{2}\pi(2Rx-x^2)^2.dx$, for $y^2=2Rx-x^2$ R being the radius of the sphere, ∴ integrating we have

$$\pi x^3 \left\{ \frac{2}{3}R^2 - \frac{1}{2}Rx + \frac{x^2}{10} \right\}$$

= the moment of inertia of a spherical segment and this integral being taken between the limits $x=0$, and $x=R$ gives

$$\pi R_3 . \left\{ \frac{2}{3}.R^2 - \frac{1}{2}R^2 + \frac{R^2}{10} \right\} = \frac{8}{15} . \pi . R^5$$

= the moment of inertia of the entire sphere with respect to a diameter, and it is very easy by means of the expression which has been given in page 180, to obtain the moment of inertia for any axis parallel to the diameter, if R is supposed to be variable in the last expression, and if ρ the density varies from the centre to the circumference, the moment of inertia of any spherical stratum whose radius= R is

$$\frac{8.5}{15} . \pi \rho R^4 . dR$$

(ρ being a function of R).

If, as is very probable, the denser strata are nearer to the centre; the function $\frac{\int\rho . R^4 dR}{\int\rho . R^2 dR}$ will be less than $\frac{3R^2}{5}$, consequently the value of f will be less than in the case of homogeneity.

30. Let us now determine the oscillations of a body when it turns very nearly about the third principal axis. We might deduce them from the integrals which we obtained in the preceding number; but it is

$\therefore$ the moment of inertia of a sphere composed of concentrical strata is equal to

$\frac{8}{3}\pi f\rho . R^4 dR$, in like manner m = the mass of the sphere $= 4\pi . \int\rho R^2 dR$

$$\therefore \pi = \frac{m}{4 . \int\rho R^2 dR} \text{ and } f = \frac{C . p}{m . r U} = \frac{8m\, p . \int\rho R^4 dR}{3.4m . r U\int\rho . R^2 dR}, = \frac{2p . \int\rho . R^4 . dR}{3r U\int\rho , R^2 . dR} -$$

we obtain the ratio of U to p from knowing the period of the earth and the time of its rotation, for the angular velocities are inversely as the angles described in the same time, ρ being by hypothesis a function of R where the density increases towards the centre $\rho = \frac{1}{\varphi(R)}$ $\therefore$ the fraction in the text becomes

$$\frac{\int\frac{R^4 . dR}{\varphi . (R)}}{\int\frac{R^2 dR}{\varphi(R)}} =$$

by partial integration

$$\frac{R^5}{5 . \varphi R} - \int\frac{R^5 . d . \varphi(R)}{5(\varphi(R))^2} + \frac{R^3}{3\varphi(R)} - \int\frac{R^3 . d\varphi(R)}{3 . (\varphi R)^2}$$

and as the numerator is more diminished than the denominator the value of the fraction which in the case of homogeneity was $\frac{3R^2}{5}$ will be diminished when the density increases towards the centre.

simpler to deduce them directly from the differential equations (D) of No. 26. The body not being actuated by any forces; these equations will become by substituting Cp, Aq, and Br, in place of their respective values p', q', r',

$$dp+\frac{(B-A)}{C}.qr.dt=0;$$

$$dq+\frac{(C-B)}{A}.rp.dt=0;$$

$$dr+\frac{(A-C)}{B}.pq.dt=0.$$

The solid being supposed to revolve very nearly about the third principal axis, q and r * are very small quantities, therefore we may reject their squares and products; consequently we shall have $dp=0$ and p will be constant. If in the other two equations we suppose

$$q=M.\sin.(nt+\gamma);\ r=M'.\cos.(nt+\gamma);$$

we shall have

* The solid being supposed to revolve very nearly about the principal axis,

$$\frac{p}{\sqrt{p^2+q^2+r^2}}=$$

the cosine of the angle which the instantaneous axis of rotation, make with the principal will be $q.p.$ equal to unity consequently, q and r will be very small because the sine of the above mentioned angle which is equal to

$$\frac{\sqrt{q^2+r^2}}{\sqrt{p^2+q^2+r^2}}$$

very nearly vanishes.

$n = p.\sqrt{\frac{(C-A.).(C-B)}{AB}}$; $M' = -M.\sqrt{\frac{A.(C-A)}{B.(C-B)}}$, M and γ*

being two constant quantities, the velocity of rotation will be $\sqrt{p^2+q^2+r^2}$ or simply p, the squares of q and r being neglected; therefore this velocity will be very nearly constant, finally the sine of the angle formed by the real axis of rotation, and the third principal axis will be $\frac{\sqrt{q^2+r^2}}{p}$.

If at the commencement of the motion we have $q=0$ and $r=0$, *i, e,* if at this instant the real axis of rotation coincides with the third principal axis; we shall have $M=0$ $M'=0$; consequently q and r will be always equal to nothing, and the axis of rotation will always coincide with the third principal axis; from which it follows that if the body commences to revolve round one of its principal axes, it will continue to revolve uniformly about the same axis. It is from this remarkable pro-

* $q = M.\sin.(nt+\gamma)$ $r = M'.\cos.(nt+\gamma)$ satisfy the preceding differential equations, for by substituting these values we obtain

$$M.n.dt.(\cos.(nt+\gamma)+\frac{(C-B)}{A}.p\,M'.dt.\cos.(nt+\gamma)=0$$

$$-M'.n.dt.\sin.(nt+\gamma)+\frac{A-C}{B}.pM.dt.\sin.(nt+\gamma)=0$$

$$\therefore Mn+\frac{(C-B)}{A}.pM'=0 \quad -M'.n+\frac{A-C}{B}.pM=0 \quad \therefore M'=$$

$$-\frac{Mn.A}{p.(C-B)}=\frac{(A-C).p.M}{Bn}\therefore n^2=$$

$$p^2.\frac{(C-A)(C-B)}{AB}\therefore M'=-M.\sqrt{\frac{A.(C-A)}{B.(C-B)}},$$

the quantities M and γ are arbitrary consequently these values are perfect integrals of the two preceding differential equations which they satisfy. (See Lacroix traite elementaire de Calcul integral, No. 297).

perty, that these axes have been termed principal axes of rotation, it appertains to them exclusively; for if the real axis of rotation is invariable on the surface of the body, we have $dp=0$, $dq=0$, $dr=0$, therefore from the preceding values of those quantities we obtain

$$\frac{(B-A)}{C}.rq=0\,;\ \frac{(C-B)}{A}.rp=0\,;\ \frac{(A-C)}{B}.pq=0.$$

In the general case where A, B, C, are unequal, two of the three quantities p, q, r, vanish in consequence of these equations, which implies that the real axis of rotation coincides with one of the principal axes.*

If two of the three quantities A, B, C, are equal, for example, if we have $A=B$; the three preceding equations will be reduced to the following, $rp=0$, $pq=0$; and they may be satisfied by supposing $p=0$. The axis of rotation in this case exists in a plane perpendicular to the third principal axis; but we have seen in No. 27, that all axes existing in this plane, are in this case principal axes.

E E

* The value of the quantities M, M', may be determined by knowing the position of the instantaneous axis of rotation at the commencement of the motion, whatever be their values at that instant they remain unaltered during the motion of the body ∴ if at the commencement of the motion, the real axis of rotation coincided with the principal axis

$$\frac{\sqrt{r^2+q^2}}{\sqrt{p^2+r^2+q^2}}=0$$

∴ q and r are respectively equal to nothing, and therefore M and M' will vanish, consequently the values of q and r will always be equal to nothing, and as p is constant and equal to the angular velocity, the body will revolve uniformly about the principal axis. If the position of the real axis of rotation is invariable on the surface of the body, p, q, r, must be constant, see No. 29, page 201, ∴ dp, dq, dr, are respectively equal to nothing ∴ their values

$$\frac{B-A}{C}.rq\ \frac{C-B}{A}.rp\ \frac{A-C}{A}.pq$$

respectively vanish, ∴ in order to satisfy these equations two of the three variable quantities p, q, r, must vanish.

Finally, if the three quantities A, B, C, are equal, the preceding equations will be satisfied, whatever may be the values of p, q, r; but in this case, all the axes of the body are principal axes.*

It follows from what precedes, that to the principal axes only belongs the property of being permanent axes of rotation; † but they do not

* When $A=B$, the first of these three equations vanishes of itself, whatever may be the values of r and q, and we shall satisfy the two last equations by supposing $p=0$, $\therefore$ the real axis of rotation is perpendicular to the third principal axis, see No. 29, notes, but as in this case all lines drawn in a plane perpendicular to the third principal axis, are principal axes, it follows that the axis of rotation is in this case a principal axis; if $A=B=C$ the three preceding equations will be identical, and the values of p, q, and r, may be assumed at pleasure, but in this case all axes are principal axes, $\therefore$ it follows universally, that if the axis of rotation remain permanently the same, it must be a principal axis.

In the general case when A B and C, are unequal, we shall be always certain that p, q, and r, and M, M', vanish at the commencement of the motion, when the impulse is made in a plane which coincides with the plane of two of the principal axes, for in this case the invariable plane to which we adverted in Note to page 184, coincides with the plane passing through two of the principal axes, and the axis of rotation or of this invariable plane will necessarily coincide with the third principal axis. See Notes, to page 188.

† It might be proved directly from the property of principal axes scilicet $S.xz.dm=0$, $Syz.dm=0$, that the pressure on the axis of rotation which is produced by the centrifugal force must vanish, when this axis is a principal axis, and that consequently, when there is a fixed point given in a body, there exists always three axes passing through this point, about which the body may revolve uniformly without a displacement of the axis, and as if these lines were entirely free; for if the body is acted upon by an initial impulse, ϖ denoting the angular velocity and r the distance of a molecule dm from the axis of rotation which we suppose to coincide with the axis z, x and y being the coordinates with respect to the axes of x and y, we have the centrifugal force $=\varpi^2 r.dm$, this force resolved parallel to x and $y=$ $\frac{\varpi^2 r.x}{r}.dm$, $\frac{\varpi^2 ry}{r}$; because $\frac{x}{r}$, $\frac{y}{r}$ are equal to the cosines of the angles which the axes of x and y make with r, $\therefore$ the sum of the forces for all the molecules of the body $=\varpi^2.Sx.dm$, $\varpi^2.Sy.dm$, and the respective sums of their moments for the axes of y and of x are $\varpi^2\ Sx.z.dm$, $\varpi^2.\ S.yz.dm$. and m being the mass of the body and $x_{,}$, $y_{,}$, being the coordinates of the centre of gravity, we have $\varpi^2.mx_{,}=\varpi^2 S.xdm$, $\varpi^2.my_{,}=\varpi^2 S.y.dm$, and if $z_{,}$ $z_{,,}$ represent the distances of the resultants $\varpi^2.mx_{,}$ $\varpi^2 my_{,}$, from the plane of the axis of $x\ y$ we have by note to No. 3, $\varpi^2 mx_{,}z_{,}=\varpi^2 Sxy.dm$, $\varpi^2.myz_{,,}=\varpi^2.Syz.dm$, when $z_{,}z_{,,}$ are equal, the resultants

possess this property in the same manner. The motion of rotation about the axis, of which the moment of inertia is intermediate between the moments of inertia of the two other axes, may be disturbed in a sensible degree by the slightest cause; so that in this motion, there is no stability.

The state of a system of bodies is termed *stable*, when the system being very slightly deranged, it deviates from the state by an indefinitely small degree, by making continual oscillations about this state. This being understood, let us suppose that the real axis of rotation deviates from the third principal axis by an indefinitely small quantity; in this case, the quantities M and M' are indefinitely small; and if n is a real quantity, the values of q and r will always remain indefinitely small, and the real axis of rotation will only make excursions of the

$\varpi^2.mx_{,}$, $\varpi^2.my_{,}$, are applied to the same point, ∴ these two forces will compose one sole force $=\varpi^2.m\sqrt{x_{,}^2+y_{,}^2}$, now if the fixed axes pass through the centre of gravity we have $x_{,}=0$ $y_{,}=0$ ∴ $\varpi^2 Sxdm$, $\varpi^2.Sydm$ respectively vanish, and if the axis of rotation is a principal axes we have $\varpi^2 S.xz.dm=0$, $\varpi^2 S.yzdm=0$, from the first equation it follows that the axes does not experience any tendency to a progressive motion, and the second equations indicate that the sum $\varpi^2.Sxzdm$ of the moments of the forces vanish, from these two conditions it follows that the forces constitute an equilibrium independently of the axis. If the fixed axis of rotation and origin of the coordinates was transferred to a different point of the body, being still a principal axis, we should have as before $S.xz.dm=0$ $Syz.dm=0$ ∴ the sum of the moments of the forces with respect to the axes of y and of x vanish as before ∴ as $x_{,}$ and $y_{,}$ have in this case a finite value $z_{,}$ and $z_{,,}$ must vanish, for $\varpi^2.mx_{,}z_{,}$, $\varpi^2.my_{,}z_{,,}$ vanish being equal to $\varpi^2.Sxzdm$, $\varpi^2.Syzdm$, ∴ the pressure $=\varpi^2.m\sqrt{x'^2+y'^2}$., which as $z_{,}$ $z_{,,}$ vanish, must exist in the plane of x, y, and must pass through the origin of the coordinates, ∴ if this point is fixed the pressure will be destroyed, and the motion will be performed about the axis as if it was fixed, for the only pressure which could displace it is destroyed, by the resistance of the fixed point.

From what precedes it appears, that when the principal axis passes through the centre of gravity, it is not necessary that any point should be fixed, in order that the motion may be perpetuated uniformly about the fixed axes, in any other case it is necessary that the origin of the coordinates be fixed.

same order * about the third principal axis. But if n was imaginary, sin. $(nt+\gamma)$, cos. $(nt+\gamma)$ will become exponential, and the expressions for q and r might then increase indefinitely, and at length cease to be very small; consequently there would be no stability in the motion of rotation of the body about the third principal axis. The value of n is real, if C is the greatest or the least of the three quantities A, B, C; for the product $(C-A).(C-B)$ is positive; but this product is negative if C is intermediate between A and B, and in this case n is imaginary; thus, the motion of rotation is stable about the two principal

* When n is a real quantity, p and q can be expressed by sines and cosines of nt, but these values are not susceptible of indefinite increase with the time, for they are periodic functions of t, and the limit of the values of sin. $(nt+\gamma)$, cos. $(nt+\gamma)$ is unity, if they are very small at the commencement of the motion, M and M' must be very small, and as these quantities are invariable, the expressions for q and r will always remain indefinitely small. If n is imaginary, sin. $(nt+\gamma)$, cos. $(nt+\gamma)$ are imaginary, and as

$$\cos.(nt+\gamma)+\sqrt{-1}.\ \sin.(nt+\gamma)=c^{+(nt+\gamma).\sqrt{-1}}$$

and

$$\cos.(nt+\gamma)-\sin.(nt+\gamma)=c^{-(nt+\gamma).\sqrt{-1}}$$

we obtain by adding and subtracting

$$\cos.(nt+\gamma)=\frac{c^{(nt+\gamma).\sqrt{-1}}+c^{-(nt+\gamma).\sqrt{-1}}}{2}$$

$$\sin.(nt+\gamma)=\frac{c^{(nt+\gamma).\sqrt{-1}}-c^{-(nt+\gamma).\sqrt{-1}}}{2.\sqrt{-1}}$$

if n is imaginary the preceding exponential expressions will become

$$\frac{c^{-nt+\gamma\sqrt{-1}}+c^{nt-\gamma.\sqrt{-1}}}{2}\qquad\frac{c^{-nt+\gamma\sqrt{-1}}-c^{nt-\gamma\sqrt{-1}}}{2\sqrt{-1}}$$

in these exponential expressions, the part which is not affected with the radical sign, is

axes of which the moments of inertia are the greatest, and the least; but not so about the other principal axis.*

proportional to the time, and therefore the values of q and r, will increase indefinitely with the time, $\therefore$ though they may have been indefinitely small at the commencement of the motion, still as there is no limit to the increase of the exponential expressions, they will at length exceed any assigned magnitude.

* It might be shewn directly by means of the equations $C^2p^2+A^2q^2+B^2r^2=k^2$: $ABC^2.p^2+A^2BCq^2+AB^2Cr^2=H^2$, that there is a limit to the increase of q and r when C is the greatest or least of the three quantities A, B, C, for if we multiply the first equation by AB, and then subduct it from the second we obtain $A^2.B(C-A)q^2+AB^2.(C-B).r^2=H^2-AB.k^2$, if at any instant the quantities q, r, are very small H^2-Ak^2 which is constant will be very small, consequently in all the changes which r and q undergo they are subjected to the same condition, and this condition requires that r and q should be always very small when $C-A$ and $C-B$ are of the same sign, because then both the terms of the first member of the preceding differential equation will be either positive or negative, and the expressions

$$\frac{H^2-AB.k^2}{A^2.B.(C-A)}, \quad \frac{H^2-ABk^2}{AB^2(C-B)},$$

are the limits to which the respective values of q and r can never attain. If $C-B$ and $C-A$ are of different signs, then the terms of the first member of the equation will be of different signs, and it is only the difference of the quantities $A^2B(C-A).q^2+AB^2.(C-B)r^2$, that is indefinitely small $\therefore$ since this difference depends on the relative values of these quantities, q and r may be very great, though the preceding residual is a quantity indefinitely small.

Philosophers have distinguished the equilibrium of stability into two species absolute and relative, in the first case the stability obtains whatever may be the oscillations of the system, in the second case it is necessary that the oscillations should be of a certain description, in order to insure the stability of the equilibrium. If a body revolving about a fixed axis passes through *several positions* of equilibrium, these will be alternately stable and instable. For if a system deviates from a position of stable equilibrium, from the nature of this equilibrium it tends to revert, but according as the system deviates more and more from its first position, this tendency will diminish, and at length it will tend to deviate from the original position, but previous to this change of tendency there must have been a position in which the system neither tended to revert, or to deviate from its original position, consequently this is a position of equilibrium, but this equilibrium is evidently one of instability, for previous to the arrival of the system at this position it tended to revert to its primary position, and when it passed this position, it tends to deviate from the primary and consequently from this second position of

Now, in order to determine the position of the principal axes in space, we shall suppose the third principal axis to coincide very nearly with the plane of x' and of y', so that θ will be a very small quantity of which we may neglect the square.

By No. 26, we shall have

$$d\varphi - d\psi = pdt\,^{*}$$

and by integrating we obtain

$$\psi = \varphi - pt - \varepsilon$$

ε being a constant arbitrary quantity. If we afterwards make

$$\sin.\,\theta.\,\sin.\,\varphi = s\,;\;\; \sin.\,\theta.\,\cos.\,\varphi = u\,;$$

from the values of q and of r which have been given in No. 26, we shall obtain, by the elemination of $d\psi$

$$\frac{ds}{dt} - pu = r\,;\;\; \frac{du}{dt} + ps = -q\,;\;\dagger$$

equilibrium, this tendency of the body to deviate from the second position of equilibrium gradually diminishes, and at length vanishes, afterward the system tends to revert to the second position of equilibrium, and where the tendency to deviate from the second position of equilibrium vanishes, is also a position of equilibrium, which is evidently an equilibrium of stability, for previous to the arrival of the system at this position it tends towards it, inasmuch as it tends to deviate from the second position, and after passing this third position of equilibrium it tends to revert to the second, and consequently to the third position of equilibrium, thus it appears that when a system has returned to its primary position, it has passed through an even number of positions of equilibrium, alternately stable and instable.

* $d\varphi - d\psi.\,\cos.\,\theta = p.dt$, but $\cos.\,\theta = 1 - \frac{\theta^2}{2} + \frac{\theta^4}{1.2.3.4} - \&c = $ when θ is very small, unity $\therefore\; d\varphi - d\psi = pdt$.

† $d\psi.\,\sin.\,\theta.\,\sin.\,\varphi - d\theta.\,\cos.\,\varphi = q\,dt\,;\; d\psi.\,\sin.\,\theta.\,\cos.\,\varphi + d\theta.\,\sin.\,\varphi. = r.dt,$

substituting in place of $d\psi$ its value $d\varphi - pdt$, we shall have

and by integrating

$$s = \epsilon.\sin.(pt+\lambda) - \frac{A.M}{C.p}.(\sin.\,nt+\gamma);$$

$$u = \epsilon.\cos.(pt+\lambda) - \frac{BM'}{Cp.}.\cos.(nt+\gamma);^*$$

$$d\varphi.\sin.\theta\sin.\varphi - p.\sin.\theta.\sin.\varphi.dt - d\theta.\cos.\varphi = q.dt;\ d\varphi.\sin.\theta.\cos.\varphi - p.\sin.\theta\cos.\varphi.dt$$

$$+d\theta.\sin.\varphi = r.dt,;$$

substituting θ in place of $\sin.\theta$, to which it is very nearly equal since the higher powers of θ may be neglected, we obtain

$$-d\varphi.\theta.\sin.\varphi + d\theta.\cos.\varphi + p.\sin.\theta.\sin.\varphi.dt = -q.dt,\ i,e,$$

$$d.(\cos.\varphi.\sin.\theta) + p.\sin.\theta.\sin.\varphi.dt = -qdt,$$

and by substituting for $\sin.\theta.\sin.\varphi.\sin.\theta.\cos.\varphi$, their values which have been given in the text, we obtain

$$\frac{du}{dt} + p.s = -q;$$

in like manner the second differential equation becomes,

$$d\varphi.\theta.\cos.\varphi + d\theta.\sin.\varphi - p.dt\ \sin.\theta.\cos.\varphi = r.dt,\ i,e,\ d.(\sin.\theta.\sin.\varphi)$$

$$-p.dt.\sin.\theta.\cos.\varphi = r.dt,$$

and by substitution, $\frac{ds}{dt} - pu = r.$

* The integrals assigned in the text are the complete values of s and u for

$$\frac{ds}{dt} = \epsilon.p.\cos.(pt+\lambda) - \frac{M}{C}.\sqrt{\frac{A}{B}.(C-A).(C-B).}\ \cos.(nt+\gamma),$$

this expression is equal to $pu+r$, for substituting in place of u and r, we shall have

$$\epsilon.p.\cos.(pt+\lambda) - \frac{B.M'p}{Cp}\cos.(nt+\gamma) + M'.\cos.(nt+\gamma) =$$

(by substituting for M' its value,) $\epsilon.p.\cos.(pt+\lambda)$

$$-\frac{M}{C}.\sqrt{\frac{A}{B}.(C-A).(C-B).}\ \ \cos.(nt+\gamma),$$

ε and λ being two new arbitrary quantities: therefore the problem is completely resolved, since the values of s and of u give the angles θ and φ in functions of the time, and ψ is determined in a function of φ and t. If ε vanishes, the plane of x' and of y' becomes the invariable plane, to which we have referred in the preceding number, the angles θ, φ and ψ. *

∴ since the integrals given in the text satisfy the differential equations

$$\frac{ds}{dt}-pu=r,\ \frac{du}{dt}+ps=-q;$$

and since there are two constant quantities introduced, these values of u and s are their complete integrals.

* When ε vanishes $s=\sin.\theta.\sin.\varphi=-\frac{A.q}{Cp}$; $u=\sin.\theta.\cos.\varphi=-\frac{B.r}{C.p}$, *i, e*,

$$\sin.\theta.\sin.\varphi=-\frac{q'}{p'},\ \sin.\theta.\cos.\varphi=-\frac{r'}{p'},$$

and those are values of the cosines of the angles which the principal axes of x'' and y'' make with the axis of the invariable plane, see notes to page 198. *In this case*

$$\frac{s}{u}=\tan.\varphi=\frac{AM}{BM'}.\tan.(nt+\gamma)\therefore\varphi=\frac{AM}{B.M'}.(nt+\gamma),$$

as φ is equal to the angle formed by the intersection of the invariable plane, and of the plane of x'', y'', with the axis of x'', if we know this angle at the commencement of the motion, or at any given epoch, we shall have the value of γ; we might in like manner find M, for

$$u^2+s^2=\sin.^2\theta.(\sin.^2\varphi+\cos.^2\varphi)=\frac{A^2M^2}{C^2p^2}+\frac{B^2M^2}{C^2p^2}\left(\frac{A.(C-A)}{B.(C-B)}\right)=\sin.^2\theta,$$

by substituting for $(\sin.^2\varphi+\cos.^2\varphi)$ unity, and for M'^2 its value.

$$\psi=\frac{AM}{BM'}.(nt+\gamma)-pt-\epsilon$$

∴ as we have already determined the values of M, M', and γ, we can determine the value of ϵ, when the value of ψ is given at the commencement of the motion; from the preceding value of ψ it appears that this angle increases proportionably to the time, ∴ the intersection of the invariable plane and the plane of $x''\ y''$ revolves about the axis of the invariable plane with an uniform angular velocity.

31. If the solid is free; the analysis of the preceding numbers will determine its motion about its centre of gravity: if the solid is constrained to move about a fixed point, it will make known the motion of rotation about this point. It now remains for us to consider the motion of a solid constrained to revolve about a fixed axis.

Let us suppose this axis to be that of x', which we will make horizontal: in this case, the last of the equations (B) of No. 25, will be sufficient to determine the motion. Moreover let us conceive that the axis of y' is horizontal, and thus that the axis of z' is vertical, and directed towards the centre of the earth, lastly let the plane which passes through the axis of y' and of z',* pass through the centre of gravity of the body, and let us conceive an axis always passing through this centre and through the origin of the coordinates. If θ represents the angle which this new axis constitutes with the axis of z; and y'', and z'', the coordinates referred to this new axis, we shall have

$$y'=y''.\cos.\theta+z''.\sin.\theta;\quad z'=z''.\cos.\theta-y''.\sin.\theta;$$

from which we may obtain

$$S.\left\{\frac{y'dz'-z'dy'}{dt}\right\}.dm=-\frac{d\theta}{dt}.S.dm.(y''^2+z''^2).\dagger$$

F F

* Since the plane passing through the axis of z', and of y', of which the former is vertical, and the latter horizontal, passes constantly through the centre of gravity, this centre must move in a vertical plane.

† As the coordinates x'', y'', z'', do not vary with the time, being always the same for the same molecule, in taking the differentials of y', z', and their respective values, with respect to the time they become

$$dy=d\theta.(z''.\cos.\theta-y''.\sin.\theta);\quad dz'=-d\theta.(z''.\sin.\theta+y''.\cos.\theta)$$

$$\therefore y'dz'-z'dy'=(y''.\cos.\theta+z''.\sin.\theta).(-d\theta.(z''.\sin.\theta+y''.\cos.\theta))-(z''.\cos.\theta-y''.\sin.\theta).$$

$$(d\theta.(z''.\cos.\theta-y''.\sin.\theta))$$

$S.dm.(y''^2+z''^2)$ is the moment of inertia of the body with respect to the axis of x': * Let this moment be equal to C. The last of the equations (B) of No. 25, will give

$$-C.\frac{d^2\theta}{dt^2}=\frac{dN''}{dt}$$

Let us suppose that the body is only solicited by the force of gravity; the values of P and of Q of No. 25, will vanish, and R will be constant, which gives

$$\frac{dN''}{dt}=S.Ry'.dm=R.\cos.\theta.S.y''.dm+R.\sin.\theta.\ S.z''.dm.$$

The axis of z'' passing through the centre of gravity of the body, we have $S.y''.dm=0$; moreover, if we name h the distance of the centre of gravity of the body, from the axis of x', we shall have $S.z''.dm=mh$, m being the entire mass of the body; therefore we shall have

$$=-d\theta.(y''.\cos.\theta+z''.\sin.\theta)^2$$

$$-d\theta(z''.\cos.\theta-y''.\sin.\theta)^2=-d\theta.(y''^2+z''^2)$$

$\therefore$ multiplying by dm, and extending the expression to all the molecules we obtain,

$$S.\frac{y'\,dz'-z'\,dy'}{dt}.dm=-C.\frac{d\theta}{dt}.$$

and since C is constant, we shall have

$$-C.\frac{d^2\theta}{dt^2}=\frac{dN''}{dt}.$$

* $y'^2+z'^2=y''^2\cos.^2\theta+z''^2\sin.\theta+2y''z''.\sin.\theta.\cos.\theta+y''^2\sin.^2\theta+z''^2\cos.^2\theta$

$$-2y'z''.\sin.\theta.\cos.\theta=y''^2+z''^2\ \therefore\ S(y'^2+z'^2).dm,$$

the moment of inertia of the body relative to the axis of

$$x'=S(z''^2+y''^2).dm=C.$$

$$\frac{dN''}{dt} = mh.\ R.\ \sin.\ \theta\ *$$

and consequently

$$\frac{d^2\theta}{dt^2} = \frac{-\ m.h.R.\ \sin.\ \theta}{C}$$

Let us now consider a second body, all whose parts are concentrated in one point, of which the distance from the axis of x', is equal to l; we shall have for this body, $C = m'l^2$, m' expressing its mass; moreover h will be equal to l; and therefore

$$\frac{d^2\theta}{dt^2} = \frac{-R}{l}.\ \sin.\ \theta\ \dagger$$

* N'' is always equal to $S.\int(Ry' - Qz').\ dt.dm$ ∴ Q vanishing we shall have

$$\frac{dN''}{dt} = S.Ry'.dm$$

and by substituting for y' we obtain the expression given in the text. In fact, since the axis of z'' passes through the centre of gravity, we have $S.y''.dm = 0$, and $S.z''.dm = mh$, See No. 15, page 91, it also appears from note to same number, page 88, that when a body is constrained to move about an axis, one of the equations (B) of No. 25, is sufficient to determine the motion of the body; ∴ by substituting $mh.\ \sin.\ \theta$. for $\sin.\ \theta.\ Sz''.dm$ we shall have

$$\frac{dN''}{dt} = mh\ R.\sin.\ \theta.$$

† For any body m' of which all the molecules are concentrated into a point at the distance equal to l from the axis of x' we have

$$\frac{d^2\theta}{dt^2} = -\ \frac{m'l.\ R}{m'l^2}\ \sin.\ \theta = -\ \frac{R}{l}\sin.\ \theta,$$

for in this case the centre of gravity, is in this point, and the moment of its inertia, is equal to $m'.l^2$;
if this body has the same motion of oscillation with the body we have first considered, the values of $\frac{d^2\theta}{dt^2}$ must be the same, *i, e,*

$$-\ \frac{mh.R.\sin.\ \theta.}{C} = -\frac{R}{l}\sin.\ \theta\ \therefore\ l = \frac{C}{mh}.$$

Consequently these two bodies will have the same motion of oscillation, if their initial angular velocities, when their centres of gravity, exist in the vertical, are the same, and if we have also $l=\frac{C}{mh}$ * The second body which we have considered is the simple pendulum, the oscillations of which are determined in No. 11, and by means of this formula we are always enabled to assign the length l of the simple pendulum of which the oscillations are isochronous, with those of the solid which we have considered in this number, and which constitutes the compound pendulum. It is thus, that the length of the simple pendulum, which vibrates in a second, is determined by observations made on compound pendulums.†

Multiplying both sides of the equation $\frac{d^2\theta}{dt^2}=-\frac{R.\sin.\theta}{l}$ by $2d\theta$, and integrating we obtain

$$\frac{d\theta^2}{dt^2}=\frac{2R}{l}.\cos.\theta+C,$$

the constant quantity C, depends on the angular velocity, and on the value of θ, at the commencement of the motion.

* From the expression $l=\frac{C}{mh}$, it appears that when the axis of rotation passes through the centre of gravity, l is infinite, and consequently the time of oscillation is infinite in this case, in fact the action of gravity being destroyed, the primitive impulse will communicate a rotatory motion which will be perpetuated for ever, if the resistance of the air be removed.

† The point which is distant from the axis of rotation by a quantity equal to l is termed the centre of oscillation of the body, and if the axis of rotation passed through this point, the centre of oscillation with respect to this new axis, will be in the former axis of rotation, for the moment of inertia with respect to the centre of gravity being equal to $C-mh^2$, the moment with respect to the new axis will be $C+ml^2-2mlh$. See note, page 182, $\therefore$ the value of l for the new axis $=\frac{C+ml^2-2mlh}{ml-mh}$ but $C=mlh$ $\therefore$ the value of l for the new axis $=\frac{ml^2-mlh}{ml-mh}=l$.

$C'=A\sin.^2\theta.\sin.^2\varphi+B.\sin.^2\theta.\cos.^2\varphi+C.\cos.^2\theta+mh^2$, see page 180, where $A,B,C,$

are the moments of inertia, relative to the principal axis, passing through the centre of gravity, we shall have

$$l = \frac{mh^2 + A.\sin.^2\theta.\sin.^2\varphi + B.\sin.^2\theta.\cos.^2\varphi + C.\cos.^2\theta}{mh}$$

$\therefore l$ will be a minimum when the quantity represented by C *in the text* is the least of the three principal moments of inertia, for in that case the other two moments vanish, let A be the least of the three moments then we shall have

$l = \frac{mh^2 + A}{mh}$, for sin. θ. cos. $\varphi = 0$, cos. $\theta = 0$, $\therefore$ when l is a minimum

$$dl = \frac{2m^2h^2 - m^2h^2 - mA}{m^2h^2}.dh = 0 \therefore h = \sqrt{\frac{A}{m}}$$

$\therefore l$ and consequently the time of oscillation will be a minimum when the axis of rotation is that principal axis, relatively to which, the moment of inertia is a minimum, and at a distance from the centre of gravity by a quantity equal to $\sqrt{\frac{A}{m}}$. The product of lh. is constant and $=$ to $\frac{C}{m}$, this fraction is equal to the square of the distance of the centre of gyration from the axis of rotation, therefore this distance is a mean proportional, between the distances of the centres, of gravity and oscillation, from the axis of rotation, and it readily appears from what precedes, that when the time of vibration is a minimum, the distance of the centre of gyration from the axis of rotation is equal to the distance of the centre of gravity from this axis, and the distance of the centre of oscillation from the same axis $= .2\sqrt{\frac{A}{m}}$. In this case, the centre of gyration, is termed the principal centre of gyration.

CHAPTER VIII.

Of the motion of fluids.

32. We may make the laws of the motion of fluids, depend on those of their equilibrium; in the same manner, as in the fifth chapter we have deduced the laws of the motion of a system of bodies, from those of the equilibrium of the system. For this purpose, let us resume the general equation of the equilibrium of fluids, which has been given in No. 17,

$$\delta p = \rho \{P.\delta x + Q.\delta y + R.\delta z\};$$

in which, the characteristic δ refers only to the coordinates of the molecule x, y, z, being independent of the time. When the fluid is in motion, the forces which would retain the molecules in equilibrio are by No. 18,

$$P - \left\{\frac{d^2x}{dt^2}\right\}; Q - \left\{\frac{d^2y}{dt^2}\right\}; R - \left\{\frac{d^2z}{dt^2}\right\};$$

(dt being supposed constant); therefore it is necessary to substitute in the preceding equation of equilibrium, these forces in place of P, Q, R. If we suppose that $P\delta x + Q.\delta y + R\delta z$ is an exact variation, represented by δV; we shall have

$$\delta V - \frac{\delta p}{\rho} = \delta x.\left(\frac{d^2x}{dt^2}\right) + \delta y.\left(\frac{d^2y}{dt^2}\right) + \delta z.\left(\frac{d^2z}{dt^2}\right);^{*} \quad (F)$$

this equation is equivalent to three distinct equations; because the variations δx, δy, δz, being independent, we are permitted to make their coefficients, separately equal to nothing.

The coordinates x, y, z, are functions of the primitive coordinates, and of the time t; † let a b c be the primitive coordinates, we shall have

$$*\delta p = \varrho\left\{\left\{P - \frac{d^2x}{dt^2}\right\}\delta x + \left\{Q - \frac{d^2y}{dt^2}\right\}.\delta y + \left\{R - \frac{d^2z}{dt^2}\right\}.\delta z\right\}$$

$$= \varrho.(P.\delta x + Q.\delta y + R\delta z) - \varrho\left\{\frac{d^2x}{dt^2}.\delta x + \frac{d^2y}{dt^2}.\delta y + \frac{d^2z}{dt^2}.\delta z\right\}. ;$$

we are permitted to consider $P\delta x + Q\delta y + R\delta z$, an exact variation where the forces which solicit the molecules, are those of attraction directed towards fixed or moveable points, or such as arise from the mutual attraction of the fluid molecules. We have seen in No. 17, that this is the condition which must be satisfied, when the molecules of the fluid, are in equilibrio by the action of the same forces.

† The position of a molecule at any instant, is known when we know the coordinates a, b, c, which determine its position at the commencement of the motion, or at any determined epoch, ∴ x, y, z, are respectively functions of a, b, c, and t, consequently we have $x = f(a, b, c, t)$, $y = F.(a, b, c, t)$; $z = \varphi.(a, b, c, t)$. and as the differences indicated by the characteristic δ refer solely to the variations of the coordinates a, b, c, being independent of the time, the expressions for δx, δy, δz, should be such as are given in the text, ∴ if it was proposed to compare the respective positions of two molecules at any given moment, the time should be considered as constant, and the expressions for δx δy δz should be those which are given in page 224, on the other hand, if we consider the motion of the *same* molecule for the time dt, the values of dx, dy, dz, deduced from the preceding expressions for x, y, z, must be taken on the hypothesis that t only varies and ∴ when $t=0$, $x=a$, $y=b$, $z=c$. If the form of the preceding functions was given, by eliminating the time from the equations which determine values of x, y, z, the two equations which result will be the equations of the curve described by the molecule, however as a b c are different for each molecule, the nature of this curve and its position will be different for each molecule, see Note page 31.

$$\delta x = \left\{\frac{dx}{da}\right\}.\delta a + \left\{\frac{dx}{db}\right\}.\delta b + \left\{\frac{dx}{dc}\right\}.\delta c;$$

$$\delta y = \left\{\frac{dy}{da}\right\}.\delta a + \left\{\frac{dy}{db}\right\}.\delta b + \left\{\frac{dy}{dc}\right\}.\delta c;$$

$$\delta z = \left\{\frac{dz}{da}\right\}.\delta a + \left\{\frac{dz}{db}\right\}.\delta b + \left\{\frac{dz}{dc}\right\}.\delta c.$$

By substituting these values in the equation (F), we may put the coefficients of δa, δb, δc, separately equal to nothing; which will give three equations of partial differences between the three coordinates of the molecule x, y, z, its primitive coordinates a,b,c, and the time t.

It remains to satisfy the condition of the continuity of the fluid.* For this purpose, let us consider at the commencement of the motion, a rectangular fluid parallelepiped, of which the three dimensions are da, db, dc. If we denote its primitive density by (ρ), its mass will be equal to $(\rho).da.db.dc$. Let this parallelepiped be represented by (A), it is easy to see, that after the time t,† it will be changed into an oblique angled parallelepiped; for all the molecules which in the primitive situation existed on any face of the

* In order to determine the condition of a fluid mass at each instant, we must know the direction of the motion of a molecule, its velocity, the pressure p, and the density ρ, but if we know the three partial velocities parallel to the coordinates, we shall have the entire velocity, and also the direction, for the partial velocities divided by the entire velocity, are proportional to the cosines of the angles which the coordinates make with the direction, see Note page 26, and page 227.

Three of the equations which are required for the determination of those sought quantities, are furnished by the equation (F); another equation from the continuity of the fluid, for though each indefinitely small portion of the fluid changes its form, and if it is compressible, its volume during the motion, still the mass must be constant, consequently the product of the volume into the density must be the same as at the commencement, $\therefore$ by equating those two values of the mass, we obtain the equation relative to the continuity of the fluid.

† After the time t, the coordinates of the summit of the parallelogram, which were a, b, c, at the commencement of the motion, will be x, y, z, or $f(a\,b\,c\,t)$, $F(a\,b\,c\,t)$, $\varphi\,(a\,b\,c\,t)$, the coordinates of that point of which the initial coordinates were $a, b, c+dc$, will be

parallelepiped (A) will still be in the same plane, at least if we neglect quantities indefinitely small of the second order; all the molecules situated on the parallel edges of (A) will be found on small right lines, equal and parallel to each other. Denoting this new parallelepiped by (B), and conceiving that through the extremities of the slice constituted, of those molecules which in the parallelepiped (A) compose the side dc, we draw two planes parallel to the plane of x and y. Then producing the edges of the second parallelepiped to meet these two planes, we shall have a new parallelepiped (C) contained between

$$f(a, b, c+\mathrm{d}c, t),\ F(a, b, c+\mathrm{d}c, t),\ \varphi\ (a, b, c+\mathrm{d}c, t)=$$

respectively to

$$x+\frac{dx}{dc}.\,\mathrm{d}c+\frac{d^2x}{2.dc^2}.\mathrm{d}c^2+\&c, y+\frac{dy}{dc}.\mathrm{d}c+\frac{d^2y}{2.dc^2}.\mathrm{d}c^2+\&c, z+\frac{dz}{dc}.\,\mathrm{d}c+\frac{dz^2}{2.dc^2}.\mathrm{d}c_2+\&c.$$

the difference between these coordinates and x, y, z, are

$$\frac{dx}{dc}.\mathrm{d}c+\frac{d^2x}{2dc^3}.\mathrm{d}c^2, \frac{dy}{dc}.\mathrm{d}c+\frac{d^2y}{2.dc^2}.\mathrm{d}c, \frac{dz}{dc}.\mathrm{d}c+\frac{d^2z}{2.dc^2}.\,\mathrm{d}c^2$$

and the square root of the sum of the squares of these three quantitities, is the value of the side of the parallelepiped which answers to the side dc of the primitive parallelepiped, extracting the square root, and neglecting the third, and higher powers of dc, this side becomes equal to

$$\frac{dz}{dc}.\,\mathrm{d}c+\frac{d^2z}{2.dc}.\,\mathrm{d}c^2,$$

in like manner it may be shewn that the quantities which in the original parallelepiped are equal to da, db, become

$$\frac{dx}{da}.\mathrm{d}a+\frac{d^2x}{da^2}.\,\mathrm{d}a^2, \frac{dy}{db}.\mathrm{d}b+\frac{d^2y}{db^2}.\,\mathrm{d}b^2,$$

the opposite sides of the figure are equal to these; for the value of x, y, z, which corresponds to the primitive coordinates $a+da, b, c$,

$$\text{are} f(a+\mathrm{d}a,\ b+c\,t) F(a+\mathrm{d}a+b, c\ t,) \varphi(a+\mathrm{d}a, b\ c\ t)=$$

$$x+\frac{dx}{da}.\,\mathrm{d}a+\frac{d^2x}{2.da^2}.\,\mathrm{d}a^2, y+\frac{dy}{da}.\mathrm{d}a+\frac{d^2y}{2.da^2}.\mathrm{d}a^2, z+\frac{dz}{da}.\mathrm{d}a+\frac{dz^2}{2.da_2}.\,\mathrm{d}a^2$$

those planes, and equal to (B); for it is manifest that what one of these planes takes from the parallelepiped (B), is added by the other plane. The two bases of the parallelepiped (C) will be parallel to the plane x, y, : its altitude contained between its bases will be equal to the difference of z, taken on the hypothesis that c * only varies ; consequently this altitude will be equal to $\left(\frac{dz}{dc}\right).\,dc.$

the values of x, y, z, which answers to the primitive coordinates $a+da$, b, $c+dc$, will be

$$f\,(a+da,\ b,\ c+dc,\ t)\ F(a+da,\ b,\ c+dc,\ t)\ \varphi(a+da,\ b,\ c+dc\ t)=$$

$$x+\frac{dx}{da}.da+\frac{d^2x}{2.\,da^2}.da^2,+\frac{dx}{dc}.dc+\frac{d^2x}{2.dc^2}.dc^2,+\&c.\,y+\frac{dy}{da}.\,da+\frac{d^2y}{2\,da^2}.da^2,\frac{dy}{dc}.dc\frac{d^2y}{2\,dc^2}.2dc^2+\&c$$

$$z+\frac{dz}{dc}.\,dc+\frac{d^2z}{2dc^2}.dc^2+\frac{dz}{da}.da+\frac{d^2z}{2.da^2}.\,da^2$$

∴ the difference of the coordinates of these points

$$=\frac{dx}{dc}.dc+\frac{d^2x}{2.dc^2}.\,dc^2,\ \frac{dy}{dc}.\,dc+\frac{d^2y}{2dc^2}.\,dc^2,\ \frac{dz}{dc}.\,dc+\frac{d^2z}{2dc^2}.\,dc^2,$$

and as these differences are equal to the corresponding differences of the opposite side of the figure, it follows that these sides must be equal, being equal to the square root of the sum of the squares of these differences, in like manner it may be proved, that the other sides are respectively equal to those to which they are opposed ; and the parallelism of these sides is a necessary consequence of their equality, from which we infer that the figure which the molecules assume is a parallelepiped. The equation of the line connecting the points whose respective coordinates are

$$f(a,b,c,t),\ F(a\,b\,c\,t),\ \varphi(a\,b\,c\,t),\ f(a+da,\ b\,c\,t),\ F(a+da,\ b,\ c\ t,),\ \varphi)a+da,\ b\ c\ t),$$

will be that of a right line, if we neglect the indefinitely small quantities of the second order, and the same is true for all lines parallel to this line, of the sum of which the face may be conceived to made up, ∴ this face may be considered as a plane.

* The difference between the values of z corresponding to the expressions

$$z=\varphi(a,\ b,\ c,\ t),\ z'=\varphi.\ (a\ b\ c+dc\ t)=\frac{dz}{dc}\ .\ dc+\left\{\frac{d^2z}{dc^2}\right\}.\frac{dc^2}{1.2}=\left\{\frac{dz}{dc}\right\}.dc$$

We shall obtain its base, by remarking that it is equal to a section of (B) made by a plane parallel to the plane of $x, y,$; let us designate this section by (ϵ). The value of z will be the same for all the molecules of which this base is constituted, therefore we shall have

$$o = \left\{\frac{dz}{da}\right\}.da + \left\{\frac{dz}{db}\right\}.db + \left\{\frac{dz}{dt}\right\}.dc.$$

Let δp, δq, be two contiguous sides of the section (ϵ), of which the first is made up of molecules which existed on the face $db.\ dc.$ of the parallelepiped (A), and of which the second is composed of molecules which existed on the face $da.\ dc.$ If we conceive two lines to be drawn through the extremities of the side δp, parallel to the axis of x, by producing them to meet that side of the parallelogram (ϵ), which is parallel to δp, they will intercept a new parallelogram (λ) equal to (ϵ), of which the base will be parallel to the axis of x. The side δp being composed of molecules which existed on the face $db.\ dc$, and relatively to which the value of z is constant; it is easy to perceive that the altitude of the parallelogram (λ) is the difference of y, on the supposition that a, z, and t are constant, consequently we have

$$dy = \left\{\frac{dy}{db}\right\}.db + \left\{\frac{dy}{dc}\right\}.dc;*$$

$$o = \left\{\frac{dz}{db}\right\}.db + \left\{\frac{dz}{dc}\right\}.dc;$$

by neglecting quantities indefinitely small of the second order. For all the molecules situated on the edge, which corresponds to dc in the original parallelepiped, projected on the axis of z, the values a and b remain the same, nor do any molecules which occur in the face $da.db$ enter in the constitution of this perpendicular, therefore it is equal to dz on the hypothesis that c only varies.

* If we conceive the molecules of the face $db.dc$ relatively to which dz is constant, to be projected on the axis of y, it is evident that the projected line is equal to the difference

from which may be obtained

$$dy = \frac{\left\{\left(\frac{dy}{db}\right).\left(\frac{dz}{dc}\right) - \left(\frac{dy}{dc}\right).\left(\frac{dz}{db}\right)\right\}.db}{\left(\frac{dz}{dc}\right)}$$

this is the expression for the altitude of the parallelogram (λ). Its base is equal to a section of this parallelogram by a plane parallel to the axis of x; this section is composed of those molecules of the parallelepiped (A), with respect to which z and y are constant; its length will be equal to the differential of x taken on the hypothesis that z, y, and t are constant, which gives the three following equations

$$dx = \left\{\frac{dx}{da}\right\}.da + \left\{\frac{dx}{db}\right\}.db + \left\{\frac{dx}{dc}\right\}.dc\,;^{*}$$

$$0 = \left\{\frac{dy}{da}\right\}.da + \left\{\frac{dy}{db}\right\}.db + \left\{\frac{dy}{dc}\right\}.dc\,;$$

$$0 = \left\{\frac{dz}{da}\right\}.da + \left\{\frac{dz}{db}\right\}.db + \left\{\frac{dz}{dc}\right\}.dc.$$

of y, on the hypothesis that a is constant, for this projection is the same for every series of molecules, which exist on the face which corresponds to the primitive face $db.dc$, and relatively to which z is the same. We obtain the expression which is given in the text for dy by eleminating dc between the two preceding equations.

* Since the parallelogram (λ) exists in the plane parallel to the axes of x, y, the value of z will be constant for this parallelogram, and since the base of (λ) is a line parallel to the axis of x the value of y will be the same for all molecules situated in this base, but since in this base molecules occur which belong to the faces $da.db$, $da.dc$, $db.dc$, a,b,c, will vary for these molecules.

In order to abridge, let us make

$$\varepsilon = \left\{\frac{dx}{da}\right\}.\left\{\frac{dy}{db}\right\}.\left\{\frac{dx}{dc}\right\} - \left\{\frac{dx}{da}\right\}.\left\{\frac{dy}{dc}\right\}.\left\{\frac{dz}{db}\right\}$$

$$+ \left\{\frac{dx}{db}\right\}.\left\{\frac{dy}{dc}\right\}.\left\{\frac{dz}{da}\right\} *$$

* Multiplying the second equation by $\left\{\frac{dz}{dc}\right\}$, and the third by $\left\{\frac{dy}{dc}\right\}$, and then subtracting we shall eliminate dc

$$\left\{\frac{dz}{dc}\right\}.\left\{\frac{dy}{da}\right\}.da + \left\{\frac{dz}{dc}\right\}.\left\{\frac{dy}{db}\right\}.db + \left\{\frac{dz}{dc}\right\}.\left\{\frac{dy}{dc}\right\}.dc = 0$$

$$\left\{\frac{dy}{dc}\right\}.\left\{\frac{dz}{da}\right\}.da + \left\{\frac{dy}{dc}\right\}.\left\{\frac{dz}{db}\right\}.db + \left\{\frac{dy}{dc}\right\}.\left\{\frac{dz}{dc}\right\}.dc = 0$$

$$\therefore \left\{\left(\frac{dz}{dc}\right).\left(\frac{dy}{da}\right) - \left(\frac{dy}{dc}\right).\left(\frac{dz}{da}\right)\right\}.da + \left\{\left(\frac{dz}{dc}\right).\left(\frac{dy}{db}\right) - \left(\frac{dy}{dc}\right).\left(\frac{dz}{db}\right)\right\}.db = 0$$

$$\therefore db = \frac{\left\{\left(\frac{dy}{dc}\right).\left(\frac{dz}{da}\right) - \left(\frac{dz}{dc}\right).\left(\frac{dy}{da}\right)\right\}}{\left(\frac{dz}{dc}\right).\left(\frac{dy}{db}\right) - \left(\frac{dy}{dc}\right).\left(\frac{dz}{db}\right)}.da$$

in like manner we can obtain

$$\left\{\left\{\frac{dz}{db}\right\}.\left\{\frac{dy}{da}\right\} - \left\{\frac{dy}{db}\right\}.\left\{\frac{dz}{da}\right\}\right\}.da + \left\{\left\{\frac{dz}{db}\right\}.\left\{\frac{dy}{dc}\right\} - \left\{\frac{dy}{db}\right\}.\left\{\frac{dz}{dc}\right\}\right\}.dc = 0$$

$$\therefore dc = \frac{\left\{\frac{dy}{db}\right\}.\left\{\frac{dz}{da}\right\} - \left\{\frac{dz}{db}\right\}.\left\{\frac{dy}{da}\right\}}{\left\{\frac{dz}{db}\right\}.\left\{\frac{dy}{dc}\right\} - \left\{\frac{dy}{db}\right\}.\left\{\frac{dz}{dc}\right\}}.da$$

$$dx = \left\{\left(\frac{dx}{da}\right) + \frac{\left\{\frac{dy}{dc}\right\}.\left\{\frac{dz}{da}\right\} - \left\{\frac{dz}{dc}\right\}.\left\{\frac{dy}{da}\right\}}{\left\{\frac{dz}{dc}\right\}.\left\{\frac{dy}{db}\right\} - \left\{\frac{dy}{dc}\right\}.\left\{\frac{dz}{db}\right\}}.\left\{\frac{dx}{db}\right\}\right.$$

$$-\left\{\frac{dx}{db}\right\}.\left\{\frac{dy}{da}\right\}.\left\{\frac{dz}{dc}\right\}+\left\{\frac{dx}{dc}\right\}.\left\{\frac{dy}{da}\right\}.\left\{\frac{dz}{db}\right\}-\left\{\frac{dx}{dc}\right\}.\left\{\frac{dy}{db}\right\}.\left\{\frac{dz}{da}\right\}$$

we shall have

$$dx=\frac{\epsilon.\,da}{\left\{\frac{dy}{db}\right\}.\left\{\frac{dz}{dc}\right\}-\left\{\frac{dy}{dc}\right\}.\left\{\frac{dz}{db}\right\}}$$

this is the value of the base of the parallelogram (λ); therefore the surface of this parallelogram will be equal to

$$\frac{\epsilon.da.db}{\left(\frac{dz}{dc}\right)}.$$

This quantity also expresses the surface of the parallelogram (ε), if we multiply it by $\left(\frac{dz}{dc}\right).dc$ we shall have $\epsilon.da.db.dc$ for the volume of the

$$+\frac{\left\{\frac{dy}{db}\right\}.\left\{\frac{dz}{da}\right\}-\left\{\frac{dz}{db}\right\}.\left\{\frac{dy}{da}\right\}}{\left\{\frac{dz}{dc}\right\}.\left\{\frac{dy}{db}\right\}-\left\{\frac{dy}{dc}\right\}.\left\{\frac{dz}{db}\right\}}.\left\{\frac{dx}{dc}\right\}\Bigg\}.da=$$

$$\Bigg\{\left\{\frac{dx}{da}\right\}.\left\{\frac{dz}{dc}\right\}.\left\{\frac{dy}{db}\right\}-\left\{\frac{dx}{da}\right\}.\left\{\frac{dy}{dc}\right\}.\left\{\frac{dz}{db}\right\}+\left\{\frac{dx}{db}\right\}.\left\{\frac{dy}{dc}\right\}.\left\{\frac{dz}{da}\right\}$$

$$-\left\{\frac{dx}{db}\right\}.\left\{\frac{dz}{dc}\right\}.\left\{\frac{dy}{da}\right\}+\left\{\frac{dx}{dc}\right\}.\left\{\frac{dy}{db}\right\}\left\{\frac{dz}{da}\right\}-\left\{\frac{dx}{dc}\right\}.\left\{\frac{dz}{da}\right\}.\left\{\frac{dy}{db}\right\}\Bigg\}.da$$

$$\div\left\{\frac{dz}{dc}\right\}.\left\{\frac{dy}{db}\right\}-\left\{\frac{dy}{dc}\right\}.\left\{\frac{dz}{db}\right\}$$

$$=\frac{\epsilon.\,da}{\left\{\frac{dz}{dc}\right\}.\left\{\frac{dy}{db}\right\}-\left\{\frac{dy}{dc}\right\}.\left\{\frac{dz}{db}\right\}}$$

= the base of the parallelogram (λ), this expression being multiplied into the value of dy gives the area of (λ), and this area being multiplied by the altitude gives the volume of (C)

parallelepipeds (C), and (B). Let ρ represent the density of the parallepiped (A), after the time t; we shall have its mass equal to $\rho\ \epsilon.da.db.dc$; and by equating this to its primitive mass $(\rho).da.db.dc$ we shall have

$$\rho\epsilon=(\rho)\ ;\ (G)$$

for the equation relative to the continuity of the fluid.

33. The equations (F) and (G) may be made to assume another form, which is in certain circumstances of more convenient application. Let u, v, and V be the velocities of a molecule of the fluid, parallel to the axes of x, of y, and of z; we shall have

$$\left\{\frac{dx}{dt}\right\}=u;\left\{\frac{dy}{dt}\right\}=v;\ \left\{\frac{dz}{dt}\right\}=V.$$

By differentiating these equations, u, v, ,V being considered as functions of the coordinates x, y, z, of the molecule, and of the time t, we shall have

$$\left\{\frac{d^2x}{dt^2}\right\}=\left\{\frac{du}{dt}\right\}+u.\left\{\frac{du}{dx}\right\}+v.\left\{\frac{du}{dy}\right\}+V.\left\{\frac{du}{dz}\right\};\ *$$

*u, v, V, are respectively unknown functions of x,y, z, and t, they depend on the coordinates x, y, z, because for a given value of t, the velocity is different in different molecules, they depend on t, because for the same values of x, y, z, the velocity varies every instant,

$$\therefore du=\left\{\frac{du}{dt}\right\}.dt+\left\{\frac{du}{dx}\right\}.dx+\left\{\frac{du}{dy}\right\}dy+\left\{\frac{du}{dz}\right\}.dz,$$

and since $dx=udt$, $dy=v.dt$ $dz=\mathrm{V}dt$,
substituting and dividing by dt, we obtain

$$\frac{du}{dt}=\left\{\frac{du}{dt}\right\}+\left\{\frac{du}{dz}\right\}.V+\left\{\frac{du}{dy}\right\}.v+\left\{\frac{du}{dx}\right\}.V,$$

$$\text{but } u=\frac{dx}{dt}\therefore\frac{du}{dt}=\frac{d^2x}{dt^2}.$$

From the values of $\frac{du}{dt},\frac{dv}{dt},\frac{dV}{dt}$, given in the text, it appears how the increment of each of the three velocities depends on the two other velocities. If we were able to determine the

$$\left\{\frac{d^2y}{dt^2}\right\} = \left\{\frac{dv}{dt}\right\} + u.\left\{\frac{dv}{dx}\right\} + v.\left\{\frac{dv}{dy}\right\} + V.\left\{\frac{dv}{dz}\right\};$$

$$\left\{\frac{d^2z}{dt^2}\right\} = \left\{\frac{dV}{dt}\right\} + u.\left\{\frac{dV}{dx}\right\} + v.\left\{\frac{dV}{dy}\right\} + V.\left\{\frac{dV}{dz}\right\}.$$

consequently the equation (F) of the preceding number will become,

$$\delta V - \frac{\delta p}{\rho} = \delta x.\left\{\left\{\frac{du}{dt}\right\} + u.\left\{\frac{du}{dx}\right\} + v.\left\{\frac{du}{dy}\right\} + V.\left\{\frac{du}{dz}\right\}\right\}$$

$$+ \delta y.\left\{\left\{\frac{dv}{dt}\right\} + u.\left\{\frac{dv}{dx}\right\} + v.\left\{\frac{dv}{dy}\right\} + V.\left\{\frac{dv}{dz}\right\}\right\}; \quad (H)$$

$$+ \delta z.\left\{\left\{\frac{dV}{dt}\right\} + u.\left\{\frac{dV}{dx}\right\} + v.\left\{\frac{dV}{dy}\right\} + V.\left\{\frac{dV}{dz}\right\}\right\}$$

In order to have the equation relative to the continuity of the fluid; let us conceive that in the value of ϵ, of the preceding number, a, b, c, were equal to x, y, z, and that x, y, z, were equal to $x+udt$, $y+vdt$, $z+V.dt$, which is equivalent to assuming the primitive coordinates a, b, c, indefinitely near to x, y, z, ; we shall have

value of u in a function of x, y, z, t, we could by means of the equations $\frac{dx}{dt}=u$, $\frac{dy}{dt}=v$, $\frac{dz}{dt}=V$ determine the position of a molecule at any instant, provided we know the initial position of this molecule, and also what function of $x\ y\ z\ t$, $u\ v$ V are, for substituting in the equations $\frac{dx}{dt}=u$, $\frac{dy}{dt}=v$, $\frac{dz}{dt}=V$ the values of $u\ v$, V, in functions of $x\ y\ zt$, and integrating, we would obtain the values of x, y, z, respectively in a function of t, the constant arbitrary quantities which are introduced are the values of x, y, z, at the commencement of the motion which by hypothesis are given, consequently the values of $x\ y\ z$ will be completely determined for *any* instant. Eliminating t between values of x, y, z, to which we have arrived, we would obtain the two equations of the curve described by the molecule, but since the initial position of each molecule is different, the form of this curve will also be different, as will be in like manner, the position.

$$\epsilon = 1 + dt.\left\{\left\{\frac{du}{dx}\right\} + \left\{\frac{dv}{dy}\right\} + \left\{\frac{dV}{dz}\right\}\right\};^{*}$$

H H

* The first coordinates being assumed indefinitely near to x, y, z, we shall have $da = dx$, and the quantity which corresponds to dx=to $dx + du.dt$, in like manner we shall have

$$\frac{dx+du.dt}{dz}, \frac{dx+du.dt}{dy}, \frac{dy+du{\cdot}dt}{dz}, \frac{dy+dv.dt}{dz}, \frac{dz+dV.dt}{dy}, \frac{dz+dV.dt}{dx}$$

respectively indefinitely small, because when $t=0$ these quantities vanish, $\therefore$ the product of any two of these quantities may be neglected, making these substitutions the expression for ϵ becomes equal to

$$\left\{\frac{dx+du.dt}{dx}\right\}.\left\{\frac{dy+dv.dt}{dy}\right\}.\left\{\frac{dz+dVdt}{dz}\right\}$$

$$-\left\{\frac{dx+du.dt}{dx}\right\}.\left\{\frac{dy+dv.dt}{dz}\right\}.\left\{\frac{dz+dV.dt}{dy}\right\}$$

$$+\left\{\frac{dx+du.dt}{dy}\right\}.\left\{\frac{dy+dv.dt}{dz}\right\}.\left\{\frac{dz+dV.dt}{dx}\right\}$$

$$-\left\{\frac{dx+du.dt}{dy}\right\}.\left\{\frac{dy+dv.dt}{dx}\right\}.\left\{\frac{dz+dV.dt}{dz}\right\}$$

$$+\left\{\frac{dx+du.dt}{dz}\right\}.\left\{\frac{dy+dv.dt}{dx}\right\}.\left\{\frac{dz+dV.dt}{dy}\right\}$$

$$-\left\{\frac{dx+du.dt}{dz}\right\}.\left\{\frac{dy+dv.dt}{dy}\right\}.\left\{\frac{dz+dV.dt}{dx}\right\}$$

the first term of this expression

$$= \left\{1+\frac{du.dt}{dx}\right\}.\left\{1+\frac{dv.dt}{dy}\right\}.\left\{1+\frac{dV.dt}{dz}\right\}$$

= by neglecting quantities indefinitely small

$$1 + \left\{\frac{du}{dx} + \frac{dv}{dy} + \frac{dV}{dz}\right\}.dt,$$

the other terms of this expression vanish. It appears from what precedes that $\epsilon\rho$ is a constant quantity independent of the time, when the fluid is incompressible $\epsilon=1$.

the equation (G) becomes,

$$\rho.\left\{\left\{\frac{du}{dx}\right\}+\left\{\frac{dv}{dy}\right\}+\left\{\frac{dV}{dz}\right\}\right\}+\rho-(\rho)=0.$$

If we consider ρ as a function of x, y, z, and t, we shall have

$$(\rho)=\rho-dt.\left\{\frac{d\rho}{dt}\right\}-udt.\left\{\frac{d\rho}{dx}\right\}-vdt.\left\{\frac{d\rho}{dy}\right\}-Vdt.\left\{\frac{d\rho}{dz}\right\};$$

therefore the preceding equation will become

$$0=\left\{\frac{d\rho}{dt}\right\}+\left\{\frac{d.\rho u}{dx}\right\}+\left\{\frac{d.\rho v}{dy}\right\}+\left\{\frac{d.\rho V}{dz}\right\};\ (K)\ ^{*}$$

* The density ϱ, the pressure p, may be shewn to be functions of $x\ y\ z,\ t$, by reasoning, analogous to that, by which u, v, V, were proved to be functions of these quantities;

$$\varrho.dt.\left\{\left\{\frac{du}{dx}\right\}+\left\{\frac{dv}{dy}\right\}+\left\{\frac{dV}{dz}\right\}\right\}$$

is the increment of ϱ on the supposition that t is constant,

$$dt.\left\{\frac{d\varrho}{dt}\right\}-u.dt.\left\{\frac{d\varrho}{dx}\right\}-v.dt.\left\{\frac{d\varrho}{dy}\right\}-V.\left\{\frac{d\varrho}{dz}\right\}$$

is the variation of ϱ on the hypothesis that x, y, z, t, vary $\therefore$ their difference

$$=\varrho.\left\{\frac{du}{dx}\right\}+u.\left\{\frac{d\varrho}{dx}\right\}+\varsigma.\left\{\frac{dv}{dy}\right\}+V.\left\{\frac{d\varrho}{dy}\right\}$$

$$+\varrho.\left\{\frac{dV}{dv}\right\}+V.\left\{\frac{d\varrho}{dz}\right\}+\left\{\frac{d\varrho}{dt}\right\}$$

$$=\left\{\frac{d.\varrho u}{dx}\right\}+\left\{\frac{d.\varrho v}{dy}\right\}+\left\{\frac{d.\varrho V}{dz}\right\}+\left\{\frac{d\varrho}{dt}\right\}$$

is the differential of the equation (G) taken with respect to the time;

this is the equation relative to the continuity of the fluid, and it is easy to perceive that it is the differential of the equation (G) of the preceding number, taken with respect to the time t.

The equation (H) is susceptible of integration in a very extensive case that is, when $u\delta x + v.\delta y + \text{V}.\delta z$ is an exact variation of x, y, z, ρ being any function whatever of the pressure p. Therefore if we re-

H H 2

when the fluid is incompressible, we have

$$\left\{\frac{d\varrho}{dx}\right\}.u + \left\{\frac{d\varrho}{dy}\right\}.v + \left\{\frac{d\varrho}{dz}\right\}.\text{V} + \left\{\frac{d\varrho}{dt}\right\}$$

$$=0;\ \varrho.\left\{\left\{\frac{du}{dx}\right\} + \left\{\frac{dv}{dy}\right\} + \left\{\frac{d\text{V}}{dz}\right\}\right\}=0;$$

for in this case both the magnitude, and density are constant, ∴ dG and $d\varrho$ are respectively equal to nothing, these two equations combined with the three, which may be derived from the equations (H), or (F), are sufficient to determine p, ϱ, and the three partial velocities, u, v, V, in functions of x, y, z, t,. When the differential coefficients $\frac{d\varrho}{dt}, \frac{d\varrho}{dx}, \frac{d\varrho}{dy}, \frac{d\varrho}{dz}$, vanish of themselves, ϱ must be a constant quantity, and the incompressible fluid will be also homogenous, ∴ in this case the number of unknown quantities is reduced to four, which is also the number of differential equations. When the fluid is elastic the number of unknown quantities will be ultimately reducible to four, for when the temperature is given $p=k.\varrho$, ∴ the equation (K) and the three equations (H) are sufficient to determine the unknown quantities, in this case

$$\frac{\delta p}{\varrho} = \frac{1}{k}.\frac{\delta\varrho}{\varrho} = \frac{1}{k}.\ \delta.\log\varrho.$$

k will not be constant when the temperature varies, but if the law of its variation is known, since for each different instant, and point of space the temperature is a given function of x,y,z,t,k will be so likewise, so that even in this case the equations (K) and H are sufficient to determine $\varrho,u,v,$V. It appears from what precedes, that we have *always* as many equations of partial differences as sought quantities, however the general integration of these equations has baffled the ingenuity of Philosophers and even granting that it is possible to effect this integration, still the determination of the arbitrary functions introduced by these integration, is extremely difficult, these functions depend partly, on the primitive state of the fluid, and partly on the equation of the exterior surface.

present this variation by $\delta\varphi$, the equation (H) will give

$$\delta V - \frac{\delta p}{\rho} = \delta.\left\{\frac{d\varphi}{dt}\right\} + \tfrac{1}{2}.\delta.\left\{\left\{\frac{d\varphi}{dx}\right\}^2 + \left\{\frac{d\varphi}{dy}\right\}^2 + \left\{\frac{d\varphi}{dz}\right\}^2\right\};$$

from which may be obtained by integrating with respect to δ,

$$V - \int\frac{\delta p}{\rho} = \left\{\frac{d\varphi}{dt}\right\} + \tfrac{1}{2}.\left\{\left\{\frac{d\varphi}{dx}\right\}^2 + \left\{\frac{d\varphi}{dy}\right\}^2 + \left\{\frac{d\varphi}{dz}\right\}^2\right\}.*$$

* If we take the differential of the equation $u\delta x + v.\delta y + V.\delta z$ with respect to t, x, y, z, we shall obtain

$$\frac{du}{dt}.dt.\delta x + \frac{dv}{dt}.dt.\delta y + \frac{dV}{dt}.dt.\delta z = \frac{d.\delta\varphi}{dt}.dt = \frac{du}{dt}.dt.\delta x + \frac{dv}{dt}.dt.\delta y + \frac{dV}{dt}.dt.\delta z$$

$$\frac{du}{dx}.dx.\delta y + \frac{dv}{dx}.dx.\delta y + \frac{dV}{dx}.dx.\delta z = \frac{d.\delta\varphi}{dx}.dx = \frac{du}{dx}.udt.\delta x + \frac{dv}{dx}.udt.\delta y + \frac{dV}{dx}udt.\delta z$$

$$\frac{du}{dy}.dy.\delta x + \frac{dv}{dy}.dy.\delta y + \frac{dV}{dz}.dy.\delta z = \frac{d.\delta\varphi}{dy}.dy = \frac{du}{dy}.v.dt.\delta x + \frac{dv}{dy}.v.dt.\delta y + \frac{dV}{dy}.v.dt.\delta z$$

$$\frac{du}{dz}.dz.\delta x + \frac{dv}{dz}.dz.\delta y + \frac{dV}{dz}.dz.\delta z = \frac{d.\delta\varphi}{dz}.dz = \frac{du}{dz}.V.dt.\delta z + \frac{dv}{dz}.V.dt.\delta y + \frac{dV}{dx}.V.dt.\delta z$$

now substituting udt, vdt, Vdt, in place of dx, dy, dz, and remarking that, $u = \frac{d\varphi}{dz}$, $v = \frac{d\varphi}{dy}$, &c. and also that $\delta.\frac{d\varphi}{dt} = \frac{d.\delta\varphi}{dt}$ we shall have

$$\delta.\left\{\frac{d\varphi}{dt}\right\} + \delta.\left\{\frac{d\varphi}{dx}\right\}.\left\{\frac{d\varphi}{dx}\right\} + \delta.\left\{\frac{d\varphi}{dy}\right\}.\left\{\frac{d\varphi}{dy}\right\} + \delta.\left\{\frac{d\varphi}{dz}\right\}.\left\{\frac{d\varphi}{dz}\right\}$$

$$= \delta.\left\{\frac{d\varphi}{dt} + \tfrac{1}{2}.\delta.\left\{\left\{\frac{d\varphi}{dx}\right\}^2 + \left\{\frac{d\varphi}{dy}\right\}^2 + \left\{\frac{d\varphi}{dz}\right\}^2\right\}\right.$$

= the sum of the last members of the preceding equations, but these by concinnating, and dividing by dt are evidently equal to the second member of the equation (H). Since the integration is only made relative to the characteristic δ, it is evident that the time is not involved in this expression. When the fluid is homogenous $\frac{\delta r}{dx}$&c. $=0$ $\therefore$ the equation of continuity is reduced to the second term, by means of this equation, and the equations $u = \frac{d\varphi}{dx}$,

It is necessary to add to this integral, a constant quantity, which is a function of t; but we may suppose that this function is contained in the function φ. This last function gives the velocity of the molecules of the fluid parallel to the axes of x, of y, and of z; for we have

$$u = \left\{\frac{d\varphi}{dx}\right\};\ v = \left\{\frac{d\varphi}{dy}\right\};\ V = \left\{\frac{d\varphi}{dz}\right\}.$$

The equation (K) relative to the continuity of the fluid, becomes

$$0 = \left\{\frac{d\rho}{dt}\right\} + \left\{\frac{d\rho}{dx}\right\}.\left\{\frac{d\varphi}{dx}\right\} + \left\{\frac{d\rho}{dy}\right\}.\left\{\frac{d\varphi}{dy}\right\} + \left\{\frac{d\rho}{dz}\right\}.\left\{\frac{d\varphi}{dz}\right\}$$

$$+\rho.\left\{\left\{\frac{d^2\varphi}{dx^2}\right\} + \left\{\frac{d^2\varphi}{dy^2}\right\} + \left\{\frac{d^2\varphi}{dz^2}\right\}\right\};$$

consequently, we shall have in the case of homogenous fluids,

$$0 = \left\{\frac{d^2\varphi}{dx^2}\right\} + \left\{\frac{d^2\varphi}{dy^2}\right\} + \left\{\frac{d^2\varphi}{dz^2}\right\}.$$

It may observed, that if the function $u\delta x + v\delta y + V.\delta z$ is an exact variationof x, y, z, at any one instant, it will always remain so. In fact, let us suppose that at any instant whatever, it is equal to $\delta\varphi$, in the subsequent instant it will be equal to

$$\delta\varphi + dt.\left\{\left\{\frac{du}{dt}\right\}.\delta x + \left\{\frac{dv}{dt}\right\}.\delta y + \left\{\frac{dV}{dt}\right\}.\delta z\right\};\ *$$

$v = \frac{d\varphi}{dy}$, $V = \frac{d\varphi}{dz}$, and the value for $f\frac{\delta p}{\rho}$, $=$ in this case $\frac{p}{\rho}$, we can determine φ and p and consequently u, v, V, in functions of $x\ y\ z$.

* From the value of $V—f.\ \frac{\delta p}{\rho}$ it appears that the pressure of a molecule, of which the density is constant, diminishes when the velocity which is equal to

therefore it will be an exact variation at this new instant, if

$$\left\{\frac{du}{dt}\right\}.\delta x+\left\{\frac{dv}{dt}\right\}.\delta y+\left\{\frac{dV}{dt}\right\}.\delta z$$

$$\sqrt{\left\{\frac{d\phi}{dx}\right\}^2+\left\{\frac{d\phi}{dy}\right\}^2+\left\{\frac{d\phi}{dz}\right\}^2}$$

is increased.

$$d.\frac{\delta\phi}{dt}.dt=\frac{d.\delta\phi}{dt}.dt=\delta.\left\{\frac{d\phi}{dt}\right\}.dt=\left\{\left\{\frac{du}{dt}\right\}\delta x+\left\{\frac{dv}{dt}\right\}.\delta y+\left\{\frac{dV}{dt}\right\}.\delta z\right\}.dt$$

substituting this value of $\delta.\left\{\frac{d\phi}{dt}\right\}$ in the expression for $\delta V-\frac{\delta p}{\varrho}$ we obtain

$$\left\{\frac{du}{dt}\right\}\delta x+\left\{\frac{dv}{dt}\right\}.\delta y+\left\{\frac{dV}{dt}\right\}.\delta z=\delta V$$

$$-\tfrac{1}{2}.\delta.\left\{\left\{\frac{d\phi}{dx}\right\}^2+\left\{\frac{d\phi}{dy}\right\}^2+\left\{\frac{d\phi}{dz}\right\}^2\right\}-\frac{\delta p}{\varrho}$$

and since each of the terms, of the second member of this equation, are exact variations of x, y, z, the first member will also be an exact variation, we suppose ϱ to be a function of p.

$$\left\{\left\{\frac{du}{dt}\right\}.\delta x+\left\{\frac{dv}{dt}\right\}.\delta y+\left\{\frac{dV}{dt}\right\}.\delta z\right\}.dt$$

is the differential of $\delta\phi$, on the supposition that the time only varies. Consequently, we are not obliged to determine ϕ in x, y, z, in order to know whether it is an exact differential or not. $\therefore$ It appears that if $u\delta x+v\delta y+V.\delta z$ be an exact variation, at the subsequent instant *its increment* will be an exact variation, $\therefore$ $\delta\phi+$this increment will be an exact variation. As in general we know the condition of the fluid at the commencement of the motion, if at this moment $u\delta x+v\delta y+V.\delta x$ is an exact variation, it will be an exact variation when $t=\pm dt$, $t=\pm 2dt$, &c. and in general whatever may the value of t. $u\delta x+v.\delta y+V.\delta z$ will be an exact variation, if when $t=0$, the fluid either has no velocity or a constant one, for in first case $u=0$, $v=0$, $V=0$ when t vanishes, $\therefore$ $u\delta x+v\delta y+V\delta z$ will be integrable for this moment, the second case will obtain when the motion is produced by an impulse on the surface of the fluid, such as that which arises from the action of a piston. For the velocities u, v, V which are communicated to each of the molecules, must be such, that if they are

is an exact variation at the first moment, but the equation (H) gives at this moment

$$\left\{\frac{du}{dt}\right\}.\delta x+\left\{\frac{dv}{dt}\right\}.\delta y+\left\{\frac{dV}{dt}\right\}.\delta z$$

$$=\delta V-\tfrac{1}{2}\delta.\left\{\left\{\frac{d\varphi}{db}\right\}^2+\left\{\frac{d\varphi}{dy}\right\}^2+\left\{\frac{d\varphi}{dz}\right\}^2\right\};$$

consequently the first member of this equation is an exact variation of x, y, z, ; therefore if the function $u\delta x+v.\delta y+V.dz$ be an exact variation at any one instant, it will be one in the next, therefore it will be an exact variation at all times.

When the motions are very small; the squares and products of u, v, V, may be neglected; and the equation (H) will then become

$$\delta V-\frac{\delta p}{\rho}=\left\{\frac{du}{dt}\right\}\delta x+\left\{\frac{dv}{dt}\right\}.\delta y+\left\{\frac{dV}{dt}\right\}.\delta z;\ ^*$$

therefore in this case $u\delta x+v\delta y+V.\delta z$, is an exact variation, provided that, as we have supposed, p is a function of ρ; therefore if we designate

destroyed by impressing on each molecule, equal velocities in an opposite direction the *entire* fluid would quiesce; ∴ in consequence of the primitive impulsion, and the velocities u, v, V, applied in an opposite direction, there must be an equilibrium, ∴ u v V must be such that $u\delta x+v\delta y+V.\delta z$ may be an exact variation, see No. 17; it appears from what precedes, that the integrability of the equation (H), and the consequent determination of p, ϱ, u, v, V, depends on the nature of the velocities, communicated to the molecules at the commencement of the motion.

* In the equation (H) u, v, V, are very small quantities, and in like manner

$$\left\{\frac{du}{dx}\right\}\left\{\frac{du}{dy}\right\}\left\{\frac{dv}{dy}\right\}\left\{\frac{dV}{dz}\right\}\ \&c.$$

∴ their product may be rejected ∴ naming this variation $\delta\varphi$ we have as before,

$$\frac{d.\delta\varphi}{dt}.=\delta\frac{d.\varphi}{dt}.=\left\{\left(\frac{du}{dt}\right).\delta x+\left(\frac{dv}{dt}\right).\delta y+\left(\frac{dV}{dt}\right).\delta z\right\};$$

$$=\delta V-\frac{\delta p}{\varrho},\ \therefore\frac{d\varphi}{dt}=V-\int\frac{\delta p}{\varrho}$$

this variation by $\delta\varphi$, we shall have

$$V - \int \frac{\delta p}{\rho} = \left\{ \frac{d\varphi}{dt} \right\};$$

and if the fluid be homogenous, the equation of continuity will become

$$0 = \left\{ \frac{d^2\varphi}{dx^2} \right\} + \left\{ \frac{d^2\varphi}{dy^2} \right\} + \left\{ \frac{d\varphi^2}{dz^2} \right\};$$

$$= \frac{d\varphi}{dt} + \frac{u^2 + v^2 + V^2}{2};$$

the expression

$$\left(\frac{d\phi}{dt}\right) + \tfrac{1}{2}.\left\{ \left(\frac{d\varphi}{dx}\right)^2 + \left(\frac{d\varphi}{dy}\right)^2 + \left(\frac{d\varphi}{dz}\right)^2 \right.$$

is the value of $V - \int \frac{\delta p}{\rho}$, when $u\delta x + v\delta y + V.\delta z$ is an exact variation, it is reduced to its first term when u, v, V, are very small quantities.

However though the form of these equations is comparatively so much simpler, than the *general equations* which have been given in page 232, still the determination of *the laws* of the small oscillations of the waves of the sea, is yet a desideratum in Physics. Philosophers have been much more successful in investigating the oscillations of the pulses of the air, and in the determination of the velocity of the propagation of sound.

The integration of

$$\left\{ \frac{d^2\varphi}{dx^2} \right\} + \left\{ \frac{d^2\varphi}{dy^2} \right\} + \left\{ \frac{d^2\varphi}{dz} \right\}$$

which is the equation relative to the continuity of the fluid, when $u\delta x + v.\delta y + V\delta z$ is an exact variation, and when the fluid is homogenous, which is consequently the simplest possible form, is extremely difficult, however it has been completed effected by Antonie Parseval.

these two equations contain the entire theory, of the very small undulations of homogeneous fluids.*

I I

* If the fluid which makes small oscillations be water, by making the axis of z vertical, $R\partial z = g.\partial z$, g representing the force of gravity, Pdx, $Q\partial y$ are = respectively to nothing, in like manner we may conceive it to be homogeneous and incompressible, consequently we shall have

$$f\frac{\partial p}{\varrho} = \frac{p}{\varrho}, \therefore \partial V - \frac{\partial p}{\varrho} = \partial.\left(\frac{d\varphi}{dt}\right) = g.\partial z - \frac{\partial p}{\varrho}, \& gz - \frac{p}{\varrho} = \left(\frac{d\varphi}{dt}\right);$$

at the surface p vanishes, $\therefore z = \frac{1}{g}.\left\{\frac{d\varphi}{dt}\right\}$, consequently when the form of φ is determined, we can derive the equation of the part of the fluid in which $p=0$, *i, e,* the equation of the surface of the fluid.

We determine φ as was already observed by means of the equation

$$\left\{\frac{d^2\varphi}{dx^2}\right\} + \left\{\frac{d^2\varphi}{dy^2}\right\} + \left\{\frac{d^2\varphi}{dx^2}\right\} = 0,$$

For, elastic fluids or those whose density varies, $p = \iota\varrho$, and if (ϱ) the density of the fluid in a state of rest, becomes in a state of motion equal to $(\varrho) + (\varrho).q$, q being a very small quantity, ϱ will be equal to $(\varrho) + (\varrho).q$, the oscillations being supposed very small, $\partial V - \frac{\partial p}{\varrho} = \partial.\left\{\frac{d\varphi}{dt}\right\}$ will become $\partial V - \iota.\frac{\partial\varrho}{\varrho} = \partial.\left\{\frac{d\varphi}{dt}\right\}$, the only force acting being that of gravity, and the motion being supposed *parallel* to the horizon, ∂V will vanish and the equation will become $-\frac{\iota.\partial\varrho}{\varrho} = \partial.\left\{\frac{d\varphi}{dt}\right\}$ = by substituting for ϱ its value, (ϱ) being supposed constant, $-\frac{\iota(\varrho).\partial q}{(\varrho).q}$; $\therefore -\iota.\log.q = \left\{\frac{d\varphi}{dt}\right\}$, the equation relative to the continuity of the fluid will become

$$0 = \left\{\frac{d(\varrho)q}{dt}\right\} + \left\{\frac{d(\varrho)q}{dx}\right\}.\left\{\frac{d\varphi}{dx}\right\} + \varrho\left\{\frac{d^2\varphi}{dx^2}\right\}; \text{for} \left\{\frac{d\varphi}{dy}\right\} \left\{\frac{d\varphi}{dz}\right\},$$

vanish, the motion being supposed to be performed in a direction parallel to the axis of x, and

34. Let us consider an homogeneous fluid mass which revolves uniformly about the axis of x. n representing the angular velocity of rotation, at a distance from the axis equal to unity, we shall have $v = -nz$; $V = ny$; * consequently the equation (H) of the preceding number, will become

$$\frac{\delta p}{\rho} = \delta V + n^2 . \{ y\delta y + z\delta z \}; \dagger$$

consequently the velocities v, V, = respectively

$$\left(\frac{d\varphi}{dz}\right), \left(\frac{d\varphi}{dz}\right), \text{vanish}; \left(\frac{d(\varrho)q}{dx}\right).\frac{d\varphi}{dx} = (\varrho).\left(\frac{dq}{dx}\right)u,$$

which is a quantity indefinitely small of the second order, ∴ it may be neglected, consequently the preceding equation becomes

$$(\varrho) \left\{ \left(\frac{dq}{dt}\right) + (1+q)\left(\frac{d^2\varphi}{dx^2}\right) \right\} = 0, \text{ but } \frac{d\varphi}{dt} = -\iota . \log . q \therefore \frac{d^2\varphi}{dt^2} = -\iota . \left\{ \frac{dq}{q.dt} \right\}$$

$$\text{consequently} - \frac{q}{\iota} . \left\{ \frac{d^2\varphi}{dt^2} \right\} + (1+q) . \left\{ \frac{d^2\varphi}{dx^2} \right\} = 0;$$

this equation is of great celebrity in the history of the integral calculus, it was first integrated by D'Alembert, in an analysis of the problem of the vibrating chord, which leads to an equation of precisely the same form.

* The linear velocity is equal to the angular velocity multiplied into the distance, ∴ at a distance represented by unity, the linear velocity $= n$, and since the angular velocity at all distances from the axis is the same, at a distance $= \sqrt{z^2+y^2}$ the linear velocity $= n . \sqrt{z^2+y^2}$, the direction of the motion being perpendicular to the radius in order to obtain the velocity parallel to the coordinates z, y, we should multiply $n . \sqrt{z^2+y^2}$ into the cosines of the angles which z and y make with the tangent, but these cosines are respectively $\frac{y}{\sqrt{z^2+y^2}}$, $\frac{-z}{\sqrt{z^2+y^2}}$, for the motion being circular, if one of the cordinates be increased, the other will be diminished ∴ $v = -nz$, $V = ny$.

† The terms corresponding to $\left\{\frac{du}{dt}\right\}$, $\left\{\frac{dv}{dt}\right\}$, $\left\{\frac{dV}{dt}\right\}$, in the equation ($H$) vanish, because the time does not enter into the values of u, v, V, in like manner u and its differential coefficients vanish, and from the values of v, V, given above, it is manifest that

which equation is possible, because its two members are exact variations. The equation (K) of the same number will become

$$0=dt.\left\{\frac{d\rho}{dt}\right\}+u.dt.\left\{\frac{d\rho}{dx}\right\}+v.dt.\left\{\frac{d\rho}{dy}\right\}+\text{V}.dt.\left\{\frac{d\rho}{dz}\right\};\ *$$

and it is manifest that this equation will be satisfied, if the fluid mass be homogeneous. The equations of the motion of fluids will therefore be satisfied, and consequently, the motion is possible.

The centrifugal force at the distance $\sqrt{y^2+z^2}$ from the axis of rotation, is equal to the square $n^2.(z^2+y^2)$ of the velocity, divided by this distance; therefore the function $n^2.(y\delta y+z.\delta z)$ † is the product of the

$\left(\frac{dv}{dy}\right)$, $\left(\frac{d\text{V}}{dz}\right)$, are equal respectively to nothing, consequently the only terms which have a finite value are V. $\left(\frac{dv}{dz}\right)$, $v.\left(\frac{d\text{V}}{dy}\right)$, which are respectively equal to $=-n^2y, -n^2z$, ∴ the equation (H) will become $\frac{\delta p}{\rho}=\delta V+n^2.(y\delta z+z\delta z)$, this equation determines the pressure when ρ is constant, or when it is a function of p.

* The equation (K) is resolvable into two parts as before,

$$\left(\frac{d\rho}{dt}\right)+u.\left(\frac{d\rho}{dx}\right)+v.\left(\frac{d\rho}{dy}\right)+\text{V}.\left(\frac{d\rho}{dz}\right)+\rho.\left\{\left(\frac{du}{dx}\right)+\left(\frac{dv}{dy}\right)+\left(\frac{d\text{V}}{dz}\right)\right\},$$

the velocity being uniform, its increment resolved parallel to the axes of x, y, z, i, e

$$\left(\frac{du}{dx}\right),\left(\frac{dv}{dy}\right),\left(\frac{d\text{V}}{dz}\right),$$

must be severally equal to nothing, this is evident for v, V, from their values which have been given above, with respect to the velocity u, it must be produced by the part of the velocity which is parallel to x, and if it was not uniform, the fluid would not have a uniform motion of rotation about the axis of x.

† The centrifugal force $=n^2.\sqrt{z^2+y^2}$, the variation of the distance $=\frac{z\delta z+y\delta y}{\sqrt{z^2+y^2}}$ ∴ $n^2.(z\delta z+y\delta y)$ is $=$ to the centrifugal force multiplied into the element of the distance.

centrifugal force, by the element of its direction; thus, if we compare the preceding equation of the motion of a fluid, with the general equation of the equilibrium of fluids, which has been given in No. 17, we may perceive that the conditions of the motion are reduced, to those of the equilibrium of the fluid mass, solicitedby the same forces, and by the centrifugal force which arises from the motion of rotation; which is sufficiently evident from the nature of the case.

If the exterior surface of the fluid mass be free, we shall have $\delta p=0$, at this surface, and consequently

$$0=\delta V+n^2.\{y\delta y+z\delta z);^*$$

Substituting for δV we obtain $\frac{\delta p}{\rho}=P.\delta x+Q.\delta y+R.\delta z+n2.y\delta y+n^2z.\delta z$, the quantity added i, e, the centrifugal force multiplied into the element of distance, being an exact variation, it follows that the expression for $\frac{\delta p}{\rho}$ will in this case be an exact variation, n is some function of the distance of the molecules from the axis of rotation, as the *time* is not involved in the preceding equation, it follows that the conditions of the motion of a fluid mass, about an axis, with a given velocity, are the same as the conditions of equilibrium of a fluid mass, the same forces as before soliciting the molecules, combined with the centrifugal force, arising from the uniform revolution about the axis. The molecules of the fluid, though they have a motion about an axis, are relatively at rest.

* At the exterior free surface $\delta p=0$, $\therefore \delta V+n^2(y\delta y+z\delta z)=0$, $\therefore$ in order that the form of the fluid, may remain the same, during the entire motion, n must be constant. If the fluid was water contained in a vessel open at its upper surface, ρ is constant, and $\delta V=g.\delta x$, the axis of rotation being supposed vertical, $\therefore$ $Q.\delta y$, $R\delta z$ vanish, and $P=g$, consequently, we shall have $\frac{p}{\rho}=-gx+n^2.\left(\frac{z^2+y^2}{2}\right)+h$ and at the free surface, we have $x=n^2.\left(\frac{z^2+y^2}{2g}\right)+\frac{h}{g}$ for the equation of this surface; if $n^2.\sqrt{z^2+y^2}$ which expresses the centrifugal force varied at the $2r-1$ power of the of the distance from the axis of rotation *i, e,* as

$$(z^2+y^2)^{\frac{2r-1}{2.}};\ n^2=a^2.(z^2+y^2)^{r-1},\ \text{and} \int.n^2.(y\delta y+z\delta z)$$

$$=a.^2\left(\frac{z^2+y^2}{4r}\right)^r,\ \therefore x=a^2\left(\frac{z^2+y^2}{2r.g}\right)^r+\frac{h}{g}$$

from which it follows that the resultant of all the forces which actuate each molecule, must be perpendicular to this surface, moreover it must be directed towards the interior of the fluid mass. If these conditions be satisfied, an homogeneous fluid mass will be in equilibrio, whatever may be the figure of the solid, which it covers.

The case which we have discussed, is one of those in which the variation $u\delta x+v\delta y+V\delta z$ * is not exact; for then this variation becomes

$\therefore$ if r is positive, x is least, when$(z^2+y^2)=0$, when $r=1$ all the molecules revolve in the same time, and $x=a^2.\left(\frac{z^2+y^2}{2g}\right)+\frac{h}{g}$ which is the equation of the concave surface of the paraboloid, of which the parameter$=\frac{2g}{a^2}$, the periodic time being equal to the force divided by the distance $=\frac{\pi}{a}$. $\therefore$ if the time of revolution, be called T, we shall have the parameter of the generating curve $=$to $\frac{2g}{\pi^2}T^2$ & $\frac{p}{\varrho}=\frac{\pi^2.(z^2+y^2)}{2T^2}+h-gx$ $\therefore x$ being the same, the pressure is greater at a greater distance from the axis of rotation.

When r is negative, at the point where $z^2+y^2=0$, x is infinite, and when$=-\frac{1}{2}$ the surface of the fluid will be such, as would be generated by the revolution of aconical hyperbola, about its asymptote, the axis of x is in this case the asymptote. The constant quantity h denotes the distance of the origin of the coordinates from the other asymptote, $\therefore$ both in this case and where the surface of the fluid is paraboloidal, the constant quantity depends on the quantity of water in the vessel. If the vessel was cylindrical, we could determine the area of the paraboloid, provided that we knew the area of the base of the cylinder, and also the points of greatest elevation and depression, for the paraboloid is half the circumscribing cylinder.

This paraboloidal figure is that which is assumed by the molecules of the fluid, in the experiment which Newton adduces, in order to shew that the effects by which *absolute* and *relative* motions are distinguished from each other, are the forces of receding from the axis of circular motion. See Princip. Math. page 10.

* $u\delta x+v\delta y+V.\delta z$ is not an exact variation in the preceding investigation, for substituting for v, and V, we obtain $v=-nz, V=ny$, $\therefore u\delta x+v.\delta y+V.\delta z=n.(y\delta z-z.\delta y)$, consequently it appears, that though the circumstance of the preceding expression being an exact variation, would facilitate very much, our investigations, still it is not *essentially* necessary, that this should be the case, in order that the motion should *be possible*. $\because$ Since in the case of the sea, revolving round with the earth round its axis, and relatively quiescing with respect to the

$-n\{z\delta y - y\delta z\}$; therefore in the theory of the flux and reflux of the sea, we are not permitted to assume, that the variation concerned is exact; since it is not so in the very simple case, in which the sea has no other motion, but that of rotation, which is common to it, and the earth.

35. Let us now determine the oscillations of a fluid mass which covers a spheroid revolving about the axis of x; and let us suppose that it is deranged from the position of equilibrium, by the action of very small forces.

At the commencement of the motion, let r represent the distance of a molecule of the fluid, * from the centre of gravity of the spheroid over which it is spread, and which we shall suppose immoveable; let θ be the angle which the radius r makes with the axis of x, and ϖ the angle which the plane passing through the axis of x and the radius r, constitutes with the plane of x and of y. Let us suppose that after the time t, the radius r is changed into $r+\alpha s$, that the angle θ is changed into $\theta+\alpha u$, and finally, that the angle ϖ is changed into $nt+\varpi+\alpha v$; αs, αu, and αv, being very small quantities, of which the squares and products may be neglected, we shall have

$$x=(r+\alpha s).\cos.(\theta+\alpha u);$$

$$y=(r+\alpha s).\sin.(\theta+\alpha u).\cos.(nt+\varpi+\alpha v);$$

$$z=(r+\alpha s).\sin.(\theta+\alpha u).\sin.(nt+\varpi+\alpha v).$$

earth, $u\delta x+v\delta y+V.\delta z$ is not an exact variation, we may conclude a *fortiori*, that it is not one, where the oscillations arise from the attractions of the sun and moon, which produce the flux and reflux of the sea.

In order to ascertain whether an incompressible fluid solicited by accelerating forces, and also by a centrifugal force, may be at the surface of a *given figure of revolution, we substitute in the equation* $0=\delta V+n^2(y\delta y+z.\delta z)$ the forces parallel to x, y, z, which would result from this hypothesis, the resulting expression should be the differential equation of the given surface, if it is not, then we may be certain that the given curve does not satisfy the equilibrium of the fluid. See Book 3. Chap III. No. 18.

* If a perpendicular is let fall from the extremity of r on the axis of x, it will be equal to $r.\sin.\theta$, and the projection of this perpendicular on the plane of y, x, is equal to the coordinate y and its value will be $r.\sin.\theta.\cos.\varpi$, and this perpendicular projected on the plane $z\,x$ will be the coordinate z, and it will be equal to $r.\sin.\theta.\sin.\varpi$.

Substituting these values in the equation (F) of No. 32, we shall obtain, the square of α being neglected, *

* Since αu, $\alpha \varrho$, $\alpha \varpi$, are very small quantities, of which the squares and products may be neglected, the time t will of the same order as α, so that αt is of the order α^2, consequently

$$\sin. \alpha u = \alpha u - \frac{\alpha^3 u^3}{1.2.3} \&c. = \alpha u, \cos. \alpha u = 1 - \frac{\alpha^2 u^2}{2} = 1 \therefore x = (r. + \alpha s). \cos. (\theta + \alpha u)$$

$$= r. \cos. \theta. \cos. \alpha u - r. \sin. \theta. \sin. \alpha u + \alpha s. \cos. \theta. \cos. \alpha u - \alpha s. \sin. \theta. \sin. \alpha u$$

= by neglecting quantities of the order α^2, $r. \cos. \theta - r. \sin. \theta. \alpha u + \alpha s. \cos. \theta$,

r and θ are independent of t,

$$\therefore \frac{dx}{dt} = -\frac{du}{dt}.\alpha r. \sin. \theta + \frac{ds}{dt}\alpha. \cos. \theta; \frac{d^2x}{dt^2} = -\frac{d^2u}{dt^2}\alpha r. \sin. \theta + \frac{d^2s}{dt^2}.\alpha \cos. \theta,$$

$$\delta x = \delta r. \cos. \theta - \delta\theta. r. \sin. \theta - \delta r. \sin. \theta. \alpha u - \delta\theta. \cos. \theta. r\alpha u - \delta\theta. \sin. \theta. \alpha s; \; \delta x. \left(\frac{d^2x}{dt^2}\right)$$

$$= -\delta r. r\alpha. \sin. \theta. \cos. \theta. \frac{d^2u}{dt^2} + \delta r. \alpha. \cos.^2 \theta. \frac{d^2s}{dt^2} + \delta\theta. r^2\alpha. \sin.^2 \theta. \frac{d^2u}{dt^2} - \delta\theta. r\alpha. \sin. \theta. \cos. \theta. \frac{d^2s}{dt^2},$$

rejecting quantities involving α^2 &c.

$$y = (r + \alpha s). \sin. (\theta + \alpha u). \cos. (nt + \varpi + \alpha v) = r. \sin. (\theta + \alpha u). \cos. (nt + \varpi + \alpha v)$$

$$+ \alpha s. \sin. (\theta + \alpha u). \cos. (nt + \varpi + \alpha v) = r. \sin. \theta. \cos. (nt + \varpi) - r. \sin. \theta. \sin. (\varpi + nt)\alpha v$$

$$+ \alpha u\, r. \cos. \theta. \cos. (\varpi + nt) + \alpha s. \sin. \theta. \cos. (\varpi + nt)$$

rejecting as before quantities of the order α^2, substituting αu, αv, for $\sin. \alpha u$, $\sin. \alpha v$, and observing that αt is of the order α^2, $\therefore y =$

$$r. \sin. \theta. \cos. \varpi - ntr. \sin. \theta. \sin. \varpi - r. \sin. \theta. \sin. \varpi\, \alpha v - nrt\alpha v. \sin. \theta. \cos. \varpi + \alpha ur. \cos. \theta. \cos. \varpi$$

$$- \alpha urnt. \cos. \theta. \sin. \varpi + \alpha s. \sin. \theta. \cos. \varpi - \alpha snt. \sin. \theta. \sin. \varpi;$$

$$\frac{dy}{dt} = -nr. \sin. \theta. \sin. \varpi - r. \sin. \theta. \sin. \varpi. \alpha. \frac{dv}{dt} - nr. \alpha v. \sin. \theta. \cos. \varpi - nrt\alpha. \frac{dv}{dt}. \sin. \theta. \cos. \varpi$$

$$\alpha r. \cos. \theta. \cos. \varpi. \frac{du}{dt} - \alpha urn \cos. \theta. \sin. \varpi - \alpha rnt. \frac{du}{dt}. \cos. \theta. \sin. \varpi$$

$$\alpha r^2.\delta\theta.\left\{\left(\frac{d^2u}{dt^2}\right)-2n.\sin.\theta.\cos.\theta.\left(\frac{dv}{dt}\right)\right\}$$

$$+\alpha r^2.\delta\varpi.\left\{\sin.^2\theta.\left(\frac{d^2v}{dt^2}\right)+2n.\sin.\theta.\cos.\theta.\left(\frac{du}{dt}\right)+\frac{2n.\sin.^2\theta}{r}.\left(\frac{ds}{dt}\right)\right\};\ (L)$$

$$+\alpha.\delta r.\left\{\left(\frac{d^2s}{dt^2}\right)-2nr.\sin.^2\theta.\left(\frac{dv}{dt}\right)\right\}$$

$$=\frac{n^2}{2}.\ \delta.\left\{(r+\alpha s).\sin.\ (\theta+\alpha u)\right\}^2+\delta V-\frac{\delta p}{\rho}.$$

$$+\ \alpha.\frac{ds}{dt}.\sin.\theta.\cos.\varpi-\alpha s\ n.\sin.\theta.\sin.\varpi-\alpha nt.\ \sin.\theta.\ \sin.\varpi.\frac{ds}{dt}$$

$$\frac{d^2y}{dt^2}=-\alpha r.\sin.\theta.\sin.\varpi.\frac{d^2v}{dt^2}-2nr.\alpha.\sin.\theta.\cos.\varpi.\frac{dv}{dt}+\alpha r.\cos.\theta.\cos.\varpi.\frac{d^2u}{dt^2}$$

$$-2\alpha rn.\cos.\theta.\ \sin.\varpi.\frac{du}{dt}+\alpha.\sin.\theta.\cos.\varpi.\frac{d^2s}{dt^2}-2\alpha n.\sin.\theta.\sin.\varpi.\frac{ds}{dt}.$$

$$\delta y=\delta r.\sin.\theta.\cos.\varpi+\delta\theta.r.\cos.\theta.\cos.\varpi-\delta\varpi.r.\sin.\theta.\sin.\varpi,$$

rejecting those quantities in the value of δy, where α occurs, for in the product of the expression for $\frac{d^2y}{dt}$ into the value of δy, these would be of the order α^2, $\therefore$ they ought to be neglected;

$$\therefore\delta y.\frac{d^2y}{dt^2}=\delta r.(-\alpha r.\sin.^2\theta.\sin.\varpi.\ \cos.\varpi)\frac{d^2v}{dt^2}-2nr\alpha.\sin.^2\theta.\cos.^2\varpi.\frac{dv}{dt}$$

$$+\alpha r.\sin.\theta.\cos.\theta.\cos.^2\varpi.\frac{d^2u}{dt^2}-2\alpha rn.\sin.\theta.\cos.\theta.\sin.\varpi.\cos.\varpi.\frac{du}{dt}$$

$$+\alpha.\ \sin.^2\theta\cos.^2\varpi.\frac{d^2s}{dt^2}-2\alpha n.(\sin.^2\theta.\sin.\varpi.\cos.\varpi).\frac{ds}{dt})$$

$$\delta\theta(-\alpha r^2\sin.\theta.\cos.\theta.\sin.\varpi.\ \cos.\varpi\frac{d^2v}{dt^2}-2nr^2\alpha.\sin.\theta.\cos.\theta.\cos.^2\varpi.\frac{dv}{dt}$$

$$+\alpha r^2.\cos.^2\theta.\cos.^2\varpi.\frac{d^2u}{dt^2}-2\alpha nr^2.\cos.^2\theta.\sin.\varpi.\cos.\varpi.\frac{du}{dt}+\alpha r.\sin.\theta.\cos.\theta.\cos.^2\varpi\frac{d^2s}{dt^2}$$

At the exterior surface of the fluid we have $\delta p = 0$; moreover in the state of equilibrium,

$$0 = \frac{n^2}{2} \delta . \{(r + \alpha s) . \sin.(\theta + \alpha u)\}^2 + (\delta V);$$

K K

$$-2\alpha nr . \sin. \theta . \cos. \theta . \sin. \varpi . \cos. \varpi . \frac{ds}{dt}\Big) + \delta\varpi \Big(\alpha r^2 . \sin.^2 \theta \sin.^2 \varpi . \frac{d^2 v}{dt^2}$$

$$+ 2nr^2 \alpha . \sin.^2 \theta \sin. \varpi . \cos. \varpi . \frac{dv}{dt} - \alpha r^2 . \sin. \theta . \cos. \theta . \sin. \varpi . \cos. \varpi . \frac{d^2 u}{dt^2}$$

$$+ 2\alpha r^2 n . \sin. \theta . \cos. \theta . \sin.^2 \varpi . \frac{du}{dt} - \alpha r . \sin.^2 \theta . \sin. \varpi . \cos. \varpi . \frac{d^2 s}{dt^2} + 2\alpha nr . \sin.^2 \theta . \sin.^2 \varpi . \frac{ds}{dt}\Big);$$

$$(r + \alpha s.) \sin.(\theta + \alpha u) . \sin.(nt + \varpi + \alpha v) = (r + \alpha s.) \sin. \theta . \sin.(nt + \varpi + \alpha v) + \alpha ur . \cos. \theta . \sin.(nt + \varpi$$

$$+ \alpha v) = r . \sin. \theta . \sin.(nt + \varpi) + r . \sin. \theta . \cos.(nt + \varpi) . \alpha v + \alpha ur . \cos. \theta . \sin.(nt + \varpi)$$

$$\alpha s . \sin.(\theta + \alpha u) . \sin.(nt + \varpi + \alpha v) \; (= \alpha s . \sin. \theta . \sin.(nt + \varpi) .)$$

$$= r . \sin. \theta . \sin. \varpi + ntr . \sin. \theta . \cos. \varpi + r . \sin. \theta . \cos. \varpi . \alpha v - r . \sin. \theta . \sin. \varpi . nt . \alpha v$$

$$+ \alpha ur . \cos. \sin. \theta . \sin. \varpi + \alpha ur . \cos. \theta . \cos. \varpi . nt + \alpha s . \sin. \theta . \sin. \varpi + \alpha s . \sin. \theta . \cos. \varpi . nt . \therefore \frac{dz}{dt} =$$

$$nr . \sin. \theta . \cos. \varpi + r . \sin. \theta . \cos. \varpi . \alpha \frac{dv}{dt} - r . \sin. \theta . \sin. \varpi . n\alpha v - r . \sin. \theta . \sin. \varpi . nt\alpha . \frac{dv}{dt}$$

$$+ \alpha r . \cos. \theta . \sin. \varpi . \frac{du}{dt} + \alpha ur . \cos. \theta . \cos. \varpi . n + \alpha r . nt . \cos. \theta . \cos. \varpi . \frac{du}{dt} + \alpha . \sin. \theta . \sin. \varpi . \frac{ds}{dt}$$

$$+ \alpha . \sin. \theta . \cos. \varpi . ns + \alpha \sin. \theta . \cos. \varpi . nt . \frac{ds}{dt}; \frac{d^2 z}{dt^2} = r\alpha . \sin. \theta . \cos. \varpi . \frac{d^2 v}{dt^2}$$

$$- nr\alpha . \sin. \theta . \sin. \varpi . \frac{dv}{dt} - nr\alpha . \sin. \theta . \sin. \varpi . \frac{dv}{dt} + \alpha r . \cos. \theta . \sin. \varpi . \frac{d^2 u}{dt^2} + \alpha nr . \cos. \theta . \cos. \varpi . \frac{du}{dt}$$

$$+ \alpha nr . \cos. \theta . \cos. \varpi . \frac{du}{dt} + \alpha . \sin. \theta . \sin. \varpi . \frac{d^2 s}{dt^2} + \alpha n . \sin. \theta . \cos. \varpi . \frac{ds}{dt} + \alpha n . \sin. \theta . \cos. \varpi . \frac{ds}{dt};$$

$$\delta z = \delta r . \sin. \theta . \sin. \varpi + \delta\theta . r . \cos. \theta . \sin. \varpi + \delta\varpi . r . \sin. \theta . \cos. \varpi,$$

neglecting those terms which involve α, for as was before mentioned, in the product

(δV) being the value of δV which corresponds to this state. Let us suppose that the fluid in question, is the sea; the variation(δV) will be the product of the gravity mlutiplied, into the element of its direction. Let g represent

$\partial z.\frac{d^2z}{dt^2}$, these quantities would produce terms of the order α^2 and would consequently be neglected. $\because\ \partial z.\frac{d^2z}{dt^2} =$

$$\partial r.\Big\{r\alpha.\sin.^2\theta.\sin.\varpi.\cos.\varpi.\frac{d^2v}{dt^2}-2nr\alpha.\sin.^2\theta.\sin.^2\varpi.\frac{dv}{dt}+\alpha r.\sin.\theta.\cos.\theta.\sin.^2\varpi.\frac{d^2u}{dt^2}$$

$$+2\alpha nr.\sin.\theta.\cos.\theta.\sin.\varpi.\cos.\varpi.\frac{du}{dt}+\alpha.\sin.^2\theta.\sin.^2\varpi.\frac{d^2s}{dt^2}+2\alpha n.\sin.^2\theta.\sin.\varpi.\cos.\varpi.\frac{ds}{dt}\Big\}$$

$$+\partial\theta.\Big(r^2\alpha\sin.\theta.\cos.\theta.\sin.\varpi.\cos.\varpi.\frac{d^2v}{dt^2}-2nr^2\alpha.\sin.\theta.\cos.\theta.\sin.^2\varpi.\frac{dv}{dt}+\alpha r^2.\cos.^2\theta.\sin.^2\varpi.\frac{d^2u}{dt^2}$$

$$nr^2.\cos.^2\theta.\sin.\varpi.\cos.\varpi.\frac{du}{dt}+\alpha r.\sin.\theta.\cos.\theta.\sin.^2\varpi.\frac{d^2s}{dt^2}+2\alpha nr.\sin.\theta.\cos.\theta.\sin.\varpi.\cos.\varpi.\frac{ds}{dt}\Big\}$$

$$\Big\{r^2\alpha.\sin.^2\theta.\cos.^2\varpi.\frac{d^2v}{dt^2}-2nr^2\alpha.\sin.^2\theta.\sin.\varpi.\cos.\varpi.\frac{dv}{dt}+\alpha r^2.\sin.\theta.\cos.\theta.\sin.\varpi.\cos.\varpi.\frac{d^2u}{dt^2}$$

$$+2\alpha nr^2.\sin.\theta.\cos.\theta.\cos.^2\varpi.\frac{du}{dt}+\alpha r.\sin.^2\theta.\sin.\varpi.\cos.\varpi.\frac{d^2s}{dt^2}+2\alpha nr.\sin.^2\theta.\cos.^2\varpi.\frac{ds}{dt}\Big\}$$

$$\therefore\ \partial x.\frac{d^2x}{dt^2}+\partial y.\frac{d^2y}{dt^2}+\partial z.\frac{d^2z}{dt^2}=$$

$$\partial r.\Big\{-r\alpha.\sin.\theta.\cos.\theta.\frac{d^2u}{dt^2}+\alpha.\cos.^2\theta.\frac{d^2s}{dt^2}-\alpha r.\sin.^2\theta.\sin.\varpi.\cos.\varpi.\frac{d^2v}{dt^2}$$

$$-2nr\alpha.\sin.^2\theta.\cos.^2\varpi.\frac{dv}{dt}+\alpha r.\sin.\theta.\cos.\theta.\cos.^2\varpi.\frac{d^2u}{dt^2}-2\alpha rn.\sin.\theta.\cos.\theta.\sin.\varpi.\cos.\varpi.\frac{du}{dt}$$

$$+\alpha.\sin.^2\theta.\cos.^2\varpi.\frac{d^2s}{dt^2}-2\alpha n.\sin.^2\theta.\sin.\varpi.\cos.\varpi.\frac{ds}{dt}$$

$$+r\alpha.\sin.^2\theta.\sin.\varpi.\cos.\varpi.\frac{d^2v}{dt^2}-2nr\alpha.\sin.^2\theta.\sin.^2\varpi.\frac{dv}{dt}+\alpha r.\sin.\theta.\cos.\theta.\sin.^2\varpi.\frac{d^2u}{dt^2}$$

$$+2\alpha nr.\sin.\theta.\cos.\theta.\sin.\varpi.\cos.\varpi.\frac{du}{dt}+\alpha.\sin.^2\theta.\sin.^2\varpi.\frac{d^2s}{dt^2}+2\alpha n.\sin.^2\theta.\sin.\varpi.\cos.\varpi.\frac{ds}{dt}\Big\}$$

the force of gravity, and αy the elevation of a molecule of water at its surface, above the surface of equilibrium, which surface we shall consider as the true level of the sea. The variation (δV) in the state of motion, will in consequence of this elevation, be increased by the quan-

(= by concinnating

$$\alpha\delta r.\left(\frac{d^2s}{dt^2}-2nr.\ \sin.^2\theta.\frac{dv}{dt}\right)\Big);+\partial\theta.\Big\{r^2\alpha.\sin.^2\theta.\frac{d^2u}{dt^2}-r\alpha.\sin.\theta.\cos.\theta.\frac{d^2s}{dt^2}$$

$$-\alpha r.^2\sin.\theta.\cos.\theta.\sin.\varpi.\cos.\varpi.\frac{d^2v}{dt^2}-2nr^2\alpha.\sin.\theta.\cos.\theta.\cos.^2\varpi.\frac{dv}{dt}$$

$$+\alpha r^2.\cos.^2\theta.\cos.2\varpi.\frac{d^2u}{dt}-2\alpha r^2n\cos.^2\theta.\sin.\varpi.\cos.\varpi.\frac{du}{dt}+\alpha r.\sin.\theta.\cos.\theta.\cos.^2\varpi.\frac{d^2s}{dt^2}$$

$$-2\alpha nr.\sin.\theta.\cos.\theta.\sin.\varpi.\cos.\varpi.\frac{ds}{dt}+r^2\alpha\sin.\theta.\cos.\theta.\sin.\varpi.\cos.\varpi.\frac{d^2v}{dt^2}$$

$$-2nr^2\alpha\sin.\theta.\cos.\theta.\sin.^2\varpi.\frac{dv}{dt}+\alpha r^2.\cos.^2\theta.\sin.^2\varpi.\frac{du^2}{dt^2}+2\alpha nr^2.\cos.^2\theta.\sin.\varpi.\cos.\varpi.\frac{du}{dt}$$

$$+\alpha r.\sin.\theta.\cos.\theta.\sin.^2\varpi.\frac{d^2s}{dt^2}+2\alpha nr.\sin.\theta..\cos.\theta.\sin.\varpi.\cos.\varpi.\frac{ds}{dt}\Big\}$$

(and by concinnating we obtain the coefficient of $\partial\theta$ = to

$$\left(r^2\alpha.\frac{d^2u}{dt^2}-2nr^2\alpha\sin.\theta.\cos.\theta.\frac{dv}{dt}\right);$$

$$\partial\varpi.\Big\{\alpha r^2.\sin.^2\theta.\sin.^2\varpi.\frac{d^2v}{dt^2}+2nr^2\alpha.\sin.^2\theta.\sin.\varpi.\cos.\varpi.\frac{dv}{dt}-\alpha r^2.\sin.\theta.\cos.\theta.\sin.\varpi.\cos.$$

$$+2\alpha r^2n.\sin.\theta.\cos.\theta.\sin.^2\varpi.\frac{du}{dt}-\alpha r.\sin.^2\theta.\sin.\varpi.\cos.\varpi.\frac{d^2s}{dt^2}+2anr.\sin.^2\theta\sin.2\varpi.\frac{ds}{dt}$$

$$+r\alpha^2.\sin.^4\theta.\cos.^2\varpi\frac{d^2v}{dt^2}-2nr^2\alpha.\sin.^2\theta.\sin.\varpi.\cos.\varpi.\frac{dv}{dt}+\alpha r^2.\sin.\theta.\cos.\theta.\sin.\varpi.\cos,$$

$$+2\alpha nr^2.\sin.\theta.\cos.\theta.\cos.^2\varpi.\frac{du}{dt}+\alpha r\sin.^2\theta.\sin.\varpi.\cos.\varpi\frac{d^2s}{dt^2}+2\alpha nr.\sin.^2\theta.\cos^2\varpi\frac{ds}{dt}\Big\}$$

tity $-\alpha g.\delta y$; because the gravity is very nearly in the direction of αy, and tends *towards* its origin; * consequently, if we denote by $\alpha\delta V'$, the part of δV relative to the new forces, which in the state of motion

concinnating as before we obtain

$$\delta\varpi.\left(\alpha r^2.\sin.^2\theta.\frac{d^2v}{dt^2}+2\alpha r^2 n.\sin.\theta.\cos.\theta.\frac{du}{dt}+2\alpha nr.\sin.^2\theta.\frac{ds}{dt},\right);$$

the body having a rotatory motion about an axis, the part of the equation (H) which corresponds to the centrifugal force arising from the rotation is by the preceding number equal to $n^2(y\delta y+z\delta z)=\frac{n^2}{2}.\delta.(y^2+z^2)=\frac{n^2}{2}.\delta.\left\{(r+\alpha s).\sin.(\theta+\alpha u)\right\}^2$ $\therefore$ the second numbers of the preceding equations, when concinnated, give the equation (L) of the text.

* At the surface of the spheroid $r=1+q\,l$, in which l is for simplicity, considered as a function of θ only, and the semi-axis minor$=1$, $\therefore$ $\delta r=q.\left(\frac{\delta l}{\delta\theta}\right)\alpha u$, q depends on the eccentricity, r receiving at the surface of the solid the increment αs, the corresponding increment of $\theta=\alpha u$. therefore the expression for r will become $1+q\,l+\alpha uq.\left(\frac{\delta l}{\delta\theta}\right)$ $\therefore \alpha s=\alpha uq.\left(\frac{dl}{d\theta}\right)$ and q being very small, s may neglected in comparison of u, and it is evidently of the order uq, *i, e*, of u multiplied into the eccentricity, and if l be considered as a function of ϖ only, we might shew that ϖ receiving an increment αv, the corresponding increment of r, is to αv, as the eccentricity multiplied into $\left(\frac{dl}{d\varpi}\right)$ is to unity. If we produce the radius r to the surface of the fluid in equilibrio; it will be represented by $1+q\,l+\gamma$, γ being the depth of the fluid, and a function of θ and ϖ, $\therefore$ θ receiving the increment αu, the corresponding increase of the radius, drawn to the surface of the fluid supposed in equilibrio, will be $q.\left(\frac{dl}{d\theta}\right).\alpha u+\left(\frac{d\gamma}{d\theta}\right).\alpha u$; when the fluid is in motion, the distance of the exterior surface from the centre, $=r'+\alpha s'$, is greater than the distance of the surface of equilibrium, from the centre of the spheroid, measured on the same radius, this last distance

$$=1+q\,l+\gamma+\alpha u.\left(q.\left(\frac{dl}{d\theta}\right)+\left(\frac{d\gamma}{d\theta}\right)\right)+\alpha v.\left(q.\left(\frac{dl}{d\varpi}\right)+\left(\frac{d\gamma}{d\varpi}\right)\right),\ r'+\alpha s'=1+q\,l+\gamma+$$

$$\alpha s'\ \therefore\ \alpha.\left(s'-u.\left(q.\left(\frac{dl}{d\theta}\right)+\left(\frac{d\gamma}{d\theta}\right)+v.q\left(\frac{dl}{d\varpi}\right)+\left(\frac{d\gamma}{d\varpi}\right)\right)\right)=\alpha y$$

$=$ the elevation of a molecule of water in the state of motion, above the surface of

agitate the molecule, and which arise either from the changes, which in the state of motion the attractions of the fluid and spheroid experience, or from the attractions of extraneous bodies; we shall have at the surface,

$$\delta V=(\delta V)-\alpha g.\delta y+\alpha.\delta V.'$$

The variation $\frac{n^2}{2}.\delta.\{(r+\alpha s).\sin.(\theta+\alpha u)\}^2$ is increased by the quantity $\alpha n^2.\delta y.r.\sin.^2\theta$, * in consequence of the elevation of the molecule of the water, above the level of the sea; but this quantity may be neglected in comparison of the term $-\alpha g.\delta y$, because the ratio $\frac{n^2.r}{g}$ of the centrifugal force at the equator, to the gravity, is a very small fraction equal to $\frac{1}{289}$. Finally, the radius r is very nearly constant at the surface of the sea, because it differs very little from a spherical surface; therefore we may make $\delta r=0$. The equation (L) will thus, become, at the surface of the sea,

$$r^2.\delta\theta\left\{\left\{\frac{d^2u}{dt^2}\right\}-2n.\sin.\theta.\cos.\theta.\left\{\frac{dv}{dt}\right\}\right\}$$

$$+r^2.\delta\varpi.\left\{\sin.^2\theta.\left\{\frac{d^2v}{dt^2}\right\}+2n.\sin.\theta.\cos.\theta.\left\{\frac{du}{dt}\right\}+\frac{2n}{r}\sin.^2\theta.\left\{\frac{ds}{dt}\right\}\right\}$$

equilibrium; it is evidently a function of θ and ϖ. q being the eccentricity, it is evident that the differential of the normal according to which the gravity acts, in case of equilibrium, differs from the differential of the radius, by a quantity which = the product of the eccentricity into the differential of N, a function of θ. ∴ at the surface of the fluid in equilibrio, $(\delta V)=g.\delta.(r'+q.N)$, at the surface of the fluid in motion, the normal corresponding to $r'+\alpha y$, has not the same direction as when in equilibrio, its variation $=\delta.(r'+qN+\alpha y+\alpha q.qN)$; the attraction of the spheroid in motion differs from the attraction of the spheroid in equilibrio by quantities of the order αy ∵ let it be equal to $\alpha yg'$, then $(g+\alpha yg').\delta(r'+qN+\alpha y+\alpha y\,q.N')=(g+\alpha y\,g').\delta(r+qN)+g.\delta\alpha y$, rejecting quantities of the order α^2, and remarking that δr is of the order $q.\delta\theta$, the first term of the second member of the preceding equation $=(\delta V)$ ∴ the second term is the quantity by which in the state of motion (δV) is increased, as has been stated in the text.

$$= -g.\delta y + \delta V';$$

the variations δy, and $\delta V'$, being taken relatively to the two variables θ, and ϖ.

Let us now, consider, the equation relative to the continuity of the fluid. For this purpose, let us conceive at the origin of the motion, a rectangular parallelepiped, of which the altitude is dr, the breadth $r.\,d\varpi.\sin.\theta.$ and the length $r.d\theta.$ * Let r', θ', ϖ', represent what r, θ, ϖ, become after the time t. By following the reasoning of No. 32, we shall find that after this interval, the volume of the molecule of the fluid, is equal to a rectangular parallelepiped, of which the height is $\left\{\frac{dr'}{dr}\right\}.dr$; of which the breadth is

$$r'.\sin'.\theta'.\left\{\left\{\frac{d\varpi'}{d\varpi}\right\}.d\varpi + \left\{\frac{d\varpi'}{dr}\right\}.dr\right\},$$

dr being eliminated, by means of the equation

$$0 = \left\{\frac{dr'}{d\varpi}\right\}.d\varpi + \left\{\frac{dr'}{dr}\right\}.dr;$$

Finally, its length is

$$r'.\left\{\left\{\frac{d\theta'}{dr}\right\}.dr + \left\{\frac{d\theta'}{d\theta}\right\}.d\theta + \left\{\frac{d\theta'}{d\varpi}\right\}.d\varpi\right\}$$

* $r\sin.\theta =$ radius of a small circle, whose plane is parallel to the equator, and as the plane of the axes of x, and y, is fixed, $r.\sin.\theta.\,d\varpi =$ the differential of the arc of this circle, to which dr is evidently perpendicular, also, the differential of the meridian$=r.d\theta$, is perpendicular both to $r.\sin.\theta.\,d\varpi$ and to dr, $\therefore$ these three differentials, constitute the parallelepiped mentioned in the text.

* When the fluid is in motion, this expression becomes, $\frac{n^2}{2}\delta.(r+\alpha s+\alpha y)\sin.(\theta+\alpha u)^2$ $\therefore$ the part which corresponds to αy, is $n^2.\alpha\delta y.(r+\alpha s+\alpha y).\sin.(\theta+\alpha u)^2 =$ by neglecting quantities of the order α^2, $n^2.\alpha\delta y.\,r.\sin.^2\theta$.

dr, and $d\varpi$, being eliminated by means of the equations

$$0=\left\{\frac{dr'}{dr}\right\}.dr+\left\{\frac{dr'}{d\theta}\right\}.d\theta+\left\{\frac{dr'}{d\varpi}\right\}.d\varpi;$$

$$0=\left\{\frac{d\varpi'}{dr}\right\}.dr+\left\{\frac{d\varpi'}{d\theta}\right\}.d\theta+\left\{\frac{d\varpi'}{d\varpi}\right\}.d\varpi.$$

Consequently, if we make

$$\begin{aligned}\epsilon'=&\left\{\frac{dr'}{dr}\right\}.\left\{\frac{d\theta'}{d\theta}\right\}.\left\{\frac{d\varpi'}{d\varpi}\right\}-\left\{\frac{dr'}{dr}\right\}.\left\{\frac{d\theta'}{d\varpi}\right\}.\left\{\frac{d\varpi'}{d\theta}\right\}\\&+\left\{\frac{dr'}{d\theta}\right\}.\left\{\frac{d\theta'}{d\varpi}\right\}.\left\{\frac{d\varpi'}{dr}\right\}\\&-\left\{\frac{dr'}{d\theta}\right\}.\left\{\frac{d\theta'}{dr}\right\}.\left\{\frac{d\varpi'}{d\varpi}\right\}+\left\{\frac{dr'}{d\varpi}\right\}.\left\{\frac{d\theta'}{dr}\right\}.\left\{\frac{d\varpi'}{d\theta}\right\}\\&-\left\{\frac{dr'}{d\varpi}\right\}.\left\{\frac{d\theta'}{d\theta}\right\}.\left\{\frac{d\varpi'}{dr}\right\};\end{aligned}$$

after the time t, the volume of the parallelepiped will be equal to $\epsilon'.r'^2.\sin.\theta.dr.d\theta.d\varpi$; * therefore if (ρ) represent the primitive density of the molecule, and ρ its density, corresponding to the time t, we shall obtain, by putting the primitive value of its mass, equal to its value after the time t,

$$\rho.\epsilon' r'^2.\sin.\theta'=(\rho).r^2.\sin.\theta;$$

this is the equation relative to the continuity of the fluid. In the case we are at present considering,

$$r'=r+\alpha s;\ \theta'=\theta+\alpha u;\ \varpi'=nt+\varpi+\alpha v;$$

* r' θ ϖ' are *generally* functions of r, θ, ϖ, and t, see page 217, notes; the reasoning is precisely the same as in page 218, substituting the coordinates r, θ, ϖ, in place of x, y, z.

consequently, we shall have by neglecting quantities of the order α^2

$$\varrho' = 1 + \alpha . \left\{ \frac{ds}{dr} \right\} + \alpha . \left\{ \frac{du}{d\theta} \right\} + \alpha . \left\{ \frac{dv}{d\varpi} \right\} . *$$

Let us suppose that after the time t, the primitive density (ρ) is changed into $(\rho) + \alpha\rho'$; the preceding equation relative to the continuity of the fluid, will give

$$0 = r^2 . \left\{ \rho' + (\varrho) . \left\{ \left\{ \frac{du}{d\theta} \right\} + \left\{ \frac{dv}{d\varpi} \right\} + \frac{u . \cos. \theta}{\sin. \theta} \right\} \right\} + (\varrho) . \left\{ \frac{d.r^2 s}{dr} \right\} .$$

36. Let us apply these results, to the oscillations of the sea. Its mass being homogeneous, ϱ' vanishes, consequently,

$$0 = \left\{ \frac{d.r^2 s}{dr} \right\} + r^2 . \left(\left\{ \frac{du}{d\theta} \right\} + \left\{ \frac{dv}{d\varpi} \right\} + \frac{u \cos. \theta}{\sin. \theta} \quad \dagger \right\} .$$

* $dr' = dr + \alpha ds$, $d\theta' = d\theta + \alpha du$, $d\varpi' = d\varpi + \alpha dv$ $\therefore \left(\frac{dr'}{dr} \right) . \left(\frac{d\theta'}{d\theta} \right) . \left(\frac{d\varpi'}{d\varpi} \right) =$

$$\left(\frac{dr + \alpha ds}{dr} \right) \times \left(\frac{d\theta + \alpha du}{d\theta} \right) \times \left(\frac{d\varpi + \alpha dv}{d\varpi} \right) = 1 + \alpha \left(\frac{ds}{dr} \right) + \alpha . \left(\frac{du}{d\theta} \right) + \alpha . \left(\frac{dv}{d\varpi} \right),$$

it is plain, that if there was no motion, the differential of any coordinate θ, with respect to another coordinate, would vanish, after the time t, this differential is of the order t $\therefore$ $\left(\frac{d\theta + \alpha du}{d\varpi} \right) \times \left(\frac{d\varpi + \alpha dv}{d\theta} \right)$ is of the order t^2 or α^2, consequently it may be neglected, from which it appears, that all the terms in expression for ϱ' after the first may be neglected.

$$\dagger \left\{ (\varrho) + \alpha\varrho' \right\} . \left\{ 1 + \alpha . \left\{ \frac{ds}{dr} \right\} + \alpha . \left\{ \frac{du}{d\theta} \right\} + \alpha . \left\{ \frac{dv}{d\varpi} \right\} \right\} .$$

$$r^2 (\sin. \theta + \alpha u . \cos \theta) \Big\} = (\varrho) . r^2 . \sin. \theta)$$

$$\left\{ (\varrho) + \alpha\varrho' \right\} . 1 + \alpha . \left\{ \frac{ds}{dr} \right\} + \alpha . \left\{ \frac{du}{d\theta} \right\} + \alpha . \left\{ \frac{dv}{d\varpi} \right\} .$$

$$(r^2 + 2\alpha s) . \sin. \theta + \alpha u . \cos. \theta) \Big\} = (\varrho) . r^2 . \sin. \theta, \ i, e,$$

Let us suppose, conformably to what appears to be the case of nature, that the depth of the sea is very small in comparison with the radius r of the terrestrial spheroid; let this depth be represented by γ, γ being a very small function of θ and ϖ, which depends on the law of this depth. If we integrate the preceding differential equation, with respect to r, from the surface of the solid which the sea covers, to the surface of the sea, * it is obvious that the value of s will be equal to a function of θ, ϖ, and t, independent of

$$(\varrho).(r^2+2\alpha rs).(\sin.\theta+\alpha u\cos.\theta)+(\varrho).r^2.\sin.\theta.\left\{\alpha.\left\{\frac{ds}{dr}\right\}+\left\{\frac{du}{d\theta}\right\}+\left\{\frac{dv}{d\varpi}\right\}\right\}$$

$$+\alpha\varrho'.r^2.\sin.\theta=(\varrho)r^2.\sin.\theta.$$

$$\therefore(\varrho).r^2.\alpha u\cos.\theta+(\varrho)2\alpha rs.\sin.\theta+(\varrho).r^2.\sin.\theta.\left\{\alpha\left\{\frac{ds}{dr}\right\}+\left\{\frac{du}{d\theta}\right\}+\left\{\frac{dv}{d\varpi}\right\}\right\}$$

$$+\alpha\varrho'.r^2.\sin.\theta=0$$

$\therefore$ dividing by $\sin.\theta$ and α, we obtain

$$r^2.\left\{(\varrho).\left\{\frac{du}{d\theta}\right\}+\left\{\frac{dv}{d\varpi}\right\}+\frac{u.\cos.\theta}{\sin.\theta}\right\}+\varrho'\Big\}+(\varrho)2rs+(\varrho)r^2.\frac{ds}{dr}$$

$$\left\{=\left\{\left\{(\varrho).\frac{2r.dr.s+r^2ds}{dr}\right\}=(\varrho)\left\{\frac{d.r^2s}{dr}\right\}.\right.\right.$$

* The depth of the sea being inconsiderable, in comparison of the terrestrial radius, we may suppose, that for this depth r^2, and the factor of r^2 in the second term, of the second member of this equation, are constant $\therefore$ integrating we obtain

$$r^2s'-r^2s=\gamma.r^2.\left(\left(\frac{du}{d\theta}\right)+\left(\frac{dv}{d\varpi}\right)+\frac{u\cos.\theta}{\sin.\theta}\right),$$

as the increment of the radius at the surface of the spheroid $=\alpha uq.\left(\frac{dl}{d\theta}\right)+\alpha vq.\left(\frac{dl}{d\varpi}\right)$ see notes to page 252, $\therefore s'$ at the surface of the sea

$$=\gamma.\left\{\left\{\frac{du}{d\theta}\right\}+\left\{\frac{dv}{d\varpi}\right\}+\frac{u.\cos.\theta}{\sin.\theta}\right\}+uq.\left\{\frac{dl}{d\theta}\right\}+vq.\left(\frac{dl}{d\varpi}\right)$$

r, together with a very small function which will be to u and to v, of the same order of smallness as the function $\frac{\gamma}{r}$; but at the surface of the solid which the sea covers, when the angles θ, and ϖ, are respectively changed into $\theta+\alpha u$, $\varpi+nt+\alpha v$, it is easy to perceive that the distance of a molecule of water, contiguous to this surface, from the centre of gravity of the earth, only varies by a quantity very small with respect to αu and αv, and of the same order, as the products of these quantities, into the eccentricity of the spheroid covered by the sea: therefore, the function, which occurs in the expression for s, independent of the value of r, is a very small quantity of the same order; thus we can generally neglect s, as inconsiderable, in comparison of u and v. Consequently, the equation of the motion of the sea, which has been given in No. 35, becomes,

$$r^2.\delta\theta.\left\{\left\{\frac{d^2u}{dt^2}\right\}-2n.\sin.\theta.\cos.\theta.\left\{\frac{dv}{dt}\right\}\right\}$$

$$+r^2\delta\varpi.\left\{\sin.^2\theta.\left\{\frac{d^2v}{dt^2}\right\}+2n.\sin.\theta.\cos.\theta.\left\{\frac{du}{dt}\right\}\right\}=-g.\delta y+\delta V'; \quad (M)$$

the equation (L) of the same number relative to any point of the interior of the fluid, gives in the state of equilibrium,

$$0=\frac{n^2}{2}.\delta.\left((r+\alpha s).\sin(\theta+\alpha u)\right)^2+(\delta V)-\frac{(\delta p)}{\rho}$$

(δV) and (δp) being the values of δV and δp, which in the state of equi-

these two last terms are to u, or v, as the product of these quantities into the eccentricity. With respect to the first term, it may be remarked that we can derive another expression for it, in terms of the difference of the eccentricities of the interior and exterior spheroids, divided by r, but this difference is evidently proportional to γ, in fact this term will be to ur as γ to r. The integral involves t because it was taken with respect to the characteristic d and not δ.

The last member of the equation (L), becomes in a state of motion, in consequence of this substitution,

librium, answer to the quantities $r+\alpha s$, $\theta+\alpha u$, $\varpi+\alpha v$. Suppose that when the fluid is in motion, we have

$$\delta V=(\delta V)+\alpha\delta V'; \ \delta p=(\delta p)+\alpha\delta p';$$

the equation (L) will give

$$\left\{\frac{d.\left(V'-\frac{p'}{\rho}\right)}{dr}\right\}=\left(\frac{d^2s}{dt^2}\right)-2nr.\sin.^2\theta.\left(\frac{dv}{dt}\right).$$

From a consideration of the equation (M), it appears that $n.\left(\frac{dv}{dt}\right)$ is of the same order as y or s, and consequently of the order $\frac{\gamma u}{r}$; the value of the first member of this equation is therefore of the same order; * thus, multiplying this value, by dr, and then integrating from the surface of the spheroid, to the surface of the sea; we shall have $V'-\frac{p'}{\rho}$ equal to a very small function, of the order $\frac{\gamma s}{r}$, plus a function of θ, ϖ, and t, independent of r, which we will denote by λ; therefore, if in the

* $\frac{n^2}{2}.\partial\left\{(r+\alpha s).\sin.(\theta+\alpha u)\right\}^2+(\partial V)-\left\{\frac{\partial p}{\rho}\right\}+\alpha.\partial V'-\alpha\frac{\partial p'}{\rho}$, the three first terms destroy each other $\therefore$ $\alpha\partial V'-\alpha\frac{\partial p'}{\rho}+$| is equal to the first member of the equation (L), and since it is an exact variation, the first member of the equation (L) will be so also, $\therefore$ $V'-\frac{p'}{\rho}$ differenced with respect to r, is equal to the term of the first member of the equation (L), which is multiplied by ∂r.

$-2.\sin.\theta.\cos.\theta=\left\{\frac{d.\cos.\theta^2}{d\theta}\right\}$ $\therefore$ in order that $-2n.\left\{\frac{dv}{dt}\right\}.\sin.\theta.\cos.\theta$ may be of the same order as $\left\{\frac{d^2u}{dt^2}\right\}$ it is necessary that $n\left\{\frac{dv}{dt}\right\}$ should be of the order y or s, which is of the order $\frac{\gamma s}{r}$

equation (L) of No. 35, we only consider the two variables θ and ϖ, it will be changed into the equation (M), with this sole difference, that the second member will be changed into $\delta\lambda$. But λ being independent of the depth of the molecule, which we consider; if we suppose this molecule very near the surface; the equation (L) must evidently coincide with the equation (M); therefore we have $\delta\lambda = \delta V' - g\delta y$, and consequently,

$$\delta.\left\{V' - \frac{p'}{\rho}\right\} = \delta V' - g\delta y;$$

the value of $\delta V'$ in the second member of this equation, being relative to the surface of the sea.* We shall find in the theory of the flux and reflux of the sea, that this value is very nearly the same for all molecules situated on the same terrestrial radius, from the surface of the solid which the sea covers, to the surface of the sea; therefore with respect to all these molecules $\frac{\delta p'}{\rho} = g.\delta y$; which gives $p' = \rho g y$, together with a function independent of θ, ϖ, and r; but at the surface of the level of the sea, the value of $\alpha p'$, is equal to the pressure of a small column of water αy, which is elevated

* $\int \frac{d^2 s}{dt^2} dr - 2\int nrdr.\sin.^2\theta \left\{\frac{dv}{dt}\right\}$ integrated between the the surface of the spheroid, and the surface of sea, gives the integral of the text, the first term is = to $\left\{\frac{d^2 s}{dt^2}\right\}\gamma$, which is a function of θ, ϖ, and t, $= \lambda$, the other term being of the order $\frac{\gamma s}{r}$ may be rejected. If we only consider the terms, which refer to θ and ϖ, the first member of the equation (L) is the same as the first member of the equation (M), near the surface, the last term of the first member of the equation (L′) vanishes ∴ the equation (L) must in this case coincide with the equation (M), but λ the member of the equation (L) does not vary ∴ we have the second member of the equation (L) = the second member of the equation (M) *i. e*, $\delta\lambda = \delta V' - g\delta y$; but $\delta\lambda = \delta.\left\{V' - \frac{p'}{\rho}\right\}$ ∴ $\delta.\left\{V' - \frac{p'}{\rho}\right\} = \delta V' - g.\delta y$, from the theory of the tides it appears that the $\delta V'$s in these two members are the same, ∴ $g\delta y = \frac{\delta p'}{\rho}$ and $p' = \rho g y' +$ a constant arbitrary quantity; when the integral is taken between the surface of spheroid, and surface of the sea, this constant arbitrary quantity may be rejected.

above this surface, and this pressure is equal to $\alpha\rho.gy$; therefore we have, in the entire of the interior of the fluid, from the surface of the spheroid covered by the sea, to the surface of the level of the sea, $p'=\rho gy$; consequently, any point of the surface of the spheroid, which is covered by the sea, is more pressed than in the state of equilibrium, by the entire weight of a column of water, contained between the surface of the sea, and the surface of level. This excess of pressure becomes negative, for those points, where the surface of the sea is depressed beneath the surface of level.

It follows from which has been stated above, that if we only consider the variations of θ and ϖ; the equation (L) will be changed into the equation (M), for all the interior molecules of the fluid. Consequently, the values of u, and v, relative to all molecules, * situated on the same terrestrial radius, are determined by the same differential equations; thus, supposing, as we shall do in the theory of the flux and reflux of the sea, that at the commencement of the motion, the values of $u, \left(\frac{du}{dt}\right), v, \left(\frac{dv}{dt}\right)$, were the same for all the molecules of the fluid, situated on the same radius, these molecules will exist the same radius, during the oscillations of the fluid. Therefore the values of r, u, and v, may be supposed very nearly the same, on the small part of the radius, comprised between the solid, which the sea covers, and the surface of the sea; thus, if we integrate with respect to r, the equation

$$0=\left\{\frac{d.r^2s}{dr}\right\}+r^2.\left\{\left\{\frac{du}{d\theta}\right\}+\left\{\frac{dv}{d\varpi}\right\}+\frac{u\cos\theta}{\sin.\theta}\right\}; \dagger$$

* At the commencement of the motion u, and v, $\left\{\frac{du}{dt}\right\}, \left\{\frac{dv}{dt}\right\}$, are the same, for all molecules situated on the same radius, ∴ after the interval dt, the corresponding values of u and v, will be the same for all molecules situated on the same radius.

† $r^2s-(r^2s)=r^2s-r^2.(s)+2r\gamma.(s)+\gamma^2(s)$ for $(r^2)=(r-\gamma)^2$
γ being a function of θ, and ϖ, when these angles are increased by the quantity $\alpha u, \alpha v$, becomes $\gamma+\alpha u.\left\{\frac{d\gamma}{d\theta}\right\}+\alpha v.\left\{\frac{d\gamma}{d\varpi}\right\}$ this is the value of γ corresponding to the angle $\theta+\alpha u$, $\varpi+nt+\alpha v$ for the surface of equilibrium, ∴ where the fluid is in motion, we must add αy to this expression.

we shall have

$$0=r^2s-(r^2s)+r^2\gamma.\left\{\left\{\frac{du}{d\theta}\right\}+\left\{\frac{dv}{d\varpi}\right\}+\frac{u.\cos.\theta}{\sin.\theta}\right\};$$

(r^2s) being the value of r^2s, at the surface of the spheroid covered by the sea. The function $r^2s-(r^2s)$ is very nearly equal to $r^2.\{s-(s)\}+2r\gamma(s)$, (s) being what s becomes at the surface of the spheroid; considering, the smallness of γ, and (s), in comparison of r, we may neglect the term $2r\gamma.(s)$; therefore, we shall have

$$r^2s-(r^2s)=r.^2\{s-(s)\}.$$

Now, the depth, of the sea, corresponding to the angles $\theta+\alpha u$, $\varpi+nt+\alpha v$, is $\gamma+\alpha\{s-(s)\}$. If the origin of the angles θ, and $nt+\varpi$, be referred to a point, and a meridian, which are fixed on the surface of the earth, which we are permitted to do, as we shall see very soon; this same depth will be $\gamma+\alpha u.$ $\left\{\frac{d\gamma}{d\theta}\right\}+\alpha v.\left\{\frac{d\gamma}{d\varpi}\right\}$, plus the elevation αy of the molecule of the fluid at the surface of the sea, above the surface of level; therefore, we shall have

If we make $\cos.\theta=\mu$, then

$$d\theta=\frac{-d\mu}{\sin.\theta},\quad d.\sqrt{1-\mu^2}=\frac{-\mu.d\mu}{\sqrt{1-\mu^2}}=\frac{-d\mu.\cos.\theta}{\sin.\theta}$$

consequently the equation of continuity, on the supposition that the sea is homogeneous becomes,

$$\left(\frac{d.r^2.s}{dr}\right)+r^2.\left(\frac{dv}{d\varpi}\right)-\frac{r^2.du}{d\mu}.\sqrt{1-\mu^2}+u\frac{d.\sqrt{1-\mu^2}}{d\mu}$$

$$-\left(\frac{d.r^2.s}{dr}\right)+r^2.\left(\frac{dv}{d\varpi}\right)-r^2.\left(\frac{d.\{u.\sqrt{1-\mu^2}\}}{d\mu}\right)$$ see Book IV. Chap. 2.

In like manner, if γ be constant, $y=-\gamma.\left\{\left\{\frac{du}{d\theta}\right\}+\left\{\frac{dv}{d\varpi}\right\}+\frac{u\cos.\theta}{\sin.\theta}\right\}=$

$$-\gamma\left\{\left\{\frac{dv}{d\varpi}\right\}+\frac{d.u.\sqrt{1-\mu^2}}{d\mu}+\frac{u.d.\sqrt{1-\mu^2}}{d\mu}\right\}=-\gamma.\left\{\left\{\frac{dv}{d\varpi}\right\}+\frac{d(u.\sqrt{1-\mu^2})}{d\mu}\right.$$

See Book IV. Chap. 1, No. 2.

$$s-(s)=y+u.\left\{\frac{d\gamma}{d\theta}\right\}+v.\left\{\frac{d\gamma}{d\varpi}\right\}.$$

Consequently the equation relative to the continuity of the fluid will become *

$$y=-\left\{\frac{d\ \gamma u}{d\theta}\right\}-\left\{\frac{d.\gamma v}{d\varpi}\right\}-\frac{\gamma u.\cos.\theta}{\sin.\theta}.\ (N)$$

It may be remarked, that in this equation, the angles θ and $nt+\varpi$ are reckoned from a point, and a meridian, which are respectively fixed on the surface of the earth, and in the equation (M), these angles are reckoned from the axis of x, and from a plane, which passing through this axis, revolves about it with a rotatory motion, expressed by n; but this axis, and this plane are not fixed on the surface of the earth, since the attraction and pressure of the fluid which covers it, as well as the rotatory motion of the spheroid, disturb a little their position. However it is easy to perceive that these perturbations † are to the values of αu, and αv, in the ratio of the mass

* Substituting for $s-(s)$, its value

$$-\gamma.\left\{\frac{du}{d\theta}\right\}-\gamma.\frac{dv}{d\varpi}-\gamma.\frac{u.\cos.\theta}{\sin.\theta}$$

and observing that

$$\left\{\frac{d.\gamma.u}{d\theta}\right\}=\gamma.\left\{\frac{du}{d\theta}\right\}+u.\left\{\frac{d\gamma}{d\theta}\right\},$$

we will arrive at the value of y, which is given in the text.

† In the state of equilibrium, neither the pressure or attraction of the ocean, can produce any motion in the spheroid covered by the sea, and it is only the stratum of water which in consequence of the attractions of the exterior bodies, and of the centrifugal force, is elevated above the surface, which can produce any effect. The effects of the pressure and attraction may be considered separately, with respect to the first, if the mean radius of the earth be supposed equal to unity, αy being the elevation, the action of the aqueous stratum is equal to the difference of the attractions of two spheroids, of which the radius of the interior $=1$, of the exterior $=1+\alpha y$, naming this difference $\alpha y.h.$ and τ its direction, $\alpha y h d\tau$ will be the expression for this attraction; multiplied into the element of its direction, τ being a function of θ, and ϖ, $d\tau$

of the sea, to the mass of the spheroid; therefore, in order to refer the angles θ, and $nt+\varpi$, to a point and meridian, which are invariable on the surface of the spheroid, in the two equations (M) and (N); we should alter u, and v, by quantities of the order $\frac{\gamma u}{r}$ and $\frac{\gamma v}{r}$, which quantities we are permitted to neglect; therefore we may suppose in these equations, that αu and αv are the motions of the fluid, in latitude and longitude.*

It may also be observed, that the centre of gravity of the spheroid being supposed immoveable, we should transfer in an opposite direction to the molecules, the forces by which it is actuated, in consequence of the reaction of the sea; but the common centre of gravity of the sea and spheroid being invariable in consequence of this reaction; it is manifest that the ratio of these forces, to those by which the molecules are solicited by the action of the spheroid, is of the same order, as the ratio of the mass of the fluid to that of the spheroid, and consequently of the order $\frac{\gamma}{r}$, therefore they may be omitted in the calculation of $\delta V'$.

$$=\left\{\frac{d\tau}{d\theta}\right\}.\alpha u+\left\{\frac{d\tau}{d\varpi}\right\}.\alpha v \therefore \alpha y.hd\tau=\alpha yh.\left\{\frac{d\tau}{d\theta}\right\}.\alpha u+\alpha yh.\left\{\frac{d\tau}{d\varpi}\right\}.\alpha v$$

The attractions are of the order αy; for if y vanished there would be no pressure or action, but y is of the order $\frac{\gamma u}{r}$. The exact effect which the attractions, and pressures of the aqueous stratum produce are calculated in Book V. Nos. 10 and 11.

* The centre of gravity of the spheroid is considered immoveable, because we do not consider the *absolute* oscillations of the molecules in space, but only their oscillations relative to the mass of the fluid. The common centre of gravity of the fluid and spheroid covered by the fluid is not affected by the mutual action of these molecules, see No. 20. With respect to the action of foreign bodies, their effect is not to be neglected, as in case of the action of the sea, if we consider the centre of gravity of the spheroid immoveable, we must transfer in a contrary direction to the molecule, the attraction which such bodies exert on the centre of gravity of the spheroid, the oscillations αy and the force which actuates the particles are of the order $\alpha\frac{d^2y}{dt^2}$, or $\alpha.q.\left\{\frac{d^2s}{dt^2}\right\}$, see preceding note.

37. Let us consider in the same manner, the motions of the atmosphere. In this investigation, we shall omit the consideration of the variation of heat in different latitudes, and different elevations, as well as all anomalous causes of perturbation, and consider only the regular causes which act upon it, as upon the ocean. Consequently, we may consider the sea as surrounded by an elastic fluid of an uniform temperature; we shall also suppose, that the density of this fluid is proportional to its pressure, which is conformable to experience. This supposition implies, * that the atmosphere has an infinite height; but it is easy to be assured, that at a very small height, its density is so small, that it may be regarded as evanescent.

This being premised, let s', u', and v', denote for the molecules of the atmosphere, what s, u v, designated, for the molecules of the sea; the equation (L) of No. 35, will then become

$$\alpha r^2.\delta\theta.\left\{\left\{\frac{d^2u'}{dt^2}\right\}-2n.\sin.\theta.\cos.\theta.\left\{\frac{dv'}{dt}\right\}\right\}$$

$$+\alpha r^2.\delta\varpi.\left\{\sin.^2\theta.\left(\frac{d^2v'}{dt^2}\right)+2n.\sin.\theta.\cos.\theta.\left(\frac{du'}{dt}\right)+\frac{2n.\sin.^2\theta}{r}.\left(\frac{ds'}{dt}\right)\right\}$$

$$+\alpha.\delta r.\left\{\left(\frac{d^2s'}{dt^2}\right)-2nr.\sin.^2\theta.\left(\frac{dv'}{dt}\right)\right\}=\frac{n}{2}.\delta.\left\{(r+\alpha s').\sin.\theta+\alpha u').\right\}^2$$

$$+\delta V-\frac{\delta p}{\rho}.$$

* According as the fluid is elevated above the surface of the earth, it becomes rarer, in consequence of its elasticity which dilates it more and more, as it is less compressed, and it would extend indefinitely, and eventually dissipate itself in space, if the molecules of its *surface* were elastic; consequently, if there is a state of rarity, in which the molecules are devoid of elasticity, the elasticity of the atmosphere must diminish in a greater ratio than the compressing force.

At first let us consider the atmosphere in a state of equilibrium, in which case s', u' and v' vanish. Then, the preceding equation, being integrated becomes,

$$\frac{n^2}{2}.r^2.\sin.^2\theta + V - \int\frac{\delta p}{\rho} = \text{constant}.$$

The pressure p being by hypothesis proportional to the density; we shall make $p = l.\,g.\,\rho$, g represents the gravity at a determined place, * which we will suppose to be the equator, and l is a constant quantity which expresses the height of the atmosphere, of which the density is throughout the same as at the surface of the sea: this height is very small relative to the radius of the terrestrial spheroid, of which it is less than the 720th part.

The integral $\int\frac{\delta p}{\rho}$ is equal to $lg.\,\log.\,\rho$; consequently the preceding equation relative to the equilibrium of the atmosphere becomes,

$$lg.\,\log.\,\rho = \text{constant} + V + \frac{n^2}{2}.r^2.\sin.^2\theta.$$

At the surface of the sea, the value of V is the same for a molecule of air, as for a molecule of water contiguous to it, because the forces which solicit each molecule, are the same; but the condition of the equilibrium of the sea requires, that we should have

$$V + \frac{n^2}{2}.r^2.\sin.^2\theta = \text{constant};$$

* An homogeneous atmosphere is an atmosphere, supposed to be of the same weight as that which actually surrounds the earth; its density being uniform, and every where equal to the density of the air at the surface of the earth. Let h be the height of the mercury in the barometer at the equator, and d its density, we shall have $l\rho = h.d.\therefore\, l = \frac{hd}{\rho}$ and by substituting for h and d and ρ their numerical values, l comes out equal to $5\frac{1}{4}$ miles very nearly, which is somewhat less than the 720th part of the radius of the equator. When the temperature is given, this height is a constant quantity, whatever be the changes which the pressure undergoes.

therefore ρ is constant at this surface, *i, e,* the density of the stratum of air contiguous to the sea, is every where the same, in the state of equilibrium.

Let R represent, the part of the radius r, comprehended between the centre of the spheroid and the surface of the sea, and r' the part comprised between this surface and a molecule of air elevated above it; r' will differ only by quantities nearly of the order $\frac{\left(\frac{n^2}{g}.r'\right)^2}{R}$, * from the *height* of this molecule above the surface of the sea; we may without sensible error neglect quantities of this order. The equation between ρ and r will give

$$lg.\ \log.\ \rho = \text{constant} + V + \frac{r'}{1}\left\{\frac{dV}{dr}\right\} + \frac{r'^2}{1.2}\left\{\frac{d^2V}{dr^2}\right\}$$

$$+\frac{n^2}{2}.\ R^2.\ \sin.\ ^2\theta + n^2\ Rr'.\ \sin.\ ^2\theta\ ;$$

the values of V, $\left(\frac{dV}{dr}\right)$and $\left(\frac{d^2V}{dr^2}\right)$ being relative to the surface of the sea, where we have,

$$\text{constant} = V + \frac{n^2}{2}.R^2.\ \sin.\ ^2\theta\ ;$$

the quantity $-\left(\frac{dV}{dr}\right) - n^2\ R.\ \sin.\ ^2\theta$, expresses the gravity at the same

* V being a function of R, θ, and ϖ, if R receive the increment r', V becomes $= V + \frac{r'}{1}.\left\{\frac{dV}{dr}\right\} + \frac{r'^2}{1.2}.\left\{\frac{d^2V}{dr^2}\right\} +$ &c. and the expression $\frac{n^2}{2}\ R^2.\ \sin.\ ^2\theta$ will be increased by the quantity $n^2\ Rr'.\ \sin.\ ^2\theta + \frac{n^2}{2}r'^2.\ \sin.\ ^2\theta$, but this last term being indefinitely small, may be rejected.

surface; which we will represent by g'. The function $\left\{\frac{d^2V}{dr}\right\}$ * being multiplied by a very small quantity r',[2] we may determine it on the hypothesis that the earth is spherical, and we may neglect the density of the atmosphere relatively to that of the earth; therefore, we shall have very nearly,

$$-\left\{\frac{dV}{dr}\right\} = g = \frac{m}{R^2};$$

m expressing the mass of the earth; consequently $\left\{\frac{d^2V}{dr^2}\right\} = -\frac{2m}{R^3} = -\frac{2g'}{R}$; therefore we shall have $lg.\ \log.\ \rho =$ constant $-r'g' - \frac{r'^2}{R}g'$; from which may be obtained

$$\rho = \Pi . c^{-\frac{r'g'}{lg}.\left\{1+\frac{r'}{R}\right\}},\ \dagger$$

*If the earth was a sphere then r', would be equal to the height of the molecule of the atmosphere above the surface of the sea, and as in the case of a spheroid the height is determined by a normal drawn to the surface from the molecule, the difference between r' and the part of this normal which is exterior to the surface, depends on the ellipticity of the spheroid, which is nearly of the order $\frac{\left(\frac{n^2 r'}{g}\right)^2}{R}$, for he afterwards supposes that the earth is at the surface of the sea very nearly spherical, ∴ the only abberration from sphericity can arise from the greater centrifugal force of the molecule of the air, the ratio of this excess of centrifugal force to gravity, for a molecule elevated at the equator, above the surface of the earth $= \frac{n^2 r'}{g}$, and the intercept at the surface between the direction of r, and the direction of a normal drawn from the molecule of the air must be evidently of the order of the ellipticity *i, e*, of the order $\frac{n^2 r'}{g}$, and the difference between r' and this height is equal to the square of this quantity divided by R very nearly.

† $\delta V = P\delta x + Q\delta y + R\delta z$, and if we refer the molecules to the polar coordinates r, θ, ϖ,

$$\delta V = \left\{\frac{dV}{dr}\right\}.\delta r + \left\{\frac{dV}{d\theta}\right\}.\delta\theta + \left\{\frac{dV}{d\varpi}\right\}.\delta\varpi, \therefore \left\{\frac{dV}{dr}\right\}$$

c being the number of which the hyperbolical logarithm is equal to unity, and Π being a constant quantity evidently equal to the density of the air at the surface of the sea. Let h and h' represent the lengths of a pendulum, which vibrates seconds at the surface of sea, under the equator, and at the latitude of the molecule of the atmosphere, which has been

is that part of the force δV, which is resolved in the direction of the radius of the earth, $\theta =$ the complement of latitude $\therefore n^2 R \sin.^2 \theta$ is the part of the centrifugal force, which acts in the direction of the terrestrial radius. The force varying inversely as the square of the distance, $V = \frac{1}{R}$, and $\frac{dV}{dr} = \frac{m}{R^2}$ see Book II. No. 12.

The earth being supposed spherical $\left\{\frac{dV}{dr}\right\}$ is nearly the same in every parallel, and $\therefore$ equal to its value at the equator, where it is equal to g very nearly; in the value of $\left\{\frac{d^2V}{dr^2}\right\}$ we substitute g' in place of $\frac{m}{R^2}$, for thus the error of the supposition that $g = \frac{m}{R^2}$ is somewhat corrected; substituting for

$$\left(\frac{dV}{dr}\right) + n^2 R.\sin.^2\theta,\ \left(\frac{d^2V}{dr^2}\right) + \frac{n^2}{2} R^2.\sin.^2\theta$$

their values and of remarking that $V + \frac{n^2}{2} R.^2 \sin.^2\theta$ is constant, we obtain the value of $lg.\log.\varrho$ which is given in the text.

The density of the atmosphere being inconsiderable with respect to that of the earth, we may without sensible error, neglect the attraction of its molecules.

The variable part of the value of ϱ is necessarily negative, for the density decreases, according as we ascend in the atmosphere;

$$\log.\varrho = \frac{\text{const}}{lg} - \frac{r'g'.}{l.g}\left(1+\frac{r'}{R}\right) \therefore \varrho = c^{\frac{\text{const}}{lg} - \frac{r'g'.}{lg}\left(1+\frac{r'}{R}\right)}$$

and at the surface of the sea $r' = 0 \therefore \varrho = c^{\frac{\text{const}}{lg}} = \Pi$ which is consequently the value of ϱ at the surface of the sea; when the times of vibration are given, the lengths of the isochronous pendulums are proportional to the forces of gravity, $\therefore \frac{g'}{g} = \frac{h'}{h}$.

considered: we shall have $\frac{g'}{g}=\frac{h'}{h}$, and consequently,

$$\rho = \Pi . c^{-\frac{r'h'}{lh}.\left\{1+\frac{r'}{R}\right\}}.\ *$$

From this expression of the density of the air, it appears that strata of the same density, are throughout equally elevated about the surface of the sea, with the exception of the quantity $\frac{r'(h'-h)}{h}$; however, in the exact determination of the heights of mountains by observations of the barometer, this quantity ought not to be neglected.

Let us now consider the atmosphere in a state of motion, and let the oscillations of a stratum of level, or of the same density in the state of equilibrium, be determined. Let $\alpha\varphi$ represent the elevation of a molecule of the fluid, above the surface of level, to which it appertains in the

* If we expand the value of ρ into a series it becomes equal to

$$1-\frac{r'h'}{lh}.\left(1+\frac{r'}{R}\right)+\frac{1}{2}.\frac{r'h'}{lh}.\left(1+\frac{r'}{R}\right)^2+\&c.$$

and neglecting higher powers of r', $=1-\frac{r'h'}{lh}$ $\therefore$ in strata of *equal elevation* above the level of the sea, the difference of density is equal to $r.\left(\frac{h'-h}{lh}\right)$; in like manner, if the density of two strata, in latitudes of which the forces are respectively equal to g and g'; *be the same*, we shall have

$$\frac{r'h'}{lh}.\left(1+\frac{r'}{R}\right)=\frac{r''.h}{l.h}.\left(1+\frac{r''}{R}\right)$$

r' and r'' being the heights which correspond to the respective latitudes, $\therefore$ neglecting quantities of the second order we shall have, when the density is given, $r'h'=r''h$ $\therefore$ $r''=\frac{r'h'}{h}$ consequently the difference between r' and $r''\left(=\frac{r'h'}{h}\right)=r'.\left(\frac{h'-h}{h}\right)$.

state of equilibrium; it is manifest that, in consequence of this elevation, the value of δV will be increased by the differential variation $-\alpha g.\delta\varphi$; thus we shall have, $\delta V = (\delta V) - \alpha g.\delta\varphi + \alpha\delta V'$; (δV) being the value of δV, which, in the state of equilibrium, corresponds to the stratum of level, and to the angles $\theta + \alpha u$, and $nt + \varpi + \alpha v$; $\delta V'$ being the part of δV, which is produced by the new forces, which in the state of motion, agitate the atmosphere.

Let $\rho = (\rho) + \alpha\rho'$, ρ being the density of the stratum of level, in the state of equilibrium. By making $\frac{l\rho'}{(\rho)} = y'$, we shall have

$$\frac{\delta p}{\rho} = \frac{lg.\delta(\rho)}{(\rho)} + \alpha g.\delta y';^{*}$$

but in the state of equilibrium we have,

$$0 = \frac{n^2}{2}.\delta.\{(r+\alpha s).\ \sin.\ (\theta+\alpha u)\}^2 + (\delta V) - \frac{lg.\delta(\rho)}{(\rho)};$$

therefore, the general equation relative to the motion of the atmosphere will become, relatively to the strata of level, with respect to which δr very nearly vanishes,

$$r.^2\delta\theta.\left\{\left\{\frac{d^2u'}{dt^2}\right\} - 2n.\ \sin.\theta.\ \cos.\ \theta.\left\{\frac{dv'}{dt}\right\}\right\}$$

$$+r^2.\delta\varpi.\left\{\sin.\ ^2\theta.\ \left\{\frac{d^2v'}{dt^2}\right\} + 2n.\ \sin.\ \theta.\ \cos.\ \theta.\left\{\frac{du'}{dt}\right\} + \frac{2n.\ \sin.\ ^2\theta}{r}.\left\{\frac{ds'}{dt}\right\}\right\}$$

$$p^{*} = l.g.\rho = lg.(\rho) + \alpha lg.\rho' \therefore \frac{\delta p}{\rho} = \frac{lg.\partial(\rho)}{(\rho)+\alpha\rho'}, + \frac{\alpha.lg.\partial\rho'}{(\rho)+\alpha\rho'}$$

= neglecting quantities of the order α^2, $lg.\ \partial(\rho)\ (.(\rho)^{-1}(\rho).^{-2}\alpha.\rho')$

$$+\alpha lg.\partial\rho'.(.(\rho^{-1}) - \rho^{-2}\alpha\rho') = lg.\ \frac{\partial(\rho)}{(\rho)} - \frac{lg.\alpha\rho'.\partial(\rho)}{(\rho^2)} + \frac{\alpha lg.\ \partial\rho'}{(\rho)} = \frac{lg.\partial(\rho)}{(\rho)}$$

$$+ \frac{lg\ \alpha\partial\rho'.(\rho) - lg\alpha\rho'.d(\rho)}{(\rho^2)} = \frac{lg.\partial(\rho)}{(\rho)} + \alpha g.\partial.\ \frac{l.\rho'}{(\rho)}\ (=\alpha g.\partial y').$$

$=\delta V'-g.\delta\varphi-g\delta y'+n^2 r.\ \sin.^2\theta.\delta.\ (s'-(s'))$,*
$\alpha\ (s')$ being the variation of r, which in the state of equilibrium corresponds to the variations $\alpha u'$, $\alpha v'$, of the angles θ, and ϖ.

Let us suppose that all the molecules, which at the commencement of the motion existed on the same radius vector, remained constantly on the same radius in a state of motion, which, as appears from what precedes, obtains in the oscillations of the sea; and let us examine whether this supposition is consistent with the equations of the motion and continuity of the atmosphere. For this purpose, it is necessary that the values of u' and of v', should be the same for all these molecules, as we shall see in the sequel, when the forces which cause this variation are determined; consequently, it is necessary that the variations $\delta\varphi$ and δy, should be the same for these molecules, and moreover that the quantities

$$2nr.\ \delta\varpi.\ \sin.^2\theta.\left\{\frac{ds'}{d\varpi}\right\},\ \text{and}\ n^2 r.\ \sin.^2\theta.\delta.\left\{s'-(s')\right\},$$

may be neglected in the preceding equation.

At the surface of the sea, we have $\varphi=y$, αy being the elevation of the surface of the sea above the surface of level. Let us examine whether the suppositions of φ equal to y, and of y constant for all molecules of the atmosphere, existing on the same radius vector, is compatible with the equation of the continuity of the fluid. This equation is by No. 35,

* $\alpha s'$ and $\alpha(s')$ being the variations of r, corresponding respectively, in the states of motion and equilibrium, to the variations $\alpha u'$ and $\alpha v'$, the expression

$$\frac{n^2}{2}.\ \partial.\left\{(r+\alpha s').\ \sin.(\theta+\alpha u')\right\}^2=\frac{n^2}{2}.\ \partial.\ \left\{\left(r+\alpha(s')+\alpha(s'-(s'))\right).\ \sin.(\theta+\alpha u)\right\}^2$$

and when we neglect quantities of the order α^2, the part of this expression, which does not occur in the equation

$$0=\frac{n^2}{2}.\ \partial.\ \left\{(r+\alpha s).\ \sin.(\theta+\alpha u)\right\}^2,\ \text{is,}\ n^2\ r.\alpha.\partial.\ \left\{(s'-(s')\right\}.\ \sin.^2\theta.$$

$$0=r^2.\left\{\rho'+(\rho).\left[\left\{\frac{du'}{d\theta}\right\}+\left\{\frac{dv'}{d\varpi}\right\}+\frac{u'\cos.\theta}{\sin.\theta}\right\}\right\}+(\rho).\left\{\frac{d.r^2s'}{dr}\right\};*$$

fiom which we obtain

$$y=-l.\left\{\left\{\frac{d.r^2s'}{r^2dr}\right\}+\left\{\frac{du'}{d\theta}\right\}+\left\{\frac{dv'}{d\varpi}\right\}+\frac{u.'\cos.\theta}{\sin.\theta}\right\}.$$

$r+\alpha s'$ is equal to the value of r at the surface of level, which corresponds to the angles $\theta+\alpha u$, and $\varpi+\alpha v$, together with the elevation of a molecule of air above this surface; the part of $\alpha s'$ which depends on the variation of the angles θ and ϖ,† being of the order $\frac{\alpha n^2.u}{g}$, may be neglected in

N N

* Dividing this equation by r^2 (ϱ) we shall obtain

$$\frac{\varrho'}{(\varrho)}\left(=\frac{y}{l}\right)=-\left(\frac{du'}{d\theta}\right)-\left(\frac{dv'}{d\varpi}\right)-\frac{u'.\cos.\theta}{\sin.\theta}-\left(\frac{d.r^2s'}{r^2\,dr}\right).$$

† The part of $\alpha s'$ which corresponds to the variations $\alpha u'$, $\alpha v'$, is of the same order as the products of these quantities by the eccentricity of the spheroid, see page 258, and the eccentricity in this case is proportional to the fraction $\frac{n^2}{g}$, consequently the variation of $\alpha s'$ which corresponds to the variation of the angles θ and ϖ, $=\frac{\alpha n^2 u}{g}$; the entire variation of $\alpha s'$ is made up of two parts, of which one is equal to the elevation of the molecule above the surface of equilibrium, on the supposition that the angles θ and ϖ are not varied, and this part of the variation of $\alpha s'=\alpha\varphi$, the other part of the variation is the part which corresponds to the variations $\alpha u'$ and $\alpha v'$ of the angles θ and ϖ, and from what precedes it appears that this part may be neglected, consequently we have

$$\alpha s'=\alpha\varphi;\left(\frac{d.r^2s'}{r^2dr}\right)=\frac{2s'}{r}+\frac{ds'}{dr}$$

the second term $=\left(\frac{d\varphi}{dr}\right)$ by substituting φ in place of y', to which it is equal, and when φ is supposed to be equal to y; its derivitive function with respect to r must vanish, φ being the same for all the molecules, situated on the same radius, y is the same order as s', or the eccen-

the preceding expression for y', consequently it may be supposed in this expression that $s' = \varphi$; by making $\varphi = y$, we shall have $\left(\frac{d\varphi}{dr}\right) = 0$, since the value of φ is then the same for all molecules situated on the same radius. Moreover, by what precedes, y is of the order l or $\frac{n^2}{g}$; therefore the expression for y' will become,

$$y' = -l.\left\{\left\{\frac{du'}{d\theta}\right\} + \left\{\frac{dv'}{d\varpi}\right\} + \frac{u'.\cos.\theta}{\sin.\theta}\right\};$$

thus, u' and v' being the same for all molecules situated primitively on the same radius, the value of y' will be the same for all these molecules. Moreover, it is manifest from what has been stated that the quantities

$$2nr.\ \delta\varpi.\ \sin.^2\theta.\left\{\frac{ds'}{dt}\right\}, \text{and } n^2 r.\sin.^2\theta.\ \delta.(s'-(s')),$$

may be neglected in the preceding equations of the motion of the atmosphere, which can then be satisfied, by supposing that u' and v' are the same for all the molecules of the atmosphere, which at the commencement of the motion existed on the same radius; therefore the supposition that all those molecules remain constantly on the same radius during the oscillations, is compatible with the equations of the motion and of the continuity of the atmospheric fluid. In this case, the oscillations of the different strata of level are the same, and may be determined by means of the equations,

tricity which is proportional to $\frac{n^2}{g}$, and this last quantity is proportional to l, see page 258 and 266, ∴ we may neglect both $\frac{2s'}{r}$ and $\frac{ds'}{dr}$ consequently we will obtain for y' the expression given in the text. It is manifest from what has been stated in notes to page 253, that $2nr.\delta\varpi\ \sin.^2\theta.\left(\frac{ds'}{dt}\right)$; $n^2.r\sin.^2\theta.\delta(s'-(s))$ may be neglected when the earth is nearly spherical.

$$r^2.\delta\theta.\left\{\left\{\frac{d^2u'}{dt^2}\right\}-2n.\sin.\theta.\cos.\theta.\left\{\frac{dv'}{dt}\right\}\right\}$$

$$+r.^2\delta\varpi.\left\{\sin.^2\theta.\left\{\frac{d^2v'}{dt^2}\right\}-2n.\sin.\theta.\cos.\theta.\left\{\frac{du'}{dt}\right\}=\delta V'-g.\delta y'-g.\delta y;\right.$$

$$y'=-l.\left\{\left\{\frac{du'}{d\theta}\right\}+\left\{\frac{dv'}{d\varpi}\right\}+\frac{u'\cos\theta}{\sin.\theta}\right\}.$$

These oscillations of the atmosphere ought to produce corresponding oscillations,, in the heights of the barometer. In order to determine these last by means of the first, we should suppose a barometer fixed at any elevation above the level of the sea. The altitude of the mercury is proportional to the pressure which the surface exposed to the action of the air experiences; therefore it may be represented by $lg.\rho$; but this surface is successively exposed to the action of different strata of level, which are alternately elevated and depressed like the surface of the sea; thus the value of ρ at the surface of the mercury varies, 1st, * because it appertains to a stratum of lovel, which in the state of equilibrium was less elevated by the quantity αy; 2dly, because the density of a stratum increases in the state of motion, by $\alpha\rho'$ or by $\frac{\alpha(\rho).y'}{l}$. In consequence of the first cause, the variation of ρ is augmented by the quantity $-\alpha y.\left(\frac{d\rho}{dr}\right)$ or $\frac{\alpha(\rho).y}{l}$ therefore the entire variation of the density ρ at the surface of the mercury, is $\alpha(\rho).\frac{(y+y')}{l}$. It follows from this, that if we represent the height of the mercury, in

* $\left(\frac{dp}{dr}\right)=lg.\left(\frac{d\rho}{dr}\right)$, in the state of equilibrium $\left(\frac{dp}{dr}\right)=g.(\rho)$ see (page 223) $\therefore\left(\frac{d\rho}{dr}\right)=\frac{g.(\rho)}{g.l}$ consequently $-\alpha y.\left(\frac{d\rho}{dr}\right)=\frac{\alpha y.(\rho)}{l},\left(\frac{d\rho}{dr}\right)$ is negative because the density increases as we ascend in the atmosphere.

The temperature of the air being supposed to remain unvaried, its specific gravity will vary as (ρ) its density, and this quantity varies as k.

the barometer, in the state of equilibrium by k; its oscillations, in the state of motion will be represented by the function $\frac{\alpha k.(y+y')}{l}$; consequently at all heights above the level of the sea, these oscillations are similar, and proportional to the altitudes of the barometer.

It only now remains, in order to *determine* the oscillations of the sea, and of the atmosphere, to know the forces which act on these respective fluids, and to integrate the preceding differential equations; which will be done in the sequel of this work.

END OF THE FIRST BOOK.

TREATISE

OF

CELESTIAL MECHANICS,

BY P. S. LAPLACE,

MEMBER OF THE NATIONAL INSTITUTE, &c.

PART THE FIRST—BOOK THE SECOND.

TRANSLATED FROM THE FRENCH, AND ELUCIDATED WITH *EXPLANATORY NOTES.*

BY THE REV. HENRY H. HARTE, F.T.C.D. M.R.I.A.

DUBLIN:

PRINTED AT THE UNIVERSITY PRESS,

FOR RICHARD MILLIKEN AND HODGES AND M'ARTHUR.

1827.

TABLE OF CONTENTS.

BOOK II.

Development of the differential equations relative to the excentricicities and position of the perihelia, in any system whatever of orbits having a small excentricity and small inclination to each other. - - - - - - - No. 55

Integration of these equations, and determination by observations, of the arbitraries of their integrals. - - - - - - - - - No. 56

The system of the orbits of the planets and satellites is stable with respect to the excentricities, that is to say, those excentricities remain always very small, and the system only oscillates about a mean state of ellipticity, from which it deviates very little. No. 57

Differential expressions of the secular variations of the excentricity and position of the perihelion. - - - - - - - - - No. 58

Integration of the differential equations relative to the nodes and inclinations of the orbits. In the motion of a system of bodies very little inclined to each other, their mutual inclinations remain always very small. - - - - - No. 59

Differential equations of the secular variations of the nodes and inclinations of the orbits; 1st, with respect to a fixed plane; 2dly, with respect to the moveable orbit of one of the bodies of the system. - - - - - - No. 60

General relations between the elliptic elements of a system of bodies, whatever may be their excentricities and respective inclinations. - - - - No. 61

Investigation of the invariable plane, or that on which the sum of the masses of the bodies of the system, multiplied respectively by the projections of the areas described by their radii vectores in a given time, is a *maximum*. Determination of the motion of two bodies, inclined to each other at any angle whatever, - - - No. 62

CHAP. VIII. *Second method of approximation of the celestial motions.* - 352

This method is founded on the variations which the elements of the motion supposed to be elliptic, experience in virtue of the secular and periodic inequalities. General method for determining these variations. The finite equations of elliptic motion and their first differentials, are the same in the variable and invariable ellipse. - No. 63

Expressions of the elements of elliptic motion, in the disturbed orbit, whatever may be its excentricity and inclination to the planes of the orbits of the disturbing masses. No. 64

Development of these expressions, in the case of orbits having a small excentricity and inconsiderable inclination to each other. First, with respect to the mean motions and the major axes; it is proved that if the squares and products of the disturbing forces be neglected, these two elements are only subject to periodic inequalities, depending on the configuration of the bodies of the system. If the mean motions of the two planets are very nearly commensurable, there may result in their mean longitude two considerable inequalities, affected with contrary signs, and inversely as the products of the masses of the bodies into the square roots of the major axes of their orbits. It is

ERRATA.

Page Line

20, 3, *for* This *read* The.

28, 7, *for* $(z''+z')^2$, *read* $(z''-z')^2$.

34, 6, *for* mm, *read* mm'.

50, 19, *for* from the M, *read* from M.

51, 12, *for* their, *read* its.

52, 16, *for* $z-z$, *read* $z-z'$.

62, 11, *for* its, *read* these.

68, 5, *for* $r.\left(\frac{d^2U}{du}\right)$, *read* $r.\left(\frac{d^2U}{du^2}\right)$.

81, last line, *for* the second $\frac{3}{2}$, *read* $\frac{5}{2}$.

96, 8, *for* supply, *read* solely.

96, 19, *for* $\frac{dy}{dx}$, *read* $\frac{dy_{,}}{dx}$.

103, 1, *for* e, *read* c.

143, 17, *for* cos. ιn, *read* cos. ιnt.

152, 19, *for* $u_{,}$, *read* v.

163, 3, *for* tan.$^2\frac{1}{2}v$, *read* tan. $\frac{1}{2}v$.

166, 17, *for* value, *read* ratio.

174, 10, *for* cos. ε. cos. ε, *read* cos. ε. cos. ε'.

174, 11, *for* e, *read* c.

174, 20, *for* sin u. sin. u'^2, *read* sin. u. sin. u'.

216, 1, *for* $\delta\varkappa''$, *read* $\delta\varkappa'''$.

219, 1, *for* $\frac{2}{r}$, *read* $-\frac{2}{r}$.

224, 20, *for* $U-V'$, *read* $U'-V'$.

240, 2, *for* the second aQ, *read* aQ'.

244, 11, *for* these, *read* the.

256, 4, *for* -0, *read* $=0$.

266, 1, *for* dR, *read* $\text{d}R$.

271, 4, *for* dt', *read* dt^2.

284, 3, for a^2, *read* α^2.

ERRATA.

Page Line

285, 11, *for* $a = \frac{a}{a'}$, *read* $\alpha = \frac{a}{a'}$.

287, 13, for $-\frac{1}{a'} - \frac{db_{\frac{1}{2}}^{(i)}}{da}\left(\frac{d\alpha}{da}\right)$, *read* $\frac{a}{a'^2} - \frac{1}{a'} . b_{\frac{1}{2}}^{(1)}$.

287, 16, dele — before $\frac{1}{a'^2}$.

299, 2, *for* $n + \epsilon$, *read* $nt + \epsilon$.

300, 7, *for* $e.$ cos. ϖ', *read* e' cos. ϖ'.

306, 5, *for* m', *read* m.

315, 1, $\int \chi'' dr$, *read* $\int \chi'' dR$.

318, 5, *for* motion, *read* motions.

323, 14, *for* $m'.\sqrt{a}$, *read* $m'.\sqrt{a'}$.

328, 20, *for* the second $b_2 - b$, *read* $b_2 - b_1$.

330, 2, *for* in u, *read* (u).

A

TREATISE

ON

CELESTIAL MECHANICS,

&c. &c.

PART I.—BOOK II.

OF THE LAW OF UNIVERSAL GRAVITATION, AND OF THE MOTIONS OF THE CENTRES OF GRAVITY OF THE HEAVENLY BODIES.

CHAPTER I.

Of the law of universal gravitation, deduced from the phenomena.

1. AFTER having developed the laws of motion, we proceed to deduce from these laws, and from those of the celestial motions, which have been given in detail in the work entitled the *Exposition of the System of the World*, the general law of these motions. Of all the phenomena, that which seems most proper, to discover it, is the elliptic motion of the planets and of the comets round the sun, let us therefore consider what this law furnishes us with on the subject. For this purpose, let

x and y represent the rectangular coordinates of a planet, in the plane of its orbit, their origin being at the centre of the sun; moreover, let P and Q represent the forces with which the planet is actuated in its relative motion round the sun, parallel to the axes of x and of y, these forces being supposed to tend towards the origin of the coordinates; finally, let dt represent the element of the time which is supposed to be constant; by the second chapter of the first book,* we shall have

$$0 = \frac{d^2x}{dt^2} + P; \quad (1)$$

$$0 = \frac{d^2y}{dt^2} + Q. \quad (2)$$

If we add the first of these equations multiplied by $-y$, to the second multiplied by x, the following equation will be obtained:

$$0 = \frac{d.(xdy-ydx)}{dt^2} + xQ-yP.$$

It is evident that $xdy-ydx$ is equal to twice the area which the radius vector of the planet describes about the sun during the instant dt; by the first law of Kepler this area is proportional to the time, consequently we have

$$xdy - ydx = cdt,$$

c being a constant quantity; hence it appears, that the differential of the first member of this equation is equal to cypher, which gives

$$xQ-yP = 0,$$

* These laws refer strictly to the motion of the centre of gravity of each planet, it is therefore the motion of this point which is determined, and by the position and velocity

it follows from this, that the forces P and Q are to each other in the ratio of x to y; and consequently their resultant must pass through the origin of the coordinates, that is, through the centre of the sun, and as the curve which the planet describes is* concave towards the sun, it is evident that the force which acts on it, must tend towards this star.

The law of the areas, proportional to the times employed in their description, leads us therefore to this first remarkable result, namely, that the force which solicits the planets and comets, is directed towards the centre of the sun.

2. Let us in the next place, determine the law according to which this force acts at different distances from this star. It is evident that as the planets and the comets alternately approach to and recede from the sun, during each revolution, the nature of the elliptic motion ought to conduct us to this law. For this purpose, let the differential equations (1) and (2) of the preceding number be resumed. If we add the first, multiplied by dx, to the second, multiplied by dy, we shall obtain

$$0 = \frac{dx.d^2x + dy.d^2y}{dt^2} + Pdx + Qdy;$$

which gives by integrating

of a planet, we always understand, unless the contrary be specified, the position and velocity of its centre of gravity; hence it is evident, that the equations of the motion of a *material point*, which have been given in the second chapter, are applicable in the present case.

* The areas being proportional to the times, the curve described is one of single curvature, (see Book I. page 28, Notes), therefore two coordinates (x, y) are sufficient to determine the circumstances of the planet's motion. As the curve described by the planet is *concave* to the sun, it is plain that in the equation $\frac{d^2x}{dt^2} = P$; $\frac{d^2x}{dt^2}$ must be taken negatively, because the force tends to diminish the coordinates. See Book I. Chapter II. page 31.

$$0=\frac{dx^2+dy^2}{dt^2}+2\int(Pdx+Qdy),*$$

the arbitrary constant being indicated by the sign of integration. Substituting instead of dt, its value $\frac{xdy-ydx}{c}$, which is given by the law of the proportionality of the areas to the time, we shall have

$$0=\frac{c^2.(dx^2+dy^2)}{(xdy-ydx)^2}+2\int(Pdx+Qdy).$$

For greater simplicity, let us transform the coordinates x and y, into a radius vector, and a traversed angle, conformably to the practice of astronomers. Let r represent a radius drawn from the centre of the sun to that of the planet, or its radius vector; and let v be the angle which it makes with the axis of x, we shall have then,

$$x=r.\cos.v;\ y=r.\sin.v;\ r=\sqrt{x^2+y^2};\dagger$$

from which may be obtained,

$$dx^2+dy^2=r^2.dv^2+dr^2;\ xdy-ydx=r^2dv.$$

If the *principal* force which acts on the planet be denoted by φ, we shall have by means of the preceding number,

$$P=\varphi.\cos.v;\ Q=\varphi.\sin.v;\ \varphi=\sqrt{P^2+Q^2};$$

which gives

$$Pdx+Qdy=\varphi dr;$$

* The equation $0=\frac{dx^2+dy^2}{dt^2}+2\int(Pdx+Qdy)$, has been already deduced in No 8; by substituting for dx^2 and dy^2 their values in terms of the polar coordinates, we obtain $\frac{dr^2}{dt^2}+\frac{r^2dv^2}{dt^2}+2\int\varphi.dr=0$; hence if φ be given in terms of r we shall immedi-diately obtain the velocity at any distance from the centre of force.

† The most obvious way of determining the position of any body, is by means of rectangular coordinates, in which case the differential equations of motion are symmetrical; however, as the polar coordinates involve directly the quantities which are required to be known in astronomical investigations, namely, the distance, longitude and latitude of a planet, astronomers make use of these coordinates in determining the circumstances of its motion, &c.

and by substitution we shall have

$$0=\frac{c^2.(r^2.dv^2+dr^2)}{r^4dv^2}+2.\int\phi dr;*$$

* $dx = dr.\cos.v - dv.\sin.v.r$, $dy = dr.\sin.v + dv.\cos.v.r$, $\because dx^2+dy^2=dr^2.(\cos.^2v+\sin.^2v) - 2dr.dvr.\sin.v.\cos.v + 2dr.dvr.\sin.v.\cos.v + dv^2.r^2.(\sin.^2v+\cos.^2v)=dr^2+dv^2.r^2$; $xdy = r.\cos.v.(dr.\sin.v + rdv.\cos.v) = rdr.\sin.v.\cos,v + dv.r^2.\cos.^2v$, $ydx=r.\sin.v.(dr.\cos.v-r.dv.\sin.v)=rdr.\sin.v.\cos.v-dvr^2.\sin.^2v$, $\because xdy-ydx=r^2.dv$; $Pdx=\phi.\cos.v.(dr.\cos.v-rdv.\sin.v)$; $Qdy=\phi.\sin.v.(dr.\sin.v+rdv.\cos.v)$, $\because Pdx+Qdy=\phi dr.(\cos.^2v+\sin.^2v)$, $+\phi dv.(r.\cos.v.\sin.v-r.\cos.v.\sin.v)$ $=\phi dr$; therefore by substituting in the equation $\frac{c^2.(dx^2+dy^2)}{(xdy-ydx)^2}+2\int(Pdx+Qdy)=0$, we obtain $\frac{c^2.(r^2dv^2+dr^2)}{r^4dv^2}+2\int\phi dr=0$; and $\because(-c^2r^2-r^4.2\int\phi dr).dv^2=c^2dr^2$; as the variables dv and dr are separated in the equation $dv=\frac{cdr}{r.\sqrt{-c^2-2r^2.\int\phi dr}}$, it can be integrated and constructed, the radical ought to be affected with the sign $\pm$, when v and r increase the same time, the sign is $+$, and in the contrary case the sign is $-$; these circumstances depend on the initial impulse of the planet. The determination of v, or of the orbit described by a body, when the law of the force ϕ is given, is called the inverse problem of central forces, the expression for dv coincides with that given by Newton in Prop. 41, Lib. 1st. Princip. for it is there demonstrated that $XY.XC=\frac{Q.IN.CX^2}{A^2.\sqrt{ABTD-Z^2}}$, from the construction it is evident that $\frac{XY}{XC}=dv$, that $IN=dr$, that $Q=c$, and finally that $A=r$, and as $Z^2\propto\frac{Q^2}{A^2}$, and $ABTD=$ the square of the velocity, $\sqrt{ABTD-Z^2}=\sqrt{-\int\phi dr-\frac{c^2}{r^2}}\because\frac{XY}{XC}=dv=\frac{Q.IN}{A^2.\sqrt{ABTD-Z^2}}$ $=\frac{cdr}{r^2.\sqrt{-c^2-2r^2\int\phi dr}}.\div$ by r.

If the force ϕ be as any power n of the distance, then $2\int\phi dr=2\int r^n dr$ (= the square of the velocity) $=b^2+\frac{2}{n+1}.r^{n+1}-\frac{2}{n+1}.a^{n+1}$ (a being the initial distance), hence

$dv=\frac{cdr}{r.\sqrt{-c^2-b^2r^2+\frac{2}{n+1}.r^{n+3}+\frac{2}{n+1}.a^n r_2}}$, as b is the velocity of projec-

from which we may obtain,

$$dv = \frac{cdr}{r.\sqrt{-c^2 - 2r^2 \int \varphi dr}}. \quad (8)$$

This equation will give by the method of quadratures, the value of v in terms of r, when φ is a known function of r, but if, this force being unknown, the nature of the curve which it makes the planet describe, be given, then, by differentiating the preceding expression of $2\int \varphi dr$, we shall have, to determine φ, the equation

tion, if p be the perpendicular on the tangent at this point, $c \propto p\, b$, and $b^2 = m^2\, a^{n+1}$, $\because dv = \frac{pbdr}{r.\sqrt{-(p^2+r^2)m^2a^{n+1} - \frac{2}{n+1}.r^{n+3} + \frac{2}{n+1}.a^{n+2}\,r^2}}$, at the apsides $p=a$, $dr=0$, and $\because r = \frac{pb}{vel.} = \frac{pb}{\sqrt{b^2 + \frac{2}{n+1}.(a^{n+1} - r^{n+1})}}$, hence $r.\sqrt{b^2 + \frac{2}{n+1}.(a^{n+1} - r^{n+1})} - pb = 0$, by squaring this equation, we get b^2r^2

$$+ \frac{2}{n+1}.a^{n+1}\,r^2 - \frac{2}{n+1}.r^{n+3} - p^2b^2 = 0.$$

When n is even, this equation may have four possible roots, when it is odd, it can only have three; but as this equation is the square of the given equation, some of the roots are introduced by the operation, so that the equation to the apsides can never have more than two possible roots, consequently no orbit can have more than two apsides, *i. e.* there are only two different distances of the apsides, but there is no limit to the number of repetitions of these, without again falling on the *same* points, if $n = -3$ or a greater negative number, the equation can have only one possible root, and the orbit but one apsid.

If in the equation $\frac{c^2}{r^2} + \frac{dr^2}{r^4.dv^2} + 2\int \varphi dr$, $\frac{1}{z}$ be substituted in place of r, it becomes $c^2.\left(\frac{dz^2}{dv^2} + z^2\right) - 2\int \varphi.\frac{dz}{z^2}$, which is a much more convenient form, particularly when the

$$\varphi = \frac{c^2}{r^3} - \frac{\frac{c^2}{2}.d.\left\{\frac{dr^2}{r^4 dv^2}\right\}}{dr}. \quad (4)^*$$

The orbits of the planets are ellipses, having the centre of the sun in one of the foci; if, in the ellipse, ϖ represents the angle which the axis major makes with the axis of x, moreover if a represents the semiaxis major, and e the ratio of the excentricity to the semiaxis major, we shall have, the origin of the coordinates being in the focus,

$$r = \frac{a.(1-e^2)}{1+e.\cos.(v-\varpi)},\dagger$$

which equation becomes that of a parabola, when $e = 1$, and a is infinite, it appertains to an hyperbola, when e is greater than unity.

law of the force being given, the nature of the orbit is required; for instance the equation in page 5 becomes, when $\frac{1}{z}$ is substituted for r then differentiated, and the result divided by $2dz$,

$c^2.\left(\frac{d^2z}{dv^2} + z^2\right) - \frac{\varphi}{z^2} = 0$, $\because \varphi = c^2z^2.\left(\frac{d^2z}{dv^2} + z^2\right)$, and as $z = \frac{1}{r} = \frac{1+e.\cos.(v-\varpi)}{a.(1-e^2)}$, $\because$ differentiating twice $\frac{d^2z}{dv^2} = -\frac{e.\cos.(v-\varpi)}{a.(1-e^2)}$, $\because \frac{d^2z}{dv^2} + z^2 = \frac{1}{a.(1-e^2)}$, $\because \varphi = \frac{c^2z^2}{a.(1-e^2)}$.

* $\frac{c^2.(r^2.dv^2+dr^2)}{r^4.dv} = \frac{c^2}{r^2} + \frac{c^2.dr^2}{r^4.dv^2} = -2\int\varphi dr$, $\because$ by differentiating and dividing by by dr we obtain $\frac{c^2}{r^3} - d.\left(\frac{c^2dr^2}{r^4dv^2}\right) = \varphi$.

† The greatest and least values of r correspond to $v-\varpi=\pi$, $v-\varpi'=0$, $\because$ they are respectively $a.(1+e)$, $a.(1-e)$, consequently they lie in directum; hence it is easy to perceive, that when φ. varies as $\frac{1}{r^2}$, the apsides are 180° distant, and *vice versa*.

This equation gives

$$\frac{dr^2}{r^4dv^2} = \frac{2}{ar.(1-e^2)} - \frac{1}{r^2} - \frac{1}{a^2.(1-e^2)};$$

and consequently

$$\varphi = \frac{c^2}{a.(1-e^2)} \cdot \frac{1}{r^2};^*$$

therefore, the orbits of the planets and comets being conic sections, the force φ is reciprocally proportional to the square of the distance of the centres of these stars from that of the sun.

Moreover we may perceive, that, if the force φ be inversely as the square of the distance, or expressed by $\frac{h}{r^2}$, h being a constant coefficient, the preceding equation of conic sections, will satisfy the differential equation (4) between r and v, which gives the expression of φ, when φ is changed into $\frac{h}{r^2}$. We have then $h = \frac{c^2}{a.(1-e^2)}$, which

* $\frac{1}{r} = \frac{1+e.\cos.(v-\varpi)}{a.(1-e^2)}$, $\therefore \frac{dr^2}{r^4dv^2} = \left(\frac{e.\sin.(v-\varpi)}{a.(1-e^2)}\right)^2$, and $\frac{a.(1-e^2)}{r} - 1, = e.\cos.(v-\varpi) \therefore \left(\frac{a.(1-e^2)}{r}\right)^2 - \frac{2a.(1-e^2)}{r} + 1 = e^2.\cos.(v-\varpi)^2 = e^2 - e^2.\sin.^2(v-\varpi)$, $\therefore \frac{dr^2}{r^4.dv^2} = -\frac{1}{r^2} + \frac{2}{a.(1-e^2)} \times \frac{1}{r} - \frac{1}{a^2.(1-e^2)}$, and the differential of the second member divided by dr will be equal to $\frac{2}{r^3} - \frac{2}{a.(1-e^2)} \cdot \frac{1}{r^2}$, consequently we have the value of

$$\varphi = \frac{c^2}{r^3} - \frac{c^2}{2} \cdot \frac{d.\left(\frac{dr^2}{r^4dv^2}\right)}{dr} = \frac{c^2}{r^3} - \frac{c^2}{r^3} + \frac{c^2}{a.(1-e^2)} \cdot \frac{1}{r^2}.$$

forms an equation of condition between the two arbitrary quantities a and e, of the equation of a conic section; therefore the three arbitrary quantities a, c, and ϖ, of this equation, are reduced two distinct quantities, and as the differential equation between r and v, is only of the second order, the finite equation of conic sections is its complete integral.*

From what precedes, it follows, that, if the curve described is a conic section, the force is in the inverse ratio of the square of the distance, and conversely, if the force be inversely as the square of the distance, the curve described is a conic section.

3. The intensity of the† force φ, with respect to *each* planet and comet depends on the coefficient $\frac{c^2}{a(1-e^2)}$; the laws of Kepler furnish us with the means of determining it. In fact, if we denote the time of the revolution of a planet by T; the area, which its radius vector describes during this time, being the surface of the planetary ellipse, it

* Conversely, when $\varphi = \frac{h}{r^2}$, the preceding equation of conic sections will satisfy the differential equation (4) between r and v, and h becomes $= \frac{c^2}{a.(1-e^2)}$, ∵ the three arbitrary quantities are reduced to two distinct ones, and this is the required number of arbitrary quantities, for the differential equation between r and v being of the second order, the number of arbitrary quantities introduced by the double integration is two, so that the equation of conic sections is the complete integral of this differential equation.

† The two first laws of Kepler, are sufficient to determine the ratio which exists between the intensities of the action of the sun on each planet, at different distances of the planet from the sun; by means of the third law we are enabled to find the relations which exist between the respective actions of the sun on *different* planets. As $\frac{c^2}{a.(1-e^2)}$, which expresses the intensity of the force for each planet, at the unity of its distance from the sun, depends on the three quantities a, c, e, which have particular values for each planet, we cannot determine without the third law, whether it changes, or remains the same, in passing from one planet to another.

will be $\pi.a^2.\sqrt{1-e^2}$,* π being the ratio of the semicircumference to the radius; but, by what precedes, the area described during the instant dt, is equal to $\frac{1}{2}.cdt$; therefore the law of the proportionality of the areas to the times of describing them, will give the following proportion:

$$\tfrac{1}{2}.cdt : \pi a^2.\sqrt{1-e^2} :: dt : T:$$

consequently

$$c = \frac{2\pi.a^2.\sqrt{1-e^2}}{T}.$$

With respect to the planets, the law of Kepler, according to which the squares of the times of their revolutions, are as the cubes of the greater axes of their ellipses, gives $T^2 = k^2.a^3$, k being the same for all the planets; therefore, we have

$$c = \frac{2\pi.\sqrt{a.(1-e^2)}}{k}.$$

$2a.(1-e^2)$ is the parameter of the orbit, and in different orbits, the values of c are proportional to the areas, described by the radii vectores in equal times; therefore these areas are as the square roots of the parameters of the orbits.

This proportion obtains also, for the orbits described by the comets, compared either among themselves, or with the orbits of the planets; this is one of the fundamental points of their theory, which corresponds so exactly to all their observed motions. The greater axes of their orbits, and the times of their revolutions, being unknown, we compute the motion of these stars, on the hypothesis that it is performed in a

* The area of the ellipse being equal to that of a circle, whose radius is a mean proportional between the semiaxes a and $a\sqrt{1-e^2}$; it must be equal to $\pi a^2.\sqrt{1-e^2}$.

parabolic orbit, and expressing their perihelion distance by D,* we suppose $c = \frac{2\pi.\sqrt{2D}}{k}$, which is equivalent to making e equal to unity, and a infinite, in the preceding expression of c; consequently, we have relatively to the comets, $T^2 = k^2.a^3$, so that we can determine the greater axes of their orbits, when the periods of their revolution are known.

The expression for c gives,

$$\frac{c^2}{a.(1-e^2)} = \frac{4\pi^2}{k^2};$$

therefore we have

$$\phi = \frac{4\pi^2}{k^2}.\frac{1}{r^2}.†$$

* The polar equation of the parabola is $r = \frac{p}{1+\cos.(v-\varpi)}$; ∵ when $v-\varpi=0$, i. e. at the perihelium, $r = \frac{a(1-e^2)}{2} = \frac{p}{2} = D$, ∵ $a(1-e^2)=2D$. Now this is the same thing, as if a was made infinite, and $e=$ to unity, in the equation, $r=a.\frac{(1-e^2)}{2}$, which expresses the distance of the nearest apsis from the focus of the ellipse, for substituting for the excentricity its value $\sqrt{a^2-b^2}$, r becomes equal to $a.\left(\frac{1}{2}-\frac{\sqrt{a^2-b^2}}{2a}\right) =$ as $(b^2 = ap)$ $\frac{a.(a-\sqrt{(a^2-ap)}}{2a}$, and as $\sqrt{a^2-ap}=a-\frac{p}{2}+(\quad).\frac{1}{a}=$ when a is infinite $a-\frac{p}{2}$, $r=\frac{a.(a-a+\frac{p}{2})}{2a} = \frac{p}{4}$, and it is evident that e is equal in this case to unity. ∵ If we suppose that the synchronous areas are as the square roots of the parameters, or $c = \frac{2\pi.\sqrt{2D}}{k}$, we will have $\frac{2\pi.\sqrt{2D}}{2k}.dt : \pi a^{\frac{3}{2}}\sqrt{2D} :: dt : T$; ∵ $T^2=k^2 a^3$.

† The constant ratio which c bears to the square root of $2D$, is that of $2\pi : k$, which is the same for all the planets; $\frac{4\pi^2}{k^2}$, or $\frac{c^2}{a.(1-e^2)}$ is the value of the

The coefficient $\frac{4\pi^2}{k^2}$, being the same for all the planets and comets, it

force φ at the unity of the distance of a planet from the sun. The *accelerating* force of the planets being the same at equal distances from the sun, it follows that the *moving* force will be proportional to the mass; and if all the planets descended at the same instant, and without any initial velocities from different points of the same spheric surface, of which the centre coincided with that of the sun, they would arrive at the surface of the sun, being supposed spheric, in the same time; here, we may perceive, a remarkable analogy between this force and the terrestrial gravity, which also impresses the same motion, on all bodies situated at equal distances from its centre.

If the apparent diameter of the sun be observed accurately with a micrometer, it will be found to vary in the subduplicate ratio of his angular velocity; from this phenomenon the equable description of areas may be inferred; for as the apparent diameters of the sun are inversely as the distance of the sun from the earth, the angular velocity of the sun must be inversely as the square of the distance of the sun from the earth, therefore the product of the diurnal motion into the square of the distance, *i. e.* the small area must be constant. If the sun's mean apparent diameter be called m, and his least apparent diameter $m-n$, his apparent diameter at any other time, will be $m-n\cos.z$, z being the angular distance of the sun from the point where his diameter is least, hence it may be inferred, that the orbit is elliptic; for as the distance is inversely as the apparent diameter, $r=\frac{B}{m-n\cos.(v-\varpi)}$, when r is greatest, $v-\varpi=0$, when least $v-\varpi=\pi$, $\because mr-nr\cos.(v-\varpi)=x(m-n)$, x being the greatest distance, and $mr=x(m-n)+nr.(\cos.v-\varpi)$, let $(m-n).\ x=nx'$, and then $mr=n(r.\cos.(v-\varpi)+x')$, $\because m:n::r.\cos.(v-\varpi)+x':r$; now $r.(\cos.(v-\varpi)$ is equal to a part of the axis intercepted between a perpendicular let fall from the sun's place on this axis, and the place the earth is supposed to occupy, and x' is a constant quantity, $\because$ producing the axis in an opposite direction from the sun, till the distance from the earth is equal to x', and erecting a perpendicular to the produced axis at the extremity of its production, $x'+r\cos.(v-\varpi)$ is equal to the distance of the sun from this perpendicular, and as it is to r the distance of the sun from the earth, in a given ratio of major inequality, namely $m:n$, it follows that the curve is an ellipse of which the directrix is a perpendicular, erected at the extremity of x'. This conclusion might also have been inferred from the polar equation to the ellipse $r=\frac{a(1-e^2)}{1+e\cos.(v-\varpi)}=a(1-e^2).(1+e\cos.(v-\varpi))^{-1}$.

Kepler directed his observations to the planet of Mars, of which the motion appeared to be more irregular, than the motion of the other planets, and by determining several distances of the planet from the sun, and tracing the orbit which passes through them all, it will appear that this orbit must be an ellipse, of which the sun occupies one of the foci, it follows that for each of these bodies, the force φ, is inversely as the square of the distance from the centre of the sun, and that it only varies from one planet to another, in consequence of the change of distance; from which it follows that it is the same for all these bodies supposed at equal distances from the sun.

We are thus conducted, by the beautiful laws of Kepler, to consider the centre of the sun as the focus of an attractive force, which, decreasing in the ratio of the square of the distance, extends indefinitely in every direction. The law of the proportionality of the areas to the times of their description, indicates that the principal force which solicits the planets and comets, is constantly directed towards the centre of the sun; the ellipticity of the planetary orbits, and the motions of the comets which are performed in orbits, which are very nearly parabolic, prove, that for each planet and for each comet, this force is in the inverse ratio of the square of the distance of these stars from the sun; finally, from the law of the squares of the periodic times proportional, to the cubes of the greater axes of their orbits, i. e. from the proportionality of the areas traced in equal times by the radii vectores in different orbits, to the square roots of the parameters of these orbits, which law involves the preceding, and is applicable to comets; it follows, that this force is the same for all the planets and comets, placed at equal distances from the sun, so that in *this* case, these bodies would fall towards the sun, with equal velocities.

4. If from the planets we pass to the consideration of the satellites, we find that the laws of Kepler being very nearly observed in their motions about their respective primary planets, they must gravitate towards the centres of these planets, in the inverse ratio of the squares of their distances from these centres; they must in like manner gravitate very nearly as their primaries towards the sun, in order that their relative motions about their respective primary planets, may be very nearly the same

can also be shewn that the angular velocities are inversely as the squares of the distances from the sun, from which it follows that the areas are proportional to the times.

as if these planets were at rest. Therefore the satellites are solicited towards their primaries and towards the sun, by forces which are inversely as the squares of the distances. The ellipticity of the orbits of the three* first satellites of Jupiter is inconsiderable; but the ellipticity of the fourth satellite is very perceptible. From the great distance of Saturn we have not been able hitherto to recognise the ellipticity of the orbits of his satellites, with the exception of the sixth, of which the orbit appears to be sensibly elliptic. But the law of the gravitation of the satellites of Jupiter, Saturn, and Uranus is principally conspicuous in the relation which exists between their mean motions, and their mean distances from the centre of these planets. This relation consists in this, that for each system of satellites, the squares of the times of their revolutions are as the cubes of their mean distances from the centre of the planet. Therefore let us suppose that a satellite describes a circular orbit, of which the radius a is equal to its mean distance from the centre of the primary, T expressing the number of seconds contained in the duration of a sidereal revolution, and π expressing as before the ratio of the semiperiphery to the radius, $\frac{2.a\pi}{T}$ will be the small arc described by the satellite in a second of time. If, the attractive force of the pla-

* The frequent recurrence of the eclipses of the satellites, enables us to determine the synodic revolution with great accuracy: and by means of this revolution, and of the motion of Jupiter, we can obtain the periodic time. The hypothesis of the orbits being very nearly circular, in the case of the first and second satellites, is confirmed by the phenomena, for the greatest elongations are always very nearly the same; besides the supposition of the uniformity of the motions, satisfies very nearly the computations of the eclipses. The distances of the satellites from the centre of Jupiter, may be found, by measuring with a micrometer, their distances from this centre, at the time of their greatest elongation, and also the diameter of Jupiter at this time, by means of which, these distances may be obtained in terms of the diameter; however they cannot be determined with the same precision as the periods of the satellites. As it is necessary in a comparison of a great number of observations, to modify the laws of circular motion, in the case of the third and fourth satellites, but especially in the case of the fourth, we conclude that the orbits of these satellites are elliptical.

net ceasing, the satellite was no longer retained in its orbit, it would recede from the centre of the planet along the tangent, by a quantity equal to the versed sine of the arc $\frac{2a\pi}{T}$, that is by the quantity* $\frac{2a\pi^2}{T^2}$; therefore this attractive force makes it to descend by this quantity, towards the primary. Relatively to another satellite, of which the mean distance from the centre of the primary is represented by a', T' being equal to the duration of a sidereal revolution, reduced into seconds, the descent in a second will be equal to $\frac{2a'\pi^2}{T'^2}$; but if we name φ, φ', the attractive forces of the planet at the distances a and a', it is manifest, that they are proportional to the quantities by which they make the two satellites to descend towards their primary in a second; therefore we have $\varphi : \varphi' :: \frac{2a\pi^2}{T^2} : \frac{2a'\pi^2}{T'^2}$.

The law of the squares of the times of the revolutions, proportional to the cubes of the mean distances of the satellites from the centre of their primary, gives

$$T^2 : T'^2 :: a^3 : a'^3 :$$

From these two proportions, it is easy to infer

$$\varphi : \varphi' :: \frac{1}{a^2} : \frac{1}{a'^2};$$

consequently, the forces φ and φ' are inversely as the squares of the distances a and a'.

* $T : 1'' :: 2a\pi$: arc described in a second, on the hypothesis that the motion is uniform, the versed sine of this arc $= \frac{4a^2\pi^2}{2aT^2}$. As the orbits of all the satellites are not elliptic, we cannot determine from the nature of the orbits, whether the force for each satellite in particular, varies inversely as the square of the distance or not.

5. The earth having but one satellite, the ellipticity of the lunar orbit is the only phenomenon, which can indicate to us the law of its attractive force; but the elliptic motion of the moon, being very sensibly deranged by the* perturbating forces, some doubts may exist, whether the law of the diminution of the attractive force of the earth, is in the inverse ratio of the square of the distance from its centre. Indeed, the analogy which exists between this force, and the attractive forces of the sun, of Jupiter, of Saturn, and of Uranus, leads us to think that it follows the same law† of diminution; but the experiments which have been instituted on terrestrial gravity, offer a direct means of verifying this law.

For‡ this purpose, we proceed to determine the lunar parallax, by

* The orbit of the moon differs sensibly from the *elliptic* form, in consequence of the action of the disturbing forces, and the variation of its apparent diameter shews, that it deviates more from the *circular* form, than the orbit of the sun. The first law of Kepler may be proved to be true, in the case of the moon, in the same manner as for the sun, namely, by a comparison of her apparent motion, with her apparent diameter. Indeed, if great accuracy is required, the observations ought to be made in the syzygies and in the quadratures; for in the other points of the orbit, the disturbing force of the sun deranges the proportionality of the areas to the times employed in their description. See Princip. Math. Lib. 1. Prop. 66. and Lib. 3, Prop. 3and 29.

† Newton demonstrates that the force which retains the moon in her orbit, is inversely as the square of the distance, in the following manner: if the distance between the apsides was 180°, the force would be inversely as the square of the distance, as has been already pointed out. See Note to page 7.

Now the apsides are observed to advance three degrees and three minutes every month, and the law of the force which would produce such an advance of the apsides, varies inversely as some power of the distance, intermediate between the square and the cube, but which is nearly sixty times nearer to the square; ∵ on the hypothesis, that the progression of the apsides, is produced by a deviation from the law of elliptical motion, the force must vary *very nearly* in the inverse ratio of the square of the distance; but if, as Newton demonstrates, the motion of the apsides arises from the disturbing force of the sun, it follows, *a fortiori*, that the force must be inversely as the square of the distance.

‡ The value of the constant part of the parallax is deduced on the hypothesis, that the force soliciting the moon, is the terrestrial gravity, diminished in the ratio of the square of

means of experiments on the length of the pendulum which vibrates seconds, and to compare it with observations made in the heavens. On the parallel of which the square* of the sine of the latitude is $\frac{1}{3}$, the space through which bodies fall by the action of gravity in a second, is, from observations on the length of the pendulum, equal to $3^{\text{metres}},65548$,

the distance; and if this parallax agrees with the observed parallax corrected for the lunar inequalities, we are justified in inferring, that the diminished terrestrial gravity and the force solliciting the moon are identically the same.

* Let unity represent the radius of a sphere equicapacious with a spheroid, its density being supposed to be the same with the mean density of this spheroid; if the greater semi-axis of the spheroid be $=1+\varrho$, and the lesser $=1-s$, we shall have for the oblong spheroid the following equation, $\frac{4\pi}{3}.1^3=\frac{4\pi}{3}(1+\varrho).(1-s)^2$, ∵ $1^3=1+\varrho-2s$ neglecting the squares and products of s and ϱ, which is permitted as the ellipticity of the spheroid is supposed to be inconsiderable, consequently we have $\varrho=2s$, ∵ in an oblong spheroid, such as would be generated by a revolution about the greater axis, the elevation of the spheroid above the equicapacious sphere is double of the depression below this sphere; and if r be the radius of the equicapacious sphere, a the greater, and b the lesser axis of the spheroid, we have $a-r=2r-2b$, ∵ $r=\frac{a+2b}{3}$; if the spheroid be oblate, i. e. such as would be generated by a revolution about the lesser axis, $\frac{4\pi}{3}.1^3=\frac{4\pi}{3}.(1-s)(1+\varrho)^2$, hence $s=2\varrho$, *i.e.* the depression in this case is equal to twice the elevation, ∵ $2a-2r=r-b$, and $r=\frac{2a+b}{3}$.

If a sphere be inscribed in a spheroid, the elevation of any point of the spheroid above the inscribed sphere, is to the *greatest* elevation of a spheroid above the inscribed sphere, *i. e.* to the difference between the radius of the equator and semiaxis, as the square of the cosine of the angular distance λ from the axis major, to the square of radius, ∵ the elevation $=(a-b)\cos.^2\lambda$, and as the equicapacious sphere is elevated above the lesser axis, and ∵ above the inscribed sphere by a quantity equal to $r-b$, the elevation of the spheroid above the *equicapacious* sphere $=(a-b)\cos.^2\lambda-r+b=(a-b).\cos.^2\lambda-\frac{2a+b}{3}+b, \left(=\frac{-2a+2b}{3}\right)$, consequently when the elevation is 0, we have $\cos.^2\lambda=\frac{2}{3}$, ∵ $\sin.^2\lambda=\frac{1}{3}$, and $\lambda=35°16'$. This situation is also remarkable for being the distance from the quadrature at which the addititious force of the sun, is equal to that part of its ablatitious force, which acts in direction of the radius of the moon's orbit.

as we shall see in the third book: we select this parallel, because the attraction of the earth on the corresponding points of its surface, is very nearly, as at the distance of the moon, equal to the mass of the earth, divided by the square of its distance from its centre of gravity. Under this parallel, the gravity is less than the attraction of the earth, by $\frac{2}{3}$* of the centrifugal force which arises from the motion of rotation at the equator; this force is the $\frac{1}{288}$th part of the force of gravity; consequently we must augment the preceding space by its 432d part, in order to obtain the entire space which is due to the action of the earth, which on this parallel, is equal to its mass divided by the square of the terrestrial radius; therefore this space will be equal to $3^{me},66394$. At the distance of the moon, it must be diminished in the ratio of the square of the radius of the spheroid of the earth, to the square of the distance of this star, to effect this, it is sufficient to multiply it by the square of the sine of the lunar parallax; therefore x representing this sine under the parallel above mentioned, we shall have $x^2.3^{me},66394$, for the height through which the moon ought to fall in a second, by the attraction of the earth. But we shall see in the theory of the moon, that the action of the sun diminishes its gravity towards the earth by a quantity, of which the constant part is†

* The centrifugal force at the equator is to the efficient part of the centrifugal force at any parallel, as the square of radius to the square of the cosine of latitude, *i. e.* in this case, as 1 to $\frac{2}{3}$, ∵ as the centrifugal force at the equator is the $\frac{1}{288}$th part of the gravity, the force at the parallel in question, will be $=\frac{2}{3}\cdot\frac{1}{288}=\frac{1}{432}$.

† m being the mass of the sun, and d its distance from the moon, a the radius of the moon's orbit, the addititious force $=\frac{ma}{d^3}$, and the part of the ablatitious force, which acts in the direction of the radius vector $=\frac{ma}{d^3}.3\sin.^2\varpi$, ϖ being the angular distance from quadrature, see Newton, Princip. Prop. 66; ∵ $\frac{ma}{d^3}(1-3\sin.^2\varpi)$ is the part of the sun's

equal to the $\frac{1}{358}$th part of this gravity; moreover, the moon, in its relative motion about the earth, is sollicited by a force equal to the sum of the masses* of the earth and moon, divided by the square of their mutual distance; it is therefore necessary to diminish the preceding space by its 358th part, and to increase it in the ratio of the sum the masses of the earth and moon, to the mass of the earth; but we shall see in the fourth book, that the mass of the moon deduced from the phenomena of the tides, is a $\frac{1}{58,7}$th part of the mass of the earth; therefore the space through which the moon descends towards the earth, in the interval of a second, is equal to $\frac{357}{358} \cdot \frac{59,7}{58,7} \cdot x^2 . 3^{me}.66394$.

Now a representing the mean radius of the lunar orbit, and T, the duration of a sidereal revolution of the moon, expressed in seconds;

disturbing force acting in the direction of the radius, which is efficient at any point; (hence it appears that it vanishes when $\sin.^2\varpi = \frac{1}{3}$, see Note, page 17); in order to obtain its mean quantity, multiply this expression by $d\varpi$ and it becomes $\frac{ma}{d^3}.(d\varpi - 3d\varpi . \sin.^2\varpi) = \frac{ma}{d^3}(d\varpi - \frac{3}{2}d\varpi + \frac{3}{2}d\varpi \cos. 2\varpi)$, and its integral $= \frac{ma}{d^3}(\varpi - \frac{3}{2}\varpi + \frac{3}{4}. \sin. 2\varpi) =$ for the entire circumference, *i.e.* when $\varpi = \pi$, $-\frac{ma}{d^3}.\frac{\pi}{2}$; ∴ the mean disturbing force $= -\frac{ma}{2d^3}$, but $\frac{m}{d^2} : F$ the force retaining the moon in its orbit $:: \frac{d}{T^2} : \frac{a}{T'^2}$ (T, T' are the periods of the sun and moon) ∴ $\frac{ma}{d^3} = \frac{T'^2 F}{T^2} = \frac{F}{179}$, for $\frac{T'^2}{T^2} = \frac{1}{179}$, and $-\frac{ma}{2d^3} = -\frac{F}{358}$, ∴ in consequence of the diminution of her gravity by the action of the disturbing force, the moon is sustained at a greater distance from the earth, than it would be if the action of the sun was removed, and as the mean area described in a given time in the primitive and disturbed orbits is the same, the radius vector is increased by a 358th part, and the angular velocity is diminished by a 179th part.

* The moon being considered as a point, if it revolved about the centre of the earth, in

$\frac{2a\pi^2}{T'^2}$ will be, as has been already observed, the versed sine of the arc which it describes during a second, and it expresses the quantity, by which the moon has descended towards the earth, in this interval. This value of a is equal to the radius of the earth, under the above mentioned parallel, divided by the sine of x; this radius is equal to 6369514me; therefore we have

$$a = \frac{6369514^{metre}}{x};$$

but in order to obtain a value of a, independent of the inequalities of the moon, it is necessary to assume for its mean parallax of which the sine is x, the part of this parallax, which is independent of these inequalities, and which has been therefore termed the *constant part of the parallax*. Thus, π representing the ratio of 355 to 113, and T' being $= 2732166''$; the mean space through which the moon descends towards the earth, will be

$$\frac{2.(355)^2.6369514^{me}}{(113)^2.x.(2732166)^2}.$$

the same time in which it revolves about the common centre of gravity of the earth and moon, the central force which should exist in the centre of the earth capable of effecting this, should be $=$ to the sum of the masses of the earth and moon; for a being the distance of the earth from the moon, and m,m' their respective masses, the distance y at which the moon would revolve round the earth by itself, considered as quiescent, is $= \frac{am^{\frac{1}{3}}}{(m+m')^{\frac{1}{3}}}$, see Prin. Math. Prop. 59, Book I. and $T'^2 = \frac{y^3}{m} = \frac{a^3}{m+m'}$, hence if a be the distance, the central force $= m+m'$, $\because$ as the versed sine of the arc described in a second is the space through which the moon descends in consequence of the combined actions of the earth and moon, this must be diminished in the ratio of $m : m+m'$ to obtain the space described in consequence of the sole action of m. The two corrections, which are here applied to the *space* through which a heavy body would descend at the latitude 35°16′, diminished in the ratio of the square of the distance, are in the *Systeme du Monde*, applied to the *versed sine* of the arc described in a second, hence it appears that they must be affected with contrary signs.

By equalling the two expressions, which we have found for this space, we shall have

$$x^3 = \frac{2.(355)^2.358.58,7.6369514}{(113)^2.357.59,7.3,66394(2732166)^2};$$

from which we obtain 10536″,2 for the constant part* of the lunar parallax, under the parallel in question. This value differs very little from the constant quantity 10540,7 which Triesnecker collected from a great number of observations of eclipses, and of † occultations of the stars by the moon; it is therefore certain that the *principal* force which retains the moon in its orbit, is the terrestrial gravity diminished in the ratio of the square of the distance; thus, the law of the diminution of gravity, which in the planets attended by several satellites, is proved by a comparison of the times of their revolutions, and of their distances, is

* In order to find the constant part of the parallax, we apply to the observed parallax, all the corrections which theory makes known, and we may perceive from this how the theory of gravity, by indicating the forces which act on the moon, furnishes us with the means of determining the mean motion, and the nature of the inequalities which act on it.

† If in a partial eclipse of the moon, the time be noted in which the two horns of the part which is not eclipsed, are observed to be in the same vertical line, it would be easy to shew that the height of the centre of the moon at this instant, will be the same as the height of the centre of the shadow; ∵ if at this instant the height of each of the horns be observed, the mean height, which will be the height of the centre of the shadow, will be the apparent height affected by the parallax; but as the centre of the shadow is diametrically opposite to the centre of the sun, the true height will be equal to the depression of the sun, which is known from the time of observation; ∵ the difference of these heights will be the parallax of the moon for the observed altitude, by means of which we can easily determine the greatest parallax; and if in a total and central eclipse, the height of the moon be observed *at the instant* that it is entirely immersed, and also when it *first* begins to emerge, the mean height will be the height of the centre of the shadow as it is affected by parallax.

In an occultation of a fixed star, the star's parallax vanishes, and the difference of apparent altitudes is = to the difference of the true altitudes + parallax in altitude of the moon; hence by the known formulæ we can obtain the true parallax. A constant ratio exists between the horizontal parallax, and the moon's apparent diameter at the same terrestrial latitude.

demonstrated for the moon, by comparing its motion with that of projectiles near the surface of the earth. It follows from this, that the origin of the distances of the sun, and of the planets, ought in the computation of their attractive forces, on bodies placed at their surface, or beyond it, to be fixed in the centre of gravity of these bodies; since this has been demonstrated to be the case for the earth, of which the attractive force is, as has been remarked, of the same nature with that of these stars.

6. The sun and the planets which are accompanied with satellites, are consequently endowed with an attractive force, which decreasing indefinitely, in the inverse ratio of the squares of the distances, comprehends all bodies in the sphere of its activity. Analogy would induce us to think, that a like force inheres generally in all the planets and in the comets; but we may be assured of it directly in the following manner. It is a constant law of nature, that one body cannot act on another, without experiencing an equal and contrary reaction; therefore the planets and comets being attracted towards the sun, they ought to attract this star according to the same law. For the same reason, the satellites attract their respective primary planets; consequently this attractive force is common to the planets, to the comets, and to the satellites, and therefore we may consider the gravitation of the heavenly bodies, towards* each other, as a general property which belongs to all the bodies of the universe.

We have seen, that it varies inversely as the square of the distance; indeed, this ratio is given by the laws of elliptic motion, which do not rigorously obtain in the celestial motions; but we should consider, that the simplest laws ought always to be preferred, unless observations compel us to abandon them; it is natural for us to suppose, in the first instance, that the law of gravitation is inversely as some power of the dis.

* Besides, it follows from the sphericity of these bodies that their molecules are united about their centres of gravity, by a force which at equal distances solicits them equally towards these points; the existence of this force is also indicated by the perturbations which the planetary motions experience.

tance, and by computation it has been found, that the slightest difference between this* power and the square, would be very perceptible in the position of the perihelia of the orbits of the planets, in which observation has indicated motions hardly perceptible, and of which we shall hereafter develope the cause. In general, we shall see throughout this treatise, that the law of gravitation inversely as the square of the distance, represents with the greatest precision all the observed inequalities of the motions of the heavenly bodies; this agreement, combined with the simplicity of this law, justifies us in assuming that it is rigorously the law of nature.

The gravitation is proportional to the masses; for it follows from No. 3, that the planets and comets being supposed at equal distances from the sun, and then remitted to their gravity towards this star, would fall through equal spaces, in the same time; consequently their gravity will be proportional to their mass. The motions almost circular of the satellites about their primaries, demonstrate that they gravitate as their primaries towards the sun, in the ratio of their masses; the slightest difference in this respect, would be perceptible in the motions of the† satellites, and observations have not indicated any inequality depending

* See No. 58 of this book; this also follows from Prop. 45, Book 1st, Prin. For if the force which is added to the force varying in the inverse ratio of the square of the distance be called X, the angular distance between the apsides $= 180.\frac{\sqrt{1+X}}{\sqrt{1+3X}} = 180.(1-X)$, the square of X being neglected, and conversely if the distance between the apsides be given, we can determine X. The force X is supposed to vary as the distance.

† See Newton Princip. Prop. 6, Book 3, where it is shewn, that if the satellite gravitated more towards the sun than the primary at equal distances from the sun, in the ratio of $d:c$, the distance of the centre of the sun from the centre of the orbit of the satellite, would be greater than the distance of the centre of the sun from the centre of the primary, in the ratio of $\sqrt{d}:\sqrt{c}$, $\because$ if the difference between d and c, was the thousandth part of the entire gravity, the distance of the centre of the orbit from the centre of the sun, would be greater than the distance of the centre of Jupiter from that of the sun, by a $\frac{1}{2000}$th part of the entire distance.

on this cause. Therefore it appears that if the comets, the planets and satellites, were placed at equal distances from the sun, they would gravitate towards this star, in the ratio of their masses; from which it follows, in consequence of the equality between action and reaction, that these stars must attract the sun, in the same ratio, and consequently their action on this star, is proportional to their* masses divided by the square of their distance from its centre.

The same law obtains on the earth; for from very exact experiments instituted by means of the pendulum, it has been ascertained, that if the resistance of the air was removed, all bodies would descend towards *its centre* with equal velocities; therefore bodies near the earth gravitate towards its centre, in the ratio of their masses, in the same manner as the planets gravitate towards the sun, and the satellites towards their primaries. This conformity of nature with itself on the earth, and in the immensity of the heavens, evinces in the most striking manner, that the

* The mutual attraction does not affect the elliptic motion of any *two* bodies when their mutual action is considered, for the relative motion is not affected when a common velocity is impressed on the bodies, ∵ if the motion which the sun has, and the action which it experiences on the part of the planet, be impressed in a contrary direction, on both the sun and the planet; the sun may be regarded as immovable, and the planet will be sollicited by a force ::' to the sum of the masses of the sun and planet, divided by the square of their mutual distance; ∵ the motion will be elliptic; but the periodic time will be less than if the planet did not act on the sun, for the ratio of the cube of the greater axis of the orbit to the square of the periodic time, is proportional to the sum of the masses of the sun and planet; however as this ratio of the square of the time to the cube of the distance, is very nearly the same for all the planets, it follows that the masses of the planets must be comparatively much smaller than the mass of the sun, which is confirmed by an estimation of their volumes. See No. 25, and Prop. 8, Lib. 3. Princip. Math. The comparative smallness of the masses is also confirmed by the laws which Kepler was enabled to announce, for these laws were deduced from observation, notwithstanding the various causes which disturb the elliptic motion; hence appears the reason why, in the commencement of this chapter, the sun was supposed to be immoveable, and to exert its action on the planets as on so many points, which do not react on the sun, neither was the mutual action of the planets on each other taken into account; the same simplifications were employed, when the motion of a satellite about its primary was considered.

gravity observed here on earth, is only a particular case of a general law, which obtains throughout the universe.

The attractive property of the heavenly bodies does not appertain to them solely in a mass, but is peculiar to each of their molecules. If the sun only acted on the centre of the earth, without attracting in particular each of its parts, there would be produced in the sea, oscillations much greater, and very different from those which we observe; therefore the gravity of the earth to the sun, is the result of the gravitations of all its molecules, which consequently attract the sun, in the ratio of their respective masses. Besides, each body on the earth gravitates towards its centre, proportionally to its mass; it reacts therefore on the earth, and attracts it in the same ratio. If this was not the case, and if any part of the earth, however small, did not attract the other part, as it is attracted by this other part, the centre of gravity of the earth would have a motion in space, in consequence of the force of gravity, which is impossible.

The celestial phenomena, compared with the laws of motion, conduct us therefore to this great principle of nature, namely, that all the molecules of matter mutually attract each other in the proportion of their masses, divided by the square of their distances. We may perceive already, in this *universal* gravitation, the cause of the perturbations, which the heavenly bodies experience; for the planets and comets being subject to their reciprocal action, ought to deviate a little from the laws of elliptic motion, which they would accurately follow, if they only obeyed the action of the sun. The satellites in like manner deranged in their motions about their primaries, by their mutual attraction, and by that of the sun, deviate from these laws. We may perceive also, that the molecules of each of the heavenly bodies, united by their attraction, should constitute a mass nearly spherical, and that the result of their action at the surface of the body, should produce all the phenomena of gravitation. We see moreover, that the motion of rotation of the heavenly bodies, should slightly alter the sphericity of their figure, and flatten them at the poles, and that then, the resultant of their mutual action, not passing accurately through their centres of gravity, ought to produce in their axes of rotation, motions similar to those, which are indicated by observation. Finally, we may perceive why the molecules of the ocean, unequally acted on by the sun and moon, ought to have an oscillatory motion, similar to the ebbing and flowing of the sea. But the developement of these different effects of universal gravitation, requires a profound analysis. In order to embrace them in all their generality, we proceed to give the differential equations of the motion of a system of bodies, subjected to their mutual attraction, and to investigate the exact integrals which may be derived from them. We will then take advantage of the facilities which the relations of the masses and distances of the heavenly bodies furnish us with, in order to obtain integrals more and more accurate, and thus to determine the celestial phenomena, with all the precision which the observations admit of.

CHAPTER II.

Of the differential equations of the motion of a system of bodies, subjected to their mutual attraction.

7. LET m, m', m'', &c. represent the masses of the different bodies of the system, considered as so many points; let x, y, z, be the rectangular coordinates of the body m; x', y', z', those of the body m', and corresponding expressions for the coordinates of the other bodies. The distance of m' from m being equal to

$$\sqrt{(x'-x)^2+(y'-y)^2+(z'-z)^2},$$

its action on m, will be, by the law of universal gravitation, equal to

$$\frac{m'}{(x'-x)^2+(y'-y)^2+(z'-z)^2}.$$

If we resolve this action, parallel to the axes of x, of y, and of z, the force parallel to the axis of x, and directed from the origin, will be

$$\frac{m'(x'-x)}{\{(x'-x)^2+(y'-y)^2+(z'-z)^2\}^{\frac{3}{2}}}\ *$$

* The force parallel to the axis of x : $\frac{m'}{(x'-x)^2+(y'-y)^2+(z'-z)^2}$ :: $x'-x)$: $\sqrt{(x'-x)^2+(y'-y)^2+(z'-z)^2}$; and if $\frac{mm'}{\sqrt{x'-x)^2+(y'-y)^2+(z'-z)^2}}$ be differenced with respect to x, and then divided by $m.dx$, it will become

$$=\frac{1}{m.dx}\cdot\left(\frac{mm'.(x'-x).dx}{((x'-x)^2+(y'-y)^2+(z-z)^2)^{\frac{3}{2}}}\right).$$

or

$$\frac{1}{m}.\left\{\frac{d.\frac{mm'}{\sqrt{(x'-x)^2+(y'-y)^2+(z'-z)^2}}}{dx}\right\}.$$

We shall have also,

$$\frac{1}{m}.\left\{\frac{d.\frac{mm''}{\sqrt{(x''-x)^2+(y''-y)^2+(z''-z)^2}}}{dx}\right\}$$

for the action of m'' on m, resolved parallel to the axis of x, and corresponding expressions for the other bodies of the system. Consequently if

$$\lambda=\frac{mm'}{\sqrt{(x'-x)^2+(y'-y)^2+(z'-z)^2}}+\frac{mm''}{\sqrt{(x''-x)^2+(y''-y)^2+(z''-z)^2}}$$

$$+\frac{m'm''}{\sqrt{(x''-x')^2+(y''-y')^2+(z''-z')^2}}+\ \&c.\ ;$$

λ representing the sum of the products of the masses m, m', m'', &c, taken two by two, and divided by their respective distances; $\frac{1}{m}.\left\{\frac{d\lambda}{dx}\right\}$ * will express the sum of the actions of the bodies m', m'', &c. on m, resolved parallel to the axis of x, and directed from the origin of

* $\frac{1}{m}.\left(\frac{d\lambda}{dx}\right)=\frac{1}{m}\left\{\frac{d.\frac{mm'}{\sqrt{(x'-x)^2+(y'-y)^2+(z'-z)^2}}}{dx}+\frac{d.\frac{mm''}{\sqrt{(x''-x)^2+(y''-y)^2+(z''-z)^2}}}{dx}+\&c.\right\}=\frac{m'.(x'-x)}{((x'-x)^2+(y'^2-y)^2+(z'-z)^2)^{\frac{3}{2}}}$ $+\frac{m''(x''-x)}{((x''-x)^2+(y''-y)^2+(z''-z)^2)^{\frac{3}{2}}}+\ \&c.$ = the sum of the actions of the bodies m', m'', m''', &c. on m, resolved parallel to the axis of x.

the coordinates. Therefore dt representing the element of the time, supposed constant; we shall have by the principles of dynamics, explained in the preceding book,

$$0 = m.\frac{d^2x}{dt^2} - \left\{\frac{d\lambda}{dx}\right\}.$$

In like manner we shall have

$$0 = m.\frac{d^2y}{dt^2} - \left\{\frac{d\lambda}{dy}\right\};$$

$$0 = m.\frac{d^2z}{dt^2} - \left\{\frac{d\lambda}{dz}\right\}.$$

If we consider, in the same manner, the action of the bodies m, m'', &c. on m'; that of the bodies m, m', on m'', and so of the rest, we shall have the following equations, namely,

$$0 = m'.\frac{d^2x'}{dt^2} - \left\{\frac{d\lambda}{dx'}\right\}; \quad 0 = m'.\frac{d^2y'}{dt^2} - \left\{\frac{d\lambda}{dy'}\right\};$$

$$0 = m'.\frac{d^2z'}{dt^2} - \left\{\frac{d\lambda}{dz'}\right\};$$

$$0 = m''.\frac{d^2x''}{dt^2} - \left\{\frac{d\lambda}{dx''}\right\}; \quad 0 = m''.\frac{d^2y''}{dt^2} - \left\{\frac{d\lambda}{dy''}\right\};$$

$$0 = m''.\frac{d^2z''}{dt^2} - \left\{\frac{d\lambda}{dz''}\right\}. \quad \&c.$$

The determination of the motions of m, m', m'', &c., depends on the integration of these differential equations; but as yet they have not been completely integrated, except in the case in which the system is composed of only two bodies. In other cases, we have not been able to obtain but a small number of perfect integrals, which we proceed to develope.

8. For this purpose, let us first consider the differential equations in x, x', x'', &c.; if we add them together, observing at the same time, that by the nature of the function λ, we have

$$0=\left\{\frac{d\lambda}{dx}\right\}+\left\{\frac{d\lambda}{dx'}\right\}+\left\{\frac{d\lambda}{dx''}\right\}+\&c.;^{*}$$

we shall obtain, $0=\Sigma.m.\frac{d^2x}{dt^2}$. We shall have also, $0=\Sigma.m.\frac{d^2y}{dt^2}$; $0=\Sigma.m.\frac{d^2z}{dt^2}$. Let X, Y, Z represent the three coordinates of the centre of gravity of the system; we shall have by the nature of this centre

$$X=\frac{\Sigma.mx}{\Sigma.m};\quad Y=\frac{\Sigma.my}{\Sigma.m};\quad Z=\frac{\Sigma.mz}{\Sigma.m};$$

therefore we shall have

$$0=\frac{d^2X}{dt^2};\quad 0=\frac{d^2Y}{dt^2};\quad 0=\frac{d^2Z}{dt^2};$$

and by integrating, we shall obtain

$$X=a+bt;\quad Y=a'+b't;\quad Z=a''+b''t;^{\dagger}$$

* Suppose that there are only three bodies, then $\Sigma.m.\frac{d^2x}{dt^2}=\left(\frac{d\lambda}{dx}\right)+\left(\frac{d\lambda}{dx'}\right)+\left(\frac{d\lambda}{dx''}\right)$ $=\frac{m'm.((x'-x)-(x'-x))}{((x'-x)^2+(y'-y)^2+(z'-z)^2)^{\frac{3}{2}}}+\frac{mm''((x''-x)-(x''-x))}{((x''-x)^2+(y''-y)^2+(z''-z)^2)^{\frac{3}{2}}}$ $+\frac{m''m'((x''-x')-(x''-x'))}{((x''-x')^2+(y''-y')^2+(z''-z')^2)^{\frac{3}{2}}}=0$; the same proof may be extended to any number of bodies.

† $X=\frac{\Sigma.mx}{\Sigma m}$, $\because$ $\frac{dX}{dt}=\Sigma.m.\frac{dx}{dt}\div\Sigma.m,$ $\frac{d^2X}{dt^2}=\Sigma.m,\frac{d^2x}{dt^2}\div\Sigma.m,=0$, and by inte-

a, a', a'', b, b', b'', being constant arbitrary quantities. We may perceive by this, that the motion of the centre of gravity of the system is rectilinear and uniform, and that consequently, it is not deranged by the reciprocal action of the bodies composing the system; which agrees with what has been demonstrated in the fifth chapter of the first book. Resuming the differential equations of the motion of these bodies, and multiplying the differential equations in y, y', y'', &c., respectively by x, x', x'', &c., and then adding them to the differential equations in x, x', x'', &c. multiplied respectively by $-y, -y', -y''$, &c.; we shall obtain

$$0 = m.\left\{\frac{xd^2y-yd^2x}{dt^2}\right\}+m'.\left\{\frac{x'.d^2y'-y'd^2x'}{dt^2}\right\}+$$

$$m''.\left\{\frac{x''d^2y''-y''d^2x''}{dt^2}\right\}+\text{\&c.}$$

$$+y.\left\{\frac{d\lambda}{dx}\right\}+y'.\left\{\frac{d\lambda}{dx'}\right\}+y''.\left\{\frac{d\lambda}{dx''}\right\}+\text{\&c.}$$

$$-x.\left\{\frac{d\lambda}{dy}\right\}-x'.\left\{\frac{d\lambda}{dy'}\right\}-x''.\left\{\frac{d\lambda}{dy''}\right\}-\text{\&c.};$$

but from the nature of the function λ, it is evident that

$$0=y.\left\{\frac{d\lambda}{dx}\right\}+y'.\left\{\frac{d\lambda}{dx'}\right\}+\text{\&c.}$$

$$-x.\left\{\frac{d\lambda}{dy}\right\}-x'.\left\{\frac{d\lambda}{dy'}\right\}-\text{\&c.};$$

grating,* $\frac{dX}{dt}=a$, and $X=at+b$, the constant quantity a depends on the velocity of the centre of gravity at the commencement of the motion, and b depends on the position of this centre, at the same instant.

consequently,* by integrating the preceding equation, we shall obtain

$$c = \Sigma.m.\left\{\frac{xdy-ydx}{dt}\right\}.$$

In like manner we shall have,

$$c' = \Sigma.m.\left\{\frac{xdz-zdx}{dt}\right\};$$

$$c'' = \Sigma.m.\left\{\frac{ydz-zdy}{dt}\right\};$$

c, c', c'', &c. being constant arbitrary quantities. These three integrals involve the principle of the conservation of areas, which has been explained in the fifth chapter of the first book.

Finally, if we multiply the differential equations in x, x', x'', &c., respectively by dx, dx', dx'', &c.; and those in y, y', y', &c. respectively by dy, dy', dy'', &c.; those in z, z', z'', &c., respectively by dz, dz', dz'', &c.; and then add them together, we shall obtain

$$0 = \Sigma.m.\frac{(dx.d^2x+dy.d^2y+dz.d^2z)}{dt^2} - d\lambda, \dagger$$

* Suppose that there are only three bodies, then $y\left(\frac{d\lambda}{dx}\right)+y'\left(\frac{d\lambda}{dx'}\right)+y''\left(\frac{d\lambda}{dx''}\right)-x\left(\frac{d\lambda}{dy}\right)-x'\left(\frac{d\lambda}{dy'}\right)-x''\left(\frac{d\lambda}{dy''}\right)=m.\left(\frac{xd^2y-yd^2x}{dt^2}\right)+m'.\left(\frac{x'd^2y'-y'd^2x'}{dt^2}\right)+m''.\left(\frac{x''d^2y''-y''d^2x''}{dt^2}\right)=\frac{mm'.(y(x'-x)-y'(x'-x))}{((x'-x)^2+(y'-y)^2+(z'-z)^2)^{\frac{3}{2}}}$

$$+\frac{mm''(y(x''-x)-y''(x''-x))}{((x''-x)^2+(y''-y)^2+(z''-z)^2)^{\frac{3}{2}}}+\frac{m''m'(\ )y'(x''-x')-y''(x''-x'))}{((x''-x')^2+(y''-y')^2+(z''-z')^2)^{\frac{3}{2}}}$$

$$-\frac{mm'(x(y'-y)-x'(y'-y))}{((x'-x)^2+(y-y)^2(z'-z)^2)^{\frac{3}{2}}}-\frac{mm''(x(y''-y)-x''(y'-y))}{((x''-x)^2+(y''-y)^2+(z''-z)^2)^{\frac{3}{2}}}$$

$$-\frac{m''m'(x'(y''-y')-x''(y''-y'))}{((x''-x')^2+(y''-y')^2+(z''-z')^2)^{\frac{3}{2}}}=0.$$

† By multiplying $\left\{\frac{d\lambda}{dx}\right\}$ $\left\{\frac{d\lambda}{dx'}\right\}$ + &c. by dx, dx', dx'', &c.; $\left\{\frac{d\lambda}{dy}\right\}$, $\left\{\frac{d\lambda}{dy'}\right\}$, +

and by integrating,

$$h = \Sigma.m.\left(\frac{dx^2+dy^2+dz^2}{dt^2}\right) - 2\lambda;$$

h being a new arbitrary quantity. This integral contains the principle of the conservation of living forces, which has been treated of in the fifth chapter of the first book.

The* seven preceding integrals are the only exact integrals, which we have hitherto been able to obtain; when the system is composed of only two bodies, the determination of their motions is reduced to differential equations of the first order, which can be integrated, as we will see in the sequel; but when the system is composed of three or a greater number of bodies, we are then obliged to recur to the methods of approximation.

9. As we can only observe the relative motions of bodies; we refer the motions of the planets and of the comets, to the centre of the sun, and the motions of the satellites, to the centre of their primaries. Therefore in order to compare the theory with observations, it is necessary to determine the relative motions of a system of bodies, about a body which is considered as the centre of their motions.

Let M represent this last body, m, m', m'', &c., being the other bodies, the relative motion of which about M, is required; Let ζ, Π and γ be the rectangular coordinates of M, $\zeta+x$, $\Pi+y$, $\gamma+z$, those of m; $\zeta+x'$, $\Pi+y'$, $\gamma+z'$, those of m', &c.; it is manifest that x, y, z, will be the coordinates of m, with respect to M; that x', y', z', will be those

&c. by dy, dy', dy'', &c. and then adding these quantities together, their aggregate is equal to the differential of λ considered as a function of x, x', &c. y, y', &c. z, z', &c., and $\because$ it is equal to $d\lambda$.

* Three of these integrals are furnished by the principle of the conservation of areas, three by the principle of the conservation of the motion of the centre of gravity, and one by the conservation of living forces.

of m' referred to the same body, and so of the rest. Let r, r', &c., represent the distances of m, m', &c. from the body M, so that

$$r = \sqrt{x^2+y^2+z^2}\,;\quad r' = \sqrt{x'^2+y'^2+z'^2}\,;\quad \&c.$$

and let us also suppose

$$\lambda = \frac{m'm}{\sqrt{(x'-x)^2+(y'-y)^2+(z'-z)^2}} +$$

$$\frac{mm''}{\sqrt{(x''-x)^2+(y''-y)^2+(z''-z)^2}}$$

$$+\frac{m'm''}{\sqrt{(x''-x')^2+(y''-y')^2+(z''-z')^2}} + \&c.$$

This being premised, the action of m on M, resolved parallel to the axis of x, and tending from the origin, will be $\frac{mx}{r^3}$; that of m' on M resolved in the same direction, will be $\frac{m'x'}{r'^3}$, and so of the other bodies of the system. Therefore, to determine ζ, we will have the following differential equation:

$$0 = \frac{d^2\zeta}{dt^2} - \Sigma.\frac{mx}{r^3}\,;$$

and in like manner,

$$0 = \frac{d^2\Pi}{dt^2} - \Sigma.\frac{my}{r^3},$$

$$0 = \frac{d^2\gamma}{dt^2} - \Sigma.\frac{mz}{r^3}.$$

The action of M on m, resolved parallel to the axis of x, and directed from the origin, will be $-\frac{Mx}{r^3}$, and the sum of the actions of the bodies m', m'', &c. on m, resolved in the same direction, will be $\frac{1}{m}.\left(\frac{d\lambda}{dx}\right)$; consequently, we will have

$$0=\frac{d^2(\zeta+x)}{dt^2}+\frac{Mx}{r^3}-\frac{1}{m}.\left\{\frac{d\lambda}{dx}\right\};*$$

and substituting in place of $\frac{d^2\zeta}{dt^2}$, its value $\Sigma.\frac{mx}{r^3}$, we will obtain

$$0=\frac{d^2x}{dt^2}+\frac{Mx}{r^3}+\Sigma.\frac{mx}{r^3}-\frac{1}{m}.\left\{\frac{d\lambda}{dx}\right\};\ (1)$$

in like manner, we will have

$$0=\frac{d^2y}{dt^2}+\frac{My}{r^3}+\Sigma.\frac{my}{r^3}-\frac{1}{m}.\left\{\frac{d\lambda}{dy}\right\};\ (2)$$

$$0=\frac{d^2z}{dt^2}+\frac{Mz}{r^3}+\Sigma.\frac{mz}{r^3}-\frac{1}{m}.\left\{\frac{d\lambda}{dz}\right\};\ (3)$$

* $\frac{1}{m}.\left\{\frac{d\lambda}{dx}\right\}$ is equal to the sum of the actions of the bodies m', m'', &c. on m, resolved parallel to the axis of x, ∵ if we add to this expression the action of M on m, which is equal to $-\frac{Mx}{r^3}$, we will have the actions of all bodies of the system on m, and ∵ by the principles of dynamics established in the first book, $\frac{d^2(\zeta+x)}{dt^2}+\frac{Mx}{r^3}-\frac{1}{m}.\left\{\frac{d\lambda}{dx}\right\}=0.$

If in the equations (1), (2), (3), we change successively the quantities m, x, y, z, into m', x', y', z'; m'', x'', y'', z'', &c.; and reciprocally, we will obtain the equations of the motion of the bodies m', m'', &c. about M.

If we multiply the differential equation in ζ, by $M+\Sigma.m.$; that in x, by m; that in x', by m', and performing similar operations on the other differential equations; by adding them together, and observing that by the nature of the function λ, we have

$$0=\left\{\frac{d\lambda}{dx}\right\}+\left\{\frac{d\lambda}{dx'}\right\}+\text{ \&c.};$$

we will obtain

$$0=(M+\Sigma.m).\frac{d^2\zeta}{dt^2}+\Sigma.m.\,\frac{d^2x}{dt^2};\ *$$

from which we obtain by integrating

* The differential equation in ζ, becomes by this multiplication, $(M+\Sigma.m.)\,\frac{d^2\zeta}{dt^2}$ $-M.\Sigma.\frac{mx}{r^3}-\Sigma.m.\Sigma.\frac{mx}{r^3}=0$; and if the differential equations in x, x', x'', &c. be multiplied by m, m', m'', &c., respectively, and then added together, their sum will be $=$ $\Sigma.m.\left\{\frac{d^2x}{dt^2}\right\}+M.\Sigma.\frac{mx}{r^3}+\Sigma.m.\Sigma.\frac{mx}{r^3}-\left\{\frac{d\lambda}{dx}\right\}-\left\{\frac{d\lambda}{dx'}\right\}-\left\{\frac{d\lambda}{dx''}\right\}-\text{\&c.}=0$, if this expression be added to the preceding, we will have, observing the quantities which destroy each other, and likewise those which are equal to cypher, $(M+\Sigma.m)\left\{\frac{d^2\zeta}{dt^2}\right\}+$ $\Sigma\,m.\left\{\frac{d^2x}{dt^2}\right\}=0$, and by integrating we have $(M+\Sigma.m.).\left\{\frac{d\zeta}{dt}\right\}+\Sigma.m.\left\{\frac{dx}{dt}\right\}=d$, $\therefore (M+\Sigma.m)\zeta+\Sigma.m.x=c+dt$, and $\therefore$ if $\frac{c}{M+\Sigma.m}=a\,\frac{d}{M+\Sigma.m}=b$, we shall have $\zeta=$ the expression given in the text.

$$\zeta = a + bt - \frac{\Sigma.m\,x}{M+\Sigma.m};$$

a and b being two constant arbitrary quantities. We will obtain also

$$\Pi = a'+b't - \frac{\Sigma.my}{M+\Sigma.m};$$

$$\gamma = a'' + b''t - \frac{\Sigma.mz}{M+\Sigma.m};$$

a', b', a'', b'', being constant arbitrary quantities: we shall thus obtain the absolute motion of M in space, when the relative motions of m, m', &c., about it, are known.

If we multiply the differential equation in x, by

$$-my+m.\frac{\Sigma.my}{M+\Sigma.m};$$

and the differential equation in y, by

$$mx-m.\frac{\Sigma.mx}{M+\Sigma.m};$$

and in like manner, the differential equation in x', by

$$-m'y'+m'.\frac{\Sigma.my}{M+\Sigma.m.};$$

and the differential equation in y', by

$$m'x' - m'.\frac{\Sigma.m.x}{M+\Sigma.m};$$

and if the same operations be performed on the coordinates of the other bodies of the system, by adding all these equations together, and observing that by the nature of the function λ,

$$0 = \Sigma.x.\left\{\frac{d\lambda}{dy}\right\} - \Sigma.y.\left\{\frac{d\lambda}{dx}\right\};$$

$$0 = \Sigma.\left\{\frac{d\lambda}{dx}\right\};\ 0 = \Sigma.\left\{\frac{d\lambda}{dy}\right\};$$

we will obtain

$$0 = \Sigma.m.\frac{(xd^2y - yd^2x)}{dt^2} - \frac{\Sigma.mx}{M + \Sigma.m}.\Sigma.m.\frac{d^2y}{dt^2} + \frac{\Sigma.my}{M + \Sigma.m}.\Sigma.m.\frac{d^2x}{dt^2};*$$

* Performing these operations, the differential equation in x becomes $= -my.\frac{d^2x}{dt^2} - M.m.\frac{yx}{r^3} - my\,\Sigma\frac{mx}{r^3} + y.\left\{\frac{d\lambda}{dx}\right\} + \frac{m}{M+\Sigma.m}.\frac{d^2x}{dt^2}.\Sigma.my. + \frac{Mmx}{r^3}.\frac{\Sigma\,my}{M+\Sigma.m} + \frac{m}{M+\Sigma.m}.\Sigma.\frac{mx}{r^3}.\Sigma.my - \frac{\Sigma.my}{M+\Sigma.m}.\left\{\frac{d\lambda}{dx}\right\}$; and corresponding operations being performed on the differential equations in x', x'', &c. we obtain, by adding them all together, $-\Sigma.my.\Sigma.\frac{d^2x}{dt^2} - M.\Sigma.m.\frac{yx}{r^3} - \Sigma.my\,\Sigma.\frac{mx}{r^3} + \Sigma.y.\left\{\frac{d\lambda}{dx}\right\} + \frac{\Sigma.my}{M+\Sigma.m}.\Sigma.m.\frac{d^2x}{dt^2} + \frac{\Sigma.my.M}{M+\Sigma.m}.\Sigma\frac{mx}{r^3} + \frac{\Sigma.m.\Sigma.my}{M+\Sigma.m}.\Sigma.\frac{mx}{r^3} - \frac{-\Sigma.my}{M+\Sigma.m}\Sigma.\left\{\frac{d\lambda}{dx}\right\}$; multiplying the differential equations in y, y', y'', &c. by $mx - m.\frac{\Sigma\,mx}{M+\Sigma.m}$, $m'x' - m'.\frac{\Sigma.mx}{M+\Sigma.m}$, &c., we obtain for the equation in y, $mx\frac{d^2y}{dt^2} + M.m.\frac{xy}{r^3} + mx.\Sigma.\frac{my}{r^3} - x.\left\{\frac{d\lambda}{dy}\right\} - \frac{m}{M+\Sigma.m}.\frac{d^2y}{dt^2}.\Sigma.mx. - \frac{mM}{M+\Sigma.m}.\frac{y}{r^3}.\Sigma.mx. - m.\frac{\Sigma.mx}{M+\Sigma.m}.\Sigma.\frac{my}{r^3} + \frac{\Sigma.mx}{M+\Sigma.m}.\left\{\frac{d\lambda}{dy}\right\}$; if the same operation be performed for the equations in y' and y'', &c. we obtain, by adding these equations, and concinnating

$$\Sigma.mx.\Sigma.\frac{d^2y}{dt^2} + M.\Sigma.\frac{m.xy}{r^3} + \Sigma.mx.\Sigma.\frac{my}{r^3} - \Sigma.x.\left\{\frac{d\lambda}{dy}\right\} - \frac{\Sigma.m.\frac{d^2y}{dt^2}.\Sigma.mx.}{M+\Sigma.m}.$$

of which equation the integral is

$$\text{Const}^{nt}. = \Sigma.m.\frac{(xdy-ydx)}{dt} - \frac{\Sigma.m.x}{M+\Sigma.m}.\Sigma.m.\frac{dy}{dt}$$

$$+\frac{\Sigma.my}{M+\Sigma.m}.\ \Sigma.m.\frac{dx}{dt};$$

or $c =$

$$M.\Sigma.m.\left\{\frac{xdy-ydx}{dt}\right\}+$$

$$\Sigma.mm'.\left\{\frac{(x'-x).(dy'-dy)-(y'-y.(dx'-dx)}{dt}\right\}; \quad (4)$$

$$-\frac{M}{M+\Sigma.m}.\Sigma.\frac{my}{r^3}.\Sigma.mx.-\frac{\Sigma.m.\Sigma.mx.}{M+\Sigma.m}.\Sigma.\frac{my}{r^3}+\frac{\Sigma.mx.\Sigma.\left\{\frac{d\lambda}{dy}\right\}}{M+\Sigma.m};$$

this equation being added to the equation obtained, by taking the sum of the equations in x, x', &c. gives

$$0=\Sigma.m.\left\{\frac{xd^2y-yd^2x}{dt^2}\right\}+\Sigma.\left\{y.\left\{\frac{d\lambda}{dx}\right\}-x.\left\{\frac{d\lambda}{dy}\right\}\right\}+$$

$$\left\{\frac{\Sigma.my.}{M+\Sigma.m}\Sigma.m.\frac{d^2x}{dt^2}-\frac{\Sigma.m.x}{M+\Sigma.m}\Sigma.m.\frac{d^2y}{dt^2}\right\}+\frac{\Sigma.mx.\Sigma.}{M+\Sigma.m}\left\{\frac{d\lambda}{dy}\right\}-\frac{\Sigma.my.\Sigma.}{M+\Sigma.m}\left\{\frac{d\lambda}{dx}\right\},$$

the quantities which destroy each other, by the opposition of signs are omitted.

$\Sigma.\left\{y.\left\{\frac{d\lambda}{dx}\right\}-x.\left\{\frac{d\lambda}{dy}\right\}\right\}=0$, and $\Sigma.\left\{\frac{d\lambda}{dx}\right\}=0$, $\Sigma.\left\{\frac{d\lambda}{dy}\right\}=0$, see page 31.

The first term of the second member of this equation is evidently an exact differential, see page 2, and the integral of the remaining terms which do not vanish $=\frac{\Sigma.my}{M+\Sigma.m}.\Sigma.m.\frac{dx}{dt}-$

$$\int\frac{\Sigma.m.dy}{M+\Sigma.m}.\Sigma.m.\frac{dx}{dt}-\frac{\Sigma.m.x}{M+\Sigma.m}.\Sigma.m.\frac{dy}{dt}+\int\frac{\Sigma.mdx}{M+\Sigma.m}.\Sigma.m.\frac{dy}{dt}.$$

c being* a constant arbitrary quantity. By a similar process we may obtain the two following integrals :

* If there are but three bodies

$$\text{const.} = m.\left\{\frac{xdy-ydx}{dt}\right\} + m'.\left\{\frac{x'dy'-y'dx'}{dt}\right\} + m''.\left\{\frac{x''dy''-y''dx''}{dt}\right\} -$$

$$\frac{mx}{M+m+m'+m''}.\frac{mdy}{dt} - \frac{m'x'.m'dy'}{(M+m+m'+m'')dt} - \frac{m''x''.m''dy''}{(M+m+m'+m'')dt} - \frac{mx.m'dy'}{(M+m+m'+m'')dt} -$$

$$\frac{mx.m''dy''}{(M+m+m'+m'')dt} - \frac{m'x'.mdy}{(M+m+m'+m'')dt} - \frac{m'x'.m''dy''}{(M+m+m'+m'').dt} - \frac{m''x''.mdy}{(M+m+m'+m'')dt} -$$

$$\frac{m''x''.m'dy'}{(M+m+m'+m'').dt} + \frac{my.mdx}{(M+m+m'+m'')dt} + \frac{m'y'.m'dx'}{(M+m+m'+m'')dt} + \frac{m''y''.m''dx''}{(M+m+m'+m'')dt}$$

$$+ \frac{my.m'dx'}{(M+m+m'+m'')dt} + \frac{my.m''dx''}{(M+m+m'+m'')dt} + \frac{m'y'.mdx}{(M+m+m'+m'')dt} + \frac{m'y'.m''dx''}{(M+m+m'+m'')dt}$$

$$+ \frac{m''y''.mdx}{(M+m+m'+m'').dt} + \frac{m''y''.m'dx'}{(M+m+m'+m'')dt}$$; multiplying both sides of this equation by $M+\Sigma.m.$ we have

$$M+\Sigma.m.\ \text{Const.} = M.\left\{m.\frac{(xdy-ydx)}{dt} + m'\frac{(x'dy'-y'dx')}{dt} + m''.\frac{(x''dy''-y''dx'')}{dt}\right\} +$$

$$mm'.\frac{(xdy-ydx+x'dy'-y'dx')}{dt} + mm''.\frac{(xdy-ydx+x''dy''-y''dx'')}{dt},$$

$$+ m'm''.\frac{(x'dy'-y'dx'+x''dy''-y''dx'')}{dt} + m^2.\frac{(xdy-ydx)}{dt} + m'^2.\frac{(x'dy'-y'dx')}{dt}$$

$$+ m''^2.\frac{(x''dy''-y''dx'')}{dt} - m^2.\frac{(xdy-ydx)}{dt} - m'^2.\frac{(x'dy'-y'dx')}{dt} - m''^2.\frac{(x''dy''-y''dx'')}{dt}$$

$$+ mm'.\frac{(ydx'-xdy')}{dt} + mm''.\frac{(ydx''-xdy'')}{dt} + mm'.\frac{(y'dx-x'dy)}{dt}$$

$$+ m'm''.\frac{(y'dx''-x'dy'')}{dt} + mm''.\frac{(y''dx-x''dy)}{dt} + m''m'.\frac{(y''dx'-x''dy')}{dt};$$ But

$$mm'.\frac{(xdy-ydx+x'dy'-y'dx')}{dt} + mm'.\frac{(ydx'-xdy')}{dt} + mm'.\frac{(y'dx-x'dy)}{dt} + \&c. =$$

$$mm'.\frac{((x'-x)(dy'-dy)-(y'-y).(dx'-dx))}{dt},$$ ∵ making the factors of mm'', $m'm''$, &c.

$$c' = M.\Sigma.m.\frac{(xdz - zdx)}{dt} +$$

$$\Sigma.mm'.\left\{\frac{(x'-x).(dz'-dz)-(z'-z).(dx'-dx)}{dt}\right\}; \quad (5)$$

$$c'' = M.\Sigma.m.\frac{(ydz - zdy)}{dt} +$$

$$\Sigma.mm'.\left\{\frac{(y'-y).(dz'-dz)-(z'-z).(dy'-dy)}{dt}\right\}; \quad (6)$$

c' and c'' being two new arbitrary quantities.

If we multiply the differential equation in x, by

$$2mdx - 2m.\frac{\Sigma.m.dx}{M+\Sigma.m};$$

the differential equation in y, by

$$2mdy - 2m.\frac{\Sigma.m.dy}{M+\Sigma.m};$$

the differential equation in z, by

$$2mdz - 2m.\frac{\Sigma.m.dz}{M+\Sigma.m};$$

and if, in like manner, we multiply the differential equation in x', by

also to coalese, and obliterating the quantities which destroy each other, we have $(M+\Sigma.m)$. Const. $= c =$ the second member of the equation in the text, it is evident that the same proof is applicable to any number of bodies.

$$2m'.dx'.-2m'.\frac{\Sigma.m.dx}{M+\Sigma.m};$$

the differential equation in y', by

$$2m'.dy'.-2m'.\frac{\Sigma.m.dy}{M+\Sigma.m};$$

the differential equation in z', by

$$2m'.dz'.-2m'.\frac{\Sigma.m.dz}{M+\Sigma.m};$$

and so of the other bodies; if we then add together these different equations, observing that

$$0=\Sigma.\left\{\frac{d\lambda}{dx}\right\};\ 0=\Sigma.\left\{\frac{d\lambda}{dy}\right\};\ 0=\Sigma.\left\{\frac{d\lambda}{dz}\right\};$$

we will obtain

$$0=2\Sigma.m.\frac{(dx.d^2x+dy.d^2y+dz.d^2z)}{dt^2}-\frac{2\Sigma.mdx}{M+\Sigma.m}.\Sigma.m.\frac{d^2x}{dt^2}.$$

$$-\frac{2\Sigma.m.dy}{M+\Sigma.m}.\Sigma.m.\frac{d^2y}{dt^2}-\frac{2\Sigma.m.dz}{M+\Sigma.m}.\Sigma.m.\frac{d^2z}{dt^2}+2M.\Sigma.\frac{mdr}{r^2}-2d\lambda;\text{*}$$

* The differential equation in x, being multiplied by this quantity becomes = $2m.\frac{dx.d^2x}{dt^2}+M.\frac{2mx\,dx}{r^3}+2mdx.\Sigma.\frac{mx}{r^3}-2.\left(\frac{d\lambda}{dx}\right)dx-\frac{2\Sigma.mdx}{M+\Sigma.m}.m.\frac{d^2x}{dt^2}-\frac{2M}{M+\Sigma.m}.\frac{mx}{r^3}\Sigma.mdx.-\frac{2m}{M+\Sigma.m}\Sigma.mdx.\Sigma.\frac{mx}{r^3}+\frac{2}{M+\Sigma\,m}.\Sigma.mdx.\left(\frac{d\lambda}{dx}\right)$, if corresponding operations be performed on the differential equations in x', x'', &c. we will obtain by adding them together,

$$2\Sigma.m.\frac{dx.d^2x}{dt^2}+M.2\Sigma.\frac{mxdx}{r^3}+2\Sigma.mdx.\Sigma.\frac{mx}{r^3}-2\Sigma.\left\{\frac{d\lambda}{dx}\right\}dx-$$

which gives by integrating

$$\text{const.} = \Sigma.m.\frac{(dx^2+dy^2+dz^2)}{dt^2} \quad \frac{-(\Sigma.mdx)^2-(\Sigma.mdy)^2-(\Sigma.mdz)^2}{(M+\Sigma.m)dt^2}$$

$$-2M.\Sigma.\frac{m}{r} - 2\lambda,$$

or

$$h=M.\Sigma.m.\frac{(dx^2+dy^2+dz^2)}{dt^2}+$$

$$\Sigma.mm'.\left\{\frac{(dx'-dx)^2+(dy'-dy)^2+(dz'-dz)^2}{dt^2}\right\}^*$$

G 2

$$\frac{2\Sigma.mdx.\Sigma.m.\frac{d^2x}{dt^2}}{M+\Sigma.m}-\frac{2M}{M+\Sigma.m}.\Sigma.mdx.\Sigma.\frac{mx}{r^3}-\frac{2.\Sigma.m}{M+\Sigma.m}.\Sigma.mdx.\Sigma.\frac{mx}{r^3}+\frac{2}{M+\Sigma.m}.\Sigma.mdx.\Sigma.$$

$\left\{\frac{d\lambda}{dx}\right\}$, this equation by reducing, and observing that $-\frac{2M}{M+\Sigma.m}.\ \Sigma.mdx.\Sigma.\frac{mx}{r^3}$ $-\frac{2\Sigma.m}{M+\Sigma.m}.\Sigma.mdx.\Sigma.\frac{mx}{r^3}=-2\Sigma.mdx.\Sigma.\frac{mx}{r^3}$, and also that $\frac{2}{M+\Sigma.m}.\ \Sigma.mdx.\Sigma,\ \frac{d\lambda}{dx}=0$, becomes

$$2\Sigma.mdx.\frac{d^2x}{dt^2}+M.2\Sigma.\frac{mxdx}{r^3}-2\Sigma.\left\{\frac{d\lambda}{dx}\right\}.dx-\frac{2\Sigma.\ mdx.\Sigma.m.\frac{d^2x}{dt^2}}{M+\Sigma.m};$$

if this equation be added to the differential equations, which result by performing corresponding operations on the equations in y, y', y'', &c. z, z', z'', &c., observing also that $2xdx+2ydy+2zdz=2rdr$, we shall obtain the differential equation of the text.

$$\Sigma.\left\{\frac{d\lambda}{dx}\right\}.dx+\Sigma.\left\{\frac{d\lambda}{dy}\right\}.dy+\Sigma.\left\{\frac{d\lambda}{dz}\right\}.dz=d\lambda$$ see page 28.

* If there are but three bodies, we have by multiplying by $(M+m+m'+m'')$; Const. $.(M+m+m'+m'')=h$; and if we only consider the coordinates parallel to the axis of x, we will have $M(mdx^2+m'dx'^2+m''dx''^2)+(m+m'+m'')$. $(mdx^2+m'dx'^2+m''dx''^2)-\overline{(m+m'+m'')dx+dx'+dx'')}^2 = M.\Sigma.mdx^2+m^2dx^2+m'^2dx'^2+m''^2dx''^2+mm'dx^2+mm'dx'^2+mm''dx^2+mm''dx''^2+m'm''dx'^2+m'm''dx''^2-m^2dx^2-m'^2dx'^2-m''^2dx''^2-2mm'dxdx'-2mm''dxdx''-2m'm''dx'dx''.=M.\Sigma.mdx^2+mm'(dx-dx')^2+(mm''.(dx-dx'')^2+m'm''.(dx'-dx'')^2, =M\Sigma\,mdx^2+\Sigma.mm'(dx'-dx)^2$; similar expressions may be obtained for the differentials of the coordinates parallel to the axes of z and y, and if to these be added $-(2M.\Sigma.m+2\lambda)$ multiplied by $M+\Sigma.m$, we will have the expression in the text.

$$-\left\{2M.\Sigma.\frac{m}{r}+2\lambda\right\}.(M+\Sigma.m); \quad (7)$$

h being a constant arbitrary quantity. These different integrals were already obtained in the fifth chapter of the first book, relatively to a system of bodies which react on each other in any manner; but considering their utility in the theory of the system of the world, we thought it necessary to demonstrate them here again.

10. The preceding being the only integrals which have been obtained in the actual state of analysis; we are compelled to recur to the methods of approximation, and to avail ourselves of the facilities which the constitution of the system of the world furnishes us with for this object. One of the greatest arises from the circumstance of the solar system being distributed into partial systems, composed of the planets and their respective satellites; these systems are so constituted that the distances of the satellites from their primaries, are considerably less than the distance of the primary from the sun; it follows from this, that the action of the sun, being very nearly the same on the primary and on the satellites, they move very nearly in the same manner, as if they were only subject to the action of the primary. The following remarkable property also follows, from this arrangement of the planets and satellites, namely, that the motion of the centre of gravity of a planet, and of its satellites, is very nearly the same,* as if all these bodies were concentrated in this centre.

In order to demonstrate this, let us suppose that the mutual distances of the bodies m, m', &c. are very small, compared with the distance of their centre of gravity, from the body M. Let

$$x=X+x_,;\ y=Y+y_,;\ z=Z+z_,;$$

$$x'=X+x'_,;\ y'=Y+y'_,;\ z=Z+z'_,;$$
&c.;

* See Princip. Math. Lib. 1st. Prop. 65.

X, Y, Z, being the coordinates of the centre of gravity of the system of bodies m, m', m'', &c.; the origin of these coordinates, as also that of the coordinates, x, y, z, x', y', z', &c., being at the centre of M. It is manifest that $x_{\prime}$, $y_{\prime}$, $z_{\prime}$, $x'_{\prime}$, &c. will be the coordinates of m, m', &c. relatively to their common centre of gravity; we shall suppose these to be very small quantities of the first order, in relation to X, Y, Z. This being premised, we will obtain, as we have seen in the first book, the force which solicits the centre of gravity of the system parallel to any right line, by taking the sum of the forces, which solicit the bodies parallel to this line, multiplied respectively by their masses, and then dividing this sum by the sum of the masses. Moreover, we have seen in the same book, that the mutual action of bodies connected together in any manner, does not derange the motion of the centre of gravity of the system; and by No. 8, the mutual attraction of those bodies, does not alter this motion, consequently, in the investigation of the forces, which actuate the centre of gravity of the system, it is sufficient to consider the action of the body M, which does not belong to this system.

The action of the body M on m, resolved parallel to the axis of x, and in a direction tending from the origin is $-\frac{Mx}{r^3}$, therefore the entire force which sollicits the centre of gravity of the system of bodies m, m', &c. parallel to this line, is*

$$\frac{-M.\Sigma.\frac{mx}{r^3}}{\Sigma.m},$$

and by substituting in place of x and of r, their values, we have

* By what has been stated in No. 20 of the first book, it appears that $\frac{d^2X}{dt^2}=\frac{\Sigma.mP}{\Sigma.m}$; now in the present case $\Sigma.m.P=-M\Sigma.\frac{mx}{r^3}$, for $P=-\frac{Mx}{r^3}$.

$$\frac{x}{r^3} = \frac{X+x_{,}}{((X+x_{,})^2+(Y+y_{,})^2+(Z+z_{,})^2)^{\frac{3}{2}}}.$$

If we neglect very small quantities of the second order, namely the squares, and the products of the variables $x_{,}$, $y_{,}$, $z_{,}$, $x'_{,}$, &c.; and if we denote by R, the distance $\sqrt{X^2+Y^2+Z^2}$, of the centre of gravity of the system, from the body M; we shall obtain

$$\frac{x}{r^3} = \frac{X}{R^3} + \frac{x_{,}}{R^3} - 3X.\frac{(Xx_{,}+Yy_{,}+Zz_{,})}{R^5},*$$

we shall have the values of $\frac{x'}{r'^3}$, $\frac{x''}{r''^3}$, &c. by distinguishing the letters x, y, z, &c. by one, two accents, &c.; but by the nature of the centre of gravity,

$$0=\Sigma.mx_{,};\ 0=\Sigma.my_{,};\ 0=\Sigma\,mz_{,};$$

therefore we will have, neglecting quantities of the second order,

$$-\frac{M.\Sigma.\frac{mx}{r^3}}{\Sigma.m} = -\frac{MX}{R^3};$$

* $\frac{X+x_{,}}{((X+x_{,})^2+(Y+y_{,})^2+(Z+z_{,})^2)^{\frac{3}{2}}} = (X+x_{,})((X+x_{,})^2+(Y+y_{,})^2+(Z+z_{,})^2)^{-\frac{3}{2}} =$ by neglecting quantities very small of the second order, $X.(X^2+2Xx_{,}+Y^2+2Yy_{,}+Z^2+2Zz_{,})^{-\frac{3}{2}}+x_{,}(X^2+Y^2+Z^2)^{-\frac{3}{2}} = X(X^2+Y^2+Z^2)^{-\frac{3}{2}} - \frac{3}{2}X.(2Xx_{,}+2Yy_{,}+2Zz_{,})R^{5}$ $+x_{,}(X^2+Y^2+Z^2)^{-\frac{3}{2}} =$ (by substituting R^2 for $X^2+Y^2+Z^2$) $\frac{X}{R^3}+\frac{x_{,}}{R^3}-3X.\frac{(Xx_{,}+Yy_{,}+Zz_{,})}{R^5}$; ∵ as $\Sigma.mx_{,}=0$, $\Sigma.my_{,}=0$, $\Sigma.mz_{,}=0$, $-\frac{M\Sigma.\frac{mx}{r^3}}{\Sigma\,m} = \left(-\frac{MX.\Sigma.m}{R^3\Sigma.m} - \frac{\Sigma.mx_{,}}{R^3.\Sigma.m} + 3X.\frac{(X\Sigma.mx_{,}+Y\Sigma.my_{,}+Z\Sigma.mz_{,})}{R^5\Sigma.m}\right) = -\frac{MX}{R^3}$, for the two last terms of the second member of this equation vanish.

consequently, the centre of gravity of the system is sollicited by the action of the body M parallel to the axis of x, in very nearly the same manner as if all bodies of the system were concentrated in this centre. The same conclusion evidently obtains for the axes of y and of z, so that the forces by which the centre of gravity of the system is actuated parallel to these axes, by the action of M, are $-\frac{MY}{R^3}$, $-\frac{MZ}{R^3}$.

When we consider the relative motion of the centre of gravity of the system about M, we should transfer in an opposite direction, the force which sollicits this body. This force resulting from the action of m, m', m'', &c. on M, resolved parallel to x, and acting in a direction tending from their origin, is $\Sigma.\frac{mx}{r^3}$; if quantities of the second order are neglected, this function is by what precedes, equal to

$$\frac{X.\Sigma.m}{R^3}.$$

In like manner, the forces by which M is sollicited, in consequence of the action of the system, parallel to the axes of y and of z, in a direction tending from the origin, are

$$\frac{Y.\Sigma.m}{R^3}, \text{ and } \frac{Z.\Sigma.m}{R^3}.$$

It appears from this, that the action of the system on the body M, is very nearly the same, as if all the bodies were condensed in their common centre of gravity. By transferring to this centre, and with a contrary sign, the three preceding forces; this point will be sollicited parallel to the axes of x, of y, and of z, in its relative motion round M, by the three following forces:

$$-(M+\Sigma.m).\frac{X}{R^3}; \quad -(M+\Sigma.m).\frac{Y}{R^3}; \quad -(M+\Sigma.m).\frac{Z}{R^3}.$$

These forces are the same as if all the bodies m, m', m'', &c. were united in their common centre of gravity;* consequently neglecting very small quantities of the second order, this centre moves as if all the bodies were concentrated in this point.

* The action of m on M resolved parallel to the axis of $x = \frac{mx}{r^3}$, ∵ the sum of the actions of all the bodies m, m', m'', &c. on M; $= \Sigma.\frac{mx}{r^3}$, = by what precedes $\frac{X.\Sigma\, m}{R^3}$; ∵ if this action be transferred to the centre of gravity, with a contrary sign, this centre in its relative motion about M, will be sollicited parallel to the axis of x, by the force $-(M+\Sigma.m).\frac{X}{R^3}$; now if all the bodies m, m', m'', &c. were concentrated in their common centre of gravity, this centre would be acted on parallel to axis of x, by the force $-(M+\Sigma.m)X$, ∵ this centre moves as if all the bodies were concentrated in it, consequently it describes very nearly an ellipse about M, the quantities which are neglected are of the order of the square and higher powers of x, and it is easy to shew, that the aberration of the force, by which the common centre of gravity is sollicited, from the inverse ratio of the square of the distance, is much less than the aberration of the forces sollicititing any of the bodies composing the system, from the inverse square of the distance. For if there are but three bodies, and if the distance of the *greatest* M from the remaining m and m', be much greater than the distance of m from m', then if R be the distance of M from the common centre of gravity of m and m', p and q the distances of this centre from m and m', respectively, and ϖ the angle which $r=p+q$, makes with R, the distance of M from m, $= R-p.\cos.\varpi$, the distance of M from m' $= R+q.\cos.\varpi$, ∵ the attraction of M on m, resolved parallel to $R = \frac{MR}{(R-p\cos\varpi)^3} = MR(R^{-3}+3R^{-4}p.\cos.\varpi+6R^{-5}p^2\cos.^2\varpi+\&c. = \frac{M}{R^2}+\frac{3Mp.\cos.\varpi}{R^3}+\frac{6Mp^2.\cos.^2\varpi)}{R^4}+\&c.$; in like manner, the action of M on m', resolved parallel to $R = \frac{MR}{(R+q.\cos.\varpi)^3}$, $= \frac{M}{R^2}-\frac{3Mq.\cos.\varpi}{R^3}+\frac{6Mq^2.\cos.^2\varpi}{R^4}$, $-$&c. now we know from what has been already established in the first book, that the accelerating force by which the centre of gravity of m and m', is sollicited in the direction of R, is obtained by dividing the sum of the motive forces, by which m and m' are sollicited in this direction, by $m+m'$, ∵ this force is = to

$$\left\{\frac{MmR}{(R-p.\cos.\varpi)^3}+\frac{Mm'R}{(R+q.\cos.\varpi)^3}\right\}.\frac{1}{m+m'} = \text{by substitution}$$

It follows from what precedes, that if there are several systems, of which the centres of gravity are at considerable distances from each other, compared with the respective distances of the bodies of each

$$\left\{\frac{Mm}{R^2}+\frac{3Mmp.\cos.\varpi}{R^3}+\frac{6Mmp^2.\cos.^2\varpi}{R^4}+\&c.+\frac{Mm'}{R^2}-\frac{3Mm'q.\cos.\varpi}{R^3}\right.$$
$$\left.+\frac{6Mm'q^2.\cos.^2\varpi}{R^4}+\&c.\right\}.\frac{1}{m+m'}=\frac{M}{R^2}.\frac{m+m'}{m+m'}+\frac{3M.\cos.\varpi}{R^3.(m+m')}.(mp-m'q)$$

$+\frac{6M\cos.^2\varpi}{R^4(m+m')}.(mp^2+m'q^2)+$ &c., the first term gives the law of elliptic motion; the second term vanishes by the nature of the centre of gravity, ∵ the third and following terms are those which cause an aberration from the law of elliptic motion in the centre of gravity. The actions of m and m' on M, resolved parallel to R, are respectively $\frac{mR}{(R-p.\cos.\varpi)^3}$, $\frac{m'R}{(R+q.\cos.\varpi)^3}$, which become by reducing, $\frac{m}{R^2}$, $\frac{m'}{R^2}$, and if these be transferred to M with a contrary sign, the entire force by which the centre is urged, is $\frac{M+m+m'}{R^2}$. It appears from this discussion that the centre of gravity of the earth and moon describes very nearly an ellipse about the sun; now a comparison of this expression, with that which gives the action of M on m, disturbed by the action of m' on M and on m, shews that the curve described by the centre of gravity, approaches much nearer to an ellipse than the curve described by m, for the force on m, acting in the direction of $R-p.\cos.\varpi$ $=\frac{M+m}{(R-p\cos.\varpi)^2}+\frac{m'.(R-p.\cos.\varpi)}{r^3}+m'.\left\{\frac{1}{(R+q.\cos.\varpi)^2}-\frac{R+q.\cos.\varpi}{r^3}\right\}.$ $\cos.\theta$, θ being the angle at which r is inclined to a radius drawn from M to m, this expression becomes by rejecting very small quantities of the second and higher orders, $\frac{M+m+m'}{(R-p.\cos.\varpi)^2}+\frac{m'.\cos.\theta}{(R+q.\cos.\varpi)^2}$, and the last term is evidently greater than $\frac{6M.\cos.^2\varpi}{R^4}.\frac{mp^2+m'q^2}{m+m'}$. The force which is perpendicular to $R-p.\cos.\varpi$ is equal to $m'.\left\{\frac{R+q.\cos.\varpi}{r^3}-\frac{1}{(R+q.\cos.\varpi)^2}\right\}.\sin.\theta=$ by reducing $\frac{m'.\sin.\theta}{(R+q.\cos.\varpi)^2}$; but if the force of M on m, be resolved parallel to r it will be $=\frac{Mp}{(R-p.\cos.\varpi)^3}$, and the force of M on m' parallel to $r=\frac{Mq}{(R+q.\cos.\varpi)^3}$, ∵ the accelerating force on the centre of gravity parallel to $r=\left\{\frac{Mmp}{(R-p.\cos.\varpi)^3}-\frac{Mm'.q}{(R+q.\cos.\varpi)^3}\right\}\frac{1}{m+m'}=\left\{\frac{Mmp}{R^3}\right.$ $\left.+\frac{3Mmp^2.\cos.\varpi}{R^4}-\frac{Mm'q}{R^3}+\frac{3Mm'q.^2\cos.\varpi}{R^4}\right\}\frac{1}{m+m'}=$ because $mp-m'q=0$, $\frac{3M\cos\varpi}{R^4(m+m')}(mp^2+m'q^2)$; the part of *this* force which is perpendicular to R disturbs the

system ; these centres will move very nearly in the same manner, as if the bodies of the respective systems were concentrated in them ; for the action of the first system on each body of the second system, is, by what precedes, very nearly the same, as if all the bodies of the first system were united in their common centre of gravity ; the action of the first system on the centre of gravity of the second, will, therefore, by what has been just established, be the same as in this hypothesis, from which we may conclude generally, that the reciprocal action of different systems, on their respective centres of gravity, is the same as if the bodies of each system

proportionality of the areas described by the centre of gravity to the times, and it is evidently less than $\frac{m'. \sin. \theta}{(R+q. \cos. \varpi)^2}$, See Princip. Math. Lib. 1. Prop. 66. Cor. 3, 4, &c.

The distance of the centre of gravity from M differs from the distance of m from M resolved parallel to R, by $p. \cos. \varpi, = \frac{m'}{m+m'}. r. \cos. \varpi.$ (by the nature of the centre of gravity). In like manner the abberration in longitude $=p. \sin. \varpi = \frac{m'}{m+m'}. r. \sin. \varpi$, ∴ it varies as the sine of the angle of elongation of M from m ; if s be the tangent of the latitude of the earth, the distance of the earth from the plane passing through M and the centre of gravity of m and m', $= sp = rs. \frac{m'}{m+m'}$, now $s = \tan. \phi. \sin. (v-\theta)$, φ being the inclination of the orbit of the moon to the above mentioned plane, and $v-\theta$ being = to the distance of the moon from her node. The distance from this plane, as seen from the $M = \frac{m'}{m+m'}. \frac{rs}{R}$. See Book 7, and Newton Princip. Math. Prop. 65, 66, 67, 68. What has been stated at the commencement of this note, shews the truth of Newton's 65 and 67 Prop. Lib. 1. And it would be easy to demonstrate, as Newton states in Prop. 64, that when the force varies as the distance, the centre of gravity describes an *accurate* ellipse about M, for the force solliciting m parallel to the axis of x, $= -Mx$, ∵ the force which solicits the centre of gravity parallel to this axis, $- \frac{M.\Sigma.mx}{\Sigma.m} = -MX - \frac{M.\Sigma mx_{,}}{\Sigma m}$, now this last term vanishes, if we add to this force, the force $\Sigma.mx = X\Sigma.m + \Sigma.m.x_{,}$ by which M is sollicited in a contrary direction, the entire force on the centre of gravity parallel to this axis $= -(M+\Sigma.m.)X$, ∵ the centre of gravity describes an accurate ellipse, and m describes an ellipse about the common centre of gravity of M and m' ; the periodic time in this ellipse depends on the number of bodies composing the system, and it varies inversly as the square root of the sum of the masses.

were concentrated in them, and that consequently those centres move, as they would do, in the case of this concentration. It is manifest, that this conclusion equally obtains, whether the bodies of each system are free, or connected together in any manner whatever, because their mutual action does not affect the motion of their common centre of gravity.

Therefore, the system of a planet and its satellites acts very nearly in the same manner on the other bodies of the solar system, as if the planet and its satellites were united in their common centre of gravity; and this centre is attracted by the several bodies of the solar system, as in this hypothesis.

Each of the heavenly bodies, being composed of an infinite number of molecules, endowed with an attractive power, and their dimensions being very small compared with its distance from the other bodies of the system of the world; its centre of gravity is attracted very nearly in the same manner, as if the entire mass was concentrated in it, and it acts itself on the several bodies of the system, as on this hypothesis; therefore in the investigation of the motion of the centre of gravity of the heavenly bodies, we may consider these bodies as so many massive points, placed in their centres of gravity. But the sphericity of the planets, and of their satellites, render this hypothesis, already very near to the truth, still more exact. In fact, these several bodies may be conceived to be made up of strata very nearly spherical, and of a density which varies according to any given law; and we now proceed to show that the action of a spherical stratum on a body, which is exterior to it, is the same as if its mass was united in its centre. For this purpose, we will establish some general propositions, relative to the attractions of spheroids, which will be very useful in the sequel.

11. Let x, y, z, represent the three coordinates of the attracted point, which we will denote by m; let dM represent a molecule of the spheroid, and x', y', z', the coordinates of this molecule, ρ denoting the density, which is a function of x', y', z', independent of x, y, z; we will have

$$dM = \rho.dx'.dy'.dz'.$$

The action of dM on m, resolved parallel to the axis of x, and tending towards the origin, will be

$$\frac{\rho.dx'.dy'.dz'.(x-x')}{((x-x')^2+(y-y')^2+(z-z')^2)^{\frac{3}{2}}};$$

and it will consequently be equal to

$$-\left\{\frac{d.\frac{\rho.dx'.dy'.dz'}{\sqrt{(x-x')^2+(y-y')^2+(z-z')^2}}}{dx}\right\};$$

therefore if V denote the integral

$$\int\frac{\rho.dx'.dy'.dz'}{\sqrt{(x-x')^2+(y-y')^2+(z-z')^2}};*$$

* The action of dM on m, is expressed by $\frac{\rho.dx'.dy'.dz'}{(x-x')^2+(y-y')^2+(z-z')^2}$, ∵ the force parallel to the axis of x: $\frac{\rho.dx'.dy'.dz'}{(x-x')^2+(y-y')^2+(z-z')^2}$ :: $(x-x')$: $\sqrt{(x-x')^2+(y-y')^2+(z-z')^2}$, consequently it is $=\frac{\rho.dx'.dy'.dz'}{((x-x')^2+(y-y')^2+(z-z')^2)^{\frac{3}{2}}}$, the expression $\frac{\rho.dx'.dy'.dz'}{\sqrt{((x-x')^2+(y-y')^2+(z-z')^2)}}$, differenced with respect to x, and divided by dx, becomes $-\frac{\rho.dx'.dy'.dz'.(x-x')}{((x-x')^2+(y-y')^2+(z-z')^2)^{\frac{3}{2}}}$; ∴ this expression or $-\left\{\frac{d.\frac{\rho.dx'.dy'.dz'}{\sqrt{(x-x')^2+(y-y')^2+(z-z')^2}}}{dx}\right\}$, expresses the actión of a molecule of the spheroid, on a point without the surface of the spheroid, consequently, if we take the sum of the corresponding expressions for all the molecules of the spheroid, *i. e.* if we take $-\left\{\frac{d.\int\frac{\rho.dx'.dy'.dz'}{\sqrt{(x-x')^2+(y-y')^2+(z-z')^2}}}{dx}\right\} = -\left\{\frac{dV}{dx}\right\}$, this quantity expresses the action of the spheroid, on the point m, resolved parallel to the axis of x; the characteristic, d refers solely to the coordinates x, y, z, it does not denote an operation the reverse of that indicated by the characteristic $\int$.

extended to the entire mass of the spheroid; $-\left\{\frac{dV}{dx}\right\}$ will represent the entire action of the spheroid on the point m, resolved parallel to the axis of x, and directed towards their origin. V is the sum of the molecules of the spheroid, divided by their respective distances from the point attracted; in order to obtain the attraction of the spheroid on this point, we should consider V as a function of three rectangular coordinates, of which one may be parallel to this line, and then take the differentlal of the function, with respect to this coordinate; the coefficient of this differential, affected with a contrary sign, will express the attraction of the spheroid parallel to the given line, and directed towards the origin of the coordinate to which it is parallel.

Denoting the function $((x-x')^2+(y-y')^2+(z-z')^2)^{-\frac{1}{2}}$, by ϵ, we will have

$$V=\int \epsilon.\rho.dx'.dy'.dz'.$$

As the integration only respects the variables x', y', z', it is manifest that we will have

$$\left\{\frac{d^2V}{dx^2}\right\}+\left\{\frac{d^2V}{dy^2}\right\}+\left\{\frac{d^2V}{dz^2}\right\}=\int \rho.dx'.dy'.dz'.$$

$$\left\{\left\{\frac{d^2\epsilon}{dx^2}\right\}+\left\{\frac{d^2\epsilon}{dy^2}\right\}+\left\{\frac{d^2\epsilon}{dz^2}\right\}\right\};$$

but we have

$$0=\left\{\frac{d^2\epsilon}{dx^2}\right\}+\left\{\frac{d^2\epsilon}{dy^2}\right\}+\left\{\frac{d^2\epsilon}{dz^2}\right\};*$$

* $\frac{d\epsilon}{dx}=\frac{-(x-x')}{((x-x')^2+(y-y')^2+(z-z')^2)^{\frac{3}{2}}}\ \therefore\ \frac{d^2\epsilon}{dx^2}=\frac{-1}{((x-x')^2+(y-y')^2+(z-z')^2)^{\frac{3}{2}}}$,

$+\frac{3(x-x')^2}{((x-x')^2+(y-y')^2+(z-z')^2)^{\frac{5}{2}}}=\frac{-(x-x')^2-(y-y')^2-(z-z')^2+3(x-x')^2}{((x-x')^2+(y-y')^2+(z-z')^2)^{\frac{5}{2}}}$, consequently we will have also

$$0=\left\{\frac{d^2V}{dx^2}\right\}+\left\{\frac{d^2V}{dy^2}\right\}+\left\{\frac{d^2V}{dz^2}\right\}; \text{(A)}$$

This remarkable equation will be extremely useful in the theory of the figure of the heavenly bodies; we may make it to assume other forms, which will in different circumstances be more convenient; for instance, let a radius be drawn from the origin of the coordinates to the point attracted, which radius we will represent by r, let θ be equal to the angle, which this radius makes with the axis of x, and ϖ the angle which the plane passing through r and this axis, makes with the plane of the coordinates x and y; we will have

$$x=r.\cos.\theta;\ y=r.\sin.\theta.\cos.\varpi;\ z=r.\sin.\theta.\sin.\varpi;$$

consequently we shall obtain

$$r=\sqrt{x^2+y^2+z^2};\ \cos.\theta=\frac{x}{\sqrt{x^2+y^2+z^2}};\ \tan.\varpi=\frac{z}{y};$$

by means of these expressions, we can obtain the partial differences of

in like manner, $\frac{d^2\zeta}{dy^2}$, $\frac{d^2\zeta}{dz^2}$, are respectively equal to

$$\frac{-(x-x')^2-(y-y')^2-(z-z')^2+3(y-y')^2}{((x-x')^2+(y-y')^2+(z-z')^2)^{\frac{5}{2}}},\quad \frac{-(x-x')^2-(y-y')^2-(z-z')^2+3(z-z')^2}{((x-x')^2+(y-y')^2+(z-z')^2)^{\frac{5}{2}}}$$

$$\therefore\ \frac{d^2\zeta}{dx^2}+\frac{d^2\zeta}{dy^2}+\frac{d^2\zeta}{dz^2}=$$

$$\frac{-3(x-x')^2-3(y-y')^2-3(z-z')^2+3(x-x')^2+3(y-y')^2+3(z-z')^2}{((x-x')^2+(y-y')^2+(z-z')^2)^{\frac{5}{2}}}=0.$$

r, θ, and ϖ, with respect to the variables x, y, z; from which we can deduce the values of $\left\{\frac{d^2V}{dx^2}\right\}$, $\left\{\frac{d^2V}{dy^2}\right\}$, $\left\{\frac{d^2V}{dz^2}\right\}$, in partial differences of V, with respect to the variables r, θ, and ϖ. As we shall have occasion frequently to consider these transformations of partial differences; it will be useful here to trace the principle of them. V being considered first as a function of the variables x, y, z, and then, of the variables r, θ, and ϖ, we have

$$\left\{\frac{dV}{dx}\right\} = \left\{\frac{dV}{dr}\right\}.\left\{\frac{dr}{dx}\right\} + \left\{\frac{dV}{d\theta}\right\}.\left\{\frac{d\theta}{dx}\right\} + \left\{\frac{dV}{d\varpi}\right\}.\left\{\frac{d\varpi}{dx}\right\}.^{*}$$

In order to obtain the partial differences, $\left\{\frac{dr}{dx}\right\}$, $\left\{\frac{d\theta}{dx}\right\}$, $\left\{\frac{d\varpi}{dx}\right\}$, it is only necessary to make x the sole variable in the preceding expressions for r, cos. θ, and tan. ϖ, consequently, if we difference these expressions, we will have

$$\left\{\frac{dr}{dx}\right\} = \cos.\theta; \left\{\frac{d\theta}{dx}\right\} = -\frac{\sin.\theta}{r}; \frac{d\varpi}{dx} = 0;$$

* $\left\{\frac{dr}{dx}\right\} = \frac{x}{\sqrt{x^2+y^2+z^2}} = \frac{x}{r} = \cos.\theta$; $-\left\{\frac{d\theta}{dx}\right\}.\sin.\theta = \frac{1}{\sqrt{x^2+y^2+z^2}} - \frac{x^2}{(x^2+y^2+z^2)^{\frac{3}{2}}} = \frac{y^2+z^2}{(x^2+y^2+z^2)^{\frac{3}{2}}}$, and as $\frac{y^2+z^2}{x^2+y^2+z^2} = \sin.^2\theta$; $\left\{\frac{d\theta}{dx}\right\} = -\frac{\sin.\theta}{r}$, by substituting for $\left\{\frac{dr}{dx}\right\}$, $\left\{\frac{d\theta}{dx}\right\}$, we obtain the value of $\left\{\frac{dV}{dx}\right\}$, which has been given in the text.

which gives

$$\left\{\frac{dV}{dx}\right\} = \cos.\theta.\left\{\frac{dV}{dr}\right\} - \frac{\sin.\theta}{r}.\left\{\frac{dV}{d\theta}\right\}.$$

By this means we can obtain the partial difference $\left\{\frac{dV}{dx}\right\}$, in partial differences of the function V, taken with respect to the variables r, θ, and ϖ. By differencing this value of $\left\{\frac{dV}{dx}\right\}$ a second time, we shall obtain the difference $\left\{\frac{d^2V}{dx^2}\right\}$ in terms of the partial differences of V, taken relatively to the variables r, θ, and ϖ. We can obtain, by a similar process, the values of $\left\{\frac{d^2V}{dy^2}\right\}$, and $\left\{\frac{d^2V}{dz^2}\right\}$.

By the preceding operations, we can transform the equation (A) into the following:

$$0 = \left\{\frac{d^2V}{d\theta^2}\right\} + \frac{\cos.\theta}{\sin.\theta}.\left\{\frac{dV}{d\theta}\right\} + \frac{\left\{\frac{d^2V}{d\varpi^2}\right\}}{\sin.^2\theta} + r.\left\{\frac{d^2.rV}{dr^2}\right\}; \quad (B)^*$$

* $\left\{\frac{dr}{dx}\right\} = \frac{x}{r}$; $\therefore \left\{\frac{d^2r}{dx^2}\right\} = \frac{1}{r} - \frac{x^2}{r^3} = \frac{y^2+z^2}{r^3} = \frac{\sin.^2\theta}{r}$; $\left\{\frac{d\theta}{dx}\right\} = -\frac{\sin.\theta}{r}$ $= -\frac{\sqrt{y^2+z^2}}{r^2}$, $\therefore \left\{\frac{d^2\theta}{dx^2}\right\} = \frac{2x.\sqrt{y^2+z^2}}{r^4} = \frac{2.\sin\theta.\cos.\theta}{r^2}$; $\left\{\frac{d\varpi}{dx}\right\}$ and $\left\{\frac{d^2\varpi}{dx^2}\right\} = 0$; $\therefore \left\{\frac{d^2V}{dx^2}\right\} = \frac{d^2V}{dr^2}.\frac{dr^2}{dx^2} + \frac{dV}{dr}.\frac{d^2r}{dx^2} + \frac{d^2V}{d\theta^2}.\frac{d\theta^2}{dx^2} + \frac{dV}{d\theta}.\frac{d^2\theta}{dx^2} =$

$$\frac{d^2V}{dr^2}.\cos.^2\theta + \frac{dV}{dr}.\frac{\sin.^2\theta}{r} + \frac{d^2V}{d\theta^2}.\frac{\sin.^2\theta}{r^2} + \frac{dV}{d\theta}.\frac{2\sin.\theta.\cos.\theta}{r^2};$$

$\left\{\frac{dr}{dy}\right\} = \frac{y}{r} = \sin.\theta.\cos.\varpi$; $\left\{\frac{d^2r}{dy^2}\right\} = \frac{1}{r} - \frac{y^2}{r^3} = \frac{x^2+z^2}{r^3} = \frac{\cos.^2\theta + \sin.^2\theta.\sin.^2\varpi}{r}$;

$-\left\{\frac{d\theta}{dy}\right\}.\sin.\theta. = -\frac{xy}{r^3}$, $\therefore \left\{\frac{d\theta}{dy}\right\} = \frac{xy}{\sqrt{y^2+z^2)}r^2}$, by substituting for $-\sin.\theta$ its value $-\frac{\sqrt{y^2+z^2}}{r}$; and by substituting $r.\cos.\theta$ for x, and $r.\sin.\theta.\cos.\varpi$ for y, we obtain,

$$\frac{xy}{\sqrt{y^2+z^2}.r^2}=\frac{\cos.\theta.\cos.\varpi}{r}\ \therefore$$

$$\left\{\frac{d^2\theta}{dy^2}\right\}=\frac{x}{\sqrt{y^2+z^2}.r^2}-\frac{xy^2}{(y^2+z^2)^{\frac{3}{2}}.r^2}-\frac{2xy^2}{\sqrt{y^2+z^2})r^4}=\frac{\cos.\theta}{\sin.\theta.r^2}-\frac{\cos.\theta.\cos.^2\varpi}{\sin.\theta.r^2}$$

$$-\frac{2\cos.\theta.\sin.\theta.\cos.^2\varpi}{r^2};\ \left\{\frac{d\varpi}{dy}\right\}=d.\frac{\tan.\varpi}{\frac{dy}{1+\tan.^2\varpi}}=-\frac{z}{y^2}\div\left\{1+\frac{z^2}{y^2}\right\}=-\frac{z}{y^2+z^2}=$$

$$-\frac{\sin.\varpi}{\sin.\theta.r};\ \left\{\frac{d^2\varpi}{dy^2}\right\}=\frac{2yz}{(y^2+z^2)^2}=\frac{2.\sin.\varpi.\cos.\varpi}{\sin.^2\theta.r^2};\ \therefore\left\{\frac{dV}{dy}\right\}=\left\{\frac{dV}{dr}\right\}.\left\{\frac{dr}{dy}\right\}$$

$$+\left\{\frac{dV}{d\theta}\right\}.\left\{\frac{d\theta}{dy}\right\}+\left\{\frac{dV}{d\varpi}\right\}.\left\{\frac{d\varpi}{dy}\right\}=\left\{\frac{dV}{dr}\right\}.\sin.\theta.\cos.\varpi+\left\{\frac{dV}{d\theta}\right\}.$$

$$\frac{\cos.\theta.\cos.\varpi}{r}-\left\{\frac{dV}{d\varpi}\right\}.\frac{\sin.\varpi}{r.\sin.\theta};\ \therefore\left\{\frac{d^2V}{dy^2}\right\}$$

$$=\left\{\frac{d^2V}{dr^2}\right\}.\left\{\frac{dr^2}{dy^2}\right\}+\left\{\frac{dV}{dr}\right\}.\left\{\frac{d^2r}{dy^2}\right\}+\left\{\frac{d^2V}{d\theta^2}\right\}.\left\{\frac{d\theta^2}{dy^2}\right\}+\left\{\frac{dV}{d\theta}\right\}.$$

$$\left\{\frac{d^2\theta}{dy^2}\right\}+\left\{\frac{d^2V}{d\varpi^2}\right\}.\left\{\frac{d\varpi^2}{dy^2}\right\}+\left\{\frac{dV}{d\varpi}\right\}.\left\{\frac{d^2\varpi}{dy^2}\right\}=\frac{d^2V}{dr^2}\sin.^2\theta.\cos.^2\varpi+\frac{dV}{dr}.$$

$$\frac{\cos.^2\theta+\sin.^2\theta.\sin.^2\varpi}{r}+\left\{\frac{d^2V}{d\theta^2}\right\}.\frac{\cos.^2\theta.\cos.^2\varpi}{r^2}+\left\{\frac{dV}{d\theta}\right\}.\left\{\frac{\cos.\theta-\cos.\theta.\cos.^2\varpi}{r^2.\sin.\theta}\right.$$

$$\left.-\frac{2\sin.\theta.\cos.\theta.\cos.^2\varpi}{r^2}\right\}+\frac{d^2V}{d\varpi^2}.\frac{\sin.^2\varpi}{r^2.\sin.^2\theta}+\frac{dV}{d\varpi}.\frac{2\sin.\varpi.\cos.\varpi}{r^2.\sin.^2\theta};\ \frac{dr}{dz}=\frac{z}{r}=$$

$$\sin.\theta.\sin.\varpi;\ \frac{d^2r}{dz^2}=\frac{1}{r}-\frac{z^2}{r^3}=\frac{x^2+y^2}{r^3}=\frac{\cos.^2\theta.+\sin.^2\theta.\cos.^2\varpi}{r},-\left\{\frac{d\theta}{dz}\right\}.\sin.\theta$$

$$=-\frac{zx}{r^2}=-\frac{\sin.\theta.\cos.\theta.\sin.\varpi}{r};\ \therefore\left\{\frac{d\theta}{dz}\right\}=\frac{\cos.\theta.\sin.\varpi}{r}=\frac{zx}{\sqrt{y^2+z^2}.r^2}\ \therefore\frac{d^2\theta}{dz^2}$$

$$=\frac{x}{\sqrt{y^2+z^2}.r^2}-\frac{z^2x}{(y^2+z^2)^{\frac{3}{2}}r^2}-\frac{2z^2x}{\sqrt{y^2+z^2}.r^4}=\frac{\cos.\theta}{r^2.\sin.\theta}-\frac{\cos.\theta.\sin.^2\varpi}{\sin.\theta.r^2}$$

$$-\frac{2\sin.\theta.\cos.\theta.\sin.^2\varpi}{r^2};\ \left\{\frac{d\varpi}{dz}\right\}=\frac{y}{y^2+z^2}=\frac{\cos.\varpi}{r.\sin.\theta};\ \frac{d^2\varpi}{dz^2}=-\frac{2zy}{(y^2+z^2)^2}=$$

$$-\frac{2\sin.\varpi.\cos.\varpi}{\sin.^2\theta.r^2};\ \left\{\frac{dV}{dz}\right\}=\left\{\frac{dV}{dr}\right\}.\left\{\frac{dr}{dz}\right\}+\left\{\frac{dV}{d\theta}\right\}.\left\{\frac{d\theta}{dz}\right\}+\left\{\frac{dV}{d\varpi}\right\}.\left\{\frac{d\varpi}{dz}\right\}$$

if cos. θ be put equal to μ, this last equation will become

$$=\left\{\frac{dV}{dr}\right\}\text{sin. }\theta.\text{ sin. }\varpi+\left\{\frac{dV}{d\theta}\right\}\frac{\text{cos. }\theta.\text{ sin. }\varpi}{r}+\left\{\frac{dV}{d\varpi}\right\}.\frac{\text{cos. }\varpi}{r.\text{sin. }\theta};\left\{\frac{d^2V}{dz^2}\right\}$$

$$=\left\{\frac{d^2V}{dr^2}\right\}.\text{ sin. }^2\theta.\text{ sin. }^2\varpi+\left\{\frac{dV}{dr}\right\}.\left\{\frac{\text{cos. }^2\theta.+\text{sin. }^2\theta.\text{ cos. }^2\varpi}{r}\right\}+\left\{\frac{d^2V}{d\theta^2}\right\}.$$

$$\frac{\text{cos. }^2\theta.\text{ sin. }^2\varpi}{r^2}+\left\{\frac{dV}{d\theta}\right\}\frac{\text{cos. }\theta-\text{cos. }\theta.\text{ sin. }^2\varpi}{r^2\text{ sin. }\theta}-\frac{2\text{ sin. }\theta}{r^2}\text{ cos. }\theta.\text{ sin. }^2\varpi\ .$$

$$+\left\{\frac{d^2V}{d\varpi^2}\right\}.\frac{\text{cos. }^2\varpi}{r^2.\text{sin. }^2\theta}-\left\{\frac{dV}{d\varpi}\right\}.\frac{2\text{ sin. }\varpi.\text{ cos. }\varpi}{r^2.\text{ sin. }^2\theta};$$

if the corresponding terms are made to coalesce in the values of $\left\{\frac{d^2V}{dx^2}\right\}+\left\{\frac{d^2V}{dy^2}\right\}$ $+\left\{\frac{d^2V}{dz^2}\right\}$, we will obtain the following expression

$$\left\{\frac{d^2V}{dr^2}\right\}.\ (\text{cos. }^2\theta+\text{sin. }^2\theta.\text{ cos. }^2\varpi+\text{sin. }^2\theta.\text{ sin. }^2\varpi)+\frac{dV}{dr}.\left\{\frac{\text{sin. }^2\theta}{r}+\right.$$

$$\left.\frac{\text{cos. }^2\theta.+\text{sin. }^2\theta.\text{ sin. }^2\varpi}{r}+\frac{\text{cos. }^2\theta+\text{sin. }^2\theta.\text{ cos. }^2\varpi}{r}\right\}+\left\{\frac{d^2V}{d\theta^2}\right\}$$

$$\frac{\text{sin. }^2\theta+\text{cos. }^2\theta.\text{ cos. }^2\varpi+\text{cos. }^2\theta.\text{ sin. }^2\varpi)}{r^2}+\left\{\frac{dV}{d\theta}\right\}.\left\{\frac{2\text{ sin. }\theta.\text{ cos. }\theta}{r^2}+\frac{\text{cos. }\theta}{r^2\text{sin. }\theta}\right.$$

$$-\frac{\text{cos. }\theta.\text{ cos. }^2\varpi}{r^2.\text{ sin. }\theta}-\frac{2\text{ sin. }\theta.\text{ cos. }\theta.\text{cos. }^2\varpi}{r^2}+\frac{\text{cos. }\theta}{r^2.\text{ sin. }\theta}-\frac{\text{cos. }\theta.\text{ sin. }^2\varpi}{r^2.\text{ sin. }\theta}$$

$$\left.-\frac{2\text{ sin. }\theta.\text{ cos. }\theta.\text{ sin. }^2\varpi}{r^2}\right\}+\left\{\frac{d^2V}{d\varpi^2}\right\}\left\{\frac{\text{sin. }^2\varpi}{r^2.\text{ sin. }^2\theta}+\frac{\text{cos. }^2\varpi}{r^2.\text{ sin. }^2\theta}\right\}+\left\{\frac{dV}{d\varpi}\right\}$$

$$\left(\frac{2\text{ sin. }\varpi.\text{ cos. }\varpi-2\text{ sin. }\varpi.\text{ cos. }\varpi}{r^2.\text{ sin. }^2\theta}\right)=\left\{\frac{d^2V}{dr^2}\right\}+2\left\{\frac{dV}{dr}\right\}.\frac{1}{r}+\left\{\frac{d^2V}{d\theta^2}\right\}.\frac{1}{r^2}$$

$+\left\{\frac{dV}{d\theta}\right\}.\frac{\text{cos. }\theta}{r^2.\text{sin. }\theta}+\left\{\frac{d^2V}{d\varpi^2}\right\}.\frac{1}{r^2.\text{ sin. }^2\theta}=0$, ∵ hence multiplying by r^2, we obtain

$\left\{\frac{d^2V}{dr^2}\right\}.\ r^2+2r.\left\{\frac{dV}{dr}\right\}+\left\{\frac{d^2V}{d\theta^2}\right\}+\left\{\frac{dV}{d\theta}\right\}.\frac{\text{cos. }\theta}{\text{sin. }\theta}+\left\{\frac{d^2V}{d\varpi^2}\right\}.\frac{1}{\text{sin. }^2\theta}=0$; but as

$$0=\left\{\frac{d.(1-\mu^2).\frac{dV}{d\mu}}{d\mu}\right\}+\frac{\left\{\frac{d^2V}{d\varpi^2}\right\}}{1-\mu^2}+r.\left\{\frac{d^2.rV}{dr^2}\right\}. \quad (C)^*$$

12. Let us now suppose, that the spheroid is a spherical stratum, the origin of the coordinates being at the centre; it is obvious that V will only depend on r, and that it will not contain μ or ϖ; the equation (C) will therefore be reduced to

$$0=\left\{\frac{d^2.rV}{dr^2}\right\};$$

from which we obtain by integrating,

$$V=A+\frac{B}{r};\dagger$$

I 2

$\left\{\frac{d^2.rV}{dr^2}\right\}=r.\left\{\frac{d^2V}{dr^2}\right\}+2.\left\{\frac{dV}{dr}\right\}$, dr being considered as constant, $\therefore r.\left\{\frac{d^2.rV}{dr^2}\right\}$ may be substituted in place of $r^2.\left\{\frac{d^2V}{dr^2}\right\}+2r.\left\{\frac{dV}{dr}\right\}$.

* If we make cos. $\theta=\mu$, then $\frac{dV}{d\theta}=\left(\frac{dV}{d\mu}\right).\left(\frac{d\mu}{d\theta}\right)$, and $\frac{d^2V}{d\theta^2}=\left(\frac{d^2V}{d\mu^2}\right).\frac{d\mu^2}{d\theta^2}+\left(\frac{dV}{d\mu}\right).\left(\frac{d^2\mu}{d\theta^2}\right)$, and as $d\theta$ is constant, and $d\mu=-d\theta.\sin.\theta$, $d^2\mu=-d\theta^2.\cos.\theta$; $\frac{d^2V}{d\theta^2}=\left(\frac{d^2V}{d\mu^2}\right).(1-\mu^2)-\left(\frac{dV}{d\mu}\right).\mu$; $\left(\frac{dV}{d\theta}\right)=\left(\frac{dV}{d\mu}\right).\frac{d\mu}{d\theta}=-\frac{dV}{d\mu}.\sqrt{1-\mu^2}$, and $\left(\frac{dV}{d\theta}\right).\frac{\cos.\theta}{\sin.\theta}=-\frac{dV}{d\mu}.\frac{\sqrt{1-\mu^2}.\mu}{\sqrt{1-\mu^2}}$ $\therefore \left(\frac{d^2V}{d\theta^2}\right)+\left(\frac{dV}{d\theta}\right).\frac{\cos.\theta}{\sin.\theta}=\frac{d^2V}{d\mu^2}.(1-\mu^2)-2\left(\frac{dV}{d\mu}\right).\mu=\frac{d((1-\mu^2\left(\frac{dV}{d\mu}\right)}{d\mu}$; hence it appears how the equation (B) may be reduced to the equation (C).

† If the attracting body be spherical, the quantity V will be always the same, when r is

A and B being two constant arbitrary quantities. Consequently we have

$$-\left\{\frac{dV}{dr}\right\}=\frac{B}{r^2}.$$

from what precedes, it is manifest, that $-\left\{\frac{dV}{dr}\right\}$ expresses the action of the spherical stratum on the point m, resolved in the direction of the radius r, and directed towards the centre of the stratum; but it is evident, that the entire action of the stratum must be in the direction of the radius; therefore $-\left\{\frac{dV}{dr}\right\}$ expresses the total action of the spherical stratum on the point m.*

First, let us suppose this point to be placed within the stratum. If it was at the centre itself, the action of the stratum would vanish; therefore when $r=o$, we have $-\left\{\frac{dV}{dr}\right\}=0$, i. e. $\frac{B}{r^2}=0$, from

the same, and it only varies when r is increased or diminished. For suppose the attracted point to move on the surface of a sphere, concentrical with the attracting body, it is evident that the value of V remains the same when the attracting body is spherical, but when this body is any other figure, V will vary from one position to another of the point moving on the spheric surface.

$$\left(\frac{d^2.rV}{dr^2}\right)=0, \because \frac{d.rV}{dr}=A, \text{ and } rV=Ar+B,$$

it appears from this equation, that if $r=0$, $B=0$.

* From what has been stated in page 42, relative to the action of a spheroid, it appears that $-\left(\frac{dV}{dr}\right)$ expresses the action of the stratum parallel to r, but it is evident that the entire action of the stratum is equivalent to this expression, for if equal elements be assumed at each side, equally distant from the direction of r, their action perpendicular to r will be destroyed, and the remaining action will be in the direction of r, and this being the case for every two corresponding elements, it is true for the entire spherical stratum.

which it follows that $B=0$, and consequently whatever may be the value of r, $-\left\{\frac{dV}{dr}\right\}=0$; from this it appears, that a point situated within a spherical stratum does not experience any action, or, which is the same thing, it is equally attracted in every direction.

If the point m exists without the spherical stratum; it is manifest that if we suppose it at an infinite distance from its centre, the action of the stratum on this point, will be the same, as if the entire mass was collected in this centre; therefore if M represent the mass of this stratum; $-\left\{\frac{dV}{dr}\right\}$ or $\frac{B}{r^2}$ will become in this case, equal to $\frac{M}{r^2}$, from which we obtain $B=M$, therefore we have universally,*

* When the point is at the centre $\frac{B}{r^2}=0$, when $r=0$, as has been already remarked, see preceding page; this is also evident from other considerations, and as B must be the same, wherever the point is assumed within the surface, B in all such cases $=0$; $\because V=A$, the value of A may be easily determined.

When the point is infinitely distant, the action is the same as if all the molecules were united in the centre of gravity of the sphere, see page 47, and in this case the action is equal to $\frac{M}{r^2}$, $\because -\left\{\frac{dV}{dr}\right\}$ or $\frac{B}{r^2}=\frac{M}{r^2}$, $\therefore B=M$; $V=A+\frac{M}{r}$, hence when the attracted point is infinitely distant, $A=0$, $\because$ it is always $=0$; and $V=\frac{B}{r}=\frac{M}{r}$.

If the attracted point be without the sphere, the attraction towards the convex part is equal to the attraction to the concave part of the surface: and when the point is on the surface, the attraction to the spherical stratum is only half of what it is, when the point is at a distance from the surface. This is immediately evident from the expression $\frac{u^2.du.d\varpi.d\theta.\sin.\theta}{f}(r-u.\cos.\theta.\phi.(f))$, which, when $\phi.(f)\propto\frac{1}{f^2}$ becomes $u^2.du.d\varpi.d\theta.\sin.\theta.\frac{r-u.\cos.\theta}{f^3}$, and it is easy to shew that this expression is the same for two elements situated on the convex and concave sides of the spherical stratum, and which lie on two lines drawn from the attracted point, and making an indefinitely small angle with each other, for $u\sin.\theta=$ a perpendicular let fall on r from the attracting element, $r-u.\cos.\theta=$

with respect to exterior points,

$$-\left\{\frac{dV}{dr}\right\} = \frac{M}{r^2};$$

that is to say, they are attracted by the spherical stratum, in the same manner, as if the entire mass was united in its centre.

A sphere being a spherical stratum, of which the radius of the interior surface vanishes; it is obvious, that its attraction on a point situated on its surface, or beyond it, is the same as if its mass was united in its centre.*

This conclusion is equally true, for globes composed of concentrical strata, of which the density varies from the centre to the surface according to any given law; for this is true for each of its strata; thus, as the sun, the planets, and the satellites may be considered, very nearly, as globes of this nature; they attract exterior bodies almost, as if their masses were concentrated in their centres of gravity, which is conformable to the result of observation, as we have seen in No. 5. Indeed, the figure of the heavenly bodies deviates a little from the spherical form; however, the difference is very small, and the error which results

part of r intercepted between attracted point and this perpendicular, and it is manifest from similar triangles that the perpendicular let fall on r, and also the intercepts between these perpendiculars and attracted point are respectively as the distances of the attracting elements from the attracted point, and $ud\theta$ is also in the same ratio in both cases, see Princip. Math. Book I. Prop. 72, $\because$ for the two elements at above mentioned, $\frac{u.d\theta.u.\sin.\theta\,(r-u.\cos.\theta)}{f^3}$ is the same for both, consequently the attractions which vary as these expressions will be equal, and this being true for every two corresponding elements existing on the same right lines, it is true for the entire stratum. Hence if the attracted point is indefinitely near to the spherical surface, its attraction to the molecule contiguous to it, is equal to its attraction to the rest of the spherical stratum; if the attracted point approaches still nearer, so as to become identified with this molecule, it will then be a part of the stratum, and its attraction will now be only half what it was previous to its contact with the stratum.

* For u being the radius of the homogeneous sphere $M = \frac{4\pi}{3}.u^3$, $\therefore -\left\{\frac{dV}{dr}\right\} =$

from the preceding supposition, is of the same order as this difference, relative to points contiguous to this surface; and with respect to those points which are at a considerable distance,* the error is of the same order as the product of this difference, by the square of the ratio of the radii of the attracting bodies to their distances from the points attracted, because we have seen, in No. 10, that the sole consideration of the great distance of the attracted points, renders the error of the preceding supposition, of the same order as the square of this ratio; the heavenly bodies, therefore attract one another very nearly as if their masses were concentrated in their centres of gravity, not only because they are at considerable distances from each other, relatively to their respective dimensions; but also because their figures differ little from the spherical form.

The property which spheres possess in the law of nature, of acttracting, as if their masses were united in their centres, is very remarkable, and it is interesting to know whether it obtains in other laws of attraction. For this purpose, it may be observed, that if the law of gravity is such, that a homogeneous sphere attracts a point placed without it, as if the entire mass was united in its centre; the same result will have place for a spherical stratum of a uniform thickness; for if we take away from a sphere, a spherical stratum of a uniform thickness, we will obtain a new sphere of a smaller radius, which will possess the property equally with the first sphere, of attracting as if the entire mass

$\frac{M}{r^2} =$ when $r = a$, $\frac{4\pi}{3} . a$; for a point which is situated within the sphere, it is evident the action of the strata between the point and exterior surface vanishes, consequently this case is reduced to the former.

* This ratio may be deduced from what has been established in No. 46, page 10; see also Systeme du Monde, page 255, and Book 3, No. 9. If the force varied as the distance, a homogeneous body of any figure will attract a particle of matter placed any where, with the same force and in the same direction, as if all the matter of the body was collected in the centre of gravity. See notes to page 50. This will appear immediately if the force of each element be resolved into other forces parallel to three rectangular co-ordinates.

was united in its centre; but it is evident, that if this property belongs to these two spheres, it must also belong to the spherical stratum which constitutes their difference. Consequently the problem reduces itself to determine the laws of attraction, according to which a spherical stratum, of an uniform and indefinitely small thickness, attracts an exterior point, as if the entire mass was collected in its centre.

Let r represent the distance of the attracted point from the centre of the spherical stratum; u the radius of this stratum, and du its thickness. Let θ be the angle, which the radius u, makes with the right line r, ϖ the angle made by the plane which passes through the two lines r and u, with a fixed plane, passing through the right line r; $u^2du.d\varpi.d\theta.\sin.\theta$,* will represent the element of the spherical stratum. If then f denote the distance of this element, from the point attracted, we will have

$$f^2=r^2-2ru.\cos.\theta+u^2.$$

Let us represent the law of the attraction, at the distance f by $\varphi(f)$, the action of the element of the stratum, resolved parallel to r, and directed towards the centre of the stratum, will be

$$u^2du.d\varpi.d\theta.\sin.\theta.\frac{(r-u.\cos.\theta)}{f}.\varphi(f);$$

but we have

$$\frac{r-u.\cos.\theta}{f}=\left\{\frac{df}{dr}\right\};$$

in consequence of which, the preceding expression assumes this form

* The three sides of the element, are du in the direction of the radius, $ud\theta$ the element of the curve in the plane passing through the radius u and r, and $u\sin.\theta.d\varpi$ the element perpendicular to this plane; see Book 3, No. 1.

$$u^2.du.d\varpi.d\theta.\ \text{sin.}\ \theta.\left\{\frac{df}{dr}\right\}.\ \varphi.(f);^*$$

therefore if we denote $\int df.\ \varphi(f)$, by $\varphi_{\prime}(f)$; we shall obtain the entire action of the spherical stratum on the point attracted, by means of the integral $u^2.du.\int d\varpi.d\theta.\ \text{sin.}\ \theta.\varphi_{\prime}(f)$, differenced with respect to r, and divided by dr.

This integral relatively to ϖ, should be taken from $\varpi = 0$, to ϖ equal to the circumference, and after this integration, it becomes

$$2\pi.u^2.du.\int d\theta.\ \text{sin.}\ \theta.\ \varphi_{\prime}(f);$$

π expressing the ratio of the semi-circumference to the radius. The value of f differenced with respect to θ, will give

$$d\theta.\ \text{sin.}\ \theta = \frac{fdf}{ru};$$

and consequently,

$$2\pi.u^2du.\int d\theta.\ \text{sin.}\ \theta.\ \varphi_{\prime}(f) = 2\pi.\frac{udu}{r}.\int fdf.\ \varphi_{\prime}(f).$$

* The attraction in the direction of $f = u^2du.d\varpi.d\theta.\ \text{sin.}\ \theta.\ \varphi(f)$, and as $r - u.\ \text{cos.}\ \theta$ = the distance of the attracted point from a perpendicular demitted from the attracting element on the direction of r, it is evident that $u^2du.d\varpi.d\theta.\ \text{sin.}\ \theta.\varphi(f).\frac{(r-u.\ \text{cos.}\ \theta)}{f}$ is equal to the action of the attracting element in the direction of r,

$$f = \sqrt{r^2 - 2ru.\ \text{cos.}\ \theta + u^2},\ \therefore df = \frac{dr.(r-u.\ \text{cos.}\ \theta) + ru.d\theta.\ \text{sin.}\ \theta + (u - r.\ \text{cos.}\ \theta)\,du}{f};$$

$$\therefore \left\{\frac{df}{dr}\right\} = \frac{r-u.\ \text{cos.}\ \theta}{f};\ \frac{df}{ru}, = \frac{d\theta.\ \text{sin.}\ \theta}{f}.$$

The integral relative to θ, must be taken from $\theta=0$, to $\theta=\pi$, and at these two limits, we have $f=r-u$, and $f=r+u$; consequently the integral relative to f, must be taken from $f=r-u$, to $f=r+u$; therefore let $\int fdf.\,\varphi_{,}(f)=\psi(f)$; we shall have*

$$\frac{2\pi.udu}{r}\cdot\int fdf.\,\varphi_{,}(f)=\frac{2\pi.udu}{r}.\left\{\psi(r+u)-\psi(r-u)\right\}.$$

The coefficient of dr, in the differential of the second member of this equation, taken with respect to r, will give the attraction of the spherical stratum, on the point attracted, and it is easy to infer from thence, that in the case of nature in which $\varphi(f)=\frac{1}{f^2}$,† this attrac-

* The action of the entire stratum, in the direction of $r=u^2du.\int d\varpi.d\theta.\sin.\theta.\left\{\frac{df}{dr}\right\}.$ $\varphi(f)=u^2du.\int d\varpi.d\theta.\sin.\theta.\frac{d.\varphi_{,}(f)}{dr}=u^2du.\int d\varpi.d\theta.\sin.\theta.\varphi_{,}(f)$ differenced with respect to r, and divided by dr, dr and $d\theta$ being independent variables. The attracting force for each molecule $=u^2.du.d\varpi.d\theta.\sin.\theta.\left\{\frac{df}{dr}\right\}.\ \varphi(f)$, ∵ in order to obtain the entire force a *triple* integration is requisite, with respect to f, to θ, and to ϖ.

In order to integrate with respect to $d\theta.\sin.\theta.\varphi_{,}(f)$, this expression is reduced to a function of f only, and as f is here considered as a function of θ *only*, r comes from under the sign of integration; by substituting $\frac{fdf}{ru}$ for $d\theta\sin.\theta$, we get $2\pi u^2du.\int d\theta.\sin.\theta.$ $\varphi_{,}(f)=\frac{2\pi u}{r}.du\int fdf.\,\varphi_{,}(f)$, and as df is only concerned as far as f is a function of θ, and as the limits between which the integral of the first member of this equation ought to be taken, are $\theta=0$, $\theta=\pi$, to which limits the corresponding values of f are $r-u$, $r+u$, *i. e.* the least and greatest values of f, it is evident that by making $\int fdf.\varphi_{,}(f)=\psi(f)$, the integral of the second member will assume the form in the text.

† $\varphi(f)=\frac{1}{f^2}$, ∵ $\int df.\,\varphi(f)=\varphi_{,}(f)=-\frac{1}{f}$, and $\int fdf.\varphi_{,}(f)=\psi(f)=-f=$ at the limits, $-r-u$, $+r-u$; ∵ $\psi(r+u)-\psi(r-u)=-2u$, consequently, the differential

tion is equal to $\frac{4\pi.u^2du}{r^2}$, that is to say, it is the same, as if the entire mass of the spherical stratum was united in its centre; which furnishes a new demonstration of the property, which we have already established, on the attraction of spheres.

Let us now determine $\varphi(f)$, from the condition that the attraction of the stratum is the same as if its mass was united in its centre. This mass is equal to $4\pi.u^2du$, and if it was collected in its centre, its action on the attracted point, will be $4\pi.u^2du.\varphi(r)$; therefore we shall have

$$2\pi.udu.\left\{\frac{d.\left\{\frac{1}{r}.[(\psi(r+u)-\psi(r-u)]\right\}}{dr}\right\}=4\pi.u^2du.\ \varphi(r);\ \text{(D)}$$

and by integrating with respect to r, we shall have

$$\psi(r+u)-\psi(r-u)=2ru.\int dr.\ \varphi(r)+rU,$$

U being a function of u, and of constant quantities, added to the integral* $2u.\int dr.\varphi(r)$. If we represent $\psi(r+u)-\psi(r-u)$, by R, we shall obtain by differentiating the preceding equation,

$$\left\{\frac{d^2R}{dr^2}\right\}=4u.\varphi(r)+2ru.\frac{d.\varphi(r)}{dr};$$

coefficient of the second member of this equation, with respect to $r=-\frac{2\pi.udu}{r^2}.(-2u)=\frac{4\pi u^2.du}{r^2}$; $4\pi u^2du=$ the mass of the spherical stratum, for $\pi u^2=$ the area of a circle whose radius $=u$, ∴ $4\pi u^2=$ the surface of the spherical stratum, and $4\pi u.^2du=$ the mass of the stratum, of which the thickness $=du$.

* Multiplying both sides by dr, and dividing by $2\pi.udu$ we obtain by integrating $\frac{\psi(r+u)-\psi(r-u)}{r}=2ud\int dr.\varphi(r)+U$.

$$\left\{\frac{d^2R}{du^2}\right\} = r.\left\{\frac{d^2U}{du^2}\right\};^*$$

but by the nature of the function R, we have

$$\left\{\frac{d^2R}{dr^2}\right\} = \left\{\frac{d^2R}{du^2}\right\};^\dagger$$

consequently,

$$2u.\left\{2\varphi(r) + \frac{r.d.\varphi(r)}{dr}\right\} = r.\left\{\frac{d^2U}{du^2}\right\};$$

or

$$\frac{2\varphi(r)}{r} + \frac{d.\varphi(r)}{dr} = \frac{1}{2u}.\left\{\frac{d^2U}{du^2}\right\}.$$

Thus, the first member of this equation being independent of u, and the second member being independent of r, each of these members

* $\left\{\frac{dR}{dr}\right\} = 2u\int dr.\varphi(r) + 2ru.\varphi(r) + U$; $\frac{d^2R}{dr^2} = 2u.\varphi(r) + 2u.\varphi(r) + \frac{2rud.\varphi(r)}{dr}$;

$\frac{dR}{du} = 2r.\int dr.\varphi(r) + r.\frac{dU}{du}$; $\frac{d^2R}{du^2} = r.\left\{\frac{d^2U}{du^2}\right\}$.

† For $\int\int df.\varphi_{,}(f) = \psi(f)$, $\because \int df.\varphi_{,}(f) = d.\psi(f)$, and $df.^2\varphi_{,}(f) + df^2 f.\varphi(f) = d^2.\psi(f)$, $\because (dr + du)^2.(\varphi_{,}(r+u) + (r+u).\varphi(r+u)) = d^2.\psi(r+u)$, $(dr - du)^2(\varphi_{,}(r-u) + (r-u).\varphi(r-u)) = d^2.\psi(r-u)$;

$$\because \frac{d^2.\psi(r+u) - d^2.\psi(r-u)}{dr^2} = \frac{d^2R}{dr^2} = \frac{d^2.\psi(r+u) - d^2.\psi(r-u)}{du^2} = \frac{d^2R}{du^2};$$

In order to obtain the attraction to a *sphere*, we should integrate the expression $\frac{2\pi.udu}{r}(\psi(r+u) - \psi(r-u)$ from $u=0$ to $u=L$, L being the radius of the sphere, and then the differential of this function taken with respect to r, and divided by dr, will give the attraction of the sphere.—See Book 12, No. 2.

must be equal to a constant arbitrary quantity, which we will denote by $3A$; therefore, we have

$$\frac{2.\varphi(r)}{r}+\frac{d.\varphi(r)}{dr}=3A;^{*}$$

from which we obtain by integrating,

$$\varphi(r)=Ar+\frac{B}{r^2};$$

B being a new arbitrary quantity. Consequently, all the laws of attraction, in which a sphere acts on an exterior point, placed at the distance r from its centre, as if the entire mass was collected in this centre, are comprised in the general formula

$$Ar+\frac{B}{r^2}.$$

In fact, it is evident, that this value satisfies the equation (D),† whatever may be the values of A and B.

If we suppose $A=0$, we shall have the law of nature, and it is evident that in the infinite number of laws which render the attraction very small at great distances, that of nature is the only one, in which

* Since u does not occur in the first member, nor r in the second member of this equation, the equality of these members can only arise from their being respectively equal to a constant quantity, independent of both u and r.

Multiplying both sides by r^2dr, we shall have

$$2r.dr.\varphi(r)+r^2.d.\varphi(r)=3Ar^2.dr. \therefore r^2.\varphi r=Ar^3+B.$$

† In this hypothesis $\int df\varphi(f)=A.\int df.f+B\int\frac{df}{f^2}=\frac{Af^2}{2}-\frac{B}{f}=\phi_{/}(f)$, and

spheres are endowed with the power of attracting, as if their masses were united in their centres.

And if a body be situated within a spherical stratum of a uniform thickness throughout, it is in this law only that the body will be equally attracted in every direction. From the foregoing analysis, it appears that the attraction of a spherical stratum, of which the thickness is expressed by du, on a point placed in its interior, is equal to

$$2\pi.udu.\left\{\frac{d.\frac{1}{r}\left\{\psi(u+r)-\psi(u-r\right\}}{dr}\right\}.$$

In order that this function should vanish, we should have

$$\psi(u+r)-\psi(u-r)=r.U,$$

U* being a function of u, independent of r, and it is easy to perceive

$$\int dff.\varphi(f)=\psi(f)=\frac{A}{2}.\int dff^3-B\int df=\frac{A}{8}.f^4-Bf;\ \because\ \psi(r+u)=\frac{A}{8}.$$

$$(r^4+4r^3u+6r^2u^2+4ru^3+u^4)-B(r+u),\text{ and }\psi(r-u)=\frac{A}{8}.(r^4-4r^3u+6r^2u^2-$$

$$4ru^3+u^4)-B(r-u),\ \therefore\ \psi(r+u)-\psi(r-u)=A.(r^3u+ru^3)-2Bu;\text{ and}$$

$$\frac{d.\left\{\frac{1}{r}.(\psi(r+u)-\psi(r-u)\right\}}{dr}=\frac{d.\left\{\frac{1}{r}.A(r^3u+ru^3)-2Bu)\right\}}{dr}$$

$$=\frac{3Ar^3u+Au^3r-Ar^3u-Au^3r+2Bu}{r^2}=2Aru+\frac{2Bu}{r^2};$$

and if we substitute for $\varphi(r)$ its value $Ar+\frac{B}{r^2}$, in the second member of the equation (D), it comes out equal to $2Aru+\frac{2Bu}{r^2}$.

* U being the constant arbitrary quantity which is introduced by the integration of

that this is the case in the law of nature, in which $\varphi(f)=\frac{B}{f^2}$. But in order to demonstrate that it only obtains in this law, we shall represent by $\psi'(f)$, the difference of $\psi(f)$, divided by df; we shall likewise denote by $\psi''(f)$, the difference of $\psi'(f)$ divided by df, and so on; we shall thus obtain by two successive differentiations of the preceding equation, with respect to r,

$$\psi''(u+r)-\psi''(u-r)=0.*$$

As this equation obtains, whatever may be the values of u and r, it follows that $\psi''(f)$ must be equal to a constant quantity, whatever may be the value of f; and that therefore $\psi'''(f)=0$; but, we have by what precedes,

$$\psi'(f)=f.\varphi_{,}(f),$$

from which we deduce

$$\psi''(f)=2.\varphi(f)+f.\varphi'(f);$$

$d.\frac{1}{r}(\psi(u+r)-\psi)u-r))$, differenced with respect to r, if $\frac{\psi(u+r)-\psi(u-r)}{r}$ is only equal to U, its differential with respect to r must vanish, for then the quantity to which this differential is equal vanishes: *i. e.* $4\pi u^2.du\,\varphi r=0$. If $\varphi(f)=\frac{B}{f^2}$, $\int df.\,\varphi(f)=\varphi_{,}(f)=-\frac{B}{f}$, and $\int df f\varphi_{,}(f)=-\int Bdf=-B(f)$, $\therefore \psi(u+r)-\psi(u-r)=B.(-r-u)-B.(-u+r)=-2Br$; $\therefore \frac{d.\left\{\frac{1}{r}.\psi(u+r-\psi(u-r)\right\}}{dr}=-\frac{d.\frac{2Br}{r}}{dr}=0$; r is less than u when the point is assumed within the sphere, $\therefore$ the limits of f must be taken $u+r$, $u-r$.

* $\frac{d.\psi(u+r)-d.\psi(u-r)}{dr}=U=\psi'(u+r)-\psi'(u-r)$; and $\psi''(u+r)-\psi''(u-r)=$

and therefore

$$0 = 2.\,\varphi(f) + f.\,\varphi'(f)\,;$$

which gives by integrating, $\varphi(f) = \frac{B}{f^2}$,* and consequently the law of nature.

13. Let us resume the equation (C) of No. 11. If this equation could be generally integrated in every case, we would obtain an expression for V, involving two arbitrary functions, which could be determined by seeking the attraction of the spheroid on a point situated in a position which facilitates this investigation, and then comparing this attraction with its general expression. But the integration of the equation (C) can only be effected in some particular cases, such as when the attracting spheroid becomes a sphere, in which case the equation is reduced to one of ordinary differences; it is also possible, in the case in which the spheroid is a cylinder, of which the base is a curve returning into itself, and of which the length is infinite: we shall see in the third book, that this particular case involves the theory of the rings of Saturn.

Let us fix the origin of the distances r, on the axis itself of the cylinder, which we shall suppose to be indefinitely extended on each side of the origin. Denoting the distance of the point attracted, from the axis by r', we shall have

$$r' = r.\sqrt{1-\mu^2}.$$

$$\frac{d^2.\psi(u+r) - d^2.\psi(u-r)}{dr^2} = \frac{d.U}{dr} = 0.$$

$\psi''(u+r)$ is always equal to $\psi''(u-r)$, now this could not always be the case unless each of them was constant.

* $\psi(f) = \int f df.\,\varphi_{\prime}(f)$; $\because$ $\psi'(f) = f.\,\varphi_{\prime}(f)$, and $\psi''(f) = \varphi_{\prime}(f) + f.\,\varphi(f)$, and $\psi'''(f) = \varphi(f) + \varphi(f) + f\varphi'(f) = 0$, multiplying by $f df$ we obtain $2f\varphi(f)\,df + f^2\varphi'(f).\,df = 0$, $\because f^2.\varphi(f) = B$, and $\varphi(f) = \frac{B}{f^2}$.

It is obvious that V depends solely on r' and ϖ, because it is the same for all points, relatively to which, these two variables are the same ;* consequently it only involves μ, inasmuch as r' is a function of this variable ; which gives

$$\left\{\frac{dV}{d\mu}\right\} = \left\{\frac{dV}{dr'}\right\}.\left\{\frac{dr'}{d\mu}\right\} = -\frac{r\mu}{\sqrt{1-\mu^2}}.\left\{\frac{dV}{dr'}\right\};$$

$$\left\{\frac{d^2V}{d\mu^2}\right\} = \frac{r^2\mu^2}{1-\mu^2}.\left\{\frac{d^2V}{dr'^2}\right\} - \frac{r}{(1-\mu^2)^{\frac{3}{2}}}.\left\{\frac{dV}{dr'}\right\};$$

thus, the equation (C) becomes,

$$0 = r'^2.\left\{\frac{d^2V}{dr'^2}\right\} + \left\{\frac{d^2V}{d\varpi^2}\right\} + r'.\left\{\frac{dV}{dr'}\right\};^*$$

* r' = a perpendicular let fall from the attracted point, on the axis of the cylinder, θ = the angle which r makes with the axis, $\because r' = r.\sin.\theta = r.\sqrt{1-\mu^2}$; if the base of the cylinder was circular, V would be always the same, when r' was the same, *i. e.* it would be a function of r' only, but as this curve may be an ellipse, or any other curve which returns into itself, V must depend also on the angle which the plane of x, y makes with the plane passing through r, and the axis of x, *i. e*, on ϖ.

* $dr' = dr.\sqrt{1-\mu^2} - \frac{r\mu.d\mu}{\sqrt{1-\mu^2}}$, $d^2r' = -\frac{dr.d\mu\mu}{\sqrt{1-\mu^2}} - \frac{dr.d\mu\mu}{\sqrt{1-\mu^2}} - \frac{r.d\mu^2}{\sqrt{1-\mu^2}}$ $- \frac{r\mu^2 d\mu^2}{(1-\mu^2)^{\frac{3}{2}}}$, $\because \frac{d^2r'}{d\mu^2} = \frac{r\mu^2 - r\mu^2 - r}{(1-\mu^2)^{\frac{3}{2}}}$; $\frac{d^2V}{d\mu^2} = \left\{\frac{d^2V}{dr'^2}\right\}.\left\{\frac{dr'^2}{d\mu^2}\right\} + \left\{\frac{dV}{dr'}\right\}.$ $\left\{\frac{d^2r'}{d\mu^2}\right\}$; $\left\{\frac{d^2V}{d\mu^2}\right\}.(1-\mu^2) - 2\mu.\left\{\frac{dV}{d\mu}\right\} + \frac{\frac{d^2V}{d\varpi^2}}{1-\mu^2} + r.\left\{\frac{d^2.rV}{dr^2}\right\}$ = by (substituting for $\left\{\frac{d^2V}{d\mu^2}\right\}$, $\left\{\frac{dV}{d\mu}\right\}$); $\frac{d^2V}{dr'^2}.\frac{r^2\mu^2(1-\mu^2)}{1-\mu^2} - \left\{\frac{dV}{dr'}\right\}.\frac{r.(1-\mu^2)}{(1-\mu^2)^{\frac{3}{2}}} + \left\{\frac{dV}{dr'}\right\}.$

from which we obtain by integrating,

$$V = \varphi(r'.\ \cos.\ \varpi + r'.\ \sqrt{-1}.\ \sin.\ \varpi) + \psi(r'.\ \cos.\ \varpi - r'.\ \sqrt{-1}.\ \sin.\ \varpi);^*$$

$\frac{2\mu^2 r}{\sqrt{1-\mu^2}} + \frac{\left\{\frac{d^2 V}{d\varpi^2}\right\}}{1-\mu^2} + r.\left\{\frac{d^2.rV}{dr^2}\right\}$; (but $d^2.rV = 2dr.dV + rd^2V$; and $dr = \frac{dr'}{\sqrt{1-\mu^2}}$;

$\therefore d^2.rV = \frac{2dr'}{\sqrt{1-\mu^2}}.\ dV + r.d^2V$, hence $r.\left\{\frac{d^2.rV}{dr^2}\right\} = \frac{2dV}{dr'}.\ r.\sqrt{1-\mu^2} + r^2.$

$(1-\mu^2).\left\{\frac{d^2V}{dr'^2}\right\}$. By substituting these values, the equation (C) becomes

$$\left\{\frac{d^2V}{dr'^2}\right\}.\ r^2\mu^2 - \left\{\frac{dV}{dr'}\right\}.\ \frac{r}{\sqrt{1-\mu^2}} + \left\{\frac{dV}{dr'}\right\}.\ \frac{2\mu^2.r}{\sqrt{1-\mu^2}}$$

$$+\frac{\left\{\frac{d^2V}{d\varpi^2}\right\}}{1-\mu^2} + \left\{\frac{d^2V}{dr'^2}\right\}.\ r^2.(1-\mu^2) + 2\left\{\frac{dV}{dr'}\right\}.\ r.\sqrt{1-\mu^2}.$$

$$= \left\{\frac{d^2V}{dr'^2}\right\}.\ r^2(\mu^2+1-\mu^2) - \left\{\frac{dV}{dr'}\right\}.\frac{r}{\sqrt{1-\mu^2}} + \left\{\frac{dV}{dr'}\right\}\frac{2r\mu^2}{\sqrt{1-\mu^2}} + \frac{\frac{d^2V}{d\varpi^2}}{1-\mu^2}$$

$+\frac{dV}{dr'}.\frac{2r.(1-\mu^2)}{\sqrt{1-\mu^2}} = 0$, and if both sides of this equation be multiplied by $1-\mu^2$, we will obtain the expression given in the text, by substituting r' for $r.\sqrt{1-\mu^2}$.

* This integral may be deduced a priori in the following manner: let $\frac{d^2V}{d\varpi^2} = r$, $\frac{d^2V}{dr'^2} = t$, $\frac{dV}{dr'} = q$, then we will have $r + r'^2.t + r'.q = 0$; the general expression $Rk^2 + Sk + T = 0$, Lacroix, tom. 2. No. 752, 753, &c. becomes $k^2 + r'^2 = 0$, $\therefore k = \pm r'.\sqrt{-1}$, and $du = \frac{du}{dr'}.\ (dr' + k.d\varpi)$, $dv = \frac{dv}{dr'}.\ (dr' + k'd\varpi)$ become by making $\frac{du}{dr'}, \frac{dv}{dr'} =$ respectively $\frac{1}{r'}$, and substituting $+\sqrt{-1}.r'$, $-\sqrt{-1}.r'$, for k and k'; $du = \frac{dr'}{r'} + \sqrt{-1}.d\varpi$, $dv = \frac{dr'}{r'} - \sqrt{-1}.\ d\varpi$, consequently $u = \log.\ r' + \sqrt{-1}.\varpi$, $v = \log.\ r' - \sqrt{-1}.$

$\varphi(r')$ and $\psi(r')$ being arbitrary functions of r', which may be deter-

L 2

ϖ, are particular integrals of the preceding differential equations; let $\frac{du}{dr'} = \frac{1}{r'} = n$; $\frac{dv}{dr'} = \frac{1}{r'} = n'$; $\frac{du}{d\varpi} = \sqrt{-1}. = m$; $\frac{dv}{d\varpi} = -\sqrt{-1}. = m'$; $q = np' + nq'$, (see Collection of Examples of differential and integral calculus, page 466,) $= \frac{p'}{r'} + \frac{q'}{r'}$; $r = -r_{\prime}' + 2s' - t$; $t = \frac{r_{\prime}'}{r'^2} + \frac{2s'}{r'^2}\ \frac{t'}{r'^2} - \frac{p'}{r'^2} - \frac{q'}{r'^2}$, $\because r + r'^2 t + r'q = -r_{\prime}' + 2s' - t' + r_{\prime}' + t' + 2s' - p' - q' + q' + q' = 0$, $\because 4s' = 0$, *i. e.* $\frac{d^2V}{dv.du} = 0$, and $V = \varphi'(u) + \psi'(v) = \varphi'(\log. r' + \sqrt{-1}.\ \varpi) + \psi'(\log. r' - \sqrt{-1}.\ \varpi)) =$ respectively, $(\varphi' \log. r' + \log. e^{\varpi.\sqrt{-1}.}) + \psi'(\log. r' - \log e^{-\varpi.\sqrt{-1}.}) = \varphi'(\log.\ (r'.(\cos.\ \varpi + \sqrt{-1}.\sin.\ \varpi)) + \psi'((\log.\ r'.(\cos.\ \varpi - \sqrt{-1}.\ \sin.\ \varpi)) = \varphi(r'.\cos.\ \varpi + r'.\sqrt{-1}.\ \sin.\ \varpi) + \psi(r'.\cos.\ \varpi - r'.\sqrt{-1}.\sin.\ \varpi)$, by substituting $\cos.\ \varpi \pm \sqrt{-1}.\ \sin.\ \varpi$ for $e^{\pm\varpi\sqrt{-1}}$, and assuming the arbitrary function $\varphi =$ the function φ'. log. This integral evidently satisfies the preceding equation, for

$$\left(\frac{dV}{dr}\right) = \frac{d.\varphi(r'.\ \cos.\ \varpi + r'.\sqrt{-1}.\sin.\ \varpi)}{d(r'.\ \cos.\ \varpi + r'\sqrt{-1}\ \ \sin.\ \varpi)} \cdot \frac{d.(r'.\cos.\ \varpi + r'\sqrt{-1}.\ \sin.\ \varpi)}{dr'}$$

$$+ d.\ \frac{\psi.(r'.\cos\ \varpi - r'.\sqrt{-1}.\ \sin.\ \varpi)}{d.(r'.\cos.\ \varpi - r'.\sqrt{-1}.\ \sin.\ \varpi)} \cdot d.\ \frac{(r'.\ \cos.\ \varpi - r'.\sqrt{-1}.\ \sin.\ \varpi)}{dr'}$$

$$\left(\frac{d^2V}{dr'^2}\right) = \frac{d^2.\varphi.(r'.\cos.\ \varpi + r'.\sqrt{-1}.\ \sin.\ \varpi)}{d.(r'.\ \cos.\ \varpi + r'\ \sqrt{-1}.\ \sin.\ \varpi)^2} \cdot \frac{d.(r'.\ \cos.\ \varpi + r'.\sqrt{-1}.\ \sin.\ \varpi)^2}{dr'^2}$$

$$+ \frac{d.\ \varphi(r'.\cos.\ \varpi + r'.\sqrt{-1}.\ \sin.\ \varpi)}{d.(r'.\cos.\ \varpi + r'\sqrt{-1}.\ \sin.\ \varpi)} \cdot \frac{d^2.(r'.\cos.\ \varpi + r'.\sqrt{-1}.\ \sin.\ \varpi)}{dr'^2}$$

$$+ \frac{d^2.\psi(r'.\cos.\ \varpi - r'.\sqrt{-1}.\ \sin\ \varpi)}{d.(r'.\ \cos.\ \varpi - r'.\sqrt{-1}.\ \sin.\ \varpi)^2} \cdot \frac{d.(r'.\ \cos.\ \varpi - r'.\sqrt{-1}.\ \sin.\ \varpi)^2}{dr'^2}$$

$$+ \frac{d.\ \psi(r'\cos.\ \varpi - r'.\sqrt{-1}.\ \sin.\ \varpi)}{d.(r'.\cos.\ \varpi - r'.\sqrt{-1}.\ \sin.\ \varpi)} \cdot \frac{d^2.(r'.\ \cos.\ \varpi - r'.\sqrt{-1}.\ \sin.\ \varpi)}{dr'^2}$$

mined, by investigating the attraction of the cylinder, when ϖ is equal to cipher, and when it becomes equal to a right angle.

$$\text{but } \frac{d.(r'.\cos.\varpi \pm r'.\sqrt{-1}.\sin.\varpi)}{dr'} = \cos.\varpi \pm \sqrt{-1}.\sin.\varpi, \therefore$$

$$\frac{d^2.(r'.\cos.\varpi \pm r'.\sqrt{-1}.\sin.\varpi)}{dr'^2} = 0;$$

$$r'.\left(\frac{dV}{dr'}\right) = \frac{d.\phi(r'.\cos.\varpi + r'.\sqrt{-1}.\sin.\varpi)}{d.(r'.(\cos.\varpi + r'.\sqrt{-1}.\sin.\varpi)}.(r'.\cos.\varpi + r'.\sqrt{-1}.\sin.\varpi)$$

$$+ \frac{d.\psi(r'.\cos.\varpi - r'.\sqrt{-1}.\sin.\varpi)}{d.(r'.\cos.\varpi - r'.\sqrt{-1}.\sin.\varpi)}.(r'.\cos.\varpi - r'.\sqrt{-1}.\sin.\varpi)$$

$$r'^2.\left(\frac{d^2V}{dr'^2}\right) = \frac{d^2.\phi(r'.\cos.\varpi + r'.\sqrt{-1}.\sin.\varpi)}{d.(r'.\cos.\varpi + r'\sqrt{-1}.\sin.\varpi)^2}.r'^2.(\cos.^2\varpi + 2\sqrt{-1}.\sin.\varpi.\cos.\varpi - \sin.^2\varpi)$$

$$+ \frac{d^2.\psi(r'.\cos.\varpi - r'.\sqrt{-1}.\sin.\varpi)}{d.(r'.\cos.\varpi - r'.\sqrt{-1}.\sin.\varpi)^2}.r'^2.(\cos.^2\varpi - 2\sqrt{-1}.\sin.\varpi.\cos.\varpi - \sin.^2\varpi)$$

$$\left(\frac{dV}{d\varpi}\right) = \frac{d.\phi(r'.\cos.\varpi + r'.\sqrt{-1}.\sin.\varpi)}{d.(r'.\cos.\varpi + r'.\sqrt{-1}.\sin.\varpi)}.\frac{d.(r'.\cos.\varpi + r'.\sqrt{-1}.\sin.\varpi)}{d\varpi}$$

$$+ \frac{d.\psi(r'.\cos.\varpi - r'.\sqrt{-1}.\sin\varpi)}{d.(r'.\cos.\varpi - r'.\sqrt{-1}.\sin.\varpi)}.\frac{d.(r'.\cos.\varpi - r'.\sqrt{-1}.\sin.\varpi)}{d\varpi},$$

$$\because \frac{d^2V}{d\varpi^2} = \frac{d^2.\phi(r'.\cos.\varpi + r'.\sqrt{-1}.\sin.\varpi)}{d.(r'.\cos.\varpi + r'.\sqrt{-1}.\sin.\varpi)^2}.\frac{d.(r'.\cos.\varpi + r'.\sqrt{-1}.\sin.\varpi)^2}{d\varpi^2},$$

$$+ \frac{d.\phi(r\cos.\varpi + r'.\sqrt{-1}.\sin.\varpi)}{d(r'.\cos.\varpi + r'.\sqrt{-1}.\sin.\varpi)}.\frac{d^2.(r.\cos.\varpi + r'.\sqrt{-1}.\sin.\varpi)}{d\varpi^2},$$

$$+ \frac{d^2.\psi(r'.\cos.\varpi - r'.\sqrt{-1}.\sin.\varpi)}{d.(r'.\cos.\varpi - r'.\sqrt{-1}.\sin.\varpi)^2}.\frac{d.(r'.\cos.\varpi - r'.\sqrt{-1}.\sin.\varpi)^2}{d\varpi^2}$$

$$+ \frac{d.\psi(r'.\cos.\varpi - r'.\sqrt{-1}.\sin.\varpi)}{d.(r'.\cos.\varpi - r'.\sqrt{-1}.\sin.\varpi)}.\frac{d^2.(r'.\cos.\varpi - r'.\sqrt{-1}.\sin.\varpi)}{d\varpi^2}$$

If the base of the cylinder is a circle, V will be evidently a function of r', independent of ϖ; the preceding equation of partial differences will consequently become,

$$o = r'^2 . \left\{\frac{d^2V}{dr'^2}\right\} + r' . \left\{\frac{dV}{dr'}\right\},$$

which gives, by integrating,

$$-\left\{\frac{dV}{dr'}\right\} = \frac{H}{r'},$$

$$\frac{d.(r'.\cos.\varpi \pm r'.\sqrt{-1}.\sin.\varpi)}{d\varpi} = -r'.\sin.\varpi \pm r'.\sqrt{-1}.\cos.\varpi.$$

$$\frac{d^2.(r'.\cos.\varpi \pm r'.\sqrt{-1}.\sin.\varpi)}{d\varpi^2} = -r'.\cos.\varpi \mp r'.\sqrt{-1}.\sin.\varpi); \because \left(\frac{d^2V}{d\varpi^2}\right)$$

$$= \frac{d^2.\varphi(r'.\cos.\varpi + r'.\sqrt{-1}.\sin.\varpi)}{d.(r'.\cos.\varpi + r'.\sqrt{-1}.\sin.\varpi)^2} . r'^2.(\sin.^2\varpi - 2\sqrt{-1}.\sin.\varpi.\cos.\varpi - \cos.^2\varpi)$$

$$+ \frac{d.\varphi(r'.\cos.\varpi + r'.\sqrt{-1}.\sin.\varpi)}{d.(r'.\cos.\varpi + r'.\sqrt{-1}.\sin.\varpi)} . (-r'.(\cos.\varpi + \sqrt{-1}.\sin.\varpi))$$

$$+ \frac{d^2.\psi(r'.\cos.\varpi - \sqrt{-1}.r'.\sin\varpi)}{d.(r'.\cos.\varpi - \sqrt{-1}.r'.\sin.^2\varpi)} . r'^2.(\sin.^2\varpi,) + 2\sqrt{-1}.\sin.\varpi.\cos.\varpi - \cos.^2\varpi).$$

$$+ \frac{d.\psi(r'.\cos.\varpi - r'.\sqrt{-1}.\sin.\varpi)}{d.(r'.\cos.\varpi - r'.\sqrt{-1}.\sin.\varpi)} . (-r'.(\cos.\varpi - \sqrt{-1}.\sin.\varpi)).$$

$\therefore r'^2\left\{\frac{d^2V}{dr'^2}\right\} + r'.\left\{\frac{dV}{dr'}\right\} + \left\{\frac{d^2V}{d\varpi^2}\right\} = 0$, when the values of $\frac{d^2V}{dr'^2}$, $\frac{dV}{dr'}$ $\frac{dV}{d\varpi^2}$ are substituted; consequently this integral satisfies the given differential equation.

When ϖ vanishes $V = \varphi(r') + \psi(r')$, and when $\varpi = 90°$, $V = \varphi(r'\sqrt{-1}) + \psi(-r'.\sqrt{-1})$, and as the attraction in the direction of $r' = \left\{\frac{dV}{dr'}\right\}$, $\varphi(r')$, and $\psi(r')$ may be determined.

H being a constant quantity. In order to determine it, we will suppose r' very great with respect to the radius of the base of the cylinder, which consideration permits us to regard the cylinder as an infinite right line. Let A represent this base, and z the distance of any point of the axis of the cylinder, from the point where r' meet this axis, the action of the cylinder supposed to be concentrated in its axis, and resolved parallel to r', will be equal to

$$\int \frac{Ar'.dz}{(r'^2+z^2)^{\frac{3}{2}}},$$

the integral being taken from $z = -\infty$, to $z = \infty$; which reduces this integral to $\frac{2A}{r'}$; this is the value of $-\left\{\frac{dV}{dr'}\right\}$, when r' is very considerable. By comparing it with the preceding expression, we obtain $H = 2A$, and it is evident that whatever may be the value of r', the action of the cylinder on an exterior point, is $\frac{2A}{r'}$.*

* If the base of the cylinder be circular, V will be always the same, when r' is given, ∴ V will be a function of r', independent of ϖ; dividing by r', and multiplying both sides by dr', we obtain

$$0 = rdr'.\left\{\frac{d^2V}{dr'^2}\right\} + \left\{\frac{dV}{dr'}\right\}.dr' = d.r'\left\{\frac{dV}{dr'}\right\}; \therefore r'.\left\{\frac{dV}{dr'}\right\} = -H.$$

$r = \sqrt{r'^2+z^2}$, ∴ the attraction in a direction perpendicular to the base, : to the attraction towards the assumed point $\left(=\frac{1}{r'^2+z^2}\right) :: r' : \sqrt{r'^2+z^2}$, hence as Adz is the differential of the area of the base; $\frac{Ar'dz}{(r'^2+z^2)^{\frac{3}{2}}}$ is the differential of the entire force and its integral $= \frac{Az}{r'.\sqrt{r'^2+z^2}}$, (see Lacroix, No. 192), when $z = \infty$ this integral becomes $\frac{A}{r'}$, and when $z = -\infty$, it becomes $-\frac{A}{r'}$; and as we want the attraction of the point to the cylinder between these two values of z, the difference of the expressions in these

If the attracted point lies within a circular cylindrical stratum, of an uniform thickness, and of an infinite length; we have also $-\left\{\frac{dV}{dr'}\right\}$

two cases, $=\frac{2A}{r'}$, must give the attraction required.

When r' is very considerable with respect to the radius of the cylinder, it is the same thing as if the mass of the cylinder was concentrated in its axis. When the point is situated within the cylinder, V is of a different form from what it is, when the point is situated without the cylinder; and as it is of the *same* form wherever the point is assumed within the cylinder, whatever it is in one case, it will be the same in all. The length of the cylinder must be infinite, otherwise the point, even when situated in the axis, would not be equally attracted in the direction of the axis.

When the base is circular, $-\left\{\frac{dV}{dr'}\right\}=\frac{H}{r'} \because -\left\{\frac{dV}{dr'}\right\}.\,dr' = H.\frac{dr'}{r'}, \because -V = H.\log.r'+C.$ The cylinder being of an infinite length, the attraction perpendicular to the axis is the only attraction which it is necessary to estimate.

Therefore the force varying inversely as the square of the distance, there are two cases in which a point is equally attracted in every direction; the first is when the point is situated in the interior of a spherical stratum, (it will be proved in the third book, that this conclusion may be extended to the case of elliptic strata, the interior and exterior surfaces being similar, and similarly situated;) the second is that in which the point is situated in the interior of a hollow cylinder, whose base is circular and length infinite.

If the cylinder was concentrated into a right line of a finite length, the attraction in a direction perpendicular to this line $=\frac{r'.dz}{(r^2+z^2)^{\frac{3}{2}}}$. of which the integral is $\frac{z}{\sqrt{(r'^2+z^2)}\,r'}$.

And if a is $=$ the length of this line, the entire attraction in a direction perpendicular to it $=\frac{a}{\sqrt{a^2+r^2}.\,r'}$; hence if a be infinite, the attraction is as $\frac{1}{r'}$; the attraction in the *direction* of a, is as $\frac{z}{(r^2+z^2)^{\frac{3}{2}}}$; $\because$ the differential of the force $=\frac{zdz}{(r^2+z^2)^{\frac{3}{2}}}$, the integral of which is $\frac{-1}{\sqrt{r^2+z^2}}+C$, when $z=0$, $C=\frac{1}{r'}$, $\because$ the entire attraction $=\frac{1}{r'}-\frac{1}{\sqrt{r^2+z^2}}=$ $\frac{\sqrt{r'^2+z^2}-r'}{r'.\sqrt{r'^2+z^2}}=$ when $z=a$; $\frac{\sqrt{r'^2+a^2}-r'}{r'.\sqrt{r'^2+a^2}}$; $\because$ the attraction in the direction of a is to the attraction in the direction of r' $\because \sqrt{r'^2+a^2}-r' : a$; hence it is easy to determine the direction in which the point would *commence* to move; it may be easily

$= \frac{H}{r'}$; and as the attraction vanishes, when the attracted point is on the axis itself of the stratum, we have $H = 0$, and consequently

shewn that a point placed in the vertex of a triangle is attracted towards the segments made by the perpendicular with a force reciprocally proportional to the secants of the angles which the base makes with the sides. For if r' be the altitude, and a, a', the segments of the base, it is evident from the expression $\frac{a}{r'.\sqrt{a^2+r'^2}}$ that the attractions to the segments a, a' are as $\frac{a}{\sqrt{a^2+r'^2}}$ to $\frac{a'}{\sqrt{a'^2+r'^2}}$, but these expressions will be evidently proportional to the reciprocals of the secants of the angles at the base of the triangle. If the attracted point exist in a perpendicular to the plane of a circle which passes through the centre, x being the distance of the attracted point from the circumference of a circle, concentrical with the given circle, the distance of the centre from this point being $=r'$, then $\pi.(x^2-r'^2)$=the area of this circle, and $2\pi x dx$ is the differential of the area, and as the attraction in the direction of r' is as $\frac{r'}{x^3}$; the differential of the attraction of the point towards the circle $=\frac{2\pi.r'.dx}{x^2}$, of which the integral is $-\frac{2\pi r'}{x}+C$, and when $x=r'$ the attraction vanishes, $\because C=2\pi$, and the corrected integral $=2\pi.\left(1-\frac{r}{x}\right)$, hence the attraction of a point situated in the vertex of a cone to all circular sections of the cone is the same, and for *similar* cones the attraction varies as the side of the cone. If the attracted point exist in the produced axis of a finite cylinder with a circular base, of which the radius $=a$, r' being as before the distance of the attracted point from any point in the axis, $\sqrt{a^2+r'^2}$ will be the distance of the circumference of the cylinder from this point, the attraction towards this circumference is as $1-\frac{r'}{\sqrt{a^2+r'^2}}$, and the differential of this attraction is as $dr'-\frac{r'dr'}{\sqrt{a^2+r'^2}}$ of which the integral $=r'-\sqrt{a^2+r'^2}$, $r_{,}$ and $r_{,,}$ being the greatest and least values of r', the attraction to the entire cylinder $=-r_{,}+r_{,,}-\sqrt{a^2+r^2_{,,}}+\sqrt{a^2+r_{,}^2}$; $r_{,}-r_{,,}=$ the length of the cylinder. If the length be infinite $r_{,,}=\sqrt{a^2+r_{,}'^2}$, $\because$ the attraction is as $r_{,}-\sqrt{a^2+r_{,}^2}$, and if a be infinite the attraction is as $r_{,}-r_{,,}$, the length of the cylinder.

a point situated in the interior of the stratum is equally attracted in every direction.

14. We may apply to the motion of a body, the equations A, B, and C, of No. 11, and then elicit from them, an equation of condition, which will be found very useful, in verifying as well the computations of the theory, as also the theory itself of universal gravitation. The differential equations (1), (2), (3) of No. 9, which determine the relative motion of m about M, may be made to assume the following form:

$$\frac{d^2x}{dt^2} = \left\{\frac{dQ}{dx}\right\};\ \frac{d^2y}{dt^2} = \left\{\frac{dQ}{dy}\right\};\ \frac{d^2z}{dt^2} = \left\{\frac{dQ}{dz}\right\};\ (i)$$

Q being equal to $\frac{M+m}{r} - \Sigma.\frac{m'.(xx'+yy'+zz')}{r'^3} + \frac{\lambda}{m}$; and it is easy to perceive that we have

$$0 = \left\{\frac{d^2Q}{dx^2}\right\} + \left\{\frac{d^2Q}{dy^2}\right\} + \left\{\frac{d^2Q}{dz^2}\right\};\ (E)^*$$

provided that the variables x', y', z', x'', &c., which Q contains, are independent of x, y and z.

* $\left\{\frac{dQ}{dx}\right\} = \frac{-(M+m).x}{(x^2+y^2+z^2)^{\frac{3}{2}}} - \Sigma.\frac{m'x'}{r'^3} + \frac{1}{m}.\left\{\frac{d\lambda}{dx}\right\}$; $\left\{\frac{dQ}{dy}\right\} = -\frac{(M+m)y}{(x^2+y^2+z^2)^{\frac{3}{2}}} - \Sigma.\frac{m'y'}{r'^3} + \frac{1}{m}.\left\{\frac{d\lambda}{dy}\right\}$; $\left\{\frac{dQ}{dz}\right\} = -\frac{(M+m)z}{(x^2+y^2+z^2)^{\frac{3}{2}}} - \Sigma.\frac{mz'}{r'^3} + \frac{1}{m}.\left\{\frac{d\lambda}{dz}\right\}$; but

$$-\frac{mx}{(x^2+y^2+z^2)^{\frac{3}{2}}} - \Sigma.\frac{m'x'}{r'^3} = -\Sigma.\frac{mx}{r^3},\quad \therefore\ \frac{d^2x}{dt^2} = -\frac{Mx}{r^3} - \Sigma.\frac{mx}{r^3} + \frac{1}{m}.$$

$\left\{\frac{d\lambda}{dx}\right\} = \left\{\frac{dQ}{dx}\right\}$; see page 35.

$$\frac{d^2Q}{dx^2} = -\frac{(M+m)}{(x^2+y^2+z^2)^{\frac{3}{2}}} + \frac{3(M+m).x^2}{(x^2+y^2+z^2)^{\frac{5}{2}}} + \frac{1}{m}.\left\{\frac{d^2\lambda}{dx^2}\right\} =$$

$$\left(\frac{-m'}{((x'-x)^2+(y'-y)^2+(z'-z)^2)^{\frac{3}{2}}} + \frac{3m'.(x'-x)^2}{((x'-x)^2+(y'-y)^2+(z'-z)^2)^{\frac{5}{2}}}\right) + \&c.$$

The variables x, y, z, may be transformed into others, which are more convenient for astronomical purposes. r being the radius drawn from the centre of M to that of m, let v represent the angle which the projection of this radius on the plane of x, and of y, makes with the axis of x; and θ, the inclination of r on the same plane; we shall have,

$$x = r.\cos.\theta.\cos.v;$$
$$y = r.\cos.\theta.\sin.v;$$
$$z = r.\sin.\theta.$$

By referring the equation (E) to these new variables, we shall have by No. 11,

$$0 = r^2.\left\{\frac{d^2Q}{dr^2}\right\} + 2r.\left\{\frac{dQ}{dr}\right\} + \frac{\left\{\frac{d^2Q}{dv^2}\right\}}{\cos.^2\theta} + \left\{\frac{d^2Q}{d\theta^2}\right\} - \frac{\sin.\theta.}{\cos.\theta.}.\left\{\frac{dQ}{d\theta}\right\}; \quad (F)$$

Multiplying the first of the equations (i) by $\cos.\theta.\cos.v$; the second, by $\cos.\theta.\sin.v$; the third, by $\sin.\theta$; and then, in order to abridge, making

$$M' = \frac{d^2r}{dt^2} - \frac{r.dv^2}{dt^2}.\cos.^2\theta - \frac{r.d\theta^2}{dt^2};$$

$$\frac{d^2Q}{dy^2} = -\frac{(M+m)}{(x^2+y^2+z^2)^{\frac{3}{2}}} + \frac{3(M+m).y^2}{(x^2+y^2+z^2)^{\frac{5}{2}}} + \frac{1}{m}.\left\{\frac{d^2\lambda}{dy^2}\right\} =$$

$$\left(\frac{-m}{(x'-x)^2+(y'-y)^2+(z'-z)^2)^{\frac{3}{2}}} + \frac{3m'(y'-y)^2}{((x'-x)^2+(y'-y)^2+(z'-z)^2)^{\frac{5}{2}}}\right) + \&c.$$

$$\frac{d^2Q}{dz^2} = -\frac{(M+m)}{(x^2+y^2+z^2)^{\frac{3}{2}}} + \frac{3(M+m).y^2}{(x^2+y^2+z^2)^{\frac{5}{2}}} + \frac{1}{m}.\left\{\frac{d^2\lambda}{dz^2}\right\} =$$

$$\left(\frac{-m'}{(x'-x)^2+(y'-y)^2+(z'-z)^2)^{\frac{3}{2}}} + \frac{3m'(z'-z)^2}{((x'-x)^2+(y-y)^2+(z'-z)^2)^{\frac{5}{2}}}\right) + \&c.$$

$$\therefore \frac{d^2Q}{dx^2} + \frac{d^2Q}{dy^2} + \frac{d^2Q}{dz^2} = \frac{-3(M+m).r^2+3(M+m).r^2}{r^5}$$

$$\frac{-3m'.(x'-x)^2+(y'-y)^2+(z'-z)^2)}{((x'-x)^2+(y-y)^2+(z'-z)^2)^{\frac{5}{2}}}$$

$+3m'.\frac{)x'-x)^2+(y'-y)^2+z'-z)^2}{((x'-x)^2+(y-y)^2+(z'-z)^2)^{\frac{5}{2}}} = 0.$ In the expression for $\frac{1}{m}.\left\{\frac{d^2\lambda}{dx^2} + \frac{d^2\lambda}{dy^2} + \frac{d^2\lambda}{dz^2}\right\}$

we shall obtain, by adding them together,

$$M' = \left\{\frac{dQ}{dr}\right\}.$$

In like manner, if we multiply the first of the equations (i), by $-r.\cos.\theta.\sin.v$; the second, by $r.\cos.\theta.\cos.v$, we shall obtain by their addition

$$N' = \left\{\frac{dQ}{dv}\right\};$$

N' being supposed equal to $\dfrac{d.\left\{r^2.\dfrac{dv}{dt}.\cos.^2\theta\right\}}{dt}$.

Finally, if we multiply the first of the equations (i), by $-r.\sin.\theta.\cos.v$; the second by $-r.\sin.\theta.\sin.v$; and if then we add them to the third, multiplied by $\cos.\theta$, we shall obtain, by making P' equal to

$$r^2.\frac{d^2\theta}{dt^2} + r^2.\frac{dv^2}{dt^2}.\sin.\theta.\cos.\theta + \frac{2r.dr.d\theta}{dt^2};$$

$$P' = \left\{\frac{dQ}{d\theta}\right\}.*$$

M 2

are only considered the first terms in each, but as the other terms are precisely of the same form, it is evident, that the sum of the three differential coefficients, for each of the other terms respectively constitute a result equal to cipher.

* $dx = dr.\cos.\theta.\cos.v - d\theta.r.\sin.\theta.\cos.v - dv.r.\cos.\theta.\sin.v$; ∵ $d^2x = d^2r.\cos.\theta.\cos.v - dr.d\theta.\sin.\theta.\cos.v - dr.dv.\cos.\theta.\sin.v - d^2\theta.r.\sin.\theta.\cos.v - d\theta.dr.\sin.\theta.\cos.v - d\theta^2.r.\cos.\theta.\cos.v + d\theta.dv.r.\sin.\theta.\sin.v - d^2v.r.\cos.\theta.\sin.v - dv.dr.\cos.\theta.\sin.v + dv.d\theta.r.\sin.\theta.\sin.v - dv^2.r.\cos.\theta.\cos.v$, ∵ $d^2x.\cos.\theta.\cos.v = d^2r.\cos.^2\theta.\cos.^2v - 2dr.d\theta.\sin.\theta.\cos.\theta.\cos.^2v - 2dr.dv.\cos.^2\theta.\sin.v.\cos.v - d^2\theta.r.\sin.\theta.\cos.\theta.\cos.^2v - d\theta^2.r.\cos.^2\theta.\cos.^2v + 2dv.d\theta.r.\sin.\theta.\cos.\theta.\sin.v.\cos.v - d^2v\,r.\cos.^2\theta.\sin.v.\cos.v - dv^2.r.\cos.^2\theta.\cos.^2v$; $dy = dr.\cos.\theta.\sin.v - rd\theta.\sin.\theta.\sin.v + rdv.\cos.\theta.\cos.v$; ∵ $d^2y = d^2r.\cos.\theta.\sin.v - dr.d\theta.\sin.\theta.\sin.v + dr.dv.\cos.\theta.\cos.v - dr.d\theta.\sin.\theta.\sin.v - rd\theta^2.\cos.\theta.\sin.v - rd\theta.dv.\sin.\theta.\cos.v - rd^2\theta.\sin.\theta.\sin.v + dr.dv.\cos.\theta.\cos.v - rdv^2.\cos.\theta.\sin.v - rdv.d\theta.\sin.\theta.\cos.v + rd^2v.\cos.\theta.\cos.v$; ∵ $d^2y.\cos.\theta.\sin.v = d^2r.\cos.^2\theta.\sin.^2v.$

The values of r, v, and θ, involve six arbitrary quantities, which are introduced by the integration of the preceding differential equa-

$-2dr.d\theta.\sin.\theta.\cos.\theta.\sin.^2v+2dr.dv.\cos.^2\theta.\sin.v.\cos.v-rd\theta^2.\cos.^2\theta.\sin.^2v-rd^2\theta$ $\sin.\theta.\cos.\theta.\sin.^2v-rdv^2.\cos.^2\theta.\sin.^2v+rd^2v.\cos^2\theta.\sin.v.\cos.v-2rd\theta.dv.\sin.\theta.\cos.\theta.$ $\sin.v.\cos.v$; $dz=dr.\sin.\theta+rd\theta.\cos.\theta$; $\because d^2z=d^2r.\sin.\theta.+2dr.d\theta.\cos.\theta+rd^2\theta.\cos.\theta$ $-rd\theta^2.\sin.\theta$; $\because d^2z.\sin.\theta=d^2r.\sin.^2\theta+2dr.d\theta.\sin.\theta.\cos.\theta+rd^2\theta.\sin.\theta.\cos.\theta-rd\theta^2.$ $\sin.^2\theta$, consequently, $\frac{d^2x}{dt^2}\cos.\theta.\cos.v+\frac{d^2y}{dt^2}\cos.\theta.\sin.v+\frac{d^2z}{dt^2}\sin.\theta=\frac{d^2r}{dt^2}-\frac{rd\theta^2}{dt^2}$ $-\frac{rdv^2}{dt^2}.\cos.^2\theta$, but $\frac{dx}{dr}=\cos.\theta.\cos.v$; $\frac{dy}{dr}=\cos.\theta.\sin.v$; $\frac{dz}{dr}=\sin.\theta.\because\frac{d^2x}{dt^2}.$ $\cos.\theta.\cos.v+\frac{d^2y}{dt^2}.\cos.\theta.\sin.v+\frac{d^2z}{dt^2}.\sin.\theta=$

$$\left\{\frac{dQ}{dx}\right\}.\left\{\frac{dx}{dr}\right\}+\left\{\frac{dQ}{dy}\right\}.\left\{\frac{dy}{dr}\right\}+\left\{\frac{dQ}{dz}\right\}.\left\{\frac{dz}{dr}\right\}=\left\{\frac{dQ}{dr}\right\}=M'.$$

In like manner, if d^2x and its value be respectively multiplied by the differential of x, on the hypothesis that v is the only variable quantity, we shall obtain; $-r.d^2x.\cos.\theta.$ $\sin.v=-rd^2r.\cos.^2\theta.\sin.v.\cos.v+2dr.d\theta.r.\sin.\theta.\cos.\theta.\sin.v.\cos.v+2dr.dv.r.\cos.^2\theta.$ $\sin.^2v+d^2\theta.r^2.\sin.v.\cos.v.\sin.\theta.\cos.\theta+d\theta^2.r^2.\cos.^2\theta.\sin.v.\cos.v+d^2v.r^2.\cos.^2\theta.$ $\sin.^2v+dv^2r^2.\cos.^2\theta.\sin.v.\cos.v-2dv\,d\theta.r^2.\sin.\theta.\cos.\theta.\sin.^2v$; and multiplying d^2y and its value by the differential of y, taken on the same hypothesis, we obtain $r.d^2y.$ $\cos.\theta.\cos.v=r.d^2r.\cos.^2\theta.\sin.v.\cos.v-2dr.d\theta.r.\sin.\theta.\cos.\theta.\sin.v.\cos.v+2dr.dv.$ $r.\cos.^2\theta.\cos.^2v-r^2d\theta^2.\cos.^2\theta.\sin.v.\cos.v-r^2d^2\theta.\sin.\theta.\cos.\theta.\sin.v.\cos.v-r^2.dv^2.$ $\cos.^2\theta.\sin.v.\cos.v+r^2d^2v.\cos.^2\theta.\cos.^2v-2r^2.d\theta.dv.\sin.\theta.\cos.\theta.\cos.^2v$; $\therefore -r.d^2x.\cos.\theta.$ $\sin.v+rd^2y.\cos.\theta.\cos.v=2rdr\,dv.\cos.^2\theta+r^2d^2v.\cos.^2\theta-2r^2dv.d\theta\,\sin.\theta.\cos.\theta.$

$=d.(r^2.dv.\cos.^2\theta)$; $\frac{dx}{dv}=-r.\cos\theta.\sin.v$; $\frac{dy}{dv}=r.\cos.\theta.\cos.v$, $\because -\left\{\frac{d^2x}{dt^2}\right\}.$

$$r.\cos.\theta.\sin.v+\left\{\frac{d^2y}{dt^2}\right\}.r.\cos.\theta.\cos.v=\left\{\frac{dQ}{dx}\right\}.\left\{\frac{dx}{dv}\right\}+\left\{\frac{dQ}{dy}\right\}.\left\{\frac{dy}{dv}\right\}$$

$=\left\{\frac{dQ}{dv}\right\}=N'$. Multiplying d^2x and its value, by the differential of x, taken on the supposition that θ is the variable quantity; $-rd^2x.\sin.\theta.\cos.v=-rd^2r.\sin.\theta.\cos.\theta.$ $\cos.^2v+2rdr.d\theta.\sin.^2\theta.\cos.^2v+2rdr.dv.\sin.\theta.\cos.\theta.\sin.v.\cos.v+r^2d\theta^2.\sin.\theta.\cos.\theta.$ $\cos.^2v-2r^2d\theta.dv.\sin.^2\theta.\sin.v.\cos.v+r^2dv^2\sin.\theta.\cos.\theta.\cos.^2v+r^2.d^2\theta.\sin.^2\theta.$ $\cos.^2v+r^2d^2v.\sin.\theta.\cos.\theta.\sin.v.\cos.v$; performing a similar operation on d^2y and its value, we obtain $-d^2y.r.\sin.\theta.\sin.v=-rd^2r.\sin.\theta.\cos.\theta.\sin.^2v+2rdr.d\theta.\sin.^2\theta.\sin.^2v$ $-2rdr.dv.\sin.\theta.\cos.\theta.\sin.v.\cos.v+r^2d\theta^2.\sin.\theta.\cos.\theta.\sin.^2v+2r^2.d\theta.dv.\sin.^2\theta.$

tions.* Let us consider any three of these which we will denote by a, b, c; the equations $M' = \left\{\frac{dQ}{dr}\right\}$ will furnish us with the three following equations:

$$\left\{\frac{d^2Q}{dr}\right\}\cdot\left\{\frac{dr}{da}\right\}+\left\{\frac{d^2Q}{dr.dv}\right\}\cdot\left\{\frac{dv}{da}\right\}+\left\{\frac{d^2Q}{dr.d\theta}\right\}\cdot\left\{\frac{d\theta}{da}\right\}=\left\{\frac{dM'}{da}\right\};$$

$$\left\{\frac{d^2Q}{dr^2}\right\}\cdot\left\{\frac{dr}{db}\right\}+\left\{\frac{d^2Q}{dr.dv}\right\}\cdot\left\{\frac{dv}{db}\right\}+\left\{\frac{d^2Q}{dr.d\theta}\right\}\cdot\left\{\frac{d\theta}{db}\right\}=\left\{\frac{dM'}{db}\right\};$$

$$\left\{\frac{d^2Q}{dr^2}\right\}\cdot\left\{\frac{dr}{dc}\right\}+\left\{\frac{d^2Q}{dr.dv}\right\}\cdot\left\{\frac{dv}{dc}\right\}+\left\{\frac{d^2Q}{dr.d\theta}\right\}\cdot\left\{\frac{d\theta}{dc}\right\}=\left\{\frac{dM'}{dc}\right\};$$

We can obtain by means of those equations, the value of $\left\{\frac{d^2Q}{dr^2}\right\}$, and if we make

$$m=\left\{\frac{dv}{db}\right\}\cdot\left\{\frac{d\theta}{dc}\right\}-\left\{\frac{dv}{dc}\right\}\cdot\left\{\frac{d\theta}{db}\right\};$$

$$n=\left\{\frac{dv}{dc}\right\}\cdot\left\{\frac{d\theta}{da}\right\}-\left\{\frac{dv}{da}\right\}\cdot\left\{\frac{d\theta}{dc}\right\};$$

sin. v. cos. v + r^2dv^2. sin. θ. cos. θ. sin. ^2v + $r^2.d^2\theta$. sin. $^2\theta$. sin. ^2v — r^2d^2v. sin. θ. cos. θ. sin. v. cos. v; and in like manner $d^2z.r$ cos. $\theta = rd^2r$. sin. θ. cos. θ + $2rdr.d\theta$. cos. $^2\theta - r^2d\theta^2$. sin. θ. cos. $\theta + r^2d^2\theta$. cos. $^2\theta$, ∵ $-\frac{d^2x.r}{dt^2}$ sin. θ. cos. $v - \frac{d^2y.r}{dt^2}$ sin. θ. sin. $v + \frac{d^2z.r}{dt^2}$. cos. $\theta = \frac{2rdr.d\theta}{dt^2} + \frac{r^2.dv^2}{dt^2}$ sin. θ. cos. $\theta + r^2.\frac{d^2\theta}{dt^2}$, but $\frac{dx}{d\theta} = r$. sin. θ. cos. v; $\frac{dy}{d\theta} = -r$. sin. θ. sin. v.

$\frac{dz}{d\theta}$ = cos. θ; and $-\left\{\frac{d^2x}{dt^2}\right\}$. r. sin. θ. cos. $v - \left\{\frac{d^2y}{dt^2}\right\}$. r. sin. θ. sin. $v + \left\{\frac{d^2z}{dt^2}\right\}r$. cos. θ.

$$=\left\{\frac{dQ}{dx}\right\}\cdot\left\{\frac{dx}{d\theta}\right\}+\left\{\frac{dQ}{dy}\right\}\cdot\left\{\frac{dy}{d\theta}\right\}+\left\{\frac{dQ}{dz}\right\}\cdot\left\{\frac{dz}{d\theta}\right\}=\left\{\frac{dQ}{d\theta}\right\}$$

$$=\frac{2r.dr.d\theta}{dt^2}+r^2.\frac{d^2\theta}{dt^2}\text{sin. }\theta.\text{ cos. }\theta+r^2.\left\{\frac{dv^2}{dt^2}\right\}=P'.$$

* The values of r, v and θ are determined by the integration of equations of the second order, ∵ two arbitrary quantities are involved in the determination of each variable.

$$p = \left\{\frac{dv}{da}\right\}.\left\{\frac{d\theta}{db}\right\} - \left\{\frac{dv}{db}\right\}.\left\{\frac{d\theta}{da}\right\};$$

$$\epsilon = \left\{\frac{dr}{dc}\right\}.\left\{\frac{dv}{db}\right\}.\left\{\frac{d\theta}{dc}\right\} - \left\{\frac{dr}{da}\right\}.\left\{\frac{dv}{dc}\right\}.\left\{\frac{d\theta}{db}\right\};$$

$$+ \left\{\frac{dr}{db}\right\}.\left\{\frac{dv}{dc}\right\}.\left\{\frac{d\theta}{da}\right\} - \left\{\frac{dr}{db}\right\}.\left\{\frac{dv}{da}\right\}.\left\{\frac{d\theta}{dc}\right\};$$

$$+ \left\{\frac{dr}{dc}\right\}.\left\{\frac{dv}{da}\right\}.\left\{\frac{d\theta}{db}\right\} - \left\{\frac{dr}{dc}\right\}.\left\{\frac{dv}{db}\right\}.\left\{\frac{d\theta}{da}\right\};$$

we shall have

$$\epsilon.\left\{\frac{d^2Q}{dr^2}\right\} = m.\left\{\frac{dM'}{da}\right\} + n.\left\{\frac{dM'}{db}\right\} + p.\left\{\frac{dM'}{dc}\right\}.*$$

* From the value of $\left\{\frac{dQ}{dr}\right\} = M'$; it is evident that M' is a function of r, v and θ, and as these coordinates are functions of a, b, c, and conversely, it follows that

$$\left\{\frac{dM'}{da}\right\} = \left\{\frac{dM'}{dr}\right\}.\left\{\frac{dr}{da}\right\} + \left\{\frac{dM'}{dv}\right\}.\left\{\frac{dv}{da}\right\} + \left\{\frac{dM'}{d\theta}\right\}.\left\{\frac{d\theta}{da}\right\} =$$

(by substituting for M' its value $\left\{\frac{dQ}{dr}\right\}$)

$$\left\{\frac{d^2Q}{dr^2}\right\}.\left\{\frac{dr}{da}\right\} + \left\{\frac{d^2Q}{dr.dv}\right\}.\left\{\frac{dv}{da}\right\} + \left\{\frac{d^2Q}{dr.d\theta}\right\}.\left\{\frac{d\theta}{da}\right\},$$

by similar operations we obtain the values of $\left\{\frac{dM'}{db}\right\}$. $\left\{\frac{dM'}{dc}\right\}$, &c. Multiplying $\left\{\frac{dM'}{da}\right\}$ and its value, by m and its value, $\left\{\frac{dM'}{db}\right\}$ and its value, by n and its value, $\left\{\frac{dM'}{dc}\right\}$ and its value, by p and its value, we obtain

$$\left\{\frac{d^2Q}{dr^2}\right\}.\left\{\frac{dr}{da}\right\}\left(\left\{\frac{dv}{db}\right\}\left\{\frac{d\theta}{dc}\right\} - \left\{\frac{dv}{dc}\right\}.\left\{\frac{d\theta}{db}\right\}\right) + \left\{\frac{d^2Q}{dr.dv}\right\}.$$

$$\left\{\frac{dv}{da}\right\}.\left(\left\{\frac{dv}{db}\right\}.\left\{\frac{d\theta}{dc}\right\} - \left\{\frac{dv}{dc}\right\}.\left\{\frac{d\theta}{db}\right\}\right) + \left\{\frac{d^2Q}{dr.d\theta}\right\}.\left\{\frac{d\theta}{da}\right\}.\left(\left\{\frac{dv}{db}\right\}.\right.$$

In like manner if we make

$$m' = \left\{\frac{dr}{dc}\right\}.\left\{\frac{d\theta}{db}\right\} - \left\{\frac{dr}{db}\right\}.\left\{\frac{d\theta}{dc}\right\};$$

$$n' = \left\{\frac{dr}{da}\right\}.\left\{\frac{d\theta}{dc}\right\} - \left\{\frac{dr}{dc}\right\}.\left\{\frac{d\theta}{da}\right\};$$

$$p' = \left\{\frac{dr}{db}\right\}.\left\{\frac{d\theta}{da}\right\} - \left\{\frac{dr}{da}\right\}.\left\{\frac{d\theta}{db}\right\};$$

$$\left\{\frac{d\theta}{dc}\right\} - \left\{\frac{dv}{dc}\right\}.\left\{\frac{d\theta}{db}\right\}\Big) = m\left\{\frac{dM'}{da}\right\}.$$

$$\left\{\frac{d^2Q}{dr^2}\right\}.\left\{\frac{dr}{db}\right\}.\Big(\left\{\frac{dv}{dc}\right\}.\left\{\frac{d\theta}{da}\right\} - \left\{\frac{dv}{da}\right\}.\left\{\frac{d\theta}{dc}\right\}\Big) + \left\{\frac{d^2Q}{dr.dv}\right\}.$$

$$\left\{\frac{dv}{db}\right\}.\Big(\left\{\frac{dv}{dc}\right\}.\left\{\frac{d\theta}{da}\right\} - \left\{\frac{dv}{da}\right\}.\left\{\frac{d\theta}{dc}\right\}\Big) + \left\{\frac{d^2Q}{dr.d\theta}\right\}.\left\{\frac{d\theta}{db}\right\}.\Big(\left\{\frac{dv}{dc}\right\}.$$

$$\left\{\frac{d\theta}{da}\right\} - \left\{\frac{dv}{da}\right\}.\left\{\frac{d\theta}{dc}\right\}\Big) = n.\left\{\frac{dM'}{db}\right\}$$

$$\left\{\frac{d^2Q}{dr^2}\right\}.\left\{\frac{dr}{dc}\right\}\Big(\left\{\frac{dv}{da}\right\}.\left\{\frac{d\theta}{db}\right\} - \left\{\frac{dv}{db}\right\}.\left\{\frac{d\theta}{da}\right\}\Big) + \left\{\frac{d^2Q}{dr.dv}\right\}.$$

$$\left\{\frac{dv}{dc}\right\}\Big(\left\{\frac{dv}{da}\right\}.\left\{\frac{d\theta}{db}\right\} - \left\{\frac{dv}{db}\right\}.\left\{\frac{d\theta}{da}\right\}\Big) + \left\{\frac{d^2Q}{dr.dv}\right\}.\left\{\frac{d\theta}{dc}\right\}.\Big(\left\{\frac{dv}{da}\right\}.$$

$$\left\{\frac{d\theta}{db}\right\} - \left\{\frac{dv}{db}\right\}.\left\{\frac{d\theta}{da}\right\}\Big) = p.\left\{\frac{dM'}{dc}\right\}.$$

Adding these three expressions together, and observing that the coefficients of $\left(\frac{d^2Q}{dr.dv}\right)$, $\left(\frac{d^2Q}{dr.d\theta}\right)$ are respectively equal to cipher, and that the coefficient of $\left(\frac{d^2Q'}{dr^2}\right) = \mathfrak{C}$, we will obtain the expression given in the text. We can by a similar process obtain the values of $\left(\frac{d^2Q}{dv^2}\right)$, $\left(\frac{d^2Q}{d\theta^2}\right)$, now if we substitute these values in the equation (F), and also M' and P', for $\left\{\frac{dQ}{dr}\right\}$, $\left\{\frac{dQ}{d\theta}\right\}$, and multiply by $\mathfrak{C}$ and $\cos^2\theta$, we will arrive at the equation (G).

the equation $N' = \left(\frac{dQ}{dv}\right)$ will give

$$\epsilon.\left\{\frac{d^2Q}{d^2v}\right\} = m'.\left\{\frac{dN'}{da}\right\} + n'.\left\{\frac{dN'}{db}\right\} + p'.\left\{\frac{dN'}{dc}\right\}.$$

Finally, if we make

$$m'' = \left\{\frac{dr}{db}\right\}.\left\{\frac{dv}{dc}\right\} - \left\{\frac{dr}{dc}\right\}.\left\{\frac{dv}{db}\right\};$$

$$n'' = \left\{\frac{dr}{dc}\right\}.\left\{\frac{dv}{da}\right\} - \left\{\frac{dr}{da}\right\}.\left\{\frac{dv}{dc}\right\};$$

$$p'' = \left\{\frac{dr}{da}\right\}.\left\{\frac{dv}{db}\right\} - \left\{\frac{dr}{db}\right\}.\left\{\frac{dv}{da}\right\};$$

The equation $P' = \left\{\frac{dQ}{d\theta}\right\}$ will give

$$\epsilon.\left\{\frac{d^2Q}{d\theta^2}\right\} = m''.\left\{\frac{dP'}{da}\right\} + n''.\left\{\frac{dP'}{db}\right\} + p''.\left\{\frac{dP'}{dc}\right\}.$$

Consequently, the equation (F) will become,

$$0 = m.r^2 \cos.^2\theta.\left\{\frac{dM'}{da}\right\} + n.r^2 \cos.^2\theta.\left\{\frac{dM'}{db}\right\} + p.r^2.\cos.^2\theta.\left\{\frac{dM'}{dc}\right\}$$

$$+ m'.\left\{\frac{dN'}{da}\right\} + n'.\left\{\frac{dN'}{db}\right\} + p'.\left\{\frac{dN'}{dc}\right\}. \text{(G)}$$

$$+ m''.\cos.\theta^2.\left\{\frac{dP'}{da}\right\} + n''.\cos.^2\theta.\left\{\frac{dP'}{db}\right\} + p''.\cos.^2\theta.\left\{\frac{dP'}{dc}\right\}.$$

$$+ \epsilon(2rM'.\cos.^2\theta - P'.\sin.\theta.\cos.\theta).$$

In the theory of the moon, we neglect the perturbations, that its action produces in the relative motion of the sun about the earth, which implies that its mass is indefinitely small. Then the variables x', y', z', which are relative to the sun, are independent of x, y, z, and the equation (G) obtains in this theory; it is therefore necessary that the values found for r, v and θ, should satisfy this equation, which furnishes us with a means of verifying these values. If the inequalities which are observed in the motion of the moon, are the result of a mutual attraction between these three bodies, namely, the sun, the earth, and the moon, the observed values of r, v and θ, deduced from observation, should satisfy the equation (G), which furnishes us with a means of verifying the theory of universal gravitation; for the mean longitudes of the moon, of its perigee, and of its ascending node, occur in these values, and a, b, c, may be assumed equal to these longitudes.

In like manner, if in the theory of the planets, we neglect the square of the disturbing forces, which we are almost always permitted to do; then, in the theory of the planet, of which the coordinates are x, y, z, we can suppose that the coordinates x', y', z', x'', &c. of the other planets, are relative to their elliptic motion, and consequently, independent of x, y, z; therefore the equation (G) obtains in this theory.*

15. The differential equations of the preceding No.

$$\left.\begin{aligned} &\frac{d^2r}{dt^2}-\frac{rdv^2}{dt^2}.\cos.^2\theta-r.\frac{d\theta^2}{dt^2}=\left\{\frac{dQ}{dr}\right\};\\ &\frac{d.(r^2.\frac{dv}{dt}.\cos.^2\theta)}{dt}=\left\{\frac{dQ}{dv}\right\};\\ &r^2.\frac{d^2\theta}{dt^2}+r^2.\frac{dv^2}{dt^2}.\sin.\theta.\cos.\theta+\frac{2rdr.d\theta}{dt^2}=\left\{\frac{dQ}{d\theta}\right\} \end{aligned}\right\};\quad (H)$$

* We arrived at the equation (G) on the supposition that x, y, z were independent of x' y', z', &c. In the case of elliptic motion x, y, z, are independent of x', y', z', and conversely, and as when the square of the perturbating force is neglected, the motion is $q.p.$ elliptic, it follows that x, y, z, are in this case independent of x', y', z'. See page 49, of the text.

are only a combination of the differential equations (i) of the same No.; but they are more convenient, and better adapted to astronomical computations. We can assign other forms to them, which may be useful in different circumstances.

Instead of the variables r and θ, let us consider u and s, u being equal to $\frac{1}{r.\cos.\theta}$, that is to unity divided by the projection of the radius vector, on the plane of x and of y; and s being equal to the tangent of θ, or to the tangent of latitude of m above the same plane, by multiplying the second of the equations (H) by $r^2dv.\cos.^2\theta$, and then integrating, we shall obtain

$$\left\{\frac{dv}{u^2.dt}\right\}^2 = h^2 + 2\int\left\{\frac{dQ}{dv}\right\}.\frac{dv}{u^2};\text{*}$$

h being a constant arbitrary quantity; consequently we have

$$dt = \frac{dv}{u^2.\sqrt{h^2 + 2\int\left\{\frac{dQ}{dv}\right\}.\frac{dv}{u^2}}}.$$

If the first of the equations (H) multiplied by $-\cos.\theta$, be added to the third multiplied by $\frac{\sin.\theta}{r}$, we shall obtain

$$-\frac{d^2.\frac{1}{u}}{dt^2} + \frac{1}{u}.\frac{dv^2}{dt^2} = u^2.\left\{\frac{dQ}{du}\right\} + us.\left\{\frac{dQ}{ds}\right\};$$

from which we deduce

There are two distinct objects, one to verify the values of r, v, θ, and the other to verify the theory of universal gravitation.

* $r^2.dv.\cos.^2\theta.\ d.(r^2.\frac{dv}{dt}.\cos.^2\theta) = \frac{dv}{u^2}\ d.\left(\frac{dv}{u^2.dt}\right) = \frac{dv}{u^2}.\left(\frac{dQ}{dv}\right) \therefore \left(\frac{dv}{u^2.dt}\right)^2$
$= h^2 + 2\int.\frac{dv}{u^2}.\left(\frac{dQ}{dv}\right).$

$$d.\left\{\frac{du}{u^2.dt}\right\}+\frac{dv^2}{u.dt}=u^2.dt.\left\{\left\{\frac{dQ}{du}\right\}+\frac{s}{u}.\left\{\frac{dQ}{ds}\right\}\right\}.$$

If we consider dv as constant, we shall obtain by substituting for dt its value, which has been already given

$$0=\frac{d^2u}{dv^2}+u+\frac{\left\{\frac{dQ}{dv}\right\}.\frac{du}{u^2dv}-\frac{dQ}{du}-\frac{s}{u}.\left\{\frac{dQ}{ds}\right\}}{h^2+2.\int\left\{\frac{dQ}{dv}\right\}.\frac{dv}{u^2}}\;*$$

* $-\frac{d^2r}{dt^2}.\cos.\theta+r.\frac{dv^2}{dt^2}.\cos.^3\theta+r.\frac{d\theta^2}{dt^2}.\cos.\theta+r.\frac{d^2\theta}{dt^2}.\sin.\theta+r.\frac{dv^2}{dt^2}.\sin.^2\theta.\cos.\theta+\frac{2dr.d\theta}{dt^2}.\sin.\theta=-\left(\frac{dQ}{dr}\right).\cos.\theta+\left(\frac{dQ}{d\theta}\right).\frac{\sin.\theta}{r}$; but $\frac{1}{u}=r.\cos.\theta$; and $d.\frac{1}{u}=dr.\cos.\theta-rd\theta.\sin.\theta$; $\because d^2.\frac{1}{u}=d^2r.\cos.\theta-2dr.d\theta.\sin.\theta.-d^2\theta.r.\sin.\theta-rd\theta^2.\cos.\theta$; $\therefore$ by concinnating and substituting $-d^2.\frac{1}{u}$, for its value, and noting that $r.\left(\frac{dv^2}{dt^2}\right).\cos.^3\theta=r.\left(\frac{dv^2}{dt^2}\right).\cos.\theta-r.\left(\frac{dv^2}{dt^2}\right).\cos.\theta.\sin.^2\theta$, we obtain $-\frac{d^2.\frac{1}{u}}{dt^2}+r.\frac{dv^2}{dt^2}.\cos.\theta.=-\left(\frac{dQ}{dr}\right).\cos.\theta+\left(\frac{dQ}{d\theta}\right).\frac{\sin.\theta}{r}$; $-\frac{du}{u^2}=dr.\cos.\theta-rd\theta.\sin.\theta$; $\left(\frac{dQ}{dr}\right)=\left(\frac{dQ}{du}\right).\left(\frac{du}{dr}\right)$, but $\frac{du}{dr}=-u^2.\cos.\theta.\therefore-\left(\frac{dQ}{dr}\right).\cos.\theta=\left(\frac{dQ}{du}\right).u^2.\cos.^2\theta$; $\left(\frac{dQ}{d\theta}\right)=\left(\frac{dQ}{du}\right).\left(\frac{du}{d\theta}\right)+\left(\frac{dQ}{ds}\right).\left(\frac{ds}{d\theta}\right)$, and as $s=\tan.\theta$; $\frac{ds}{d\theta}=(1+s^2)$; $\left(\frac{du}{d\theta}\right)=r.\sin.\theta.u^2\therefore\left(\frac{dQ}{d\theta}\right).\frac{\sin.\theta}{r}=\left(\frac{dQ}{du}\right).\left(\frac{du}{d\theta}\right).\frac{\sin.\theta}{r}+\left(\frac{dQ}{ds}\right).\left(\frac{ds}{d\theta}\right).\frac{\sin.\theta}{r}=\left(\frac{dQ}{du}\right).\sin.^2\theta.u^2+\left(\frac{dQ}{ds}\right).(1+s^3).\frac{\sin.\theta}{r}$; $\sin.\theta=\frac{s}{\sqrt{1+s^2}}$; and $\frac{1}{r}=\frac{u}{\sqrt{1+s^2}}\therefore\left(\frac{dQ}{ds}\right).(1+s^2)\frac{\sin.\theta}{r}=\left(\frac{dQ}{ds}\right).us$, and making the two cofficients of $\left(\frac{dQ}{du}\right)$ to coalesce, we obtain $\frac{d^2\frac{1}{u}}{dt^2}+\frac{dv^2}{u.dt^2}=u^2.(\sin.^2\theta+\cos.^2\theta)$.

In the same manner, by treating dv as if it was constant, the third of the equations (H), will become

$$0=\frac{d^2s}{dv^2}+s+\frac{\frac{ds}{dv}.\left\{\frac{dQ}{dv}\right\}-(1+s^2)\left\{\frac{dQ}{ds}\right\}-us.\left\{\frac{dQ}{du}\right\}^*}{u^2.\left(h^2+2\int\left\{\frac{dQ}{dv}\right\}.\frac{dv}{u^2}\right)}.$$

$\left(\frac{dQ}{du}\right)+us.\left(\frac{dQ}{ds}\right)$. Substituting for dt we obtain

$$d.\left(\frac{du}{dv}.\sqrt{h^2+2\int\left(\frac{dQ}{dv}\right).\frac{dv}{u^2}}\right)+dv.u.\sqrt{h^2+2\int\left(\frac{dQ}{dv}\right).\frac{dv}{u^2}}$$

$$=\frac{dv}{\sqrt{h^2+2\int\left(\frac{dQ}{dv}\right).\frac{dv}{u^2}}}\left(\left(\frac{dQ}{du}\right)+\frac{s}{u}.\left(\frac{dQ}{ds}\right)\right)=\frac{d^2u}{dv}.\sqrt{h^2+2\int\left(\frac{dQ}{dv}\right).\frac{dv}{u^2}}$$

$$\frac{+du.dv.\left(\frac{dQ}{dv}\right).\frac{1}{u^2}}{dv.\sqrt{h^2+2\int\left(\frac{dQ}{dv}\right).\left(\frac{dv}{u^2}\right)}}+dv.u.\sqrt{h^2+2\int\left(\frac{dQ}{dv}\right).\frac{dv}{u^2}}=$$

$\frac{dv}{\sqrt{h^2+2\int\left\{\frac{dQ}{dv}\right\}.\frac{dv}{u^2}}}.\left\{\left\{\frac{dQ}{du}\right\}+\frac{s}{u}\left\{\frac{dQ}{ds}\right\}\right\}$, $\therefore$ dividing by dv, and the radical quantity we obtain the expression which is given in the text.

* $d\theta=\frac{ds}{1+s^2}$, $\therefore d^2\theta=\frac{d^2s}{1+s^2}-\frac{2sds^2}{(1+s^2)^2}$; $r^2=\frac{1+s^2}{u^2}$, $\therefore r^2.\frac{d^2\theta}{dt^2}=\frac{d^2s}{u^2dt^2}-\frac{2s}{(1+s^2)}$ $\frac{ds^2}{u^2.dt^2}$, (sin. θ. cos. $\theta=\frac{s}{1+s^2}$, $\therefore r^2.\frac{dv^2}{dt^2}$. sin. θ. cos. $\theta=\frac{s}{u^2}.\frac{dv^2}{dt^2}$; $2rdr=\frac{2sds}{u^2}$ $-\frac{2du.(1+s^2)}{u^3}$, $\therefore 2rdr.d\theta=\frac{2s\cdot ds^2}{(1+s^2)u^2}-\frac{2du.ds}{u^3}$; but $r^2.\frac{d^2\theta}{dt^2}=\frac{r^2}{dt}.d.\left\{\frac{d\theta}{dt}\right\}=\frac{r^2}{dt}.$ $\left\{\frac{d^2\theta}{dt}-\frac{d\theta.d^2t}{dt^2}\right\}$; $\therefore$ by substituting for $d^2\theta$, $d\theta$ and r^2 their values already given, and for $-\frac{d^2t}{dt^2}$ its value

$$\frac{d.\left(u^2.\sqrt{h^2+2\int\left\{\frac{dQ}{dv}\right\}.\frac{dv}{u^2}}\right.}{dv}=\frac{2udu}{dv}.\sqrt{h^2+2\int\left\{\frac{dQ}{dv}\right\}.\frac{dv}{u^2}}$$

Therefore in place of the three differential equations (H), we shall have the following:

$$dt = \frac{dv}{u.\sqrt{h^2 + 2\int\left\{\frac{dQ}{dv}\right\}.\frac{dv}{u^2}}};$$

$$0 = \frac{d^2u}{dv^2} + u + \frac{\left\{\frac{dQ}{dv}\right\}.\frac{du}{u^2dv} - \left\{\frac{dQ}{du}\right\} - \frac{s}{u}.\left\{\frac{dQ}{ds}\right\}}{h^2 + 2\int\left\{\frac{dQ}{dv}\right\}.\frac{dv}{u^2}} \qquad (K)$$

$$0 = \frac{d^2s}{dv^2} + s + \frac{\frac{ds}{dv}.\left\{\frac{dQ}{dv}\right\} - us.\left\{\frac{dQ}{dv}\right\} - (1+s^2).\left\{\frac{dQ}{ds}\right\}}{u^2.\left\{h^2 + 2.\int\left\{\frac{dQ}{dv}\right\}.\frac{dv}{u^2}\right\}}.$$

By making these equations to assume the following form, we avoid fractions and radicals,

$$\left.\frac{+u^2.\frac{dQ}{dv}.\frac{dv}{u^2}}{dv.\sqrt{h^2+2\int\left\{\frac{dQ}{dv}\right\}.\frac{dv}{u^2}}}\right\},$$ the third equation (H) becomes =

$$\left\{\frac{d^2s}{u^2.dt^2} - \frac{2s.ds^2}{(1+s^2).u^2.dt^2}. + \left\{\frac{ds}{u^2}.\frac{2u.du}{dv.dt}\right\}\right.$$

$$\left\{\sqrt{h^2+2\int\left\{\frac{dQ}{dv}\right\}.\frac{dv}{u^2}}\right\} + \frac{\frac{ds}{u^2}.u^2.\frac{dQ}{dv}.\frac{dv}{u^2}}{dt.dv.\sqrt{h^2+2\int\left\{\frac{dQ}{dv}\right\}.\left\{\frac{dv}{u^2}\right\}}} + \frac{s}{u^2}.\frac{dv^2}{dt^2}$$

$$\left. + \frac{2sds^2}{(1+s^2).u^2.dt^2} - \frac{2du.ds}{u^3.dt^2} = \left\{\frac{dQ}{du}\right\}.\left\{\frac{du}{d\theta}\right\} + \left\{\frac{dQ}{ds}\right\}.\left\{\frac{ds}{d\theta}\right\}\right\}$$ = oy substituting for dt its value, and calling $\sqrt{h^2+2\int\left\{\frac{dQ}{dv}\right\}.\left\{\frac{dv}{u^2}\right\}.}$ p $\frac{d^2s}{dv^2}.u^2.p^2 - \frac{2s}{(1+s^2)}.$

$$\frac{ds^2.u^2}{dv^2}.p^2 + \frac{ds}{dv^2}.2udu.p^2 + \frac{ds}{dv^2}.\frac{dQ}{dv}.dv + s.u^2.p^2 + \frac{2s.ds^2}{1+s^2}.\frac{u^2.p^2}{dv^2}$$

$\frac{-2du.u\,ds.p^2}{dv^2} = +\left\{\frac{dQ}{du}\right\}.su + \left\{\frac{dQ}{ds}\right\}.(1+s^2)$; equal evidently to the third equation (K).

$$0=\frac{d^2t}{dv^2}+\frac{2du.dt}{u.dv^2}+u^2.\left\{\frac{dQ}{dv}\right\}.\frac{dt^3}{dv^3};^*$$

$$0=\left\{\frac{d^2u}{dv^2}+u.\right\}.\left\{1+\frac{2}{h}.\int\left\{\frac{dQ}{dv}\right\}.\frac{dv}{u^2}\right\}$$

$$+\frac{1}{h^2}\left\{\left\{\frac{dQ}{dv}\right\}.\frac{du}{u^2.dv}-\left\{\frac{dQ}{du}\right\}-\frac{s}{u}.\left\{\frac{dQ}{ds}\right\}\right\}; \qquad \text{(L)}$$

$$0=\left\{\frac{d^2s}{dv^2}+s\right\}.\left\{1+\frac{2}{h^2}.\int\left\{\frac{dQ}{dv}\right\}.\frac{dv}{u^2}\right\}$$

$$+\frac{1}{h^2u^2}.\left\{\frac{ds}{dv}.\left\{\frac{dQ}{dv}\right\}-us.\left\{\frac{dQ}{du}\right\}-(1+s^2).\left\{\frac{dQ}{ds}\right\}\right\}.$$

By making use of other coordinates, we might form new systems of differential equations; suppose, for example, that the coordinates x and y, of the equations (i) of No. 14, are transformed into others, relative to two moveable axes situated in the plane of these coordinates, and of which the first indicates the mean longitude of the body m, the second lying perpendicular to it. Let $x_{,}$ and $y_{,}$ represent the coordinates of m, relatively to these axes, and let $nt+\varepsilon$ denote the mean longitude of m, or

* By differentiating the first of the equations (K), we obtain d^2t

$$=\frac{-2du\,dv}{u^3.\sqrt{(h^2+2\int\left\{\frac{dQ}{dv}\right\}.\frac{dv}{u^2}}}-\frac{dv^2.\frac{dQ}{dv}}{u^4(h^2+2\int\left\{\frac{dQ}{dv}\right\}.\frac{dv}{u^2}\right\}^{\frac{3}{2}}}$$; and by substituting $\frac{dt}{dv}, \frac{dt^3}{dv^3}$,

for their values, $d^2t=-\frac{2du}{u}.\,dt-\dfrac{dt^2.\left\{\frac{dQ}{dv}\right\}}{\sqrt{h^2+2\int\left\{\frac{dQ}{dv}\right\}.\frac{dv}{u^2}}}\;\dfrac{=dt^3.\left\{\frac{dQ}{dv}\right\}.u^2;}{dv}$ ∴

dividing by dv^2; we obtain $\frac{d^2t}{dv^2}=\frac{2du.dt}{udv^2}-\frac{dt^3}{dv^3}.u^2.\left\{\frac{dQ}{dv}\right\}$, in the second and third equations, the second should be multiplied by the denominator, and then divided by h^2, the third should be multiplied by the denominator, and afterwards divided by $h^2.u^2$.

the angle which the moveable axis of $x_{,}$ makes with the axis of x; we shall have

$$x = x_{,}.\cos.(nt+\varepsilon) - y_{,}.\sin.(nt+\varepsilon);$$
$$y = x_{,}.\sin.(nt+\varepsilon) + y_{,}.\cos.(nt+\varepsilon);$$

from which we collect, on the supposition that dt is constant,

$$d^2x.\cos.(nt+\varepsilon) + d^2y.\sin.(nt+\varepsilon) = d^2x_{,} - n^2x_{,}.dt^2 - 2ndy_{,}.dt;$$
$$d^2y.\cos.(nt+\varepsilon) - d^2x.\sin.(nt+\varepsilon) = d^2y_{,} - n^2y_{,}^2.dt^2 + 2ndx_{,}.dt.$$

By substituting in Q, in place of x and of y, their preceding values, we will obtain

$$\left\{\frac{dQ}{dx}\right\} = \left\{\frac{dQ}{dx_{,}}\right\}.\cos.(nt+\varepsilon) - \left\{\frac{dQ}{dy_{,}}\right\}.\sin.(nt+\varepsilon);$$
$$\left\{\frac{dQ}{dy}\right\} = \left\{\frac{dQ}{dx_{,}}\right\}.\sin.(nt+\varepsilon) + \left\{\frac{dQ}{dy_{,}}\right\}.\cos.(nt+\varepsilon);$$

This being premised, the differential equations (i) will give the three following;

$$0 = \frac{d^2x_{,}}{dt^2} - n^2x_{,} - 2n.\frac{dy_{,}}{dt} - \left\{\frac{dQ}{dx_{,}}\right\};*$$
$$0 = \frac{d^2y_{,}}{dt^2} - n^2y_{,} + 2n.\frac{dx_{,}}{dt} - \left\{\frac{dQ}{dy_{,}}\right\};$$
$$0 = \frac{d^2z}{dt^2} - \left\{\frac{dQ}{dz}\right\}.$$

* $dx = dx_{,}.\cos.(nt+\varepsilon) - dy_{,}.\sin.(nt+\varepsilon) - nx_{,}.dt.\sin.(nt+\varepsilon) - ny_{,}.dt.\cos.(nt+\varepsilon).$

$dy = dx_{,}.\sin.(nt+\varepsilon) + dy_{,}.\cos.(nt+\varepsilon) + nx_{,}.dt.\cos.(nt+\varepsilon) - ny_{,}.dt.\sin.(nt+\varepsilon).$

$d^2x = d^2x_{,}.\cos.(nt+\varepsilon) - d^2y_{,}.\sin.(nt+\varepsilon) - 2ndx_{,}.dt.\sin.(nt+\varepsilon) - 2ndy_{,}.dt.\cos.(nt+\varepsilon).$
$- n^2x_{,}.dt^2.\cos.(nt+\varepsilon) + n^2y_{,}.dt^2.\sin.(nt+\varepsilon).$

$d^2y = d^2x_{,}.\sin.(nt+\varepsilon) + d^2y_{,}.\cos.(nt+\varepsilon) + 2ndx_{,}.dt.\cos.(nt+\varepsilon) - 2ndy_{,}.dt.\sin.(nt+\varepsilon)$
$- n^2x_{,}.dt^2.\sin.(nt+\varepsilon) - n^2y_{,}.dt^2.\cos.(nt+\varepsilon).$

$\because\ d^2x.\cos.(nt+\varepsilon) + d^2y.\sin.(nt+\varepsilon) = d^2x_{,} - 2ndy_{,}.dt - n^2x_{,}.dt^2.$

After having deduced the differential equations of a system of bodies subject to their mutual attraction, and also the only exact integrals, which we have hitherto been able to obtain, being determined; it remains for us to integrate these equations by successive approximations. In the solar system, the heavenly bodies move very nearly as if they were only subject to the principal force which actuates them, and the disturbing forces are inconsiderable; we are therefore permitted in a first approximation, solely to consider the mutual action of two bodies, namely, that of a planet or of a comet, and of the Sun, in the theory of the planets, and of the comets; and the mutual action of a planet and its satellite, in the theory of the satellites. We will, therefore, commence with determining rigorously the motion of two bodies which attract each other; this first approximation will conduct us to a second, in which we will consider the first power of the disturbing forces; afterwards we will take into account, the squares and products of these forces; and proceeding in this manner, we will determine the celestial motions with all the precision which the observations admit of.

$$d^2y.\cos.(nt+\epsilon)-d^2x.\sin.(nt+\epsilon)=d^2y_{,}+2ndx_{,}.dt-n^2y_{,}.dt^2.$$

$$\frac{dQ}{dx}=\left\{\frac{dQ}{dx_{,}}\right\}.\left\{\frac{dx_{,}}{dx}\right\}+\left\{\frac{dQ}{dy_{,}}\right\}.\left\{\frac{dy_{,}}{dx}\right\};\text{ but }\left\{\frac{dx_{,}}{dx}\right\}=\cos.(nt+\epsilon);\ \left\{\frac{dy_{,}}{dx}\right\}$$

$$=-\sin.(nt+\epsilon)\ \because\ \left\{\frac{dQ}{dx}\right\}=\left\{\frac{dQ}{dx_{,}}\right\}.\cos.(nt+\epsilon)-\left\{\frac{dQ}{dy_{,}}\right\}.\sin.(nt+\epsilon).$$

$x_{,}=x.\cos.(nt+\epsilon)+y.\sin.(nt+\epsilon)$; $y_{,}=y.\cos.(nt+\epsilon)-x.\sin.(nt+\epsilon)$; hence may be inferred the values of $\frac{dx_{,}}{dx}$, $\frac{dy_{,}}{dx}$, &c. &c.

$\frac{d^2x}{dt^2}.\cos.(nt+\epsilon)=\left\{\frac{dQ}{dx}\right\}.\cos.(nt+\epsilon)=\left\{\frac{dQ}{dx_{,}}\right\}.\cos.^2(nt+\epsilon)-\left\{\frac{dQ}{dy_{,}}\right\}.\sin.(nt+\epsilon).$ $\cos.(nt+\epsilon)$; $\frac{d^2y}{dt^2}.\sin.(nt+\epsilon)=\left\{\frac{dQ}{dy}\right\}.\sin.(nt+\epsilon)=\left\{\frac{dQ}{dx_{,}}\right\}.\sin.^2(nt+\epsilon)+\left\{\frac{dQ}{dy_{,}}\right\}.$ $\sin.(nt+\epsilon).\cos.(nt+\epsilon)$. $\therefore\ \frac{d^2x}{dt^2}.\cos.(nt+\epsilon)+\frac{d^2y}{dt^2}.\sin.(nt+\epsilon)=\frac{d^2x_{,}}{dt^2}-n^2x_{,}.dt-$ $2ndy_{,}dt=\left\{\frac{dQ}{dx_{,}}\right\}.$

CHAPTER III.

First approximation of the celestial motions, or the theory of elliptic motion.

16. It has been already demonstrated in the first Chapter, that a body attracted to a fixed point, by a force which is inversely as the square of the distance, describes a conic section; but in the relative motion of the body m about M, if this last body be considered at rest, we should transfer to m in an opposite direction, the action which m exercises on M; therefore, in this relative motion, m is sollicited towards M by a force which is equal to the sum of the masses divided by the square of their distance, consequently the body m describes a conic section about M. But the importance of this subject in the theory of the system of the world, requires that it should be resumed under new points of view.

For this purpose, let us consider the equations (K) of No. 15. If $M+m$ be made $=\mu$, it is evident from No. 14, that if we only consider the reciprocal action of M on m, Q is equal to $\frac{\mu}{r}$ or to $\frac{\mu u}{\sqrt{1+s^2}}$, the equations (K) will consequently become,

$$dt = \frac{dv}{h.u^2};$$

$$0=\frac{d^2u}{dv^2}+u-\frac{\mu}{h.^2(1+s^2)^{\frac{3}{2}}};^*$$

$$0=\frac{d^2s}{dv^2}+s.$$

The area described by the projection of the radius vector, during the element of time dt, being equal to $\frac{1}{2}.\frac{dv}{u^2}$;† the first of these equations indicates that this area is proportional to this element, and that consequently in a finite time, it is proportional to the time. By integrating the last equation we obtain

$$s=\gamma.\ \sin.\ (v-\theta),‡$$

* $\left\{\frac{dQ}{du}\right\}=\frac{\mu}{\sqrt{1+s^2}}$, $\left\{\frac{dQ}{ds}\right\}=\frac{-\mu us}{(1+s^2)^{\frac{3}{2}}}$, $\left\{\frac{dQ}{dv}\right\}=0$; therefore if these values of $\left\{\frac{dQ}{dv}\right\}$, $\left\{\frac{dQ}{ds}\right\}$, $\left\{\frac{dQ}{du}\right\}$ be substituted in the equations (K); the second of these equations becomes

$$\frac{d^2u}{dv^2}+u-\frac{\frac{dQ}{du}-\frac{s}{u}.\frac{dQ}{ds}}{h^2}=\frac{d^2u}{dv^2}+u-\frac{\mu}{h^2\sqrt{1+s^2}}+\frac{\mu.s^2}{h^2(1+s^2)^{\frac{3}{2}}}=\frac{d^2u}{dv^2}$$

$+u-\frac{\mu}{h^2(1+s^2)^{\frac{3}{2}}}$, and the third equation becomes $\frac{d^2s}{dv^2}+s-$

$$\frac{\frac{\mu us}{\sqrt{1+s^2}}+\frac{\mu us}{\sqrt{1+s^2}}}{u^2.h^2}=\frac{d^2s}{dv^2}+s.$$

† $\frac{1}{2}.\frac{dv}{u^2}=\frac{1}{2}.dv.r^2.\cos.^2\theta=$ the element of the area described in a given time by the projection of the radius vector; see page 4.

‡ $\frac{d^2s}{dv^2}+s=0$; $\because \frac{d^2s.ds}{dv^2}+sds=0$, therefore by integrating $\frac{ds^2}{dv^2}+s^2=c$, it is evident that $s=\sin.\ v$, or $s=\cos.\ v$, and that $\because s=a\ \sin.\ v$, or $s=b.\ \cos.\ v$, and consequently $s=a.\ \sin.\ v+b.\ \cos.\ v$. will satisfy the given equation, and be its complete integral; as it contains two independent arbitrary quantities. Now, $a\sin.v+b.\cos.v$. may be reduced to the form $\gamma\sin(v-\theta)$, by assuming $a=\gamma.\cos.\theta$, $b=-\gamma.\sin\theta$, which gives $a.\sin.v+b.\cos.v=\gamma.(\sin.v.\cos.\theta-\cos.v.\sin.\theta)=\gamma.\sin.(v-\theta)$, and it may be shewn that $\gamma.\sin.(v-\theta)$, likewise satisfies this equation. It is also

γ and θ being two arbitrary quantities. Finally, the second equation gives by its integration

$$u = \frac{\mu}{h^2.(1+\gamma^2)} \left\{ \sqrt{1+s^2} + e. \cos. (v-\varpi) \right\} = \frac{\sqrt{1+s^2}}{r};^*$$

e and ϖ being two new arbitrary quantities. By substituting in this

evident, that $s = a. \sin. (v-\theta) + b. \cos. (v-\theta)$ will satisfy the equation $\frac{d^2s}{dv^2} + s = 0$, and may be used when convenient, but in this case a, b and θ, must be selected in such a manner, that they may be reduced to two *independent* quantities.

* In the equation $\frac{d^2u}{dv^2} + u - \frac{\mu}{h^2.(1+s^2)^{\frac{3}{2}}}$, let $P = \frac{\mu}{h^2(1+s^2)^{\frac{3}{2}}}$, and $u = a. \sin. (v-\theta) + b. \cos. (v-\theta)$ will be the complete integral of the equation $\frac{d^2u}{dv^2} + u = 0$; and $a \sin. (v-\theta)$ and $b. \cos. (v-\theta)$ will respectively satisfy the equation $\frac{d^2u}{dv^2} + u = 0$; now if the expression $a. \sin. (v-\theta) + b. \cos. (v-\theta)$ be regarded as the integral of the differential equation $\frac{d^2u}{dv^2} + v - P = 0$; a and b must in this case be functions of the variables v, and as there is only one equation to verify by means of a and b, we can impose certain conditions on them which will facilitate their determination; supposing them to be functions of v in the equation $u = a. \sin. (v-\theta) + b. \cos. (v-\theta)$, we shall have

$$du = adv. \cos. (v-\theta) - b. dv. \sin. (v-\theta) + da. \sin. (v-\theta) + db. \cos. (v-\theta);$$

but as there are two quantities to be determined, and as the proposed question furnishes us with but one condition, we are at liberty to select the other condition; for this purpose let

$$da. \sin. (v-\theta) + db. \cos. (v-\theta) = 0;$$

then $du = dv. (a. \cos. (v-\theta) - b. \sin. (v-\theta))$; and consequently,

$$d^2u = - dv^2. (a. \sin. (v-\theta) + b. \cos. (v-\theta)) + dv. da. \cos. (v-\theta) - dv.db. \sin. (v-\theta);$$

and this value of d^2u being substituted in the equation $\frac{d^2u}{dv^2} + u - \frac{\mu}{h^2(1+s^2)^{\frac{3}{2}}}$ gives, $adv^2. (\sin. (v-\theta) - \sin. (v-\theta)) + bdv^2. (\cos. (v-\theta) - \cos. (v-\theta)) + da.dv. \cos. (v-\theta) - db.dv. \sin. (v-\theta) - Pdv^2 = 0$; $\therefore da.dv. \cos^2. (v-\theta) - db.dv. \sin. (v-\theta). \cos. (v-\theta)$

expression for u, in place of s, its value in terms of v, and then substituting this expression, in the equation $dt = \frac{dv}{h.u^2}$; the integral of the resulting equation will give t in a function of v; therefore we shall have v, u and s, in functions of the time.

$-P.\cos.(v-\theta).dv^2 = 0$; and if this equation be divided by dv, and then added to the equation $da.\sin^2.(v-\theta) + db.\sin(v-\theta).\cos.(v-\theta) = 0$, we shall have $da = P.\cos.(v-\theta).dv$, of which the integral is $a = a' + \int P.\cos.(v-\theta).dv$; in like manner if the same equations be respectively multiplied by $\cos.(v-\theta)$, $\sin.(v-\theta)$, we obtain by subtracting the second, divided by dv, from the first; $db = -P.\sin.(v-\theta)dv$; and $\because b = b' - \int P.\sin.(v-\theta).dv$. Therefore $u = a.\sin.(v-\theta) + b.\cos.(v-\theta) = a'.\sin.(v-\theta) + \sin.(v-\theta)\int P.\cos.(v-\theta)dv. + b'.\cos.(v-\theta) - \cos.(v-\theta).\int P.\sin.(v-\theta)dv$; a' and b' are the values of a and b when $P=0$;

$$P = \frac{\mu}{h^2(1+s^2)^{\frac{3}{2}}} = \text{(by substituting for } s^2 \text{ its value)} \frac{\mu}{h^2(1+\gamma^2.\sin.^2(v-\theta))^{\frac{3}{2}}}, \text{ therefore}$$

$$\sin.(v-\theta)\int P.\cos.(v-\theta)dv = \frac{\mu.\sin.(v-\theta)}{h^2}.\int\frac{\cos.(v-\theta).dv}{(1+\gamma^2.\sin.^2(v-\theta))^{\frac{3}{2}}}, \text{ but}$$

$$\int\frac{\cos.(v-\theta)dv}{h^2(1+\gamma^2.\sin.^2(v-\theta))^{\frac{3}{2}}} = \frac{\sin.(v-\theta)}{h^2(1+\gamma^2.\sin.^2(v-\theta))^{\frac{1}{2}}}, \text{ for } d.\frac{\sin.(v-\theta)}{h^2(1+\gamma^2.\sin.^2(v-\theta))^{\frac{1}{2}}}$$

$$= \frac{\cos.(v-\theta).dv}{h^2(1+\gamma^2.\sin.^2(v-\theta))^{\frac{1}{2}}} - \frac{\gamma^2.\sin^2(v-\theta).\cos.(v-\theta).dv}{h^2(1+\gamma^2.\sin.^2(v-\theta))^{\frac{3}{2}}} = \text{by reducing to a com-}$$

mon denominator $\frac{\cos.(v-\theta).dv}{h^2(1+\gamma^2.\sin.^2(v-\theta))^{\frac{3}{2}}}$; consequently $\frac{\mu.\sin.(v-\theta)}{h^2}$.

$$\int\frac{\cos.(v-\theta).dv}{(1+\gamma^2.\sin.^2(v-\theta))^{\frac{3}{2}}} = \frac{\mu}{h^2}.\frac{\sin.^2(v-\theta)}{(1+\gamma^2.\sin.^2(v-\theta))^{\frac{1}{2}}}.$$

$$-\cos.(v-\theta).\int P.\sin.(v-\theta).dv =$$

$$-\mu.(\cos.(v-\theta).\int\frac{\sin.(v-\theta).dv}{h^2(1+\gamma^2.\sin.^2(v-\theta))^{\frac{3}{2}}}, \text{ and } \int\frac{\sin.(v-\theta).dv}{h^2(1+\gamma^2.\sin.^2(v-\theta))^{\frac{3}{2}}}$$

$$= \frac{-1}{(1+\gamma^2)}.\frac{\cos.(v-\theta)}{h^2(1+\gamma^2.\sin.^2(v-\theta))^{\frac{1}{2}}}, \text{ for } \frac{1}{1+\gamma^2}.d.\frac{\cos.(v-\theta)}{h^2(1+\gamma^2.\sin.^2(v-\theta))^{\frac{1}{2}}}$$

$$= -\frac{1}{1+\gamma^2}.\frac{\sin.(v-\theta).dv}{h^2(1+\gamma^2.\sin.^2(v-\theta))^{\frac{1}{2}}} - \frac{1}{1+\gamma^2}.\gamma^2.\frac{\sin.(v-\theta).\cos.^2(v-\theta).dv}{h^2(1+\gamma^2.\sin.^2(v-\theta))^{\frac{3}{2}}}$$

$$= \text{by reducing} - \frac{1}{1+\gamma^2}.\frac{(\sin.(v-\theta)+\gamma^2.\sin.(v-\theta)(\sin.^2(v-\theta)+\cos.^2(v-\theta)).dv}{h^2(1+\gamma^2.\sin.^2(v-\theta))^{\frac{3}{2}}}$$

The calculus may be considerably simplified, by observing that the value of s indicates that the orbit exists entirely* in a plane of which γ is the tangent of the inclination to a fixed plane, and of which θ represents the longitude of the node, reckoned from the origin of the angle v. Consequently, if we refer the motion of m to this plane, we shall have $s=0$, and $\gamma = 0$, which gives

$$u = \frac{1}{r} = \frac{\mu}{h^2}\left\{1+e.\cos.(v-\varpi)\right\}.$$

This is the equation of an ellipse, in which the origin of the radii is at the focus: $\frac{h^2}{\mu.(1-e^2)}$, is the semiaxis major, which we will represent by a; e is the ratio of the excentricity to the semiaxis major;

$$= -\frac{1}{1+\gamma^2}\cdot\frac{\sin.(v-\theta).(1+\gamma^2).dv}{h^2(1+\gamma^2.\sin.^2(v-\theta))^{\frac{3}{2}}} = -\frac{\sin.(v-\theta).dv}{h^2(1+\gamma^2.\sin.^2(v-\theta))^{\frac{3}{2}}},$$

$$\therefore \frac{\mu.\sin.(v-\theta).\int\cos.(v-\theta).dv}{h^2(1+\gamma^2.\sin.^2(v-\theta))^{\frac{3}{2}}} - \frac{\mu.\cos.(v-\theta)\int\sin.(v-\theta).dv}{h^2(1+\gamma^2.\sin.^2(v-\theta))^{\frac{3}{2}}}$$

$$= \frac{\mu\sin.^2(v-\theta)}{h^2(1+\gamma^2.\sin^2(v-\theta))^{\frac{1}{2}}} + \frac{1}{1+\gamma^2},\frac{\mu\cos.^2(v-\theta)}{h^2.(1+\gamma^2.\sin.^2(v-\theta))^{\frac{1}{2}}} =$$

$$\mu.\frac{(\sin.^2(v-\theta)+\cos.^2(v-\theta)+\gamma^2.\sin.^2(v-\theta)}{(1+\gamma)^2.h^2(1+\gamma^2.\sin.^2(v-\theta)^{\frac{1}{2}}} = \mu.\frac{(1+\gamma^2.\sin.^2(v-\theta))^{\frac{1}{2}}}{(1+\gamma^2).h^2}$$

$= \mu.\frac{(1+s^2)^{\frac{1}{2}}}{(1+\gamma^2)h^2}$, $\therefore u = a'.\sin.(v-\theta)+b'.\cos.(v-\theta)+\mu.\frac{(1+s^2)^{\frac{1}{2}}}{(1+\gamma^2)h^2}$, and as e'. $\cos.(v-\varpi)$ satisfies the equation $\frac{d^2u}{dv^2}+u=0$, we may write this function instead of $a'.\sin.(v-\theta)+b'.(\cos.(v-\theta)$, and as e' is arbitrary we can assume it equal to $\frac{\mu}{h^2.(1+\gamma^2}$. e, by means of which the expression for u will assume the form given in the text.

* γ is evidently equal to the tangent of latitude, when $v-\theta=90$, and consequently it is in this case equal to the inclination of the orbit, and as $\sin.(v-\theta) = \frac{s}{\gamma} = s.$ cotangent of inclination; the orbit described must be a plane, for this equation expresses the relation between the two sides, and *invariable* angle of a spherical triangle.

finally, ϖ is the longitude of the perihelium. The equation $dt = \frac{dv}{h.u^2}$ becomes, by substituting in place of u^2,

$$dt = \frac{a^{\frac{3}{2}}.(1-e^2)^{\frac{3}{2}}.\,dv}{\sqrt{\mu}.\,(1+e.\cos.(v-\varpi))^2}.^*$$

Let us expand the second member of this equation, into a series proceeding according to the cosines of the angle $v-\varpi$, and of its multiples. For this purpose, we will commence by expanding $\frac{1}{1+e.\cos.(v-\varpi)}$ into a similar series. By making

$$\lambda = \frac{e}{1+\sqrt{1-e^2}};$$

we shall have

$$\frac{1}{1+e.\cos.(v-\varpi)} = \frac{1}{\sqrt{1-e^2}}\left\{\frac{1}{1+\lambda.\,c^{(v-\varpi).\sqrt{-1}}} - \frac{\lambda.c^{-(v-\varpi).\sqrt{-1}}}{1+\lambda.c^{-(v-\varpi).\sqrt{-1}}}\right\};\dagger$$

* $\frac{1}{u} = r = \frac{h^2}{\mu(1+e.\cos.(v-\varpi))} = \frac{a(1-e^2)}{1+e.\cos.(v-\varpi)}$, $\because a = \frac{h^2}{\mu(1-e^2)}$; hence $h = \sqrt{a}.\sqrt{\mu(1-e^2)}$, and $dt = \frac{dv}{h.u^2} = \frac{dv.h^3}{\mu^2(1+e.\cos.(v-\varpi))^2} = \frac{dv.\,a^{\frac{3}{2}}.\mu^{\frac{3}{2}}.(1-e^2)^{\frac{3}{2}}}{\mu^2.(1+e.\cos.(v-\varpi))^2}$.

† By reducing the coefficient of $\frac{1}{\sqrt{1-e^2}}$, in the second member of this equation to the same denominator, it becomes equal to

$$\frac{1-\lambda^2}{\sqrt{1-e^2}.(1+\lambda^2+\lambda(c^{(v-\varpi)\sqrt{-1}}+c^{-(v-\varpi).\sqrt{-1}}))}$$

but $c^{(v-\varpi)\sqrt{-1}} - c^{-(v-\varpi)\sqrt{-1}} = 2\cos.(v-\varpi)$, $\because$ this second member $=$

e being the number of which the hyperbolical logarithm is equal to unity. By expanding the second member of this equation, into a series; namely, the first term relatively to the powers of $c^{(v-\varpi)\sqrt{-1}}$ and the second term relatively to the powers $c^{-(v-\varpi)\sqrt{-1}}$, and then substituting in place of the imaginary exponentials their expressions in sines and cosines; we shall find

$$\frac{1}{1+e.\cos.(v-\varpi)}=\frac{1}{\sqrt{1-e^2}}.^{*}$$

$$(1-2\lambda.\cos.(v-\varpi)+2\lambda^2.\cos.2(v-\varpi)-2\lambda^3.\cos.3.(v-\varpi)+\&c.);$$

By representing the second member of this equation by φ, and making $q=\frac{1}{e}$, we shall have generally,

$\frac{1-\lambda^2}{\sqrt{1-e^2})(1+\lambda^2+\lambda.\cos.(v-\varpi))}$; and from the equation $\lambda=\frac{e}{(1+\sqrt{1-e^2})}$, we obtain $1-\lambda^2=\frac{2(1+\sqrt{1-e^2}-e^2)}{(1+\sqrt{1-e^2})^2}$, and $1+\lambda^2=\frac{2(1+\sqrt{1-e^2})}{(1+\sqrt{1-e^2})^2}$; ∵ by substituting for $1-\lambda^2$, and $1+\lambda^2$ we obtain $\frac{2(1-e^2+\sqrt{1-e^2})}{2.\sqrt{1-e^2}(1+\sqrt{1-e^2}).(1+e.\cos.(v-\varpi))}=\frac{1}{1+e.\cos.(v-\varpi)}$.

* The expression of the first term gives the following series:

$$1-\lambda c^{(v-\varpi)\sqrt{-1}}+\lambda^2.c^{2(v-\varpi).\sqrt{-1}}-\lambda^3.c^{3(v-\varpi).\sqrt{-1}}+\lambda^4.c^{4(v-\varpi).\sqrt{-1}}-\&c;$$

the expansion of the second term gives

$$-\lambda.c^{-(v-\varpi).\sqrt{-1}}(1-\lambda.c^{-(v-\varpi).\sqrt{-1}}+\lambda^2.c^{-2(v-\varpi)\sqrt{-1}}-\lambda^3.c^{-3(v-\varpi)\sqrt{-1}}$$
$$+\lambda^4.c^{-4(v-\varpi)\sqrt{-1}}+\&c.;)$$

making the factors of the same powers of λ to coalesce in the two series, and observing that $\lambda^i(c^{i(v-\varpi).\sqrt{-1}}+c^{-i(v-\varpi)\sqrt{-1}})=\lambda^i.\cos.i(v-\varpi)$, we will obtain the value of $\frac{1}{1+e.\cos.(v-\varpi)}$, which is given in the text.

$$\frac{1}{(1+e.\cos.(v-\varpi))^{m+1}} = \pm\frac{e^{-m-1}.d.^m\left\{\frac{\varphi}{q}\right\}}{1.2.3.........m.dq^m};*$$

in which dq is supposed to be constant, and the sign is + or —, according as m is even or odd. From this, it is easy to to infer, that if we make

$$\frac{1}{(1+e.\cos.(v-\varpi))^2} = (1-e^2)^{-\frac{3}{2}}$$

$$(1+E^{(1)}.\cos.(v-\varpi)+E^{(2)}.\cos.2(v-\varpi)+E^{(3)}.\cos.3(v-\varpi)+\&c.);$$

we shall have, whatever may be the value of i,

$$E^{(i)} = \pm\frac{2e^i(1+i.\sqrt{1-e^2})}{(1+\sqrt{1-e^2})^i};\dagger$$

the sign being +, if i is even, and — if i is odd; therefore if n be

* Substituting $\frac{1}{q}$ for e we obtain $\frac{1}{1+e.\cos.(v-\varpi)} = \frac{q}{q+\cos.(v-\varpi)} = \varphi$, ∵ $\frac{1}{(q+\cos.(v-\varpi))} = \frac{\varphi}{q}$, and $d.\frac{1}{q+\cos.(v-\varpi)} \div dq = \frac{-1}{(q+\cos.(v-\varpi))^2} = \frac{d.\left\{\frac{\varphi}{q}\right\}}{dq}$; and $\frac{d^2.\left\{\frac{\varphi}{q}\right\}}{dq^2} = d\frac{-1}{(q+\cos.(v-\varpi))^2} \div dq = \frac{2}{(q+\cos.(v-\varpi))^3}$, and $\frac{d^3.\left\{\frac{\varphi}{q}\right\}}{dq^3} = d.\frac{2}{(q+\cos.(e-\varpi))^3} \div dq = \frac{-2.3}{(q+\cos.(v-\varpi))^4}$: hence generally we obtain $\frac{d^m\left\{\frac{\varphi}{q}\right\}}{dq^m} = \frac{\pm.1.2.3.......m}{(q+\cos.(v-\varpi))^{m+1}} = \frac{\pm 1.2.3.......me^{m+1}}{(1+e.\cos.(v-\varpi))^{m+1}}$.

† Substituting $\frac{1}{q}$ for e, in the value of φ, we obtain $\frac{\varphi}{q} = \frac{1}{\sqrt{q^2-1}}.(1-2\lambda.\cos.(v-\varpi)+2\lambda^2.\cos.2(v-\varpi)-2\lambda^3.\cos.3(v-\varpi)+\&c.)$ ∵ $\frac{1}{(1+e.\cos.v-\varpi))^2} = e^{-2}.\frac{d.\left\{\frac{\varphi}{q}\right\}}{dq}$ = the

supposed equal to $a^{-\frac{3}{2}}.\sqrt{\mu}$, we shall have

$$ndt = dv.\,(1 + E^{(1)}.\cos.(v-\varpi) + E^{(2)}.\cos.2(v-\varpi) + E^{(3)}.\cos.3(v-\varpi) + \&c.);$$

and by integrating

$$nt + \epsilon = v + E^{(1)}.\sin.(v-\varpi) + \tfrac{1}{2}.E^{(2)}.\sin.2(v-\varpi) + \tfrac{1}{3}E^{(3)}.\sin.3(v-\varpi) + \&c.$$

ϵ being a constant arbitrary quantity. This expression for $nt+\epsilon$ is very converging* when the orbits have a very small excentricity, such as the orbits of the planets and of the satellites; and we can, by the

preceding series differenced with respect to q, and divided by e^2; the differential of the i term $= e^{-2}d.\frac{1}{\sqrt{(q^2-1)}}2\lambda^i = 2e^{-2}d.\frac{1}{\sqrt{q^2-1}}.\left\{\frac{1}{(q+\sqrt{q^2-1})^i}\right\} \div dq = \pm$ $2e.^{-2}\frac{q}{(q^2-1)^{\frac{3}{2}}}.\frac{1}{(q+\sqrt{q^2-1})^i} \pm 2e^{-2}\frac{1}{\sqrt{q^2-1}}.i.\frac{\left\{1+\frac{q}{\sqrt{q^2-1}}\right\}}{(q+\sqrt{q^2-1})^{i+1}} =$

$$\pm 2e^{-2}.\left\{\frac{q}{(q^2-1)^{\frac{3}{2}}}.\frac{1}{(q^2+\sqrt{q^2-1})^i}\right\} \pm \frac{e^{-2}.i}{q^2-1}.\frac{(q+\sqrt{q^2-1})}{(q+\sqrt{q^2-1})^{i+1}};$$

= by simplifying and reducing to a common denominator,

$\pm 2e^{-2}.\frac{(q+i\sqrt{q^2-1})}{(q^2-1)^{\frac{3}{2}}.(q+\sqrt{q^2-1})^i}$, which becomes, by substituting $\frac{1}{e}$ for q,

$\pm\frac{2e^i(1+i\sqrt{1-e^2})}{(1-e^2)^{\frac{3}{2}}(1+\sqrt{1-e^2})^i}$, the expression given in the text.

* $(1-e^2)^{\frac{3}{2}}$ occurs both in the numerator and also in the denominator of the value of $n.dt$, as is evident from the value of dt given in page 101, compared with the preceding expression; when the excentricity of the orbit is inconsiderable, e which expresses the ratio of the excentricity to the semiaxis major will be very small, ∴ the value of $E^{(i)}$, in which e^i occurs as a factor will be very small, and perpetually less and less.

reversion of series, conclude the value of v in terms of t; we will effect this, in the subsequent N[os.]

When* the planet returns to the same point in its orbit, v is increased by the circumference which is always represented by 2π; naming T the periodic time, we shall have

$$T = \frac{2\pi}{n} = \frac{2\pi . a^{\frac{3}{2}}}{\sqrt{\mu}},$$

This value of T may be easily deduced from the differential expression for dt, without recurring to series. In fact, let us resume the equation $dt = \frac{dv}{h.u^2}$, or $dt = \frac{r^2.dv}{h}$. From it, we obtain $T = \int \frac{r^2.dv}{h}$; $\int r^2.dv$ is double the surface of the ellipse, and consequently it is equal to $2\pi.\ a^2.\sqrt{1-e^2}$; moreover, h^2 is equal to $\mu a.\ (1-e^2)$; thus we shall obtain the same expression for T, as has been given above.

If the masses of the planets be neglected relatively to that of the sun, we have $\sqrt{\mu} = \sqrt{M}$; the value of μ is then the same for all the planets; T is therefore proportional to $a^{\frac{3}{2}}$, and consequently, the squares of the periodic times, are as the cubes of the greater axes of the orbits. It is evident, that the same law obtains in the motions of the satellites about their primary, their masses being neglected relatively to that of the primary.

17. The equations of the motion of two bodies, which attract each

* When the planet returns to the same point, the terms of this equation will become

$$n(t+T)+\varepsilon = v+2\pi+E^{(1)}.\sin.((v-\varpi)+2\pi)+E^{(2)}.\sin.2((v-\varpi)+2\pi)+\&c.$$

if this equation be taken from the equation $nt+\varepsilon =$

$v+E^{(1)}.\sin.(v-\varpi)+E^{(2)}.\sin.2(v-\varpi)+E^{(3)}.\sin.3(v-\varpi)+\&c.$ the difference will be $nT=2\pi$.

other in the inverse ratio of the squares of the distances, may be also integrated in the following manner: the equations (1), (2), (3), of No. 9, become, when we only consider the action of the two bodies M and m,

$$\left.\begin{aligned} 0 &= \frac{d^2x}{dt^2} + \frac{\mu.x}{r^3} \\ 0 &= \frac{d^2y}{dt^2} + \frac{\mu.y}{r^3} \\ 0 &= \frac{d^2z}{dt^2} + \frac{\mu.z}{r^3} \end{aligned}\right\}. \qquad (O)$$

(μ being equal to $M + m$).

The integrals of these equations will give the three coordinates x, y, z, of the body m, referred to the centre of M, in a function of the time, and then by No. 9, we can obtain the coordinates ξ, Π and γ of the body M, referred to a fixed point, by means of the equations

$$\xi = a + bt - \frac{mx}{M+m}; \; \Pi = a' + b't - \frac{my}{M+m}; \; \gamma = a'' + b''t - \frac{mz}{M+m}.$$

Finally, we shall have the coordinates of m, referred to the same fixed point, by adding ξ to x, Π to y, and γ to z; by this means we shall obtain the relative motions of the bodies M and m, and also their absolute motion in space. Therefore every thing depends on the integration of the differential equations (O).

For this purpose, it may be observed, that if there is given between the n variables $x^{(1)}$, $x^{(2)}$, $x^{(3)}$ ....$x^{(n)}$, and the variable t, of which the difference is supposed to be constant, a number n of differential equations determined by the following:

$$0 = \frac{d^i x^{(s)}}{dt^i} + \frac{A.d^{i-1}x^{(s)}}{dt^{i-1}} + \frac{B.d^{i-2}x^{(s)}}{dt^{i-2}} + \ldots\ldots H.x^{(s)},*$$

* In every equation of the same form as that in the text, if the $x^{(n-i+1)}$, $x^{(n-i+2)}$,

in which we suppose that s is successively equal to 1, 2, 3, ...n; A, B, ...H being functions of the variables $x^{(1)}$, $x^{(2)}$, $x^{(3)}$, ...$x^{(n)}$, and of t, symmetrical with respect to the variables $x^{(1)}, x^{(2)}, \ldots\ldots x^{(n)}$, that is such, that they remain the same when any one of these variables is changed into the other, and vice versa, we can suppose

$$x^{(1)} = a.^{(1)} x^{(n-i+1)} + b^{(1)}. x^{(n-i+2)} \ldots\ldots\ldots + h.^{(1)}. x^{(n)};$$
$$x^{(2)} = a.^{(2)} x^{(n-i+1)} + b^{(2)}. x^{(n-1+2)} \ldots\ldots\ldots + h.^{(2)} x^{(n)};$$
$$\ldots \quad \ldots \quad \ldots \quad \ldots \quad \ldots \quad \ldots \quad \ldots \quad \ldots \quad \ldots$$
$$x^{(n-i)} = a^{(n-i)}. x^{(n-i+1)} + b^{(n-i)}. x^{(n-i+2)} \ldots\ldots + h^{(n-i)} x^{(n)},$$

$a^{(1)}$, $b^{(1)}$......$h^{(1)}$; $a^{(2)}$, $b^{(2)}$, &c. being arbitrary quantities of which the number is equal to $i(n-i)$. It is evident that these values satisfy the proposed system of differential equations: moreover, they reduce these equations, to i differential equations between the i variables $x^{(n-i+1)}$, $x^{(n-i+2)}$......$x^{(n)}$. Their integrals will introduce i^2 new

$x^{(n-i+3)}$,.........$x^{(n)}$, quantities satisfy this equation; then their sum will also satisfy the same equation, as will appear by substitution, and we are at liberty to assume $x^{(1)} = a^{(1)}. x^{(n-i+1)} + b^{(b)}. x^{(n-i+2)} \ldots h^{(1)} x^{n}$. In each of the values of $x^{(1)}$, $x^{(2)}$, ...$x^{(n)}$, there are i arbitrary quantities; ∵ in the sum of all the values of the $n-i$ quantities these are $i.(n-i)$ arbitrary quantities. In the integration of a differential equation of the i order, there are i arbitrary quantities introduced. ∴ In the integration of i differential equations of the i order, there must be in all, i^2 arbitrary quantities.

This theorem is evidently applicable to the differential equations (O); for these equations are symmetrical with respect to x, y, z, and remain the same, when any one of the variables is changed into another; ∵ as x, y, z, correspond to $x^{(i)}$, $x^{(n-i+1)}$, $x^{(n-i+2)}$, &c. in the theorem, we are at liberty to assume one of them z equal to the other two, multiplied respectively by arbitrary quantities.

arbitrary variables, which combined with the $i.(n-i)$ variables, already given, will constitute the arbitrary quantities, which would be produced by the integration of the proposed differential equations.

The application of this theorem, to the equations (O), gives $z=ax+by$, a and b being two arbitrary quantities. This equation is that of a plane passing through the origin of the coordinates; consequently, the orbit of m exists entirely in the same plane.

The equations (O) give

$$\left.\begin{aligned} 0 &= d.\left\{r^3.\frac{d^2x}{dt^2}\right\} + \mu.dx \\ 0 &= d.\left\{r^3.\frac{d^2y}{dt^2}\right\} + \mu.dy \\ 0 &= d.\left\{r^3.\frac{d^2z}{dt^2}\right\} + \mu.dz \end{aligned}\right\}; \quad (O')$$

but by differentiating twice successively, the equation $rdr = xdx+ydy+zdz$, we obtain

$$r.d^3r+3dr.d^2r=x.d^3x+y.d^3y+z.d^3z$$
$$+3.(dx.\,d^2x+dy.d^2y+dz.d^2z),$$

and consequently,

$$d.\left\{r^3.\frac{d^2r}{dt^2}\right\}=r^2.\left\{x.\frac{d^3x}{dt^2}+y.\frac{d^3y}{dt^2}+z.\frac{d^3z}{dt^2}\right\}*$$
$$+\ 3r^2.\left\{dx.\frac{d^2x}{dt^2}+dy.\frac{d^2y}{dt^2}+dz.\frac{d^2z}{dt^2}\right\}.$$

By substituting in the second member of this equation, in place of d^3x, d^3y, d^3z, their values determined by the equations (O′), and then,

* $rd^2r+dr^2=xd^2x+yd^2y+zd^2z+dx^2+dy^2+dz^2$, $\because$ $rd^3r+3drd^2r=xd^3x+yd^3y+zd^3z+3dx.d^2x+3dy.d^2y+3dz.d^2z$, and multiplying by r^2 we obtain the expression in the text.

in place of d^2x, d^2y, d^2z, their values given by the equations (O); we shall find

$$0 = d.\left\{r^3.\frac{d^2r}{dt^2}\right\} + \mu.dr.^*$$

The comparison of this equation with the equations (O′), will give, in consequence of the theorem which has been announced above, ($\frac{dx}{dt}, \frac{dy}{dt}, \frac{dz}{dt}, \frac{dr}{dt}$, being considered as corresponding to the particular variables $x^{(1)}, x^{(2)}, x^{(3)}, x^{(4)}$, and r being supposed a function of the time t;)

$$dr = \lambda.\ dx + \gamma.dy\,;$$

λ, γ, being constant arbitrary quantities; and by integrating,

$$r = \frac{h^2}{\mu} + \lambda x + \gamma y,^\dagger$$

$\frac{h^2}{\mu}$ being a constant quantity. This equation combined with the following:

$$z = ax + by\,;\ r^2 = x^2 + y^2 + z^2,$$

* From the equation (O′) we obtain $r^3.x.\frac{d^3x}{dt^3} = -3r^2.x.\frac{d^2x}{dt^2}.\ dr - \mu x dx$, and by substituting for $\frac{d^2x}{dt^2}$, we have $r^3x.\frac{d^3x}{dt^3} = 3\frac{\mu.x^2}{r}dr - \mu x dx$; $\therefore$ the second member of the preceding equation $= +3\mu.\frac{(x^2+y^2+z^2)}{r^2}.\ dr - \mu.\frac{(xdx+ydy+zdz)}{r} - 3\frac{\mu r^2}{r^3}(xdx+ydy+zdz)$, hence the second member is reduced to $-\mu.dr$, which combined with the member at the right hand side, gives the expression in the text.

† It is clear from an inspection of the equations (O′) that the theorem already announced, is applicable to them, and to this last equation, since any one of these variables may be changed into the other without affecting the constant quantties, $\because \frac{dr}{dt} = \lambda.\frac{dx}{dt} + \gamma.\frac{dy}{dt}$.

gives an equation of the second degree, between either x and y, x and z, or y and z, consequently the three projections of the curve described by m, about M, are lines of the second order, and therefore as all the points of this curve exist in the same plane, it is itself a line of the second order, or a conic section. It is easy to prove from the nature of this species of curves, that when the radius vector r is expressed by a linear function of the coordinates x, y; the origin of the coordinates must be* in the focus of the section. Now from the equation, $r = \frac{h^2}{\mu} + \lambda . x + \gamma . y$, we can obtain, in consequence of the equations (O),

$$0 = \frac{d^2r}{dt^2} + \mu . \frac{\left\{ r - \frac{h^2}{\mu} \right\}}{r^3}.$$

By multiplying this equation by dr, and then integrating, we shall obtain

$$r^2 . \frac{dr^2}{dt^2} - 2\mu . r + \frac{\mu r^2}{a'} + h^2 = 0, \dagger$$

a' being a constant arbitrary quantity. From which may be obtained

$$dt = \frac{rdr}{\sqrt{\mu} \sqrt{2r - \frac{r^2}{a'} - \frac{h^2}{\mu}}};$$

this equation will give r in a function of t; and as by what precedes,

* It is a distinguishing property of the foci of conic sections, that if their equation be expressed by means of polar coordinates, these coordinates will be linear, when the origin is at the focus.

† $\frac{d^2r}{dt^2} = \lambda . \frac{d^2x}{dt^2} + \gamma . \frac{d^2y}{dt^2} = -\mu . \left\{ \frac{\lambda x}{r^3} + \frac{\gamma . y}{r^3} \right\} = -\mu . \frac{\left\{ r - \frac{h^2}{\mu} \right\}}{r^3}$. Multiplying by dr, we obtain, $\frac{d^2 r dr}{dt^2} = -\mu . \frac{dr}{r^2} + h^2 . \frac{dr}{r^3}$; and by integrating $\frac{dr^2}{dt^2} = \frac{2\mu}{r} - \frac{h^2}{r^2} + \frac{\mu}{a'}$.

x, y, z, are determined in functions of r; we shall have the coordinates of m, in functions of the time.

18. We might arrive at these several equations, by the following method, which has this advantage, that it determines the arbitrary quantities in functions of the coordinates x, y, z, and of their first differences; which will be extremely useful in what follows.

Let us suppose that $V =$ constant, is an integral of the first order of the equations (O), V being a function of x, y, z, $\frac{dx}{dt}$, $\frac{dy}{dt}$, $\frac{dz}{dt}$: Let x', y', z', represent these three last quantities, and then the equation $V =$ constant, will give by its differentiation,

$$0 = \left\{\frac{dV}{dx}\right\}.\frac{dx}{dt} + \left\{\frac{dV}{dy}\right\}.\frac{dy}{dt} + \left\{\frac{dV}{dz}\right\}.\frac{dz}{dt}$$
$$+ \left\{\frac{dV}{dx'}\right\}.\frac{dx'}{dt} + \left\{\frac{dV}{dy'}\right\}.\frac{dy'}{dt} + \left\{\frac{dV}{dz'}\right\}.\frac{dz'}{dt};*$$

but the equations (O) give

$$\frac{dx'}{dt} = -\frac{\mu x}{r^3}; \quad \frac{dy'}{dt} = -\frac{\mu y}{r^3}; \quad \frac{dz'}{dt} = -\frac{\mu z}{r^3};$$

consequently, we have the following identical equation, of partial differences,

$$0 = x'.\left\{\frac{dV}{dx}\right\} + y'.\left\{\frac{dV}{dy}\right\} + z'.\left\{\frac{dV}{dz}\right\} - \frac{\mu}{r}.$$
$$\left\{\left\{x.\left\{\frac{dV}{dx'}\right\} + y.\left\{\frac{dV}{dy'}\right\} + z.\left\{\frac{dV}{dz'}\right\}\right\}\right\}; \qquad (I)$$

It is manifest, that every function of x, y, z, x', y', z', which, substituted in place of (V) in this equation, renders it identically nothing,

* As V is in an immediate function of the six variables, x, y, z, x', y', z', its differential coefficient with respect to another variable t, must be equal to the several differential coefficients of V, considered as a function of x, y, z, x', y', z', multiplied respectively, into the differential coefficients of these variables, considered as a functions of t.

becomes, when it is put equal to a constant arbitrary quantity, an integral of the first order of the equations (O).

Let us suppose

$$V = U + U' + U'' + \&c.$$

U being a function of the three variables x, y, z; U' being a function of the six variables x, y, z, x', y', z', but of the first order relatively to x', y', z'; U'' being a function of the same variables, and of the second order relatively to x', y', z', and so of the rest. Substituting this value in the equation (I), and comparing separately, first, the terms in which x', y', z', does not occur; secondly, those which involve the first power of these variables; thirdly, those which contain their squares, and their products, and so on of the rest; we shall have

$$0 = x.\left\{\frac{dU'}{dx'}\right\} + y.\left\{\frac{dU'}{dy'}\right\} + z.\left\{\frac{dU'}{dz'}\right\};$$

$$\left.\begin{array}{l}
x'.\left\{\frac{dU}{dx}\right\} + y'.\left\{\frac{dU}{dy}\right\} + z'.\left\{\frac{dU}{dz}\right\} = \frac{\mu}{r^3}.\left(x.\left\{\frac{dU''}{dx'}\right\} + y.\left\{\frac{dU''}{dy'}\right\} + z.\left\{\frac{dU''}{dz'}\right\}\right); \\
x'.\left\{\frac{dU'}{dx}\right\} + y'.\left\{\frac{dU'}{dy}\right\} + z'.\left\{\frac{dU'}{dz}\right\} = \frac{\mu}{r^3}.\left(x.\left\{\frac{dU'''}{dx'}\right\} + y.\left\{\frac{dU'''}{dy'}\right\} + z.\left\{\frac{dU'''}{dz'}\right\}\right); \\
x'.\left\{\frac{dU''}{dx}\right\} + y'.\left\{\frac{dU''}{dy}\right\} + z'.\left\{\frac{dU''}{dz}\right\} = \frac{\mu}{r^3}.\left(x.\left\{\frac{dU''''}{dx'}\right\} + y.\left\{\frac{dU''''}{dy'}\right\} + z.\left\{\frac{dU''''}{dz'}\right\}\right); \\
\&c.
\end{array}\right\} \quad (I')$$

The integral of the first of these equations is, as we know by the theory of equations of partial differences,

$$U' = \text{func.}\ (xy' - yx',\ xz' - zx',\ yz' - zy',\ x,\ y,\ z.)^{*}$$

As the value of U' must be linear with respect to x', y', z', we shall suppose it of the following form :

$$U' = A.(xy' - yx') + B.(xz' - zx') + C.(yz' - zy')\ ;$$

$A, B, C,$ being constant arbitrary quantities. Let the value of V be continued as far as the term U'', so that U''', U'''', &c. may vanish ; the third of the equations (I′) will become

$$0 = x'.\left\{\frac{dU'}{dx}\right\} + y'.\left\{\frac{dU'}{dy}\right\} + z'.\left\{\frac{dU'}{dz}\right\}.$$

The preceding value of U' satisfies also this equation. The fourth of the equations (I′) becomes

$$0 = x'.\left\{\frac{dU''}{dx}\right\} + y'.\left\{\frac{dU''}{dy}\right\} + z'.\left\{\frac{dU''}{dz}\right\};$$

The integral of which equation, is

$$U'' = \text{funct.}\ (xy' - yx',\ xz' - zx',\ yz' - zy',\ x',\ y',\ z').^{\dagger}$$

This function ought to satisfy the second of the equations (I′), and

* For the integration of this equation see Euler Integral Calculus, tome 3, chapter 3, No. , and Lacroix Traité Complete, Tom. 2, No. 634.

† F' being the derivative function of U', $\frac{dU}{dx'} = -(y+z).\ F'$, $\frac{dU'}{dy'} = (x-z).\ F'$; $\frac{dU'}{dz'} = (x+y).\ F'$; $\because x.\frac{dU'}{dx'} + y.\frac{dU'}{dy'} + z.\frac{dU'}{dz'} = (-x.(y+z) + y.(x-z) + z.(x+y)).F' = 0$; $\frac{dU''}{dx} = (y'+z').\ F''$; $\frac{dU''}{dy} = (z'-x').\ F''$; $\frac{dU''}{dz} = -(x'+y').\ F''$; $\therefore x'.\frac{dU''}{dx} + y'.\frac{dU''}{dy} + z'.\frac{dU''}{dz} = (x'.(y'+z') + y'.(z'-x') - z'.(x'+y')).F'' = 0$; Multiplying the first member by dt, and substituting we obtain $\left\{\frac{dU}{dx}.\frac{dx}{dt} + \frac{dU}{dy}.\frac{dy}{dt} + \frac{dU}{dz}.\frac{dz}{dt}\right\}.d = dU.$

the first member of this equation multiplied by dt, is evidently equal to dU; therefore the second member must be an exact differential of a function of x, y, z. But it is evident that we can satisfy at once this condition, the nature of the function U'', and the supposition that this function is of the second order in z', y', x'; by making

$$U'' = (Dy'-Ex').(xy'-yx') + (Dz'-Fx').$$
$$(xz'-zx') + (Ez'-Fy').(yz'-zy') + G.(x'^2+y'^2+z'^2);$$

D, E, F, G, being constant arbitrary quantities; and then r being equal to $\sqrt{x^2+y^2+z^2}$, we have

$$U = -\frac{\mu}{r}.(Dx+Ey+Fz+2G);^*$$

* $$\frac{dU''}{dx'} = -D.(yy'+zz')+E.(2yx'-xy')+F.(2x'z-xz')+2Gx',$$
$$\frac{dU''}{dy'} = D.(2y'x-yx')-E.(xx'+zz')+F.(2zy'-yz')+2Gy',$$
$$\frac{dU''}{dz'} = D.(2z'x-zx')+E.(2yz'-zy')-F.(xx'+yy')+2Gz'.$$
$$\therefore \frac{\mu}{r^3}\left\{x.\frac{dU''}{dx'}+y.\frac{dU''}{dy'}+z.\frac{dU''}{dz'}\right\} =$$
$$-D.((yxy'+zxz')+E.(2yx.x'-x^2y')+F.(2zx.x'-x^2z'+2Gxx')\frac{\mu}{r^3}$$
$$+D.((2xyy'-y^2x')-E.(xyx'+zyz')+F.(2zy.y'-y^2z')+2Gyy')\frac{\mu}{r^3}$$
$$+D.((2xzz'-z^2x')+E.(2yzz'-z^2y')-F.(xzx'+yzy')+2Gzz')\frac{\mu}{r^3},$$

= by concinnating and omitting those terms which destroy each other, $(-D.(y^2+z^2)x'-E.(x^2+z^2).y'-F.(x^2+z^2)z'+D.(xy)y'+D.(xz)z'+E.(yx)x'+E(yz)z'+F.(zx)x'+F.(zy)y'+2G.(xx'+yy'+zz'))\frac{\mu}{r^3}$ = (by observing that $y^2+z^2=r^2-x^2$; $x^2+z^2=r^2-y^2$ &c) the value of U, differenced with respect to x, y, z, successively, for

$$\frac{dU}{dx} = -\frac{\mu}{r}.D+\frac{\mu}{r^3}.Dx^2+\frac{\mu}{r^3}(Eyx+Fzx+2Gx) = -\frac{\mu}{r^3}.(D.(y^2+z^2)-Eyx-$$

consequently we can obtain, by this means, the values of U, U', U''; and the equation $V =$ constant, will become

$$\text{const.} = -\frac{\mu}{r}.(Dx+Ey+Fz+2G)+(A+Dy'-Ex').(xy'-yx')^{*}$$
$$+(B+Dz'-Fx').(xz'-zx')+(C+Ez'-Fy').(yz'-zy')$$
$$+G.(x'^2+y'^2+z'^2).$$

This equation satisfies the equation (I), and consequently the dif-

$Fzx-2Gx)$; $\frac{dU}{dy}=-\frac{\mu}{r}.E+\frac{\mu}{r^3}.Ey^2+\frac{\mu}{r^3}.(Dxy+Fyz+2Gy)=-\frac{\mu}{r^3}.(E(x^2+z^2)-D.xy-F.yz-2Gy)$, $\frac{dU}{dz}=-\frac{\mu}{r}.F+\frac{\mu}{r^3}.Fz^2+\frac{\mu}{r^3}(Dxz+Eyz+2Gz)=-\frac{\mu}{r^3}.(F(x^2+y^2)-Dxz-Eyz-2Gz)$, $\therefore$ if these equations be multiplied by x', y', z', respectively, the sum of the terms at the left hand side will be equal to dU, and the sum of those on the right hand, will coincide with those already given.

* This equation evidently satisfies the equation (I), for

$$\frac{dV}{dx}=-\frac{\mu}{r}.D.+\frac{\mu}{r^3}.(Dx^2+Exy+Fxz+2Gx)+Ay'+Dy'^2-Ex'y'+Bz'+Dz'^2-Fx'z'$$

$$\frac{dV}{dy}=-\frac{\mu}{r}.E+\frac{\mu}{r^3}.(Ey^2+Dxy+Fyz+2Gy)-Ax'-Dy'x'+Ex'^2+Cz'+Ez'^2-Fy'z',$$

$$\frac{dV}{dz}=-\frac{\mu}{r}.F+\frac{\mu}{r^3}.(Fz^2+Dxz+Eyz+2Gz)-Bx'-Dz'x'+Fx'^2-Cy'-Ez'y'+Fy'^2.$$

$$\therefore x'.\frac{dV}{dx}+y'.\frac{dV}{dy}+z'.\frac{dV}{dz}=.$$

$$-\frac{\mu}{r^3}(D)y^2+z^2)-Exy-Fxz-2Gx).x'.+Ay'x'+Dy'^2x'-Ex'^2y'+Bz'x+Dz'^2x'-Fx'^2z',$$

$$-\frac{\mu}{r^3}.(E(x^2+z^2)-Dxy-Fyz-2Gy)y'-Ay'x'-Dy'^2x'+Ex'^2y'+Cz'y'+Ez'^2y'-Fy''^2z'.$$

$$-\frac{\mu}{r^3}.(F(x^2+y^2)-Dxz-Eyz+2Gz)z'-Bx'z'-Dz'^2x'+Fx'^2z'-Cy'z'-Ez'^2y'+Fy'^2z'.$$

= by obliterating the quantities which destroy each other

$$-\frac{\mu}{r^3}.(D(y^2+z^2)-Exy-Fxz-2Gx)x'+E((x^2+z^2)-Dxy-Fyz-2Gy)y'+F(x^2+y^2)-Dxz-Eyz$$
$$-2Gz)z';\ \frac{dV}{dx'}=-E(xy'-yx')-y(A+Dy'-Ex')-F(xz'-zx')-z(B+Dz'-Fx')+2Gx',$$

ferential equations (O), whatever may be the arbitrary quantities A, B, C, D, E, F, G. Supposing them all to vanish first, with the exception of A; 2dly, with the exception of B; 3dly, with the exception of C, &c., and restoring $\frac{dx}{dt}$, $\frac{dy}{dt}$, $\frac{dz}{dt}$, in place of x', y', z', we shall obtain the integrals

$$\left.\begin{array}{l}
c = \frac{xdy - ydx}{dt}; \; c' = \frac{xdz - zdx}{dt}; \; c'' = \frac{ydz - zdy}{dt}; \\
0 = f + x.\left\{\frac{\mu}{r} - \frac{(dy^2 + dz^2)}{dt^2}\right\} + \frac{ydy.dx}{dt^2} + \frac{zdz.dx}{dt^2};^* \\
0 = f' + y.\left\{\frac{\mu}{r} - \frac{(dx^2 + dz^2)}{dt^2}\right\} + \frac{xdx.dy}{dt^2} + \frac{zdz.dy}{dt^2}; \\
0 = f'' + z.\left\{\frac{\mu}{r} - \frac{(dx^2 + dy^2)}{dt^2}\right\} + \frac{xdx.dz}{dt^2} + \frac{ydy.dz}{dt^2}; \\
0 = \frac{\mu}{a} - \frac{2\mu}{r} + \frac{dx^2 + dy^2 + dz^2}{dt^2};
\end{array}\right\} ; \; (P)$$

c, c', c'', f, f', f'', and a being constant arbitrary quantities.

$$\frac{dV}{dy'} = D(xy' - yx') + x(A + Dy' - Ex') - F(yz' - zy') - z(C + Ez' - Fy') + 2Gy',$$
$$\frac{dV}{dz'} = D(xz' - zx') + x(B + Dz' - Fx') + E(yz' - zy') + y(C + Ez' - Fy') + 2Gz',$$

Multiplying these three equations by x, y, z, respectively, and observing that those terms, of which one factor is the product of two of the coordinates, x, y, z, destroy each other, we obtain, by concinnating $\frac{dV}{dx'}x + \frac{dV}{dy'}.y + \frac{dV}{dz'}.z = -E(x^2 + z^2)y' - D(y^2 + z^2)x' - F(y^2 + x^2)z' + E(yx) + Fxz + 2Gx)x' + (Dxy + Fzy + 2Gy)y' + (Dxz + Eyz + 2Gz)z'$, and this expression, when multiplied by $\frac{\mu}{r^3}$ is identical with the preceding value of $x'\frac{dV}{dx} + y'.\frac{dV}{dy} + z'.\frac{dV}{dz}$.

* Supposing all the constant quantities but A to vanish, the preceding equation becomes const. $= A(xy' - yx')$; supposing them all except D to vanish, we shall have const. =

The differential equations (O) can only have six* distinct integrals of the first order, by means of which, if the differences dx, dy, dz, be eliminated, we shall obtain the three variables x, y, z, in functions of the time t; therefore one at least of the seven preceding integrals should occur in the six others. We may perceive even, *a priori*, that two of these integrals must occur in the five remaining. In fact, as the sole element of the time, occurs in these integrals; they are not sufficient to determine the variables x, y, z, in functions of the time, and consequently they are inadequate to the complete determination of the motion of m about M. We proceed to examine how it happens that these integrals are only equivalent to five distinct integrals.

If we multiply the fourth of the equations (P) by $\frac{zdy-ydz}{dt}$, and then add it to the fifth, multiplied by $\frac{xdz-zdx}{dt}$; we shall obtain

$$0=f.\frac{(zdy-ydz)}{dt}+f'.\frac{(xdz-zdx)}{dt}+z.\frac{(xdy-ydx)}{dt}.$$

$$\left\{\frac{\mu}{r}-\frac{(dx^2+dy^2)}{dt^2}\right\}+\frac{(xdy-ydx)}{dt}.\left\{\frac{xdx.dz}{dt^2}+\frac{ydy.dz}{dt^2}\right\}.\dagger$$

$-\frac{\mu}{r}.Dx+Dy'(xy'-yx')+Dz'.(xz'-zx')$; $\because \frac{\text{const.}}{D}=f=-x.\left(\frac{\mu}{r}+(y'^2+z'^2)\right)-yy'.x'-zz'x'$ which will be equal to the fourth of the equations (P), by substituting for x', y', z', their values. Supposing G to be the only constant arbitrary quantity, we obtain, const. $=G\left(-\frac{2\mu}{r}+(x'^2+y'^2+z'^2)\right)$; $\because$ making $\frac{\text{const.}}{G}=\frac{\mu}{a}$, and substituting for x'. y', z', we obtain the expression given in the text.

* As the differential equations (O) are of the second order, and since the complete integration of each equation furnishes two constant arbitrary quantities, the entire number cannot exceed six.

† Performing this multiplication and addition, we obtain

$$-fc''+\frac{\mu}{r}\frac{(xzdy-xydz)}{dt}\frac{-xzdy^3-xzdy.dz^2+xydy^2.dz+xydz^3}{dt^3}+\frac{zydy^2.dx+z^2dxdydz}{dt^3}$$

By substituting in place of $\frac{xdy-ydx}{dt}, \frac{xdz-zdx}{dt}, \frac{ydz-zdy}{dt}$ their values, which have been determined by the three first of the equations (P), we shall have

$$0 = \frac{f'c'-fc''}{c} + z.\left\{\frac{\mu}{r} - \left\{\frac{dx^2+dy^2}{dt^2}\right\}\right\} + \frac{xdx.dz}{dt^2} + \frac{ydy.dz}{dt^2}.$$

This equation coincides with the sixth of the integrals (P), by making $f'' = \frac{f'c'-fc''}{c}$, or $0 = fc'' - f'c' + f''c$. Thus the sixth of the integrals (P), results from the five preceding, and the six arbitrary quantities c, c', c'', f, f', f'', are connected together by the preceding equation.

If we take the squares of the values of f, f', f'', which are determined by the equations (P), and then add them together, we shall obtain

$$\frac{-y^2.dx.dy.dz - yz.d^2z.dx}{dt^3} + f'.c' + \frac{\mu}{r}\frac{(xy.dz-yzdx)}{dt}\frac{-yx.dx^2.dz - yx.dz^3}{dt^3}$$

$$+\frac{yz.dx^3+yz.dz^2.dx}{dt^3} + \frac{x^2.dx.dy.dz+x.zdz^2.dy}{dt^3} - \frac{xz.dx^2.dy}{dt^3} - \frac{z^2.dx.dy.dz}{dt^3} =$$ by making factors to coalesce $-fc''+f'c'+z.\frac{\mu}{r}\frac{(xdy-ydx)}{dt} - z.\frac{x.dy}{dt}\frac{(dy^2+dz^2)}{dt^2} + z.\frac{xdy}{dt}\frac{(dz^2-dx^2)}{dt^2} + \frac{xy.dz}{dt}\frac{(dy^2+dz^2)}{dt^2} - \frac{xy.dz}{dt}\frac{(dx^2+dz^2)}{dt^2} + z.\frac{y.dx}{dt}\frac{(dy^2-dz^2)}{dt^2} + z.\frac{y.dx}{dt}\frac{(dz^2+dx^2)}{dt} + (z^2-y^2)\frac{dx.dy\,dz}{dt^3} + (x^2-z^2).\frac{dx.dy.dz}{dt^3} =$ after all reductions, and obliterating quantities which destroy each other, $f\frac{(zdy-ydz)}{dt} + f'.\frac{(xdz-zdx)}{dt} + \frac{z\mu}{r}.\frac{(xdy-ydx)}{dt} - z.\frac{(xdy-ydx)}{dt}.\frac{(dx^2+dy^2)}{dt^2} + \frac{xdy}{dt}.\left\{\frac{ydy.dz}{dt^2} + \frac{xdx.dz}{dt^2}\right\} - \frac{ydx}{dt}.\left\{\frac{xdx\,dz}{dt^2} + \frac{ydy.dz}{dt^2}\right\}$ which is the expression in the text.

$$l-\mu^2=\left(r^2.\left\{\frac{dx^2+dy^2+dz^2}{dt^2}\right\}-\left\{\frac{rdr}{dt}\right\}^2\right\}.\left\{\frac{dx^2+dy^2+dz^2}{dt^2}-\frac{2\mu}{r}\right);^*$$

in which l^2 is, for the sake of abridging, put equal to $f^2+f'^2+f''^2$; but if we take the square of the values of c, c', c'', which are given by the same equations. and then add them together, we shall have, by making $c^2+c'^2+c''^2=h^2$;

$$* f^2=\frac{\mu^2x^2}{r^2}+x^2\frac{(dy^4+2dy^2.dz^2+dz^4)}{dt^4}-\frac{2\mu x^2}{r}.\frac{(dy^2+dz^2)}{dt^2}$$
$$+\frac{y^2dy^2.dx^2+z^2dz^2.dx^2}{dt^4}+\frac{2yz.dy.dz.dx^2}{dt^4}+\frac{2\mu x}{r}\frac{(ydy.dx+zdz.dx)}{dt^2}-2x.\frac{(dy^2+dz^2)}{dt^2}.$$
$$\frac{(ydy.dx+zdz.dx)}{dt^2};f'^2=\frac{\mu^2y^2}{r^2}+y^2.\frac{(dx^4+2dx^2.dz^2+dz^4)}{dt^4}-\frac{2\mu y^2}{r}\frac{(dx^2+dz^2)}{dt^2}$$
$$+\frac{x^2dx^2.dy^2+z^2dz^2.dy^2}{dt^4}+\frac{2xz.dx.dz.dy^2}{dt^4}+\frac{2\mu y}{r}\frac{(xdx.dy+zdz.dy)}{dt^2}-2y.\frac{dx^2+dz^2}{dt^2}.$$
$$\frac{(xdx.dy+zdz.dy)}{dt^2};f''^2=\frac{\mu^2z^2}{r^2}+z^2.\frac{(dx^4+2dx^2.dy^2.+dy^4)}{dt^4}-\frac{2\mu}{r}z^2.\frac{(dx^2+dy^2)}{dt^2}$$
$$+\frac{x^2dx^2.dz^2+y^2dy^2.dz^2}{dt^4}+\frac{2xy.dx.dy.dz^2}{dt^4}+\frac{2\mu}{r}.z.\frac{(xdx.dz+ydy.dz)}{dt^2}-2z.$$
$$\frac{(dx^2+dy^2)}{dt^2}.\frac{(xdx.dz+ydy.dz)}{dt^2},\ \because\text{ we obtain } f^2+f'^2+f''^2-\mu^2.=$$
$$x^2.\frac{(dy^4+2dy^2.dz^2+dz^4)}{dt^4}+y^2\frac{(dx^4+2dx^2.dz^2+dz^4)}{dt^4}+z^2.\frac{(dx^4+2dx^2.dy^2+dy^4)}{dt^4}$$
$$-\frac{2\mu}{r}.x^2.\frac{(dy^2+dz^2)}{dt^2}-\frac{2my^2}{r}\frac{(dx^2+dz^2)}{dt^2}-\frac{2\mu.z^2}{r}.\frac{(dx^2+dy^2)}{dt^2}$$
$$+\frac{y^2dy^2}{dt^2}\frac{(dx^2+dz^2)}{dt^2}+\frac{x^2dx^2}{dt^2}\frac{(dy^2+dz^2)}{dt^2}+\frac{z^2dz^2}{dt^2}\frac{(dy^2+dx^2)}{dt^2}$$
$$+2yz.\frac{dy.dz}{dt^2}.\frac{dx^2}{dt^2}+\frac{2xz.dx.dz}{dt^2}.\frac{dy^2}{dt^2}+\frac{2yz.dy.dz}{dt^2}.\frac{dx^2}{dt^2}.$$
$$\frac{2\mu}{r}\left\{xy.\frac{dy.dx}{dt^2}+xz.\frac{dx.dz}{dt^2}+xy.\frac{dx.dy}{dt^2}+yz.\frac{dy.dz}{dt^2}+xz.\frac{dx\,dz}{dt^2}+yz.\frac{dy.dz}{dt^2}\right\}$$

$$r^2.\left\{\frac{dx^2+dy^2+dz^2}{dt^2}\right\}-\left\{\frac{rdr}{dt}\right\}^2 = h^2;^*$$

consequently, the preceding equation will become,

$$\left\{-2xy.\frac{dx.dy}{dt^2}-2xz.\frac{dx.dz}{dt^2}\right\}.\frac{dy^2+dz^2}{dt^2}+\left\{-2xy.\frac{dy.dx}{dt^2}-2yz.\frac{dy.dz}{dt^2}\right\}.$$

$$\left\{\frac{dx^2+dz^2}{dt^2}\right\}+\left\{-2xz.\frac{dx\,dz}{dt^2}-2yz.\frac{dy.dz}{dt^2}\right\}.\left\{\frac{dx^2+dy^2}{dt^2}\right\}=$$

$$(x^2+y^2+z^2).\frac{(dx^4+dy^4+dz^4+2dx^2.dy^2+2dx^2dz^2+2dy^2.dz^2)}{dt^4}-x^2.$$

$$\frac{(dx^4+2dx^2.dy^2+2dx^2.dz^2)}{dt^4}-y^2.\frac{(dy^4+2dx^2.dy^2+2dy^2.dz^2)}{dt^4}-z^2.\frac{(dz^4+2dz^2.dx^2+2dz^2dy^2)}{dt^4}$$

$$-\left(2xy.\frac{dx.dy}{dt^2}+2z.\frac{dx.dz}{dt^2}+2yz.\frac{dy.dz}{dt^2}\right.\;x.\;\frac{(dx^2+dy^2+dz^2)}{dt^2}-\frac{2\mu}{r}.(x^2+y^2+z^2).$$

$$\frac{(dx^2+dy^2+dz^2)}{dt^2}+\frac{2\mu}{r}\,\frac{(x^2.dt^2+y^2dy^2+z^2dz^2+2xy.dx.dy)}{dt^4}+\frac{(2xz.dx.dz+2yz.dy.dz)}{dt^2}$$

$$+y^2.\frac{(dy^2.dx^2+dy^2.dz^2)}{dt^4}+x^2.\frac{(dx^2.dy^2+dx^2.dz^2)}{dt^4}+z^2.\frac{(dz^2dy^2+dz^2.dx^2)}{dt^4}=$$ (by obliterating the quantities which destroy each other, and observing that $r^2dr^2=x^2dx^2+y^2dy^2+z^2dz^2+2xy.dx\,dy+2xz.dx.dz+2yz.dy.dz$

$$r^2.\frac{dx^4+dy^4+dz^4+2dx^2.dy^2+2dx^2.dz^2+2dy^2.dz^2)}{dt^4}(-x^2.dx^4-y^2dy^4-z^2dz^4$$

$$\left\{-\frac{2xy.dx.dy}{dt^2}-\frac{2xz.dz.dy}{dt^2}-\frac{2yz.dy.dz^2}{dt^2}\right\}.\left\{\frac{dx^2+dy^2+dz^2}{dt^2}\right\}-\frac{2\mu}{r}.r^2+\frac{2\mu}{r}.$$

$\left\{\frac{rdr}{dt^2}\right\}^2$, which may be evidently reduced to the expression in the text.

* Squaring these equations and then adding them together, gives

$$x^2.\frac{(dy^2+dz^2)}{dt^2}+y^2.\frac{(dx^2+dz^2)}{dt^2}+z^2.\frac{(dx^2+dy^2}{dt^2}-\frac{2xy.dy(dx}{dt^2}-\frac{2xz.dx.dz}{dt^2}$$

$$-\frac{2yz.dy.dz}{dt^2}=(x^2+y^2+z^2).\frac{(dx^2+dy^2+dz^2)}{dt^2}-\frac{x^2.dx^2}{dt^2}-\frac{y^2dy^2}{dt^2}-\frac{z^2.dz^2}{dt^2}$$

$$-\frac{2xy.dx.dy}{dt^2}-\frac{2xz.dxdz}{dt^2}-\frac{2yz.dy.dz}{dt^2}=r^2.\frac{(dx^2+dy^2+dz^2)}{dt^2}-\left\{\frac{rdr}{dt}\right\}^2.$$

$$0=\frac{dx^2+dy^2+dz^2}{dt^2}-\frac{2\mu}{r}+\frac{\mu^2-l^2}{h^2}.$$

The comparison of this equation, with the last of the equations (P), will give the following equation of condition

$$\frac{\mu^2-l^2}{h^2}=\frac{\mu}{a}.$$

Therefore it follows, that the last of the equations (P), occurs in the six first, which are themselves only equivalent to five distinct integrals, the seven arbitrary quantities c, c', c'', f, f', f'', and a being connected by the two preceding equations of condition. From hence it results, that we shall obtain the most general expression for V, which satisfies the equation (I), by assuming for this expression, an arbitrary function of the values of c, c', c'', f, and f', which are determined by the five first of the equations (P).

19. Although these integrals are inadequate to the determination of x, y, z, in functions of the time, they nevertheless determine the species of the curve described by m, about M. In fact, if we multiply the first of the equations (P), by z, the second by $-y$, and the third by x, we shall obtain, by their addition,

$$0=cz-c'y+c''x,\text{*}$$

which is the equation of a plane, of which the position depends on the constant quantities c, c', c''.

If we multiply the fourth of the equations (P) by x; the fifth by y, and the sixth by z, we shall obtain

* Performing this multiplication the members at the right hand side of the equation will disappear, for they become

$$cz-c'y+c''x=\frac{xz\,dy-yz.dx}{dt}\cdot\frac{-xy.dz+zy.dx}{dt}\;\frac{+yx.dz-zx.dy}{dt}=0.$$

$$0 = fx + f'y + f''z + \mu r - r^2.\frac{(dx^2 + dy^2 + dz^2)}{dt^2} + \frac{r^2.dr^2}{dt^2};$$

but by the preceding number we have,

$$r^2.\frac{(dx^2 + dy^2 + dz^2)}{dt^2} - \frac{r^2.dr^2}{dt^2} = h^2;$$

consequently,

$$0 = \mu r - h^2 + fx + f'y + f''z.$$

This equation, combined with the following, namely,

$$0 = c''x - c'y + cz\,;\; r^2 = x^2 + y^2 + z^2\,;$$

gives the equation of conic sections, the origin of r being at the focus. From this it follows,* that the planets and the comets describe very nearly conic sections about the sun, this star existing in one of the foci, and these stars move in such a manner, that the areas described by the radii vectores, increase proportionally to the time. In fact, if dv re-

R 2

* Performing this multiplication, and then adding the products together, we obtain

$$fx + f'y + f''z = \frac{\mu}{r}.(x^2+y^2+z^2) - (x^2+y^2+z^2)\frac{(dx^2+dy^2+dz^2)}{dt^2} + x^2.\frac{dx^2}{dt^2}$$
$$+ y^2.\frac{dy^2}{dt^2} + z^2.\frac{dz^2}{dt^2} + 2xy.\frac{dx.dy}{dt} + 2xz.\frac{dx}{dt}.\frac{dz}{dt} + 2yz.\frac{dy}{dt}.\frac{dz}{dt} = \mu r - r^2.$$
$$\frac{(dx^2+dy^2+dz^2)}{dt^2} + r^2.\frac{dr^2}{dt^2}.$$

From the first of these equations we obtain $\mu^2.r^2 = h^4 - 2h^2.(fx + f'.y + f''.z) + f^2x^2 + f'^2y^2 + f''^2z^2 + 2ff'.xy + 2ff''.xz + 2f'.f''.yz$, and by means of the equation $0 = c''x - c'y + cz$, and $r^2 = x^2 + y^2 + z^2$, we can eliminate, z^2 and z, and then substituting for r^2 its value, we arrive at an equation of the second degree between y and x, by similar process we obtain equations of the second degree between x and z, y and z, from which it follows that the curve described is a conic section; and as the value of r is given in a linear function of the coordinates x, y, z, the origin must be at the focus.

represents the indefinitely small angle, intercepted between the radii r and $r+dr$, we shall have

$$dx^2+dy^2+dz^2=r^2dv^2+dr^2;*$$

the equation

$$r^2.\frac{(dx^2+dy^2+dz^2)}{dt^2}-\frac{r^2dv^2}{dt^2}=h^2.$$

will consequently become, $r^4dv^2=h^2dt^2$; therefore

$$dv=\frac{hdt}{r^2}.$$

From this it appears that the elementary area $\frac{1}{2}rdv$, described by the radius vector r, is proportional to the element of time dt, consequently the area described in a finite time, is proportional to this time. It also appears, that the angular motion of m about M, is at each point of the orbit, inversely proportional to the square of the radius vector; and as we can, without sensible error, assume very short intervals of time, for the indefinitely small moments; by means of the preceding

* The differential of the curve $= ds=\sqrt{dx^2+dy^2+dz^2} =$ the hypothenuse of a right angle triangle, of which one side $= dr$, and the other side about the right angle $= rdv$, $\because dx^2+dy^2+dz^2 = ds^2 = dr^2+r^2.dv^2$.

As h varies as the square root of the parameter, it follows that the angular velocity $\frac{dv}{dt}$ varies as the square root of the synchronous areas divided by the square of the distance, see page 10; hence the angular velocity in a conic section is to that in a circle at the same distance r, as $h :: \sqrt{r}$; $\because$ they are equal at the extremity of the focal ordinate; substituting for h its value $\frac{2\pi a^2\sqrt{1-e^2}}{T}$; $\frac{dv}{dt}$ will be $\frac{2\pi a^2\sqrt{1-e^2}}{T.r^2}$; if a body describes a circle at the unity of distance in a time equal to T, then the angular velocity in the circle $=\frac{2\pi}{T}=$ the mean angular velocity in the ellipse, consequently, when the angular velocity in the ellipse is equal to the mean angular velocity, we have $\frac{2\pi}{T}=\frac{2\pi a^2.\sqrt{1-e^2}}{T.r^2}$, and $\because r=a.(1-e^2)^{\frac{1}{4}}$, $=$ a mean proportional between the semiaxes; in this position the equation of the centre is a maximum.

equation, we can obtain the horary motions of the planets and comets in different parts of their orbits.

The elements of the conic section described by m, are the constant arbitrary quantities of its motion; they are consequently functions of the preceding arbitrary quantities c, c', c'', f, f', f'', and $\frac{\mu}{a}$; we now proceed to determine these functions. Let θ represent the angle which the intersection of the plane of the orbit with the plane of x and of y, constitutes with the axis of x, which intersection is termed the *line of the nodes*; let φ be the mutual inclination of these two planes. If x' and y' represent the coordinates of m, referred to the line of the nodes, as axis of the abscissæ; we shall have

$$x' = x.\cos.\theta + y.\sin.\theta;$$
$$y' = y.\cos.\theta - x.\sin.\theta.$$

We have also

$$z = y'.\tan.\varphi;$$

consequently we shall have

$$z = y.\cos.\theta.\tan.\varphi - x.\sin.\theta.\tan.\varphi.$$

The comparison of this equation with the following,

$$0 = c''x - c'y + cz;$$

will give

$$c' = c.\cos.\theta.\tan.\varphi;$$
$$c'' = c.\sin.\theta.\tan.\varphi;\text{*}$$

from which may be obtained

* A comparison of these equations, gives $y.\cos.\theta.\tan.\varphi - x.\sin.\theta.\tan.\varphi = \frac{c'}{c}$. $y - \frac{c''}{c}.x \because \frac{c'}{c} = \cos.\theta.\tan.\varphi$; $\frac{c''}{c} = \sin.\theta.\text{tang}.\varphi$, $\because \frac{c'^2 + c''^2}{c^2} = \text{tang}.^2\varphi$.— See page 3, and page 34 of 1st Book.

$$\tan.\theta = \frac{c''}{c'};$$

$$\tan.\varphi = \frac{\sqrt{c'^2+c''^2}}{c}.$$

By means of the preceding equations, the positions of the nodes, and the inclination of the orbit are determined in functions of the constant arbitrary quantities, c, c', c''. At the perihelium, we have

$$rdr = 0; \text{ or } xdx + ydy + zdz = 0;$$

let therefore X, Y, Z, represent the coordinates of the planet at this point; and from the fourth and fifth of the equations (P), of the preceding No. may be obtained,

$$\frac{Y}{X} = \frac{f'}{f}.*$$

But if we name I the longitude of the projection of the perihelium, on the plane of x and of y, this longitude being reckoned from the axis of x, we have

$$\frac{Y}{X} = \tan.\ I;$$

consequently,

$$\text{tang. } I = \frac{f'}{f};$$

this equation determines the position of the axis major of the conic section.

* Substituting $-xdx$ for $ydy + zdz$, and $-ydy$ for $xdx + zdz$ in the two last terms of the second member of this equation, and they will become

$$0 = f + X\left\{\frac{\mu}{r} - \frac{(dX^2+dY^2+dZ^2)}{dt^2}\right.; \; 0 = f' + Y\left\{\frac{\mu}{r} - \frac{dX^2+dY^2+dZ^2}{dt^2}\right\}$$

∴ multiplying the first by Y, and the second by X, and then subtracting, we obtain the expression given in the text.

If by means of the last of the equations (P), $\frac{dx^2+dy^2+dz^2}{dt^2}$ be eliminated from the equation $r^2.\frac{(dx^2+dy^2+dz^2)}{dt^2} - \frac{r^2dr^2}{dt^2} = h^2$, we shall obtain

$$2\mu r - \frac{\mu r^2}{a} - \frac{r^2.dr^2}{dt^2} = h^2;$$

but dr vanishes at the extremities of the greater axis; therefore at these points we have,

$$0 = r^2 - 2ar + \frac{ah^2}{\mu}.$$

The sum of the two values of r in this equation, is the axis major of the conic section, and their difference is equal to twice the excentricity; thus, a is the semiaxis* major of the orbit, or the mean distance of m from M; and $\sqrt{1-\frac{h^2}{\mu a}}$ is the ratio of the excentricity to the semi-axis major. Let e represent this ratio; and by the pre-

* The coefficient of r with its sign changed is the sum of the two values of r, and their difference is equal to twice the radical, and ∵ = to $2a.\sqrt{1-\frac{h^2}{\mu a}}$, and $\sqrt{1-\frac{h^2}{\mu a}}$ is the ratio of the excentricity to a; $\sqrt{\mu^2-\frac{\mu h^2}{a}} = \mu e$

$\mu.\left\{\mu-\frac{h^2}{a}\right\} = \mu^2e^2 = l^2$; $dr = ae.\sin. udu$, ∵ $rdr = a^2.e.\sin. udu.(1-e\cos. u)$,

$2r - \frac{r^2}{a} = a.((2-2e.\cos. u)-(1+e^2.\cos.^2 u-2e.\cos. u)) = a.(1-e^2.\cos.^2 u)$, and

∵ $2r - \frac{r^2}{a} - a.(1-e^2) = ae^2.(1-\cos.^2 u) = ae^2.\sin.^2 u$, and therefore

$$\frac{rdr}{\sqrt{\mu}.\sqrt{2r-\frac{r^2}{a}-a.(1-e^2)}}(=dt) = \frac{a^2.e.\sin. u.(1-e\cos. u)\,du}{\sqrt{\mu}.\sqrt{ae^2.\sin.^2 u}} = \frac{a^{\frac{3}{2}}}{\sqrt{\mu}}.$$
$(1-e\cos. u)\,du.$

ceding number, we have

$$\frac{\mu}{a} = \frac{\mu^2 - l^2}{h^2};$$

therefore $\mu e = l$. Thus, we can know all the elements which determine the nature of the conic section, and its position in space.

20. The three finite equations found in the preceding number, between x, y, z, and r, give x, y, z, in functions of r; thus, in order to determine these coordinates in a function of the time, it is sufficient to have the radius vector r, in a similar function, which requires a new integration. For this purpose, let us resume the equation

$$2\mu r - \frac{\mu r^2}{a} - \frac{r^2.dr^2}{dt^2} = h^2;$$

by the preceding number, we have,

$$h^2 = \frac{a}{\mu}.(\mu^2 - l_2) = a\mu.(1-e_2);$$

therefore we shall obtain

$$dt = \frac{rdr}{\sqrt{\mu}.\sqrt{2r - \frac{r^2}{a} - a.(1-e^2)}}.$$

In order to integrate this equation, let $r = a.(1-e.\cos.u)$, we shall have

$$dt = \frac{a^{\frac{3}{2}}.du}{\sqrt{\mu}}.(1-e\cos.u).$$

from which may be obtained by integrating,

$$t + T = \frac{a^{\frac{3}{2}}}{\sqrt{\mu}}.(u-e\sin.u); \quad \text{(S)}$$

T being a constant arbitrary quantity. This equation determines u, and consequently r in a function of t; and as x, y, z are determined in functions of r; we shall obtain the values of these coordinates, for any instant whatever.

We have thus completely integrated the differential equations (O) of No. 17; this integration introduces the six arbitrary quantities a, e, I, θ, φ, and T: the two first depend on the nature of the orbit; the three following depend on its position in space; and the last is relative to the position of the body m, at a determined period, or, what comes to the same thing, it depends on the instant of its transit through the perihelium.

Let us refer the coordinates of the body m, to other coordinates which are more convenient for the usages of astronomy, and for this purpose, let v represent the angle which the radius vector r makes with the greater axis, reckoning from the perihelium; the equation of the ellipse will be

$$r = \frac{a.(1-e^2)}{1+e.\cos. v}.$$

The equation $r=a.(1-e\cos. u)$, of the preceding number, indicates that u vanishes at the perihelium, so that this point is the origin of the two angles u and v; it is easy to shew, that the angle u is formed by the greater axis of the orbit, and by the radius drawn from its centre, to the point where the circumference described on the greater axis as diameter, meets the ordinate drawn from the body m, perpendicular to the greater axis. This angle is termed the *excentric anomaly*, and the angle v is the *true anomaly*. A comparison of the two values of r, gives

$$1-e.\cos. u = \frac{1-e^2}{1+e.\cos. v};$$

from which may be obtained

$$\text{tang.}\tfrac{1}{2}.v = \sqrt{\frac{1+e}{1-e}}.\ \text{tang.}\ \tfrac{1}{2}\ u.^{*}$$

If the origin of the time t be fixed at the very moment of the passage, through the perihelium, T will vanish; and by making, in order to abridge, $\frac{\sqrt{\mu}}{a^{\frac{3}{2}}} = n$, we shall have, $nt = u - e.\ \text{sin}.\ u$.

By collecting together the equations of the motion of m, about M, we shall have

$$\left.\begin{array}{l} nt = u - e.\text{sin}.\ u, \\ r = a.(1-e.\ \text{cos}.\ u) \\ \text{tan}.\ \tfrac{1}{2}\ v = \sqrt{\frac{1+e}{1-e}}.\ \text{tan}.\ \tfrac{1}{2}\ u. \end{array}\right\}; \qquad (f)$$

the angle nt being what is termed the *mean anomaly*. The first of these equations determines u in a function of the time t, and the two remaining equations will give r and v, when u shall be determined. The equation between u and v is transcendental, and can only be resolved by approximation. Fortunately, from the circumstances of the celestial motions, the approximation is very rapid. In fact, the orbits of the celestial bodies are either almost circular, or extremely ex-

* $\frac{\text{sin}.\ a + \text{sin}.\ b}{\text{cos}.\ a + \text{cos}.\ b} = \text{tan}.\ \frac{(a+b)}{2}$, let $b = 0$, and $\frac{\text{sin}.\ a}{1+\text{cos}.\ a} = \text{tan}.\ \frac{a}{2}$, i. e. $\frac{\sqrt{1-\text{cos}.^2 a}}{1+\text{cos}.\ a} = \frac{\sqrt{1-\text{cos}.\ a}}{\sqrt{1+\text{cos}.\ a}} = \text{tan}.\ \frac{a}{2}$; now $e.\ \text{cos}.\ u = e\,\frac{(e+\text{cos}.\ v)}{1+e.\ \text{cos}.\ v}$, and $\text{cos}.\ v = \frac{\text{cos}.\ u - e}{1-e.\ \text{cos}.\ u}$; $\because \text{tan}.\ \frac{v}{2} = \frac{\sqrt{1-\text{cos}.\ v}}{\sqrt{1+\text{cos}.\ v}} = \frac{\sqrt{1+\frac{e-\text{cos}.\ u}{1-e\ \text{cos}.\ u}}}{\sqrt{1+\frac{-e+\text{cos}.\ u}{1-e\ \text{cos}.\ u}}} = \frac{\sqrt{1+e-e.\ \text{cos}.\ u - \text{cos}\ u}}{\sqrt{1-e-e.\ \text{cos}.\ u+\text{cos}.\ u}} = \frac{\sqrt{(1+e).(1-\text{cos}\ u)}}{\sqrt{(1-e).(1+\text{cos}.\ u)}} = \frac{\sqrt{1+e}}{\sqrt{1-e}}\ \text{tan}.\ \frac{u}{2}$.

centric, and in these two cases, we can determine u in terms of t, by very convergent formulæ, which we proceed to develope. We shall give for this purpose, some general theorems on the reduction of functions into series, which will be extremely useful in the sequel.

21. Let u be any function of α, which it is required to expand into a series proceeding according to the powers α; this series being supposed to be represented by

$$u = \text{u} + \alpha q_1, + \alpha^2.q_2 + \alpha^3 q_3, \ldots\ldots\ldots + \alpha^n q_n + \alpha^{n+1}.\,q_{n+1}. +, \ \&c.$$

u, q, q_2, &c., being quantities independent of α; it is evident that u is what u becomes, when α is supposed to be equal to cypher, and that, whatever be the value of n,

$$\left\{\frac{d^n u}{d\alpha^n}\right\} = 1.2.3\ldots\ldots\ldots n.q_n + 2.3\ldots\ldots\ldots(n+)1.\alpha q_{n+1} + \ \&c.$$

the difference $\left\{\frac{d^n u}{d\alpha^n}\right\}$, being taken on the hypothesis, that in u every thing is made to vary which ought to vary with α. Consequently, if we suppose that after the differentiations, $\alpha = 0$, in the expression of $\left\{\frac{d^n u}{d\alpha}\right\}$; we shall have

$$q_n = \frac{\left\{\frac{d^n u}{d\alpha^n}\right\}}{1.2.3\ldots\ldots n}$$

If u is a function of the two quantities α and α', and it is proposed to expand it into a series, proceeding according to the powers and products of α and α'; this series being represented by

$$\begin{aligned} u = \text{u} &+ \alpha.q_{1,0} + \alpha^2.q_{2,0} + \ \&c. \\ &+ \alpha'.q_{0,1} + \alpha\alpha'.q_{1,1} + \ \&c. \\ &+ \alpha'^2.q_{0,2} + \ \&c. \end{aligned}$$

the coefficient $q_{n,n'}$ of the product $\alpha^n.\alpha'^{n'}$, will be in like manner equal to

$$\frac{\left\{\frac{d^{n+n'}u}{d\alpha^n.d\alpha'^{n'}}\right\}}{1.2.3......n.1.2.3......n'};$$

α and α' being supposed to vanish after the differentiations.

In general, if u is a function of α, α', α'', &c., and if it is proposed to expand u into a series, ranged according to the powers and products of α, α', α'', &c., the term of this series, of which the factor is the product $\alpha^n.\alpha'^{n'}.\alpha''^{n''}......$ will be $\alpha^n.\alpha'^{n'}.\alpha''^{n''}...... q_{n.n'.n''}$, we shall have

$$q_{n.n'.n''\&c.......} = \frac{\left\{\frac{d^{n+n'+n''+\&c.}u}{d\alpha^n.d\alpha'^{n'}.d\alpha''^{n''}\ \&c.}\right\}}{1.2.3......n.1.2.3......n'.1.2.3......n''.\ \&c.};$$

provided α, α', α'', &c., are supposed to vanish after the differentiations.

Let us now suppose that u is a function of α, α', α'', &c., and of the variables t, t', t'', &c.; if by the nature of this function, or by an equation of partial differences which represents it, we have obtained

$$\left\{\frac{d^{n+n'+\&c.}u}{d\alpha^n.\,d\alpha'^{n'}.\ \&c.}\right\}$$

in a function of u and of its differences, taken with respect to t, t', &c.; F representing this function, when u is changed into u, u being what u becomes when α, α', &c. vanish, it is manifest that we shall obtain $q_{n,n'}$, &c. by dividing F by the product $1.2.3...n.\ 1.2.3...n'$, &c.; therefore we shall obtain the law of the series according to which u is expanded.

In the next place, let u be equal to any function of $t+\alpha$, $t'+\alpha'$, $t''+\alpha''$, &c., which we will represent by $\varphi(t+\alpha,\ t'+\alpha',\ t''+\alpha'')$, in this case the mth difference of u, taken with respect to α, and divided by $d\alpha^m$, is evidently equal to this same difference, taken with respect to t, and divided by dt_m. The same equality obtains between the differences taken relatively to α' and t', or relatively to α'' and t'', &c.; hence it follows, that in general, we have

$$\left\{\frac{d^{n+n'+n''+\&c.}u}{d\alpha^n.d\alpha'^{n'}.d\alpha''^{n''}.\&c.}\right\}=\left\{\frac{d^{n+n'+n''+\&c.}u}{dt^n.dt'^{n'}.dt''^{n''}}\right\}.$$

If in the second member of this equation, u be changed into u, that is, into $\varphi(t, t', t'', \&c.)$; we shall have, by what precedes,

$$q_{n,n',n'',\&c.}=\left\{\frac{d^{n+n'+n''+\&c.}.\varphi(t,t',t'',\&c.)}{1.2.3\ldots n.\ 1.2.3\ldots n'.\ 1.2.3\ldots n''.\ \&c.}\right\}$$

If u is a function of t and α, only, we shall have

$$q_n=\frac{d^n.\varphi(t)}{1.2.3\ldots n.dt^n},$$

therefore

$$\varphi(t+\alpha)=\varphi(t)+\frac{\alpha.d.\varphi(t)}{dt}+\frac{\alpha^2}{1.2}.\frac{d.\varphi(t)}{dt^2}+\frac{\alpha^3}{1.2.3}.\frac{d^3\varphi(t)}{dt^3}+\&c.\quad (i)$$

Let us in the next place suppose that u, instead of being given immediately in α and t, as in the preceding case, is a function of x, x being given by the equation of partial differences, $\left\{\frac{dx}{d\alpha}\right\}=z.\left\{\frac{dx}{dt}\right\}$, in which z is any function whatever of x.

In order to reduce u into a series proceeding according to the powers of α, the value of $\left\{\frac{d^nu}{d\alpha^n}\right\}$ must be determined in the case in which $\alpha=0$; but in consequence of the proposed equation of partial differences, we have

$$\left\{\frac{du}{d\alpha}\right\} = \left\{\frac{du}{dx}\right\}.\left\{\frac{dx}{d\alpha}\right\} = z.\left\{\frac{du}{dx}\right\}.\left\{\frac{dx}{dt}\right\};$$

therefore, we shall have

$$\left\{\frac{du}{d\alpha}\right\} = \frac{d.\int z.du}{dt};^{*} \qquad (k)$$

This equation being differenced with respect to α, gives

$$\left\{\frac{d^2u}{d\alpha^2}\right\} = \frac{d^2.\int z.du}{d\alpha.dt},^{\dagger}$$

but the equation (k) gives, by changing u into $\int z.du$,

$$\left\{\frac{d.\int z.du}{d\alpha}\right\} = \left\{\frac{d\int z^2.du}{dt}\right\};$$

consequently

$$\left\{\frac{d^2u}{d\alpha^2}\right\} = \frac{d^2.\int z^2.du}{dt^2}.$$

This equation being differenced again with respect to α, gives

$$\left\{\frac{d^3u}{d\alpha^3}\right\} = \frac{d^3.\int z^2.du}{d\alpha.dt^2};$$

but the equation (k) gives, by changing u into $\int z^2du$

$$\left\{\frac{d\int z^2.du}{d\alpha}\right\} = \left\{\frac{d\int z^3.du}{dt}\right\};$$

* Let $\int zdu = u'$, then $\frac{du'}{d\alpha} = \frac{du'}{dx}.\frac{dx}{d\alpha} = z.\frac{du'}{dx}.\frac{dx}{dt} = z.\frac{du'}{dt} = d.\frac{\int z.du'}{dt}$ and by substituting for du' its value, we obtain $\frac{d.\int z.du}{d\alpha} = \frac{d.\int z^2.du}{dt}$.

† As the characteristic $\int$ indicates an operation, the reverse of that denoted by d, we can remove the sign $\int$, by depressing the index of d by unity.

therefore

$$\left\{\frac{d^3u}{d\alpha^3}\right\} = \left\{\frac{d^3.fz^3.du}{dt^3}\right\}.$$

By continuing this process, it is easy to infer generally

$$\left\{\frac{d^nu}{d\alpha^n}\right\} = \left\{\frac{d^n.fz^n.du}{dt^n}\right\} = \left\{\frac{d^{n-1}.z^n.\left\{\frac{du}{dt}\right\}}{dt^{n-1}}\right\}.$$

Les us now suppose that by making $\alpha=0$, we have $x = T$, T being a function t; we shall substitute this value of x, in z, and in u.

Let Z and u represent what these quantities then become; we shall have on the hypothesis that $\alpha=0$,

$$\left\{\frac{d^nu}{d\alpha^n}\right\} = \frac{d^{n-1}.Z^n.\frac{d\text{u}}{dt}}{dt^{n-1}},$$

and consequently, by what precedes, we shall obtain,

$$q_n = \frac{d^{n-1}Z^n.\frac{d\text{u}}{dt}}{1.2.3\ldots n.dt^{n-1}};$$

which gives

$$u = \text{u} + \alpha.Z.\frac{d\text{u}}{dt} + \frac{\alpha^2}{1.2}.\frac{d.\left\{Z^2.\frac{d\text{u}}{dt}\right\}}{dt} + \frac{\alpha^3}{1.2.3}.\frac{d^2.\left\{Z^3.\frac{d\text{u}}{dt}\right\}}{dt^2} + \&c; \text{(P)}$$

It only now remains to determine what function of t and α, x represents; which will be effected by the integration of the equation of partial differences $\left\{\frac{dx}{d\alpha}\right\} = z.\left\{\frac{dx}{dt}\right\}$. For this purpose, we shall observe, that

$$dx = \left\{\frac{dx}{dt}\right\}.dt + \left\{\frac{dx}{d\alpha}\right\}.d\alpha;$$

and by substituting in place of $\left\{\frac{dx}{d\alpha}\right\}$, its value $z.\left\{\frac{dx}{dt}\right\}$ we will obtain

$$dx = \left\{\frac{dx}{dt}\right\}.(dt+zd\alpha) = \frac{dx}{dt}.\left(d.(t+\alpha z) - \alpha.\left\{\frac{dz}{dx}\right\}\right.$$

therefore, we shall have

$$dx = \frac{\frac{dx}{dt}.d.(t+\alpha z)}{1+\alpha.\left\{\frac{dz}{dx}\right\}.\left\{\frac{dx}{dt}\right\}};^{*}$$

which gives by its integration, $x=\varphi(t+\alpha z)$, $\varphi(t+\alpha z)$ being an arbitrary function of $t+\alpha z$; so that the quantity which we have termed T, is equal to $\varphi(t)$. Consequently, as often as there exists between α and x, an equation reducible to the form $x=\varphi(t+\alpha z)$; the value of u will be determined by the formula (P) in a series proceeding according to the powers of α.

* $zd\alpha = d.\alpha z - \alpha.\frac{dz}{dx}.dx$, therefore, by substituting this value of $zd\alpha$, we obtain the expression for dx given in the text; now as dx is an exact differential, the member, at the right hand side of the equation must be also an exact differential, consequently, $\frac{dx}{dt} \div \left(1+\alpha.\frac{dz}{dx}.\frac{dx}{dt}\right)$, must be equal to $\varphi'(t+\alpha z)$, φ' denoting the derivative function of φ.

z being by hypothesis a function of x, let it equal $F(x)$ and we shall have $x = \varphi(t+\alpha F(x))$, and it is easy to obtain from this expression the proposed differential equation of partial differences, for

$$\frac{dx}{d\alpha} = \varphi'(t+\alpha F(x)).\left\{(F(x))+\alpha F'(x).\frac{dx}{d\alpha}\right\};\ \frac{dx}{dt} = \varphi'(t+\alpha F(x))\left\{1+\alpha F'(x).\frac{dx}{dt}\right\};$$

and by eliminating $\varphi'(t+\alpha F(x))$, and reducing, we shall obtain

$$\frac{dx}{d\alpha} = F(x).\frac{dx}{dt};$$

Let us now suppose, that u is a function of the two variables x and x', these variables being given by the equations of partial differences

$$\left\{\frac{dx}{d\alpha}\right\} = z.\left\{\frac{dx}{dt}\right\}; \quad \left\{\frac{dx'}{d\alpha}\right\} = z'.\left\{\frac{dx'}{dt}\right\};$$

in which z and z' are any functions whatever of x and x'. It is easy to be assured that the integrals of these equations are respectively

$$x = \varphi(t + \alpha z); \quad x' = \psi(t' + \alpha' z');^*$$

$\varphi(t+\alpha z)$, and $\psi(t'+\alpha' z')$ being arbitrary functions, the one of $t+\alpha z$,

and as u is supposed to be equal to $\varphi(x)$,

$$\frac{du}{d\alpha} = \varphi'(x).\frac{dx}{d\alpha}; \quad \frac{du}{dt} = \varphi'(x).\frac{dx}{dt};$$

hence, by eliminating $\varphi(x)$ we obtain $\frac{du}{d\alpha}\cdot\frac{dx}{dt} = \frac{du}{dt}\cdot\frac{dx}{d\alpha}$, and by substituting for $\frac{dx}{d\alpha}$ its value $F(x).\frac{dx}{dt}$, and making $F(x) = z$, we obtain after all reductions $\frac{du}{d\alpha} = z.\frac{du}{dt}$, when $x = t + \alpha F(x)$; $x = t$ when $\alpha = 0$; $\frac{dx}{dt} = 1$; u, Z, and $\frac{du}{dt}$ become respectively $\psi(t)$, $F(t)$, and $\psi'(t)$, consequently, the equation (P) will become $\psi(t) + \psi'(t).F(t)\frac{\alpha}{1} + \frac{d.(\psi(t).F(t)^2)}{dt^2}\frac{\alpha^2}{1.2} + \frac{d^2.(\psi'(t).F(t)^3)}{dt^3}\cdot\frac{\alpha^3}{1.2.3} +$ &c., if in the preceding equation, $\alpha = 1$, then we shall have $x = t + F(x)$, and the preceding series becomes $\psi(x) = \psi t + \psi'(t).F(t) + \frac{1}{1.2}\cdot\frac{d(\psi'(t).F(t)^2)}{d\alpha} +$ &c., which Lagrange first announced in 1772, an epoch deservedly celebrated in the history of science for the many beautiful applications of this series, if $F(x) = 1$, then $x = F(t+\alpha)$, and ∵ $u = \psi(x)$.

* Let $z = F(x\,x')$; $z' = F_{,}(x\,x')$; ∵ $x = \varphi(t + \alpha.\,F(x\,x'))$, $x' = \psi(t' + \alpha'.\,F_{,}(x\,x'))$, if the functions indicated by F, $F_{,}$, be defined, and if the form of the preceding equations permits us to eliminate, the values of z' and z, may be respectively obtained in terms of α, t, α', t', we may ∵ regard x, x', as functions of those four quantities.

$$\frac{dx}{dt} = \varphi'(t + \alpha.\,F(x\,x')).(1 + \alpha.\frac{dF}{dt}); \quad \frac{dx}{d\alpha} = \varphi'(t + \alpha.\,F(x\,x')).(F + \alpha.\,\frac{dF}{d\alpha});$$

and the other of $t'+\alpha'z'$. Moreover, we have

$$\left\{\frac{du}{d\alpha}\right\} = z.\left\{\frac{du}{dt}\right\}; \quad \left\{\frac{du}{d\alpha'}\right\} = z'.\left\{\frac{du}{dt'}\right\}.$$

$$\frac{dx}{dt'}=\varphi'(t+\alpha\, F(x,x')).(1+\alpha.\frac{dF}{dt'}) ; \frac{dx}{d\alpha'} = \varphi'(t+\alpha.\, F(x,x')).\alpha.\frac{dF}{d\alpha'} ;$$

$$\frac{dx'}{dt} = \psi'(t'+\alpha'.\, F_{,}(x,x'))\,\alpha.\,\frac{dF_{,}}{dt}; \frac{dx'}{d\alpha} = \psi'(t'+\alpha'.\, F(x,x')).\alpha'.\,\frac{dF_{,}}{d\alpha} ;$$

$$\frac{dx'}{dt'} = \psi(t'+\alpha'.\, F_{,}(x,x')).(1+\alpha'.\,\frac{dF_{,}}{dt'}); \frac{dx'}{d\alpha'} = \psi'(t'+\alpha'.F_{,}(x,x')).\,\alpha'.\,\frac{dF_{,}}{d\alpha'} ,$$

$$\frac{dx'}{dt'} = \psi(t'+\alpha'.F'(x'x')).(1+\alpha'.\,\frac{dF'}{dt'}); \frac{dx'}{d\alpha'} = \psi'(t'+\alpha'.F'(x,x')).\alpha'.\,\frac{dF_{,}}{d\alpha'} ,$$

when α, α' vanish, we have $\frac{dx}{dt} = \varphi'(t)$, $\frac{dx}{d\alpha} = \varphi'(t').\ F_{,}$;

$$\frac{dx}{dt'}=0; \ \frac{dx}{d\alpha'}=0; \ \frac{dx'}{d\alpha}=0; \ \frac{dx}{dt'} = \psi'(t'); \ \frac{dx'}{d\alpha'} = \psi'(t').\ F_{,};$$

in this case $x=\varphi(t)$; $x'=\psi(t')$, $\therefore$ u is a function of t, t', only; as u is only an explicit function of x, x', we shall have

$$\frac{du}{d\alpha} = \frac{du}{dx}.\frac{dx}{d\alpha} + \frac{du}{dx'}.\frac{dz}{d\alpha};\ \text{and when } \alpha \text{ and } \alpha' \text{ vanish } \frac{dx}{d\alpha} = \varphi'(t)\ F.$$

$\frac{dx'}{d\alpha}=0$; $\because$ $\frac{du}{d\alpha}=\frac{du}{dx}.\ \varphi'(t).\ F$; $\frac{du}{d\alpha'} = \frac{du}{dx}.\frac{dx}{d\alpha'} + \frac{du}{dx'}.\frac{dx'}{d\alpha'}$, and when a, $a'=0$,

$\frac{dx}{d\alpha'}=0$; $\frac{dx'}{d\alpha'} = \psi'(t').\ F$, and $\because$ $\frac{du'}{d\alpha} = \frac{du}{dx'}.\ \psi'(t').\ F_{,}$; $\varphi'(t) = \frac{dx}{dt}$; $\psi'(t) = \frac{dx}{dt'}$;

$\therefore$ $\frac{du}{d\alpha} = \frac{du}{dx}.\frac{dx}{dt}.F = \frac{du}{dt}.\ F$; $\frac{du}{du'} = \frac{du}{d\alpha'}.\frac{dx'}{dt'}.\ F_{,} = \frac{du}{dt'}.\ F_{,}$. $\therefore$ by substituting z for F we obtain $\frac{du}{d\alpha} - z.\,\frac{du}{dt} = 0$ when $x=\varphi(t+\alpha z)$, conversely, when this differential equation obtains, we can determine the value of $x=\varphi(t+\alpha z)$.

As u depends explicitly only on x, t', α', and as α' is one of the independent variables in differencing u with respect to α, it is only necessary to have respect to x, $\because$ the reasoning of the preceding page is applicable in this case.

When α is equal to cipher $\frac{du}{d\alpha} = z.\frac{du}{dt}$, $\because$ in this case we may substitute $\frac{du}{d\alpha}$ for $z.\,\frac{du}{dt}$.

This being premised, if we conceive that x' is eliminated from u and from z, by means of the equation $x' = \psi(t' + \alpha' z')$; u and z will become functions of x, α' and t' without α or t; therefore we shall obtain, by what goes before,

$$\left\{\frac{d^n u}{d\alpha^n}\right\} = \left\{\frac{d^{n-1}.z^n.\left\{\frac{du}{dt}\right\}}{dt^{n-1}}\right\}.$$

If we suppose $\alpha = 0$ after the differentiations, and if besides, we make $x = \varphi(t + \alpha z^n)$ in the second member of this equation $x = \varphi(t + \alpha z^n)$, and consequently $\left\{\frac{du}{d\alpha}\right\} = z^n.\left\{\frac{du}{dt}\right\}$, we shall have on these suppositions,

$$\left\{\frac{d^n u}{d\alpha^n}\right\} = \left\{\frac{d^{n-1}.\left\{\frac{du}{d\alpha}\right\}}{dt^{n-1}}\right\};$$

and consequently,

$$\left\{\frac{d^{n+n'}u}{d\alpha^n.d\alpha'^{n'}}\right\} = \frac{\left\{\frac{d^{n-1}.(d.\left\{\frac{d^{n'}.u}{d\alpha'^{n'}}\right\}}{d\alpha}\right\}}{dt^{n-1}}.$$

We shall have in like manner,

$$\left\{\frac{d^{n'}.u}{d\alpha'^{n'}}\right\} = \left\{\frac{d^{n'-1}.\left\{\frac{du}{d\alpha}\right\}}{dt^{n-1}}\right\}.$$

If we suppose a' to vanish after the differentiations, and if besides we suppose that in the second member of this equation, $x' = \psi(t' + a'z'^{n'})$; we shall obtain

$$\left\{\frac{d^{n+n'}.u}{d\alpha^n.d\alpha'^{n'}}\right\} = \left\{\frac{d^{n+n'-2}\left\{\frac{d^2u}{d\alpha.d\alpha'}\right\}}{dt^{n-1}.dt'^{n'-1}}\right\};$$

provided that we make α and α' to vanish after the differentiations, and also that we suppose in the second member of this equation

$$x=\varphi(t+\alpha z^{n});\quad x'=\psi(t'+\alpha' z'^{n'});$$

which comes to supposing in the second member as well as in the first

$$x=\varphi(t+\alpha z);\quad x'=\psi(t+\alpha' z'),$$

and to change in the partial difference $\left\{\frac{d^2u}{d\alpha.d\alpha'}\right\}$, of this second member z into z^{n}, and z' into $z'^{n'}$. Thus, we shall have on those suppositions, and also by changing z into Z, z' into Z', and u into u,

$$q_{n,n'}=\left\{\frac{d^{n+n'-2}.\left\{\frac{du}{d\alpha.d\alpha'}\right\}}{1.2.3\ldots\ldots n.\ 1.2.3\ldots\ldots n'.\ dt^{n-1}.dt'^{n'-1}}\right\}.$$

By following on this reasoning, it is easy to infer, that if we have r equations,

$$\begin{aligned}x&=\varphi(t+\alpha z);\\ x'&=\psi(t'+\alpha' z');\\ x''&=\Pi(t''+\alpha'' z'');\\ &\text{\&c.}\end{aligned}$$

z, z', z'', &c., being any functions whatever of x, x', x'', &c.; u being supposed to be a function of the same variables, we shall have generally

$$q_{n,n',n'',\text{\&c.}}=\left\{\frac{d^{n+n'+n''+\text{\&c.}-r}.\left\{\frac{d^{r}u}{d\alpha.d\alpha'.d\alpha''.\ \text{\&c.}}\right\}}{1.2.3\ldots n.1.2.3\ldots n'.1.2.3\ldots n''.\text{\&c.}dt^{n-1}.dt'^{n'-1}.dt''^{n''-1}}\right\};$$

provided that in the partial difference $\left\{\frac{d^{r}u}{d\alpha.d\alpha'.d\alpha''.\ \text{\&c.}}\right\}$, we change z into z^{n}, z' into $z'^{n'}$, &c., and that afterwards we change z into Z, z' into Z', z'' into Z'', &c., and u into u′.

If there is but one variable x, we shall have

$$\left\{\frac{du}{d\alpha}\right\} = z. \left\{\frac{du}{dt}\right\};$$

therefore

$$q_n = \frac{d^{n-1}.\left(z^n.\left\{\frac{du}{dt}\right\}\right)}{1.2.3.\ldots\ldots n.dt^{n-1}}$$

If there are two variables x and x'; we shall have

$$\left\{\frac{du}{d\alpha}\right\} = z. \left\{\frac{du}{dt}\right\};^{*}$$

this equation differenced with respect to α', gives

$$\left\{\frac{d^2u}{d\alpha.d\alpha'}\right\} = \left\{\frac{dz}{d\alpha'}\right\}.\left\{\frac{du}{dt}\right\} + z.\left\{\frac{d^2u}{d\alpha'.dt}\right\};$$

but we have $\left\{\frac{du}{d\alpha'}\right\} = z'.\left\{\frac{du}{dt'}\right\}$; and if in this equation z is substituted in place of u, we have $\left\{\frac{dz}{d\alpha'}\right\} = z'.\left\{\frac{dz}{dt}\right\}$; therefore

$$\left\{\frac{d^2u}{d\alpha.d\alpha'}\right\} = z.\left\{\frac{d.z'.\left\{\frac{du}{dt'}\right\}}{dt}\right\} + z'.\left\{\frac{dz}{dt'}\right\}.\left\{\frac{du}{dt}\right\}.$$

* By substituting z^n for z, &c. we have made the coefficient $\frac{d^{n+n'}u}{d\alpha^n.d'\alpha^{n'}} = q_{n,n'}$ to depend on a coefficient of the second order, and the differentiations relative to t and t' will not be difficult when α, α' are = to cipher.

$$\frac{du}{d\alpha'} = z'.\frac{du}{dt'}, \therefore z.\frac{du^2}{d\alpha'.dt} = z.d.\left(z'.\left\{\frac{du}{dt'}\right\}\right) = zz'.\left\{\frac{d^2u}{dt.dt'}\right\} + z.\frac{dz'}{dt}.\frac{du}{dt},$$

$\therefore$ by substituting z^n, $z'^{n'}$, for z, z', respectively, we obtain the expression which is given in the text.

If we suppose α and α' equal to nothing, in the second member of this equation, and if we change z into Z^n, z' into $Z'^{n'}$, and u into u; we shall obtain the value of $\left\{\frac{d^2u}{d\alpha.d\alpha'}\right\}$, on the same suppositions; hence we obtain

$$q_{n,n'} = \frac{d^{n+n'-2}.\left\{\begin{array}{l} Z^n.\ Z'^{n'}.\ \left\{\frac{d^2\mathrm{u}}{dt.dt'}\right\} + Z'^{n'}.\left\{\frac{d.Z^n}{dt'}\right\}.\left\{\frac{d\mathrm{u}}{dt}\right\} \\ + Z^n.\left\{\frac{d.Z'^{n'}}{dt}\right\}.\left\{\frac{d\mathrm{u}}{dt}\right\} \end{array}\right\}}{1.2.3\ldots\ldots n.dt^{n-1}.\ 1.2.3\ldots\ldots n'.dt'^{n'-1}}.$$

by proceeding in this manner the value of $q_{n,n',n''}$, &c., for any number of variables whatever, may be obtained.

Although we have supposed that u, z, z', z'', &c., are functions of x, x', x'', &c., without t, t', t'', &c.; we can however suppose, that they contain these last variables: but then denoting these variables by $t_{,}$, $t'_{,}$, $t''_{,}$, &c., it is necessary to suppose $t_{,}$, $t'_{,}$, $t''_{,}$, constant in the differentiations, and after these operations to restore t, t', &c., in place of $t_{,}$, $t'_{,}$, &c.

22. Let us apply these results to the elliptic motion of the planets; and for this purpose, let the equations (f) of No. 20, be resumed. The equation $nt = u - e.\ \sin.\ u$, or $u = nt + e.\ \sin.\ u$, being compared with $x = \varphi(t + az)$; x will be changed into u, t into nt, and a into e, z into $\sin\ u$, and $\varphi(t+az)$ into $nt+e.\ \sin\ u$, consequently, the formula (P) of the preceding number will become

$$\psi(u) = \psi(nt) + e.\ \psi'(nt).\ \sin.\ nt + \frac{e^2}{1.2}.\ d.\frac{(\psi'(nt).\ \sin.\ ^2nt)}{ndt} + \frac{e^3}{1.2.3}.\ *$$

$$d^2.\frac{(\psi'(nt).\ \sin.\ ^3nt)}{n^2dt^2}. + \ \&c.;\ (q)$$

* If in the equation $u = nt + e,\ \sin.\ u$ it be required to develope $\psi\ (u)$ into a series arranged according to the powers of e, then applying the preceding formula, besides the changes indicated in the text, u will be changed into $\psi(u)$.

$\psi'(nt)$ being equal to $\frac{d.\psi(nt)}{ndt}$. In order to expand this formula, it is to be observed that c being the number of which the hyperbolical logarithm is unity, we have

$$\sin^{i}.nt = \left\{\frac{c^{nt.\sqrt{-1}} - c^{-nt.\sqrt{-1}}}{2\sqrt{-1}}\right\}^{i}; \quad \cos.^{i}nt = \left\{\frac{c^{nt.\sqrt{-1}} + c^{-nt.\sqrt{-1}}}{2}\right\}^{i*};$$

i being any number whatever. If we expand the second members of these equations, and then substitute, in place of $c^{rnt.\sqrt{-1}}$ and of $c^{-rnt.\sqrt{-1}}$, their values cos. $rnt. + \sqrt{-1}$ sin. $rnt.\sqrt{-1}$, and cos. $rnt.$ $- \sqrt{-1}$ sin. $rnt.\sqrt{-1}$, r being any number whatever; we will obtain the i powers of sin. nt and of cos. nt, evolved according to the sines and cosines of the angles nt of its multiples; this being premised, we shall find

$$\sin.\,nt + \frac{e}{1.2}.\sin.^{2}nt + \frac{e^2}{1.2.3}.\sin.^{3}nt + \frac{e^3}{1.2.3.4}.\sin.^{4}nt + \&c.$$

$$= \sin.\,nt - \frac{e}{1.2.2}(\cos.\,2nt - 1)$$

$$- \frac{e^2}{1.2.3.2^2}(\sin.\,3nt - 3\sin.\,nt)$$

$$+ \frac{e^3}{1.2.3.4.2^3}\left(\cos.\,4nt - 4\cos.\,2nt + \tfrac{1}{2}.\frac{4.3}{1.2}\right)$$

$$+ \frac{e^4}{1.2.3.4.5.2^4}\left(\sin.\,5nt - 5\sin.\,3nt + \frac{5.4}{1.2}.\sin.\,nt\right)$$

$$- \frac{e^5}{1.2.3.4.5.6.2^5}\left(\cos.\,6nt - 6\cos.\,4nt + \frac{6.5}{1.2}.\cos.\,2n - \tfrac{1}{2}.\frac{6.5.4}{1.2.3}\right)$$

$$- \&c.$$

* See Lacroix, Traite Complete, Tome I, page 76, 95, of the Introduction.

Let P* represent this function; if it be multiplied by $\psi'(nt)$ and then if each of its terms be differenced, with respect to t, as often as there are units in the power of e, by which it is multiplied, dt being supposed constant; and if then these differentials be divided by the corresponding power of ndt, the formula (q) will become

$$\psi u = \psi(nt) + eP').$$

P representing the sum of these differentials thus divided.

* The series P is always the same where the equation $u = nt + e.$ sin. nt obtains, whatever be the form of the function indicated by ψ; therefore when the form of ψ is given, the expression for $\psi(u)$ will be obtained by performing the operations indicated in the text.

When the value of P, is multiplied by $e.$ cos. nt, the form of the terms multiplied into the even powers of e, will be cos. $i.\ nt.$ sin. $s.\ nt$, and the expansion of this product is effected by the formula sin. $a.$ cos. $b = \text{sin.} \frac{(a+b) + \text{sin.}\ (a-b)}{2}$, therefore the terms multiplied by the even powers will be the sines. The form of the terms multiplied into the odd powers of e, will cos. $in.$ cos. snt the developement of which is effected by the formula cos. $a.$ cos. $b = \frac{\text{cos.}\ (a+b) + \text{cos.}\ (a-b)}{2}$, consequently the terms multiplied by the odd powers of e will be the cosines. If any term of the form $Ke^{2r}.$ sin. $snt.$ be differenced as often as there are units in $2r$, it is evident that when this term is divided by $\overline{ndt)}^{2r}$, the resulting terms will be $Ke^{2r}.\ s^{2r}.$ sin. snt, for as the terms are alternately cos. snt, sin. snt. when the number of differentiations is even the last term must be sin. snt, and as s is introduced as a factor at each successive differentiation when the number of differentiations is 2^r, s^{2r} will be a factor of this last term, the first term is + cos. int, and the signs of the subsequent terms are minus and plus in pairs, ∴ the signs of the successive differential coefficients including the first, are plus minus, minus plus, plus minus; i. e. + —, — +, + —, &c.; hence it appears, that when r is an odd number, the sign of the last term will be —, and when r is an even number, the last term will be +. In a term of the form of the $Ke^{2r+1}.$ cos. snt the number of differentiations being odd, the last term must be of the form $Ke^{2r+1}.\ s^{2r+1}.$ sin. snt, the signs of the terms in this case are alternately minus and plus in pairs, i. e. — —, + +, — —, + +, and as the sign of sin. snt, is the opposite of the sign of the penultimate term, when r is even this sign is evidently —, and when r is odd this sign is +.

It would be easy by this method to obtain the values of the angle u, and of the sines and cosines of this angle, and of its multiples. If for example, we suppose $\psi(u) = \sin. iu$; we shall obtain $\psi'(nt) = i \cos. int$. The preceding value of P, must be multiplied by $i. \cos. int$, and the product should be expanded into sines and cosines of the angle nt, and of its multiples. The sines will be multiplied by the even powers of e, and the cosines will be multiplied by the odd powers of e. Then any term of the form $Ke^{2r}. \sin. snt$ will be changed into $\pm Ke^{2r}. s^{2r}$, $\sin. snt$, the sign $+$ having place, if r is even, and the sign $-$ obtaining, if r is odd. In like manner any term of the form $Ke^{2r+1}. \cos. snt$. will be changed into $\mp Ke^{2r+1}. s^{2r+1}. \sin. snt$, the sign $-$ having place if r is even, and the sign $+$ obtaining, if r be odd. The sum of all these terms will be the value of P', and we shall obtain

$$\sin. iu = \sin. int + eP'.$$

If $\psi(u)$ be supposed equal to u*, $\psi'(nt)$ will be equal to unity, and we will find

$$u = nt + e. \sin. nt + \frac{e^2}{1.2.2}. 2 \sin. 2nt + \frac{e^3}{1.2.3.2^2}.(3^2. \sin. 3nt - 3 \sin. nt)$$

$$+ \frac{e^4}{1.2.3.4.2^3}.(4^3.\sin.4nt - 4.2^3.\sin.2nt)$$

$$+ \frac{e^5}{1.2.3.4.5.2^4} (5^4. \sin. 5nt - 5.3 .$$

$$\sin. 3nt + \frac{5.4}{1.2}. \sin. nt).$$

* If $\psi(u) = u$, then $\psi(nt) = nt$, and $\psi'(nt) = \frac{ndt}{ndt} - 1$, the series P' becomes sin. nt

$$- \frac{e}{1.2.2}. d. \frac{\cos. (2nt - 1)}{ndt} - \frac{e^2}{1.2.3.2^2}. d^2. \frac{(\sin. 3nt - 3 \sin. nt)}{(ndt)^2} - \frac{e^3}{1.2.3.4.2^3}.$$

$$d^3. \frac{(\cos. 4nt - 4 \cos. 2nt + \frac{4}{2}. \frac{4.3}{1.2}}{(ndt)^3}$$ + &c. which will be reduced to the expression in the text, by performing the prescribed differentiations.

This series is very converging for the planets. u being thus determined for any instant; the corresponding values of r and v, will be given by means of the equations (f) of N°. 20; but we can obtain these last quantities directly in converging series, in the following manner:

For this purpose, it may be remarked, that by No. 20, we have $r = a(1-e\cos. u)$; and if in the formula (q), we suppose $\psi(u) = 1 - e.\cos. u$, we shall have $\psi'(nt) = e.\sin. nt$, and consequently

$$1-e.\cos. u = 1-e.\cos. nt + e^2.\sin.^2 nt + \frac{e^3}{1.2}.\frac{d.\sin.^3 nt}{ndt} + \frac{e^4}{1.2.3}.\frac{d^2.\sin.^4 nt}{n^2.dt^2} + \&c.$$

Therefore by the preceding analysis, we shall obtain

$$\frac{r}{a} = 1 + \frac{e^2}{2} - e.\cos. nt - \frac{e^2}{2}\cos. 2nt^*$$
$$-\frac{e^3}{1.2.2^2}.(3.\cos. 3nt - 3.\cos. nt)$$
$$-\frac{e^4}{1.2.3.2^3}.(4^2.\cos. 4nt - 4.2^2.\cos. 2nt)$$
$$-\frac{e^5}{1.2.3.4.2^4}.(5^3.\cos. 5nt - 5.3^3.\cos. 3nt + \frac{5.4}{1.2}.\cos. nt)$$

* Since $\psi(u) = 1-e.\cos. u$, $\psi(nt) = 1-e.\cos. nt$; by substituting for $\sin.^2 nt$, $\sin.^3 nt$ &c. their values, the expression for $1-e.\cos. u$ becomes $1-e.\cos. nt + \frac{e^2}{2}.(1-\cos. 2nt) + \frac{e^3}{1.2}.d.\frac{(-\sin. 3nt + 3\sin. nt)}{4ndt} + \frac{e^4}{1.2.3}.d^2.\frac{(\cos. 4nt - 4\cos. 2nt + 3)}{8(ndt)^2}$ +&c., now when the differentiations indicated by the characteristics d, d^2, &c. are performed, the resulting terms only contain cos. nt, and its multiples, for those terms, in which the differentiation is performed an odd number of times, involve the sines of nt and of its multiples, therefore the resulting terms are cosines, and where the cosines of nt, and of its multiples are to be operated upon, the differentiation must be performed an even number of times, ∴ the resulting terms are in this case also cosines. The reason why in terms of the form $Ke^{2r}.\sin. snt$ the resulting quantity becomes $Ke^{2r}.s^{-r}.\sin. snt$, is the same as that assigned for a similar expression in the preceding page.

$$-\frac{e^6}{1.2.3.4.5.2^5}.(6^4.\cos.6nt-6.4^4.\cos.4nt+\frac{6.5}{1.2}.2^4.\cos.2nt).$$

Let us now consider the third of the equations (f) of No. 20; by means of it we obtain

$$\frac{\sin.\frac{1}{2}v}{\cos.\frac{1}{2}v}=\sqrt{\frac{1+e}{1-e}}.\frac{\sin.\frac{1}{2}u}{\cos.\frac{1}{2}u}.$$

By substituting in this equation, in place of the sines and of the cosines, their values expressed in imaginary exponentials, we shall have

$$\frac{c^{v.\sqrt{-1}}-1}{c^{v.\sqrt{-1}}+1}=\sqrt{\frac{1+e}{1-e}}\left\{\frac{e^{u.\sqrt{-1}}-1}{e^{u.\sqrt{-1}}+1}\right\};*$$

and by supposing

$$\lambda=\frac{e}{1+\sqrt{1-e^2}};$$

we shall have

* $\text{Sin.}\frac{1}{2}v=\frac{c^{\frac{v}{2}\sqrt{-1}}-c^{-\frac{v}{2}\sqrt{-1}}}{2.\sqrt{-1}}$, $\cos.\frac{1}{2}v=\frac{c^{\frac{v}{2}\sqrt{-1}}+c^{-\frac{v}{2}\sqrt{-1}}}{2}$, ∵ substituting these expressions for $\sin.\frac{v}{2}\cos.\frac{v}{2}$, in the expression $\frac{\sin.\frac{v}{2}}{\cos.\frac{v}{2}}$, multiplying both numerator and denominator by $c^{\frac{v}{2}\sqrt{-1}}$, and performing similar operations on $\frac{\sin.\frac{u}{2}}{\cos.\frac{u}{2}}$, we shall have the expression in the text.

$$c^{v.\sqrt{-1}} = c^{u.\sqrt{-1}}.\left\{\frac{1-\lambda.c^{-u.\sqrt{-1}}}{1-\lambda.c^{u.\sqrt{-1}}}\right\};*$$

and consequently,

$$v = u + \frac{\log.(1-\lambda.c^{-u\sqrt{-1}}) - \log.(1-\lambda.c^{u\sqrt{-1}})}{\sqrt{-1}};$$

from which may be obtained, by reducing the logarithms into series,†

* $\because c^{v.\sqrt{-1}} - 1 = c^{u.\sqrt{-1}}\frac{(1-\lambda c^{-u.\sqrt{-1}})}{1-\lambda c^{u.\sqrt{-1}}} - 1 = \frac{(1+\lambda).(c^{u.\sqrt{-1}}-1)}{1-\lambda c^{u.\sqrt{-1}}}$; and

$c^{v.\sqrt{-1}} + 1 = c^{u.\sqrt{-1}}\frac{(1-\lambda c^{-u.\sqrt{-1}})}{1-\lambda c^{u.\sqrt{-1}}} + 1 = \frac{(1-\lambda)(c^{u.\sqrt{-1}}+1)}{1-\lambda c^{u.\sqrt{-1}}}$, $\because \frac{c^{v.\sqrt{-1}}-1}{c^{v.\sqrt{-1}}+1}$

$= \frac{(1+\lambda).(c^{u.\sqrt{-1}}-1)}{(1-\lambda).(c^{u.\sqrt{-1}}+1)}$; $1+\lambda = \frac{1+e+\sqrt{1-e^2}}{1+\sqrt{1-e^2}} = \sqrt{1+e}.\frac{(\sqrt{1+e}+\sqrt{1-e})}{1+\sqrt{1-e^2}}$; $(1-\lambda)$

$= \frac{1-e+\sqrt{1-e^2}}{1+\sqrt{1-e^2}} = \sqrt{1-e}.\frac{(\sqrt{1-e}+\sqrt{1+e})}{1+\sqrt{1-e^2}}$, $\because$ by substituting these values of $1+\lambda$ and $1-\lambda$, we obtain

$\frac{c^{v.\sqrt{-1}}-1}{c^{v.\sqrt{-1}}+1} = \frac{\sqrt{1+e}\,(\sqrt{1-e}+\sqrt{1+e}).}{\sqrt{1-e}(\sqrt{1+e}+\sqrt{1-e}.)}.\frac{(c^{u.\sqrt{-1}}-1)}{(c^{u.\sqrt{-1}}+1)} = \frac{\sqrt{1+e}}{\sqrt{1-e}}.\frac{c^{u.\sqrt{-1}}-1}{c^{u.\sqrt{-1}}+1}.$

† $\text{Log.}\,c^{v.\sqrt{-1}} = v.\sqrt{-1} = \log.c^{u.\sqrt{-1}} + \log.(1-\lambda.c^{-u.\sqrt{-1}}) - \log.(1-\lambda.c^{u.\sqrt{-1}}) = u.\sqrt{-1} + \log.(1-\lambda.c^{-u.\sqrt{-1}}) - \log.(1-\lambda.c^{u.\sqrt{-1}})$; $\log.(1-\lambda.c^{-u\sqrt{-1}})$
$= -\frac{\lambda}{1}c^{-\sqrt{-1}} - \frac{\lambda^2}{2}.c^{-2u.\sqrt{-1}} - \frac{\lambda^3}{3}.c^{-3u.\sqrt{-1}} - \&c. - \log.(1-\lambda).c^{u.\sqrt{-1}}$
$= \frac{\lambda}{1}.c^{u\sqrt{-1}} + \frac{\lambda^2}{2}.c^{2u.\sqrt{-1}} + \frac{\lambda^3}{3}.c^{3u.\sqrt{-1}} + \&c.$; $\therefore \log.(1-\lambda).c^{-u.\sqrt{-1}} -$
$\log.(1-\lambda).c^{u.\sqrt{-1}} = \frac{\lambda}{1}.(c^{u.\sqrt{-1}} - c^{-u.\sqrt{-1}}) + \frac{\lambda^2}{2}.(c^{2u.\sqrt{-1}} - c^{-2u.\sqrt{-1}}) + \frac{\lambda^3}{3}.$

$$v = u + 2\lambda.\,\sin.\,u + \frac{2\lambda^2}{2}.\,\sin.\,2u + \frac{2\lambda^3}{3}.\,\sin.\,3u + \frac{2\lambda^4}{4}.\,\sin.\,4u + \&c.$$

by what goes before, we have u, sin. u, sin. $2u$, &c. in a series arranged according to the powers of e, and expanded into sines and cosines of the angle nt and its multiples, therefore in order to obtain v expressed in a similar series, it is only necessary to expand the successive powers of l into a series ranged according to the powers of e.

The equation $u = 2 - \frac{e^2}{u}$, will give by the formula (p) of the preceding number,

$$\frac{1}{u^i} = \frac{1}{2^i} + \frac{i.e^2}{2^{i+2}} + \frac{i.(i+3)}{1.2}.\,\frac{e^4}{2^{i+4}} + \frac{i.(i+3).(i+5)}{1.2.3}.\,\frac{e^6}{2^{i+6}} + \&c.;$$

and as we have,

$$u = 1 + \sqrt{1-e^2};\ \text{we shall have}$$

$$^*\lambda^i = \frac{e^i}{2^i}\left\{1 + i.\left(\frac{e}{2}\right)^2 + \frac{i.(i+3)}{1.2}.\left(\frac{e}{2}\right)^4 + \frac{i.(i+3).(i+5)}{1.2.3}.\left(\frac{e}{2}\right)^6 + \&c.\right\}$$

This being premised, we shall find by continuing the approximation to

$(c^{3u.\sqrt{-1}} - c^{-3u.\sqrt{-1}}) + \&c.$, ∵ dividing by $\sqrt{-1}$, and substituting $2\sqrt{-1}$ sin. su. for $c^{su.\sqrt{-1}} - c^{-su.\sqrt{-1}}$, we obtain the expression which is given in the text.

* The equation $u = 2 - \frac{e^2}{u}$, being compared with the expression $x = \phi(t + \alpha x)$ gives $z = F(x) = \frac{1}{u}$, $\alpha = -e^2$, $t = 2$, and $\psi(x) = \frac{1}{u^i}$, ∵ when $\psi(x) = \frac{1}{u^i}$, $\psi(t) = \frac{1}{2^i}$, $\psi'(t) = \frac{-i}{2^{i+1}}$, $F(t) = \frac{1}{2}$, consequently $\frac{1}{u^i} = \frac{1}{2^i} + \frac{ie^2}{2^{i+2}} + \frac{i.(i+3)}{1.2}.\,\frac{e^4}{2^{i+4}} + \frac{i.(i+3).(i+5)}{1.2.3}.\,\frac{e^6}{2^{i+6}} + \&c.$

From the equation $u = 2 - \frac{e^2}{u}$ we obtain $u^2 - 2u = -e^2$, $\therefore \frac{1}{u} = 1 + \sqrt{1-e^2} = \frac{\lambda}{e}$ hence $\lambda^i = \frac{e^i}{u^i}$ = the expression given in the text. And if $i = 1$, $\lambda = \frac{e}{2}\left(1 + \left(\frac{e}{2}\right)^2\right.$

quantities of the order i^6 inclusively,

$$v = nt + \left\{2e - \frac{1}{4}.e^3 + \frac{5}{96}.e^5\right\}.\sin.nt + \left\{\frac{5}{4}.e^2 - \frac{11}{24}.e^4 + \frac{17}{192}.e^6\right\}.\sin.2nt.$$

$$+ \left\{\frac{13}{12}.e^3 - \frac{43}{64}.e^5\right).\sin.3nt + \left\{\frac{103}{96}.e^4 - \frac{451}{480}.e^6\right\}.\sin.4nt,^*$$

$$+ \frac{1097}{960}.e^5.\sin.5nt + \frac{1223}{960}.e^6.\sin.6nt.$$

$+ \left\{\frac{1+3}{1.2}\right\}.\frac{e^4}{2^4} = \frac{e}{2} + \frac{e^3}{8} + \frac{e^5}{16}$, (as the approximation is not carried beyond the fifth powers), $\lambda^2 = \frac{e^2}{2^2}\left\{1 + 2\left\{\frac{e}{2}\right\}^2 + \frac{2(2+3)}{1.2}.\left\{\frac{e}{2}\right\}^4 = \frac{e^2}{4} + \frac{e^4}{8} + \frac{5}{4}.\right.$ $\frac{e^6}{16}$; $\lambda^3 = \frac{e^3}{2^3}.\left(1+3.\left\{\frac{e}{2}\right\}^2\right) = \frac{e^3}{8} + \frac{3}{8}.\frac{e^5}{4}$; $\lambda^4 = \frac{e^4}{2^4}.\left(1+4.\left\{\frac{e}{2}\right\}^2\right) = \frac{e^4}{16}$ $+ \frac{e^6}{16}$; $\lambda^6 = \frac{e^6}{64}$.

* When u is expressed in the manner prescribed in the text, the five first terms are those given in the preceding page; and as the approximation is carried to the sixth powers of e, we must add the additional term which is

$$\frac{e^6}{1.2.3.4.5.6.2^5}.(6^5.\sin.6nt - 6.4^5.\sin.4nt + \frac{6.5}{1.2}.2^5.\sin.2nt);$$

If to these terms expressing the value of u, be added the values of $2\lambda.\sin.u$, $2\lambda^2.\sin.2u$, &c., reduced into a series ranged according to the powers of e, and developed into sines and cosines of the angle nt and its multiples, we shall have

$2\lambda.\sin.u = \left\{e + \frac{e^3}{4} + \frac{e^5}{8}\right\}.\sin.nt. + \left\{\frac{e^2}{2} + \frac{e^4}{8} + \frac{e^6}{16}\right\}.\sin.2nt + \left\{\frac{e^3}{8}\right.$ $\left.+ \frac{e^5}{32}\right\}.(3.\sin.3nt - \sin.nt) + \left\{\frac{e^4}{48} + \frac{e^6}{192}\right\}.(4^2.\sin.4nt - 2^2.\sin.2nt) + \frac{e^5}{384}.$ $(5^3.\sin.5nt - 3.3^3.\sin 3nt + 2.\sin.nt) + \frac{e^6}{3840}.(6^4.\sin.6nt + 4.4^4.\sin.4nt +$ $5.2^4.\sin.2nt)$; $\frac{2\lambda^2}{2}.\sin.2u = \left\{\frac{e^2}{4} + \frac{e^4}{8} + \frac{5e^6}{64}\right\}.\sin.2nt + \left\{\frac{e^3}{4} + \frac{e^5}{8}\right\}$ $(\sin.3nt - \sin.nt) + \left\{\frac{e^4}{14} + \frac{e^6}{32}\right\}.(4.\sin.4nt - 4\sin.2nt) + \frac{e^5}{96}.(5^2.\sin.5nt -$

The angles v and nt are here reckoned from the perihelium, but if we wish to count them from aphelium, it is evident that to effect this, it is only necessary to make e negative in the preceding expressions of r and v. It will also be sufficient to augment in those expressions, the angle nt, by the semicircumference, which renders the sines and cosines of the odd multiples of nt negative, consequently, as the results of these two methods ought to be identical, it is necessary that in the expressions of r and of v, the sines and cosines of the odd multiples of nt, should be multiplied by the odd powers of e, and that the sines and cosines of the even multiples of the same angle, should be multiplied by the even powers of this quantity. This is, in fact, confirmed *à posteriori* by the calculus.

Let us suppose that in place of reckoning the angle v, from the perihelium, we fix its origin at any point whatever; it is evident that this angle will be increased by a constant quantity, which we will denote by ϖ, and which will express the longitude of the perihelium.

$3.3^2.\sin.3nt+4\sin.nt)+\frac{e^6}{768}.(6^3.\sin.6nt-4.4^3.\sin.4nt+7.2^3.\sin.2nt)$; $\frac{2\lambda^3}{3}.\sin.3u=\left\{\frac{e^3}{12}+\frac{e^5}{16}\right\}.\sin.3nt+\left\{\frac{e^6}{8}+\frac{3e^5}{32}\right\}.(\sin.4nt-\sin.2nt)+\frac{e^5}{32}.(5.\sin.5nt-2.3.\sin.3nt+\sin.nt)+\frac{e^6}{192}.(6^2.\sin.6nt-3.4^2.\sin.4nt+3.2^2.\sin.2nt)$; $\frac{2\lambda^4}{4}.\sin.4u=\left\{\frac{e^4}{32}+\frac{e^6}{32}\right\}.\sin.4nt+\frac{e^5}{16}.(\sin.5nt-\sin.3nt)+\frac{e^6}{64}.(6.\sin.6nt-2.4.\sin.4nt+2.\sin.2nt)$; $\frac{2\lambda^5}{5}.\sin.5u=\frac{e^5}{80}.\sin.5nt+\frac{e^6}{16}.(\sin.6nt-\sin.4nt)$. If the several factors of sin. nt, sin. $2nt$, &c., be collected and arranged, they will give the respective terms of the value of v, for instance, the factors which multiply sin. nt, are, taking into account the value of u which is given in page 145).

$$\left(2e-\frac{e^3}{8}+\frac{e^3}{4}-\frac{e^3}{8}+\frac{e^5}{8}-\frac{e^3}{4}-\frac{e^5}{32}\frac{e^5}{192}-\frac{e^5}{8}+\frac{e^5}{24}+\frac{e^5}{32}+\frac{e^5}{192}\right\}.\sin.nt.$$

$=\left(2e-\frac{e^3}{4}+\frac{5e^5}{96}\right\}.\sin.nt$; the factors of sin. $2nt$ are $\frac{e^2}{2}+\frac{e^2}{4}+\frac{e^2}{2}+\frac{e^4}{6}+\frac{e^4}{6}+\frac{e^4}{8}+\frac{e^4}{12}+\frac{e^4}{8}-\frac{e^4}{4}-\frac{e^4}{8}$, &c. See page 145.

If instead of fixing the origin of t, at the moment of the passage through the perihelium, we fix it at any instant whatever; the angle nt will be increased by a constant quantity, which we will denote by $\varepsilon - \varpi$; and consequently the preceding expressions of $\frac{r}{a}$, and of v will become

$$\frac{r}{a} = 1 + \tfrac{1}{2}e^2 - (e - \frac{3}{8}e^3).\cos.(nt+\varepsilon-\varpi) - \left(\frac{1}{2}e^2 - \frac{1}{3}e^4\right).$$
$$\cos. 2.(nt + \varepsilon - \varpi) - \&c.;$$
$$v = nt + \varepsilon + (2e - \frac{1}{4}e^3).\sin.(nt+\varepsilon-\varpi) + \left(\frac{5}{4}e^2 - \frac{11}{24}e^4\right).$$
$$\sin. 2(nt + \varepsilon - \varpi) + \&c.;$$

v is the true longitude of the planet, and $nt + \varepsilon$ is its mean longitude, these two longitudes being referred to the plane of the orbit.

Let us now refer the motion of the planet, to a fixed plane, a little inclined to that of the orbit. Let φ represent the mutual inclination of these two planes, and θ the longitude of the ascending node of the orbit, reckoned on the fixed plane; let ϵ be this longitude reckoned on the fixed plane of the orbit, so that θ is the projection of ϵ; also let $v_{,}$ be the projection of v on the fixed plane. We shall have

$$\tan.(v_{,} - \theta) = \cos.\varphi.\tan.(v - \epsilon).$$

This equation gives $v_{,}$ in terms of $u_{,}$ and vice versa; but we can have these two angles, each in terms of the other, in very converging series, by the following method. The series

$$\tfrac{1}{2}v = \tfrac{1}{2}u + \lambda.\sin. u + \frac{\lambda^2}{2}.\sin. 2u + \frac{\lambda^3}{3}.\sin. 3u + \&c.$$

has been already deduced from the equation

$$\text{tang.}\ \tfrac{1}{2}v = \sqrt{\frac{1+e}{1-e}}.\ \text{tang.}\ \tfrac{1}{2}u.$$

by making

$$\lambda = \frac{\sqrt{\frac{1+e}{1-e}} - 1}{\sqrt{\frac{1+e}{1-e}} + 1}.$$

If $\frac{1}{2}v$, be changed into $v_{,}-\theta$; $\frac{1}{2}u$ into $u - \epsilon$; and $\sqrt{\frac{1+e}{1-e}}$ into $\cos\varphi$; we shall have

$$\lambda = \frac{\cos.\ \varphi - 1}{\cos.\ \varphi + 1} = -\text{tan.}^2 \frac{1}{2}\ \varphi;\dagger$$

the equation between $\frac{1}{2}v$ and $\frac{1}{2}u$, will be changed into an equation be-

* By making e negative in the equation $r = \frac{a.(1-e^2)}{1+e.\cos.v}$, v will be equal to cipher, when $r = a.(1+e)$, *i. e.* at the aphelium, ∵ it is from this point that the angle v is reckoned.

Since the results must be identically the same, when v is reckoned from perihelium and aphelium, and since the signs of the odd multiples are necessarily changed, in order that these expressions may remain the same as before, the sign of the factors which multiply these odd multiples, must be changed at the same time, *i. e.* these factors must be odd powers of e.

† $1 - 2\sin.^2\frac{1}{2}\varphi = \cos.\ \varphi$; $2\cos.^2\frac{1}{2}\varphi - 1 = \cos.\varphi$, ∴ $\frac{\cos.\ \varphi - 1}{\cos.\ \varphi + 1} = -\text{tang.}^2\frac{1}{2}\varphi$, $\frac{\frac{\sqrt{1+e}}{\sqrt{1-e}} - 1}{\frac{\sqrt{1+e}}{\sqrt{1-e}} + 1} = \frac{\sqrt{1+e} - \sqrt{1-e}}{\sqrt{1+e} + \sqrt{1-e}}$, multiplying both numerator and denominator by $\sqrt{1+e} + \sqrt{1-e}$, we obtain after all reductions $\frac{2e}{2+2\sqrt{1-e^2}} = \frac{e}{1+\sqrt{1-e^2}} = \lambda$;

tween $v_{,}-\theta$ and $v-\epsilon$, and the preceding series will give

$$v_{,}-\theta = v-\epsilon - \tan{}^2\tfrac{1}{2}\varphi.\ \sin.\ 2(v-\epsilon) + \tfrac{1}{2}.\ \tan.\ {}^4\tfrac{1}{2}\varphi.\ \sin.\ 4(v-\epsilon)$$
$$-\tfrac{1}{3}.\ \tan.\ {}^6\tfrac{1}{2}\varphi.\ \sin.\ 6.(v-\epsilon) + \&c.$$

If in the equation between $\frac{1}{2}v$ and $\frac{1}{2}u$, we change $\frac{1}{2}v$ into $v-\epsilon$, $\frac{1}{2}u$ into $v_{,}-\theta$, and $\sqrt{\frac{1+e}{1-e}}$ into $\frac{1}{\cos.\ \varphi}$; we will obtain

$$\lambda = \tan.\ {}^2\tfrac{1}{2}\varphi,^*$$

and

$$v-\epsilon = v_{,}-\theta + \tan.\ {}^2\tfrac{1}{2}\varphi.\ \sin.\ 2(v_{,}-\theta) + \tfrac{1}{2}.\ \tan.\ {}^4\tfrac{1}{2}\varphi.\ \sin.\ 4(v_{,}-\theta)$$
$$+\tfrac{1}{3}.\ \tan.\ {}^6\tfrac{1}{2}\varphi.\ \sin.\ 6(v_{,}-\theta) + \&c.$$

It is evident from an inspection of the two preceding series, that they may be converted one into the other, by changing the sign of the tan. ${}^2\frac{1}{2}\varphi$, and by changing the angles, $v_{,}-\theta$, and $v-\epsilon$, the one into the other. We will obtain $v_{,}-\theta$, in a function of the sines and cosines of the angle nt and its multiples, by observing that by what goes before, we have,

$$v = nt + \varepsilon + eQ,$$

(Q being a function of the sine of the angle $nt+\epsilon-\varpi$, and of its multiples); and that the formula (i) of No. 21, gives, whatever may be the value of i,

$2(v-\epsilon)$ being substituted for u, and observing that when $-\text{tang.}\ \frac{{}^2 1}{2}.\ v$ is substituted for λ, the even multiples of two are positive, and the odd multiples negative, we obtain the expression which is given in the text.

* In this case $$\frac{\frac{1}{\cos.\ \varphi}-1}{\frac{1}{\cos.\ \varphi}+1} = \frac{1-\cos.\ \varphi}{1+\cos.\ \varphi} = \frac{\sin.\ \frac{{}^2 1}{2}\varphi}{\cos.\ \frac{{}^2 1}{2}\varphi} = \tan.\ \frac{{}^2 1}{2}\varphi.$$

$$\sin. i.(v-\varpi)=\sin. i.(nt+\varepsilon-\varpi+eQ)=\left\{1-\frac{i^2e^2.Q^2}{1.2}+\frac{i^4e^4.Q^4}{1.2.3.4}-\&c.\right\}^*$$
$$.\sin. i.(nt+\varepsilon-\varpi)$$
$$+\left\{ieQ-\frac{i^3e^3.Q^3}{1.2.3}+\frac{i^5.e^5.Q^5}{1.2.3.4.5}-\&c\right\}$$
$$.\cos. i.(nt+\varepsilon-\varpi).$$

Finally, s being the tangent of the latitude of the planet, above the fixed plane, we have

$$s=\tan. \varphi. \sin. (v_,-\theta);$$

and if $r_,$ represents the radius vector r projected on the fixed plane, we shall have

$$r_,=r.(1+s^2)^{-\frac{1}{2}}=r(1-\tfrac{1}{2}s^2+\tfrac{3}{8}.s^4-\&c.);\dagger$$

by this means we are enabled to determine $v_,$ r, and s in converging series of sines, and cosines of the angle nt, and of its multiples.

23. Let us now consider the orbits which are very eccentric, such as are those of the comets; and for this purpose let the equations of No. 20, be resumed, namely

$$r=\frac{a.(1-e^2)}{1+e.\cos. v};$$

$$nt=u-e.\sin. u;$$

$$\tan. \tfrac{1}{2}v=\sqrt{\frac{1+e}{1-e}}.\tan. \tfrac{1}{2}u.$$

x 2

* By the formulæ of No. 21, if the function sin. $i.(nt+\varepsilon-\varpi)$ receive the increment ieQ, the value of this function so increased, will be the successive differential coefficients of sin. $i.(nt+\varepsilon-\varpi)$, (which are ultimately its sines and cosines) multiplied into the successive powers of ieQ, and divided by the products $1.2.3...r$; and these terms being concinnated, give the expression in the text.

† $s. \cot. \varphi=\sin. (v_,-\theta)$, $\because s=\text{tang}. \varphi. \sin. (v_,-\theta)$; $r'=r\cos. \text{lat.}=\frac{r}{\sqrt{1+s^2}}$, $=r.(1-\frac{1}{2}s^2+\frac{3}{8}s^4-\&c.)$.

In the case of very excentric orbits, e differs very little from unity; therefore let us suppose, $1-e=\alpha$, α being very small. If we name D, the perihelium distance of the comet; we shall have $D=a.(1-e)=\alpha a$; therefore the expression of r will become

$$r=\frac{(2-\alpha).D}{2.\cos.^2\tfrac{1}{2}v-\alpha.\cos.v}=\frac{D}{\cos.^2\tfrac{1}{2}v.\left\{1+\frac{\alpha}{2-\alpha}\tan.^2\tfrac{1}{2}v\right\}};\text{*}$$

which gives, by reducing into a series,

$$r=\frac{D}{\cos.^2\tfrac{1}{2}v}\left\{1-\frac{\alpha}{2-\alpha}.\tan.^2\tfrac{1}{2}v+\left\{\frac{\alpha}{2-\alpha}\right\}^2.\tan.^4\tfrac{1}{2}v-\&c.\right\}$$

In order to have the ratio of v to the time t, we will observe that the expression of the arc in terms of the tangent, gives

$$u=2.\tan.\tfrac{1}{2}u.\left(1-\tfrac{1}{3}.\tan.^2\tfrac{1}{2}u+\tfrac{1}{5}.\tan.^4\tfrac{1}{2}u-\&c.\right);\dagger$$

but we have

$$\tan.\tfrac{1}{2}u=\sqrt{\frac{\alpha}{2-\alpha}}.\tan.\tfrac{1}{2}v;$$

therefore we shall have

$$u=2.\sqrt{\frac{\alpha}{2-\alpha}}.\tan.\tfrac{1}{2}v.\left\{1-\tfrac{1}{3}\left(\frac{\alpha}{2-\alpha}\right).\tan.^2\tfrac{1}{2}.v+\tfrac{1}{5}.\left(\frac{\alpha}{2-\alpha}\right)^2.\tan.^4\tfrac{1}{2}v-\&c.\right\}$$

* $e^2=\alpha^2-2\alpha+1$; $\because r=\dfrac{a.(1-\alpha^2+2\alpha-1)}{1+2.\cos.^2\tfrac{1}{2}v-1-2\alpha.\cos.^2\tfrac{1}{2}v+\alpha}=$

$$\frac{\alpha.a.(2-\alpha)}{2.\cos.^2\tfrac{1}{2}v+\alpha(1-2\cos.^2\tfrac{1}{2}v)}=\frac{D.(2-\alpha)}{2.\cos.^2\tfrac{1}{2}v-\alpha.\cos.^2\tfrac{1}{2}v+\alpha.\sin.^2\tfrac{1}{2}v}$$

$=\dfrac{D.(2-\alpha)}{\cos.^2\tfrac{1}{2}v(2-\alpha)+\alpha.\sin.^2\tfrac{1}{2}v}$; dividing the numerator and denominator by $2-\alpha$, we obtain the expression in the text.

† $\text{tang.}\tfrac{1}{2}u=\dfrac{\sqrt{1-e}}{\sqrt{1+e}}.\text{tang.}\tfrac{1}{2}v=\dfrac{\sqrt{\alpha}}{\sqrt{2-\alpha}}.\text{tang.}\tfrac{1}{2}v$;

we have likewise

$$\sin. u = \frac{2 \tan. \frac{1}{2}u}{1+\tan.^2\frac{1}{2}u} = 2. \tan. \tfrac{1}{2}u.(1 - \tan.^2\tfrac{1}{2}u + \tan.^4\tfrac{1}{2}u - \&c.);^*$$

from which may be obtained

$$e. \sin. u = 2(1-\alpha).\sqrt{\frac{\alpha}{2-\alpha}}.\tan. \tfrac{1}{2}v.\left\{1 - \frac{\alpha}{2-\alpha}.\tan.^2\tfrac{1}{2}v + \left\{\frac{\alpha}{2-\alpha}\right\}^2.\tan.^4\tfrac{1}{2}v - \&c.\right\}$$

These values of u and of $e. \sin. u$, being substituted in the equation $nt = u - e. \sin. u$, will determine, in a very converging series, the time t, in a function of the anomaly v; but previous to making this substitution, it may be observed that by No. 20, $n = a.^{-\frac{3}{2}}\sqrt{\mu}$, and as $D = \alpha a$, we shall have

$$\frac{1}{n} = \frac{D^{\frac{3}{2}}}{\alpha^{\frac{3}{2}}.\sqrt{\mu}}.$$

This being premised, we shall find

$$t = \frac{2D^{\frac{3}{2}}}{\sqrt{(2-\alpha).\mu}}.\tan. \tfrac{1}{2}v.\left\{1 + \frac{\left\{\frac{2}{3} - \alpha\right\}}{2-\alpha}.\tan.^2\tfrac{1}{2}v - \frac{\left\{\frac{4}{5} - \alpha.\right\}.\alpha}{(2-\alpha)^2}\tan.^4\tfrac{1}{2}v + \&c.\right\}.\dagger$$

* $$\frac{2 \tan. \frac{1}{2}u}{1+\text{tang.}^2\frac{1}{2}u} = \frac{\frac{2.\sin.\frac{1}{2}u}{\cos.\frac{1}{2}u}}{1+\frac{\sin.^2\frac{1}{2}u}{\cos.^2\frac{1}{2}u}} = \frac{2\sin.\frac{1}{2}u.\cos.\frac{1}{2}u}{\sin.^2\frac{1}{2}u+\cos.^2\frac{1}{2}u} = \sin. u.$$

† $n = \frac{\sqrt{\mu}}{a^{\frac{3}{2}}}$, $\frac{D}{\alpha} = a$, $\therefore n = \frac{\alpha^{\frac{3}{2}}\sqrt{\mu}}{D^{\frac{3}{2}}}$; $t = \frac{u - e.\sin. u}{n} = \frac{D^{\frac{3}{2}}}{\alpha^{\frac{3}{2}}\sqrt{\mu}}\left\{\frac{2\sqrt{\alpha}}{\sqrt{2-\alpha}}\right.$ $\left.(\tan.\tfrac{1}{2}v(1 - \frac{1}{3}\left\{\frac{\alpha}{2-\alpha}\right\}.\tan.^2\tfrac{1}{2}v + \frac{1}{5}\left\{\frac{\alpha}{2-\alpha}\right\}^2.\text{tang.}^4\tfrac{1}{2}v - \&c.) - 2.(1-\alpha.)\sqrt{\frac{\alpha}{2-\alpha}}.\right.$

If the orbit be parabolical, $\alpha = 0$, and consequently

$$r = \frac{D}{\cos.^2 \frac{1}{2}v};$$

$$t = \frac{D^{\frac{3}{2}}}{\sqrt{\mu}} \sqrt{2}.\ (\tan.\ \tfrac{1}{2}v + \tfrac{1}{3}.\ \tan.^3 \tfrac{1}{2}v).*$$

The time t, the distance D, and the sum μ of the masses of the sun and of the comet, are heterogeneous quantities, and in order to render them comparable, they should be divided by the respective units of their species. Let therefore the mean distance of the sun from the earth represent the unity of the distance, so that D may be expressed in parts of this distance. It may then be remarked, that if T be called the time of a sidereal revolution of the earth, which we will suppose to depart from the perihelium, we shall have in the equation $nt = u - e.\ \sin.\ u$, $u = 0$, at the commencement of the revolution, and $u = 2\pi$, at its completion, π being the semicircumference of which the the radius is unity; therefore we shall have $nT = 2\pi$; but we have $n = a^{-\frac{3}{2}}. \sqrt{\mu} = \sqrt{\mu}$, because $a = 1$; therefore

$$\sqrt{\mu} = \frac{2\pi}{T}.$$

The value of μ is not exactly the same, in the case of the earth and of the comet; since, in the first case, it expresses the sum of the masses of the

$\tan.\ \frac{1}{2}v(1 - \frac{\alpha}{2-\alpha}.\ \tan.^2 \frac{1}{2}v + \left\{\frac{\alpha}{2-\alpha}\right\}^2.\ \text{tang}.^4 \frac{1}{2}v - \&c.) \Big\}$, if the parts which destroy each other in this expression be obliterated, and if $\alpha^{\frac{3}{2}}$ which occurs both in the numerator and denominator, of the part which remains, be likewise obliterated, the resulting quantity will be value of t given in the text.

* It appears from this value of t, that the times in which different comets moving in parabolick orbits, describe equal angels about the sun placed in the focus, are in the sesquiplicate ratio of the perihelium distance. See Newton, Prop. 37, Book 3, and also No. 27.

sun and earth; in place of which, in the second case, it expresses the sum of the masses of the sun and comet; but the masses of the earth, and of the comet, being much less than that of the sun, they may be neglected, and we may suppose that μ is the same for all these bodies, and that it expresses the mass of the sun. Therefore by substituting in place of $\sqrt{\mu}$, its value $\frac{2\pi}{T}$ in the preceding expression of t; we shall have

$$t = \frac{D^{\frac{3}{2}}.\ T}{\pi.\sqrt{2}}.\ (\tan.\ \tfrac{1}{2}v + \tfrac{1}{3}.\ \tan.\ ^{3}\tfrac{1}{2}v).$$

This equation contains no quantities which are not comparable with each other, it will easily determine t, whenever μ will be known; but in order to determine v, by means of t, we must solve an equation of the third degree which admits of but one real root. We may dispense with the resolution, by making a table of the values of v, corresponding to those of t, in a parabola of which the perihelium distance is equal to unity, or equal to the mean distance of the earth from the sun. This table will give the time which corresponds to the anomaly v, in any parabola of which D represents the perehelium distance, by multiplying by $D^{\frac{3}{2}}$, the time which answers to the same anomaly, in the table. We shall obtain the anomaly v, which answers to the time, by dividing t by $D^{\frac{3}{2}}$, and then seeking in the table, the anomaly which answers to the quotient of this division.

Let us now suppose that the anomaly v, which corresponds to the time t, in a very eccentric ellipse, is required. If quantities of the order α^2 be neglected, and of $1-e$ be substituted, instead of α; the preceding ex-

When this equation is reduced to an original form there will be only one mutation of sign; $\because$ there will be only one real and affirmative root; when u and D are given, r and t may be obtained immediately by the solution of a simple equation.

pression of t in v, in the ellipse, will give

$$t = \frac{D^{\frac{3}{2}}.\sqrt{2}}{\sqrt{\mu}} \left\{ \begin{array}{l} \tan.\ \tfrac{1}{2}v + \tfrac{1}{3}.\ \tan.\ ^{3}\tfrac{1}{2}v \\ +(1-e).\ \tan.\ \tfrac{1}{2}v.(\tfrac{1}{4} - \tfrac{1}{4}.\ \tan.\ ^{2}\tfrac{1}{2})v - \tfrac{1}{5}.\ \tan.\ ^{4}\tfrac{1}{2}v) \end{array} \right\}^{*}$$

We should seek, in the table of the motion of comets, the anomaly which answers to the time t, in a parabola of which D represents the perehelium distance; let U represent this anomaly, $U+x$ being the true anomaly in the ellipse, corresponding to the same time, x being a very small angle. If we substitute in the preceding equation $U+x$ in place of v, and then reduce the second member of this equation into a series arranged according to the powers of x; we shall obtain by neglecting the square of x, and the product of x into $1-e$,

$$t = \frac{D^{\frac{3}{2}}.\sqrt{2}}{\sqrt{\mu}} \left\{ \begin{array}{l} (\tan.\ \tfrac{1}{2}U + \tfrac{1}{3}.\ \tan.\ ^{3}\tfrac{1}{2}U) + \dfrac{x}{2.\ \cos.\ ^{4}\tfrac{1}{2}U} \\ + \dfrac{1-e}{4}.\ \tan.\ \tfrac{1}{2}U.(1 - \tan.\ ^{2}\tfrac{1}{2}U - \tfrac{4}{5}.\ \tan.\ ^{4}\tfrac{1}{2}U) \end{array} \right\}^{*};$$

* $\dfrac{2D^{\frac{3}{2}}}{\sqrt{\mu.(2-\alpha)}} = \dfrac{2D^{\frac{3}{2}}}{\sqrt{\mu}} \left\{ 2^{-\frac{1}{2}} + \dfrac{2^{-\frac{3}{2}}.\alpha}{2} \right\}$ (neglecting the square and higher powers of α) $= \dfrac{\sqrt{2}.D^{\frac{3}{2}}}{\sqrt{\mu}}. \left\{ 1 + \dfrac{\alpha}{4} \right\}$, ∵ the value of t becomes $=$

$$\frac{\sqrt{2}.D^{\frac{3}{2}}}{\sqrt{\mu}}.\left(1+\frac{\alpha}{4}\right).\ \text{tang.}\ \tfrac{1}{2}v \left\{ 1 + \left(\tfrac{1}{3} - \frac{\alpha}{3}\right).\ \tan.\ ^{2}\tfrac{1}{2}v - (\tfrac{4}{5} - \alpha).\alpha.2.^{-2}\text{tang.}\ ^{3}\tfrac{1}{2}v \right\}$$

$$= \frac{\sqrt{2}.D^{\frac{3}{2}}}{\sqrt{\mu}} \left\{ .\text{tang.}\ \tfrac{1}{2}v + \frac{\alpha}{4}.\ \text{tang.}\ \tfrac{1}{2}v + \tfrac{1}{3}.\ \text{tang.}\ ^{3}\tfrac{1}{2}v + \frac{\alpha}{4.3}.\ \tan.\ ^{3}\tfrac{1}{2}v - \frac{\alpha}{3}.\ \text{tang.}\ ^{3}\tfrac{1}{2}v - \right.$$

$$\left. \frac{4\alpha}{5}2^{-2}.\ \text{tang.}\ ^{4}\tfrac{1}{2}v \right\} = \frac{\sqrt{2}.D^{\frac{3}{2}}}{\sqrt{\mu}}.\ (\text{tang.}\ \tfrac{1}{2}v + \tfrac{1}{3}.\ \text{tang.}\ ^{3}\tfrac{1}{2}v + (1-e).\ \text{tang.}\ \tfrac{1}{2}v(\tfrac{1}{4} + (\tfrac{1}{12} - \tfrac{1}{3}).$$

tang. $^{2}\tfrac{1}{2}v) - \tfrac{1}{5}$. tang. $^{4}\tfrac{1}{2}.\ v)$; $1-e$ being substituted for α.

* Substituting $U + x$ for v; this equation becomes

$$t = \frac{D^{\frac{3}{2}}}{\sqrt{\mu}}\sqrt{2}.\ (\text{tang.}\ \tfrac{1}{2}(U+x) + \tfrac{1}{3}.\ \tan.\ ^{3}\tfrac{1}{2}(U+x) + (1-e)\ \tan.\ \tfrac{1}{2}(U+x).(\tfrac{1}{4} - \tfrac{1}{4}.\ \text{tang.}\ ^{2}\tfrac{1}{2}$$

but by hypothesis, we have

$$t=\frac{D^{\frac{3}{2}}\sqrt{2}}{\sqrt{\mu}}.\left(\tan.\tfrac{1}{2}U+\tfrac{1}{3}.\tan.{}^{3}\tfrac{1}{2}U\right);^{*}$$

$$(U+x)-\tfrac{1}{3}.\tan.{}^{4}(U+v))=\frac{D^{\frac{3}{2}}}{\sqrt{\mu}}\sqrt{2}\left\{\frac{\text{tang.}\,\frac{1}{2}U+\tan.\,\frac{1}{2}x}{1-\tan.\frac{U}{2}.\,\text{tang.}\frac{x}{2}}+\tfrac{1}{3}\left\{\frac{\tan.\,\frac{1}{2}U+\text{tang.}\,\frac{1}{2}x}{1-\text{tang.}\,\frac{U}{2}.\,\tan.\frac{x}{2}}\right\}^{3}\right.$$

$$+\frac{(1-e).\,\tan.\frac{U}{2}+\tan.\frac{x}{2}}{1-\tan.\frac{U}{2}.\,\tan.\frac{x}{2}}\left\{\tfrac{1}{4}-\left\{\frac{\tfrac{1}{4}.\,\text{tang.}\frac{U}{2}+\tan.\frac{x}{2}}{1-\tan.\frac{U}{2}.\,\tan.\frac{x}{2}}\right\}^{2}-\tfrac{1}{3}\right.$$

$$\left.\left\{\frac{\tan.\frac{U}{2}+\tan.\frac{x}{2}}{1-\tan.\frac{U}{2}.\tan.\frac{x}{2}}\right\}^{4}\right\}=\frac{D^{\frac{3}{2}}\sqrt{2}.}{\sqrt{\mu}}.\left(\tan.\frac{U}{2}+\tan.\frac{x}{2}+\tan.\frac{x}{2}.\,\tan.\frac{{}^{2}U}{2}+\tfrac{1}{3}(\tan.\frac{{}^{3}U}{2}\right.$$

$$\left.+3\tan.\frac{{}^{2}U}{2}.\,\tan.\frac{x}{2}+3\tan.\frac{{}^{4}U}{2}.\,\tan.\frac{x}{2}\right)+(1-e).\tan.\frac{U}{2}\left(\tfrac{1}{4}-\tfrac{1}{4}\tan.\frac{{}^{2}U}{2}-\tfrac{1}{3}.\right.$$

$$\left.\tan.\frac{{}^{4}U}{2}\right)=\frac{D^{\frac{3}{2}}\sqrt{2}}{\sqrt{\mu}}\left(\tan.\frac{U}{2}+\tfrac{1}{3}\tan.\frac{{}^{3}U}{2}+\tan.\frac{x}{2}\left(1+2.\,\tan.\frac{{}^{2}U}{2}+\tan.\frac{{}^{4}U}{2}\right)\right.$$

$+\frac{1-e}{4}.\,\tan.\frac{U}{2}.\left(1-\tan.\frac{{}^{2}U}{2}-\tfrac{4}{3}\tan.\frac{{}^{3}U}{2}\right)$, and since $\tan.\frac{x}{2}=\frac{x}{2}$, when x^2, x^3, &c. are rejected, and $1+2\tan.\frac{{}^{2}U}{2}+\tan.\frac{{}^{4}U}{2}=\left(1+\tan.\frac{{}^{2}U}{2}\right)^{2}=\frac{1}{\cos.\frac{{}^{4}U}{2}}$, by substituting $\frac{x}{\cos.\frac{{}^{4}U}{2}}$ for $\tan.\frac{x}{2}.\left(1+2\tan.\frac{{}^{2}U}{2}+\tan.\frac{{}^{4}U}{2}\right)$, we shall have the expression given in the text.

* Therefore the two last terms of the second member of this equation are equal to cipher, consequently $\frac{x}{2\cos.\frac{{}^{4}U}{2}}=\frac{1-e}{4}.\,\tan.\frac{U}{2}\left(-1+\tan.\frac{{}^{2}U}{2}+\tfrac{4}{3}.\,\tan.\frac{{}^{4}U}{2}\right)$; $\because x$ or $\sin.x=\frac{1-e}{4}.\,\tan.\frac{U}{2}\left(-2.\cos.\frac{{}^{4}U}{2}+2\sin.\frac{{}^{2}U}{2}.\cos.\frac{{}^{2}U}{2}+\tfrac{8}{3}\sin.\frac{{}^{4}U}{2}\right)$, (by substituting for $\tan.\frac{U}{2}$ its value); $=\frac{1-e}{4}\left(\tan.\frac{U}{2}\left(-2.\cos.\frac{{}^{4}U}{2}+2\cos.\frac{{}^{2}U}{2}-2\cos.\frac{{}^{4}U}{2}+\tfrac{8}{3}\right.\right.$

therefore by substituting in place of the small arc x, its sine, we shall obtain

$$\sin. x = \frac{1}{10}.(1-e).\tan.\tfrac{1}{2}U.(4-3.\cos.^2\tfrac{1}{2}U-6.\cos.^4\tfrac{1}{2}.U).$$

Thus, by constructing a table of the logarithms of the expression,

$$\frac{1}{10}.\tan.\tfrac{1}{2}U.(4-3.\cos.^2\tfrac{1}{2}U-6.\cos.^4\tfrac{1}{2}U);$$

it will be sufficient to add to them the logarithm of $1-e$, in order to obtain that of $\sin. x$; consequently if this correction be made to the anomaly U, computed for the parabola, we will have the corresponding anomaly in a very eccentric ellipse.

24. It remains for us to consider the motion in an hyperbolic orbit. For this purpose, it may be observed that in the hyperbola, the semi-axismajor a becomes negative, and the excentricity e surpasses unity. If therefore in the equation (f) of No. 20, we make $a=-a'$, and $u=\dfrac{u'}{\sqrt{-1}}$, and then substitute in place of the sines and cosines, their values in imaginary exponentials; the first of these equations will give

$$\frac{t.\sqrt{\mu}}{a^{\frac{3}{2}}} = \frac{e}{2}.(c^{u'}-c^{-u'})-u'.\text{*}$$

$\left(1-2.\cos\frac{^2U}{2}+\cos.\frac{^4U}{2}\right)\Big) = \frac{1-e}{4}.\tan.\frac{U}{2}\Big(-4.\cos.\frac{^4U}{2}+2\cos.\frac{^2U}{2}+\frac{8}{5}$
$\left(1-2\cos.\frac{^2U}{2}+\cos.\frac{^4U}{2}\right)=\frac{1-e}{4}.\tan.\frac{U}{2}.\Big(\frac{8}{3}-\frac{20}{3}\cos.\frac{^4U}{2}-\frac{6}{3}.\cos.\frac{^2U}{2}+$
$\frac{8}{3}\cos.\frac{^4U}{2}\Big)=$ evidently the expression given in the text.

* $nt=u-e\sin.u$, (n in this case $=\dfrac{\sqrt{\mu}}{\sqrt{-a^3}}\Big)=\dfrac{\sqrt{\mu}}{a^{\frac{3}{2}}.\sqrt{-1}}$; $\because nt=-\dfrac{u'}{\sqrt{-1}}+e.\sin.\dfrac{u'}{\sqrt{-1}}$;

The second will become

$$r = a'.(\tfrac{1}{2}.\, e.\, (c^{u'} + c^{-u'}) - 1);^{*}$$

finally, if we make a corresponding change in the sign of the radical of the third equation, in order that v may increase with t, and consequently with u'; we shall have

$$\tan.\tfrac{1}{2}v = \sqrt{\frac{e+1}{e+1}}.\left\{\frac{c^{u'}-1}{c^{u'}+1}\right\}.^{\dagger}$$

Let us suppose that in these formulæ, $u' = \log.\tan.\,(\tfrac{1}{4}\pi + \tfrac{1}{2}\varpi,)$ π being the semicircumference of which the radius is equal to unity, and the preceding logarithm being hyperbolic; we shall have

$$\frac{t.\sqrt{\mu}}{a'^{\frac{3}{2}}} = e.\,\text{tang}.\,\varpi - \log.\tan.\,(\tfrac{1}{4}\pi + \tfrac{1}{2}\varpi);^{\ddagger}$$

$$\sin.\frac{u'}{\sqrt{-1}} = \frac{c^{u'} - c^{-u'}}{2\sqrt{-1}};\ \therefore \frac{\sqrt{\mu}}{a'^{\frac{3}{2}}}.\,t = -u' + e.\,\frac{c^{u'} - c^{-u'}}{2}.$$

* $r = a(1 - e\cos.u)$, becomes $r' = -a'(1-e)\left(\dfrac{c^{u'} + c^{-u'}}{2}\right).$

† $$\text{Tang}.\frac{v}{2} = \frac{\sqrt{1+e}}{\sqrt{1-e}}.\frac{\sin.\dfrac{u'}{2.\sqrt{-1}}}{\cos.\dfrac{u'}{2.\sqrt{-1}}} = \frac{\sqrt{1+e}}{\sqrt{1-e}}.\frac{c^{\frac{u'}{2}} - c^{\frac{-u'}{2}}}{c^{\frac{u'}{2}} + c^{\frac{-u}{2}}} = \frac{\sqrt{e+1}}{\sqrt{e-1}}.$$

$$\frac{c^{u'}-1}{c^{u'}+1}.$$

‡ $$\text{Tang}.\left(\frac{\pi}{4} + \frac{\varpi}{2}\right) = c^{u'} \text{ and } \frac{1}{\tan.\left(\frac{\pi}{4} + \frac{\varpi}{2}\right)} = \cot.\left(\frac{\pi}{4} + \frac{\varpi}{2}\right) = c^{-u'};\ \therefore$$

$$c^{u'} - c^{-u'} = \tan.\left(\frac{\pi}{4} + \frac{\varpi}{2}\right) - \cot.\left(\frac{\pi}{4} + \frac{\varpi}{2}\right) = \frac{\sin.\left(\frac{\pi}{4} + \frac{\varpi}{2}\right)}{\cos.\left(\frac{\pi}{4} + \frac{\varpi}{2}\right)} - \frac{\cos.\left(\frac{\pi}{4} + \frac{\varpi}{2}\right)}{\sin.\left(\frac{\pi}{4} + \frac{\varpi}{2}\right)}$$

$$r = a'.\left\{\frac{e}{\cos.\varpi} - 1\right\};$$

$$\tan.\tfrac{1}{2}v = \sqrt{\frac{e+1}{e-1}}.\tan.\tfrac{1}{2}\varpi.$$

The arc. $\frac{t.\sqrt{\mu}}{a'^{\frac{3}{2}}}$ is the mean angular motion of the body m, during the time t, supposed to move in a circle about M, at a distance equal to a'. This arc may easily be determined by reducing it into parts of the radius; the first of the preceding equations will give by trials, the value of the angle ϖ, corresponding to the time t; the two other equations will then give the corresponding values of r and of v.

25. T expressing the sidereal revolution of a planet of which a is the mean distance from the sun; the first of the equations (f) of No. 20, will give $T = 2\pi$; but by the same number we have $\frac{\sqrt{\mu}}{a^{\frac{3}{2}}} = n$; there-

$$= \frac{\sin.^2\left(\frac{\pi}{4}+\frac{\varpi}{2}\right) - \cos.^2\left(\frac{\pi}{4}+\frac{\varpi}{2}\right)}{\sin.\left(\frac{\pi}{4}+\frac{\varpi}{2}\right).\cos.\left(\frac{\pi}{4}+\frac{\varpi}{2}\right)} = -2\,\frac{\cos.\left(\frac{\pi}{2}+\varpi\right)}{\sin.\left(\frac{\pi}{2}+\varpi\right)} = -2\cot.\left(\frac{\pi}{2}+\varpi\right) = 2.$$

$\tan g.\varpi$; $\therefore$ by substituting this expression for $\frac{c^{u'} - c^{-u'}}{2}$; we obtain the value of $\frac{t.\sqrt{\mu}}{a'^{\frac{3}{2}}}$ given in the text. $c^{u'} + c^{-u'} = \tan.\left(\frac{\pi}{4}+\frac{\varpi}{2}\right) + \cot.\left(\frac{\pi}{4}+\frac{\varpi}{2}\right) = 2\,\text{sec}^{nt}.\varpi$

$$= \frac{2}{\cos\varpi};\ \therefore r' = a'\left(\tfrac{1}{2}e(c^{u} + c^{-u'}) - 1\right) = a'.\left(\frac{e}{\cos.\varpi} - 1\right);\ \text{tang}.\frac{v}{2} = \frac{\sqrt{e+1}}{\sqrt{e-1}}.$$

$$\frac{\tan.\left(\frac{\pi}{4}+\frac{\varpi}{2}\right) - 1}{\tan.\left(\frac{\pi}{4}+\frac{\varpi}{2}\right) + 1} = \frac{\sqrt{e+1}}{\sqrt{e-1}}.\ \frac{\sin.\left(\frac{\pi}{4}+\frac{\varpi}{2}\right) - \cos.\left(\frac{\pi}{4}+\frac{\varpi}{2}\right)}{\sin.\left(\frac{\pi}{4}+\frac{\varpi}{2}\right) + \cos.\left(\frac{\pi}{4}+\frac{\varpi}{2}\right)} = \frac{\sqrt{e+1}}{\sqrt{e-1}}.$$

$$\frac{2\cos.\frac{\pi}{4}.\sin.\frac{\varpi}{2}}{2\sin.\frac{\pi}{4}.\cos.\frac{\varpi}{2}} = \frac{\sqrt{e+1}}{\sqrt{e-1}}.\ \cot.\frac{\pi}{4}.\text{tang}.\frac{\varpi}{2} =,\ (\text{as }\cot.\frac{\pi}{4} = 1),\ \frac{\sqrt{e+1}}{\sqrt{e-1}}.\tan.\frac{\varpi}{2}.$$

fore we shall have

$$T = \frac{2\pi . a^{\frac{3}{2}}}{\sqrt{\mu}}.$$

If the masses of the planets, relatively to that of the sun, be neglected; μ will express the mass of this star, and this quantity will be the same for all the planets; thus, for a second planet, of which a' and T' express the mean distances from the sun, and the time of the sidereal revolution; we shall have in like manner

$$T' = \frac{2\pi . a'^{\frac{3}{2}}}{\sqrt{\mu}};$$

consequently we shall have

$$T^2 : T'^2 :: a^3 : a'^3;$$

that is to say, the squares of the times of the revolutions of different planets, are to each other, as the cubes of the greater axes of their orbits; this is one of the laws discovered by Kepler. It appears from the preceding analysis, that this law is not rigorously true, and that it only obtains when we neglect the action of the planets, on each other, and on the sun.

If we assume for the measure of the time, the mean motion of the earth, and for the unit of distance, its mean distance from the sun; T will in this case be equal to 2π, and we will have $a = 1$; therefore the preceding expression for T will give $\mu = 1$; from which it follows that the mass of the sun ought then to be taken for the unity of mass. We can thus, in the theory of the planets and of the comets, suppose $\mu = 1$, and assume for the unity of distance, the mean distance of the earth from the sun; but then, the time t is measured by corresponding arc of the mean sidereal motion of the earth.

The equation

$$T = \frac{2\pi . a^{\frac{3}{2}}}{\sqrt{\mu}}$$

enables us to determine, in a very simple manner, the ratios of the masses of the planets which are accompanied by satellites, to the mass of the sun. In fact, M representing this mass, if we neglect the mass m of the planet relatively to that of M; we shall have

$$T=\frac{2\pi.a^{\frac{3}{2}}}{\sqrt{M}}.$$

If we afterwards consider a satellite of any planet m'; and if p represent the mass of this satellite, and h its mean distance from the centre of m', and T, the time of its sidereal revolution, we shall have

$$\text{T}=\frac{2\pi.h^{\frac{3}{2}}}{\sqrt{m'+p}};$$

therefore,

$$\frac{m'+p}{M}=\frac{h^3}{a^3}.\left(\frac{T}{\text{T}}\right)^2.$$

This equation gives the ratio of the sum of the masses of the planet m' and of its satellite, to the mass M of the sun; if therefore the mass of the satellite be neglected in comparison with that of its primary, or if we suppose that the ratio of these masses is known; we will obtain the value of the mass of the planet, to that of the sun. We will give, in the theory of the planets, the values of the masses of the planets about which satellites have been observed to revolve.

CHAPTER IV.

Determination of the elements of Elliptic Motion.

26. After having treated of the general theory of elliptic motion, and of the mode of computing it by converging series, in the two cases of nature, namely, in that of orbits very nearly circular, and in the case of very eccentric orbits; it now remains for us to determine the elements of of these orbits. If the circumstances of the primitive motions of the heavenly bodies were given, we could easily deduce the elements from them. In fact, if we name V the velocity of m, in its relative motion about M; we shall have

$$V^2 = \frac{dx^2+dy^2+dz^2}{dt^2};$$

and the last of the equations (p) of No. 18, will give

$$V^2 = \mu.\left\{\frac{2}{r} - \frac{1}{a}\right\}.$$

In order to make μ to disappear from this expression; let U denote the velocity which m would have, if it described about M, a circle of which the radius is equal to the unity of distance. In this hypothesis, we have $r = a = 1$, and consequently $U^2 = \mu$; therefore

$$V^2 = U^2.\left\{\frac{2}{r} - \frac{1}{a}\right\}.$$

This equation will give the semiaxis major a, of the orbit, by means of the primitive velocity of m, and of its primitive distance from M. a is positive in the ellipse; it is infinite in the parabola, and negative in the hyperbola; therefore the orbit described by m, is an ellipse, a parabola, or an hyperbola, according as V is less, equal to or greater than $U.\sqrt{\frac{2}{r}}$. It is remarkable that the direction of the primitive motion, does not at all influence the species of conic section.*

In order to determine the excentricity of the orbit, it may be observed, that if ϵ represent the angle which the direction of the relative motion of m, makes with the radius vector r; we have $\frac{dr^2}{dt^2} = V^2.\cos.^2\epsilon$. By substituting in place of V^2, its value $\mu.\left\{\frac{2}{r}-\frac{1}{a}\right\}$, we shall have

$$\frac{dr^2}{dt^2} = \mu.\left\{\frac{2}{r}-\frac{1}{a}\right\}.\cos.^2\epsilon;\dagger$$

* From the equation $\frac{1}{a} = \frac{2}{r} - \frac{V^2}{U^2}$, it appears that when V and r are given, the axis major and therefore the periodic time are constantly the same. Hence since $U.\sqrt{\frac{1}{r}}$ = the velocity in a circle at the same distance, it follows that in the ellipse the velocity at any point is to that in a circle at the same distance in a less ratio than that of $\sqrt{2}:1$, in a parabola, it is in the ratio of $\sqrt{2}:1$; and in the hyperbola it is in a greater ratio than that of $\sqrt{2}:1$. See Princip. Math. Prop. 16. In the ellipse when the velocity of projection diminishes, the distance increases, and when V vanishes, r becomes equal to $2a$, in this case the excentricity e becomes equal to unity. In the hyperbola, the limit of the velocity, when r is infinite, is $U^2\frac{1}{a}$ = the velocity in a circle, at the distance of a transverse semiaxis from focus.

It is also manifest that when the distance is equal to the semiaxis major, the velocity is equal to that in a circle at the same distance, and that in general the velocity in an ellipse, is to the velocity in a circle at the same distance in the subduplicate ratio of the distance from the other focus to the semiaxis; for it is as $\sqrt{2a-r}:\sqrt{a}$.

† $\frac{dr}{dt}$ = the velocity resolved in the direction of the radius, ∴ it is equal to V, multiplied into the cosine of the angle which the radius vector makes with the curve or tangent, *i. e.* it is equal to $V.\cos\epsilon$.

but by No. 19, we have

$$2\mu r-\frac{\mu r^2}{a}-\frac{r^2.dr^2}{dt^2}=\mu a.(1-e^2);$$

therefore we shall have

$$a\,(1-e^2)=r^2.\sin.^2\epsilon.\left\{\frac{2}{r}-\frac{1}{a}\right\};$$

by means of this equation, we can determine ae the excentricity of the orbit.

From the polar equation of a conic section, namely

$$r=\frac{a.(1-e^2)}{1+e.\cos.v},$$

we obtain

$$\cos.v=\frac{a.(1-e^2)-r}{er}.$$

Substituting for $\frac{dr^2}{dt^2}$ its value, we shall have $2\mu r-\frac{\mu r^2}{a}-\mu\left(\frac{2}{r}-\frac{1}{a}\right)r^2.\cos.^2\epsilon=\mu a.(1-e^2)$, $\therefore\left(2r-\frac{r^2}{a}\right).(1-\cos.^2\epsilon)=a(1-e^2)=$ the parameter; hence it appears that when the distance and axis major are given, the parameter varies as the square of the sine of projection. Since $V^2=\frac{dr^2+r^2.dv^2}{dt^2}$, see page 4, $a(1-e^2)=r^2.\frac{r^2.dv^2}{dt^2}$, $\because$ the parameter depends on that part of the velocity which acts perpendicularly to the radius vector, it is termed the paracentrick velocity, and it is evidently a maximum at the extremity of the focal ordinate.

From the expression $a\,(1-e^2)=r^2.\sin.^2\epsilon\left(\frac{2}{r}-\frac{1}{a}\right)$, it follows that $\sin.^2\epsilon$ varies inversely as $r.\left(\frac{2a-r}{a}\right)$, but the sum of the two factors is given, being equal to $2a$, $\because$ the product is a maximum, and consequently the sine of projection is the least possible, when the distance from the focus is equal to the semiaxis major.

We shall thus obtain the angle v, which the radius vector r constitutes with the perihelion distance, consequently we have the position of the perihelion. The equations (f) of No. 20, will make known the angle u, and by means of it, the instant of the passage through the perihelion.

In order to determine the position of the orbit, with respect to a fixed plane passing through the centre of M, supposed immoveable; let φ represent the inclination of the orbit on this plane, and ϵ the angle which the radius r constitutes with the line of the nodes; moreover let z be the primitive elevation of m, above the fixed plane, which elevation we suppose to be known; we shall have

$$r.\,\sin.\,\epsilon.\,\sin.\,\varphi = z;$$

so that the inclination φ of the orbit will be known, when we shall have determined ϵ. For this purpose, let λ represent the angle, which the primitive direction of the relative motion of m, makes with the fixed plane, which angle we suppose to be known; if we consider the triangle formed by this direction produced to meet the line of the nodes, by this last line, and by the radius r; l representing the side of the triangle which is opposed to the angle ϵ, we shall have

$$l = \frac{r.\,\sin.\,\epsilon}{\sin.\,(\epsilon+\iota)};$$

we have also $\frac{z}{l} = \sin.\,\lambda$; therefore we shall have

$$\tan.\,\epsilon = \frac{z.\,\sin.\,\iota}{r.\,\sin.\,\lambda - z.\,\cos.\,\iota}.*$$

* $r.\,\sin.\,\epsilon = a$ perpendicular let fall from the extremity of r, on the line of the nodes, and $z =$ this perpendicular multiplied into the sine of φ. The supplement of the angle which the primitive direction makes with the line of the nodes $= \epsilon+\iota$, $\therefore l : r :: \sin.\,\epsilon : \sin.\,(\epsilon+\iota)$;

$\therefore l = \frac{r.\,\sin\,\epsilon}{\sin.\,\iota.\,\cos.\,\epsilon + \sin.\,\epsilon.\,\cos.\,\iota} = \frac{r.\,\tan.\,\epsilon}{\sin.\,\iota + \tan.\,\epsilon.\,\cos.\,\iota} = \frac{z}{\sin.\,\lambda}$, $\therefore (r.\,\sin.\,\lambda - z.\,\cos.\,\iota).$ $\tan\,\epsilon = z.\,\sin.\,\iota.$

The elements of the orbit of the planet being determined by these formulæ, in functions of the coordinates r and z, of the velocity of the planet and of the direction of its motion; the variations of these elements, corresponding to the variations which are supposed to take place in its velocity and in its direction may be obtained; it will be easy, by the methods which will be given in the sequel, to infer the differential variations of these elements, arising from the action of disturbing forces.

Let us resume the equation

$$V^2 = U^2 . \left\{ \frac{2}{r} - \frac{1}{a} \right\}.$$

In the circle $a = r$, and consequently $V = U . \sqrt{\frac{1}{r}}$; from which it appears, that the velocities of the planets in different circles are reciprocally as the square roots of their radii.

In the parabola, $a = \infty$, $\therefore$ $V = U . \sqrt{\frac{2}{r}}$; therefore the velocities in different points of the orbit, are in this case reciprocally as the square roots of the radii vectores, and the velocity in each point is to that which the planet would have, if it described a circle whose radius was equal to the radius vector r, as $\sqrt{2} : 1$.

An ellipse, of which the minor axis is indefinitely small, is changed into a right line; and in this case, V expresses the velocity of m, if it descended in a right line towards M. Let us suppose that m sets out from a state of repose, and that its primitive distance from M is r; let us moreover suppose, that having attained the distance r', it has acquired the velocity V'; the preceding expression for the velocity, will give the two following equations:

$$0 = \frac{2}{r} - \frac{1}{a}; \quad V'^2 = U^2 . \left\{ \frac{2}{r'} - \frac{1}{a} \right\};$$

from which we obtain

$$V'=U.\sqrt{\frac{2.(r-r')}{rr'}};$$

this is the expression of the relative velocity acquired by m, in departing from the distance r, and in falling towards M, through the height $r-r'$. We can easily determine by means of this formula, from what height a body m, which moves in a conic section, ought to fall towards M, in order to acquire, in departing from the extremity of the radius vector r, a relative velocity equal to that which it has at this extremity; for V expressing this last velocity, we have

$$V^2=U^2.\left\{\frac{2}{r}-\frac{1}{a}\right\};$$

but the square of the velocity acquired in falling through the height $r-r'$, is $\frac{2U^2.(r-r')}{rr'}$; by equating these two expressions, we shall have

$$r-r'=\frac{r.(2a-r)}{4a-r}.*$$

* By equating these expressions we have $\frac{2a-r}{ar}=\frac{2r-2r'}{rr'}$, $\therefore$ $(2a-r)r'=2a.(r-r')$; and consequently $(4a-r)\,r'=2ar$; $\therefore r'=\frac{2ar}{4a-r}$, and $r-r'=\frac{2ar-r^2}{4a-r}$, in the ellipse $4a-r$ is greater than twice $2a-r$, $\therefore$ $r-r'$ is less than $\frac{r}{2}$; in the parabola a being infinite, $r-r'=\frac{r}{2}$, in the hyperbola $r-r'=\frac{r\,(2a+r)}{4a+r}$, and as in this case $4a+r$ is less than twice $2a+r$, $r-r'$ is greater than $\frac{r}{2}$.

In order to determine the space through which a body must fall externally, so that it may acquire the velocity which it has in a conic section, $r'-r$ must be substituted for $r-r'$, and then we equate $\frac{2(r'-r)}{rr'}$ to $\frac{2a-r)}{ar}$, from which we obtain $2ar'-2ar=$

In the circle $a=r$, and then $r-r'=\frac{1}{3}r$; in the ellipse, we have $r-r'\angle\frac{1}{2}r$; a being infinite in the parabola, we have $r-r'=\frac{1}{2}r$; and in the hyperbola, in which a is negative, we have $r-r'>\frac{1}{2}r$.

27. The equation

$$0=\frac{dx^2+dy^2+dz^2}{dt^2}-\mu.\left\{\frac{2}{r}-\frac{1}{a}\right\}$$

is remarkable, in that it determines the velocity independently of the eccentricity of the orbit. It is contained in a more general equation, which exists between the axis major of the orbit, the chord of the elliptic arc, the sum of its extreme radii vectores, and the time employed to describe this arc. In order to arrive at this last equation, we will resume the equations of elliptic motion, which have been given in No. 20; μ being supposed for the sake of simplicity equal to unity. These equations will consequently become

$$r=\frac{a.(1-e^2)}{1+e.\cos. v};$$
$$r=a.(1-e.\cos. u);$$
$$t=a^{\frac{3}{2}}.(u-e.\sin. u).$$

Let us suppose that r, v, and t correspond to the first extremity of the elliptic arc, and that r', v', and t' correspond to the other extremity; we will have

$$r'=\frac{a.(1-e^2)}{1+e.\cos. v'};$$
$$r'=a.(1-e.\cos. u');$$
$$t'=a^{\frac{3}{2}}.(u'-e.\sin. u').$$

$$\text{Let } t'-t=T;\quad \frac{u'-u}{2}=\beta;\quad \frac{u'+u}{2}=\beta';\quad r'+r=R;$$

$2ar'-r'r$, ∵ in an ellipse r' is $=$ to the axis major, in a circle it is $=$ to the diameter, it is infinite in the parabola; and in the hyperbola r' becomes $=-2a$.

subtracting the expression of t, from that of t', and observing at the same time that

$$\sin. u' - \sin. u = 2. \sin. \mathfrak{E}. \cos. \mathfrak{E}';$$

we shall have

$$T = 2a^{\frac{3}{2}}. (\mathfrak{E} - e. \sin. \mathfrak{E}. \cos \mathfrak{E}').$$

If we add together the two expressions of r and of r' in terms of u and u', and if we observe that

$$\cos. u' + \cos. u = 2 \cos. \mathfrak{E}. \cos. \mathfrak{E}';$$

we shall have

$$R = 2a.(1 - e. \cos. \mathfrak{E}. \cos. \mathfrak{E}).$$

Now, let e represent the chord of the elliptic arc, we have

$$c^2 = r^2 + r'^2 - 2rr'. \cos. (v - v');$$

but from the two equations

$$r = \frac{a.(1-e^2)}{1+e. \cos. v}; \; r = a.(1 - e. \cos. u),$$

we obtain

$$\cos. v = \frac{a.(\cos. u - e)}{r}; \; \sin. v = \frac{a.\sqrt{1-e^2}. \sin. u}{r}.$$

In like manner we have

$$\cos. v' = \frac{a.(\cos. u' - e)}{r}; \; \sin. v' = \frac{a.\sqrt{1-e^2}. \sin. u'}{r'};$$

therefore we shall have

$$rr'. \cos. (v - v') = a^2.(e - \cos. u).(e - \cos. u') + a^2.(1-e^2). \sin. u. \sin. u'^2;$$

and consequently

$$c^2 = 2a^2.(1-e^2).(1 - \sin. u. \sin. u' - \cos. u. \cos. u')$$
$$+ a^2e^2.(\cos. u - \cos. u')^2;$$

but we have

$$\sin. u. \sin. u' + \cos. u'. \cos. u = 2 \cos.^2\varepsilon - 1;$$
$$\cos. u - \cos. u' = 2. \sin. \varepsilon. \sin. \varepsilon';$$

therefore

$$c^2 = 4a^2. \sin.^2\varepsilon.(1 - e^2. \cos.^2\varepsilon');^*$$

consequently we will by this means obtain the three following equations,

$$R = 2a.(1 - e. \cos. \varepsilon. \cos. \varepsilon');$$
$$T = 2a^{\frac{3}{2}}. (\varepsilon - e. \sin. \varepsilon. \cos. \varepsilon');$$
$$c^2 = 4a^2. \sin.^2\varepsilon.(1 - e^2. \cos.^2\varepsilon').$$

* $u' = \varepsilon' + \varepsilon$, $u = \varepsilon' - \varepsilon$; $\therefore \sin. u' = \sin. \varepsilon'. \cos. \varepsilon + \sin. \varepsilon. \cos. \varepsilon'$; $\sin. u = \sin. \varepsilon'. \cos. \varepsilon - \sin. \varepsilon. \cos. \varepsilon'$; $\therefore \sin. u' - \sin. u = 2. \sin. \varepsilon. \cos. \varepsilon'$, hence $T = t' - t = a^{\frac{3}{2}}. (u' - u - e. (\sin. u' - \sin. u)$ = the expression in the text. $\text{Cos.}\, u' = \cos. \varepsilon'. \cos. \varepsilon - \sin. \varepsilon. \sin. \varepsilon'$, $\cos. u = \cos. \varepsilon. \cos. \varepsilon' + \sin. \varepsilon. \sin. \varepsilon'$, $\therefore \cos. u + \cos. u' = 2. \cos. \varepsilon'. \cos. \varepsilon$, and $r' + r = R = a.(2 - e. (\cos. u' + \cos. u)$ = the expression given in the text. $v - v'$ is evidently equal to the angle contained between r and r'.

$1 + e. \cos. v = \frac{a.(1 - e^2)}{r}$; $\therefore e. \cos. v = \frac{a.(1 - e^2) - a.(1 - e. \cos. u)}{r}$, (by substituting for r its value) $= \frac{ae.(\cos. u - e)}{r}$; $\therefore \cos\, v = \frac{a.(\cos. u - e)}{r}$; $\sin.^2 v =$ $\frac{a^2.(1 - 2e. \cos. u + e^2. \cos.^2 u) - \cos.^2 u + 2e. \cos. u - e^2)}{r^2} = \frac{a^2.(1 - \cos.^2 u - e^2.(\sin.^2 u)}{r^2}$ $= \frac{a^2.(1 - e^2). \sin.^2 u}{r^2}$, consequently $\cos. (v - v') = \cos. v'. \cos. v + \sin. v. \sin. v' =$ $\frac{a^2.(\cos. u - e).(\cos. u' - e) + a^2.(1 - e^2) \sin. u. \sin u'}{rr'}$; $r^2 + r'^2 = a^2.(2 - 2e.(\cos. u + \cos. u') + e^2.(\cos.^2 u + \cos.^2 u'))$, $\therefore r^2 + r'^2 - 2rr'. \cos. (v - v') = a^2.(2 - 2e.(\cos. u + \cos. u') + e^2. (\cos.^2 u + \cos.^2 u') - 2a^2(e^2 - e.(\cos. u + \cos. u') + \cos. u. \cos. u') - 2a^2. \sin. u. \sin. u' + 2a^2.e^2. \sin. u. \sin. u'$ = by reduction $2a^2.(1 - e^2). (1 - \sin. u. \sin. u') - \cos. u. \cos. u' + a^2.e^2. (\cos.^2 u + \cos.^2 u') - 2a^2.e^2. \cos. u. \cos. u'$.

$\text{Cos.}\, u. \cos. u' + \sin. u. \sin. u' = \cos. 2\varepsilon = \cos. \varepsilon^2 - \sin. \varepsilon^2 = 2. \cos.^2\varepsilon - 1.$

$\therefore c^2 = 2a^2(1 - e^2).(1 + 1. - 2. \cos.^2\varepsilon) + a^2.e^2.(4. \sin.^2\varepsilon. \sin.^2\varepsilon' = 4a^2.(1 - e^2).(1 - \cos.^2\varepsilon) + 4a^2.e^2. \sin.^2\varepsilon. \sin.^2\varepsilon' = 4a^2.(1 - e^2). \sin.^2\varepsilon + 4a^2.e^2. \sin.^2\varepsilon - 4a^2.e^2. \sin. \varepsilon^2. \cos.^2\varepsilon' = 4a^2. \sin.^2\varepsilon.(1 - e^2. \cos.^2\varepsilon').$

The first of these equations gives

$$e.\cos.\,\epsilon' = \frac{2a - R}{2a.\cos.\,\epsilon};$$

by substituting this value of $e.\cos.\,\epsilon'$, in the two others, we shall have

$$T = 2a^{\frac{3}{2}}\left\{\epsilon + \left(\frac{R-2a}{2a}\right).\ \tan.\,\epsilon\right\};$$

$$c^2 = 4a^2.\ \tan.^2\epsilon.\left\{\cos.^2\epsilon - \left(\frac{2a-R}{2a}\right)^2\right\}.$$

These two equations do not involve the excentricity e; and if in the first we substitute in place of ϵ, its value given by the second, we shall obtain T in a function of c, R and a. It appears from this, that the time T depends only on the axis major, the chord c, and the sum R of the extreme radii vectores.

If we make

$$z = \frac{2a - R + c}{2a};\quad z' = \frac{2a - R - c}{2a},$$

the last of the preceding equations will give

$$\cos.\,2\epsilon = zz' + \sqrt{(1-z^2).(1-z'^2)};$$

from which may be obtained,

$$2\,\epsilon = \text{arc.}\cos.\,z' - \text{arc.}\cos.\,z;\text{*}$$

* $\frac{c^2}{4a^2} = \sin.^2\epsilon - \left(\frac{2a-R}{2a}\right)^2.\,\frac{\sin.^2\epsilon}{\cos.^2\epsilon}$, let $\frac{c^2}{4a^2} = n$, $\frac{2a-R}{2a} = m$, and as $\sin.^2\epsilon = 1 - \cos.^2\epsilon$, $\therefore n.\cos.^2\epsilon = \cos.^2\epsilon - \cos.^4\epsilon - m^2 + m^2.\cos.^2\epsilon$, $\therefore \cos.^4\epsilon + (n - m^2 - 1).\cos.^2\epsilon = -m^2$, and solving this equation $\cos.^2\epsilon = \frac{-(n-m^2-1)}{2} \pm \frac{\sqrt{(n-m^2-1)^2 - 4m^2}}{2}$, and as $\cos.\,2\epsilon = 2\cos.^2\epsilon - 1$, we have $\cos.\,2\epsilon = -n + m^2 \pm \sqrt{(n-m^2-1)^2 - 4m^2}$, and substituting for n and m, we obtain;

arc. cos. z denotes here the arc, of which the cosine is z; consequently we have

$$\tan.\ \varepsilon = \frac{\sin.\,(\text{arc. cos. } z') - \sin.\,(\text{arc. cos. } z)}{z + z'};$$

we have likewise $z + z' = \dfrac{2a - R}{a}$; therefore the expression of T will become, (by observing, that if T is the duration of the sidereal revolution of the earth, of which the mean distance from the sun is taken for unity, we have by No. 16, $T = 2\pi$);

$$\mathrm{T} = \frac{a^{\frac{3}{2}}.T}{2\pi}.\,(\text{arc. cos. } z' - \text{arc. cos. } z - \sin.\,(\text{arc. cos. } z') + \sin.\,(\text{arc. cos. } z)). \qquad (a)$$

As the same cosine may appertain to several arcs, this expression of

$$\frac{\overline{2a - R}^2 - c^2}{4a^2} \pm \left(\frac{c^4 + (2a-R)^4 - 2c^2.(2a-R)^2}{(2a)^4} - \frac{2c^2 - 2\,(2a-R)^2}{4a^2} + 1\right)^{\frac{1}{2}} = \cos.\,2\varepsilon,$$

the part of this *radical* of which the denominator $(2a)^4 = z^2.z'^2$,

for $z^2 = \dfrac{(2a-R)^2 + c^2 + 2.\,c.(2a-R)}{(2a)^2}$ and $z'^2 = \dfrac{(2a-R)^2 + c^2 - 2.\,c.(2a-R)}{(2a)^2}$; and the part of this radical of which the denominator is $4a^2 = -z^2 - z'^2 = -(2a - R)^2 - c^2 - (2a-R)^2 - c^2 + 2c.(2a-R) - 2c.(2a-R)$, the part without the radical is evidently equal to zz', $\therefore$ by substituting we shall find the cosine of $2\varepsilon = zz' + \sqrt{z^2 z'^2 - z^2 - z'^2 + 1}$. which is evidently equal to the expression given in the text.

Let z, z' represent the cosines of two arcs, and the cosine of the difference of these arcs will be $= zz' + \sqrt{1 - z^2.\,(1 - z'^2)} = \cos.\,2\varepsilon$, $\therefore$ $2\varepsilon =$ the difference of two arcs of which the cosines are z and z'.

$\text{Sin. } a - \sin.\,b = 2.\cos.\,\dfrac{(a+b)}{2}.\,\sin.\,\dfrac{(a-b)}{2}$, $\cos.\,a + \cos.\,b = 2.\cos.\,\dfrac{(a+b)}{2}.\,\cos.\,\dfrac{(a-b)}{2}$

$\therefore\ \dfrac{\sin.\,a - \sin.\,b}{\cos.\,a + \cos.\,b} = \dfrac{\sin.\,\frac{(a-b)}{2}}{\cos.\,\frac{(a-b)}{2}} = \text{tang.}\,\dfrac{(a-b)}{2}$, from this formula may be inferred the value of $\tan.\,\varepsilon$, which is given in the text.

T is ambiguous, and it is necessary carefully to distinguish the arcs to which the cosines z and z' belong.

In the parabola, the semiaxis major a is infinite, and we have

$$\text{arc. cos. } z' - \text{sin. (arc. cos. } z') = \frac{1}{6} \cdot \left(\frac{R+c}{a}\right)^{\frac{3}{2}} *$$

By making c negative, we obtain the value of the arc. cos. z—sin. (arc. cos. z); the formula (a) will therefore give for the time T, employed to describe the arc subtended by the chord c,

$$\mathrm{T} = \frac{T}{12\pi} \cdot \left((r + r' + c)^{\frac{3}{2}} \mp (r + r' - c)^{\frac{3}{2}}\right);$$

The sign — having place, when the two extremities of the parabolic

* Arc. cos. z'—sin. arc. cos. z'=arc. sin. $\sqrt{1-z'^2} - \sqrt{1-z'^2}$ = by expressing the arc, in terms of the sine, $\sqrt{1-z'^2} + \frac{(1-z'^2)^{\frac{3}{2}}}{2.3} + \text{\&c.} - \sqrt{1-z'^2}$

$$= \left(\frac{(4a^2-(2a-R)^2+2c.(2a-R)-c^2)}{(2.3.4a^2)}\right)^{\frac{3}{2}} = \frac{((4Ra-R^2+4ac-2cR-c^2))^{\frac{3}{2}}}{(2.3.4a^2)}$$

$$= \text{when } a \text{ is } \infty, \ \frac{(4a.(R+c))^{\frac{3}{2}}}{(2.3.4a^2)}.$$

In the expression for arc. sin. $\sqrt{1-z'^2}$, the approximation is not continued beyond the second term, because the subsequent terms disappear in the value of T, when a is supposed to be infinite. The second term of the value of T vanishes when c passes through the focus, and T is less when the angle formed by r,r' is turned towards the perehelion, than when the second term vanishes, it is manifest that the sign of the second term must be in this case negative, and positive in every other case.

The second term of the second member of this equation vanishes when the extremities of the arc described, are bounded by the focal ordinates, ∴ the time of describing the parabolic arc intercepted between vertex and focal ordinate varies in the sesquiplicate ratio of the parameter. See Newton, Princip. Vol. 3, Lem. 9, 10. Indeed it appears from the value of T, that the time of describing any parabolic arc, of which the chord passes through the focus, varies in the sesquiplicate ratio of the chord.

arc are situated on the same side of the axis of the parabola, or when one of them being situated below, the angle formed by the two radii vectores, is turned towards the perehelion, it is necessary to make use of the sign $+$ in every other case. T being equal to $365^{\text{days}}, 25638$, we have $\frac{T}{2\pi} = 9^{\text{days}}, 688754$.

In the hyperbola, a is negative; z and z' become greater than unity; the arcs, arc. cos. z, and arc. cos. z' are imaginary, and their hyperbolic logarithms are,

$$\text{arc. cos. } z = \frac{1}{\sqrt{-1}} \cdot \log. (z+\sqrt{z^2-1});$$

$$\text{arc. cos. } z' = \frac{1}{\sqrt{-1}} \cdot \log. (z'+\sqrt{z'^2-1});$$

consequently the formula (a) becomes by changing a into $-a$,

$$T = \frac{a^{\frac{3}{2}}T}{2\pi} \cdot (\sqrt{z'^2-1} \mp \sqrt{z^2-1} - \log. (z'+\sqrt{z'^2-1}) \pm \log. (z+\sqrt{z^2-1}).$$

The formula (a) determines the time, of rectilinear descent of a body towards the focus, when it departs with a given velocity, from a given distance; it is sufficient for this purpose, to suppose that the ellipse which it then describes, is infinitely compressed. If, for example, we suppose that the body departs from a state of rest, at the distance $2a$ from the focus, and that the time T, which it employs to describe the distance c is sought; in this case $R=2a+r$; $r=2a-c$; which gives $z'=-1$; $z=\frac{c-a}{a}$; the formula (a) will consequently give

$$T = \frac{a^{\frac{3}{2}}T}{2\pi} \left\{ \pi - \text{arc. cos. } \left(\frac{c-a}{a}\right) + \sqrt{\frac{2ac-c^2}{a^2}} \right\}.$$

There* is, however an essential difference between the elliptic motion towards the focus, and the motion in an ellipse infinitely compressed. In the first case, the body arrives at the focus, passes beyond it, and elongates itself to the distance from which it commenced to move; in the second case the body having attained the focus, returns to the point from which it set out. A tangential velocity at the aphelion, ever so small, suffices to produce this difference, which does not influence the time employed by the body in descending towards the focus.

28. As the circumstances of the primitive motions of the heavenly bodies are not known from observation, the elements of their orbit cannot be determined by the formulæ of No. 26. In order to effect this object, we should compare together their respective positions observed at different epochs; which presents considerable difficulties, as these bodies are not observed from the centre of their motions. Indeed, with respect to the planets, we can, by means of their oppositions and conjunctions, obtain their longitude such as it would be observed from the centre itself of the sun; and this consideration, combined with the small excentricity, and small inclination of their orbits to the ecliptic, simplifies very much the determination of their elements. Besides,

* $R = 2a + r = 4a - c$, $\therefore z' = \frac{2a - 4a + c - c}{2a} = -1$, $z = \frac{2a - 4a + 2c}{2a} = \frac{c - 2a}{2a}$;

If a be infinite $T = T.\frac{a^{\frac{3}{2}}}{2\pi}.(\pi - \pi + \sqrt{\frac{2ac}{a^2}} = \frac{a^{\frac{3}{2}}\sqrt{c}}{\pi.\sqrt{2}.\,a^{\frac{1}{2}}} = T\frac{\sqrt{c}}{\sqrt{2}\,\pi}$;

arc. cos. $\frac{c - a}{a}$ = arc. sin. $= \sqrt{\frac{2ac - c^2}{a^2}}$, $\therefore$ as $\pi -$ arc. sin. $= \sqrt{\frac{2ac - c^2}{a^2}}$, and arc. sin. $= \sqrt{\frac{2ac - c^2}{a^2}}$ have the same sine, T varies in an ellipse as the arc — sin.; which agrees with Newton's conclusion; Princip. Math. Lib. 1. Prop. 37. See Prony Mechanique Analytique, Tom. 2. No. 914, and Euler's Mechanics, No. 272, 672.

If $c = 2a$ the time of falling to the centre will be equal to $\frac{a^{\frac{3}{2}}T}{2\pi}.\pi$.

in the actual state of astronomy, the elements* of these orbits require only very slight corrections; and as the variations of the distances of the planets from the earth are not at any time sufficiently great to render them invisible to us, we can observe them perpetually, and by a comparison of a great number of observations, correct the elements of their orbits, and also the errors themselves to which the observations are liable. This method cannot be applied in the case of the comets, as they are only visible near their perehelion; and if the observations which are made on them during the time of their appearance, are inadequate to the determination of their elements, we have not then any means of following these stars in imagination, through the immensity of space; so that when the lapse of ages brings them back towards the sun, it is impossible for us to recognise them; it is therefore of the greatest consequence to be able to determine by observations made during the time of the appearance of a comet, the elements of its orbits; but the rigorous solution of this problem surpasses the powers of analysis, and we are obliged to recur to methods of approximation, in order to obtain the first values of these elements, which we can afterwards correct with all the precision which the observations admit of.

If we employ observations which are at a considerable distance from each other, the eliminations would lead to impracticable computations; it is therefore necessary to restrict ourselves to the consideration of near observations; and even with this restriction, the problem presents considerable difficulties. It has appeared to me, after mature reflection, that instead of employing directly the observations themselves, it would be more advantageous to deduce from them data, which offer a simple and exact result; and I am satisfied that the geocentric latitude and longitude of the comet, at a given moment, and their first and second

* In the present state of Astronomy, the motions of the planets may be considered as very accurately known, and the object of these observations is to determine them with still greater accuracy. And when the elements have been determined under the most favourable circumstances, *i. e.* in those in which they have the greatest influence, they should be afterwards corrected simultaneously, by the method of *the equations of condition.*

differences divided by corresponding powers of the element of the time, are those which best satisfy this condition; for by means of these data, we can determine rigorously, and with facility, the elements, without having recourse to any integration, and by the sole consideration of the differential equations of the orbit. This mode of considering the problem permits us also to employ a great number of neighbouring observations, and by this means, to embrace a considerable interval between the extreme observations, which is very useful in diminishing the influence of the errors, to which these observations are always liable, in consequence of the nebulosity which surrounds the comets. I proceed now to present the formulæ, by means of which the first differences of the longitude and latitude may be deduced from any number of neighbouring observations; I will afterwards determine the elements of the orbit of the comet by means of these differences. Finally, I will point out the means which have appeared to me the simplest, for correcting these elements, by three observations, made at a considerable distance from each other.

29. Let at any given epoch, α be the geocentric longitude of a comet, and θ its northern geocentric latitude, the southern latitudes being supposed negative. If we denote by s, the number of days which have elapsed since this epoch; the geocentric longitude and latitude of the comet, after this interval, will be expressed in consequence of the formula (i) of No. 21, by the two following series,

$$\alpha+s.\left(\frac{d\alpha}{ds}\right)+\frac{s^2}{1.2}.\left(\frac{d^2\alpha}{ds^2}\right)+\frac{s^3}{1.2.3}.\left(\frac{d^3\alpha}{ds^3}\right)+\&c;$$

$$\theta+s.\left(\frac{d\theta}{ds}\right)+\frac{s^2}{1.2}.\left(\frac{d^2\theta}{ds^2}\right)+\frac{s^3}{1.2.3}.\left(\frac{d^3\theta}{ds^3}\right)+\&c;$$

The values of α, $\left(\frac{d\alpha}{ds}\right)$, $\left(\frac{d^2\alpha}{ds^2}\right)$, &c; θ, $\left(\frac{d\theta}{ds}\right)$, &c. may be determined by means of several observed geocentric longitudes and latitudes.

In order to obtain them in the simplest manner, let us consider the infinite series which expresses the geocentric longitudes. The coefficients of the powers of s, in this series, may be determined by the condition that it ought to represent each observed longitude, when we substitute for s, the number of days which corresponds to it; we shall by this means obtain as many equations as there are observations; and if the number of these last be n, we cannot determine by their means, in the infinite series, but n quantities α, $\left(\frac{d\alpha}{dt}\right)$, &c. However, it ought to be observed, that s being supposed very small, we can neglect the terms* multiplied by s^n, s^{n+1}, &c., so that the infinite series is reduced to the n first terms, which we are able to determine by the n observations. These determinations are only approximative, and their accuracy will depend on the smallness of the terms which we have neglected; they will be always more exact, in proportion to the smallness of s, and to the greater number of observations employed. Therefore the question is reduced to a problem in the theory of interpolations, namely to find an entire and rational function of s, of such a nature, that when we substitute for s, the number of days which correspond to each observation, this function is changed into the observed longitude.

Let β, β', β'', represent the observed longitudes of the comet, and

* As the values of the differential coefficients in the series expanded according to the formula of No. 21, are independent of the value of the increments, these values will remain, when the increment varies; and there are as many series of the form $\alpha + \frac{s}{1}\left(\frac{d\alpha}{ds}\right) + \frac{s^2}{1.2}\cdot\left(\frac{d^2\alpha}{ds^2}\right) +$ &c. as there are observations; if s be very small, it may be proved that the terms of the series after the n first diminish very rapidly, and consequently may be neglected; and as there will remain but n terms, if we have n observations we have as many observations as unknown quantities; if the number of observations be increased, a greater number of coefficients can be determined, and if s become less, the value of the terms which are rejected will be less.

i, i', i'', the number of days which intervene between them and the given epoch; these numbers ought to be supposed negative, for the observations anterior to this epoch. By making

$$\frac{\text{ϐ}'-\text{ϐ}}{i'-i} = \delta\text{ϐ}\,; \quad \frac{\text{ϐ}''-\text{ϐ}}{i''-i'} = \delta\text{ϐ}'\,; \quad \frac{\text{ϐ}'''-\text{ϐ}''}{i'''-i''} = \delta\text{ϐ}''\,; \ \&c.\,;$$

$$\frac{\delta\text{ϐ}'-\delta\text{ϐ}}{i''-i} = \delta^2\text{ϐ}\,; \frac{\delta\text{ϐ}''-\delta\text{ϐ}'}{i'''-i'} = \delta^2\text{ϐ}'\,; \ \&c.$$

$$\frac{\delta^2\text{ϐ}'-\delta^2\text{ϐ}}{i'''-i} = \delta^3\text{ϐ} \ \&c.$$

&c.;

the function sought will be

$$\text{ϐ} + (s-i).\delta\text{ϐ} + (s-i).(s-i').\delta^2\text{ϐ} + (s-i).(s-i').(s-i'').\delta^3\text{ϐ} + \&c.\,;$$

for it is easy to be assured, that if we make successively, $s=i$, $s=i'$, $s=i''$, &c. this function will be converted into ϐ, ϐ′, ϐ″, &c.

Now, the comparison of the preceding function, with the following:

$$\alpha + s.\left(\frac{d\alpha}{ds}\right) + \frac{s^2}{1.2}\left(\frac{d^2\alpha}{ds^2}\right) + \&c.\,;$$

will give, by putting the coefficients of similar powers of s equal to each other,

$$\alpha = \text{ϐ} - i.\ \delta\text{ϐ} + i.\ i'.\delta^2\text{ϐ} - i.i'.\ i''.\ \delta^3\text{ϐ} + \&c.\,;$$

$$\left(\frac{d\alpha}{ds}\right) = \delta\text{ϐ} - (i+i').\ \delta^2\text{ϐ} + (ii'+ii''+i'i'').\ \delta^3\text{ϐ} - \&c.$$

$$\tfrac{1}{2}.\left(\frac{d^2\alpha}{ds^2}\right) = \delta^2\text{ϐ} - (i+i'+i'').\delta^3\text{ϐ} + \&c.\,;*$$

the ulterior differences of α will be useless to us. The coefficients of

* These equations evidently obtain from the principle of indeterminate coefficients, and it is manifest that the greater the number of observations the more accurately will they be determined, and the less i', i'', i''', &c. are, the more rapid will be the convergence of the series.

these expressions are alternately positive and negative; the coefficient of $\delta^r \beta$ is, abstracting from the sign, the product of r into r, of the r quantities $i, i', i'', i^{(r-1)}$, in the value of α; it is the sum of the products of the same quantities, $r-1$, into $r-1$, in the value of $\left(\frac{d\alpha}{ds}\right)$; finally it is the sum of the products of the quantities, $r-2$, into $r-2$, in the value of $\frac{1}{2}\cdot\left(\frac{d^2\alpha}{ds^2}\right)$.

If $\gamma, \gamma', \gamma''$, &c. represent the observed geocentric latitudes of the comet, we shall obtain the values of θ, $\left(\frac{d\theta}{ds}\right)$, $\left(\frac{d^2\theta}{ds^2}\right)$ &c.; by changing in the preceding expressions for α, $\left(\frac{d\alpha}{ds}\right)$, $\left(\frac{d^2\alpha}{ds^2}\right)$, &c., the quantities β, β', β'', &c. into $\gamma, \gamma', \gamma''$, &c.

These expressions will be more exact, according as the number of observations is increased, and as the intervals which separate them, are less; we could therefore* employ all the neighbouring observations of the selected epoch, provided that they were exact; but the errors to which they are always liable, would lead to an erroneous result; therefore in order to diminish the influence of these errors, the interval between the extreme observations should be increased, in proportion as a greater number of observations is employed. We are able in this manner, with five observations, to embrace an interval of thirty-five or forty degrees, which ought to lead to very approximate values of the geocentric longitudes and latitudes, and of their first and second differences. If the epoch which we select, is such that there exists an equal number of observations before and after it, so that each longitude which follows, has a corresponding longitude which precedes it by the same interval; this condition will render the

* The number of observations will of itself produce an increase in the error, $\therefore$ in order that the error may be distributed over a greater number of degrees, we must increase the interval between the extreme observations.

values of α, $\left(\frac{d\alpha}{ds}\right)$, $\left(\frac{d^2\alpha}{ds^2}\right)$ more accurate,* and it is easy to perceive

* When the observations are assumed at different sides of the epoch which is selected i', i''', i''''', &c. are negative when i, i'', i'''', &c. are positive, and vice versa. In the values of α, which are given above, the terms after the first, are negative and positive in pairs and in the values of $\frac{d\alpha}{ds}$, $\frac{d^2\alpha}{ds^2}$. the coefficients of $d\zeta$, $d^2\zeta$, &c. are less than when all the observations are made at the same side of the selected epoch, ∴ the convergence of the terms will be more rapid, and the terms which are omitted are of less consequence.

Let the number of observations be odd, and $=2r+1$, and let i be the number of days between each observation, and let the epoch from which we count be the instant of the mean observation when $\alpha=\zeta^{(r)}$, then we have

$$\frac{d\alpha}{ds}=\frac{1}{2i}\cdot\left\{\begin{array}{l}\Delta\zeta^{(r)}+\Delta\zeta^{(r-1)}-\frac{1}{1.2.3}\cdot\left\{\Delta^3\zeta^{(r-1)}+\Delta^3\zeta^{(r-2)}\right\}\\ +\frac{2^2}{1.2.3.4.5}\cdot\left\{\Delta^5\zeta^{(r-2)}+\Delta^5\zeta^{(r-3)}\right\}\\ -\frac{2^2.3^2}{1.2.3.4.5.6.7}\left\{\Delta^7\zeta^{(r-3)}+\Delta^7\zeta^{(r-4)}\right\}\\ +\ \&c.\end{array}\right.$$

$$\frac{d^2\alpha}{ds^2}=\frac{\Delta^2\zeta^{(r-1)}}{2.i^2}-\frac{1}{2.3.4.i^2}\cdot\Delta^4.\zeta^{(r-4)}$$

$$\frac{+2^2}{1.2.3.4.5.6.i^2}\cdot\Delta^6\zeta^{(r-3)}-\frac{2^2.3^2}{2.3.4.5.6.7.8i.^2}\cdot\Delta^8.\zeta^{(r-4)}+\&c.$$

Δ is the characteristic of finite differences, so that $\Delta.\zeta^{(r)}=\zeta^{(r+1)}-\zeta^{(r)}$.

If the number of observations be even, and equal to $2r$, we should assume for the epoch, the mean time between the first and last observation, and then we shall have

$$\alpha=\tfrac{1}{2}\cdot\left\{\begin{array}{l}\zeta^{(r)}+\zeta^{(r-1)}-\frac{1}{2.4}\cdot\Delta^2(\zeta^{(r-1)}+\zeta^{(r-2)})\\ +\frac{3^2}{2.4.6.8}\cdot\Delta^4(\zeta^{(r-2)}+\zeta^{(r-3)})\\ -\frac{3^2.5^2}{2.4.6.8.10.12}\cdot\Delta^6.(\zeta^{(r-3)}+\zeta^{r-4})\end{array}\right\}$$

$$\frac{d\alpha}{ds}=\frac{\Delta\zeta^{(r-1)}}{i^2}-\frac{1}{4.6.i}\cdot\Delta^3.\zeta^{(r-2)}+\frac{3^2}{4.6.8.10.i}\cdot\Delta^3.\zeta^{(r-3}-\&c.;$$

that new observations assumed at equal intervals, and at opposite sides of this epoch, will cause quantities to be added to those values, which will be, with respect to their last terms, of the same order, as the ratio of $s^2.\left(\frac{d^2\alpha}{ds^2}\right)$ to α. This symmetric disposition obtains when all the observations being equidistant, we fix the epoch in the middle of the interval contained between them; it is therefore advantageous to employ corresponding observations.

In general it will be always useful to fix the epoch towards the middle of this interval; because that the number of days which separates the extreme observations, being less considerable, the approximations are more convergent. The calculus will be likewise simplified by fixing the epoch at the very instant of one of the observations; for then the values of α and of θ will be immediately given.

When, by the preceding process, we have determined, $\left(\frac{d\alpha}{ds}\right)$, $\left(\frac{d^2\alpha}{ds^2}\right)$, $\left(\frac{d\theta}{ds}\right)$, $\left(\frac{d^2\theta}{ds^2}\right)$; we can deduce in this manner the first and second differences of α and θ, divided by the corresponding powers of the element of the time. If the masses of the planets and of the comets, are neglected in comparison with that of the sun assumed to represent the unity of the mass; if, moreover, we assume for the unity of distance, its mean distance from the earth; the mean motion of the earth round the sun, will be, by No. 23, the measure of the time t; let, therefore λ represent the number of seconds which the earth de-

$$\frac{d^2\alpha}{1.2.ds^2} = \frac{1}{4.i^2}.\ \Delta^2.(\beta^{(r-1)}+\beta^{(r)}) - \frac{3^2}{4.6.8.i^2}.\ \Delta^4.(\beta^{(r-2)}+\beta^{(r-3)})$$

$$\frac{+259}{4.6.8.10.12.i^2}.\ \Delta^6.(\beta^{(r-3)}+\beta^{(r-4)}) - \&c.;$$

It is easy to prove these theorems from the theory of finite differences. See Lacroix, Tom. 3.

scribes in a day, in consequence of its mean sidereal motion; the time t corresponding to the number s of days, will be λs; therefore we shall have

$$\left(\frac{d\alpha}{dt}\right)=\frac{1}{\lambda}\cdot\left(\frac{d\alpha}{ds}\right),\ \left(\frac{d^2\alpha}{dt^2}\right)=\frac{1}{\lambda^2}\cdot\left(\frac{d^2\alpha}{ds^2}\right).$$

Observations give in logarithms of the tables, log. $\lambda=4,0394622$; moreover, log. $\lambda^2=$log. $\lambda+$log. $\frac{\lambda}{R}$, R being the radius of the circle, reduced into seconds; from this it appears that log. $\lambda^2=2,2750444$; therefore, if the values of $\left(\frac{d\alpha}{ds}\right)$, and of $\left(\frac{d^2\alpha}{ds^2}\right)$, be reduced into seconds; the logarithms of $\left(\frac{d\alpha}{ds}\right)$ and of $\left(\frac{d^2\alpha}{d^2s}\right)$ will be obtained, by subducting from the logarithms of these values, the logarithms, 4,0394622, and 2,2750444. We shall obtain in like manner, the the logarithm of $\left(\frac{d\theta}{dt}\right)$, and of $\left(\frac{d^2\theta}{dt^2}\right)$; by subtracting respectively the same logarithms, from the logarithms of their values reduced into seconds.

As the precision of the following results depends on the accuracy of the values of α, $\left(\frac{d\alpha}{dt}\right)$, $\left(\frac{d^2\alpha}{dt^2}\right)$, θ, $\left(\frac{d\theta}{dt}\right)$, and $\left(\frac{d^2\theta}{dt^2}\right)$, and as their formation is very simple, the observations ought to be selected and multiplied in such a manner, as to obtain them with the greatest possible precision. We now proceed to the determination of the elements of the orbit of the comet by means of these values, and in order to generalize these results, we will consider the motion of a system of bodies actuated by any forces whatever.

30. Let x, y, z, be the rectangular coordinates of the first body; x', y', z', those of the second body, and so on of the rest. Let us conceive that the first body is sollicited parallel to the axis of x, of y, and of z, by the forces X, Y, and Z, which forces we will suppose

to tend to diminish these variables. Let us conceive, in like manner, that the second body is sollicited parallel to the same axes, by the forces X', Y', Z', and so of the rest. The motions of all these bodies will be given by differential equations of the second order,

$$0=\frac{d^2x}{dt^2}+X;\quad 0=\frac{d^2y}{dt^2}+Y;\quad 0=\frac{d^2z}{dt^2}+Z;$$

$$0=\frac{d^2x'}{dt^2}+X';\quad 0=\frac{d^2y'}{dt^2}+Y';\quad 0=\left(\frac{d^2z'}{dt^2}\right)+Z'.$$

&c.

If the number of bodies is n, the number of these equations will be $3n$, and their finite integrals will involve $6n$ arbitrary quantities, which will be the elements of the orbits of these different bodies.*

In order to determine these elements by means of observations, we should transform the coordinates of each body into others, of which the origin will be at the observer. Therefore supposing a plane, of which the position may remain always parallel to itself, to pass through the eye of the observer, while the observer moves on a given curve, let ρ, ρ', ρ'', represent the distances of the observer from the different bodies, projected on this plane; and α, α', α'', &c., the apparent longitudes of these bodies, referred to the same plane, and θ, θ', θ'', their apparent latitudes. The variables x, y, z, will be given in a function of ρ, α, θ, and of the coordinates of the observer. In like manner, x', y', z', will be given in functions of ρ', α', θ', and of the coordinates of the observer, and so of the rest. Moreover, if we suppose that the forces X, Y, Z, X', Y', Z', &c., arise from the reciprocal action of the bodies of the system, and from the action of foreign bodies; they will be given in functions of ρ, ρ', ρ'', &c.; α, α',

* Each body furnishes three equations, and consequently the n bodies furnish $3n$ equations, and as in the integration of each differential equation of the second order, two arbitrary quantities are introduced, the total number of arbitrary quantities must be $6n$.

α'', &c.; $\theta, \theta', \theta''$, &c.; and of known quantities; consequently the preceding differential equations will be between these new variables, and their first and second differences; now observations make known, for a given time instant, the values of α, $\left(\frac{d\alpha}{dt}\right)$, $\left(\frac{d^2\alpha}{dt^2}\right)$, θ, $\left(\frac{d\theta}{dt}\right)$, $\left(\frac{d^2\theta}{dt^2}\right)$; α', $\left(\frac{d\alpha'}{dt}\right)$, $\left(\frac{d^2\alpha'}{dt^2}\right)$, &c.; therefore, the quantities which remain unknown, are $\varrho, \varrho', \varrho''$, &c., their first and second differences. These unknown quantities are $3n$ in number, and as we have $3n$ differential equations, we can determine them. There is also this advantage connected with this method, that the first and second differences of ϱ, ϱ', ϱ'', &c. occur in these equations, in a linear form.

The quantities $\alpha, \theta, \varrho, \alpha', \theta', \varrho'$, &c., and their first differentials divided by dt, being known; we shall have for any given instant, the the values of x, y, z, x', y', z', &c., and of their first differentials divided by dt. These values being* substituted in the $3n$ integrals of the preceding differential equations, and in the first differences of these integrals will give $6n$ equations, by means of which we can determine the $6n$ arbitrary quantities of these integrals, or the elements of the orbits of these different bodies.

31. Let us apply this method to the motion of the comets. For this purpose it may be observed, that the principal force which actuates them, being the attraction of the sun, we may abstract from the consideration of every other force. However, if the comet passes sufficiently near to any large planet, to experience a sensible perturbation, the preceding method would still make known its velocity, and its distance from the earth; but this case being of rare occurrence, we shall only consider, in the subsequent researches, the action of the sun.

* The number of unknown quantities for each body is three, namely ϱ, $\frac{d\varrho}{dt}$, $\frac{d^2\varrho}{dt^2}$, therefore there are $3n$ unknown quantities in the system of n bodies.

Assuming the mass of the sun to represent the unity of mass, and its mean distance from the earth, the unity of distance, and moreover placing the origin of the coordinates x, y, z, of a comet of which the radius is r, at the sun; the differential equations (O) of No. 17, will become, (the mass of the comet, in comparison with that of the sun being neglected)

$$\left.\begin{aligned} 0 &= \frac{d^2x}{dt^2} + \frac{x}{r^3}; \\ 0 &= \frac{d^2y}{dt^2} + \frac{y}{r^3}; \\ 0 &= \frac{d^2z}{dt^2} + \frac{z}{r^3}; \end{aligned}\right\}. \quad (k)$$

Let us now suppose that the plane of x and of y, is the plane of the ecliptic; that the axis of x is the line drawn from the centre of the sun to the first point of Aries, at a given epoch; that the axis of y is the line drawn from the centre of the sun to the first point of Cancer, at the same epoch; that the positive z' are on the same side with the north pole of the ecliptic; and finally, that x' and y' are the coordinates of the earth, and R its radius vector; this being premised,

Let the coordinates x, y, z, be transformed into others relative to the observer; and for this purpose let α represent the geocentric longitude of the comet, θ its geocentric latitude, and ϱ its distance from the earth projected on the ecliptic; we shall have

$$x = x' + \varrho.\cos.\alpha; \quad y = y' + \varrho.\sin.\alpha; \quad z = \varrho.\tan.\theta.$$

If from the first of the equations (k), multiplied by sin. α, be subtracted the second multiplied by cos. α, we shall have

$$0 = \sin.\alpha.\frac{d^2x}{dt^2} - \cos.\alpha.\frac{d^2y}{dt^2} + \frac{x.\sin.\alpha - y.\cos.\alpha}{r^3} \; *$$

* $\frac{dx}{dt} = \frac{dx'}{dt} + \frac{d\varrho}{dt}.\cos.\alpha - \varrho.\sin.\alpha.\frac{d\alpha}{dt}$; $\therefore \frac{d^2x}{dt^2}.\sin.\alpha = \frac{d^2x'}{dt^2}.\sin.\alpha + \frac{d^2\varrho}{dt^2}.$

hence we deduce, by substituting for x and y their preceding values

$$\sin.\ \alpha.\ \frac{d^2x'}{dt^2} - \cos.\ \alpha.\ \frac{d^2y'}{dt^2} + \frac{x'.\ \sin.\ \alpha - y'.\ \cos.\ \alpha}{r^3}.$$

$$-2.\left\{\frac{d\varrho}{dt}\right\}.\left\{\frac{d\alpha}{dt}\right\} - \varrho.\ \left\{\frac{d^2\alpha}{dt^2}\right\}.$$

The earth being retained in its orbit, as the comet, by the attraction of the sun, we have

$$0 = \frac{d^2x'}{dt^2} + \frac{x'}{R^3}\ ;\ 0 = \frac{d^2y'}{dt^2} + \frac{y'}{R^3}\ ;$$

consequently,

$$\sin.\ \alpha.\frac{d^2x'}{dt^2} - \cos.\ \alpha.\ \frac{d^2y'}{dt^2} = \frac{y'.\ \cos.\ \alpha - x'.\ \sin.\ \alpha}{R^3}\ ;$$

therefore, we shall have

$$0 = (y'.\ \cos.\ \alpha - x'.\ \sin.\ \alpha).\left\{\frac{1}{R^3} - \frac{1}{r^3}\right\} - 2.\left\{\frac{d\varrho}{dt}\right\}.\left\{\frac{d\alpha}{dt}\right\} - \varrho.\ \left\{\frac{d\alpha^2}{dt^2}\right\}.$$

Let A be the longitude of the earth, as seen from the sun; we shall have

$$x' = R.\ \cos.\ A\ ;\ y' = R.\ \sin.\ A\ ;$$

therefore

$$y'.\ \cos.\ \alpha - x'.\ \sin.\ \alpha = R.\ \sin.\ (A - \alpha)\ ;$$

the preceding equation will consequently become,

$\sin.\ \alpha.\ \cos.\ \alpha - 2.\frac{d\varrho}{dt}.\frac{d\alpha}{dt}.\ \sin.^2\alpha - \varrho.\ \sin.\ \alpha.\ \cos.\ \alpha.\ \frac{d\alpha^2}{dt^2} - \varrho.\ \sin.^2\alpha.\ \frac{d^2\alpha}{dt^2}\ ;\ \frac{dy}{dt} = \frac{dy'}{dt}$ $+ \frac{d\varrho}{dt}.\ \sin.\ \alpha + \varrho.\ \cos.\ \alpha.\ \frac{d\alpha}{dt}\ ;\ \therefore\ \frac{d^2y}{dt^2}.\ \cos.\ \alpha = \frac{d^2y'}{dt^2}.\ \cos.\ \alpha + \frac{d^2\varrho}{dt^2}.\ \sin.\ \alpha.\ \cos.\ \alpha$ $+ 2.\ \frac{d\varrho}{dt}.\ \frac{d\alpha}{dt}.\ \cos.^2\alpha - \varrho.\ \sin.\ \alpha.\ \cos.\ \alpha.\ \frac{d\alpha^2}{dt^2} + \varrho.\ \cos.^2\alpha.\frac{d^2\alpha}{dt^2}$, by subtracting this equation from the value of $\frac{d^2x}{dt^2}.\ \sin.\ \alpha$, observing the quantities which destroy each other, and also those which coalesce, we arive at the expression given in the text.

$$\left\{\frac{d\varrho}{dt}\right\}=\frac{R.\sin.(A-\alpha)}{2.\left\{\frac{d\alpha}{dt}\right\}}.\left\{\frac{1}{R^3}-\frac{1}{r^3}\right\}-\frac{\varrho.\left\{\frac{d^2\alpha}{dt^2}\right\}}{2.\left\{\frac{d\alpha}{dt}\right\}}. \quad (1)$$

Let us now investigate a second expression for $\left\{\frac{d\varrho}{dt}\right\}$. For this purpose multiplying the first of the equations (k), by tan. θ. cos. α; the second by tan. θ. sin. α; and then subtracting the third equation, from the sum of these two products; we shall have

$$0=\tan.\theta.\left\{\cos.\alpha.\frac{d^2x}{dt^2}+\sin.\alpha.\frac{d^2y}{dt^2}\right\}+\tan.\theta.\left\{\frac{x.\cos.\alpha+y.\sin.\alpha}{r^3}\right\}$$
$$-\frac{d^2z}{dt^2}-\frac{z}{r^3}.$$

This equation will become, by substituting for x, y, z, their values,

$$0=\tan.\theta.\left\{\left\{\frac{d^2x'}{dt^2}+\frac{x'}{r^3}\right\}.\cos.\alpha+\left\{\frac{d^2y'}{dt^2}+\frac{y'}{r^3}\right\}.\sin.\alpha.\right\}-{}^{*}$$
$$\frac{2.\left\{\frac{d\theta}{dt}\right\}.\left\{\frac{d\varrho}{dt}\right\}.}{\cos.^2\theta}$$

* $\frac{d^2x}{dt^2}=\frac{d^2x'}{dt^2}+\frac{d^2\varrho}{dt^2}.\cos.\alpha-2.\frac{d\varrho}{dt}.\frac{d\alpha}{dt}.\sin.\alpha-\varrho.\cos.\alpha.\frac{d\alpha^2}{dt^2}-\varrho.\sin.\alpha.\frac{d^2\alpha}{dt^2}$

$\frac{d^2y}{dt^2}=\frac{d^2y'}{dt^2}+\frac{d^2\varrho}{dt^2}.\sin.\alpha+2.\frac{d\varrho}{dt}.\frac{d\alpha}{dt}.\cos.\alpha-\varrho.\sin.\alpha.\frac{d\alpha^2}{dt^2}+\varrho.\cos.\alpha.\frac{d^2\alpha}{dt^2}$

$\therefore\frac{d^2x}{dt^2}.\cos.\alpha+\frac{d^2y}{dt^2}.\sin.\alpha=\frac{d^2x'}{dt^2}.\cos.\alpha+\frac{d^2y'}{dt^2}.\sin.\alpha+\frac{d^2\varrho}{dt^2}-\varrho.\frac{d\alpha^2}{dt^2}.$

$$\frac{x.\cos.\alpha+y.\sin.\alpha}{r^3}=\frac{x'.\cos.\alpha+y'.\sin.\alpha}{r^3}+\frac{\varrho}{r^3},$$

$z=\varrho.\tan.\theta\therefore\frac{dz}{dt}=\frac{d\varrho}{dt}.\text{tang.}\theta+\varrho.\frac{d\theta}{\cos.^2\theta};\ \frac{d^2z}{dt^2}=\frac{d^2\varrho}{dt^2}.\tan.\theta+$

$2.\frac{d\varrho}{dt}.\frac{d\theta}{dt}.\frac{1}{\cos.^2\theta}+\frac{d^2\theta}{dt^2}.\frac{\varrho}{\cos.^3\theta}+\frac{2\varrho}{\cos.^3\theta}.\frac{d\theta^2}{dt^2}.\sin.\theta$, this expression being subtracted from the preceding multiplied into tan. θ, gives $0=$

$$-\varrho.\left\{\frac{\left\{\frac{d^2\theta}{dt^2}\right\}}{\cos.^2\theta}+2.\frac{\left\{\frac{d\theta}{dt}\right\}^2.\sin.\theta}{\cos.^3\theta}+\left\{\frac{d\alpha}{dt}\right\}^2.\tan.\theta\right\};$$

but we have

$$\left\{\frac{d^2x'}{dt^2}+\frac{x'}{r^3}\right\}.\cos.\alpha+\left\{\frac{d^2y'}{dt^2}+\frac{y'}{r^3}\right\}.\sin.\alpha=(x'.\cos.\alpha+y'.\sin.\alpha).$$

$$\left\{\frac{1}{r^3}-\frac{1}{R^3}\right\}=R.\cos.(A-\alpha).\left\{\frac{1}{r^3}-\frac{1}{R^3}\right\};$$

therefore

$$\left\{\frac{d\varrho}{dt}\right\}=-\tfrac{1}{2}\varrho.\left\{\frac{\left\{\frac{d^2\theta}{dt^2}\right\}}{\left\{\frac{d\theta}{dt}\right\}}+2.\left\{\frac{d\theta}{dt}\right\}.\operatorname{tang}.\theta+\frac{\left\{\frac{d\alpha}{dt}\right\}^2.\sin.\theta.\cos.\theta.}{\left\{\frac{d\theta}{dt}\right\}}\right\}$$

$$+\frac{R.\sin.\theta.\cos.\theta.\cos.(A-\alpha)}{2.\left\{\frac{d\theta}{dt}\right\}}.\left\{\frac{1}{r^3}-\frac{1}{R^3}\right\};^{*}\qquad(2)$$

if this value of $\frac{d\varrho}{dt}$ be subtracted from the first, and if we suppose

$$\mu'=\frac{\left\{\frac{d\alpha}{dt}\right\}.\left\{\frac{d^2\theta}{dt^2}\right\}-\left\{\frac{d\theta}{dt}\right\}.\left\{\frac{d^2\alpha}{dt^2}\right\}+2.\left\{\frac{d\alpha}{dt}\right\}.\left\{\frac{d\theta}{dt}\right\}^2.\tan.\theta+\left\{\frac{d\alpha}{dt}\right\}^3.\sin.\theta.\cos.\theta.}{\left\{\frac{d\alpha}{dt}\right\}.\sin.\theta.\cos.\theta.\cos.(A-\alpha)+\left\{\frac{d\theta}{dt}\right\}.\sin.(A-\alpha)}; \dagger$$

$$\tan.\theta.\left(\frac{d^2x'}{dt^2}.\cos.\alpha+\frac{d^2y'}{dt^2}.\sin.\alpha.+\frac{x'}{r^3}.\cos.\alpha+\frac{y'}{r^3}.\sin.\alpha.\right)+\frac{\varrho.\tan.\theta}{r^3}-$$

$$\frac{d^2\varrho}{dt^2}.\tan.\theta-2.\frac{d\varrho}{dt}.\frac{d\theta}{dt}.\frac{1}{\cos.^2\theta}-\frac{d^2\theta}{dt^2}.\frac{\varrho}{\cos.^2\theta}-\frac{2\varrho}{\cos.^3\theta}.\frac{d\theta^2}{dt^2}.\sin.\theta-\frac{d\alpha^2}{dt^2}.\tan.\theta.$$

$$-\frac{\varrho.\tan.\theta}{r^3}.$$

* This value of $\frac{d\varrho}{dt}$ is derived immediately from the preceding equations, by multiplying the entire expression, by $\cos.^2\theta$. and dividing by $\frac{d\theta}{dt}$, and observing that $\tan.\theta=\frac{\sin.\theta}{\cos.\theta}$.

† If the two values of $\frac{d\varrho}{dt}$, be multiplied by $\frac{d\alpha}{dt}.\frac{d\theta}{dt}$, and if the second be then sub-

we shall obtain

$$\varrho = \frac{R}{\mu'} \left\{ \frac{1}{r^3} - \frac{1}{R^3} \right\}. \quad (3)$$

The projected distance ϱ, of the comet from the earth, being always positive; this equation shews that the distance r of the comet from the sun is greater or less than the distance R of the earth from the sun, according as μ' is positive or negative; these two distances are equal, if $\mu' = 0$.

We can, by the sole inspection of the celestial globe, determine the sign of μ'; and consequently, whether the comet is nearer or farther than the earth from the sun. For this purpose, let us conceive a great circle, which passes through two geocentric positions of the comet, indefinitely near to each other. Let γ represent the inclination of this circle to the ecliptic, and λ, the longitude of its ascending node; we shall have

$$\text{tan. } \gamma . \text{ sin. } (\alpha - \lambda) = \text{tang. } \theta;$$

from which may be obtained

$$d\theta . \text{ sin. } (\alpha - \lambda) = d\alpha . \text{ sin. } \theta . \text{ cos. } \theta . \text{ cos. } (\alpha - \lambda);$$

differentiating a second time, we shall have

$$0 = \left\{\frac{d\alpha}{dt}\right\} . \frac{d^2\theta}{dt^2} - \frac{d\theta}{dt} . \frac{d^2\alpha}{dt^2} + 2 . \left\{\frac{d\alpha}{dt}\right\} . \left\{\frac{d\theta}{dt}\right\}^2 . \text{ tang. } \theta$$

tracted from the first, the quantity by which ϱ is multiplied is the numerator of the value of μ', and the quantity independent of ϱ, is its denominator.

If r be less than R, $\frac{1}{r^3} - \frac{1}{R^3}$ is positive, $\therefore$ in this case μ' must be positive; if r is greater than R, then $\frac{1}{r^3} - \frac{1}{R^3}$ is negative, $\therefore$ μ' must in this case be negative; when $r = R$, $\mu' = \frac{R}{\varrho} . \left(\frac{1}{r^3} - \frac{1}{R^3}\right) = 0$.

$$+\left\{\frac{d\alpha}{dt}\right\}^3 . \sin.\ \theta .\ \cos.\ \theta ;^*$$

$d^2\theta_{,}$ being the value of $d^2\theta$, which it would have, if the apparent motion of the comet continued in the great circle. Consequently the value of μ' becomes, by substituting for $d\theta$, its value $\frac{d\alpha .\ \sin.\ \theta .\ \cos.\ \theta .\ \cos.\ (\alpha - \lambda)}{\sin.\ (\alpha - \lambda)}$;

$$\mu' = \frac{\left\{\left\{\frac{d^2\theta}{dt^2}\right\} - \left\{\frac{d^2\theta_{,}}{dt^2}\right\}\right\} . \sin.(\alpha - \lambda)}{\sin.\ \theta .\ \cos.\ \theta .\ \sin.\ (A - \lambda)} ;\dagger$$

The function $\frac{\sin.\ (\alpha - \lambda)}{\sin.\ \theta .\ \cos.\ \theta}$ is constantly positive; therefore the value of μ' is positive or negative, according as $\left\{\frac{d^2\theta}{dt^2}\right\} - \left\{\frac{d^2\theta_{,}}{dt^2}\right\}$ has the same or a contrary sign, to $\sin.\ (A - \lambda)$; $A - \lambda$ is equal to two right angles, plus the distance of the sun from the ascending node of the

* $d\alpha .\ \cos.\ (\alpha - \lambda) .\ \tan.\ \gamma = \frac{d\theta}{\cos.^2\theta}$, $\therefore d\alpha . \frac{\cos.\ (\alpha - \lambda) .\ \tan.\ \theta}{\sin.\ (\alpha - \lambda)} = \frac{d\theta}{\cos.^2\theta}$, $\therefore d\alpha .\ \cos.\ (\alpha - \lambda) .\ \sin.\ \theta .\ \cos.\ \theta = d\theta .\ \sin.\ (\alpha - \lambda)$; hence

$d^2\theta_{,} .\ \sin.\ (\alpha - \lambda) + d\alpha .\ d\theta .\ \cos.\ (\alpha - \lambda) = d^2\alpha .\ \sin.\ \theta .\ \cos.\ \theta .\ \cos.\ (\alpha - \lambda) + d\alpha .\ d\theta .\ \cos.^2\theta .\ \cos.\ (\alpha - \lambda) - d\alpha .\ d\theta .\ \sin.^2\theta .\ \cos.\ (\alpha - \lambda) - d\alpha^2 .\ \sin.\ \theta .\ \cos.\ \theta .\ \sin.\ (\alpha - \lambda)$, by substituting for $\sin.\ (\alpha - \lambda)$ its value $\frac{d\alpha}{d\theta} .\ \sin.\ \theta .\ \cos.\ \theta .\ \cos.\ (\alpha - \lambda)$, we obtain $\frac{d^2\theta_{,} .\ d\alpha}{d\theta} .\ \sin.\ \theta .\ \cos.\ \theta .\ \cos.\ (\alpha - \lambda) + d\alpha . d\theta .\ (\cos.\ (\alpha - \lambda) = d^2\alpha .\ \sin.\ \theta .\ \cos.\ \theta .\ \cos.\ (\alpha - \lambda) + d\alpha . d\theta .\ \cos.^2\theta .\ \cos.\ (\alpha - \lambda) - d\alpha . d\theta .\ \sin.^2\theta .\ \cos.\ (\alpha - \lambda) - \frac{d\alpha^3}{d\theta} .\ \sin.^2\theta .\ \cos.^2\theta .\ \cos.\ (\alpha - \lambda)$; dividing both sides of this equation by $\frac{\sin.\ \theta .\ \cos.\ \theta}{d\theta} .\ \cos.\ (\alpha - \lambda)$, we obtain the expression which is given in the text.

† By substituting for $\frac{2d\alpha}{dt} . \frac{d\theta^2}{dt^2} .\ \text{tang.}\ \theta + \left(\frac{d\alpha}{dt}\right)^3 .\ \sin.\ \theta .\ \cos.\ \theta$. its value given in the preceding equation, and for $d\theta$ its value, we obtain $\mu' =$

$\left(\frac{d^2\theta}{dt^2} - \frac{d^2\theta_{,}}{dt^2}\right) .\ \sin.\ (\alpha - \lambda)$ divided by $\sin.\ \theta .\ \cos.\ \theta .\ (\sin.\ (\alpha - \lambda) .\ \cos.\ (A - \alpha) + \cos.\ (\alpha - \lambda)$, $\sin.\ (A - \alpha))$; $= (\sin.\ \theta .\ \cos.\ \theta .\ \sin.\ (\alpha - \lambda + A - \alpha) = \sin.\ \theta .\ \cos.\ \theta .\ \sin.\ (A - \lambda)$.

great circle; hence it is easy to infer that μ' will be positive or negative, according as in a third geocentric position of the comet, indefinitely near* to the two first, the comet deviates from this great circle from the very side in which the sun exists, or from the opposite side. Let us conceive, therefore, that a great circle of the sphere passes through two geocentric positions of the comet, indefinitely near to each other; if in a third consecutive geocentric position indefinitely near to the two first, the comet deviates from this great circle, from the same side as the sun, or from the opposite side, it will be nearer or farther than the earth from the sun, it will be equally distant, if it continues to appear in this great circle; thus the different inflexions of its apparent route will throw some light on the variations of its distances from the sun.

In order to eliminate r from the equation (3), so that this equation may only involve the unknown ρ, it is to be observed that we have $r^2 = x^2+y^2+z^2$, and by substituting in place of x, y, z, their values in terms of ρ, α and θ; we shall have

$$r^2 = x'^2 + y'^2 + 2\rho.(x'.\cos.\alpha + y'.\sin.\alpha) + \frac{\rho^2}{\cos.^2\theta};\dagger$$

* $A = 180 + a$ (= the sun's longitude, as seen from the earth) and $\therefore A - \lambda = 180 + a - \lambda = 180 +$ the distance of the sun from the ascending node of the great circle, $\therefore$ when a is $> \lambda$ the sign of sin. $(A-\lambda)$ is negative, and if $\frac{d^2\theta}{dt^2} - \frac{d^2\theta,}{dt^2}$ be also negative, the comet in the third position must deviate from the great circle from the very direction in which the sun appears as seen from the earth, if a be $\angle \lambda$, then sin. $(A-\lambda)$ is positive, $\therefore$ if $\frac{d^2\theta}{dt^2} - \frac{d^2\theta,}{dt^2}$ be also positive, it is evident that the comet must be nearer than the earth to the sun, and $\therefore$ that in the third position, the comet must deviate from the great circle, from the direction in which the sun appears from the earth; on the contrary, if sin. $(A-\lambda)$ be negative, and $\frac{d^2\theta}{dt^2} - \frac{d^2\theta,}{dt^2}$ positive, in order that this may obtain, in this situation of the bodies, it is necessary that in the third position the comet should deviate from the great circle, from the opposite side to that in which the sun appears, as seen from the earth. See Memoirs of the Academy of Berlin, for the years 1772, and 1778.

† $x^2 = x'^2 + 2\rho.x'.\cos.\alpha + \rho^2.\cos.^2\alpha$; $y^2 = y'^2 + 2ry'.\sin.\alpha + \rho^2.\sin.^2\alpha$; $z^2 = \rho^2$

but we have $x'=R.\cos. A$; $y'=R.\sin. A$; therefore

$$r^2=\frac{\varrho^2}{\cos.^2\theta}+2R.\varrho.\cos.(A-\alpha)+R^2.$$

By squaring the members of the equation (3), when arranged under the following form,

$$r^3.(\mu'.R^2\varrho+1)=R^3;$$

we shall obtain, by substituting in place of r^2, its value,

$$\left(\frac{\varrho^2}{\cos.^2\theta}+2R\varrho.\cos.(A-\alpha)+R^2\right)^3.(\mu'.R^2\varrho+1)^2=R^6; \quad (4)$$

In this* equation, ϱ is the only unknown quantity, and it ascends to the seventh degree, because the term which is entirely known in the first member being equal to R^6, the entire equation is divisible by ϱ. Having by this means determined ϱ, we will obtain $\left\{\frac{d\varrho}{dt}\right\}$ by means of the equations (1) and (2). By substituting, for example in the equation (1), instead of $\frac{1}{r^3}-\frac{1}{R^3}$, its value $\frac{\mu'\rho}{R}$, which is given by the equation (3); we shall have

$$\left\{\frac{d\varrho}{dt}\right\}=\frac{-\varrho}{2.\left\{\frac{d\alpha}{dt}\right\}}.\left\{\left\{\frac{d^2\alpha}{dt^2}\right\}+\mu'.\sin.(A-\alpha)\right\}.$$

The equation (4) is frequently susceptible of several real and positive roots; by making its second member to coalesce with the first, and then dividing by ϱ, its last term will be

$\tan.^2\theta$. $\therefore x^2+y^2+z^2=x'^2+y'^2+2\varrho.(x'.\cos. a+y'.\sin. a)+\varrho^2.(1+\tan.^2\theta)=\left(\frac{\varrho^2}{\cos.^2\theta}\right.$.

Multiplying both sides of equation (3) by $\mu'.R^3.r^3$, and we obtain $\mu'.R^3.\varrho.r^3=R^4-R.r^3$, $\therefore r^3.(\mu'.R^2\varrho+1)=R^3$; $\therefore$ substituting for r^3 its value we obtain $\left(\frac{\varrho^2}{\cos.^2\theta}+2R\varrho.\cos.(A-\alpha)+R^2\right)^{\frac{3}{2}}.(\mu'R^2.\varrho+1)=R^3$.

* R^6 occurs on both sides of this equation with the same sign, therefore it may be omitted, and as the remaining quantity is divisible by ϱ, it may be depressed to the seventh degree.

$$2.\ R^5.\ \cos.\ {}^6\theta.\ (\mu'.R^3+3.\ \cos.\ (A-\alpha))\ ;^*$$

Thus the equation in ρ, being of the seventh degree, it will have at least two roots which are real and positive, if $\mu'.\ R^3+3.\ \cos.\ (A-\alpha)$ is positive ;† for by the nature of the problem, it must always have a positive root, and it is evident from the nature of equations that when this is the case the number of its positive roots cannot be odd. Each real and positive value of ρ, gives a different conick section for the orbit of the comet ; therefore we will have as many curves which satisfy three neighbouring observations, as ρ will have real and positive values, and in order to determine the true orbit of the comet, we must have recourse to a new observation.

32. The value of ρ, deduced from the equation (4) would be rigorously exact, if α, $\left(\frac{d\alpha}{dt}\right)$, $\left(\frac{d^2\alpha}{dt^2}\right)$, θ, $\left(\frac{d\theta}{dt}\right)$, $\left(\frac{d^2\theta}{dt^2}\right)$, were exactly known ; but these are only approximate values. Indeed, we can by the method already laid down approach to them nearer and nearer, by employing a considerable number of observations, which has also the advantage, of enabling us to consider intervals sufficiently great, and thus to compensate by each other, the errors of observations. But this method is liable to the analytic inconvenience of employing more than three observations, in aproblem in which three is sufficient. We can obviate this inconvenience in the following manner, which at the same

* This equation when expanded becomes

$\left(\frac{\rho^2}{\cos.\ ^2\theta}+2R\rho.\ \cos.(A-\alpha)\right)^3+3.\left(\frac{\rho^2}{\cos.\ ^2\theta}+2R\rho.\ \cos.\ (A-\alpha)\right)^2.\ R^2+3.\left(\frac{\rho^2}{\cos.\ ^2\theta}+\right.$ $\left.2R\rho.\ \cos.\ (A-\alpha)\right).R^4+R^6).(\mu'^2.R^4\rho^2+2\mu R^2\rho+1)=R^6$, when R^6 is obliterated, and this expression is multiplied by $\cos.\ ^6\theta$, and divided by ρ, the absolute quantity is evidently equal to $(2R.\ \cos.\ (A-\alpha).\ 3R^4+2\mu R^8).\ \cos.\ ^6\theta$.

† This equation being of the seventh dimension, when the absolute quantity is positive it must have one real negative root, and from the nature of the problem it has one real affirmative root, ∴ as impossible roots enter questions by pairs, the number of those in the proposed equation cannot exceed four; consequently, in order that the sign of the absolute quantity may be positive, the remaining real root must be positive.

time that it only employs three observations, will render our solution as accurate as we please.

For this purpose let us suppose that α and θ represent the geocentric longitude and latitude of the intermediate observations; by substituting in place of x, y, z, their values $x'+\rho.\cos.\alpha$; $y'+\rho.\sin.\alpha$; and $\rho.\text{tang}.\theta$; they will give $\left\{\frac{d^2\rho}{dt^2}\right\}$, $\left\{\frac{d^2\alpha}{dt^2}\right\}$ and $\left\{\frac{d^2\theta}{dt^2}\right\}$, in functions of ρ, α, and θ, of their first differences and of known quantities. By differentiating these functions, we will obtain, $\left\{\frac{d^3\rho}{dt^3}\right\}$, $\left\{\frac{d^3\alpha}{dt^3}\right\}$ and $\left\{\frac{d^3\theta}{dt^3}\right\}$, in functions of ρ, α, θ, and of their first and second differences. We can eliminate the second difference of ρ, by means of its value, and its first difference, by means of the equation (2) of the preceding number. By continuing to difference successively, the values of $\left\{\frac{d^3\alpha}{dt^3}\right\}$, $\left\{\frac{d^3\theta}{dt^3}\right\}$, and then by eliminating the differences of α and θ, superior to the second, and all the differences of ρ, we will obtain the values of $\left\{\frac{d^3\alpha}{dt^3}\right\}$, $\left\{\frac{d^4\alpha}{dt^4}\right\}$, &c., $\left\{\frac{d^3\theta}{dt^3}\right\}$, $\left\{\frac{d^4\theta}{dt^4}\right\}$, &c., in functions of ρ, α, $\left\{\frac{d\alpha}{dt}\right\}$, θ, $\left\{\frac{d\theta}{dt}\right\}$, $\left\{\frac{d^2\theta}{dt^2}\right\}$; this being premised, let α, α', α'', be the three observed geocentric longitudes of the comet; θ, θ', θ'', its three corresponding geocentric latitudes; let i be the number of days which intervene between the first and second observation, and i', the number which separates the second observation from the third; finally, let λ be the arc which the earth describes in a day by its mean sidereal motion; by No. 29, we shall have

$$\alpha_{,}=\alpha-i.\lambda.\left(\frac{d\alpha}{dt}\right)+\frac{i^2.\lambda^2}{1.2}.\left(\frac{d^2\alpha}{dt^2}\right)-\frac{i^3.\lambda^3}{1.2.3}.\left(\frac{d^3\alpha}{dt^3}\right)+\&c.;$$

$$\alpha'=\alpha+i'\lambda.\left(\frac{d\alpha}{dt}\right)+\frac{i'^2.\lambda^2}{1.2}.\left(\frac{d^2\alpha}{dt^2}\right)+\frac{i'^3.\lambda^3}{1.2.3}.\left(\frac{d^3\alpha}{dt^3}\right)+\&c.;$$

$$\theta_{,}=\theta-i.\lambda.\left(\frac{d\theta}{dt}\right)+\frac{i^2.\lambda^2}{1.2}.\left(\frac{d^2\theta}{dt^2}\right)-\frac{i^3.\lambda^3}{1.2.3}.\left(\frac{d^3\theta}{dt^3}\right)+\&c.;$$

$$\theta'=\theta+i'.\lambda.\left(\frac{d\theta}{dt}\right)+\frac{i'^2.\lambda^2}{1.2}.\left(\frac{d^2\theta}{dt^2}\right)+\frac{i'^3.\lambda^3}{1.2.3}.\left(\frac{d^3\theta}{dt^3}\right)+\&c.$$

By substituting in these series, for $\left\{\frac{d^3\alpha}{dt^3}\right\}$, $\left\{\frac{d^4\alpha}{dt^4}\right\}$, &c. $\left\{\frac{d^3\theta}{dt^3}\right\}$, $\left\{\frac{d^4\theta}{dt^4}\right\}$, &c., their values obtained by the preceding method; we shall have four equations between the five unknown quantities ρ, $\left\{\frac{d\alpha}{dt}\right\}$, $\left\{\frac{d^2\alpha}{dt^2}\right\}$, $\left\{\frac{d\theta}{dt}\right\}$, $\left\{\frac{d^2\theta}{dt^2}\right\}$. These equations will be always more exact, according as we consider a greater number of terms in the preceding series. By this means we shall obtain, $\left\{\frac{d\alpha}{dt}\right\}$, $\left\{\frac{d^2\alpha}{dt^2}\right\}$, $\left\{\frac{d\theta}{dt}\right\}$ and $\left\{\frac{d^2\theta}{dt^2}\right\}$, in functions of ρ and of known quantities; and by substituting them in the equation (4) of the preceding number, it will only involve the unknown quantity ρ. In fine, this method which has been detailed here, merely in order to shew how by means of three observations only we can obtain continually approaching values of ρ, would require in practice, very troublesome computations, and it is at the same time more exact and more simple, to consider a greater number, by the method explained in No. 29.

33. When the values of ρ and of $\left\{\frac{d\rho}{dt}\right\}$ shall have been determined, we can obtain those of x, y, z, $\left(\frac{dx}{dt}\right)$, $\left(\frac{dy}{dt}\right)$ and $\left(\frac{dz}{dt}\right)$ by means of the equations $x=R.\cos.A+\rho.\cos.\alpha$; $y=R.\sin.A+\rho.\sin.\alpha$; $z=\rho.\text{tang}.\theta$; and of their differentials divided by dt,

$$\left(\frac{dx}{dt}\right)=\left(\frac{dR}{dt}\right).\ \cos.\ A-R.\left(\frac{dA}{dt}\right).\ \sin.\ A+\left(\frac{d\rho}{dt}\right).\ \cos.\ \alpha-\rho.\left(\frac{d\alpha}{dt}\right).\ \sin.\ \alpha\ ;$$

$$\left(\frac{dy}{dt}\right)=\left(\frac{dR}{dt}\right).\ \sin.\ A+R.\left(\frac{dA}{dt}\right).\ \cos.\ A+\left(\frac{d\rho}{dt}\right).\ \sin.\ \alpha+\rho.\left(\frac{d\alpha}{dt}\right).\ \cos.\ \alpha\ ;$$

$$\left(\frac{dz}{dt}\right)=\left(\frac{d\rho}{dt}\right).\ \tan.\ \theta+\frac{\rho.\left(\frac{d\theta}{dt}\right)}{\cos.^2\theta}.$$

The values of $\left(\frac{dA}{dt}\right)$ and of $\left(\frac{dR}{dt}\right)$ are given by the theory of the motion of the earth: in order to facilitate their computation, let E represent the eccentricity of the earth's orbit, and H the longitude of its perihelion; by the nature of the elliptic motion we have,

$$\left(\frac{dA}{dt}\right)=\frac{\sqrt{1-E^2}}{R^2};\ R=\frac{1-E^2}{1+E.\cos.(A-H)}.^*$$

These two equations give

$$\left(\frac{dR}{dt}\right)=\frac{E.\sin.(A-H)}{\sqrt{1-E^2}};$$

let R' represent the radius vector of the earth corresponding to A, the longitude of this planet, increased by a right angle; we shall have

$$R'=\frac{1-E^2}{1-E.\sin.(A-H)};$$

from which may be obtained

$$E.\sin.(A-H)=\frac{R'-1+E^2}{R'};$$

* $\frac{dA}{dt}$ being equal to the angular velocity of the earth, it is equal to the square root of the parameter divide by the square of the distance, $\therefore$ it is equal to $\frac{\sqrt{1-E^2}}{R^2}$.

consequently

$$\left(\frac{dR}{dt}\right)=\frac{R'+E^2-1}{R'.\sqrt{1-E^2}}.*$$

If we neglect the square of the excentricity of the terrestrial orbit, which is very small, we shall have

$$\left(\frac{dA}{dt}\right)=\frac{1}{R^2}\ ;\ \left(\frac{dR}{dt}\right)=R'-1\ ;$$

the preceding values of $\left(\frac{dx}{dt}\right)$ and $\left(\frac{dy}{dt}\right)$ will consequently become

$$\left(\frac{dx}{dt}\right)=(R'-1).\cos.A-\frac{\sin.A}{R}+\left(\frac{d\varrho}{dt}\right).\cos.\alpha-\varrho.\left(\frac{d\alpha}{dt}\right).\sin.\alpha.$$

$$\left(\frac{dy}{dt}\right)=(R'-1).\sin.A+\frac{\cos.A}{R}+\left(\frac{d\varrho}{dt}\right).\sin.\alpha+\varrho.\left(\frac{d\alpha}{dt}\right).\cos.\alpha\ ;$$

R, R' and A being given immediately by the tables of the sun, the computation of the six quantities x, y, z, $\left(\frac{dx}{dt}\right)$, $\left(\frac{dy}{dt}\right)$, and $\left(\frac{dz}{dt}\right)$ will be easy, when ϱ, and $\left(\frac{d\varrho}{dt}\right)$ will be known. The elements of the orbit of the comet can be deduced from them, in the following manner.

* $\frac{dR}{dt}=\frac{dA}{dt}.\frac{(1-E^2).E.\sin.(A-H)}{(1+E.\cos.A-H)^2}=\frac{\sqrt{1-E^2}}{(1-E^2)^2}.(1+E.\cos.(A-H)^2.$

$\frac{(1-E^2).E.\sin.(A-H)}{(1+E.\cos.(A-H)^2}=\frac{E.\sin.(A-H)}{\sqrt{1-E^2}}$; $R'=\frac{1-E^2}{1+E.\cos.(A+90-H)}$

$=\frac{1-E^2}{1-E.\sin.(A-H)}$; $=(1-E^2).(1-E.\sin.(A-H))^{-1}=$ (when the square of E is neglected) $1+E.\sin.(A-H)$, $\therefore R'-1(=E.\sin.(A-H))$ is equal $\left(\frac{dR}{dt}\right)$, when E^2 is neglected.

The indefinitely small sector, which the projection of the radius vector of the comet on the plane of the ecliptic, describes during the element of time dt, is $\frac{xdy-ydx}{2}$; and it is manifest that this sector is positive or negative according as the motion of the comet is direct or retrograde; thus, the sign of the quantity $x.\left(\frac{dy}{dt}\right)-y.\left(\frac{dx}{dt}\right)$, will indicate the direction of the motion of the comet.

In order to determine the position of the orbit, let us name φ, its inclination to the ecliptic, and I the longitude of the node, which will be the ascending one, if the motion of the comet be direct; we shall have

$$z=y.\cos. I.\tan\varphi-x.\sin. I.\tan.\varphi.$$

This equation, combined with its differential, gives

$$\tan. I=\frac{y.\left(\frac{dz}{dt}\right)-z.\left(\frac{dy}{dt}\right)}{x.\left(\frac{dz}{dt}\right)-z.\left(\frac{dx}{dt}\right)};*$$

* $z=\tan.\varphi.$ multiplied into the distance of z from the line of the nodes, and if the axis of x be a line drawn to the first point of Aries, this last distance $=y.\cos. I-x.\sin. I.$

$$dz=dy.\cos. I.\tan.\varphi-dx.\sin. I.\tan.\varphi;\ \because\ \frac{y.\frac{dz}{dt}-z.\frac{dy}{dt}}{x.\frac{dz}{dt}-z.\frac{dx}{dt}}=$$

$$\frac{\left(y.\frac{dy}{dt}.\cos. I-y.\frac{dx}{dt}.\sin. I-y.\frac{dy}{dt}.\cos. I+x.\frac{dy}{dt}.\sin. I\right).\tan.\varphi.}{\left(x.\frac{dy}{dt}.\cos. I-x.\frac{dx}{dt}.\sin. I-y.\frac{dx}{dt}.\cos. I+x.\frac{dx}{dt}.\sin. I\right).\tan.\varphi.}$$

$$=\frac{\left(x.\frac{dy}{dt}-y.\frac{dx}{dt}\right).\sin. I.}{\left(x.\frac{dy}{dt}-y.\frac{dx}{dt}\right).\cos. I.}=\tan. I.$$

$=\tan. I.$

$$\tan.\,\varphi = \frac{y.\left(\frac{dz}{dt}\right) - z.\left(\frac{dy}{dt}\right)}{\sin.I.\left\{x.\left(\frac{dy}{dt}\right) - y.\left(\frac{dx}{dt}\right)\right\}}$$

φ must be always positive and less than a right angle; this condition determines the sign of sin. I; but the tangent of I, and the sign of its sine being determined, the angle I is entirely determined. This angle is equal to the longitude of the ascending node of the orbit, provided that the motion is direct, but if the motion is retrograde, we must add to it two right angles, in order to obtain the longitude of this node. It will be simpler to consider only the direct motions, by making φ the inclination of the orbits to vary, from *zero* to two right angles; for it is manifest, that then the retrograde motions correspond to an inclination greater than a right angle. In this case, tan. φ is of the same sign as $x.\left(\frac{dy}{dt}\right) - y.\left(\frac{dx}{dt}\right)$, which determines sin. I, and consequently the angle I, which expresses always the longitude of the ascending node.

a and ea representing the semiaxis major, and excentricity of the orbit, we have, by N°s. 18 and 19, μ being supposed $=1$,

By substituting we obtain $\dfrac{\left(y.\frac{dz}{dt} - z.\frac{dy}{dt}\right)}{\sin.I.\left(x.\frac{dy}{dt} - y.\frac{dx}{dt}\right)} =$

$$\frac{y.\frac{dy}{dt}.\cos.I - y.\frac{dx}{dt}.\sin.I - y.\frac{dy}{dt}.\cos.I + x.\frac{dy}{dt}.\sin.I).\tan.\varphi.)}{\left(x.\frac{dy}{dt} - y.\frac{dx}{dt}\right).\sin.I.}$$

$$= \frac{\left(x.\frac{dy}{dt} - y.\frac{dx}{dt}\right).\sin.I.\tan.\varphi.}{\left(x.\frac{dy}{dt} - y.\frac{dx}{dt}\right).\sin.I.} = \tan.\varphi.$$

$$\frac{1}{a}=\frac{2}{r}-\left(\frac{dx}{dt}\right)^2-\left(\frac{dy}{dt}\right)^2-\left(\frac{dz}{dt}\right)^2;$$

$$a.(1-e^2)=2r-\frac{r^2}{a}-\left\{x.\left(\frac{dx}{dt}\right)+y.\left(\frac{dy}{dt}\right)+z.\left(\frac{dz}{dt}\right)\right\}^2.$$

The first of these equations determines the semiaxis major of the orbit, and the second determines its excentricity. The sign of the function $x.\left(\frac{dx}{dt}\right)+y.\left(\frac{dy}{dt}\right)+z.\left(\frac{dz}{dt}\right)$ makes known whether the comet has already passed through its perihelion; for if this function is negative, it approaches towards it; in the contrary case, it has already passed this point.

Let T represent the interval of time comprised between the epoch which we have selected, and the passage of the comet through the perehelion; the two first of the equations (f) of No. 20, will give, by observing that μ being supposed equal to unity, we have $n=a^{-\frac{3}{2}}$,

$$r=a.(1-e.\cos.u);\quad T=a^{\frac{3}{2}}.(u-e.\cos.u).$$

The first of these equations gives the angle u, and the second makes known the time T. This time added or subtracted from the epoch, according as the comet approaches or departs from the perihelion, will give the instant of its passage through this point. The values of x and of y, determine the angle which the projection of the radius vector r makes with the axis of x, and as we know the angle I made by this axis, with the line of the nodes, we shall have the angle which this last line constitutes with the projection of r; from which may be obtained, by means of the inclination φ of the orbit, the angle which the line of the nodes makes with the radius r. But the angle u being known, we shall have by means of the third of the equations (f), of No. 20, the angle v, which this radius forms, with the line of the apsides; therefore we will have the angle comprised between the two lines, of the apsides and the nodes, and, consequently, the position of the perihelion. All the elements of the orbit will be thus determined.

34. These elements are given, by what precedes, in functions of ρ $\left(\frac{d\rho}{dt}\right)$, and of known quantities; and as $\left(\frac{d\rho}{dt}\right)$ is given in ρ, by No. 31; the elements of the orbit will be functions of ρ, and of known quantities. If one of them was given, we would have a new equation, by means of which we could determine ρ; this equation will have a common divisor with the equation (4) of No. 31; and seeking this divisor by the ordinary method we will arrive at an equation of the first degree in ρ, we shall have besides, an equation of condition between the data of the observations, and this equation will be that which should have place, in order that the given element might belong to the orbit of the comet.

Let us now apply this consideration to nature. For this purpose, we may observe that the orbits of the comets are very elongated ellipses, which are sensibly confounded with a parabola, in that part of their orbit in which these stars are visible; therefore we may suppose without sensible error, that $a = \infty$, and $\frac{1}{a} = 0$; consequently the expression for $\frac{1}{a}$ of the preceding No. will give,

$$0 = \frac{2}{r} - \frac{(dx^2 + dy^2 + dz^2)}{dt^2}.$$

If we afterwards substitute, instead of $\left(\frac{dx}{dt}\right)$, $\left(\frac{dy}{dt}\right)$, $\left(\frac{dz}{dt}\right)$ their values, which are found in the same No.; we shall have, after all reductions, and by neglecting the square of $R'-1$,

$$0 = \left(\frac{d\rho}{dt}\right)^2 + \rho^2 . \left(\frac{d\alpha}{dt}\right)^2 + \left\{ \left(\frac{d\rho}{dt}\right) . \tan. \theta + \rho . \frac{\left(\frac{d\theta}{dt}\right)}{\cos.^2 \theta} \right\}^2$$

$$+2.\left(\frac{d\varrho}{dt}\right)\left\{(R'-1).\cos.(A-\alpha)-\frac{\sin.(A-\alpha)}{R}\right\} \quad (5)$$

$$+2\varrho.\left(\frac{d\alpha}{dt}\right).\left\{(R'-1).\sin.(A-\alpha)+\frac{\cos.(A-\alpha)}{R}\right\}+\frac{1}{R^2}-\frac{2}{r};$$

by substituting in this equation, instead of $\left(\frac{d\varrho}{dt}\right)$ its value

$$\frac{-\varrho}{2.\left(\frac{d\alpha}{dt}\right).\left\{\left(\frac{d^2\alpha}{dt^2}\right)+\mu'.\sin.(A-\alpha)\right\}}$$

which has been found in No. 31; and then by making

$$4.\left(\frac{d\alpha}{dt}\right)^2.B=4.\left(\frac{d\alpha}{dt}\right)^4+\left\{\left(\frac{d^2\alpha}{dt^2}\right)+\mu'.\sin.(A-\alpha)\right\}^2$$

$$+\left\{\frac{\tan.\theta.\left(\frac{d^2\alpha}{dt^2}\right)+\mu'.\tan.\theta.\sin.(A-\alpha)-2.\left(\frac{d\alpha}{dt}\right).\left(\frac{d\theta}{dt}\right)}{\cos.^2\theta}\right\}^2;$$

$$C=\frac{\left\{\left(\frac{d^2\alpha}{dt^2}\right)+\mu'.\sin.(A-\alpha)\right\}}{\left(\frac{d\alpha}{dt}\right)}.\left\{\frac{\sin.(A-\alpha)}{R}-(R'-1).\cos.(A-\alpha)\right\}$$

* By making this substitution, the equation (5) becomes

$$4.\frac{\varrho^2}{\frac{d\alpha^2}{dt^2}}\left(\frac{d^2\alpha}{dt^2}+\mu'.\sin.(A-\alpha)\right)^2+\varrho^2.\left(\frac{d\alpha}{dt}\right)^2+\varrho^2.\left\{\frac{\left(\frac{d^2\alpha}{dt^2}+\mu.\sin.(A-\alpha)\right).\tan.\theta.-2.\left(\frac{d\alpha}{dt}\right)}{}\right.$$

$$\left.+\frac{\left(\frac{d\theta}{dt}\right)}{\cos.^2\theta}\right\}^2-\frac{\varrho}{\frac{d\alpha}{dt}}\left(\frac{d^2\alpha}{dt^2}+\mu'.\sin.(A-\alpha)\right).(R'-1).\cos.(A-\alpha)-\sin.\frac{(A-\alpha)}{R}\Big)'$$

$$+2\varrho.\left(\frac{d\alpha}{dt}\right)\left\{(R'-1).\sin.(A-\alpha)+\frac{\cos.(A-\alpha)}{R}\right\}+\frac{1}{R^2}-\frac{2}{r}.$$

It is evident from an inspection of this expression, that B is equal to the quantity by which ϱ^2 is multiplied, and that C is equal to the corresponding factor of ϱ.

$$+2.\left(\frac{d\alpha}{dt}\right).\left\{(R'-1).\sin.(A-\alpha)+\frac{\cos.(A-\alpha)}{R}\right\};$$

we shall have

$$0=B.\rho^2+C.\rho+\frac{1}{R^2}-\frac{2}{r};$$

and consequently

$$r^2.\left\{B.\rho^2+C.\rho+\frac{1}{R^2}\right\}^2=4;$$

this equation is only of the sixth degree, and in* this respect it is simpler than the equation (4) of No. 31; but it is peculiar to the parabola, on the contrary, the equation (4) is applicable to every species of conic section.

35. We may perceive by the preceding analysis, that the determination of the parabolic orbits of comets, leads to more equations† than unknown quantities, we can, by different combinations of these equations, form as many different methods of calculating these orbits. Let us investigate those from which we ought to expect the greatest precision in the results, or which participate the least in the errors of observations.

It is principally on the values of the second differences $\left(\frac{d^2\alpha}{dt^2}\right)$ and $\left(\frac{d^2\theta}{dt^2}\right)$, that these errors have a sensible influence; in fact, it is necessary, in order to determine them, to take the finite differences of the geocentric longitudes and latitudes of the comet, observed during a

* This equation is of the sixth degree for ρ^4 and r^2 occurs in it, and if we substitute for r^2 its value, in terms of ρ; ρ^6 will be the highest dimension of ρ which occurs in it.

† The reason why there are more equations than unknown quantities in this case, is because the axis major is supposed to be infinite.

very short interval of time; but these differences being less than the first differences, the errors of observation are a greater aliquot part of them; besides, the formulæ of No. 29, which determine, by the comparison of observations, the values of α, θ, $\left(\frac{d\alpha}{dt}\right)$, $\left(\frac{d\theta}{dt}\right)$, $\left(\frac{d^2\alpha}{dt^2}\right)$, and $\left(\frac{d^2\theta}{dt^2}\right)$, determine with greater precision the four first of these quantities, than the two last; it is therefore advantageous to rely as little as possible on the second differences of α and of θ; and as we cannot reject them all at once, the method which only employs the greatest ought to lead to the most exact results; this being premised,

Let the equations which have been found in the N°s. 31 and 34, be resumed

$$r^2 = \frac{\rho^2}{\cos.^2\theta} + 2R\rho.\cos.(A-\alpha) + R^2;$$

$$\left(\frac{d\rho}{dt}\right) = \frac{R.\sin.(A-\alpha)}{2.\left(\frac{d\alpha}{dt}\right)}.\left\{\frac{1}{R^3} - \frac{1}{r^3}\right\} - \frac{\rho.\left(\frac{d^2\alpha}{dt^2}\right)}{2.\left(\frac{d\alpha}{dt}\right)}; \qquad \text{(L)}$$

$$\left(\frac{d\rho}{dt}\right) = -\tfrac{1}{2}\rho.\left\{\frac{\left(\frac{d^2\theta}{dt^2}\right)}{\left(\frac{d\theta}{dt}\right)} + 2.\left(\frac{d\theta}{dt}\right).\tan.\theta + \frac{\left(\frac{d\alpha}{dt}\right)^2.\sin.\theta.\cos.\theta}{\left(\frac{d\theta}{dt}\right)}\right\}$$

$$+ R.\frac{\sin.\theta.\cos.\theta.\cos.(A-\alpha)}{2.\left(\frac{d\theta}{dt}\right)}.\left\{\frac{1}{r^3} - \frac{1}{R^3}\right\};$$

$$0 = \left(\frac{d\rho}{dt}\right)^2 + \rho^2.\left(\frac{d\alpha}{dt}\right)^2 + \left\{\frac{\left(\frac{d\rho}{dt}\right).\tan.\theta + \rho.\left(\frac{d\theta}{dt}\right)}{\cos.^2\theta}\right\}^2$$

$$+ 2.\left(\frac{d\rho}{dt}\right).\left\{(R'-1).\cos.(A-\alpha) - \frac{\sin.(A-\alpha)}{R}.\right\}$$

$$+2\rho.\left(\frac{d\alpha}{dt}\right).\left\{(R'-1).\sin.(A-\alpha)+\frac{\cos.(A-\alpha)}{R}\right\}+\frac{1}{R^2}-\frac{2}{r}.$$

If we wish to reject $\left(\frac{d^2\theta}{dt^2}\right)$, it is only necessary to consider the first, the second, and the fourth of these equations; eliminating $\left(\frac{d\rho}{dt}\right)$, from the last, by means of the second, we will obtain an equation which freed from fractions will contain a term multiplied by $r^6.\rho^2$, and other terms affected with even and odd powers of ρ and of r. If all the terms affected with the even powers of r, be reduced into one member, and likewise all the terms affected with the odd powers of r;* the term multiplied by $r^6.\rho^2$ will produce one multiplied by $r^{12}.\rho^4$; therefore by substituting instead of r^2, its value given by the first of the equations (L), we shall have a final equation of the sixteenth degree in ρ. But instead of forming this equation, in order afterwards to resolve it, it will be simpler to satisfy by trials, the three preceding equations.

If we wish to reject $\left(\frac{d^2\alpha}{dt^2}\right)$; we must consider the first, the third and the fourth of the equations (L). These three equations would also lead us to a final equation of the sixteenth degree in ρ, which can be easily satisfied by trials.

The two preceding methods appear to me the most exact which can be employed in the determination of the parabolic orbits of the comets; it is even indispensably requisite to recur to them, if the motion of the comet in longitude or in latitude is insensible, or too small for the errors of the observations not to alter sensibly its second difference; in this case we should reject that one of the equations (L), which contains this difference. But although in these methods, we

EE 2

* By squaring each member, we get rid of the odd powers of r, and the value of any even power will be obtained by means of the first of the equations (L).

only employ three of the preceding equations; yet the fourth is useful, in order to determine amongst all the real and positive values of ρ, which satisfy the system of the three other equations, that which ought to be admitted.

36. The elements of the orbit of a comet, determined by what precedes, would be exact, if the values of α, θ, and of their first and second differences, were rigorously correct; because we have taken into account in a very simple manner, the excentricity of the earth's orbit, by means of the radius vector R' of the earth, corresponding to its true anomaly, increased by a right angle; we are only permitted to neglect the square of this excentricity, as being too small a fraction for its omission to influence sensibly the results. But θ, α, and their differences, are always liable to some inaccuracy, as well on account of the errors of observation, as because these differences are collected from the observations in an approximate manner. It is therefore necessary to correct these elements by means of three observations at considerable intervals from each other, which may be effected in an indefinite number of ways; for if we know very nearly two quantities relative to the motion of a comet, such as the radii vectores corresponding to the two observations, or the position of the node, and the inclination of its orbit, by computing the observations, at first with these quantities, and then with other quantities which differ very little from them; the law of the differences between these results, will easily make known the corrections which those quantities ought to undergo. But among the binary combinations of quantities relative to the motion of the comets, there is one of which the calculation is the simplest, and which on this account deserves to be preferred; and in a problem so complicated, it is a matter of importance, to spare the computer every superfluous operation. The two elements which have appeared to me to afford this advantage, are the perihelion distance, and the instant of the passage of the comet through this point; for they not only may be readily deduced from the values of ρ and of $\left(\frac{d\rho}{dt}\right)$; but it also

is very easy to correct them by observations, without being obliged, at each variation which they are made to undergo, to determine the other corresponding elements of the orbit.

Let us resume the equation which has been found in No. 19,

$$a.(1-e^2)=2r-\frac{r^2}{a}-\frac{r^2.dr^2}{dt^2};$$

$a.(1-e^2)$ is the semiparameter of the conic sections of which a is the semiaxis major, and ea the excentricity; in the parabola, where a is infinite, and ea equal to unity, $a.(1-e^2)$ is equal to twice the perihelion distance; let D equal this distance, the preceding equation becomes, relatively to this curve,

$$D=r-\tfrac{1}{2}.\left\{\frac{rdr}{dt}\right\}^2.$$

$\frac{rdr}{dt}$ is equal to $\frac{\frac{1}{2}d.r^2}{dt^2}$; by substituting in place of r^2, its value $\frac{\varrho^2}{\cos.^2\theta}+2R\varrho.\cos.(A-\alpha)+R^2$, and instead of $\left\{\frac{dR}{dt}\right\}$ and of $\left\{\frac{dA}{dt}\right\}$, their values found in No. 33, we shall have

$$\frac{rdr}{dt}=\frac{\varrho}{\cos.^2\theta}.\left\{\left\{\frac{d\varrho}{dt}\right\}+\varrho.\left\{\frac{d\theta}{dt}\right\}.\tan.\theta\right\}+R.\left\{\frac{d\varrho}{dt}\right\}.\cos.(A-\alpha)^*$$

$$+\varrho.\left\{(R'-1).\cos.(A-\alpha)-\frac{\sin.(A-\alpha)}{R}\right\}$$

$$+\varrho.R.\left\{\frac{d\alpha}{dt}\right\}.\sin.(A-\alpha)+R.(R'-1).$$

* $\frac{rdr}{dt}=\frac{\varrho.d\varrho}{\cos.^2\theta.dt}+\varrho^2.\frac{\sin.\theta}{\cos.^3\theta}.\left(\frac{d\theta}{dt}\right)+\cos.(A-\alpha).\left\{\varrho.\left(\frac{dR}{dt}\right)+R.\left(\frac{d\varrho}{dt}\right)\right\}$ $-R\varrho.\sin.(A-\alpha)\left\{\left(\frac{dA}{dt}\right)-\left(\frac{d\alpha}{dt}\right)\right\}+R.\left(\frac{dR}{dt}\right)$; and by substituting $R'-1$ for $\left(\frac{dR}{dt}\right)$,

Let P represent this quantity; if it is negative the radius vector r goes on diminishing, and consequently the comet* tends towards its perihelion; but it moves from it, if P is positive. We have then

$$D = r - \tfrac{1}{2}.\,P^2;$$

the angular distance v of the comet from the perihelion will be determined by the polar equation of the parabola

$$\cos.^2 \tfrac{1}{2}v = \frac{D}{r};$$

finally, the time employed to describe the angle v will be obtained, by the table of the motion of comets. This time added or subtracted from that of the epoch, according as P is negative or positive, will give themoment of the passage through the perihelion.

37. These different results being collected together, will give the following method, for determining the parabolick orbits of comets.

A general method for determining the Orbits of the Comets.

This method will be divided into two parts; in the first, we will give the means of obtaining very nearly the perihelion distance of the comet, and the instant of its passage through the perihelion; in the second, we will determine exactly all the elements of the orbit, these quantities being supposed to be very nearly known.

and $\frac{1}{R^2}$ for $\left(\frac{dA}{dt}\right)$ we shall have $\frac{rdr}{dt} = \frac{\rho}{\cos.^2\theta}\left\{\left(\frac{d\rho}{dt}\right) + \rho.\frac{\sin.\theta}{\cos.\theta}.\left(\frac{d\theta}{dt}\right)\right\} + \cos.(A-\alpha).$

$\rho.(R'-1) + \cos.(A-\alpha).\,R.\frac{d\rho}{dt} - \frac{R.\rho.\sin.(A-\alpha)}{R^{\frac{1}{2}}} + R\rho.\sin.(A-\alpha).\left(\frac{d\alpha}{dt}\right) + R.(R'-1).$

An approximate determination of the perihelion distance of a Comet, and of the instant of its passage through perihelion.

Let three, four, or five, &c. observations of the comet be selected as nearly as possible* equi-distant from each other; with four observations we can embrace an interval of 30°; with five observations, an interval of 36°, or 40°, and so on of the rest; but it is necessary always that the interval comprised between the observations should be more considerable, as they are more numerous, in order to diminish the influence of their errors; this being premised,

Let β, β', β'', &c. be the successive geocentrick longitudes of the comet; γ, γ', γ'', the corresponding latitudes, these latitudes being supposed positive or negative, according as they are north or south. Let the difference $\beta'-\beta$ be divided by the number of days which separates the first from the second observation; in like manner, the difference $\beta''-\beta'$ be divided by the number of days which separates the second from the third observation; we will also divide the difference $\beta'''-\beta''$, by the number of days which separates the third from the fourth observation, and so of the rest. Let $\delta\beta$, $\delta\beta'$, $\delta\beta''$, be these quotients; let the difference $\delta\beta'-\delta\beta$, be divided by the number of days which separates the first observation from the third; in like manner let the difference $\delta\beta''-\delta\beta'$, be divided by the number of days which separates the second observation from the

* The precision which might be expected from an increased number of observations would not (as M. Laplace has since ascertained) compensate for the errors to which the observations are liable, and also for the greater length of the calculus; he therefore proposes in the 15th Book, to employ only three observations, and by fixing the epoch at the intermediate observation, to render the extreme observations at such inconsiderable distances from each other, that for the interval which separates them, the preceding data may be supposed very nearly the same; an additional advantage in having the intervals short is, that the differences superior to the second are inconsiderable, and may therefore be neglected.

fourth; and $\delta\varepsilon'-\delta\varepsilon''$, by the number of days which separates the third observation from the fifth; and so of the rest. Let $\delta^2\varepsilon$, $\delta^2\varepsilon'$, $\delta^2\varepsilon''$, represent these quotients.

Dividing the difference $\delta^2\varepsilon'-\delta^2\varepsilon$, by the number of days which separates the first observation from the fourth; and in like manner $\delta^2\varepsilon''-\delta^2\varepsilon'$, by the number of days which intervenes between the second and fifth observation, and so of the rest. Let $\delta^3\varepsilon$, $\delta^3\varepsilon'$, &c. represent these quotients. Let these operations be continued till we arrive at $\delta^{n-1}.\varepsilon$, n being the number of observations employed.

This being performed, let an observation which is a mean, or very nearly so between the instants of the extreme observations be selected, and let i, i', i'', i''', &c. represent the number of days by which it precedes each observation, i, i', i'', being supposed to be negative for the observations which are anterior to this epoch; the longitude of the comet, after a small number z of days reckoned from the epoch, will be expressed by the following formula:

$$\varepsilon-i.\delta\varepsilon+i.i'.\delta^2\varepsilon-i.i'.i''.\delta^3\varepsilon+\&c.$$

$$+z.(\delta\varepsilon-(i+i').\delta^2\varepsilon+(i.i'+i.i''+i'.i''.).\delta^3\varepsilon-(i.i'.i''+i.i'.i'''+i.i''.i'''+ i'.i''.i''').\delta^4\varepsilon+\ \&c.);\qquad (p)$$

$$+z^2.(\delta^2\varepsilon-(i+i'+i'').\ \delta^3\varepsilon+i.i'+i.i''.+i.i'''+i'.i''+i'.i''').d^4\varepsilon-\&c.).$$

The coefficients of $-\delta\varepsilon$, $+\delta^2\varepsilon$, $-\delta^3\varepsilon$, &c. in the part which is independent of z, are, 1st. the number i; 2dly. the product of the two numbers i and i'; 3dly. the product of the three numbers i, i', i'', &c.

The coefficients of $-\delta^2\varepsilon$, $+\delta^3\varepsilon$, $-\delta^4\varepsilon$, &c. in the part multiplied by z are, 1st. the sum of the two numbers i and i; 2dly. the sum of the binary products of the three numbers i, i', i''; 3dly. the sum of the products of the four numbers i, i', i'', i''', &c. taken three by three.

The coefficients of $-\delta^3\varepsilon$, $+\delta^4\varepsilon$, $-\delta^5\varepsilon$, &c. in the part multiplied by z^2, are 1st. the sum of the three numbers i, i', i''; 2dly. the sum of the products of the four numbers i, i', i'', i''', taken two by two; 3dly. the sum of the products of the five numbers, i, i', i'', i''', i'''', &c. taken three by three.

In place of forming these products, it would be as simple to develope the function

$$\beta + (z-i).\,\delta\beta + (z-i).(z-i').\,\delta^2\beta + (z-i').(z-i'').(z-i''').\,\delta^3\beta + \&c.$$

the powers of z superior to the second, which the preceding formulæ would give, being rejected.

If we perform similar operations on the observed geocentrick latitudes of the comet; its geocentrick latitude after the number z of days, reckoned from the epoch, will be expressed by the formula (p), by changing β into γ; and let (q) represent what this formula becomes after this change; this being premised, α will be the part independent of z, in the formula (p); θ will be the part independent of z, in the formula (q).

If the coefficient of z be reduced to seconds, in the formula (p), and if the logarithm 4,0394622 be subducted from the tabular logarithm of this nnmber of seconds; it will give the logarithm of a number which we will denote by a.

And if the coefficient of z^2 in the same formula be reduced to seconds, and if the logarithm 1,9740144 be then subtracted from this number of seconds, it will give the logarithm of a number, which we will denote by b.

The coefficients of z and of z^2 being in like manner reduced to seconds in the formula (q), and then the logarithms 4,0394622, and 1,9740144 being subtracted from the logarithms of these numbers respectively, will give the logarithms of two numbers, which we will denote by h and l.

The accuracy of this method depends on the precision of the values of a, b, h, l; and as their formation is very simple, we should select and multiply the observations, so as to obtain them with all the precision which the observations admit of. It is easy to perceive that these values are the quantities $\left(\frac{d\alpha}{dt}\right)$, $\left(\frac{d^2\alpha}{dt^2}\right)$, $\left(\frac{d\theta}{dt}\right)$ and $\left(\frac{d^2\theta}{dt^2}\right)$, which for greater simplicity we have expressed by the preceding letters.

If the number of observations be odd, we can fix the epoch at the instant of the mean observation; this enables us to dispense with the computation of the parts independent of z, in the two preceding formulæ; for it is evident that these values are then respectively equal to the longitude and latitude of the mean observation.

The values of α, a, b, θ, h and l, being thus determined; the longitude of the sun at the instant which we select for the epoch, must next be determined; let this longitude be equal to E, R being the corresponding distance of the sun from the earth, and R' the distance which answers to E increased by a right angle, the following equations will be obtained,

$$r^2 = \frac{x^2}{\cos.^2\theta} - 2R.x.\cos.(E-\alpha) + R^2; \quad (1)$$

$$\dot{y} = \frac{R.\sin.(E-\alpha)}{2a}.\left\{\frac{1}{r^3} - \frac{1}{R^3}\right\} - \frac{b.x}{2a}; \quad (2)$$

$$\left.\begin{array}{l} y = -x.\left\{h.\tan.\theta + \frac{l}{2h} + \frac{a^2.\sin.\theta.\cos.\theta}{2h}\right\} \\ + \frac{R.\sin.\theta.\cos.\theta}{2h}.\cos.(E-\alpha).\left\{\frac{1}{R^3} - \frac{1}{r^3}\right\} \end{array}\right\}.$$

$$0 = y^2 + a^2.x^2 + \left\{y.\tan.\theta + \frac{h.x}{\cos.^2\theta}\right\}^2 + 2y.\left\{\frac{\sin.(E-\alpha)}{R} - (R'-1).\right.$$
$$\left.\cos.(E-\alpha)\right) \quad (4)$$

* All the observations made in the interval between the extreme observations may be made use of in determining α a, b, θ, h, and l; for if each observation be expressed in a linear function of these data, there will be more equations than unknown quantities; the first final equation will be obtained if each equation be multiplied by the coefficient the first unknown quantity, the second final equation will be obtained by a similar process, and so on; and the data will be given by a resolution of these equations with a precision which will be greater, as more observations are made use of. This advantage is peculiar to this methed. (See Connaissance des Temps, Année 1824.)

$$-2ax.((R'-1).\sin.(E-\alpha)+\frac{\cos.(E-\alpha)}{R}+\frac{1}{R^2}+\frac{2}{r}.$$

In order to deduce from these equations, the values of the unknown quantities x, y, and r; we must consider, in the first place, whether, abstracting from the sign, b is greater or less than l. In the first case, we employ the equations (1), (2) and (4). We make a first supposition for x, by supposing it, for example, equal to unity; and from this we conclude, by means of the equations (1) and (2), the values of r and of y. We substitute then, these values in the equation (4), and if the remainder vanishes, it shews that the value of x has been rightly assumed; but if this remainder be negative, the value of x must be increased, and it must be diminished, if this remainder be positive. By this means, we shall obtain by a small number of trials, the values of x, y, and r. But as these unknown quantities are susceptible of several real and positive values, it is necessary to select that value which satisfies exactly or very nearly the equation (3).

Since the publication of this book M. Laplace has ascertained that the best means of diminishing the influence which the errors of observation have on their results, consists in combining the equations (2) and (3), by multiplying the first by a^2, and the second by h^2, and then adding the products together, by means of which the following equation will be obtained,

$$\left.\begin{array}{l} y=\dfrac{a\sin.(E-a)-h.\sin.\theta.\cos.\theta.\cos.(E-a).R}{2.(a^2+h^2)}.\left(\dfrac{1}{r^3}-\dfrac{1}{R^3}\right. \\ -\dfrac{x.h^3.\text{tang}.\theta+\frac{1}{2}al.+\frac{1}{2}.h.l+\frac{1}{2}.a^2h.\sin.\theta.\cos\theta}{a^2+h^2} \end{array}\right\} \quad (5)$$

This equation combined with the equations (1), (4), will give the values of x, y, r. By making a first hypothesis for x, the equations (a) will give the corresponding values of r, and then the equation (5) will give y. Now if the value of x has been properly assumed, these values, when substituted in the equation (4) ought to satisfy it; if this equation is not satisfied, a second value of x should be taken, and so on. Hence the perehelion distance D, and the instant of the passage through the perehelion, may be determined.

In the second case, *i. e.*, if we have $l > b$, we must employ the equations (1), (3), and (4), and then the equation (2) will serve to veri y the values deduced from these equations.

Having by this means obtained the values of x, y, and r; let P be assumed

$$= \frac{x}{\cos.^2\theta}.\left\{y + h.\, x.\, \tan.\, \theta\right\} - Ry.\, \cos.\, (E-\alpha)$$

$$+ x.\left\{\frac{\sin.\, (E-\alpha)}{R} - (R'-1).\, \cos.\, (E-\alpha)\right\} - R.ax.\, \sin.\, (E-\alpha)$$

$$+ R.(R'-1).$$

The perihelion distance D of the comet will be determined by the equation

$$D = r - \tfrac{1}{2}.\, P^2;$$

the cosine of its anomaly v will be given by the equation

$$\cos.^2 \tfrac{1}{2}.v = \frac{D}{r};$$

and from this we infer, by the table of the motion of the comets, the time employed to describe the angle v. In order to obtain the instant of the passage through the perihelion, this time should be added to the epoch, if P is negative, and subtracted from it, if P is positive, because, in the first case, the comet approaches the perihelion, and in the second case, it moves from it.

Having thus determined very nearly the perihelion distance of the comet, and the instant of its passage through the perihelion, we can correct them by the following method, which has the advantage of being independent of an approximative knowledge of the other elements of the orbit.

An exact determination of the elements of the orbit, when we know very nearly the perihelion distance of the Comet, and the instant of its passage through the perihelion.

In the first place, three observations of the comet, at a considerable distance from each other, should be selected, and then from the perihelion distance of the comet, and from the instant of its passage through the perihelion, as data which are determined by what precedes, we compute three anomalies of the comet, and the radii vectores which correspond to the instants of the three observations. Let v, v', v'', represent these anomalies, (those which precede the passage through the perihelion being supposed negative); moreover, let r, r', r'', represent the corresponding radii vectores of the comet; $v'-v$, $v''-v$, will be the angles contained between r and r', and between r, and r''; let U be the first of these angles, and U' the second.

Likewise let α, α', α'', represent the three observed geocentrick longitudes of the comet, referred to a fixed equinox; θ, θ', θ'', its three geocentrick latitudes, the southern latitudes being supposed to be negative; let ϵ, ϵ', ϵ'', be its three corresponding heliocentrick longitudes; and ϖ, ϖ', ϖ'', its three heliocentrick latitudes, finally, let E, E', E'', be the three corresponding longitudes of the sun; and R, R', R'', its three distances from the centre of the earth.

Let us suppose that the letter S indicates the centre of the sun;

T that of the earth ; C the centre of the comet, and C', its projection on the plane of the ecliptic. The angle STC', is the difference of the geocentrick longitudes of the sun and of the comet; by adding the logarithm of the cosine of this angle, to the logarithm of the co-sine of the geocentrick latitude of the comet,* we will obtain the logarithm of the cosine of the angle STC; therefore in the triangle STC there will be given the side ST or R; the side SC or r, and the angle STC; we can thus by trigonometry obtain the angle CST. The heliocentrick latitude of the comet will then be obtained by means of the equation

$$\sin.\varpi = \frac{\sin.\theta.\sin.CST}{\sin.CTS}.\dagger$$

The angle TSC' is the side of a right angled spherical triangle, of which the hypothenuse is the angle TSC, and of which one of the sides is the angle ϖ; from which we can easily obtain the angle TSC', and consequently, the heliocentrick longitude ϵ of the comet.

In like manner, ϖ', ϵ', ϖ'', ϵ''; and the values of ϵ, ϵ', ϵ'', will determine whether the motion of the comet is direct or retrograde.

If we conceive the two arcs of latitude ϖ, ϖ', to meet in the pole of the ecliptic, they will make an angle equal to $\epsilon'-\epsilon$; and in the spherical triangle formed by this angle, and by the sides $\frac{\pi}{2}-\varpi$, and $\frac{\pi}{2}-\varpi'$,

* If E be the longitude of the sun, $STC'=\alpha-E$, and in the right angled spherical triangle, of which one side is the measure of $\alpha-E$, and the other side about the right angle the measure of θ, the hypothenuse will be equal to the measure of the angle at the earth between the sun and comet *i. e.* equal to STC, ∴ by Napier's rules we have $\cos.(\alpha-E).\cos.\theta=\cos.STC$.

† $\sin.CST:CTS:$ distance of comet from earth $: r :: \sin.\varpi : \sin.\theta$, ∴ $\sin.\varpi=\frac{\sin.\theta.\sin.CST}{\sin.CTS}$.

π being the semicircumference, the side opposite to the angle $\beta'—\beta$, will be the angle at the sun, contained between the radii vectores r and r'. It may be easily determined, by spherical trigonometry, or by the following formula:

$$\sin.^2 \tfrac{1}{2} V. = \cos.^2 \tfrac{1}{2}. (\varpi + \varpi') — \cos.^2 \tfrac{1}{2} (\beta' — \beta). \cos. \varpi. \cos. \varpi',^*$$

in which V represents this angle; so that if we name A, the angle of which the square of the sine is $\cos.^2 \tfrac{1}{2}.(\beta — \beta). \cos. \varpi. \cos. \varpi'$, and which can be readily derived from the tables, we shall obtain

$$\sin.^2 \tfrac{1}{2} V = \cos. (\tfrac{1}{2}\varpi + \tfrac{1}{2}\varpi' + A). \cos. (\tfrac{1}{2}\varpi + \tfrac{1}{2}\varpi' — A).$$

Naming in like manner V' the angle constituted by the two radii vectores r and r', we will have

$$\sin.^2 \tfrac{1}{2} V' = \cos. (\tfrac{1}{2}\varpi + \tfrac{1}{2}\varpi' + A'). \cos. (\tfrac{1}{2}\varpi + \tfrac{1}{2}\varpi' — A'),$$

A' being what A becomes, when ϖ' and β' are changed into ϖ'' and β''. Now, if the perihelion distance of the comet, and the moment of its passage through the perihelion were accurately determined, and if the

* This expression may be easily derived from the known formulæ of spherical trigonometry, for if we assume $B = (\beta' — \beta)$; $C = \frac{\pi}{2} — \varpi$; $C' = \frac{\pi}{2} — \varpi'$; we shall have, cos. B

$$= \frac{\cos V — \cos. C. \cos. C'}{\sin. C. \sin. C'}; \therefore 1 — \cos. B = 2 \sin.^2 \frac{1}{2}. B$$

$$= \frac{\sin C. \sin. C' — \cos. V + \cos C. \cos. C'}{\sin C. \sin. C'} = \frac{\cos. (C — C') — \cos V}{\sin. C. \sin. C'};$$

$\therefore 2 \sin.^2 \tfrac{1}{2} B. \sin C. \sin. C' = \cos. (C—C') — \cos. V = 2 \sin.^2 \tfrac{1}{2}. V — 2 \sin.^2 \tfrac{1}{2} (C — C')$, and since $\sin.^2 \tfrac{1}{2} B = 1 — \cos.^2 \tfrac{1}{2} B$; and $\sin.^2 \tfrac{1}{2} (C — C') = \sin.^2 \tfrac{1}{2} (C + C') — \sin. C. \sin. C$, we shall have $(2 — 2 \cos.^2 \tfrac{1}{2}. B). \sin. C. \sin. C' = 2 \sin.^2 \tfrac{1}{2} V — 2 \sin.^2 \tfrac{1}{2} (C + C) + 2. \sin. C. \sin. C'$. $\therefore \sin.^2 \tfrac{1}{2} V = \sin. \tfrac{1}{2} (C + C') — \cos.^2 \tfrac{1}{2} B. \sin. C. \sin. C'$; which will give the expression in the text when their values are substituted for B, C, C'.

observations were rigorous, we would have

$$V = U; \ V' = U;$$

but as this can never be the case, we will suppose

$$m = U - V; \ m' = U' - V'.$$

(It is to be observed here, that the computation of the triangle STC, gives for the angle CST two different* values. Most frequently, the nature of the cometary motion will make known which of them ought to be employed, especially if these two values are very different; for then one of them will place the comet farther than the other from the earth, and it will be easy to determine, by the apparent motion of the comet at the instant of observation, which ought to be selected. But any uncertainty which remains on this account may be removed, by taking care to select that value which renders V and V' very little different from U and U'.)

Then we will make a second hypothesis, in which the instant of the transit through the perihelion remaining the same as before the perihelion distance varies by a small quantity; .*e g.* by a five hundreth part of its value, and then we seek in this hypothesis the values of $U - V$, and of $U' - V'$; let then

$$n = U - V; \ n' = U - V'.$$

Finally, we make a third supposition in which, the distance of the perihelion remaining the same as in the first hypothesis, we make to vary by half of a day, more or less, the instant of the passage through the perihelion. And then let the values of $U - V$, and of $U' - V'$ be investigated on this new hypothesis. Let in this case

$$p = U - V; \ p' = U' - V'.$$

This being premised, if u represents the number by which the sup-

* The values of CST, are CST, and $180 - 2\,STC - CST$.

posed variation in the perihelion distance should be multiplied, in order to obtain the true distance, and t the number by which the supposed variation in the instant of the passage through the perihelion should be multiplied, in order to obtain the true instant; we shall have the two following equations,

$$(m-n).\ u+(m-p).\ t=m;$$
$$(m'-n').\ u+(m'-p').\ t=m';$$

by means of which equations we obtain the values of u and of t, and consequently the corrected distance of the perihelion, and true instant of the passage of the comet through the perihelion.

The preceding corrections suppose that the elements determined by the first approximation, are sufficiently accurate to enable us to treat their errors as indefinitely small. Both if the second approximation does not appear to be sufficient, we must recur to a third, by operating on the elements already corrected, as we have done on their first values; it is solely necessary in addition to secure that they undergo small variations. It will also suffice to compute by these corrected elements the values of $U-V$, and of $U'-V'$; by representing them by M and N, and substituting them in place of m and m', in the second members of the two preceding equations; we shall have by this means two new equations which will give the values of u and of t, relative to the corrections of these new elements.*

Having by this method obtained the accurate distance of the peri-

* If in place of computing U, U', V, V', on the three hypothesis mentioned in the text, they were computed on the five following hypotheses, 1st, with the elements found in the first approximation; 2dly, by making the perihelion distance to vary by a very small quantity; 3dly, by making it to vary by twice the same quantity; 4thly, the same perihelion distance as in the first hypothesis being preserved, by making the instant of the passage

helion, and the true instant of the passage of the comet through the perihelion; the other elements of the orbit may be inferred in the following manner.

Let j be the longitude of the node which will be the ascending one, if the motion of the comet be direct, and φ the inclination of the orbit; we shall obtain by a comparison of the first and last observation,

$$\tan. j = \frac{\tan. \varpi. \sin. \beta'' - \tan. \varpi''. \sin. \beta}{\tan. \varpi. \cos. \beta'' - \tan. \varpi''. \cos. \beta};^{*}$$

$$\tan. \varphi = \frac{\tan. \varpi''}{\sin. (\beta'' - j)}.$$

As we can thus compare two by two, the three observations, it

through the perehelion to vary by a very small quantity; 5thly, by making the same instant to vary by twice this quantity. Let m, m', m'', m''', m'''', be the values of $U-V$; n, n', n'', n''', n'''', the values of $U'-V'$; in order to determine in this case the value of $\dot{n}$, and t, the two following equations should be formed

$$(4m'-3m-m'')u+(m''-2m'+m)u^2+(4m'''-3m-m'''').t$$
$$+(m''''-2m'''-m)t^2=2m;\ (4n'-3n-n'').u+)n''-2n'+n).u^2$$
$$+(4n'''-3n-n'''').\,t+(n''''2n'''+n).t^2=2n.$$

The values of u and of t which satisfy those equations, are much more precise than the preceding. Although this precision is for the most part unnecessary, it is however indispensably necessary to form these equations, when the terms depending on the second differences will be of the same order as those which depend on the first differences, as for instance, when the radius vector is very nearly at right angles to the visual ray from the earth to the comet; in which case the angle SCT is very nearly equal to a right angle; on the other hand, if SCT was $= 45°$, the two values of SCT would be very nearly equal.

* Let I be the inclination of the orbit to the plane of the ecliptic, and we shall have

$$\text{rad. sin.}\ (\beta - j) = \cot. I. \tan. \varpi = \text{rad. sin.}\ (\beta'' - j) = \cot. I. \text{tang.}\ \varpi''.\ \text{therefore}$$

will be more exact to select those which give to the preceding fractions, the greatest numerators and the greatest denominators.

Tan. j may appertain to the two angles j and $j+\pi$, j being the smallest of the positive angles to which its value belongs; in order to determine which of these two angles we ought to select, it may be observed that φ is positive and less than a right angle; and that thus sin. $(\text{ϐ}''-j)$ must have the same sign as tan. ϖ''. This condition determines the angle j, and this angle will give the position of the ascending node, if the motion of the comet is direct; but if its motion be retrograde, we should add two right angles to the angle j, in order to have the position of this node.

The hypothenuse of the spherical triangle of which $\text{ϐ}''-j$ and ϖ'' are the sides, is the distance of the comet, from its ascending node in the third observation; and the difference between v'' and this hypothenuse is the interval between the node and the perihelion, reckoned on the orbit.

If we wish to give to the cometary theory all the precision which the observations admit of, it ought to be established on a comparison of all the best observations, which can be effected in the following manner: denoting by one, two strokes, &c. the letters m, n, p, relative to the second observation, to the third, &c. compared all with the first observation, we shall form the following equations,

$$(m-n).\,u+(m-p).\,t=m;$$

$$(m'-n').\,u+(m'-p').\,t=m';$$

$$(m''-n'').\,u+(m''-p'').\,t=m'';$$

&c.

$\frac{\sin.\text{ϐ}.\cos.j-\cos.\text{ϐ}.\sin.j}{\tan.\varpi}=\frac{\sin.\text{ϐ}''.\cos.j-\cos.\text{ϐ}''.\sin.j}{\tan.\varpi''}$; ∴ dividing by cos. j. we have $\frac{\sin.\text{ϐ}-\cos.\text{ϐ}.\tan.j}{\tan.\varpi}=\frac{\sin.\text{ϐ}''-\cos.\text{ϐ}''.\tan.j}{\tan.\varpi''}$, hence we derive the expression for tan. j, which is given in the text.

If then these equations be combined in the most advantageous manner, in order to determine u and t, we will have the corrections of the perihelion distance, and of the instant of the transit through the perihelion deduced from all the observations compared together. From these values, we can deduce the values of β, β', β'', &c. ϖ, ϖ', ϖ'', &c., and we shall have

$$\tan. j=\frac{\tan.\varpi.(\sin.\beta'+\sin.\beta''+\&c.)-\sin.\beta.(\tan.\varpi'+\tan.\varpi''+\&c.)}{\tan.\varpi.(\cos.\beta'+\cos.\beta''+\&c.)-\cos.\beta.(\tan.\varpi'+\tan.\varpi''+\&c.)}\;;\,*$$

$$\tan.\varphi=\frac{\tan.\varpi'+\tan.\varpi''+\&c.}{\sin.(\beta'-j)+\sin.(\beta''-j)+\&c.}.$$

38. There is a case, of rare occurrence indeed, in which the orbit of a comet can be determined in a rigorous and simple manner; namely, when the comet has been observed in the two nodes. The right line which joins these two observed positions, passes then through the centre of the sun, and coincides with the line of the nodes. The length of this line can be determined by the time which intervenes between the two observations; T representing this time reduced to decimals of a day, and c denoting the right line in question, we shall have, by N°. 27,

$$c=\tfrac{1}{2}\sqrt{\frac{T^2}{(9^d,688724)^2}}.$$

Now let β be the heliocentrick longitude of the comet, at the instant of the first observation; and r its radius vector, ρ its distance from the earth, and α its geocentrick longitude. Also let R be the radius of the orbit of the earth, and E the corresponding longitude of the sun at the same instant; we shall have

* By composition of ratios we obtain these values of $\tan. j$, $\tan.\varphi$, which are more accurate than the preceding.

$$r.\sin.\,\epsilon = \rho.\sin.\,\alpha - R.\sin.\,E;$$

$$r.\cos.\,\epsilon = \rho.\cos.\,\alpha - R.\cos.\,E.$$

$\pi+\epsilon$ will be the heliocentrick longitude of the comet, at the instant of the second observation; and if we denote by one stroke the quantities r, α, ρ, R and E, relative to the same instant, we shall have

$$r'.\sin.\,\epsilon = R'.\sin\,E' - \rho'.\sin.\,\alpha'.$$
$$r'.\cos.\,\epsilon = R'.\cos.\,E' - \rho'.\cos.\,\alpha'.$$

These four equations give

$$\tan.\,\epsilon = \frac{\rho.\sin.\,\alpha - R.\sin.\,E}{\rho.\cos.\,\alpha - R.\cos.\,E} = \frac{\rho'.\sin.\,\alpha'. - R'.\sin.\,E'}{\rho'.\cos.\,\alpha' - R'.\cos.\,E'};$$

hence we obtain

$$\rho' = \frac{RR'.\sin.\,(E-E') - R.\rho.\sin.\,(\alpha-E')}{\rho.\sin.\,(\alpha'-\alpha) - R.\sin.\,(\alpha'-E)}.$$

We have afterwards

$$(r+r').\sin.\,\epsilon = \rho.\sin.\,\alpha - \rho'.\sin.\,\alpha' - R.\sin.\,E + R'.\sin.\,E'.$$

$$(r+r').\cos.\,\epsilon = \rho.\cos.\,\alpha - \rho'.\cos.\,\alpha' - R.\cos.\,E + R'.\cos.\,E'.$$

By squaring these two equations, and adding them together, we shall obtain, (c being substituted in place of $r+r'$)

$$\begin{aligned} c^2 = {} & R^2 - 2RR'.\cos.\,(E'-E) + R'^2 \\ & + 2\rho.(R'.\cos.\,(\alpha-E') - R.\cos.\,(\alpha-E)) \\ & + 2\rho'.(R.\cos.\,(\alpha'-E) - R'.\cos.\,(\alpha'-E')) \\ & + \rho^2 - 2\rho\rho'.\cos.\,(\alpha'-\alpha) + \rho'^2. \end{aligned}$$

If in this equation, we substitute instead of ρ' its preceding values given in terms of ρ, we shall have an equation in ρ of the fourth degree, which can be resolved by the known methods; but it will be simpler to suppose ρ equal to some given value, to infer from it the value of ρ', then to substitute these values in the preceding equation, and see whether they satisfy it. A few trials will serve to determine with accuracy, ρ and ρ'.

By means of these quantities we can obtain c, r and r'. And v representing the angle which the radius r makes with the perihelion distance denoted by D; $\pi - v$ will be the angle formed by this same distance, and by the radius r', thus we will obtain by No. 23,

$$r = \frac{D}{\cos.^2\frac{1}{2}v}; \quad r' = \frac{D}{\sin.^2\frac{1}{2}v};$$

consequently*

$$\tan.^2\tfrac{1}{2}v = \frac{r}{r'}; \quad D = \frac{rr'}{r+r'}.$$

Therefore we shall have v the anomaly of the comet at the instant of the first observation, and its perihelion distance D, hence it is easy to infer the position of the perihelion, and the instant of the passage of the comet through this point. Thus, of the five elements of the orbit of the comet, four are known, namely, the perihelion distance, the position of the perihelion, the instant of the transit of the comet through this point, and the position of the node. It only remains to find out the inclination of the orbit; but for this purpose it will be necessary to recur to a third observation, which will also be useful in indicating amongst the different real and positive roots of the equation in ρ, that of which we ought to make use.

38. The hypothesis of the parabolick motion of the comets, is not rigorously true, it is even very improbable, considering the infinite number of cases which give an elliptic or a hyperbolic motion, relatively to those which determine a parabolic motion. Besides, a comet which moves

* Dividing r and its value by r' and its value respectively, we have $\frac{r}{r'} = \frac{\sin.^2\frac{1}{2}v}{\cos.^2\frac{1}{2}v}\cdot\frac{D}{D}$, and also we have $\frac{1}{r} + \frac{1}{r'} = \frac{r'+r}{rr'} = \frac{1}{D}$.

in either a parabolic or an hyperbolick orbit, would be only visible once; therefore we may with great appearance of probability suppose, that the comets which describe these curves, if any such ever existed, have long since disappeared, so that at the present day, we only observe those, which moving in orbits returning into themselves, are perpetually brought back, after greater or less intervals, into the regions of space, near to the sun. We can by the following method, determine nearly within an interval of some years, the duration of their revolutions, when we shall have made a great number of very accurate observations before and after the passage through the perihelion.

For this purpose, let us suppose that we had four or a greater number of accurate observations, which may embrace all the visible part of the orbit, and that we have determined by the preceding method, the parabola, which satisfies very nearly these observations. Let v, v', v'', v''', &c., be the corresponding anomalies, r, r', r'', r''', &c., the corresponding radii vectores. Let also

$$v'-v=U;\ v''-v=U';\ v'''-v=U'';\ \&c.;$$

this being agreed upon, we compute by the preceding method, with the parabola already found, the values of U, U', U'', &c., V, V', V'', &c.; let

$$m=U-V;\ m'=U'-V';\ m''=U''-V'';\ m'''=U'''-V''';\ \&c.$$

Afterwards, suppose the perihelion distance in this parabola, to vary by a very small quantity; and let in this hypothesis,

$$n=U-V;\ n'=U'-V';\ n''=U''-V'';\ n'''=U'''-V''';\ \&c.$$

We then make a third hypothesis, in which the same distance of the perihelion being preserved, as in the first, the instant of the passage through the perihelion is varied by a very small quantity; let then

$$p=U-V;\ p'=U'-V';\ p''=U''-V'';\ p'''=U'''-V''';\ \&c.$$

Finally, we will compute with the perihelion distance, and the instant of the passage of the comet through the perihelion of the first hypothesis, the angle v, and the radius vector r, on the hypothesis that the orbit is elliptic, and that the difference $1 - e$ between its excentricity, and unity, is equal to a very small quantity, for example, to a 50th part. In order to obtain the value of the angle v on this hypothesis, it will suffice, by No. 23, to add to the anomaly v, computed in the parabola of the first hypothesis, a small angle of which the sine is

$$\tfrac{1}{10}.\ (1 - e).\ \text{tang.}\ \tfrac{1}{2}v.\ (4 - 3.\ \cos.^2\tfrac{1}{2}v - 6.\ \cos.^4\tfrac{1}{2}v).^*$$

By substituting then in the equation

$$r = \frac{D}{\cos.^2\frac{1}{2}v}.\left\{1 - \frac{(1-e)}{2}\ .\ \tan.^2\tfrac{1}{2}v\right\};$$

in place of v, this anomaly thus computed in the ellipse; we will obtain the corresponding radius vector. In a similar manner we can compute, v', r', v'', r'', v''', r''', &c.; by means of which we can obtain the values of U, U', U'', U''', &c., and by No. 37, those of V, V', V'', &c. Let in this case

$$q = U - V;\ q' = U' - V';\ q'' = U'' - V'';\ q''' = U''' - V''';\ \&c.$$

Lastly, let u denote the number by which we must multiply the supposed variation in the distance of the perihelion, in order to obtain the true distance; and t the number by which the supposed variation in the instant of the transit through the perihelion must be multiplied. in order to obtain the true instant; and s the number by which the

* When the orbit is supposed elliptic, we must have at least four observations; and then if the arc observed be considerable, and particularly if it is greater than 90°, the ellipticity will be very sensible, and the periodic time may be determined with tolerable precision, if the four observations be made with all the precision of modern observations. If the square of α be neglected, the expression for r will be $\frac{D}{\cos.^2\frac{1}{2}v}\left(1 - \frac{\alpha}{2-\alpha}\ .\ \tan.^2 v\right)$ which becomes the expression in the text when $1-e$ is substituted for α.

supposed value of $1-e$ must be multiplied, in order to obtain the accurate value, we will thus form the following equations,

$$(m-n).\ u+(m-p).\ t+(m-q).\ s=m$$
$$(m'-n').\ u+(m'-p').\ t+(m'-q').\ s=m'$$
$$(m''-n'').\ u+(m''-p'').\ t+(m''-q'').\ s=m''$$
$$(m'''-n''').\ u+(m'''-p''').\ t+(m'''-q''').\ s=m''';$$
&c.

The values of u, t, s, may be determined by means of these equations, from which we can infer the true distance of the perihelion, the true instant of the transit of the comet through the perihelion, and the true value of $1-e$. Let D be the perihelion distance, and a the semiaxis major of the orbit; we shall have $a=\frac{D}{1-e}$; the time of the comets sidereal revolution will be expressed by a number of sidereal years, equal to $a^{\frac{3}{2}}$, or to $\left(\frac{D}{1-e}\right)^{\frac{3}{2}}$, the mean distance of the sun from the earth being taken for unity. Afterwards by N°. 37, we shall get the inclination of the orbit, and the position of the node.

Whatever be the precision of the observations, they will always leave some uncertainty as to the duration of the comets revolution. The most exact method to determine it, consists in comparing the observations of a comet, in two consecutive revolutions; but this means is not practicable, except when the lapse of time brings the comet back towards its perihelion.*

CHAPTER V.

General methods for determining, by successive approximations, the motions of the heavenly bodies.

40. In the first approximation of the motions of the heavenly bodies, we have only considered the principal forces which actuate them, and from thence the laws of the elliptic motion have been deduced. We will consider, in the following investigations, the forces which disturb this motion. In consequence of the action of these forces, it is only requisite to add small terms to the differential equations of the elliptic motion, of which we have previously determined the finite integrals: it is necessary now to determine, by successive approximations, the integrals of the same equations, increased by the terms which arise from the action of the disturbing forces. For this object, we here subjoin a general method, which is applicable whatever be the number and the degree of the differential equations, of which it is proposed to find the perpetually approaching integrals.

Let us suppose that we have between the n variables y, y', y'', &c. and the variable t, of which the element dt may be considered as constant, the n differerential equations

$$0=\frac{d^iy}{dt^i}+P+\alpha Q;$$

$$0=\frac{d^iy'}{dt^i}+P'+\alpha Q';$$

&c.

P, Q, P', Q', &c. being functions of t, y, y', &c.; and of their differences continued to the order $i-1$ inclusively, and α being a very small constant coefficient, which, in the theory of the celestial motions, is of the order of the disturbing forces. Let us in the next place suppose that we have obtained the finite integrals of these equations, when Q, Q', &c. vanish; by differencing each, $i-1$ times in succession, they will constitute with their differentials, in equations by means of which we can determine by elimination, the arbitrary quantities c, c', c'', &c. in functions of t, y, y', y'', &c. and of their differentials to the order $i-1$. Therefore, if V, V', V'', &c. represent these functions, we shall have*

$$c=V;\; c'=V';\; c''=V'';\; \&c.$$

These equations are the in integrals of the order $i-1$, which the differential equations ought to have, and which their finite integrals furnish by the elimination of the differences of these variables.

Now, by differentiating the preceding integrals of the order $i-1$, we shall have

$$0=dV;\; 0=dV';\; 0=dV'';\; \&c.$$

but it is evident that these last equations being differentials of the order i, without involving arbitrary quantities; they can be no other than the sums of the equations

$$0=\frac{d^iy}{dt^i}+P;\; 0=\frac{d^iy'}{dt^i}+P';\; \&c.$$

HH 2

* In *every* differential equation of the order i, the number of *first* integrals is equal to i, these integrals are of the order $i-1$, and therefore they only contain the $i-1$ differential coefficients $\frac{dy}{dt}$, $\frac{d^2y}{dt^2}$ ...... $\frac{d^{i-1}y}{d^{i-1}t}$; and if these could be eliminated we would have the 1th integral, or the primitive equation, which corresponds to the proposed differential equation; consequently, if we have n differential equations, the number of first integrals, or of integrals of the order $i-1$, must be in, from which if the differential coefficients of the variables y, y', y'', &c. could be eliminated we would obtain the n finite integrals of the proposed equations.

multiplied respectively by suitable factors, in order that these sums may be exact differences; therefore representing the factors which ought to multiply these equations respectively in order to form the equation $dV = 0$, by Fdt, $F'dt$, &c., and in like manner, representing by Hdt, $H'dt$, &c. the factors which ought respectively to multiply the same equations, in order to constitute the equation $0 = dV'$; and so of the rest, we shall have

$$dV = F.dt.\left\{\frac{d^iy}{dt^i} + P\right\} + F'.dt.\left\{\frac{d^iy'}{dt^i} + P'\right\} + \&c.;$$

$$dV' = H.dt.\left\{\frac{d^iy}{dt^i} + P\right\} + H'.dt.\left\{\frac{d^iy'}{dt^i} + P'\right\} + \&c.;$$

F, F', &c. H, H', &c. are functions of t, y, y', y'', &c. and of their differences to the order $i-1$: it is easy to determine them, when V, V', &c. are known; for F is evidently the coefficient of $\frac{d^iy}{dt^i}$, in the differential of V; F' is the coefficient of $\frac{d^iy'}{dt^i}$, in the same differential, and so on of the rest. In like manner, H, H', &c. are the coefficients of $\frac{d^iy}{dt^i}$, $\frac{d^iy'}{dt^i}$, &c. in the differential of V'; consequently, as the functions of V, V', &c. are supposed to be known, by differencing them solely with respect to $\frac{d^{i-1}y}{dt^{i-1}}$, $\frac{d^{i-1}y'}{dt^{i-1}}$, &c. we will obtain the factors by which the differential equations

$$0 = \frac{d^iy}{dt^i} + P; \quad 0 = \frac{d^iy'}{dt^i} + P'; \quad \&c.$$

should be multiplied in order to obtain the exact differences; this being premised, let us resume the differential equations

$$0 = \frac{d^iy}{dt^i} + P + \alpha.Q; \quad 0 = \frac{d^iy'}{dt^i} + P' + \alpha Q'; \quad \&c.$$

The first being multiplied by Fdt, the second by $F'dt$, and so of the rest, and then added together, will give

$$0 = dV + \alpha.dt.(FQ + F'Q' + \text{\&c.});$$

in like manner will have,

$$0 = dV' + \alpha.dt.(HQ + H'Q' + \text{\&c.});$$
&c.

hence we obtain by integrating,

$$c - \alpha.\int dt.(FQ + F'Q' + \text{\&c.}) = V;$$
$$c' - \alpha.\int dt.(HQ + H'Q' + \text{\&c.}) = V';$$
&c.;

we will have by this means in differential equations which will be of the same form as when Q, Q', &c. are equal to nothing, with this sole difference, that the arbitrary quantities, c, c', c'', &c. must be changed into

$$c - \alpha.\int dt.(FQ + F'Q' + \text{\&c.}); \; c' - \alpha.\int dt.(HQ + H'Q' + \text{\&c.}); \; \text{\&c.}$$

Now if, on the hypothesis of Q, Q', &c. equal to zero, we eliminate from the in integrals of the order $i-1$, the differences of the variables y, y', &c.; we shall have the n finite integrals of the proposed equations; consequently, the integrals of the same equations, when Q, Q', &c. do not vanish, will be had, by changing in the first integrals c, c', &c. into

$$c - \alpha.\int dt.(FQ + F'Q' + \text{\&c.}); \; c' - \alpha.\int dt.(HQ + H'Q' + \text{\&c.})$$

41. If the differentials

$$dt.(FQ + FQ' + \text{\&c.}), \; dt.(HQ + H'Q' + \text{\&c.}) \; \text{\&c.}$$

were exact, we could obtain by the preceding method the finite integrals of the proposed differential equations; but this does not obtain except in some particular cases, of which the most extensive and the most interesting, is that in which these equations are linear. Let us, therefore, suppose that P, P', &c. are linear functions of y, y', &c. and of their differences to the order $i-1$, without any term independent of these variables, and at first let us consider the case, in which Q, Q', &c. vanish. The differential equations being linear, their successive integrals will be also linear, so that $c = V$, $c' = V'$, being the in integrals of the order $i-1$, of the differential linear equations

$$0 = \frac{d^i y}{dt^i} + P; \quad 0 = \frac{d^i y'}{dt^i} + P'; \text{ \&c.}$$

V, V', &c. may be considered as linear functions of y, y', &c. and of their differences, to the order $i-1$. In order to demonstrate this, let us suppose, that in the expressions of y, y', &c. the constant arbitrary quantity c is equal to a determinate quantity, added to an indeterminate δc; the constant quantity c', is equal to a determinate quantity added to the indeterminate, $\delta c'$, &c.; these expressions being reduced into series, arranged with respect to the powers and products of δc, $\delta c'$, &c., we will have by the formula of No. 21,

$$y = Y + \delta c.\left(\frac{dY}{dc}\right) + \delta c'.\left(\frac{dY}{dc'}\right) + \text{\&c.}$$
$$+ \frac{\delta c^2}{1.2}.\left(\frac{d^2 Y}{dc^2}\right) + \text{\&c.};$$

$$y' = Y' + \delta c.\left(\frac{dY'}{dc}\right) + \delta c'.\left(\frac{dY'}{dc'}\right) + \text{\&c.}$$
$$+ \frac{\delta c^2}{1.2}.\left(\frac{d^2 Y'}{dc^2}\right) + \text{\&c.};$$

&c.

Y, Y', $\left(\frac{dY}{dc}\right)$, &c. being functions of t, without arbitrary quantities. By substituting these values in the proposed differential equations, it is manifest that δc, $\delta c'$, &c. being indeterminate, the coefficients of the first powers of each of them, must vanish in those different equations; but these equations being linear, we shall have evidently the terms affected with the first powers of δc, $\delta c'$, &c., by substituting $\left(\frac{dY}{dc}\right).\delta c+\left(\frac{dY'}{dc'}\right).\delta c'+$ &c. in place of y, &c. $\left(\frac{dY'}{dc'}\right).\delta c+\left(\frac{dY'}{dc'}\right).\delta c'+$ &c. in place of y', &c. These expressions of y, y', &c. satisfy separately the proposed differential equations; and as they contain the in arbitrary quantities δc, $\delta c'$, &c. they are their complete integrals. Therefore it follows that the arbitrary quantities exist in a linear form, in the expressions of y, y', &c. and consequently also, in their differentials; hence it is easy to infer that the variables y, y', &c. and their differences may be supposed to exist in a linear form, in the successive integrals of the proposed differential equations.

It follows from what has been stated that F, F', &c. being the coefficients of $\frac{d^iy}{dt^i}$, $\frac{d^iy'}{dt^i}$, &c. in the differential of V, H, H' &c. being the coefficients of the same differences, in the differential of V'; and so of the rest; these quantities are functions of the sole variable t. Therefore, if we suppose Q, Q', &c. to be functions of t only, the differences $dt.(FQ+F'Q'+\text{&c.})$; $dt.(HQ+H'Q'+\text{&c.})$; will be exact.

From the above results a simple means of obtaining the integrals of any number n of linear differential equations of the order i, and which involve any terms αQ, $\alpha Q'$, &c. which are functions of the sole variable t; when we know how to integrate the same equations, in the case in which these terms vanish; for then, if we difference their n finite integrals, $i-1$ times in succession, we shall have in equations which will give by elimination, the values of the in arbitrary quantities c, c', &c., in functions of t, y, y', &c., and of the differences of these variable quantities to the order $i-1$. We will thus form, the in equations, $c=V$, $c'=V'$, &c.; this being premised, F, F', &c. will be the coefficients of $\frac{d^{i-1}y}{dt^{i-1}}$, $\frac{d^{i-1}y'}{dt^{i-1}}$, &c., in V; H, H', &c., will be the coefficients of the same differences in V', and so of the rest; therefore, we will obtain the finite integrals of the linear differential equations,

$$0=\frac{d^2y}{dt^2}+P+\alpha.Q\,;\ 0=\frac{d^2y'}{dt^2}+P'+\alpha.Q\,;\ \&c.,$$

by changing in the finite integrals of these equations deprived of their last terms αQ, $\alpha Q'$, &c., the arbitrary quantities c, c', &c., into $c-\alpha.\int dt.(FQ+F'Q'+\&c.)$, $c'-\alpha.\int dt.(HQ+H'Q'+\&c.)$; &c.

Let us, for example, consider the linear differential equation

$$0=\frac{d^2y}{dt^2}+a^2y+\alpha.Q.$$

The finite integral of the equation $0=\frac{d^2y}{dt^2}+a^2y$ is

$$y=\frac{c}{a}.\ \sin.\, at+\frac{c'}{a}.\ \cos.\, at\,;$$

c and c' being arbitrary quantities. By differentiating this integral we obtain

$$\frac{dy}{dt}=c.\ \cos.\, at-c'.\ \sin.\, at.$$

If this differential be combined with the integral itself, we can form two integrals of the first order,

$$c=ay.\ \sin.\, at+\frac{dy}{dt}.\ \cos.\, at\,;$$

$$c'=ay.\ \cos.\, at-\frac{dy}{dt}.\ \sin.\, at\,;$$

thus we shall have in this case,

$$F=\cos.\, at\,;\ H=-\sin.\, at\,;$$

therefore, the complete integral of the proposed will be

$$y = \frac{c}{a} . \sin. at + \frac{c'}{a} . \cos. at - \frac{\alpha . \sin. at}{a} . \int Q. dt. \cos. at +$$

$$\frac{\alpha . \cos. at}{a} . \int Q.dt. \sin. at.$$

It is easy to perceive that if Q is composed of terms of the form $K. \begin{matrix}\sin.\\ \cos.\end{matrix} (mt + \epsilon)$, each of these terms will produce in the value of y, the corresponding term

$$\frac{\alpha K}{m^2 - a^2} . \begin{matrix}\sin.\\ \cos.\end{matrix} (mt + \epsilon)^*$$

* If Q be of the form $\sin. (mt + \epsilon)$ then we shall have $-\int Q.dt. \cos. at = -\int \sin.(mt + \epsilon). dt. \cos. at$, which by partial integration becomes

$$\frac{1}{a} . \sin. (mt + \epsilon). \sin. at - \frac{m}{a} . \int \cos.(mt + \epsilon). \sin. at.dt. (= -\frac{m}{a^2} . \cos. (mt + \epsilon). \cos. at$$

$$-\frac{m^2}{a^2} . \int \sin. (mt + \epsilon). \cos. at.dt. \left(= \frac{m^2}{a^3} . \sin. (mt + \epsilon). \sin. at - \frac{m^3}{a^3} . \int \cos.(mt + \epsilon) \sin. at.dt. \right)$$

$$\left(= -\frac{m^3}{a^4} . \cos.(mt + \epsilon). \cos. at - \frac{m^4}{a^4} . \int \sin.(mt + \epsilon). \cos. at.dt. \right) =$$

$$\frac{m^4}{a^5} . \sin.)mt + \epsilon). \sin. at - \frac{m^5}{a^5} . \int \cos. (mt + \epsilon). \sin. at.dt;$$

now if the factors of $\sin. at$, and of $\cos. at$, be collected respectively, we shall obtain

$$-\frac{\alpha . \sin. at}{a} . \int \sin. (mt + \epsilon). \cos. at.dt = \sin. (mt + \epsilon). \sin.^2 at. \alpha. (a^{-2} + a^{-4}.m^2 + a^{-6}.m^4 + \&c.)$$

$$- \cos. (mt + \epsilon). \sin. at. \cos. at. \alpha. (a^{-3}.m + a^{-5}.m^3 + a^{-7}.m^5 + \&c.)$$

and if the term $\int. \sin. (mt + \epsilon). \sin. at.dt$, be expanded into a series by a similar process we shall have

$$\frac{\alpha . \cos. at}{a} . \int. \sin. (mt + \epsilon). \sin. at.dt = \sin. (mt + \epsilon). \cos.^2 at. \alpha.$$

$$(a^{-2} + a^{-4}.m^2 + a^{-6}.m^4 + \&c.) + \cos. (mt + \epsilon). \sin. at. \cos. at. a. (a^{-3}m + a.^{-5}.m^3 + a^{-7}.m^5 + \&c.)$$

If m is equal to a, the term $K.\begin{smallmatrix}\sin.\\ \cos.\end{smallmatrix}(mt+\epsilon)$ will produce in y, 1st, the term $-\frac{\alpha K}{4a^2}.\begin{smallmatrix}\sin.\\ \cos.\end{smallmatrix}(at+\epsilon)$, which being comprized in the two terms $\frac{c}{a}.\sin.at+\frac{c'}{a}.\cos.at$, may be neglected; 2dly, the term $\pm\frac{\alpha Kt}{2a}.\begin{smallmatrix}\cos.\\ \sin.\end{smallmatrix}(at+\epsilon)$, the sign + obtaining, if the term of the expression of Q is a sine, and the sign — having place,* if this term is a cosine. It appears from what has been stated above, how the arc t is produced without the signs of sine or cosine, in the values of y, y', &c. by the

∴ adding these two expressions, and observing that $a^{-2}+a^{-4}.m^2+a^{-6}.m^4+$ &c. $=\frac{1}{a^2-m^2}$, we shall arrive at the expression given in the text.

* The parts under the sign of integration in this case are respectively $\int.\sin.(at+\epsilon).\cos.at.dt$, $\int.\sin.(at+\epsilon).\sin.at.dt) = \int.\sin.at.\cos.at.\cos.\epsilon.dt + \int.\cos.^2at.dt.\sin.\epsilon$, $\int.\sin.^2at.\cos.\epsilon.dt + \int.\sin.at.\cos.at\sin.\epsilon.dt$, and these expressions are $=\frac{1}{2}\int.\sin.2.at.\cos.\epsilon.dt+\frac{1}{2}\int.\cos.2at.\sin.\epsilon.dt+\frac{1}{2}\int\sin.\epsilon.dt$, and $-\frac{1}{2}\int.\cos.2at.\cos.\epsilon.dt+\frac{1}{2}\int.\cos.\epsilon.dt+\frac{1}{2}\int.\sin.2.at.\sin.\epsilon.dt$, and by integrating these expressions become $\frac{-1}{4a}.\cos.2at.\cos.\epsilon+\frac{1}{4a}.\sin.2at.\sin.\epsilon+\frac{1}{2}.\sin.\epsilon.t$, $-\frac{1}{4a}.\sin.2at.\cos.\epsilon+\frac{1}{2}\cos.\epsilon.t-\frac{1}{4a}.\cos.2.at.\sin.\epsilon$, and if the three first terms be multiplied by $-\frac{\alpha.\sin.at}{a}$, and the three last by $\frac{\alpha.\cos.at}{a}$ they become respectively

$+\frac{\alpha}{4a^2}.\sin.at.\cos.2at.\cos.\epsilon-\frac{\alpha}{4a^2}.\sin.2at.\sin.at.\sin.\epsilon-\frac{\alpha}{2a}.\sin.at.\sin.\epsilon.t-\frac{\alpha}{4a^2}.\sin.2at.\cos.at.\cos.\epsilon+\frac{\alpha}{2a}.\cos.at.\cos.\epsilon.t-\frac{\alpha}{4a^2}.\cos.at.\cos.2at.\sin.\epsilon=$ $+\frac{\alpha}{4a^2}.\sin.at.(\cos.2at.\cos.\epsilon-\sin.2at.\sin.\epsilon)-\frac{\alpha}{4a^2}.\cos.at.(\sin.2at.\cos\epsilon+\cos.2at.\sin.\epsilon)+\frac{\alpha}{2a}.(\cos.at.\cos.\epsilon-\sin.at.\sin.\epsilon)=\frac{\alpha}{4a^2}.\sin.at.\cos.(2at+\epsilon)-\cos.at.\sin.(2at+\epsilon))=\frac{-\alpha}{4a^2}.\sin.(at+\epsilon)+\frac{\alpha t}{2a}.\cos.(at+\epsilon)$.

successive integrations, although the differential equations do not contain it under this form. It is evident that this will be the case as often as the functions FQ, $F'Q'$, &c. HQ, $H'Q'$, &c. contain constant terms.

42. If the differences $dt.(FQ+$ &c.), $dt.(HQ+$ &c., are not exact, the preceding analysis will not give their rigorous integrals; but it suggests a simple means of obtaining integrals more and more approaching, when α is very small, and when the values of y, y', &c. on the hypothesis of α being equal to cypher, are known. By differentiating these values, $i-1$ times in succession, we will obtain the following differential equations of the order $i-1$,

$$c = V; \; c' = V'; \; \&c.$$

The cofficients of $\frac{d^iy}{dt^i}$, $\frac{d^iy'}{dt^i}$, in the differentials of V, V', &c. being the values of F, F', &c. H, H', &c.; we will substitute them in the differential functions

$$dt.(FQ+F'Q'+ \&c.); \; dt.(HQ+H'Q'+ \&c.)^*$$

Afterwards, we must substitute, in place of y, y', &c., their first approximate values; which will give their differences in functions of t, and of the arbitrary quantities c, c', &c. Let $T.dt$, $T'dt$, &c., be

* Let $y = \phi.(t, c, c', c'', \&c.)$ be the value of y, when $\alpha=0$, which being substituted in place of y, in the function $dt.(FQ+F'Q')$, $dt.(HQ+H'Q')+$ &c. these functions will depend on t, and $c_{,}$, $c'_{,}$, $c''_{,}$, &c. $\because y = \phi.(t_{,}, c-\alpha\int Tdt, c'-\alpha\int T'dt, \&c.)$, and if this value of y be also substituted in $dt.(FQ+F'Q'+\&c.)$, $dt.(HQ+H'Q'+\&c.)$, they will become $= T_{,}dt$, $T'_{,}dt$, &c.; hence $y=\phi.(t, c-\alpha.\int T_{,}dt. \; c'-\alpha.\int T'_{,}.dt, \&c.)$

The successive powers of α must necessarily occur in these approaching values of y. This method corresponds to the method of continued substitutions adopted by Newton.

these functions. If in the first approximate values of y, y', &c., we change the arbitrary quantities c, c', &c. respectively into $c - \alpha.\int Tdt$; $c' - \alpha.\int T'dt$, &c. we will have the second approximate values of those variables.

These second values being substituted again, in the differential functions

$$dt.(FQ + \&c.)\,;\ dt.(HQ + \&c.)\,;\ \&c.$$

it is manifest that these functions are then what Fdt, $F'dt$, become, when the arbitrary quantities c, c', c'', &c. are changed into $c - \alpha.\int Tdt$; $c' - \alpha.\int T'dt$, &c. Therefore, let F, F', &c. be what T, T'. &c. become in consequence of these changes; we shall have the third approximate values of y, y', &c.; by changing in the first, c, c', &c. respectively into $c - \alpha.\int T_{,}d.$ $c' - \alpha.\int T'_{,}.dt$; &c.

In like manner, $T_{,,}$, $T'_{,,}$, &c. representing what $T_{,}$, $T'_{,}$, &c. become when $c_{,}$, $c'_{,}$, &c. are changed into $c - \alpha.\int T_{,}dt$, $c' - \alpha.\int T'_{,}dt$, &c.: we shall have the fourth approximate values of y, y', &c. by changing in the first approaching values of these variables, c, c', into $c - \alpha.\int T_{,,}.dt$, $c' - \alpha.\int T'_{,,}.dt$, &c.; and so on of the rest.

We shall see in the sequel, that the determination of the celestial motions depends almost always on differential equations of the form

$$0 = \frac{d^2y}{dt^2} + a^2y + \alpha Q,^*$$

Q being an entire and rational function of y, and of the sines and cosines of angles increasing proportionably to the time represented by t. The following is the easiest means of integrating this equa-

* Let $Q = y.\cos.2t$, and we have $0 = \frac{d^2y}{dt^2} + a^2.y + \alpha y.\cos.2t$, let $\alpha = 0$, and we shall have $0 = \frac{d^2y}{dt^2} + a^2.y$; of which the integral is $\frac{c}{a}.\sin.at + \frac{c'}{a}.\cos.at$, which value

tion. We suppose, in the first place, α equal to nothing, and by the preceding number we will obtain a first value of y.

This value being substituted in Q, it will by this means become an entire and rational function of the sines and cosines of angles proportional to the time t. Afterward by integrating the differential equation we will obtain a second value of y, approximate as far as quantities of the order α inclusively.

This value being substituted in $Q_{,}$; will give, by integrating the differential equation, a third approximate value of y, and so on of the rest.

This manner of integrating by approximation, the differential equations of the celestial motions, although the simplest of all, is however liable to the inconvenience of giving in the expressions of the variables y, y', &c., the arcs of circles without the signs of the *sine* and *cosine*, even in the case in which these arcs do not exist in the accurate values of these variables; in fact, we may conceive, that if these values involve the sines and cosines of angles of the order αt, these sines and cosines ought to be exhibited in the form of a series, in the approximate values which are found by the preceding method; because these last values are arranged according to the powers of α. This expansion into a series of the sines and cosines of angles of the order αt, ceases to be exact, when in the progress of time, the arc αt becomes considerable; consequently the approximate values of y, y', &c., cannot be extended to an indefinite time. As it is* of consequence to have values

being substituted for y in $ay.\cos.\ 2t$, the differential equation $\frac{d^2y}{dt^2}+a^2y+\alpha y.\cos.\ 2t$, can be integrated by the method pointed out in the preceding page.

* It would seem at first sight only necessary to substitute for the arc t and its powers their developements deduced from the series $t=\sin.\ t+\frac{\sin.\ t^3}{1.2.3}+\frac{3.\ \sin.\ t^5}{2.3.4.5}+$ &c. but it is to be considered, that when t exceeds a quadrant the series ceases to be exact, ∵ this series cannot be substituted for any arc *whatever*.

which embrace the past as well as future ages; the reversion of the arcs of a circle, which the approximate values contain, to the functions which would produce them by their expansion into a series, is a very delicate problem, and of great interest in analysis. The following is a very simple and general method of resolving it.

43. Let us consider the differential equation of the order i,

$$0 = \frac{d^i y}{dt^i} + P + \alpha Q;$$

α being a very small quantity, and P and Q being algebraic functions of y, $\frac{dy}{dt} \ldots\ldots \frac{d^{i-1}y}{dt^{i-1}}$, and of the sines and cosines of angles increasing proportionably to t. Let us suppose that we have the complete integral of this differential equation, in the case of $\alpha = 0$, and that the value of y, determined by this integral, does not involve the arc t, without the signs *sine* and *cosine*; let us afterwards suppose, that this equation being integrated by the preceding method of approximation, when α does not vanish, gives

$$y = X + t.Y + t^2.Z + t^3.S + \&c.$$

X, Y, Z, &c., being periodic functions of t, which involve the i arbitrary quantities c, c', c'', &c.; and the powers of t, in this expression of y, extending to infinity by the successive approximations. It is manifest that the coefficients of these powers will always decrease with greater rapidity, as α is smaller. In the theory of the motions of the heavenly bodies, α expresses the order of the disturbing forces relatively to the principal forces which actuate them.

If the preceding value of y, be substituted in the function $\frac{d^i y}{dt^i} + P + \alpha Q$; it will assume the following form, $k + k't + k''t^2 + \&c.$; k, k', k'', being periodic functions of t; but by hypothesis the value of y

satisfies the differential equation

$$0 = \frac{d^iy}{dt^i} + P + \alpha Q;$$

therefore we ought to have identically

$$0 = k + k't + k''t^2 + \&c.$$

If k, k', k'', &c., do not vanish, this equation will give by the reversion of series, the arc t, in a function of the sines and cosines of angles proportionable to t; therefore α being supposed to be indefinitely small, we would have t equal to a finite function of the sines and cosines of similar angles, which is impossible; consequently, the functions k, k', &c., are identically equal to cypher.

Now, if the arc t is only elevated to the first power under the sign *sine* and *cosine*, as is the case in the theory of the celestial motions,* this arc will not be produced by the successive differences of y; therefore by substituting the preceding value of y, in the function $\frac{d^iy}{dt^i} + P + \alpha Q$ the function $K + K't +$ &c., into which it is transformed, will not contain the arc t, without the sines *sin.*, and *cos.*, but as far as it is already contained in y; thus, by changing in the expression of y, the arc t, without the periodic signs; into $t - \theta$, θ being a constant quantity, the function $k + k't +$ &c., will be changed into $k + k'.(t - \theta) +$ &c.; and because this last function is identically equal to nothing, in consequence of the identical equations $k = 0$, $k' = 0$, &c.; it follows that the expression†

$$y = X + (t - \theta).\ Y + (t - \theta)^2.\ Z + \&c.,$$

* If a term of the form $\sin.(at^n)$ occurred in the value of y, then in the successive differences of y, powers of the arc t will be produced.

† The values of Y, Z, &c. in this second value of y are different from the quantities represented by Y, Z, &c. in the first value of y.

satisfies also the differential equation

$$0 = \frac{d^i y}{dt^i} + P + \alpha Q.$$

Although this second value of y seems to involve $i + 1$ arbitrary quantities, namely the i arbitrary quantities c, c', c'', &c., and the arbitrary θ; however, it can only contain the number i of arbitrary quantities which are really distinct. It is therefore necessary, that by suitable transformation in the constant quantities c, c', c'', &c., the arbitrary quantity θ should disappear from this second expression of y, and that, consequently, it should coincide with the first. This consideration furnishes us with means of making the arcs of circle which exist without the periodic signs to disappear.

The second expression of y, may be made to assume the following form:

$$y = X + (t - \theta).\ R.$$

As we have supposed that θ disappears from y, we will have $\left(\frac{dy}{d\theta}\right) = 0$, and consequently

$$R = \frac{dX}{d\theta} + (t - \theta).\left(\frac{dR}{d\theta}\right).*$$

This equation being differenced successively, will give

* If $\phi.(t,\ \theta,\ t - \theta)$ be expanded by the formula of No. 21, it will become $\phi.(t,\ \theta) + \frac{d.\phi.(t,\ \theta)}{d\theta}.\ (t - \theta) + \frac{d^2.\phi.(t,\ \theta)}{d\theta^2}\ .\ (t - \theta)^2 + \&c. =$ (as $\phi.(t,\ \theta,) = X$) the expression in the text.

$$\left(\frac{dy}{d\theta}\right) = \left(\frac{dX}{d\theta}\right) + (t - \theta)\left(\frac{dR}{d\theta}\right) - R.$$

See an example of this method in Chapter 7, Article 53.

$$2.\left(\frac{dR}{d\theta}\right)=\left(\frac{d^2X}{d\theta^2}\right)+(t-\theta).\left(\frac{d^2R}{d\theta^2}\right);$$

$$3.\left(\frac{d^2R}{d\theta^2}\right)=\left(\frac{d^3X}{d\theta^3}\right)+(t-\theta).\left(\frac{d^3R}{d\theta^3}\right);$$

&c.

hence it is easy to infer by eliminating R, and its differentials, from the preceding expression of y, that

$$y=X+\frac{(t-\theta)}{1}.\left(\frac{dX}{d\theta}\right)+\frac{(t-\theta)^2}{1.2}.\left(\frac{d^2X}{d\theta^2}\right)+\frac{(t-\theta)^3}{1.2.3}.\left(\frac{d^3X}{d\theta^3}\right)+\text{\&c.}$$

X is a function of t, and of the constant quantities c, c', c'', &c.; and as these constants are functions of θ,' X is a function of t and of θ, which we can represent by $\varphi.(t, \theta)$. The expression of y is, by the formula (i) of N°. 21, the expansion of the function $\varphi.(t, \theta+t-\theta)$, according to the powers of $t-\theta$; therefore we have $y=\varphi.(t, t)$; it follows from this that the value of y will be had by changing θ into t, in X. The proposed problem is by this means reduced to the determination of X, in a function of t, and of θ, and consequently to the determination of c, c', c'', &c., in functions of θ.

For this purpose, let the equation

$$y+X+(t-\theta).\ Y+(t-\theta)^2.\ Z+(t-\theta)^3.\ S+\ \text{\&c.}$$

be resumed. The constant quantity θ being supposed to disappear from this value of y, we have the identical equation

$$0=\left(\frac{dX}{d\theta}\right)-Y+(t-\theta).\left\{\left(\frac{dY}{d\theta}\right)-2Z\right\}+(t-\theta)^2.\left\{\left(\frac{dZ}{d\theta}\right)-3S\right\}+\text{\&c.}\quad (a)$$

By applying to this equation the same reasoning as in the case of the equation $0=k+k't+k''t^2+$ &c., it will appear that the coefficients of the successive powers of $(t-\theta)$, must of themselves be equal to zero. The functions X, Y, Z, &c., do not involve θ, except as far as it is contained in c, c', &c.; so that in order to constitute the partial differences $\left(\frac{dX}{d\theta}\right)$, $\left(\frac{dY}{d\theta}\right)$, $\left(\frac{dZ}{d\theta}\right)$, &c., it is sufficient merely to make c, c', &c., vary in these functions, which gives

$$\left(\frac{dX}{d\theta}\right)=\left(\frac{dX}{dc}\right).\frac{dc}{d\theta}+\left(\frac{dX}{dc'}\right).\frac{dc'}{d\theta}+\left(\frac{dX}{dc''}\right).\frac{dc''}{d\theta}+\&c.;$$
$$\left(\frac{dY}{d\theta}\right)=\left(\frac{dY}{dc}\right).\frac{dc}{d\theta}+\left(\frac{dY}{dc'}\right).\frac{dc'}{d\theta}+\left(\frac{dY}{dc''}\right).\frac{dc''}{d\theta}+\&c.;$$
&c.

Now it may happen that some of the arbitrary quantities c, c', c'', &c., multiply the arc t in the periodic functions X, Y, Z, &c.; the differentiation of these functions relatively to θ, or which comes to the same thing, relatively to these arbitrary quantities, will develope this arc, and make it issue from without the signs of the periodic functions; the differences $\left(\frac{dX}{d\theta}\right)$, $\left(\frac{dY}{d\theta}\right)$, $\left(\frac{dZ}{d\theta}\right)$, &c., will then be of the following form:

$$\left(\frac{dX}{d\theta}\right)=X'+t.X'';$$
$$\left(\frac{dY}{d\theta}\right)=Y'+t.Y'';$$
$$\left(\frac{dZ}{d\theta}\right)=Z'+t.Z'';$$
&c.,

in which X', X'', Y', Y'', Z', Z'', &c., are periodic functions of t, and moreover involve the arbitrary quantities c, c', c'', &c., and their first differences divided by $d\theta$, which differences do not occur in these functions, except under a linear form; we shall therefore, have

$$\left(\frac{dX}{d\theta}\right)=X'+\theta X''+(t-\theta).X'';$$
$$\left(\frac{dY}{d\theta}\right)=Y'+\theta Y''+(t-\theta.\ Y';$$

$$\left(\frac{dZ}{d\theta}\right) = Z' + \theta Z'' + (t-\theta).\, Z'' ;$$
&c.

This value being substituted in the equation (a), will give

$$\begin{aligned} 0 = {} & X' + \theta X'' - Y \\ & + (t-\theta).\,(Y' + \theta Y'' + X'' - 2Z) \\ & + (t-\theta)^2.\,(Z' + \theta Z'' + Y'' - 3S) + \text{\&c.} \end{aligned}$$

hence we deduce, by putting the coefficients of the powers of $t-\theta$, separately equal to nothing,

$$\begin{aligned} 0 &= X' + \theta.\, X'' - Y ; \\ 0 &= Y' + \theta.\, Y'' + X'' - 2Z ; \\ 0 &= Z' + \theta.\, Z'' + Y'' - 3S ; \end{aligned}$$
&c.

The first of these equations, being differenced $i-1$ times in succession, with respect to t, will give a corresponding number of equations between the arbitrary quantities c, c', c'', &c., and their first differences divided by dt; the resulting equations being afterwards integrated, with respect to θ, will give these constant quantities in functions of θ. The sole inspection of the first of the preceding equations will almost always suffice to determine the differential equations in c, c', c'', &c., by comparing separately the coefficients of the sines and of the cosines which it contains; because it is manifest that the values of c, c', &c. being independent of t, the differential equations which determine them ought to be equally independent of this quantity. The simplicity which this consideration produces in the computation, is one of the principal advantages of this method. Most frequently these equations can only be integrated by successive approximation, which may introduce the arc θ, without the periodic signs, in the values of c, c', &c., even when this arc does not occur in the rigorous integrals; but we can make it to disappear by the method which we have laid down.

It may happen that the first of the preceding equations, and its $i-1$ differentials in t, do not give a number i of distinct equations, between the quantities c, c', c'', &c., and their differences. In this case, we should recur to the second and subsequent equations.

When the values of c, c', c'', &c., shall have been determined in functions of θ; we can substitute them in X, and by changing afterwards θ into t, we will have the value of y, in which no function of the arcs of a circle occur, which are not affected by periodic signs, when this is possible. If this value still preserves them, it will be a proof that they existed in the exact integrals.

44. Let us now consider any number n of differential equations

$$0=\frac{d^iy}{dt^i}+P+\alpha.Q;\quad 0=\frac{d^iy'}{dt^i}+P'+\alpha Q;\ \&c.$$

P, Q, P', Q', &c., being functions of y, y', &c., and of their differentials, continued to the order $i-1$, and of the sines and cosines of angles increasing proportionably to the variable t, of which the difference is supposed to be constant. Let us suppose that the approximate integrals of these equations are

$$y=X+t.Y+t^2.Z+t^3S+\&c.;$$
$$y'=X_{,}+t.Y_{,}+t^2.Z_{,}+t^3S_{,}+\&c.;$$

X, Y, Z, &c., $X_{,}$, $Y_{,}$, $Z_{,}$, &c., being periodic functions of t, and containing the in arbitrary quantities c, c', c'', &c., we will have, as in the preceding number,

$$0=X'+\theta.\,X''-Y;$$
$$0=Y'+\theta.\,Y''+X''-2Z;$$
$$0=Z'+\theta.\,Z''+Y''-3S;$$
$$\&c.$$

The value of y' will in like manner give equations of the following form :

$$0 = X_{,}' + \theta.\, X_{,}'' + Y_{,};$$
$$0 = Y_{,}' + \theta.\, Y_{,}'' + X_{,}'' - 2Z_{,};$$
$$\&c.$$

The values of y'', y''', &c., will furnish similar equations. By means of these different equations we can determine the values of c, c', c'', &c., in functions of θ, those equations being selected, which are the simplest and most approximative: by substituting these values in X, $X_{,}$, &c., and afterwards changing θ into t, we will have the values of y, y', &c., not containing the arcs of a circle *without the periodic signs*, when this is possible.

45. Let us resume the method which has been explained in N°. 40. It follows from it, that if in place of supposing the parameters c, c', c'', &c., constant, we make them to vary, so that we may have

$$dc = -\alpha dt.\,(FQ + F'Q' + \&c.);$$
$$dc' = -\alpha dt.\,(HQ + H'Q' + \&c.),$$
$$\&c.$$

we will have always the in integrals of the order $i-1$, namely

$$c = V;\ c' = V';\ c'' = V'';\ \&c.$$

as in the case of α equal to zero; hence it follows, that not only the finite integrals, but also all the equations in which only differences of an order inferior to i, enter, preserve the same form in the case of α equal to nothing, and of a being any finite value whatever; because these equations can result solely from a comparison of the preceding integrals of the order $i-1$. Consequently, we can equally, in these two cases, difference $i-1$ times in succession the finite integrals, without making c, c', &c., to vary; and as we are at liberty to make all, vary at once, there results an equation of condition between the parameters c, c', &c., and their differences.

In the two cases namely, of α equal to nothing, and of α being any quantity whatever, the values of y, y', y'', &c., and of their differences to the order $i-1$ inclusively, are the same functions of t, and of the parameters c', c'', &c.; let, therefore, Y be any function of the variables, y, y', y'', &c., and of their differentials inferior to the order $i-1$, and let us name T, the function of t, into which it is changed, when we substitute in place of those variables and of their differences, their values in t. We can difference the equation $Y=T$, by considering the parameters c, c', c'', &c., as constant; we can even assume the partial difference of Y, relatively to one only, or to several of the variables y, y', &c., provided that we only make to vary that part of T, which varies with them. In all these differentiations the parameters c, c', c'', &c., may be always regarded as constant; because, by substituting for y, y', &c., and their differences, their values in t, we will have equations identically nothing, in the two cases of α equal to nothing, of α having any finite value whatever.

When the differential equations are of the order $i-1$, it is no longer permitted, in differentiating them, to treat the parameters c, c', c'', &c., as if they were constant. In order to difference those equations, let us consider the equation $\varphi=0$, φ being a differential function of the order $i-1$, and which contains the parameters c, c', c'', &c.: let $\delta\varphi$ be the difference of this function taken on the supposition that c, c', &c., as well as the differences dy^{i-1}, $d^{i-1}y'$, &c., are constant. Let S be the coefficient of $\frac{d^iy}{dt^{i-1}}$ in the entire difference of φ: let S' be the coefficient of $\frac{d^iy'}{dt^{i-1}}$, in this same difference, and so of the rest. The equation $\varphi=0$, being differenced, will give

$$0 = \delta\varphi + \left(\frac{d\varphi}{dc}\right).dc + \left(\frac{d\varphi}{dc'}\right).dc' + \&c. + S.\frac{d^iy}{dt^{i-1}} + \&c.;$$

by substituting in place of $\frac{d^iy}{dt^{i-1}}$, its value $-dt.(P+\alpha.Q)$; in place of $\frac{d^iy'}{dt^{i-1}}$, its value $-dt.(P'+\alpha Q')$, &c.; we shall have

$$0 = \delta\varphi + \left(\frac{d\varphi}{dc}\right).\, dc + \left(\frac{d\varphi}{dc'}\right).\, dc' + \&c.$$
$$-dt\,(SP+S'P'+\ \&c.) - \alpha.dt.(SQ+S'Q'+\ \&c.)\,;\ (t)$$

The parameters c, c', c'', &c., are constant on the hypothesis that α vanishes; thus we have

$$0 = \delta\varphi - dt.\ (SP+S'P'+\ \&c.)$$

If we substitute in this equation, in place of c, c', c'', &c., their values V, V', V'', &c., we will have a differential equation of the order $i-1$, without arbitraries, which is impossible unless the terms of this equation are identically equal to cypher. Therefore the function

$$\delta\varphi - dt.(SP+S'P'+\ \&c.)$$

becomes identically equal to nothing, in consequence of the equations $c = V$, $c' = V'$, &c.; and as the same equations also obtain when the parameters c, c', c'', &c., are variable, it is manifest, that in this case also, the preceding function is identically equal to nothing, the equation (t) will consequently become

$$0 = \left(\frac{d\varphi}{dc}\right).\, dc + \left(\frac{d\varphi}{dc'}\right).\, dc' + \&c.$$
$$-\ \alpha.dt.(SQ + S'Q'+\ \&c.)\,:\ (x)$$

It appears from this, that in order to difference the equation $\varphi = 0$, it is sufficient to make the parameters c, c', c'', &c., and the differences $d^{i-1}y$, $d^{i-1}y'$, &c., to vary in φ, and after the differentiations to substitute $-\alpha Q$, $-\alpha Q'$, &c., in place of the quantities $\frac{d^iy}{dt^i}$, $\frac{d^iy'}{dt^i}$, &c.

Let $\psi = 0$, be a finite equation between y, y', &c., and the variable t; if we denote by $\delta\psi$, $\delta^2\psi$, &c., the successive differences of ψ, taken on the supposition that c, c', &c., are constant; by what goes before we shall have, even in the case in which c, c', &c., are variable, the following equations:

$$\psi = 0;\ \delta\psi = 0;\ d^2\psi = 0 \ldots\ldots\ldots d^{i-1}\psi = 0;$$

therefore, by changing successively in the equation (x), the function φ into ψ, $\delta\psi$, $d^2\psi$, &c., we shall have

$$0 = \left(\frac{d\psi}{dc}\right) . dc + \left(\frac{d\psi}{dc'}\right) . dc' + \&c.;$$

$$0 = \left(\frac{d.\delta\psi}{dc}\right) . dc + \left(\frac{d.\delta\psi}{dc'}\right) . dc' + \&c.$$

... ...

$$0 = \left(\frac{d.\delta^{i-1}.\psi}{dc}\right) . dc + \left(\frac{d.\delta^{i-1}.\psi}{dc'}\right) . dc' + \&c.$$

$$- \alpha dt. \left\{ Q. \left(\frac{d\psi}{dy}\right) + Q'. \left(\frac{d\psi}{dy'}\right) + \&c. \right\}.$$

Thus the equations $\psi = 0$, $\psi' = 0$, &c., being supposed to be the n finite integrals of the differential equations,

$$0 = \frac{d^iy}{dt^i} + P;\ 0 = \frac{d^iy'}{dt^i} + P';\ \&c.;$$

we will have the in equations by means of which the parameters c, c', c'', &c., may be determined without the necessity of forming for this purpose the equations $c = V$, $c' = V'$, &c., but when the integrals will be under this last form, the determination of c, c', &c., will be more simple.

45. This method of making the parameters to vary is of the greatest use in analysis, and in its applications. In order to shew a new application of it, let us consider the differential equation

$$0 = \frac{d^iy}{dt^i} + P;$$

P being a function of t, y, of its differences to the order $i-1$, and of the quantities q, q', &c., which are functions of t. Let us suppose that we have the finite integral of this equation on the hypothesis that q, q', &c., are constant, and let $\varphi=0$ represent this integral, which will contain the i arbitrary quantities c, c', &c., let $\delta\varphi$, $\delta^2\varphi$, $\delta^3\varphi$, &c., denote the successive differences of φ, taken on the supposition that q, q', &c., and also the parameters c, c', &c., are constant. If all these quantities are supposed to vary, the difference of φ will be

$$\delta\varphi+\left\{\frac{d\varphi}{dc}\right\}.\,dc+\left\{\frac{d\varphi}{dc'}\right\}.\,dc'+\text{\&c.}+\left\{\frac{d\varphi}{dq}\right\}.\,dq+\left\{\frac{d\varphi}{dq'}\right\}.\,dq'+\text{\&c.}$$

therefore, by making

$$0=\left\{\frac{d\varphi}{dc}\right\}.\,dc+\left\{\frac{d\varphi}{dc'}\right\}.\,dc'+\text{\&c.}+\left\{\frac{d\varphi}{dq}\right\}.\,dq+\left\{\frac{d\varphi}{dq'}\right\}.\,dq'+\text{\&c.};$$

$\delta\varphi$ will be yet the first difference of φ when c, c' &c., q, q', &c., are variable. If in like manner we make,

$$0=\left\{\frac{d.\delta\varphi}{dc}\right\}.\,dc+\left\{\frac{d.\delta\varphi}{dc'}\right\}.\,dc'+\text{\&c.}+\left\{\frac{d.\delta\varphi}{dq}\right\}.\,dq+\left\{\frac{d.\delta\varphi}{dq'}\right\}.\,dq'+\text{\&c.};$$

... ...

$$0=\left\{\frac{d.\delta^{i-1}\varphi}{dc}\right\}.\,dc+\left\{\frac{d.\delta^{i-1}\varphi}{dc'}\right\}.\,dc'+\text{\&c.}$$
$$+\left\{\frac{d.\delta^{i-1}\varphi}{dq}\right\}dq+\left\{\frac{d.\delta^{i-1}\varphi}{dq'}\right\}dq'+\text{\&c.};$$

$\delta^2\varphi$, $\delta^3\varphi$.........$\delta^i\varphi$, will be also the second, third, ...i^{th} differences of φ, when c, c', &c., q, q', &c. are supposed to be variable.

Now, in the case of c, c', &c., q, q', &c., being constant, the differential equation

$$0=\frac{d^iy}{dt^i}+P,$$

is the result of the elimination of the parameters, c, c', &c., by means of the equations

$$\varphi = 0;\ \delta\varphi = 0;\ \delta^2\varphi = 0;\ \ldots\ldots\ldots\delta^i\varphi = 0;$$

thus, as these last equations obtain even when q, q', &c., are supposed to be variable, the equation $\varphi = 0$, satisfies also, in this case the proposed differential equation, provided that the parameters c, c', &c., are determined by means of the preceding i differential equations; and as their integration gives i constant arbitrary quantities, the function φ will contain these arbitrary quantities, and the equation $\varphi = 0$, will be the complete integral of the proposed.

This method of making the constant arbitrary quantities to vary can be employed with advantage, when the quantities q, q', &c. vary with great slowness, because this consideration generally renders the integration by approximation, of the differential equations which determine the parameters c, c', c'', &c., much easier.

CHAPTER VI.

The second approximation of the celestial motions, or the theory of their perturbations.

46. Let us now apply the preceding methods to the perturbations of the motions of the heavenly bodies, in order to infer from them the simplest expressions of their periodic and secular inequalities. For this purpose, let the differential equations (1), (2) and (3), of No. 9, be resumed, which determine the relative motion of m about M. Let

$$R = m'.\frac{(xx'+yy'+zz')}{(x'^2+y'^2+z'^2)^{\frac{3}{2}}} + m''.\frac{(xx''+yy''+zz'')}{(x''^2+y''^2+z''^2)^{\frac{3}{2}}} + \&c. - \frac{\lambda}{m};$$

λ being by the number cited, equal to

$$\frac{mm'}{((x'-x)^2+(y'-y)^2+(z'-z)^2)^{\frac{1}{2}}} + \frac{mm''}{((x''-x)^2+(y''-y)^2+(z''-z)^2)^{\frac{1}{2}}}$$

$$+\frac{m'm''}{((x''-x')^2+(y''-y')^2+(z''-z')^2)^{\frac{1}{2}}} + \&c.;$$

Moreover, if we suppose $M+m=\mu$; and $r=\sqrt{x^2+y^2+z^2}$; $r'=\sqrt{x'^2+y'^2+z'^2}$; &c., we will have

$$\left.\begin{aligned} 0 &= \frac{d^2x}{dt^2} + \frac{\mu.x}{r^3} + \left\{\frac{dR}{dx}\right\} \\ 0 &= \frac{d^2y}{dt^2} + \frac{\mu.y}{r^3} + \left\{\frac{dR}{dy}\right\} \\ 0 &= \left\{\frac{d^2z}{dt^2}\right\} + \frac{\mu.z}{r^3} + \left\{\frac{dR}{dz}\right\} \end{aligned}\right\}; \quad (P)$$

The sum of these three equations multiplied respectively by dx, dy, dz, gives by their integration,

$$0=\frac{dx^2+dy^2+dz^2}{dt^2}-\frac{2\mu}{r}+\frac{\mu}{a}+2\int dR\,; \qquad (Q)$$

the differential dR being solely relative to the coordinates x, y, z, of the body m, and a being a constant arbitrary quantity, which when R vanishes, becomes by N°s. 18 and 19, the semiaxis major of the ellipse described by m about M.

The equations (P) multiplied respectively by x, y, z, and added to the integral (Q), will give*

$$0=\tfrac{1}{2}.\frac{d^2r^2}{dt^2}-\frac{\mu}{r}+\frac{\mu}{a}+2.\int dR$$
$$+x.\left\{\frac{dR}{dx}\right\}+y.\left\{\frac{dR}{dy}\right\}+z.\left\{\frac{dR}{dz}\right\}; \qquad (R)$$

Now, we may conceive that the disturbing masses m', m'', &c., are multiplied by a coefficient α; and then the value of r will be a function of the time t and of α. If this function be expanded with respect to the powers of α; and if α be made $=1$, after this expansion, it will be ranged according to the powers and products of the disturbing masses. Let the characteristic δ, placed before a quantity, denote the differential of this quantity, taken with respect to α, and divided by $d\alpha$. When the value of δr shall have been determined in a series arranged according to the powers of α, we will have the radius r, by multiplying this series by $d\alpha$, then integrating it with respect to α, and adding to this integral a function of t, independent of α, which function is evidently the value of r when the perturbating forces vanish, and when consequently the curve described is a conic section. The determination of r is therefore reduced to the forming and integrating the differential equation which determines δr.

* $\frac{1}{2}\frac{d^2r^2}{dt^2}=\frac{1}{2}.\frac{d^2.(x^2+y^2+z^2)}{dt^2}=x.\frac{d^2x}{dt^2}+y.\frac{d^2y}{dt^2}+z.\frac{d^2z}{dt^2}+\frac{dx^2+dy^2+dz^2}{dt^2}$.

For this purpose, let us resume the differential equation (R), and let us make for greater simplicity,

$$x.\left\{\frac{dR}{dx}\right\}+y.\left\{\frac{dR}{dy}\right\}+z.\left\{\frac{dR}{dz}\right\}=r.R';$$

differentiating it with respect to α, we will have

$$0=\frac{d^2.r\delta r}{dt^2}+\frac{\mu.r\delta r}{r^3}+2\int\delta.\mathrm{d}R+\delta.rR'; \quad \text{(S)}$$

naming dv the indefinitely small arc intercepted between the two radii vectores r and $r+dr$; the element of the curve described by m about M, will be $\sqrt{dr^2+r^2dv^2}$; therefore we will have $dx^2+dy^2+dz^2=dr^2+r^2dv^2$; and the equation (Q) will become

$$0=\frac{r^2dv^2+dr^2}{dt^2}-\frac{2\mu}{r}+\frac{\mu}{a}+2.\int\mathrm{d}R.$$

eliminating $\frac{\mu}{a}$, from this equation, by means of the equation (R), we shall have*

$$\frac{r^2dv^2}{dt^2}=\frac{r.d^2r}{dt^2}+\frac{\mu}{r}+r.R';$$

hence we deduce by differentiating with respect to α,

$$\frac{2r^2.dv.d\delta v}{dt^2}=\frac{rd^2.\delta r-\delta rd^2r}{dt^2}-\frac{3\mu.r\delta r}{r^3}+r.\delta R'-R'.\delta r.$$

By substituting in this equation, in place of $\frac{\mu.r\delta r}{r^3}$ its value deduced

* Substituting for $\frac{\mu}{a}$ its value given by the equation (R), we obtain $\frac{r^2.dv^2}{dt^2}+\frac{dr^2}{dt^2}-\frac{dr^2}{dt^2}-\frac{r.d^2r}{dt^2}+\frac{\mu}{r}-2\int\mathrm{d}R-rR'-\frac{2\mu}{r}+2\int\mathrm{d}R=0$; which by obliterating quantities which destroy each other becomes the expression in the text; and its differential with respect to α is obtained by dividing by r^2, and then differentiating.

from the equation (S), we will have

$$d.\delta v = \frac{d.(dr.\delta r + 2r.d\delta r) + dt^2.(3.\int\delta.dR + 2r.\ \delta R + R'.\delta r)}{r^2.dv.};^{*} \qquad \text{(T)}$$

We can obtain, by means of the equations (S) and (T), the values of δr and of δv as accurately as we please; but it ought to be observed, that dv being the angle intercepted between the radii r and $r+dr$, the integral v of these angles does not exist in one and the same plane. In order to deduce from it value of the angle described about M, by the projection of the radius vector R on the fixed plane, let $v_{,}$ represent this last angle, and let s denote the tangent of the latitude of m above this plane; $r.(1+s^2)^{-\frac{1}{2}}$ will be the expression of the projected radius vector, and the square of the element of the curve described by m, will be

$$\frac{r^2 dv_{,}^2}{1+s^2} + dr^2 + \frac{r^2 ds^2}{(1+s^2)^2};^{\dagger}$$

but the square of this element is $r^2 dv^2 + dr^2$; therefore we will obtain, by putting these two expressions equal to each other,

$$dv_{,} = \frac{dv\sqrt{(1+s^2) - \frac{ds^2}{dv^2}}}{\sqrt{1+s^2}}.$$

Thus $dv_{,}$ can be determined by means of dv when s will be known.

* $\frac{d.r\delta r}{dt} = \frac{dr.\delta r}{dt} + \frac{r.d\delta r}{dt}$; $\frac{d^2.r.\delta r}{dt^2} = \frac{d^2r.\delta r}{dt^2} + \frac{2dr.d\delta r}{dt^2} + \frac{r.d^2\delta r}{dt^2}$, $\therefore -\frac{3\mu.r\delta r}{r^3}$ $= +\frac{3d^2r.\delta r}{dt^2} + \frac{6dr.d\,\delta r}{dt^2} + \frac{3r\,d^2\delta r}{dt^2} + 6\int\delta.dR + 3\delta.rR'$, and $\frac{2r^2.dv.d.\delta v}{dt^2} =$ $\frac{r.d^2.\delta r - \delta r.d^2r}{dt^2} + \frac{3d^2r\,\delta r}{dt^2} + \frac{6\,d.r.d\delta r}{dt^2} + \frac{3r.d^2\delta r}{dt^2} + 6\int\delta.dR + 3r.\delta R' + 3R'.\delta r + r.\delta R'$ $- R'.\delta r$; $\therefore \frac{r^2dv.d\delta v}{dt^2} = \frac{2r.d^2.\delta r}{dt^2} + \frac{d^2.r.\delta r}{dt^2} + \frac{3d.r.d\delta r}{dt^2}$ $= \frac{d(dr.\delta.r + 2r.d\delta r) + dt^2.(3\int\delta\,dR + 2r.\delta R' + R'.dr)}{dt^2}$.

† s being equal to the tangent of latitude, $\frac{ds}{1+s^2}$ is equal to the differential of the latitude, and $\frac{r^2}{1+s^2}\cdot\frac{ds^2}{1+s^2} + \frac{r^2}{1+s^2}\cdot dv_{,}^2 + dr^2 = r^2.dv^2 + dr^2$.

If the fixed plane is assumed to be the plane of the ordit of m at a given epoch, s and $\frac{ds}{dv}$ will be manifestly of the order of the perturbating forces; therefore, by neglecting the square and the products of these forces, we shall have $v = v_{,}$. In the theory of the planets and comets, these squares and products may be neglected, with the exception of certain terms of this order, which particular circumstances render sensible, and which can be easily determined by means of the equations (S) and (T). These last equations assume a simpler form when we only take into account the first power of the perturbating forces. In fact, we can then consider δv and δr as the parts of r and v arising from these forces; and δR, $\delta.rR'$, are what R and rR', become, when we substitute in place of the coordinates of these bodies their values relative to the elliptic motion:* they can be denoted by these last quantities, subject to this condition. Consequently, the equation S becomes,

$$0 = \frac{d^2.r\delta r}{dt^2} + \frac{\mu.r\delta r}{r^3} + 2.\int dR + rR'.$$

The fixed plane of x and of y being supposed to be that of the orbit of m, at a given epoch, z will be of the order of perturbating forces, and because the square of these forces is neglected, the quantity $z.\left\{\frac{dR}{dz}\right\}$ may likewise be neglected. Moreover, the radius r only

* In the equation (R) when coordinates relative to the elliptic motion are substituted in place of the coordinates of the body, the three first terms vanish; consequently if in place of r in the equation (R) be substituted, a radius r' (which is relative to the elliptic motion) plus an indefinitely small quantity $\delta r'$ which is the effect of the disturbing forces, then the equation (R) becomes $=\frac{1}{2}.\frac{d^2.(r'+\delta r')^2}{dt^2} - \frac{\mu}{r'+\delta r'} + \frac{\mu}{a} + 2\int dR + rR' =$ $\frac{1}{2}.\frac{d^2r'}{dt^2} - \frac{\mu}{r'} + \frac{\mu}{a} + \frac{d^2.r'\delta r'}{dt^2} + \frac{\mu.\delta r'}{r^3} + 2\int dR + rR'$, in this case the three first terms are $=$ to cypher, and the three last are what (S) is reduced to; when dR and rR' are substituted for $\delta.dR$ and $\delta.rR'$.

differs from its projected value by quantities of the order s^2. The angle which this radius makes with the axis of x, differs only from its projection by quantities of the same order; therefore this angle may be supposed equal to v, and we have, excepting quantities of the same order,

$$x = r.\cos. v\,;\; y = r.\sin. v\,;$$

hence we deduce*

$$x.\left\{\frac{dR}{dx}\right\} + y.\left\{\frac{dR}{dy}\right\} = r.\left\{\frac{dR}{dr}\right\};$$

and consequently, $r.R' = r.\left\{\frac{dR}{dr}\right\}$. It is easy to be assured by differentiation, that if we neglect the square of the perturbating force, the preceding differential equation will give, in consequence of the two first equations (P)

$$r.\delta r = \frac{x.\int y dt.\left\{2.\int dR + r.\left\{\frac{dR}{dr}\right\}\right\} - y.\int x dt.\left\{2.\int dR + r.\left\{\frac{dR}{dr}\right\}\right\}}{\left\{\frac{xdy - ydx}{dt}\right\}}.\dagger$$

* $\frac{dR}{dr} = \frac{dR}{dx}.\frac{dx}{dr} + \frac{dR}{dy}.\frac{dr}{dy} = \cos. v.\frac{dR}{dx} + \sin. v.\frac{dR}{dy}$ multiplying both sides by r, and substituting x for $r.\cos. v$, and y for $r\sin. v$, we shall have the value of rR'.

† Add to the first of the equations (P) multiplied into $r.\delta r$, the equation (S) multiplied into $-x$, and we shall have

$$0 = r.\delta r.\left(\frac{d^2x}{dt^2} + \frac{\mu x}{r^3} + \left(\frac{dR}{dx}\right)\right) - \frac{x.d^2.r\delta r}{dt^2} - \frac{\mu x r.\delta r}{r^3} - 2x.\int dR - x.rR',$$

in like manner if the second of the equations (P) be multiplied by $r.\delta r$, and then added to the equation (S) multiplied into $-y$ we shall have

$$0 = r.\delta r.\left(\frac{d^2y}{dt^2} + \frac{\mu y}{r^3} + \left(\frac{dR}{dy}\right)\right) + y.\frac{d^2\delta.rdr}{dt^2} + \frac{\mu y r.\delta r}{r^3} + 2y\int dR + y.rR';$$

now if these equations be respectively integrated, and then the integral of the first multi-

In the second member of this equation the coordinates may refer to the elliptic motion, which gives $\left\{\frac{xdy-ydx}{dt}\right\}$ constant, and equal by N°. 19, to $\sqrt{\mu.a(1-e^2)}$, ae being the excentricity of the orbit of m. If we substitute in the expression of $r\delta r$, in place of x and of y, their values $r.\cos.v$, and $r.\sin.v$, and instead of $\frac{xdy-ydx}{dt}$, the quantity $\sqrt{\mu a.(1-e^2)}$; and if finally we observe that by N°. 20, we have $\mu = n^2.a^3$; we will obtain

$$\delta r = \frac{\left\{\begin{array}{l} a.\cos.v.\int ndt.\,r.\sin.v.\left\{2.\int dR+r.\left\{\frac{dR}{dr}\right\}\right\} \\ -a.\sin.v.\int ndt.\,r.\cos.v.\left\{2.\int dR+r.\left\{\frac{dR}{dr}\right\}\right\}\end{array}\right\}}{\mu.\sqrt{1-e^2}}; \quad (X)$$

the equation (T) gives by integrating and neglecting the square of the perturbating forces;

plied into y. be added to the second multiplied into $-x$, we shall obtain obliterating the quantities which destroy each other

$$r\delta r.y.\frac{dx}{dt} + y\int r\delta r.\left(\frac{dR}{dx}\right) - \frac{xy\,dr.\delta r}{dt} - 2y\int dt.x.dR - y\int x.rR$$
$$- r\delta r.x.\frac{dy}{dt} - x\int r.\delta r.\left(\frac{dR}{dx}\right) + \frac{xy.dr.\delta r}{dt} + 2x\int dt.ydR + x\int y.r.R',$$

∴ neglecting quantities of the same order as the square of the disturbing force, we have $r.\delta r.\frac{ydx-xdy}{dt} = x.\int ydt.(2dR + rR') - y.\int x.dt.(2dR + rR')$, which becomes the expression in the text, when $r.\left(\frac{dR}{dr}\right)$ is substituted for $r.R'$, and by substituting for x and y their respective values $r.\cos.v$, $r\sin.v$, this equation is divisible by r; now $\frac{xdy-ydx}{dt}$ $= \sqrt{\mu.a.(1-e^2)}$, and $\sqrt{\mu} = n.a^{\frac{3}{2}}$: consequently $\frac{an}{\mu.\sqrt{1-e^2}} = \frac{1}{na^{\frac{1}{2}}.\sqrt{1-e^2}} =$ $\frac{1}{\sqrt{\mu a.(1-e^2)}}$.

$$\delta v = \frac{\frac{2r.d.\delta r + dr.\delta r}{a^2.ndt} + \frac{3a}{\mu}.\int\int ndt.dR + \frac{2a}{\mu}.\int n.dt.r.\left\{\frac{dR}{dr}\right\}}{\sqrt{1-e^2}}; \quad (Y)^*$$

By means of this equation the perturbations of the motions of m in longitude can be easily determined, when those of the radius vector shall have been determined.

It now remains to determine the perturbations of the motion in latitude. For this purpose, we shall resume the third of the equations (P), and by integrating it as we have integrated the equation (S), and making $z = r\delta s$, we shall have

$$\delta s = \frac{a.\cos.v.\int ndt.r.\sin.v.\left\{\frac{dR}{dz}\right\} - a.\sin.v.\int ndt.r.\cos.v.\left\{\frac{dR}{dz}\right\}^{\dagger}}{\mu.\sqrt{1-e^2}}; \quad (Z)$$

δs is the latitude of m above the plane of the primitive orbit: if we

* $\delta v = \frac{dr.\delta r + 2rd.\delta r}{\sqrt{\mu.a.(1-e^2)}} + \frac{\int\int dt^2.3.(dR + 2r.\left(\frac{dR}{dr}\right)}{\sqrt{\mu.a.(1-e^2)}} =$ the expression in the text; $R'\delta r$ is omitted as being of the order of the squares of the disturbing forces.

† Multiplying the third of the equations (P) by x, and subtracting it from the first multiplied by z, and then integrating, we shall obtain neglecting quantities of the order of the square of the disturbing forces

$$z.\frac{dx}{dt} - x.\frac{dz}{dt} = -\int x.dt.\left(\frac{dR}{dz}\right),$$

in like manner subtracting the second of the equations (P) multiplied into z from the third multiplied into y, we shall obtain by integrating,

$$y.\frac{dz}{dt} - z.\frac{dy}{dt} = \int y.dt.\left(\frac{dR}{dz}\right),$$

and multiplying the first of these equations by y, and the second by x, we obtain by adding them together

would wish to refer the motion of m, on a plane a little inclined to this orbit; by naming s its latitude, when it is supposed to exist on this plane, $s+\delta s$ will be very nearly the latitude of m above the proposed plane.

47. The formulæ (X), (Y) and (Z), have the advantage of exhibiting the perturbations under a finite form; which is very useful in the theory of the comets, in which these perturbations can only be determined by quadratures. But in consequence of the little excentricity and inclination of the respective orbits of the planets, we are permitted to expand their perturbations, in converging series of the sines and cosines of angles increasing proportionably to the time, and to form tables of them which may serve for an indefinite time. Then, instead of the preceding expressions of δr and δs, it is more convenient to make use of differential equations which determine these variables. By arranging these equations with respect to the powers and to the products of the excentricities and inclinations of the orbits, we can always reduce the determination of the values of δr and δs, to the integration of equations of the form

$$0=\frac{d^2y}{dt^2}+n^2y+Q;$$

the integration of this species of differential equation has been given in N°. 42. But we can immediately give this very simple form, to the preceding differential equations, by the following method.

Resuming the equation (R) of the preceding number, and in order to abridge making,

$$Q=2.\int dR+r.\left\{\frac{dR}{dr}\right\};$$

$$z.\left(y.\frac{dx}{dt}-x.\frac{dy}{dt}\right)=x\int y.dt.\left(\frac{dR}{dz}\right)-y\int x.dt.\left(\frac{dR}{dz}\right),$$

and by substituting for $\frac{ydx-xdy}{dt}$ its value $\sqrt{\mu.a.(1-e^2)}$, and for x and y their values $r.\cos. v$, $r.\sin. v$, we obtain the expression which is given in the text.

it thus becomes,

$$0=\tfrac{1}{2}.\frac{d^2.r^2}{dt^2}-\frac{\mu}{r}+\frac{\mu}{a}+Q; \quad (R')$$

In the case of elliptic motion, in which $Q=0$, r^2 is by the N°. 22, a function of $e.\cos.(nt+\varepsilon-\varpi)$, ae being the excentricity of the orbit, and $nt+\varepsilon-\varpi$ being the mean anomaly of the planet m. Let $e.\cos.(nt+\varepsilon-\varpi)=u$; and let us suppose that $r^2=\varphi(u)$; we shall have

$$0=\frac{d^2u}{dt^2}+n^2u.*$$

In the case of the disturbed motion we can also suppose $r^2=\varphi(u)$; but u will be no longer equal to $e.\cos.(nt+\varepsilon-\varpi)$; it will therefore be given by the preceding differential equation increased by a term depending on the disturbing forces. In order to determine this term, it ought to be observed, that if we make $u=\psi(r^2)$, we shall have

$$\frac{d^2u}{dt^2}+n^2.u=\frac{d^2.r^2}{dt^2}.\psi'.(r^2)+\frac{4r^2dr^2}{dt^2}.\psi''.(r^2)+n^2.\psi.(r^2),\dagger$$

$\psi'.(r^2)$ being the differential of $\psi.(r^2)$ divided by $d.(r^2)$ and $\psi''.(r^2)$ being the differential of $\psi'.(r^2)$, divided by $d.r^2$. The equation (R′) gives $\frac{d^2.r^2}{dt^2}$ equal to a function of r, plus a function depending on the disturbing force. If we multiply this equation by $2rdr$, and then in-

* $\frac{du}{dt}=-e.n.\sin.(nt+\varepsilon-\varpi)$; $\frac{d^2u}{dt^2}=-en^2.\cos.(nt+\varepsilon-\varpi)$, therefore $\frac{d^2u}{dt^2}+n^2u=-en^2.\cos.(nt+\varepsilon-\varpi)+e.n^2.\cos.(nt+\varepsilon-\varpi)=0$;

† $\frac{du}{dt}=\frac{dr^2}{dt}.\psi'.(r^2)$, $\therefore\frac{d^2u}{dt^2}=\frac{d^2r^2}{dt^2}.\psi'.(r^2)+\left(\frac{dr^2}{dt}\right)^2.\psi''.(r^2)$, and by substituting for dr^2 its value $2rdr$, we obtain the expression for $\frac{d^2u}{dt^2}+n^2.u$, which is given in the text.

tegrate it; we shall have $\frac{r^2dr^2}{dt^2}$ equal to a function of r, plus a function depending on the disturbing force. By substituting these values of $\frac{d^2r}{dt^2}$ and of $\frac{r^2dr^2}{dt^2}$, in the preceding expression of $\frac{d^2u}{dt^2}+n^2u$; the function of r independent of the disturbing force will disappear of itself, because the terms are identically equal to nothing, when this force vanishes, therefore we shall obtain the value of $\frac{d^2u}{dt^2}+n^2u$, by substituting in its expression, in place of $\frac{d^2r}{dt^2}$ and of $\frac{r^2dr^2}{dt^2}$, the parts of their expressions which depend on the disturbing force. But, if we only consider these parts, the equation (R') and its integral, give

$$\frac{d.^2r}{dt^2}=-2Q;$$

$$\frac{4r^2.dr^2}{dt^2}=-8.\int Qrdr;$$

therefore,

$$\frac{d^2u}{dt^2}+n^2u=-2Q.\psi'.(r^2)-8.\ \psi''.(r^2).\int Q.rdr.$$

Now, from the equation $u=\psi.(r^2)$ we deduce $du=2rdr.\ \psi'.(r^2)$; the equation $r^2=\varphi.(u)$, gives $2rdr=du.\ \varphi'.(u)$, and consequently

$$\psi'.(r^2)=\frac{1}{\varphi'.(u)}.$$

By differentiating this last equation, and by substituting $\varphi'.(u)$ instead of $\frac{2rdr}{du}$, we shall have

$$\psi''.(r^2) = \frac{-\varphi''.(u)}{\varphi'.(u)^3},$$

$\varphi''.(u)$ being equal to $\frac{d.\varphi'.(u)}{du}$, in like manner as $\varphi'.(u)$ is equal to $\frac{d.\varphi.(u)}{du}$. This being premised, if we make

$$u = e.\cos.(nt+\varepsilon-\varpi)+\delta u,$$

the differential equation in u will become

$$0 = \frac{d^2.\delta u}{dt^2} + n^2.\delta u - \frac{4.\varphi''.(u)}{\varphi'.(u)^3}.\int Q.du.\,\varphi'.(u) + \frac{Q}{\varphi'.(u)};\dagger$$

and if we neglect the square of the disturbing force, u may be supposed to be equal to $e.\cos.(nt+\varepsilon-\varpi)$, in the terms depending on Q.

The value of $\frac{r}{a}$ found in N°. 22, gives, by carrying the precision to quantities of the order e^2 inclusively,

$$r = a.(1+e^2-u.(1-\tfrac{3}{2}e^2)-u^2-\tfrac{3}{2}u^3);$$

hence we deduce

$$r^2 = a^2.(1+2e^2-2u.(1-\tfrac{1}{2}e^2)-u^2-u^3) = \varphi.(u).\ddagger$$

If this value of $\varphi(u)$ be substituted in the differential equation in δu,

† Substituting in place of u its value, the part which involves the cosine will be equal to nothing, as is evident from the preceding page; the other part is what is given in the text.

‡ $\frac{r}{a}$ = (as powers of e higher than the third are rejected) $1+\frac{1}{2}e^2-(e-\frac{3}{8}e^3).\cos.(nt+\varepsilon-\varpi)-\frac{1}{2}e^2.\cos.2(nt+\varepsilon-\varpi)-\frac{3}{8}e^3.\cos.3(nt+\varepsilon-\varpi)$; $\cos.2(nt+\varepsilon-\varpi)=\frac{2u^2}{e^2}-1$, $\cos.3(nt+\varepsilon-\varpi) = \cos.2(nt+\varepsilon-\varpi).\cos.(nt+\varepsilon-\varpi)-\sin.2(nt+\varepsilon-\varpi).\sin.(nt+\varepsilon-\varpi) = \frac{2u^3}{e^3}-\frac{u}{e}+\frac{2u^3}{e^3}-\frac{2u}{e}; = \frac{4u^3}{e^3}-\frac{3u}{e}$; $\therefore\ \frac{r}{a} = 1+\frac{e^2}{2}-(e-\frac{3}{8}e^3)\frac{u}{e}-\frac{1}{2}e^2$.

and if we then restore in place of Q, its value $2.\int dR + r.\left\{\frac{dR}{dr}\right\}$, and $e.\cos.(nt+\varepsilon-\varpi)$, instead of u, we shll have, as far as quantities of the order e^3,

$$0 = \frac{d^2.\delta u}{dt} + n^2.\delta u$$

$$-\frac{1}{a^2}.\ (1 + \tfrac{1}{4}e^2 - e.\cos.(nt+\varepsilon-\varpi) - \tfrac{1}{4}e^2.\cos.(2nt+2\varepsilon-2\varpi)).$$

$$\left\{(2.\int dR + r.\left\{\frac{dR}{dr}\right\}\right\};^{*} \qquad (X')$$

$$-\frac{2e}{a^2}.\int ndt.[\sin.(nt+\varepsilon-\varpi).\ [1 + e.\cos.(nt+\varepsilon-\varpi)].$$

$$\left\{2.\int dR + r.\left\{\frac{dR}{dr}\right\}\right].$$

When δu shall have been determinined, by means of this differential equation; δr will be obtained by differentiating the expression of r, with respect to the characteristic δ, which gives

$$\delta r = -a\delta u.(1+\tfrac{3}{4}e^2+2e.\cos.(nt+\varepsilon-\varpi)+\tfrac{9}{4}e^2.\cos.(2nt+2\varepsilon-2\varpi)).$$

This value of δr will give the value of δv by means of the formula (Y) of the preceding number.

$\left(\frac{2u^2}{e^2}-1\right)-\frac{3}{8}e^3.\left(\frac{4u^3}{e^3}-\frac{3u}{e}\right)=1+\frac{1}{2}e^2+\frac{1}{2}e^2-\left(1-\frac{12}{8}e^2\right).u-u^2-\frac{12}{8}u^3\Big)$;

$\frac{r^2}{a^2}=(1+e^2-(1-\frac{3}{2}e^2)u)^2+2(1+e^2-u(1-\frac{3}{2}e^2).(u^2+\frac{3}{2}u^3)+(u^2+\frac{3}{2}u^3)^2$, as u involves e, powers of u higher than the third may be neglected, $\therefore \frac{r^2}{a^2}=1+2e^2-2(u(1-\frac{3}{2}e^2)$ $-2ue^2+u^2-2u^2+2.u^3-\frac{3}{2}2.u^3$.

* $\varphi'.(u)=\frac{2rdr}{du}=-2a^2(1-\frac{1}{2}e^2+u+\frac{3}{2}u^2)$, $\because \frac{1}{\varphi'.(u)}=-\frac{1}{2a^2}.(1-\frac{1}{2}e^2+u+\frac{3}{2}u^2)^{-1}$ $=-\frac{1}{2a^2}.(1+\frac{1}{2}e^2-u-\frac{3}{2}u^2+u^2)$, because powers of u higher than the second are rejected, inasmuch as they would involve powers of e higher than the third, when their

It now remains to determine δs; but if the formulæ (X) and (Z) of the preceding number be compared together, it will appear that δr is changed into δs, by changing in its expression $2.\int dR + r.\left\{\frac{dR}{dr}\right\}$ into $\left\{\frac{dR}{dz}\right\}$; hence it follows, that in order to obtain δs, it is sufficient to effect this change in the differential equation of δu, and afterwards to substitute the value of δu given by this equation, and which we will denote by $\delta u'$, in the expression of δr. Thus, we shall have,

$$0 = \frac{d^2.\delta u'}{dt^2} + n^2.\delta u'$$

$$-\frac{1}{a^2}.\left(1+\tfrac{1}{4}e^2 - e.\cos.(nt+\varepsilon-\varpi) - \tfrac{1}{4}e^2.\cos.(2nt+2\varepsilon-2\varpi)\right).\left(\frac{dR}{dz}\right)$$

$$-\frac{2e}{a^2}.\int ndt.\left(\sin.(nt+\varepsilon-\varpi).(1+e.\cos.(nt+\varepsilon-\varpi)).\left(\frac{dR}{dz}\right)\right); \quad (Z)$$

values are substituted in place of u, hence substituting for u and u^2 their values, namely, $e.\cos.(nt+\varepsilon-\varpi)$, $\frac{e^2}{2}.\cos.2(nt+\varepsilon-\varpi)+\frac{e^2}{2}$, $\frac{2Q}{\varphi'.(u)} = \left(2\int dR + r.\left(\frac{dR}{dr}\right)\right).\left(-\frac{2}{2a^2}\right.$ $\left(1+\frac{1}{2e^2}-\frac{1}{4e^2}-e.\cos.(nt+\varepsilon-\varpi)-\frac{e^2}{4}.\cos.(2nt+2\varepsilon-2\varpi)\right)$; $\varphi''.(u) = d.\frac{\varphi'.(u)}{du} = -2a^2(1+3u)$; and $\frac{1}{\varphi'(u)^3} = -\frac{1}{8a^6}.(1+\frac{3}{2}e^2-3u)$, the other terms are omitted because powers of e higher than the third would occur when we substitute for du and $\varphi'.(u)$

$\therefore \frac{\varphi'.(u)}{\varphi'.(u)^3} = \frac{-2a^2}{-8a^6}.(1+3u).(1-3u)$

$=$ (omitting terms which would by their multiplication produce powers of e higher than the third) $\frac{1}{4a^4}$; $du = -e.ndt.\sin.(nt+\varepsilon-\varpi)$; $\varphi'.(u) = -2a^2.(1+e.\cos.(nt+\varepsilon-\varpi))$, hence substituting for $\varphi''.(u)$, $\frac{1}{\varphi'.(u)^3}$, and $du.\varphi'.(u)$, their values just given we obtain the last term of the equation (X′).

$\delta r = -a.(\delta u.(1-\frac{3}{2}e^2+2u+\frac{9}{2}.u^2)$, $\frac{9}{2}u^2 = \frac{9}{4}.\cos.2(nt+\varepsilon-\varpi)+\frac{9}{4}e^2$, $\therefore \delta r = -a\delta u.(1+\frac{3}{4}.e^2+2e.\cos.(nt+\varepsilon+\varpi)+\frac{9}{4}.\cos.(2nt+2\varepsilon-2\varpi)$.

$$\delta s = -a\delta u'.(1+\tfrac{3}{4}e^2+2e.\cos.(nt+\epsilon-\varpi)+\tfrac{9}{4}e^2.\cos.(2nt+2\epsilon-2\varpi)).$$

The system of equations (X′), (Y′), (Z′), will give, in a very simple manner, the troubled motion of m, if we only consider the first power of the perturbating force. The consideration of the terms due to this power being very nearly sufficient in the theory of the planet; we now proceed to deduce from them formulæ which may be conveniently applied in determining the motion of these bodies.

48. For this purpose, it is necessary to expand the function R into a series. If we only consider the action of m on m', we have, by N°. 46,

$$R=\frac{m.(xx'+yy'+zz')}{(x'^2+y'^2+z'^2)^{\frac{3}{2}}}-\frac{m'}{((x'-x)^2+(y'-y)^2+(z'-z)^2)^{\frac{1}{2}}}.$$

This function is entirely independent of the position of the plane of x and of y, for as the radical $\sqrt{(x'-x)^2+(y'-y)^2+(z'-z)^2}$, expresses the distance of m from m', it is independent of it, consequently the function $x^2+y^2+z^2+x'^2+y'^2+z'^2-2xx'-2yy'-2zz'$ is equally independent of it; but the squares $x^2+y^2+z^2$, and $x'^2+y'^2+z'^2$, of the radii vectores do not all depend on this position, therefore the quantity $xx'+yy'+zz'$, does not depend on it, and consequently the function R is independent of it. Let us suppose that in this function

$$x=r.\cos.v;\quad y=r.\sin.v;$$
$$x'=r'.\cos.v';\quad y'=r'.\sin.v';$$

we shall have

$$R=m'.\frac{(rr'.\cos.(v'-v)+zz')}{(r'^2+z'^2)^{\frac{3}{2}}}-\frac{m'}{(r^2-2rr'.\cos.(v'-v)+r'^2+(z'-z)^2)^{\frac{1}{2}}}.$$

As the orbits of the planets are very nearly circular, and inclined at small angles to each other, the plane of x and of y may be so selected, that z and z' shall be very small. In this case, r and r' differ very little from the greater semiaxes a and a' of the elliptic orbits; therefore we can suppose that

$$r = a.(1+u_{,}); \quad r' = a'.(1+u'_{,});$$

$u_{,}$ and $u'_{,}$ being small quantities. As the angles v and v' differ little from the mean longitudes $nt+\varepsilon$, and $n't+\varepsilon'$; we may suppose that

$$v = nt+\varepsilon+v_{,}; \quad v' = n't+\varepsilon'+v'_{,},$$

$v_{,}$ and $v'_{,}$ being very small quantities. Hence it appears that if R be arranged into a series proceeding according to the powers and products of $u_{,}$, $v_{,}$, z, $u'_{,}$, $v'_{,}$, and z'; this series will be very converging.

Let

$$\frac{a}{a'^2}.\cos.(n't-nt+\varepsilon'-\varepsilon)-(a^2-2aa'.\cos.(n't-nt+\varepsilon'-\varepsilon)+a'^2)^{-\frac{1}{2}}$$
$$=\tfrac{1}{2}.A^{(0)}+A^{(1)}.\cos.(n't-nt+\varepsilon'-\varepsilon)+A^{(2)}.\cos.2.(n't-nt+\varepsilon'-\varepsilon)$$
$$+A^{(3)}.\cos.3.(n't-nt+\varepsilon'-\varepsilon)+\&c.;$$

this series may be made to assume the following form, namely, $\tfrac{1}{2}.\Sigma.A^{(i)}.\cos.i.(n't-nt+\varepsilon'-\varepsilon)$. the characteristic Σ of finite integrals being relative to the number i, which ought to extend to all entire numbers from $i=-\infty$ to $i=\infty$; the value $i=0$, being also comprised in this infinite number of values; but then it ought to be observed, that in this case $A^{(-i)}=A^{(i)}$. This form has not only the advantage of enabling us to express, in a very simple manner, the preceding series, but also the product of this series, by the sine or the cosine of any angle $ft+\varpi$; for it is easy to see that this product is equal to

$$\tfrac{1}{2}.\Sigma.A^{(i)}.\begin{matrix}\sin.\\ \cos.\end{matrix}(i.(n't-nt+\varepsilon'-\varepsilon)+ft+\varpi)^{*}$$

* Let $w = n'-nt+\varepsilon'-\varepsilon$, and $ft+\varpi=p$, we shall have $\cos.i.(n'-nt+\varepsilon'-\varepsilon).\cos.(ft+\varpi)) = \cos.iw.\cos.p$, now $\cos.(-iw)=\cos.iw)$, $\sin.-iw=-\sin.iw)$, $(-i.\sin.(-iw)=i.\sin.iw$, ∵ if i' denote the positive values of i, we shall have $\cos.iw.\cos.p = 2\cos.i'w.\cos.p = \cos.(p+i'w)+\cos.(p-i'w)$; $\cos.iw.\sin.p = 2\cos.i'w.\sin.p = \sin.(p+i'w)+\sin.(p-i'w)$; $i.\sin.iw.\cos.p=2i'.\sin.i'w.\cos.p=i'.\sin.(p+i'w)-i'.\sin.(p-i'w)$; $i.\sin.(iw.\sin.p=2i.\sin.i'w.\sin.p=-i'.\cos.(p+i'w)+i.\cos.(p-i'w)$; in the second member of these equations, the first term is changed into the second when i has a negative value, ∵ if i is indifferently positive or negative, the second member is contained in the first; hence we have $\cos.iw.\cos.p=\tfrac{1}{2}.\cos.(iw+p)$. &c. See note page 290.

This property will also enable us to express in a very commodious manner the perturbations of the motions of the planets. Let, in like manner

$$(a^2 - 2aa'.\cos.(n't-nt+\varepsilon'-\varepsilon)+a'^2)^{-\frac{3}{2}}$$
$$=\tfrac{1}{2}.\Sigma.\,B^{(i)}.\cos.\,i.(n't-nt+\varepsilon'-\varepsilon);$$

$B^{(-i)}$ being equal to $B^{(i)}$. This being premised, we shall have by the theorems of N°. 21,

$$R=\frac{m'}{2}.\,\Sigma.\,A^{(i)}.\cos.\,i.(n't-nt+\varepsilon'-\varepsilon)^*$$
$$+\frac{m'}{2}.\,u_{,}.\,\Sigma.a.\left(\frac{dA^{(i)}}{da}\right).\cos.\,i.(n't-nt+\varepsilon'-\varepsilon)$$
$$+\frac{m'}{2}.\,u'_{,}.\Sigma.a'.\left(\frac{dA^{(i)}}{da'}\right).\cos.\,i.(n't-nt+\varepsilon'-\varepsilon)$$
$$-\frac{m'}{2}.\,(v'_{,}-v_{,}).\Sigma.i.\,A^{(i)}.\sin.\,i.(n't-nt+\varepsilon'-\varepsilon)$$
$$+\frac{m'}{4}.\,u_{,}^2.\Sigma.a^2.\left(\frac{d^2.A^{(i)}}{da^2}\right).\cos.\,i.(n't-nt+\varepsilon'-\varepsilon)$$

* Substituting for r, r', v, v', their values, the constant part of the value of R will become $\frac{m'.aa'.\cos.(n't-nt+\varepsilon'-\varepsilon)+zz'}{(a'^2+z^2)^{\frac{3}{2}}}-\frac{m'}{(a^2-2aa'.\cos.(n't-nt+\varepsilon'-\varepsilon)+a'^2+(z'-z)^2)^{\frac{1}{2}}}$,

which becomes (by reducing, and observing that terms higher than of the order of the square of the disturbing forces are neglected) $=m'.(aa'.\cos.((n't-nt+\varepsilon'-\varepsilon)+zz'.(a'^{-3}-\frac{3}{2}a'^{-5}z^2)$

$$-\frac{m'}{(a^2-2aa'.\cos.(n't-nt+\varepsilon'-\varepsilon)+a'^2)^{\frac{1}{2}}}+\frac{\frac{m'}{2}.(z'-z)^2}{(a^2-2aa'.\cos.(n't-nt+\varepsilon'-\varepsilon)+a'^2)^{\frac{3}{2}}};$$

$$=\frac{m'}{2}.\,\Sigma.A^{(i)}.\cos.\,i.(n't-nt+\varepsilon'-\varepsilon)+\frac{m'.zz'}{a'^3}-\frac{\frac{3}{2}m'.az^2.\cos.(n't-nt+\varepsilon'-\varepsilon)}{a'^4}$$
$$+\frac{m'}{4}.\,(z'-z)^2.\Sigma.\,B^{(i)}.\cos.\,i.(n't-nt+\varepsilon'-\varepsilon);$$

now if a, a', $nt+\varepsilon$, $n't+\varepsilon'$, be supposed to be increased by u', $u'_{,}$, $v_{,}$, $v'_{,}$ respectively, the value of R will be given by the formula of N°. 21, in the manner expressed in the text.

$$+\frac{m'}{2}.(u_{,}u_{,}'.\Sigma aa'.\left(\frac{d^2.A^{(i)}}{da.da'}\right).\cos.i.(n't-nt+\epsilon'-\epsilon)$$

$$+\frac{m'}{4}.u_{,}'^2.\Sigma.a'^2.\left(\frac{d^2.A^{(i)}}{da'^2}\right).\cos.i.(n't-nt+\epsilon'-\epsilon)$$

$$-\frac{m'}{2}.(v_{,}'-v_{,}).u_{,}.\Sigma.ia.\left(\frac{dA^{(i)}}{da}\right).(\sin.i.(n't-nt+\epsilon'-\epsilon)$$

$$-\frac{m'}{2}.(v_{,}'-v').u_{,}'.\Sigma.ia'.\left(\frac{dA^{(i)}}{da'}\right).\sin.i.(n't-nt+\epsilon'-\epsilon)$$

$$-\frac{m'}{4}.(v_{,}'-v_{,})^2.\Sigma.i^2.A^{(i)}.\cos.i.(n't-nt+\epsilon'-\epsilon)$$

$$+\frac{m'.zz'}{a'^3}-\frac{3m'.az'^2}{2a'^4}.\cos.(n't-nt+\epsilon'-\epsilon)$$

$$+m'.\frac{(z'-z)^2}{4}.\Sigma.B^{(i)}.\cos.i.(n't-nt+\epsilon'-\epsilon)$$

$$+\&c.$$

If in this expression of R, the values relative to the elliptic motion, are substituted in place of $u_{,}$, $u_{,}'$, $v_{,}$, $v_{,}'$, z and z', which values are functions of the sines and cosines of the angles $nt+\epsilon$, $n't+\epsilon'$, and of their multiples; k will be expressed by an infinite series of cosines of the form $m'k.\cos.(i'n't-int+A)$,* i and i' being entire numbers.

It is evident that the action of the bodies m'', m''', &c., on m, will produce in R, terms analogous to those which result from the action of m', and that we shall obtain them, by changing in the preceding expression of R, all that which is relative to m', into the same quantities relative to m'', m''', &c.

Let any term $m'k.\cos.(i'n't-int+A)$ of the expression for R, be considered. If the orbits were circular, and existed in the same

* The form of this function is always that of a cosine, for the values of u', $u_{,}'$, are expressed by series of the cosines of $nt+\epsilon$, $n't+\epsilon'$, and of their multiples, which are multiplied into a function of the form $\Sigma.\cos.i.(n't-nt+\epsilon'-\epsilon)$, the value of $v-v_{,}'$ is expressed by a series involving $\sin.(nt+\epsilon)$; $\sin.(n't+\epsilon')$; and their multiples, and this is multiplied into a function of the form $\Sigma.\sin.i.(n't-nt+\epsilon'-\epsilon)$.

plane, we would have $i' = i$, therefore i' cannot surpass i, or be surpassed by it, but by means of the sines and cosines of the expressions of $u_{,}$, $v_{,}$, z, $u'_{,}$, $v'_{,}$, z' which by combining with the sines and cosines of the angle $n't - nt + \epsilon' - \epsilon$, and of its multiples, would produce sines and cosines of angles in which i' is different from i.

If we consider the excentricities and inclinations of the orbits, as very small quantities of the first order, it results from the formulæ of N°. 22, that in the expressions of $u_{,}$ $v_{,}$ z or rs, s being the tangent of the latitude of m, the coefficient of the sine or of the cosine of an angle, such as $f.(nt+\epsilon)$, is expressed by a series, of which the first term is of the order f, the second term of the order $f+2$, the third of the order* $f+4$; and so of the rest. The same obtains for the coefficient of the sine and cosine of the angle $f'(n't+\epsilon')$, in the expressions of $u'_{,}$, $v'_{,}$. z'. It follows from this, that i and i' being supposed positive, and i' greater than i: the coefficient k in the term of $m'k.\cos.(i'n't - int + A)$, is of the order $i' - i$, and that in the series which expresses it, the first term is of the order $i' - i$, the second term is of the order $i' - i + 2$, and so of the rest, so that this series is very converging. If i be greater than i', the terms of the series will be successively of the orders $i - i'$, $i - i' + 2$, &c.

* It is evident from inspection of the series in pages 150, 152, that when all the coefficients of the function $\cos. f.(nt+\epsilon)$ are collected together, they will constitute a series of the form $e^{f} \pm e^{f+2} \pm e^{f+4} \pm e^{f+6}$, &c., hence multiplying $\cos. f.(nt+\epsilon)$ into $\cos. i.(n't - nt + \epsilon' - \epsilon)$ the product will be of the form of

$$\frac{\cos. i.(n't - nt + \epsilon' - \epsilon) + f.(n't + \epsilon'))}{2},$$

$=$ by making $f' + i = i'$

$$\frac{\cos.(i'n't - int + A)}{2};$$

which is to be multiplied into the series e^{f}, ϵ^{f+2}, ϵ^{f+4}, &c., $=$ (as $f = i' - i =$), $e^{i'-i}$, $e^{i'-i+2}$, &c.

Let ϖ denote the longitude of the perihelion of the orbit of m, and θ the longitude of its node; and in like manner let ϖ' denote the longitude of the perihelion of the orbit of m', and θ' that of its node; these longitudes being reckoned on a plane very little inclined to that of its orbit. It follows from the formulæ of N°. 22, that in the expressions of $u_{,}$, $v_{,}$ and z, the angle $nt+\varepsilon$ is always accompanied by $-\varpi$, or by $-\theta$; and that in the expressions of $u'_{,}$, $v'_{,}$, and z', the angle $n't+\varepsilon'$ is always accompanied by $-\varpi'$, or by $-\theta'$, hence it follows that the term $m'k.\cos.(i'n't-int+A)$ is of the following form

$$m'k.\cos.(i'n't-int+i'\varepsilon'-i\varepsilon-g\varpi-g'\varpi'-g''\theta-g'''\theta'),$$

g, g', g', g''', being entire numbers, positive or negative, and such that we have

$$0=i'-i-g-g'-g''-g'''.$$

This also follows from considering, that the value of R, and its different terms are independent of the position of the right line, from which we reckon the longitudes. Moreover, in the formulæ of N°. 22, the coefficient of the sine and cosine of the angle ϖ, has always for factor the excentricity e of the orbit of m, the coefficient of the sine and cosine of the angle 2ϖ, has for factor the square of this excentricity, and so of the rest. In like manner, the coefficient of the sine and cosine of the angle θ, has for factor $\text{tang.}\tfrac{1}{2}\varphi$, φ being the inclination of the orbit of m on a fixed plane. The coefficient of the sine and cosine of the angle 2θ, has for factor $\text{tang.}^{2}\tfrac{1}{2}\varphi$, and so of the rest; from this it follows, that the coefficient k has for factor, $e^{g}.e'^{g'}.\text{tang.}^{g''}(\tfrac{1}{2}\varphi).\text{tang.}^{g'''}(\tfrac{1}{2}\varphi)$ the numbers g, g', g'', g''', being taken positively in the exponents of these factors. If all these numbers are positive in themselves, this factor will be of the order $i'-i$, in consequence of the equation

$$0=i'-i-g-g'-g''-g''';$$

but if one of them, such as g, be negative and equal to $-g$, this factor will be of the order $i'-i+2g$.* Therefore, if we only preserve, among the terms of k, those which depending on the angle $i'n't-int$, are of the order $i'-i$, and neglect all those which depending on the same angle, are of the orders $i'-i+2$, $i'-i+4$, &c.; the expression of k will be constituted in the following manner:

$$H.e^{g}.e'^{g'}.\text{tang.}^{g''}(\tfrac{1}{2}\varphi).\text{tang.}^{g'''}(\tfrac{1}{2}\varphi').\cos.(i'n't-int$$
$$+i'\varepsilon'-i\varepsilon-g.\varpi-g'.\varpi'-g''.\theta-g'''.\theta')$$

H being a coëfficient independent of the excentricities and of the inclinations of the orbits, and the numbers g, g', g'', g''', being all positive, and such that their sum is equal to $i'-i$.

If we substitute in R, $a.(1+u_{,})$, in place of r,' we shall have

$$r.\left(\frac{dR}{dr}\right)=a.\left(\frac{dR}{da}\right).$$

If in this same function, we substitute in place of $u_{,}$, $v_{,}$ and z, their values given by the formulæ of N°. 22, we shall have

$$\left(\frac{dR}{dv}\right)=\left(\frac{dR}{d\varepsilon}\right).$$

provided we suppose that $\varepsilon-\varpi$, and $\varepsilon-\theta$ are constant, in the differential of R, taken relatively to ε; for then $u_{,}$, $v_{,}$, and z are constant in this differential, and as we have $v=nt+\varepsilon+v_{,}$, it is evident that the preceding equation has place. We can therefore easily obtain the values of $r.\left(\frac{dR}{dr}\right)$ and of $\left(\frac{dR}{dv}\right)$, which occur in

* For in this case $i'-i+2g=g+g'+g''+g'''$.

' $r=a.(1+u)$; $\frac{dr}{da}=1+u$, $\frac{dR}{da}=\frac{dR}{dr}.\frac{dr}{da}$, $=\frac{dr}{da}.(1+u)$, $\therefore a.\left(\frac{dR}{da}\right)=r.\left(\frac{dR}{dr}\right)$.

the differential equations of the preceding numbers, when we shall have obtained the value of R expanded into a series of the cosines of angles increasing proportionally to the time. It will also be very easy to determine the differential dR, by taking care that the angle nt, solely varies in the expression of R, the angle $n't$ being supposed to be constant; because dR is the difference of R, taking on the supposition, that the coordinates of m', which are functions of $n't$, are constant.

49. The difficulty of the expansion of R into a series, is reduced to the determination of the quantities $A^{(i)}$, $B^{(i)}$, and their differences, taken relatively to a and a'. For this purpose, let us consider generally the function $(a^2-2aa'.\cos.\theta+a'^2)^{-s}$, and let us expand it according to the cosines of the angle θ, and of its multiples. By making $\frac{a}{a'}=\alpha$, it will become $a'^{-2s}.(1-\alpha.\cos.\theta+\alpha)^{-s}$. Let

$$(1-2\alpha.\cos.\theta+\alpha^2)^{-s}=\tfrac{1}{2}.b_s^{(0)}+b_s^{(1)}.\cos.\theta+b_s^{(2)}.\cos.2\theta. \\ +b_s^{(3)}.\cos.3\theta+\&c.$$

$b_s^{(0)}$, $b_s^{(1)}$, $b_s^{(2)}$, &c., being functions of α and s. If we take the logarithmic differences of the two members of this equation, with respect to the variable θ, we shall have

$$\frac{-2s.\alpha.\sin.\theta}{1-2\alpha.\cos.\theta+\alpha^2}=\frac{-b_s^{(1)}.\sin.\theta-2b_s^{(2)}.\sin.2\theta-\&c.}{\tfrac{1}{2}.b_s^{(0)}+b_s^{(1)}.\cos.\theta+b_s^{(2)}.\cos.2\theta+\&c.},$$

by multiplying transversely, and comparing together like cosines, we find generally

$$b_s^{(i)}=\frac{(i-1).(1+\alpha^2).b_s^{(i-1)}-(i+s-2).\alpha.b_s^{(i-2)}}{(i-s).\alpha};\quad (a)$$

by this means the values of $b_s^{(2)}$, $b_s^{(3)}$, &c., will be given, when $b_s^{(0)}$, $b_s^{(1)}$, are known.

s being changed into $s+1$ in the preceding expression of $(1-2\alpha.\cos.\theta)+\alpha^2)^{-s-1}$, we shall have

$$(1-2\alpha.\cos.\theta+\alpha^2)^{-s-1}=\tfrac{1}{2}.b^{(0)}_{s+1}.+b^{(1)}_{s+1}\cos.\theta+b^{(2)}_{s+1}.\cos.2\theta.$$
$$+b^{(3)}_{s+1}.\cos.3\theta+\&c.$$

By multiplying the two members of this equation, by $1-2\alpha.\cos.\theta+\alpha^2$, and by substituting in place of $(1-2\alpha.\cos.\theta+\alpha^2)^{-s}$, its value in a series, we shall have

$$\tfrac{1}{2}.b^{(0)}_s+b^{(1)}_s.\cos.\theta+b^{(2)}_s.\cos.2\theta+\&c.$$
$$=(1-2\alpha.\cos.\theta+\alpha^2).(\tfrac{1}{2}.b^{(0)}_{s+1}+b^{(1)}_{s+1}.\cos.\theta+b^{(2)}_{s+1}.\cos.2\theta+b^{(3)}_{s+1}.\cos.3\theta+\&c.);$$

from which may be obtained, by a comparison of similar cosines

$$b^{(i)}_s=(1+\alpha^2).b^{(i)}_{s+1}-\alpha.b^{(i-1)}_{s+1}-\alpha.b^{(i+1)}_{s+1}.*$$

The formula (a) gives

$$b^{i+1}_{s+1}=\frac{i.(1+\alpha^2).b^{(i)}_{s+1}-(i+s).\alpha.b^{(i-1)}_{s+2}}{(i-s).\alpha};$$

the preceding expression of $b^{(i)}_s$, will therefore become

$$b^{(i)}_s=\frac{2s.\alpha.b^{(i-1)}_{s+1}-s.(1+\alpha^2).b^{(i)}_{s+1}}{i-s}.$$

When this transverse multiplication is performed we must substitute for $\cos.\theta.\sin.^2(\theta)$, $\sin.\theta.\cos.^{(i)}\theta$, their values in terms of $\frac{\sin.(i+1).\theta}{2}+\frac{\sin.(i-1)\theta}{2}$; hence we obtain $-s\alpha b^{(i-2)}_s.\sin.(i-1).\theta-s\alpha b^{(i)}_s.\sin.(i-1).\theta-(1+\alpha^2).(i-1).b^{i-1}_s,\sin.(i-1).\theta+\alpha i b^{(i)}_s.\sin.(i-1).\theta.+\alpha.(i-2).b^{(i-2)}_s.\sin.(i-1).\theta=0$ $\therefore b^{i}_s.\alpha.(i-s)=(1+\alpha^2).(i-1).b^{(i-1)}_s-\alpha.(i-2+s).b^{i-2}_s$.

* To obtain this value of $b^{(i)}_s$, it is to be remarked that $\cos.\theta.\cos.i\theta=\frac{\cos.(i+1).\theta+\cos.(i-1).\theta}{2}$, hence multiplying the two factors of the second member of this equation, the coefficient of $\cos.i\theta$ is $(1+\alpha^2)\,b^{(i)}_{s+1}-\alpha b^{(i+1)}_{s+1}-\alpha b^{(i-1)}_{s+1}$.

By changing i into $i+1$, in this equation, we shall have

$$b_s^{(i+1)}=\frac{2s.\alpha.b_{s+1}^{(i)}-s.(1+\alpha^2).\,b_{s+1}^{(i+1)}}{i-s+1};$$

and if we substitute in place of $b_{s+1}^{(i+1)}$, its preceding value, we will have

$$b_s^{(i+1)}=\frac{s.(i+s).\,\alpha.(1+\alpha^2).\,b_{s+1}^{(i-1)}+s.(2(i-s).\,\alpha^2-i.(1+\alpha^2)^2).\,b_{s+1}^{(i)}}{(i-s).(i-s+1).\alpha}.$$

These two expressions of $b_s^{(i)}$, and of $b_s^{(i+1)}$, give

$$b_{s+1}^{(i)}=\frac{\frac{(i+s)}{s}.\,(1+\alpha^2).\,b_s^{(i)}-2.\,\frac{(i-s+1)}{s}.\,\alpha b_s^{(i+1)}}{(1-\alpha^2)^2};\quad (b)$$

by substituting for $b_s^{(i+1)}$, its value deduced from the equation (a), we shall have

$$b_{s+1}^{(i)}=\frac{\frac{(s-i)}{s}.\,(1+\alpha^2).\,b_s^{(i)}+\frac{2(i+s-1)}{s}.\,\alpha.b_s^{(i-1)}}{(1-\alpha^2)^2};\quad (c)^*$$

which expression might have been inferred from the preceding by changing i into $-i$, and by remarking that $b_s^{(i)}=b_s^{(-i)}$. We shall consequently obtain by means of this formula, the values of $b_{s+1}^{(0)}$, $b_{s+1}^{(1)}$, $b_{s+1}^{(2)}$, &c., when the values of $b_s^{(0)}$, $b_s^{(1)}$, $b_s^{(2)}$, &c., will have been known.

In order to abridge, let λ denote the function $1-2\alpha.\cos.\theta+\alpha^2$, by differentiating with respect to α, the equation

$$\lambda^{-s}=\tfrac{1}{2}.\,b_s^{(0)}.+b_s^{(1)}\cos.\theta+b_s^{(2)}.\cos.2\theta+\ \&c.;$$

we will obtain

$$-2s.(\alpha-\cos.\theta).\,\lambda^{-s-1}=\tfrac{1}{2}.\,\frac{db_s^{(0)}}{d\alpha}+\frac{db_s^{(1)}}{d\alpha}.\cos.\theta+\frac{db_s^{(2)}}{d\alpha}.\cos.2\theta+\&c.;$$

* Hence if we know the coefficients of the multiple cosines in the series which is equivalent to $(1-2\alpha.\cos.\theta+\alpha^2)^{-s}$, we know the coefficients of the multiple cosines in the series which is equivalent to $(1-2\alpha.\cos.\theta+\alpha^2)^{-s-1}$.

but we have

$$-\alpha+\cos.\,\theta=\frac{1-\alpha^2-\lambda}{2\alpha};$$

therefore we shall have

$$\frac{s.(1-\alpha^2)}{\alpha}\,.\,\lambda^{-s-1}-\frac{s.\lambda^{-s}}{\alpha}=\tfrac{1}{2}.\frac{db_s^{(0)}}{d\alpha}+\frac{db_s^{(1)}}{d\alpha}.\cos.\,\theta+\ \&c.\,;$$

hence we deduce generally

$$\frac{db_s^{(i)}}{d\alpha}=\frac{s.(1-\alpha^2)}{\alpha}\,.\,b_{s+1}^{(i)}-\frac{s.b_s^{(i)}}{\alpha}.\text{*}$$

By substituting in place of $b_{s+1}^{(i)}$ its value given by the formula (b), we will obtain

$$\frac{db_s^{(i)}}{d\alpha}=\left\{\frac{i+(i+2s).\alpha^2}{\alpha.(1-\alpha^2)}\right\}.\,b_s^{(i)}-\frac{2.(i-s+1)}{1-\alpha^2}.\,b_s^{(i+1)}.\dagger$$

This equation being differentiated, will give

$$\frac{d^2b_s^{(i)}}{d\alpha^2}=\left\{\frac{i+(i+2s).\alpha^2}{\alpha.(1-\alpha^2)}\right\}.\frac{db_s^{(i)}}{d\alpha}+\left\{\frac{2.(i+s).(1+\alpha^2)}{(1-\alpha^2)^2}-\frac{i}{\alpha^2}\right\}.\,b_s^{(i)}.$$

$$-\,2.\frac{(i-s+1)}{1-\alpha^2}.\frac{db_s^{(i+1)}}{d\alpha}-4.\frac{(i-s+1).\alpha}{(1-\alpha^2)^2}.\,b_s^{(i+1)}.$$

* Substituting for λ^{-s-1}, λ^{-s}, their values given in the preceding page, the coefficient of cos. $i\theta$, in the value of λ^{-s-1} is $\mathfrak{b}_{s+1}^{i}$, and the coefficient of the same quantity in the value of λ^{-s} is $\mathfrak{b}_s^{(i)}$.

† Differencing the coefficient of $\mathfrak{b}_s^{(i)}$ with respect to α it becomes

$$\frac{-i.(1-\alpha^2)+2\alpha^2 i}{\alpha^2.(1-\alpha^2)^2}+\frac{(i+2s).(1-\alpha^2)+2\alpha^2.(i+2s)}{(1-\alpha^2)^2}=$$

$$-\frac{i.(1-3\alpha^2)}{\alpha^2.(1-\alpha^2)^2}+\frac{(i+2s).\alpha^2.(1-\alpha^2)}{\alpha^2.(1-\alpha^2)^2}+\frac{2\alpha^2.(i+2s)}{(1-\alpha^2)^2}=-\frac{i.(1-2\alpha^2+\alpha^4)}{\alpha^2.(1-\alpha^2)^2}$$

$$+\frac{(1+\alpha^2).2(s+i)}{(1-\alpha^2)^2}.$$

By differentiating again, we will obtain

$$\frac{d^3b_s^{(i)}}{d\alpha^3}=\left\{\frac{i+(i+2s).\alpha^2}{\alpha.(1-\alpha^2)}\right\}.\frac{d^2b_s^{(i)}}{d\alpha^2}+2.\left\{\frac{2.(i+s).(1+\alpha^2)}{(1-\alpha^2)^2}-\frac{i}{a^2}\right\}.\frac{db_s^{(i)}}{d\alpha}$$

$$+\left\{\frac{4(i+s).\alpha(3+\alpha^2)}{(1-a^2)^3}+\frac{2i}{\alpha^3}\right\}.b_s^{(i)}-\frac{2.(i-s+1)}{1-\alpha^2}.\frac{d^2.b_s^{(i+1)}}{d\alpha^2}$$

$$-\frac{8.(i-s+1).\alpha}{(1-\alpha^2)^2}.\frac{db_s^{(i+1)}}{d\alpha}-\frac{4.(i-s+1).(1+3\alpha^2)}{(1-\alpha^2)^3}.b_s^{(i+1)}.$$

It appears from this that in order to determine the values of $b_s^{(i)}$, and of its successive differentials, it is sufficient to know those of $b_s^{(0)}$, and of $b_s^{(1)}$. These two quantities may be determined in the following manner:

Let c represent the number of which the hyperbolical logarithm is unity; the expression of λ^{-s}, may be made to assume the following form:

$$\lambda^{-s}=(1-\alpha.c^{\theta\sqrt{-1}})^{-s}.(1-\alpha.c^{-\theta.\sqrt{-1}})^{-s}.$$

By expanding the second member of this equation, with respect to the powers of $c^{\theta.\sqrt{-1}}$, and of $c^{-\theta.\sqrt{-1}}$, it is evident that the two exponential quantities $c^{i\theta\sqrt{-1}}$, and $c^{-i\theta\sqrt{-1}}$ will have the same coefficients which we will denote by k. The sum of the two terms $k.c^{i\theta.\sqrt{-1}}$, and $k.c^{-i\theta.\sqrt{-1}}$ is $2k$. cos. $i\theta$; this will be the value of $b_s^{(i)}$. cos. $i\theta$; therefore we will obtain $b_s^{(i)}=2k$. Now the expression of λ^{-s} is equal to the product of the two series

$$1+s\alpha.c^{\theta.\sqrt{-1}}+\frac{s.(s+1)}{1.2}.\alpha^2.c^{2\theta.\sqrt{-1}}+\text{\&c.};$$

$$1+s\alpha.c^{-\theta.\sqrt{-1}}+\frac{s.(s+1)}{1.2}.\alpha^2.c^{-2\theta\sqrt{-1}}+\text{\&c.}$$

these two series being multiplied, the one by the other, will give, in the case of $i=0$,*

$$k=1+s^2\alpha^2+\left\{\frac{s.(s+1)}{1.2}\right\}^2.\alpha^4+\text{\&c.};$$

and in the case of $i=1$,

$$k=\alpha.\left\{s+s.\frac{s.(s+1)}{1.2}.\alpha^2+\frac{s.(s+1)}{1.2}.\frac{s.(s+1).(s+2)}{1.2.3}.\alpha^4+\text{\&c.};\right\}$$

consequently,

$$b_s^{(0)}=2.\left\{1+s^2.\alpha^2+\left\{\frac{s.(s+1)}{1.2}\right\}^2.\alpha^4+\left\{\frac{s.(s+1).(s+2)^2}{1.2.3}\right\}.\alpha^6+\text{\&c.};\right\}$$

$$b_s^{(1)}=2\alpha.\left\{s+s.\frac{s.(s+1)}{1.2}.\alpha^2+\frac{s.(s+1)}{1.2}.\frac{s.(s+1).(s+2)}{1.2.3}.\alpha^4+\text{\&c.}\right\}$$

In order that this series may converge, it is necessary that α should be less than unity; this may be always effected by assuming α equal to the ratio of the smaller of the distances a and a' to the greater, and as we have already supposed $\alpha=\frac{a}{a'}$, we will assume that a is less than a'.

In the theory of the motions of the bodies m, m', m'', &c., it is necessary to know the values of $b_s^{(0)}$, and of $b_s^{(1)}$, when $s=\frac{1}{2}$, and $s=\frac{3}{2}$. In these two cases these values do not converge rapidly unless α is a very small fraction. These series converge with greater rapidity when $s=-\frac{1}{2}$, and we have

$$\tfrac{1}{2}b_{-\frac{1}{2}}^{(0)}=1+(\tfrac{1}{2})^2.\alpha^2+\left(\frac{1.1}{2.4}\right)^2.\alpha^4+\left(\frac{1.1.3}{2.4.6}\right)^2.\alpha^6+\left(\frac{1.1.3.5}{2.4.6.8}\right)^2.\alpha^8+\text{\&c.}$$

$$b_{-\frac{1}{2}}^{(1)}=-\alpha.\left\{1-\frac{1.1}{2.4}.\alpha^2-\frac{1}{4}.\frac{1.1.3}{2.4.6}.\alpha^4-\frac{1.3}{4.6}.\frac{1.1.3.5}{2.4.6.8}.\alpha^6-\frac{1.3.5}{4.6.8}.\frac{1.1.3.5.7}{2.4.6.8.10}.\alpha^8-\text{\&c.}\right\}.$$

* $i=0$ when equal powers of $b^{\theta.\sqrt{-1}}$, and $c^{-\theta.\sqrt{-1}}$, are multiplied together and, $i=1$, when powers of $b^{\theta.\sqrt{-1}}$, are multiplied into powers of $c^{-\sqrt{-1}}$, which are less by unit than these. This is evident from the value of k.

In the theory of the planets and of the satellites, it will be sufficient to assume the sum of the first eleven or twelve terms, the subsequent being neglected, or more accurately, by summing* them as a geometric progression of which the ratio is $1-\alpha^2$. When $b^{(0)}_{-\frac{1}{2}}$, $b^{(1)}_{-\frac{1}{2}}$, shall have been thus determined we will obtain $b^{(0)}_{-\frac{1}{2}}$ by making $i=0$, and $s=-\frac{1}{2}$, in the formula (b), and we will find

$$b^{(0)}_{\frac{1}{2}}=\frac{(1+\alpha^2).\,b^{(0)}_{-\frac{1}{2}}+6.\alpha.b^{(1)}_{-\frac{1}{2}}}{(1-\alpha^2)^2}.$$

If in the formula (c), we suppose $i=1$, and $s=-\frac{1}{2}$, we will have

$$b^{(1)}_{\frac{1}{2}}=\frac{2.\alpha b^{(0)}_{-\frac{1}{2}}+3.(1+\alpha^2).\,b^{(1)}_{-\frac{1}{2}}}{(1-\alpha^2)^2}.$$

By means of these values of $b^{(0)}_{\frac{1}{2}}$, and of $b^{(1)}_{\frac{1}{2}}$, we will obtain by the preceding formula, the values of $b^{(i)}_{\frac{1}{2}}$, and of its partial differences, whatever may be the number i, from which we may we may conclude the values of $b^{(i)}_{\frac{3}{2}}$, and of its differences. The values of $b^{(0)}_{\frac{3}{2}}$, and of $b^{(1)}_{\frac{3}{2}}$ may be determined very simply, by the following formulæ;

$$b^{(0)}_{\frac{3}{2}}=\frac{b^{(0)}_{-\frac{1}{2}}}{(1-\alpha^2)^2}\;;\quad b^{(1)}_{\frac{3}{2}}=-3.\frac{b^{(1)}_{-\frac{1}{2}}}{(1-\alpha^2)^2}.\dagger$$

* For if $(1-\alpha^2)^{-1}$ be expanded to a series, the sum of the remaining terms will be very nearly equal to this series multiplied into the eleventh term.

† By formula (b) $b^{(0)}_{\frac{3}{2}}=\frac{(1+\alpha^2).\,b^{(0)}_{\frac{1}{2}}-2\alpha b^{1}_{\frac{1}{2}}}{(1-\alpha^2)^2}$; substituting for $b^{0}_{\frac{1}{2}}$, $b^{(1)}_{\frac{1}{2}}$, their values we obtain $b^{0}_{\frac{3}{2}}=\frac{(1+\alpha^2)^2.b^{0}_{-\frac{1}{2}}+6\alpha.(1+\alpha^2).\,b^{(1)}_{-\frac{1}{2}}-4\alpha^2.b^{(0)}_{-\frac{1}{2}}-6\alpha.(1+\alpha^2).\,b^{(1)}_{-\frac{1}{2}}}{(1-\alpha^2)^4}=\frac{(1-\alpha^2)^2 b^{(0)}_{-\frac{1}{2}}}{(1-\alpha^2)^4}$ $\frac{b^{(0)}_{-\frac{1}{2}}}{(1-\alpha^2)^2}$; in a similar manner we obtain the value of $b^{(1)}_{\frac{3}{2}}$.

$$\frac{d^2A^{(1)}}{da^2}=\frac{1}{a'^2}.\frac{d^2b^{(1)}_{\frac{1}{2}}}{d\alpha^2}.\frac{d\alpha}{da}=-\frac{1}{a'^3}.\frac{d^2b^{(1)}_{\frac{1}{2}}}{d\alpha^2}$$

Now, in order to obtain the quantities $A^{(0)}$, $A^{(1)}$, &c., and their differences, it may be remarked that by the preceding number, the series

$$\tfrac{1}{2}.A^{(0)} + A^{(1)}.\cos.\theta + A^{(2)}.\cos.2\theta + \text{\&c.}$$

results from the expansion of the function

$$\frac{a.\cos.\theta}{a'^2} - (a^2 - 2aa'.\cos.\theta + a'^2)^{-\frac{1}{2}},$$

in a series ranged according to the cosines of the angle θ and of its multiples; by making $\frac{a}{a'} = \alpha$, this same function is reduced to

$$-\frac{1}{2a'}.b_{\frac{1}{2}}^{(0)} + \left(\frac{a}{a'^2} - \frac{1}{a'}.b_{\frac{1}{2}}^{(1)}\right).\cos.\theta - \frac{1}{a'}.b_{\frac{1}{2}}^{(2)}.\cos.2\theta - \text{\&c.}$$

which gives generally

$$A^{(i)} = -\frac{1}{a'}.b_{\frac{1}{2}}^{(i)};$$

when i is zero, or greater than unity, abstracting from the sign. In the case of $i = 1$, we have

$$A^{(1)} = -\frac{1}{a'}.\frac{db_{\frac{1}{2}}^{(i)}}{d\alpha}.\left(\frac{d\alpha}{da}\right);$$

we have then

$$\frac{dA^{(i)}}{d\alpha} = -\frac{1}{\alpha'}.\frac{db_{\frac{1}{2}}^{(i)}}{d\alpha}.\left(\frac{d\alpha}{da}\right);$$

but we have $\left(\frac{d\alpha}{da}\right) = \frac{1}{a'}$; therefore

$$\frac{dA^{(i)}}{d\alpha} = -\frac{1}{\alpha'^2}.\frac{db^{(i)}}{d\alpha};$$

and in the case of $i = 1$, we have

$$\left(\frac{dA^{(i)}}{da}\right) = -\frac{1}{a'^2}.\left(1 - \frac{db_{\frac{1}{2}}^{(i)}}{d\alpha}\right).$$

Finally, even in the case of $i=1$, we have,

$$\left(\frac{d^2A^{(i)}}{da^2}\right)=-\frac{1}{a'^3}\cdot\frac{d^2b_{\frac{1}{2}}^{(i)}}{d\alpha^2};$$

$$\left(\frac{d^3A^{(i)}}{da^3}\right)=-\frac{1}{a'^4}\cdot\frac{d^3b_{\frac{1}{2}}^{(i)}}{d\alpha^3};$$

&c.

In order to obtain the differences of $A^{(i)}$ relative to a' it may be observed, that $A^{(i)}$ being an homogeneous function of a and a', of the dimension -1, we have by the nature of this kind of functions,

$$a.\left(\frac{dA^{(i)}}{da}\right)+a'.\left(\frac{dA^{(i)}}{da'}\right)=-A^{(i)},$$

hence we deduce

$$a'.\left(\frac{dA^{(i)}}{da'}\right)=-A^{(i)}-a.\left(\frac{dA^{(i)}}{da}\right);$$

$$a'.\left(\frac{d^2A^{(i)}}{da.da'}\right)=-2.\left(\frac{dA^{(i)}}{da}\right)-a.\left(\frac{d^2A^{(i)}}{da^2}\right);$$

$$a'^2.\left(\frac{d^2A^{(i)}}{da'^2}\right)=2.A^{(i)}+4a.\left(\frac{dA^{(i)}}{da}\right)+a^2.\left(\frac{d^2A^{(i)}}{da^2}\right);$$

$$a'^2.\left(\frac{d^3A^{(i)}}{da.da'^2}\right)=6.\left(\frac{dA^{(i)}}{da}\right)+6a.\left(\frac{d^2A^{(i)}}{da^2}\right)+a^2.\left(\frac{d^3A^{(i)}}{da^3}\right);$$

$$a'^3.\left(\frac{d^3A^{(i)}}{da'^3}\right)=-6.A^{(i)}-18a.\left(\frac{dA^{(i)}}{da}\right)-9a^2.\left(\frac{d^2A^{(i)}}{da^2}\right)-a^3.\left(\frac{d^3A^{(i)}}{da}\right);$$

&c.

$B^{(i)}$ and its differences will be obtained by observing that by the preceding number, the series

$$\tfrac{1}{2}.\,B^{(0)}+B^{(1)}.\cos.\theta+B^{(2)}.\cos.\theta+\text{\&c.}$$

is the expansion of the function $a^{-\frac{3}{2}}.\,(1-2a.\cos.\theta+a^2)^{-\frac{3}{2}}$ according to the cosines of the angle θ and of its multiples; but this function thus expanded, is equal to

$$a'^{-3}.\left(\tfrac{1}{2}.\,b^{(0)}_{\frac{3}{2}}+b^{(1)}_{\frac{3}{2}}.\cos.\theta+b^{(2)}_{\frac{3}{2}}.\cos.2\theta+\&c.\right);$$

therefore we have generally

$$B^{(i)}=\frac{1}{a'^3}.\,b^{(i)}_{\frac{3}{2}};$$

hence we obtain

$$\left(\frac{dB^{(i)}}{da}\right)=\frac{1}{a'^4}.\frac{db^{(i)}_{\frac{3}{2}}}{d\alpha};\quad\left(\frac{d^2B^{(i)}}{da^2}\right)=\frac{1}{a'^5}.\frac{d^2b^{(i)}_{\frac{3}{2}}}{d\alpha^2};\quad\&c.$$

Moreover, $B^{(i)}$ being an homogeneous function of a and of a', of the dimension -3, we have

$$a.\left\{\frac{dB^{(i)}}{da}\right\}+a'.\left\{\frac{dB^{(i)}}{da'}\right\}=-3B^{(i)};$$

from which it is easy to infer the partial differences of $B^{(i)}$ teken relatively to a', by means of its partial differences relatively to a.

In the theory of the perturbations of m' by the action of m, the values of $A^{(i)}$ and of $B^{(i)}$ are the same as above, with the exception of $A^{(1)}$, which in this theory becomes $\frac{a'}{a^2}-\frac{1}{a'}.\,b^{(1)}_{\frac{1}{2}}$. Thus the computation of the values of $A^{(i)}$, $B^{(i)}$, and of their differences, serves at once for the theories of the two bodies m and m'.

50. After this digression on the expansion of R into a series, let us resume the differential equations (X'), (Y') and (Z') of N°s. 46 and 47; and let us determine by their means, the values of δr, δv, and δs, the approximation being extended to quantities of the order of the excentricities and of the inclinations of the orbits.

If in the elliptic orbits, we suppose

$$r=a.(1+u_{,});\quad r'=a'.(1+u'_{,});$$
$$v=nt+\varepsilon+v_{,};\quad v'=n't+\varepsilon'+v'_{,};$$

by N°. 22 we shall have

$$u_{,}=-e.\cos.(nt+\varepsilon-\varpi);\quad u'_{,}=-e'.\cos.(n't+\varepsilon'-\varpi')$$
$$v_{,}=2e.\sin.(nt+\varepsilon-\varpi);\quad v'_{,}=2e'.\sin.(n't+\varepsilon'-\varpi');$$

$nt+\varepsilon$, $n't+\varepsilon'$ being the mean longitudes of m and m'; a and a' being the greater semiaxes of their orbits; e and e' being the ratios of the excentricities to the greater semiaxes; finally, ϖ and ϖ' being the longitudes of their perihelions. All these longitudes, may be referred indifferently to the planes themselves of the orbits, or to a plane which is very little inclined to them; because quantities of the order of the squares and products of the excentricities and of the inclinations are neglected. The preceding values being substituted, in the expression of R of N°. 48, will give

$$R=\frac{m'}{2}.\ \Sigma.\ A^{(i)}.(\cos.\ i.\ (n't-nt+\varepsilon'-\varepsilon)^{*}$$

* As the approximation is carried only as far as terms involving the first power of the excentricity, the only terms in the general expression for R which are to be considered, are the four first. Now as $A^{(i)}=A^{(-i)}$ and $\left(\frac{dA^{(i)}}{da}\right)=\left(\frac{dA^{(-i)}}{da}\right)$, and $\cos.i.w=\cos.(-i.w)$ w representing $(n't-nt+\varepsilon'-\varepsilon)$, and $\sin.(-i.w)=-\sin.iw$, we shall have generally (i' representing the positive values of i, and n representing $(nt+\varepsilon-\varpi)$), $\cos.i.w.\cos.n=2\cos.i'.w.\cos.n=\cos.(i'.w+n)+\cos.(i'.w-n)$, and $i.\sin.i.w.\sin.n=2i'.\sin.i'w.\sin.n=+i'.\cos.((i'.w+n)-i'.\cos.(n-i'.w)$ See page 274, Notes). Hence substituting for $n_{,}$ its value, $(nt+\varepsilon-\varpi)$, and observing that $\cos.i.(n't-nt+\varepsilon'-\varepsilon.)\cos.(nt+\varepsilon-\varpi)$

$$=\cos.i'.(n't-nt+\varepsilon'-\varepsilon)+nt+\varepsilon-\varpi)+\cos.i'.(n't-nt+\varepsilon'-\varepsilon)-(nt+\varepsilon-\varpi)),$$

and also that when $2e.\sin.(nt+\varepsilon-\varpi)$ is substituted for $v'_{,}$, $\sin.i.(n't-nt+\varepsilon'-\varepsilon)$.

$$\sin.(nt+\varepsilon-\varpi)=\cos.i.(n't-nt+\varepsilon'-\varepsilon)+nt+\varepsilon-\varpi)-\cos.$$

$i'.(n't-nt+\varepsilon'-\varepsilon)-nt-\varepsilon-\varpi)$, we obtain the second term in the expression; in like manner the third term is obtained, by taking the index $i-1$; in the third term the circular part is

$$-\frac{m'}{2}.\,\Sigma.\left\{a.\left\{\frac{dA^{(i)}}{da}\right\}+2i.A^{(i)}\right\}.\,e.\cos.(i.(n't-nt+\varepsilon'-\varepsilon)+nt+\varepsilon-\varpi)$$

$$-\frac{m'}{2}.\,\Sigma.\left\{a'.\left\{\frac{dA^{(i-1)}}{da'}\right\}-2.(i-1).A^{(i-1)}.\right\}e'\cos.(i.(n't-nt+\varepsilon'-\varepsilon)+nt+\varepsilon-\varpi');$$

the sign Σ of finite integrals, extending to all integral values positive and negative of i, the value $i=0$ being comprehended among them. From which we obtain

$$2.\int dR+r.\left(\frac{dR}{dr}\right)=$$

$$2m'.g+\frac{m'}{2}\,a.\left\{\frac{dA^{(0)}}{da}\right\}+\frac{m'}{2}.\Sigma.\left\{a.\left\{\frac{dA^{(i)}}{da}\right\}+\frac{2n}{n-n'}.\,A^{(i)}\right\}$$
$$\cos.\,i.(n't-nt+\varepsilon'-\varepsilon)$$

$$-\frac{m'}{2}.\left\{a^2.\left\{\frac{d^2A^{(0)}}{da^2}\right\}+3a\left\{\frac{dA^{(0)}}{da}\right\}\right\}.\,e.\,(\cos.\,nt+\varepsilon-\varpi)$$

$$-\frac{m'}{2}.\left\{aa'\left\{\frac{d^2A^{(1)}}{da.da'}\right\}+2a.\left\{\frac{dA^{(1)}}{da}\right\}+2a'.\left\{\frac{dA^{(1)}}{da'}\right\}+4A^{(1)}\right\}.$$
$$e'.\cos.\,(nt+\varepsilon-\varpi')$$

$$-\frac{m'}{2}.\Sigma.\left\{\begin{matrix}a^2.\left\{\frac{d^2A^{(i)}}{da^2}\right\}+(2i+1).\,a.\left\{\frac{dA^{(i)}}{da}\right\}\\+\frac{2.(i-1).n}{i.(n-n')-n}.\left\{a.\left\{\frac{dA^{(i)}}{da}\right\}+2i.A^{(i)}\right\}\end{matrix}\right\}.$$
$$e.\cos.\,(i.(n't-nt+\varepsilon'-\varepsilon)+nt+\varepsilon-\varpi);$$

made to assume a more symmetrical form, for it becomes by performing the prescribed operations, $\cos.(i-1).(n't-nt+\varepsilon'-\varepsilon)+n't+\varepsilon'-\varpi')$, which is evidently identical with the expression $\cos.i.(n't-nt+\varepsilon'-\varepsilon)+nt+\varepsilon-\varpi')$, besides the values when $i=0$, are comprized in this expression.

$$-\frac{m'}{2}.\,\Sigma.\left\{\begin{array}{l} aa'.\left\{\frac{d^2A^{(i-1)}}{da.da'}\right\}-2.(i-1)a.\left\{\frac{dA^{(i-1)}}{da}\right\} \\ \frac{2.(i-1).n}{i.(n-n')-n}.\left\{a'.\left\{\frac{dA^{(i-1)}}{da'}\right\}-2.(i-1)A^{(i-1)}\right\} \end{array}\right\}.^{*}$$

$$e'.\cos.\,(i.(n't-nt+\varepsilon'-\varepsilon)+nt+\varepsilon-\varpi');$$

The sign Σ extending in this and the following formulæ to all the integral values of i, positive and negative, the sole value $i=0$ being

* When the value of $i=0$, is excepted out of the positive and negative values of i, we shall have

$$\frac{dR}{dr}=\frac{m'}{2}.\frac{dA^{(0)}}{da}+\frac{m'}{2}.\frac{d.\Sigma A^{(i)}}{da}.\cos.i.(n't-nt+\varepsilon'-\varepsilon)-\frac{m'}{2}.a.\frac{d^2A^{(0)}}{da^2}.e.\cos.(nt+\varepsilon-\varpi)$$

$$-\frac{m'}{2}.\Sigma.\left(a.\frac{d^2A^{(i)}}{da^2}+2i.\frac{dA^{(i)}}{da}\right)e.\cos.i.(n't-nt+\varepsilon'-\varepsilon)+nt-\varepsilon-\varpi)$$

$$-\frac{m'}{2}.\left(a'.\frac{d^2A^{(1)}}{da'.da}+\frac{2.dA^{(1)}}{da}\right)e'.\cos.(nt+\varepsilon-\varpi')-\frac{m'}{2}.\Sigma.a'.\frac{d^2A^{i-1}}{da.da'}-2(i-1).$$

$$\left.\frac{dA^{(i-1)}}{da}\right)e'.\cos.i.(n't-nt+\varepsilon'-\varepsilon)+nt+\varepsilon-\varpi'),$$ $\therefore$ substituting for r its value, $a.(1-e.)$.

$\cos.(nt+\varepsilon-\varpi)$, we shall have $r.\left(\frac{dR}{dr}\right)=\frac{m'}{2}.a.\frac{dA^{(0)}}{da}-\frac{m'}{2}.\frac{dA^{(0)}}{da}.$

$$e.\cos.(nt+\varepsilon-\varpi)+\frac{m'}{2}.\ a.\frac{d\Sigma A^{(i)}}{da}.\cos.i.(n't-nt+\varepsilon'-\varepsilon)-\frac{m'}{2}.a.\frac{d\Sigma A^{(i)}}{da}.e.\cos.i.$$
$$(n't-nt+\varepsilon'-\varepsilon)+nt+\varepsilon-\varpi)$$

$$-\frac{m'}{2}\left(\Sigma a^2.\frac{d^2A}{da^2}+2ia.\frac{dA}{da}\right).e.\cos.i.(n't-nt'+\varepsilon'-\varepsilon)+nt+\varepsilon-\varpi)$$

$$-\frac{m'}{2}.a^2.\frac{d^2A^{(0)}}{da^2}.e.\cos.(nt+\varepsilon-\varpi)$$

$$-\frac{m'}{2}.a'.a.\left(\frac{d^2A^{(1)}}{da'.da}+a.\frac{2dA^{(1)}}{da}\right).e'.\cos.(nt+\varepsilon-\varpi')$$

$$-\frac{m'}{2}.\Sigma.\left(a^2a'.\frac{dA^{(i-1)}}{da'}-2(i-1)\,d.\frac{A^{(i-)}}{da}\right)e'.\cos.((n't-nt+\varepsilon'-\varepsilon)+nt+\varepsilon-\varpi)$$

(the remaining terms are omitted because e^2 occurs)

excepted, because the terms in which $i=0$, are extricated from this sign: mg is a constant quantity added to the integral $\int dR$. Therefore by making

$$C=\tfrac{1}{2}a^3.\left\{\frac{d^2A^{(0)}}{da^2}\right\}+3a^2.\left\{\frac{dA^{(0)}}{da}\right\}+6ag;$$

$$D=\tfrac{1}{2}a^2a'.\left\{\frac{d^2A^{(1)}}{dada'}\right\}+a^2.\left\{\frac{dA^{(1)}}{da}\right\}+aa'.\left\{\frac{dA^{(1)}}{da'}\right\}+2aA^{(1)};$$

$$C^{(i)}=\tfrac{1}{2}a^3.\left\{\frac{d^2A^{(i)}}{da^2}\right\}+\frac{(2i+1)}{2}.a^2.\left\{\frac{dA^{(i)}}{da}\right\}$$
$$+\frac{(i.(n-n')-3n)}{2.(i.(n-n')-n)}.\left\{a^2.\left\{\frac{dA^{(i)}}{da}\right\}+\frac{2n}{n-n'}.aA^{(i)}\right\}$$
$$+\frac{(i-1).n}{i.(n-n')-n}.\left\{a^2.\left\{\frac{dA^{(i)}}{da}\right\}+2i.aA^{(i)}\right\};$$

$$D^{(i)}=\tfrac{1}{2}a^2a'.\left\{\frac{d^2A^{(i-1)}}{da.da'}\right\}-(i-1).a^2.\left\{\frac{dA^{(i-1)}}{da}\right\}$$

$$dR=+\frac{m'}{2}.indt.\Sigma A^{(i)}.\sin.i.(n't-nt+\epsilon'-\epsilon)+\frac{m'}{2}.ndta.\frac{dA^{(0)}}{da}.e.\sin.(nt+\epsilon-\varpi)$$
$$+\frac{m'}{2}(n-in).dt.\Sigma.\left(a.\left(\frac{dA^{(i)}}{da}\right)+2iA^{(i)}\right)e.\sin.i.(n't-nt+\epsilon'-\epsilon)+nt+\epsilon-\varpi)$$
$$+\frac{m'}{2}.ndt.\left(\Sigma a'.\frac{dA^{(1)}}{da'}+2A^{(1)}\right)e'.\sin.(nt+\epsilon-\varpi')+\frac{m'}{2}.(1-i),n)dt.(\Sigma a'.\frac{dA^{(i-1)}}{da'}$$
$$-2.(i-1).A^{(i-1)})\,e'.\sin.i.(n't-nt+\epsilon'-\epsilon)+nt+\epsilon-\varpi'),\ \therefore\ 2\int dR$$
$$=2m'g-\frac{m'}{2}.\frac{2n}{n'-n}.\Sigma.A^{(i)}.\cos.i.(n't-nt+\epsilon'-\epsilon)-\frac{m'}{2}.2a.\frac{dA^0}{da}.e.\cos.(nt+\epsilon-\varpi)-\frac{m'}{2}.$$
$$\frac{2.(n-in)}{in'-in+n}.\left(\Sigma a.\frac{dA^{(i)}}{da}+2iA^{(i)}.\right)e.\cos.i.(n't-nt+\epsilon'-\epsilon)+nt+\epsilon-\varpi)-\frac{m'}{2}.2a'.$$
$$\left(\frac{dA^{(1)}}{da'}+4A^{(1)}\right).e'.\cos.(nt+\epsilon-\varpi')-\frac{m'}{2}.\frac{2.(i-1).n)}{i.(n'-n)+n}.\left(\Sigma a'.\frac{dA^{(i-1)}}{da'}-2.(i-1).A^{(i-1)}.\right)$$

$e'.\cos.i.(n't-nt+\epsilon'-\epsilon)+nt+\epsilon-\varpi')$, $\because$ by reducing we obtain $2\int dR+r.\frac{dR}{dr}=$ the expression which is given in the text.

$$+\frac{(i-1).n}{i.(n-n')-n}.\left\{aa'.\left\{\frac{dA^{(i-1)}}{da'}\right\}-2.(i-1).aA^{(i-1)}\right\};$$

the sum of the masses $M+m$ being assumed equal to unity, and $\frac{M+m}{a^3}$ being supposed equal to n^2; the equation (X′) will become

$$0=\frac{d^2.\delta u}{dt^2}+n^2.\delta u-2n^2.m'ag-\frac{n^2m'}{2}.a^2.\left\{\frac{dA^{(0)}}{da}\right\}*$$

* The equation (X′) becomes by neglecting the square of the excentricity, $\frac{d^2.\delta u}{dt^2}+n^2.\delta u-n^2a.(1-e.\cos.(nt+\epsilon-\varpi)).\left(2\int dR+r.\frac{dR}{dr}\right)-2ean^2.\int ndt.(\sin.(nt+\epsilon-\varpi).\left(2\int dR+r.\frac{dR}{dr}\right)$; ($n^2a$ being substituted for $\frac{1}{a^2}$ and $M+m$ being by hypothesis $=1$).

By substituting for $2\int dR+r\frac{dR}{dr}$, its value, this equation becomes $=$

$$\frac{d^2.\delta u}{dt^2}+n^2.\delta u-2n^2.m'ag-\frac{n^2.m'}{2}.a^2.\left(\frac{dA^{(0)}}{da}\right)-\frac{n^2m'}{2}.\left(\Sigma a^2.\frac{dA^{(i)}}{da}+\frac{2n}{n-n'}.aA^{(i)}.\right)\cos.$$

$$i.(n't-nt+\epsilon'-\epsilon)+\frac{n^2m'}{2}.\left(a^3.\frac{d^2A^0}{da^2}+3a^2.\frac{dA^{(0)}}{da}\right).e.\cos.(nt+\epsilon-\varpi)+$$

$$\left((n^2a).(2m'g+\frac{m'}{2}).a.\frac{dA^{(0)}}{da}+2an^2.(2m'g+\frac{m'}{2}.a.\frac{dA^{(0)}}{da})\right).e.\cos.(nt+\epsilon-\varpi);\ (=n^2m'.Ce.$$

$$\cos.(nt+\epsilon-\varpi))+n^2a.\frac{m'}{2}\left(aa'.\frac{d^2A^{(1)}}{da.da'}+2a.\frac{dA^{(1)}}{da}+2a'.\frac{dA^{(1)}}{da'}+4A^{(1)}\right)e'.(\cos.nt+$$

$$\epsilon-\varpi')=(n^2m'.De'.\cos.(nt+\epsilon-\varpi').$$

$$+\frac{m'}{2}.n^2a\Sigma.\left\{\begin{matrix}a^2.\frac{d^2A^{(i)}}{da^2}+(2i+1).a.\frac{dA^{(i)}}{da}\\ \frac{2.(i-1).n}{i.(n-n')-n}\left(a.\frac{dA^{(i)}}{da}+2iA^{(i)}\right)\end{matrix}\right\}e.\cos.(i.(n't-nt+\epsilon'-\epsilon)+nt+\epsilon-\varpi)$$

$$+\frac{m'}{2}.n^2a.\left(\Sigma a.\frac{dA^{(i)}}{da}+\frac{2n}{n-n'}.A^{(i)}.\right)e.\cos.i.(n't-nt+\epsilon-\epsilon)+nt+\epsilon-\varpi)$$

$$-2an^2.e.\int ndt.(\sin.i.(n't-nt+\epsilon'-\epsilon)+nt+\epsilon-\varpi)\left(\frac{m'}{2}.\Sigma a.\frac{d.A^{(i)}}{da}+\frac{2n}{n-n'}A^{(i)}\right)=\left(\frac{m'}{2}.\right.$$

$$-\frac{n^2m'}{2}.\ \Sigma.\ \left\{a^2.\left(\frac{dA^{(i)}}{da}\right)+\frac{2n}{n-n'}.\,aA^{(i)}\right\}.\ \cos.\ i.(n't-nt+\epsilon'-\epsilon)$$

$$+n^2m'.\ C.e.\cos.\ (nt+\epsilon-\varpi)+n^2m'.\ De'.\cos.\ (nt+\epsilon-\varpi')$$

$$+n^2m'.\Sigma.C^{(i)}.e.\cos.(i.(n't-nt+\epsilon'-\epsilon)+nt+\epsilon-\varpi).$$

$$+n^2m'.\Sigma\ D^{(i)}.e'\cos.\ (i.(n't-nt+\epsilon'-\epsilon)+nt+\epsilon-\varpi');$$

and by integrating

$$\delta u=2m'ag+\frac{m'^2}{2}.\ a^2.\left(\frac{dA^{(0}}{da}\right)$$

$$-\frac{m'}{2}.\ n^2.\ \Sigma.\frac{\left\{a^2.\left(\frac{dA^{(i)}}{da}\right)+\frac{2n}{n-n'}.\ aA^{(i)}\right\}'}{i^2.(n-n')^2-n^2}.\ \cos.\ i.(n't-nt+\epsilon'-\epsilon)$$

$$+m'f_{,}.e\cos.\ (nt+\epsilon-\varpi)+m'f'_{,}.\ e'.\cos.\ (nt+\epsilon-\varpi')$$

$$-\frac{m'}{2}.\ C.nt.\ e.\sin.(nt+\epsilon-\varpi)-\frac{m}{2}.\ D.\,nt.\ e'.\sin.\ (nt+\epsilon-\varpi')$$

$$+m'.\Sigma.\frac{C^{(i)}.n^2}{(i.(n-n')-n)^2-n^2}.\ e.\cos.\ (i.(n't-nt+\epsilon'-\epsilon)+nt+\epsilon-\varpi)$$

$$+m'.\Sigma.\ \frac{D^{(i)}.n^2}{(i.(n-n')-n)^2-n^2}.\ e'.\cos.\ (i.(n't-nt+\epsilon'-\epsilon)+nt+\epsilon-\varpi'),$$

$$2an^2.\left(\frac{n}{i.(n'-n)+n}\right).\Sigma a.\frac{dA^{(i)}}{da}+\left(\frac{2n}{n-n'}\right).\ A^{(i)}.\Big)e.\cos.i.(n't-nt+\epsilon'-\epsilon)+nt+\epsilon-\varpi)\Big)$$

which added to the preceding term becomes, by changing the signs of the numerator and denominator of $\frac{2n}{i.(n'-n)+n}$

$$\frac{m'}{2}\left(.\ n^2.\frac{i.(n-n')-3n}{i.(n-n')-n}.\ \Sigma a^2.\frac{dA^{(i)}}{da}+\frac{4na}{n-n'}.\ A^{(i)}\right).\ e.\cos.\ (i.(n't-nt+\epsilon'-\epsilon)+nt+\epsilon-\varpi)$$

and by adding this quantity to $\frac{m'}{2}.\ n^2a.\left(\Sigma.a^2.\frac{d^2A^{(i)}}{da^2}+(2i+1).a.\frac{dA^{(i)}}{da}\right)$, it will appear that he coefficient of $n^2m'.e'.\cos.\ (i.(n't-nt+\epsilon'-\epsilon)+nt+\epsilon-\varpi)$ is equal to $C^{(i)}$; it is evident from an inspection of the coefficients of $e^2.\cos.\ (nt+\epsilon-\varpi')$, $e'.\cos.\ i.(n't-nt+\epsilon'-\epsilon)+nt+\epsilon-\varpi')$ that they are respectively equal to D, and $D^{(i)}$.

$f_{,}$ and $f'_{,}$ being two arbitrary quantities.

The expression for δr in δu which has been found in N°. 47, will give

$$\frac{\delta r}{a} = -2m'.ag - \frac{m'}{2}.a^2.\left(\frac{dA^{(0)}}{da}\right)$$

$$+\frac{m'}{2}.n^2\Sigma.\left\{\frac{a^2.\left\{\frac{dA^{(i)}}{da}\right\}+\frac{2n}{n-n'}.aA^{(i)}}{i^2.(n-n')^2-n^2}\right\}.\cos.i.(n't-nt+\varepsilon'-\varepsilon)$$

$$-m'.fe.\cos.(nt+\varepsilon-\varpi)-m'f'e'.\cos.(nt+\varepsilon-\varpi')$$

$$+\tfrac{1}{2}.m'C.nt.e.\sin.(nt+\varepsilon-\varpi)+\tfrac{1}{2}.m'.D.nte'.\sin.(nt+\varepsilon-\varpi').$$

$$+m'.n^2\Sigma.\left\{\begin{matrix}\left\{\frac{\left\{a^2.\left\{\frac{dA^{(i)}}{da}\right\}+\frac{2n}{n-n'}.aA^{(i)}\right.}{i^2.(n-n')^2-n^2}-\frac{C^{(i)}}{(i.(n-n')-n)^2-n^2)}\right\}\\ (e.\cos.(i.(n't-nt+\varepsilon'-\varepsilon)+nt+\varepsilon-\varpi)\end{matrix}\right\}$$

$$-m'.n^2.\Sigma.\frac{D^{(i)}}{i.(n-n')-n)^2-n^2}.e'.\cos.(i.(n't-nt+\varepsilon'-\varepsilon)+nt+\varepsilon-\varpi');$$

f and f' being two arbitrary quantities depending on $f_{,}$ and $f'_{,}$.

This value of δr, substituted in the formula (Y) of N°. 46, will give δv, or the perturbations of the motion of the planet in longitude; but it may be observed, that nt expressing the mean motion of m, the term proportional to the time must disappear from the expression of δv. This condition determines the constant quantity g, and we find

$$g = -\tfrac{1}{3}a.\left\{\frac{dA^{(0)}}{da}\right\}.*$$

The introduction of the arbitrary quantities f and f', might have

* As nt must vanish from this expression, by substituting for dR and $\int r.\frac{dR}{dr}$ their values in the expression for δv given in page 263, and then integrating, the terms involving nt are $3am'gnt$ and $2\,\frac{m'}{2}.a^2nt.\left(\frac{dA^{(0)}}{da}\right)$, hence we will have $3m'g = -\frac{2m'}{2}.a.\frac{dA^{(0)}}{da}$.

been dispensed with, by supposing them to be comprised in the elements e and ϖ of elliptic motion; but then the expression for δv, would have involved terms depending on the mean anomaly, which would not have been included in those which are given by the elliptic motion: now it is more convenient to make those terms to disappear from the expression for the longitude, in order to introduce them into the expression for the radius vector; $f_{,}$ and $f'_{,}$ will be so determined as to satisfy this condition. This being premised, by substituting in place of

$a'.\left\{\frac{dA^{(i-1)}}{da'}\right\}$ its value $-A^{(i-1)}-a.\left\{\frac{dA^{(i-1)}}{da}\right\}$, we shall obtain

$$C=a^2.\left(\frac{dA^{(0)}}{da}\right)+\tfrac{1}{2}.a^3.\left(\frac{d^2A^{(0)}}{da^2}\right);$$

$$D=aA^{(1)}-a^2.\left(\frac{dA^{(1)}}{da}\right)-\tfrac{1}{3}a^3.\left(\frac{d^2A^{(1)}}{da^2}\right);$$

$$D^{(i)}=\frac{i-1).(2i-1).n}{n-i.(n-n')}.aA^{(i-1)}+\frac{(i^2.(n-n')-n)}{n-i.(n-n')}.a^2.\left(\frac{dA^{(i-1)}}{da}\right)$$
$$-\tfrac{1}{2}a^3.\left(\frac{d^2A^{(i-1)}}{da^2}\right);$$

$$f_{,}=\tfrac{2}{3}a^2.\left(\frac{dA^{(0)}}{da}\right)+\tfrac{1}{4}a^3.\left(\frac{d^2A^{(0)}}{da^2}\right)$$

$$f'_{,}=\tfrac{1}{4}.\left\{a.A^{(1)}-a^2.\left(\frac{dA^{(1)}}{da}\right)+a^3.\left(\frac{d^2A^{(1)}}{da^2}\right)\right\};$$

moreover let $E^{(i)}=$

$$-\frac{3n}{n-n'}.aA^{(i)}+\frac{i^2.(n-n').(n+i.(n-n'))-3n^2)}{i^2.(n-n')^2-n^2}$$

$$\times\left\{a^2.\left(\frac{dA^{(i)}}{da}\right)+\frac{2n}{n-n'}.aA^{(i)}\right\}+\tfrac{1}{2}a^3.\left(\frac{d^2A^{(i)}}{da^2}\right);$$

$$F^{(i)}=\frac{(i-1).n}{n-n'}.\,aA^{(i)}+\frac{\frac{in}{2}.\,(n+i(n-n'))-3n^2)}{i^2.(n-n')^2-n^2}$$

$$\times\left\{a^2.\left(\frac{dA^{(i)}}{da}\right)+\frac{2n}{n-n'}.\,aA^{(i)}\right\}-\frac{2n^2E^{(i)}}{n^2-(n-i.(n-n'))^2}\;;$$

$$G^{(i)}=\frac{(i-1).(2i-1).na.A^{(i-1)}+(i-1).na^2.\left(\frac{dA^{(i-1)}}{da}\right)}{2.(n-i.(n-n'))}$$

$$-\frac{2n^2.D^{(i)}}{n^2-(n-i.(n-n'))^2}\;;$$

we shall have

$$\frac{\delta r}{a}=\frac{m'}{6}.\,a^2.\left(\frac{dA^{(0)}}{da}\right)+\frac{m'.n^2}{2}.\,\Sigma.\left\{\frac{a.\left(\frac{dA^{(i)}}{da}\right)+\frac{2n}{n-n'}.\,aA^{(i)}}{i^2.(n-n')^2-n^2}\right\}.\cos.i.(n't-nt+\varepsilon'-\varepsilon)$$

$$-m'.fe.\cos.(nt+\varepsilon-\varpi)-m'.f'e'.\cos.(nt+\varepsilon-\varpi')$$

$$+\tfrac{1}{2}m'.C.nt.e.\sin.(nt+\varepsilon-\varpi)+\tfrac{1}{2}m'.D.nt.e'.\sin.(nt+\varepsilon-\varpi')$$

$$+n^2.m'.\Sigma.\left\{\begin{array}{l}\frac{*\;E^{(i)}}{n^2-(n-i(n-n'))^2}.e.\cos.(i.(n't-nt+\varepsilon'-\varepsilon)+nt+\varepsilon-\varpi)\\+\frac{D^{(i)}}{n^2-(n-i.(n-n'))^2}.e'.\cos.(i.(n't-nt+\varepsilon'-\varepsilon)+nt+\varepsilon-\varpi')\end{array}\right\}\;;$$

$$\delta v=\frac{m'}{2}.\,\Sigma.\left\{\frac{n^2}{i.(n-n')^2}.\,a.A^{(i)}+\frac{2n^3.\left\{a^2.\left\{\frac{dA^{(i)}}{da}\right\}+\frac{2n}{n-n'}.\,aA^{(i)}\right\}}{i.(n-n').(i^2.(n-n')^2-n)^2}\right\}.$$

$$\sin.i.(n't-nt+\varepsilon'-\varepsilon),$$

$$+m'.C.nt.e.\cos.(nt+\varepsilon-\varpi)+m'D.nt.e'.\cos.(nt+\varepsilon-\varpi')$$

* If to the value of $C^{(i)}$ be added the terms $\pm\left(\frac{2i+1}{}\right).\frac{2n}{n-n'}.\,aA^{(i)},\pm$

$$+nm'.\Sigma.\left\{\begin{array}{l}\dfrac{F^{(i)}}{n-i.(n-n')}.\ e.\sin.\ (i.(n't-nt+\varepsilon'-\varepsilon)+nt+\varepsilon-\varpi)\\ +\dfrac{G^{(i)}}{n-i.(n-n')}.\ e'.\sin.\ (i.(n't-nt+\varepsilon'-\varepsilon)+n+\varepsilon-\varpi')\end{array}\right\};$$

in these expressions the integral sign Σ extends to the whole values of i both positive and negative, the sole value $i=0$ being excepted.

It may be observed here, that in the very case in which the series represented by $\Sigma.A^{(i)}.\cos.\ i.(n't-nt+\varepsilon'-\varepsilon)$ converges slowly, the expressions of $\frac{\delta r}{a}$, and of δv, may be rendered converging by means of the divisors which they acquire. This observation is extremely important,

$$\frac{(i-1).n}{i.(n-n')-n}.\frac{2n}{n-n'}.\ aA^{(i)} \text{ it will become } =\tfrac{1}{2}.\frac{d^2A^{(i)}}{da^2}+\frac{2i+1}{2}\left(a^2.\frac{dA^{(i)}}{da}\right.$$

$$\left.+\frac{2n}{n-n'}.\ aA^{(i)}\right)-\left(\frac{2i+1}{2}\right)\frac{2n}{n-n'}.\ aA^{(i)}+\frac{i.(n-n')-3n}{2.(i.(n-n')-n}.$$

$$\left(a^2.\left(\frac{dA^{(i)}}{da}\right)+\frac{2n}{n-n'}.\ aA^{(i)}\right)+\frac{(i-1).n}{i(n-n')-n}.\left(a^2.\frac{dA^{(i)}}{da}+\frac{2n}{n-n'}.\ aA^{(i)}\right)-\frac{2.(i-1)n}{n-n'}$$

$aA^{(i)}$; now by reducing the two terms which constitute the factor of $e.\cos.\ i.(n't-nt+\varepsilon'-\varepsilon)+nt+\varepsilon-\varpi)$ in page 296, to a common denominator, it will become $=$ to

$$(2i^2.(n-n')^2-4in.(n-n')-2i.(i^2.(n-n')^2+2i.n^2-i^2.(n-n')^2+n^2-i^2.(n-n')^2+2in.(n-n')$$

$$+3n^2-2in.(i.(n-n')+2in.(n-n')-2in^2+2n^2).\left(a^2.\frac{dA^{(i)}}{da}+\frac{2n}{n-n'}.\ aA^{(i)}\right) \text{ (divided by}$$

$$2i.^2((n-n')^2-n^2))+\frac{4in+2n-4i.n+4n}{2(n-n')}.\ aA^{(i)}=-2i^2.n-n').\ i.(n-n')+n)+6n^2$$

$\left(a^2.\frac{dA^{(i)}}{da}+\frac{2n}{n-n'}.\ aA^{(i)}\right)$. divided by $2i^2.(n-n')^2-n^2)+\frac{6n}{2.(n-n')}.\ aA^{(i)}$. ; which is evidently equal to $E^{(i)}$.

because without it it would be impossible to express analytically the reciprocal perturbations of the planets, the ratio of whose distances from the sun, differ little from unity.

These expressions may be made to assume the following form, which will be extremely useful in the sequel; let

$$h = e.\sin.\varpi;\ h' = e'\sin.\varpi';$$
$$l = e.\cos.\varpi;\ \ l' = e.\cos.\varpi';$$

we shall have

$$\frac{\delta r}{a} = \frac{m'}{6}.a^2.\left(\frac{dA^{(0)}}{da}\right) + \frac{m'n^2}{2}.\Sigma.\left\{\frac{a^2.\left(\frac{dA^{(i)}}{da}\right) + \frac{2n}{n-n'}.aA^{(i)}}{i^2.(n-n')^2-n^2}\right\}.$$
$$\cos.i.(n't-nt+\varepsilon'-\varepsilon)$$
$$-m'.(hf+h'f').\cos.nt+\varepsilon)-m'.(lf+l'f').\sin.(nt+\varepsilon)$$
$$+\frac{m'}{2}.(l.C+l'D).nt.(\sin.(nt+\varepsilon)-\frac{m'}{2}.(h.C+h'D).nt.\cos.(nt+\varepsilon)$$
$$+n^2m'.\Sigma.\left\{\begin{array}{l}\frac{hE^{(i)}+h'.D^{(i)}}{n^2-(n-i.(n-n'))^2}.\sin.(i.(n't-nt+\varepsilon'-\varepsilon)+nt+\varepsilon)\\ +\frac{(l.E^{(i)}+l'.D^{(i)}}{n^2-(n'-.(n-n'))^2}.\cos.(i.(n't-nt+\varepsilon'-\varepsilon)+nt+\varepsilon)\end{array}\right\};$$

$$\delta v = \frac{m'}{2}.\Sigma.\left\{\frac{n^2}{i.(n-n')^2}.aA^{(i)} + 2n^3\frac{\left\{a^2.\left(\frac{dA^{(i)}}{da}\right) + \frac{2n}{n-n'}.aA^{(i)}\right\}}{i.(n-n').(i^2.(n-n')^2-n^2)}\right\}.$$
$$\sin.i.(n't-nt+\varepsilon'-\varepsilon').$$
$$+m'.(h.C+h'.D).nt.\sin.(nt+\varepsilon)+m'.(l.C+l'.D).nt.\cos.(nt+\varepsilon)$$
$$+n.m'.\Sigma.\left\{\begin{array}{l}\frac{l.F^{(i)}+l'.G^{(i)}}{n-i.(n-n')}.\sin.(i.(n't-nt+\varepsilon'-\varepsilon)+nt+\varepsilon)\\ -\frac{(h.F^{(i)}+h'.G^{(i)})}{n-i.(n-n')}.\cos.(i.(n't-nt+\varepsilon'-\varepsilon)+nt+\varepsilon)\end{array}\right\};$$

these expressions of δr and δv being added to the values of r and of v, relative to the elliptic motion, will give the entire values of the radius vector of m, and of its motion in longitude.

51. Let us at present, consider the motion of m, in latitude. For this purpose let the formula (Z') of N°. 47, be resumed; and if the product of the inclinations, by the excentricities of the orbits, be neglected it becomes

$$0 = \frac{d^2\delta u'}{dt^2} + n^2.\delta u' - \frac{1}{a^2}.\left(\frac{dR}{dz}\right);^*$$

the expression for R of N°. 48, gives, by assuming for the fixed plane, the plane of the primitive orbit of m,

$$\left(\frac{dR}{dz}\right) = \frac{m'z'}{a'^3} - \frac{m'z'}{2}.\ \Sigma.\ B^{(i)}.\cos.\ i.(n't - nt + \epsilon' - \epsilon);$$

the value of i comprehending all whole numbers both positive and negative, including $i = 0$. Let γ represent the tangent of the inclination of the orbit of m', to the primitive orbit of m, and Π the longitude of the ascending node of the first of these orbits, on the second; we shall have very nearly,

$$z' = a'.\gamma.\ \sin.(n't + \epsilon' - \Pi);\dagger$$

which gives

$$\left(\frac{dR}{dz}\right) = \frac{m'}{a'^2}.\ \gamma.\ \sin.\ (n't + \epsilon' - \Pi) - \frac{m'}{2}.\ a'.B^{(1)}.\ \gamma.\ \sin.\ (nt + \epsilon - \Pi)$$

* When the primitive orbit of m is assumed as the fixed plane, the differential of the two last terms in the value of R (which is given in page 276) with respect to z, becomes (when quantities of the order m'^2 are neglected) the expression which is given in the text.

† When quantities of the higher orders of the inclinations are neglected, we may substitute for sin. $(n't + \epsilon' - \Pi)$, the longitude on the fixed plane, and we can also assume the distance of the planet from the centre of its orbit, equal to the mean distance a',; under these restrictions it will readily appear that the tangent of latitude of m' above the fixed plane $= \gamma.\sin.(n't + \epsilon' - \Pi)$, and $\therefore z' = a'.\gamma.\sin.(n't + \epsilon' - \Pi)$.

$$-\frac{m'}{2}.\ a'.\Sigma.B^{(i-1)}.\gamma.\ \sin.\ (i.(n't-nt+\varepsilon'-\varepsilon)+nt+\varepsilon-\Pi),$$

the value of i, in this and the following expressions extending to all whole numbers, as well positive as negative, the sole value $i=0$* being excepted. The differential equation in $\delta u'$, will consequently become, by multiplying the value of $\left(\frac{dR}{dz}\right)$, by n^2a^3. which is equal to unity,

$$0=\frac{d^2.\delta u'}{dt^2}+n^2.\delta u'-m'.n.\frac{a}{a'^2}.\ \gamma.\ \sin.\ (n't+\varepsilon'-\Pi)$$

$$+\frac{m'n^2}{2}.\ aa'.\ B^{(1)}.\ \gamma.\ \sin.\ (nt+\varepsilon-\Pi)$$

$$+\frac{m'n^2}{2}.\ aa'.\ \Sigma.B^{(i-1)}.\gamma.\ \sin.(i.(n't-nt+\varepsilon'-\varepsilon)+nt+\varepsilon-\Pi);$$

from which we obtain, by integrating, and by remarking that by N°. 47, $\delta s=-a.\delta u'$,

$$\delta s=-\frac{m'.n^2}{n^2-n'^2}.\ \frac{a^2}{a'^2}.\ \gamma.\sin.\ (n't+\varepsilon'-\Pi)$$

$$-\frac{m'.a^2,a'}{4}.\ B^{(1)}.\ nt.\ \gamma.\ \cos.\ (nt+\varepsilon-\Pi)\dagger$$

* When this value of z' is multiplied into $\Sigma.B^{(i)}.\cos.\ i.(n't-nt+\varepsilon'-\varepsilon)$, it becomes, when $i=1$, equal to $B^{(1)}.\sin.(n't-nt+\varepsilon'-\varepsilon)+n't+\varepsilon'-\Pi)+B^{(1)}.\sin.(nt+\varepsilon-\Pi)$, and when $i=0$ it becomes $=B^{(0)}.\sin.\ (n't+\varepsilon'-\Pi)$; now had this product been expressed generally $-\frac{m'}{2}.a'.\Sigma.B^{(i)}.\gamma.\sin.(i.(n't-nt+\varepsilon'-\varepsilon)+nt+\varepsilon-\Pi)$, it would not answer to the two cases in which $i=1$, and in which $i=0$; hence we see the reason why this product is resolved into parts in the expression for $\left(\frac{dR}{dz}\right)$, and also why the value $i=0$, is excepted out of the values of i.

† This differential equation is integrated in the manner prescribed in N°. 41.

$$+\frac{m'.n^2.a^2.a'}{2}.\ \Sigma.\ \frac{B^{(i-1)}}{n^2-(n-i.(n-n'))^2}.\ \gamma.\sin.(i.(n't-nt+\varepsilon'-\varepsilon)+nt+\varepsilon-\Pi).$$

In order to obtain the latitude of m, above a fixed plane, a little inclined to the plane of its primitive orbit, naming φ the inclination of this orbit on the fixed plane, and θ the longitude of its ascending node on the same plane, it will be sufficient to add to δs, the quantity tan. φ. sin. $(v-\theta)$, or tan. φ. sin. $(nt+\varepsilon-\theta)$, the excentricity of the orbit being neglected.* Let φ' and θ' represent what φ and θ become relatively to m'. If m moved in the primitive orbit of m', the tangent of latitude will be tan. φ'. sin. $(nt+\varepsilon-\theta')$; it will be tan. φ. sin. $(nt+\varepsilon-\theta)$, if m continued to move on its primitive orbit. The difference of these two tangents is very nearly the tangent of the latitude of m, above the plane of the primitive orbit, it being supposed to move on the plane of the primitive orbit of m'; therefore we have

$$\tan.\ \varphi'.\ \sin.\ (nt+\varepsilon-\theta')-\tan.\ \varphi.\ \sin.\ (nt+\varepsilon-\theta)=\gamma.\ \sin.\ (nt+\varepsilon-\Pi).$$

Let

$$\tan.\ \varphi.\ \sin.\ \theta=p;\qquad \tan.\ \varphi'.\ \sin.\ \theta'=p';$$
$$\tan.\ \varphi.\ \cos.\ \theta=q;\qquad \tan.\ \varphi'.\ \cos.\ \theta'=q';$$

we shall obtain

$$\gamma.\ \sin.\ \Pi=p'-p;\qquad \gamma.\ \cos.\ \Pi=q'-q;$$

and consequently, if s denote the latitude of m above the fixed plane, we shall have very nearly,

$$s=q.\ \sin.\ (nt+\varepsilon)-p.\ \cos.\ (nt+\varepsilon)$$
$$-\frac{m'.a^2a'}{4}.\ (p'-p).\ B^{(1)}.\ nt.\ \sin.\ (nt+\varepsilon)$$

* This expression for the latitude of m above the fixed plane, which is a *little* inclined to the plane of its primitive orbit, is true when quantities of the higher orders are neglected.

$$-\frac{m'.a^2a'}{4}.(q'-q).B^{(1)}.nt.\cos.(nt+\varepsilon)$$

$$-\frac{m'n^2}{n^2-n'^2}\cdot\frac{a^2}{a'^2}\cdot((q'-q).\sin.(n't+\varepsilon')-(p'-p).\cos.(n't+\varepsilon'))$$

$$+\frac{m'.n^2.a^2.a'}{2}.\Sigma.\left\{\begin{array}{l}\dfrac{(q'-q).B^{(i-1)}}{n^2-(n-i.(n-n'))^2}.\sin.(i.(n't-nt+\varepsilon'-\varepsilon)+nt+\varepsilon)\\ \dfrac{-(p'-p).B^{(i-1)}}{n^2-(n-i.(n-n'))^2}.\cos.(i.(n't-nt+\varepsilon'-\varepsilon)+nt+\varepsilon)\end{array}\right\}.$$

52. Let us now sum up the formulæ which we have investigated. If (r) and (v) represent the parts of the radius vector and of the longitude v of the orbit, which depend on the elliptic motion; we will have

$$r=(r)+\delta r;\ v=(v)+\delta v;$$

The preceding value of s will be the latitude of m above the fixed plane; but it will be more exact to employ instead of its two first terms which are independent of m', the value of the latitude which would obtain in case that m did not depart from the plane of ts primitive orbit. These expressions contain the entire theory of the planets, when the squares and products of the excentricities and of the inclinations of the orbits are neglected, which we are in most cases permitted to do. They have besides the advantage of appearing under a very simple form, which enables easily to perceive the law of their different terms.

Sometimes it will be necessary to recur to terms depending on the squares and the products of the excentricities and of the inclinations, and even on higher powers and products. These terms may be determined by means of the preceding analysis: the consideration which renders them necessary will always facilitate their determination. The approximations in which we will have occasion to take them into account, will introduce new terms depending on new arguments. These will again reproduce the arguments which the preceding approximations give, but with coefficients which are smaller and smaller according to the following law, which it is easy to infer from the expansion of R into a series, and which has been given in N°. 48; *an argument which in the successive approximations is found for the first time among quantities of any order r, is only produced again by quantities of the orders $r+2$, $r+4$, &c.*

It follows from this that the coefficients of the terms of the form $t. \begin{smallmatrix}\sin.\\ \cos.\end{smallmatrix} (nt+\varepsilon)$, which occur in the expressions of r, v, and s, are approximate as far as quantities of the third order, that is to say, the approximation in which we only consider the squares and products of the excentricities and of the inclinations of their orbits, will add nothing to their values; therefore they have all the required accuracy; this observation is the more important, in as much as the secular variations of the orbits depend on these coefficients.

The different terms of the perturbations of r, v, s, are comprised in the form

$$k. \begin{smallmatrix}\sin.\\ \cos.\end{smallmatrix} \left\{ i.(n't-nt+\varepsilon'-\varepsilon)+rnt+r\varepsilon \right\},$$

r being either a positive integral number, or equal to cypher, and k being a function of the excentricities and of the inclinations of the orbits, of the order r, or of a superior order: we are enabled by means of this, to determine of what order a term depending on a given angle is.

It is manifest that the action of the bodies m'', m''', &c., only cause to be added to the preceding values of r, v and s, terms analogous to those which result from the action of m', and that if we neglect the square of the perturbating force, the sum of all these terms will give the complete values of r, v and s. This follows from the nature of the formulæ (X'), (Y') and (Z'),* which are linear with respect to quantities which depend on the perturbating force.

Finally, we shall obtain the perturbation of m', produced by the action of m', by changing in the preceding formulæ, a, n, h, l, ϵ, ϖ, p, q, and m', into a', n', h', l', ϵ', ϖ', p', q', and m, and *vice versa.*

* When quantities of the order of the square of the perturbating forces are neglected, the formulæ X', Y', Z', are linear with respect to the perturbating force, from which it follows, that the variation of the sum is equal to the sum of the variations.

CHAPTER VII.

Of the secular inequalities of the celestial motions.

53. The perturbating forces which disturb the elliptic motion introduce into the expressions of r, $\frac{dv}{dt}$ and of s, which are given in the preceding chapter, the time without the signs of the *sine* and *cosine*, or under the form of arcs of circles, which increasing indefinitely, must at length render these expressions erroneous; it is therefore essentially necessary to make these arcs to disappear, and to obtain the functions which produce them by their expansion into a series. There has been given for this object, in the fifth chapter, a general method, from which it follows, that these arcs arise from the variations of the elliptic motion, which are then functions of the time. These variations being performed with extreme slowness, have been termed *secular inequalities.* Their theory is one of the most interesting points in the system of the world: we proceed to present it here, in all the detail which its importance requires.

By the preceding chapter we have

$$r = a.\left\{\begin{array}{l} 1 - h.\sin.(nt+\varepsilon) - l.\cos(nt+\varepsilon) - \&c. \\ +\frac{m'}{2}.(l.C+l'.D).nt.\sin.(nt+\varepsilon) \\ -\frac{m'}{2}.(h.C+h'.D).nt.\cos.(nt+\varepsilon)+m'S. \end{array}\right\};$$

$$\frac{dv}{dt} = n+2nh.\sin.(nt+\varepsilon)+2nl.\cos.(nt+\varepsilon)+\&c.$$

$$- m'.(l.C+l'D).n^2t.\sin.(nt+\epsilon)$$
$$+ m'.(h.C+h'D).n^2t.\cos.(nt+\epsilon)+m'.T;$$
$$s = q.\sin.(nt+\epsilon) - p.\cos.(nt+\epsilon) + \&c.$$
$$-\frac{m'}{4}.a^2.a'.(p'-p).B^{(1)}.nt.\sin.(nt+\epsilon)$$
$$-\frac{m'}{4}.a^2.a'.(q'-q).B^{(1)}.nt.\cos.(nt+\epsilon)+m'.\chi;$$

S, T, χ, being periodic functions of the time t. Let us at first consider the expression of $\frac{dv}{dt}$, and compare it with the expression of y of No. 43. As the arbitrary quantity n multiplies the arc t, under the periodic signs, in the expression for $\frac{dv}{dt}$; we must employ the following equations, which have been found in N°. 43,

$$0 = X' + \theta.X'' - Y;$$
$$0 = Y' + \theta.Y'' + X'' - 2Z;$$

let us consider what X, X', X'', Y, &c. become in this case; the expression of $\frac{dv}{dt}$, being compared with that of y of the above cited N°. gives

$$X = n + 2nh.\sin.(nt+\epsilon) + 2nl.\cos.(nt+\epsilon) + m'.T;$$
$$Y = m'.n^2.(h.C+h'D).\cos.(nt+\epsilon) - m'n^2.(l.C+l'.D).\sin.(nt+\epsilon).$$

The product of the partial differences of the constant quantities, into the disturbing masses being neglected,* which we are permitted

* Since the product of the partial differences of the constants into the disturbing masses are neglected, it will not be necessary to take into account the periodic function $m'.T$; the second and third terms of the value of X involve nt under the periodic signs, ∴ differencing the arbitraries contained under the signs with respect to n, we obtain the value of X'', which is given in the text.

to do, because these differences are of the order of the masses, we shall have by N°. 43,

$$X' = \left(\frac{dn}{d\theta}\right).(1+2h.\sin.(nt+\varepsilon)+2l.\cos.(nt+\varepsilon))$$

$$+2n.\left(\frac{d\varepsilon}{d\theta}\right).(h.\cos.(nt+\varepsilon)-l.\sin.(nt+\varepsilon))$$

$$+2n.\left(\frac{dh}{d\theta}\right).\sin.(nt+\varepsilon)+2n.\left(\frac{dl}{d\theta}\right).\cos.(nt+\varepsilon);$$

$$X''=2n.\left(\frac{dn}{d\theta}\right).(h.\cos.(nt+\varepsilon)-l.\sin.(nt+\varepsilon)).$$

The equation $0 = X' + \theta.X'' - Y$, will consequently become

$$0=\left(\frac{dn}{d\theta}\right).(1+2h.\sin.(nt+\varepsilon)+2l.\cos.(nt+\varepsilon))$$

$$+2n.\left(\frac{dh}{d\theta}\right).\sin.(nt+\varepsilon)+2n.\left(\frac{dl}{d\theta}\right).\cos.(nt+\varepsilon)$$

$$+2n.\left\{\theta.\left(\frac{dn}{d\theta}\right)+\left(\frac{d\varepsilon}{d\theta}\right)\right\}.(h.\cos.(nt+\varepsilon)-l.\sin.(nt+\varepsilon))$$

$$-m'.n^2.(h.C+h'.D).\cos.(nt+\varepsilon)+m'.n^2.(l.C+l'.D).\sin.nt+\varepsilon).$$

The coefficients of the corresponding sines and cosines, being put separately equal to nothing, we shall have

$$0=\left(\frac{dn}{d\theta}\right)$$

$$0=\left(\frac{dh}{d\theta}\right)-l.\left(\frac{d\varepsilon}{d\theta}\right)+\frac{m'.n}{2}.(l.C+l'.D);$$

$$0=\left(\frac{dl}{d\theta}\right)+h.\left(\frac{d\varepsilon}{d\theta}\right)-\frac{m'.n}{2}.(h.C+h'.D).$$

If these equations be integrated, and if in their integrals, θ be changed into t, we shall have by N°. 43, the value of the arbitrary quantities, in functions of t, and we can efface the arcs of the circle from the expressions for $\frac{dv}{dt}$ and for r, but instead of this change we can all at once change θ into t, in these differential equations. The first of these equations indicates that n is constant, and as the arbitrary quantity a of the expressions for r depends upon it, in consequence of the equations $n^2 = \frac{1}{a^3}$; a is likewise constant. The two other equations are not sufficient to determine h, l, ϵ. We shall have a new equation by observing, that the expression for $\frac{dv}{dt}$, gives by integrating, $\int ndt$, for the value of the mean longitude of m; but we have supposed that this longitude is equal to $nt+\epsilon$; therefore we have $nt+\epsilon = \int ndt$, which gives

$$t.\frac{dn}{dt} + \frac{d\epsilon}{dt} = 0;$$

and as $\frac{dn}{dt} = 0$; we shall have also $\frac{d\epsilon}{dt} = 0$. Thus the two arbitrary quantities n and ϵ are constant; the arbitrary quantities h and l will be consequently determined by means of the differential equations,

$$\frac{dh}{dt} = -\frac{m'.n}{2}.(l.\,C + l'.D); \quad (1)$$

$$\frac{dl}{dt} = \frac{m'.n}{2}.(h.\,C + h'.D); \quad (2)$$

The consideration of the expression of $\frac{dv}{dt}$ being sufficient to determine the values of n, a, h, l and ϵ; we may perceive *a priori*, that the differential equation between the same quantities, which results from the expression for r, must coincide with the preceding. We may be easily assured of this *a posteriori*, by applying to this expression the method of N°. 43.

Let us now consider the expression of s. By comparing it with the expression of y in the N°. already cited; we shall have

$$X = q.\sin.(nt+\varepsilon) - p.\cos.(nt+\varepsilon) + m'.\chi$$

$$Y = \frac{m'.n}{4}.a^2.a'.B^{(1)}.(p-p').\sin.(nt+\varepsilon)$$
$$+\frac{m'.n}{4}.a^2.a'.B^{(1)}.(q-q').\cos.(nt+\varepsilon).$$

n and ε being constant, as is evident from what precedes; by N°. 43, we have

$$X' = \left(\frac{dq}{d\theta}\right).\sin.(nt+\varepsilon) - \left(\frac{dp}{d\theta}\right).\cos.(nt+\varepsilon)$$
$$X'' = 0.$$

The equation $0 = X' + \theta.X'' - Y$ consequently becomes,

$$0 = \left(\frac{dq}{d\theta}\right).\sin.(nt+\varepsilon) - \left(\frac{dp}{d\theta}\right).\cos.(nt+\varepsilon)$$
$$-\frac{m'.n}{4}.a^2a'.B^{(1)}.(p-p').\sin.(nt+\varepsilon)$$
$$-\frac{m'.n}{4}.a^2.a'.B^{(1)}.(q-q').\cos.(nt+\varepsilon);$$

from this we deduce, by comparing the coefficients of corresponding sines and cosines, and by changing θ into t, in order to obtain p and q directly in functions of t,

$$\frac{dp}{dt} = -\frac{m'.n}{4}.a^2.a'.B^{(1)}.(q-q'); \qquad (3)$$
$$\frac{dq}{dt} = -\frac{m'.n}{4}.a^2.a'.B^{(1)}.(p-p'); \qquad (4)$$

After that p and q shall have been determined by these equations, if we substitute them in the preceding expression of s, by obliterating the terms which contain the arcs of a circle, we will have

$$s = q.\sin.(nt+\varepsilon) - p.\cos.(nt+\varepsilon) + m'.\chi.$$

54. The equation $\frac{dn}{dt} = 0$, to which we have arrived, is of great importance in the theory of the system of the world, in that it indicates that the mean motions of the heavenly bodies, and the greater axes of their orbits are invariable; but this equation is only accurate as far as quantities of the order $m'.h$, inclusively. If quantities of the order $m'.h^2$, or of the superior orders, would produce in $\frac{dv}{dt}$, a term of the form* $2kt$, k being a function of the elements of the orbits of m and of m'; a term of the order kt^2 would be produced in the expression of v, which by changing the longitudes of m, proportionably to the square of the time, would at length become extremely sensible. The equation $\frac{dn}{dt} = 0$, would no longer obtain, but in place of this equation there would be obtained by the preceding number $\frac{dn}{dt} = 2k$; it is therefore of importance to ascertain whether there exists in the expressions for v terms of the form kt^2. We proceed to demonstrate that if we only consider the first power of the disturbing masses, however far we extend the approximations relative to the powers of the excentricities and the inclinations of the orbits; the expression of v will not involve terms of this kind.

For this purpose let the formula (X) of No. 46 be resumed,

$$\delta r = \frac{a.\cos.v.\int ndt.\,r.\sin.v.\left\{2\int dR + r.\left\{\frac{dR}{dr}\right\}\right\}}{\mu.\sqrt{1-e^2}}$$

* If the value of v contained a term of the order kt^2, there would exist in the expression of $\frac{dv}{dt}$, the term $2kt$, and consequently this term would exist in X, so that in comparing coefficients of corresponding terms, we would have $\frac{dn}{dt} = 2k$.

$$\frac{-a.\sin. v.\int ndt.\, r.\cos. v.\left\{2\int \mathrm{d}R+r.\left\{\frac{\mathrm{d}R}{dr}\right\}\right\}}{\mu.\sqrt{1-e^2}}.$$

Let us consider the part of δr which involves terms multiplied by t^2, or for greater generality, let us consider the terms, which being multiplied by the sine or cosine* of the angle $\alpha t+\epsilon$, in which α is very small, have at the same time α^2 for a divisor. It is evident that α being supposed $=0$, there will result a term multiplied by t^2, so that the first case is contained in the second. The terms which have α^2 for a divisor can only be produced by a double integration; therefore they must be produced by the part of δr, which involves the double integral sign $\int$. Let us first examine the term

$$\frac{2a.\cos. v.\int ndt.(r.\sin. v\int \mathrm{d}R)}{\mu.\sqrt{1-e^2}}.$$

The origin of the angle i being fixed at the perihelion, we have in the elliptic orbit, by No. 20,

$$r=\frac{a.(1-e^2)}{1+e.\cos. v},$$

and consequently

$$\cos. v=\frac{a.(1-e^2)-r}{er};$$

hence we deduce by differencing

$$r^2.dv.\sin. v=\frac{a.(1-e^2)}{e}\,dr;\dagger$$

* α must be very small, because the sine is supposed to increase with great slowness; it is evident that if α be supposed equal to nothing, the double integrations would produce a term proportional to the square of the time.

† $-dv.\sin. v=\frac{-er.dr-e.a.((1-e^2)+r).dr}{e^2r^2}=-\frac{a.(1-e^2)}{er^2}.dr.$

but by No. 19, we have

$$r^2.dv = dt.\sqrt{\mu a.(1-e^2)} = a^2.ndt.\sqrt{1-e^2};$$

consequently,

$$\frac{andt.\,r.\,\sin.\,v}{\sqrt{1-e^2}} = \frac{rdr}{e}.$$

The term $\frac{2a.\cos.\,v.\int ndt.(r.\sin.\,v.\int \mathrm{d}R)}{\mu.\sqrt{1-e^2}}$, will therefore become

$$\frac{2.\cos.\,v}{\mu.e}.\int (rdr.\int \mathrm{d}R), \text{ or } \frac{\cos.\,v}{\mu.e}.(r^2.\int \mathrm{d}R - \int r^2.\mathrm{d}R).$$

It is evident that as this last function does not contain any double integrals, there cannot arise any term which has α^2 for a divisor.

Let us now consider the term

$$-\frac{2a.\sin.\,v\int ndt.\,(r.\cos.\,v\int \mathrm{d}R)}{\mu.\sqrt{1-e^2}};$$

of the expression of δr. By substituting for cos. v, its preceding value in r, this term becomes

$$\frac{2.\sin.\,v.\int ndt.(r-a.(1-e^2)).\int \mathrm{d}R}{\mu e.\sqrt{1-e^2}}.$$

By N°. 22, we have

$$r = a.(1+\tfrac{1}{2}e^2 + e\chi'),$$

χ' being an infinite series of the cosines of the angle $nt+\epsilon$, and its multiples; therefore we shall have

$$\frac{\int ndt}{e}.\,(r-a.(-e^2)).\int \mathrm{d}R = a.\int ndt.(\tfrac{3}{2}e+\chi').\int \mathrm{d}R.^*$$

* $r - a.(1-e^2) = a.(1+\frac{1}{2}e^2+e.\chi') - a.(1-e^2) = a.(\frac{3}{2}e^2+e.\chi')$.

Denoting by χ'' the integral $\int \chi' ndt$, we will have

$$a.\int ndt.(\tfrac{3}{2}e+\chi')\int dR = \tfrac{3}{2}ae.\int ndt.\int dR + a\chi''.\int dR - a.\int \chi''.dk.$$

As these two last terms do not involve the double sign of integration, no term which has α^2 for a denominator can arise from it; therefore if we only consider terms of this kind, we will have

$$-\frac{2a.\sin.v.\int ndt.(r.\cos.v.\int dR}{\mu.\sqrt{1-e^2}} = \frac{3a^2.e.\sin.v.\int ndt.\int dR}{\mu.\sqrt{1-e^2}}$$

$$= \frac{dr}{ndt}.\frac{3a}{\mu}.\int ndt.\int dR;$$

and the radius r will become

$$(r)+\left(\frac{dr}{ndt}\right).\frac{3a}{\mu}.\int ndt.\int dR;$$

(r) and $\left(\frac{dr}{ndt}\right)$ being the values of r and $\frac{dr}{ndt}$ in the case of elliptic motion. Thus, in order to consider in the expression of the radius vector, the part of the perturbations, which is divided by α^2, it will be sufficient to increase the mean longitude $nt+\varepsilon$, by the quantity $\frac{3a}{\mu}.\int ndt.\int dR$, in the expression for the mean longitude in the case of the elliptic motion.

Let us now examine whether this part of the perturbations should be taken into account in the expression for the longitude v. The formula (Y) of N°. 46, gives by substituting $\frac{3a}{\mu}.\frac{dr}{ndt}.\int ndt.\int dR$ in place of δr, when the terms divided by α^2 are only considered

$$\delta v = \frac{\left\{\frac{2rd^2r+dr^2}{a^2n^2dt^2}+1\right\}}{\sqrt{1-e^2}}.\frac{3a}{\mu}.\int ndt.\int dR;$$

but by what goes before, we have

$$\delta r = \frac{ae.ndt.\ \sin. v}{\sqrt{1-e^2}}\ ;\ r^2 dv = a^2 ndt.\ \sqrt{1-e^2}\ ;$$

hence it is easy to conclude, by substituting for cos. v, its value, which has been already given* in terms of r

$$\frac{\left\{\frac{2rd^2r+dr^2}{a^2n^2dt^2}+1\right\}}{\sqrt{1-e^2}} = \frac{dv}{ndt}\ ;$$

therefore if we only consider the part of the perturbations, of which the divisor is α^2, the longitude v will become

$$(v) + \left(\frac{dv}{ndt}\right).\frac{3a}{\mu}.\int ndt.\int dR\ ;$$

(v) and $\left(\frac{dv}{ndt}\right)$ being the parts of v and of $\frac{dv}{ndt}$ which are relative to

* $r.d^2.r = \frac{r.ae.n.dt.\ \cos.\ v.dv}{\sqrt{1-e^2}}$ equal by substituting for cos. v; $\frac{(a.(a.(1-e^2)-r).ndt.dv}{\sqrt{1-e^2}}$,

$\therefore\ \frac{2rd^2r}{a^2n^2dt^2.\sqrt{1-e^2}} = \frac{2a^2.ndt.\sqrt{1-e^2}.\ dv}{a^2n^2dt^2.\sqrt{1-e^2}} - \frac{2ar.ndt.dv}{(1-e^2).a^2n^2dt^2}$; $dr^2 = \frac{a^2e^2n^2dt^2}{1-e^2}$

$-\frac{(a^2e^2n^2dt^2.(a^2.(1-e^2)^2-2ar.(1-e^2)+r^2)}{e^2.r^2.(1-e^2)}$, $\therefore \frac{dr^2}{a^2.n^2dt^2.\sqrt{1-e^2}} = \frac{e^2}{(1-e^2)^{\frac{3}{2}}} - \frac{a^2.\sqrt{1-e^2}}{r^2}$

$+\frac{2a}{r.\sqrt{1-e^2}} + \frac{1}{(1-e^2)^{\frac{3}{2}}}$, $\therefore \frac{\frac{2rd^2r+dr^2}{a^2n^2dt^2}}{\sqrt{1-e^2}} = \frac{2dv}{ndt} - \frac{2rdv}{(1-e^2)andt} + \frac{e^2}{(1-e^2)^{\frac{3}{2}}}$

$-\frac{a^2.\sqrt{1-e^2}}{r^2} + \frac{2a}{r.\sqrt{1-e^2}} - \frac{1}{(1-e^2)^{\frac{3}{2}}} + \frac{1}{\sqrt{1-e^2}}$; now $-\frac{2rdv}{(1-e^2).andt} + \frac{2a}{r.\sqrt{1-e^2}}$

$= -\frac{2r^2dv+2a^2ndt.\sqrt{1-e^2}}{(1-e^2).r.andt} = 0$, and $\frac{e^2}{(1-e^2)^{\frac{3}{2}}} + \frac{1}{\sqrt{1-e^2}} - \frac{1}{(1-e^2)^{\frac{3}{2}}} = 0$, $\because$ since

$-\frac{a^2.\sqrt{1-e^2}}{r^2} = -\frac{dv}{ndt}$, the preceding expression becomes equal to $\frac{dv}{n.dt}$.

the elliptic motion. Therefore in order to consider this part of the perturbations in the expression for the longitude of m, we should follow the same rule as we have given, when considering the expression of the radius vector, that is to say, it is necessary to increase in the elliptic expression of the true longitude, the mean longitude $nt+\epsilon$ by the quantity $\frac{3a}{\mu}.\int ndt.\int dR$.

The constant part of the expression for $\left(\frac{dv}{ndt}\right)$, being expanded into a series of the cosines of the angle $nt+\epsilon$ and of its multiples, is reduced to unity, as we have seen in N°. 22; hence arises the term $\frac{3a}{\mu}.\int ndt.\int dR$ in the expression for the longitude. If dR contains the constant term $km'.ndt$, this term would produce $\frac{3}{2}.\frac{am'}{\mu}.k.n^2t^2$, in the expression for the longitude v. Therefore in order to ascertain whether such terms exist in this expression, we must consider whether dR contains a constant term.

When the excentricities of the orbits and their mutual inclinations to each other are small, R can be reduced always into an infinite series of the sines and cosines of angles proportional to the time t. They can be generally represented by the term $km'.\cos.(i'n't+int+A)$, i and i' being integral numbers, either positive or negative, or equal to cypher. The differential of this term taken solely with respect to the mean motion of m, is $-ikm'.ndt.\sin.(i'n't+int+A)$; this is the part of dR, which is relative to this term: it cannot be constant unless we have $0=i'n'+in$; but this supposes that the mean motions of the bodies m and m' are commensurable with each other; and as this is not the case in the solar system, we ought to infer from it, that the value of dR does not contain constant terms; and that consequently if we only consider the first power of the perturbating masses, the mean motions of the celestial bodies are uniform, or what comes to the same thing, $\frac{dn}{dt} = 0$. The value of a being connected with that of n, by means of the equation $n^2 = \frac{\mu}{a}$; it follows that if we do not take into account periodic quantities, the greater axes of the orbits are constant.

If the mean motions of the bodies m and m', though not exactly commensurable are very nearly so; there will exist in the theory of their motions, inequalities of a very long period, and which may become very sensible, on account of the smallness of the divisor α^2. We will see in the sequel that this obtains in the case of Jupiter and Saturn. The preceding analysis will give in a very simple manner, the part of the perturbations which depend on this divisor. It follows from it, that then it is sufficient to make the mean longitude $nt + \varepsilon$ or $\int ndt$ vary by the quantity $\frac{3an}{\mu}.\int ndt.dR$; which comes to make n, in the integral $\int ndt$, increase by the quantity $\frac{3an}{\mu}.\int dR$; the orbit of m being considered as a variable ellipse, we have $n^2 = \frac{\mu}{a^3}$; therefore the preceding variation of n must introduce in the semiaxis major of the orbit, the variation* $-\frac{2a^2 \int dR}{\mu}$.

If in the value of $\frac{dv}{dt}$ we carry the approximation as far as quantities of the order of the squares of the perturbating masses, terms proportional to the times will arise; but by attentively considering the differential equations of the motion of the bodies m, m', m'', &c.; it will readily appear that these terms are at the same time of the order of the squares and of the products of the excentricities and of

* From the equation $n^2 = \frac{\mu}{a^3}$ we have $da = -\frac{2na^4 dn}{3\mu}$ substituting $\frac{3an}{\mu}.\int dR$ for dn, and we have $da = -\frac{2n^2a^5.\int dR}{\mu^2} = -\frac{2a^2}{\mu}.\int dR$.

the inclinations of the orbits. However, as every thing which affects the mean motion, may at length become very sensible, we will consider in the sequel those terms, and we shall see that they produce the secular equations which have been observed in the motion of the moon.

55. Let us now resume the equations (1) and (2) of No. 55, and let

$$(0, 1) = -\frac{m'nC}{2}; \quad \boxed{0, 1} = \frac{m'.n.D}{2};$$

they will become

$$\frac{dh}{dt} = (0, 1).\, l - \boxed{0, 1}.\, l';$$

$$\frac{dl}{dt} = -(0, 1).\, h + \boxed{0, 1}.\, h'.$$

The expressions of $(0, 1)$ and of $\boxed{0, 1}$ may be determined very simply in the following manner. By substituting in place of C, and of D, their values, which have been determined in N°. 50, there will be obtained

$$(0, 1) = -\frac{m'.n}{2}.\left\{a^2.\left(\frac{dA^{(0)}}{da}\right) + \tfrac{1}{2}a^3.\left(\frac{d^2A^{(0)}}{da^2}\right)\right\};$$

$$\boxed{0, 1} = \frac{m'.n}{2}.\left\{a.A^{(1)} - a^2.\left(\frac{dA^{(1)}}{da}\right) - \tfrac{1}{2}.a^3,\left(\frac{d^2A^{(1)}}{da^2}\right)\right\}.$$

By N°. 49, we have

$$a^2.\left(\frac{dA^{(0)}}{da}\right) + \tfrac{1}{2}a^3.\left(\frac{d^2A^{(0)}}{da^2}\right) = -\alpha^2.\frac{db_{\frac{1}{2}}^{(0)}}{d\alpha} - \tfrac{1}{2}\alpha^3.\frac{d^2b_{\frac{1}{2}}^{(0)}}{d\alpha^2};$$

we will readily obtain by the same N°. $\frac{db_{\frac{1}{2}}^{(0)}}{d\alpha}, \frac{d^2b_{\frac{1}{2}}^{(0)}}{d\alpha^2}$, in functions of $b_{\frac{1}{2}}^{(0)}$, and of $b_{\frac{1}{2}}^{(1)}$; and these quantities are given in linear functions of $b_{-\frac{1}{2}}^{(0)}$. and of $b_{-\frac{1}{2}}^{(1)}$; this being premised we shall find

$$a^2.\left(\frac{dA^{(0)}}{da}\right) + \tfrac{1}{2}a^3.\left(\frac{d^2A^{(0)}}{da^2}\right) = \frac{3\alpha^2.b_{-\frac{1}{2}}^{(1)}}{2.(1-\alpha^2)^2};$$

therefore

$$(0, 1) = -\frac{3m'.n.\alpha^2.b^{(1)}_{-\frac{1}{2}}}{4.(1-\alpha^2)^2},$$

let

$$(a^2-2aa'.\cos\theta+a'^2)^{\frac{1}{2}} = (a, a') + (a, a)'.\cos.\theta + (a.a'')''.\cos.2\theta + \&c.$$

by No. 49, we shall have

$$(aa') = \tfrac{1}{2}a'.b^{(0)}_{-\frac{1}{2}};^* \quad (a, a)' = (a'.b^{(1)}_{-\frac{1}{2}}), \ \&c.$$

therefore we shall have

$$(0, 1) = -\frac{3m'.na^2.a'.(a.a')'}{4.(a'^2-a^2)^2}.$$

consequently by N°. 49, we obtain

$$a\mathrm{A}^{(1)} - a^2.\left\{\frac{d\mathrm{A}^{(1)}}{da}\right\} - \tfrac{1}{2}a^3.\left\{\frac{d^2\mathrm{A}^{(1)}}{da^2}\right\} = -\alpha.\left\{b^{(1)}_{\frac{1}{2}} - \alpha.\frac{db^{(1)}_{\frac{1}{2}}}{d\alpha} - \tfrac{1}{2}\alpha^2.\frac{d^2b^{(1)}_{\frac{1}{2}}}{d\alpha^2}\right\};$$

by substituting in place of $b^{(1)}_{\frac{1}{2}}$ and of its differences, their values in $b^{(0)}_{-\frac{1}{2}}$, and $b^{(1)}_{-\frac{1}{2}}$, the preceding function will be found equal to

$$-3\alpha.\frac{((1+\alpha^2).b^{(1)}_{-\frac{1}{2}}+\frac{1}{2}\alpha.b^{(0)}_{-\frac{1}{2}})}{(1-\alpha^2)^2};$$

therefore

$$\boxed{0, 1} = -\frac{3\alpha.m'n.((1+\alpha^2).b^{(1)}_{-\frac{1}{2}}+\frac{1}{2}\alpha.b^{(0)}_{-\frac{1}{2}})}{2.(1'^2-\alpha^2)^2};$$

or

$$\boxed{0, 1} = -\frac{3m'.an.((a^2+a'^2).(a,a')+a.a'.(a,a'))}{2.(a'^2-a^2)^2},$$

we shall obtain by this means very simple expressions for $(0, 1)$ and for $\boxed{0, 1}$, and it is easy to conclude by the values in a series for $b^{(0)}_{-\frac{1}{2}}$, and for $b^{(1)}_{-\frac{1}{2}}$, which are given in N°. 49, that these expressions are positive, if n be positive, and negative, if n be negative.

Naming $(0, 2)$ and $\boxed{0, 2}$ what $(0, 1)$ and $\boxed{0, 2}$ become, when a' and m' are changed into a''' and m'', and in like manner let $(0, 3)$ and $\boxed{0, 3}$ represent what these same quantities become when a' and m' are changed into a''' and m'''; and so on. Moreover let h'', l'', h''', l''', denote what

h and l become relative to the bodies m', m''', &c.; we shall obtain in consequence of the combined actions of the different bodies m', m'', m''', &c. on m,

$$\frac{dh}{dt} = ((0, 1) + (0, 2) + (0, 3) + \&c.)).\, l - \boxed{0, 1}.l' - \boxed{0, 2}.l'' - \&c.;$$

$$\frac{dl}{dt} = -((0, 1) + (0, 2) + (0, 3) + \&c.).\, h + \boxed{0, 1}.h' + \boxed{0, 2}.h'' + \&c..$$

It is manifest that $\frac{dh'}{dt}$, $\frac{dl'}{dt}$; $\frac{dh''}{dt}$, $\frac{dl''}{dt}$, &c., will be determined by expressions similar to those of $\frac{dh}{dt}$ and of $\frac{dl}{dt}$, and that it is easy to infer them from the preceding by changing successively, that which is relative to m, into that which refers to m', m'', &c., and *vice versa*. Let therefore

$$(1, 0),\ \boxed{1, 0}; \quad (1, 2),\ \boxed{1, 2};\ \&c.$$

be what

$$(0, 1),\ \boxed{0, 2}; \quad (0, 2),\ \boxed{0, 2};\ \&c.$$

become when we change in them that which is relative to m, into that which is relative to m', and conversely; let also

$$(2, 0),\ \boxed{2, 0}; \quad (2, 1),\ \boxed{2, 1};\ \&c.$$

be what

$$(0, 2),\ \boxed{0, 1}; \quad (0, 1),\ \boxed{0, 1}$$

become when that which is relative to m, is changed into that which is relative to m', and conversely, and so of the rest. The preceding

* In this case $(1-2a.\cos.\theta+a^2)^{-s} = (1-2a.\cos.\theta+a^2)^{\frac{1}{2}}$, $\because s = -\frac{1}{2}$; see page 278: $\because$ the first term in the expansion of $a'^{-2s}.(1-2a.\cos.\theta+a^2)^{-s}$ becomes (when $s = -\frac{1}{2}$.) $a'.b^{(0)}_{-\frac{1}{2}}$, and the coefficient of $\cos.\theta = a'.b^{(1)}_{-\frac{1}{2}}$.

differential equations referred successively to the bodies m, m', m'', &c. will give for the determination of h, l, h', l', h'', l'', &c. the following system of equations,

$$\left.\begin{aligned}
\frac{dh}{dt}&=((0,1)+(0,2)+(0,3)+\&c.).l-\boxed{0,1}.l'-\boxed{0,2}.l''-\boxed{0,3}.l'''-\&c.\\
\frac{dl}{dt}&=-((0,1)+(0,2)+(0,3)+\&c.).h+\boxed{0,1}h'+\boxed{0,2}.h''+\boxed{0,3}.h'''+\&c.\\
\frac{dh'}{dt}&=((1,0)+(1,2)+(1,3)+\&c.)l'-\boxed{1,0}.l-\boxed{1,2}.l''-\boxed{1,3}.l'''-\&c.\\
\frac{dl'}{dt}&=-((1,0)+(1,2)+(1,3)+\&c.)h'+\boxed{1,0}.h+\boxed{1,0}.h''+\boxed{1,3}.h'''+\&c.\\
\frac{dh''}{dt}&=((2,0)+(2,1)+(2,3)+\&c.)l''-\boxed{2,0}.l-\boxed{2,1}.l'-\boxed{2,3}.l'''-\&c.\\
\frac{dl''}{dt}&=-((2,0)+(2,1)+(2,3)+\&c.)h''+\boxed{2,0}.h+\boxed{2,1}.h'+\boxed{2,3}.h'''+\&c.
\end{aligned}\right\};(A)$$

The quantities $(0, 1)$ and $(1, 0)$, $\boxed{0,1}$ and $\boxed{1,0}$ have remarkable relations, which will very much facilitate the computation, and which will be useful in the sequel. By what precedes we have,

$$(0,1)=-\frac{3m'.na^2.a'.(a,a')'}{4(a'^2-a^2)^2}.$$

If in this expression for $(0, 1)$, m' be changed into m, n into n', a into a', and *vice versa*; we shall have the expression of $(1, 0)$ which will be consequently

$$(1,0)=-\frac{3m.n'a'^2.a.(a'.a)'}{4(a'^2-a^2)^2};$$

but we have $(a', a)'=(a, a')'$, because each of these quantities results from the expansion of the function $(a^2-2aa'.\cos.\theta+a'^2)^{\frac{1}{2}}$ into a series arranged according to the cosines of the angle θ and of its multiples; therefore we will have

$$(0,1)\,m.n'a'=(1,0).\,m'.na;$$

but, when the masses m, and m', &c., are neglected with respect to M,

$$n^2 = \frac{M}{a^3}; \; n'^2 = \frac{M}{a'^3}; \; \text{\&c.}$$

therefore

$$(0,1).m.\sqrt{a} = (1,0).m'.\sqrt{a'};$$

by means of this equation we can easily obtain $(1,0)$ when $(0,1)$ will be determined. In like manner we have

$$\boxed{0,1}\; m.\sqrt{a} = \boxed{1,0}\; m'.\sqrt{a'}.$$

These two equations will also subsist when n and n' have contrary signs; that is to say, when the two bodies m and m' revolve in contrary directions; but then we must give the sign of n to the radical $\sqrt{a}$, and the sign of n' to the radical $\sqrt{a'}$.

The following equations result evidently from the two preceding:

$$(0,2)\; m.\sqrt{a} = (2,0)\; m''.\sqrt{a''}; \; \boxed{0,2}\; m.\sqrt{a} = \boxed{2,0}.\; m''.\sqrt{a''}; \; \text{\&c.}$$

$$(1,2)\; m'.\sqrt{a} = (2,1)\; m''.\sqrt{a''}; \; \boxed{1,2} m'.\sqrt{a'} = \boxed{2,1}.\; m''.\sqrt{a''}; \; \text{\&c.}$$

56. Now in order to integrate the equations (A) of the preceding number, let

$$h = N.\sin.(gt+\epsilon); \; l = N.\cos.(gt+\epsilon);$$
$$h' = N'.\sin.(gt+\epsilon); \; l' = N'.\cos.(gt+\epsilon);$$

these values being substituted in the equation (A), will give

$$\left.\begin{array}{l} Ng = ((0,1)+(0,2)+\text{\&c.}).N - \boxed{0,1}.\,N' - \boxed{0,2}\,N'' - \text{\&c.} \\ N'g = ((1,0)+(1,2)+\text{\&c.}).N' - \boxed{1,0}.\,N' - \boxed{1,2}.\,N'' - \text{\&c.} \\ N'g = ((2,0)+(2,1)+\text{\&c.}).N'' - \boxed{2,0}.\,N - \boxed{2,1}.\,N' - \text{\&c.} \end{array}\right\}; \quad (B)^*$$

&c.

* In general, the number of these algebraic equations is equal to that of the coefficients

The number of bodies m, m', m'', &c., being equal to i, the number of these equations will be also i, and by eliminating the constant quantities N, N' &c., we will have a final equation in g, of the degree i, which can easily be obtained in the following manner:

Naming φ the function

$$
\begin{aligned}
& N^2.\,m.\sqrt{a}.(g-(0,1)-(0,2)-\&c.) \\
& +N'^2 m'.\sqrt{a'}.(g-(1,0)-(1,2)-\&c.) \\
& +\&c. \\
& +2N.\,m.\sqrt{a}.(\boxed{0,1}.\,N'+\boxed{0,1}.\,N''+\&c.) \\
& +2N'.m'.\sqrt{a'}.(\boxed{1,2}.N''+\boxed{1,3}.\,N'''+\&c.) \\
& +2N''.m''.\sqrt{a''}.(\boxed{2,3}.N''+\&c.) \\
& +\&c.
\end{aligned}
$$

In consequence of the relations which are given in the preceding number, the equations (B) are reduced to the following $\left(\frac{d\varphi}{dN}\right)=0$; $\left(\frac{d\varphi}{dN'}\right)=0$; $\left(\frac{d\varphi}{dN''}\right)=0$, &c,; therefore N, N', N'', &c. being considered as so many variables, φ will be a *maximum*. Moreover, φ being an homogeneous function of these variables of the second dimension; we have

$$N.\left(\frac{d\varphi}{dN}\right)+N'.\left(\frac{d\varphi}{dN'}\right)+\&c.=2\varphi;$$

therefore in consequence of the preceding equations, $\varphi=0$.

Now, we can determine in the following manner the *maximum* of the function φ. First, let this function be differenced relatively to N, and then substitute in φ, in place of N its value deduced from the equation

N, N', &c.; by means of the operations performed on the function φ, the ratio of these coefficients is obtained; one of them remains undetermined.

$\left(\frac{d\varphi}{dN}\right)=0$; this value will be a linear function of the quantities N', N'', &c.; in this manner we shall obtain a rational function, which is both integral and homogeneous, of the second dimension in N', N'', &c., let $\varphi^{(1)}$ be this function. By differencing $\varphi^{(1)}$ relatively to N', and by substituting in $\varphi^{(1)}$ in place of $N^{(1)}$ its value deduced from the equation $\left(\frac{d\varphi^{(1)}}{dN'}\right)=0$; we shall obtain an homogeneous function, which will be likewise of the second dimension in N'', N''', &c. let $\varphi^{(2)}$ be this function. By continuing this operation, we will arrive at a function $\varphi^{(i-1)}$ of the second dimension, in $N^{(i-1)}$, and which will consequently be of the form $(N^{(i-1)})^2.k$; k being a function of g, and of constant quantities. If the differential of $\varphi^{(i-1)}$ taken with respect to $N^{(i-1)}$, be put equal to cypher, we shall have $k=0$; this will give an equation in g of the degree i, of which the different roots will give so many different systems for the indeterminate quantities N, N', N'', &c.; the indeterminate $N^{(i-1)}$ will be the arbitrary quantity of each system, we shall obtain immediately, the ratio of the other indeterminate quantities N, N', &c. of the same system to this, by means of the preceding equations taken in an reverse order, namely

$$\left(\frac{d\varphi^{(i-2)}}{dN^{i-2}}\right)=0;\ \left(\frac{d\varphi^{(i-3)}}{dN^{i-3}}\right)=0;\ \&c.$$

Let g, g_1, g_2, be the i roots of the equation in g; let N, N', N'', &c. be the system of indeterminate quantities relative to the root g; let N, $N_{\prime}'$, $N_{\prime}''$, &c. be the system of indeterminate quantities relative to the root $g_{\prime}$, and so on of the rest: by the known theory of differential linear equations we will have

$$h=N.\sin.(gt+\epsilon)+N_1.\sin.(g_{\prime}t+\epsilon_{\prime})+N_2.\sin.(g_2t+\epsilon_2)+\ \&c.;$$
$$h'=N'.\sin.(gt+\epsilon)+N_1'.\sin.(g_{\prime}t+\epsilon_{\prime})+N_2'.\sin.(g_2t+\epsilon_2)+\ \&c.;$$
$$h''=N''.\sin.(gt+\epsilon)+N_1''.\sin.(g_{\prime}t+\epsilon_{\prime})+N_2''.\sin.(g_2t+\epsilon_2)+\ \&c.;$$
&c.

ε, ε_1, ε_2, being constant arbitrary quantities. The values of l, l', l'', &c. will be obtained by changing in the expressions for h, h', h'', &c. the sines into the cosines. These different values contain twice as many arbitrary quantities, as there are roots g, g_1, g_2, &c.; for each system of indeterminate quantities contains one arbitrary quantity, and besides, there are i arbitrary quantities ε, ε_1, ε_2, &c.; these values are consequently the complete integrals of the equations (A) of the preceding number.

It is only now required to determine the constant quantities N, $N_{,}$, &c. N', $N'_{,}$. &c. ε, $\varepsilon'_{,}$, &c. These constant quantities are not given immediately by observation; but they make known at a given epoch, the excentricities e, e. &c. of the orbits, and the longitudes ϖ, ϖ', &c. of their perihelious, and consequently the values of h, h', &c. l, l, &c; thus we shall derive from them the values of the preceding constant quantities. For this purpose it may be observed, that if we multiply the first, third, and fifth, &c. of the differential equations (A) of the preceding number, by $Nm.\sqrt{a}$, $N'm'.\sqrt{a'}$, &c. respectively, we will have in consequence of the equations (B), and of the relations found in the preceding number, between (0, 1) and (1, 0), (0, 2) and (2, 0), &c.

$$N.\frac{dh}{dt}.m.\sqrt{a}+N'.\frac{dh'}{dt}.m'.\sqrt{a'}+N''.\frac{dh''}{dt}.m''.\sqrt{a''}+\text{\&c.})^*$$

$$=g.(N.l.m.\sqrt{a}+N'.l'.m.\sqrt{a'}+N''.l''.m''.\sqrt{a''}+\text{\&c.})$$

* Multiplying the first of the equations (A) by $N.m.\sqrt{a}$, and the third by $N'.m'.\sqrt{a'}$, we shall obtain by adding them together,

$N.\frac{dh}{dt}.m.\sqrt{a}+N'.\frac{dh'}{dt}.m'.\sqrt{a'} = (0,1)+(0,2)+(0,3)+\text{\&c.})\,l.N.m.\sqrt{a} - \boxed{0,1}.l'.N.m.\sqrt{a} - \text{\&c.} + ((1,0)+(1,2)+(1,3)+\text{\&c.})\,l'.N'.m'.\sqrt{a'} - \boxed{1,0}.l.N'.m'.\sqrt{a'} - \text{\&c.} = (\text{as } \boxed{0,1}.m.\sqrt{a} = \boxed{1,0}\,m'.\sqrt{a'},)\ l.m.\sqrt{a}.((0,1)+(0,2)+(0,3)+\text{\&c.})\,N - \boxed{0,1}.N' - \text{\&c.}) + l'.m'.\sqrt{a'}.((1,0)+(1,2)+(1,3)+\text{\&c.}\ N'.$

By substituting in this equation, in place of h, h', h'', &c. l, l', l'', &c. their preceding values; we will have by comparing the coefficients of the same cosines,

$$0 = N.N_{,}.m.\sqrt{a} + N'.N'_{,}.m'.\sqrt{a'} + N''.N''_{,}.m''.\sqrt{a''} + \text{\&c.};$$
$$0 = N.N_{2}.m.\sqrt{a} + N'.N'_{2}.m'.\sqrt{a'} + N''.N''_{2}.m''.\sqrt{a''} + \text{\&c.}$$

&c.

This being premised, if the preceding values of h, h', &c., be multiplied by $N.m.\sqrt{a}$, $N'.m'.\sqrt{a'}$, &c., respectively, we will have in consequence of these last equations,

$$N.mh.\sqrt{a} + N'.m'h'.\sqrt{a'} + N''.m''h''.\sqrt{a''} + \text{\&c.}$$
$$= (N^2.m.\sqrt{a} + N'^2.m'.\sqrt{a'} + N''^2.m''.\sqrt{a''} + \text{\&c.}).\ \sin.\ (gt+\epsilon).$$

we shall have in like manner,

$$N.ml.\sqrt{a} + N'm'.l'.\sqrt{a'} + N''.m''l''.\sqrt{a''} + \text{\&c.}$$
$$= (N^2.m.\sqrt{a} + N'^2.m'.\sqrt{a'} + N''^2.m''.\sqrt{a''} + \text{\&c.})\ \cos.\ (gt+\epsilon).$$

The commencement of the time being fixed at an epoch, for which the values of h, l, h', l', &c. are supposed to be known; the two preceding equations give

— $[\overline{1,0}].N$ — &c.) $= (N.lm.\sqrt{a} + N'.l'm'.\sqrt{a'} + \text{\&c.})\,g$; now by substituting for $\frac{dh}{dt} + \frac{dh'}{dt} +$&c. l, l', &c. we obtain; $m.\sqrt{a}.\,(N^2.g.\cos.(gt+\epsilon) + NN_{,}g_{,}.\cos.(g_{,}t+\epsilon_{,}) + NN_{2}g_{2}.\cos.(g_{2}t+\epsilon_{2})) +$ &c. $+ m'.\sqrt{a'}.\,(N'^2.g.\cos.(gt+\epsilon) + N'N'_{,}.g_{,}.\cos.(g_{,}t+\epsilon_{,}) + NN'_{2}.g_{2}.\cos.(g_{2}t+\epsilon_{2}) + \text{\&c.}) = g)N^2.\,m.\sqrt{a}.\cos.(gt+\epsilon) + NN_{,}\cos.(g_{,}t+\epsilon_{,}) + NN'_{2}.\cos.(g_{2}t+\epsilon_{2}) + m'.\sqrt{a'}.N'^2.\cos.(gt+\epsilon) + N'N'_{,}.\cos.(g_{,}t+\epsilon) + N'N'_{2}.\cos.(g_{2}t+\epsilon_{2}) +$ &c.) From hence it follows, that in order for this equation always to obtain, we must have $NN_{,}m.\sqrt{a} + N'N'_{,}.m'.\sqrt{a'} + \text{\&c.} = 0$.

$$\tan. \epsilon = \frac{N.hm.\sqrt{a} + N'.h'.m'.\sqrt{a'} + N''.h''m''.\sqrt{a''} + \&c.}{N.lm.\sqrt{a} + N'.l'.m'.\sqrt{a'} + N''.l''m''.\sqrt{a''} + \&c.} \;*$$

This expression of tan. ϵ does not contain any indeterminate quantity; for although the constant quantities N, N', N'', depend on the indeterminate quantity $N^{(i-1)}$; yet, as, their ratio to this indeterminate quantity is known by what precedes, it must disappear from the tan. ϵ. ϵ being thus determined, we shall obtain $N^{(i-1)}$, by means of one of the two equations which determine tan. ϵ, and from it we infer the system of indeterminates N, N', N'', &c., relative to the root g. And if in the preceding expressions, this root be successively changed into g_1, g_2, g_3, &c., the values of the arbitrary quantities relative to each of these roots will be obtained.

These values being substituted in the expressions for h, l, h', l', &c. the excentricities e, e', &c. of the orbits may be deduced from them, as also the longitudes ϖ, ϖ', &c., of their perihelions, by means of the equations

$$e^2 = h^2 + l^2\,; \quad e'^2 = h'^2 + l'^2\,; \;\&c.$$

$$\tan.\, \varpi = \frac{h}{l}\,; \quad \tan.\, \varpi' = \frac{h'}{l'}\,; \;\&c.$$

thus we shall have

$$e^2 = N^2 + N_1^2 + N_2^2 + \;\&c. + 2NN_1.\cos.\,((g_1 - g).t + \epsilon_1 - \epsilon)^*$$

$$+ 2NN_2.\cos.\,((g_2 - g).t + \epsilon_2 - \epsilon) + 2N_1N_2.\cos.(g_2 - g_1).t + \epsilon_2 - \epsilon) + \&c.$$

This quantity is always less than $(N + N_1 + N_2 + \;\&c.)^2$, when

* By fixing the origin at the epoch when h, h', l, l', &c. are known, gt vanishes, therefore the coefficients of $N.m.\sqrt{a} + N'.m'.\sqrt{a'} + \&c.$ are sin. ϵ, cos. ϵ.

* The coefficients by which $2NN$ is multiplied in the values of $h^2 + l^2$ are sin. $(gt + \epsilon)$. sin. $(g_1t + \epsilon_1)$, cos. $(gt + \epsilon)$. cos. $(g_1t + \epsilon_1)$, and the sum of these two $=$ cos. $(g_1 - g)$. $t + \epsilon_1 - \epsilon)$.

the roots $g, g_{,}$, &c., are all real and unequal, the quantities $N, N_{,}$, &c., being supposed to be positive. In like manner we shall have

$$\tan. \varpi = \frac{N.\sin.(gt+\epsilon)+N_1.\sin.(g_1t+\epsilon_1)+N_2.\sin.(g_2t+\epsilon_2)+\&c.}{N.\cos.(gt+\epsilon)+N_1.\cos.(g_1t+\epsilon_1)+N_2.\cos.(g_2t+\epsilon_2)+\&c.},$$

hence it is easy to infer

$$\tan.(\varpi-gt-\epsilon) = \frac{N_1.\sin.((g_1-g).t+\epsilon_1-\epsilon))+N_2.\sin.((g_2-g).t+\epsilon_2-\epsilon))+\&c.}{N+N_1.\cos.((g_1-g).t+\epsilon_1-\epsilon))+N_2.\cos.((g_2-g).t+\epsilon_2-\epsilon))+\&c.}.$$

When the sum $N_1, +N_2, +$&c. of the coefficients of the cosines of this denominator, taken positively, is less than N; tang. $(\varpi-gt-\epsilon)$ can never become infinite; therefore the angle $\varpi-gt-\epsilon$ can never attain the fourth part of a circumference; so that in this case, the true mean motion of the perihelion is equal to gt.

57. From what precedes it follows, that the excentricities of the orbits, and the positions of the greater axes are subject to considerable variations, which change at length the nature of these orbits, and as their periods depend on the roots g, g, g_2, &c., they embrace relatively to the planets, a great number of ages. The excentricities may therefore be considered as of variable ellipticities, and the motions of the perihelions as not altogether uniform. These variations are very consider-

$$* \ \text{Tan.}(\varpi-(gt+\epsilon)) = \frac{\tan.\varpi-\tan.(gt+\epsilon)}{1+\tan.\varpi.\tan.(gt+\epsilon)} = \frac{\frac{h}{l}-\tan.(gt+\epsilon)}{1+\frac{h}{l}.\tan.(gt+\epsilon)} =$$

$\frac{h.\cos.(gt+\epsilon)-l.\sin.(gt+\epsilon)}{l.\cos.(gt+\epsilon)+h.\sin.(gt+\epsilon)}$, now by substituting for h and l their values, and observing that $\sin.(gt+\epsilon).\cos.(g_{,}t+\epsilon_{,})-\sin.(g_{,}t+\epsilon_{,}).\cos.(gt+\epsilon)=\sin.((g_{,}-g).t+(\epsilon_{,}-\epsilon))$, the numerator of this fraction becomes $N.\sin.(gt+\epsilon).\cos.(gt+\epsilon)+N_{,}.\sin.(g_{,}t+\epsilon_{,}).\cos.(gt+\epsilon)+$ &c.$-N.\sin.(gt+\epsilon).\cos.(gt+\epsilon)-N_{,}.\sin.(gt+\epsilon).\cos.(g_{,}t+\epsilon_{,})-$ &c. $=$ $N_{,}.\sin.((g'-g).t+(\epsilon'-\epsilon)+N_{,,}.\sin.(g_{,,}-g).t+(\epsilon_{,,}-\epsilon))+$ &c., and the denominator becomes $N.\sin.^2(gt+\epsilon)+N.\cos.^2(gt+\epsilon)+N_{,}.\sin.(gt+\epsilon).\sin.(g_{,}t+\epsilon_{,})+N_{,}.\cos.(gt+\epsilon).\cos.(g_{,}t+\epsilon_{,})+$&c. $=N+N_{,}.\cos.(g-g_{,}).t+(\epsilon-\epsilon_{,})+$ &c.

able in the satellites of Jupiter, and we shall see in the sequel that they explain the remarkable inequalities which are observed in the third satellite. But are there limits to the variations of the excentricities, and do the orbits always differ very little from circles? It is of great moment to investigate this question. We have already observed, that if the roots of the equation in g, are all real and unequal, the excentricity e of the orbit of m is always less than the sum $N+N_1+N_2+$ &c. of the coefficients of the sines of the expression for h, taken positively; and as these coefficients are supposed to be very small, the value of e will be always inconsiderable. It is therefore evident, that if we only consider the secular variations, the orbits of the bodies m, m', m'', &c. will undergo slight changes in their compression, deviating inconsiderably from the circular form; but the positions of the greater axes will experience considerable variations. These axes will be always of the same magnitude, and the mean motions which depend on them will be always uniform, as we have seen in N°. 54. The preceding results, which are founded on the small excentricities of the orbits, will invariably subsist, and may be extended to future and past ages; so that we can affirm, that at any assigned period, the orbits of the planets and of the satellites have not been very excentrick, at least, if we only consider their mutual action. But this would not be the case if any of the roots g, g_1, g_2. &c., were equal or imaginary: the sines and cosines of the expressions of h, l, h', l', &c, corresponding to these roots, will then be changed into arcs of circles, or into exponentials; and as these quantities increase indefinitely with the time, the orbits will eventually become very excentrick; the stability of the planetary system will then be destroyed, and the results to which we have arrived will cease to have place. It is therefore very interesting to determine whether the roots g, g_1, g_2, &c., are all real and unequal. This may be demonstrated very simply in the case of nature, in which the bodies m, m', m'', &c., revolve in the same direction.

Resuming the equations (A) of N°. 55, and multiplying the first by

$m.\sqrt{a}.h$; the second by $m.\sqrt{a}.l$; the third by $m'.\sqrt{a'}.h'$; the fourth by $m'.\sqrt{a'}.l'$, &c., and then adding them together; the coefficients of $h.l$, $h'.l$, $h''.l''$. &c., will vanish in this sum; the coefficient of $h'.l-h.l'$, will be $\boxed{0,1}.m.\sqrt{a}-\boxed{1,0}.m'.\sqrt{a'}$. and it will be equal to nothing, in virtue of the equation $\boxed{0,1}.m.\sqrt{a}=\boxed{1,0}.m'.\sqrt{a'}$, which has been found in N°. 55. The coefficients of $h''.l-h.l''$. $h''.l'-h'.l''$ will vanish for the same reason; therefore the sum of the equations (A) thus prepared, will be reduced to the following equation:

$$\frac{(hdh+ldl)}{dt}.m.\sqrt{a}+\frac{(h'dh'+l'dl')}{dt}.m'.\sqrt{a'}+\text{\&c.}=0;$$

and consequently to the following,

$$0=ede.m.\sqrt{a}+e'de'.m'.\sqrt{a'}+\text{\&c.}$$

By integrating this equation, and remarking that by N°. 54, the greater axes a, a', a'', of the orbits are constant, we will have

$$e^2.m.\sqrt{a}+e'^2.m'.\sqrt{a'}+e''^2.m''.\sqrt{a''}+\text{\&c.}=\text{constant}; \quad (u).$$

Now the bodies m, m', m'', &c., being supposed to revolve in the same direction, the radicals $\sqrt{a}$, $\sqrt{a'}$, $\sqrt{a''}$; &c., ought to be taken positively in the preceding equation, as has been observed in N°. 55; therefore all the terms of the first member of this equation are positive, and consequently each of them is less than the constant of the second member; but if we suppose that at any given epoch, the excentricities are very small, this constant quantity will be very small; therefore each of the terms of the equations will always remain very small, and cannot increase indefinitely; consequently, the orbits will be always very nearly circular.

The case which we have now examined, is that of the planets and of the satellites of the solar system; because all these bodies revolve in the same direction, and the excentricities of their orbits are at this present epoch very inconsiderable. In order to remove every doubt on this important result, it may be observed that if the equation which determines g, contains imaginary roots, some of the sines and of the cosines of the expressions of h, l, h', l', &c., will be changed into exponentials; thus the expressions for h will contain a finite number of terms of the form $P.c^{ft}$, c being the number of which the hyperbolic logarithm is equal to unity, and P being a real quantity, because h or e. sin. ϖ is a real quantity. Let $Q.c^{ft}$, $P'.c^{ft}$, $Q'.c^{ft}$, $P''.c^{ft}$, &c., be the corresponding terms of l, h', l', h'', &c.; Q, P', Q, P'', &c., being also real quantities: the expression of e^2 will contain the term $(P^2+Q^2).c^{2ft}$; the expression of e'^2 will contain the term $(P'^2+Q'^2).\,c^{2ft}$, and so on of the rest: consequently the first member of the equation (u) will contain the term

$$((P^2+Q^2).m.\sqrt{a}+(P'^2+Q'^2).m'.\sqrt{a'}+(P''^2+Q''^2).m''.\sqrt{a''}+\&c.).\,c^{2ft}$$

If c^{ft} be the greatest of the exponentials which h, l, h', l', &c., contain, that is to say, in which f is the most considerable; c^{2ft} will be the greatest of the exponentials, which the first member of the preceding equation will contain; therefore the preceding term cannot be destroyed by any other term of this first member; consequently in order that this member may be reduced to a constant quantity, it is necessary that the coefficient of c^{2ft} should vanish, which gives

$$0=(P^2+Q^2).m.\sqrt{a}+(P'^2+Q'^2).\,m'.\sqrt{a'}+(P''^2+Q''^2).m''.\sqrt{a''}+\&c.$$

When $\sqrt{a}$, $\sqrt{a'}$, $\sqrt{a''}$, &c., have the same sign, or what comes to the same thing, when the bodies m, m', m'', &c., revolve in the same direction, this equation is impossible, unless we suppose $P=0$, $Q=0$, $P'=0$, &c.; hence it follows, that the quantities h, l, h', l', &c., do not contain exponential quantities, and that consequently the equation in g does not contain imaginary roots.

If this equation have equal roots, the expressions of h, l, h', l', &c., contain, as we know, arcs of circles, and we would have in the expression for h, a finite number of terms of the form $P.t^r$. Let $Q.t^r$,

$P't^r$, $Q't^r$, &c., be the corresponding terms for l, h', l'. &c.; P, Q, P', &c., being real quantities; the first member of the equation in u will contain the term*

$$(P^2+Q^2), m.\sqrt{a}+(P'^2+Q'^2). m'.\sqrt{a'}+(P''^2+Q''^2).m''.\sqrt{a''}, \&c.)\ t^{2r}.$$

If t^r be the highest power of t, which the values of h, l, h', l', &c. contain; t^{2r} will be the highest power of t, contained in the first member of the equation (u); thus in order that this member may be reduced to a constant quantity, it is necessary that we have

$$0=(P^2+Q^2).m.\sqrt{a}+(P'^2+Q'^2).m'.\sqrt{a'}+\ \&c.$$

consequently $P=0$, $Q=0$, $P'=0$, $Q'=0$, &c. It follows therefore that the expressions of h, l, h', l', &c., do not contain either exponential quantities, or arcs of circles, and that consequently all the roots of the equation in g are real and unequal.

The system of the orbits of m, m', m'', &c., is therefore perfectly stable, relatively to their excentricities; these orbits only oscillate about a mean state of ellipticity, from which they deviate a little, the greater axes remaining the same: their excentricities are always subject to this condition, namely, that the sum of their squares multiplied respectively by the masses of the bodies, and by the square roots of their greater axes is constantly the same.

58. When, by what precedes, the values of e, and of ϖ shall have been determined; let them be substituted in all the terms of the expressions for r, and $\frac{dv}{dt}$, which are given in the preceding numbers, the terms which contain the time t, without the signs *sine* and *cosine*,

* See Lacroix, tom. 2, No. 613, for the truth of the assertion will be immediately apparent, in the first case, if in place of the sines and cosines their imaginary exponentials be substituted, or if in the second, the equal roots be supposed to differ by very small indeterminate quantities.

being effaced. The elliptic part of these expressions will be the same as in the case of the undisturbed orbit; with this sole difference, that the excentricity and the position of the perihelion will be variable; but the period of these variations being very long, on account of the smallness of the masses m, m', m'', relatively to M; we can suppose these variations proportional to the time, for a long interval, which for the planets may be extended to several ages, before and after the epoch which we select for the origin of the time. It is useful, for astronomical purposes, to have under this form the secular variations of the excentricities of the perihelions of their orbits; they can be easily inferred from the preceding formulæ. In fact, the equation $e^2 = h^2 + l^2$, gives $ede = hdh + ldl$; and if we only consider the action of m', we have, by N°. 55,

$$\frac{dh}{dt} = (0, 1).l - \boxed{0, 1}.l';$$

$$\frac{dl}{dt} = -(0, 1).h + \boxed{0, 1}.h';$$

therefore

$$\frac{ede}{dt} = \boxed{0, 1}.(h'l - hl');$$

but we have $h'l - hl' = e.e'. \sin. (\varpi' - \varpi)$; therefore we shall have

$$\frac{de}{dt} = \boxed{0, 1}. e'. \sin. (\varpi' - \varpi);$$

consequently, if we only take into account the reciprocal action of the bodies m', m'', &c. we shall have

$$\frac{de}{dt} = \boxed{0, 1}. e'. \sin. (\varpi' - \varpi) + \boxed{0, 2}\, e''. \sin. (\varpi'' - \varpi) + \&c.$$

$$\frac{de'}{dt} = \boxed{1,\ }. e. \sin. (\varpi - \varpi') + \boxed{1, 2}. e''. \sin. (\varpi'' - \varpi') + \&c.$$

* $h = e. \sin. \varpi$, $h' = e'. \sin. \varpi'$; $l = e. \cos. \varpi$; $l' = e' \cos. \varpi'$, ∵ $h'l - hl' = ee'. \sin. (\varpi - \varpi)$.

$$\frac{de''}{dt} = \boxed{2,0}\,.\,e.\sin.\,(\varpi - \varpi'') + \boxed{2,1}\,.\,e'\sin.\,(\varpi' - \varpi'' + \&c.\,;$$

&c.

The equation $\text{tang.}\,\varpi = \frac{h}{l}$, gives by differenceing it

$$e^2.d\varpi = l.dh - h.dl.$$

If the action of m', be only considered, by substituting for dh and dl their values, we shall have

$$\frac{e^2 d\varpi}{dt} = (0,1).\,(h^2 + l^2) - \boxed{0,1}\,.\,(hh' + ll')\,;\,^{*}$$

which gives

$$\frac{d\varpi}{dt} = (0,1) - \boxed{0,1}\,.\,\frac{e'}{e}.\cos.\,(\varpi' - \varpi)\,;$$

therefore we shall have, in consequence of the reciprocal actions of the bodies, m, m', m'', &c.;

$$\frac{d\varpi}{dt} = (0,1) + (0,2) + \&c. - \boxed{0,1}\,.\,\frac{e'}{e}.\cos.\,(\varpi' - \varpi) -$$

$$\boxed{0,2}\,.\,\frac{e''}{e}.\cos.\,(\varpi'' - \varpi) - \&c.\,;$$

$$\frac{d\varpi'}{dt} = (1,0) + (1,2), + \&c. - \boxed{1,0}\,.\,\frac{e}{e'}.\cos.\,(\varpi - \varpi') -$$

$$\boxed{1,2}\,.\,\frac{e''}{e'}.\cos.\,(\varpi'' - \varpi') - \&c.\,;$$

* $\frac{d\varpi}{\cos.^2\varpi} = \frac{ldh - hdl}{l^2}$; but from the equation $\text{tang.}\,\varpi = \frac{h}{l}$, we have $\cos.^2\varpi = \frac{l^2}{h^2+e^2} = \frac{l^2}{e^2}$, $\therefore$ by substituting we have the expression in the text.

$$\frac{d\varpi''}{dt}=(2,0)+(2,1)+\&c.-\boxed{2,0}.\frac{e}{e''}.\cos.(\varpi-\varpi'')-$$

$$\boxed{2,1}.\frac{e'}{e''}.\cos.(\varpi'-\varpi'')-\&c.$$

&c.

These values of $\frac{de}{dt}$, $\frac{de'}{dt}$, &c.; $\frac{d\varpi}{dt}$, $\frac{d\varpi'}{dt}$, &c., being multiplied by the time t, the differential expressions of the secular variations of the excentricities and of the perihelions will be had; and these expressions, which are only rigorously true, when t is indefinitely small, can however serve for a long interval, relatively to the planets. Their comparison with accurate observations, which are made at considerable intervals from each other, is the most exact means of determining the masses of the planets, which have no satellites. For any time t, the excentricity e is equal to $e+t.\left(\frac{de}{dt}\right)+\frac{t^2}{1.2}.\frac{d^2e}{dt^2}+\&c$; e, $\frac{de}{dt}$, $\frac{d^2e}{dt^2}$, &c. being relative to the origin of the time t, or to the epoch. The preceding value of $\frac{de}{dt}$ will give by differencing it, and by observing that a, a', &c., are constant, the values of $\frac{d^2e}{dt^2}$, $\frac{d^3e}{dt^3}$, &c., we can therefore continue as far as we please the preceding series, and by a similar process, the series relative to ϖ; but in the case of the planets, it will be sufficient, in the comparison of the most ancient observations of which we are in possession, to take into account the square of the time, in the expressions in series of e, e', &c., ϖ, ϖ', &c.

59. Let us now consider the equations relative to the position of the orbits, and for this purpose let the equations (3) and (4) of N°. 53, be resumed,

$$\frac{dp}{dt}=\frac{m'n}{4}.a^2a'.B^{(1)}.(q-q');$$

$$\frac{dq}{dt}=\frac{m'n}{4}.a^2a'.B^{(1)}.(p-p').$$

By No. 49, we have,

$$a^2 a'.B^{(1)} = \alpha^2.\ b^{(1)}_{\frac{3}{2}};$$

and by the same number we have

$$b^{(1)}_{\frac{3}{2}} = -\frac{3.b^{(1)}_{-\frac{1}{2}}}{(1-\alpha^2)^2};$$

therefore we shall have

$$\frac{m'n}{4}.\ a^2 a'.B^{(1)} = -\frac{3m'.n.\alpha^2 b^{(1)}_{-\frac{1}{2}}}{4.(1-\alpha^2)^2}.$$

The second member of this equation is that which we have designated by (0, 1) in N°. 55; consequently we shall have

$$\frac{dp}{dt} = (0,1).\ (q'-q);$$

$$\frac{dq}{dt} = (0,1).\ (p-p');$$

hence it is easy to infer, that the values of q, p, q', p', &c., will be determined by the following system of differential equations,

$$\left.\begin{aligned}
\frac{dq}{dt} &= ((0,1)+(0,2)+\&c.).p-(0,1).p'-(0,2).p''-\&c. \\
\frac{dp}{dt} &= -((0,1)+(0,2)+\&c.).q+(0,1).q'+(0,2).q''+\&c. \\
\frac{dq'}{dt} &= ((1,0)+(1,2)+\&c.).p'-(1,0).p-(1,2).p''-\&c. \\
\frac{dp'}{dt} &= -((1,0)+(1,2)+\&c.)q'+(1,0).q+(1,2).q''+\&c. \\
\frac{dq''}{dt} &= ((2,0)+(2,1)+\&c.).p''-(2,0).p-(2,1).p'-\&c. \\
\frac{dp''}{dt} &= -((2,0)+(2,1)+\&c.).q''+(2,0).q+(2,1).q'+\&c. \\
&\&c.
\end{aligned}\right\}; \quad (C)$$

This system of equations is similar to that of the equations (A) of N°. 55; it would coincide altogether with it, if in the equations A, h, l, h', l', &c., be changed into q, p, q', p', &c., and if we suppose $\boxed{0, 1}$. $=(0, 1)$; $\boxed{1, 0}=(1, 0)$, &c.; consequently, the analysis which we have employed in N°. 56, in order to integrate the equation (A), is applicable to the equations (C). Therefore let us suppose

$$q=N.\cos.(gt+\epsilon)+N_1.\cos.(g_1t+\epsilon_1)+N_2.\cos.(g_2t+\epsilon_2)+\&c.;$$
$$p=N.\sin.(gt+\epsilon)+N_1.\sin.(g_1t+\epsilon_1)+N_2.\sin.(g_2t+\epsilon_2)+\&c.;$$
$$q'=N'.\cos.(gt+\epsilon)+N_1'.\cos.(g_1t+\epsilon_1)+N_2'.\cos.(g_2t+\epsilon_2)+\&c.;$$
$$p'=N'.\sin.(gt+\epsilon)+N_1'.\sin.(g\,t+\epsilon_1)+N'_2.\sin.(g_2t+\epsilon_2)+\&c.;$$
$$\&c.$$

and by the method given in N°. 56, an equation in g of the degree i, may be obtained, of which the different roots will be g, g_1, g_2, &c. It is easy to see that one of these roots vanishes, because the equations (C) will be satisfied by supposing p, p', p'', &c., equal and constant, and also q, q', q'', &c., but this requires that one of the roots of the equation in g should vanish, and thus the equation is depressed to the degree $i-1$. The arbitrary quantities N, N_1, N_2, &c., ϵ, ϵ_1, ϵ_2, &c., may be determined by the method detailed in N°. 56. Finally, by an analysis similar to that of No. 57, we shall find

$$\text{const.}=(p^2+q^2).\,m.\sqrt{a}+(p'^2+q'^2).\,m'.\sqrt{a'}+\&c.;$$

from which may be inferred, as in the above cited N°. that the expressions of p, q, p', q', &c., do not contain either arcs of a circle, or exponential quantities, when the bodies m, m', m'', &c., revolve in the same direction: and that consequently all the roots of the equation in g, are real and unequal.

Two other integrals of the equations in C may be obtained. In fact, if the first of these equations be multiplied by $m.\sqrt{a}$, the third by $m'.\sqrt{a'}$, the fifth by $m''.\sqrt{a''}$, &c, we shall have in consequence of the relations found in N°. 55,

$$0 = \frac{dq}{dt} \cdot m.\sqrt{a} + \frac{dq'}{dt} \cdot m'.\sqrt{a'} + \&c.$$

which being integrated, gives

$$\text{constant} = q.m.\sqrt{a} + q'.m'.\sqrt{a'} + \&c. \quad (1)$$

In the same manner we shall find

$$\text{constant} = p.m.\sqrt{a} + p'.m'.\sqrt{a'} + \&c. \quad (2)$$

Naming φ the inclination of the orbit of m, on the fixed plane, and θ the longitude of the ascending node of this orbit on the same plane; the latitude of m will be very nearly, tang. φ. sin. $(nt+\varepsilon-\theta)$. By comparing* this value, with the following, $q.\sin.(nt+\varepsilon) - p.\cos.(nt+\varepsilon)$ we will have

$$p = \text{tang.}\,\varphi.\,\sin.\,\theta\,; \quad q = \text{tang.}\,\varphi.\,\cos.\,\theta\,;$$

hence we deduce

$$\text{tang.}\,\varphi = \sqrt{p^2+q^2}\,; \quad \text{tang.}\,\theta = \frac{p}{q}\,;$$

therefore the inclination of the orbit of m, and the position of its node, may be obtained by means of the value of p and of q. If we denote successively by one stroke, two strokes, &c., relatively to m', m'', &c., the values of tang. φ, and of tang. θ, the inclinations of the orbits of

* $d.\tan.\varpi.\left(=\frac{d\varpi}{\cos.^2\varpi}\right) = \frac{ldh-hdl}{l^2}$, ∵ as $l^2 = e^2.\cos.^2\varpi$, we obtain $e^2 d\varpi = ldh - hdl$; as $hh'+ll' - ee'.\cos.(\varpi'-\varpi)$; if $\frac{e^2 d\varpi}{dt} = (0,1).(h^2+l^2) - [\overline{0,1}].(hh'+ll')$, be divided by $e^2 = h^2+l^2$ we shall have the value of $\frac{d\varpi}{dt}$ which is given in the text.

* This is the value of s, or of the latitude very nearly, when periodic quantities are neglected, in fact the values of φ and θ, which are derived from a comparison of the two values of s, are the mean values, only affected with secular inequalities; see N°. 53.

m', m'', &c., and the positions of their nodes, will be had by means of the quantities p', q'. p'', q'', &c.

The quantity $\sqrt{p^2+q^2}$, is less than the sum N, N_1, N_2, + &c. of the coefficients of the sines of the expression for q; therefore these coefficients being very small, because by hypothesis, the orbit is inclined by a very small angle to the fixed plane, its inclination to this plane will be always inconsiderable; hence it follows, that the system of the orbits is always stable relative to their inclinations, as well as relative to their excentricities. The inclinations of the orbits may therefore be considered as variable quantities comprised between determinate limits, and the motions of the nodes as not being altogether uniform. These variations are very sensible in the satellites of Jupiter, and we shall see in the sequel that they explain the singular phenomena, which are observed in the inclination of the orbit of the fourth satellite.

From the preceding expressions for p and q, results the following theorem:

That if a circle be conceived, of which the inclination to the fixed plane is N, and of which $gt+\epsilon$ is the longitude of its ascending node; and if on this first circle a second be conceived inclined to it by an angle equal to $N_{,}$, $g_{,}t+\epsilon_{,}$ being the longitude of its intersection with the second circle, and so of the rest; the position of the last circle will be that of the orbit of m.

The same construction being applied to the expressions of h and of l of N°. 56; it will appear that the tangent of the inclination of the last circle on the fixed plane, is equal to the excentricity of the orbit of m, and that the longitude of the intersection of this circle with the same plane, is equal to that of the perihelion of the orbit of m.

60.* It is useful for astronomical purposes to obtain the differential variations of the nodes and of the inclinations of the orbits. For this purpose let the equations of the preceding N°. be resumed, namely,

* It should be observed, that the differential expressions which are given in this N°., are relative to the secular variations of the nodes and of the inclinations of the orbits.

$$\text{tang.}\ \varphi = \sqrt{p^2+q^2}; \quad \text{tang}\ \theta = \frac{p}{q}.$$

By differentiating, there will be obtained,

$$d\varphi = dp.\ \text{sin.}\ \theta + dq.\ \text{cos.}\ \theta\ ;\ ^*$$

$$d\theta = \frac{dp.\ \text{cos.}\ \theta - dq.\ \text{sin.}\ \theta}{\text{tang.}\ \varphi}.$$

Substituting for dp and dq, their values, which have been given by the equations (C) of the preceding N°., we will have

$$\frac{d\varphi}{dt} = (0, 1).\ \text{tang.}\ \varphi'.\ \text{sin.}\ (\theta - \theta') + (0, 2).\ \text{tang.}\ \varphi''.\ \text{sin.}\ (\theta - \theta'') + \&c.$$

$$\frac{d\theta}{dt} = -((0, 1) + (0, 2) + \&c.) + (0, 1).\frac{\text{tang.}\ \varphi'}{\text{tang.}\ \varphi}.\ \text{cos.}\ (\theta - \theta')\ ^*$$

$$+ (0, 2).\frac{\text{tang.}\ \varphi''}{\text{tang.}\ \varphi}.\ \text{cos.}\ (\theta - \theta'') + \&c.\ ;$$

* $d.\ \text{tan.}\ \varphi = \frac{d\varphi}{\text{cos.}^2\varphi} = \frac{pdp+qdq}{\sqrt{p^2+q^2}}$ = by substituting for p and q their values, and neglecting $\frac{1}{\text{cos.}^2\varphi}$, the expression in the text. $d.\ \text{tan.}\ \theta = \frac{d\theta}{\text{cos.}^2\theta} = d\theta.\left(\frac{p^2+q^2}{q^2}\right) = \frac{q.dp - p.dq}{q^2}$, which becomes, by substituting for p and q their values, and multiplying by q^2, $d\theta.\ \text{tan.}^2\varphi = dp.\ \text{cos.}\ \theta.\ \text{tan.}\ \varphi - dq.\ \text{sin.}\ \theta.\ \text{tan.}\ \varphi$.

† When this substitution is made, the first term in the expression for $dp.\ \text{sin.}\ \theta$ becomes equal to the first term of the expression for $dq.\ \text{cos.}\ \theta$, and affected with a contrary sign, consequently they destroy each other. The second terms of these expressions are respectively $(0, 1).\ \text{tan}\ \varphi'.\ \text{cos.}\ \theta'.\ \text{sin.}\ \theta - (0, 1).\ \text{tan.}\ \varphi'.\ \text{sin.}\ \theta'.\ \text{cos.}\ \theta = (0, 1).\ \text{tan.}\ \varphi'.\ \text{sin.}\ (\theta - \theta')$; by a similar process the third and following terms are obtained. The first term in the value of $dp.\ \text{cos.}\ \theta = -((0, 1) + (0, 2) + (0, 3) + (0, 4) + \&c.,)\ \text{tan.}\ \varphi.\ \text{cos.}^2\theta$, and the second term $= (0, 1).\ \text{tan.}\ \varphi'.\ \text{cos.}\ \theta'.\ \text{cos.}\ \theta$; in like manner the first term of the value of $-dq\ \text{sin.}\ \theta$ is $-((0, 1), + (0, 2) + (0, 3) + \&c.\ \text{tan}\ \varphi\ \text{sin.}^2\theta$, and the second term $= -(0, 1).\ \text{tan.}\ \varphi'.\ \text{sin.}\ \theta'.\ \text{sin.}\ \theta$, &c., by making these terms respectively to coalesce, they become $-((0, 1) + (0, 2) + (0, 3) + \&c.) + (0, 1).\ \frac{\text{tan.}\ \varphi'}{\text{tan.}\ \varphi}.\ (\text{cos.}\ \theta.\ \text{cos.}\ \theta' + \text{sin.}\ \theta.\ \text{sin.}\ \theta')$. If there are only

In like manner we will have

$$\frac{d\varphi'}{dt} = (1, 0).\,\text{tang.}\,\varphi.\,\sin.\,(\theta'-\theta)+(1, 2).\,\text{tang.}\,\varphi''.\,\sin.\,(\theta'-\theta'')+\&c.;$$

$$\frac{d\theta'}{dt} = -((1, 0)+(1, 2)+\&c.)+(1, 0).\frac{\text{tang.}\,\varphi}{\text{tang.}\,\varphi'}.\cos.\,(\theta'-\theta)$$

$$+(1, 2).\,\frac{\text{tang.}\,\varphi''}{\text{tang.}\,\varphi'}.\cos.\,(\theta'-\theta'')+\,\&c.$$

&c.

Astronomers refer the celestial motions to the moveable orbit of the earth; in fact, it is from the plane of this orbit that they are observed; it is therefore of consequence to know the variations of the nodes and of the inclinations of the orbits, with respect to the ecliptic. Suppose, therefore, that it were required to determine the differential variations of the nodes, and of the inclinations of the orbits, with respect to the orbit of one of the bodies m, m', m'', &c., for example, relatively to the orbit of m. It is evident that $q.\sin.(n't+\varepsilon')-p.\cos.(n't'+\varepsilon')$ will be the latitude of m' above the fixed plane, if it was in motion on the orbit of m. Its latitude above the same plane, is $q'.\sin.(n't+\varepsilon')-p'.\cos.(n't+\varepsilon')$; now the difference of those two latitudes, is very nearly the latitude of m' above the orbit of m; therefore $\varphi'_{\prime}$ representing the inclination, $\theta'_{\prime}$ being the longitude of the node of the orbit of m' on the orbit of m, by what goes before

two bodies m, m', the nodes of each of them will regrade on the fixed ecliptic, when $\frac{\tan.\varphi}{\tan.\varphi'}.\cos.(\theta'-\theta)$, $\frac{\tan.\varphi'}{\tan.\varphi}.\cos.(\theta-\theta')$ are respectively less than unity; if one of them, as, for instance, the first, be greater than unity, this can only arsise from $\tan.\varphi$ being greater than $\tan.\varphi'$, therefore the second must be less than unity; consequently, the nodes of one of the orbits must *always* regrade. It appears also from this expression, that if the distance between the ascending nodes of the two planets be greater than 90°, the nodes must regrade. It is likewise evident that if $\theta-\theta$ is greater than 180, the inclination increases, and that it diminishes when this inclination is less than 180; the variation is greater according as the distance between the nodes approaches to 90, and according as φ increases. See Princep. Matth. Lib. I. Prop. 66, Cor. 11.

there will be obtained

$$\text{tang.}\,\varphi'_{,}=\sqrt{(p'-p)^2+(q'-q)^2}\,;\quad \text{tang.}\,\theta'_{,}=\frac{p'-p}{q'-q}.^{*}$$

If the fixed plane be assumed to be that of the orbit of m, at a given epoch; for this epoch p and q will be respectively $=0$; however the differentials dp, dq, will not vanish; thus we shall have

$$d\varphi'_{,}=(dp'-dp).\,\text{sin.}\,\theta'+(dq'-dq).\,\text{cos.}\,\theta'\,;\dagger$$

$$d\theta'_{,}=\frac{(dp'-dp).\,\text{cos.}\,\theta'-(dq'-dq).\,\text{sin.}\,\theta'}{\text{tang.}\,\varphi'}.$$

By substituting for dp, dq, dp', dq', &c., their values given by the equation (C) of the preceding N°, there will be obtained

$$\frac{d\varphi'_{,}}{dt}=((1,2)-(0,2)).\,\text{tang.}\,\varphi''.\,\text{sin.}\,(\theta'-\theta'')\,\ddagger$$

* Neglecting quantities of the second and higher orders, the differences of the expressions for the tangents of these latitudes, which in the present case may be substituted for the latitudes themselves, is equal to $(q'-q).\,\text{sin.}\,(n't+\varepsilon')-(p'-p).\,\text{cos.}\,(n't+\varepsilon')=\text{tan.}\,\varphi'_{,}.\,\text{sin.}\,(n't+\varepsilon'-\theta'_{,})$, $\because q-q'=\text{tan.}\,\varphi'_{,}.\,\text{cos.}\,\theta'_{,}$; $p'-p=\text{tan}\,\varphi'_{,}.\,\text{sin.}\,\theta'_{,}$; hence we get the values of $\varphi'_{,}$. and $\text{tan.}^2\theta'_{,}$ as before.

† $d.\,\text{tan.}\,\varphi'_{,}=d\varphi'_{,}=$ (as p and q vanish) $\frac{(dp'-dp).p'+(dq'-dq).dq'}{\sqrt{p'^2+q'^2}}$, which by substituting for p' and q', their values $\text{tan.}\,\varphi'.\,\text{sin.}\,\theta'$, $\text{tan.}\,\varphi'.\,\text{cos.}\,\theta'$. becomes the expression in the text. Similarly by substituting $\frac{d\theta'_{,}}{\text{cos.}^2\theta'_{,}}=\frac{(dp'-dp).\,q'-(dq'-dq).\,p'}{q'^2}$; but $\frac{1}{\text{cos.}^2\theta''_{,}}=\frac{q'^2+p'^2}{q'^2}$, $\because d\theta'_{,}=\frac{(dp'-dp).\,\text{cos.}\,\theta'-(dq'-dq).\,\text{sin.}\,\theta'}{\text{tan.}\,\varphi'}$.

‡ $dp'.\,\text{sin.}\,\theta'=-((1,0)+(1,2)+\&c.)\;\text{tan.}\,\varphi'.\,\text{cos.}\,\theta'.\,\text{sin.}\,\theta'+(1,2),\,\text{tan.}\,\varphi''.\,\text{cos.}\,\theta''.\,\text{sin.}\,\theta'+\&c.$; $-dp.\,\text{sin.}\,\theta'=-(0,1).\,\text{tan.}\,\varphi'.\,\text{cos.}\,\theta'\,\text{sin.}\,\theta'-(0,2).\,\text{tan.}\,\varphi''.\,\text{cos.}\,\theta''.\,\text{sin}\cdot\theta'-\&c.)$; $dq'.\,\text{cos.}\,\theta'=((1,0)+(1,2)+\&c.).\,\text{tan.}\,\varphi'.\,\text{sin.}\,\theta'.\,\text{cos.}\,\theta'-(1,2).\,\text{tan.}\,\varphi''_{,}.\,\text{sin.}\,\theta''.\,\text{cos.}\,\theta'-\&c.)-dq.\,\text{cos.}\,\theta'=(0,1).\,\text{tan.}\,\varphi'\cdot\text{sin.}\,\theta'\,\text{cos.}\,{}'\theta+(0,2).\,\text{tan.}\,\varphi''.\,\text{cos.}\cdot\theta+\&c.$; hence, obliterating the terms which destroy each other, and making corresponding factors of tan. φ'', tan. φ''', &c., to coalesce, we obtain the expressions which are giveen in the text. Since p and $q=0$, the coefficients of these terms are neglectcd in the vhluc of $\frac{dp}{dt}$, $\frac{dq}{dt}$, $\frac{dp'}{dt}$, &c.

$$((1,3)-(0,3)).\text{tang. }\varphi''.\sin.(\theta'-\theta'')+\&c.$$

$$\frac{d\theta'}{dt}=-((1,0)+(1,2)+(1,3)+\&c.)-(0,1)$$

$$+((1,2)-(0,2))\frac{\text{tang. }\varphi''}{\text{tang. }\varphi'}.\cos.(\theta'-\theta'')$$

$$+((1,3)-(0,3))\frac{\text{tang. }\varphi''}{\text{tang. }\varphi'}.\cos.(\theta'-\theta''')+\&c.$$

It is easy to infer from these expressions, the variations of the nodes and of the inclinations of the orbits of the other bodies, m'', m'', &c., on the moveable orbit of m.

61. The integrals previously found of the differential equations which determine the variations of the elements of the orbits, are only approximative, and the relations which they indicate between all these elements, have place only on the hypothesis that the excentricities of the orbits and their inclinations are very small. But the integrals (4), (5), (6) and (7), to which we have arrived in N°. 9, give the same relations, whatever may be the excentricities and the inclinations. For this purpose, it may be observed, that $\frac{xdy-ydx}{dt}$ is double of the area described in the time dt, by the projection of the radius vector of the planet m, on the plane of x and of y. In the elliptic motion, if the mass of the planet be neglected, relatively to that of the sun, which is assumed equal to unity, we have by N°s. 19 and 20, relatively to the plane of the orbit of m,

$$\frac{xdy-ydx}{dt}=\sqrt{a.(1-e^2)^2}.$$

In order to refer the area of the orbit to a fixed plane, it is necessary to multiply it by the the cosine of the inclination of φ, of the orbit to this plane; therefore with respect to this plane we will have

$$\frac{xdy-ydx}{dt}=\cos.\varphi.\sqrt{a.(1-e^2)}=\sqrt{\frac{a.(1-e^2)}{1+\text{tang}.\varphi^2}}.$$

In like manner we have

$$\frac{x'dy'-y'dx'}{dt}=\sqrt{\frac{a'.(1-e'^2)}{1+\text{tang}.^2\varphi'}};$$

&c.

These values of $xdy-ydx$, $x'dy'-y'dx'$, &c., may be employed, when we do not take into account the inequalities of the motion of the planets, provided that the elements e, e', &c., φ, φ', &c., are considered as variable, in consequence of the secular inequalities; therefore the equation (4) of N°. (9). will then give

$$c=m.\sqrt{\frac{a.(1-e^2)}{1+\text{tang}.^2\varphi}}+m'.\sqrt{\frac{a'.(1-e'^2)}{1+\text{tang}.\varphi'^2}}+\&c.$$

$$+\Sigma.mm'.\left\{\frac{(x'-x).(dy'-dy)-(y'-y).(dx'-dx)}{dt}\right\}.$$

This last term, which is always of the order mm', being neglected, we shall have

$$c=m.\sqrt{\frac{a.(1-e^2)}{1+\text{tang}.^2\varphi}}+m'.\sqrt{\frac{a'.(1-e'^2)}{1+\text{tang}.^2\varphi'}}+\&c.$$

Therefore, whatever changes may be produced in the progress of time, in the values of e, e', &c., φ, φ', &c., in consequence of the secular variations; these values ought always to satisfy the preceding equation.

If the very small quantities of the order e^4, $e^2\varphi^2$, be neglected, this equation will give

$$c=m.\sqrt{a}+m'.\sqrt{a'}+\&c.-\tfrac{1}{2}.m.\sqrt{a}.(e^2+\text{tang}.^2\varphi)$$

$$-\tfrac{1}{2}.m'.\sqrt{a'}.(e'^2+\text{tang}.^2\varphi')-\&c.;$$

and consequently, if the squares of e, e', φ, &c., be neglected, we shall have $m.\sqrt{a} + m'.\sqrt{a'} +$ &c., constant. It has appeared already, that if only the first powers* of the disturbing force be taken into account, a, a', &c., will be separately constant; the preceding equation will therefore give, when the very small quantities of the order e^4, or $e^2\varphi^2$, are neglected,

$$\text{const.} = m.\sqrt{a}.\,(e^2 + \text{tang.}^2\varphi^2) + m'.\sqrt{a'}.\,(e'^2 + \text{tang.}^2\varphi') + \&c.;$$

on the supposition that the orbits are very nearly circular, and inclined to each other at small angles, the secular variations of the excentricities of the orbits, are by N°. 55, determined by means of differential equations independent of the inclinations, and which are therefore the same as if the orbits existed in the same plane; but on this hypothesis, $\varphi = 0$, $\varphi' = 0$, &c.; consequently, the preceding equation becomes

$$\text{const.} = e^2.m\sqrt{a} + e'^2.m'.\sqrt{a'} + e''^2.m''.\sqrt{a''} + \&c.$$

this equation has been already obtained in N°. 57.

In like manner, the secular variations of the inclinations of the orbits, are by N°. 59, determined by means of differential equations independent of the excentricities, and which are therefore the same as if the orbits were circular; but on this hypothesis, $e = 0$, $e' = 0$, &c.; therefore

$$\text{const.} = m.\sqrt{a}.\,\text{tang.}\,\varphi^2 + m'.\sqrt{a'}.\,\text{tang.}\,\varphi'^2 + m''.\sqrt{a''}.\,\text{tang.}\,\varphi^{2\prime\prime} + \&c.$$

which equation has been obtained in N°. 59.

If we suppose, as in this last number, that

$$p = \text{tang.}\,\varphi.\,\sin.\,\theta; \quad q = \text{tang.}\,\varphi.\,\cos.\,\theta;$$

It is easy to be assured, when the inclination of the orbit of m, on the plane of x and y, is φ, θ being the longitude of its ascending node, reckoned from the axis of x; that the cosine of the inclination of

* See No. 54, page 324.

this orbit on the plane of x and z, will be

$$\frac{q}{\sqrt{1+\tan.^2\varphi}}.^{*}$$

This quantity being multiplied by $\frac{xdy-ydx}{dt}$, or by its equivalent value $\sqrt{a.(1-e^2)}$, the value of $\frac{xdz-zdx}{dt}$, will be obtained; therefore the equation (5) of N°. 9, will give, when quantities of the order m^2 are neglected,

$$c'=m.q.\sqrt{\frac{a.(1-e^2)}{1+\tan.^2\varphi}}+m'.q'.\sqrt{\frac{a'.(1-e'^2)}{1+\tan.^2\varphi'}}+\&c.$$

In like manner the equation (6) of N°. 9, will give

$$c''=mp.\sqrt{\frac{a.(1-e^2}{1+\tan.^2\varphi}}+m'.p'.\sqrt{\frac{a'.(1-e'^2)}{1+\tan.^2\varphi'}}+\&c.$$

If quantities of the order e^3, or $e^2\varphi$, are neglected in these two equations; they become

$$\text{constant} = mq.\sqrt{a}+m'q'.\sqrt{a'}+\&c.\dagger$$
$$\text{constant} = mp.\sqrt{a}+m'p'.\sqrt{a'}+\&c.$$

which equations have been already obtained in N°. 59.

Finally, the equation (7) of No. 9, when quantities of the order

* $\cos.\varphi = \frac{1}{\sqrt{1+\tan.^2\varphi}}$, ∵ by substituting for q its value $\tan.\varphi.\cos.\theta$, we obtain $\frac{q}{\sqrt{1+\tan.^2\varphi}} = \sin.\varphi.\cos.\theta$, which is the cosine of the inclination of the orbit of m to the plane x, z.

† $\tan.\varphi$, $\tan.\varphi'$, being of the order e, the quantities which are neglected are of the order e^3, and of higher orders.

mm' are neglected, will give, by remarking that by N°. 18, $\frac{\mu}{a} = \frac{2\mu}{r} - \frac{(dx^2+dy^2+dz^2)}{dt^2}$,

$$\text{constant} = \frac{m}{a} + \frac{m'}{a'} + \frac{m''}{a''} + \&c.^*$$

These different equations subsist with respect to those inequalities of very long periods, which may affect the elements of the orbits of m, m', &c. It has been remarked in N°. 54, that the relation of the mean motions of these bodies may introduce into the expressions of the greater axes of the orbits considered as variable, inequalities of which the arguments being proportional to the time, increase with great slowness, and which as they have for divisors the coefficients of the time t, may at length become sensible. But it is evident, that if we only take into account the terms which have similar divisors, the orbits being considered as ellipses of which the elements vary in consequence of these terms, the integrals (4), (5), (6) and (7) of N°. 9, will always give the relations which we have found between these elements; because that the terms of the order mm' which have been neglected in order to infer these relations, have not for divisors the very small coefficients of which we have spoken; or at least, they only contain them multiplied by a power of the disturbing force, superior to that which has been taken into account.

62. It has been remarked in N°ˢ. 21 and 22, of the first book, that in the motion of a system of bodies, there exists an invariable plane,

* When quantities of the order mm' are neglected, we have (M being considered as unity) $h = \Sigma m. \frac{dx^2+dy^2+dz^2}{dt^2} - \frac{2\Sigma m}{r}$, now we have $\mu = 1+m$, ∵ if the expression $\frac{\mu}{a} = \frac{2\mu}{r} - \left(\frac{dx^2+dy^2+dz^2}{dt^2}\right)$ be multiplied by m, it will give when quantities of the order m^2 are neglected, $\frac{m}{a} = \frac{2m}{r} - m.\frac{(dx^2+dy^2+dz^2)}{dt^2}$, ∵ by making similar substitutions for the bodies m', m'', &c., we obtain the expression which is given in the text.

which preserves always a parallel position, and which the following condition enable us to find easily, at all times, namely, that the sum of the masses of the system respectively multiplied by the projections of the areas described by the radii vectores in a given time, is a *maximum*. It is principally in the theory of the solar system, that the investigation of this plane is important, in consequence of the proper motions of the stars, and of the ecliptic, which render the exact determination of the celestial motions a matter of great difficulty to astronomers. Naming γ the inclination of this invariable plane, to the plane of x and of y, and Π the longitude of its ascending node, it follows, from what has been demonstrated in N°s. 21 and 22, of the first book, that we will have

$$\tan.\ \gamma.\ \sin.\ \Pi=\frac{c''}{c};\ \tan.\ \gamma.\ \cos.\ \Pi=\frac{c'}{c};$$

consequently,

$$\tan.\ \gamma.\sin.\Pi=\frac{m.\sqrt{a.(1-e^2}.\ \sin.\ \varphi.\ \sin.\ \theta+m'.\sqrt{a'.(1-e'^2)}.\ \sin.\ \varphi'.\ \sin.\ \theta'+\&c.}{m.\sqrt{a.(1-e^2}.\ \cos.\ \varphi+m'.\sqrt{a'.(1-e'^2)}.\ \cos.\ \varphi'+\ \&c.}*$$

$$\tan.\gamma.\cos.\Pi=\frac{m.\sqrt{a.(1-e^2)}.\sin.\varphi.\cos.\theta+m'.\sqrt{a'.(1-e'^2)}.\ \sin.\varphi'.\ \cos.\theta'+\&c.}{m.\sqrt{a.(1-e^2)}.\ \cos.\ \varphi+m'.\sqrt{a'.(1-e^2)}.\ \cos.\ \varphi'+\ \&c.}.$$

The two angles γ and Π may be easily determined, by means of these values. It is evident that in order to determine accurately the invariable plane, it is necessary to know the masses of the comets and the elements of their orbits; fortunately, their masses appear to be very small, so that their action on the planets may be neglected without any sensible error; but time will give us fuller information on this point. It may be remarked here, that with respect to the invariable* plane, the values of p, q, p', q', &c. do not contain constant terms; for it is

* Since $\frac{1}{1+\tan.\ ^2\varphi}=\cos.\ ^2\varphi$ we obtain $c''=m.\sqrt{a.(1-e^2)}.\ \sin.\ \varphi\ \sin.\ \theta+\ \&c.$, by substituting for p, its value $\tan.\ \varphi.\ \sin.\ \theta$.

evident from the equations (C), of N°. 59, that these terms are the same for p, p', p'', &c., and that they are also the same for q, q', q'', &c. and as relatively to the invariable plane, the constant quantities of the first member of the equations (1) and (2) of N°. 59, vanish; in consequence of these equations, the constant terms must vanish from the expressions of p, p', &c., q, q', &c.

Let us now consider the motion of two orbits, which are inclined at any angle to each other, by N°. 61, we will have,

$$c' = \sin. \varphi. \cos. \theta.\ m.\sqrt{a.(1-e^2)} + \sin. \varphi'. \cos. \theta'.\ m'.\sqrt{a'.(1-e'^2)};$$
$$c'' = \sin. \varphi. \sin. \theta.\ m.\sqrt{a.(1-e^2)} + \sin. \varphi'. \sin. \theta'.\ m'.\sqrt{a'.(1-e'^2)};$$

Let us suppose that the fixed plane to which the motion of the orbits is referred, is the invariable plane of which we have treated, and with respect to which the constant quantities of the first members of these equations vanish, as has been remarked in N°s. 21 and 22 of the first book. The angles φ and φ' being positive, the preceding equations give the following:

$$m.\sqrt{a.(1-e^2)}. \sin. \varphi = m'.\sqrt{a'.(1-e'^2)}. \sin. \varphi':$$
$$\sin. \theta = -\sin. \theta'; \quad \cos. \theta = -\cos. \theta';$$

hence we infer that $\theta' = \theta +$ the semicircumference; consequently the nodes of the orbits are on the same line; but the ascending node of one coincides with the descending node of the other; so that the mutual inclination of these two orbits is equal to $\varphi+\varphi'$.

By. N°. 61, we have

$$c = m.\sqrt{a.(1-e^2)}. \cos. \varphi + m'.\sqrt{a'.(1-e'^2)}. \cos. \varphi';$$

this equation being combined with the preceding one between $\sin. \varphi$ and $\sin. \varphi'$, gives*

* These constants must vanish, for they are in fact equal to c' and c'', which in the case of the invariable plane are equal to cypher.

$$2mc.\cos.\varphi.\sqrt{a.(1-e^2)}=c^2+m^2a.(1-e^2)-m'^2a'.(1-e'^2).$$

If the orbits be supposed to be circular, or at least of such a small excentricity, that the squares of the excentricities may be neglected, the preceding equations will give φ equal to a constant quantity; therefore the inclinations of the planes of the orbits to the fixed plane, and to each other, will be constant, and these three planes will always have a common intersection. It follows from this, that the mean instantaneous variation of this intersection, is always the same; because it is only a function of those inclinations. When they are very small, it may be easily proved by N°. 60, and in virtue of the relation just found† between sin. φ, and sin. φ', that for the time t, the motion of this intersection is $-((0,1)+(1,0)).\,t$.

The position of the invariable plane, to which the motion of the planets has been referred, may be easily determined for any given instant; as it is only requisite to divide the angle of the mutual inclination of the orbits into two angles φ, and φ', such that the preceding equation may obtain between sin. φ, and sin. φ'. Therefore denoting this mutual inclination by ϖ, we shall have

$$\tan.\varphi=\frac{m'.\sqrt{a'.(1-e'^2)}.\sin.\varpi}{m.\sqrt{a.(1-e^2)}+m'.\sqrt{a'.(1-e'^2)}.\cos.\varpi}.‡$$

* Multiplying both sides of this equation by $2m.\sqrt{a.(1-e^2}.\cos.\varphi$, we obtain $2mc.\cos.\varphi.\sqrt{a.(1-e^2}=2m^2.a\,(1-e^2).\cos{}^2\varphi+2m.m'.\cos.\varphi.\cos.\varphi'.\sqrt{a.(1-e^2)}.\sqrt{a'(1-e'^2)}$, which will coincide with the second member of this equation, if we substitute for c^2 its value, and observe that $m^2a.(1-e^2).\sin.{}^2\varphi=m'^2a'.(1-e'^2).\sin.{}^2\varphi'$.

† When φ and φ' are very small the nodes must regrade. See page 342.

‡ If one of the angles be φ, then we have $\sin.\varphi.\,m.\sqrt{a.(1-e^2)}=\sin.(\varpi-\varphi).\,m'.\sqrt{a'.(1-e'^2)}=(\sin.\varpi.\cos.\varphi-\sin.\varphi.\cos.\varpi).\,m'.\sqrt{a'.(1-e'^2)}$, ∴ dividing by cos. φ. $\tan.\varphi.(m.\sqrt{a.(1-e^2)}+\cos.\varpi.m'.\sqrt{a'.(1-e'^2)})=\sin.\varpi.\,m'.\sqrt{a'.(1-e'^2)}$.

CHAPTER VIII.

Second method of approximation of the Celestial Motions.

63. It has been observed in the second chapter, that the coordinates of the heavenly bodies, referred to the foci of the principal forces which actuate them, are determined by differential equations of the second order. These equations have been integrated in the third Chapter, the principal forces being solely taken into account, and it has been shewn that in this case, the orbits are conic sections, of which the elements are the constant arbitrary quantities introduced by the integrations. As the action of the disturbing forces, cause only very small inqualities, to be added to the elliptic motion; it is natural to endeavour to reduce to the laws of this motion, the disturbed motion of the heavenly bodies. If the method of approximation explained in N°. 45, be applied to the differential equations of elliptic motion, increased by small terms due to the action of the disturbing forces; we can still consider the celestial motions in the reentrant orbits as being elliptical; but the elements of this motion will be variable; and their variations can be obtained by this method. It follows from it that the equations of the motion, being differentials of the second order, not only their finite integrals, but also the indefinitely small integrals of the first order, are the same as in the case of invariable ellipses; so that we can differentiate the finite equations, the elements of this motion being considered as constant. It likewise results from the same method, that the equations of this motion, which are differentials of the first order, may be differenced, the elements of

the orbits, and the first differences of the coordinates being solely made to vary; provided that in place of the second differences of the coordinates, we only substitute that part of their values, due to the disturbing forces. These results may be immediately inferred from the consideration of elliptic motion.

For this purpose, conceive an ellipse passing through a planet, and through the element of the curve which it describes, the centre of the sun being supposed to exist in one of the foci. This ellipse is that which the planet would invariably describe, if the distubing forces ceased to act on it. Its elements are constant during the interval of dt; but they vary from one instant to another. Let therefore $V=0$, be the finite equation of the invariable ellipse, V being a function of the rectangular coordinates, x, y, z, and of the parameters c, c', c'', &c., which last are functions of the elements of elliptic motion. This equation will also obtain in the case of the variable ellipse; but the parameters c, c', &c., will be no longer constant. However, since this ellipse appertains to the element of the curve described by the planet, during the instant dt; the equation $V=0$, will also obtain for the first and last point of this element, c, c', &c., being considered as constant.

This equation can therefore be differenced once, x, y, z, being solely made to vary, which gives

$$0=\left(\frac{dV}{dx}\right).dx+\left(\frac{dV}{dy}\right).dy+\left(\frac{dV}{dz}\right).dz; \qquad (i)^{*}$$

* In consequence of the mutual action of the planets on each other, it is necessary to add to the differential equations of their motion, terms which render the accurate integration of the resulting equations impossible in the present state of analysis, we are therefore obliged to have recourse to approximations; fortunately the terms resulting from the action of the disturbing forces are extremely small, for they are multiplied by the masses of the planets, or rather by their ratio to that of the sun; therefore if the differential equations, deprived of these terms, were integrated, the *constant* arbitrary quantities in this case, would only

Hence we see the reason why the finite equations of the invariable ellipse, may, in the case of the variable ellipse, be differenced once, the parameters being considered as constant. For the same reason, every differential equation of the first order, which belongs to the invariable ellipse, obtains equally for the variable; for let $V'=0$, be an equation of this order, V' being a function of x, y, z, $\frac{dx}{dt}$, $\frac{dy}{dt}$, $\frac{dz}{dt}$, and of the parameters c, c', &c. It is evident that these quantities are the same for the variable ellipse, as for the invariable ellipse, which coincides with it, during the instant dt.

Now, if we consider the planet at the end of the time dt, or at the commencement of the subsequent instant; the function V' will not vary from the ellipse relative to the instant dt, to the consecutive ellipse, except in consequence of the variation of the parameters, since

differ by a very small quantity, from the arbitrary quantities which the integration of the complete equations would furnish, if such integration could be effected; for since the two equations differ only by these small terms, the difference between the arbitrary quantities must depend on the disturbing force, and therefore must be extremely small; hence the expressions of the constant arbitrary quantities, which would be furnished by the integration of the imperfect or elliptical equations, may be assumed to express the *variable* arbitrary quantities, provided that the variations of those latter are determined by means of the difference between the two sets of equations; therefore the elements of elliptic motion, which would be constant if the planet was subject to the sole action of the sun, are liable to small variations; and although the motion is no longer elliptic, still it may be considered as such, during each indefinitely small portion of time, and the variable ellipse in which the planet may be considered to move during each instant, will be osculatory to the true orbit of the planet; in fact, since the equation $V=0$, has place for the first and last point of the curves described by the planet during the instant dt, the expressions for the coordinates x, y, z, will be the same: consequently the curves to which they belong are similar, but in one case the curve is an ellipse, $\because$ the curve of which x, y, z, are the coordinates when c, c', c'', &c., are variable, must be similar to the former, and $\because$ an ellipse, and if the disturbing forces ceased to act, the planet would describe this ellipse; but as c, c', c'', &c., have different values for each subsequent instant, the ellipses which would be respectively described if the disturbing forces ceased to act during these instants, must be different, so that they constitute a series of ellipses of curvature to the orbits of the planets.

the coordinates x, y, z, relative to the end of the first instant, are the same in the case of the two ellipses; thus the function V being equal to cypher, we have

$$0 = \left(\frac{dV}{dc}\right).dc + \left(\frac{dV}{dc'}\right).dc' + \left(\frac{dV}{dc''}\right).dc'' + \text{\&c.} \quad (i')$$

This equation may be also inferred from the equation $V = 0$, by making to vary at once, x, y, z, c, c', &c.; for if the equation (i) be subtracted from this differential, we shall have the equation (i').

By differentiating the equation (i), we shall have a new equation in dc, dc', &c., which combined with the equation (i') will enable us to determine the parameters c, c', &c.

It is thus that the geometers who first occupied themselves with the theory of the celestial motions, have determined the variations of the nodes and of the inclinations of the orbits; but this differentiation may be simplified in the following manner.

Let us consider generally the differential equation of the first order $V' = 0$, which equation, as we have seen, appertains equally to the variable ellipse and to the invariable ellipse, which, during the interval dt, coincides with it. In the following instant, this equation agrees equally to the two ellipses, but with this difference, that c, c', &c., remain the same in the case of the invariable ellipse, whilst they change with the variable ellipse. Let V'' be what V' becomes, when the ellipse is supposed invariable; let $V'_{,}$ be what this same function becomes, in the case of the variable ellipse. It is evident that in order to obtain V'', we must change in V', the coordinates x, y, z, which are relative to the commencement of the first instant dt, into those which are relative to the commencement of the second instant; it is necessary then to increase the first differences dx, dy, dz, respectively by the quantities d^2x, d^2y, d^2z, relatively to the invariable ellipse, the element dt of the time, being supposed constant.

In like manner, in order to obtain $V'_{,}$, it is necessary to change in V' the coordinates x, y, z, into those which are relative to the commencement of the second instant, and which are likewise the same in the two ellipses; it is necessary afterwards to increase dx, dy, dz, respectively by the quantities d^2x, d^2y, d^2z; finally, it is necessary to change the parameters c, c', &c., into $c+dc$, $c'+dc'$, $c''+dc''$, &c.

The values of d^2x, d^2y, d^2z, are not the same in the two ellipses; they are increased in the case of the variable ellipse, by quantities which are due to the action of the disturbing forces. It thus appears that the two functions V' and $V'_{,}$ only differ in this, that in the second, the parameters c, c', &c., are increased by dc, dc', &c.; and the values of d^2x, d^2y, d^2z, relative to the invariable ellipse, are increased by the quantities which are due to the disturbing forces.

We shall therefore obtain $V'_{,}-V''$ by differencing on the supposition of x, y, z, being constant, &c., and of dx, dy, dz, c, c', c'', &c., being variable, provided that in this differential, we substitute for d^2x, d^2y, d^2z, &c., the parts of their values, which arise solely from the action of the disturbing forces.

Now, if in the function $V''-V'_{,}$ we substitute in place of d^2x, d^2y, d^2z, their values relative to elliptic motions, we shall have a function of x, y, z, $\frac{dx}{dt}$, $\frac{dy}{dt}$, $\frac{dz}{dt}$, c, c', &c., which, in the case of the invariable* ellipse, is equal to cypher; this function is therefore likewise nothing in

* When in $V''-V'$, the values of $\frac{d^2x}{dt^2}$, $\frac{d^2y}{dt^2}$, $\frac{d^2z}{dt^2}$, due to the elliptic motion are substituted, the terms of the resulting equation must be identically equal to cypher; but in the case of $V'_{,}-V$, the values of $\frac{d^2x}{dt^2}$, $\frac{d^2y}{dt^2}$, $\frac{d^2z}{dt^2}$ must be increased by the quantities due to the action of the disturbing forces; so that after substitution, the resulting expression may be resolved into two distinct equations, one of which would obtain, if there were no dis-

the case of the variable ellipse. We have evidently in this last case, $V_{,}$ $-V'=0$; for this equation is the differential of $V'=0$; by subtracting from it the equations $V''-V'=0$, we shall have $V_{,}'-V''=0$; consequently we can in this case difference the equation $V'=0$, dx, dy, dz, c, c', &c., being solely made to vary, provided that for d^2x, d^2y, d^2z, be substituted the parts of their values, relative to the disturbing forces. These results are precisely the same as those which we obtained in N°. 45, from considerations purely analytic; but considering their great importance, it was deemed right to deduce them here from the consideration of elliptic motion. This being premised,

64. Let the equations (P) of N°. 46 be resumed,

$$\left.\begin{aligned} 0&=\frac{d^2x}{dt^2}+\frac{\mu.x}{r^3}+\left(\frac{dR}{dx}\right);\\ 0&=\frac{d^2y}{dt^2}+\frac{\mu.y}{r^3}+\left(\frac{dR}{dy}\right);\\ 0&=\frac{d^2z}{dt^2}+\frac{\mu.z}{r^3}+\left(\frac{dR}{dz}\right);\end{aligned}\right\}\quad(P)$$

If we suppose $R=0$, we shall have the equations of elliptic motion, which were integrated in the third chapter.

In N°. 18, the seven following integrals were obtained,

$$\left.\begin{aligned} &c=\frac{xdy-ydx}{dt};\; c'=\frac{xdz-zdz}{dt};\; c''=\frac{ydz-zdy}{dt};\\ &0=f+x.\left\{\frac{\mu}{r}-\left(\frac{dy^2+dz^2}{dt}\right)\right\}+\frac{ydy.dx}{dt^2}+\frac{zdz.dx}{dt^2};\\ &0=f'+y.\left\{\frac{\mu}{r}-\left(\frac{dx^2+dz^2}{dt^2}\right)\right\}+\frac{xdx.dy}{dt^2}+\frac{zdz.dy}{dt^2};\\ &0=f''+z.\left\{\frac{\mu}{r}-\left(\frac{dx^2+dy^2}{dt^2}\right)\right\}+\frac{xdx.dz}{dt^2}+\frac{ydy.dz}{dt^2};\\ &0=\frac{\mu}{a}-\frac{2\mu}{r}+\left(\frac{dx^2+dy^2+dz^2}{dt^2}\right).\end{aligned}\right\}\quad(p)$$

turbing forces, and by means of the other the variations af the parameter, may be obtained, these equations are respectively equal to V'' and $V_{,}-V''$.

These integrals give the arbitrary quantities, in functions of the coordinates and of their first differences; their form is extremely commodious for determining the variations of these arbitrary quantities. The three first integrals give, by differencing them, and by making the parameters c, c', c'', &c., and the first differences of the coordinates solely to vary,

$$dc=\frac{xd^2y-yd^2x}{dt};\quad dc'=\frac{xd^2z-zd^2x}{dt};\quad dc''=\frac{yd^2z-zd^2y}{dt};$$

By substituting in place of d^2x, d^2y, d^2z, the parts of their values which are due to the actions of the disturbing forces, and which in virtue the differential equations (P), are $-dt^2.\left(\frac{dR}{dx}\right)$, $-dt^2.\left(\frac{dR}{dy}\right)$, $-dt^2.\left(\frac{dR}{dz}\right)$; we shall have

$$dc=dt.\left\{y.\left(\frac{dR}{dx}\right)-x.\left(\frac{dR}{dy}\right)\right\};$$
$$dc'=dt.\left\{z.\left(\frac{dR}{dx}\right)-x.\left(\frac{dR}{dz}\right)\right\};$$
$$dc''=dt.\left\{z.\left(\frac{dR}{dy}\right)-y.\left(\frac{dR}{dz}\right)\right\}.$$

We have seen in N°s. 18, and 19, that the parameters c, c', c'', &c., determine the three elements of the elliptic orbit, namely, φ the inclination of the orbit on the plane of x and y, and θ the longitude of its node, by means of the equations

$$\tan.\varphi=\frac{\sqrt{c'^2+c''^2}}{c};\quad \tan.\theta=\frac{c''}{c'};$$

and the semiparameter $a.(1-e^2)$ of the ellipse, by means of the equation

$$\mu a.(1-e^2)=c^2+c'^2+c''^2;$$

These same equations obtain also in the case of the variable ellipse, provided that c, c', c'', are determined by means of the preceding differential equations. In this manner the parameter of the variable ellipse, its inclination to the fixed plane of x and y, and the position of its node may be obtained.

By means of the three first equations (p), we have deduced in N°. 19 the finite integral $0 = c''x - c'y + cz$; this equation, and also its first differential, $0 = c''dx - c'dy + cdz$, taken on the supposition that c, c', c'', are constant, obtain in case of the disturbed ellipse.

If the fourth, the fifth, and sixth of the integrals (p) be differenced, the parameters f, f', f'', and the differences dx, dy, dz, being considered as the sole variables, and if then we substitute, in place of d^2x, d^2y, d^2z, the quantities $-dt^2.\left(\frac{dR}{dx}\right)$, $-dt^2.\left(\frac{dR}{dy}\right)$ $-dt^2.\left(\frac{dR}{dz}\right)$, we shall have

$$df = dy.\left\{y.\left(\frac{dR}{dx}\right) - x.\left(\frac{dR}{dy}\right)\right\} + dz.\left\{z.\left(\frac{dR}{dx}\right) - x.\left(\frac{dR}{dz}\right)\right\}.^*$$
$$+ (ydx - xdy).\left(\frac{dR}{dy}\right) + (zdx - xdz).\left(\frac{dR}{dz}\right);$$

$$df' = dx.\left\{x.\left(\frac{dR}{dy}\right) - y.\left(\frac{dR}{dx}\right)\right\} + dz.\left\{z.\left(\frac{dR}{dy}\right) - y.\left(\frac{dR}{dz}\right)\right\}$$

* Differentiating under these restrictions we have

$$df = -2x\frac{(dy.d^2y + dz.d^2z)}{dt^2} + ydx.\frac{d^2y}{dt^2} + ydy.\frac{d^2x}{dt^2} + zdz.\frac{d^2x}{dt^2} + zdx.\frac{d^2z}{dt^2},$$

$\therefore$ by ordering the terms we have

$$df = dy.\left(y.\frac{d^2x}{dt^2} - x.\frac{d^2y}{dt^2}\right) + dz.\left(z.\frac{d^2x}{dt^2} - x.\frac{d^2z}{dt^2}\right) + (ydx - xdy).\frac{d^2y}{dt^2} +$$

$(zdx - xdz).\frac{d^2z}{dt^2}$, which becomes the expression in the text, when $\left(\frac{dR}{dx}\right)$, $\left(\frac{dR}{dy}\right)$, $\left(\frac{dR}{dz}\right)$, are substituted for $\frac{d^2x}{dt^2}$, $\frac{d^2y}{d^2y}$, $\frac{d^2z}{dt^2}$.

$$+(xdy-ydx).\left\{\frac{dR}{dx}\right\}+(zdy-ydz).\left\{\frac{dR}{dz}\right\};$$

$$df''=dx.\left\{x.\left\{\frac{dR}{dz}\right\}-z.\left\{\frac{dR}{dx}\right\}\right\}+dy.\left\{y.\left\{\frac{dR}{dz}\right\}-z.\left\{\frac{dR}{dy}\right\}\right\}$$

$$+(xdz-zdx).\left\{\frac{dR}{dx}\right\}+(ydz-zdy).\left\{\frac{dR}{dy}\right\}.$$

Finally, the seventh of the integrals (p), when differenced with the same restrictions, will give the variations of the semiaxis major a, by means of the equation $d.\frac{\mu}{a}=2.dR$, the differential dR being* referred solely to the coordinates x, y, z, of the body m.

The values of f, f', f'', determine the longitude of the projection of the perihelion of the orbit, on the fixed plane, and the ratio of the excentricity to the semiaxis major; for I being the longitude of this projection, we have by N°. 19,

$$\tan. I=\frac{f}{f'},$$

* Differentiating the seventh equation under the same restrictions, we obtain $d.\frac{\mu}{a}=-2.\left(\frac{d^2x}{dt^2}.dx+\frac{d^2y}{dt^2}.dy+\frac{d^2z}{dt^2}.dz\right)=\frac{dR}{dx}.dx+\frac{dR}{dy}.dy+\frac{dR}{dz}.dz=dR.$ See N°. 46.

By means of this expression, Lagrange ascertained that the mean motions were invariable, if the first power of the disturbing masses be only considered, the approximation being extended to any power of the excentricities and inclinations. From the extreme simplicity of this expression of the differential of the major axis, the determination of the longitude is a very easy problem. In the supplement to the third book, Laplace investigated the simplest form of which the other elements were susceptible, and he has succeeded in assigning such a form to them, that they only depend on partial differences of the same function, taken with respect to these elements, and what is particularly remarkable, the coefficients of these differences do not involve the time, and are solely functions of the elements themselves.

and e being the ratio of the excentricity to the semiaxis major, we have by the same number

$$\mu e = \sqrt{f^2 + f'^2 + f''^2}.$$

This ratio may also be determined, by dividing the semiparameter $a.(1-e^2)$, by the semiaxis major a, and by taking the quotient from unity, the value of e^2 will be obtained.

The integrals (p) have given by elimination, in N°. 19, the finite integral, $0 = \mu r - h^2 + fx + f'y + f''z$; this equation obtains also in the case of the disturbed ellipse, and it determines at each instant the nature of the variable ellipse, we can difference it, f, f', f'', being considered as constant quantities, which gives

$$0 = \mu dr + fdx + f'dy + f''dz.$$

The semiaxis major a determines the mean motion of m, or more accurately, that which in the troubled orbit, corresponds to the mean motion in the invariable orbit; for by N°. 20, we have $n = a^{-\frac{3}{2}}.\sqrt{\mu}$; moreover, if we denote by ζ the mean motion of m, we have in the invariable elliptic orbit $d\zeta = ndt$; this equation obtains equally for the variable ellipse, since it is a differential of the first order. By differencing, we shall have $d^2\zeta = dn.dt$; but we have

$$dn = \frac{3an}{2\mu}.\ d.\ \frac{\mu}{a} = \frac{3an.\mathrm{d}R}{\mu},\text{*}$$

therefore

$$d^2\zeta = \frac{3an.dt.\mathrm{d}R}{\mu};$$

* $dn = -\frac{3}{2}.\sqrt{\mu}.\frac{da}{a^{\frac{5}{2}}} = \frac{3}{2}.\sqrt{\frac{\mu}{a}}.d.\frac{1}{a} = \left(\text{as } \sqrt{\frac{\mu}{a}} = na\right)\frac{3an}{2\mu}.d.\frac{\mu}{a}.$

and by integrating

$$\zeta = \frac{3}{\mu} \cdot \iint an.dt.\text{d}R.$$

Finally, it has been observed in N°. 18, that the integrals (p) are only equivalent to five distinct integrals, and that they furnish between the seven parameters c, c', c'', f, f', f'', and e the two following equations of condition,

$$0 = fc'' - f'c' + f''c;$$

$$0 = \frac{\mu}{a} + \frac{f^2 + f'^2 + f''^2 - \mu^2}{c^2 + c'^2 + c''^2};$$

these equations obtain also in the case of the variable ellipse, provided that the parameters be determined by what precedes. We can likewise be assured of this *a posteriori.*

We have thus determined five elements of the disturbed orbit, namely its inclination, the position of its nodes, the semiaxis major (which gives the mean motion), its excentricity, and the position of the perihelion. It now remains for us to determine the sixth element of the elliptic motion, namely, that which in the undisturbed ellipse corresponds to the position of m, at a given epoch. For this purpose, let the expression for dt of N°. 18 be resumed,

$$\frac{dt.\sqrt{\mu}}{a^{\frac{3}{2}}} = \frac{dv.(1-e^2)^{\frac{3}{2}}}{(1+e.\cos.(v-\varpi))^2}.$$

This equation being expanded into a series, gave in the number already cited,

$$ndt = dv.(1 + E^{(1)}.\cos.(v-\varpi) + E^{(2)}.\cos.2.(v-\varpi) + \&c.):$$

which being integrated on the supposition that e and ϖ are constant, will give

$$\int ndt + \epsilon = v + E^{(1)}.\sin.(v-\varpi) + \frac{E^{(2)}}{2}.\sin.2.(v-\varpi) + \&c.$$

ϵ being an arbitrary quantity. This integral is relative to the invariable ellipse; in order to extend it to the disturbed ellipse, it is necessary when we make all the terms to vary, even to the arbitrary quantities ϵ, e and ϖ, which it contains, that its differential should coincide with the preceding; which gives

$$d\epsilon = de. \left\{ \left\{ \frac{dE^{(1)}}{de} \right\}. (\sin. (v-\varpi) + \tfrac{1}{2}. \left\{ \frac{dE^{(2)}}{de} \right\}. \sin. 2.(v-\varpi) + \&c. \right\}$$

$$-d\varpi.(E^{(1)}. \cos. (v-\varpi) + E^{(2)}. \cos. 2.(v-\varpi) + \&c.).$$

$v-\varpi$ is the true anomaly of m, reckoned on the orbit, and ϖ is the longitude of the perihelion, also reckoned on the orbit. I the longitude of the projection of the perihelion, on a fixed plane has been already determined; but by N°. 22, we have by changing v into ϖ, and $v_{\prime}$ into I in the expression for $v-\epsilon$ of that N°.,

$$\varpi-\epsilon = I-\theta + \text{tang.}^2 \tfrac{1}{2}\varphi. \sin. 2(I-\theta) + \&c.$$

If then v and $v_{\prime}$ be supposed equal to cypher, in this same expression, we have

$$\epsilon = \theta + \text{tang.}^2 \tfrac{1}{2}\varphi. \sin. 2\theta + \&c.$$

therefore

$$\varpi = I + \text{tang.}^2 \tfrac{1}{2}\varphi.(\sin. 2\theta + \sin. 2(I-\theta)) + \&c.;$$

which gives

$$d\varpi = dI(1 + 2 \tan.^2 \tfrac{1}{2}\varphi. \cos. 2.(I-\theta) + \&c.)$$
$$+ 2d\theta. \text{tang.}^2 \tfrac{1}{2}\varphi.(\cos. 2\theta - \cos. 2.(I-\theta) + \&c.$$
$$+ \frac{d\varphi. \tan. \frac{1}{2}\varphi}{\cos.^2 \frac{1}{2}\varphi}. (\sin. 2\theta + \sin. 2.(I-\theta) + \&c.)$$

consequently, the values of dI, $d\theta$ and $d\varpi$ being determined by what goes before; we shall have that of $d\varpi$, by means of which, the value of $d\epsilon$ will be obtained.

Hence it follows, that the expressions in series of the radius vector, of its projection on the fixed plane, of the longitude reckoned either on the fixed plane or on that of the orbit, and of the latitude, which have been determined in N°. 22, in the case of the invariable ellipse, obtain equally in the case of the disturbed ellipse, provided that nt be changed into $\int ndt$, and that the elements of the variable ellipse be determined by the preceding formulæ. For, since the finite equations between r, v, s, x, y, z, and $\int ndt$, are the same in the two cases; and since the expressions in series of N°. 22, result from those equations by operations purely analytic, and altogether independent of the constancy or variability of the elements; it is evident that these expressions obtain also in the case of variable elements.

When the ellipses are extremely excentric, as is the case in the orbits of the comets, the preceding analysis should be changed a little. The inclination φ of the orbit on the fixed plane, θ the longitude of its ascending node, the semiaxis major a, the semiparameter $a.(1-e^2)$, the excentricity e, and I the longitude of the perihelion on a fixed plane, may be determined by what goes before. But the values of ϖ, and of $d\varpi$ being given in series arranged according to the powers of tan. $\frac{1}{2}\varphi$, it is necessary in order to render them convergent, to select the fixed plane, such that tang. $\frac{1}{2}\varphi$ may be inconsiderable, and the simplest mode of effecting this, is to assume for the fixed plane, that of the orbit of m, at a given epoch.

The preceding value of $d\varepsilon$ is expressed in a series which is only convergent, when the excentricity of the orbit is inconsiderable, it cannot therefore be employed in the present case. In order to remedy this, let us resume the equation

$$\frac{dt.\sqrt{\mu}}{a^{\frac{3}{2}}}=\frac{dv.(1-e^2)^{\frac{3}{2}}}{(1+e.\cos.(v-\varpi))^2}.$$

If we make $1-e=\alpha$, we have by the analysis of N°. 23, in the case of the invariable ellipse,

$$t+T=\frac{2a^{\frac{3}{2}}(1-e^2)^{\frac{3}{2}}}{(2-\alpha)^2.\sqrt{\mu}}.\tan.\tfrac{1}{2}(v-\varpi)\left\{1+\frac{\frac{3}{2}-\alpha}{2-\alpha}.\tan.^2\tfrac{1}{2}.(v-\varpi)+\&c.\right\};$$

T being an arbitrary quantity. In order to extend this equation to the variable ellipse, it is necessary to difference it, T, the semiparameter $a.(1-e^2)$, α and ϖ being considered as the sole variables. By this means we shall obtain a differential equation, which will enable us to determine T; and the finite equations which obtain in the case of the the invariable ellipse, will likewise subsist in the case of the disturbed ellipse.

65. Let us particularly consider the variations of the elements of the orbit of m, in the case of the orbits having a small excentricity, and small inclination to each other. In N°. 48, we have shewn how to develope R in that case, into a series of sines and cosines of the form $m'.k.\cos.(in't-int+A)$, k and A being functions of the excentricities and of the inclinations of the orbits, of the positions of their nodes and of their perihelions, of the longitudes of the bodies at a given epoch, and of the greater axes. When the ellipses are variable all these quantities may be supposed to vary agreeably to what precedes, it is necessary moreover, to change in the preceding term the angle $i'n't-int$ into $i'\int n'dt-i\int ndt$, or what comes to the same thing, into $i'\zeta'-i\zeta$.

Now, by the preceding number we have

$$\frac{\mu}{a}=2\int dR;$$

$$\zeta=\int ndt=\frac{3}{\mu}.\iint andt.dR.$$

The difference dR being taken solely with respect to the coordinates x, y, z, of the body m, we should not make to vary in the term $m'k.\cos.(i'\zeta'-i\zeta+A)$ of the expression for R, developed into a series, only that part which depends on the motion of this body; besides, R being a finite function of x, y, z, x', y', z', we can by N°. 63 suppose the elements of the orbit constant in the differential dR, it is therefore sufficient to make ζ to vary in the preceding term, and as the difference of ζ is ndt, we shall have $i.m'.kndt.$ sin. $(i'\zeta' - i\zeta + A)$ for the term of dR, which corresponds to the preceding term of R. Thus, by having regard only to this term, we shall have

$$\frac{1}{a} = \frac{2i.m'}{\mu}.\int kndt.\ \text{sin.}\ (i'\zeta' - i\zeta + A);$$

$$\zeta = \frac{3i.m'}{\mu}.\iint akn^2dt^2.\ \text{sin.}\ (i'\zeta' - i\zeta + A).$$

If the squares and products of the disturbing masses be neglected, we can in the integration of these terms, suppose the elements of elliptic motion constant, which changes ζ into nt, and ζ' into $n't$; hence we deduce

$$\frac{1}{a} = -\frac{2im'n.k}{\mu.(i'n'-in)}.\ \text{cos.}\ (i'n't - int + A);$$

$$\zeta = -\frac{3im'.an^2k}{\mu.(i'n-in)^2}.\ \text{sin.}\ (i'n't - int + A).$$

It appears* from this, that if $i'n' - in$ does not vanish, the quantities a and ζ only contain periodical inequalities, the approximation being continued as far as the first power of the disturbing force; but as i' and i are integral numbers, the equation $i'n' - in = 0$, cannot have place when the mean motions† of m and of m' are incommensurable,

* This conclusion which was first shewn by Laplace to be true, when the approximation was continued as far as the first power of the disturbing force, and as far as the products of four dimensions of the excentricities and inclinations, was shewn by Lagrange to be true, taking into account any power of the excentricity and inclination; and it was further extended by Poisson, and afterwards by Laplace and Lagrange, who proved, that even continuing the approximation as far as the squares of the disturbing forces, no inequalities, but those which are periodic affect the major axis; and in general, that the stability of the planetary system is not deranged, when the squares of the masses, and all powers of the excentricities and inclinations, are taken into account. See N°. 54.

† The equation $i'n' - in = 0$, would therefore suppose an unique case, among an infinity of others equally possible, besides the disturbing action of m' is solely considered in

which is the case of the planets, and we may assume in general, since n and n'. are constant arbitrary quantities susceptible of all possible values, that their exact ratio, number to number, is extremely improbable.

We are consequently brought to this remarkable conclusion, namely, that the greater axes of the orbits of the planets and their mean motions, are only subject to periodic inequalities depending on their mutual configuration; and consequently, if these quantities be neglected, their greater axes are constant, and their mean motions are uniform: which result accords with that which was previously deduced in another manner, in N°. 54.

If the mean motions nt and $n't$ without being accurately commensurable, are yet very nearly in the ratio of i' to i; the divisor $i'n'-in$ will be extremely small, and there would result in ζ and ζ', inequalities which increasing with extreme slowness, may give ground to observers, to think that the mean motions of the bodies m and m', are not uniform. We shall see in the theory of Jupiter and Saturn, that this is the case relatively to those two planets; their mean motions are such that twice that of Jupiter, is very nearly equal to five times that of Saturn; so that $5n'-2n$ is not the seventy-fourth part of n. The smallness of this divisor renders the term of the expression for ζ, which depends on the angle $5n't-2nt$ extremely sensible, although it is of the order $i'-i$, or of the third order,* with respect to the ex-

this case, but strictly speaking R is a function of the actions of all the planets m', m'', m''', &c., ∵ the form of the angle will be $(in+i'n'+i''n''+\&c.)t+A$, so that the similar equation of mean motion would suppose $in+i'n'+i'n''+\&c.=0$, which is even more improbable than the equation $i'n'-in=0$, besides, if this last equation obtained, when there were only three bodies, it would cease to exist when the action of the other planets was taken into account.

* As $i'=5$, and $i=2$, $i'-i=3$, and consequently, the periodic function is multiplied by quantities of the third order, with respect to the excentricities and inclinations. If the axis major is subject to an inequality increasing proportionally to the time, the mean longitude has one increasing proportionally to the square of the time. See N°. 54.

centricities and inclinations of the orbits, as has been observed in N°. 48. The preceding analysis gives the most sensible part of these inequalities; for the variation of the mean longitude depends on two integrations; while the variations of the other elements of elliptic motion depend only on one integration; consequently, the terms of the expression for the mean longitude are those solely, which can have the square of $(i'n'-in)$ for a divisor; therefore taking into account these terms solely, which considering the smallness of this divisor, must be the most considerable, it will be sufficient in the expressions for the radius vector, the longitude, and the latitude, to increase by these terms the mean longitude.

When we have inequalities of this kind, which the action of m' produces in the mean motion of m; it is easy to infer the corresponding inequalities produced by the action of m on the mean motion of m'. In fact, if we only consider the mutual action of the three bodies M, m and m'; the formula (7) of N°. 9. gives

$$\text{const.} = m.\frac{(dx^2+dy^2+dz^2)}{dt^2} + m'.\frac{(dx'^2+dy'^2+dz'^2)}{dt^2}$$

$$-\frac{((mdx+m'dx')^2+(mdy+m'dy')^2+(mdz+m'dz')^2)}{(M+m+m').dt^2} \qquad (a)$$

$$-\frac{2Mm}{\sqrt{x^2+y^2+z^2}}-\frac{2Mm'}{\sqrt{x'^2+y'^2+z'^2}}-\frac{2mm'}{\sqrt{(x'-x)^2+(y'-y)^2+(z'-z)^2}}.$$

The last of the integrals (p) of the preceding number, gives by substituting for $\frac{\mu}{a}$, the integral $2\int dR$

$$\frac{dx^2+dy^2+dz^2}{dt^2}=\frac{2.(M+m)}{\sqrt{x^2+y^2+z^2}}-2\int dR.$$

If we then call R' what R becomes, when the action of m on m' is considered, we shall have

$$R' = \frac{m.(xx'+yy'+zz')}{(x^2+y^2+z^2)^{\frac{3}{2}}} - \frac{m}{\sqrt{(x'-x)^2+(y'-y)^2+(z'-z)^2}}$$

$$\frac{dx'^2+dy'^2+dz'^2}{dt^2} = \frac{2.(M+m')}{\sqrt{x'^2+y'^2+z'^2}} - \int \text{d}'R';$$

the differential characteristic d' only referring to the coordinates x', y', z', of the body m'. By substituting in the equation (a) in place of $\frac{dx^2+dy^2+dz^2}{dt^2}$ and of $\frac{dx'^2+dy'^2+dz'^2}{dt^2}$, these values, we shall have

$$m\int \text{d}R + m'\int \text{d}'R = \text{const.}$$

$$-\frac{((m.dx+m'dx')^2+(m.dy+m'.dy')^2+(m.dz+m'.dz')^2)}{2.(M+m+m')dt^2}$$

$$+\frac{m^2}{\sqrt{x^2+y^2+z^2}} + \frac{m'^2}{\sqrt{x'^2+y'^2+z'^2}}.$$

It is evident that the second member of this equation does not contain terms of the order of the squares and of the products of the masses m and m', which have for a divisior $i'n'-in$; therefore if we only consider such terms, we shall have

$$m\int \text{d}R + m'\int \text{d}'R' = 0;$$

hence if we only take into account those terms, of which the divisor is $(i'n'-in)^2$, we shall have

$$\frac{3\iint a'n'dt\text{d}'R'}{M+m'} = -\frac{m.(M+m).a'n'}{m'.(M+m').an} \cdot \frac{3\iint andt.\text{d}R}{M+m};$$

but we have

$$\zeta = \frac{3.\iint andt.\text{d}R}{M+m}; \quad \zeta' = \frac{3.\iint a'n'dt.\text{d}'R'}{M+m'};$$

consequently

$$m'.(M+m').an\zeta'+m.(M+m).a'n'))=0;$$

moreover

$$n=\frac{\sqrt{M+m}}{a^{\frac{3}{2}}};\quad n'=\frac{\sqrt{M+m'}}{a'^{\frac{3}{2}}};$$

therefore m and m' being neglected in comparison with M, we shall have

$$m.\sqrt{a}.\,\zeta+m'.\sqrt{a'}\,\zeta'=0;$$

or

$$\zeta'=-\frac{m.\sqrt{a}}{m'.\sqrt{a'}}\cdot\zeta.$$

Thus the inequalities of ζ, which have for a divisor $(i'n'-in)^2$ will make known those of ζ', which have the same divisor. These inequalities are, as we have seen, affected with contrary signs, if n and n' have the same sign, or what comes to the same thing, if the two bodies m and m' revolve in the same direction; they are besides in a constant ratio to each other; hence it follows, that if they appear to accelerate the mean motion of m, they will appear to retard that of m', according to the same law, and the apparent acceleration of m, will be to the apparent retardation of m', as $m'.\sqrt{a'}$ to $m.\sqrt{a}$. The acceleration of the mean motion of Jupiter, and the retardation of the mean motion of Saturn, which the comparison of ancient with modern observations made known to Halley, being very nearly in this ratio; I have inferred from the preceding theorem, that they are owing to the mutual action of these two planets; and since it has been demonstrated, that this action cannot produce any change in the mean motions, independent of the configuration of the planets, I did not hesitate to admit that there exists in the theory of Jupiter and Saturn, a great periodic inequality of a very long period. And observing then that five times the mean motion of Saturn, minus twice that of Jupiter, is very nearly equal to cypher, it appeared to me very probable that the cause of the phenomena observed by Halley, was an inequality depending on this argument. The determination of this inequality verified my conjecture.

The period of the argument $(i'n't-int)$, being supposed very long, the elements of the orbits m' and m experience in this interval sensible variations, which it is essentially necessary to consider in the double integral $\int\int akn^2.dt^2.\sin.(i'n't-int+A)$. For this purpose, we shall make the function $k.\sin.(i'n't-int+A)$ assume the form $Q.\sin.(i'n't-int+i'\epsilon'-i\epsilon)+Q'.\cos.(i'n't-int+i'\epsilon'-i\epsilon)$; Q and Q' being functions of the elements of the orbits, we shall have consequently

$$\int\int akn^2.dt^2.\sin.(i'n't-int+A)=\text{*}$$

$$-\frac{n^2a.\sin.(i'n't-int+i'\epsilon'-i\epsilon)}{(i'n'-in)^2}\left\{Q-\frac{2dQ'}{(i'n'-in).dt}-\frac{3d^2Q}{(i'n'-in)^2.dt^2}\right.$$

$$\left.+\frac{4d^3Q'}{(i'n'-in)^3dt^3}+\&c.\right\}$$

3 B 2

* Substituting for A its value $i'\epsilon'-i\epsilon-g\varpi-g'\varpi-g''\theta-g'''\theta$; $\sin.(in't-int+A)=\sin.(in't-int+i'\epsilon-i\epsilon).\cos.(g\varpi+g\varpi'+g''\theta+g'''\theta')-\cos.(in't-int+i'\epsilon-i\epsilon).\sin.(g\varpi+g'\varpi'+g''\theta+g'''\theta)$, hence the value of $k.\sin.(in't-int+A)$ will be given; calling $in't-int+i'\epsilon'-i\epsilon$, $ft+b$, the quantity to be integrated becomes $\int dt.\int dt.\sin.(ft+b)Q+\int dt.\int dt.\cos.(ft+b).Q'$, now one integration gives $\int dt.\sin.(ft+b).Q=-\frac{Q}{f}.\cos.(ft+b)+\frac{1}{f}\int.\cos.(ft+b).dt.\frac{dQ}{dt}.\left(=\frac{1}{f^2}.\frac{dQ}{dt}.\sin.(ft+b)+\frac{1}{f^2}.\int.\sin.(ft+b).dt.\frac{d^2Q}{dt^2}+\&c.\right.$ $=\frac{Q}{f}.\cos.(ft+b)-\frac{1}{f^2}.\frac{dQ}{dt}.\sin.(ft+b)+\frac{1}{f^3}.\frac{d^2Q}{dt^2}.\cos.(ft+b)+\frac{1}{f^4}.\frac{d^3Q}{dt^3}.\sin.(ft+b)+\&c.$; in like manner we can obtain by partial integration, $\int dt.\cos.(ft+b).Q'=\frac{Q'}{f}.\sin(ft+b)+\frac{1}{f^2}.\frac{dQ'}{dt^2}.\cos.(ft+b)-\frac{1}{f'}.\frac{d^2Q'}{dt^2}.\sin.(ft+b)-\&c.$, in order to obtain the second integrals, *i.e.* $\int dt.\int dt.\sin.(ft+b)$, each of the terms of the preceding series into which the first integrals may be resolved, should be multiplied by dt, and then integrated in the same manner as $\int dt.\sin.(ft+b).Q$, and if all the factors of $\sin.(ft+b)$, and $\cos.(ft+b)$ be respectively collected, we shall obtain by substituting for f and b, the expression given in the text.

$$-\frac{n^2a.\cos.(i'n't-int+i'\iota'-i\iota)}{(i'n'-in)^2}\left\{Q'+\frac{2dQ}{(i'n'-in).dt}-\frac{3d^2Q'}{(i'n'-in).^2dt}\right.$$
$$\left.-\frac{4d^3Q}{(i'n'-in)^3.dt^3}+\&c.\right\}.$$

In consequence of the slowness of the secular variations of the elliptic elements, the terms of these two series decrease with great rapidity. We may therefore only consider the two first terms in each series. If then we substitute in place of the elements of the orbits, their values arranged according to the powers of the time, the first power being the only one which is retained; the preceding double integral may be transformed into one sole term of the form

$$(F+E.t).\sin.(i'n't-int+A+H.t).$$

Relatively to Jupiter and Saturn, this expression will serve for several centuries before and after the instant, which may have been selected for the epoch.

The great inequalities of which we have been speaking, produce some sensible terms among those which depend on the second power of the disturbing masses. In fact, if in the formula

$$\zeta=\frac{3im'}{\mu}.\int\int akn^2.dt^2.\sin.(i'\zeta'-i\zeta+A);$$

we substitute for ζ and ζ' their values

$$nt-\frac{3i.m'.an^2k}{\mu.(i'n'-in)^2}.\sin.(i'n't-int+A);$$
$$n't'+\frac{3i.mank^2}{\mu.(i'n'-in)^2}\frac{\sqrt{a}}{\sqrt{a'}}.\sin.(i'n't-int+A),$$

there will result among the terms of the order m^2, the following

$$-\frac{9i^2.m'^2.a^2.n^4.k^2}{8.\mu^2.(i'n'-in)^4}\frac{(im'.\sqrt{a'}+i'm.\sqrt{a}}{m^{2\prime}.\sqrt{a'}}.\sin.2.(i'n't-int+A),^*$$

* Assuming $p=\frac{3im'.n^2ak}{\mu.(i'n'-in)^2}$, and $p'=\frac{3i.m.an^2k}{\mu.(i'n'-in)^2}.\frac{\sqrt{a}}{\sqrt{a'}}$, the value of $\zeta=E$.

There will result in the value of ζ' a corresponding term, which is to the preceding in the ratio of $m.\sqrt{a}$ to $-m'.\sqrt{a'}$, it is therefore

$$\frac{9.i^2.m'^2a^2.n^4.k^2}{8.\mu^2.(i'n'-in)^4}\left\{im'.\sqrt{a'} + i'.m.\sqrt{a}.\right\}\frac{m.\sqrt{a}}{m'^2.a'}.\ \text{sin. } 2.(i'n't-int+A).$$

66. It may happen, that the most sensible inequalities of mean motion occur among the terms of the order of the squares of the disturbing masses. If we suppose three bodies m, m', m'', to revolve about M, the expression for dR relative to terms of this order, will contain inequalities of the form $k.\text{sin.}\,(int-i'n't+i''n''t+A)$, now if the mean motions of m, m', m'', &c., are such that $in-i'n'+i''n''$, may be supposed a very small fraction of n, there will result a very sensible inequality in the value of ζ. This inequality may even render rigorously equal to cypher, the quantity $in-i'n'+i'n''$, and thus establish an equation of condition between the mean motions and the mean longitudes of the three bodies m, m', m''; this remarkable case obtains in the system of the satellites of Jupiter. We proceed to develope the analysis of it.

If we suppose M to represent the unity of mass, and if m, m', m'', be neglected in comparison with M, we shall have

$$n^2=\frac{1}{a^3},\ n'^2=\frac{1}{a'^3};\ n''^2=\frac{1}{a''^3};$$

$\int\int dt^2.\,\text{sin.}\,(in't-int+(p'-p).\,\text{sin.}\,(in't-int-A)+A)\ (a)$, now if p', p be supposed to be very small, we shall have $\text{sin.}\,((p'-p).\,\text{sin.}\,(in't-int+A))=(p'-p).\,\text{sin.}\,(i'n't-int+A)$, and the cosine of the same quantity $=1$, in each case these expressions are true, for the first power of the disturbing force; ∵ in the expression (a) a term occurs $=E.\,\text{cos.}(i'n't-int+A)\,(i'p'+ip).\,\text{sin.}\,(i'n't-int-A)=\frac{E}{2}.\,(i'p'+ip).\,\text{sin. } 2.(in't-int+A)$, now $i'p'+ip=\frac{3ian^2k.(i'm.\sqrt{a}+im'.\sqrt{a'}}{\mu.(i'n'-in)^2.\sqrt{a'}}$, and $E=\frac{3im'^2.akn^2}{\mu.m'}$, ∵ the coefficient of $\text{sin. } 2.(n't-nt+A)=\frac{9i^2.m'^2.a^2n^2.k^2}{2\mu^2,(i'n'-in)^2}.\frac{(i'm.\sqrt{a}+i'm'.\sqrt{a'}}{m'.\sqrt{a'}})$, and when the double integration is performed, there will result the expression given in the text.

we have also

$$d\zeta = ndt;\ d\zeta' = n'dt;\ d\zeta'' = n''dt;$$

consequently

$$\frac{d^2\zeta}{dt} = -\frac{3}{2}.n^{\frac{1}{3}}.\frac{da}{a^2};\quad \frac{d^2\zeta'}{dt} = -\frac{3}{2}.n'^{\frac{1}{3}}.\frac{da'}{a'^2};\quad \frac{d^2\zeta''}{dt} = -\frac{3}{2}.n''^{\frac{1}{3}}.\frac{da''}{a''^2}.$$

It has been observed in N°. 61, that if we only consider inequalities which have very long periods, we have

$$\text{constant} = \frac{m}{a} + \frac{m'}{a'} + \frac{m''}{a''};$$

which gives

$$0 = m.\frac{da}{a^2} + m'.\frac{da'}{a'^2} + m''.\frac{da''}{a''^2}.$$

It has been also observed in the same number, that if the squares of the excentricities and of the inclinations of the orbits be neglected, we have

$$\text{constant} = m.\sqrt{a} + m'.\sqrt{a'} + m''.\sqrt{a''};$$

which gives

$$0 = \frac{mda}{\sqrt{a}} + \frac{m'.da'}{\sqrt{a'}} + \frac{m''.da''}{\sqrt{a''}}.$$

From these different equations it is easy to infer

$$\frac{d^2\zeta}{dt} = -\frac{3}{2}.n^{\frac{1}{3}}.\frac{da}{a^2}.\ *$$

$$\frac{d^2\zeta'}{dt} = \frac{3}{2}.\frac{m.n'^{\frac{4}{3}}}{m'.n}.\left(\frac{n-n''}{n'-n''}\right).\frac{da}{a^2}$$

$$\frac{d^2\zeta''}{dt} = -\frac{3}{2}\frac{m.n''^{\frac{4}{3}}}{m''.n}.\left(\frac{n-n'}{n'-n''}\right).\frac{da}{a^2}.$$

* $n^{\frac{2}{3}} = \frac{1}{a}$, $\therefore -\frac{2}{3}.\frac{dn}{n^{\frac{1}{3}}} = \frac{da}{a^2}$, and $\frac{d^2\zeta}{dt} = dn = -\frac{3}{2}.n^{\frac{1}{3}}.\frac{da}{a^2}$; in like manner

Finally, the equation $\frac{\mu}{a} = 2\int dR$, of N°. 64, gives

$$-\frac{da}{a^2} = 2dR.$$

It is therefore only requisite to determine dR.

By N°. 46 we have,

$$R = \frac{m'.r}{r'^2}.\cos.(v'-v) - m'.(r^2 - 2rr'.\cos.(v'-v) + r'^2)^{-\frac{1}{2}}$$

$$+\frac{m''.r}{r''^2}.\cos.(v''-v) - m''.(r^2 - 2rr''.\cos.(v''-v) + r''^2)^{-\frac{1}{2}}$$

the squares and the products of the inclinations of the orbits being neglected. If this function be developed into a series arranged according to the powers of the cosines of $v'-v$, of $v''-v$, and of their multiples: we shall have an expression of the following form,

$$R = \frac{m'}{2}.(r,r')^{(0)} + m'.(r,r')^{(1)}.\cos.(v'-v) + m'.(r,r')^{(2)}.\cos.2.(v'-v)$$
$$+ m'.(r,r')^{(3)}.\cos.3.(v'-v) + \&c.$$

$$+\frac{m''}{2}.(r,r'')^{(0)} + m''.(r,r'')^{(1)}.\cos.(v''-v) + m''.(r,r'')^{(2)}.\cos.2.(v''-v)$$
$$+ m''.(r,r'')^{(3)}.\cos.3(v''-v) + \&c.$$

$n^{\frac{4}{3}} = n^2.n^{-\frac{2}{3}} = n^2.a.$

$\frac{mda}{a^2} + \frac{m'da'}{a'^2} = -\frac{m''da''}{a''^2} = \left(\text{as } n = \frac{1}{a^{\frac{3}{2}}}\right)\frac{mn''da}{\sqrt{a}} + \frac{m'n''.da'}{\sqrt{a'}}$, therefore multiplying both sides by $nn' = a^{-\frac{3}{2}}.a'^{-\frac{5}{2}}$, we shall obtain $\frac{m.nn'.da}{a^2} + \frac{m'nn'.da'}{a'^2} = \frac{mn'n''.da}{a^2} + \frac{m'nn''.da'}{a'^2}$; $\therefore$ $\frac{da'}{a'^2} = \frac{m.n'.(n-n'')}{m'.n.(n'-n'')}.\frac{da}{a^2}$, $\therefore \frac{d^2\zeta'}{dt} = -\frac{3}{2}.n'^{\frac{1}{3}}.\frac{da'}{a'^2} = \frac{3}{2}.\frac{m.n'^{\frac{4}{3}}}{m'.n}.\frac{(n-n'')}{(n''-n')}.\frac{da}{a^2}$, the expression for $\frac{d^2\zeta''}{dt}$ may be obtained in a similar manner.

hence we obtain

$$dR=\left\{\begin{array}{l} dr.\left\{\begin{array}{l}\frac{m'}{2}.\left\{\frac{d.(r,r')^{(0)}}{dr}\right\}+m'.\left\{\frac{d.(r,r')^{(1)}}{dr}\right\}.\cos.(v'-v)+m'.\\ \qquad\left\{\frac{d.(r,r')^{(2)}}{dr}\right\}.\cos.2.(v'-v)+\&c.\\ \frac{m''}{2}.\left\{\frac{d.(r,r'')^{(0)}}{dr}\right\}+m''.\left\{\frac{d.(r,r'')^{(1)}}{dr}\right\}.\cos.(v''-v)+m''.\\ \qquad\left\{\frac{d.(r,r'')^{(2)}}{dr}\right\}.\cos.2.(v''-v)+\&c.\end{array}\right\}\\ +dv.\left\{\begin{array}{l}m'.(r,r')^{(1)}.\sin.(v'-v)+2m'.(r,r')^{(2)}.\sin.2.(v'-v)+\&c.\\ +m''.(r,r'')^{(1)}.\sin.(v''-v)+2m''.(r,r'')^{(2)}.\sin.2.(v''-v)+\&c.\end{array}\right\}\end{array}\right\}$$

Suppose agreeably to what is indicated by observations, in the system of the three first satellites of Jupiter, that $n-2n'$, and $n'-2n''$. are very small fractions of n, and that their difference $(n'-2n')-(n'-2n'')$, or $n-3n'+2n''$ is incomparably less than each of them. It results from the expressions of $\frac{\delta r}{a}$, and of δv, of N°. 50, that the action of m' produces in the radius vector, and in the longitude of m, a very sensible inequality, depending on the argument $2.(n't-nt+\varepsilon'-\varepsilon)$. The terms relative to this inequality ,have for a divisor $4.(n'-n)^2-n^2$, or $(n-2n').(3n-2n')$. and this divisor is extremely small in consequence of the smallness of the factor $n-2n'$. It appears also from a consideration of the same expressions, that the action of m produces in the radius vector, and in the longitude of m', an inequality depending on the argument $(n't-nt+\varepsilon'-\varepsilon)$, and which as it has for a divisor $(n'-n)^2-n^2$ or $n.(n-2n')$ is extremely sensible. It appears in like manner, that the action of m'' on m' produces in the same quantities a considerable inequality, depending on the argument $2.(n''t-n't+\varepsilon''-\varepsilon')$. Finally, we may perceive that the action of m', produces in the longitude and radius vector of m'' a considerable inequality, depending on the argument $n''t-n't+\varepsilon''-\varepsilon'$. These inequalities have been recognized by observations, we shall develope them in detail in the theory of the satellites of Jupiter; their magnitude relative to the other inequalities permits us to neglect the latter in the present question. Let us therefore suppose

$$\delta r = m'.E'.\cos.2.(n't - nt + \varepsilon' - \varepsilon);$$
$$\delta v = m'.F.\sin.2.(n't - nt + \varepsilon' - \varepsilon);$$
$$\delta r' = m''.E''.\cos.2.(n''t - n't + \varepsilon'' - \varepsilon') + m.G.\cos.(n't - nt + \varepsilon' - \varepsilon);$$
$$\delta v' = m''.F''.\sin.2.(n''t - n't + \varepsilon'' - \varepsilon') + m.H.\sin.(n't - nt + \varepsilon' - \varepsilon);$$
$$\delta r'' = m'.G''.\cos.(n''t - n't + \varepsilon'' - \varepsilon');$$
$$\delta v'' = m'.H'.\sin.(n''t - n't + \varepsilon'' - \varepsilon').$$

It is necessary now to substitute in the preceding expression for dR, instead of r, v, r', v', r'', v'', the values of $a + \delta r$, $nt + \varepsilon + \delta v$, $a' + \delta r'$, $n't + \varepsilon' + \delta v'$, $a'' + \delta r''$, $n''t + \varepsilon'' + \delta v''$, and only to retain the terms depending on the argument $nt - 3n't + 2n''t + \varepsilon - 3\varepsilon' + 2\varepsilon''$, it is easy to see that the substitution of the values of δr, δv, $\delta r''$, $\delta v''$, cannot produce any such term. Therefore it can only arise from the substitution of the values of $\delta r'$, and of $\delta v'$; the term $m'.(r,r')^{(1)}.\,dv.\sin.(v' - v)$ of the expression of dR, produces the following quantity:

$$-\frac{m'.m''.ndt}{2}.\left\{E''.\frac{d.(a,a')^{(1)}}{da'} - F''.(a,a')^{(1)}\right).\sin.nt - 3n't + 2n''t + \varepsilon - 3\varepsilon' + 2\varepsilon'').^{*}$$

And it is the only quantity of this kind, which the expression of dR

* $(r,r')^{(1)} = (a,a')^{(1)} + \frac{d.(a,a')^{(1)}}{da}.\delta r + \frac{d.(a,a')^{(1)}}{da'}.\delta r' + \&c.$; $\sin.(v' - v) = \sin.(n't + \varepsilon' + \delta v' - nt - \varepsilon - \delta v) = \sin.(n't - nt + \varepsilon' - \varepsilon) + \cos.(n't - nt + \varepsilon' - \varepsilon).\delta v'\ \&c.$; by substituting for $\delta r'$, we shall have $\frac{d.(a,a')^{(1)}}{da'}.\delta r' = \frac{d.(a,a')^{(1)}}{da'}.\ m''E''.\cos.(2.(n''t - n't + \varepsilon'' - \varepsilon')$, which when multiplied into $\sin.(n't - nt + \varepsilon' - \varepsilon)$ gives a term of the form $-m''.E''.\sin.(nt - 3n't + 2n''t + \varepsilon - 3\varepsilon' + 2\varepsilon'')$, in like manner by substituting for $\delta v'$, we obtain $\cos.(n't - nt + \varepsilon - \varepsilon').\delta v' = -m''.F''.\sin.(nt - 3n't + 2n''t + \varepsilon - 3\varepsilon' + 2\varepsilon'')$, hence if we substitute for dv its value, there will result in the term $m'.(r,r')^{(1)}.\,dv.\sin.(v' - v)$, the expression which is given in the text.

contains. The expressions of $\frac{\delta r}{a}$ and of δv of N°. 50, being applied to the action of m'' on m', give, when the terms which have $n'-2n''$ for a divisor are retained, and observing that n'' is very nearly equal to $\frac{n'}{2}$,

$$\frac{E''}{a'}=\frac{\frac{1}{2}n'^2.\left\{a'^2.\left\{\frac{d.(a'_{,}a'')^{(2)}}{da'}\right\}+\frac{2n'}{n'-n''}.a'.(a'_{,}a'')^{(2)}\right\}}{(n'-2n'').(3n'-2n'')} \;*$$

$$F''=\frac{2E''}{a'};$$

therefore we shall have

$$\mathrm{d}R=\frac{m'.m''.ndt}{2}.E''.\left\{\frac{2.(a_{,}a')^{(1)}}{a'}-\left(\frac{d.(a_{,}a')^{(1)}}{da'}\right)\right\}$$

$$\times\sin.(nt-3n't+2n''t+\epsilon-3\epsilon'+2\epsilon'')=-\tfrac{1}{2}.\frac{da}{a^2}.$$

This value of $\frac{da}{a^2}$ being substituted in the values of $\frac{d^2\zeta}{dt}$, $\frac{d^2\zeta'}{dt}$, and $\frac{d^2\zeta''}{dt}$, will give, because n is very nearly equal to $2n'$, and n' is very nearly equal to $2n''$;

* In page 296, if we substitute for $\frac{dA^{(2)}}{da'}$, $A^{(2)}$, their values, the coefficient of cos. $2.(n''t-n't+\epsilon''-\epsilon')$ becomes $=\frac{\frac{m''}{2}.n'^2.a'^2.\frac{d.(a'_{,}a'')^{(2)}}{da'}+\frac{2n'}{n'-n''}.a'.(a'_{,}a'')^{(2)}}{(n'-2n'').(3n'-2n'')}=\frac{m''E''}{a'}$;

in like manner the coefficient of sin. $2.(n''t-n't+\epsilon''-\epsilon')$ in the expression for $\delta v'$, given in page 298, $=\frac{2n'^2.a'^2.\frac{d.(a'_{,}a'')^{(2)}}{da'}+\frac{2n'}{n'-n''}.a'.(a'_{,}a'')^{(2)}}{\frac{2n'}{2}.(n'-2n'').(3n'-2n'')}=F''=\frac{2E''}{a'}$.

$$\frac{d^2\zeta}{dt^2}-\frac{3d^2\zeta'}{d_{t}^{2}}+\frac{2d^2\zeta''}{dt^2}=6n^2.\sin.(nt-2nt'+2n''t''+\epsilon-3\epsilon'+2\epsilon'');*$$

(6 being made, in order to abridge, equal to

$$\frac{3}{2}.E'.\left\{2.(a,a')^{(1)}-a'.\left\{\frac{d.(a,a')^{(1)}}{da'}\right\}\right\}.\left\{\frac{a}{a'}.m'.m''+\frac{9}{4}.m.m''+\frac{a''}{4a'}.m.m'\right\};$$

Or more accurately,

$$\frac{d^2\zeta}{dt^2}-\frac{3d^2\zeta'}{dt^2}+\frac{2d^2\zeta''}{dt^2}=6.\,n^2.\sin.(\zeta-3\zeta'+2\zeta''+\epsilon-3\epsilon'+2\epsilon'');$$

so that if we assume

$$V=\zeta-3\zeta'+2\zeta''+\epsilon-3\epsilon'+2\epsilon'',$$

we shall have

$$\frac{d^2V}{dt^2}=6.n^2.\sin.V.$$

As the mean distances a, a', a'', and also the quantity n vary very little, we can in this equation consider $6n^2$ as a constant quantity. By integrating it, we obtain

3 C 2

* $\frac{d^2\zeta}{dt^2}=-\frac{3}{2}.n^{\frac{1}{3}}\frac{da}{a^2}$, therefore multiplying by n, we obtain the coefficient of $\frac{da}{a^2}=-\frac{3}{2}.n^{\frac{4}{3}}=-\frac{3}{2}.n^2a$, therefore by substituting for $\frac{da}{a^2}$, we obtain $\frac{d^2\zeta}{dt^2}=\frac{3}{2}.E''.\left(\frac{2.(a,a')^{(1)}}{a'}-\frac{d.(a,a')^{(1)}}{da'}\right).n^2.m'm''a.\sin.(nt-2n't+3n''t+\epsilon-3\epsilon'-2\epsilon'')$; in like manner the coefficient of $\frac{da}{a^2}$ in the value of $\frac{d^2\zeta'}{dt^2}=\frac{3}{2}.\frac{mn'^{\frac{4}{3}}}{m'.n}.\frac{3\frac{n'}{2}}{\frac{n}{2}}=\frac{9}{2}.\frac{mn'^2a'}{m'.n}$, which being multiplied into $m''m'ndt$, gives (by substituting for n'^2, its value $\left(\frac{n}{2}\right)^2$) — $\frac{3d^2\zeta'}{dt^2}=\frac{3}{2}.E''.\left(\frac{2.(a,a')^{(1)}}{a'}-\frac{d.(a,a')^{(1)}}{da'}\right)\frac{9}{4}.n^2.m.m''.\sin.(nt-3n't+2n''t+\epsilon-3\epsilon'+2\epsilon'')$. The value of $\frac{2d^2\zeta''}{dt^2}$ may be obtained in a similar manner.

$$dt = \frac{\pm dV}{\sqrt{c - 2\text{Є}n^2 . \cos. V}},$$

c being a constant arbitrary quantity. From the different values of which this constant is susceptible, the three following cases arise.

If c be positive and greater than $\pm 2\text{Є}n^2$, the angle V will increase continually; and this will be the case, if, at the commencement of the motion $(n - 3n' + 2n'')^2$ is greater* than $\pm 2\text{Є}n^2.(1 \mp \cos. V)$, the superior, or lower signs having place according as Є is positive or negative. It is easy to be assured, and shall we point it out particularly in the theory of the satellites of Jupiter, that Є is a positive quantity relative to the three first satellites; therefore, supposing $\mp \varpi = \pi - V$,† (π being the semicircumference) we shall have

$$dt = \frac{d\varpi}{\sqrt{c + 2\text{Є}n^2 . \cos. \varpi}}.$$

In the interval from $\varpi = 0$, to $\varpi = \frac{\pi}{2}$; the radical $\sqrt{c + 2\text{Є}n^2 . \cos. \varpi}$ is greater than $\sqrt{2\text{Є}n^2}$, when c is equal to or greater than $2\text{Є}n^2$; therefore, the time t in which the angle ϖ passes from zero to a right angle, is less than $\frac{\pi}{2n . \sqrt{2\text{Є}}}$. The value of Є depends on the masses m, m', m''. The inequalities which have been observed in the motions of the three first satellites of Jupiter, and which we have already adverted to, assign relations between their masses and that of Jupiter, from which it

* If c be positive and greater than $\pm 2\text{Є}n^2$, the angle V must always increase, for the quantity under the radical sign can never be equal to cypher; $c - 2\text{Є}n^2 . \cos. V = \left(\frac{dV}{dt}\right)^2 = (n - 3n' + 2n'')^2$, if this quantity be greater than $\pm 2\text{Є}n^2.(1 \mp \cos. V)$, $c - 2\text{Є}n^2 . \cos. V$ must be greater than $\pm 2 . \text{Є}n^2 . (1 \mp \cos. V)$; i. e. c must be greater than $2\text{Є}n^2$.

† By making $\mp \varpi = \pi - V$, we get rid of the ambiguity of sign in the value of dt.

follows that $\frac{\pi}{2n.\sqrt{2\text{C}}}$ is less than* two years, as we shall see in the theory of these satellites. Therefore the angle ϖ passes from zero to a right angle in less than two years; now from observations made on Jupiter's satellites, it appears that since their discovery, the angle ϖ has been either equal to cypher, or insensible, consequently the case which we have examined, is not that of the three first satellites of Jupiter.

If the constant c is less than $\pm 2\text{C}n^2$, the angle V will only oscillate, it will never attain to two right angles, if C be negative, since then the radical $\sqrt{c-2\text{C}n^2. \cos. V}$ will become imaginary;† it will be never equal to cypher, if C is positive. In the first case, its value will be alternately greater or less than cypher; in the second case, it will be alternately greater or less than two right angles. From all observations made on the three first satellites of Jupiter, it appears that this second case, is that of these stars, therefore the value of C ought to be positive relatively to them, and as the theory of gravity assigns a positive value to C, we ought to consider this phenomenon as an additional confirmation of this theory.

Since according to observation, the angle ϖ in the equation

* As $n=\frac{2\pi}{P}$, P being the time of revolution of the first satellite, we have $t \angle \frac{P}{4.\sqrt{2\text{C}}}$; the value of C depends on the masses m, m', m'', and also on n, n', n'', these last are had by knowing the periodic times of the three first satellites, and the first are determined by their effects in producing certain inequalities, and are obtained in the same manner as the masses of Venus, Mercury, and Mars, are determined from certain effects which they produce on the earth's orbit.

† When c is negative and less than $\mp 2\text{C}n^2$, the radical is evidently imaginary when $V=\pi$; ∵ V can never be $=$ to π, and it must be alternately positive and negative, its mean value being equal to *cypher*. If C is positive, the radical is evidently imaginary when $V=0$; ∵ in this case V can never be $=0$, its value is therefore periodic, and in its mean state is equal to π.

$$dt = \frac{d\varpi}{\sqrt{c + 2\text{б}n^2 . \cos. \varpi}},^*$$

must be always very small, we can suppose $\cos. \varpi = 1 - \frac{1}{2}\varpi^2$, and the preceding equation will give by integrating it,

$$\varpi = \lambda . \sin. (nt.\sqrt{\text{б}} + \gamma),$$

λ and γ being two constant arbitrary quantities, which can be determined by observation alone. . Hitherto, it has not indicated this inequality, which proves that it is extremely small.

From the preceding analysis the following consequences may be inferred. Since the angle $nt - 3n't + 2n''t + \epsilon - 3\epsilon' - 2\epsilon''$ only oscillates on one side or other of two right angles, its mean value is equal to two right angles; therefore we shall have, if we only consider mean quantities, $n - 3n' + 2n'' = 0$; that is to say, *the mean motion of the first satellite plus twice that of the third, minus three times that of the second, is exactly and constantly equal to cypher.* It is not necessary that this equality should accurately obtain at the commencement, which would be extremely improbable, it is sufficient that it should be nearly the case, and that $n - 3n' + 2n''$, should be, abstracting from the sign, less than† $\lambda . n . \sqrt{\text{б}}$; and then the mutual attraction of these three satellites would have rendered this relation rigorously exact. We have therefore $n - 3n' + 2n''$ equal to two right angles; hence, the mean longitude of the first satellite, minus three times the mean longitude of the second, plus twice that of the third is exactly and constantly equal to

* The equation $\frac{dt}{\sqrt{c + 2\text{б}n^2 . \cos. \varpi}}$, is that of a pendulum whose length is $\frac{2g}{\text{б}i^2}$, i. being the number of seconds in a revolution of the first satellite, the amplitude of the arc of vibration being $-\frac{c}{2\text{б}i^2}$.

† Or in other words, at the origin of the motion, it should be comprized within the limits $\pm \lambda . n . \sqrt{\text{б}}$.

two right angles. In consequence of this theorem, the preceding values of $\delta r'$ and $\delta v'$ are reduced to the following,

$$\delta r' = (m.G - m'.E''). \cos. (n't - nt + \varepsilon' - \varepsilon);^*$$
$$\delta v' = (m.H - m'F''). \sin. (n't - nt + \varepsilon' - \varepsilon).$$

The two inequalities in the motion of m', arising from the action of m and of m''. are consequently confounded into one, and will be always combined. It follows also, that the three first satellites can never be eclipsed together; they cannot be seen together from Jupiter, neither in opposition nor in conjunction with the sun; for it is easy to perceive that the preceding theorems obtain equally for the mean synodic motions, and the mean synodic longitudes of the three satellites. These two theorems likewise obtain, notwithstanding the changes which the mean motions of the satellites may experience, either from a cause similar to that which alters the mean motion of the moon, or from the resistance of a very rare medium. It is evident that if these different causes operated it would be merely requisite to add to the value of $\frac{d^2V}{dt^2}$, a quantity of the form $\frac{d^2\psi}{dt^2}$, which can only become sensible by integrations; supposing therefore $V = \pi - \varpi$, and ϖ very small, the differential equation in V will become

$$0 = \frac{d^2\varpi}{dt^2} + \beta n^2.\varpi + \frac{d^2\psi}{dt^2}.$$

As the period of the angle $nt.\sqrt{\beta}$ embraces but a very few number of years, while the quantities contained† in $\frac{d^2\psi}{dt^2}$ are either constant or

* For $2n''t + 2\varepsilon'' - 2n't - 2\varepsilon' = \pi + n't - ut + \varepsilon' - \varepsilon$, $\therefore$ $m''.E''. \cos. 2.(n''t - n't + \varepsilon'' - \varepsilon') = -m''.E''. \cos. (n't - nt + \varepsilon' - \varepsilon)$, in a similar manner, for the value of $m''.F''. \sin. 2.(n''t - n't + \varepsilon'' - \varepsilon')$ may be sabstituted $-m''.F''. \sin. (n't - nt + \varepsilon' - \varepsilon)$.

† The period of the variation of ϖ, and $\therefore$ of V will be determined by means of the

extend to several centuries, we shall obtain very nearly, by integrating the preceding equation

$$\varpi = \lambda.\ \sin.\ (nt.\sqrt{\mathfrak{C}}+\gamma) - \frac{d^2\psi}{\mathfrak{C}n^2.dt^2}.$$

Thus the value of ϖ will be always extremely small, and the secular equations of the mean motions of the three first satellites will be coordinated by the mutual action of these stars, so that the secular equation of the first plus twice that of the third, minus three times that of the second, is equal to cypher.

The preceding theorems establish between the six constants n, n', n'', ε, ε', ε'', two equations of condition by means of which these arbitrary quantities are reduced to four. However they are replaced by the two arbitrary quantities λ and γ, of the value of ϖ. This value is distributed between the three satellites in such a manner, that naming p, p', p'', the coefficients of sin. $(nt.\sqrt{\mathfrak{C}}+\gamma)$ in the expressions for v, v', v''; those coefficients are in the ratio of the preceding values of $\frac{d^2\zeta}{dt^2}$, $\frac{d^2\zeta'}{dt^2}$, $\frac{d^2\zeta''}{dt^2}$, and moreover, we have $p-3p'+2p''=\lambda$. Hence, results in the mean motions of the three first satellites of Jupiter, an inequality which differs for each of them in the value of its coefficient, and which produces in these motions a species of vibration the extent of which is arbitrary. It appears from observation that it is insensible.

67. Let us now consider the variations of the excentricities and

equation $nt.\sqrt{\mathfrak{C}} = 2\pi$, ∵ as $nP=2\pi$, $t=\frac{P}{\sqrt{\mathfrak{C}}}$; hence the two limits of t depend on those of $\mathfrak{C}$.

The integral of the equation $\frac{d^2\varpi}{dt^2}+\mathfrak{C}n^2.\varpi=0$, is $\varpi=\lambda'.\ \sin.\ (nt.\sqrt{\mathfrak{C}}+\gamma)$; nd in the equation $\varpi=\lambda.\ \sin.\ (nt.\sqrt{\mathfrak{C}}+\gamma)-\frac{d^2\psi}{\mathfrak{C}.n^2.dt^2}$; the mean value of $\frac{d\varpi}{dt}$, and ∵ of $n-3n'+2n'')=0$.

perihelias of the orbits. For this purpose, let the expressions of df, df', df'', found in N°. 64, be resumed: naming r the radius vector of m, projected on the plane of x, and of y; v the angle which this projection makes with the axis of x, and s the tangent of latitude of m above the same plane; we shall have

$$x = r.\cos.v;\ y = r.\sin.v;\ z = rs;$$

hence it is easy to conclude

$$x.\left\{\frac{dR}{dy}\right\} - y.\left\{\frac{dR}{dx}\right\} = \left\{\frac{dR}{dv}\right\};$$

$$x.\left\{\frac{dR}{dz}\right\} - z.\left\{\frac{dR}{dx}\right\} = (1+s^2).\cos.v.\left\{\frac{dR}{ds}\right\} - rs.\cos.v.\left\{\frac{dR}{dr}\right\} + s.\sin.v.\left\{\frac{dR}{dv}\right\};^*$$

$$y.\left\{\frac{dR}{dz}\right\} - z.\left\{\frac{dR}{dy}\right\} = (1+s^2).\sin.v.\left\{\frac{dR}{ds}\right\} - rs.\sin.v.\left\{\frac{dR}{dr}\right\} - s.\cos.v.\left\{\frac{dR}{dv}\right\},$$

moreover, by N°. 64, we have

* $\left(\frac{dR}{dx}\right) = \left(\frac{dR}{dr}\right).\frac{dr}{dx} + \left(\frac{dR}{dv}\right).\frac{dv}{dx} + \left(\frac{dR}{ds}\right).\frac{ds}{dx}$, $\left(\frac{dR}{dy}\right) = \left(\frac{dR}{dr}\right).\frac{dr}{dy} + \left(\frac{dR}{dv}\right).\frac{dv}{dy} + \left(\frac{dR}{ds}\right).\frac{ds}{dy}$; $r = \sqrt{x^2+y^2}$, $\frac{x}{r} = \cos.v$, $-\frac{dv}{dx}.\sin v = \frac{y^2}{r^3}$; $s = \frac{z}{\sqrt{x^2+y^2}}$, $\therefore \frac{ds}{dx} = -\frac{z.x}{r^3}$; $\frac{dv}{dy}.\cos.v = \frac{x^2}{r^3}$; $\frac{ds}{dy} = -\frac{zy}{r^3}$; hence $x.\frac{dR}{dy} - y.\frac{dR}{dx} = \left(\frac{dR}{dr}\right).\frac{xy-yx}{r} + \left(\frac{dR}{dv}\right).\left(\frac{x^2+y^2}{r^2}\right) + \left(\frac{dR}{ds}\right).\left(\frac{xyz-xyz}{r^3}\right) = \left(\frac{dR}{dv}\right)$, in like manner $x.\left(\frac{dR}{dz}\right) - z.\left(\frac{dR}{dx}\right) = \frac{dR}{ds}\left(\frac{r.\cos.v}{r} + \frac{r^3.s^2.\cos.v}{r^3}\right) - \frac{dR}{dr}.r.\cos.v.s. + \frac{dR}{dv}.\frac{rs.\sin.v}{r}$ = the expression in the text, and by a similar process the remaining terms may be obtained.

$$xdy-ydx=cdt; \quad xdz-zdx=c'dt, \quad ydz-zdy=c''dt;$$

these differential equations in f, f', f'', will consequently become

$$df=-dy.\left\{\frac{dR}{dv}\right\}-dz.\left\{(1+s^2).\cos.v.\left\{\frac{dR}{ds}\right\}-rs.\cos.v.\left\{\frac{dR}{dr}\right\}+s.\sin.v.\left\{\frac{dR}{dv}\right\}\right\}$$

$$-cdt.\left\{\sin.v.\left\{\frac{dR}{dr}\right\}+\frac{\cos.v}{r}\left\{\frac{dR}{dv}\right\}-\frac{s.\sin.v}{r}.\left\{\frac{dR}{ds}\right\}\right\}-\frac{c'.dt}{r}.\left\{\frac{dR}{ds}\right\};$$

$$df'=dx.\left\{\frac{dR}{dv}\right\}-dz.\left\{(1+s^2).\sin.v.\left\{\frac{dR}{ds}\right\}-rs.\sin.v.\left\{\frac{dR}{dr}\right\}-s.\cos.v.\left\{\frac{dR}{dv}\right\}\right\}$$

$$+cdt.\left\{\cos.v.\left\{\frac{dR}{dr}\right\}-\frac{\sin.v}{r}.\left\{\frac{dR}{dv}\right\}-\frac{s.\cos.v}{r}.\left\{\frac{dR}{ds}\right\}\right\}-\frac{c''.dt}{r}.\left\{\frac{dR}{ds}\right\};$$

$$df''=dx.\left\{(1+s^2).\cos.v.\left\{\frac{dR}{ds}\right\}-r.s.\cos.v.\left\{\frac{dR}{dr}\right\}+s.\sin.v.\left\{\frac{dR}{dv}\right\}\right\}$$

$$+dy.\left\{(1+s^2).\sin.v.\left\{\frac{dR}{ds}\right\}-r.s.\sin.v.\left\{\frac{dR}{dr}\right\}-s.\cos.v.\left\{\frac{dR}{dv}\right\}\right\}$$

$$+c'.dt.\left\{\cos.v.\left\{\frac{dR}{dr}\right\}-\frac{\sin.v}{r}\left\{\frac{dR}{dv}\right\}-\frac{s.\cos.v}{r}.\left\{\frac{dR}{ds}\right\}\right\}$$

$$+c''dt.\left\{\sin.v.\left\{\frac{dR}{dr}\right\}+\frac{\cos.v}{r}.\left\{\frac{dR}{dv}\right\}-\frac{s.\sin.v}{r}.\left\{\frac{dR}{ds}\right\}\right\}.$$

The quantities c', c'' depend, as we have seen in N°. 64, on the inclination of the orbit of m to the fixed plane, so that these quantities become equal to zero, if this inclination is nothing; besides it is easy to perceive, from the nature of R, that $\left\{\frac{dR}{ds}\right\}$ is of the order of the inclinations of the orbits; therefore the products and the squares of the inclinations of the orbits being neglected, the preceding expressions for df, and df', will become

$$df = -dy.\left(\frac{dR}{dv}\right) - cdt.\left\{\sin. v.\left(\frac{dR}{dr}\right) + \frac{\cos. v}{r}\left(\frac{dR}{dv}\right)\right\};$$

$$df' = dx.\left(\frac{dR}{dv}\right) + cdt.\left\{\cos. v.\left(\frac{dR}{dr}\right) - \frac{\cos. v}{r}.\left(\frac{dR}{dv}\right)\right\};$$

but we have

$$dx = d.(r. \cos. v);\ dy = d.(r. \sin. v);\ cdt = xdy - ydx = r^2 dv;$$

therefore we shall have

$$df = -(dr. \sin. v + 2rdv. \cos. v).\left(\frac{dR}{dv}\right) - r^2.dv. \sin. v.\left(\frac{dR}{dr}\right);^*$$

$$df' = (dr. \cos. v - 2rdv. \sin. v).\left(\frac{dR}{dv}\right) + r^2.dv. \cos. v.\left(\frac{dR}{dr}\right).$$

These equations will be more exact, if we assume for the fixed plane of x and y, that of the orbit of m at a given epoch; for then c', c'', and s, are of the order of the disturbing forces; consequently the quantities which are neglected are of the order of the squares of the disturbing forces multiplied by the square of the respective inclination of the two orbits of m and of m'.

The values of r, dr, dv, $\left(\frac{dR}{dr}\right)$, $\left(\frac{dR}{dv}\right)$ remain evidently the same, whatever be the position of the point from which the longitudes are reckoned; but if v be diminished by a right angle, sin v will be changed into $-\cos. v$, and cos. v will be changed into sin v, consequently the expression for df will be changed into that of df'; hence it follows, that if the value of df be developed into a series of the sines and cosines of angles increasing proportionally to the time, the value of df' will

3 D 2

* $\frac{cdt. \cos. v}{r} = rdv. \cos. v$, ∵ the coefficient of $\left(\frac{dR}{dv}\right)$ in the value of df is $2rdv. \cos. v$.

be obtained by diminishing in the first, the angles ϵ, ϵ', ϖ, ϖ', θ and θ', by a right angle.

The quantities f and f' determine the position of the perihelion and the excentricity of the orbit; in fact, we have seen in N°. 64, that

$$\text{tan.}\, I = \frac{f'}{f},$$

I being the longitude of the perihelion referred to the fixed plane. When this plane is that of the primitive orbit of m, we have (as far as quantities of the order of the squares of the disturbing forces multiplied by the square of the respective inclination of the orbits) $I = \varpi$, ϖ being the longitude of the perihelion reckoned on the orbit, therefore we shall then have

$$\text{tang.}\, \varpi = \frac{f'}{f};$$

which gives,

$$\text{sin.}\, \varpi = \frac{f'}{\sqrt{f^2 + f'^2}}; \quad \text{cos.}\, \varpi = \frac{f}{\sqrt{f + f'^2}};$$

hence results, by N°. 64,

$$\mu e = \sqrt{f^2 + f'^2 + f''^2}; \quad f'' = \frac{f'c' - fc''}{c};$$

Thus c' and c'' being on the preceding hypothesis of the order of the disturbing forces, f'' is of the same order, and neglecting the terms of the square of these forces, we shall have $\mu e = \sqrt{f^2 + f'^2}$. If in the expressions of sin. ϖ, cos. ϖ, we substitute instead of $\sqrt{f^2 + f'^2}$, its value μe, we shall have

$$\mu e.\, \text{sin.}\, \varpi = f'; \quad \mu e.\, \text{cos.}\, \varpi = f;$$

these two equations will determine the excentricity and the position of the perihelion, and we can easily infer

$$\mu^2.ede = f.df + f'df' \,;\quad \mu^2.e^2.d\varpi = fdf' - f'df.^*$$

By assuming for the plane of x and of y, that of the orbit of m; we shall have by N°s. 19 and 20, in the case of invariable ellipses,

$$r = \frac{a.(1-e^2)}{1+e.\cos.(v-\varpi)} \,;\quad dr = \frac{r^2.dv.\, e.\sin.(v-\varpi)}{a.(1-e^2)} \,;$$

$$r^2dv = a^2ndt.\sqrt{1-e^2} \,;$$

and by N°. 63, these equations subsist also in the case of variable ellipses; the expressions of df and of df' consequently become

$$df = -\frac{andt}{\sqrt{1-e^2}}.\left(2.\cos.v + \tfrac{3}{2}e.\cos.\varpi + \tfrac{1}{2}e.\cos.(2v-\varpi)\right).\left(\frac{dR}{dv}\right)\dagger$$

$$-\, a^2ndt.\sqrt{1-e^2}.\sin.v.\left(\frac{dR}{dr}\right) \,;$$

$$df' = -\frac{andt}{\sqrt{1-e^2}}.(2.\sin.v + \tfrac{3}{2}.e.\sin.\varpi + \tfrac{1}{2}.e.\sin.(2v-\varpi).\left(\frac{dR}{dv}\right)$$

$$+\, a^2ndt.\sqrt{1-e^2}.\cos.v.\left(\frac{dR}{dr}\right) \,;$$

therefore

* $\mu^2.e^2 = f^2 + f'^2$; $\therefore \mu^2.ede = fdf + f'df'$; $\tan.\varpi = \frac{f'}{f}$, $\therefore \frac{d\varpi}{\cos.^2\varpi} = \frac{fdf' - f'df}{f^2}$, $\therefore$ substituting for f^2, we have $\mu^2e^2.d\varpi = fdf' - f'df$.

† Substituting for dr and r^2dv, we obtain $df = -\frac{r^2.dv.e.\sin.(v-\varpi).\sin.v}{a.(1-e^2)} - \frac{2a^2.ndt.\sqrt{1-e^2}.(\cos.v.(1+e).\cos.(v-\varpi)}{a.(1-e^2)} = -\frac{andt}{\sqrt{1-e^2}}.(2.\cos.v + e.\sin.v.\sin.(v-\varpi) + 2e.\cos.v.\cos.(v-\varpi)$; $e.\sin.v.\sin.(v-\varpi) = e.\sin.^2v.\cos.\varpi - e.\sin.v.\cos.v.\sin.\varpi$. $2e.\cos.v.\cos.(v-\varpi) - 2e.\cos.^2v.\cos.\varpi + 2e.\sin.v.\cos.v.\sin.\varpi = e.(\sin.^2v + \cos.^2v).\cos.\varpi + e.\cos.v.(\cos.v.\cos.\varpi + \sin.v.\sin.\varpi) = e.\cos.v\,\cos.(v-\varpi) = e.\frac{\cos.(2v-\varpi)}{2} + e.\frac{\cos.\varpi}{2}$, $\therefore$ by making similar terms to coalesce we obtain the expression given in the text, we can in a similar manner derive the other expressions.

$$ed\varpi = -\frac{andt}{\mu.\sqrt{1-e^2}}.\ \sin.(v-\varpi).(2+e.\cos.(v-\varpi)).\left(\frac{dR}{dv}\right)^*$$

$$+\frac{a^2.ndt.\sqrt{1-e^2}}{\mu}.\ \cos.(v-\varpi).\left(\frac{dR}{dr}\right);$$

$$de = -\frac{andt}{\mu.\sqrt{1-e^2}}.(2.\cos.(v-\varpi)+e+e.\cos.^2(v-\varpi)).\left(\frac{dR}{dv}\right)$$

$$-\frac{a^2ndt}{\mu}.\sqrt{1-e^2}.\sin.(v-\varpi).\left(\frac{dR}{dr}\right).$$

This expression for de may be made to assume a form which in several circumstances is more commodious. For this purpose, it may be observed, that $dr.\left(\frac{dR}{dr}\right) = \mathrm{d}R - dv.\left(\frac{dR}{dv}\right)$, by substituting in place of r, and dr their preceding values, we shall have

$$r^2.dv.\ e.\sin.(v-\varpi).\left(\frac{dR}{dr}\right) = a.(1-e^2).\ \mathrm{d}R - a.(1-e^2).\ dv.\left(\frac{dR}{dv}\right);$$

but we have

$$r^2.dv = a^2ndt.\sqrt{1-e^2};\ dv = \frac{ndt.(1+e.\cos.(v-\varpi))^2}{(1-e^2)^{\frac{3}{2}}};$$

$$^*fdf' = -\frac{\mu e.andt}{\sqrt{1-e^2}}.\ 2.\sin.v.\cos.\varpi + \frac{3}{2}.\ e.\sin.\varpi.\cos.\varpi + \tfrac{1}{2}e.\sin.(2v-\varpi).\cos.\varpi.\left(\frac{dR}{dv}\right)$$

$$+\mu.ea^2.ndt.\sqrt{1-e^2}.\cos.v.\cos.\varpi.\left(\frac{dR}{dr}\right)$$

$$f'.df = -\frac{\mu e.andt}{\sqrt{1-e^2}}.\ 2.\cos.v.\sin.\varpi + \frac{3}{2}.\ e.\sin.\varpi.\cos.\varpi + \tfrac{1}{2}e.\sin.\varpi.\cos.(2v-\varpi).\left(\frac{dR}{dv}\right)$$

$$-\mu e.a^2.ndt.\sqrt{1-e^2}.\sin.v.\sin.\varpi.\left(\frac{dR}{dr}\right);$$

$$\because \mu^2e^2.d\varpi = fdf' - f'df = -\frac{\mu e.andt}{\sqrt{1-e^2}}.\ 2.\sin.(v-\varpi) + \tfrac{1}{2}.e.\sin.(2v-2\varpi).\left(\frac{dR}{dv}\right).$$

$$+\mu e.a^2ndt.\sqrt{1-e^2}.\cos.(v-\varpi).\left(\frac{dR}{dr}\right),$$

therefore,

$$a^2ndt.\sqrt{1-e^2}.\ \sin.\ (v-\varpi).\left(\frac{dR}{dr}\right)$$

$$=\frac{a.(1-e^2)}{e}.\ \mathrm{d}R-\frac{andt}{e.\sqrt{1-e^2}}.\ (1+e.\cos.\ (v-\varpi))^2.\left(\frac{dR}{dv}\right);$$

therefore the preceding expression for dv will give

$$ede=\frac{andt.\sqrt{1-e^2}}{\mu}.\left(\frac{dR}{dv}\right)-\frac{a.(1-e^2)}{\mu}.\ \mathrm{d}R.$$

This formula may be also obtained in a very simple manner, by the following method. By N°. 64, we have

$$\frac{dc}{dt}=y.\left(\frac{dR}{dx}\right)-x.\left(\frac{dR}{dy}\right)=-\left(\frac{dR}{dv}\right);$$

but by the same number we have $c=\sqrt{\mu a.(1-e^2)}$, which gives

$$dc=-\frac{da.\sqrt{\mu a(1-e^2)}}{2a}-\frac{ede.\sqrt{\mu a}}{\sqrt{1-e^2}};$$

therefore†

$$ede=\frac{andt.\sqrt{1-e^2}}{\mu}.\left(\frac{dR}{dv}\right)+a.(1-e^2).\ \frac{da}{2a^2};$$

then by N°. 64, we have

$$\frac{\mu da}{2a^2}=-\mathrm{d}R;$$

which is evidently equal to the expression given in the text, the value of dc may be obtained in a similar manner.

† Dividing both sides by $\frac{\sqrt{\mu}}{\sqrt{1-e^2}}$, and observing that $an=\frac{\sqrt{\mu}}{a^{\frac{1}{2}}}$, and $\because\sqrt{\mu a}=\frac{\mu}{an}$, we obtain the value of ede, which is given in the text.

thus we shall obtain the same expression for ede, as has been given above.

68. It has been observed in N°. 65, that if the squares of the disturbing forces are neglected, the variations of the greater axis and of the mean motion only contain periodic quantites, depending on the mutual configuration of the bodies m, m', m'', &c. This is not the case with respect to the variations of the excentricities and of the inclinations: their differential expressions contain terms which are independent of this configuratión, and which if they were rigorously constant would produce by integration terms proportional to the time, which would at length render the orbits extremely excentric, and very much inclined to each other; consequently, the preceding approximations which depend on the small excentricity and inclination of the orbits, would become inadequate and even erroneous. But the terms which being apparently constant, enter into the differential expressions of the excentricities and inclinations, are functions of the elements of the orbits; so that in fact they vary with extreme slowness in consequence of the changes which these elements experience. We may conceive therefore that there ought to result from them considerable inequalities, independent of the mutual configuration of the bodies of the system, the periods of which depend on the ratios of the masses m, m', m''.&c., to the mass M. These inequalities under the denomination of *secular inequalities*, have been already considered in Chapter VII. In order to determine them by this method, let the value of df, given in the preceding number, be resumed

$$df = -\frac{andt}{\sqrt{1-e^2}}.(2.\cos. v + \tfrac{3}{2}.e.\cos.\varpi + \tfrac{1}{2}.e.\cos.(2v-\varpi)).\left(\frac{dR}{dv}\right)$$

$$-a^2ndt.\sqrt{1-e^2}.\sin. v.\left(\frac{dR}{dr}\right).$$

In the developement of this equation we shall neglect the squares and products of the excentricities and of the inclinations of the orbits; and amongst the terms depending on the excentricities and inclinatiens, we shall only retain those which are constant. Let us then suppose, as in N°. 48,

$$r = a.(1+u_{,}); \quad r' = a'.(1+u'_{,}),$$
$$v = nt+\varepsilon+v_{,} \quad v' = n't+\varepsilon'+v'_{,}.$$

This being premised, if we substitute in place of R, its value found in N°. 48, observing that by the same N°. we have

$$\left\{\frac{dR}{dr}\right\} = \frac{a}{r}.\left\{\frac{dR}{da}\right\} = (1-u_{,}).\left\{\frac{dR}{da}\right\}$$

finally, if we substitute in place of $u_{,}$, $u'_{,}$, $v_{,}$, $v'_{,}$, their values

$$-e.\cos.(nt+\varepsilon-\varpi), \; -e'.\cos.(n't+\varepsilon'-\varpi'), \; 2e.\sin.(nt+\varepsilon-\varpi),$$
$$2e'.\sin.(n't+\varepsilon'-\varpi'),$$

which are given in N°. 22, and if among the terms which depend on the first power of the excentricities, we only retain those which are constant, we shall find (the squares of the inclinations and excentricities being neglected,)

$$df = \frac{am'ndt}{2}.\,e.\sin.\varpi.\left\{a.\left\{\frac{dA^{(0)}}{da}\right\} + a^2.\left\{\frac{d^2A^{(0)}}{da^2}\right\}\right\}^{*}$$
$$+am'ndt.\,e'.\sin.\varpi'.\left\{A^{(1)} + \tfrac{1}{2}a.\left\{\frac{dA^{(1)}}{da}\right\} + \tfrac{1}{2}a'.\left\{\frac{dA^{(1)}}{da'}\right\} + \tfrac{1}{4}aa'.\left\{\frac{d^2A^{(1)}}{da.da'}\right\}\right\}$$
$$-am'ndt.\Sigma.\left\{i.A^{(i)} + \tfrac{1}{2}a.\left\{\frac{dA^{(i)}}{da}\right\}\right\}.\sin.(i.(n't-nt+\varepsilon'-\varepsilon)+nt+\varepsilon);$$

* Sin. $v = \sin.(nt-\varepsilon+v_{,}) = \sin.(nt+\varepsilon).\cos.v_{,} + \cos.(nt+\varepsilon).\sin.v_{,}$, now $\sin.v_{,} = v_{,} - \frac{v_{,}^3}{3} +$ &c., $\cos.v_{,} = 1 - \frac{v_{,}^2}{2} +$ &c., hence substituting for $v_{,}$ its value $2.e.\sin.(nt+\varepsilon-\varpi)$, and neglecting the square of e, we obtain $\sin.(nt+\varepsilon+v_{,}) = \sin.(nt+\varepsilon) + \cos.(nt+\varepsilon)$.

The integral sign Σ extending in this expression, as in the value of R of N°. 48, to all entire values of i, as well positive as negative, the value $i = 0$ being included.

$2e. \sin. (nt + \varepsilon - \varpi)$, differencing R with respect to a, and retaining those terms only in which the first power of the excentricity or inclination can occur, and from which we may obtain constant quantities, the first term of the expression for $\frac{dR}{da}$ (differenced under these restrictions) will give $\frac{dA^{(0)}}{da}$, the second term will give $\frac{dA^{(0)}}{da}$, and also $a. \frac{d^2A^{(0)}}{da^2}$, $\because (1 - u_{\prime}).\left(\frac{dR}{da}\right) = (1 + e. \cos. (nt + \varepsilon - \varpi).\left(\left(\frac{dA^{0}}{da}\right) - \left(\left(\frac{dA^{(0)}}{da}\right) - a. \left(\frac{d^2A^{(0)}}{da^2}\right)\right)\right.$. $e. \cos. (nt + \varepsilon - \varpi)$, now this quantity should be multiplied into $\sin. v$, or into $\sin. (nt + \varepsilon) + \cos. (nt + \varepsilon)$. $2e. (\sin.(nt + \varepsilon - \varpi)$; hence, performing this operation, neglecting the square of e, and we shall have the coefficient of $\frac{dA^{(0)}}{da} = 2.e. \cos. (nt + \varepsilon). \sin. (nt + \varepsilon - \varpi) + e. \cos. (nt + \varepsilon - \varpi). \sin. (nt + \varepsilon) - e. \cos. (nt + \varepsilon - \varpi). \sin. (nt + \varepsilon) = 2e. \cos. (nt + \varepsilon). \sin. (nt + \varepsilon - \varpi) = e. \sin. (2) (nt + \varepsilon) - \varpi) - e. \sin. \varpi$; in like manner, the coefficient of $-a. \frac{d^2A}{da^2}$, is $e. \sin. (nt + \varepsilon). \cos. (nt + \varepsilon - \varpi) = \frac{e}{2}. \sin. 2.(nt + \varepsilon) - \varpi) + \frac{e}{2}. \sin. \varpi$; hence, by multiplying by $\frac{m'}{2}$, see N°. 48, the constant part of the second term of the value of $df = \frac{n^2m'n}{2} . dt. e. \sin. \varpi. \left(\left(\frac{dA^{(0)}}{da}\right) + \frac{a}{2}.\left(\frac{d^2A^{(0)}}{da^2}\right).\right)$, in like manner, to obtain the coefficient of $e'. \sin. \varpi'$, let the third and fourth terms of the value of R be differenced with respect to a, (i being equal to unity), which will give $-a'. \left(\frac{d^2A^{(1)}}{da.da'}\right). e'. \cos. (n't - nt + \varepsilon' - \varepsilon). \cos. (n't + \varepsilon' - \varpi')$; $-A^{(1)}. 2.e'. \sin. (n't + \varepsilon' - \varpi'). \sin. (n't - nt + \varepsilon' - \varepsilon)$; $\sin. (nt + \varepsilon)$ is the only part of the value of $\sin. v$, into which these quantities can be multiplied without introducing powers of e greater than the first, $\because$ when for these quantities equivalent expressions are substituted, determined by the equations of the form $\cos. a. \cos. b = \frac{\cos. (a + b) + \cos. (a - b)}{2}$. $\sin. a. \sin. b = \cos. \frac{(a + b)}{2} - \cos. \frac{(a - b)}{2}$; we shall obtain the second and fourth terms of the second line of the value of df; in order to obtain the first and third terms, let the third and fourth terms be differenced, when $i = 1$, considering ε as the variable, for we have $\left(\frac{dR}{dv}\right) = \left(\frac{dR}{d\varepsilon}\right)$, and then these terms become $\frac{m'}{2}. u_{\prime}'. a'. \frac{dA^{(1)}}{da'}. \sin. (n't - nt + \varepsilon' - \varepsilon)$; $+ \frac{m'}{2}. v_{\prime}'A^{(1)}$.

By the preceding number, the value of df' will be obtained, if the angles ϵ, ϵ', ϖ, and ϖ', be diminished by a right angle in that of f; hence we deduce

$$df' = -\frac{am'ndt}{2}.\ e.\ \cos.\ \varpi.\ \left\{a.\left\{\frac{dA^{(0)}}{da}\right\} + \tfrac{1}{2}a^2.\left\{\frac{d^2A^{(0)}}{da^2}\right\}\right\}$$

$$-\ am'ndt.\ e'.\ \cos.\ \varpi'.\ \left\{A^{(1)} + \tfrac{1}{2}a.\left\{\frac{dA^{(1)}}{da}\right\} + \tfrac{1}{2}a'.\left\{\frac{dA^{(1)}}{da'}\right\} + \tfrac{1}{4}.\left\{\frac{d^2A^{(1)}}{da.da'}\right\}\right\}$$

$$+\ am'ndt.\Sigma.\left\{iA^{(i)} + \tfrac{1}{2}a.\left\{\frac{dA^{(i)}}{da}\right\}\right\}.\ \cos.\ (i.(n't - nt + \epsilon' - \epsilon) + nt + \epsilon\}.$$

Let us name, in order to abridge, X the part of the expression of df, contained under the sign Σ, and Y the part of the expression of df' contained under the same sign. Moreover, let us make as in N°. 55,

$$(0,\ 1) = -\frac{m'.n}{2}.\left\{a^2.\left\{\frac{d.A^{(0)}}{da}\right\} + \tfrac{1}{2}a^3.\left\{\frac{d^2A^{(0)}}{da^2}\right\}\right\};$$

$$\boxed{0,\ 1} = \frac{m'.n}{2}.\left\{aA^{(1)} - a^2.\left\{\frac{dA^{(1)}}{da}\right\} - \tfrac{1}{2}a^3.\left\{\frac{d^2A^{(1)}}{da^2}\right\}\right\}.$$

It should be then observed, that the coefficient of $e'dt.\ \sin.\ \varpi'$, in the expression of df, is reduced to $\boxed{0,\ 1}$, when we substitute in it,, in place of the partial differences of $A^{(1)}$ in a', their values in partial differences relative to a; finally, let, as in N°. 50,

cos. $(n't - nt + \epsilon' - \epsilon)$, when we substitute for u_i' and v_i' their values, and proceed as before, we shall obtain, after the resulting quantities are multiplied by 2. cos. $(nt + \epsilon)$. (the only part of the value of cos. v which can be taken into account): the first and third terms of the coefficient of e'. sin. ϖ'; in order to obtain the variable part of the value of df, e, e', do not occur; the first term of the value of R, must be differentiated with respect to v, or, what is the same thing with respect to ϵ, and then multiplied into 2. cos. $(nt + \epsilon)$, this same term should be also differenced with respect to a, and then multiplied into sin. $(nt + \epsilon)$.

$$e.\sin.\varpi = h;\quad e'.\sin.\varpi' = h',$$
$$e.\cos.\varpi = l;\quad e'.\cos.\varpi' = l';$$

which by the preceding number, gives $f=\mu l$; $f'=\mu h$; or simply, $f=l$; $f'=h$, the mass of M being assumed as unity, and the mass m being neglected relatively to M; we shall have

$$\frac{dh}{dt} = (0,1).l - \boxed{0,1}.l' + am'.n.Y;$$
$$\frac{dl}{dt} = -(0,1).h + \boxed{0,1}.h'. - am'.n.X.$$

Hence it is easy to infer, that if the sum of the terms analogous to $am'nY$ be named (Y), which terms arise from the action of each of the bodies m', m'', &c. on m; if in like manner, the sum of the terms analogous to $-am'nX$, arising from the same action, be called (X), finally, if we denote by one, two, &c., strokes, what the quantities (X), (Y), h and l become relatively to the bodies m', m'', &c.; we shall obtain the following system of differential equations:

$$\frac{dh}{dt} = ((0,1)+(0,2)+\&c.).l - \boxed{0,1}.l' - \boxed{0,2}.l'' - \&c. + (Y);$$
$$\frac{dl}{dt} = -((0,1)+(0,2)+\&c.).h + \boxed{0,1}.h' + \boxed{0,2}.h'' + \&c. + (X);$$
$$\frac{dh'}{dt} = ((1,0)+(1,2)+\&c.)l' - \boxed{1,0}.l - \boxed{1,2}.l'' - \&c. + (Y');$$
$$\frac{dl'}{dt} = -((1,0)+(1,2)+\&c.)h' + \boxed{1,0}.h + \boxed{1,2}.h'' + \&c. + (X').$$
&c.

In order to integrate these equations, let it be observed that each of the quantities h, l, h', l', &c., is made up of two parts, the one depending on the mutual configuration of the bodies m, m', &c., the other independent of this configuration, containing the secular variations of these quantities. We shall obtain the first part, if we consider that when we have regard to it solely, h, l, h', l', &c., are of the order of the disturbing masses, and consequently $(0, 1).h$, $(0, 1).l$, are of the order of the squares of these masses. Neglecting quantities of this order, we shall have

$$\frac{dh}{dt}=(Y); \quad \frac{dl}{dt}=(X);$$

$$\frac{dh'}{dt}=(Y'); \quad \frac{dl'}{dt}=(X');$$

therefore,

$$h=\int(Y).dt; \quad l=\int(X).dt; \quad h'=\int(Y').dt; \quad l'=\int(X').dt; \quad \&c.$$

If these integrals be taken, the elements of the orbits being considered constant; and if Q be what $\int(Q).dt$ then becomes, and if δQ be the variation of Q, arising from that of the elements, we shall have

$$\int(Y).dt=Q-\int\delta Q;$$

But as Q is of the order of the perturbating masses, and as the variations of the elements are of the same order, δQ is of the order of the squares of these masses, therefore, if quantities of this order be neglected, we shall have

$$\int(Y).dt=Q.$$

We can therefore take the integrals $\int(Y).dt$, $\int(X).dt$, $\int(Y').dt$, &c., on the hypothesis that the elements of the orbits are constant, provided that we consider these elements as variable in the integrals; by this means we shall obtain in a very simple manner, the periodic parts of the expressions of h, l, h', &c.

In order to obtain the parts of these expressions, which contain the secular inequalities, it is to be remarked, that they are furnished by the integration of the preceding differential equations deprived of their last terms (Y), (X), &c.; for it is evident that the substitution of the periodic parts of h, l, h', &c., will make these terms to disappear. But if these equations be deprived of their last terms, they will coincide with the differential equations (A) of N°. 55, which we have already discussed in detail.

69. It has been observed in N°. 65, that if the mean motions nt and $n't$ of the two bodies m and m', are very nearly in the ratio of i to i', so that $i'n'-in$, may be a very small quantity, very sensible inequalities may result in the mean motions of these bodies. This ratio of the mean motions may also produce sensible variations in the excentricities of the orbits and in the positions of their perihelias; in order to determine them, let the equation found in N°. 57 be resumed,

$$ede = \frac{andt.\sqrt{1-e^2}}{\mu}.\left\{\frac{dR}{dv}\right\} - \frac{a.(1-e^2)}{\mu}.\ dR.$$

It follows from what has been stated in N°. 48, that if we assume for the fixed plane, that of the orbit of m at a given epoch, which permits us to neglect in R, the inclination φ of the orbit of m on this plane; all the terms of the expression for R which depend on the angle $i'n't-int$, will be comprized in the following form,

$$mk.\cos.\ (i'n't-int+i'\varepsilon'-i\varepsilon-g\varpi-g'\varpi'-g''\theta');$$

i, i', g, g', g'', being integral numbers, such that we have $0=i'-i-g-g'-g''$. The coefficient R has for factor $e^g.\ e'^{g'}.\ (\tan.\ \frac{1}{2}\varphi')^{g''}$, g, g', g'', being taken positively in these exponents; moreover, if we suppose that i' and i are positive, and i' greater than i, we have seen in N°. 48, that the terms of R which depend on the angle $i'n't-int$ are of the order $i'-i$, and or of an order higher by two, by four, &c. unities; if therefore we only consider the terms of the order $i'-i$, R will be of the form $e^g.\ e'^{g'}.\ (\tan.\ \frac{1}{2}\varphi')^{g''}.\ Q$, Q being a function independent of the excentricities and of the respective inclinations of the orbits. The numbers g, g', g'', contained under the sign *cos.* are then positive; for if one of them, g, for example, was negative and equal to $-f$, k would be of the order $f+g'+g''$; but the equation $0=i'-i-g-g'-g''$, gives $f+g'+g''=i'-i+2f$; thus k would be of an order higher than $i'-i$, which is contrary to the hypothesis. This being premised by

N°. 48, we have $\left\{\frac{dR}{dv}\right\}=\left\{\frac{dR}{d\varepsilon}\right\}$, provided* that in this last partial difference we make $\varepsilon-\varpi$ equal to a constant quantity, therefore the term of $\left\{\frac{dR}{dv}\right\}$ which corresponds to the preceding term of R is

$$m'.(i+g).\,k.\,\sin.\,(i'n't-int+i'\varepsilon'-i'\varepsilon-g\varpi-g'\varpi'-g''\theta').$$

The corresponding term of dR is

$$m'.\,ink.dt.\,\sin.\,(i'n't-int+i'\varepsilon'-i\varepsilon-g\varpi-g'\varpi'-g'\theta'),$$

if therefore we only take such terms into account, neglecting the square of e in comparison to unity, the preceding expression for ede will give

$$de=\frac{m'.andt}{\mu}.\,\frac{gk}{e}.\,\sin.\,(i'n't-int+i'\varepsilon'-i\varepsilon-g\varpi-g'\varpi'-g''\theta').$$

but we have

$$\frac{gk}{e}=ge^{g-1}.\,e'^{g'}.\,(\text{tang.}\,\tfrac{1}{2}\varphi')^{g''}.\,Q=\frac{dk}{de};$$

therefore we shall obtain by integrating

$$e=-\frac{m'an}{\mu.(i'n'-in)}.\left\{\frac{dk}{de}\right\}.\,\cos.\,(i'n't-int+i'\varepsilon'-i\varepsilon-g\varpi-g'\varpi'-g''\theta').$$

Now, if the sum of all the terms of R, which depend on the angles $i'n't-int$ be represented by the following quantity,

$$m'P.\,\sin.\,(i'n't-int+i'\varepsilon'-i\varepsilon)+m'.P'.\,\cos.\,(i'n't-int+i'\varepsilon'-i\varepsilon);$$

the corresponding part of e will be

* Hence $-\varpi=\zeta-\varepsilon$, ∴ $-g\varpi=\zeta-g\varepsilon$, therefore if we substitute this quantity for $g\varpi$, and then take the value of $\frac{dR}{d\varepsilon}$, we shall obtain the expression for $\left(\frac{dR}{dv}\right)$, corresponding to the value of R.

$$\frac{m'.an}{\mu.(i'n'-in)}.\left\{\left\{\frac{dP}{de}\right\}.\sin.\left\{i'n't-int+i'\epsilon'-i\epsilon\right)+\left\{\frac{dP}{de}\right\}.\right.$$
$$\cos.\,(i'n't-int+i'\epsilon'-i\epsilon)).$$

This inequality may become extremely sensible if the coefficient $i'n'-in$ is very small, as is the case in the theory of Jupiter and of Saturn. Indeed, it has for a divisor only the first power $i'n'-in$, while the corresponding inequality of the mean motion has for a divisor the second power of this quantity, as has been observed in N°. 65; but $\left\{\frac{dP}{de}\right\}$ and $\left\{\frac{dP'}{de}\right\}$ being of an order inferior to P and to P', the inequality of the excentricity may be considerable, and even surpass that of mean motion, if the excentricities e and e' be very small; we shall see examples of this, in the theory of the satellites of Jupiter.

Let us now determine the corresponding inequality of the motion of the perihelion. For this purpose, let us resume the two equations,

$$ede=\frac{fdf+f'df'}{\mu^2};\quad e^2d\varpi=\frac{fdf'-f'df}{\mu^2},$$

which were obtained in N°. 67. These equations give

$$df=\mu de.\cos.\varpi-\mu ed\varpi.\sin.\varpi;$$

hence, if we only consider the angle $i'n't-int+i'\epsilon'-i\epsilon-g\varpi-g'\varpi'-g''\theta'$, we shall have

$$df=m'.andt.\left\{\frac{dk}{de}\right\}.\cos.\varpi.\sin.(i'n't-int+i'\epsilon'-i\epsilon-g\varpi-g'\varpi'-g''\theta')$$
$$-\mu e.d\varpi.\sin.\varpi.$$

Let

$$-m'.andt.\left\{\left\{\frac{dk}{de}\right\}+k'.\right\}.\cos.(i'n't-int+i'\epsilon-i\epsilon-g-\varpi-g'\varpi'-g'\theta')^{*}$$

* By multiplying by sin. ϖ, we shall have $df=$
$-m'andt.\left(\frac{dk}{de}\right).(\cos.\varpi.\sin.(i'n't-int+i'\epsilon'-i\epsilon-g\varpi-g'\varpi'-g''\theta')+\sin.\varpi.\cos.(i'n't-int+$

represent the part of $\mu ed\varpi$, which depends on the same angle, we shall have

$$df = m'.andt. \left\{ \left\{ \frac{dk}{dc} \right\} + \tfrac{1}{2}k'. \right\}. \sin.(i'n't—int+i'\epsilon'-i\epsilon-(g-1).\varpi-g'\varpi-g''\theta')$$

$$—m'.\frac{andt}{2}.\ k'.\sin.(i'n't—int+i'\epsilon'—i\epsilon—(g+1).\ \varpi—g'\varpi'—g''\theta').$$

It is easy to perceive from the last of the expressions of df, given in N°. 67, that the coefficient of this last sine, has for a factor $e^{g+1}.e'^{g'}.(\tan.\frac{1}{2}\varphi)^{g''}$; k' is therefore of an order superior by two units, to that of $\left\{ \frac{dk}{de} \right\}$; consequently, if it be neglected in comparison to $\left\{\frac{dk}{de}\right\}$, we shall have

$$—\frac{m'.andt}{\mu}.\left\{\frac{dk}{de}\right\}.\ \cos.(i'n't—int+i'\epsilon—i\epsilon—g\varpi—g'\varpi'—g''\theta'),$$

for the term of $ed\varpi$, which corresponds to the term

$$m'.k.\ \cos.(i'n't—int—int+i\epsilon'—i\epsilon—g\varpi—g'\varpi'—g''\theta'),$$

of the expression of R. It follows from this, that the part of ϖ which corresponds to the part of R expressed by

$$m'.P.\sin.(i'n't—int+i'\epsilon'—i\epsilon)+m'.P'.\cos.(i'n't—int+i'\epsilon'—i\epsilon),$$

is equal to

$$\frac{m'an}{\mu.(i'n'—in).e}.\left\{\left\{\frac{dP}{de}\right\}.\ \cos.(i'n't—int+i'\epsilon'—i\epsilon)—\left\{\frac{dP'}{de}\right\}\right.$$
$$\left.\sin.(i'n't—int+i'\epsilon—i\epsilon)\right\},$$

we shall by this means obtain, in a very simple manner, the variations of

$$i'\epsilon—i\epsilon—g\varpi—g'\varpi'—g'\theta').)$$

$$—m'andt.k'.\ \sin.\varpi.\ \cos.(i'n't—int+i'\epsilon'—i\epsilon—g\varpi—g'\varpi'—g''\theta') =$$

$$—m'andt.\ \frac{dk'}{dc}.\ \sin.(i'nt—int—i'\epsilon'—i\epsilon—(g—1).\ \varpi—g'\varpi'—g''\theta'),$$

and the two terms into the value of the coefficient of $—\frac{mandtk'}{\mu}$ are obtained from the formula $\sin.a.\cos.b = \frac{\sin.(a+b)+\sin.(a—b)}{2}$.

the excentricity and of the perihelion, which depend on the angle $i'n't - int + i'\epsilon' - i\epsilon$. They are connected with the variation ζ of the mean motion, which corresponds to it, in such a manner, that the variation of the excentricity is

$$\frac{1}{3in}.\left\{\frac{d^2\zeta}{de.dt}\right\};^*$$

and the variation of the longitude of the perihelion is

$$\frac{(i'n' - in)}{3in.e}.\left\{\frac{d\zeta}{de}\right\}.$$

The corresponding variation of the excentricity of the orbit of m', due to the action of m, will be

$$-\frac{1}{3i'n'.e'}.\left\{\frac{d^2\zeta'}{de'.dt}\right\}.$$

and the variation of the longitude of its perihelion will be

$$-\frac{(i'n' - in)}{3i'n'.e'}.\left\{\frac{d\zeta'}{de'}\right\},$$

And as by N°. 65, we have $\zeta' = -\frac{m.\sqrt{a}}{m'.\sqrt{a'}}.\zeta$ these variations will be

$$\frac{m.\sqrt{a}}{3i'n'.m'.\sqrt{a'}}.\left\{\frac{d^2\zeta}{de'.dt}\right\}, \text{ and } \frac{(i'n' - in).m.\sqrt{a}}{3i'n'.e'.m'.\sqrt{a'}}.\left\{\frac{d\zeta}{de'}\right\}.$$

When the quantity $i'n' - in$ is very small, the inequality depending on the angle $i'n't - int$ produces a sensible one in the expression of the

* $\zeta = \frac{3m'an^2i}{(i'n' - in)^2.\mu}.((P.\cos.(i'n't - int + i'\epsilon' - i\epsilon) - P'.\sin.i'n't - int + i'\epsilon' - i\epsilon))$ differencing ζ, first with respect to e and then with respect to t, the coefficient becomes $\frac{3m'an^2.i}{(i'n' - in).\mu}$, and the variable part is the same as the variable part of the expression for de, hence the ratio of de to $\left(\frac{d^2\zeta}{de.dt}\right)$ is that of 1 to $3in$; in like manner it may be shewn, that the ratio of $d\varpi$ to $\left(\frac{d\zeta}{de}\right)$, is that of $\frac{1}{e}$. to $\frac{3in}{(i'n' - in)}$.

mean motion, among the terms depending on the squares of the disturbing masses; the analysis of them has been given in N°. 65.

This same inequality produces in the expressions of de and $d\varpi$, terms of the order of the squares of those masses, which being solely functions of the elements of the orbits, have a sensible influence on the secular variations of these elements. Let us consider for instance, the expression of de depending on the angle $i'n't—int$. By what precedes, we have

$$de = -\frac{m'.an.dt}{\mu}.\left\{\left\{\frac{dP}{de}\right\}.\cos.(i'n't—int+i'\varepsilon'—i\varepsilon) — \left\{\frac{dP'}{de}\right\}.\sin.(i'n't—int+i'\varepsilon'—i\varepsilon)\right\}.$$

By N°. 65, the mean motion nt ought to be increased by

$$\frac{3m'.an.^2i'}{(i'n'—in)^2.\mu}.\left\{P.\cos.(i'n't—int+i'\varepsilon'—i\varepsilon—P'.\sin.(i'n't—int+i'\varepsilon'—i\varepsilon)\right\},$$

and the mean motion $n't$ ought to be increased by

$$-\frac{3m'.an^2i'}{(i'n'—in)^2.\mu}.\frac{m.\sqrt{a}}{m'.\sqrt{a'}}.\{P.\cos.(i'n't—int+i'\varepsilon'—i\varepsilon)— P'.\sin.(i'n't—int+i'\varepsilon'—i\varepsilon)\}.$$

In consequence of these increments, the value of de will be increased by the function

$$-\frac{3m'.a^2.in^3.dt}{2\mu^2.\sqrt{a'}.(i'n'—in)^2}.im'.\sqrt{a'}+i'm.\sqrt{a}).\left\{P.\left\{\frac{dP'}{de}\right\}—P'.\left\{\frac{dP}{de}\right\}\right\}.$$

and the value of $d\varpi$ will be increased by the function

$$\frac{3m'.a^2.in^3.dt}{2\mu^2.\sqrt{a'}.(i'n'—in)^2.e}.(i.m'.\sqrt{a'}+i'.m.\sqrt{a})P.\left\{\frac{dP}{de}\right\}+P'.\left\{\frac{dP'}{de}\right\}.$$

we shall find in like manner, that the value of de' will be increased by the function

$$-\frac{3ma^2.\sqrt{a}.in^3.dt}{2\mu^2.a'.(i'n'-in)^2}.(im'.\sqrt{a'}+i'.m.\sqrt{a}).\left\{P.\left\{\frac{dP'}{de'}\right\}-P'.\left\{\frac{dP}{de'}\right\}\right\};^*$$

and that the value of $d\varpi'$, will be increased by the function

$$\frac{3ma^2.\sqrt{a}.in^3.dt}{2\mu^2a'.(i'n'-in)^2e'}.(im'.\sqrt{a'}+i'.m.\sqrt{a}).\left\{P.\left\{\frac{dP}{de'}\right\}+P'.\left\{\frac{dP'}{de'}\right\}\right\}.$$

These different terms are sensible in the theory of Jupiter and Saturn, and in that of the satellites of Jupiter. The variations of e, e', ϖ and ϖ', relative to the angle $i'n't-int$ may also introduce some constant terms of the order of the squares of the disturbing masses, into the differentials de, de', $d\varpi$, and $d\varpi'$, and depending on the variations of e, e', ϖ and ϖ' relative to the same angle; it will be easy by means of the preceding analysis to take them into account. Finally, it will be easy by our analysis to determine the terms of the expressions of e, ϖ, ϵ' and ϖ', which depending on the angle $i'n't-int+i'\epsilon'-i\epsilon$ have

* Let the increment of $nt=d.(nt)=p.(P.\cos.A-P'.\sin.A)$, and the increment of $d.(n't)=-\frac{m.\sqrt{a}}{m'.\sqrt{a'}}.p.(P.\cos.A-P'.\sin.A)$, then we have $d.(i'n't-int)=\left(-\frac{i'm.\sqrt{a}}{m'.\sqrt{a'}}-i\right).p.(P.\cos.A-P'.\sin.A)$, calling this quantity Δ, and substituting it for $d.(i'n't-int)$ in the value of de, given in this page, we shall have the factor $\frac{dP}{de}.\cos.(A+\Delta)-\frac{dP'}{de}.\sin.(A+\Delta)$, then by developing and remarking that $\sin.\Delta=\Delta$, and $\cos.\Delta=1$ $q.p.$, the preceding expression becomes $\frac{dP}{de}.\cos.A-\frac{dP'}{de}.\sin.A-\frac{dP}{de}.\sin.A.\left(-\frac{i'm.\sqrt{a}}{m'.\sqrt{a'}}-i\right).p.(P.\cos.A-P'.\sin.A)+\frac{dP_{\prime}}{de}.\cos.A.\left(-\frac{i'm.\sqrt{a}}{m'.\sqrt{a'}}-i\right).p.(P.\cos.A-P'.\sin.A)$. as $\sin.A.\cos.A$, contain only periodic functions, the quantities multiplied by them, or any powers of them, need not be considered at present; but as $\sin.^2A=\frac{1}{2}-\frac{1}{2}.\cos.2A$; $\cos.^2A=\frac{1}{2}+\frac{1}{2}.\cos.2A$; we shall obtain (by substituting for $\sin.^2A$, $\cos.^2A$), two terms which do not involve periodic functions, and which when concinnated, become the quantity by which de is said in text to be augment

not $i'n'-in$ for a divisor, and those, which depending on the same angle and on double of this angle, are of the order of the square of the disturbing forces. These terms are sufficiently considerable in the theory of Jupiter and of Saturn to induce us to have regard to them; we shall develope them in the requisite detail, when this theory will be more particularly discussed in the 8th Book.

70. In order to determine the variations of the nodes and of the inclinations of the orbits, let the equations of N°. 64, be resumed

$$dc = dt.\left\{y.\left\{\frac{dR}{dx}\right\} - x.\left\{\frac{dR}{dy}\right\}\right\};$$

$$dc' = dt.\left\{z.\left\{\frac{dR}{dx}\right\} - x.\left\{\frac{dR}{dz}\right\}\right\};$$

$$dc'' = dt.\left\{z.\left\{\frac{dR}{dy}\right\} - y.\left\{\frac{dR}{dz}\right\}\right\};$$

If the action of m' be solely considered, the value of R, of N°. 46, gives

$$y.\left\{\frac{dR}{dx}\right\} - x.\left\{\frac{dR}{dy}\right\} = m'.(x'y - y'x).\left\{\frac{1}{(x'^2+y'^2+z'^2)^{\frac{3}{2}}} - \frac{1}{((x'-x)^2+(y'-y)^2+(z'-z)^2)^{\frac{3}{2}}}\right\}$$

$$z.\left\{\frac{dR}{dx}\right\} - x.\left\{\frac{dR}{dz}\right\} = m'.(x'z - z'x).\left\{\frac{1}{(x'^2+y'^2+z'^2)^{\frac{3}{2}}} - \frac{1}{((x'-x)^2+(y'-y)^2+(z'-z)^2)^{\frac{3}{2}}}\right\}$$

$$z.\left\{\frac{dR}{dy}\right\} - y.\left\{\frac{dR}{dz}\right\} = m'.(y'z - z'y).\left\{\frac{1}{(x'^2+y'^2+z'^2)^{\frac{3}{2}}} - \frac{1}{((x'^2-x)^2+(y'-y)^2+(z'-z)^2)^{\frac{3}{2}}}\right\}$$

Let now

$$\frac{c''}{c}=p;\quad \frac{c'}{c}=q;$$

by N°. 64, the two variables p and q will determine the tangent of the inclination φ of the orbit of m, and the longitude θ of its node, by means of the equations

$$\tan.\varphi=\sqrt{p^2+q^2};\quad \tan.\varphi=\frac{p}{q}.$$

Naming p', q', p'', q'', &c., what p and q become relatively to the bodies m', m'', &c.. we shall have by N°. 64,

$$z=qy-px;\quad z'=q'y'-p'x';\ \&c.$$

The preceding value of p being differenced, gives

$$\frac{dp}{dt}=\frac{1}{c}.\left\{\frac{dc''-pdc}{dt}\right\};$$

by substituting in place of dc and of dc'', their values, we shall have*

$$\frac{dp}{dt}=\frac{m'}{c}.((q-q').yy'+(p'-p).x'y).\left\{\frac{1}{(x'^2+y'^2+z'^2)^{\frac{3}{2}}}\right.$$

$$\left.-\frac{1}{((x'-x)^2+(y'-y)^2+(z'-z)^2)^{\frac{3}{2}}}\right\};$$

* $c''x-c'y=-cz$, $\therefore -z=\frac{c''}{c}.x-\frac{c'}{c}.y=px-qy$; $\frac{dp}{dt}=\left(c.\frac{dc''}{dt}-c''.\frac{dc}{dt}\right).\div c^2=$

$$\frac{1}{c}.\left(\frac{dc''}{dt}-\frac{c''.dc}{c.dt}\right),\ \therefore \frac{dp}{dt}=\frac{m'}{c}.((y'z-z'y)-p.(x'y-y'x)).\left(\frac{1}{(x'^2+y'^2+z'^2)^{\frac{3}{2}}}-\right.$$

$\left.\frac{1}{((x'-x)^2+(y'-y)^2+(z'-z)^2)^{\frac{3}{2}}}\right)$; therefore if we substitute for z and z' their values, we will obtain by concinnating and obliterating those terms which destroy each other, the expression for $\frac{dp}{dt}$, which is given in the text.

in like manner, we shall find

$$\frac{dq}{dt}=\frac{m'}{c}.\left((p'-p).xx'+(q-q').xy'\right).\left\{\frac{1}{(x'^2+y'^2+z'^2)^{\frac{3}{2}}}\right.$$

$$\left.-\frac{1}{((x'-x)^2+(y'-y)^2+(z'-z)^2)^{\frac{3}{2}}}\right\}.$$

If in place of x, y, x', y', their values $r.\cos.v$, $r.\sin.v$, $r'.\cos.v'$, $r'.\sin.v'$, be substituted; we shall have

$$(q-q').yy'+(p'-p).x'y=\left\{\frac{q'-q}{2}\right\}.rr'.((\cos.v'+v)-\cos.(v'-v))^*$$

$$+\left\{\frac{p'-p}{2}\right\}.rr'.(\sin.(v'+v)-\sin.(v'-v));$$

$$(p'-p).xx'+(q-q').xy'=\left\{\frac{p'-p}{2}\right\}.rr'.(\cos.(v'+v)+\cos.(v'-v)).$$

$$+\left\{\frac{q-q'}{2}\right\}.rr'.(\sin.(v'+v)+\sin.(v'-v)).$$

The excentricities and inclinations of the orbits being neglected, we have

$$r=a;\ v=nt+\epsilon;\ r'=a';\ v'=n't+\epsilon';$$

which gives

$$\frac{1}{(x'^2+y'^2+z'^2)^{\frac{3}{2}}}-\frac{1}{((x'-x)^2+(y'-y)^2+(z'-z)^2)^{\frac{3}{2}}}=\frac{1}{a'^3}$$

$$-\frac{1}{(a'^2-2aa'.\cos.(n't-nt+\epsilon'-\epsilon+a^2)^{\frac{3}{2}}}.$$

Moreover, by N°. 48, we have

$$\frac{1}{(a^2-2aa'.\cos.(n't-nt+\epsilon'-\epsilon)+a'^2)^{\frac{3}{2}}}=\tfrac{1}{2}.\Sigma B^{(i)}.\cos.i.(n't-nt+\epsilon'-\epsilon);$$

* $rr'.\cos.v.\cos.v'=\frac{rr'}{2}\cos.(v+v')+\cos.(v-v)$, $rr'.\sin.v.\cos.v'=\frac{rr'}{2}.(\sin.(v+v')+\sin.(v-v))$.

the integral sign Σ extending to all entire values of i, positive as well as negative, the value $i=0$ being included; by this means, we shall have, neglecting the terms of the order of the squares and products of the excentricities and inclinations of the orbits,

$$\frac{dp}{dt}=\frac{(q'-q)}{2c}.\frac{m'a}{a'^2}(\cos.(n't+nt+\varepsilon'+\varepsilon)-\cos.(n't-nt+\varepsilon'-\varepsilon))$$

$$+\frac{(p'-p)}{2c}.\frac{m'a}{a'^2}.(\sin.(n't+nt+\varepsilon'+\varepsilon)-\sin.(n't-nt+\varepsilon'-\varepsilon))^*$$

$$+\frac{(q'-q)}{4c}.m'.aa'\Sigma B^{(i)}.(\cos.[(i+1).(n't-nt+\varepsilon'-\varepsilon)]-\cos.(i+1).$$
$$(n't-nt+\varepsilon'-\varepsilon)+2nt+2\varepsilon])$$

$$+\frac{(p'-p)}{4c}.m.aa'.\Sigma B^{(i)}.(\sin.[(i+1).(n't-nt+\varepsilon'-\varepsilon)]-\sin.(i+1).$$
$$(n't-nt+\varepsilon'-\varepsilon)+2nt+2\varepsilon]);$$

$$\frac{dq}{dt}=\frac{(p'-p)}{2c}.\frac{m'.a}{a'^2}.(\cos.(n't+nt+\varepsilon'+\varepsilon)+\cos.(n't-nt+\varepsilon'-\varepsilon))$$

$$+\frac{(q'-q)}{2c}.\frac{m'.a}{a'^2}.\sin.(n't+nt+\varepsilon'+\varepsilon)+\sin.(n't-nt+\varepsilon'-\varepsilon))$$

$$+\frac{(p-p')}{4c}.m.a'a.\Sigma B^{(i)}.(\cos.[(i+1).(n't-nt+\varepsilon'-\varepsilon)]+\cos.(i+1).$$
$$(n't-nt+\varepsilon'-\varepsilon)\dot{+}2nt+2\varepsilon)]$$

* The value of the third term in the expression for $\frac{dp}{dt}$ will be had by observing that $\frac{\cos.(v\pm v')}{2}.\frac{1}{2}.\Sigma.B^{(i)}.\cos.i.(n't-nt+\varepsilon'-\varepsilon)=\frac{\Sigma.B^{(i)}}{4}.(\cos.(i.(n't-nt+\varepsilon'-\varepsilon)+n't+nt+\varepsilon'+\varepsilon)+\cos.i.(n't-nt+\varepsilon'-\varepsilon)-n't-nt-\varepsilon'-\varepsilon))-\cos.i.(n't-nt+\varepsilon'-\varepsilon)+n't-nt+\varepsilon'-\varepsilon)-\cos.(i.(n't-nt+\varepsilon'-\varepsilon)-n't-nt+\varepsilon+\varepsilon')$; therefore, if we concinnate the terms of this expression, we shall obtain by observing that $\cos.i.(n't-nt+\varepsilon'-\varepsilon)+n't+nt+\varepsilon'+\varepsilon)=\cos.(i+1)\,n't-nt+\varepsilon'-\varepsilon)+2nt+2\varepsilon)$, and also that $\cos.i.(n't-nt+\varepsilon-\varepsilon)+n't-nt+\varepsilon'-\varepsilon)=\cos.(i+1).(n't-nt+\varepsilon'-\varepsilon)$, the expression given in the text.

$$+\frac{(q'-q)}{4c}.\,m'.aa'.\Sigma B^{(i)}.(\sin.[(i+1).(n't-nt+\varepsilon'-\varepsilon)]+\sin.\,(i+1).$$
$$(n't-nt+\varepsilon'-\varepsilon)+2nt+2\varepsilon]).$$

The value $i=-1$ gives in the expression of $\frac{dp}{dt}$, the constant quantity $\frac{(q'-q)}{4c}.\,m'.aa'.B^{(-1)}$, all the other terms of the expression of $\frac{dp}{dt}$ are periodic, if P represents their sum, we shall have by N°. 48,

$$\frac{dp}{dt}=\frac{q'-q}{4c}.\,m'.aa'B^{(1)}+P,$$

($B^{(1)}$ being equal to $B^{(-1)}$).

By the same method, we shall find, that if we denote by Q the sum of all the periodic terms of the expression of $\frac{dq}{dt}$, we shall have

$$\frac{dq}{dt}=\frac{(p-p')}{4c}.\,m'.aa'.B^{(1)}+Q.$$

If the squares of the excentricities and of the inclinations of the orbits, be neglected, we shall have by N°. 64, $c=\sqrt{\mu a}$. If then μ be supposed $=1$, we have $n^2a^3=1$, which gives $c=\frac{1}{an}$; the quantity $\frac{m'.aa'.B^{(1)}}{4c}$, thus becomes $\frac{m'.a^2a'.nB^{(1)}}{4}$, which by N°. 59 is equal to $(0,1)$; hence we shall have

$$\frac{dp}{dt}=(0.\,1).(q'-q)+P;$$
$$\frac{dq}{dt}=(0,\,1).(p-p')+Q.$$

It follows from this, that if (P) and (Q) denote the sum of all the functions P and Q, relative to the action of the different bodies

m', m'', &c., on m, and if in like manner (P'), (Q'), (P''), (Q''), &c., denote what (P) and (Q) become, when the quantities relative to m are changed into those which refer to m', m'', &c., and conversely; we shall have for the determination of the variables p, q, p', q', p'', q'', &c., the following system of differential equations,

$$\frac{dp}{dt}=-((0,1)+(0,2)+\&c.)q+(0,1).q'+(0,2).q''+\&c.+(P);$$

$$\frac{dq}{dt}=((0,1)+(0,2)+\&c.).p-(0,1).p'-(0,2).p''-\&c.+(Q);$$

$$\frac{dp'}{dt}=-((1,0)+(1,2)+\&c.).q'+(1,0).q+(1,2).q''+\&c.+(P')$$

$$\frac{dq'}{dt}=((1,0)+(1,2)+\&c.).p'-(1,0).p-(1,2).p''-\&c.+(Q'),$$

&c.

From the analysis of N°. 68, it appears that the periodic parts of p, q, p', q', &c., are

$$p=\int(P).dt;\quad q=\int(Q).dt$$
$$p'=\int(P').dt;\quad q'=\int(Q').dt,$$

we shall afterwards obtain the secular parts of the same quantities, by integrating the preceding differential equations, deprived of their last terms (P), (Q), (P'), &c.; and then we shall light on the equations (C) of N°. 59, which have been already discussed with sufficient detail to dispense with our reverting to this object.

71. Let the equations of N°. 64 be resumed, namely,

$$\tan.\varphi=\frac{\sqrt{c'^2+c''^2}}{c};\quad \tan.\theta=\frac{c''}{c'};$$

from them may be deduced

$$\frac{c'}{c}=\tan.\varphi.\cos.\theta;\quad \frac{c''}{c}=\tan.\varphi.\sin.\theta;$$

differentiating, we shall have

$$d.\ \tan.\ \varphi=\frac{1}{c}.\ (dc'.\ \cos.\ \theta+dc''.\ \sin.\ \theta-dc.\ \tan.\ \varphi)\ ;^*$$

$$d\theta.\ \tan.\ \varphi=\frac{1}{c}.\ (dc''.\ \cos.\ \theta-dc'.\ \sin.\ \theta).$$

If in these equations, we substitute in place of $\frac{dc}{dt}$, $\frac{dc'}{dt}$, $\frac{dc''}{dt}$, their values $y.\left\{\frac{dR}{dx}\right\}-x.\left\{\frac{dR}{dy}\right\}$, $z.\left\{\frac{dR}{dx}\right\}-x.\left\{\frac{dR}{dz}\right\}$, $z.\left\{\frac{dR}{dy}\right\}-y.\left\{\frac{dR}{dz}\right\}$, and in place of these last quantities, their values furnished in N°. 67, and if moreover, we observe that $s=\tan.\ \varphi.\ \sin.\ (v-\theta)$; we shall have

$$\dagger d.\ \tan.\varphi=\frac{dt.\ \tan.\ \varphi.\ \cos.\ (v-\theta)}{c}.\left\{r.\left\{\frac{dR}{dr}\right\}.\ \sin.\ (v-\theta)+\left\{\frac{dR}{dv}\right\}.\ \cos.\ (v-\theta)\right\}$$
$$-\frac{(1+s^2).dt}{c}.\ \cos.\ (v-\theta).\ \left\{\frac{dR}{ds}\right\};$$

* Hence $\cos.\ \theta=\frac{c'}{\sqrt{c'^2+c''^2}}$. $\sin.\ \theta=\frac{c''}{\sqrt{c'^2+c''^2}}$, $\because d.\ \tan.\ \varphi=\frac{\frac{dc'.c'+dc''.c''}{c.\sqrt{c'^2+c''^2}}-dc.\frac{\sqrt{c'^2+c''^2}}{c^2}}{}$

$=$ by substituting $\cos.\ \theta$, $\sin.\ \theta$, for their respective values, the expression which is given in the text.

$$d.\ \tan.\ \theta=\frac{d\theta}{\cos.^2\theta}=\frac{dc''.c'-dc'c''}{c'^2},\ \because\frac{d\theta.\sqrt{c'^2+c''^2}}{c}=\frac{dc''}{c}.\left(\frac{c'}{\sqrt{c'^2+c''^2}}-\frac{dc'.c''}{c'.\sqrt{c'^2+c''^2}}\right).$$

† Multiplying the value of dc', given in page 385, by $\cos.\ \theta$, and that of dc'' by $\sin.\ \theta$, we shall obtain by adding them together $(1+s^2).\ \cos.\ (v-\theta).\left(\frac{dR}{ds}\right)-rs.\ \cos.\ (v-\theta).\left(\frac{dR}{dr}\right)+s.\ \sin.(v-\theta).\left(\frac{dR}{dv}\right)-\frac{dR}{dv}.\ \tan.\ \varphi=d\ \tan.\ \varphi$, hence by substituting for s its value, we shall obtain the expression given in the text.

$$d\theta. \tan.\varphi = \frac{dt.\tan.\varphi.\sin.(v-\theta)}{c}.\left\{ r.\left\{\frac{dR}{dr}\right\}.\sin.(v-\theta)+\left\{\frac{dR}{dv}\right\}.\cos.(v-\theta)\right\}$$

$$-\frac{(1+s^2).dt}{c}.\sin.(v-\theta).\left\{\frac{dR}{ds}\right\}.$$

These two differential equations will determine directly the inclination of the orbit and the motion of the nodes. They give

$$\sin.(v-\theta).\ d.\tan.\varphi - d\theta.\cos.(v-\theta).\tan.\varphi = 0\ ;^*$$

this equation may be also deduced from the equation $s = \tan.\varphi.\sin.(v-\theta)$; in fact, as this last equation is finite, we may by N°. 63, difference it, either by considering φ and θ as constant, or by treating them as if they were variable; so that its differential, taken by making φ and θ the sole variables, vanishes; hence results the preceding differential equation.

Suppose now, that the inclination of the fixed plane to that of the orbit should be extremely small; so that the square of s and of the tan. φ, may be neglected, we shall have

$$d.\tan.\varphi = -\frac{dt}{c}.\cos.(v-\theta).\left\{\frac{dR}{ds}\right\};$$

$$d\theta.\tan.\varphi = -\frac{dt}{c}.\sin.(v-\theta).\left\{\frac{dR}{ds}\right\};$$

by making, as before,

$$p = \tan.\varphi.\sin.\theta.;\ q = \tan.\varphi.\cos.\theta;$$

we shall have, in place of the two preceding differential equations, the following

$$dq = -\frac{dt}{c}.\cos.v.\left\{\frac{dR}{ds}\right\};$$

* By multiplying the first equation by sin. $(v-\theta)$, and the second by cos. $(v-\theta)$, their second members become indentically equal to each other, therefore the first members will be also equal to each other.

$$dp = -\frac{dt}{c}.\sin. v\ \left\{\frac{dR}{ds}\right\};$$

but $s = q.\sin. v - p.\cos. v$, hence

$$\left\{\frac{dR}{ds}\right\} = \frac{1}{\sin. v}.\left\{\frac{dR}{dq}\right\},\quad \left\{\frac{dR}{ds}\right\} = -\frac{1}{\cos. v}.\left\{\frac{dR}{dp}\right\};\dagger$$

therefore

$$dq = \frac{dt}{c}.\left\{\frac{dR}{dp}\right\};$$

$$dp = -\frac{dt}{c}.\left\{\frac{dR}{dq}\right\}.$$

We have seen in N°. 48, that the function R is independent of the fixed plane of x and of y; supposing, therefore, that all the angles of this function are referred to the orbit of m, it is evident that R will be a function of these angles, and of the respective inclination of these two orbits, which inclination we shall denote by $\varphi'_{,}$. Let $\theta'_{,}$ be the longitude of the node of the orbit of m' on the orbit of m, and let us suppose that $m'k\ \tan. (\varphi'_{,})^g. \cos. (i'n't - int + A - g.\theta'_{,})$ is a term in the value of R, depending on the angle $i'n't - int$: by N°. 60 we shall have

$$\tan. \varphi'_{,}.\sin. \theta'_{,} = p' - p;\quad \tan. \varphi'_{,}.\cos. \theta'_{,} = q' - q,$$

hence we deduce

$$(\tan. \varphi'_{,})^g.\sin. g\theta'_{,} = \frac{((q'-q)+(p'-p).\sqrt{-1})^g - ((q'-q)-(p'-p).\sqrt{-1})^g}{2.\sqrt{-1}};$$

* $dq = \cos. \theta. d.\tan. \varphi - d\theta.\sin. \theta.\tan. \varphi = -\frac{dt}{c}.(\cos. v.\cos. \theta + \sin. v.\sin. \theta).\cos. \theta.$ $\left(\frac{dR}{ds}\right) + \frac{dt}{c}.(\sin. v.\cos. \theta - \cos. v.\sin. \theta).\sin. \theta.\left(\frac{dR}{ds}\right) = -\frac{dt}{c}.\cos. v.\left(\frac{dR}{ds}\right)$; $\left(\frac{dR}{ds}\right) = \left(\frac{dR}{dq}\right).\left(\frac{dq}{ds}\right)$ but $\frac{dq}{ds} = \frac{1}{\sin. v}$, $\therefore \left(\frac{dR}{ds}\right) = \frac{dR}{dq}.\frac{1}{\sin. v}$.

$$\tan.(\varphi_{,}')^{g}\cos.g\theta_{,}' = \frac{((q'-q)+(p'-p).\sqrt{-1})^{g}+((q'-q)-(p'-p).\sqrt{-1})^{g}}{2};*$$

If we only consider the preceding term of the value of R, we shall have

$$\left\{\frac{dR}{dp}\right\} = -g.\,(\tan.\,\varphi_{,}')^{g-1}.\,m'k.\,\sin.(i'n't - int + \mathrm{A} - (g-1).\,\theta_{,}');$$

$$\left\{\frac{dR}{dq}\right\} = -g.(\tan.\,\varphi_{,}')^{g-1}.\,m'k.\,\cos.\,(i'n't - int + \mathrm{A} - (g-1).\theta_{,}').$$

If these values be substituted in the preceding expressions of dp and of dq, and if we observe that we have very nearly, $c = \frac{\mu}{an}$; we shall obtain

$$p = \frac{g.m'k.an}{\mu.(i'n' - in)}.\,(\tan.\,\varphi_{,}')^{g-1}.\,\sin.\,(i'n't - int + \mathrm{A} - (g-1).\theta_{,}');$$

$$q = \frac{g.m'.k.an}{\mu.(i'n' - in)}.\,(\tan.\,\varphi_{,}')^{g-1}.\,\cos.\,(i'n't - int + \mathrm{A} - (g-1).\theta_{,}').$$

and if these values be substituted in the equation $s = q.\sin.\,v - p.\cos.\,v$, we shall have

$$s = -\frac{g.m'.k.an}{\mu.(i'n' - in)}.\,(\tan.\,\varphi_{,}')^{g-1}.\,\sin.\,(i'n't - int + \mathrm{A} - (g-1).\theta_{,}').$$

* $\sin.\,\theta_{,}' = \frac{p'-p}{\sqrt{(p-p)^2+(p'-q)^2}}$, $\cos.\,\theta_{,}' = \frac{q'-q}{\sqrt{(p'-p)^2+(q'-q)^2}}$, $\because$

$\overline{\cos.\,\theta_{,}' + \sqrt{-1}.\,\sin.\,\theta_{,}'}\big)^{g} = \cos.\,g\theta_{,}' + \sqrt{-1}.\,\sin.\,g\theta = \left(\frac{(q'-q)+\sqrt{-1}.(p'-p)}{\sqrt{(p'-p)^2+(q'-q)^2}}\right)^{g}$, hence we obtain by multiplying by $\tan.\,\varphi_{,}'$, and its values, the expressions for $\tan.\,\varphi_{,}'^{g}.\,\sin.\,g\theta_{,}'$, $\tan.\,\varphi_{,}'^{g}.\,\cos.\,g\theta_{,}'$, which are given in the text; now $m'k.(\tan.\,\varphi_{,}')^{g}.\,\cos.\,(i'n't - int + \mathrm{A} - g\theta_{,}') = m'k.\,(\tan.\,\varphi_{,}')^{g}.\,(\cos.\,g\theta.\,\cos.(i'n't - int + \mathrm{A}) + \sin.\,g\theta.\,\sin.\,(i'n't - int + \mathrm{A})$, if we substitute for $(\tan.\,\varphi_{,}')^{g}.\,\cos.\,g\theta_{,}'$, $(\tan.\,\varphi_{,}')^{g}.\,\sin.\,g\theta''$, and their difference with respect to p and q, we will obtain the expressions for $\frac{dR}{dp}$, $\frac{dR}{dq}$, which are given in the text.

This expression of $s_{,}$ is the variation of the latitude corresponding to the preceding term of R, it is evident that it is the same whatever may be the fixed plane to which the motions of m and of m' may be referred, provided that its inclination to the plane of the orbits be inconsiderable; therefore we shall by this means obtain that part of the expression for the latitude, which becomes sensible from the smallness of the divisor $i'n'-in$. Indeed this inequality of the latitude involves only the first power of this divisor, and in this respect it is less sensible than the corresponding inequality of the mean longitude, which contains the square of this divisor; but on the other hand, tan. $\varphi_{,}'$ occurs affected with a power which is less by unity; which remark corresponds to that made in 69, on the corresponding inequality of the excentricities of the orbits. It thus appears that all these inequalities are connected with each other, and the corresponding part of R, by very simple expressions.

If the preceding expressions of p and of q be differenced, and if in the value of $\frac{dp}{dt}$ and of $\frac{dq}{dt}$, which result, the angles nt and $n't$ be increased by the inequalities of the mean motions, depending on the angle $i'n't-int$; there will result in these differentials; quantities which are solely functions of the elements of the orbits, and which may sensibly influence the secular variations of the inclinations and of the nodes, although being of the order of the squares of the disturbing masses; which is analogous to what has been stated in N°. 69, relative to the secular variations of the excentricities and aphelias.

72. It remains for us to consider the variation of the longitude ϵ of the epoch. By N°. 64, we have

$$d\epsilon = de.\left\{\left\{\frac{dE^{(1)}}{de}\right\}\right\}.\sin.(v-\varpi)+\tfrac{1}{2}.\left\{\frac{dE^{(2)}}{de}\right\}.\sin.2.(v-\varpi)+\&c.$$

$$-d\varpi.((E^{(1)}.\cos.(v-\varpi)+E^{(2)}.\cos.2.(v-\varpi)+\&c.);$$

If for $E^{(1)}$, $E^{(2)}$, &c. be substituted their values in series arranged according to the powers of e, which series it is easy to infer from the general expression for $E^{(i)}$, given in N°. 16, we shall have

$$d\epsilon = -2de.\sin.(v-\varpi)+2e.d\varpi.\cos.(v-\varpi)$$
$$+ede.(\tfrac{3}{2}+\tfrac{1}{2}e^2+\&c.).\sin.2.(v-\varpi)-e^2.d\varpi.(\tfrac{3}{2}+\tfrac{1}{4}e^2+\&c.)\cos.2(v-\varpi)^*$$
$$-e^2de.(1+\&c.).\sin.3.(v-\varpi)+e^3.d\varpi.(1+\&c.).\cos.3.(v-\varpi)$$
$$+\&c.$$

If for de, and $ed\varpi$, their values, given in N°. 67, be substituted, we shall find, when the approximation is carried as far as quantities of the order e^2 inclusively,

$$d\epsilon = \frac{a^2.ndt}{\mu}.\sqrt{1-e^2}.\,(2-\tfrac{3}{2}e.\cos.(v-\varpi)+e^2.\cos.2.(v-\varpi).\left\{\frac{dR}{dr}\right\}$$
$$-\frac{andt}{\mu.\sqrt{1-e^2}}.\,e.\sin.(v-\varpi).(1+\frac{e}{2}.\cos.(v-\varpi)).\left\{\frac{dR}{dv}\right\}.$$

The general expression for $d\epsilon$ contains terms of the form $m'.k.ndt.\cos.(i'n't-int+\text{A})$, and consequently the expression for ϵ contains terms of the form $\frac{m'.kn}{i'n'-in}.\sin.(i'n't-int+\text{A})$; but it is easy to be assured that the coefficient k in these terms is of the order $i'-i$, and that consequently, these terms are of the same order as those of the mean longitude which depend on the same angle. The latter have for divisor the square of $i'n'-in$; we have seen that we can neglect in respect to them, the corresponding terms of ϵ when $i'n'-in$ is a very small quantity.

If in the terms of the expressions of $d\epsilon$, which are solely functions

* By N°. 16, $E^{(i)} = \pm\,\frac{2e^i.(1+e\sqrt{1-e^2})}{(1+\sqrt{1-e})^i}$, $\therefore \log.E^{(i)} = 2i.\log.e+\log.(1+e.\sqrt{1-e^2})$ $-i.\log.(1+\sqrt{1-e^2})$, then by differentiating and substituting for $E^{(i)}$ its value, we can obtain the expression which is given in the text.

of the elements of the orbits, we substitute in place of these elements the secular parts of their values, it is evident that there will result in them constant terms, and other terms affected with the sines and cosines of the angles on which the secular variations of the excentricities and of the inclinations of the orbits depend. The constant terms will produce in the expression of ε, terms proportional to the time, which will be confounded with the mean motion of m. As to the terms affected by the sine and cosine, they will acquire by integration, in the expression of ε, very small divisors of the same order as the disturbing forces; so that these terms being at once multiplied and divided by these disturbing forces, they may become sensible, although of the order of the squares and products of the excentricities and inclinations. We shall see in the theory of the planets that these terms are insensible, but they are extremely sensible in the theory of the moon and of the satellites of Jupiter, indeed it is on these terms that their secular equations depend.

We have seen in N°. 65, that the mean motion of m has for expression $\frac{3}{\mu}\int\int andt.\, \mathrm{d}R$, and that if we only consider the first power of the disturbing masses, $\mathrm{d}R$ involves only periodic quantities; but if we take into account the squares and products of these masses, this differential may contain terms which are solely functions of the elements of the orbits. By substituting in place of these elements the secular parts of their values, there will result terms affected with the sines and cosines of angles, on which the secular variations of the orbits depend. These terms will acquire in the expression of the mean motion, by the double integration, very small divisors, which will be of the order of the squares and products of the disturbing masses; so that being simultaneously multiplied and divided by the squares and products of these masses, they may become sensible, although being of the order of the squares and products of the excentricities and inclinations of the orbits. We shall see that these terms are likewise insensible in the theory of the planets.

73. The elements of the orbit of m, being determined by what precedes, they should be substituted in the expressions for the radius vector, for the longitude, and latitude, which have been given in N°. 22; the values of these three variables will thus be obtained by means of which astronomers determine the position of the heavenly bodies. By reducing these values into a series of sines and cosines, we shall obtain a series of inequalities, from which tables may be formed, and thus the position of m at any instant may be computed with great facility. This method, founded on the variation of parameters, is extremely useful in the investigation of those inequalities, which from their relations with the mean motions of the bodies of the system, acquire great divisors, and by this means become very sensible. This species of inequalities affects principally the elliptic elements of the orbits; therefore by determining the variations which result from them in these elements, and by substituting them in the expressions of elliptic motion, we shall obtain in the simplest manner possible, all the inequalities which those divisors render sensible.

The preceding method is likewise useful in the theory of comets; these stars are only perceived for a very small part of their course, and observations solely make known the part of the ellipse, which may be confounded with the arc of the orbit which they describe during their apparition. Therefore, if the nature of the orbit, considered as a variable ellipse, be determined, we shall have the changes which this ellipse undergoes in the interval between two consecutive appearances of the same comet; we can therefore, announce its return, and when it reappears, compare the theory with observations.

After having given the methods and formulæ for determining by successive approximations, the motions of the centres of gravity of the heavenly bodies, it remains for us to apply them to the different bodies of the solar system; but as the ellipticity of these bodies influences in a sensible manner, the motions of several of them among each other, it is requisite, previously to proceeding to the numerical applications, to treat of the figure of the heavenly bodies, of which the investigation is equally interesting, on its own account, as that of their motions.

END OF THE SECOND BOOK.

Lightning Source UK Ltd.
Milton Keynes UK
UKHW020633090223
416652UK00001B/376